Acknowledgement

I dedicate this transcription to the most important people in my life – *i manggåfahu* (my family): *asaguåhu* (my wife) Josephine "Fena" Marie Manibusan-Punzalan, *famagohonhu* (my children and grandson): Brandon Joseph Manibusan Punzalan & Sherezada Young-Punzalan, and my first-born grandson Jayden Joseph; Bryant Joshua Manibusan Punzalan & Melissa Gutierrez-Punzalan; Bernard Timothy Punzalan II; Flaka Marie Punzalan; and of course the entire Punzalan and Manibusan clans! Throughout my journey of researching and documenting our families' Chamorro heritage they have been continuously very patient, understanding and supportive of my time and effort on the Chamorro Roots Genealogy Project™.

The entire Chamorro Roots Genealogy Project™ is dedicated to *i Taotao Håya* (the Chamorro people with roots) from the Mariana Islands for the documentation, preservation and perpetuation of our unique identity as a people.

I am also grateful for the continued efforts and support of:

> Elizabeth "Lisa" Martinez Bitanga for proofreading these census transcriptions. Lisa continues to provide selfless support and contributions as a primary associate researcher and collaborator on the Chamorro Roots Genealogy Project.
>
> Lourdes "Lou" Mata Torre Montez for helping to transcribe the census and also for helping to moderate the Facebook group "Chamorro Roots ~ *Håle' Chamoru*," where many discussions on our culture, language, traditions and families occur. In addition, Lou has been helping to index a collection of nicknames into a unique Chamorro Nickname Dictionary database that many members of the Facebook group have contributed. As of this writing there have been over 650 entries so perhaps this nickname dictionary just might be published one day with a Chamorro Clan Name Dictionary.

About this transcription

The transcription of the 1930 population census of Guam is a product of the Chamorro Roots Genealogy Project™. Like its predecessor, the *1920 Census Population Census of Guam: Transcribed*, that I published in 2012, this book begins with an overview and some of my observations of the census in general. There are no copies of the original images included within this book; with the exception of a modified copy of the title page. Each census page contained herein is simply a transcription from what was handwritten and transcribed into a type written format. It serves as a tool to make it a little easier for fellow genealogy researchers during the course of their work.

TABLE OF CONTENTS

TRANSCRIBED CENSUS SHEETS

Overview

The 1930 census is the second census that was taken from the formerly titled U.S. Bureau of the Census (now known as the Census Bureau), since Guam became a U.S. Territory in 1898. Census day began on January 1, 1930; however, the actual enumeration of the census for Guam did not commence until April 2, 1930 with the final recording ending on June 25, 1930. The population schedule used for Guam is distinct and differs from the population schedule used for a State.

Copies of the *Fifteenth Census of the United States: 1930-Population, The Island of Guam* are on Microfilm[1] # T1224-2629 and can be purchased at the National Archives and Records Administration website (www.archives.gov). Digital images may also be accessed at the Chamorro Roots Genealogy Project database and website (www.chamorroroots.com). Other methods of accessing the copies of census records include other genealogy websites and some major public libraries in the U.S.

Like the 1920 Census, each enumerated census is actually comprised of two sets; totaling 50 names. The first sheet set contains individuals from 1 through 25 (referred to as Sheet A), and then a subsequent sheet allows the enumerator to record individuals from 26 to 50 (Sheet B). Therefore, as you view the beginning forms of each district, the forms will normally begin with Sheet 1A, followed by Sheet 1B, Sheet 2A, Sheet 2B and so on. I intentionally excluded some sheets that were blank ("B" sheets) when the Enumerators completed the enumeration of a particular area on a Sheet "A."

There is also another number that appears to be stamped on the upper right side of the form. This number is a numerical sequence number for the entire Guam census records to help arrange and organize the records. These stamped numbers also served as the basis for my attempt to reconcile the population numbers officially recorded and presented by the Census Bureau. Be mindful that these numbers are assigned on to the first document of each set (individuals 1 through 25 – Sheet A); however, within this transcription the second sheet is labeled with a "B" after the number. The stamped numbers were helpful to organize and transcribe the information into the Chamorro Roots database. Some on-line genealogy sites have not been able to accurately organize this feature image by image and the pitfall to that can result in an erroneous transcription of family composition when family information is split between census sheets.

[1] Microfilm roll # T1224-2629 contains copies of the Census for Guam and American Samoa.

Population Summary

Census publications regarding the population statistics of Guam for the 1930 census recorded an official total population count of 18,509. However, after transcribing and reconciling the data there were actually 18,512 names recorded in the census, which leaves a difference of three (3): two additional names were found in District 11 (Municipality of Sumay) and one in District 13 (Naval Reservations and Ships).

This is the first time the military and their families were included in the decennial census for Guam. In the 1920 census the military were recorded separately as an entity and are not located within the Census records for Guam.

Thirteen primary districts were recorded for Guam and are comprised of the following localities, population count, number of census sheets and enumerators:

1930 Population: Island of Guam		
District - Municipality	**Population**	**Enumerators**
District 1 – Agana	1,710	Pauline L. Dees & Joaquin Torres
District 2 – Agana	2,064	Arthur W. Jackson
District 3 – Agana	1,827	Tomas A. Calvo
District 4 – Agana	3,089	Vicente Tydingco
District 5 - Agana	2,352	Jose Kamminga & Margarito Palting
District 6 –Agat	887	Pedro C. Charfauros
District 7 – Asan	559	Joaquin Torres
District 8 – Inarajan	1,176	Francisco G. Lujan & Cayetano A. Quinata
District 9 – Merizo	1,101	Manuel Charfauros
District 10 – Piti	928	Joaquin Torres
District 11 – Sumay	1,211	Joaquin C. Diaz
District 12 – Yona	489	Cayetano A. Quinata
District 13 – Military[2]	1,119	Susan W. Bradley[3]
Total	**18,512**	

[2] No actual municipality was used for the Military; however, the Place Name given was Naval Reservations and Ships.

[3] She was either Governor Bradley's wife or daughter.

GUAM

MUNICIPALITIES AND PRINCIPAL TOWNS

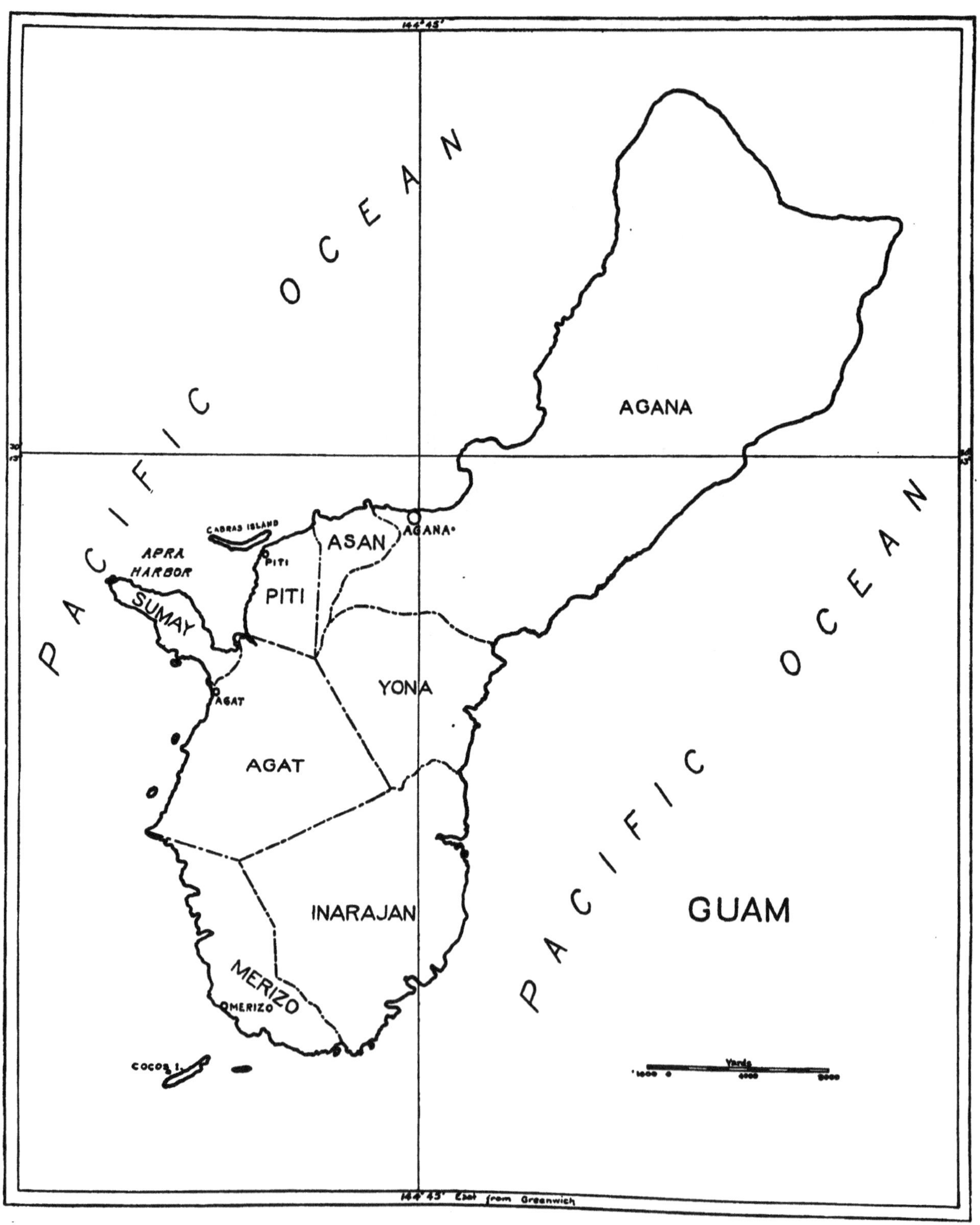

Source: *U.S. Census Bureau. (1931). Population-Agriculture: Final Bulletin - Guam. Retrieved February 9, 2012 from: http://www2.census.gov/prod2/decennial/documents/41169168ch2.pdf*

District 1, Municipality of Agana

Agana City: San Nicolas [area]			
		Total District 1	**1,710**
Castillo St	79	Maria Ana de Austria St[4]	52
Dr Hessler St[5]	229	Marshall St	10
Esperanza St	212	Minondo St	42
General Tererro St[6]	143	Paseo	92
Gerona St	95	Pazos St[7]	7
Hernan Cortez St[8]	43	San Jorge St	25
Isabel la Catolica St	218	San Juan de Letran St[9]	189
La Paz St	62	San Nicolas St	54
Madrid St	45	San Ramon St	37
Magallanes St	76		

District 2, Municipality of Agana

Agana City: Padre Palomo and San Antonio			
		Total District 2	**2,064**
Total Padre Palomo St Area	**349**	**Total San Antonio Area[10]**	**1,715**
		Barrigada Road	150
		Cerinola St	21
		Dela Corte St	428
		Luchana St	78
		Mongmong Road	265
		Padre Palomo	296
		San Victores	280
		Santiago	64
		Trafalgar	108
		[illegible street name]	25

---

[4] Parts of Mariana de Austria Street are also found in District 3, San Ignacio Urban and Togae Agana Urban.
[5] Parts of Dr. Hessler Street are also found in District 3, San Ignacio Urban.
[6] Parts of General Terrero Street are also found in District 3, San Ignacio Urban.
[7] Parts of Pazos Street are also found in District 3, San Ignacio Urban.
[8] Parts of Hernan Cortez Street are also found in District 3, San Ignacio Urban.
[9] Parts of San Juan de Letran Street are also found in District 3, San Ignacio Urban.
[10] Like the 1920 census, the San Antonio area for the 1930 census included residents of the Barrigada Road and Mongmong.

District 3, Municipality of Agana

Agana City: San Ignacio, Bilibic and Togae			
		Total District 3	**1,827**
San Ignacio Urban Total	**836**	**Bilibic Urban Total**	**592**
Dr. Hessler St	71	Soledad St	592
Fragua St	46		
General Terrero	19	**Togae Agana Urban Total**	**399**
Hernan Cortez St[11]	190	Colosa St	19
Mariana de Austria St	102	Lepanto St	93
Numancia St	29	Mariana de Austria St	64
Padre Aniceto St	22	Pavia St	70
Pazos Street	28	San Quintin St	90
San Ignacio St	72	Togae	63
San Juan de Letran	103		
Santa Cruz[12]	85		
Travesia de Gomez St	38		
Zaragosa St	31		

District 4, Municipality of Agana

Agana City: Anigua, Julale and Santa Cruz			
		Total District 4	**3,089**
Anigua Urban Total	**538**	**Santa Cruz [area] Total**	**1,647**
Agana Piti Road	538	Bailen St	67
		Cristobal Colon St	186
Julale [area] Total	**904**	Hernan Cortez St	171
Cristobal Colon St	190	Legaspi St	246
Hernan Cortez St	218	Pizarro St	213
Legaspi St	209	Sagunto St	376
Pizarro St	188	San Ignacio St	165
Santa Cruz St	99	Santa Cruz St	223

District 5, Municipality of Agana

Barrigada, Dededo, Machananao, Sinajana, Tutujan and Yigo			
		Total District 5	**2,352**
Barrigada Barrio Total	**701**	**Machananao Barrio Total**	**135**
Barrigada Barrio	366	**Sinajana Barrio Total**	**380**
[no street name]	335	**Tutujan Barrio Total**	**148**
Dededo Barrio Total	**760**	**Yigo Barrio Total**	**228**

[11] Parts of Hernan Cortez Street are also found in District 4, Agana, Julale and Santa Cruz areas.

[12] The majority of Santa Cruz Street residents are found in District 4, Agana, Julale and Santa Cruz areas.

District 6, Municipality of Agat

Agat Town, Chandia, Fena, Inaso, Omo, Opagat			
		Total District 6	**887**
Agat Town Total	**609**	**Omo Barrio Total**	**22**
Cerain St	281	**Opagat Barrio Total**	**35**
Legaspi St	103	**Pasqual Barrio Total**	**16**
Pareno St	225	**Sagua Barrio Total**	**19**
Chandia Barrio Total	**22**	**Salinas Barrio Total**	**86**
Fena Barrio Total	**21**	**Tumat Barrio Total**	**23**
Inaso Barrio Total	**34**		

District 7, Municipality of Asan

Asan Town and Libugon Barrio			
		Total District 7	**559**
Asan Town Total	**538**	**Libugon Barrio Total**	**21**
Agana-Piti Road	538	Radio Hill Road	21

District 8, Municipality of Inarajan

Bubulao, Inarajan Town, Malolos, Talofofo and Talofofo Barrio			
		Total District 8	**1,176**
Bubulao Total	**12**	**Talofofo Total**	**49**
Inarajan Town Total	**812**	**Talofofo Barrio Total**	**272**
Malolos Barrio Total	**31**		

District 9, Municipality of Merizo

Merizo Town and Umatac Barrio			
		Total District 9	**1,101**
Merizo Town Total	**710**	**Umatac Barrio Total**	**391**
Rosario St	325	San Dionisio St	303
San Dimas St	200	Nino Perdido St	51
[no street name]	185	[no street name]	37

District 10, Municipality of Piti

Piti Town, Singensong and Tepungan			
		Total District 10	**928**
Piti Town Total	**387**	**Sinengsong Barrio Total**	**178**
Agana-Piti Road	349	Piti-Sumay Road	178
Piti-Sumay Road	38	**Tepungan Barrio Total**	**363**
		Agana-Piti Road	363

District 11, Municipality of Sumay

Sumay			
		Total District 11	**1,211**
[no street listed]	181	Togai St	145
General Prin St	263	Velasco St	161
Guadalupe St	121	Vicente Gomez St	123
Quintero St	217		

District 12, Municipality of Yona

Yona	Total District 12	489

District 13, Naval Reservations & Ships

Naval Reservations & Ships			
		Total District 13	**1,119**
[unknown/illegible]	23	Piti Quarters	4
Commissary Store	16	Quarters Sumay	2
Government House	5	Radio	34
Marine Barracks	529	Rudes Hill	7
Marine Quarters	53	U.S. Naval Hospital	82
Naval Station Guam	9	U.S. Naval Station	67
Navy [illegible]	16	U.S.S Gold Star	143
Navy Station	3	U.S.S Penguin	40
Navy Yard, Piti	64	U.S.S. R.L. Barnes	22

Interesting Facts, Observations & Tips

Race[13]

Race	Transcribed	Official	Difference
Cha - Chamorro	16,503	16,402	101
Chin – Chinese	191	203	-12
Fil – Filipino	339	365	-26
Jap – Japanese	292	297	-5
Neg – Negro[14]	9	37	-28
PR – Puerto Rican	1		1
Span – Spanish	7		7
W - White	1,167	1,205	-38
W part – Part White	1		1
W Span – White Spanish	2		2
Total Population	18,512	18,509	3

[13] I compared my transcription with the official race count and noted some variable differences.
[14] The official census category reported "Negro and other colored."

Age Range[15]

Age/Range	0	1	2	3	4	5	6	7	8	9	
	704	660	626	628	557	543	498	464	448	488	
0-17 yrs	**10**	**11**	**12**	**13**	**14**	**15**	**16**	**17**			**Total**
	447	429	465	400	423	431	341	358			**8,910**
Age/Range	**18**	**19**	**20**	**21**	**22**	**23**	**24**	**25**	**26**	**27**	
	385	416	393	365	391	346	305	322	333	269	
18-37 yrs	**28**	**29**	**30**	**31**	**32**	**33**	**34**	**35**	**36**	**37**	**Total**
	272	319	292	242	217	210	228	221	243	177	**5,946**
Age/Range	**38**	**39**	**40**	**41**	**42**	**43**	**44**	**45**	**46**	**47**	
	182	223	183	124	166	134	142	143	148	121	
38-57 yrs	**48**	**49**	**50**	**51**	**52**	**53**	**54**	**55**	**56**	**57**	**Total**
	132	114	129	74	110	92	110	85	109	95	**2,616**
Age/Range	**58**	**59**	**60**	**61**	**62**	**63**	**64**	**65**	**66**	**67**	
	80	82	110	56	80	74	78	66	54	53	
58-77 yrs	**68**	**69**	**70**	**71**	**72**	**73**	**74**	**75**	**76**	**77**	**Total**
	54	35	49	13	21	15	10	15	9	8	**962**
Age/Range	**78**	**79**	**80**	**81**	**82**	**83**	**84**	**85**	**86**	**87**	
	11	8	15	4	2	5	2	4	1	2	
78-98 yrs	**88**	**89**	**90**	**91**		**92-95**		**96**	**97**	**98**	**Total**
	5	3	6	3		0		1	3	2	**77**

Gender & Average Age

Gender	Count	Avg. Age
Females	8,860	22
Males	9,652	21
Illegible		1
Total	**18,512**	**21**

Oldest Residents

Julian C. Marcelo, a Filipino gentleman residing with his family in District 4, Agana-Piti Road, Agana, was 98 years old and is the oldest recorded male for the 1930 Census of Guam. The oldest female was Satunina Fernandez, a Chamorro, age 98, residing with her family in District 1, Gerona Street, Agana.

Newborns & Children[16]

There were 704 babies recorded with the age of less than one year. Nearly half the entire population (48%) of the names and information I was able to transcribe are children aged 17 and below.

[15] One person's age was illegible.

[16] The age transcription for children seven years and young appear in decimal format within this transcription vice the original recording of their age in years and months.

Top 10 Common Names

There are approximately 1,287 unique surnames transcribed from the census. Below are the top ten most common surnames, first names and the number of times each occurs in this transcription; from highest to lowest. These top ten common names are not much different from those observed from the 1920 Census.

COMMON SURNAMES	
Surname	**#**
Cruz	1,223
Santos	557
San Nicolas	429
Leon Guerrero	406
Perez	406
Castro	351
Salas	351
Camacho	350
Sablan	316
Mendiola	315

COMMON FIRST NAMES			
Male	**#**	**Female**	**#**
Jose	1,505	Maria	1,530
Juan	937	Ana	780
Jesus	726	Rosa	414
Vicente	669	Dolores	384
Francisco	532	Carmen	230
Joaquin	477	Rita	228
Antonio	393	Antonia	221
Pedro	333	Concepcion	211
Manuel	302	Josefa	201
Ignacio	202	Isabel	176

And not so surprising as well, is a list of the top 10 common surnames with first names and number occurrences found in my transcription that often presents a genealogy research challenge when very little information on the individuals is available.

COMMON LAST NAMES WITH FIRST NAMES	#
Cruz, Jose	124
Cruz, Maria	113
Cruz, Juan	75
Cruz, Ana	55
Santos, Jose	49
Cruz, Jesus	48
Cruz, Vicente	46
Santos, Maria	44
Leon Guerrero, Maria	42
Cruz, Francisco	39

Potential Duplicate Recording of Individuals

There appears to be duplicate recordings of the some individuals and families; based on the names and ages. In addition, some individuals, particularly those who may have served as Cooks or Servants at other households may have been inadvertently recorded twice. It also seems that the reason some family members may have been recorded twice and at separate locations is because they may have maintained one permanent residence and the other residence may have been for farming. This transcription identifies at least 68 people listed below may have been recorded twice in the 1930 Census of Guam.

NAME	AGE	CENSUS INFORMATION (POSSIBLE DUPLICATE)
Ada, Maria M.	15	District 1 | Municipality of Agana : Agana City (San Nicolas) | Sheet 8B/8B | Line 29 District 5 | Municipality of Agana : Machananao Barrio | Sheet 207B/30B | Line 30
Afaisen, Susana T.	54/ 59	District 5 | Municipality of Agana : Sinajana Barrio | Sheet 221/44A | Line 7 District 8 | Municipality of Agana : Inarajan Town | Sheet 253/10A | Line 18
Aguigui, Enrique C.	24	District 6 | Municipality of Agat : Agat Town | Sheet 231B/4B | Line 43 District 11 | Municipality Sumay : Sumay Town | Sheet 254/4A | Line 23
Aguon, Antonio I.	20/ 24	District 4 | Municipality of Agana : Agana City (Santa Cruz) | Sheet 155/41A | Line 4 District 5 | Municipality of Agana : Barrigada Barrio | Sheet 210/33A | Line 8
Aguon, Francisco L. (Son)	14	District 1 | Municipality of Agana : Agana City (San Nicolas) | Sheet 12B/12B District 12 | Municipality of Yona : Yona Municipality | Sheet 283B/8B | Line 41
Aguon, Pedro T.	55/ 66	District 1 | Municipality of Agana : Agana City (San Nicolas) | Sheet 12B/12B | Line 31 District 12 | Municipality of Yona : Yona Municipality | Sheet 283B/8B | Line 39
Aguon, Sabina I.	63	District 4 | Municipality of Agana : Agana City (Santa Cruz) | Sheet 155/41A | Line 3 District 5 | Municipality of Agana : Barrigada Barrio | Sheet 210/33A | Line 7
Aguon Vicente L.	18/ 17	District 1 | Municipality of Agana : Agana City (San Nicolas) | Sheet 12B/12B | Line 33 District 12 | Municipality of Yona : Yona Municipality | Sheet 283B/8B | Line 40
Aguon, Vicente T.	63	District 4 | Municipality of Agana : Agana City (Santa Cruz) | Sheet 155/41A | Line 2 District 5 | Municipality of Agana : Barrigada Barrio | Sheet 210/33A | Line 6
Anderson, Antonio Q	67/ 68	District 3 | Municipality of Agana : Agana City (San Ignacio Urban) | Sheet 105/28A | Line 10 District 5 | Municipality of Agana : Barrigada Barrio | Sheet 213B/36B | Line 39
Anderson, Joaquina M	67/ 68	District 3 | Municipality of Agana : Agana City (San Ignacio Urban) | Sheet 105/28A | Line 10 District 5 | Municipality of Agana : Barrigada Barrio | Sheet 213B/36B

NAME	AGE	CENSUS INFORMATION (POSSIBLE DUPLICATE)
		| Line 39
Anderson, Juan	27	District 3 | Municipality of Agana : Agana City (San Ignacio Urban) | Sheet 105/28A | Line 14 District 5 | Municipality of Agana : Barrigada Barrio | Sheet 213B/36B | Line 43
Anderson, Pedro M.	26/ 35	District 3 | Municipality of Agana : Agana City (San Ignacio Urban) | Sheet 105/28A | Line 23 District 5 | Municipality of Agana : Barrigada Barrio | Sheet 213B/36B | Line 44
Anderson, Rita	31/ 37	District 3 | Municipality of Agana : Agana City (San Ignacio Urban) | Sheet 105/28A | Line 12 District 5 | Municipality of Agana : Barrigada Barrio | Sheet 213B/36B | Line 41
Anderson, Ramona	31	District 3 | Municipality of Agana : Agana City (San Ignacio Urban) | Sheet 105/28A | Line 13 District 5 | Municipality of Agana : Barrigada Barrio | Sheet 213B/36B | Line 42
Arceo, Felicita S.	12	District 3 | Municipality of Agana : Agana City (San Ignacio Urban) | Sheet 98/21A | Line 17 District 3 | Municipality of Agana : Agana City (San Ignacio Urban) | Sheet 97/20A | Line 24
Babauta, Antonio B.	20/ 22	District 5 | Municipality of Agana : Yigo Barrio | Sheet 205B/28B | Line 31 District 11 | Municipality Sumay : Sumay Town | Sheet 255/5A | Line 20
Babauta, Felix SN.	21	District 6 | Municipality of Agat : Agat Town | Sheet 232B/5B | Line 50 District 11 | Municipality Sumay : Sumay Town | Sheet 275/25A | Line 15
Bautista, Ana A.	26	District 2 | Municipality of Agana : Agana City (Part of San Antonio) | Sheet 52B/17B | Line 31 District 5 | Municipality of Agana : Sinajana Barrio | Sheet 223/46A | Line 7
Bautista, Jose A.	2.3/ 2.7	District 2 | Municipality of Agana : Agana City (Part of San Antonio) | Sheet 52B/17B | Line 33 District 5 | Municipality of Agana : Sinajana Barrio | Sheet 223/46A | Line 9
Bautista, Juan A	4.5	District 2 | Municipality of Agana : Agana City (Part of San Antonio) | Sheet 52B/17B | Line 32 District 5 | Municipality of Agana : Sinajana Barrio | Sheet 223/46A | Line 8
Bautista, Manuel S	29	District 2 | Municipality of Agana : Agana City (Part of San Antonio) | Sheet 52B/17B | Line 30

NAME	AGE	CENSUS INFORMATION (POSSIBLE DUPLICATE)
		District 5 | Municipality of Agana : Sinajana Barrio | Sheet 223/46A | Line 6
Bautista, Maria A	.3/.4	District 2 | Municipality of Agana : Agana City (Part of San Antonio) | Sheet 52B/17B | Line 34 District 5 | Municipality of Agana : Sinajana Barrio | Sheet 223/46A | Line 10
Borja, Gravela/Grabela L	20/ 19	District 2 | Municipality of Agana : Agana City (Part of San Antonio) | Sheet 51B/16B | Line 38 District 2 | Municipality of Agana : Agana City (Part of San Antonio) | Sheet 59B/24B | Line 44
Cepeda, Juan C	58/ 59	District 1 | Municipality of Agana : Agana City (San Nicolas) | Sheet 16/16A | Line 7 District 12 | Municipality of Yona : Yona Municipality | Sheet 284B/9B | Line 27
Cepeda, Pancracio M	25	District 1 | Municipality of Agana : Agana City (San Nicolas) | Sheet 9/9A | Line 7 District 5 | Municipality of Agana : Yigo Barrio | Sheet 203/26A | Line 8
Chargualaf, Consolacion	14	District 10 | Municipality of Piti : Piti Town | Sheet 293b/1B | Line 26 District 11 | Municipality Sumay : Sumay Town | Sheet 263/13A | Line 24
Diaz, Concepcion/ Concepcion L	5/6	District 2 | Municipality of Agana : Agana City (Part of San Antonio) | Sheet 52B/17B | Line 27 District 5 | Municipality of Agana : Sinajana Barrio | Sheet 223/46A | Line 13
Diaz, Francisco/ Francisco L	2.3	District 2 | Municipality of Agana : Agana City (Part of San Antonio) | Sheet 52B/17B | Line 28 District 5 | Municipality of Agana : Sinajana Barrio | Sheet 223/46A | Line 14
Diaz, Juan B	31	District 2 | Municipality of Agana : Agana City (Part of San Antonio) | Sheet 52/17A | Line 25 District 5 | Municipality of Agana : Sinajana Barrio | Sheet 223/46A | Line 11
Diaz, Rosa L	23	District 2 | Municipality of Agana : Agana City (Part of San Antonio) | Sheet 52B/17B | Line 26 District 5 | Municipality of Agana : Sinajana Barrio | Sheet 223/46A | Line 12
Diaz, Veronica/ Veronica L	.3	District 2 | Municipality of Agana : Agana City (Part of San Antonio) | Sheet 52B/17B | Line 29 District 5 | Municipality of Agana : Sinajana Barrio | Sheet 223/46A | Line 15
Flores, Alfred G	7	District 2 | Municipality of Agana : Agana City (Part of San Antonio) | Sheet 43B/8B | Line 35

NAME	AGE	CENSUS INFORMATION (POSSIBLE DUPLICATE)
		District 5 | Municipality of Agana : Barrigada Barrio | Sheet 215B/38B | Line 34
Flores, Candelaria C	22	District 1 | Municipality of Agana : Agana City (San Nicolas) | Sheet 13B/13B | Line 48 District 5 | Municipality of Agana : Barrigada Barrio | Sheet 213/36A | Line 16
Flores, Pedro G	10	District 2 | Municipality of Agana : Agana City (Part of San Antonio) | Sheet 43B/8B | Line 34 District 5 | Municipality of Agana : Barrigada Barrio | Sheet 215B/38B | Line 33
Flores, Tomasa C	.1/.3	District 1 | Municipality of Agana : Agana City (San Nicolas) | Sheet 13B/13B | Line 49 District 5 | Municipality of Agana : Barrigada Barrio | Sheet 213/36A | Line 17
Leon Guerrero, Antonia F	7	District 1 | Municipality of Agana : Agana City (San Nicolas) | Sheet 26/26A | Line 1 District 5 | Municipality of Agana : Yigo Barrio | Sheet 206/29A | Line 14
Leon Guerrero, Dolores F	41/ 42	District 1 | Municipality of Agana : Agana City (San Nicolas) | Sheet 25B/25B | Line 49 District 5 | Municipality of Agana : Yigo Barrio | Sheet 206/29A | Line 12
Leon Guerrero, Maria F	8/9	District 1 | Municipality of Agana : Agana City (San Nicolas) | Sheet 25B/25B | Line 50 District 5 | Municipality of Agana : Yigo Barrio | Sheet 206/29A | Line 13
Leon Guerrero, Vicente LG	40	District 1 | Municipality of Agana : Agana City (San Nicolas) | Sheet 25B/25B | Line 48 District 5 | Municipality of Agana : Yigo Barrio | Sheet 206/29A | Line 11
Manibusan, Regina L	14/ 15	District 1 | Municipality of Agana : Agana City (San Nicolas) | Sheet 15B/15B | Line 34 District 4 | Municipality of Agana : Agana City (Santa Cruz) | Sheet 172B/58B | Line 40
Mantanona, Atanacio I/Atanasio I	34/ 35	District 1 | Municipality of Agana : Agana City (San Nicolas) | Sheet 20B/20B | Line 37 District 12 | Municipality of Yona : Yona Municipality | Sheet 279B/4B | Line 28
Muna, Felicita/Felicita D	10/ 11	District 2 | Municipality of Agana : Agana City (Part of San Antonio) | Sheet 43/8A | Line 15 District 2 | Municipality of Agana : Agana City (Part of San Antonio) | Sheet 76/41A | Line 7

NAME	AGE	CENSUS INFORMATION (POSSIBLE DUPLICATE)
Okiyama, Jesus/Jesus C.	16/ 17	District 3 | Municipality of Agana : Agana City (San Ignacio Urban) | Sheet 101B/24B | Line 41 District 6 | Municipality of Agat : Agat town | Sheet 229B/2B | Line 37
Okiyama, Maria/Maria C	3/ 2.9	District 3 | Municipality of Agana : Agana City (San Ignacio Urban) | Sheet 101B/24B | Line 42 District 6 | Municipality of Agat : Agat town | Sheet 229B/2B | Line 38
Pangelinan, Vicente T	66	District 1 | Municipality of Agana : Agana City (San Nicolas) | Sheet 12/12A | Line 13 District 5 | Municipality of Agana : Barrigada Barrio | Sheet 216B/39B | Line 34
Pereda, Margarita C	12	District 3 | Municipality of Agana : Agana City (San Ignacio Urban) | Sheet 90/13A | Line 7 District 4 | Municipality of Agana : Agana City (Santa Cruz) | Sheet 150/36A | Line 20
Perez, Victoria T	4.2/ 5	District 2 | Municipality of Agana : Agana City (Part of San Antonio) | Sheet 48B/13B | Line 36 District 9 | Municipality of Merizo : Merizo Town | Sheet 274B/5B | Line 26
Quidachay, Timoteo Q	5/6	District 2 | Municipality of Agana : Agana City (Part of San Antonio) | Sheet 72B/37B | Line 50 District 5 | Municipality of Agana : Barrigada Barrio | Sheet 178B/1B | Line 34
Quintanilla, Manuel P	36	District 2 | Municipality of Agana : Agana City (Part of Padre Palomo) | Sheet 42/7A | Line 22 District 5 | Municipality of Agana : Yigo Barrio | Sheet 203/26A | Line 7
Quitugua, Ana SN	33	District 1 | Municipality of Agana : Agana City (San Nicolas) | Sheet 13B/13B | Line 32 District 5 | Municipality of Agana : Yigo Barrio | Sheet 206/29A | Line 24
Quitugua, Francisco B	50	District 1 | Municipality of Agana : Agana City (San Nicolas) | Sheet 13B/13B | Line 31 District 5 | Municipality of Agana : Yigo Barrio | Sheet 206/29A | Line 23
Quitugua, Silvestre SN	9	District 1 | Municipality of Agana : Agana City (San Nicolas) | Sheet 13B/13B | Line 34 District 5 | Municipality of Agana : Yigo Barrio | Sheet 206B/29A | Line 1
Quitugua, Teofila SN/Theofila SN	6	District 1 | Municipality of Agana : Agana City (San Nicolas) | Sheet 13B/13B | Line 35 District 5 | Municipality of Agana : Yigo Barrio | Sheet 206B/29A | Line 2

NAME	AGE	CENSUS INFORMATION (POSSIBLE DUPLICATE)
Rosario, Pedro C	31	District 1 | Municipality of Agana : Agana City (San Nicolas) | Sheet 8/8A | Line 20 District 5 | Municipality of Agana : Barrigada Barrio | Sheet 210/33A | Line 23
Sahagon, Magdalena Q	33/ 34	District 2 | Municipality of Agana : Agana City (Part of San Antonio) | Sheet 50B/15B | Line 49 District 5 | Municipality of Agana : Dededo Barrio | Sheet 188B/11B | Line 36
Salas, Felix S	14	District 4 | Municipality of Agana : Agana City (Julale) | Sheet 137B/22B | Line 28 District 8 | Municipality of Agana : Talofofo Barrio | Sheet 266/23A | Line 18
Salas, Trinidad LG	12/ 13	District 6 | Municipality of Agat : Inaso Barrio | Sheet 249/22A | Line 11 District 11 | Municipality Sumay : Sumay Town | Sheet 254/4A | Line 4
San Nicolas, Isabel P	15	District 1 | Municipality of Agana : Agana City (San Nicolas) | Sheet 3B/3B | Line 47 District 1 | Municipality of Agana : Agana City (San Nicolas) | Sheet 22B/22B | Line 27
Shimizu, Joaquin/Joaquin T	23/ 22	District 2 | Municipality of Agana : Agana City (Part of San Antonio) | Sheet 75/40A | Line 5 District 3 | Municipality of Agana : Agana City (San Ignacio Urban) | Sheet 100B/23B | Line 43
Taitano, Alfred F./Alfred J.	20	District 2 | Municipality of Agana : Agana City (Part of Padre Palomo) | Sheet 39B/4B | Line 49 District 5 | Municipality of Agana : Barrigada Barrio | Sheet 213/36A | Line 23
Taitano, George/George F.	16	District 2 | Municipality of Agana : Agana City (Part of Padre Palomo) | Sheet 40/5A | Line 1 District 5 | Municipality of Agana : Barrigada Barrio | Sheet 213/36A | Line 25
Taitano, Herminia/Herminia F.	13/ 16	District 2 | Municipality of Agana : Agana City (Part of Padre Palomo) | Sheet 40/5A | Line 2 District 5 | Municipality of Agana : Barrigada Barrio | Sheet 213B/36B | Line 26
Taitano, Robert/Robert F	18	District 2 | Municipality of Agana : Agana City (Part of Padre Palomo) | Sheet 39B/4B | Line 50 District 5 | Municipality of Agana : Barrigada Barrio | Sheet 213/36A | Line 24
Taitano, Teddy/Teodoro F.	9/ 14	District 5 | Municipality of Agana : Barrigada Barrio | Sheet 213B/36B | Line 27

NAME	AGE	CENSUS INFORMATION (POSSIBLE DUPLICATE)
		District 7 | Municipality of Asan : Asan Town | Sheet 236B/5B | Line 50
Ungacta, Antonio/Antonio C	22/ 21	District 4 | Municipality of Agana : Agana City (Santa Cruz) | Sheet 162B/48B | Line 30 District 5 | Municipality of Agana : Barrigada Barrio | Sheet 211B/34B | Line 33
Ungacta, Domingo P	58/ 52	District 4 | Municipality of Agana : Agana City (Santa Cruz) | Sheet 162B/48B | Line 28 District 5 | Municipality of Agana : Barrigada Barrio | Sheet 211B/34B | Line 32
Yamanak, Josefina M	14/ 15	District 3 | Municipality of Agana : Agana City (San Ignacio Urban) | Sheet 100B/23B | Line 44 District 8 | Municipality of Agana : Talofofo Barrio | Sheet 263B/20B | Line 28
Yamasaki, Vicenta/Vicenta T	10/ 12	District 2 | Municipality of Agana : Agana City (Part of San Antonio) | Sheet 57/22A | Line 20 District 5 | Municipality of Agana : Tutujan Barrio | Sheet 227B/50B | Line 36

Surname Spelling Variations

And as a final observation during this transcription project are varied spellings of some surnames. This is just something to you may want to be aware of if you are searching on these names.

Surname Spelling Variations

Agualo	**Aguon**	**Benavente**	**Blas**	**Carbullido**	**Cheguina**	**Espinosa**
Aguajlo	Agoun	Benabente	Blas	Carbuillido	Chequina	Espenosa
Agualo	Aguon	Benavente	Blaz	Carbullido	Chiguina	Espinosa
		Benevente			Chiquina	

Fejeran	**Guevara**	**Gutierrez**	**Ignacio**	**Indalecio**	**Isezaki**	**Kamminga**
Fejeran	Guevera	Gutierres	Ignacio	Indalecio	Isezaki	Kaminga
Fejerang	Guevarra	Gutierrez	Ignasio	Indelecio	Ishizaki	Kamminga
	Guivara					

Manalisay	**Marion**	**Martinez**	**Megofna**	**Mesa**	**Nangauta**	**Naputi**
Manalisay	Marion	Martines	Megofna	Mesa	Nangauta	Napute
Manilisay	Marrion	Martinez	Migofna	Meza	Nanguata	Naputi

Onedera	**Pangelinan**	**Pereira**	**Quitugua**	**Respicio**	**Rodriguez**	**Sahagon**
Onedera	Pangelinan	Peraira	Quidagua	Respecio	Rodrigues	Sahagon
Onidera	Pangilinan	Pereira	Quitugua	Respicio	Rodriguez	Sahagun

Salucnamnam	**Siguenza**	**Sococo**	**Soriano**	**Sipingco**	**Taianao**	**Taijeron**
Salubnamnam	Sigenza	Sococo	Soriano	Sipingco	Taeanao	Taijeran
Saluboramnam	Siguenza	Socoro	Suriano	Sy-pingco	Taianao	Taijeron

Taijito	**Taitague**	**Taitingfong**	**Tedtaotao**	**Techaira**	**Uncangco**	**Unsiog**
Taijito	Taitague	Taitingfong	Tedtaotao	Techaira	Uncangco	Unsiog
Taijto	Taitajgue	Taitingfon	Tertaotao	Tichaira	Uncango	Unsiok
					Unchangco	

Won Pat
Won Pat
Wongpat
Wong-Pat

Sources

U.S. Census Bureau. (1930). 15th Census Population 1930, American Samoa and Guam, microfilm # T1224-2629. National Archives and Records Administration.

U.S. Census Bureau. (1930). Instructions to Enumerators. Retrieved February 9, 2012 from: http://www.census.gov/history/www/through_the_decades/census_instructions/1930_instructions.html

U.S. Census Bureau. (1931). Population-Agriculture: Final Bulletin - Guam. Retrieved February 9, 2012 from: http://www2.census.gov/prod2/decennial/documents/41169168ch2.pdf

District 1
Municipality of Agana

San Nicolas

(CHAMORRO ROOTS GENEALOGY PROJECT™ TRANSCRIPTION)
(BERNARD T. PUNZALAN / HTTP://WWW.CHAMORROROOTS.COM)

DEPARTMENT OF COMMERCE-BUREAU OF THE CENSUS
WASHINGTON

FIFTEENTH CENSUS OF THE UNITED STATES: 1930-POPULATION

THE ISLAND OF GUAM

Sheet No. 1

1

District **Municipality of Agana**
Name of Place **Agana City (San Nicolas)**
[Proper name and, also, name of class, as city, town, village, barrio, etc]

Enumeration District No. 1
Enumerated by me on **April 2, 1930** Pauline L. Dees
Enumerator

	PLACE OF ABODE			NAME	RELATION	PERSONAL DESCRIPTION				EDUCATION		NATIVITY		OCCUPATION
	Street, avenue, road, etc.	Number of dwelling house is order of visitation	Number of family in order of visitation	of each person whose place of abode on April 1, 1930, was in this family. Enter surname, first, then given name and middle initial. If any. Include every person living on April 1, 1930. Omit children born since April 1, 1930.	Relationship of this Person to the head of the family.	Sex	Color or race	Age at last birthday	Single, married, widowed or divorced	Attended school any time since Sept. 1, 1929	Whether able to read and write.	Place of birth of this person.	Whether able to speak English.	
	1	2	3	4	5	6	7	8	9	10	11	12	13	14
1		1	1	Sablan, Pedro P	Head	M	Cha	61	M	N	Y	Saipan	Y	Carpenter
2		1	1	Sablan, Ana S	Wife	F	Cha	53	M	N	Y	Guam	N	None
3		1	1	Sablan, Felix S	Son	M	Cha	23	S	N	Y	Guam	Y	Farm laborer
4		1	1	Sablan, Juan S	Son	M	Cha	18	S	N	Y	Guam	Y	Carpenter
5		1	1	Sablan, Efiginia B	Granddaughter	F	Cha	6	S	N		Guam		None
6		1	1	Leon Guerrero, Rosalia S	Granddaughter	F	Cha	13	S	N	Y	Guam	Y	None
7		1	1	Leon Guerrero, Gregorio S	Grandson	M	Cha	15	S	N	Y	Guam	Y	Farm laborer
8		1	1	Leon Guerrero, Maria	Granddaughter	F	Cha	13	S	N	Y	Guam	Y	None
9		1	1	Leon Guerrero, Brigida S	Granddaughter	F	Cha	11	S	Y	Y	Guam	Y	None
10		1	1	Leon Guerrero, Jesus S	Grandson	M	Cha	10	S	Y	Y	Guam	N	None
11		1	2	Apuron, Manuel T	Head	M	Cha	26	M	N	Y	Guam	Y	Chauffeur
12		1	2	Apuron, Ana S	Wife	F	Cha	21	M	N	Y	Guam	Y	None
13		1	3	Sablan, Gregorio S	Head	M	Cha	37	Wd	N	Y	Guam	Y	Carpenter
14		1	3	Sablan, Maria S	Daughter	F	Cha	15	S	Y	Y	Guam	Y	None
15		1	3	Sablan, Segundo S	Son	M	Cha	13	S	Y	Y	Guam	Y	None
16		1	3	Sablan, Augusto S	Son	M	Cha	12	S	Y	Y	Guam	Y	None
17		1	3	Sablan, Francisco S	Son	M	Cha	10	S	Y	Y	Guam	Y	None
18		1	3	Sablan, Matilde S	Daughter	F	Cha	5	S	N		Guam		None
19		2	4	Hughes, William R	Head	M	W	39	M	N	Y	Virginia	Y	Foreman
20		2	4	Hughes, Joaquina U	Wife	F	Cha	40	M	N	Y	Guam	Y	None
21		2	4	Hughes, Rose B	Daughter	F	Cha	8	S	Y		Guam		None
22		2	4	Hughes, Virginia	Daughter	F	Cha	6	S	Y		Guam		None
23		2	4	Hughes, Helen	Daughter	F	Cha	5	S	N		Guam		None
24		2	4	Hughes, Maud	Daughter	F	Cha	4	S	N		Guam		None
25		2	4	Hughes, Betty	Daughter	F	Cha	1.5	S	Y		Guam		None

(CHAMORRO ROOTS GENEALOGY PROJECT™ TRANSCRIPTION)
(BERNARD T. PUNZALAN / HTTP://WWW.CHAMORROROOTS.COM)

DEPARTMENT OF COMMERCE-BUREAU OF THE CENSUS
WASHINGTON

FIFTEENTH CENSUS OF THE UNITED STATES: 1930-POPULATION

THE ISLAND OF GUAM

Sheet No. 1B

1B

District **Municipality of Agana**
Name of Place **Agana City (San Nicolas)**
[Proper name and, also, name of class, as city, town, village, barrio, etc]

Enumeration District No. **1**
Enumerated by me on **April 2, 1930** Pauline L. Dees
Enumerator

	PLACE OF ABODE			NAME	RELATION	PERSONAL DESCRIPTION				EDUCATION		NATIVITY		OCCUPATION
	Street, avenue, road, etc.	Number of dwelling house in order of visitation	Number of family in order of visitation	of each person whose place of abode on April 1, 1930, was in this family. Enter surname, first, then given name and middle initial. If any. Include every person living on April 1, 1930. Omit children born since April 1, 1930.	Relationship of this Person to the head of the family.	Sex	Color or race	Age at last birthday	Single, married, widowed or divorced	Attended school any time since Sept. 1, 1929	Whether able to read and write.	Place of birth of this person.	Whether able to speak English.	
	1	2	3	4	5	6	7	8	9	10	11	12	13	14
26	Paseo	2	4	Hughes, William R jr.	Son	M	Cha	.7	S	N		Guam		None
27		3	5	Santos, Maria S	Head	F	Cha	72	Wd	N	Y	Guam	N	None
28		4	6	Tanaka, Rosa S	Head	F	Cha	43	Wd	N	Y	Guam	N	None
29		4	6	Tanaka, Rosalia S	Daughter	F	Jap	18	S	N	Y	Guam	Y	None
30		4	6	Tanaka, Carmen S	Daughter	F	Jap	17	S	N	Y	Guam	Y	None
31		4	6	Tanaka, Emeterio S	Son	M	Jap	16	S	N	Y	Guam	Y	None
32		4	6	Tanaka, Tomas S	Son	M	Jap	14	S	Y	Y	Guam	Y	None
33		4	6	Tanaka, Asuncion S	Daughter	F	Jap	13	S	Y	Y	Guam	Y	None
34		4	6	Tanaka, Remedios S	Daughter	F	Jap	12	S	Y	Y	Guam	Y	None
35		4	6	Tanaka, Jesus S	Son	M	Jap	11	S	Y	Y	Guam	Y	None
36		4	7	Cruz, Beatrice T	Head	F	Cha	19	M	N	Y	Guam	Y	None
37		4	7	Cruz, Matilde T	Daughter	F	Cha	1.8	S	N		Guam		None
38		4	7	Cruz, Teresita T	Daughter	F	Cha	.5	S	N		Guam		None
39		5	8	Diaz, Joaquin T	Head	M	Cha	28	M	N	Y	Guam	Y	Chauffeur
40		5	8	Diaz, Maria T	Wife	F	Cha	22	M	N	Y	Guam	Y	None
41		5	8	Diaz, Alfonsina T	Daughter	F	Cha	4.6	S	N		Guam		None
42		5	8	Diaz, Cecilia T	Daughter	F	Cha	3.3	S	N		Guam		None
43		5	8	Diaz, Juan T	Son	M	Cha	2.1	S	N		Guam		None
44		5	8	Diaz, Joaquin T	Son	M	Cha	.3	S	N		Guam		None
45		6	9	Scott, Sarah M	Head	F	W	43	M	N	Y	Minnesota	Y	None
46		6	9	Scott, James R jr.	Son	M	W	3.1	S	N		California	Y	None
47		7	10	Flores, Rita B	Head	F	Cha	66	Wd	N	Y	Guam	N	None
48		7	10	Flores, Manuel B	Son	M	Cha	45	S	N	Y	Guam	Y	Farmer
49		7	10	Flores, Joaquin B	Son	M	Cha	25	S	N	Y	Guam	Y	Cable operator
50		8	11	Mendiola, Joaquin B	Head	M	Cha	42	M	N	Y	Guam	Y	Farmer

DEPARTMENT OF COMMERCE-BUREAU OF THE CENSUS
WASHINGTON

FIFTEENTH CENSUS OF THE UNITED STATES: 1930-POPULATION

THE ISLAND OF GUAM

Sheet No. 2A

District **Municipality of Agana**
Name of Place **Agana City (San Nicolas)**
[Proper name and, also, name of class, as city, town, village, barrio, etc]

Enumeration District No. **1**
Enumerated by me on **April 3, 1930** Pauline L. Dees, Enumerator

	PLACE OF ABODE			NAME	RELATION	PERSONAL DESCRIPTION				EDUCATION		NATIVITY		OCCUPATION
	Street, avenue, road, etc.	Number of dwelling house is order of visitation	Number of family in order of visitation	of each person whose place of abode on April 1, 1930, was in this family. Enter surname, first, then given name and middle initial. If any. Include every person living on April 1, 1930. Omit children born since April 1, 1930.	Relationship of this Person to the head of the family.	Sex	Color or race	Age at last birthday	Single, married, widowed or divorced	Attended school any time since Sept. 1, 1929	Whether able to read and write.	Place of birth of this person.	Whether able to speak English.	
	1	2	3	4	5	6	7	8	9	10	11	12	13	14
1	Paseo	8	11	Mendiola, Maria P	Wife	F	Cha	35	M	N	Y	Guam	N	None
2		8	11	Mendiola, Pedro P	Son	M	Cha	14	S	Y	Y	Guam	Y	None
3		8	11	Mendiola, Antonio P	Son	M	Cha	13	S	Y	Y	Guam	Y	None
4		8	11	Mendiola, Soledad P	Daughter	F	Cha	11	S	Y	Y	Guam	Y	None
5		8	11	Mendiola, Vicente P	Son	M	Cha	9	S	Y		Guam		None
6		8	11	Mendiola, Francisco P	Son	M	Cha	1.1	S	N		Guam		None
7		8	12	Evangelista, Apolonio E	Head	M	Cha	45	M	N	Y	Guam	N	Farmer
8		8	12	Evangelista, Josefa M	Wife	F	Cha	46	M	N	Y	Guam	N	None
9		8	12	Evangelista, Jose M	Son	M	Cha	25	S	N	Y	Guam	Y	Farm laborer
10		8	12	Evangelista, Jesus M	Son	M	Cha	19	S	N	Y	Guam	Y	None
11		8	12	Evangelista, Ana M	Daughter	F	Cha	17	S	N	Y	Guam	Y	None
12		8	12	Evangelista, Vicente M	Son	M	Cha	15	S	Y	Y	Guam	Y	None
13		9	13	Mendiola, Filomena U	Head	F	Cha	49	Wd	N	Y	Guam	N	None
14		9	14	Palomo, Joaquin B	Head	M	Cha	29	M	N	Y	Guam	Y	Farmer
15		9	14	Palomo, Joaquina M	Wife	F	Cha	25	M	N	Y	Guam	Y	None
16		9	14	Palomo, Maria M	Daughter	F	Cha	8	S	Y		Guam		None
17		9	14	Palomo, Joaquin M	Son	M	Cha	6	S	N		Guam		None
18		9	14	Palomo, Vicente M	Son	M	Cha	3.8	S	N		Guam		None
19		9	14	Palomo, Concepcion M	Daughter	F	Cha	1.3	S	N		Guam		None
20		9	14	Cruz, Maria T	Servant	F	Cha	18	S	N	N	Guam	N	Cook
21		10	15	Arriola, Vicente R	Head	M	Cha	73	M	N	Y	Guam	N	Farmer
22		10	15	Arriola, Simona M	Wife	F	Cha	56	M	N	Y	Guam	N	None
23		10	16	Hines, Fabian D	Head	M	Neg	46	M	N	Y	Porto Rico	Y	Chauffeur
24		10	16	Hines, Maria C	Wife	F	Cha	47	M	N	N	Guam	N	None
25		10	16	Hines, Eloisa C	Daughter	F	Neg	23	s	N	Y	Saipan	Y	Cook

(CHAMORRO ROOTS GENEALOGY PROJECT™ TRANSCRIPTION)
(BERNARD T. PUNZALAN / HTTP://WWW.CHAMORROROOTS.COM)

DEPARTMENT OF COMMERCE-BUREAU OF THE CENSUS
WASHINGTON

FIFTEENTH CENSUS OF THE UNITED STATES: 1930-POPULATION

THE ISLAND OF GUAM

Sheet No. 2B

2B

District **Municipality of Agana**
Name of Place **Agana City (San Nicolas)**
[Proper name and, also, name of class, as city, town, village, barrio, etc]

Enumeration District No. **1**
Enumerated by me on **April 3, 1930** Pauline L. Dees
Enumerator

	PLACE OF ABODE			NAME	RELATION	PERSONAL DESCRIPTION				EDUCATION		NATIVITY		OCCUPATION
	Street, avenue, road, etc.	Number of dwelling house is order of visitation	Number of family in order of visitation	of each person whose place of abode on April 1, 1930, was in this family. Enter surname, first, then given name and middle initial. If any. Include every person living on April 1, 1930. Omit children born since April 1, 1930.	Relationship of this Person to the head of the family.	Sex	Color or race	Age at last birthday	Single, married, widowed or divorced	Attended school any time since Sept. 1, 1929	Whether able to read and write.	Place of birth of this person.	Whether able to speak English.	
	1	2	3	4	5	6	7	8	9	10	11	12	13	14
26	Paseo	10	16	Hines, Adolfo C	Son	M	Neg	19	S	N	Y	Guam	Y	Laborer
27		10	16	Hines, Arturo C	Son	M	Neg	17	S	N	Y	Guam	Y	Laborer
28		10	16	Hines, Bibiana C	Daughter	F	Neg	13	S	Y	Y	Guam	Y	None
29		10	16	Hines, Aurora C	Daughter	F	Neg	9	S	Y		Guam		None
30		10	16	Camacho, Aleandra	Motherin-law	F	Cha	78	Wd	N	Y	Guam	N	None
31		11	17	Mesa, Jose G	Head	M	Cha	43	M	N	Y	Guam	Y	Musician
32		11	17	Mesa, Dolores LG	Wife	F	Cha	39	M	N	Y	Guam	N	None
33		11	17	Mesa, Antonio LG	Son	M	Cha	19	S	N	Y	Guam	Y	Cook's helper
34		11	17	Mesa, Jose LG	Son	M	Cha	17	S	N	Y	Guam	Y	Farmer
35		11	17	Mesa, Juan LG	Son	M	Cha	15	S	Y	Y	Guam	Y	None
36		11	17	Mesa, Jesusa LG	Daughter	F	Cha	12	S	Y	Y	Guam	Y	None
37		11	17	Mesa, Fernando LG	Son	M	Cha	8	S	Y		Guam		None
38		11	17	Mesa, Beatrice LG	Daughter	F	Cha	7	S	Y		Guam		None
39		11	17	Mesa, Jesus LG	Son	M	Cha	4.8	S	N		Guam		None
40		11	17	Mesa, Alfredo LG	Son	M	Cha	3.7	S	N		Guam		None
41		11	17	Mesa, Vicente LG	Son	M	Cha	.3	S	N		Guam		None
42		12	18	Untalan, Luis B	Head	M	Cha	46	M	N	Y	Guam	Y	Farmer
43	Castillo	12	18	Untalan, Ignacia M	Wife	F	Cha	44	M	N	Y	Guam	N	None
44		12	18	Untalan, Juan M	Son	M	Cha	17	S	N	Y	Guam	Y	Farm laborer
45		12	18	Untalan, Jose M	Son	M	Cha	15	S	Y	Y	Guam	Y	None
46		12	18	Untalan, Jesus M	Son	M	Cha	13	S	Y	Y	Guam	Y	None
47		12	18	Untalan, Maria M	Daughter	F	Cha	10	S	Y	Y	Guam	Y	None
48		12	18	Untalan, Vicente M	Son	M	Cha	8	S	Y		Guam		None
49		12	18	Untalan, Manuel M	Son	M	Cha	6	S	N		Guam		None
50		12	18	Untalan, Fidela M	Daughter	F	Cha	3.3	S	N		Guam		None

(CHAMORRO ROOTS GENEALOGY PROJECT™ TRANSCRIPTION)
(BERNARD T. PUNZALAN / HTTP://WWW.CHAMORROROOTS.COM)

DEPARTMENT OF COMMERCE-BUREAU OF THE CENSUS
WASHINGTON

FIFTEENTH CENSUS OF THE UNITED STATES: 1930-POPULATION

THE ISLAND OF GUAM

Sheet No. 3A

District **Municipality of Agana**
Name of Place **Agana City (San Nicolas)**
[Proper name and, also, name of class, as city, town, village, barrio, etc]

Enumeration District No. **1**
Enumerated by me on **April 4, 1930** Pauline L. Dees, Enumerator

	PLACE OF ABODE			NAME	RELATION	PERSONAL DESCRIPTION				EDUCATION		NATIVITY		OCCUPATION
	Street, avenue, road, etc.	Number of dwelling house is order of visitation	Number of family in order of visitation	of each person whose place of abode on April 1, 1930, was in this family. Enter surname, first, then given name and middle initial. If any. Include every person living on April 1, 1930. Omit children born since April 1, 1930.	Relationship of this Person to the head of the family.	Sex	Color or race	Age at last birthday	Single, married, widowed or divorced	Attended school any time since Sept. 1, 1929	Whether able to read and write.	Place of birth of this person.	Whether able to speak English.	
	1	2	3	4	5	6	7	8	9	10	11	12	13	14
1	Castillo	12	18	Untalan, Rita M	Daughter	F	Cha	.6	S	N		Guam	N	None
2		13	19	Colner, Concepcion U	Head	F	Cha	31	M	N	Y	Guam	N	Teacher
3		13	19	Colner, Andy	Husband	M	W	35	M	N	Y	Austria	N	None
4		13	19	Colner, Mary U	Daughter	F	Cha	8	S	Y		Guam		None
5		13	19	Colner, Howard U	Son	M	Cha	7	S	Y		Guam		None
6		13	19	Colner, Ruth U	Daughter	F	Cha	6	S	Y		Guam		None
7		13	19	Colner, Frank U	Son	M	Cha	4.8	S	N		Guam		None
8		14	20	Rojas, Francisco A	Head	M	Cha	35	M	N	Y	Guam	Y	Farmer
9		14	20	Rojas, Antonia LG	Wife	F	Cha	32	M	N	Y	Guam	Y	None
10		14	20	Rojas, Carmen LG	Daughter	F	Cha	6	S	N		Guam		None
11		14	20	Rojas, Asuncion LG	Daughter	F	Cha	5	S	N		Guam		None
12		14	20	Rojas, Maria LG	Daughter	F	Cha	3	S	N		Guam		None
13		14	20	Rojas, Vergenia LG	Daughter	F	Cha	1.3	S	N		Guam		None
14		15	21	Blas, Manuel C	Head	M	Cha	40	M	N	Y	Guam	Y	Plumber
15		15	21	Blas, Ana C	Wife	F	Cha	37	M	N	Y	Guam	N	None
16		15	21	Blas, Ana C	Daughter	F	Cha	16	S	Y	Y	Guam	Y	None
17		15	21	Blas, Joaquin C	Son	M	Cha	14	S	Y	Y	Guam	Y	None
18		15	21	Blas, Vicente C	Son	M	Cha	12	S	Y	Y	Guam	Y	None
19		15	21	Blas, Natividad C	Daughter	F	Cha	10	S	Y	Y	Guam	Y	None
20		15	21	Blas, Maria C	Daughter	F	Cha	7	S	Y		Guam		None
21		15	21	Blas, Juan C	Son	M	Cha	5	S	N		Guam		None
22		15	21	Blas, Barbara C	Daughter	F	Cha	2.0	S	N		Guam		None
23		15	22	Cepeda, Pedro LG	Head	M	Cha	61	Wd	N	Y	Guam	Y	Farmer
24		15	22	Cepeda, Joaquina M C	Daughter	F	Cha	19	S	N	Y	Guam	Y	None
25		15	22	Cepeda, Vicente C	Son	M	Cha	17	S	N	Y	Guam	Y	Farm laborer

(CHAMORRO ROOTS GENEALOGY PROJECT™ TRANSCRIPTION)
(BERNARD T. PUNZALAN / HTTP://WWW.CHAMORROROOTS.COM)

DEPARTMENT OF COMMERCE-BUREAU OF THE CENSUS
WASHINGTON

FIFTEENTH CENSUS OF THE UNITED STATES: 1930-POPULATION

THE ISLAND OF GUAM

Sheet No. 3B

3B

District **Municipality of Agana** — Enumeration District No. **1**

Name of Place **Agana City (San Nicolas)** — Enumerated by me on **April 5, 1930** Pauline L. Dees, Enumerator

[Proper name and, also, name of class, as city, town, village, barrio, etc]

	PLACE OF ABODE			NAME	RELATION	PERSONAL DESCRIPTION				EDUCATION		NATIVITY		OCCUPATION
	Street, avenue, road, etc.	Number of dwelling house is order of visitation	Number of family in order of visitation	of each person whose place of abode on April 1, 1930, was in this family. Enter surname, first, then given name and middle initial. If any. Include every person living on April 1, 1930. Omit children born since April 1, 1930.	Relationship of this Person to the head of the family.	Sex	Color or race	Age at last birthday	Single, married, widowed or divorced	Attended school any time since Sept. 1, 1929	Whether able to read and write.	Place of birth of this person.	Whether able to speak English.	
	1	2	3	4	5	6	7	8	9	10	11	12	13	14
26	Castillo	15	22	Cepeda, Alfredo C	Son	M	Cha	15	S	Y	Y	Guam	Y	None
27		16	23	Barnham, Minnie	Head	F	W	39	M	N	Y	New Jersey	Y	None
28		17	24	Womack, Edgar	Head	M	W	62	M	N	Y	Georgia	Y	Foreman
29		17	24	Womack, Leonarda	Wife	F	Fil	39	M	N	Y	Philippines	Y	None
30		17	24	Womack, Magdalena	Stepdaughter	F	Fil	16	S	Y	Y	Philippines	Y	None
31		17	24	Womack, Francisca	Stepdaughter	F	Fil	10	S	Y	Y	Philippines	Y	None
32		18	25	Pangelinan, Nicolasa A	Head	F	Cha	29	M	N	Y	Guam	Y	None
33		19	26	Venesiano, Ana G	Head	F	Cha	46	M	N	Y	Guam	Y	None
34		19	26	Venesiano, Rosa G	Daughter	F	Cha	27	S	N	Y	Guam	Y	None
35		19	26	Venesiano, Patrick G	Son	M	Cha	17	S	N	Y	Guam	Y	None
36		19	26	Venesiano, Enrique G	Son	M	Cha	19	S	Y	Y	Guam	Y	None
37		20	17	Cruz, Jose C	Head	M	Cha	54	M	N	N	Guam	N	Farmer
38		20	17	Cruz, Ana R	Wife	F	Cha	51	M	N	Y	Guam	N	None
39		20	17	Flores, Juan A	Lodger	M	Cha	31	M	N	Y	Guam	Y	Chauffeur
40		20	17	Flores, Rosa C	Lodger	F	Cha	30	M	N	Y	Guam	Y	None
41		21	28	San Nicolas, Jose C	Head	M	Cha	60	M	N	Y	Guam	N	Farmer
42		21	28	San Nicolas, Maria P	Wife	F	Cha	57	M	N	Y	Guam	N	None
43		21	28	San Nicolas, Maria P	Daughter	F	Cha	34	S	N	Y	Guam	Y	None
44		21	28	San Nicolas, Ana P	Daughter	F	Cha	25	S	N	Y	Guam	Y	None
45		21	28	San Nicolas, Juan P	Son	M	Cha	22	S	N	Y	Guam	Y	Farm laborer
46		21	28	San Nicolas, Rosa P	Daughter	F	Cha	18	S	N	Y	Guam	Y	None
47		21	28	San Nicolas, Isabel P	Daughter	F	Cha	15	S	N	Y	Guam	Y	None
48		21	28	Pangelinan, Ana G	Sisterinlaw	F	Cha	46	S	N	Y	Guam	Y	None
49		22	29	Walton, Genevieve V	Head	F	Cha	30	M	N	Y	Missouri	Y	None
50		22	29	McGretty, Ann	Sisterinlaw	F	Cha	32	S	N	Y	Missouri	Y	None

DEPARTMENT OF COMMERCE-BUREAU OF THE CENSUS
WASHINGTON

FIFTEENTH CENSUS OF THE UNITED STATES: 1930-POPULATION

THE ISLAND OF GUAM

Sheet No. 4A

District **Municipality of Agana**
Name of Place **Agana City (San Nicolas)**
[Proper name and, also, name of class, as city, town, village, barrio, etc]

Enumeration District No. **1**
Enumerated by me on **April 5, 1930** Pauline L. Dees
Enumerator

	PLACE OF ABODE			NAME	RELATION	PERSONAL DESCRIPTION				EDUCATION		NATIVITY		OCCUPATION
	Street, avenue, road, etc.	Number of dwelling house is order of visitation	Number of family in order of visitation	of each person whose place of abode on April 1, 1930, was in this family. Enter surname, first, then given name and middle initial. If any. Include every person living on April 1, 1930. Omit children born since April 1, 1930.	Relationship of this Person to the head of the family.	Sex	Color or race	Age at last birthday	Single, married, widowed or divorced	Attended school any time since Sept. 1, 1929	Whether able to read and write.	Place of birth of this person.	Whether able to speak English.	
	1	2	3	4	5	6	7	8	9	10	11	12	13	14
1	Castillo	23	30	Blasiar, Caroline H	Head	F	W	32	M	N	Y	Nevada	Y	None
2		24	31	Guerrero, Francisco V	Head	M	Cha	38	M	N	Y	Guam	N	Farmer
3		24	31	Guerrero, Maria R	Wife	F	Cha	35	M	N	Y	Guam	Y	None
4		24	31	Guerrero, Rosalia R	Daughter	F	Cha	15	S	N	Y	Guam	Y	None
5		24	31	Guerrero, Joaquin R	Son	M	Cha	14	S	Y	Y	Guam	Y	None
6		24	31	Guerrero, Ana R	Daughter	F	Cha	11	S	Y	Y	Guam	Y	None
7		24	31	Guerrero, Vicenta R	Daughter	F	Cha	5	S	N		Guam		None
8		24	31	Guerrero, Francisca R	Daughter	F	Cha	3.3	S	N		Guam		None
9		24	31	Guerrero, Jorge R	Son	M	Cha	1	S	N		Guam		None
10		25	32	Blaz, Jose C	Head	M	Cha	42	M	N	Y	Guam	N	Farmer
11		25	32	Blaz, Pedro G	Son	M	Cha	17	S	N	Y	Guam	Y	Farm laborer
12		25	32	Blaz, Ana G	Wife	F	Cha	35	M	N	Y	Guam	Y	None
13		25	32	Blaz, Joaquin G	Son	M	Cha	18	S	N	Y	Guam	Y	None
14		25	32	Blaz, Antonia G	Daughter	F	Cha	15	S	Y	Y	Guam	Y	None
15		25	32	Blaz, Jose G	Son	M	Cha	14	S	Y	Y	Guam	Y	None
16		25	32	Blaz, Francisco G	Son	M	Cha	12	S	Y	Y	Guam	Y	None
17		25	32	Blaz, Isabel G	Daughter	F	Cha	11	S	Y	Y	Guam	Y	None
18		25	32	Blaz, Ana G	Daughter	F	Cha	10	S	Y	Y	Guam	Y	None
19		25	32	Blaz, Matilde G	Daughter	F	Cha	9	S	Y		Guam		None
20		25	32	Blaz, Maria G	Daughter	F	Cha	7	S	Y		Guam		None
21		25	32	Blaz, Jesus G	Son	M	Cha	5.9	S	N		Guam		None
22	San Nicolas	26	33	Santos, Rosa S	Head	F	Cha	65	Wd	N	N	Guam	N	None
23		26	33	Santos, Joaquina S	Daughter	F	Cha	34	S	N	N	Guam	Y	Cook
24		26	33	Santos, Jose R	Son	M	Cha	29	S	N	Y	Guam	Y	Cook
25		26	33	Santos, Nicolas S	Grandson	M	Cha	15	S	Y	Y	Guam	Y	None

DEPARTMENT OF COMMERCE-BUREAU OF THE CENSUS
WASHINGTON

FIFTEENTH CENSUS OF THE UNITED STATES: 1930-POPULATION

THE ISLAND OF GUAM

Sheet No. 4B

4B

District **Municipality of Agana**
Name of Place **Agana City (San Nicolas)**
[Proper name and, also, name of class, as city, town, village, barrio, etc]

Enumeration District No. **1**
Enumerated by me on **April 5, 1930** Pauline L. Dees
Enumerator

	PLACE OF ABODE: Street, avenue, road, etc.	Number of dwelling house in order of visitation	Number of family in order of visitation	NAME of each person whose place of abode on April 1, 1930, was in this family. Enter surname, first, then given name and middle initial. If any. Include every person living on April 1, 1930. Omit children born since April 1, 1930.	RELATION Relationship of this Person to the head of the family.	PERSONAL DESCRIPTION: Sex	Color or race	Age at last birthday	Single, married, widowed or divorced	EDUCATION: Attended school any time since Sept. 1, 1929	Whether able to read and write.	NATIVITY Place of birth of this person.	Whether able to speak English.	OCCUPATION
	1	2	3	4	5	6	7	8	9	10	11	12	13	14
26	Hernan Cortez	27	34	San Nicolas, Margarita	Head	F	Cha	50	Wd	N	Y	Guam	N	None
27		27	34	San Nicolas, Vicenta C	Daughter	F	Cha	25	S	N	Y	Guam	Y	None
28		27	34	San Nicolas, Josefina C	Grand daughter	F	Cha	1.7	S	N		Guam		None
29		27	34	San Nicolas, Alfredo C	Grandson	M	Cha	.7	S	N		Guam		None
30		28	35	Cruz, Enrique M	Head	M	Cha	29	M	N	Y	Guam	Y	Laborer
31		28	35	Cruz, Maria SN	Wife	F	Cha	28	M	N	Y	Guam	Y	None
32		28	35	Cruz, Juan SN	Son	M	Cha	2.7	S	N		Guam		None
33		28	35	Cruz, Rosario SN	Daughter	F	Cha	.5	S	N		Guam		None
34		29	36	Flores, Ignacio C	Head	M	Cha	66	M	N	Y	Guam	N	Farmer
35		29	36	Flores, Rita C	Wife	F	Cha	57	M	N	Y	Guam	N	None
36		29	36	Flores, Juan C	Son	M	Cha	28	S	N	Y	Guam	Y	Farm laborer
37		29	36	Flores, Josefa C	Daughter	F	Cha	24	S	N	Y	Guam	Y	None
38		29	36	Flores, Nicolasa C	Daughter	F	Cha	32	S	N	Y	Guam	Y	None
39		29	36	Flores, Jose C	Son	M	Cha	21	S	N	Y	Guam	Y	Carpenter
40		29	36	Flores, Juaquina C	Daughter	F	Cha	16	S	N	Y	Guam	Y	None
41		30	37	Sablan, Manuel C	Head	M	Cha	65	M	N	Y	Guam	Y	Farmer
42		30	37	Sablan, Theresa P	Daughter	F	Cha	29	S	N	Y	Guam	Y	None
43		30	37	Sablan, Cecelia S	Grand daughter	F	Cha	8	S	Y		Guam		None
44		30	37	Sablan, Dorothea S	Grand daughter	F	Cha	7	S	Y		Guam		None
45		30	37	Sablan, Diana S	Grand daughter	F	Cha	6	S	N		Guam		None
46		30	37	Sablan, Josefina S	Grand daughter	F	Cha	4	S	N		Guam		None
47		30	37	Sablan, Patricia S	Grand daughter	F	Cha	3	S	N		Guam		None
48		30	37	Sablan, Emiliana S	Grand daughter	F	Cha	.3	S	N		Guam		None
49		31	38	Manibusan, Filomena T	Head	F	Cha	63	S	N	Y	Guam	N	None
50		31	38	Manibusan, Rosa T	Sister	F	Cha	46	S	N	Y	Guam	Y	None

(CHAMORRO ROOTS GENEALOGY PROJECT™ TRANSCRIPTION)
(BERNARD T. PUNZALAN / HTTP://WWW.CHAMORROROOTS.COM)

DEPARTMENT OF COMMERCE-BUREAU OF THE CENSUS
WASHINGTON

FIFTEENTH CENSUS OF THE UNITED STATES: 1930-POPULATION

THE ISLAND OF GUAM

Sheet No. 5A

District **Municipality of Agana**
Name of Place **Agana City (San Nicolas)**
[Proper name and, also, name of class, as city, town, village, barrio, etc]

Enumeration District No. **1**
Enumerated by me on **April 7, 1930** Pauline L. Dees, Enumerator

	PLACE OF ABODE			NAME	RELATION	PERSONAL DESCRIPTION				EDUCATION		NATIVITY		OCCUPATION
	Street, avenue, road, etc.	Number of dwelling house in order of visitation	Number of family in order of visitation	of each person whose place of abode on April 1, 1930, was in this family. Enter surname, first, then given name and middle initial. If any. Include every person living on April 1, 1930. Omit children born since April 1, 1930.	Relationship of this Person to the head of the family.	Sex	Color or race	Age at last birthday	Single, married, widowed or divorced	Attended school any time since Sept. 1, 1929	Whether able to read and write.	Place of birth of this person.	Whether able to speak English.	
	1	2	3	4	5	6	7	8	9	10	11	12	13	14
1	Hernan Cortez	32	39	Palacios, Jose T	Head	M	Cha	46	M	N	Y	Guam	Y	Farmer
2		32	39	Palacios, Maria C	Wife	F	Cha	42	M	N	Y	Guam	Y	None
3		32	39	Palacios, Francisco C	Son	M	Cha	20	S	N	Y	Guam	Y	Draftsman
4		32	39	Palacios, Jose C	Son	M	Cha	18	S	N	Y	Guam	Y	Farmer
5		32	39	Palacios, Josefina C	Daughter	F	Cha	17	S	N	Y	Guam	Y	None
6		32	39	Palacios, Maria C	Daughter	F	Cha	16	S	N	Y	Guam	Y	None
7		32	39	Palacios, Francisca C	Daughter	F	Cha	15	S	Y	Y	Guam	Y	None
8		32	39	Palacios, Maria T	Mother	F	Cha	77	M	N	Y	Guam	Y	None
9		32	40	Cruz, Vicente B	Head	M	Cha	21	S	N	Y	Guam	Y	Farm laborer
10		32	40	Tenorio, Ignacio T	Nephew	M	Cha	15	S	N	Y	Guam	Y	None
11		33	41	Carlyle, Bessie E	Head	F	W	35	M	N	Y	New Mexico	Y	Teacher
12		34	42	Sargent, Sara K	Head	F	W	31	M	N	Y	Pennsylvania	Y	None
13		34	42	Sargent, Annette	Daughter	F	W	8	S	Y		Pennsylvania	Y	None
14		35	43	Bordallo, Tomas A	Head	M	W	24	M	N	Y	Guam	Y	Salesman
15		35	43	Bordallo, Concepcion T	Wife	F	W	21	M	N	Y	Guam	Y	None
16		35	43	Bordallo, Alfredo T	Son	M	W	1.4	S	N		Guam		None
17		35	43	Reyes, Juan	Employee	M	Cha	20	S	N	Y	Guam	Y	Salesman
18		35	43	Leon Guerrero, Baltazar B	Servant	M	Cha	15	S	N	Y	Guam	Y	Houseboy
19	General Terrero	36	44	McGann, Catherine W	Head	F	W	45	M	N	Y	Alabama	Y	None
20		36	44	McGann, James Jr. H	Son	M	W	4.2	S	N		Alabama		None
21		37	45	Flores, Manuel G	Head	M	Cha	44	M	N	Y	Guam	Y	Clerk
22		37	45	Flores, Remedios D	Wife	F	Cha	40	M	N	Y	Guam	Y	None
23		37	45	Flores, Francisco D	Son	M	Cha	19	S	Y	Y	Guam	Y	None
24		37	45	Flores, Enrique D	Son	M	Cha	16	S	Y	Y	Guam	Y	None
50		38	46	Pangelinan, Manuel B	Head	M	Cha	30	M	N	Y	Guam	Y	Teacher

(CHAMORRO ROOTS GENEALOGY PROJECT™ TRANSCRIPTION)
(BERNARD T. PUNZALAN / HTTP://WWW.CHAMORROROOTS.COM)

DEPARTMENT OF COMMERCE-BUREAU OF THE CENSUS
WASHINGTON

FIFTEENTH CENSUS OF THE UNITED STATES: 1930-POPULATION

THE ISLAND OF GUAM

Sheet No. 5B

5B

District Municipality of Agana
Name of Place Agana City (San Nicolas)
[Proper name and, also, name of class, as city, town, village, barrio, etc]

Enumeration District No. 1
Enumerated by me on April 7, 1930 Pauline L. Dees
Enumerator

	PLACE OF ABODE			NAME	RELATION	PERSONAL DESCRIPTION				EDUCATION		NATIVITY		OCCUPATION
	Street, avenue, road, etc.	Number of dwelling house is order of visitation	Number of family in order of visitation	of each person whose place of abode on April 1, 1930, was in this family. Enter surname, first, then given name and middle initial. If any. Include every person living on April 1, 1930. Omit children born since April 1, 1930.	Relationship of this Person to the head of the family.	Sex	Color or race	Age at last birthday	Single, married, widowed or divorced	Attended school any time since Sept. 1, 1929	Whether able to read and write.	Place of birth of this person.	Whether able to speak English.	
	1	2	3	4	5	6	7	8	9	10	11	12	13	14
26	General Terrero	38	46	Pangelinan, Elena D	Wife	F	Cha	20	M	N	Y	Guam	Y	None
27		39	47	Hong-Yee, Nieves P	Head	F	Cha	36	M	N	Y	Guam	Y	None
28		39	47	Hong-Yee, Jose P	Son	M	Chin	18	S	N	Y	Guam	Y	Dish washter
29		39	47	Hong-Yee, Joaquin P	Son	M	Chin	17	S	N	Y	Guam	Y	Farmer
30		39	47	Hong-Yee, Isabel P	Daughter	F	Chin	15	S	N	Y	Guam	Y	None
31		39	47	Hong-Yee, Jesus P	Son	M	Chin	13	S	Y	Y	Guam	Y	None
32		39	47	Hong-Yee, Francisco P	Son	M	Chin	3.9	S	N		Guam		None
33		39	47	Hong-Yee, Maria P	Daughter	F	Chin	2.3	S	N		Guam		None
34		40	48	Guerrero, Juan F	Head	M	Cha	55	M	N	Y	Guam	N	Farmer
35		40	48	Guerrero, Ana LG	Wife	F	Cha	57	M	N	Y	Guam	N	None
36		40	48	Guerrero, Pedro LG	Son	M	Cha	19	S	N	Y	Guam	Y	Surveyor
37		40	48	Guerrero, Antonia LG	Daughter	F	Cha	18	S	N	Y	Guam	Y	None
38		40	48	Guerrero, Juan LG	Son	M	Cha	17	S	N	Y	Guam	Y	Farmer
39		40	48	Guerrero, Francisca LG	Daughter	F	Cha	15	S	N	Y	Guam	Y	None
40		41	49	Perez, Concepcion S	Head	F	Cha	32	S	N	Y	Guam	Y	Wash woman
41		41	49	Blas, Natividad P	Niece	F	Cha	21	S	N	Y	Guam	Y	House girl
42		41	49	Blas, Josefa P	Niece	F	Cha	16	S	N	Y	Guam	Y	House girl
43		41	49	Blas, Carmen P	Niece	F	Cha	12	S	Y	Y	Guam	Y	None
44		41	49	Blas, Maria P	Niece	F	Cha	1.9	S	N		Guam		None
45		42	50	Crisostomo, Vicente P	Head	M	Cha	31	M	N	Y	Guam	Y	Blacksmith
46		42	50	Crisostomo, Maria R	Wife	F	Cha	28	M	N	Y	Guam	Y	None
47		42	50	Crisostomo, Luisa R	Daughter	F	Cha	3.9	S	N		Guam		None
48		42	50	Crisostomo, Attemio R	Son	M	Cha	2.2	S	N		Guam		None
49		42	50	Crisostomo, Jose R	Son	M	Cha	.1	S	N		Guam		None
50		43	51	Leon Guerrero, Maria R	Head	F	Cha	41	S	N	Y	Guam	N	None

DEPARTMENT OF COMMERCE-BUREAU OF THE CENSUS
WASHINGTON

FIFTEENTH CENSUS OF THE UNITED STATES: 1930-POPULATION

THE ISLAND OF GUAM

Sheet No. 6A

District **Municipality of Agana**
Name of Place **Agana City (San Nicolas)**
[Proper name and, also, name of class, as city, town, village, barrio, etc]

Enumeration District No. 1
Enumerated by me on **April 8, 1930** Pauline L. Dees, Enumerator

	PLACE OF ABODE: Street, avenue, road, etc.	Number of dwelling house in order of visitation	Number of family in order of visitation	NAME of each person whose place of abode on April 1, 1930, was in this family. Enter surname, first, then given name and middle initial. If any. Include every person living on April 1, 1930. Omit children born since April 1, 1930.	RELATION Relationship of this Person to the head of the family.	PERSONAL DESCRIPTION: Sex	Color or race	Age at last birthday	Single, married, widowed or divorced	EDUCATION: Attended school any time since Sept. 1, 1929	Whether able to read and write.	NATIVITY Place of birth of this person.	Whether able to speak English.	OCCUPATION
	1	2	3	4	5	6	7	8	9	10	11	12	13	14
1	General Terrero	43	51	Leon Guerrero, Antonia R	Daughter	F	Cha	7	S	Y		Guam		None
2		43	51	Leon Guerrero, Ramon G	Nephew	M	Cha	8	S	Y		Guam		None
3		44	52	Torres, Jose M	Head	M	Cha	49	M	N	Y	Guam	Y	Retail merchant
4		44	52	Torres, Maria C	Wife	F	Cha	43	M	N	Y	Guam	Y	None
5		44	52	Torres, Francisco C	Son	M	Cha	23	S	N	Y	Guam	Y	Asst Manager
6		44	52	Torres, Jose C	Son	M	Cha	19	S	N	Y	Guam	Y	Secretary
7		44	52	Torres, Felix C	Son	M	Cha	18	S	N	Y	Guam	Y	None
8		44	52	Torres, Maria C	Daughter	F	Cha	16	S	N	Y	Guam	Y	None
9		44	52	Verlardo, Evelyn C	Adopted daughter	F	Fil	4.7	S	N		Guam		None
10		44	52	Taimanglo, Ingracia Q	Servant	F	Cha	16	S	N	Y	Guam	Y	House girl
11		45	53	Kamminga, Francisco R	Head	M	W	34	M	N	Y	Guam	Y	Chauffeur
12		45	53	Kamminga, Rita T	Wife	F	Cha	35	M	N	Y	Guam	Y	None
13		45	54	Zafra, Oliva C	Head	F	Cha	23	D	N	Y	Guam	Y	Nurse
14		45	54	Castro, Sylvia Maria	Daughter	F	Cha	.8	S	N		Guam		None
15	San Nicolas Street	46	55	Leon Guerrero, Joaquina S	Head	F	Cha	30	Wd	N	Y	Guam	Y	None
16		46	55	Leon Guerrero, Josefina S	Daughter	F	Cha	11	S	Y	Y	Guam	Y	None
17		46	55	Leon Guerrero, Balbino S	Son	M	Cha	9	S	Y		Guam		None
18		46	55	Leon Guerrero, Lourdes S	Daughter	F	Cha	7	S	Y		Guam		None
19		46	55	Leon Guerrero, Carlos S	Son	M	Cha	5	S	N		Guam		None
20		46	55	Leon Guerrero, Rosario S	Daughter	F	Cha	3.5	S	N		Guam		None
21		46	56	San Nicolas, Juan R	Head	M	Cha	48	Wd	N	Y	Guam	Y	None
22		47	57	Mesa, Vicente B	Head	M	Cha	42	M	N	Y	Guam	Y	Farm laborer
23		47	57	Mesa, Antonia W	Wife	F	Cha	26	M	N	Y	Guam	Y	None
24		47	57	Mesa, Jose W	Son	M	Cha	.4	S	N		Guam		None
25		47	57	Cruz, Francisco A	Godson	M	Cha	10	S	Y	Y	Guam	Y	None

(CHAMORRO ROOTS GENEALOGY PROJECT™ TRANSCRIPTION)
(BERNARD T. PUNZALAN / HTTP://WWW.CHAMORROROOTS.COM)

DEPARTMENT OF COMMERCE-BUREAU OF THE CENSUS
WASHINGTON

FIFTEENTH CENSUS OF THE UNITED STATES: 1930-POPULATION

THE ISLAND OF GUAM

Sheet No. 6B

6B

District **Municipality of Agana**
Name of Place **Agana City (San Nicolas)**
[Proper name and, also, name of class, as city, town, village, barrio, etc]

Enumeration District No. **1**
Enumerated by me on **April 8, 1930** Pauline L. Dees
Enumerator

	PLACE OF ABODE			NAME	RELATION	PERSONAL DESCRIPTION				EDUCATION		NATIVITY		OCCUPATION
	Street, avenue, road, etc.	Number of dwelling house is order of visitation	Number of family in order of visitation	of each person whose place of abode on April 1, 1930, was in this family. Enter surname, first, then given name and middle initial. If any. Include every person living on April 1, 1930. Omit children born since April 1, 1930.	Relationship of this Person to the head of the family.	Sex	Color or race	Age at last birthday	Single, married, widowed or divorced	Attended school any time since Sept. 1, 1929	Whether able to read and write.	Place of birth of this person.	Whether able to speak English.	
	1	2	3	4	5	6	7	8	9	10	11	12	13	14
26	SN	54	58	Mesa, Jose S	Head	M	Cha	72	M	N	Y	Guam	N	Farmer
27		54	58	Mesa, Juliana B	Wife	F	Cha	77	M	N	Y	Guam	N	None
28	Gerona Street	48	59	Camacho, Maria M	Head	F	Cha	44	Wd	N	Y	Guam	Y	None
29		48	59	Camacho, Maria M	Daughter	F	Cha	21	S	N	Y	Guam	Y	None
30		48	59	Camacho, Jose M	Son	M	Cha	19	S	N	Y	Guam	Y	Farmer
31		48	59	Camacho, Ana M	Daughter	F	Cha	15	S	N	Y	Guam	Y	None
32		48	59	Camacho, Pedro M	Son	M	Cha	12	S	Y	Y	Guam	Y	None
33		48	59	Camacho, Vicente M	Son	M	Cha	10	S	Y	Y	Guam	Y	None
34		48	59	Camacho, Francisca M	Daughter	F	Cha	9	S	Y		Guam		None
35		48	59	Camacho, Dolores M	Daughter	F	Cha	7	S	Y		Guam		None
36		48	59	Camacho, Jesus M	Son	M	Cha	5	S	Y		Guam		None
37		48	59	Camacho, Aduardo M	Son	M	Cha	2	S	N		Guam		None
38		49	60	Arriola, Juana F	Head	F	Cha	66	Wd	N	Y	Guam	Y	None
39		49	60	Arriola, Antonio F	Son	M	Cha	29	S	N	Y	Guam	Y	Farmer
40		50	61	Palomo, Jesus LG	Head	M	Cha	40	M	N	Y	Guam	Y	Tw swish
41		50	61	Palomo, Irene L	Wife	F	Cha	43	M	N	Y	Guam	Y	None
42		50	61	Palomo, Rita L	Daughter	F	Cha	6	S	N		Guam		None
43		50	61	Palomo, Maria L	Daughter	F	Cha	4.4	S	N		Guam		None
44		50	61	Palomo, Joaquin L	Son	M	Cha	2	S	N		Guam		None
45		50	61	Palomo, Jose L	Son	M	Cha	.3	S	N		Guam		None
46		50	61	Mantanona, Vicenta L	Mother-in-law	F	Cha	78	S	N	Y	Guam	N	None
47		51	62	Aquiningoc, Maria F	Head	F	Cha	31	M	N	Y	Guam	Y	None
48		51	62	Aquiningoc, Josefa F	Daughter	F	Cha	10	S	Y	Y	Guam	Y	None
49		51	62	Aquiningoc, Juan F	Son	M	Cha	8	S	Y		Guam		None
50		51	62	Aquiningoc, Albano F	Son	M	Cha	2.8	S	N		Guam		None

DEPARTMENT OF COMMERCE-BUREAU OF THE CENSUS
WASHINGTON

FIFTEENTH CENSUS OF THE UNITED STATES: 1930-POPULATION

THE ISLAND OF GUAM

Sheet No. 7A

District **Municipality of Agana**
Name of Place **Agana City (San Nicolas)**
[Proper name and, also, name of class, as city, town, village, barrio, etc]

Enumeration District No. **1**
Enumerated by me on **April 8, 1930** Pauline L. Dees, Enumerator

	PLACE OF ABODE			NAME	RELATION	PERSONAL DESCRIPTION				EDUCATION		NATIVITY		OCCUPATION
	Street, avenue, road, etc.	Number of dwelling house is order of visitation	Number of family in order of visitation	of each person whose place of abode on April 1, 1930, was in this family. Enter surname, first, then given name and middle initial. If any. Include every person living on April 1, 1930. Omit children born since April 1, 1930.	Relationship of this Person to the head of the family.	Sex	Color or race	Age at last birthday	Single, married, widowed or divorced	Attended school any time since Sept. 1, 1929	Whether able to read and write.	Place of birth of this person.	Whether able to speak English.	
	1	2	3	4	5	6	7	8	9	10	11	12	13	14
1	Gerona Street	51	62	Aquiningoc, Jesus F	Son	M	Cha	.8	S	N		Guam		None
2	Gerona Street	52	63	Perez, Jesus S	Head	M	Cha	40	M	N	Y	Guam	N	Carpenter
3	Gerona Street	52	63	Perez, Concepcion D	Wife	F	Cha	31	M	N	Y	Saipan	N	None
4	Gerona Street	52	63	Perez, Pilar S D	Daughter	F	Cha	18	S	N	Y	Guam	Y	None
5	Gerona Street	52	63	Perez, Candelario S D	Son	M	Cha	17	S	N	Y	Guam	Y	Farmer
6	Gerona Street	52	63	Perez, Jose S D	Son	M	Cha	15	S	Y	Y	Guam	Y	Carpenter
7	Gerona Street	52	63	Perez, Celia D	Daughter	F	Cha	9	S	Y		Guam		None
8	Gerona Street	52	63	Perez, Remedio D	Daughter	F	Cha	7	S	Y		Guam		None
9	Gerona Street	52	63	Perez, Antonio D	Son	M	Cha	5	S	N		Guam		None
10	Gerona Street	52	63	Perez, Juan D	Son	M	Cha	4.8	S	N		Guam		None
11	Gerona Street	52	63	Perez, Helena D	Daughter	F	Cha	3.4	S	N		Guam		None
12	Gerona Street	52	63	Perez, Gregorio D	Son	M	Cha	.1	S	N		Guam		None
13	Gerona Street	53	64	Perez, Jose M	Head	M	Cha	42	M	N	Y	Guam	Y	Farmer
14	Gerona Street	53	64	Perez, Dolores F	Wife	F	Cha	35	M	N	Y	Guam	Y	None
15	Gerona Street	53	64	Perez, Jose F	Son	M	Cha	15	S	N	Y	Guam	Y	Farm laborer
16	Gerona Street	53	64	Perez, Emiliana F	Daughter	F	Cha	14	S	Y	Y	Guam	Y	None
17	Gerona Street	53	64	Perez, Juan F	Son	M	Cha	12	S	Y	Y	Guam	Y	None
18	Gerona Street	53	64	Perez, Francisco F	Son	M	Cha	9	S	Y		Guam		None
19	Gerona Street	53	64	Perez, Joaquin F	Son	M	Cha	7	S	N		Guam		None
20	Gerona Street	53	64	Perez, Maria F	Daughter	F	Cha	3.3	S	N		Guam		None
21	Gerona Street	53	64	Perez, Vicente F	Son	M	Cha	.2	S	N		Guam		None
22	Dr. Hessier Street	54	65	Leon Guerrero, Vicenta de LG	Head	F	Cha	68	Wd	N	Y	Guam	Y	None
23	Dr. Hessier Street	54	65	Leon Guerrero, Ana de LG	Daughter	F	Cha	33	S	N	Y	Guam	Y	None
24	Dr. Hessier Street	54	66	Taitingfong, Ramon C	Head	M	Cha	31	M	N	Y	Guam	Y	Machinist
25	Dr. Hessier Street	54	66	Taitingfong, Maria de LG	Wife	F	Cha	35	M	N	Y	Guam	Y	None

DEPARTMENT OF COMMERCE-BUREAU OF THE CENSUS
WASHINGTON

FIFTEENTH CENSUS OF THE UNITED STATES: 1930-POPULATION

THE ISLAND OF GUAM

Sheet No. 7B

7B

District **Municipality of Agana**
Name of Place **Agana City (San Nicolas)**
[Proper name and, also, name of class, as city, town, village, barrio, etc]

Enumeration District No. **1**
Enumerated by me on **April 10, 1930** Pauline L. Dees
Enumerator

	PLACE OF ABODE			NAME	RELATION	PERSONAL DESCRIPTION				EDUCATION		NATIVITY		OCCUPATION
	Street, avenue, road, etc.	Number of dwelling house is order of visitation	Number of family in order of visitation	of each person whose place of abode on April 1, 1930, was in this family. Enter surname, first, then given name and middle initial. If any. Include every person living on April 1, 1930. Omit children born since April 1, 1930.	Relationship of this Person to the head of the family.	Sex	Color or race	Age at last birthday	Single, married, widowed or divorced	Attended school any time since Sept. 1, 1929	Whether able to read and write.	Place of birth of this person.	Whether able to speak English.	
	1	2	3	4	5	6	7	8	9	10	11	12	13	14
26	Dr. Hessler Street	54	66	Taitingfong, Rafael de LG	Son	M	Cha	7	S	N		Guam		None
27		54	66	Taitingfong, Jose de LG	Son	M	Cha	6	S	N		Guam		None
28		54	66	Taitingfong, Ramon de LG	Son	M	Cha	3.3	S	N		Guam		None
29		54	66	Taitingfong, Concepcion de LG	Daughter	F	Cha	.3	S	N		Guam		None
30		54	66	Leon Guerrero, Juaquina S	Servant	F	Cha	15	S	N	Y	Guam	Y	House girl
31		55	67	Leon Guerrero, Ana S	Head	F	Cha	60	Wd	N	Y	Guam	Y	None
32		55	67	Leon Guerrero, Vicente S	Son	M	Cha	29	S	N	Y	Guam	Y	Machinist
33		55	67	Leon Guerrero, Ana S	Daughter	F	Cha	23	S	N	Y	Guam	Y	None
34		55	67	Leon Guerrero, Jose S	Son	M	Cha	21	S	N	Y	Guam	Y	Farmer
35		55	67	Leon Guerrero, Vicenta S	Daughter	F	Cha	16	S	N	Y	Guam	Y	None
36		56	68	Taitano, Juan M	Head	M	Cha	61	M	N	Y	Guam	Y	Farmer
37		56	68	Taitano, Catalina C	Wife	F	Cha	65	M	N	Y	Guam	N	None
38		56	68	Taitano, Juan C	Son	M	Cha	28	S	N	Y	Guam	Y	Farm laborer
39		56	68	Lujan, Catalina C	Grand daughter	F	Cha	16	S	N	Y	Guam	Y	None
40		56	69	Francisco, Jesus C	Head	M	Cha	27	M	N	Y	Guam	Y	Farmer
41		56	69	Francisco, Maria T	Wife	F	Cha	26	M	N	Y	Guam	Y	None
42		56	69	Francisco, Fidela T	Daughter	F	Cha	3.9	S	N		Guam		None
43		56	69	Francisco, Maria T	Daughter	F	Cha	1.5	S	N		Guam		None
44		56	69	Francisco, Catalina T	Daughter	F	Cha	.3	S	N		Guam		None
45		57	70	Artero, Pascual S	Head	M	W	55	Wd	N	Y	Spain	Y	Farmer
46		57	70	Artero, Antonio C	Son	M	Cha	24	S	N	Y	Guam	Y	Farm laborer
47		57	70	Artero, Isabel C	Daughter	F	Cha	23	S	N	Y	Guam	Y	None
48		57	70	Artero, Maria C	Daughter	F	Cha	21	S	N	Y	Guam	Y	None
49		57	70	Artero, Consulasion C	Daughter	F	Cha	19	S	N	Y	Guam	Y	None
50		57	70	Artero, Pascual C	Son	M	Cha	17	S	Y	Y	Guam	Y	None

(CHAMORRO ROOTS GENEALOGY PROJECT™ TRANSCRIPTION)
(BERNARD T. PUNZALAN / HTTP://WWW.CHAMORROROOTS.COM)

DEPARTMENT OF COMMERCE-BUREAU OF THE CENSUS
WASHINGTON

FIFTEENTH CENSUS OF THE UNITED STATES: 1930-POPULATION

THE ISLAND OF GUAM

Sheet No. 8A

District **Municipality of Agana**
Name of Place **Agana City (San Nicolas)**
[Proper name and, also, name of class, as city, town, village, barrio, etc]

Enumeration District No. **1**
Enumerated by me on **April 10, 1930** Pauline L. Dees
Enumerator

	PLACE OF ABODE			NAME	RELATION	PERSONAL DESCRIPTION				EDUCATION		NATIVITY		OCCUPATION
	Street, avenue, road, etc.	Number of dwelling house is order of visitation	Number of family in order of visitation	of each person whose place of abode on April 1, 1930, was in this family. Enter surname, first, then given name and middle initial. If any. Include every person living on April 1, 1930. Omit children born since April 1, 1930.	Relationship of this Person to the head of the family.	Sex	Color or race	Age at last birthday	Single, married, widowed or divorced	Attended school any time since Sept. 1, 1929	Whether able to read and write.	Place of birth of this person.	Whether able to speak English.	
	1	2	3	4	5	6	7	8	9	10	11	12	13	14
1	Dr. Hessler Street	57	70	Artero, Jose C	Son	M	Cha	15	S	Y	Y	Guam	Y	None
2		57	71	Artero, Jesus C	Head	M	Cha	26	M	N	Y	Guam	Y	Farm laborer
3		57	71	Artero, Eugenia V	Wife	F	Fil	26	M	N	Y	Philippine Island	Y	None
4		57	71	Artero, Jesus V	Son	M	Cha	3.8	S	N		Guam		None
5		57	71	Artero, Pedro V	Son	M	Cha	1	S	N		Guam		None
6		58	72	Walton, Marie F	Head	F	W	29	M	N	Y	New York	Y	None
7		58	72	Walton, Eugene L	Son	M	W	7	S	Y		Virgin Islands		None
8		59	73	Perez, Gregorio D	Head	M	Cha	28	M	N	Y	Guam	Y	Clerk
9		59	73	Perez, Enriqueta G	Wife	F	Fil	25	M	N	Y	Guam	Y	None
10		59	73	Perez, Maria G	Daughter	F	Cha	6	S	Y		Guam		None
11		59	73	Perez, Vicente G	Son	M	Cha	4.3	S	N		Guam		None
12		59	73	Perez, Gregorio G	Son	M	Cha	.5	S	N		Guam		None
13		60	74	Camacho, Vicente P	Head	M	Cha	50	M	N	Y	Guam	Y	Judge
14		60	74	Camacho, Trinidad C	Wife	F	Cha	45	M	N	Y	Guam	Y	None
15		60	74	Manibusan, Maria C	Niece	F	Cha	25	S	N	Y	Guam	Y	None
16		60	74	Manibusan, Isabel C	Niece	F	Cha	20	S	N	Y	Guam	Y	None
17		60	74	Manibusan, Julita B	Niece	F	Cha	7	S	Y		Guam		None
18		61	75	Rosario, Josefa C	Head	F	Cha	55	Wd	N	Y	Guam	N	None
19		61	75	Rosario, Terza C	Daughter	F	Cha	34	S	N	Y	Guam	Y	None
20		61	75	Rosario, Pedro C	Son	M	Cha	31	S	N	Y	Guam	Y	Farmer
21		61	75	Rosario, Jesus C	Son	M	Cha	22	S	N	Y	Guam	Y	Farm laborer
22		61	75	Rosario, Domingo C	Son	M	Cha	21	S	N	Y	Guam	Y	Farm laborer
23		61	75	Rosario, Remedios R	Granddaughter	F	Cha	17	S	N	Y	Guam	Y	None
24		61	75	Rosario, Magdalena C	Daughter	F	Cha	16	S	N	Y	Guam	Y	None
25		62	76	Epstein, Esther B	Head	F	W	32	M	N	Y	Colorado	Y	None

(CHAMORRO ROOTS GENEALOGY PROJECT™ TRANSCRIPTION)
(BERNARD T. PUNZALAN / HTTP://WWW.CHAMORROROOTS.COM)

DEPARTMENT OF COMMERCE-BUREAU OF THE CENSUS
WASHINGTON
FIFTEENTH CENSUS OF THE UNITED STATES: 1930-POPULATION
THE ISLAND OF GUAM

Sheet No. 8B

8B

District Municipality of Agana
Name of Place Agana City (San Nicolas)
[Proper name and, also, name of class, as city, town, village, barrio, etc]

Enumeration District No. 1
Enumerated by me on April 11, 1930 Pauline L. Dees
Enumerator

	PLACE OF ABODE			NAME	RELATION	PERSONAL DESCRIPTION				EDUCATION		NATIVITY		OCCUPATION
	Street, avenue, road, etc.	Number of dwelling house is order of visitation	Number of family in order of visitation	of each person whose place of abode on April 1, 1930, was in this family. Enter surname, first, then given name and middle initial. If any. Include every person living on April 1, 1930. Omit children born since April 1, 1930.	Relationship of this Person to the head of the family.	Sex	Color or race	Age at last birthday	Single, married, widowed or divorced	Attended school any time since Sept. 1, 1929	Whether able to read and write.	Place of birth of this person.	Whether able to speak English.	
	1	2	3	4	5	6	7	8	9	10	11	12	13	14
26	Dr. Hessler Street	62	76	Epstein, Minna C	Daughter	F	W	9	S	Y		Colorado	Y	None
27		63	77	Ada, Vicente B	Head	M	Cha	76	M	N	Y	Guam	N	Mason
28		63	77	Ada, Maria M	Wife	F	Cha	75	M	N	Y	Guam	N	None
29		63	77	Ada, Maria M	Niece	F	Cha	15	S	N	Y	Guam	Y	None
30		63	78	Ada, Regino M	Head	M	Cha	50	Wd	N	Y	Guam	Y	Blacksmith
31		63	78	Ada, Antonio C	Son	M	Cha	15	S	Y	Y	Guam	Y	None
32		63	78	Ada, Jose C	Son	M	Cha	12	S	Y	Y	Guam	Y	None
33		63	78	Ada, Ana C	Daughter	F	Cha	10	S	Y	Y	Guam	Y	None
34		64	79	Manibusan, Vicente T	Head	M	Cha	55	M	N	Y	Guam	Y	Farmer
35		64	79	Manibusan, Ana M	Wife	F	Cha	54	M	N	Y	Guam	N	None
36		64	79	Manibusan, Dolores M	Daughter	F	Cha	21	S	N	Y	Guam	Y	None
37		64	79	Manibusan, Juan M	Son	M	Cha	20	S	N	Y	Guam	Y	Carpenter
38		64	79	Manibusan, Maria M	Daughter	F	Cha	16	S	N	Y	Guam	Y	None
39		64	79	Manibusan, Trinidad M	Daughter	F	Cha	14	S	N	Y	Guam	Y	None
40		64	80	Aquiningoc, Isabel M	Head	F	Cha	28	M	N	Y	Guam	Y	None
41		65	81	Torres, Juan E	Head	M	Cha	58	M	N	Y	Guam	N	Farmer
42		65	81	Torres, Dolores P	Wife	F	Cha	59	M	N	Y	Guam	N	None
43		65	81	Torres, Ana P	Daughter	F	Cha	27	S	N	Y	Guam	Y	None
44		65	81	Torres, Gregorio P	Son	M	Cha	22	S	N	Y	Guam	Y	Farm laborer
45		65	81	Torres, Joaquina P	Daughter	F	Cha	20	S	N	Y	Guam	Y	None
46		65	81	Torres, Antonio P	Son	M	Cha	15	S	Y	Y	Guam	Y	None
47		65	81	Torres, Jose P	Son	M	Cha	13	S	Y	Y	Guam	Y	None
48		65	82	Camacho, Jose M	Head	M	Cha	31	M	N	Y	Guam	N	Machinist
49		65	82	Camacho, Rosa T	Wife	F	Cha	29	M	N	Y	Guam	N	None
50		66	83	Santos, Jesus R	Head	M	Cha	36	M	N	Y	Guam	N	Cook

(CHAMORRO ROOTS GENEALOGY PROJECT™ TRANSCRIPTION)
(BERNARD T. PUNZALAN / HTTP://WWW.CHAMORROROOTS.COM)

DEPARTMENT OF COMMERCE-BUREAU OF THE CENSUS
WASHINGTON

FIFTEENTH CENSUS OF THE UNITED STATES: 1930-POPULATION

THE ISLAND OF GUAM

Sheet No. 9A

District **Municipality of Agana**
Name of Place **Agana City (San Nicolas)**
[Proper name and, also, name of class, as city, town, village, barrio, etc]

Enumeration District No. **1**
Enumerated by me on **April 11, 1930** Pauline L. Dees
Enumerator

	PLACE OF ABODE			NAME	RELATION	PERSONAL DESCRIPTION				EDUCATION		NATIVITY		OCCUPATION
	Street, avenue, road, etc.	Number of dwelling house in order of visitation	Number of family in order of visitation	of each person whose place of abode on April 1, 1930, was in this family. Enter surname, first, then given name and middle initial. If any. Include every person living on April 1, 1930. Omit children born since April 1, 1930.	Relationship of this Person to the head of the family.	Sex	Color or race	Age at last birthday	Single, married, widowed or divorced	Attended school any time since Sept. 1, 1929	Whether able to read and write.	Place of birth of this person.	Whether able to speak English.	
	1	2	3	4	5	6	7	8	9	10	11	12	13	14
1	Dr. Hessler Street	66	83	Santos, Ignacia M	Wife	F	Cha	29	M	N	Y	Guam	Y	None
2		66	83	Santos, Henry M	Son	M	Cha	4.2	S	N		Guam		None
3		66	83	Santos, Jose M	Son	M	Cha	3.2	S	N		Guam		None
4		66	83	Santos, Florencio M	Son	M	Cha	.3	S	N		Guam		None
5		67	84	Cepeda, Natibida M	Head	F	Cha	59	Wd	N	Y	Guam	Y	None
6		67	84	Cepeda, Ignacia M	Daughter	F	Cha	25	S	N	Y	Guam	Y	House-girl
7		67	84	Cepeda, Pancracio M	Son	M	Cha	25	S	N	N	Guam	N	Farmer
8		67	84	Cepeda, Antonia M	Daughter	F	Cha	22	S	N	N	Guam	N	Farm-laborer
9		67	84	Cepeda, Antonio M	Son	M	Cha	18	S	N	Y	Guam	Y	None
10		67	84	Cepeda, Vicente M	Son	M	Cha	16	S	N	Y	Guam	Y	None
11		67	84	Cepeda, Leon M	Son	M	Cha	13	S	Y	Y	Guam	Y	None
12		67	84	Cepeda, Maria M	Grand daughter	F	Cha	7	S	Y		Guam		None
13		67	84	Cepeda, Charlie F	Grandson	M	Cha	2	S	N		Guam		None
14		68	85	Toves, Rosa R	Head	F	Cha	41	M	N	Y	Guam	Y	None
15		68	85	Toves, Amanda F	Adopted daugther	F	Cha	18	S	N	Y	Guam	Y	Dressmaker
16		68	85	Toves, Antonio F	Adopted son	M	Cha	21	S	N	Y	Guam	Y	Silversmith
17		68	85	Crisostomo, Augustia	Servant	F	Cha	9	S	Y		Guam		None
18		68	85	Ninaisen, Maria	Servant	F	Cha	15	S	N	Y	Guam	N	Cook
19		69	86	Cruz, Francisco M	Head	M	Cha	48	M	N	Y	Guam	Y	Machinist
20		69	86	Cruz, Asuncion P	Wife	F	Cha	42	M	N	Y	Guam	Y	None
21		69	86	Cruz, Augusto P	Son	M	Cha	18	S	N	Y	Guam	Y	Salesman
22		69	86	Cruz, Serafina P	Daughter	F	Cha	17	S	N	Y	Guam	Y	None
23		69	86	Cruz, Antonia P	Daughter	F	Cha	11	S	Y	Y	Guam	Y	None
24		69	86	Cruz, Francisco P	Son	M	Cha	9	S	Y		Guam		None
25		69	86	Cruz, Jose P	Son	M	Cha	7	S	Y		Guam		None

(CHAMORRO ROOTS GENEALOGY PROJECT™ TRANSCRIPTION)
(BERNARD T. PUNZALAN / HTTP://WWW.CHAMORROROOTS.COM)

DEPARTMENT OF COMMERCE-BUREAU OF THE CENSUS
WASHINGTON

FIFTEENTH CENSUS OF THE UNITED STATES: 1930-POPULATION

THE ISLAND OF GUAM

Sheet No. 9B

9B

District **Municipality of Agana**
Name of Place **Agana City (San Nicolas)**
[Proper name and, also, name of class, as city, town, village, barrio, etc]

Enumeration District No. 1
Enumerated by me on **April 11, 1930** Pauline L. Dees
Enumerator

	PLACE OF ABODE			NAME	RELATION	PERSONAL DESCRIPTION				EDUCATION		NATIVITY		OCCUPATION
	Street, avenue, road, etc.	Number of dwelling house in order of visitation	Number of family in order of visitation	of each person whose place of abode on April 1, 1930, was in this family. Enter surname, first, then given name and middle initial. If any. Include every person living on April 1, 1930. Omit children born since April 1, 1930.	Relationship of this Person to the head of the family.	Sex	Color or race	Age at last birthday	Single, married, widowed or divorced	Attended school any time since Sept. 1, 1929	Whether able to read and write.	Place of birth of this person.	Whether able to speak English.	
	1	2	3	4	5	6	7	8	9	10	11	12	13	14
26	Dr. Hessler Street	69	86	Cruz, Carmen P	Daughter	F	Cha	6	S	Y		Guam		None
27		69	86	Cruz, Jesus P	Son	M	Cha	3.8	S	N		Guam		None
28		69	86	Atoigue, Joaquina P	Servant	F	Cha	17	S	N	Y	Guam	N	Cook
29		70	87	Manibusan, Juan R	Head	M	Cha	65	M	N	Y	Guam	N	Farmer
30		70	87	Manibusan, Ana C	Wife	F	Cha	28	M	N	Y	Guam	Y	None
31		70	87	Manibusan, Ana C	Daughter	F	Cha	2.8	S	N		Guam		None
32		70	87	Manibusan, Juan C	Son	M	Cha	.8	S	N		Guam		None
33		71	88	Sablan, Rosa G	Head	F	Cha	21	M	N	Y	Guam	Y	Teacher
34		71	88	Sablan, Raymond G	Son	M	Cha	1.4	S	N		Guam		None
35		71	88	Quichocho, Josefa Q	Servant	F	Cha	18	S	N	Y	Guam	Y	Cook
36	Isabel La Catolica	72	89	Franquez, Joaquin I	Head	M	Cha	30	S	N	Y	Guam	Y	Clerk
37		72	89	Franquez, Ana I	Sister	F	Cha	28	Wd	N	Y	Guam	Y	None
38		72	89	Franquez, Remedios I	Sister	F	Cha	26	S	N	Y	Guam	Y	None
39		73	90	Franquez, Maria G	Head	F	Cha	29	M	N	Y	Guam	Y	None
40		73	90	Franquez, Francisco G	Son	M	Cha	8	S	Y		Guam		None
41		73	90	Franquez, Carmen G	Daughter	F	Cha	5	S	N		Guam		None
42		73	90	Franquez, Jesus G	Son	M	Cha	2.5	S	N		Guam		None
43		74	91	Rosario, Maria S	Head	F	Cha	43	S	N	Y	Guam	Y	None
44		74	91	Rosario, Carmen S	Sister	F	Cha	39	S	N	Y	Guam	Y	None
45		74	91	Rosario, Gregorio S	Nephew	M	Cha	15	S	Y	Y	Guam	Y	None
46		74	91	Rivera, Isabel R	Niece	F	Cha	25	S	N	Y	Guam	Y	None
47		74	91	Rivera, Jesus R	Nephew	M	Cha	22	S	N	Y	Guam	Y	Clerk
48		74	91	Taitano, Angel R	Nephew	M	Cha	17	S	Y	Y	Guam	Y	None
49		75	92	Mendiola, Benigno C	Head	M	Cha	56	M	N	Y	Guam	N	Farmer
50		75	92	Mendiola, Consolasion F	Wife	F	Cha	55	M	N	Y	Guam	N	None

DEPARTMENT OF COMMERCE-BUREAU OF THE CENSUS
WASHINGTON

FIFTEENTH CENSUS OF THE UNITED STATES: 1930-POPULATION

THE ISLAND OF GUAM

Sheet No. 10A

District **Municipality of Agana**
Name of Place **Agana City (San Nicolas)**
[Proper name and, also, name of class, as city, town, village, barrio, etc]

Enumeration District No. **1**
Enumerated by me on **April 12, 1930** Pauline L. Dees, Enumerator

	PLACE OF ABODE			NAME	RELATION	PERSONAL DESCRIPTION				EDUCATION		NATIVITY		OCCUPATION
	Street, avenue, road, etc.	Number of dwelling house is order of visitation	Number of family in order of visitation	of each person whose place of abode on April 1, 1930, was in this family. Enter surname, first, then given name and middle initial. If any. Include every person living on April 1, 1930. Omit children born since April 1, 1930.	Relationship of this Person to the head of the family.	Sex	Color or race	Age at last birthday	Single, married, widowed or divorced	Attended school any time since Sept. 1, 1929	Whether able to read and write.	Place of birth of this person.	Whether able to speak English.	
	1	2	3	4	5	6	7	8	9	10	11	12	13	14
1	Isabel La Catolica	75	92	Mendiola, Vicente F	Son	M	Cha	26	S	N	Y	Guam	Y	Farm laborer
2		75	92	Mendiola, Jose F	Son	M	Cha	24	S	N	Y	Guam	Y	House-boy
3		75	92	Mendiola, Rosa F	Daughter	F	Cha	16	S	Y	Y	Guam	Y	None
4		75	92	Franquez, Josefa L	Sister-in-law	F	Cha	77	S	N	Y	Guam	N	None
5		76	93	Torres, Luis E	Head	M	Cha	45	M	N	Y	Guam	Y	Farmer
6		76	93	Torres, Consolacion N	Wife	F	Cha	48	M	N	N	Guam	N	None
7		76	93	Torres, Jesus N	Son	M	Cha	29	S	N	Y	Guam	Y	Farm laborer
8		76	93	Torres, Maria N	Daughter	F	Cha	28	S	N	Y	Guam	Y	None
9		76	93	Torres, Tomas N	Son	M	Cha	19	S	N	Y	Guam	Y	Farm laborer
10		76	93	Torres, Remedio N	Daughter	F	Cha	15	S	N	Y	Guam	Y	None
11		76	93	Torres, Luis N	Son	M	Cha	14	S	Y	Y	Guam	Y	None
12		76	93	Nededog, Nicolasa N	Sister-in-law	F	Cha	68	S	N	N	Guam	N	None
13		77	94	Flores, Rosa G	Head	F	Cha	46	S	N	Y	Guam	Y	None
14		77	94	Flores, Francisca	Daughter	F	Cha	12	S	Y	Y	Guam	Y	None
15		78	95	Flores, Manuel T	Head	M	Cha	69	Wd	N	Y	Guam	N	None
16		78	95	Flores, Juan M	Son	M	Cha	29	S	N	Y	Guam	N	Farmer
17		78	95	Flores, Jesus M	Son	M	Cha	18	S	N	Y	Guam	Y	Salesman
18		78	95	Flores, Manuel M	Son	M	Cha	16	S	Y	Y	Guam	Y	None
19		79	96	Perez, Atanasio T	Head	M	Cha	55	M	N	Y	Hong Kong	Y	Chief Clerk
20		79	96	Perez, Carmen D	Wife	F	Cha	37	M	N	Y	Guam	Y	None
21		79	96	Perez, Maria T	Daughter	F	Cha	27	S	N	Y	Guam	Y	None
22		79	96	Perez, Isabel T	Daughter	F	Cha	25	S	N	Y	Guam	Y	Teacher
23		79	96	Perez, Beatrice T	Daughter	F	Cha	23	S	N	Y	Guam	Y	None
24		79	96	Perez, Brigida T	Daughter	F	Cha	18	S	N	Y	Guam	Y	None
25		79	96	Perez, David T	Grandson	M	Cha	1.8	S	N		Guam		None

DEPARTMENT OF COMMERCE-BUREAU OF THE CENSUS
WASHINGTON

FIFTEENTH CENSUS OF THE UNITED STATES: 1930-POPULATION

THE ISLAND OF GUAM

Sheet No. 10B

10B

District **Municipality of Agana**
Name of Place **Agana City (San Nicolas)**
[Proper name and, also, name of class, as city, town, village, barrio, etc]

Enumeration District No. **1**
Enumerated by me on **April 12, 1930** Pauline L. Dees
Enumerator

	PLACE OF ABODE			NAME	RELATION	PERSONAL DESCRIPTION				EDUCATION		NATIVITY		OCCUPATION
	Street, avenue, road, etc.	Number of dwelling house is order of visitation	Number of family in order of visitation	of each person whose place of abode on April 1, 1930, was in this family. Enter surname, first, then given name and middle initial. If any. Include every person living on April 1, 1930. Omit children born since April 1, 1930.	Relationship of this Person to the head of the family.	Sex	Color or race	Age at last birthday	Single, married, widowed or divorced	Attended school any time since Sept. 1, 1929	Whether able to read and write.	Place of birth of this person.	Whether able to speak English.	
	1	2	3	4	5	6	7	8	9	10	11	12	13	14
26	Isabel La Catolica	79	96	Perez, Daniel T	Grandson	M	Cha	.5	S	N		Guam		None
27		80	97	Brady, Mary R	Head	F	W	39	M	Y		Guam	Y	None
28		80	97	Brady, John A	Son	M	W	6	S	Y		Guam		None
29	San Nicolas	81	98	Ito, Genge	Head	F	Jap	49	Wd	N	Y	Japan	N	Tailor
30		81	98	Ito, Jesus S	Son	M	Jap	10	S	Y	Y	Guam	Y	None
31		81	98	Ito, Vicente S	Son	M	Jap	9	S	Y		Guam		None
32	San Juan de Letran	82	99	Gunn, Anna R	Head	F	W	29	M	N	Y	Rhode Island	Y	None
33		82	99	Gunn, Emmette Jr. F	Son	M	W	7	S	Y		California		None
34		82	99	Gunn, James D	Son	M	W	5	S	N		California		None
35		83	100	Watson, Charles L	Head	M	W	27	M	N	Y	California	Y	Radio engineer
36		83	100	Watson, Mary E	Wife	F	W	26	M	N	Y	Ohio	Y	None
37		83	100	Watson, Ann L	Daughter	F	W	.8	S	N		California	Y	None
38		84	101	Vulte, Elizabeth	Head	F	W	36	M	N	Y	Kansas	Y	None
39	San Nicolas	85	102	Takano, Vicente K	Head	M	Jap	45	M	N	Y	Japan	Y	Merchant (R&W)
40		85	102	Takano, Dolores SN	Wife	F	Cha	33	M	N	Y	Guam	Y	None
41		85	102	Takano, Luis SN	Son	M	Jap	15	S	Y	Y	Guam	Y	None
42		85	102	Takano, Carlos SN	Son	M	Jap	13	S	Y	Y	Guam	Y	None
43		85	102	Takano, Jesus SN	Son	M	Jap	8	S	Y		Guam		None
44		85	102	Takano, Jose SN	Son	M	Jap	7	S	N		Guam		None
45		85	102	Takano, Josefina SN	Daughter	F	Jap	5	S	N		Guam		None
46		85	102	Takano, Rosario SN	Daughter	F	Jap	1.4	S	N		Guam		None
47		85	102	Takano, Vicente SN	Son	M	Jap	.3	S	N		Guam		None
48		85	102	San Nicolas, Maria D	Sisterinlaw	F	Cha	37	S	N	Y	Guam	N	None
49		85	102	San Nicolas, Ana D	Sisterinlaw	F	Cha	20	S	N	Y	Guam	Y	None
50		85	102	San Nicolas, Regina D	Sisterinlaw	F	Cha	16	S	Y	Y	Guam	Y	None

DEPARTMENT OF COMMERCE-BUREAU OF THE CENSUS
WASHINGTON

FIFTEENTH CENSUS OF THE UNITED STATES: 1930-POPULATION

THE ISLAND OF GUAM

Sheet No. 11A

District **Municipality of Agana**
Name of Place **Agana City (San Nicolas)**
[Proper name and, also, name of class, as city, town, village, barrio, etc]

Enumeration District No. **1**
Enumerated by me on **April 13, 1930** Pauline L. Dees
Enumerator

	PLACE OF ABODE			NAME	RELATION	PERSONAL DESCRIPTION				EDUCATION		NATIVITY		OCCUPATION
	Street, avenue, road, etc.	Number of dwelling house is order of visitation	Number of family in order of visitation	of each person whose place of abode on April 1, 1930, was in this family. Enter surname, first, then given name and middle initial. If any. Include every person living on April 1, 1930. Omit children born since April 1, 1930.	Relationship of this Person to the head of the family.	Sex	Color or race	Age at last birthday	Single, married, widowed or divorced	Attended school any time since Sept. 1, 1929	Whether able to read and write.	Place of birth of this person.	Whether able to speak English.	
	1	2	3	4	5	6	7	8	9	10	11	12	13	14
1	San Nicolas Street	86	103	Duenas, Jose C	Head	M	Cha	44	M	N	Y	Guam	Y	Farmer
2		86	103	Duenas, Concepcion C	Wife	F	Cha	40	M	N	Y	Guam	Y	None
3		86	103	Duenas, Jose C	Son	M	Cha	19	S	Y	Y	Guam	Y	Salesman
4		86	103	Duenas, Eduardo C	Son	M	Cha	16	S	Y	Y	Guam	Y	Clerk
5		86	103	Duenas, Alfredo C	Son	M	Cha	14	S	Y	Y	Guam	Y	None
6		86	103	Duenas, Carmen C	Daughter	F	Cha	12	S	Y	Y	Guam	Y	None
7		86	103	Duenas, Cristobal C	Son	M	Cha	9	S	Y		Guam		None
8		86	103	Duenas, Concepcion C	Daughter	F	Cha	7	S	Y		Guam		None
9		86	103	Duenas, Isabel C	Daughter	F	Cha	5	S	N		Guam		None
10		86	103	Duenas, Estella C	Daughter	F	Cha	3.4	S	N		Guam		None
11		86	103	Duenas, Eliza C	Daughter	F	Cha	1.2	S	N		Guam		None
12		86	103	Duenas, Juliana R	Daughter in law	F	Cha	20	M	N	Y	Guam	Y	None
13	General Terrero Street	87	104	Ichihara, Kamekichi	Head	M	Jap	44	M	N	Y	Japan	N	Carpenter
14		87	104	Ichihara, Dolores SM	Wife	F	Cha	44	M	N	Y	Saipan	N	None
15		87	104	Ichihara, Jose SM	Son	M	Jap	18	S	N	Y	Guam	Y	None
16		87	104	Ichihara, Joaquin SM	Son	M	Jap	15	S	N	Y	Guam	Y	None
17		87	104	Ichihara, Francisco SM	Son	M	Jap	13	S	Y	Y	Guam	Y	None
18		87	104	Ichihara, Maria SM	Daughter	F	Jap	10	S	Y	Y	Guam	Y	None
19		87	104	Ichihara, Ana SM	Daughter	F	Jap	8	S	Y		Guam		None
20		87	104	Ichihara, Jesus SM	Son	M	Jap	4.9	S	N		Guam		None
21		87	104	Ichihara, Juan SM	Son	M	Jap	1.6	S	N		Guam		None
22		88	105	Francisco, Jose P	Head	M	Cha	66	M	N	Y	Guam	N	Farmer
23		88	105	Francisco, Rita F	Wife	F	Cha	49	M	N	N	Guam	N	None
24		88	105	Francisco, Jose F	Son	M	Cha	12	S	Y	Y	Guam	Y	None
25		88	105	Francisco, Ignacio F	Son	M	Cha	10	S	Y	Y	Guam	Y	None

DEPARTMENT OF COMMERCE-BUREAU OF THE CENSUS
WASHINGTON

FIFTEENTH CENSUS OF THE UNITED STATES: 1930-POPULATION

THE ISLAND OF GUAM

Sheet No. 11B

11B

District **Municipality of Agana**
Name of Place **Agana City (San Nicolas)**
[Proper name and, also, name of class, as city, town, village, barrio, etc]

Enumeration District No. **1**
Enumerated by me on **April 13, 1930** Pauline L. Dees
Enumerator

	PLACE OF ABODE			NAME	RELATION	PERSONAL DESCRIPTION				EDUCATION		NATIVITY		OCCUPATION
	Street, avenue, road, etc.	Number of dwelling house is order of visitation	Number of family in order of visitation	of each person whose place of abode on April 1, 1930, was in this family. Enter surname, first, then given name and middle initial. If any. Include every person living on April 1, 1930. Omit children born since April 1, 1930.	Relationship of this Person to the head of the family.	Sex	Color or race	Age at last birthday	Single, married, widowed or divorced	Attended school any time since Sept. 1, 1929	Whether able to read and write.	Place of birth of this person.	Whether able to speak English.	
	1	2	3	4	5	6	7	8	9	10	11	12	13	14
26	General Terrero Street	88	105	Francisco, Candelaria F	Daughter	F	Cha	9	S	Y		Guam		None
27		88	105	Francisco, Josefa F	Daughter	F	Cha	8	S	Y		Guam		None
28		88	105	Francisco, Jesus F	Son	M	Cha	6	S	N		Guam		None
29		88	105	Flores, Josefa C	Sisterinlaw	F	Cha	69	S	N	N	Guam	N	None
30		89	106	Blas, Joaquin F	Head	M	Cha	31	M	N	Y	Guam	Y	Cook
31		89	106	Blas, Asencsion R	Wife	F	Cha	28	M	N	Y	Guam	Y	None
32		89	106	Blas, Antonia R	Daughter	F	Cha	10	S	Y	Y	Guam	Y	None
33		89	106	Blas, Jesus R	Son	M	Cha	5	S	N		Guam		None
34		89	106	Blas, Maria R	Daughter	F	Cha	1.5	S	N		Guam		None
35		89	106	Blas, Beatriz R	Daughter	F	Cha	0	S	N		Guam		None
36		90	107	Blas, Dolores T	Head	F	Cha	17	M	N	Y	Guam	Y	None
37		90	107	Blas, Estella G	Daughter	F	Cha	7	S	Y		Guam		None
38		90	107	Blas, Jose G	Son	M	Cha	4.5	S	N		Guam		None
39		90	107	Blas, Maria G	Daughter	F	Cha	3.3	S	N		Guam		None
40		90	107	Atoigue, Vicente A	Servant	M	Cha	19	S	N	Y	Guam	Y	Farm laborer
41		91	108	Castro, Lucia C	Head	F	Cha	35	S	N	Y	Guam	Y	Washerwoman
42		91	108	Castro, Rosario C	Daughter	F	Cha	14	S	Y	Y	Guam	Y	None
43		91	108	Castro, Concepcion C	Daughter	F	Cha	11	S	Y	Y	Guam	Y	None
44		91	108	Castro, Jose C	Son	M	Cha	9	S	Y		Guam		None
45		91	108	Castro, Maria C	Daughter	F	Cha	6	S	N		Guam		None
46		91	108	Castro, Florencia C	Daughter	F	Cha	4.6	S	N		Guam		None
47		91	108	Castro, Leonora C	Daughter	F	Cha	2.8	S	N		Guam		None
48		91	108	Castro, Vicenta C	Mother	F	Cha	68	S	N	Y	Guam	N	None
49		92	109	Asano, Yoshijiro	Head	M	Jap	45	M	N	Y	Japan	Y	Barber
50		92	109	Asano, Maria F	Wife	F	Cha	36	M	N	Y	Guam	Y	None

DEPARTMENT OF COMMERCE-BUREAU OF THE CENSUS
WASHINGTON

FIFTEENTH CENSUS OF THE UNITED STATES: 1930-POPULATION

THE ISLAND OF GUAM

Sheet No. 12A

District Municipality of Agana
Name of Place Agana City (San Nicolas)
[Proper name and, also, name of class, as city, town, village, barrio, etc]

Enumeration District No. 1
Enumerated by me on April 13, 1930 Pauline L. Dees, Enumerator

	PLACE OF ABODE			NAME	RELATION	PERSONAL DESCRIPTION				EDUCATION		NATIVITY	Whether able to speak English.	OCCUPATION
	Street, avenue, road, etc.	Number of dwelling house is order of visitation	Number of family in order of visitation	of each person whose place of abode on April 1, 1930, was in this family. Enter surname, first, then given name and middle initial. If any. Include every person living on April 1, 1930. Omit children born since April 1, 1930.	Relationship of this Person to the head of the family.	Sex	Color or race	Age at last birthday	Single, married, widowed or divorced	Attended school any time since Sept. 1, 1929	Whether able to read and write.	Place of birth of this person.		
	1	2	3	4	5	6	7	8	9	10	11	12	13	14
1	General Terrero Street	92	109	Asano, Oliva F	Daughter	F	Jap	15	S	Y	Y	Guam	Y	None
2		92	109	Asano, Isabel F	Daughter	F	Jap	11	S	Y	Y	Guam	Y	None
3		92	109	Asano, Rita F	Daughter	F	Jap	10	S	Y	Y	Guam	Y	None
4		92	109	Asano, Vicente F	Son	M	Jap	8	S	Y		Guam		None
5		92	109	Asano, Ignacio F	Son	M	Jap	3.3	S	N		Guam		None
6		92	109	Asano, Jose F	Son	M	Jap	1.8	S	N		Guam		None
7		93	110	Aguon, Juan T	Head	M	Cha	47	M	N	Y	Guam	Y	Gardener
8		93	110	Aguon, Joaquina SN	Wife	F	Cha	44	M	N	Y	Guam	Y	None
9		93	110	Aguon, Gregorio SN	Son	M	Cha	9	S	Y		Guam		None
10		93	110	Aguon, Cristobal SN	Son	M	Cha	6	S	N		Guam		None
11		93	110	Aguon, Fidela SN	Daughter	F	Cha	4.5	S	N		Guam		None
12		93	110	Aguon, Juan SN	Son	M	Cha	.4	S	N		Guam		None
13		94	111	Pangelinan, Vicente T	Head	M	Cha	66	M	N	Y	Guam	Y	Farmer
14		94	111	Pangelinan, Ignacia C	Wife	F	Cha	49	M	N	Y	Guam	Y	None
15		94	111	Pangelinan, Francisco C	Son	M	Cha	31	S	N	Y	Guam	Y	Farm laborer
16		94	112	Cruz, Juan G	Head	M	Cha	77	M	N	Y	Guam	N	None
17		94	112	Cruz, Dolores G	Wife	F	Cha	74	M	N	Y	Guam	N	None
18		95	113	Blaz, Gregorio B	Head	M	Cha	64	Wd	N	Y	Guam	Y	None
19		95	113	Blaz, Juan A	Son	M	Cha	30	S	N	Y	Guam	N	Carpenter
20		95	113	Blaz, Jose A	Son	M	Cha	29	S	N	Y	Guam	N	Farmer
21		95	113	Blaz, Juliana A	Daughter	F	Cha	27	S	N	Y	Guam	Y	None
22		95	113	Blaz, Alice A	Daughter	F	Cha	19	S	N	Y	Saipan	Y	None
23		96	114	Camacho, Jose D	Head	M	Cha	39	M	N	Y	Guam	Y	Farmer
24		96	114	Camacho, Ana SN	Wife	F	Cha	39	M	N	Y	Guam	Y	None
25		96	114	Camacho, Gregorio SN	Son	M	Cha	20	S	N	Y	Guam	Y	Machinist

DEPARTMENT OF COMMERCE-BUREAU OF THE CENSUS
WASHINGTON
FIFTEENTH CENSUS OF THE UNITED STATES: 1930-POPULATION

THE ISLAND OF GUAM

Sheet No. 12B

12B

District **Municipality of Agana**
Name of Place **Agana City (San Nicolas)**
[Proper name and, also, name of class, as city, town, village, barrio, etc]

Enumeration District No. **1**
Enumerated by me on **April 14, 1930** Pauline L. Dees
Enumerator

	PLACE OF ABODE			NAME	RELATION	PERSONAL DESCRIPTION				EDUCATION		NATIVITY		OCCUPATION
	Street, avenue, road, etc.	Number of dwelling house is order of visitation	Number of family in order of visitation	of each person whose place of abode on April 1, 1930, was in this family. Enter surname, first, then given name and middle initial. If any. Include every person living on April 1, 1930. Omit children born since April 1, 1930.	Relationship of this Person to the head of the family.	Sex	Color or race	Age at last birthday	Single, married, widowed or divorced	Attended school any time since Sept. 1, 1929	Whether able to read and write.	Place of birth of this person.	Whether able to speak English.	
	1	2	3	4	5	6	7	8	9	10	11	12	13	14
26	General Terrero Street	96	114	Camacho, Jose SN	Son	M	Cha	17	S	N	Y	Guam	Y	House boy
27		96	114	Camacho, Pedro SN	Son	M	Cha	16	S	Y	Y	Guam	Y	None
28		96	114	Camacho, Jesus SN	Son	M	Cha	10	S	Y	Y	Guam	Y	None
29		96	114	Camacho, Francisco SN	Son	M	Cha	2.4	S	N		Guam		None
30		96	114	San Nicolas, Maria C	Step Motherinlaw	F	Cha	73	Wd	N	Y	Guam	N	None
31		97	115	Aguon, Pedro T	Head	M	Cha	55	Wd	N	N	Guam	N	Farmer
32		97	115	Aguon, Jesus L	Son	M	Cha	23	S	N	Y	Guam	Y	Farm laborer
33		97	115	Aguon, Vicente L	Son	M	Cha	18	S	N	Y	Guam	Y	Farm laborer
34		97	115	Aguon, Francisco L	Son	M	Cha	14	S	Y	Y	Guam	Y	None
35		97	116	Blaz, Manuel A	Head	M	Cha	34	M	N	Y	Guam	Y	Farmer
36		97	116	Blaz, Trinidad A	Wife	F	Cha	21	M	N	Y	Guam	Y	None
37		97	116	Blaz, Maria A	Daughter	F	Cha	3	S	N		Guam		None
38		97	116	Blaz, Matilde A	Daughter	F	Cha	2.2	S	N		Guam		None
39		98	117	Manibusan, Luis P	Head	M	Cha	34	M	N	N	Guam	N	Farm laborer
40		98	117	Manibusan, Ana A	Wife	F	Cha	34	M	N	Y	Guam	Y	None
41		98	117	Manibusan, Pedro A	Son	M	Cha	12	S	Y	Y	Guam	Y	None
42		98	117	Manibusan, Maria A	Daughter	F	Cha	6	S	N		Guam		None
43		98	117	Manibusan, Rosa A	Daughter	F	Cha	3.8	S	N		Guam		None
44		98	117	Manibusan, Ana A	Daughter	F	Cha	1.1	S	N		Guam		None
45		98	118	Aguon, Jose T	Head	M	Cha	65	Wd	N	Y	Guam	N	Farmer
46		99	119	Taitano, Jesus R	Head	M	Cha	24	M	N	Y	Guam	Y	Barber
47		99	119	Taitano, Rosa M	Wife	F	Cha	20	M	N	N	Guam	N	None
48		99	119	Taitano, Jesus M	Son	M	Cha	.3	S	N		Guam		None
49		99	119	Taitano, Antonio R	Brother	M	Cha	12	S	Y	Y	Guam	Y	None
50		100	120	Camacho, Francisco L	Head	M	Cha	55	M	N	Y	Guam	Y	Farmer

DEPARTMENT OF COMMERCE-BUREAU OF THE CENSUS
WASHINGTON

FIFTEENTH CENSUS OF THE UNITED STATES: 1930-POPULATION

THE ISLAND OF GUAM

Sheet No. 13A

District **Municipality of Agana**
Name of Place **Agana City (San Nicolas)**
[Proper name and, also, name of class, as city, town, village, barrio, etc]

Enumeration District No. 1
Enumerated by me on **April 14, 1930** Pauline L. Dees
Enumerator

	PLACE OF ABODE			NAME	RELATION	PERSONAL DESCRIPTION				EDUCATION		NATIVITY		OCCUPATION
	Street, avenue, road, etc.	Number of dwelling house is order of visitation	Number of family in order of visitation	of each person whose place of abode on April 1, 1930, was in this family. Enter surname, first, then given name and middle initial. If any. Include every person living on April 1, 1930. Omit children born since April 1, 1930.	Relationship of this Person to the head of the family.	Sex	Color or race	Age at last birthday	Single, married, widowed or divorced	Attended school any time since Sept. 1, 1929	Whether able to read and write.	Place of birth of this person.	Whether able to speak English.	
	1	2	3	4	5	6	7	8	9	10	11	12	13	14
1	General Terrero Street	100	120	Camacho, Vicenta R	Wife	F	Cha	60	M	N	N	Guam	N	None
2		100	120	Camacho, Maria R	Daughter	F	Cha	23	S	N	Y	Guam	Y	None
3		100	120	Camacho, Mariano R	Son	M	Cha	19	S	Y	Y	Guam	Y	Farm laborer
4		101	121	Santos, Filomena Q	Head	F	Cha	54	Wd	N	Y	Guam	N	None
5		101	121	Santos, Ignacio Q	Son	M	Cha	19	S	N	Y	Guam	Y	Farm laborer
6		101	121	Santos, Francisco Q	Son	M	Cha	15	S	Y	Y	Guam	Y	None
7		102	122	Eclavea, Lucio Q	Head	M	Fil	67	M	N	Y	Philippine Is.	N	Farmer
8		102	122	Eclavea, Tomasa R	Wife	F	Cha	59	M	N	N	Guam	N	None
9		102	122	Eclavea, Antonio R	Son	M	Fil	19	S	N	Y	Guam	Y	Surveyor
10	Gerona Street	103	123	Rosario, Vicente F	Head	M	Cha	73	M	N	N	Guam	N	None
11		103	123	Rosario, Trudis C	Wife	F	Cha	66	M	N	Y	Guam	Y	Farmer
12		103	124	Rosario, Francisco C	Head	M	Cha	33	M	N	Y	Guam	Y	Farmer
13		103	124	Rosario, Maria C	Wife	F	Cha	27	M	N	Y	Guam	Y	None
14		103	124	Rosario, Vicente C	Son	M	Cha	8	S	Y		Guam		None
15		103	124	Rosario, Francisco C	Son	M	Cha	4.7	S	N		Guam		None
16		103	124	Rosario, Jose C	Son	M	Cha	3	S	N		Guam		None
17		103	124	Rosario, Maria C	Daughter	F	Cha	1.5	S	N		Guam		None
18		103	124	Fernandez, Satunina	Grandmother	F	Cha	98	Wd	N	Y	Guam	N	None
19		104	125	Camacho, Jose O	Head	M	Cha	65	M	N	Y	Guam	N	Farmer
20		104	125	Camacho, Isabel D	Wife	F	Cha	62	M	N	N	Guam	N	None
21		104	126	Borja, Luis Q	Head	M	Cha	30	M	N	N	Guam	N	Laborer
22		104	126	Borja, Maria C	Wife	F	Cha	24	M	N	Y	Guam	Y	None
23		104	126	Borja, Jose C	Son	M	Cha	3.7	S	N		Guam		None
24		104	126	Borja, Rosa C	Daughter	F	Cha	0	S	N		Guam		None
25		105	127	Taitano, Mariano B	Head	M	Cha	45	M	N	Y	Guam	Y	Farmer

(CHAMORRO ROOTS GENEALOGY PROJECT™ TRANSCRIPTION)
(BERNARD T. PUNZALAN / HTTP://WWW.CHAMORROROOTS.COM)

DEPARTMENT OF COMMERCE-BUREAU OF THE CENSUS
WASHINGTON

FIFTEENTH CENSUS OF THE UNITED STATES: 1930-POPULATION

THE ISLAND OF GUAM

Sheet No. 13B

13B

District **Municipality of Agana**
Name of Place **Agana City (San Nicolas)**
[Proper name and, also, name of class, as city, town, village, barrio, etc]

Enumeration District No. **1**
Enumerated by me on **April 15, 1930** Pauline L. Dees
Enumerator

	PLACE OF ABODE			NAME	RELATION	PERSONAL DESCRIPTION				EDUCATION		NATIVITY		OCCUPATION
	Street, avenue, road, etc.	Number of dwelling house is order of visitation	Number of family in order of visitation	of each person whose place of abode on April 1, 1930, was in this family. Enter surname, first, then given name and middle initial. If any. Include every person living on April 1, 1930. Omit children born since April 1, 1930.	Relationship of this Person to the head of the family.	Sex	Color or race	Age at last birthday	Single, married, widowed or divorced	Attended school any time since Sept. 1, 1929	Whether able to read and write.	Place of birth of this person.	Whether able to speak English.	
	1	2	3	4	5	6	7	8	9	10	11	12	13	14
26	Gerona Street	105	127	Taitano, Trinidad C	Wife	F	Cha	50	M	N	N	Guam	N	None
27		105	127	Taitano, Maria C	Daughter	F	Cha	17	S	N	Y	Guam	Y	None
28		105	127	Taitano, Antonio C	Son	M	Cha	15	S	Y	Y	Guam	Y	None
29		105	127	Taitano, Jose C	Son	M	Cha	13	S	Y	Y	Guam	Y	None
30		105	127	Taitano, Faustina C	Daughter	F	Cha	12	S	Y	Y	Guam	Y	None
31		106	128	Quitugua, Francisco B	Head	M	Cha	49	M	N	Y	Guam	Y	Farmer
32		106	128	Quitugua, Ana SN	Wife	F	Cha	33	M	N	Y	Guam	Y	None
33		106	128	Quitugua, Jose SN	Son	M	Cha	10	S	Y	Y	Guam	Y	None
34		106	128	Quitugua, Silvestre SN	Son	M	Cha	9	S	Y		Guam		None
35		106	128	Quitugua, Theofila SN	Daughter	F	Cha	6	S	N		Guam		None
36		107	129	Cruz, Jose F	Head	M	Cha	29	M	N	Y	Guam	Y	Farmer
37		107	129	Cruz, Josefina C	Wife	F	Cha	30	M	N	Y	Guam	Y	None
38		107	129	Cruz, Antonio C	Son	M	Cha	5	S	N		Guam		None
39		107	129	Cruz, Jose C	Son	M	Cha	3.9	S	N		Guam		None
40		107	129	Cruz, Rosa C	Daughter	F	Cha	2.3	S	N		Guam		None
41		107	130	Santos, Vicente C	Head	M	Cha	22	S	N	Y	Guam	Y	Laborer
42		108	131	Camacho, Manuel SN	Head	M	Cha	45	M	N	Y	Guam	N	Farmer
43		108	131	Camacho, Ana M	Wife	F	Cha	44	M	N	Y	Guam	N	None
44		108	131	Camacho, Manuel M	Son	M	Cha	21	S	N	Y	Guam	Y	Farm laborer
45		108	131	Camacho, Ana M	Daughter	F	Cha	20	S	N	Y	Guam	Y	Laundress
46		108	131	Camacho, Alfonso M	Son	M	Cha	17	S	Y	Y	Guam	Y	None
47		108	131	Camacho, Francisco M	Son	M	Cha	15	S	N	Y	Guam	Y	Farm laborer
48		108	132	Flores, Candelaria C	Head	F	Cha	22	M	N	Y	Guam	N	None
49		108	132	Flores, Tomasa C	Daughter	F	Cha	.1	S	N		Guam		None
50		109	133	Baza, Jose B	Head	M	Cha	64	M	N	N	Guam	N	None

DEPARTMENT OF COMMERCE-BUREAU OF THE CENSUS
WASHINGTON

FIFTEENTH CENSUS OF THE UNITED STATES: 1930-POPULATION

THE ISLAND OF GUAM

Sheet No. 14A

District **Municipality of Agana**
Name of Place **Agana City (San Nicolas)**
[Proper name and, also, name of class, as city, town, village, barrio, etc]

Enumeration District No. **1**
Enumerated by me on **April 15, 1930** Pauline L. Dees
Enumerator

	PLACE OF ABODE			NAME	RELATION	PERSONAL DESCRIPTION				EDUCATION		NATIVITY		OCCUPATION
	Street, avenue, road, etc.	Number of dwelling house is order of visitation	Number of family in order of visitation	of each person whose place of abode on April 1, 1930, was in this family. Enter surname, first, then given name and middle initial. If any. Include every person living on April 1, 1930. Omit children born since April 1, 1930.	Relationship of this Person to the head of the family.	Sex	Color or race	Age at last birthday	Single, married, widowed or divorced	Attended school any time since Sept. 1, 1929	Whether able to read and write.	Place of birth of this person.	Whether able to speak English.	
	1	2	3	4	5	6	7	8	9	10	11	12	13	14
1	Gerona Street	109	133	Baza, Ramona C	Wife	F	Cha	67	M	N	N	Guam	N	None
2		110	134	Santos, Jose T	Head	M	Cha	47	M	N	Y	Guam	N	Farmer
3		110	134	Santos, Milagro C	Wife	F	Cha	42	M	N	Y	Guam	N	None
4		110	134	Santos, Gregorio C	Son	M	Cha	18	S	Y	Y	Guam	Y	None
5		110	134	Santos, Jesus C	Son	M	Cha	15	S	Y	Y	Guam	Y	None
6		110	134	Santos, Manuel C	Son	M	Cha	9	S	Y		Guam		None
7		110	134	Santos, Pedro C	Son	M	Cha	8	S	N		Guam		None
8		110	135	Santos, Miguel C	Head	M	Cha	22	M	N	Y	Guam	Y	Farm laborer
9		110	135	Santos, Maria R	Wife	F	Cha	20	M	N	Y	Guam	Y	None
10		110	135	Santos, Pedro R	Son	M	Cha	.9	S	N		Guam		None
11	Dr. Hessler Street	111	136	Roberto, Francisco S	Head	M	Cha	36	M	N	Y	Guam	N	Farmer
12		111	136	Roberto, Ana G	Wife	F	Cha	36	M	N	Y	Guam	N	None
13		111	136	Roberto, Gregorio G	Son	M	Cha	18	S	Y	Y	Saipan	Y	None
14		111	136	Roberto, Antonio G	Son	M	Cha	16	S	Y	Y	Saipan	Y	None
15		111	136	Roberto, Jose G	Son	M	Cha	13	S	Y	Y	Saipan	Y	None
16		111	136	Roberto, Amparo G	Daughter	F	Cha	11	S	Y	Y	Saipan	Y	None
17		111	136	Roberto, Pedro G	Son	M	Cha	5	S	N		Saipan		None
18		111	136	Roberto, Francisca G	Daughter	F	Cha	2.1	S	N		Saipan		None
19		112	137	Torres, Vicente A	Head	M	Cha	75	M	N	Y	Guam	Y	Farmer
20		112	137	Torres, Dolores H	Wife	F	Cha	60	M	N	Y	Guam	N	Farmer
21		112	137	Torres, Felix H	Son	M	Cha	32	S	N	Y	Guam	Y	Farm laborer
22		112	137	Torres, Maria H	Daughter	F	Cha	28	S	N	Y	Guam	Y	None
23		112	137	Torres, Josefina H	Daughter	F	Cha	26	S	N	Y	Guam	Y	None
24		112	137	Torres, Dolores H	Daughter	F	Cha	25	S	N	Y	Guam	Y	None
25		112	137	Torres, Jesus H	Son	M	Cha	22	S	N	Y	Guam	Y	Farm laborer

DEPARTMENT OF COMMERCE-BUREAU OF THE CENSUS
WASHINGTON

FIFTEENTH CENSUS OF THE UNITED STATES: 1930-POPULATION

THE ISLAND OF GUAM

Sheet No. 14B

14B

District Municipality of Agana
Name of Place Agana City (San Nicolas)
[Proper name and, also, name of class, as city, town, village, barrio, etc]

Enumeration District No. 1
Enumerated by me on April 16, 1930 Pauline L. Dees
Enumerator

	PLACE OF ABODE			NAME	RELATION	PERSONAL DESCRIPTION				EDUCATION		NATIVITY		OCCUPATION
	Street, avenue, road, etc.	Number of dwelling house is order of visitation	Number of family in order of visitation	of each person whose place of abode on April 1, 1930, was in this family. Enter surname, first, then given name and middle initial. If any. Include every person living on April 1, 1930. Omit children born since April 1, 1930.	Relationship of this Person to the head of the family.	Sex	Color or race	Age at last birthday	Single, married, widowed or divorced	Attended school any time since Sept. 1, 1929	Whether able to read and write.	Place of birth of this person.	Whether able to speak English.	
	1	2	3	4	5	6	7	8	9	10	11	12	13	14
26	Dr. Hessler Street	112	138	Torres, Luis H	Head	M	Cha	41	Wd	N	Y	Guam	Y	Farmer
27		112	138	Torres, Maria P	Daughter	F	Cha	15	S	Y	Y	Guam	Y	None
28		112	138	Torres, Josefina P	Daughter	F	Cha	12	S	Y	Y	Guam	Y	None
29		113	139	Blas, Josefa B	Head	F	Cha	28	M	N	Y	Guam	Y	None
30		113	139	Blas, Rebeca B	Daughter	F	Cha	8	S	Y		Guam		None
31		113	139	Blas, Antonia B	Daughter	F	Cha	6	S	N		Guam		None
32		113	139	Blas, Josefina B	Daughter	F	Cha	4	S	N		Guam		None
33		113	139	Blas, Carmen B	Daughter	F	Cha	4.6	S	N		Guam		None
34		113	139	Blas, Rosa B	Daughter	F	Cha	1.6	S	N		Guam		None
35		113	140	Blas, Rebeca C	Head	F	Cha	65	Wd	N	N	Guam	Y	None
36		113	140	Camacho, Carmen P	Sister	F	Cha	78	S	N	N	Guam	Y	None
37		114	141	Camacho, Jose SN	Head	M	Cha	47	M	N	N	Guam	N	Farmer
38		114	141	Camacho, Carmen C	Wife	F	Cha	46	M	N	Y	Guam	N	None
39		114	141	Camacho, Vicente C	Son	M	Cha	22	S	N	N	Guam	N	Farm laborer
40		114	141	Camacho, Jesus C	Son	M	Cha	15	S	Y	Y	Guam	Y	None
41		114	141	Camacho, Beatrice C	Daughter	F	Cha	13	S	Y	Y	Guam	Y	None
42		114	141	Camacho, Maria C	Daughter	F	Cha	11	S	Y	Y	Guam	Y	None
43		114	142	Manibusan, Joaquin P	Head	M	Cha	28	M	N	Y	Guam	Y	Farmer
44		114	142	Manibusan, Trinidad C	Wife	F	Cha	26	M	N	Y	Guam	N	None
45		114	142	Manibusan, Carmen C	Daughter	F	Cha	2.1	S	N		Guam		None
46		114	142	Manibusan, Jesus C	Son	M	Cha	.3	S	N		Guam		None
47		115	143	Villagomez, Jose C	Head	M	Cha	34	M	N	Y	Guam	Y	Farmer
48		115	143	Villagomez, Antonia U	Wife	F	Cha	35	M	N	Y	Guam	Y	Midwife
49		115	143	Villagomez, Delfin U	Son	M	Cha	8	S	Y		Guam		None
50		115	143	Villagomez, Prudencio U	Son	M	Cha	7	S	Y		Guam		None

DEPARTMENT OF COMMERCE-BUREAU OF THE CENSUS
WASHINGTON

FIFTEENTH CENSUS OF THE UNITED STATES: 1930-POPULATION

THE ISLAND OF GUAM

Sheet No. 15A

District **Municipality of Agana**

Name of Place **Agana City (San Nicolas)**
[Proper name and, also, name of class, as city, town, village, barrio, etc]

Enumeration District No. **1**

Enumerated by me on **April 16, 1930** Pauline L. Dees, Enumerator

	PLACE OF ABODE			NAME	RELATION	PERSONAL DESCRIPTION				EDUCATION		NATIVITY		OCCUPATION
	Street, avenue, road, etc.	Number of dwelling house in order of visitation	Number of family in order of visitation	of each person whose place of abode on April 1, 1930, was in this family. Enter surname, first, then given name and middle initial. If any. Include every person living on April 1, 1930. Omit children born since April 1, 1930.	Relationship of this Person to the head of the family.	Sex	Color or race	Age at last birthday	Single, married, widowed or divorced	Attended school any time since Sept. 1, 1929	Whether able to read and write.	Place of birth of this person.	Whether able to speak English.	
	1	2	3	4	5	6	7	8	9	10	11	12	13	14
1	Dr. Hessler Street	115	143	Villagomez, Jose U	Son	M	Cha	5	S	N		Guam		None
2		115	143	Villagomez, Jorge U	Son	M	Cha	4	S	N		Guam		None
3		115	143	Villagomez, Carlos U	Son	M	Cha	2.3	S	N		Guam		None
4		115	143	Villagomez, Juan U	Son	M	Cha	.7	S	N		Guam		None
5		116	144	Aguon, Joaquin LG	Head	M	Cha	59	M	N	Y	Guam	N	Farmer
6		116	144	Aguon, Soledad O	Wife	F	Cha	55	M	N	Y	Guam	N	None
7		116	144	Aguon, Concepcion O	Daughter	F	Cha	25	S	N	Y	Guam	Y	None
8		116	144	Aguon, Ignacio O	Son	M	Cha	19	S	N	Y	Guam	Y	Farm laborer
9		116	144	Aguon, Ramon O	Son	M	Cha	13	S	Y	Y	Guam	Y	None
10		116	144	Aguon, Felicidad O	Daughter	F	Cha	10	S	Y	Y	Guam	Y	None
11		116	144	Camacho, Maria O	Sisterinlaw	F	Cha	42	S	N	Y	Guam	N	None
12		117	145	Pangelinan, Jose G	Head	M	Cha	29	M	N	Y	Guam	Y	Farmer
13		117	145	Pangelinan, Maria A	Wife	F	Cha	30	M	N	Y	Guam	N	None
14		117	145	Pangelinan, Carmen A	Daughter	F	Cha	8	S	Y		Guam		None
15		117	145	Pangelinan, Pedro A	Son	M	Cha	6	S	N		Guam		None
16		117	145	Pangelinan, Enrique A	Son	M	Cha	5	S	N		Guam		None
17		117	145	Pangelinan, Vicente A	Son	M	Cha	3.6	S	N		Guam		None
18		117	145	Pangelinan, Margarita A	Daughter	F	Cha	1	S	N		Guam		None
19		118	146	Blaz, Antonio C	Head	M	Cha	37	M	N	Y	Guam	Y	Farmer
20		118	146	Blaz, Angelina E	Wife	F	Cha	32	M	N	Y	Guam	N	None
21		118	146	Blaz, Jesus E	Son	M	Cha	12	S	Y	Y	Guam	Y	None
22		118	146	Blaz, Jose E	Son	M	Cha	11	S	Y	Y	Guam	Y	None
23		118	146	Blaz, Ana E	Daughter	F	Cha	8	S	Y		Guam		None
24		118	146	Blaz, Maria E	Daughter	F	Cha	5	S	N		Guam		None
25		118	146	Blaz, Joaquin E	Son	M	Cha	1.3	S	N		Guam		None

DEPARTMENT OF COMMERCE-BUREAU OF THE CENSUS
WASHINGTON

FIFTEENTH CENSUS OF THE UNITED STATES: 1930-POPULATION

THE ISLAND OF GUAM

Sheet No. 15B

15B

District **Municipality of Agana**
Name of Place **Agana City (San Nicolas)**
[Proper name and, also, name of class, as city, town, village, barrio, etc]

Enumeration District No. **1**
Enumerated by me on **April 17, 1930** Pauline L. Dees
Enumerator

	PLACE OF ABODE			NAME	RELATION	PERSONAL DESCRIPTION				EDUCATION		NATIVITY		OCCUPATION
	Street, avenue, road, etc.	Number of dwelling house is order of visitation	Number of family in order of visitation	of each person whose place of abode on April 1, 1930, was in this family. Enter surname, first, then given name and middle initial. If any. Include every person living on April 1, 1930. Omit children born since April 1, 1930.	Relationship of this Person to the head of the family.	Sex	Color or race	Age at last birthday	Single, married, widowed or divorced	Attended school any time since Sept. 1, 1929	Whether able to read and write.	Place of birth of this person.	Whether able to speak English.	
	1	2	3	4	5	6	7	8	9	10	11	12	13	14
26	Dr. Hessler Street	118	146	Perez, Conelio E	Fatherinlaw	M	Cha	79	Wd	N	N	Guam	Y	None
27		119	147	Desa, Josefa B	Head	F	Cha	58	Wd	N	N	Guam	N	None
28		119	147	Desa, Maria D	Daughter	F	Cha	32	D	N	Y	Guam	Y	None
29		120	148	Dydasco, Maria M	Head	F	Cha	25	M	N	Y	Guam	Y	None
30		120	148	Dydasco, Maria M	Daughter	F	Cha	4.3	S	N		Guam		None
31		120	148	Dydasco, Oscar M	Son	M	Cha	3.3	S	N		Guam		None
32		120	148	Dydasco, Gale M	Son	M	Cha	2.3	S	N		Guam		None
33		120	148	Dydasco, Ester M	Daughter	F	Cha	1.1	S	N		Guam		None
34		120	148	Manibusan, Regina L	Sisterinlaw	F	Cha	14	S	Y	Y	Guam		None
35		121	149	Cepeda, Jose C	Head	M	Cha	57	M	N	Y	Guam	N	Farmer
36		121	149	Cepeda, Maria R	Wife	F	Cha	54	M	N	N	Guam	N	None
37		121	149	Cepeda, Vicente R	Son	M	Cha	18	S	N	Y	Guam	Y	Machinist
38		121	149	Cepeda, Paz R	Son	M	Cha	12	S	Y	Y	Guam	Y	None
39		122	150	McLean, Elsa N	Head	F	W	31	M	N	Y	Massachusetts	Y	None
40		123	151	Finona, Joaquin R	Head	M	Cha	45	M	N	Y	Guam	N	None
41		123	151	Finona, Antonia R	Wife	F	Cha	45	M	N	N	Guam	N	None
42		123	151	Finona, Estella R	Daughter	F	Cha	13	S	Y	Y	Guam	Y	None
43		123	151	Finona, Maria R	Daughter	F	Cha	11	S	Y	Y	Guam	Y	None
44		123	151	Finona, Rosa R	Daughter	F	Cha	9	S	Y		Guam		None
45		123	151	Finona, Engracia R	Daughter	F	Cha	8	S	Y		Guam		None
46		123	151	Finona, Elena R	Daughter	F	Cha	5	S	N		Guam		None
47		123	151	Finona, Beatres R	Daughter	F	Cha	2.9	S	N		Guam		None
48		123	151	Finona, Ana F	Sister	F	Cha	43	S	N	N	Guam	N	Washerwoman
49		124	152	Blas, Jose B	Head	M	Cha	45	M	N	Y	Guam	N	Carpenter
50		124	152	Blas, Rita B	Wife	F	Cha	22	M	N	Y	Guam	N	None

DEPARTMENT OF COMMERCE-BUREAU OF THE CENSUS
WASHINGTON

FIFTEENTH CENSUS OF THE UNITED STATES: 1930-POPULATION

THE ISLAND OF GUAM

Sheet No. 16A

District **Municipality of Agana**
Name of Place **Agana City (San Nicolas)**
[Proper name and, also, name of class, as city, town, village, barrio, etc]

Enumeration District No. **1**
Enumerated by me on **April 17, 1930** Pauline L. Dees
Enumerator

	PLACE OF ABODE			NAME	RELATION	PERSONAL DESCRIPTION				EDUCATION		NATIVITY		OCCUPATION
	Street, avenue, road, etc.	Number of dwelling house is order of visitation	Number of family in order of visitation	of each person whose place of abode on April 1, 1930, was in this family. Enter surname, first, then given name and middle initial. If any. Include every person living on April 1, 1930. Omit children born since April 1, 1930.	Relationship of this Person to the head of the family.	Sex	Color or race	Age at last birthday	Single, married, widowed or divorced	Attended school any time since Sept. 1, 1929	Whether able to read and write.	Place of birth of this person.	Whether able to speak English.	
	1	2	3	4	5	6	7	8	9	10	11	12	13	14
1	Dr. Hessler Street	124	152	Blas, Flora U	Daughter	F	Cha	19	S	Y	Y	Guam	Y	Washerwoman
2		124	152	Blas, Concepcion U	Daughter	F	Cha	16	S	N	Y	Guam	Y	Washerwoman
3		124	152	Blas, Dolores U	Daughter	F	Cha	12	S	Y	Y	Guam	Y	None
4		124	152	Blas, Rosa U	Daughter	F	Cha	8	S	Y		Guam		None
5		124	152	Blas, Heyne B	Son	M	Cha	3.5	S	N		Guam		None
6		124	152	Blas, Juan B	Son	M	Cha	1.3	S	N		Guam		None
7		125	153	Cepeda, Juan C	Head	M	Cha	59	M	N	Y	Guam	N	Farmer
8		125	153	Cepeda, Josefa B	Wife	F	Cha	60	M	N	Y	Guam	N	None
9		125	153	Cepeda, Rosa B	Daughter	F	Cha	26	S	N	Y	Guam	Y	None
10		125	153	Cepeda, Ana B	Daughter	F	Cha	21	S	N	Y	Guam	Y	None
11		125	153	Cepeda, Manuel B	Son	M	Cha	19	S	N	Y	Guam	Y	None
12		125	154	Pangelinan, Dolores C	Head	F	Cha	27	N	Y		Guam	Y	None
13		125	154	Pangelinan, Henry C	Son	M	Cha	1.7	N			Saipan		None
14		125	154	Pangelinan, Henry S	Brotherinlaw	M	Cha	13	Y	Y	Y	Saipan	Y	None
15	Magallanes Street	126	155	Flores, Jose D	Head	M	Cha	66	M	N	Y	Guam	Y	Farmer
16		126	155	Flores, Dolores SN	Wife	F	Cha	55	M	N	N	Guam	N	None
17		126	155	Flores, Ana SN	Daughter	F	Cha	19	S	N	N	Guam	Y	None
18		126	155	Flores, Jose SN	Son	M	Cha	16	S	Y	Y	Guam	Y	None
19		126	155	Flores, Joaquin SN	Son	M	Cha	13	S	Y	Y	Guam	Y	None
20		127	156	Salas, Jose C	Head	M	Cha	48	M	N	Y	Guam	N	Farmer
21		127	156	Salas, Manuela SN	Wife	F	Cha	48	M	N	Y	Guam	Y	None
22		127	156	Salas, Bartola SN	Daughter	F	Cha	18	S	N	Y	Guam	Y	None
23		127	156	Salas, Jesus SN	Son	M	Cha	16	S	N	Y	Guam	Y	Farm laborer
24		127	156	Salas, Theresa SN	Daughter	F	Cha	14	S	N	Y	Guam	Y	None
25		127	156	Salas, Ana SN	Daughter	F	Cha	12	S	Y	Y	Guam	Y	None

DEPARTMENT OF COMMERCE-BUREAU OF THE CENSUS
WASHINGTON
FIFTEENTH CENSUS OF THE UNITED STATES: 1930-POPULATION

THE ISLAND OF GUAM

Sheet No. 16B

16B

District **Municipality of Agana**
Name of Place **Agana City (San Nicolas)** [Proper name and, also, name of class, as city, town, village, barrio, etc]

Enumeration District No. **1**
Enumerated by me on **April 17, 1930** Pauline L. Dees, Enumerator

	PLACE OF ABODE			NAME	RELATION	PERSONAL DESCRIPTION				EDUCATION		NATIVITY		OCCUPATION
	Street, avenue, road, etc.	Number of dwelling house in order of visitation	Number of family in order of visitation	of each person whose place of abode on April 1, 1930, was in this family. Enter surname, first, then given name and middle initial. If any. Include every person living on April 1, 1930. Omit children born since April 1, 1930.	Relationship of this Person to the head of the family.	Sex	Color or race	Age at last birthday	Single, married, widowed or divorced	Attended school any time since Sept. 1, 1929	Whether able to read and write.	Place of birth of this person.	Whether able to speak English.	
	1	2	3	4	5	6	7	8	9	10	11	12	13	14
26	Magallanes Street	127	156	Salas, Joaquin SN	Son	M	Cha	9	S	Y		Guam		None
27		127	156	Salas, Elias SN	Son	M	Cha	7	S	Y		Guam		None
28		128	157	Castro, Maria C	Head	F	Cha	62	Wd	N	Y	Guam	N	None
29		128	157	Castro, Mariano C	Son	M	Cha	39	S	N	Y	Guam	Y	Farmer
30		128	157	Castro, Jesus C	Son	M	Cha	32	S	N	Y	Guam	Y	Farm laborer
31		128	157	Castro, Trinidad C	Daughter	F	Cha	28	S	N	Y	Guam	Y	None
32		128	157	Castro, Juan C	Son	M	Cha	26	S	N	Y	Guam	Y	Clerk
33		128	157	Castro, Vicente C	Son	M	Cha	20	S	N	N	Guam	N	None
34		129	158	Alvarez, Concepcion R	Head	F	Cha	23	M	N	Y	Guam	Y	None
35		129	158	Alvarez, Maria R	Daughter	F	Cha	4.3	S	N		Guam		None
36		130	159	Camacho, Francisco S	Head	M	Cha	54	M	N	Y	Guam	Y	Farmer
37		130	159	Camacho, Rosa S	Wife	F	Cha	55	M	N	Y	Guam	Y	None
38		130	159	Camacho, Maria S	Daughter	F	Cha	29	S	N	Y	Guam	Y	Seamstress
39		130	159	Camacho, Manuela S	Daughter	F	Cha	25	S	N	Y	Guam	Y	Seamstress
40		130	159	Camacho, Ana S	Daughter	F	Cha	22	S	N	Y	Guam	Y	None
41		130	159	Camacho, Gregorio S	Son	M	Cha	21	S	N	Y	Guam	Y	Messenger
42		130	159	Camacho, Concepcion S	Daughter	F	Cha	15	S	Y	Y	Guam	Y	None
43		130	159	Camacho, Jesus S	Son	M	Cha	13	S	Y	Y	Guam	Y	None
44		130	159	Camacho, Rosario S	Daughter	F	Cha	11	S	Y	Y	Guam	Y	None
45		130	159	Pangelinan, Maria S	Sisterinlaw	F	Cha	54	Wd	N	Y	Guam	N	None
46		131	160	Baza, Ignacia B	Head	F	Cha	45	S	N	Y	Guam	N	Washerwoman
47		131	160	Baza, Juan B	Son	M	Cha	21	S	N	Y	Guam	Y	Carpenter
48		131	160	Baza, Maria B	Daughter	F	Cha	19	S	N	Y	Guam	Y	None
49		131	160	Baza, Rosa B	Daughter	F	Cha	9	S	Y		Guam		None
50		131	160	Baza, Maria A	Mother	F	Cha	72	S	N	Y	Guam	N	None

(CHAMORRO ROOTS GENEALOGY PROJECT™ TRANSCRIPTION)
(BERNARD T. PUNZALAN / HTTP://WWW.CHAMORROROOTS.COM)

DEPARTMENT OF COMMERCE-BUREAU OF THE CENSUS
WASHINGTON

FIFTEENTH CENSUS OF THE UNITED STATES: 1930-POPULATION

THE ISLAND OF GUAM

Sheet No. 17A

District **Municipality of Agana**
Name of Place **Agana City (San Nicolas)**
[Proper name and, also, name of class, as city, town, village, barrio, etc]

Enumeration District No. **1**
Enumerated by me on **April 18, 1930** Pauline L. Dees
Enumerator

	PLACE OF ABODE			NAME	RELATION	PERSONAL DESCRIPTION				EDUCATION		NATIVITY		OCCUPATION
	Street, avenue, road, etc.	Number of dwelling house is order of visitation	Number of family in order of visitation	of each person whose place of abode on April 1, 1930, was in this family. Enter surname, first, then given name and middle initial. If any. Include every person living on April 1, 1930. Omit children born since April 1, 1930.	Relationship of this Person to the head of the family.	Sex	Color or race	Age at last birthday	Single, married, widowed or divorced	Attended school any time since Sept. 1, 1929	Whether able to read and write.	Place of birth of this person.	Whether able to speak English.	
	1	2	3	4	5	6	7	8	9	10	11	12	13	14
1	Magallanes Street	132	161	Cruz, Juan G	Head	M	Cha	22	M	N	Y	Guam	Y	Carpenter
2		132	161	Cruz, Isabel M	Wife	F	Cha	22	M	N	Y	Guam	Y	None
3		132	161	Cruz, Josefa M	Daughter	F	Cha	1.5	S	N		Guam		None
4		133	162	Camacho, Juan S	Head	M	Cha	48	M	N	Y	Guam	N	Farmer
5		133	162	Camacho, Joaquina C	Wife	F	Cha	45	M	N	Y	Guam	N	None
6		133	162	Camacho, Gregorio C	Son	M	Cha	22	S	N	Y	Guam	Y	Laborer
7		133	162	Camacho, Manuela C	Daughter	F	Cha	16	S	N	Y	Guam	Y	None
8		133	162	Camacho, Vicenta C	Daughter	F	Cha	15	S	Y	Y	Guam	Y	None
9		133	162	Camacho, Carmen C	Daughter	F	Cha	10	S	Y	Y	Guam	Y	None
10		133	162	Camacho, Ramon C	Son	M	Cha	8	S	Y		Guam		None
11		133	162	Camacho, Juan C	Son	M	Cha	6	S	N		Guam		None
12		133	162	Camacho, Rosario C	Daughter	F	Cha	1.3	S	N		Guam		None
13		134	163	Blas, Joaquina R	Head	F	Cha	43	M	N	Y	Guam	Y	None
14		134	163	Blas, Rosalia R	Daughter	F	Cha	12	S	Y	Y	Guam	Y	None
15		134	163	Blas, Tomas R	Son	M	Cha	11	S	Y	Y	Guam	Y	None
16		134	163	Blas, Francisco R	Son	M	Cha	6	S	N		Guam		None
17		134	163	Blas, Cornelia R	Daughter	F	Cha	4.9	S	N		Guam		None
18		134	163	Leon Guerrero, Ana R	Sister	F	Cha	41	S	N	N	Guam	N	None
19		134	163	Leon Guerrero, Rita R	Niece	F	Cha	8	S	Y		Guam	Y	None
20		134	164	Toves, Jose T	Head	M	Cha	21	S	N	Y	Guam	Y	Farm laborer
21		134	165	Siguenza, Jose P	Head	M	Cha	56	M	N	N	Guam	N	Farmer
22		134	165	Siguenza, Maria C	Wife	F	Cha	44	M	N	N	Guam	N	None
23		134	165	Siguenza, Juan C	Son	M	Cha	10	S	Y	Y	Guam	Y	None
24		134	165	Farfan, Jose C	Nephew	M	Cha	18	S	N	Y	Guam	Y	Messenger
25		134	165	Farfan, Jesus C	Nephew	M	Cha	16	S	Y	Y	Guam	Y	None

(CHAMORRO ROOTS GENEALOGY PROJECT™ TRANSCRIPTION)
(BERNARD T. PUNZALAN / HTTP://WWW.CHAMORROROOTS.COM)

DEPARTMENT OF COMMERCE-BUREAU OF THE CENSUS
WASHINGTON

FIFTEENTH CENSUS OF THE UNITED STATES: 1930-POPULATION

THE ISLAND OF GUAM

Sheet No. 17B

17B

District **Municipality of Agana**

Name of Place **Agana City (San Nicolas)**

[Proper name and, also, name of class, as city, town, village, barrio, etc]

Enumeration District No. **1**

Enumerated by me on **April 18, 1930** Pauline L. Dees, Enumerator

	PLACE OF ABODE			NAME	RELATION	PERSONAL DESCRIPTION				EDUCATION		NATIVITY		OCCUPATION
	Street, avenue, road, etc.	Number of dwelling house is order of visitation	Number of family in order of visitation	of each person whose place of abode on April 1, 1930, was in this family. Enter surname, first, then given name and middle initial. If any. Include every person living on April 1, 1930. Omit children born since April 1, 1930.	Relationship of this Person to the head of the family.	Sex	Color or race	Age at last birthday	Single, married, widowed or divorced	Attended school any time since Sept. 1, 1929	Whether able to read and write.	Place of birth of this person.	Whether able to speak English.	
	1	2	3	4	5	6	7	8	9	10	11	12	13	14
26	Magallanes Street	134	165	Farfan, Rosa C	Niece	F	Cha	14	S	Y	Y	Guam	Y	None
27		134	165	Farfan, Ignacio C	Nephew	M	Cha	10	S	Y	Y	Guam	Y	None
28		135	166	Cabrera, Enrique V	Head	M	Cha	39	M	N	Y	Guam	Y	Laborer
29		135	166	Cabrera, Dolores C	Wife	F	Cha	36	M	N	N	Guam	N	Washerwoman
30		135	166	Cabrera, Ana C	Daughter	F	Cha	14	S	Y	Y	Guam	Y	None
31		135	166	Cabrera, Jesus C	Son	M	Cha	7	S	Y		Guam		None
32		135	166	Cabrera, Jose C	Son	M	Cha	5	S	N		Guam		None
33		135	166	Cabrera, Maria C	Daughter	F	Cha	2.6	S	N		Guam		None
34		135	166	Cabrera, Rosalia C	Daughter	F	Cha	.3	S	N		Guam		None
35		136	167	Sablan, Maria S	Head	F	Cha	29	M	N	Y	Guam	N	None
36		137	168	Garcia, Juan A	Head	M	Cha	27	M	N	Y	Guam	Y	Farmer
37		137	168	Garcia, Maria S	Wife	F	Cha	29	M	N	Y	Guam	Y	None
38		137	168	Garcia, Francisco S	Son	M	Cha	3.5	S	N		Guam		None
39		137	169	Salas, Antonio SN	Head	M	Cha	21	M	N	Y	Guam	Y	Farm laborer
40		137	169	Salas, Rosa C	Wife	F	Cha	24	M	N	Y	Guam	Y	None
41	Isabel la Catolica Street	138	170	Lansdowne, Florence H	Head	F	W	36	M	N	Y	South Dakota	Y	None
42		138	170	Lansdowne, Kenneth R	Son	M	W	7	S	Y		California		None
43		138	170	Lansdowne, Jessie P	Daughter	F	W	2.6	S	N		Virginia		None
44		139	171	Landmark, Elenora O	Head	F	W	35	M	N	Y	Oregon	Y	None
45		140	172	Duenas, Gregorio A	Head	M	Cha	36	M	N	Y	Guam	Y	Silversmith
46		140	172	Duenas, Manuela F	Wife	F	Cha	33	M	N	Y	Guam	Y	None
47		140	172	Duenas, Enrique F	Son	M	Cha	14	S	Y	Y	Guam	Y	None
48		140	172	Duenas, Joaquin F	Son	M	Cha	13	S	Y	Y	Guam	Y	None
49		140	172	Duenas, Antonio F	Son	M	Cha	12	S	Y	Y	Guam	Y	None
50		140	172	Duenas, Francisco F	Son	M	Cha	9	S	N		Guam		None

DEPARTMENT OF COMMERCE-BUREAU OF THE CENSUS
WASHINGTON

FIFTEENTH CENSUS OF THE UNITED STATES: 1930-POPULATION

THE ISLAND OF GUAM

Sheet No. 18A

District **Municipality of Agana**
Name of Place **Agana City (San Nicolas)**
[Proper name and, also, name of class, as city, town, village, barrio, etc]

Enumeration District No. **1**
Enumerated by me on **April 19, 1930** Pauline L. Dees, Enumerator

	PLACE OF ABODE			NAME	RELATION	PERSONAL DESCRIPTION				EDUCATION		NATIVITY		OCCUPATION
	Street, avenue, road, etc.	Number of dwelling house is order of visitation	Number of family in order of visitation	of each person whose place of abode on April 1, 1930, was in this family. Enter surname, first, then given name and middle initial. If any. Include every person living on April 1, 1930. Omit children born since April 1, 1930.	Relationship of this Person to the head of the family.	Sex	Color or race	Age at last birthday	Single, married, widowed or divorced	Attended school any time since Sept. 1, 1929	Whether able to read and write.	Place of birth of this person.	Whether able to speak English.	
	1	2	3	4	5	6	7	8	9	10	11	12	13	14
1	Isabel la Catolica Street	140	172	Duenas, Juan F	Son	M	Cha	6	S	N		Guam		None
2		140	172	Duenas, Jesus F	Son	M	Cha	4.9	S	N		Guam		None
3		140	172	Duenas, Manuel F	Son	M	Cha	1.9	S	N		Guam		None
4		140	172	Duenas, Gregorio F	Son	M	Cha	.2	S	N		Guam		None
5		140	172	Duenas, Dometila A	Mother	F	Cha	73	Wd	N	Y	Guam	N	None
6		141	173	Anderson, Vicenta R	Head	F	Cha	26	M	N	Y	Guam	Y	None
7		142	174	Duenas, Vicente A	Head	M	Cha	40	M	N	Y	Guam	Y	Farmer
8		142	174	Duenas, Ana B	Wife	F	Cha	36	M	N	Y	Guam	N	None
9		142	174	Duenas, Juan B	Son	M	Cha	22	S	N	Y	Guam	Y	Carpenter
10		142	174	Duenas, Joaquin B	Son	M	Cha	17	S	N	Y	Guam	Y	Farm laborer
11		142	174	Duenas, Catalina B	Daughter	F	Cha	12	S	Y	Y	Guam	Y	None
12		142	174	Duenas, Josefina B	Daughter	F	Cha	9	S	Y		Guam		None
13		142	174	Duenas, Vicente B	Son	M	Cha	4.8	S	N		Guam		None
14		142	174	Duenas, Remedios B	Daughter	F	Cha	1.2	S	N		Guam		None
15		143	175	Pereda, Antonio S	Head	M	Cha	53	Wd	N	Y	Guam	N	Machinist
16		143	175	Pereda, Juan LG	Son	M	Cha	19	S	N	Y	Guam	Y	Time keeper
17		143	175	Pereda, Concepcion LG	Daughter	F	Cha	17	S	N	Y	Guam	Y	None
18		143	175	Pereda, Joaquin LG	Son	M	Cha	15	S	Y	Y	Guam	Y	None
19		143	175	Pereda, Luisa LG	Daughter	F	Cha	9	S	Y		Guam		None
20		143	175	Pereda, Maria LG	Daughter	F	Cha	5	S	N		Guam		None
21		143	176	Leon Guerrero, Ramon B	Head	M	Cha	82	Wd	N	Y	Guam	N	None
22		143	176	Leon Guerrero, Dolores A	Daughter	F	Cha	26	S	N	Y	Guam	Y	Dressmaker
23		143	176	Leon Guerrero, Carmen A	Grand daughter	F	Cha	.2	S	N		Guam		None
24		144	177	Troy, Ruth M	Head	F	W	32	M	N	Y	Pennsylvania	Y	Teacher
25		145	178	Salas, Ignacio Q	Head	M	Cha	37	M	N	Y	Guam	Y	Farmer

DEPARTMENT OF COMMERCE-BUREAU OF THE CENSUS
WASHINGTON

FIFTEENTH CENSUS OF THE UNITED STATES: 1930-POPULATION

THE ISLAND OF GUAM

Sheet No. 18B

18B

District Municipality of Agana
Name of Place Agana City (San Nicolas)
[Proper name and, also, name of class, as city, town, village, barrio, etc]

Enumeration District No. 1
Enumerated by me on April 19, 1930 Pauline L. Dees
Enumerator

	PLACE OF ABODE			NAME	RELATION	PERSONAL DESCRIPTION				EDUCATION		NATIVITY		OCCUPATION
	Street, avenue, road, etc.	Number of dwelling house is order of visitation	Number of family in order of visitation	of each person whose place of abode on April 1, 1930, was in this family. Enter surname, first, then given name and middle initial. If any. Include every person living on April 1, 1930. Omit children born since April 1, 1930.	Relationship of this Person to the head of the family.	Sex	Color or race	Age at last birthday	Single, married, widowed or divorced	Attended school any time since Sept. 1, 1929	Whether able to read and write.	Place of birth of this person.	Whether able to speak English.	
	1	2	3	4	5	6	7	8	9	10	11	12	13	14
26	Isabel la Catolica Street	145	178	Salas, Ana B	Wife	F	Cha	33	M	N	Y	Guam	Y	None
27		145	178	Salas, Francisco S	Son	M	Cha	13	S	Y	Y	Guam	Y	None
28		145	178	Salas, Maria S	Daughter	F	Cha	10	S	Y	Y	Guam	Y	None
29		145	178	Salas, Mercedes S	Daughter	F	Cha	8	S	Y		Guam		None
30		145	178	Salas, Josefina B	Daughter	F	Cha	1.7	S	N		Guam		None
31		146	179	Herrero, Francisco L	Head	M	Cha	35	M	N	Y	Guam	Y	Chauffeur
32		146	179	Herrero, Josefa SN	Wife	F	Cha	34	M	N	Y	Guam	Y	None
33		146	179	Herrero, Soledad SN	Daughter	F	Cha	14	S	Y	Y	Guam	Y	None
34		146	179	Herrero, Jose SN	Son	M	Cha	12	S	Y	Y	Guam	Y	None
35		146	179	Herrero, Ana SN	Daughter	F	Cha	9	S	Y		Guam		None
36		146	179	Herrero, Ingracia SN	Daughter	F	Cha	5	S	N		Guam		None
37		146	179	Herrero, Juan SN	Son	M	Cha	2.8	S	N		Guam		None
38		146	179	Herrero, Luis SN	Son	M	Cha	.9	S	N		Guam		None
39		146	180	San Nicolas, Joaquin	Head	M	Cha	68	M	N	Y	Guam	N	None
40		146	180	San Nicolas, Felicita L	Wife	F	Cha	66	M	N	Y	Guam	N	None
41		147	181	Julian, Marie E	Head	F	W	29	M	N	Y	Virginia	Y	None
42		147	181	Julian, Vivian M	Daughter	F	W	9	S	Y		Virginia		None
43		147	182	Nelson, Ana G	Head	F	W	24	M	N	Y	New York	Y	None
44		147	182	Nelson, Edward R	Son	M	W	3.5	S	N		Pennsylvania		None
45		148	183	Leon Guerrero, Jesus P	Head	M	Cha	24	M	N	Y	Guam	Y	Chauffeur
46		148	183	Leon Guerrero, Rofina LG	Wife	F	Cha	25	M	N	Y	Guam	Y	None
47		148	183	Leon Guerrero, Pedro LG	Son	M	Cha	.8	S	N		Guam		None
48		149	184	Martinez, Vicente P	Head	M	Cha	26	M	N	Y	Guam	Y	Machinist
49		149	184	Martinez, Concepcion C	Wife	F	Cha	24	M	N	Y	Guam	Y	None
50		149	184	Martinez, Lourdes C	Daughter	F	Cha	1.3	S	N		Guam		None

(CHAMORRO ROOTS GENEALOGY PROJECT™ TRANSCRIPTION)
(BERNARD T. PUNZALAN / HTTP://WWW.CHAMORROROOTS.COM)

DEPARTMENT OF COMMERCE-BUREAU OF THE CENSUS
WASHINGTON

FIFTEENTH CENSUS OF THE UNITED STATES: 1930-POPULATION

THE ISLAND OF GUAM

Sheet No. 19A

District **Municipality of Agana**
Name of Place **Agana City (San Nicolas)**
[Proper name and, also, name of class, as city, town, village, barrio, etc]

Enumeration District No. 1
Enumerated by me on **April 21, 1930** Pauline L. Dees, Enumerator

	PLACE OF ABODE			NAME	RELATION	PERSONAL DESCRIPTION				EDUCATION		NATIVITY		OCCUPATION
	Street, avenue, road, etc.	Number of dwelling house in order of visitation	Number of family in order of visitation	of each person whose place of abode on April 1, 1930, was in this family. Enter surname, first, then given name and middle initial. If any. Include every person living on April 1, 1930. Omit children born since April 1, 1930.	Relationship of this Person to the head of the family.	Sex	Color or race	Age at last birthday	Single, married, widowed or divorced	Attended school any time since Sept. 1, 1929	Whether able to read and write.	Place of birth of this person.	Whether able to speak English.	
	1	2	3	4	5	6	7	8	9	10	11	12	13	14
1	Isabel la Catolica Street	149	185	Camacho, Jose S	Head	M	Cha	17	S	N	Y	Guam	Y	Farm laborer
2		150	186	Castro, Jose C	Head	M	Cha	41	M	N	Y	Guam	Y	Farmer
3		150	186	Castro, Ana S	Wife	F	Cha	38	M	N	Y	Guam	Y	Midwife
4		150	186	Castro, Delfina S	Daughter	F	Cha	13	S	Y	Y	Guam	Y	None
5		150	186	Castro, Pilar S	Daughter	F	Cha	10	S	Y	Y	Guam	Y	None
6		150	186	Castro, Ramon S	Son	M	Cha	6	S	N		Guam		None
7		150	186	Castro, Juan S	Son	M	Cha	3.8	S	N		Guam		None
8		150	186	Castro, Maria S	Daughter	F	Cha	1.8	S	N		Guam		None
9		151	187	Cepeda, Ana C	Head	F	Cha	56	S	M	Y	Guam	N	None
10		152	188	Rosario, Guadalupe S	Head	F	Cha	29	M	N	Y	Guam	Y	None
11		152	188	Rosario, Priscilla M	Daughter	F	Cha	4.9	S	N		Guam		None
12		152	188	Rosario, Sylvia J	Daughter	F	Cha	1.8	S	N		Guam		None
13		153	189	Garrido, Jose P	Head	M	Cha	33	M	N	Y	Guam	Y	Machinist
14		153	189	Garrido, Agueda A	Wife	F	Cha	31	M	N	Y	Guam	Y	None
15		153	189	Garrido, Clotilda A	Daughter	F	Cha	13	S	Y	Y	Guam	Y	None
16		153	189	Garrido, Magdalena A	Daughter	F	Cha	11	S	Y	Y	Guam	Y	None
17		153	189	Garrido, Jose A	Son	M	Cha	9	S	Y		Guam		None
18		153	189	Garrido, Ana A	Daughter	F	Cha	6	S	N		Guam		None
19		154	190	San Nicolas, Vicente L	Head	M	Cha	81	Wd	N	N	Guam	N	None
20		154	190	San Nicolas, Dolores C	Daughter	F	Cha	51	S	N	Y	Guam	Y	None
21		154	191	San Nicolas, Enrique R	Head	M	Cha	26	M	N	Y	Guam	Y	Machinist
22		154	191	San Nicolas, Ana G	Wife	F	Cha	25	M	N	Y	Guam	Y	None
23		154	191	San Nicolas, Francisco G	Son	M	Cha	5	S	N		Guam		None
24		154	191	San Nicolas, Mattina G	Daughter	F	Cha	4.3	S	N		Guam		None
25		154	191	San Nicolas, Jose G	Son	M	Cha	3.3	S	N		Guam		None

DEPARTMENT OF COMMERCE-BUREAU OF THE CENSUS
WASHINGTON

FIFTEENTH CENSUS OF THE UNITED STATES: 1930-POPULATION

THE ISLAND OF GUAM

Sheet No. 19B

19B

District **Municipality of Agana**
Name of Place **Agana City (San Nicolas)**
[Proper name and, also, name of class, as city, town, village, barrio, etc]

Enumeration District No. **1**
Enumerated by me on **April 21, 1930** Pauline L. Dees
Enumerator

	PLACE OF ABODE			NAME	RELATION	PERSONAL DESCRIPTION				EDUCATION		NATIVITY		OCCUPATION
	Street, avenue, road, etc.	Number of dwelling house is order of visitation	Number of family in order of visitation	of each person whose place of abode on April 1, 1930, was in this family. Enter surname, first, then given name and middle initial. If any. Include every person living on April 1, 1930. Omit children born since April 1, 1930.	Relationship of this Person to the head of the family.	Sex	Color or race	Age at last birthday	Single, married, widowed or divorced	Attended school any time since Sept. 1, 1929	Whether able to read and write.	Place of birth of this person.	Whether able to speak English.	
	1	2	3	4	5	6	7	8	9	10	11	12	13	14
26	Isabel la Catolica Street	154	191	San Nicolas, Ettmina G	Daughter	F	Cha	.9	S	N		Guam		None
27		255	192	Borja, Ignacio Q	Head	M	Cha	25	N	Y		Guam	Y	Messenger
28		255	192	Borja, Matilde S	Wife	F	Cha	18	N	Y		Guam	Y	None
29		255	193	Santos, Jesus T	Head	M	Cha	44	M	N	Y	Guam	N	Farmer
30		255	193	Santos, Dolores T	Wife	F	Cha	45	M	N	Y	Guam	N	None
31		255	193	Santos, Jose T	Son	M	Cha	14	S	N	Y	Guam	Y	Farm laborer
32		255	193	Santos, Joaquin T	Son	M	Cha	13	S	Y	Y	Guam	Y	None
33		255	193	Santos, Crisanta T	Daughter	F	Cha	10	S	Y	Y	Guam	Y	None
34		255	193	Santos, Julita T	Daughter	F	Cha	7	S	Y		Guam		None
35		255	193	Santos, Catalina T	Daughter	F	Cha	5	S	N		Guam		None
36		255	193	Santos, Segundo B	Grandson	M	Cha	2.9	S	N		Guam		None
37		156	194	Franquez, Pedro I	Head	M	Cha	43	M	N	Y	Guam	Y	Plumber
38		156	194	Franquez, Ana C	Wife	F	Cha	38	M	N	Y	Guam	N	None
39		156	194	Franquez, Pedro C	Son	M	Cha	18	S	Y	Y	Guam	Y	Apprentice
40		156	194	Franquez, Rita C	Daughter	F	Cha	16	S	N	Y	Guam	Y	None
41		156	194	Franquez, Maria C	Daughter	F	Cha	14	S	Y	Y	Guam	Y	None
42		156	194	Franquez, Isabel C	Daughter	F	Cha	12	S	Y	Y	Guam	Y	None
43		157	195	Leon Guerrero, Juan S	Head	M	Cha	35	M	N	Y	Guam	Y	Farmer
44		157	195	Leon Guerrero, Concepcion B	Wife	F	Cha	34	M	N	N	Guam	Y	None
45		157	195	Leon Guerrero, Maria B	Daughter	F	Cha	14	S	N	Y	Guam	Y	None
46		157	195	Leon Guerrero, Tomas B	Son	M	Cha	10	S	Y	Y	Guam	Y	None
47		157	195	Leon Guerrero, Francisca B	Daughter	F	Cha	7	S	Y		Guam		None
48		157	195	Leon Guerrero, Isabel B	Daughter	F	Cha	5	S	N		Guam		None
49		157	195	Leon Guerrero, Juan B	Son	M	Cha	3.7	S	N		Guam		None
50		157	195	Leon Guerrero, Cecelia B	Daughter	F	Cha	1.4	S	N		Guam		None

DEPARTMENT OF COMMERCE-BUREAU OF THE CENSUS
WASHINGTON

FIFTEENTH CENSUS OF THE UNITED STATES: 1930-POPULATION

THE ISLAND OF GUAM

Sheet No. 20A

District **Municipality of Agana**
Name of Place **Agana City (San Nicolas)**
[Proper name and, also, name of class, as city, town, village, barrio, etc]

Enumeration District No. **1**
Enumerated by me on **April 21, 1930** Pauline L. Dees
Enumerator

	PLACE OF ABODE			NAME	RELATION	PERSONAL DESCRIPTION				EDUCATION		NATIVITY		OCCUPATION
	Street, avenue, road, etc.	Number of dwelling house in order of visitation	Number of family in order of visitation	of each person whose place of abode on April 1, 1930, was in this family. Enter surname, first, then given name and middle initial. If any. Include every person living on April 1, 1930. Omit children born since April 1, 1930.	Relationship of this Person to the head of the family.	Sex	Color or race	Age at last birthday	Single, married, widowed or divorced	Attended school any time since Sept. 1, 1929	Whether able to read and write.	Place of birth of this person.	Whether able to speak English.	
	1	2	3	4	5	6	7	8	9	10	11	12	13	14
1	Isabel la Catolica Street	157	196	Borja, Susana Q	Head	F	Cha	57	Wd	N	N	Guam	N	None
2		157	196	Borja, Antonio Q	Son	M	Cha	32	S	N	N	Guam	N	Farmer
3		157	196	Borja, Cresencia Q	Daughter	F	Cha	19	S	N	N	Guam	N	None
4		158	197	Reyes, Jose R	Head	M	Cha	58	M	N	Y	Guam	N	Farmer
5		158	197	Reyes, Rita Q	Wife	F	Cha	44	M	N	Y	Guam	N	None
6		159	198	Guevara, Fernando SN	Head	M	Cha	36	M	N	N	Guam	Y	Carpenter
7		159	198	Guevara, Isabel C	Wife	F	Cha	34	M	N	Y	Guam	Y	None
8		159	198	Guevara, Maria C	Daughter	F	Cha	13	S	Y	Y	Guam	Y	None
9		159	198	Guevara, Enriqueta C	Daughter	F	Cha	12	S	Y	Y	Guam	Y	None
10		159	198	Guevara, Jose C	Son	M	Cha	10	S	Y	Y	Guam		None
11		159	198	Guevara, Jesus C	Son	M	Cha	8	S	Y		Guam		None
12		159	198	Guevara, Rosa C	Daughter	F	Cha	6	S	Y		Guam		None
13		160	199	San Miguel, Jose M	Head	M	Cha	58	M	N	Y	Guam	N	None
14		160	199	San Miguel, Vicenta B	Wife	F	Cha	52	M	N	Y	Guam	N	None
15		161	200	Borja, Jose B	Head	M	Cha	33	M	N	Y	Guam	N	Farmer
16		161	200	Borja, Joaquin G	Wife	F	Cha	24	M	N	Y	Guam	N	None
17		161	200	Borja, Maria G	Daughter	F	Cha	5	S	N		Guam		None
18		161	200	Borja, Vicente G	Son	M	Cha	3.4	S	N		Guam		None
19		161	200	Borja, Pedro G	Son	M	Cha	1.5	S	N		Guam		None
20		161	200	Borja, Ignacia G	Mother	F	Cha	60	S	N		Guam		None
21		162	201	Delgado, Jose D	Head	M	Cha	30	M	N	Y	Guam	Y	Farmer
22		162	201	Delgado, Josefa C	Wife	F	Cha	26	M	N	Y	Guam	Y	None
23		162	201	Delgado, Francisco C	Son	M	Cha	9	S	Y		Guam		None
24		162	201	Delgado, Rosario C	Daughter	F	Cha	3.8	S	N		Guam		None
25		162	201	Delgado, Isabel C	Daughter	F	Cha	.1	S	N		Guam		None

(CHAMORRO ROOTS GENEALOGY PROJECT™ TRANSCRIPTION)
(BERNARD T. PUNZALAN / HTTP://WWW.CHAMORROROOTS.COM)

DEPARTMENT OF COMMERCE-BUREAU OF THE CENSUS
WASHINGTON

FIFTEENTH CENSUS OF THE UNITED STATES: 1930-POPULATION

THE ISLAND OF GUAM

Sheet No. 20B

20B

District Municipality of Agana
Name of Place Agana City (San Nicolas)
[Proper name and, also, name of class, as city, town, village, barrio, etc]

Enumeration District No. 1
Enumerated by me on April 22, 1930 Pauline L. Dees
Enumerator

	PLACE OF ABODE			NAME	RELATION	PERSONAL DESCRIPTION				EDUCATION		NATIVITY		OCCUPATION
	Street, avenue, road, etc.	Number of dwelling house is order of visitation	Number of family in order of visitation	of each person whose place of abode on April 1, 1930, was in this family. Enter surname, first, then given name and middle initial. If any. Include every person living on April 1, 1930. Omit children born since April 1, 1930.	Relationship of this Person to the head of the family.	Sex	Color or race	Age at last birthday	Single, married, widowed or divorced	Attended school any time since Sept. 1, 1929	Whether able to read and write.	Place of birth of this person.	Whether able to speak English.	
	1	2	3	4	5	6	7	8	9	10	11	12	13	14
26	Isabel la Catolica Street	163	202	San Nicolas, Vicente S	Head	M	Cha	43	M	N	Y	Guam	Y	Electrician
27		163	202	San Nicolas, Remedios T	Wife	F	Cha	39	M	N	N	Guam	N	None
28		163	202	San Nicolas, Maria T	Daughter	F	Cha	15	S	Y	Y	Guam	Y	None
29		163	202	San Nicolas, Guadalupe T	Daughter	F	Cha	14	S	Y	Y	Guam	Y	None
30		163	202	San Nicolas, Manuela T	Daughter	F	Cha	10	S	Y	Y	Guam	Y	None
31		163	202	San Nicolas, Jesus T	Son	M	Cha	9	S	Y		Guam		None
32		163	202	San Nicolas, Ana T	Daughter	F	Cha	6	S	N		Guam		None
33		163	202	San Nicolas, Beatres T	Daughter	F	Cha	5	S	N		Guam		None
34		163	202	San Nicolas, Vicente T	Son	M	Cha	4.3	S	N		Guam		None
35		163	202	San Nicolas, Conelia T	Daughter	F	Cha	1.8	S	N		Guam		None
36		163	202	Mantanona, Carmen T	Niece	F	Cha	10	S	Y	Y	Guam	Y	None
37		163	203	Mantanona, Atanasio I	Head	M	Cha	35	Wd	N	N	Guam	N	Farm laborer
38		164	204	Flores, Juan G	Head	M	Cha	33	M	N	Y	Guam	Y	Farmer
39		164	204	Flores, Nicolasa C	Wife	F	Cha	30	M	Y	Y	Guam	Y	None
40		164	204	Flores, Beatres C	Daughter	F	Cha	14	S	Y	Y	Guam	Y	None
41		164	204	Flores, Juan C	Son	M	Cha	12	S	Y	Y	Guam	Y	None
42		164	204	Flores, Ana C	Daughter	F	Cha	11	S	Y	Y	Guam	Y	None
43		164	204	Flores, Joaquin C	Son	M	Cha	9	S	Y		Guam		None
44		164	204	Flores, Margarita C	Daughter	F	Cha	6	S	N		Guam		None
45		164	204	Flores, Carlos C	Son	M	Cha	3.5	S	N		Guam		None
46		164	204	Flores, Rosalia C	Daughter	F	Cha	.4	S	N		Guam		None
47		164	204	Cruz, Apolanaria	Motherinlaw	F	Cha	74	Wd	N	N	Guam	N	None
48		165	205	Castro, Vicenta S	Head	F	Cha	56	S	N	N	Guam	N	Washerwoman
49		165	205	Castro, Dolores S	Mother	F	Cha	87	Wd	N	N	Guam	N	None
50		166	206	Franquez, Jose I	Head	M	Cha	46	M	N	N	Guam	Y	Carpenter

DEPARTMENT OF COMMERCE-BUREAU OF THE CENSUS
WASHINGTON

FIFTEENTH CENSUS OF THE UNITED STATES: 1930-POPULATION

THE ISLAND OF GUAM

Sheet No. 21A

District **Municipality of Agana**
Name of Place **Agana City (San Nicolas)**
[Proper name and, also, name of class, as city, town, village, barrio, etc]

Enumeration District No. **1**
Enumerated by me on **April 22, 1930** Pauline L. Dees
Enumerator

	PLACE OF ABODE			NAME	RELATION	PERSONAL DESCRIPTION				EDUCATION		NATIVITY		OCCUPATION
	Street, avenue, road, etc.	Number of dwelling house is order of visitation	Number of family in order of visitation	of each person whose place of abode on April 1, 1930, was in this family. Enter surname, first, then given name and middle initial. If any. Include every person living on April 1, 1930. Omit children born since April 1, 1930.	Relationship of this Person to the head of the family.	Sex	Color or race	Age at last birthday	Single, married, widowed or divorced	Attended school any time since Sept. 1, 1929	Whether able to read and write.	Place of birth of this person.	Whether able to speak English.	
	1	2	3	4	5	6	7	8	9	10	11	12	13	14
1	Isabel la Catolica Street	166	206	Franquez, Maria T	Wife	F	Cha	42	M	N	Y	Guam	Y	None
2		166	206	Franquez, Maria T	Daughter	F	Cha	29	S	N	Y	Guam	Y	None
3		166	206	Franquez, Ana T	Daughter	F	Cha	17	S	N	Y	Guam	Y	Teacher
4		166	206	Franquez, Jose T	Son	M	Cha	15	S	Y	Y	Guam	Y	None
5		166	206	Franquez, Manuel T	Son	M	Cha	12	S	Y	Y	Guam	Y	None
6		166	206	Franquez, Remedios T	Daughter	F	Cha	9	S	Y		Guam		None
7		167	207	Reyes, Maria C	Head	M	Cha	62	S	N	Y	Guam	N	None
8		167	207	Reyes, Vicente C	Wife	F	Cha	21	S	N	Y	Guam	Y	Teacher
9		167	207	Taitano, Madalena C	Niece	F	Cha	8	S	Y		Guam		None
10		167	208	Paulino, Trinidad R	Head	F	Cha	32	M	N	Y	Guam	Y	None
11		167	208	Paulino, Cristobal R	Son	M	Cha	8	S	Y		Guam		None
12		167	208	Paulino, Maria R	Daughter	F	Cha	5	S	N		Guam		None
13		167	208	Paulino, Bernabe R	Son	M	Cha	3.5	S	N		Guam		None
14		167	208	Paulino, Ana R	Daughter	F	Cha	1.6	S	N		Guam		None
15		168	209	Mesa, Mariano C	Head	M	Cha	26	M	N	Y	Guam	Y	Carpenter
16		168	209	Mesa, Francisca R	Wife	F	Cha	29	M	N	Y	Guam	Y	None
17		168	209	Mesa, Juan R	Son	M	Cha	2.7	S	N		Guam		None
18		168	209	Mesa, Josefina R	Daughter	F	Cha	1.6	S	N		Guam		None
19		168	209	Mesa, Jose R	Son	M	Cha	.1	S	N		Guam		None
20	Marshall Street	169	210	Cruz, Jesus C	Head	M	Cha	68	Wd	N	N	Guam	N	Farmer
21		169	210	Cruz, Ignacio T	Son	M	Cha	17	S	N	Y	Guam	Y	Machinist
22		169	210	Cruz, Jesus T	Son	M	Cha	14	S	Y	Y	Guam	Y	None
23		169	210	Cruz, Rosa T	Daughter	F	Cha	11	S	Y		Guam	Y	None
24		169	210	Cruz, Joaquin T	Son	M	Cha	9	S	Y		Guam		None
25		169	210	Cruz, Jose T	Son	M	Cha	6	S	N		Guam		None

DEPARTMENT OF COMMERCE-BUREAU OF THE CENSUS
WASHINGTON

FIFTEENTH CENSUS OF THE UNITED STATES: 1930-POPULATION

THE ISLAND OF GUAM

Sheet No. 21B

21B

District **Municipality of Agana**
Name of Place **Agana City (San Nicolas)**
[Proper name and, also, name of class, as city, town, village, barrio, etc]

Enumeration District No. **1**
Enumerated by me on **April 23, 1930** Pauline L. Dees, Enumerator

	PLACE OF ABODE			NAME	RELATION	PERSONAL DESCRIPTION				EDUCATION		NATIVITY		OCCUPATION
	Street, avenue, road, etc.	Number of dwelling house is order of visitation	Number of family in order of visitation	of each person whose place of abode on April 1, 1930, was in this family. Enter surname, first, then given name and middle initial. If any. Include every person living on April 1, 1930. Omit children born since April 1, 1930.	Relationship of this Person to the head of the family.	Sex	Color or race	Age at last birthday	Single, married, widowed or divorced	Attended school any time since Sept. 1, 1929	Whether able to read and write.	Place of birth of this person.	Whether able to speak English.	
	1	2	3	4	5	6	7	8	9	10	11	12	13	14
26	Marshall Street	170	211	Blas, Joaquin T	Head	M	Cha	62	M	N	Y	Guam	N	Farmer
27		170	211	Blas, Maria C	Wife	F	Cha	62	M	N	Y	Guam	N	None
28		170	211	Blas, Concepcion C	Daughter	F	Cha	26	S	N	Y	Guam	Y	None
29		170	211	Blas, Pedro C	Son	M	Cha	16	S	Y	Y	Guam	Y	None
30	Minondo Street	171	212	Dydasco, Rosa T	Head	F	Cha	51	M	N	Y	Guam	N	None
31		171	212	Dydasco, Jose T	Son	M	Cha	27	S	N	Y	Guam	Y	Carpenter
32		171	212	Dydasco, Joaquin T	Son	M	Cha	23	S	N	Y	Guam	Y	Carpenter
33		171	212	Dydasco, Felix T	Son	M	Cha	17	S	N	Y	Guam	Y	Clerk
34		171	212	Dydasco, Gregorio T	Son	M	Cha	13	S	Y	Y	Guam	Y	None
35		171	212	Dydasco, Juan T	Son	M	Cha	12	S	Y	Y	Guam	Y	None
36		172	212	Flores, Jose R	Head	M	Cha	30	M	N	Y	Guam	Y	Farmer
37		172	212	Flores, Maria B	Wife	F	Cha	29	M	N	Y	Guam	Y	None
38		172	212	Flores, Guadalupe B	Daughter	F	Cha	9	S	Y		Guam		None
39		172	212	Flores, Remedios B	Daughter	F	Cha	7	S	Y		Guam		None
40		172	212	Flores, Maria B	Daughter	F	Cha	6	S	N		Guam		None
41		172	212	Flores, Jose B	Son	M	Cha	3.9	S	N		Guam		None
42		172	212	Flores, Cecelia B	Daughter	F	Cha	2.5	S	N		Guam		None
43		173	214	Cruz, Joaquina T	Head	F	Cha	35	M	N	Y	Guam	Y	None
44		173	214	Cruz, Trinidad T	Daughter	F	Cha	11	S	Y	Y	Guam	Y	None
45		173	214	Cruz, Donecio T	Son	M	Cha	10	S	Y	Y	Guam	Y	None
46		173	214	Cruz, Jose T	Son	M	Cha	6	S	N		Guam		None
47		173	214	Cruz, Manuel T	Son	M	Cha	3.9	S	N		Guam		None
48		173	214	Cruz, Francisco T	Son	M	Cha	1.2	S	N		Guam		None
49		174	216	Tenorio, Pilajia A	Head	F	Cha	29	M	N	Y	Guam	N	None
50		174	216	Tenorio, Delfina T	Niece	F	Cha	12	S	Y	Y	Guam	Y	None

(CHAMORRO ROOTS GENEALOGY PROJECT™ TRANSCRIPTION)
(BERNARD T. PUNZALAN / HTTP://WWW.CHAMORROROOTS.COM)

DEPARTMENT OF COMMERCE-BUREAU OF THE CENSUS
WASHINGTON

FIFTEENTH CENSUS OF THE UNITED STATES: 1930-POPULATION

THE ISLAND OF GUAM

Sheet No. 22A

District **Municipality of Agana**
Name of Place **Agana City (San Nicolas)**
[Proper name and, also, name of class, as city, town, village, barrio, etc]

Enumeration District No. **1**
Enumerated by me on **April 23, 1930** Pauline L. Dees
Enumerator

	PLACE OF ABODE			NAME	RELATION	PERSONAL DESCRIPTION				EDUCATION		NATIVITY		OCCUPATION
	Street, avenue, road, etc.	Number of dwelling house in order of visitation	Number of family in order of visitation	of each person whose place of abode on April 1, 1930, was in this family. Enter surname, first, then given name and middle initial. If any. Include every person living on April 1, 1930. Omit children born since April 1, 1930.	Relationship of this Person to the head of the family.	Sex	Color or race	Age at last birthday	Single, married, widowed or divorced	Attended school any time since Sept. 1, 1929	Whether able to read and write.	Place of birth of this person.	Whether able to speak English.	
	1	2	3	4	5	6	7	8	9	10	11	12	13	14
1	Minondo Street	174	216	Tenorio, Ana T	Niece	F	Cha	2	S	N		Guam		None
2		176	216	Quichocho, Tomasa C	Head	F	Cha	21	S	N	Y	Guam	Y	None
3		175	217	Flores, Carmen S	Head	F	Cha	42	Wd	N	Y	Guam	Y	Farmer
4		175	217	Flores, Mariano S	Son	M	Cha	20	S	N	Y	Guam	Y	Machinist
5		175	217	Flores, Jose S	Son	M	Cha	19	S	N	Y	Guam	Y	Clerk
6		176	218	Castro, Pedro C	Head	M	Cha	35	M	N	Y	Guam	Y	Carpenter
7		176	218	Castro, Concepcion R	Wife	F	Cha	33	M	N	Y	Guam	Y	None
8		176	218	Castro, Francisco R	Son	M	Cha	8	S	Y		Guam		None
9		176	218	Castro, Maria R	Daughter	F	Cha	6	S	N		Guam		None
10		176	218	Castro, Vicente R	Son	M	Cha	5	S	N		Guam		None
11		176	218	Castro, Dorothea R	Daughter	F	Cha	4.5	S	N		Guam		None
12		176	218	Castro, Virginia R	Daughter	F	Cha	2.8	S	N		Guam		None
13		176	218	Castro, Ojenia R	Daughter	F	Cha	1.7	S	N		Guam		None
14		177	219	Flores, Guillermo S	Head	M	Cha	32	M	N	Y	Guam	Y	Farmer
15		177	219	Flores, Rita de L.	Wife	F	Cha	38	M	N	Y	Guam	Y	None
16		177	219	Flores, Guillermo de L.	Son	M	Cha	11	S	Y	Y	Guam	Y	None
17		177	219	Flores, Ruth de L.	Daughter	F	Cha	9	S	Y		Guam		None
18		177	219	Flores, Elizabeth de L.	Daughter	F	Cha	7	S	Y		Guam		None
19		177	219	Flores, Antonia de L.	Daughter	F	Cha	6	S	N		Guam		None
20		177	219	Flores, David de L.	Son	M	Cha	3.9	S	N		Guam		None
21		177	219	Flores, Jose de L.	Son	M	Cha	.8	S	N		Guam		None
22	San Juan de Letran	178	220	Diaz, Francisca P	Head	F	Cha	54	Wd	N	Y	Guam	N	None
23		178	220	Pangelinan, Ana R	Sister	F	Cha	49	S	N	Y	Guam	N	None
24		178	220	Pangelinan, Jose R	Brother	M	Cha	46	S	N	Y	Guam	N	Farmer
25		178	220	Pangelinan, Juana R	Sister	F	Cha	44	S	N	Y	Guam	N	None

(CHAMORRO ROOTS GENEALOGY PROJECT™ TRANSCRIPTION)
(BERNARD T. PUNZALAN / HTTP://WWW.CHAMORROROOTS.COM)

DEPARTMENT OF COMMERCE-BUREAU OF THE CENSUS
WASHINGTON

FIFTEENTH CENSUS OF THE UNITED STATES: 1930-POPULATION

THE ISLAND OF GUAM

Sheet No. 22B

22B

District **Municipality of Agana**
Name of Place **Agana City (San Nicolas)**
[Proper name and, also, name of class, as city, town, village, barrio, etc]

Enumeration District No. **1**
Enumerated by me on **April 23, 1930** Pauline L. Dees
Enumerator

	PLACE OF ABODE			NAME	RELATION	PERSONAL DESCRIPTION				EDUCATION		NATIVITY		OCCUPATION
	Street, avenue, road, etc.	Number of dwelling house is order of visitation	Number of family in order of visitation	of each person whose place of abode on April 1, 1930, was in this family. Enter surname, first, then given name and middle initial. If any. Include every person living on April 1, 1930. Omit children born since April 1, 1930.	Relationship of this Person to the head of the family.	Sex	Color or race	Age at last birthday	Single, married, widowed or divorced	Attended school any time since Sept. 1, 1929	Whether able to read and write.	Place of birth of this person.	Whether able to speak English.	
	1	2	3	4	5	6	7	8	9	10	11	12	13	14
26	San Juan de Letran	178	220	Pangelinan, Joaquina R	Sister	F	Cha	39	S	N	Y	Guam	N	None
27		178	220	San Nicolas, Isabel P	Niece	F	Cha	15	S	N	Y	Guam	N	None
28		178	220	Reyes, Luis SA	Ward	M	Cha	11	S	Y	Y	Guam	Y	None
29		179	221	Siguenza, Carmen M	Head	F	Cha	35	M	N	Y	Guam	Y	Midwife
30		179	221	Siguenza, Luis M	Son	M	Cha	8	S	Y		Guam		None
31		179	221	Siguenza, Jesus M	Son	M	Cha	5	S	N		Guam		None
32		179	221	Siguenza, Rosa M	Daughter	F	Cha	4.2	S	N		Guam		None
33		179	221	Siguenza, Carmen M	Daughter	F	Cha	2.2	S	N		Guam		None
34		179	221	Siguenza, Remedios M	Daughter	F	Cha	1.3	S	N		Guam		None
35		179	221	Siguenza, Dolores S	Motherinlaw	F	Cha	63	Wd	N	Y	Guam	N	None
36		180	222	Manibusan, Lorenzo SN	Head	M	Cha	45	M	N	Y	Guam	Y	Farmer
37		180	222	Manibusan, Regina A	Wife	F	Cha	46	M	N	Y	Guam	N	None
38		180	222	Manibusan, Jose A	Son	M	Cha	16	S	Y	Y	Guam	Y	None
39		180	222	Manibusan, Lorenzo A	Son	M	Cha	15	S	Y	Y	Guam	Y	None
40		180	222	Manibusan, Juan A	Son	M	Cha	13	S	Y	Y	Guam	Y	None
41		181	223	Cabrera, Concepcion C	Head	F	Cha	38	S	N	Y	Guam	N	Midwife
42		181	223	Cabrera, Francisco C	Son	M	Cha	14	S	Y	Y	Guam	Y	None
43		181	223	Cabrera, Vicente C	Son	M	Cha	10	S	Y	Y	Guam	Y	None
44		181	223	Cabrera, Jesus C	Son	M	Cha	4.5	S	N		Guam		None
45		182	224	Siguenza, Consolacion C	Head	F	Cha	34	M	N	Y	Guam	Y	None
46		182	224	Siguenza, Emilia C	Daughter	F	Cha	11	S	Y	Y	Guam	Y	None
47		182	224	Siguenza, Pedro C	Son	M	Cha	10	S	Y	Y	Guam	Y	None
48		182	224	Siguenza, Oliva C	Daughter	F	Cha	6	S	Y		Guam		None
49		182	224	Siguenza, Fidela C	Daughter	F	Cha	5	S	N		Guam		None
50		182	224	Siguenza, Josefina C	Daughter	F	Cha	3.1	S	N		Guam		None

(CHAMORRO ROOTS GENEALOGY PROJECT™ TRANSCRIPTION)
(BERNARD T. PUNZALAN / HTTP://WWW.CHAMORROROOTS.COM)

DEPARTMENT OF COMMERCE-BUREAU OF THE CENSUS
WASHINGTON

FIFTEENTH CENSUS OF THE UNITED STATES: 1930-POPULATION

THE ISLAND OF GUAM

Sheet No. 23A

District Municipality of Agana
Name of Place Agana City (San Nicolas)
[Proper name and, also, name of class, as city, town, village, barrio, etc]

Enumeration District No. 1
Enumerated by me on April 24, 1930 Pauline L. Dees, Enumerator

	PLACE OF ABODE			NAME	RELATION	PERSONAL DESCRIPTION				EDUCATION		NATIVITY		OCCUPATION
	Street, avenue, road, etc.	Number of dwelling house is order of visitation	Number of family in order of visitation	of each person whose place of abode on April 1, 1930, was in this family. Enter surname, first, then given name and middle initial. If any. Include every person living on April 1, 1930. Omit children born since April 1, 1930.	Relationship of this Person to the head of the family.	Sex	Color or race	Age at last birthday	Single, married, widowed or divorced	Attended school any time since Sept. 1, 1929	Whether able to read and write.	Place of birth of this person.	Whether able to speak English.	
	1	2	3	4	5	6	7	8	9	10	11	12	13	14
1	San Juan de Letran	183	225	Lizama, Felix F	Head	M	Cha	23	M	N	Y	Guam	Y	Cook
2		183	225	Lizama, Concepcion D	Wife	F	Cha	19	M	N	Y	Guam	Y	None
3		184	226	Finona, Rita G	Head	F	Cha	57	Wd	N	N	Guam	N	None
4		184	226	Finona, Jesus G	Son	M	Cha	27	S	N	Y	Guam	Y	Farmer
5		185	227	Quitugua, Jose A	Head	M	Cha	48	M	N	Y	Guam	N	Farmer
6		185	227	Quitugua, Milagro P	Wife	F	Cha	47	M	N	Y	Guam	N	None
7		185	227	Quitugua, Maria P	Daughter	F	Cha	26	S	N	Y	Guam	Y	None
8		185	227	Quitugua, Ignacio P	Son	M	Cha	21	S	N	Y	Guam	Y	Teacher
9		185	227	Quitugua, Vicente P	Son	M	Cha	18	S	N	Y	Guam	Y	Teacher
10		185	227	Quitugua, Joaquin P	Son	M	Cha	16	S	N	Y	Guam	Y	None
11		185	228	Quitugua, Jose P	Head	M	Cha	23	M	N	Y	Guam	Y	Laborer
12		185	228	Quitugua, Josefina M	Wife	F	Cha	21	M	N	Y	Guam	Y	None
13		185	228	Quitugua, Pedro M	Son	M	Cha	3.3	S	N		Guam		None
14		185	228	Quitugua, Honoria M	Daughter	F	Cha	2.3	S	N		Guam		None
15		186	229	Franquez, Vicente I	Head	M	Cha	48	M	N	Y	Guam	Y	Silversmith
16		186	229	Franquez, Felicita M	Wife	F	Cha	27	M	N	Y	Guam	Y	None
17		186	229	Franquez, Emiliana P	Daughter	F	Cha	22	S	N	Y	Guam	Y	None
18		186	229	Franquez, Maria P	Daughter	F	Cha	20	S	N	Y	Guam	Y	None
19		186	229	Franquez, Rita C	Daughter	F	Cha	15	S	Y	Y	Guam	Y	None
20		186	229	Franquez, Antonia C	Daughter	F	Cha	13	S	Y	Y	Guam	Y	None
21		186	229	Franquez, Remedios C	Daughter	F	Cha	11	S	Y	Y	Guam	Y	None
22		186	229	Franquez, Lorenzo C	Son	M	Cha	9	S	Y		Guam		None
23		186	229	Franquez, Josefina C	Daughter	F	Cha	7	S	Y		Guam		None
24		186	229	Franquez, Jose C	Son	M	Cha	6	S	N		Guam		None
25		186	229	Franquez, Patricia M	Daughter	F	Cha	2.9	S	N		Guam		None

(CHAMORRO ROOTS GENEALOGY PROJECT™ TRANSCRIPTION)
(BERNARD T. PUNZALAN / HTTP://WWW.CHAMORROROOTS.COM)

DEPARTMENT OF COMMERCE-BUREAU OF THE CENSUS
WASHINGTON

FIFTEENTH CENSUS OF THE UNITED STATES: 1930-POPULATION

THE ISLAND OF GUAM

Sheet No. 23B

23B

District Municipality of Agana
Name of Place Agana City (San Nicolas)
[Proper name and, also, name of class, as city, town, village, barrio, etc]

Enumeration District No. 1
Enumerated by me on April 24, 1930 Pauline L. Dees
Enumerator

	PLACE OF ABODE			NAME	RELATION	PERSONAL DESCRIPTION				EDUCATION		NATIVITY		OCCUPATION
	Street, avenue, road, etc.	Number of dwelling house in order of visitation	Number of family in order of visitation	of each person whose place of abode on April 1, 1930, was in this family. Enter surname, first, then given name and middle initial. If any. Include every person living on April 1, 1930. Omit children born since April 1, 1930.	Relationship of this Person to the head of the family.	Sex	Color or race	Age at last birthday	Single, married, widowed or divorced	Attended school any time since Sept. 1, 1929	Whether able to read and write.	Place of birth of this person.	Whether able to speak English.	
	1	2	3	4	5	6	7	8	9	10	11	12	13	14
26	San Juan de Letran	186	229	Franquez, Mercedes M	Daughter	F	Cha	1.7	S	N		Guam		None
27		187	230	Stuart, Sarah C	Head	F	W	27	M	N	Y	Guam	Y	None
28		187	230	Stuart, James Jr. A	Son	M	W	5	S	N		Guam		None
29		187	230	Stuart, Thomas R	Son	M	W	2.9	S	N		Haiti		None
30		187	230	Stuart, Jerome C	Son	M	W	.5	S	N		South Carolina		None
31		188	231	Villagomez, Elena C	Head	F	Cha	52	S	N	Y	Guam	Y	Washerwoman
32		188	231	Villagomez, Rosa C	Sister	F	Cha	50	S	N	Y	Guam	Y	Washerwoman
33		188	231	Villagomez, Juana C	Sister	F	Cha	47	S	N	Y	Guam	Y	Washerwoman
34		188	231	Villagomez, Maria C	Niece	F	Cha	12	S	N	Y	Guam	Y	None
35		189	232	Pablo, Jose C	Head	M	Cha	34	M	N	Y	Guam	Y	Farmer
36		189	232	Pablo, Maria P	Wife	F	Cha	30	M	N	Y	Guam	Y	None
37		189	232	Pablo, Juan P	Son	M	Cha	11	S	Y	Y	Guam	Y	None
38		190	233	Clark, Ruth V	Head	F	W	27	M	N	Y	England	Y	Pianist
39		190	233	Clark, Gordon T	Son	M	W	4.3	S	N		California		None
40		190	233	Clark, Rodney A	Son	M	W	2.9	S	N		California		None
41		191	234	Toves, Joaquin C	Head	M	Cha	27	M	N	Y	Guam	Y	Farmer
42		191	234	Toves, Ann Q	Wife	F	Cha	28	M	N	Y	Guam	Y	None
43		191	234	Toves, Juan Q	Son	M	Cha	4.3	S	N		Guam		None
44		191	234	Toves, Teresa Q	Daughter	F	Cha	1.7	S	N		Guam		None
45		192	235	Cruz, Joaquin C	Head	M	Cha	52	M	N	Y	Guam	N	Farmer
46		192	235	Cruz, Ignacia G	Wife	F	Cha	37	M	N	Y	Guam	N	None
47		192	235	Cruz, Jesus G	Son	M	Cha	18	S	N	Y	Guam	N	Farm laborer
48		192	235	Cruz, Jose G	Son	M	Cha	13	S	Y	Y	Guam	Y	None
49		192	235	Cruz, Isabel G	Daughter	F	Cha	11	S	Y	Y	Guam	Y	None
50		192	235	Cruz, Rosalia G	Daughter	F	Cha	9	S	Y		Guam		None

(CHAMORRO ROOTS GENEALOGY PROJECT™ TRANSCRIPTION)
(BERNARD T. PUNZALAN / HTTP://WWW.CHAMORROROOTS.COM)

DEPARTMENT OF COMMERCE-BUREAU OF THE CENSUS
WASHINGTON

FIFTEENTH CENSUS OF THE UNITED STATES: 1930-POPULATION

THE ISLAND OF GUAM

Sheet No. 24A

District **Municipality of Agana**
Name of Place **Agana City (San Nicolas)**
[Proper name and, also, name of class, as city, town, village, barrio, etc]

Enumeration District No. **1**
Enumerated by me on **April 25, 1930** Pauline L. Dees
Enumerator

	PLACE OF ABODE			NAME	RELATION	PERSONAL DESCRIPTION				EDUCATION		NATIVITY		OCCUPATION
	Street, avenue, road, etc.	Number of dwelling house is order of visitation	Number of family in order of visitation	of each person whose place of abode on April 1, 1930, was in this family. Enter surname, first, then given name and middle initial. If any. Include every person living on April 1, 1930. Omit children born since April 1, 1930.	Relationship of this Person to the head of the family.	Sex	Color or race	Age at last birthday	Single, married, widowed or divorced	Attended school any time since Sept. 1, 1929	Whether able to read and write.	Place of birth of this person.	Whether able to speak English.	
	1	2	3	4	5	6	7	8	9	10	11	12	13	14
1	San Juan de Letran	192	235	Cruz, Joaquin G	Son	M	Cha	6	S	Y		Guam		None
2		192	235	Cruz, Francisco G	Son	M	Cha	3.9	S	N		Guam		None
3		193	236	Atoigue, Rita T	Head	F	Cha	50	M	N	Y	Guam	N	None
4		193	236	Atoigue, Asuncion T	Daughter	F	Cha	25	S	N	Y	Guam	Y	Cook
5		193	236	Atoigue, Antonio T	Son	M	Cha	20	S	N	Y	Guam	Y	Laborer
6		193	236	Atoigue, Antonia T	Daughter	F	Cha	15	S	N	Y	Guam	Y	None
7		193	236	Atoigue, Teresa T	Daughter	F	Cha	11	S	Y	Y	Guam	Y	None
8		193	236	Toves, Maria S	Mother	F	Cha	67	Wd	N	N	Guam	N	None
9		194	237	Muna, Juan D	Head	M	Cha	54	M	N	Y	Guam	Y	Farmer
10		194	237	Muna, Maria T	Wife	F	Cha	48	M	N	N	Guam	N	None
11		194	237	Muna, Juan F	Son	M	Cha	20	S	N	Y	Guam	Y	Farm laborer
12		194	237	Muna, Dolores F	Daughter	F	Cha	15	S	N	Y	Guam	Y	None
13		194	237	Muna, Vicente T	Son	M	Cha	15	S	N	Y	Guam	Y	Farm laborer
14		194	238	Muna, Joaquin F	Head	M	Cha	23	M	N	Y	Guam	Y	Cook
15		194	238	Muna, Ana G	Wife	F	Cha	24	M	N	Y	Guam	Y	None
16		194	238	Muna, Rosa G	Daughter	F	Cha	.3	S	N		Guam		None
17		194	238	Quichocho, Ignacia T	Niece	F	Cha	1.9	S	N		Guam		None
18		195	239	Simpson, Elvia H	Head	F	W	30	M	N	Y	Texas	Y	None
19		195	239	Simpson, Kirkpatrick	Son	M	W	8	S	Y		Texas		None
20		196	240	Rosario, Luisa LG	Head	F	Cha	65	Wd	N	Y	Guam	N	None
21		196	240	Rosario, Ana LG	Daughter	F	Cha	48	S	N	Y	Guam	N	Washerwoman
22		196	240	Rosario, Vicente LG	Son	M	Cha	45	S	N	Y	Guam	Y	Farmer
23	Maria Ana de Austria	197	241	Palumbo, Theena C	Head	F	W	33	M	N	Y	Guam	Y	None
24		197	241	Hazeltime, Laura V	Ward	F	W	10	S	Y	Y	Guam	Y	None
25		198	242	Siguenza, Vicente S	Head	M	Cha	45	M	N	Y	Guam	Y	Blacksmith

(CHAMORRO ROOTS GENEALOGY PROJECT™ TRANSCRIPTION)
(BERNARD T. PUNZALAN / HTTP://WWW.CHAMORROROOTS.COM)

DEPARTMENT OF COMMERCE-BUREAU OF THE CENSUS
WASHINGTON

FIFTEENTH CENSUS OF THE UNITED STATES: 1930-POPULATION

THE ISLAND OF GUAM

Sheet No. 24B

24B

District Municipality of Agana
Name of Place Agana City (San Nicolas)
[Proper name and, also, name of class, as city, town, village, barrio, etc]

Enumeration District No. 1
Enumerated by me on April 25, 1930 Pauline L. Dees
Enumerator

	PLACE OF ABODE			NAME	RELATION	PERSONAL DESCRIPTION				EDUCATION		NATIVITY		OCCUPATION
	Street, avenue, road, etc.	Number of dwelling house is order of visitation	Number of family in order of visitation	of each person whose place of abode on April 1, 1930, was in this family. Enter surname, first, then given name and middle initial. If any. Include every person living on April 1, 1930. Omit children born since April 1, 1930.	Relationship of this Person to the head of the family.	Sex	Color or race	Age at last birthday	Single, married, widowed or divorced	Attended school any time since Sept. 1, 1929	Whether able to read and write.	Place of birth of this person.	Whether able to speak English.	
	1	2	3	4	5	6	7	8	9	10	11	12	13	14
26	Maria Ana de Austria	198	242	Siguenza, Dolores C	Wife	F	Cha	34	M	N	Y	Guam	Y	None
27		198	242	Siguenza, Jose C	Son	M	Cha	15	S	Y	Y	Guam	Y	None
28		198	242	Siguenza, Juan C	Son	M	Cha	13	S	Y	Y	Guam	Y	None
29		198	242	Siguenza, Vicente C	Son	M	Cha	11	S	Y	Y	Guam	Y	None
30		198	242	Siguenza, Dolores C	Daughter	F	Cha	7	S	Y		Guam		None
31		198	242	Siguenza, Gregorio C	Son	M	Cha	5	S	N		Guam		None
32		198	242	Siguenza, Jesus C	Son	M	Cha	2.7	S	N		Guam		None
33		198	242	Siguenza, Maria C	Daughter	F	Cha	.5	S	N		Guam		None
34		199	243	Pangelinan, Jose C	Head	M	Cha	40	M	N	Y	Guam	Y	Carpenter
35		199	243	Pangelinan, Antonia B	Wife	F	Cha	36	M	N	Y	Guam	Y	Dressmaker
36		199	243	Pangelinan, Francisca B	Daughter	F	Cha	9	S	Y		Guam		None
37		199	243	Pangelinan, Jose B	Son	M	Cha	8	S	Y		Guam		None
38		199	243	Pangelinan, Joaquin B	Son	M	Cha	5	S	N		Guam		None
39		199	243	Pangelinan, Nicolas B	Son	M	Cha	2.6	S	N		Guam		None
40		199	243	Pangelinan, Consolacion B	Daughter	F	Cha	.6	S	N		Guam		None
41		199	243	Pangelinan, Francisco B	Father	M	Cha	65	Wd	N	Y	Guam	Y	Carpenter
42		200	244	Perez, Daniel L	Head	M	Cha	36	M	N	Y	Guam	Y	Teacher
43		200	244	Perez, Rosa C	Wife	F	Cha	33	M	N	Y	Guam	Y	Teacher
44		200	244	Perez, Gerado C	Son	M	Cha	14	S	Y	Y	Guam	Y	None
45		200	244	Perez, Dorothea C	Daughter	F	Cha	13	S	Y	Y	Guam	Y	None
46		200	244	Perez, Maria C	Daughter	F	Cha	10	S	Y	Y	Guam	Y	None
47		200	244	Perez, Vicente C	Son	M	Cha	8	S	Y		Guam		None
48		200	244	Perez, Eulogia C	Daughter	F	Cha	4.8	S	N		Guam		None
49		200	244	Perez, Theodoro C	Son	M	Cha	2.5	S	N		Guam		None
50		201	245	Cruz, Demetrio G	Head	M	Cha	27	M	N	Y	Guam	Y	Blacksmith

DEPARTMENT OF COMMERCE-BUREAU OF THE CENSUS
WASHINGTON

FIFTEENTH CENSUS OF THE UNITED STATES: 1930-POPULATION

THE ISLAND OF GUAM

Sheet No. 25A

District **Municipality of Agana**
Name of Place **Agana City (San Nicolas)**
[Proper name and, also, name of class, as city, town, village, barrio, etc]

Enumeration District No. 1
Enumerated by me on **April 26, 1930** Pauline L. Dees, Enumerator

	PLACE OF ABODE			NAME	RELATION	PERSONAL DESCRIPTION				EDUCATION		NATIVITY		OCCUPATION
	Street, avenue, road, etc.	Number of dwelling house in order of visitation	Number of family in order of visitation	of each person whose place of abode on April 1, 1930, was in this family. Enter surname, first, then given name and middle initial. If any. Include every person living on April 1, 1930. Omit children born since April 1, 1930.	Relationship of this Person to the head of the family.	Sex	Color or race	Age at last birthday	Single, married, widowed or divorced	Attended school any time since Sept. 1, 1929	Whether able to read and write.	Place of birth of this person.	Whether able to speak English.	
	1	2	3	4	5	6	7	8	9	10	11	12	13	14
1	Maria Ana de Austria	201	245	Cruz, Teresa D	Wife	F	Cha	24	M	N	Y	Guam	Y	None
2		201	245	Cruz, Edward D	Son	M	Cha	3.3	S	N		Guam		None
3		201	245	Cruz, Felicita D	Daughter	F	Cha	2.2	S	N		Guam		None
4		201	245	Cruz, Guadalup D	Daughter	F	Cha	1	S	N		Guam		None
5		202	246	de Tobes, Eliza C	Head	F	Cha	25	M	N	Y	Guam	Y	None
6		202	246	de Tobes, Juan C	Son	M	Cha	3.5	S	N		Guam		None
7		202	246	Cruz, Ana G	Sisterinlaw	F	Cha	15	S	Y	Y	Guam	Y	None
8		203	247	de Leon, Jose M	Head	M	Cha	55	M	N	Y	Guam	Y	Carpenter
9		203	247	de Leon, Francisca I	Wife	F	Cha	52	M	N	Y	Guam	Y	None
10		203	248	de Leon, Dolores A	Head	F	Cha	17	M	N	Y	Guam	Y	None
11		204	249	Iglesias, Enrique T	Head	M	Cha	40	M	N	Y	Guam	Y	Bookkeeper
12		204	249	Iglesias, Josefa A	Wife	F	Cha	40	M	N	Y	Guam	Y	Musician
13		204	249	Iglesias, Antonio A	Son	M	Cha	19	S	N	Y	Guam	Y	Sailor
14		204	249	Iglesias, Maria A	Daughter	F	Cha	17	S	N	Y	Guam	Y	None
15		204	249	Iglesias, Tomas A	Son	M	Cha	14	S	Y	Y	Guam	Y	None
16		204	249	Iglesias, Isabel A	Daughter	F	Cha	10	S	Y	Y	Guam	Y	None
17		204	249	Iglesias, Jesus A	Son	M	Cha	3.3	S	N		Guam		None
18		205	250	de Leon, Ana D	Head	F	Cha	30	M	N	Y	Guam	Y	None
19		205	250	de Leon, Juanita D	Daughter	F	Cha	9	S	Y		Guam		None
20		205	250	de Leon, Francisca D	Daughter	F	Cha	5	S	N		Guam		None
21		205	250	de Leon, Gregorio D	Son	M	Cha	4.3	S	N		Guam		None
22		205	250	de Leon, Jesus D	Son	M	Cha	3.3	S	N		Guam		None
23		205	250	de Leon, Tomas D	Son	M	Cha	1.5	S	N		Guam		None
24		206	251	Aflague, Vicente T	Head	M	Cha	33	M	N	Y	Guam	Y	Silversmith
25		206	251	Aflague, Ana C	Wife	F	Cha	34	M	N	Y	Guam	Y	None

(CHAMORRO ROOTS GENEALOGY PROJECT™ TRANSCRIPTION)
(BERNARD T. PUNZALAN / HTTP://WWW.CHAMORROROOTS.COM)

DEPARTMENT OF COMMERCE-BUREAU OF THE CENSUS
WASHINGTON

FIFTEENTH CENSUS OF THE UNITED STATES: 1930-POPULATION

THE ISLAND OF GUAM

Sheet No. 25B

25B

District **Municipality of Agana**
Name of Place **Agana City (San Nicolas)**
[Proper name and, also, name of class, as city, town, village, barrio, etc]

Enumeration District No. 1
Enumerated by me on **April 26, 1930** Pauline L. Dees
Enumerator

	PLACE OF ABODE			NAME	RELATION	PERSONAL DESCRIPTION				EDUCATION		NATIVITY		OCCUPATION
	Street, avenue, road, etc.	Number of dwelling house is order of visitation	Number of family in order of visitation	of each person whose place of abode on April 1, 1930, was in this family. Enter surname, first, then given name and middle initial. If any. Include every person living on April 1, 1930. Omit children born since April 1, 1930.	Relationship of this Person to the head of the family.	Sex	Color or race	Age at last birthday	Single, married, widowed or divorced	Attended school any time since Sept. 1, 1929	Whether able to read and write.	Place of birth of this person.	Whether able to speak English.	
	1	2	3	4	5	6	7	8	9	10	11	12	13	14
26	San Juan de Letran	206	251	Aflague, Vicente C	Son	M	Cha	8	S	Y	Y	Guam	Y	None
27		206	251	Aflague, Maria C	Daughter	F	Cha	7	S	Y		Guam		None
28		206	251	Aflague, Ana C	Daughter	F	Cha	3	S	N		Guam		None
29		206	251	Aflague, Eugenia C	Daughter	F	Cha	0	S	N		Guam		None
30		206	251	Quintanilla, Joaquin SN	Servant	M	Cha	19	S	N	Y	Guam		Apprentice Silversmith
31		207	252	Suarez, Antonio C	Head	M	Cha	52	M	N	Y	Guam	Y	Commissioner
32		207	252	Suarez, Teresa M	Wife	F	Cha	27	M	N	Y	Guam	Y	None
33		207	252	Suarez, Guadalupe M	Daughter	F	Cha	12	S	Y	Y	Guam	Y	None
34		207	252	Suarez, Ana M	Daughter	F	Cha	10	S	Y	Y	Guam	Y	None
35		207	252	Suarez, Rosa M	Daughter	F	Cha	8	S	Y		Guam		None
36		207	252	Suarez, Antonio D	Daughter	F	Cha	6	S	N		Guam		None
37		207	252	Suarez, Francisco M	Son	M	Cha	3.5	S	N		Guam		None
38		207	252	Suarez, Maria A	Daughter	F	Cha	1.9	S	N		Guam		None
39		207	252	Borja, Maria G	Aunt	F	Cha	60	S	N	Y	Guam	N	None
40		208	253	Duenas, Juan M	Head	M	Cha	67	Wd	N	Y	Guam	N	None
41		208	253	Duenas, Joaquin D	Son	M	Cha	33	S	N	Y	Guam	N	Laborer
42		208	253	Duenas, Remedios D	Daughter	F	Cha	27	S	N	Y	Guam	Y	None
43		208	253	Duenas, Josefa D	Daughter	F	Cha	24	S	N	Y	Guam	Y	None
44		208	253	Duenas, Juan D	Son	M	Cha	19	S	N	Y	Guam	Y	Chauffeur
45		208	253	Duenas, Vicente D	Son	M	Cha	13	S	Y	Y	Guam	Y	None
46		209	254	Wood, Anne S	Head	F	W	28	M	N	Y	Pennsylvania	Y	None
47		210	255	Quitugua, Joaquin A	Head	M	Cha	40	S	N	Y	Guam	Y	Farmer
48	Dr. Hesler Street	211	256	Leon Guerrero, Vicente LG	Head	M	Cha	40	M	N	N	Guam	Y	Farmer
49		211	256	Leon Guerrero, Dolores F	Wife	F	Cha	41	M	N	N	Guam	Y	None
50		211	256	Leon Guerrero, Maria F	Daughter	F	Cha	8	S	Y		Guam		None

DEPARTMENT OF COMMERCE-BUREAU OF THE CENSUS
WASHINGTON

FIFTEENTH CENSUS OF THE UNITED STATES: 1930-POPULATION

THE ISLAND OF GUAM

Sheet No. 26A

District **Municipality of Agana**
Name of Place **Agana City (San Nicolas)**
[Proper name and, also, name of class, as city, town, village, barrio, etc]

Enumeration District No. 1
Enumerated by me on **April 26, 1930** Pauline L. Dees
Enumerator

	PLACE OF ABODE			NAME	RELATION	PERSONAL DESCRIPTION				EDUCATION		NATIVITY		OCCUPATION
	Street, avenue, road, etc.	Number of dwelling house in order of visitation	Number of family in order of visitation	of each person whose place of abode on April 1, 1930, was in this family. Enter surname, first, then given name and middle initial. If any. Include every person living on April 1, 1930. Omit children born since April 1, 1930.	Relationship of this Person to the head of the family.	Sex	Color or race	Age at last birthday	Single, married, widowed or divorced	Attended school any time since Sept. 1, 1929	Whether able to read and write.	Place of birth of this person.	Whether able to speak English.	
	1	2	3	4	5	6	7	8	9	10	11	12	13	14
1		211	256	Leon Guerrero, Antonia F	Daughter	F	Cha	7	S	Y		Guam		None
2	San Nicolas St.	212	257	Mesa, Jesus G	Head	M	Cha	29	M	N	Y	Guam	Y	Chauffeur
3		212	257	Mesa, Ana C	Wife	F	Cha	26	M	N	Y	Guam	Y	None
4		212	257	Mesa, Antonio C	Son	M	Cha	3.8	S	N		Guam		None
5		212	257	Mesa, William C	Son	M	Cha	2.9	S	N		Guam		None
6		212	257	Mesa, Edward C	Son	M	Cha	1.3	S	N		Guam		None
7	Dr. Hesler	212	257	Mesa, Teresita C	Daughter	F	Cha	0.1	S	N		Guam		None
8	San Juan de Letran	213	258	Garrido, Ignacio L	Head	M	Cha	60	M	N	Y	Guam	Y	Farmer
9		213	258	Garrido, Magdalena P	Wife	F	Cha	63	M	N	Y	Guam	N	None
10		214	259	Kamminga, Jose	Head	M	Cha	39	M	N	Y	Guam	Y	Teacher
11		214	259	Kamminga, Maria F	Wife	F	Cha	38	M	N	Y	Guam	N	Retail merchant
12		214	259	Kamminga, Magdalena F	Daughter	F	Cha	18	S	N	Y	Guam	Y	Saleswoman
13		214	259	Kamminga, Gaily F	Son	M	Cha	17	S	N	Y	Guam	Y	Barber
14		214	259	Kamminga, Joaquina F	Daughter	F	Cha	16	S	N	Y	Guam	Y	None
15		214	259	Kamminga, Maria F	Daughter	F	Cha	14	S	Y	Y	Guam	Y	None
16		214	259	Kamminga, Jose F	Son	M	Cha	12	S	Y	Y	Guam	Y	None
17		214	259	Kamminga, Lorenzo F	Son	M	Cha	11	S	Y	Y	Guam	Y	None
18		214	259	Kamminga, David F	Son	M	Cha	9	S	Y		Guam		None
19		214	259	Kamminga, Henry F	Son	M	Cha	5	S	N		Guam		None
20		214	259	Kamminga, Johannes F	Son	M	Cha	4.8	S	N		Guam		None
21		214	259	Kamminga, Frank F	Son	M	Cha	.9	S	N		Guam		None
22		214	259	Kamminga, Joaquina H	Mother	F	Cha	75	Wd	N	Y	Guam	N	None
23		215	260	Miller, Margaret H	Head	F	W	24	M	N	Y	Maryland	Y	None
24		216	261	Torres, Jose U	Head	M	Cha	26	M	N	Y	Guam	Y	Farmer
25		216	261	Torres, Rosa A	Wife	F	Cha	26	M	N	Y	Guam	Y	None

DEPARTMENT OF COMMERCE-BUREAU OF THE CENSUS
WASHINGTON

FIFTEENTH CENSUS OF THE UNITED STATES: 1930-POPULATION

THE ISLAND OF GUAM

Sheet No. 26B

26B

District Municipality of Agana
Name of Place Agana City (San Nicolas)
[Proper name and, also, name of class, as city, town, village, barrio, etc]

Enumeration District No. 1
Enumerated by me on April 27, 1930 Pauline L. Dees, Enumerator

	PLACE OF ABODE			NAME	RELATION	PERSONAL DESCRIPTION				EDUCATION		NATIVITY		OCCUPATION
	Street, avenue, road, etc.	Number of dwelling house is order of visitation	Number of family in order of visitation	of each person whose place of abode on April 1, 1930, was in this family. Enter surname, first, then given name and middle initial. If any. Include every person living on April 1, 1930. Omit children born since April 1, 1930.	Relationship of this Person to the head of the family.	Sex	Color or race	Age at last birthday	Single, married, widowed or divorced	Attended school any time since Sept. 1, 1929	Whether able to read and write.	Place of birth of this person.	Whether able to speak English.	
	1	2	3	4	5	6	7	8	9	10	11	12	13	14
26	San Juan	216	261	Torres, Ramon A	Son	M	Cha	2.1	S	N		Guam		None
27		216	261	Torres, Jose A	Son	M	Cha	0	S	N		Guam		None
28	Dr. Hessler	217	262	Kamminga, Gaily R	Head	M	Cha	36	M	N	Y	Guam	Y	Machinist
29		217	262	Kamminga, Elvira S	Wife	F	Cha	25	M	N	Y	Guam	Y	None
30		217	262	Kamminga, Remedios S	Daughter	F	Cha	4.4	S	N		Guam		None
31		217	262	Kamminga, John S	Son	M	Cha	2.7	S	N		Guam		None
32		217	262	Baza, Jose C	Servant	M	Cha	15	S	N	Y	Guam	Y	Houseboy
33	Pazos St.	218	263	Dees, Pauline L	Head	F	W	37	M	N	Y	Canada	Y	None
34		218	263	Dees, Louis L. D	Son	M	W	8	S	Y		Canada		None
35		218	263	Dees, Julia I. L	Daughter	F	W	2	S	N		Maryland		None
36	San Juan de Letran St.	219	264	Acfalle, Santiago A	Head	M	Cha	30	M	N	Y	Guam	Y	None
37		219	265	Agualo, Luis S	Head	M	Cha	32	M	N	Y	Guam	Y	Mechanic
38		219	266	Aguigui, Juan A	Head	M	Cha	20	S	N	Y	Guam	N	None
39		219	267	Camacho, Cecilio G	Head	M	Cha	23	S	N	Y	Guam	Y	None
40		219	268	Chiguina, Antonio M	Head	M	Cha	20	S	N	N	Guam	N	None
41		219	269	Charfauros, Juan L	Head	M	Cha	56	Wd	N	Y	Guam	N	None
42		219	270	Castro, Jose LG	Head	M	Cha	30	S	N	Y	Guam	Y	Cook
43		219	271	Cruz, Antonio B	Head	M	Cha	31	S	N	Y	Guam	Y	None
44		219	272	Cruz, Felix C	Head	M	Cha	30	S	N	Y	Guam	Y	None
45		219	273	Cruz, Felix F	Head	M	Cha	22	S	N	Y	Guam	Y	None
46		219	274	Cruz, Jesus E	Head	M	Cha	22	S	N	Y	Guam	Y	None
47		219	275	Crua, Juan LG	Head	M	Cha	20	S	N	N	Guam	N	None
48		219	276	Fejerang, Cerile A	Head	M	Cha	38	M	N	Y	Guam	Y	None
49		219	277	Laguana, Jose I	Head	M	Cha	22	S	N	Y	Guam	Y	Chauffeur
50		219	278	Leon Guerrero, Juan LG	Head	M	Cha	22	S	N	N	Guam	N	None

(CHAMORRO ROOTS GENEALOGY PROJECT™ TRANSCRIPTION)
(BERNARD T. PUNZALAN / HTTP://WWW.CHAMORROROOTS.COM)

DEPARTMENT OF COMMERCE-BUREAU OF THE CENSUS
WASHINGTON

FIFTEENTH CENSUS OF THE UNITED STATES: 1930-POPULATION

THE ISLAND OF GUAM

Sheet No. 27A

District Municipality of Agana
Name of Place Agana City (San Nicolas)
[Proper name and, also, name of class, as city, town, village, barrio, etc]

Enumeration District No. 1
Enumerated by me on April 27, 1930 Pauline L. Dees
Enumerator

	PLACE OF ABODE			NAME	RELATION	PERSONAL DESCRIPTION				EDUCATION		NATIVITY		OCCUPATION
	Street, avenue, road, etc.	Number of dwelling house is order of visitation	Number of family in order of visitation	of each person whose place of abode on April 1, 1930, was in this family. Enter surname, first, then given name and middle initial. If any. Include every person living on April 1, 1930. Omit children born since April 1, 1930.	Relationship of this Person to the head of the family.	Sex	Color or race	Age at last birthday	Single, married, widowed or divorced	Attended school any time since Sept. 1, 1929	Whether able to read and write.	Place of birth of this person.	Whether able to speak English.	
	1	2	3	4	5	6	7	8	9	10	11	12	13	14
1	San Juan de Letran	219	279	Lizama, Jose Q	Head	M	Cha	21	S	N	N	Guam	Y	None
2		219	280	Mafnas, Ignacio M	Head	M	Cha	19	S	N	Y	Guam	Y	None
3		219	281	Manibusan, Luis P	Head	M	Cha	30	M	N	N	Guam	N	None
4		219	282	Mantanona, Juan P	Head	M	Cha	25	M	N	Y	Guam	Y	None
5		219	283	Paulino, Bernabe C	Head	M	Cha	39	M	N	Y	Guam	Y	Plumber
6		219	284	Rosario, Ignacio P	Head	M	Cha	62	M	N	Y	Guam	N	None
7		219	285	Rosario, Vicente B	Head	M	Cha	30	M	N	Y	Guam	Y	Chauffeur
8		219	286	San Agustin, Jose C	Head	M	Cha	32	S	N	Y	Guam	Y	Carpenter
9		219	287	San Nicolas, Jose F	Head	M	Cha	33	S	N	Y	Guam	Y	None
10		219	288	Santos, Froilan T	Head	M	Cha	29	S	N	Y	Guam	Y	None
11		219	289	Santos, Jesus SN	Head	M	Cha	25	M	N	Y	Guam	N	None
12		219	290	Santos, Vicente SN	Head	M	Cha	28	S	N	Y	Guam	N	None
13		219	291	Taimanglo, Joaquin T	Head	M	Cha	33	S	N	Y	Guam	Y	None
14		220	282	Hare, Agnes D	Head	F	W	36	M	N	Y	At Sea US Flag	Y	None
15		220	282	Hare, Aloha D	Daughter	F	W	13	S	N	Y	California	Y	None
16		221	293	Goodwin, Sula C	Head	F	W	22	M	N	Y	Sweden	Y	None
17		222	294	Waidner, Pauline	Head	F	W	26	M	N	Y	Indiana	Y	None
18		223	295	Kunkol, Elan M	Head	F	Cha	31	M	N	Y	Indiana	Y	Teacher
19		223	295	Kunkol, Helen E	Daughter	F	Cha	6	S	Y		Indiana		None
20		223	295	Kunkol, Edward K	Son	M	Cha	3.8	S	N		California		None
21		224	296	Darling, Janice R	Head	F	W	29	M	N	Y	Florida	Y	None
22		224	296	Darling, Richard O	Son	M	W	4.8	S	Y		Florida		None
23		225	297	Wigle, Iva SN	Head	F	W	28	M	N	Y	New Jersey	Y	None
24		226	298	Cloughley, Janet W	Head	F	W	32	M	N	Y	Kansas	Y	None
25		226	298	Cloughley, Constance J	Daughter	F	W	4	S	N		California		None

DEPARTMENT OF COMMERCE-BUREAU OF THE CENSUS
WASHINGTON

FIFTEENTH CENSUS OF THE UNITED STATES: 1930-POPULATION

THE ISLAND OF GUAM

Sheet No. 27B

District Municipality of Agana
Name of Place Agana City (San Nicolas)
[Proper name and, also, name of class, as city, town, village, barrio, etc]

Enumeration District No. 1
Enumerated by me on June 9, 1930 Pauline L. Dees
Enumerator

	PLACE OF ABODE			NAME	RELATION	PERSONAL DESCRIPTION				EDUCATION		NATIVITY		OCCUPATION
	Street, avenue, road, etc.	Number of dwelling house is order of visitation	Number of family in order of visitation	of each person whose place of abode on April 1, 1930, was in this family. Enter surname, first, then given name and middle initial. If any. Include every person living on April 1, 1930. Omit children born since April 1, 1930.	Relationship of this Person to the head of the family.	Sex	Color or race	Age at last birthday	Single, married, widowed or divorced	Attended school any time since Sept. 1, 1929	Whether able to read and write.	Place of birth of this person.	Whether able to speak English.	
	1	2	3	4	5	6	7	8	9	10	11	12	13	14
26	Pazos St.	227	299	Dinamore, Marie C	Head	F	W	28	M	N	Y	Illinois	Y	None
27		228	300	Cafy, Ora E	Head	F	W	30	M	N	Y	California	Y	None
28		228	300	Cafy, Phyllis G	Daughter	F	W	8	S	Y	Y	California		None
29		228	300	Cafy, Robert A	Son	M	W	6	S	Y		Illinois		None
30				Here ends the enumeration of San Nicolas Barrio in Enumeration District Number One, Guam.										
31														
32														
33														
34														
35														
36														
37														
38														
39														
40														
41														
42														
43														
44														
45														
46														
47														
48														
49														
50														

DEPARTMENT OF COMMERCE-BUREAU OF THE CENSUS
WASHINGTON

FIFTEENTH CENSUS OF THE UNITED STATES: 1930-POPULATION

THE ISLAND OF GUAM

Sheet No. 28A

District **Municipality of Agana**
Name of Place **Agana City (San Nicolas)**
[Proper name and, also, name of class, as city, town, village, barrio, etc]

Enumeration District No. 1
Enumerated by me on **April 26, 1930** Joaquin Torres, Enumerator

	PLACE OF ABODE			NAME	RELATION	PERSONAL DESCRIPTION				EDUCATION		NATIVITY		OCCUPATION
	Street, avenue, road, etc.	Number of dwelling house is order of visitation	Number of family in order of visitation	of each person whose place of abode on April 1, 1930, was in this family. Enter surname, first, then given name and middle initial. If any. Include every person living on April 1, 1930. Omit children born since April 1, 1930.	Relationship of this Person to the head of the family.	Sex	Color or race	Age at last birthday	Single, married, widowed or divorced	Attended school any time since Sept. 1, 1929	Whether able to read and write.	Place of birth of this person.	Whether able to speak English.	
	1	2	3	4	5	6	7	8	9	10	11	12	13	14
1	San Ramon St.	275	308	Caseda, Bernabe	Head	M	W	37	S	N	Y	Spain	Y	Missionary
2		275	308	Sanguesa, Francisco J	Lodger	M	W	56	S	N	Y	Spain	Y	Missionary
3		275	308	Vera, Roman M	Lodger	M	W	51	S	N	Y	Spain	Y	Missionary
4		275	308	Madrid, Jose M	Lodger	M	W	72	S	N	Y	Spain	N	Lay Brother
5		275	308	Abarguza, Pacifico	Lodger	M	W	57	S	N	Y	Spain	N	Lay Brother
6		275	308	Imbuluzqueta, Cripsin	Lodger	M	W	51	S	N	Y	Spain	N	Lay Brother
7		276	314	Olaiz, Joaquin P Z	Head	M	W	58	S	N	Y	Spain	Y	Bishop
8		276	314	Begona, Jesus	Servant	M	W	33	S	N	Y	Spain	N	Lay Brother
9		277	315	Leon Guerrero, Antonia B	Head	F	Cha	67	Wd	N	Y	Guam	N	Retail merchant
10		277	315	Leon Guerrero, Ana B	Daughter	F	Cha	47	S	N	Y	Guam	Y	None
11		277	315	Leon Guerrero, Maria B	Daughter	F	Cha	45	S	N	Y	Saipan Island	Y	None
12		277	315	Leon Guerrero, Exsaperanza B	Daughter	F	Cha	38	S	N	Y	Guam	Y	None
13		277	315	Leon Guerrero, Vicente C	Grandson	M	Cha	19	S	N	Y	Guam	Y	Servant
14		277	315	Leon Guerrero, Joaquin C	Grandson	M	Cha	17	S	N	Y	Guam	Y	Servant
15		277	315	Leon Guerrero, Silvestre C	Grandson	M	Cha	15	S	Y	Y	Guam	Y	None
16		277	316	Leon Guerrero, Joaquin B	Head	M	Cha	35	Wd	N	Y	Saipan Island	Y	Farmer
17		277	316	Leon Guerrero, Ester F	Daughter	F	Cha	13	S	N	Y	Guam	Y	None
18		277	317	Leon Guerrero, Gonzalo A	Head	M	Cha	36	M	N	Y	Saipan Island	Y	Clerk
19		277	317	Leon Guerrero, Maria A	Wife	F	Cha	35	M	N	Y	Guam	Y	None
20		277	317	Leon Guerrero, Gonzalo A	Son	M	Cha	13	S	Y	Y	Guam	Y	None
21		277	317	Leon Guerrero, Linea A	Daughter	F	Cha	11	S	Y	Y	Guam	Y	None
22		277	317	Leon Guerrero, Caridad A	Daughter	F	Cha	10	S	Y	Y	Guam		None
23		277	317	Leon Guerrero, Joaquin A	Son	M	Cha	8	S	Y		Guam		None
24		277	317	Leon Guerrero, Jose A	Son	M	Cha	6	S	Y		Guam		None
25		277	317	Leon Guerrero, Josefina A	Daughter	F	Cha	4.3	S	N		Guam		None

(CHAMORRO ROOTS GENEALOGY PROJECT™ TRANSCRIPTION)
(BERNARD T. PUNZALAN / HTTP://WWW.CHAMORROROOTS.COM)

DEPARTMENT OF COMMERCE-BUREAU OF THE CENSUS
WASHINGTON
FIFTEENTH CENSUS OF THE UNITED STATES: 1930-POPULATION

THE ISLAND OF GUAM

Sheet No. 28B

28B

District Municipality of Agana
Name of Place Agana City (San Nicolas)
[Proper name and, also, name of class, as city, town, village, barrio, etc]

Enumeration District No. 1
Enumerated by me on April 26, 1930 Joaquin Torres
Enumerator

	PLACE OF ABODE			NAME	RELATION	PERSONAL DESCRIPTION				EDUCATION		NATIVITY		OCCUPATION
	Street, avenue, road, etc.	Number of dwelling house is order of visitation	Number of family in order of visitation	of each person whose place of abode on April 1, 1930, was in this family. Enter surname, first, then given name and middle initial. If any. Include every person living on April 1, 1930. Omit children born since April 1, 1930.	Relationship of this Person to the head of the family.	Sex	Color or race	Age at last birthday	Single, married, widowed or divorced	Attended school any time since Sept. 1, 1929	Whether able to read and write.	Place of birth of this person.	Whether able to speak English.	
	1	2	3	4	5	6	7	8	9	10	11	12	13	14
26	San Ramon St.	277	317	Leon Guerrero, Ana A	Daughter	F	Cha	2.1	S	N		Guam		None
27		277	317	Leon Guerrero, Carmen A	Daughter	F	Cha	.7	S	N		Guam		None
28		278	318	Flores, Dolores R	Head	F	Cha	29	M	N	Y	Guam	Y	None
29		278	318	Flores, Lagrimas R	Daughter	F	Cha	3.2	S	N		Guam		None
30		279	319	Torres, Luis LG	Head	M	Cha	32	Wd	N	Y	Guam	Y	Silversmith
31		279	319	Torres, Ana E	Daughter	F	Cha	10	S	Y	Y	Guam	Y	None
32		279	319	Torres, Luis E	Son	M	Cha	8	S	Y		Guam		None
33		279	319	Torres, Concepcion E	Daughter	F	Cha	7	S	Y		Guam		None
34		279	319	Torres, Ignacio E	Son	M	Cha	5	S	N		Guam		None
35		279	319	Torres, Flora E	Daughter	F	Cha	4.4	S	N		Guam		None
36		279	319	Torres, Jose E	Son	M	Cha	3.7	S	N		Guam		None
37		279	319	Aguon, Luisa T	Cousin	F	Cha	64	S	N	N	Guam	N	None
38	Madrid St.	280	320	Brown, Frank	Head	M	W	42	M	N	Y	New York	Y	:abor [illegible]
39		280	320	Brown, Teodora S	Wife	F	Cha	27	M	N	Y	Guam	Y	None
40		280	320	Brown, Charles S	Son	M	Cha	4.7	S	N		Guam		None
41		280	320	Brown, Emma S	Daughter	F	Cha	4.9	S	N		Guam		None
42		280	320	Brown, Helen S	Daughter	F	Cha	3	S	N		Guam		None
43		281	321	Taitano, Rita C	Head	F	Cha	57	Wd	N	Y	Guam	N	None
44		281	321	Taitano, Miguel C	Son	M	Cha	21	S	N	Y	Guam	Y	Laborer
45		281	321	Taitano, Jose C	Son	M	Cha	18	S	N	Y	Guam	Y	Farm laborer
46		281	321	Taitano, Antonio C	Son	M	Cha	15	S	Y	Y	Guam	Y	None
47		281	322	Cruz, Isabel T	Head	F	Cha	24	M	N	Y	Guam	Y	None
48		281	322	Cruz, Jose T	Son	M	Cha	9	S	Y		Guam		None
49		281	322	Taitano, David C	Son	M	Cha	2.1	S	N		Guam		None
50		281	322	Taitano, Edward P	Son	M	Cha	.8	S	N		Guam		None

(CHAMORRO ROOTS GENEALOGY PROJECT™ TRANSCRIPTION)
(BERNARD T. PUNZALAN / HTTP://WWW.CHAMORROROOTS.COM)

DEPARTMENT OF COMMERCE-BUREAU OF THE CENSUS
WASHINGTON

FIFTEENTH CENSUS OF THE UNITED STATES: 1930-POPULATION

THE ISLAND OF GUAM

Sheet No. 29A

29

District Municipality of Agana
Name of Place Agana City (San Nicolas)
[Proper name and, also, name of class, as city, town, village, barrio, etc]

Enumeration District No. 1
Enumerated by me on April 28, 1930 Joaquin Torres, Enumerator

	PLACE OF ABODE			NAME	RELATION	PERSONAL DESCRIPTION				EDUCATION		NATIVITY		OCCUPATION
	Street, avenue, road, etc.	Number of dwelling house is order of visitation	Number of family in order of visitation	of each person whose place of abode on April 1, 1930, was in this family. Enter surname, first, then given name and middle initial. If any. Include every person living on April 1, 1930. Omit children born since April 1, 1930.	Relationship of this Person to the head of the family.	Sex	Color or race	Age at last birthday	Single, married, widowed or divorced	Attended school any time since Sept. 1, 1929	Whether able to read and write.	Place of birth of this person.	Whether able to speak English.	
	1	2	3	4	5	6	7	8	9	10	11	12	13	14
1	Madrid St.	282	323	Romero, Rita G	Head	F	Cha	48	Wd	N	Y	Guam	Y	None
2		282	323	Aflague, Francisca G	Daughter	F	Cha	27	M	N	Y	Guam	Y	Telephone operator
3		282	323	Aflague, Manuel G	Grandson	M	Cha	11	S	Y	Y	Guam	Y	None
4		282	323	Aflague, Rita G	Grand daughter	F	Cha	9	S	Y		Guam		None
5		282	323	Aflague, Joaquin G	Grandson	M	Cha	8	S	Y		Guam		None
6		282	323	Aflague, Norberto G	Grandson	M	Cha	6	S	Y		Guam		None
7		282	323	Aflague, Ricardo G	Grandson	M	Cha	4.3	S	N		Guam		None
8		283	324	Unpingco, Eliza A	Head	F	Cha	29	M	N	Y	Guam	Y	None
9		283	324	Unpingco, Gloria R	Daughter	F	Cha	3.3	S	N		Guam		None
10		283	324	Unpingco, Juan R	Son	M	Cha	0.3	S	N		Guam		None
11		283	324	Reyes, Rosario R	Niece-in-law	F	Cha	8	S	Y		Guam		None
12		284	325	Taitingfong, Maria C	Head	F	Cha	57	Wd	N	N	Guam	N	None
13		284	325	Baza, Jose C	Son	M	Cha	26	S	N	Y	Guam	Y	Laborer
14		284	325	Taitingfong, Juan C	Son	M	Cha	17	S	N	Y	Guam	Y	Farm laborer
15		285	326	Aflague, Francisco S	Head	M	Cha	40	M	N	Y	Guam	Y	Farmer
16		285	326	Aflague, Rosa SM	Wife	F	Cha	41	M	N	N	Guam	N	None
17		285	326	Aflague, Pilar SM	Daughter	F	Cha	18	S	Y	Y	Guam	Y	None
18		285	326	Aflague, Fructoso SM	Son	M	Cha	17	S	Y	Y	Guam	Y	None
19		285	326	Aflague, Tomas SM	Son	M	Cha	15	S	Y	Y	Guam	Y	None
20		285	326	Aflague, Dolores SM	Daughter	F	Cha	13	S	Y	Y	Guam	Y	None
21		285	326	Aflague, Josefina SM	Daughter	F	Cha	12	S	Y	Y	Guam	Y	None
22		285	326	Aflague, Inocencio SM	Son	M	Cha	11	S	Y	Y	Guam	Y	None
23		285	326	Aflague, Rosa SM	Daughter	F	Cha	9	S	Y		Guam		None
24		285	326	Aflague, Enrique SM	Son	M	Cha	8	S	Y		Guam		None
25		285	326	Quichocho, Rafael Q	Lodger	M	Cha	29	S	N	Y	Guam	Y	Servant

(CHAMORRO ROOTS GENEALOGY PROJECT™ TRANSCRIPTION)
(BERNARD T. PUNZALAN / HTTP://WWW.CHAMORROROOTS.COM)

DEPARTMENT OF COMMERCE-BUREAU OF THE CENSUS
WASHINGTON

FIFTEENTH CENSUS OF THE UNITED STATES: 1930-POPULATION

THE ISLAND OF GUAM

Sheet No. 29B

29B

District **Municipality of Agana**
Name of Place **Agana City (San Nicolas)**
[Proper name and, also, name of class, as city, town, village, barrio, etc]

Enumeration District No. **1**
Enumerated by me on **April 28, 1930** Joaquin Torres, Enumerator

	PLACE OF ABODE: Street, avenue, road, etc.	Number of dwelling house in order of visitation	Number of family in order of visitation	NAME of each person whose place of abode on April 1, 1930, was in this family. Enter surname, first, then given name and middle initial. If any. Include every person living on April 1, 1930. Omit children born since April 1, 1930.	RELATION Relationship of this Person to the head of the family.	PERSONAL DESCRIPTION: Sex	Color or race	Age at last birthday	Single, married, widowed or divorced	EDUCATION: Attended school any time since Sept. 1, 1929	Whether able to read and write.	NATIVITY Place of birth of this person.	Whether able to speak English.	OCCUPATION
	1	2	3	4	5	6	7	8	9	10	11	12	13	14
26	Madrid St.	286	327	Rosario, Teresa G	Head	F	Cha	56	M	N	Y	Guam	Y	None
27		286	327	Rosario, Joaquin C	Stepson	M	Cha	28	S	N	Y	Guam	Y	Barber
28		286	327	Rosario, Silvestre C	Stepson	M	Cha	24	S	N	Y	Guam	Y	Farm laborer
29		286	327	Rosario, Ignacio L	Stepson	M	Cha	20	S	N	Y	Guam	Y	Carpenter
30		286	327	Rosario, Milagro L	Stepdaughter	F	Cha	18	S	N	Y	Guam	Y	None
31		286	327	Rosario, Manuel L	Stepson	M	Cha	17	S	N	Y	Guam	Y	Farm laborer
32		286	327	Rosario, Rosa L	Stepdaughter	F	Cha	16	S	Y	Y	Guam	Y	None
33	San Jorge St.	287	328	Miner, Joaquina A	Head	F	Cha	42	Wd	N	Y	Guam	Y	None
34		287	328	Miner, Clara A	Daughter	F	Cha	26	S	N	Y	Guam	Y	Laundress
35		287	328	Miner, Leoniza A	Daughter	F	Cha	5	S	N		Guam		None
36		287	328	Cruz, Antonio A	Nephew	M	Cha	23	S	N	Y	Guam	Y	Barber
37		287	328	Cruz, Ignacio A	Nephew	M	Cha	20	S	N	Y	Guam	Y	Farm laborer
38		287	328	Cruz, Dolores A	Niece	F	Cha	19	S	Y	Y	Guam	Y	None
39		288	329	Cruz, Juan S	Head	M	Cha	54	M	N	Y	Guam	N	Farmer
40		288	329	Cruz, Ana R	Wife	F	Cha	30	M	N	Y	Guam	Y	None
41		288	329	Cruz, Maria R	Daughter	F	Cha	9	S	Y		Guam		None
42		288	329	Cruz, Juliana R	Daughter	F	Cha	7	S	Y		Guam		None
43		288	329	Cruz, Juan R	Son	M	Cha	5	S	N		Guam		None
44		288	329	Cruz, Vicenta R	Daughter	F	Cha	3.9	S	N		Guam		None
45		288	329	Cruz, Antonio R	Son	M	Cha	1.3	S	N		Guam		None
46		288	329	Cruz, Pedro R	Brother	M	Cha	40	S	N	N	Guam		Farm laborer
47		289	330	Quintanilla, Felicita C	Head	F	Cha	37	M	N	Y	Guam		Laundress
48		289	330	Quintanilla, Dolores C	Daughter	F	Cha	13	S	Y	Y	Guam		None
49		289	330	Quintanilla, Gregorio C	Son	M	Cha	9	S	Y		Guam		None
50		290	331	Taitano, Concepcion C	Head	F	Cha	25	M	N	Y	Guam		None

DEPARTMENT OF COMMERCE-BUREAU OF THE CENSUS
WASHINGTON

FIFTEENTH CENSUS OF THE UNITED STATES: 1930-POPULATION

THE ISLAND OF GUAM

Sheet No. 30A

District **Municipality of Agana**
Name of Place **Agana City (San Nicolas)**
[Proper name and, also, name of class, as city, town, village, barrio, etc]

Enumeration District No. **1**
Enumerated by me on **April 28, 1930** Joaquin Torres
Enumerator

	PLACE OF ABODE: Street, avenue, road, etc.	Number of dwelling house in order of visitation	Number of family in order of visitation	NAME of each person whose place of abode on April 1, 1930, was in this family. Enter surname, first, then given name and middle initial. If any. Include every person living on April 1, 1930. Omit children born since April 1, 1930.	RELATION Relationship of this Person to the head of the family.	PERSONAL DESCRIPTION: Sex	Color or race	Age at last birthday	Single, married, widowed or divorced	EDUCATION: Attended school any time since Sept. 1, 1929	Whether able to read and write.	NATIVITY Place of birth of this person.	Whether able to speak English.	OCCUPATION
	1	2	3	4	5	6	7	8	9	10	11	12	13	14
1	San Jorge St.	290	331	Castro, Joaquina C	Mother	F	Cha	62	Wd	N	Y	Guam	N	None
2		290	331	Castro, Juan C	Brother	M	Cha	26	S	N	Y	Guam	Y	Tailor
3		291	332	Miyasaki, Tornogoro	Head	M	Jap	52	M	N	Y	Japan	N	Cook
4		291	332	Miyasaki, Rita SN	Wife	F	Cha	29	M	N	Y	Guam	N	None
5		291	332	Miyasaki, Pedro SN	Son	M	Jap	4.8	S	N		Guam		None
6		291	332	Miyasaki, Maria SN	Daughter	F	Jap	2.9	S	N		Guam		None
7		291	332	Miyasaki, Dolores SN	Daughter	F	Jap	0	S	N		Guam		None
8	La Paz St.	292	333	Reyes, Vicente G	Head	M	Cha	31	M	N	Y	Guam	Y	Farmer
9		292	333	Reyes, Francisca B	Wife	F	Cha	21	M	N	Y	Guam	Y	None
10		292	333	Reyes, Vicente B	Son	M	Cha	5	S	N		Guam		None
11		292	333	Reyes, Maria B	Daughter	F	Cha	3.8	S	N		Guam		None
12		292	333	Reyes, Fermin B	Son	M	Cha	1.5	S	N		Guam		None
13		293	334	Duenas, Tomasa E	Head	F	Cha	26	M	N	Y	Guam	Y	None
14		294	335	Tedpaogo, Nicolasa A	Head	F	Cha	47	M	N	N	Guam	N	Laundress
15		294	335	Acfalle, Felicidad A	Daughter	F	Cha	22	M	N	Y	Guam	Y	Laundress
16		294	335	Acfalle, Josefina A	Grand daughter	F	Cha	3.7	S	N		Guam		None
17		294	335	Acfalle, Dorothy R A	Grand daughter	F	Cha	1.2	S	N		Guam		None
18		295	336	Reyes, Ignacio G	Head	M	Cha	38	M	N	Y	Guam	N	Farmer
19		295	336	Reyes, Maria T	Wife	F	Cha	38	M	N	N	Guam	N	None
20		295	336	Reyes, Julia T	Daughter	F	Cha	4.1	S	N		Guam		None
21		295	336	Reyes, Antonio T	Son	M	Cha	2.8	S	N		Guam		None
22		295	336	Reyes, Rosario T	Daughter	F	Cha	1.5	S	N		Guam		None
23		296	337	Camacho, Josefa A	Head	F	Cha	62	Wd	N	N	Guam	N	None
24		296	337	Camacho, Josefa A	Step daughter	F	Cha	34	S	N	N	Guam	Y	Dressmaker
25		296	337	Camacho, Felix A	Stepson	M	Cha	23	S	N	Y	Guam	Y	Carpenter

(CHAMORRO ROOTS GENEALOGY PROJECT™ TRANSCRIPTION)
(BERNARD T. PUNZALAN / HTTP://WWW.CHAMORROROOTS.COM)

DEPARTMENT OF COMMERCE-BUREAU OF THE CENSUS
WASHINGTON
FIFTEENTH CENSUS OF THE UNITED STATES: 1930-POPULATION

THE ISLAND OF GUAM

Sheet No. 30B

30B

District **Municipality of Agana**
Name of Place **Agana City (San Nicolas)**
[Proper name and, also, name of class, as city, town, village, barrio, etc]

Enumeration District No. **1**
Enumerated by me on **April 28, 1930** Joaquin Torres
Enumerator

	PLACE OF ABODE			NAME	RELATION	PERSONAL DESCRIPTION				EDUCATION		NATIVITY		OCCUPATION
	Street, avenue, road, etc.	Number of dwelling house is order of visitation	Number of family in order of visitation	of each person whose place of abode on April 1, 1930, was in this family. Enter surname, first, then given name and middle initial. If any. Include every person living on April 1, 1930. Omit children born since April 1, 1930.	Relationship of this Person to the head of the family.	Sex	Color or race	Age at last birthday	Single, married, widowed or divorced	Attended school any time since Sept. 1, 1929	Whether able to read and write.	Place of birth of this person.	Whether able to speak English.	
	1	2	3	4	5	6	7	8	9	10	11	12	13	14
26	La Paz St.	286	337	Camacho, Antonia A	Step daughter	F	Cha	18	S	N	Y	Guam	Y	None
27		286	337	Aguon, Maria T	Aunt	F	Cha	87	S	N	N	Guam	N	None
28		286	337	Cepeda, Josefa D	Aunt-in-law	F	Cha	86	Wd	N	N	Guam	N	None
29		297	338	Leon Guerrero, Carlos B	Head	M	Cha	39	M	N	Y	Saipan Island	Y	Machinist
30		297	338	Leon Guerrero, Magdalena C	Wife	F	Cha	22	M	N	Y	Guam	Y	None
31		297	338	Leon Guerrero, Isidro C	Son	M	Cha	3.8	S	N		Guam		None
32		297	338	Leon Guerrero, Carlos C	Son	M	Cha	2.2	S	N		Guam		None
33		297	338	Leon Guerrero, Francisco C	Son	M	Cha	0.4	S	N		Guam		None
34		298	339	Aflague, Isabel P	Head	F	Cha	29	M	N	Y	Guam	Y	None
35		298	339	Aflague, Ignacio P	Son	M	Cha	9	S	Y		Guam		None
36		298	339	Aflague, Jose P	Son	M	Cha	4.8	S	N		Guam		None
37		298	339	Aflague, Ana V P	Daughter	F	Cha	1.8	S	N		Guam		None
38		299	340	Reyes, Mariano G	Head	M	Cha	22	S	N	Y	Guam	Y	Farmer
39		300	341	Reyes, Francisco G	Head	M	Cha	27	M	N	Y	Guam	Y	Chauffeur
40		300	341	Reyes, Manuela M	Wife	F	Cha	20	M	N	Y	Guam	Y	None
41		301	342	Salas, Nicolas Q	Head	M	Cha	42	M	N	Y	Guam	N	Farmer
42		301	342	Salas, Maria F	Wife	F	Cha	36	M	N	Y	Guam	Y	None
43		302	343	Blas, Juan C	Head	M	Cha	41	M	N	Y	Guam	Y	Farmer
44		302	343	Blas, Dolores C	Wife	F	Cha	37	M	N	Y	Guam	Y	None
45		302	343	Blas, Esperanza C	Daughter	F	Cha	17	S	N	Y	Guam	Y	None
46		302	343	Blas, Francisca C	Daughter	F	Cha	15	S	Y	Y	Guam	Y	None
47		302	343	Blas, Teresa C	Daughter	F	Cha	12	S	Y	Y	Guam	Y	None
48		302	343	Blas, Jose C	Son	M	Cha	10	S	Y	Y	Guam	Y	None
49		302	343	Blas, Dolores C	Daughter	F	Cha	7	S	Y		Guam		None
50		302	343	Blas, Juan C	Son	M	Cha	3.6	S	N		Guam		None

(CHAMORRO ROOTS GENEALOGY PROJECT™ TRANSCRIPTION)
(BERNARD T. PUNZALAN / HTTP://WWW.CHAMORROROOTS.COM)

DEPARTMENT OF COMMERCE-BUREAU OF THE CENSUS
WASHINGTON

FIFTEENTH CENSUS OF THE UNITED STATES: 1930-POPULATION

THE ISLAND OF GUAM

Sheet No. 31A

District **Municipality of Agana**
Name of Place **Agana City (San Nicolas)**
[Proper name and, also, name of class, as city, town, village, barrio, etc]

Enumeration District No. **1**
Enumerated by me on **April 29, 1930** Joaquin Torres
Enumerator

	PLACE OF ABODE			NAME	RELATION	PERSONAL DESCRIPTION				EDUCATION		NATIVITY		OCCUPATION
	Street, avenue, road, etc.	Number of dwelling house is order of visitation	Number of family in order of visitation	of each person whose place of abode on April 1, 1930, was in this family. Enter surname, first, then given name and middle initial. If any. Include every person living on April 1, 1930. Omit children born since April 1, 1930.	Relationship of this Person to the head of the family.	Sex	Color or race	Age at last birthday	Single, married, widowed or divorced	Attended school any time since Sept. 1, 1929	Whether able to read and write.	Place of birth of this person.	Whether able to speak English.	
	1	2	3	4	5	6	7	8	9	10	11	12	13	14
1	La Paz St.	303	344	Quichocho, Jesus Q	Head	M	Cha	43	M	N	N	Guam	N	Farmer
2		303	344	Quichocho, Joaquina C	Wife	F	Cha	47	M	N	N	Guam	N	None
3		303	344	Quichocho, Julia C	Daughter	F	Cha	17	S	N	Y	Guam	Y	None
4		303	344	Quichocho, Jesus C	Son	M	Cha	12	S	Y	Y	Guam	Y	None
5		303	344	Castro, Marcos A	Father-in-law	M	Cha	73	Wd	N	N	Guam	N	None
6		304	345	Ninete, Joaquin C	Head	M	Cha	36	M	N	Y	Guam	Y	Laborer
7		304	345	Ninete, Rosalia P	Wife	F	Cha	38	M	N	N	Guam	N	None
8		304	345	Ninete, Pedro P	Son	M	Cha	12	S	Y	Y	Guam	Y	None
9		304	345	Ninete, Vicente P	Son	M	Cha	11	S	Y	Y	Guam	Y	None
10		304	345	Ninete, Maria P	Daughter	F	Cha	8	S	Y		Guam		None
11		304	345	Ninete, Joaquin P	Son	M	Cha	4.8	S	N		Guam		None
12		304	345	Ninete, Jesus P	Son	M	Cha	2.8	S	N		Guam		None
13		304	345	Ninete, Antonio P	Son	M	Cha	0.8	S	N		Guam		None
14		305	346	Ninete, Jose C	Head	M	Cha	41	M	N	Y	Guam	N	Farmer
15		305	346	Ninete, Guillerma M	Wife	F	Cha	41	M	N	N	Guam	N	None
16		305	346	Ninete, Ignacio M	Son	M	Cha	17	S	N	Y	Guam	Y	Farm laborer
17		305	346	Ninete, Maria M	Daughter	F	Cha	14	S	N	Y	Guam	Y	None
18		305	346	Ninete, Rosario M	Daughter	F	Cha	13	S	Y	Y	Guam	Y	None
19		305	346	Ninete, Segundo M	Son	M	Cha	3.8	S	N		Guam		None
20	Esperanza St	306	347	Herrero, Maria C	Head	F	Cha	68	S	N	Y	Guam	N	None
21		306	347	Herrero, Consuelo C	Sister	F	Cha	53	S	N	N	Guam	N	None
22		307	348	Herrero, Tomas C	Head	M	Cha	56	M	N	Y	Guam	Y	Farmer
23		307	348	Herrero, Maria C	Wife	F	Cha	46	M	N	Y	Guam	N	None
24		307	348	Herrero, Dolores C	Daughter	F	Cha	22	S	N	Y	Guam	Y	None
25		307	348	Herrero, Julia C	Daughter	F	Cha	18	S	N	Y	Guam	Y	None

(CHAMORRO ROOTS GENEALOGY PROJECT™ TRANSCRIPTION)
(BERNARD T. PUNZALAN / HTTP://WWW.CHAMORROROOTS.COM)

DEPARTMENT OF COMMERCE-BUREAU OF THE CENSUS
WASHINGTON

FIFTEENTH CENSUS OF THE UNITED STATES: 1930-POPULATION

THE ISLAND OF GUAM

Sheet No. 31B

31B

District **Municipality of Agana**
Name of Place **Agana City (San Nicolas)**
[Proper name and, also, name of class, as city, town, village, barrio, etc]

Enumeration District No. 1
Enumerated by me on April 29, 1930 Joaquin Torres
Enumerator

	PLACE OF ABODE			NAME	RELATION	PERSONAL DESCRIPTION				EDUCATION		NATIVITY		OCCUPATION
	Street, avenue, road, etc.	Number of dwelling house is order of visitation	Number of family in order of visitation	of each person whose place of abode on April 1, 1930, was in this family. Enter surname, first, then given name and middle initial. If any. Include every person living on April 1, 1930. Omit children born since April 1, 1930.	Relationship of this Person to the head of the family.	Sex	Color or race	Age at last birthday	Single, married, widowed or divorced	Attended school any time since Sept. 1, 1929	Whether able to read and write.	Place of birth of this person.	Whether able to speak English.	
	1	2	3	4	5	6	7	8	9	10	11	12	13	14
26	Esperanza St	307	348	Herrero, Angel C	Son	M	Cha	19	S	N	Y	Guam	Y	Servant
27		307	348	Herrero, Alfredo C	Son	M	Cha	14	S	N	Y	Guam	Y	Farm laborer
28		307	348	Herrero, Edward C	Son	M	Cha	12	S	Y	Y	Guam	Y	None
29		307	348	Herrero, Carlos C	Son	M	Cha	9	S	Y		Guam		None
30		308	349	Iglesias, Luis G	Head	M	Cha	51	M	N	N	Guam	N	Farmer
31		308	349	Iglesias, Maria C	Wife	F	Cha	49	M	N	N	Guam	N	None
32		308	349	Iglesias, Maria C	Daughter	F	Cha	11	S	Y	Y	Guam	Y	None
33		308	349	Iglesias, Jesus C	Son	M	Cha	9	S	Y		Guam		None
34		308	349	Iglesias, Oliva C	Daughter	F	Cha	5	S	Y		Guam		None
35		309	350	Castro, Vicente M	Head	M	Cha	49	M	N	Y	Guam	N	Farmer
36		309	350	Castro, Gertrudes M	Wife	F	Cha	46	M	N	N	Guam	N	None
37		309	350	Castro, Jose M	Brother	M	Cha	41	M	N	N	Guam	N	None
38		309	351	Crisostomo, Juan P	Head	M	Cha	43	Wd	N	Y	Guam	N	Farmer
39		309	351	Crisostomo, Miguel C	Son	M	Cha	14	S	Y	Y	Guam	Y	None
40		310	352	San Nicolas, Jose T	Head	M	Cha	40	M	N	Y	Guam	Y	Carpenter
41		310	352	San Nicolas, Maria C	Wife	F	Cha	46	M	N	Y	Guam	N	None
42		310	352	San Nicolas, Joaquin C	Son	M	Cha	20	S	N	Y	Guam	Y	Farm laborer
43		310	352	San Nicolas, Jose C	Son	M	Cha	18	S	N	Y	Guam	Y	Laborer
44		310	352	San Nicolas, Maria C	Daughter	F	Cha	10	S	Y	Y	Guam	Y	None
45		310	352	San Nicolas, Concepcion C	Daughter	F	Cha	2.3	S	N		Guam		None
46		310	353	Castro, Manuel S	Head	M	Cha	36	Wd	N	Y	Guam	N	Farmer
47		310	353	Castro, Trinidad L	Daughter	F	Cha	11	S	Y	Y	Guam	Y	None
48		310	353	Castro, Ignacio L	Son	M	Cha	9	S	Y		Guam		None
49		311	354	Castro, Jesus S	Head	M	Cha	24	M	N	Y	Guam	N	Laborer
50		311	354	Castro, Joaquina S	Wife	F	Cha	25	M	N	N	Guam	N	None

DEPARTMENT OF COMMERCE-BUREAU OF THE CENSUS
WASHINGTON

FIFTEENTH CENSUS OF THE UNITED STATES: 1930-POPULATION

THE ISLAND OF GUAM

Sheet No. 32A

District **Municipality of Agana**
Name of Place **Agana City (San Nicolas)**
[Proper name and, also, name of class, as city, town, village, barrio, etc]

Enumeration District No. **1**
Enumerated by me on **April 29, 1930** Joaquin Torres, Enumerator

	PLACE OF ABODE			NAME	RELATION	PERSONAL DESCRIPTION				EDUCATION		NATIVITY		OCCUPATION
	Street, avenue, road, etc.	Number of dwelling house is order of visitation	Number of family in order of visitation	of each person whose place of abode on April 1, 1930, was in this family. Enter surname, first, then given name and middle initial. If any. Include every person living on April 1, 1930. Omit children born since April 1, 1930.	Relationship of this Person to the head of the family.	Sex	Color or race	Age at last birthday	Single, married, widowed or divorced	Attended school any time since Sept. 1, 1929	Whether able to read and write.	Place of birth of this person.	Whether able to speak English.	
	1	2	3	4	5	6	7	8	9	10	11	12	13	14
1	Esperanza St	311	354	Castro, Esperanza S	Daughter	F	Cha	1.8	S	N		Guam		None
2		311	354	Castro, Jose S	Son	M	Cha	.5	S	N		Guam		None
3		312	355	Quidachay, Vicente B	Head	M	Cha	32	M	N	Y	Guam	Y	Farmer
4		312	355	Quidachay, Trinidad T	Wife	F	Cha	37	M	N	Y	Guam	N	None
5		312	355	Quidachay, Juan T	Son	M	Cha	7	S	Y		Guam		None
6		312	355	Quidachay, Jesus T	Son	M	Cha	5	S	N		Guam		None
7		312	355	Quidachay, Maria T	Son	M	Cha	3.4	S	N		Guam		None
8		312	355	Quidachay, Isabel T	Daughter	F	Cha	0.5	S	N		Guam		None
9		312	355	Quidachay, Remedio B	Sister	F	Cha	20	S	N		Guam		None
10		312	355	Quidachay, Antonio B	Brother	M	Cha	18	S	N	Y	Guam	Y	None
11		312	355	San Nicolas, Adela T	Step daughter	F	Cha	15	S	N	Y	Guam	Y	None
12		313	356	Rosario, Jesus C	Head	M	Cha	33	M	N	Y	Guam	Y	Laborer
13		313	356	Rosario, Ana C	Wife	F	Cha	29	M	N	Y	Guam	N	None
14		313	356	Rosario, Vicente C	Son	M	Cha	5	S	N		Guam		None
15		313	356	Rosario, Maria C	Daughter	F	Cha	1.8	S	N		Guam		None
16		314	357	Cepeda, Marcela C	Head	F	Cha	48	Wd	N	N	Guam	N	Laundress
17		314	357	Cepeda, Ana C	Daughter	F	Cha	25	S	N	Y	Guam	Y	Laundress
18		314	357	Cepeda, Jose C	Son	M	Cha	14	S	Y	Y	Guam	Y	Farm laborer
19		315	358	Delgado, Jose M	Head	M	Cha	42	M	N	Y	Guam	Y	Gardener
20		315	358	Delgado, Maria C	Wife	F	Cha	38	M	N	Y	Guam	N	None
21		315	358	Delgado, Jesus C	Son	M	Cha	15	S	Y	Y	Guam	Y	None
22		315	358	Delgado, Jose C	Son	M	Cha	12	S	Y	Y	Guam	Y	None
23		315	358	Delgado, Ana C	Daughter	F	Cha	11	S	Y	Y	Guam	Y	None
24		315	358	Delgado, Vicente C	Son	M	Cha	3.9	S	N		Guam		None
25		315	358	Delgado, Mercedes C	Daughter	F	Cha	2.4	S	N		Guam		None

(CHAMORRO ROOTS GENEALOGY PROJECT™ TRANSCRIPTION)
(BERNARD T. PUNZALAN / HTTP://WWW.CHAMORROROOTS.COM)

DEPARTMENT OF COMMERCE-BUREAU OF THE CENSUS
WASHINGTON

FIFTEENTH CENSUS OF THE UNITED STATES: 1930-POPULATION

THE ISLAND OF GUAM

Sheet No. 32B

32B

District **Municipality of Agana**
Name of Place **Agana City (San Nicolas)**
[Proper name and, also, name of class, as city, town, village, barrio, etc]

Enumeration District No. **1**
Enumerated by me on **April 30, 1930** Joaquin Torres, Enumerator

	PLACE OF ABODE			NAME	RELATION	PERSONAL DESCRIPTION				EDUCATION		NATIVITY		OCCUPATION
	Street, avenue, road, etc.	Number of dwelling house is order of visitation	Number of family in order of visitation	of each person whose place of abode on April 1, 1930, was in this family. Enter surname, first, then given name and middle initial. If any. Include every person living on April 1, 1930. Omit children born since April 1, 1930.	Relationship of this Person to the head of the family.	Sex	Color or race	Age at last birthday	Single, married, widowed or divorced	Attended school any time since Sept. 1, 1929	Whether able to read and write.	Place of birth of this person.	Whether able to speak English.	
	1	2	3	4	5	6	7	8	9	10	11	12	13	14
26	Esperanza St	316	359	Camacho, Jose A	Head	M	Cha	30	M	N	Y	Guam	Y	Machinist
27		316	359	Camacho, Maria SN	Wife	F	Cha	27	M	N	N	Guam	N	None
28		316	359	Camacho, Jose SN	Son	M	Cha	9	S	Y		Guam		None
29		316	359	Camacho, Ramon SN	Son	M	Cha	4.9	S	N		Guam		None
30		316	359	Camacho, Jesus SN	Son	M	Cha	1.8	S	N		Guam		None
31		317	360	Quichocho, Carmela N	Head	F	Cha	39	Wd	N	N	Guam	N	Laundress
32		317	360	Quichocho, Pedro N	Son	M	Cha	17	S	N	N	Guam	N	Farm laborer
33		317	360	Quichocho, Jose N	Son	M	Cha	11	S	Y	Y	Guam	Y	None
34		317	360	Quichocho, Francisca N	Mother	F	Cha	65	Wd	N	N	Guam	N	None
35		318	361	Namauleg, Joaquin N	Head	M	Cha	41	M	N	Y	Guam	Y	Farmer
36		318	361	Namauleg, Rosa E	Wife	F	Cha	34	M	N	Y	Guam	N	None
37		318	361	Namauleg, Jesus E	Son	M	Cha	13	S	Y	Y	Guam	Y	None
38		318	361	Namauleg, Maria E	Daughter	F	Cha	12	S	Y	Y	Guam		None
39		318	361	Namauleg, Antonio E	Son	M	Cha	7	S	Y		Guam		None
40		318	361	Namauleg, Gregorio E	Son	M	Cha	1.3	S	N		Guam		None
41		319	362	Aguon, Maria C	Head	F	Cha	52	Wd	N	N	Guam	N	None
42		319	362	Aguon, Josefina C	Daughter	F	Cha	20	S	N	Y	Guam	Y	Servant
43		319	362	Aguon, Nicolas C	Son	M	Cha	18	S	N	Y	Guam	Y	Servant
44		319	362	Aguon, Simeon C	Son	M	Cha	14	S	Y	Y	Guam	Y	None
45		319	362	Aguon, Juan C	Son	M	Cha	11	S	Y	Y	Guam	Y	None
46		319	363	Mendiola, Joaquina A	Head	F	Cha	29	M	N	Y	Guam	N	Laundress
47		319	363	Mendiola, Gloria A	Daughter	F	Cha	10	S	Y	Y	Guam	Y	None
48		319	364	Charfauros, Mariana A	Head	F	Cha	25	Wd	N	Y	Guam	Y	Laundress
49		319	364	Charfauros, Ramon A	Son	M	Cha	9	S	Y		Guam		None
50		319	364	Charfauros, Joaquin A	Son	M	Cha	5	S	N		Guam		None

DEPARTMENT OF COMMERCE-BUREAU OF THE CENSUS
WASHINGTON

FIFTEENTH CENSUS OF THE UNITED STATES: 1930-POPULATION

THE ISLAND OF GUAM

Sheet No. 33A

District **Municipality of Agana**
Name of Place **Agana City (San Nicolas)**
[Proper name and, also, name of class, as city, town, village, barrio, etc]

Enumeration District No. 1
Enumerated by me on April 30, 1930 Joaquin Torres, Enumerator

	PLACE OF ABODE: Street, avenue, road, etc.	Number of dwelling house in order of visitation	Number of family in order of visitation	NAME of each person whose place of abode on April 1, 1930, was in this family. Enter surname, first, then given name and middle initial. If any. Include every person living on April 1, 1930. Omit children born since April 1, 1930.	RELATION Relationship of this Person to the head of the family.	PERSONAL DESCRIPTION: Sex	Color or race	Age at last birthday	Single, married, widowed or divorced	EDUCATION: Attended school any time since Sept. 1, 1929	Whether able to read and write.	NATIVITY Place of birth of this person.	Whether able to speak English.	OCCUPATION
	1	2	3	4	5	6	7	8	9	10	11	12	13	14
1	Esperanza St	319	364	Charfauros, Carlos A	Son	M	Cha	.3	S	N		Guam		None
2		320	365	Gogo, Venancio G	Head	M	Cha	39	M	N	Y	Guam	N	Laborer
3		320	365	Gogo, Maria C	Wife	F	Cha	35	M	N	Y	Guam	N	None
4		320	365	Gogo, Rosario C	Daughter	F	Cha	11	S	Y	Y	Guam	Y	None
5		320	365	Gogo, Jose C	Son	M	Cha	8	S	Y		Guam		None
6		320	365	Gogo, Catalina C	Daughter	F	Cha	6	S	Y		Guam		None
7		320	365	Gogo, Lourdes C	Daughter	F	Cha	1.1	S	N		Guam		None
8		321	366	Sablan, Jose C	Head	M	Cha	37	M	N	Y	Agrigan Island	Y	Carpenter
9		321	366	Sablan, Maria G	Wife	F	Cha	30	M	N	Y	Guam	Y	None
10		321	366	Sablan, Jesus G	Son	M	Cha	9	S	Y		Guam		None
11		321	366	Sablan, Silvia G	Daughter	F	Cha	6	S	N		Guam		None
12		321	366	Sablan, Antonio G	Son	M	Cha	4.7	S	N		Guam		None
13		321	366	Sablan, Gregorio G	Son	M	Cha	3.3	S	N		Guam		None
14		321	366	Sablan, Felipa N G	Daughter	F	Cha	1.9	S	N		Guam		None
15		322	367	Castro, Ramon S	Head	M	Cha	38	M	N	Y	Guam	N	Farmer
16		322	367	Castro, Ana SN	Wife	F	Cha	48	M	N	N	Guam	N	None
17		322	367	Castro, Jesus SN	Son	M	Cha	6	S	N		Guam		None
18		323	368	Espinosa, Dolores F	Head	M	Cha	62	Wd	N	Y	Guam	N	None
19		323	368	Quintanilla, Ana F	Daughter	F	Cha	29	Wd	N	Y	Guam	Y	Midwife
20		323	369	Pangelinan, Consuelo E	Head	F	Cha	22	M	N	Y	Guam	Y	None
21		323	369	Pangelinan, Valentino E	Son	M	Cha	4.6	S	N		Guam		None
22		323	369	Pangelinan, Pricilia E	Daughter	F	Cha	2.8	S	N		Guam		None
23		323	369	Pangelinan, Erotida E	Daughter	F	Cha	.4	S	N		Guam		None
24		324	370	Mendiola, Maria C	Head	F	Cha	64	S	N	N	Guam	N	Laundress
25		324	370	Mendiola, Rosa C	Sister	F	Cha	59	S	N	N	Guam	N	Laundress

(CHAMORRO ROOTS GENEALOGY PROJECT™ TRANSCRIPTION)
(BERNARD T. PUNZALAN / HTTP://WWW.CHAMORROROOTS.COM)

DEPARTMENT OF COMMERCE-BUREAU OF THE CENSUS
WASHINGTON

FIFTEENTH CENSUS OF THE UNITED STATES: 1930-POPULATION

THE ISLAND OF GUAM

Sheet No. 33B

33B

District **Municipality of Agana**
Name of Place **Agana City (San Nicolas)**
[Proper name and, also, name of class, as city, town, village, barrio, etc]

Enumeration District No. **1**
Enumerated by me on **April 30, 1930** Joaquin Torres
Enumerator

	PLACE OF ABODE			NAME	RELATION	PERSONAL DESCRIPTION				EDUCATION		NATIVITY		OCCUPATION
	Street, avenue, road, etc.	Number of dwelling house in order of visitation	Number of family in order of visitation	of each person whose place of abode on April 1, 1930, was in this family. Enter surname, first, then given name and middle initial. If any. Include every person living on April 1, 1930. Omit children born since April 1, 1930.	Relationship of this Person to the head of the family.	Sex	Color or race	Age at last birthday	Single, married, widowed or divorced	Attended school any time since Sept. 1, 1929	Whether able to read and write.	Place of birth of this person.	Whether able to speak English.	
	1	2	3	4	5	6	7	8	9	10	11	12	13	14
26	Esperanza St	324	370	Mendiola, Jose M	Nephew	M	Cha	38	S	N	N	Guam	N	Farm laborer
27		324	370	Delgado, Jesus M	Nephew	M	Cha	34	S	N	Y	Guam	Y	Laborer
28		325	371	Castro, Jose A	Head	M	Cha	70	M	N	Y	Guam	N	None
29		325	371	Castro, Feliza S	Wife	F	Cha	65	M	N	N	Guam	N	None
30		325	371	Castro, Jose S	Son	M	Cha	19	S	N	Y	Guam	Y	Farm laborer
31		325	371	Espenosa, Jose C	Grandson	M	Cha	21	S	N	Y	Guam	Y	Laborer
32		326	372	Aguigui, Antonia C	Head	F	Cha	64	Wd	N	N	Guam	N	None
33		326	372	Espenosa, Juan C	Son	M	Cha	18	S	N	Y	Guam	Y	Laborer
34		326	373	Espenosa, Joaquin C	Head	M	Cha	28	M	N	Y	Guam	Y	Laborer
35		326	373	Espenosa, Maria C	Wife	F	Cha	25	M	N	Y	Guam	Y	None
36		326	373	Espenosa, Antonio C	Son	M	Cha	5	S	N		Guam		None
37		326	373	Espenosa, Barceliza C	Daughter	F	Cha	1.9	S	N		Guam		None
38		326	373	Espenosa, Ana C	Daughter	F	Cha	0	S	N		Guam		None
39		327	374	Santos, Jesus C	Head	M	Cha	51	M	N	Y	Guam	Y	Chauffeur
40		327	374	Santos, Dolores C	Wife	F	Cha	49	M	N	Y	Guam	N	None
41		327	374	Santos, Remedios C	Daughter	F	Cha	16	S	N	Y	Guam	Y	None
42		327	374	Santos, Juan C	Son	M	Cha	10	S	Y	Y	Guam	Y	None
43		327	374	Santos, Ana C	Daughter	F	Cha	8	S	Y		Guam		None
44		328	375	Gogo, Juan S	Head	M	Cha	62	M	N	Y	Guam	N	None
45		328	375	Gogo, Consolacion N	Wife	F	Cha	59	M	N	N	Guam	N	None
46		328	376	Guevara, Juan D	Head	M	Cha	24	M	N	Y	Guam	Y	Chauffeur
47		328	376	Guevara, Ana G	Wife	F	Cha	26	M	N	Y	Guam	N	None
48		328	376	Guevara, Juan G	Son	M	Cha	.5	S	N		Guam		None
49		329	377	Rivera, Juan SN	Head	M	Cha	23	M	N	Y	Guam	Y	Machinist
50		329	377	Rivera, Ros G	Wife	F	Cha	22	M	N	Y	Guam	Y	None

DEPARTMENT OF COMMERCE-BUREAU OF THE CENSUS
WASHINGTON

FIFTEENTH CENSUS OF THE UNITED STATES: 1930-POPULATION

THE ISLAND OF GUAM

Sheet No. 34A

District Municipality of Agana
Name of Place Agana City (San Nicolas)
[Proper name and, also, name of class, as city, town, village, barrio, etc]

Enumeration District No. 1
Enumerated by me on April 30, 1930 Joaquin Torres
Enumerator

	PLACE OF ABODE			NAME	RELATION	PERSONAL DESCRIPTION				EDUCATION		NATIVITY		OCCUPATION
	Street, avenue, road, etc.	Number of dwelling house is order of visitation	Number of family in order of visitation	of each person whose place of abode on April 1, 1930, was in this family. Enter surname, first, then given name and middle initial. If any. Include every person living on April 1, 1930. Omit children born since April 1, 1930.	Relationship of this Person to the head of the family.	Sex	Color or race	Age at last birthday	Single, married, widowed or divorced	Attended school any time since Sept. 1, 1929	Whether able to read and write.	Place of birth of this person.	Whether able to speak English.	
	1	2	3	4	5	6	7	8	9	10	11	12	13	14
1	Esperanza St	329	377	Rivera, Ignacio G	Son	M	Cha	3.4	S	N		Guam		None
2		329	377	Rivera, Juan G	Son	M	Cha	1.9	S	N		Guam		None
3		329	377	Rivera, Florencia G	Daughter	F	Cha	.5	S	N		Guam		None
4		330	378	Gogo, Veronica S	Head	F	Cha	28	M	N	Y	Guam	Y	None
5		330	378	Gogo, Virginia S	Daughter	F	Cha	12	S	Y	Y	Guam	Y	None
6		330	378	Gogo, Maria S	Daughter	F	Cha	9	S	Y		Guam		None
7		330	378	Gogo, Beatris S	Daughter	F	Cha	5	S	N		Guam		None
8		330	378	Gogo, Enrique S	Son	M	Cha	3.7	S	N		Guam		None
9		330	378	Gogo, Consolacion S	Daughter	F	Cha	0.9	S	N		Guam		None
10		331	379	Ninete, Ignacio C	Head	M	Cha	43	M	N	Y	Guam	N	Laborer
11		331	379	Ninete, Maria C	Wife	F	Cha	41	M	N	Y	Guam	N	Laundress
12		331	379	Ninete, Ana C	Daughter	F	Cha	15	S	N	Y	Guam	Y	None
13		331	379	Ninete, Gregorio C	Son	M	Cha	14	S	Y	Y	Guam	Y	None
14		331	379	Ninete, Ignacio C	Son	M	Cha	10	S	Y	Y	Guam	Y	None
15		331	379	Ninete, Maria C	Daughter	F	Cha	4.7	S	N		Guam		None
16		332	380	Camacho, Jose S	Head	M	Cha	61	M	N	Y	Guam	N	Farmer
17		332	380	Camacho, Ana C	Wife	F	Cha	64	M	N	N	Guam	N	None
18		332	380	Camacho, Pedro C	Son	M	Cha	26	S	N	Y	Guam	Y	Carpenter
19		333	381	Lujan, Vicente R	Head	M	Cha	52	M	N	Y	Guam	N	Farmer
20		333	381	Lujan, Rosa C	Wife	F	Cha	45	M	N	Y	Guam	N	None
21		333	381	Lujan, Vicente N	Son	M	Cha	18	S	N	Y	Guam	Y	Cook
22		333	381	Mendiola, Ignacio C	Stepson	M	Cha	9	S	Y		Guam		None
23		334	382	Roberto, Jose C	Head	M	Cha	30	M	N	Y	Guam	Y	Laborer
24		334	382	Roberto, Vicenta M	Wife	F	Cha	24	M	N	N	Guam	N	None
25		334	382	Roberto, Lidia M	Daughter	F	Cha	.5	S	N		Guam		None

DEPARTMENT OF COMMERCE-BUREAU OF THE CENSUS
WASHINGTON

FIFTEENTH CENSUS OF THE UNITED STATES: 1930-POPULATION

THE ISLAND OF GUAM

Sheet No. 34B

34B

District **Municipality of Agana**
Name of Place **Agana City (San Nicolas)**
[Proper name and, also, name of class, as city, town, village, barrio, etc]

Enumeration District No. 1
Enumerated by me on **May 1, 1930** Joaquin Torres
Enumerator

	PLACE OF ABODE			NAME	RELATION	PERSONAL DESCRIPTION				EDUCATION		NATIVITY		OCCUPATION
	Street, avenue, road, etc.	Number of dwelling house is order of visitation	Number of family in order of visitation	of each person whose place of abode on April 1, 1930, was in this family. Enter surname, first, then given name and middle initial. If any. Include every person living on April 1, 1930. Omit children born since April 1, 1930.	Relationship of this Person to the head of the family.	Sex	Color or race	Age at last birthday	Single, married, widowed or divorced	Attended school any time since Sept. 1, 1929	Whether able to read and write.	Place of birth of this person.	Whether able to speak English.	
	1	2	3	4	5	6	7	8	9	10	11	12	13	14
26	Esperanza St	335	383	Shimoda, Juana C	Head	F	Cha	54	Wd	N	N	Guam	N	None
27		336	384	Garrido, Manuel G	Head	M	Cha	38	M	N	Y	Guam	Y	Laborer
28		336	384	Garrido, Maria S	Wife	F	Cha	36	M	N	Y	Guam	Y	None
29		336	384	Garrido, Gonzalo S	Son	M	Cha	7	S	Y		Guam		None
30		336	384	Garrido, Maria S	Daughter	F	Cha	6	S	N		Guam		None
31		336	384	Garrido, Jesusa S	Daughter	F	Cha	3.2	S	N		Guam		None
32		336	384	Garrido, Leocadia C	Daughter	F	Cha	1.3	S	N		Guam		None
33		336	384	Gumataotao, Juana S	Step daughter	F	Cha	12	S	Y	Y	Guam	Y	None
34		336	384	Gumataotao, Jose S	Stepson	M	Cha	9	S	Y		Guam		None
35		336	385	Ulloa, Francisco I	Head	M	Cha	22	M	N	Y	Guam	Y	Laborer
36		336	385	Ulloa, Teresa C	Wife	F	Cha	21	M	N	Y	Guam	Y	None
37		336	385	Ulloa, Roman C	Son	M	Cha	0	S	N		Guam		None
38		337	386	Mendiola, Vicente G	Head	M	Cha	35	Wd	N	Y	Guam	Y	Laborer
39		337	386	Mendiola, Juan L	Son	M	Cha	1	S	Y		Guam		None
40		337	386	Mendiola, Juliana G	Mother	F	Cha	73	Wd	N	N	Guam	N	None
41		338	387	Tenorio, Manuel N	Head	M	Cha	29	M	N	Y	Guam	Y	Laborer
42		338	387	Tenorio, Ana M	Wife	F	Cha	21	M	N	N	Guam	N	None
43		338	387	Tenorio, Jose M	Son	M	Cha	3.1	S	N		Guam		None
44		338	387	Tenorio, Angel M	Son	M	Cha	1.8	S	N		Guam		None
45		338	387	Tenorio, Florencia M	Daughter	F	Cha	0.4	S	N		Guam		None
46		339	388	Mantanona, Rita T	Head	F	Cha	26	M	N	Y	Guam	N	Laundress
47		339	388	Mantanona, Felix T	Son	M	Cha	4.8	S	N		Guam		None
48		339	388	Mantanona, David T	Son	M	Cha	1	S	N		Guam		None
49		340	389	Damian, Justo	Head	M	Fil	48	M	N	Y	Philippine Is.	Y	Farmer
50		340	389	Damian, Petronila B	Wife	F	Fil	46	M	N	N	Malay Peninsula	Y	None

DEPARTMENT OF COMMERCE-BUREAU OF THE CENSUS
WASHINGTON

FIFTEENTH CENSUS OF THE UNITED STATES: 1930-POPULATION

THE ISLAND OF GUAM

Sheet No. 35A

District **Municipality of Agana**
Name of Place **Agana City (San Nicolas)**
[Proper name and, also, name of class, as city, town, village, barrio, etc]

Enumeration District No. 1
Enumerated by me on May 1, 1930 Joaquin Torres, Enumerator

	PLACE OF ABODE			NAME	RELATION	PERSONAL DESCRIPTION				EDUCATION		NATIVITY		OCCUPATION
	Street, avenue, road, etc.	Number of dwelling house is order of visitation	Number of family in order of visitation	of each person whose place of abode on April 1, 1930, was in this family. Enter surname, first, then given name and middle initial. If any. Include every person living on April 1, 1930. Omit children born since April 1, 1930.	Relationship of this Person to the head of the family.	Sex	Color or race	Age at last birthday	Single, married, widowed or divorced	Attended school any time since Sept. 1, 1929	Whether able to read and write.	Place of birth of this person.	Whether able to speak English.	
	1	2	3	4	5	6	7	8	9	10	11	12	13	14
1	Esperanza St	340	389	Damian, Florentino B	Son	M	Fil	18	S	N	Y	Guam	Y	Farm laborer
2		340	389	Damian, Engracio B	Son	M	Fil	15	S	N	Y	Guam	Y	Farm laborer
3		340	389	Damian, Priscila B	Daughter	F	Fil	14	S	Y	Y	Guam	Y	None
4		340	389	Damian, Andres B	Son	M	Fil	12	S	Y	Y	Guam	Y	None
5		340	389	Damian, Celestina B	Daughter	F	Fil	9	S	Y		Guam		None
6		340	389	Damian, Sixta B	Daughter	F	Fil	8	S	Y		Guam		None
7		341	390	Evangelista, Pedro E	Head	M	Cha	40	M	N	Y	Guam	Y	Mason
8		341	390	Evangelista, Rosalia T	Wife	F	Cha	36	M	N	Y	Guam	Y	None
9		341	390	Evangelista, Pedro T	Son	M	Cha	18	S	N	Y	Guam	Y	Farm laborer
10		341	390	Evangelista, Manuel T	Son	M	Cha	14	S	N	Y	Guam	Y	Farm laborer
11		341	390	Evangelista, Dolores T	Daughter	F	Cha	9	S	Y		Guam		None
12		341	390	Evangelista, Jose T	Son	M	Cha	8	S	Y		Guam		None
13		341	390	Evangelista, Juan T	Son	M	Cha	6	S	Y		Guam		None
14		341	390	Evangelista, Rosario T	Daughter	F	Cha	4.7	S	N		Guam		None
15		341	390	Evangelista, Rosa T	Daughter	F	Cha	2.8	S	N		Guam		None
16		341	390	Evangelista, Jesus T	Son	M	Cha	.4	S	N		Guam		None
17		341	390	Charfauros, Carmen C	Cousin-in-law	F	Cha	27	S	N		Guam		Servant
18		342	391	Lujan, Manuel N	Head	M	Cha	21	M	N	Y	Guam	Y	Farmer
19		342	391	Lujan, Dolores C	Wife	F	Cha	18	M	N	Y	Guam	N	None
20		343	392	Castro, Pedro S	Head	M	Cha	33	M	N	N	Guam	N	Farmer
21		343	392	Castro, Asencion C	Wife	F	Cha	35	M	N	N	Guam	N	None
22		343	392	Castro, Jose C	Son	M	Cha	7	S	Y		Guam		None
23		343	392	Castro, Gregorio C	Son	M	Cha	5	S	N		Guam		None
24		343	392	Castro, Juan C	Son	M	Cha	2.8	S	N		Guam		None
25		344	393	Cruz, Jose C	Head	M	Cha	30	S	N	Y	Guam	Y	Silversmith

DEPARTMENT OF COMMERCE-BUREAU OF THE CENSUS
WASHINGTON

FIFTEENTH CENSUS OF THE UNITED STATES: 1930-POPULATION

THE ISLAND OF GUAM

Sheet No. 35B

District Municipality of Agana
Name of Place Agana City (San Nicolas)
[Proper name and, also, name of class, as city, town, village, barrio, etc]

Enumeration District No. 1
Enumerated by me on May 1, 1930 Joaquin Torres
Enumerator

	PLACE OF ABODE			NAME	RELATION	PERSONAL DESCRIPTION				EDUCATION		NATIVITY		OCCUPATION
	Street, avenue, road, etc.	Number of dwelling house is order of visitation	Number of family in order of visitation	of each person whose place of abode on April 1, 1930, was in this family. Enter surname, first, then given name and middle initial. If any. Include every person living on April 1, 1930. Omit children born since April 1, 1930.	Relationship of this Person to the head of the family.	Sex	Color or race	Age at last birthday	Single, married, widowed or divorced	Attended school any time since Sept. 1, 1929	Whether able to read and write.	Place of birth of this person.	Whether able to speak English.	
	1	2	3	4	5	6	7	8	9	10	11	12	13	14
26	Esperanza St	345	394	Manley, Albert R	Head	M	Cha	21	S	N	Y	Guam	Y	Chauffeur
27		345	394	Manley, Jose R	Brother	M	Cha	19	S	N	Y	Guam	Y	Laborer
28		345	394	Manley, Enrique R	Brother	M	Cha	18	S	N	Y	Guam	Y	Laborer
29		345	394	Manley, Manuel R	Brother	M	Cha	16	S	N	Y	Guam	Y	Farm laborer
30		345	394	Manley, William R	Brother	M	Cha	14	S	Y	Y	Guam		None
31		345	394	Manley, Frank R	Brother	M	Cha	5	S			Guam		None
32				Here ends the enumeration of Agana City (San Ramon)										
33														
34														
35														
36														
37														
38														
39														
40														
41														
42														
43														
44														
45														
46														
47														
48														
49														
50														

District 2
Municipality of Agana

Padre Palomo
San Antonio

(CHAMORRO ROOTS GENEALOGY PROJECT™ TRANSCRIPTION)
(BERNARD T. PUNZALAN / HTTP://WWW.CHAMORROROOTS.COM)

DEPARTMENT OF COMMERCE-BUREAU OF THE CENSUS
WASHINGTON

FIFTEENTH CENSUS OF THE UNITED STATES: 1930-POPULATION

THE ISLAND OF GUAM

Sheet No. 1A

District Municipality of Agana
Name of Place Agana City (Part of Padre Palomo)
[Proper name and, also, name of class, as city, town, village, barrio, etc]

Enumeration District No. 2
Enumerated by me on April 2, 1930 Arthur W. Jackson, Enumerator

	PLACE OF ABODE			NAME	RELATION	PERSONAL DESCRIPTION				EDUCATION		NATIVITY		OCCUPATION
	Street, avenue, road, etc.	Number of dwelling house in order of visitation	Number of family in order of visitation	of each person whose place of abode on April 1, 1930, was in this family. Enter surname, first, then given name and middle initial. If any. Include every person living on April 1, 1930. Omit children born since April 1, 1930.	Relationship of this Person to the head of the family.	Sex	Color or race	Age at last birthday	Single, married, widowed or divorced	Attended school any time since Sept. 1, 1929	Whether able to read and write.	Place of birth of this person.	Whether able to speak English.	
	1	2	3	4	5	6	7	8	9	10	11	12	13	14
1	Padre Palomo Street	1	1	D'Angelo, Guisippe	Head	M	W	50	S	N	Y	Italy	Y	1st Music USNR
2		2	2	San Agustin, Pedro SA	Head	M	Cha	39	M	N	N	Guam	N	Farmer
3		2	2	San Agustin, Josefa B	Wife	F	Cha	36	M	N	N	Guam	N	None
4		2	2	San Agustin, Ana B	Daughter	F	Cha	18	S	N	Y	Guam	Y	None
5		2	2	San Agustin, Asuncion B	Daughter	F	Cha	16	S	N	Y	Guam	Y	None
6		2	2	San Agustin, Vicente B	Son	M	Cha	15	S	Y	Y	Guam	Y	Farm laborer
7		2	2	San Agustin, Dolores B	Daughter	F	Cha	13	S	Y	Y	Guam	Y	None
8		2	2	San Agustin, Remedio B	Daughter	F	Cha	11	S	Y	Y	Guam	Y	None
9		2	2	San Agustin, Rosario B	Daughter	F	Cha	9	S	Y		Guam		None
10		2	2	San Agustin, Maria B	Daughter	F	Cha	7	S	Y		Guam		None
11		2	2	San Agustin, Ramon B	Son	M	Cha	5.3	S	N		Guam		None
12		2	2	San Agustin, Carmen B	Daughter	F	Cha	3.8	S	N		Guam		None
13		2	2	San Agustin, Josefa B	Daughter	F	Cha	1.7	S	N		Guam		None
14		2	2	San Agustin, Dolores B	Mother	F	Cha	60	Wd	N	N	Guam	N	None
15		2	2	San Agustin, Juan B	Brother	M	Cha	29	S	N	Y	Guam	N	Laborer
16		3	3	Rosario, Ana T	Head	F	Cha	56	Wd	N	N	Guam	N	None
17		3	3	Taitingfong, Joaquin S	Son	M	Cha	22	S	N	Y	Guam	Y	Farmer
18		3	3	Rosario, Manuel T	Son	M	Cha	16	S	Y	Y	Guam	Y	None
19		3	3	Rosario, Ana T	Daughter	F	Cha	14	S	Y	Y	Guam	Y	None
20		3	3	Rosario, Rufina T	Daughter	F	Cha	12	S	Y	Y	Guam	Y	None
21		3	3	Rosario, Pedro T	Son	M	Cha	9	S	Y		Guam		None
22		3	3	Rosario, Helen T	Daughter	F	Cha	6	S	N		Guam		None
23		3	3	Rivera, Antonio R	Daughter	F	Cha	19	Wd	N	Y	Guam	Y	None
24		3	3	Rivera, Loreta R	Grand daughter	F	Cha	1.2	S	N		Guam		None
25		3	3	Santos, Jose S	Servant	M	Cha	18	S	N	Y	Guam	Y	Servant

DEPARTMENT OF COMMERCE-BUREAU OF THE CENSUS
WASHINGTON

FIFTEENTH CENSUS OF THE UNITED STATES: 1930-POPULATION

THE ISLAND OF GUAM

Sheet No. 1B

36B

District **Municipality of Agana**
Name of Place **Agana City (Part of Padre Palomo)**
[Proper name and, also, name of class, as city, town, village, barrio, etc]

Enumeration District No. **2**
Enumerated by me on **April 2, 1930** Arthur W. Jackson, Enumerator

	PLACE OF ABODE			NAME	RELATION	PERSONAL DESCRIPTION				EDUCATION		NATIVITY		OCCUPATION
	Street, avenue, road, etc.	Number of dwelling house in order of visitation	Number of family in order of visitation	of each person whose place of abode on April 1, 1930, was in this family. Enter surname, first, then given name and middle initial. If any. Include every person living on April 1, 1930. Omit children born since April 1, 1930.	Relationship of this Person to the head of the family.	Sex	Color or race	Age at last birthday	Single, married, widowed or divorced	Attended school any time since Sept. 1, 1929	Whether able to read and write.	Place of birth of this person.	Whether able to speak English.	
	1	2	3	4	5	6	7	8	9	10	11	12	13	14
26	Padre Palomo Street	3	4	Taitinfong, Felix S	Head	M	Cha	30	M	N	Y	Guam	N	Farmer
27		3	4	Taitinfong, Felisa C	Wife	F	Cha	27	M	N	Y	Guam	N	None
28		3	4	Taitinfong, Josefa C	Daughter	F	Cha	8	S	Y		Guam		None
29		3	4	Taitinfong, Rosa C	Daughter	F	Cha	5	S	N		Guam		None
30		3	4	Taitinfong, Rafael C	Son	M	Cha	4	S	N		Guam		None
31		3	4	Taitinfong, Ana C	Daughter	F	Cha	1.3	S	N		Guam		None
32		4	5	Alicto, Natividad C	Head	F	Cha	49	M	N	N	Guam	N	None
33		4	5	Alicto, Melchor C	Son	M	Cha	17	S	Y	Y	Guam	Y	None
34		4	5	Alicto, Pedro C	Son	M	Cha	15	S	Y	Y	Guam	Y	None
35		4	5	Alicto, Felix C	Son	M	Cha	13	S	Y	Y	Guam	Y	None
36		4	6	Manibusan, Jesus M	Head	M	Cha	25	M	N	Y	Guam	Y	Farmer
37		4	6	Manibusan, Antonia C	Wife	F	Cha	22	M	N	Y	Guam	Y	None
38		4	6	Manibusan, Vicente C	Son	M	Cha	2.2	S	N		Guam		None
39		4	6	Manibusan, Matilida C	Daughter	F	Cha	1.5	S	N		Guam		None
40		5	7	Jackson, Arthur W	Head	M	W	50	M	N	Y	New York	Y	Atty-at-law
41		5	7	Jackson, Dolores K	Wife	F	W	49	M	N	Y	Guam	Y	None
42		5	7	Jackson, Arthur K	Son	M	W	15	S	N	Y	Guam	Y	None
43		5	7	Jackson, Henry K	Son	M	W	12	S	Y	Y	Guam	Y	None
44		6	8	Nerona, Maria G	Head	F	Fil	56	Wd	N	Y	Guam	N	None
45		6	8	Guevara, Rosa SN	Sist-in-law	F	Cha	56	Wd	N	N	Guam	N	None
46		7	9	Kamminga, Jose H	Head	M	Cha	29	M	N	Y	Guam	Y	Auto mechanic
47		7	9	Kamminga, Maria SN	Wife	F	Cha	29	M	N	Y	Guam	Y	Midwife
48		7	9	Kamminga, Virginia SN	Daughter	F	Cha	4.1	S	N		Guam		None
49		7	9	Kamminga, Gaily SN	Son	M	Cha	3.5	S	N		Guam		None
50		7	9	Kamminga, Henry SN	Son	M	Cha	2.1	S	N		Guam		None

DEPARTMENT OF COMMERCE-BUREAU OF THE CENSUS
WASHINGTON

FIFTEENTH CENSUS OF THE UNITED STATES: 1930-POPULATION

THE ISLAND OF GUAM

Sheet No. 2A

District **Municipality of Agana**
Name of Place **Agana City (Part of Padre Palomo)**
[Proper name and, also, name of class, as city, town, village, barrio, etc]

Enumeration District No. **2**
Enumerated by me on **April 3, 1930** Arthur W. Jackson
Enumerator

	PLACE OF ABODE			NAME	RELATION	PERSONAL DESCRIPTION				EDUCATION		NATIVITY		OCCUPATION
	Street, avenue, road, etc.	Number of dwelling house is order of visitation	Number of family in order of visitation	of each person whose place of abode on April 1, 1930, was in this family. Enter surname, first, then given name and middle initial. If any. Include every person living on April 1, 1930. Omit children born since April 1, 1930.	Relationship of this Person to the head of the family.	Sex	Color or race	Age at last birthday	Single, married, widowed or divorced	Attended school any time since Sept. 1, 1929	Whether able to read and write.	Place of birth of this person.	Whether able to speak English.	
	1	2	3	4	5	6	7	8	9	10	11	12	13	14
1	Padre Palomo Street	8	10	Jackson, Frank K	Head	M	W	23	M	N	Y	California	Y	Chauffeur
2		8	10	Jackson, Rosie M	Wife	F	Cha	19	M	N	Y	Guam	Y	None
3		8	10	Jackson, Irene R	Daughter	F	Cha	.2	S	N		Guam		None
4		9	11	Sablan, Jesus D	Head	M	Cha	46	M	N	N	Guam	N	Farmer
5		9	11	Sablan, Josefa B	Wife	F	Cha	40	M	N	N	Guam	N	None
6		9	11	Sablan, Francisco B	Son	M	Cha	22	S	N	Y	Guam	Y	Farm laborer
7		9	11	Sablan, Manuela B	Daughter	F	Cha	19	S	N	Y	Guam	Y	None
8		9	11	Sablan, Maria B	Daughter	F	Cha	17	S	N	Y	Guam	Y	None
9		9	11	Sablan, Enrique B	Son	M	Cha	15	S	N	Y	Guam	Y	None
10		9	11	Sablan, Jose B	Son	M	Cha	11	S	Y	Y	Guam	Y	None
11		9	11	Sablan, Vicente B	Son	M	Cha	10	S	Y	Y	Guam	Y	None
12		9	11	Sablan, Vicenta B	Daughter	F	Cha	8	S	Y		Guam		None
13		9	11	Sablan, Felicita B	Daughter	F	Cha	1.9	S	N		Guam		None
14		9	11	Sablan, Epifanio B	Son	M	Cha	.8	S	N		Guam		None
15		10	12	Sablan, Joaquin D	Head	M	Cha	42	M	N	Y	Guam	Y	Carpenter
16		10	12	Sablan, Amalia R	Wife	F	Cha	40	M	N	Y	Guam	N	None
17		10	12	Sablan, Ramon R	Son	M	Cha	20	S	Y	Y	Guam	Y	None
18		10	12	Sablan, Margarita R	Daughter	F	Cha	17	S	N	Y	Guam	Y	None
19		10	12	Sablan, Rosalie R	Daughter	F	Cha	15	S	N	Y	Guam	Y	None
20		10	12	Sablan, Antonio R	Son	M	Cha	13	S	Y	Y	Guam	Y	None
21		10	12	Sablan, Isabel R	Daughter	F	Cha	11	S	Y	Y	Guam	Y	None
22		10	12	Sablan, Ana R	Daughter	F	Cha	9	S	Y		Guam		None
23		10	12	Sablan, Remedios R	Daughter	F	Cha	5	S	N		Guam		None
24		10	12	Sablan, Marta R	Daughter	F	Cha	3.1	S	N		Guam		None
25		10	12	Sablan, Emelia R	Daughter	F	Cha	1.6	S	N		Guam		None

(CHAMORRO ROOTS GENEALOGY PROJECT™ TRANSCRIPTION)
(BERNARD T. PUNZALAN / HTTP://WWW.CHAMORROROOTS.COM)

DEPARTMENT OF COMMERCE-BUREAU OF THE CENSUS
WASHINGTON

FIFTEENTH CENSUS OF THE UNITED STATES: 1930-POPULATION

THE ISLAND OF GUAM

Sheet No. 2B

37B

District Municipality of Agana
Name of Place Agana City (Part of Padre Palomo)
[Proper name and, also, name of class, as city, town, village, barrio, etc]

Enumeration District No. 2
Enumerated by me on April 3, 1930 Arthur W. Jackson, Enumerator

	PLACE OF ABODE			NAME	RELATION	PERSONAL DESCRIPTION				EDUCATION		NATIVITY		OCCUPATION
	Street, avenue, road, etc.	Number of dwelling house in order of visitation	Number of family in order of visitation	of each person whose place of abode on April 1, 1930, was in this family. Enter surname, first, then given name and middle initial. If any. Include every person living on April 1, 1930. Omit children born since April 1, 1930.	Relationship of this Person to the head of the family.	Sex	Color or race	Age at last birthday	Single, married, widowed or divorced	Attended school any time since Sept. 1, 1929	Whether able to read and write.	Place of birth of this person.	Whether able to speak English.	
	1	2	3	4	5	6	7	8	9	10	11	12	13	14
26	Padre Palomo Street	11	13	Sablan, Manuel D	Head	M	Cha	48	M	N	Y	Guam	N	Farmer
27		11	13	Sablan, Rosa P	Wife	F	Cha	49	M	N	Y	Guam	N	Laundress
28		11	13	Sablan, Jose P	Son	M	Cha	17	S	Y	Y	Guam	Y	Farmer
29		11	13	Sablan, Jesus P	Son	M	Cha	18	S	N	Y	Guam	Y	Clerk
30		11	13	Sablan, Joaq. P	Son	M	Cha	15	S	Y	Y	Guam	Y	None
31		11	13	Sablan, Maria P	Daug	F	Cha	11	S	Y	Y	Guam	Y	None
32		11	13	Sablan, Ana P	Daug	F	Cha	5	S	N		Guam		None
33		12	14	Meno, Maria N	Head	F	Cha	26	S	N	Y	Guam	Y	Laundress
34		12	14	Meno, Antonio N	Son	M	Cha	7	S	Y		Guam		None
35		12	14	Delgado, Luis D	Cousin	M	Cha	13	S	Y	Y	Guam	Y	None
36		13	15	Salas, Jose	Head	M	Cha	33	M	N	Y	Guam	Y	Draftsman
37		13	15	Salas, Clotilde S	Wife	F	Cha	33	M	N	Y	Guam	N	Household
38		13	15	Salas, Elpidia S	Daug	F	Cha	12	S	Y	Y	Guam	Y	None
39		13	15	Salas, Otelia S	Daug	F	Cha	10	S	Y	Y	Guam	Y	None
40		13	15	Salas, Francisco S	Son	M	Cha	8	S	Y		Guam		None
41		13	15	Salas, Geraldo S	Son	M	Cha	7	S	Y		Guam		None
42		13	15	Salas, Dorotea S	Daug	F	Cha	1.2	S	N		Guam		None
43		13	15	Salas, Sergio S	Son	M	Cha	1.3	S	N		Guam		None
44		13	15	Palacios, Antonio S	Servt	M	Cha	16	S	N		Guam		None
45		14	16	Garrido, Jose B	Head	M	Cha	50	M	N	Y	Guam	Y	Carpenter
46		14	16	Garrido, Vicenta T	Wife	F	Cha	53	M	N	Y	Guam	N	None
47		14	16	Garrido, Manuel T	Son	M	Cha	27	S	N	Y	Guam	Y	Mechanic
48		14	16	Garrido, Jesus T	Son	M	Cha	15	S	Y	Y	Guam	Y	Farm laborer
49		14	16	Garrido, Maria T	Daug	F	Cha	12	S	Y	Y	Guam	Y	None
50		14	16	Garrido, Juan T	Son	M	Cha	9	S	Y		Guam		None

DEPARTMENT OF COMMERCE-BUREAU OF THE CENSUS
WASHINGTON

FIFTEENTH CENSUS OF THE UNITED STATES: 1930-POPULATION

THE ISLAND OF GUAM

Sheet No. 3A

District **Municipality of Agana**
Name of Place **Agana City (Part of Padre Palomo)**
[Proper name and, also, name of class, as city, town, village, barrio, etc]

Enumeration District No. **2**
Enumerated by me on **April 3, 1930** Arthur W. Jackson
Enumerator

	PLACE OF ABODE			NAME	RELATION	PERSONAL DESCRIPTION				EDUCATION		NATIVITY		OCCUPATION
	Street, avenue, road, etc.	Number of dwelling house is order of visitation	Number of family in order of visitation	of each person whose place of abode on April 1, 1930, was in this family. Enter surname, first, then given name and middle initial. If any. Include every person living on April 1, 1930. Omit children born since April 1, 1930.	Relationship of this Person to the head of the family.	Sex	Color or race	Age at last birthday	Single, married, widowed or divorced	Attended school any time since Sept. 1, 1929	Whether able to read and write.	Place of birth of this person.	Whether able to speak English.	
	1	2	3	4	5	6	7	8	9	10	11	12	13	14
1	Padre Palomo Street	15	17	San Agustin, Alejandro C	Head	M	Cha	66	S	N	N	Guam	N	None
2		15	17	San Agustin, Jesus SN	Nephew	M	Cha	16	S	N	Y	Guam	Y	Laborer
3		15	17	San Agustin, Jose H	Nephew	M	Cha	16	S	N	N	Guam	Y	Laborer
4		15	18	San Agustin, Dolores E	Head	F	Cha	54	S	N	N	Guam	N	None
5		15	18	San Agustin, Mariano SN	Son	M	Cha	26	S	N	Y	Guam	Y	App. Printer
6		15	18	San Agustin, Jose SA	Son	M	Cha	22	S	N	Y	Guam	Y	Farmer
7		15	18	Baza, Elisabal A	Niece	F	Cha	15	S	Y	Y	Guam	Y	None
8		15	18	Baza, Emeterio A	Nephew	M	Cha	13	S	Y	Y	Guam	Y	None
9		16	19	Rivera, Jose U	Head	M	Cha	49	M	Y	Y	Guam	Y	Laborer
10		16	19	Rivera, Carmen A	Wife	F	Cha	44	M	N	Y	Guam	N	None
11		16	19	Rivera, Asuncion A	Daughter	F	Cha	17	S	N	Y	Guam	Y	None
12		16	19	Rivera, Juana A	Daughter	F	Cha	12	S	Y	Y	Guam	Y	None
13		16	19	Rivera, Josefa A	Daughter	F	Cha	11	S	Y	Y	Guam	Y	None
14		16	19	Rivera, Magdalena A	Daughter	F	Cha	10	S	Y	Y	Guam	Y	None
15		16	19	Rivera, Rosa A	Daughter	F	Cha	9	S	Y		Guam		None
16		16	19	Rivera, Elizabal A	Daughter	F	Cha	4.8	S	N		Guam		None
17		16	19	Rivera, Jose A	Son	M	Cha	.3	S	N		Guam		None
18		17	20	Benevente, Jose R	Head	M	Cha	43	M	N	N	Guam	N	Farmer
19		17	20	Benevente, Candaleria C	Wife	F	Cha	48	M	N	N	Guam	N	None
20		17	20	Benevente, Francisco C	Son	M	Cha	18	S	N	Y	Guam	Y	Laborer
21		17	20	Benevente, Maria C	Daughter	F	Cha	17	S	N	Y	Guam	Y	None
22		17	20	Benevente, Ana C	Daughter	F	Cha	15	S	Y	Y	Guam	Y	None
23		17	20	Benevente, Rosalia C	Daughter	F	Cha	8	S	Y		Guam		None
24		17	20	Benevente, Jose C	Son	M	Cha	6	S	N		Guam		None
25		17	20	Benevente, Tomasa C	Daughter	F	Cha	3.2	S	N		Guam		None

DEPARTMENT OF COMMERCE-BUREAU OF THE CENSUS
WASHINGTON

FIFTEENTH CENSUS OF THE UNITED STATES: 1930-POPULATION

THE ISLAND OF GUAM

Sheet No. 3B

District **Municipality of Agana**
Name of Place **Agana City (Part of Padre Palomo)**
[Proper name and, also, name of class, as city, town, village, barrio, etc]

Enumeration District No. **2**
Enumerated by me on **April 3, 1930** Arthur W. Jackson, Enumerator

	PLACE OF ABODE			NAME	RELATION	PERSONAL DESCRIPTION				EDUCATION		NATIVITY		OCCUPATION
	Street, avenue, road, etc.	Number of dwelling house is order of visitation	Number of family in order of visitation	of each person whose place of abode on April 1, 1930, was in this family. Enter surname, first, then given name and middle initial. If any. Include every person living on April 1, 1930. Omit children born since April 1, 1930.	Relationship of this Person to the head of the family.	Sex	Color or race	Age at last birthday	Single, married, widowed or divorced	Attended school any time since Sept. 1, 1929	Whether able to read and write.	Place of birth of this person.	Whether able to speak English.	
	1	2	3	4	5	6	7	8	9	10	11	12	13	14
26	Padre Palomo Street	17	20	Benevente, Juan C	Son	M	Cha	2.2	S	N		Guam		None
27		18	21	Untalan, Jesus P	Head	M	Cha	27	M	N	Y	Guam	Y	Carpenter
28		18	21	Untalan, Rita T	Wife	F	Cha	26	M	N	Y	Guam	N	None
29		18	21	Untalan, Jose T	Son	M	Cha	1.3	S	N		Guam		None
30		18	21	Untalan, Juan T	Son	M	Cha	.7	S	N		Guam		None
31		19	22	Perez, Juan LG	Head	M	Cha	49	M	N	N	Guam	Y	Carpenter
32		19	22	Perez, Dolores A	Wife	F	Cha	29	M	N	Y	Guam	N	None
33		19	22	Perez, Joaquin C	Son	M	Cha	17	S	Y	Y	Guam	Y	Laborer
34		19	22	Perez, Josefina C	Daughter	F	Cha	13	S	N	Y	Guam	Y	None
35		19	22	Perez, Benancio C	Son	M	Cha	11	S	Y	Y	Guam	Y	None
36		19	22	Perez, Alfreda C	Daughter	F	Cha	10	S	Y	Y	Guam	Y	None
37		19	22	Perez, Maria C	Daughter	F	Cha	9	S	Y		Guam		None
38		19	22	Perez, Remedio C	Daughter	F	Cha	8	S	Y		Guam		None
39		19	22	Perez, Josefa C	Daughter	F	Cha	7	S	Y		Guam		None
40		19	22	Perez, Eduardo C	Son	M	Cha	.8	S	N		Guam		None
41		20	23	Perez, Matias LG	Head	M	Cha	43	M	N	Y	Guam	Y	Carpenter
42		20	23	Perez, Josefa P	Wife	F	Cha	30	M	N	Y	Guam	Y	None
43		20	23	Palomo, Asuncion M	Servant	F	Cha	19	S	N	Y	Guam	Y	None
44		20	23	Palomo, Antonio R	Nephew	M	Cha	5	S	N		Guam		None
45		21	24	Mesa, Juana C	Head	F	Cha	50	Wd	N	N	Guam	N	Laundress
46		21	24	Mesa, Jesus C	Son	M	Cha	25	S	N	N	Guam	N	Farmer
47		22	25	Taguacta, Manuel R	Head	M	Cha	60	M	N	Y	Guam	Y	Farmer
48		22	25	Taguacta, Rosa B	Wife	F	Cha	63	M	N	N	Guam	N	None
49		22	25	Taguacta, Jose B	Son	M	Cha	36	S	N	Y	Guam	Y	Farm laborer
50		22	25	Taguacta, Mariano B	Son	M	Cha	20	S	N	Y	Guam	Y	Farm laborer

DEPARTMENT OF COMMERCE-BUREAU OF THE CENSUS
WASHINGTON

FIFTEENTH CENSUS OF THE UNITED STATES: 1930-POPULATION

THE ISLAND OF GUAM

Sheet No. 4A

District **Municipality of Agana**
Name of Place **Agana City (Part of Padre Palomo)**
[Proper name and, also, name of class, as city, town, village, barrio, etc]

Enumeration District No. **2**
Enumerated by me on **April 4, 1930** Arthur W. Jackson
Enumerator

	PLACE OF ABODE			NAME	RELATION	PERSONAL DESCRIPTION				EDUCATION		NATIVITY		OCCUPATION
	Street, avenue, road, etc.	Number of dwelling house in order of visitation	Number of family in order of visitation	of each person whose place of abode on April 1, 1930, was in this family. Enter surname, first, then given name and middle initial. If any. Include every person living on April 1, 1930. Omit children born since April 1, 1930.	Relationship of this Person to the head of the family.	Sex	Color or race	Age at last birthday	Single, married, widowed or divorced	Attended school any time since Sept. 1, 1929	Whether able to read and write.	Place of birth of this person.	Whether able to speak English.	
	1	2	3	4	5	6	7	8	9	10	11	12	13	14
1	Padre Palomo Street	23	26	Taguacta, Joaquin B	Head	M	Cha	27	M	N	Y	Guam	Y	Cook
2		23	26	Taguacta, Rosa SA	Wife	F	Cha	20	M	N	Y	Guam	Y	None
3		23	26	Taguacta, Pedro SA	Son	M	Cha	.2	S	N		Guam		None
4		23	26	Benavente, Carmen G	Aunt	F	Cha	60	S	N	N	Guam	N	None
5		23	26	Duenas, Jose B	Cousin	M	Cha	16	S	N	Y	Guam	Y	Servant
6		23	26	Duenas, Josefa B	Cousin	F	Cha	11	S	Y	Y	Guam	Y	None
7		24	27	Sablan, Jose B	Head	M	Cha	22	M	Y	Y	Guam	Y	Carpenter
8		24	27	Sablan, Tomasa Q	Wife	F	Cha	26	M	N	Y	Guam	Y	None
9		24	27	Sablan, Jesus Q	Son	M	Cha	2.3	S	N		Guam		None
10		24	27	Quichocho, Jesusa Q	Step-daug	F	Cha	5	S	N		Guam		None
11		25	28	Flores, Jesus P	Head	M	Cha	44	S	N	Y	Guam	Y	Carpenter
12		26	29	Blaz, Lorenzo L	Head	M	Cha	50	M	N	Y	Guam	N	Fisherman
13		26	29	Blaz, Maria M	Wife	F	Cha	37	M	N	Y	Guam	N	None
14		26	29	Blaz, Maria M	Daughter	F	Cha	16	S	N	Y	Guam	Y	None
15		26	29	Blaz, Consulo M	Daughter	F	Cha	12	S	Y	Y	Guam	Y	None
16		26	29	Blaz, Asuncion M	Daughter	F	Cha	11	S	Y	Y	Guam	Y	None
17		26	29	Blaz, Lorenzo M	Son	M	Cha	9	S	Y		Guam		None
18		26	29	Blaz, Magi M	Daughter	F	Cha	5	S	N		Guam		None
19		26	29	Blaz, Josefina M	Daughter	F	Cha	3.3	S	N		Guam		None
20		26	29	Blaz, Tomasa M	Son	M	Cha	.2	S	N		Guam		None
21		27	30	Mesa, Tomas E	Head	M	Cha	65	M	N	Y	Guam	N	Farmer
22		27	30	Mesa, Dolores C	Wife	F	Cha	53	M	N	N	Guam	N	None
23		27	30	Mesa, Jose C	Son	M	Cha	28	S	N	Y	Guam	Y	Fisherman
24		27	30	Mesa, Jose C	Son	M	Cha	21	S	N	Y	Guam	Y	Farm laborer
25		27	30	Sablan, Antonio Q	Lodger	M	Cha	5	S	N		Guam		None

DEPARTMENT OF COMMERCE-BUREAU OF THE CENSUS
WASHINGTON

FIFTEENTH CENSUS OF THE UNITED STATES: 1930-POPULATION

THE ISLAND OF GUAM

Sheet No. 4B

District **Municipality of Agana**
Name of Place **Agana City (Part of Padre Palomo)**
[Proper name and, also, name of class, as city, town, village, barrio, etc]

Enumeration District No. 2
Enumerated by me on **April 4, 1930** Arthur W. Jackson, Enumerator

	PLACE OF ABODE			NAME	RELATION	PERSONAL DESCRIPTION				EDUCATION		NATIVITY		OCCUPATION
	Street, avenue, road, etc.	Number of dwelling house is order of visitation	Number of family in order of visitation	of each person whose place of abode on April 1, 1930, was in this family. Enter surname, first, then given name and middle initial. If any. Include every person living on April 1, 1930. Omit children born since April 1, 1930.	Relationship of this Person to the head of the family.	Sex	Color or race	Age at last birthday	Single, married, widowed or divorced	Attended school any time since Sept. 1, 1929	Whether able to read and write.	Place of birth of this person.	Whether able to speak English.	
	1	2	3	4	5	6	7	8	9	10	11	12	13	14
26	Padre Palomo Street	27	30	Mesa, Joaquin C	Son	M	Cha	16	S	N	Y	Guam	Y	Farm laborer
27		27	30	Mesa, Rosa F	[illegible]	F	Cha	44	M	Y	Y	Guam	N	Laundress
28		28	31	Mesa, Maria U	Head	F	Cha	40	M	N	Y	Guam	N	None
29		28	31	Mesa, Jose U	Son	M	Cha	8	S	Y		Guam		None
30		28	31	Mesa, Maria U	Daughter	F	Cha	6	S	N		Guam		None
31		28	31	Mesa, Jesus U	Son	M	Cha	3.4	S	N		Guam		None
32		29	32	Quichocho, Joaquina Q	Head	F	Cha	55	M	N	N	Guam	N	None
33		29	32	Quichocho, Beatrice Q	Daughter	F	Cha	20	S	N	Y	Guam	Y	None
34		29	32	Quichocho, Francisco Q	Son	M	Cha	17	S	N	Y	Guam	Y	Farmer
35		30	33	Borja, Jose V	Head	M	Cha	52	M	N	Y	Guam	N	Farmer
36		30	33	Borja, Maria SN	Wife	F	Cha	54	M	N	N	Guam	N	None
37		30	34	Taitinfong, Jose S	Head	M	Cha	27	M	N	N	Guam	N	Farmer
38		30	34	Taitinfong, Rosa B	Wife	F	Cha	19	M	N	Y	Guam	N	None
39		30	34	Taitinfong, Ana B	Daughter	F	Cha	2.1	S	N	Y	Guam		None
40		31	35	Reyes, Jesus R	Head	M	Cha	35	M	N	N	Guam	N	Laborer
41		31	35	Reyes, Maria SA	Wife	F	Cha	32	M	N	Y	Guam	N	None
42		31	35	Reyes, Francisco SA	Son	M	Cha	11	S	Y		Guam	Y	None
43		31	35	Reyes, Luis SA	Son	M	Cha	9	S	Y		Guam		None
44		31	35	Reyes, Isabel SA	Daughter	F	Cha	8	S	Y		Guam		None
45		32	36	Taitinfong, Jose B	Head	M	Cha	48	M	N	Y	Guam	N	Farmer
46		32	36	Taitinfong, Maria D	Wife	F	Cha	29	M	N	Y	Guam	N	None
47		33	37	Taitano, Ramon SN	Head	M	Cha	48	M	N	Y	Guam	Y	Laborer
48		33	37	Taitano, Carmen P	Wife	F	Cha	29	M	N	Y	Guam	Y	None
49		33	37	Taitano, Alfred F	Son	M	Cha	20	S	N	Y	Guam	Y	Farm laborer
50		33	37	Taitano, Robert F	Son	M	Cha	18	S	N	Y	Guam	Y	Farm laborer

DEPARTMENT OF COMMERCE-BUREAU OF THE CENSUS
WASHINGTON

FIFTEENTH CENSUS OF THE UNITED STATES: 1930-POPULATION

THE ISLAND OF GUAM

Sheet No. 5A

District Municipality of Agana
Name of Place Agana City (Part of Padre Palomo)
[Proper name and, also, name of class, as city, town, village, barrio, etc]

Enumeration District No. 2
Enumerated by me on April 4, 1930 Arthur W. Jackson
Enumerator

	PLACE OF ABODE			NAME	RELATION	PERSONAL DESCRIPTION				EDUCATION		NATIVITY		OCCUPATION
	Street, avenue, road, etc.	Number of dwelling house in order of visitation	Number of family in order of visitation	of each person whose place of abode on April 1, 1930, was in this family. Enter surname, first, then given name and middle initial. If any. Include every person living on April 1, 1930. Omit children born since April 1, 1930.	Relationship of this Person to the head of the family.	Sex	Color or race	Age at last birthday	Single, married, widowed or divorced	Attended school any time since Sept. 1, 1929	Whether able to read and write.	Place of birth of this person.	Whether able to speak English.	
	1	2	3	4	5	6	7	8	9	10	11	12	13	14
1	Padre Palomo Street	33	37	Taitano, George F	Son	M	Cha	16	S	N	Y	Guam	Y	Farm laborer
2		33	37	Taitano, Herminia F	Daughter	F	Cha	13	S	Y	Y	Guam	Y	None
3		33	37	Taitano, Arthur F	Son	M	Cha	9	S	Y	Y	Guam	Y	None
4		34	38	Camacho, Vicente D	Head	M	Cha	31	M	N	Y	Guam	Y	Blacksmith
5		34	38	Camacho, Ana A	Wife	F	Cha	36	M	N	Y	Guam	N	None
6		34	38	Camacho, Ana A	Daughter	F	Cha	6	S	Y		Guam		None
7		34	38	Camacho, Pedro A	Son	M	Cha	5	S	N		Guam		None
8		34	38	Camacho, Vicente A	Son	M	Cha	4.3	S	N		Guam		None
9		34	38	Camacho, Amparo A	Daughter	F	Cha	.8	S	N		Guam		None
10		35	39	Lujan, Ana C	Head	F	Cha	25	M	N	Y	Guam	N	None
11		35	39	Lujan, Jesus C	Son	M	Cha	4.7	S	N		Guam		None
12		35	39	Lujan, Brigida C	Daughter	F	Cha	2.3	S	N		Guam		None
13		35	39	Jesus, Angela C	Mother	F	Cha	57	M	N	N	Guam	N	None
14		36	40	Acosta, Mariano C	Head	M	Cha	66	M	N	N	Guam	N	Farmer
15		36	40	Acosta, Isabel LG	Wife	F	Cha	47	M	N	N	Guam	N	None
16		36	40	Acosta, Maria LG	Daughter	F	Cha	7	S	Y		Guam		None
17		37	41	Leon Guerrero, Ignacio F	Head	M	Cha	31	M	N	Y	Guam	Y	Farmer
18		37	41	Leon Guerrero, Vicenta T	Wife	F	Cha	31	M	N	Y	Guam	N	None
19		37	41	Leon Guerrero, Dolores T	Daughter	F	Cha	8	S	Y		Guam		None
20		37	41	Leon Guerrero, Juan T	Son	M	Cha	4.4	S	N		Guam		None
21		37	41	Leon Guerrero, Leonia T	Daughter	F	Cha	2.1	S	N		Guam		None
22		37	41	Leon Guerrero, Justo T	Son	M	Cha	.8	S	N		Guam		None
23		37	41	Cruz, Jose LG	Nephew	M	Cha	14	S	N	Y	Guam	Y	Farmer
24		37	41	Cruz, Remedios LG	Niece	F	Cha	12	S	Y	Y	Guam	Y	None
25		37	41	Cruz, Joaquin LG	Nephew	M	Cha	12	S	Y	Y	Guam	Y	None

(CHAMORRO ROOTS GENEALOGY PROJECT™ TRANSCRIPTION)
(BERNARD T. PUNZALAN / HTTP://WWW.CHAMORROROOTS.COM)

DEPARTMENT OF COMMERCE-BUREAU OF THE CENSUS
WASHINGTON

FIFTEENTH CENSUS OF THE UNITED STATES: 1930-POPULATION

THE ISLAND OF GUAM

Sheet No. 5B

District Municipality of Agana
Name of Place Agana City (Part of Padre Palomo)
[Proper name and, also, name of class, as city, town, village, barrio, etc]

Enumeration District No. 2
Enumerated by me on April 4, 1930 Arthur W. Jackson
Enumerator

	PLACE OF ABODE			NAME	RELATION	PERSONAL DESCRIPTION				EDUCATION		NATIVITY		OCCUPATION
	Street, avenue, road, etc.	Number of dwelling house is order of visitation	Number of family in order of visitation	of each person whose place of abode on April 1, 1930, was in this family. Enter surname, first, then given name and middle initial. If any. Include every person living on April 1, 1930. Omit children born since April 1, 1930.	Relationship of this Person to the head of the family.	Sex	Color or race	Age at last birthday	Single, married, widowed or divorced	Attended school any time since Sept. 1, 1929	Whether able to read and write.	Place of birth of this person.	Whether able to speak English.	
	1	2	3	4	5	6	7	8	9	10	11	12	13	14
26	Padre Palomo Street	38	42	Cruz, Jose A	Head	M	Cha	47	M	N	Y	Guam	N	Farmer
27		38	42	Cruz, Ana A	Wife	F	Cha	35	M	N	Y	Guam	N	None
28		38	42	Cruz, Vicente A	Son	M	Cha	14	S	Y	Y	Guam	Y	None
29		38	42	Cruz, Francisco A	Son	M	Cha	13	S	Y	Y	Guam	Y	None
30		38	42	Cruz, Maria A	Daughter	F	Cha	10	S	Y	Y	Guam	N	None
31		38	42	Cruz, Gregorio A	Son	M	Cha	8	S	Y		Guam		None
32		38	42	Cruz, Juan A	Son	M	Cha	7	S	Y		Guam		None
33		38	42	Cruz, Rosario A	Daughter	F	Cha	5	S	N		Guam		None
34		38	42	Cruz, Felix A	Son	M	Cha	1.2	S	N		Guam		None
35		38	42	Taitinfong, Dominga A	Mother in-law	F	Cha	70	S	N	N	Guam	N	None
36		39	43	Duenas, Luis P	Head	M	Cha	66	M	N	Y	Guam	N	None
37		39	43	Duenas, Josefa B	Wife	F	Cha	60	M	N	Y	Guam	N	None
38		39	43	Duenas, Pedro B	Son	M	Cha	19	S	Y	Y	Guam	Y	Student
39		39	43	Duenas, Jesus B	Son	M	Cha	15	S	Y	Y	Guam	N	None
40		40	44	Manibusan, Benigno C	Head	M	Cha	38	M	Y	Y	Guam	Y	Blacksmith
41		40	44	Manibusan, Joaquina B	Wife	F	Cha	35	M	N	Y	Guam	Y	None
42		40	44	Manibusan, Jesus B	Son	M	Cha	13	S	Y	Y	Guam	Y	None
43		40	44	Manibusan, Juan B	Son	M	Cha	10	S	Y	Y	Guam	N	None
44		40	44	Manibusan, Antonio B	Son	M	Cha	7	S	Y		Guam		None
45		40	44	Manibusan, Eduardo B	Son	M	Cha	4.6	S	N		Guam		None
46		40	44	Manibusan, Maria B	Daughter	F	Cha	3.1	S	N		Guam		None
47		40	44	Manibusan, Lourdes B	Daughter	F	Cha	1.7	S	N		Guam		None
48		40	45	Cruz, Pedro C	Head	M	Cha	55	S	N	N	Guam	N	Farmer
49		41	46	Quintanilla, Juan C	Head	M	Cha	26	M	N	Y	Guam	Y	Farmer
50		41	46	Cruz, Natividad Q	Aunt	F	Cha	60	S	N	N	Guam	N	None

(CHAMORRO ROOTS GENEALOGY PROJECT™ TRANSCRIPTION)
(BERNARD T. PUNZALAN / HTTP://WWW.CHAMORROROOTS.COM)

DEPARTMENT OF COMMERCE-BUREAU OF THE CENSUS
WASHINGTON

FIFTEENTH CENSUS OF THE UNITED STATES: 1930-POPULATION

THE ISLAND OF GUAM

Sheet No. 6A

41

District **Municipality of Agana**
Name of Place **Agana City (Part of Padre Palomo)**
[Proper name and, also, name of class, as city, town, village, barrio, etc]

Enumeration District No. 2
Enumerated by me on **April 5, 1930** Arthur W. Jackson, Enumerator

	PLACE OF ABODE			NAME	RELATION	PERSONAL DESCRIPTION				EDUCATION		NATIVITY		OCCUPATION
	Street, avenue, road, etc.	Number of dwelling house is order of visitation	Number of family in order of visitation	of each person whose place of abode on April 1, 1930, was in this family. Enter surname, first, then given name and middle initial. If any. Include every person living on April 1, 1930. Omit children born since April 1, 1930.	Relationship of this Person to the head of the family.	Sex	Color or race	Age at last birthday	Single, married, widowed or divorced	Attended school any time since Sept. 1, 1929	Whether able to read and write.	Place of birth of this person.	Whether able to speak English.	
	1	2	3	4	5	6	7	8	9	10	11	12	13	14
1	Padre Palomo Street	41	46	Quintanilla, Maria G	Wife	F	Cha	28	M	N	Y	Guam	Y	None
2		42	47	Aguajlo, Concepcion C	Head	F	Cha	35	M	N	Y	Guam	Y	None
3		42	47	Aguajlo, Francisco C	Son	M	Cha	10	S	Y	Y	Guam	Y	None
4		42	47	Aguajlo, Maria C	Daughter	F	Cha	8	S	Y		Guam		None
5		42	47	Aguajlo, Ana C	Daughter	F	Cha	7	S	N		Guam		None
6		42	47	Aguajlo, Catalina C	Daughter	F	Cha	2	S	N		Guam		None
7		42	47	Aguajlo, Ignacia C	Daughter	F	Cha	1	S	N		Guam		None
8		42	47	Toves, Juan A	Lodger	M	Cha	12	S	Y	Y	Guam	Y	None
9		43	48	Crisostomo, Mecaila C	Head	F	Cha	50	Wd	N	N	Rota	Y	None
10		43	48	Crisostomo, Vicente C	Son	M	Cha	20	S	N	Y	Guam	Y	Farmer
11		43	49	Santos, Jesus Q	Head	M	Cha	33	M	N	Y	Guam	N	Farmer
12		43	49	Santos, Vicenta C	Wife	F	Cha	29	M	N	Y	Guam	N	Launcress
13		43	49	Santos, Maria C	Daughter	F	Cha	11	S	Y	Y	Guam		None
14		43	49	Santos, Luis C	Son	M	Cha	8	S	Y		Guam		None
15		43	49	Santos, Lourdes C	Daughter	F	Cha	7	S	N		Guam		None
16		43	49	Santos, Vicente C	Son	M	Cha	5	S	N		Guam		None
17		43	49	Santos, Juan C	Son	M	Cha	2.5	S	N		Guam		None
18		44	50	Acosta, Joaquin A	Head	M	Cha	69	M	N	N	Guam	N	Farmer
19		44	50	Acosta, Beatris D	Wife	F	Cha	55	M	N	N	Guam	N	None
20		44	50	Crisostomo, Antonio C	Nephew	M	Cha	15	S	Y	Y	Guam	Y	None
21		45	51	Arriola, Vicente T	Head	M	Cha	34	M	N	Y	Guam	Y	Ex. of Titles
22		45	51	Arriola, Soledad C	Wife	F	Cha	25	M	N	Y	Guam	Y	None
23		45	51	Arriola, Joaquin C	Son	M	Cha	4.8	S	N		Guam		None
24		45	51	Arriola, Francisco C	Son	M	Cha	.1	S	N		Guam		None
25		45	51	Cruz, Catalina F	Servant	F	Cha	13	S	N	Y	Guam	Y	Servant

DEPARTMENT OF COMMERCE-BUREAU OF THE CENSUS
WASHINGTON

FIFTEENTH CENSUS OF THE UNITED STATES: 1930-POPULATION

THE ISLAND OF GUAM

Sheet No. 6B

41B

District **Municipality of Agana**
Name of Place **Agana City (Part of Padre Palomo)**
[Proper name and, also, name of class, as city, town, village, barrio, etc]

Enumeration District No. **2**
Enumerated by me on **April 5, 1930** Arthur W. Jackson, Enumerator

	PLACE OF ABODE			NAME	RELATION	PERSONAL DESCRIPTION				EDUCATION		NATIVITY		OCCUPATION
	Street, avenue, road, etc.	Number of dwelling house in order of visitation	Number of family in order of visitation	of each person whose place of abode on April 1, 1930, was in this family. Enter surname, first, then given name and middle initial. If any. Include every person living on April 1, 1930. Omit children born since April 1, 1930.	Relationship of this Person to the head of the family.	Sex	Color or race	Age at last birthday	Single, married, widowed or divorced	Attended school any time since Sept. 1, 1929	Whether able to read and write.	Place of birth of this person.	Whether able to speak English.	
	1	2	3	4	5	6	7	8	9	10	11	12	13	14
26	Padre Palomo Street	46	52	Flores, Antonio C	Head	M	Cha	40	M	N	Y	Guam	Y	Farmer
27		46	52	Flores, Maria C	Wife	F	Cha	38	M	N	N	Guam	N	None
28		46	52	Flores, Vicenta C	Daughter	F	Cha	17	S	N	Y	Guam	Y	None
29		46	52	Flores, Dolores C	Daughter	F	Cha	15	S	Y	Y	Guam	Y	None
30		46	52	Flores, Jose C	Son	M	Cha	12	S	Y	Y	Guam	Y	None
31		46	52	Flores, Antonio C	Son	M	Cha	17	S	Y	N	Guam	Y	None
32		46	52	Flores, Natividad C	Daughter	F	Cha	9	S	Y		Guam		None
33		46	52	Flores, Isabel C	Daughter	F	Cha	5	S	N		Guam		None
34		46	52	Flores, Ana C	Daughter	F	Cha	1.5	S	N		Guam		None
35		47	53	Torre, Jesus C	Head	M	Cha	32	M	N	Y	Guam	Y	Farmer
36		47	53	Torre, Amparo SN	Wife	F	Cha	26	M	N	Y	Guam	Y	None
37		47	53	Torre, Luis SN	Son	M	Cha	2.3	S	N		Guam		None
38		47	53	Torre, Gregorio SN	Son	M	Cha	1.4	S	N		Guam		None
39		47	53	Dydasco, Vicente A	Uncle	M	Cha	52	S	N	N	Guam	N	Laborer
40		47	53	San Nicolas, Maria D	Sist in law	F	Cha	31	S	N	N	Guam	Y	None
41		48	54	Marion, Eduardo B	Head	M	Cha	24	M	N	Y	Guam	Y	Laborer
42		48	54	Marion, Maria L	Wife	F	Cha	23	M	N	Y	Guam	Y	None
43		48	54	Marion, Jesus L	Son	M	Cha	5	S	N		Guam		None
44		48	54	Marion, Henry L	Son	M	Cha	2.3	S	N		Guam		None
45		48	54	Marion, Silvia L	Daughter	F	Cha	.2	S	N		Guam		None
46		48	54	Crisostomo, Jesus C	Lodger	M	Cha	9	S	Y		Guam		None
47		48	54	Cruz, Nicolas M	Servant	M	Cha	9	S	Y		Guam		None
48		49	55	Perez, Jesus F	Head	M	Cha	45	M	N	Y	Guam	Y	Farmer
49		49	55	Perez, Margarita D	Wife	F	Cha	39	M	N	Y	Guam	Y	None
50		49	55	Perez, Maria D	Daughter	F	Cha	19	S	N	Y	Guam	Y	None

(CHAMORRO ROOTS GENEALOGY PROJECT™ TRANSCRIPTION)
(BERNARD T. PUNZALAN / HTTP://WWW.CHAMORROROOTS.COM)

DEPARTMENT OF COMMERCE-BUREAU OF THE CENSUS
WASHINGTON

FIFTEENTH CENSUS OF THE UNITED STATES: 1930-POPULATION

THE ISLAND OF GUAM

Sheet No. 7A

District **Municipality of Agana**
Name of Place **Agana City (Part of Padre Palomo)**
[Proper name and, also, name of class, as city, town, village, barrio, etc]

Enumeration District No. 2
Enumerated by me on **April 5, 1930** Arthur W. Jackson, Enumerator

	PLACE OF ABODE			NAME	RELATION	PERSONAL DESCRIPTION				EDUCATION		NATIVITY		OCCUPATION
	Street, avenue, road, etc.	Number of dwelling house is order of visitation	Number of family in order of visitation	of each person whose place of abode on April 1, 1930, was in this family. Enter surname, first, then given name and middle initial. If any. Include every person living on April 1, 1930. Omit children born since April 1, 1930.	Relationship of this Person to the head of the family.	Sex	Color or race	Age at last birthday	Single, married, widowed or divorced	Attended school any time since Sept. 1, 1929	Whether able to read and write.	Place of birth of this person.	Whether able to speak English.	
	1	2	3	4	5	6	7	8	9	10	11	12	13	14
1	Padre Palomo Street	49	55	Perez, Francisco D	Son	M	Cha	16	S	Y	Y	Guam	Y	None
2		50	56	Punzalan, Antonia	Head	F	Cha	26	M	N	Y	Guam	Y	None
3		50	56	Punzalan, Antonio A	Son	M	Fil	7	S	Y		Guam		None
4		50	56	Punzalan, Jose A	Son	M	Fil	4.5	S	N		Guam		None
5		50	56	Punzalan, Nieves A	Daughter	F	Fil	2.3	S	N		Guam		None
6		50	56	Punzalan, Emelia A	Daughter	F	Fil	.8	S	N		Guam		None
7		51	57	Perez, Rosa C	Head	F	Cha	57	M	N	N	Guam	N	Farmer
8		51	57	Perez, Jesus C	Son	M	Cha	26	S	N	Y	Guam	Y	Cook
9		51	58	Perez, Jose C	Head	M	Cha	24	M	N	Y	Guam	Y	Farmer
10		51	58	Perez, Josefa C	Wife	F	Cha	18	M	N	Y	Guam	Y	None
11		51	58	Quitugua, Juan	Nephew	M	Cha	6	S	N		Guam		None
12		52	59	Adriano, Joaquin G	Head	M	Cha	57	Wd	N	N	Guam	N	None
13		52	59	Adriano, Maria G	Daughter	F	Cha	19	S	N	Y	Guam	Y	None
14		53	60	Yokoi, Jose T	Head	M	Jap	44	M	N	Y	Japan	Y	Retail merchant
15		53	60	Yokoi, Maria Q	Wife	F	Cha	34	M	N	Y	Guam	Y	None
16		53	60	Yokoi, Gertrudes Q	Daughter	F	Jap	15	S	Y	Y	Guam	Y	None
17		53	60	Yokoi, Emelia Q	Daughter	F	Jap	11	S	Y	Y	Guam	Y	None
18		53	60	Yokoi, Juan Q	Son	M	Jap	10	S	Y	Y	Guam		None
19		53	60	Yokoi, Jose Q	Son	M	Jap	7	S	Y		Guam		None
20		53	60	Yokoi, Francisco Q	Son	M	Jap	6	S	N		Guam		None
21		53	60	Yokoi, Agueda Q	Daughter	F	Jap	3.2	S	N		Guam		None
22		53	60	Quintanilla, Manuel P	Bro-in-law	M	Cha	36	S	N	Y	Guam	N	Farmer
23		53	60	Yoshida, Shitaro	Boarder	M	Jap	46	S	N	Y	Japan	N	None
24		54	61	Baza, Manuel C	Head	M	Cha	30	M	N	Y	Guam	Y	Barber
25		54	61	Baza, Maria LG	Wife	F	Cha	32	M	N	Y	Guam	N	None

(CHAMORRO ROOTS GENEALOGY PROJECT™ TRANSCRIPTION)
(BERNARD T. PUNZALAN / HTTP://WWW.CHAMORROROOTS.COM)

DEPARTMENT OF COMMERCE-BUREAU OF THE CENSUS
WASHINGTON

FIFTEENTH CENSUS OF THE UNITED STATES: 1930-POPULATION

THE ISLAND OF GUAM

Sheet No. 7B

42B

District **Municipality of Agana**
Name of Place **Agana City (Part of Padre Palomo)**
[Proper name and, also, name of class, as city, town, village, barrio, etc]

Enumeration District No. 2
Enumerated by me on **April 7, 1930** Arthur W. Jackson, Enumerator

	PLACE OF ABODE			NAME	RELATION	PERSONAL DESCRIPTION				EDUCATION		NATIVITY		OCCUPATION
	Street, avenue, road, etc.	Number of dwelling house in order of visitation	Number of family in order of visitation	of each person whose place of abode on April 1, 1930, was in this family. Enter surname, first, then given name and middle initial. If any. Include every person living on April 1, 1930. Omit children born since April 1, 1930.	Relationship of this Person to the head of the family.	Sex	Color or race	Age at last birthday	Single, married, widowed or divorced	Attended school any time since Sept. 1, 1929	Whether able to read and write.	Place of birth of this person.	Whether able to speak English.	
	1	2	3	4	5	6	7	8	9	10	11	12	13	14
26	Padre Palomo Street	54	61	Baza, Jose LG	Son	M	Cha	9	S	Y		Guam		None
27		54	61	Baza, Isabel LG	Daughter	F	Cha	8	S	Y		Guam		None
28		54	61	Baza, Rosario LG	Daughter	F	Cha	6	S	N		Guam		None
29		54	61	Baza, Francisco LG	Son	M	Cha	4	S	N		Guam		None
30		54	61	Baza, Jesus LG	Son	M	Cha	2.3	S	N		Guam		None
31		55	62	Naputi, Jesus N	Head	M	Cha	46	M	N	Y	Guam	Y	Cook
32		55	62	Naputi, Ana B	Wife	F	Cha	41	M	N	Y	Guam	N	None
33		55	62	Naputi, Jose B	Son	M	Cha	20	S	N	Y	Guam	Y	Cook
34		55	62	Naputi, Maria B	Daughter	F	Cha	17	S	N	Y	Guam	Y	None
35		55	62	Naputi, Rosa B	Daughter	F	Cha	14	S	Y	Y	Guam	Y	None
36		55	62	Naputi, Jesus B	Son	M	Cha	10	S	Y	Y	Guam	Y	None
37		55	62	Naputi, Ana B	Daughter	F	Cha	10	S	Y	Y	Guam	Y	None
38		55	62	Naputi, Asuncion B	Daughter	F	Cha	8	S	Y		Guam		None
39		55	62	Naputi, Joaquin B	Son	M	Cha	6	S	Y		Guam		None
40		55	62	Naputi, Brigida B	Daughter	F	Cha	4.3	S	N		Guam		None
41		55	62	Naputi, Rosalia B	Daughter	F	Cha	2.3	S	Y		Guam		None
42		55	62	Naputi, Catalina B	Daughter	F	Cha	.1	S	Y		Guam		None
43		55	62	Benavente, Jesus H	Servant	M	Cha	17	S	N	N	Guam	Y	Servant
44		56	62	Gumabon, Ariston G	Head	M	Fil	65	M	N	Y	Phil Islands	Y	Barber
45		56	62	Gumabon, Carmen N	Wife	F	Cha	54	M	N	N	Guam	N	None
46		56	62	Gumabon, Vicente N	Son	M	Fil	20	S	Y	Y	Guam	Y	Barber
47		56	62	Meno, Josefa B	Head	F	Cha	28	S	N	Y	Guam	Y	Laundress
48		56	62	Meno, Jose M	Son	M	Cha	.8	S	N		Guam		None
49		56	62	Gumabon, A M	Nephew	M	Cha	6	S	N		Guam		None
50					Here ends the enumeration of Dist 1 Padre Palomo									None

DEPARTMENT OF COMMERCE-BUREAU OF THE CENSUS
WASHINGTON

FIFTEENTH CENSUS OF THE UNITED STATES: 1930-POPULATION

THE ISLAND OF GUAM

Sheet No. 8A

District Municipality of Agana
Name of Place Agana City (Part of San Antonio)
[Proper name and, also, name of class, as city, town, village, barrio, etc]

Enumeration District No. 2
Enumerated by me on April 7, 1930 Arthur W. Jackson
Enumerator

	PLACE OF ABODE			NAME	RELATION	PERSONAL DESCRIPTION				EDUCATION		NATIVITY		OCCUPATION
	Street, avenue, road, etc.	Number of dwelling house is order of visitation	Number of family in order of visitation	of each person whose place of abode on April 1, 1930, was in this family. Enter surname, first, then given name and middle initial. If any. Include every person living on April 1, 1930. Omit children born since April 1, 1930.	Relationship of this Person to the head of the family.	Sex	Color or race	Age at last birthday	Single, married, widowed or divorced	Attended school any time since Sept. 1, 1929	Whether able to read and write.	Place of birth of this person.	Whether able to speak English.	
	1	2	3	4	5	6	7	8	9	10	11	12	13	14
1	Dela Corte	57	65	Jesus, Lucas SN	Head	M	Cha	47	M	N	N	Guam	N	Farmer
2		57	65	Jesus, Maria C	Wife	F	Cha	62	M	N	N	Guam	N	None
3		57	65	Cruz, Manuel D	Fath-in-law	M	Cha	89	Wd	N	Y	Guam	N	None
4		57	65	Iglesias, Juana I	Aunt	F	Cha	85	Wd	N	N	Guam	N	None
5		57	65	San Nicolas, Rosa C	Lodger	F	Cha	15	S	N	Y	Guam	N	None
6		57	65	San Nicolas, Maria C	Lodger	F	Cha	12	S	Y	Y	Guam	Y	None
7		57	65	San Nicolas, Beatrice C	Lodger	F	Cha	11	S	Y	Y	Guam	Y	None
8		57	65	Cruz, Teresa C	Lodger	F	Cha	14	S	Y	Y	Guam	Y	None
9		58	66	Cruz, Vicente A	Head	M	Cha	49	M	N	Y	Guam	N	Fisherman
10		58	66	Cruz, Ana D	Wife	F	Cha	47	M	N	N	Guam	N	None
11		58	66	Cruz, Felix D	Son	M	Cha	23	S	N	Y	Guam	Y	Laborer
12		58	66	Cruz, Engracia D	Daughter	F	Cha	16	S	N	Y	Guam	Y	None
13		58	66	Cruz, Geronimo D	Son	M	Cha	14	S	N	Y	Guam	N	None
14		58	66	Dydasco, Joaquin A	Bro-in-law	M	Cha	52	S	Y	Y	Guam	Y	Carpenter
15		58	66	Muna, Felicita	Niece	F	Cha	10	S	Y	Y	Guam	Y	None
16		59	67	Aguajlo, Juan S	Head	M	Cha	26	M	N	Y	Guam	Y	Policeman
17		59	67	Aguajlo, Maria P	Wife	F	Cha	25	M	N	Y	Guam	Y	None
18		59	67	Camacho, Juan P	Step-son	M	Cha	4.6	S	N		Guam		None
19		60	68	Perez, Mariano T	Head	M	Cha	48	M	N	Y	Guam	N	Farmer
20		60	68	Perez, Antonia S	Daughter	F	Cha	16	S	N	Y	Guam	Y	None
21		61	69	Meno, Maria G	Head	F	Cha	34	M	N	Y	Guam	Y	Farmer
22		61	69	Meno, Vicente G	Son	M	Cha	9	S	Y		Guam		None
23		61	69	Meno, Nicolasa G	Daughter	F	Cha	8	S	Y		Guam		None
24		61	69	Meno, Tomas G	Son	M	Cha	4.3	S	Y		Guam		None
25		61	69	Perez, Antonia C	Servant	M	Cha	14	S	Y	Y		Y	Servant

(CHAMORRO ROOTS GENEALOGY PROJECT™ TRANSCRIPTION)
(BERNARD T. PUNZALAN / HTTP://WWW.CHAMORROROOTS.COM)

DEPARTMENT OF COMMERCE-BUREAU OF THE CENSUS
WASHINGTON

FIFTEENTH CENSUS OF THE UNITED STATES: 1930-POPULATION

THE ISLAND OF GUAM

Sheet No. 8B

43B

District **Municipality of Agana**
Name of Place **Agana City (Part of San Antonio)**
[Proper name and, also, name of class, as city, town, village, barrio, etc]

Enumeration District No. 2
Enumerated by me on **April 7, 1930** Arthur W. Jackson, Enumerator

	PLACE OF ABODE			NAME	RELATION	PERSONAL DESCRIPTION				EDUCATION		NATIVITY		OCCUPATION
	Street, avenue, road, etc.	Number of dwelling house in order of visitation	Number of family in order of visitation	of each person whose place of abode on April 1, 1930, was in this family. Enter surname, first, then given name and middle initial. If any. Include every person living on April 1, 1930. Omit children born since April 1, 1930.	Relationship of this Person to the head of the family.	Sex	Color or race	Age at last birthday	Single, married, widowed or divorced	Attended school any time since Sept. 1, 1929	Whether able to read and write.	Place of birth of this person.	Whether able to speak English.	
	1	2	3	4	5	6	7	8	9	10	11	12	13	14
26	Dela Corte	61	69	Gogue, Ramona W	Mother	F	Cha	67	Wd	N	N	Guam	N	None
27		62	70	Tajalle, Justo C	Head	M	Cha	26	M	N	Y	Guam	N	Machinist
28		62	70	Tajalle, Concepcion G	Wife	F	Cha	21	M	N	Y	Guam	N	None
29		62	70	Tajalle, Maria G	Daug	F	Cha	2.3	S	N	Y	Guam		None
30		62	70	Tajalle, Jose G	Son	M	Cha	1.3	S	N	Y	Guam		None
31		63	71	Takai, Arezo V	Head	M	Jap	57	M	N		Japan	N	Baker
32		63	71	Takai, Francisca F	Wife	F	Cha	47	M	N		Guam	N	None
33		63	71	Quidachay, Vicenta	Boarder	F	Cha	3.8	S	N		Guam		None
34		63	71	Flores, Pedro G	Nephew	M	Cha	10	S	Y	Y	Guam	Y	None
35		63	71	Flores, Alfred G	Nephew	M	Cha	7	S	Y		Guam		None
36		64	72	Palomo, Ignacio D	Head	M	Cha	69	M	N	Y	Guam	N	None
37		64	72	Palomo, Francisca T G	Wife	F	Cha	58	M	N	Y	Guam	N	None
38		64	72	Palomo, Vicente G	Son	M	Cha	25	S	N	Y	Guam	Y	Teacher
39		64	72	Palomo, Silvestre G	Son	M	Cha	22	S	N	Y	Guam	Y	None
40		64	72	Palomo, Jose G	Son	M	Cha	20	S	N	Y	Guam	Y	Farmer
41		64	72	Palomo, Maria G	Daug	F	Cha	17	S	N	Y	Guam	Y	None
42		64	73	Castro, Mariano LG	Head	M	Cha	25	M	N	Y	Guam	Y	Auto mech
43		64	73	Castro, Ana P	Wife	F	Cha	23	M	N	Y	Guam	Y	Teacher
44		65	74	Pablo, Antonio E	Head	M	Cha	48	M	N	Y	Guam	N	Farmer
45		65	74	Pablo, Getrudes B	Wife	F	Cha	44	M	N	N	Guam	N	None
46		65	74	Pablo, Jesus B	Son	M	Cha	20	S	N	Y	Guam	Y	Farm lab
47		65	74	Pablo, Magdalena B	Daug	F	Cha	16	S	N	Y	Guam	Y	None
48		65	74	Pablo, Concepcion B	Daug	F	Cha	12	S	N	Y	Guam	Y	Laborer
49		65	74	Pablo, Vicente R	Son	M	Cha	9	S	Y		Guam		None
50		65	74	Pablo, Rosario R	Daug	F	Cha	7	S	Y		Guam		None

DEPARTMENT OF COMMERCE-BUREAU OF THE CENSUS
WASHINGTON

FIFTEENTH CENSUS OF THE UNITED STATES: 1930-POPULATION

THE ISLAND OF GUAM

Sheet No. 9A

District **Municipality of Agana**
Name of Place **Agana City (Part of San Antonio)**
[Proper name and, also, name of class, as city, town, village, barrio, etc]

Enumeration District No. **2**
Enumerated by me on **April 8, 1930** Arthur W. Jackson
Enumerator

	PLACE OF ABODE			NAME	RELATION	PERSONAL DESCRIPTION				EDUCATION		NATIVITY		OCCUPATION
	Street, avenue, road, etc.	Number of dwelling house is order of visitation	Number of family in order of visitation	of each person whose place of abode on April 1, 1930, was in this family. Enter surname, first, then given name and middle initial. If any. Include every person living on April 1, 1930. Omit children born since April 1, 1930.	Relationship of this Person to the head of the family.	Sex	Color or race	Age at last birthday	Single, married, widowed or divorced	Attended school any time since Sept. 1, 1929	Whether able to read and write.	Place of birth of this person.	Whether able to speak English.	
	1	2	3	4	5	6	7	8	9	10	11	12	13	14
1	Dela Corte	65	74	Pablo, Maria B	Daughter	F	Cha	3.8	S	N		Guam		None
2		65	75	Pablo, Jose B	Head	M	Cha	22	M	N	Y	Guam	Y	Laborer
3		65	75	Pablo, Maria B	Wife	F	Cha	22	M	N	Y	Guam	Y	None
4		65	75	Pablo, Emelia R	Daughter	F	Cha	.2	S	N		Guam		None
5		66	76	Rosario, Maria M	Head	F	Cha	31	M	N	Y	Guam	Y	None
6		66	76	Rosario, Julia M	Daughter	F	Cha	9	S	N		Guam		None
7		66	76	Rosario, Dolores M	Daughter	F	Cha	7	S	N		Guam		None
8		66	76	Rosario, Barbara M	Daughter	F	Cha	4.8	S	N		Guam		None
9		66	76	Rosario, Juan M	Son	M	Cha	1.6	S	N		Guam		None
10		67	77	Naputi, Josefa R	Head	F	Cha	35	Wd	N	Y	Guam	N	None
11		67	77	Naputi, Jose R	Son	M	Cha	4	S	N		Guam		None
12		67	77	Rosario, Juliana B	Mother	F	Cha	68	Wd	N	N	Guam	N	None
13		68	78	Gomez, Silvestre J	Head	M	Neg	74	Wd	N	N	Massachusetts	N	None
14		69	79	Sablan, Vicenta D	Head	F	Cha	84	Wd	N	N	Guam	N	None
15		69	79	Sablan, Josefa D	Daughter	F	Cha	63	S	N	N	Guam	N	Weaver
16		69	79	Sablan, Felisa D	Daughter	F	Cha	62	S	N	N	Guam	N	Weaver
17		69	79	Sablan, Dolores D	Daughter	F	Cha	55	S	N	N	Guam	N	Weaver
18		70	80	Guerrero, Maria M	Head	F	Cha	39	S	N	Y	Guam	N	Laundress
19		70	80	Guerrero, Soledad M	Sister	F	Cha	31	S	N	Y	Guam	N	Laundress
20		70	80	Guerrero, Ana M	Sister	F	Cha	26	S	N	Y	Guam	N	Laundress
21		70	80	Guerrero, Jesus M	Brother	M	Cha	22	S	N	Y	Guam	N	Farmer
22		70	80	Blas, Mariano G	Nephew	M	Cha	13	S	Y	Y	Guam	Y	None
23		70	80	Guerrero, Vicente M	Nephew	M	Cha	5	S	N		Guam		None
24		71	81	Taitinfong, Teresa T	Head	F	Cha	55	S	N	N	Guam		None
25		71	81	Taitinfong, Juan S	Grandson	M	Cha	6	S	N		Guam		None

DEPARTMENT OF COMMERCE-BUREAU OF THE CENSUS
WASHINGTON

FIFTEENTH CENSUS OF THE UNITED STATES: 1930-POPULATION

THE ISLAND OF GUAM

Sheet No. 9B

44B

District **Municipality of Agana**
Name of Place **Agana City (Part of San Antonio)**
[Proper name and, also, name of class, as city, town, village, barrio, etc]

Enumeration District No. 2
Enumerated by me on April 8, 1930 Arthur W. Jackson, Enumerator

	PLACE OF ABODE: Street, avenue, road, etc.	Number of dwelling house in order of visitation	Number of family in order of visitation	NAME of each person whose place of abode on April 1, 1930, was in this family. Enter surname, first, then given name and middle initial. If any. Include every person living on April 1, 1930. Omit children born since April 1, 1930.	RELATION Relationship of this Person to the head of the family.	PERSONAL DESCRIPTION: Sex	Color or race	Age at last birthday	Single, married, widowed or divorced	EDUCATION: Attended school any time since Sept. 1, 1929	Whether able to read and write.	NATIVITY Place of birth of this person.	Whether able to speak English.	OCCUPATION
	1	2	3	4	5	6	7	8	9	10	11	12	13	14
26	Dela Corte	71	81	Taitinfong, Romona S	Grandaughter	F	Cha	3.5	S	N		Guam		None
27		72	82	Quitugua, Jose Q	Head	M	Cha	47	M	N	Y	Guam	N	Farmer
28		72	82	Quitugua, Magdalena I	Wife	F	Cha	45	M	N	Y	Guam	N	None
29		72	82	Quitugua, Maria I	Daughter	F	Cha	16	S	Y	Y	Guam	Y	None
30		72	82	Mendiola, Quintino M	Servant	M	Cha	12	S	Y	Y	Guam	Y	None
31		73	83	Taitano, Vicente M	Head	M	Cha	63	Wd	N	Y	Guam	N	Fisherman
32		73	84	Taitano, Catalina	Head	F	Cha	29	M	N	Y	Guam	Y	None
33		73	84	Taitano, Lillian A	Daughter	F	Cha	10	S	Y	Y	Guam	Y	None
34		73	84	Taitano, David A	Son	M	Cha	7	S	Y		Guam		None
35		73	84	Taitano, Catherine A	Daughter	F	Cha	5	S	N		Guam		None
36		73	84	Taitano, Luke A	Son	M	Cha	4.4	S	N		Guam		None
37		73	84	Taitano, Miguel A	Son	M	Cha	2.5	S	N		Guam		None
38		73	85	Perez, Vicente B	Head	M	Cha	78	M	N	Y	Guam	N	None
39		73	85	Perez, Josefa C	Wife	F	Cha	51	M	N	N	Guam	N	None
40		74	86	Flores, Jose C	Head	M	Cha	26	M	N	Y	Guam	Y	Farmer
41		74	86	Flores, Magdalena T	Wife	F	Cha	27	M	N	Y	Guam	Y	School teacher
42		74	86	Flores, Henry T	Son	M	Cha	.3	S	N		Guam		None
43		74	86	Salas, Evelyn T	Niece	F	Cha	20	S	N	Y	Guam	Y	School teacher
44		75	87	Toves, Antonio LG	Head	F	Cha	60	M	N	N	Guam	N	Farmer
45		75	87	Toves, Ana Q	Wife	F	Cha	58	M	N	N	Guam	N	None
46		75	87	Toves, Juan Q	Son	M	Cha	25	S	N	Y	Guam	Y	Farm laborer
47		75	87	Toves, Rita Q	Daughter	F	Cha	18	S	N	Y	Guam	Y	None
48		75	88	Borja, Maria T	Head	F	Cha	28	M	N	Y	Guam	Y	None
49		75	88	Borja, Jose T	Son	M	Cha	3.6	S	N		Guam		None
50		75	88	Borja, Rosario T	Daughter	F	Cha	1.3	S	N		Guam		None

DEPARTMENT OF COMMERCE-BUREAU OF THE CENSUS
WASHINGTON

FIFTEENTH CENSUS OF THE UNITED STATES: 1930-POPULATION

THE ISLAND OF GUAM

Sheet No. 10A

District Municipality of Agana
Name of Place Agana City (Part of San Antonio)
[Proper name and, also, name of class, as city, town, village, barrio, etc]

Enumeration District No. 2
Enumerated by me on April 8, 1930 Arthur W. Jackson
Enumerator

	PLACE OF ABODE			NAME	RELATION	PERSONAL DESCRIPTION				EDUCATION		NATIVITY		OCCUPATION
	Street, avenue, road, etc.	Number of dwelling house is order of visitation	Number of family in order of visitation	of each person whose place of abode on April 1, 1930, was in this family. Enter surname, first, then given name and middle initial. If any. Include every person living on April 1, 1930. Omit children born since April 1, 1930.	Relationship of this Person to the head of the family.	Sex	Color or race	Age at last birthday	Single, married, widowed or divorced	Attended school any time since Sept. 1, 1929	Whether able to read and write.	Place of birth of this person.	Whether able to speak English.	
	1	2	3	4	5	6	7	8	9	10	11	12	13	14
1	Dela Corte	76	89	Guerrero, Nieves C	Head	F	Cha	62	Wd	N	N	Guam	N	None
2		76	89	Guerrero, Nicolas G	Son	M	Cha	39	D	N	Y	Guam	Y	Farmer
3		76	89	Guerrero, Francisco G	Step-son	M	Cha	36	S	N	Y	Guam	Y	Farmer
4		76	90	Crisostomo, Josefa D	Head	F	Cha	36	S	N	Y	Guam	N	None
5		76	90	Crisostomo, Antonio C	Son	M	Cha	14	S	Y	Y	Guam	Y	None
6		76	90	Crisostomo, Tomas C	Son	M	Cha	12	S	Y	Y	Guam	Y	None
7		76	90	Crisostomo, Manuela C	Daughter	F	Cha	8	S	Y		Guam		None
8		76	90	Crisostomo, Rafael C	Son	M	Cha	6	S	N		Guam		None
9		76	90	Crisostomo, Ana C	Daughter	F	Cha	5	S	N		Guam		None
10		76	90	Crisostomo, Maria C	Daughter	F	Cha	4.3	S	N		Guam		None
11		76	90	Crisostomo, Vicente C	Son	M	Cha	.5	S	N		Guam		None
12		77	91	Alvarez, Jose G	Head	M	Cha	59	M	N	Y	Guam	N	Farmer
13		77	91	Alvarez, Soledad G	Wife	F	Cha	52	M	N	N	Guam	N	None
14		77	91	Guerrero, Maria L	Niece	F	Cha	17	S	N	Y	Guam	Y	None
15		77	91	Guerrero, Silvestre L	Nephew	M	Cha	15	S	N	Y	Guam	Y	Farm laborer
16		78	92	Cruz, Ignacio G	Head	M	Cha	30	M	N	Y	Guam	Y	Farmer
17		78	92	Cruz, Carlota K	Wife	F	Cha	27	M	N	Y	Guam	Y	None
18		78	92	Cruz, Juan I	Son	M	Cha	3.5	S	N		Guam		None
19		78	92	Cruz, Lucia I	Daughter	F	Cha	.2	S	N		Guam		None
20		79	93	Cruz, Ana G	Head	F	Cha	40	Wd	N	N	Guam	N	None
21		79	93	Cruz, Andrea G	Daughter	F	Cha	24	S	N	Y	Guam	Y	None
22		79	93	Cruz, Juan G	Son	M	Cha	23	S	N	Y	Guam	Y	Laborer
23		79	93	Cruz, Manuel G	Son	M	Cha	21	S	N	Y	Guam	Y	Farmer
24		79	93	Cruz, Antonio G	Son	M	Cha	17	S	N	Y	Guam	Y	None
25		80	94	Cruz, Pedro G	Head	M	Cha	26	M	N	Y	Guam	Y	Farmer

DEPARTMENT OF COMMERCE-BUREAU OF THE CENSUS
WASHINGTON

FIFTEENTH CENSUS OF THE UNITED STATES: 1930-POPULATION

THE ISLAND OF GUAM

Sheet No. 10B

District **Municipality of Agana**
Name of Place **Agana City (Part of San Antonio)**
[Proper name and, also, name of class, as city, town, village, barrio, etc]

Enumeration District No. 2
Enumerated by me on **April 9, 1930** Arthur W. Jackson, Enumerator

	PLACE OF ABODE			NAME	RELATION	PERSONAL DESCRIPTION				EDUCATION		NATIVITY		OCCUPATION
	Street, avenue, road, etc.	Number of dwelling house is order of visitation	Number of family in order of visitation	of each person whose place of abode on April 1, 1930, was in this family. Enter surname, first, then given name and middle initial. If any. Include every person living on April 1, 1930. Omit children born since April 1, 1930.	Relationship of this Person to the head of the family.	Sex	Color or race	Age at last birthday	Single, married, widowed or divorced	Attended school any time since Sept. 1, 1929	Whether able to read and write.	Place of birth of this person.	Whether able to speak English.	
	1	2	3	4	5	6	7	8	9	10	11	12	13	14
26	Dela Corte	80	94	Cruz, Maria T	Wife	F	Cha	36	M	N	Y	Guam	N	None
27		80	94	Cruz, Luisa T	Daughter	F	Cha	4.8	S	N		Guam		None
28		80	94	Toves, Jose B	Father in-law	M	Cha	65	M	N	Y	Guam	N	None
29		81	95	Ulloa, Mariano C	Head	M	Cha	33	M	N	Y	Guam	Y	Printer
30		81	95	Ulloa, Joaquina C	Wife	F	Cha	31	M	N	Y	Guam	Y	None
31		81	95	Ulloa, Maria C	Daughter	F	Cha	12	S	Y	Y	Guam	Y	None
32		81	95	Ulloa, Vicente C	Son	M	Cha	10	S	Y	Y	Guam	Y	None
33		81	95	Ulloa, Ana C	Daughter	F	Cha	9	S	Y		Guam		None
34		81	95	Ulloa, Lourdes C	Daughter	F	Cha	5	S	Y		Guam		None
35		81	95	Ulloa, Jesus C	Son	M	Cha	.3	S	N		Guam		None
36		82	96	Camacho, Jose R	Head	M	Cha	36	S	N	Y	Guam	N	Farmer
37		82	96	Camacho, Maria R	Mother	F	Cha	63	Wd	N	N	Guam	N	None
38		82	96	Camacho, Candaleria R	Sister	F	Cha	26	S	N	Y	Guam	N	None
39		82	96	Camacho, Jose R	Nephew	M	Cha	7	S	Y		Guam		None
40		82	96	Camacho, Maria C	Niece	F	Cha	2.3	S	N		Guam		None
41		83	97	Meno, Vicente M	Head	M	Cha	37	M	N	N	Guam	N	Farmer
42		83	97	Meno, Vicenta P	Wife	F	Cha	47	M	N	N	Guam	N	None
43		83	97	Meno, Jose P	Son	M	Cha	17	S	N	Y	Guam	Y	None
44		83	97	Meno, Isabel P	Daughter	F	Cha	15	S	N	Y	Guam	Y	None
45		83	97	Meno, Jesus P	Son	M	Cha	12	S	Y	Y	Guam	Y	None
46		83	97	Meno, Felix P	Son	M	Cha	10	S	Y	Y	Guam	Y	None
47		83	97	Meno, Ignacio P	Son	M	Cha	9	S	Y		Guam		None
48		83	97	Meno, Francisca P	Daughter	F	Cha	4.5	S	Y		Guam		None
49		84	98	Untalan, Pedro P	Head	M	Cha	34	M	N	Y	Guam	Y	Clerk
50		84	98	Untalan, Emeliana P	Wife	F	Cha	33	M	N	Y	Guam	Y	None

DEPARTMENT OF COMMERCE-BUREAU OF THE CENSUS
WASHINGTON

FIFTEENTH CENSUS OF THE UNITED STATES: 1930-POPULATION

THE ISLAND OF GUAM

Sheet No. 11A

District **Municipality of Agana**
Name of Place **Agana City (Part of San Antonio)**
[Proper name and, also, name of class, as city, town, village, barrio, etc]

Enumeration District No. **2**
Enumerated by me on **April 9, 1930** Arthur W. Jackson
Enumerator

	PLACE OF ABODE			NAME	RELATION	PERSONAL DESCRIPTION				EDUCATION		NATIVITY		OCCUPATION
	Street, avenue, road, etc.	Number of dwelling house is order of visitation	Number of family in order of visitation	of each person whose place of abode on April 1, 1930, was in this family. Enter surname, first, then given name and middle initial. If any. Include every person living on April 1, 1930. Omit children born since April 1, 1930.	Relationship of this Person to the head of the family.	Sex	Color or race	Age at last birthday	Single, married, widowed or divorced	Attended school any time since Sept. 1, 1929	Whether able to read and write.	Place of birth of this person.	Whether able to speak English.	
	1	2	3	4	5	6	7	8	9	10	11	12	13	14
1	Dela Corte	84	98	Untalan, Maria D	Daughter	F	Cha	20	S	N	Y	Guam	Y	None
2		84	98	Benavente, Cristobal D	Nephew	M	Cha	4.2	S	N		Guam		None
3		84	98	Delgado, Rosa	Servant	F	Cha	10	S	Y	Y	Guam	Y	Servant
4		85	99	Cepedes, Josefa S	Head	F	Fil	35	M	Y	Y	Guam	Y	None
5		85	99	Cepedes, Leopaldo S	Son	M	Fil	5	S	Y		Guam		None
6		85	99	Cepedes, Gregorio S	Son	M	Fil	4.5	S	N		Guam		None
7		85	99	Cepedes, Crecencia S	Daughter	F	Fil	3.5	S	N		Guam		None
8		85	99	Cepedes, Samuel S	Son	M	Fil	1.8	S	N		Guam		None
9		85	99	Sanchez, Candido A	Father	M	Fil	71	M	N	Y	Phil Islands	Y	None
10		85	99	Sanchez, Emeteria A	Mother	F	Fil	67	M	N	Y	Phil Islands	Y	None
11		86	100	Toves, Jose C	Head	M	Cha	36	M	N	Y	Guam	Y	Laborer
12		86	100	Toves, Carmen F	Wife	F	Cha	26	M	N	Y	Guam	N	None
13		86	100	Toves, Concepcion F	Daughter	F	Cha	7	S	Y		Guam		None
14		86	100	Toves, Josefina F	Daughter	F	Cha	6	S	N		Guam		None
15		86	100	Toves, Jesus F	Son	M	Cha	3.3	S	N		Guam		None
16		86	100	Toves, Jose F	Son	M	Cha	1.5	S	N		Guam		None
17		87	101	Sanchez, Ana C	Head	F	Cha	38	M	N	Y	Guam	N	None
18		87	101	Sanchez, Engracia C	Daughter	F	Fil	17	S	Y	Y	Guam	Y	None
19		87	101	Sanchez, Isabel C	Daughter	F	Fil	15	S	Y	Y	Guam	Y	None
20		87	101	Sanchez, Segundo C	Son	M	Fil	11	S	Y	Y	Guam	Y	None
21		87	101	Sanchez, Francisco C	Son	M	Fil	10	S	Y	Y	Guam	Y	None
22		87	101	Sanchez, Maria C	Daughter	F	Fil	8	S	Y		Guam		None
23		87	101	Sanchez, Dolores C	Daughter	F	Fil	7	S	Y		Guam		None
24		87	101	Sanchez, Ceriaco C	Son	M	Fil	4.8	S	N		Guam		None
25		87	101	Sanchez, Gloria C	Daughter	F	Fil	1.3	S	N		Guam		None

(CHAMORRO ROOTS GENEALOGY PROJECT™ TRANSCRIPTION)
(BERNARD T. PUNZALAN / HTTP://WWW.CHAMORROROOTS.COM)

DEPARTMENT OF COMMERCE-BUREAU OF THE CENSUS
WASHINGTON

FIFTEENTH CENSUS OF THE UNITED STATES: 1930-POPULATION

THE ISLAND OF GUAM

Sheet No. 11B

46B

District Municipality of Agana
Name of Place Agana City (Part of San Antonio)
[Proper name and, also, name of class, as city, town, village, barrio, etc]

Enumeration District No. 2
Enumerated by me on April 9, 1930 Arthur W. Jackson, Enumerator

	PLACE OF ABODE			NAME	RELATION	PERSONAL DESCRIPTION				EDUCATION		NATIVITY		OCCUPATION
	Street, avenue, road, etc.	Number of dwelling house is order of visitation	Number of family in order of visitation	of each person whose place of abode on April 1, 1930, was in this family. Enter surname, first, then given name and middle initial. If any. Include every person living on April 1, 1930. Omit children born since April 1, 1930.	Relationship of this Person to the head of the family.	Sex	Color or race	Age at last birthday	Single, married, widowed or divorced	Attended school any time since Sept. 1, 1929	Whether able to read and write.	Place of birth of this person.	Whether able to speak English.	
	1	2	3	4	5	6	7	8	9	10	11	12	13	14
26	Dela Corte	87	101	Sanchez, Brigida C	Daughter	F	Fil	1	S	N		Guam		None
27		88	102	Hines, Cristobal C	Head	M	Neg	21	M	N	Y	Guam	Y	Chauffeur
28		88	102	Hines, Joaquina T	Wife	F	Cha	30	M	N	Y	Guam	N	None
29		88	102	Hines, Margarita T	Daughter	F	Cha	.3	S	N		Guam		None
30		89	103	San Agustin, Juan C	Head	M	Cha	47	F	N	Y	Guam	Y	Farmer
31		89	103	San Agustin, Maria S	Wife	F	Cha	44	F	N	Y	Guam	N	None
32		89	103	San Agustin, George S	Son	M	Cha	14	S	Y	Y	Guam	Y	None
33		89	103	San Agustin, Pedro S	Son	M	Cha	11	S	Y	Y	Guam	Y	None
34		89	103	San Agustin, Alberto S	Son	M	Cha	8	S	Y		Guam		None
35		89	103	San Agustin, Patricia S	Daughter	F	Cha	3.8	S	N		Guam		None
36		90	104	Guerrero, Vicente LG	Head	M	Cha	56	M	N	Y	Guam	N	Carpenter
37		90	104	Guerrero, Maria C	Wife	F	Cha	43	M	N	Y	Guam	N	None
38		90	104	Guerrero, Juan B	Son	M	Cha	19	S	N	Y	Guam	Y	Clerk
39		90	104	Guerrero, Joaquin C	Son	M	Cha	13	S	Y	Y	Guam	Y	None
40		90	104	Guerrero, Francisco C	Son	M	Cha	11	S	Y	Y	Guam	Y	None
41		90	104	Guerrero, Enrique C	Son	M	Cha	9	S	Y		Guam		None
42		90	104	Guerrero, Vicente C	Son	M	Cha	7	S	Y		Guam		None
43		90	104	Guerrero, Jesus C	Son	M	Cha	5	S	N		Guam		None
44		90	104	Guerrero, Carlos C	Son	M	Cha	1.5	S	N		Guam		None
45		91	105	Guerrero, Antonio C	Head	M	Cha	46	M	N	N	Guam	N	Fisherman
46		91	105	Guerrero, Ana B	Wife	F	Cha	48	M	N	Y	Guam	N	None
47		91	105	Guerrero, Jose B	Son	M	Cha	26	S	N	Y	Guam	Y	Barber
48		91	105	Guerrero, Juan B	Son	M	Cha	23	S	N	Y	Guam	Y	Farmer
49		91	105	Guerrero, Antonio B	Son	M	Cha	22	S	N	Y	Guam	Y	Laborer
50		91	105	Guerrero, Vicente B	Son	M	Cha	19	S	N	Y	Guam	Y	Laborer

DEPARTMENT OF COMMERCE-BUREAU OF THE CENSUS
WASHINGTON

FIFTEENTH CENSUS OF THE UNITED STATES: 1930-POPULATION

THE ISLAND OF GUAM

Sheet No. 12A

District **Municipality of Agana**
Name of Place **Agana City (Part of San Antonio)**
[Proper name and, also, name of class, as city, town, village, barrio, etc]

Enumeration District No. 2
Enumerated by me on **April 10, 1930** Arthur W. Jackson, Enumerator

	PLACE OF ABODE			NAME	RELATION	PERSONAL DESCRIPTION				EDUCATION		NATIVITY		OCCUPATION
	Street, avenue, road, etc.	Number of dwelling house is order of visitation	Number of family in order of visitation	of each person whose place of abode on April 1, 1930, was in this family. Enter surname, first, then given name and middle initial. If any. Include every person living on April 1, 1930. Omit children born since April 1, 1930.	Relationship of this Person to the head of the family.	Sex	Color or race	Age at last birthday	Single, married, widowed or divorced	Attended school any time since Sept. 1, 1929	Whether able to read and write.	Place of birth of this person.	Whether able to speak English.	
	1	2	3	4	5	6	7	8	9	10	11	12	13	14
1	Dela Corte	91	105	Guerrero, Vicente B	Son	M	Cha	19	S	N	Y	Guam	Y	Laborer
2		91	105	Guerrero, Maria B	Daughter	F	Cha	17	S	N	Y	Guam	Y	None
3		91	105	Guerrero, Francisco B	Son	M	Cha	13	S	Y	Y	Guam	Y	None
4		91	105	Guerrero, Candaleria B	Daughter	F	Cha	10	S	Y	Y	Guam	Y	None
5		91	105	Guerrero, Concepcion B	Daughter	F	Cha	8	S	Y		Guam		None
6		91	105	Guerrero, Jesus B	Son	M	Cha	5	S	N		Guam		None
7		91	105	Guerrero, Rita B	Daughter	F	Cha	1.3	S	N		Guam		None
8		91	105	Torre, Consolacion C	Lodger	F	Cha	25	S	N		Guam		None
9		92	106	Manibusan, Joaquin T	Head	M	Cha	59	Wd	N	Y	Guam	N	Farmer
10		92	107	Manibusan, Jose M	Head	M	Cha	27	M	N	Y	Guam	N	Farmer
11		92	107	Manibusan, Juana LG	Wife	F	Cha	26	M	N	Y	Guam	Y	None
12		92	107	Manibusan, Felisa LG	Daughter	F	Cha	2.7	S	N		Guam		None
13		92	107	Manibusan, Rufina LG	Daughter	F	Cha	1.7	S	N		Guam		None
14		92	107	Manibusan, Juan M	Brother	M	Cha	26	S	N		Guam		Farmer
15		92	107	Manibusan, Antonio M	Brother	M	Cha	23	S	N	Y	Guam	Y	None
16		92	107	Manibusan, Maria M	Sister	F	Cha	22	S	N	Y	Guam	Y	None
17		93	108	Blaz, Dolores C	Head	M	Cha	49	Wd	N	Y	Guam	N	None
18		93	108	Blaz, Rita C	Daughter	F	Cha	21	S	N	Y	Guam	Y	None
19		93	108	Blaz, Jose C	Son	M	Cha	19	S	N	Y	Guam	Y	None
20		93	108	Blaz, Jesus C	Son	M	Cha	17	S	N	Y	Guam	Y	None
21		93	108	Blaz, Concepcion C	Daughter	F	Cha	14	S	N	Y	Guam	Y	None
22		93	109	Pocaigue, Francisco P	Head	M	Cha	28	M	N	Y	Guam	Y	Farmer
23		93	109	Pocaigue, Ana B	Wife	F	Cha	27	M	N	Y	Guam	Y	None
24		93	109	Pocaigue, Antonia B	Daughter	F	Cha	3.8	S	N		Guam		None
25		93	109	Pocaigue, Rosabela B	Daughter	F	Cha	1.9	S	N		Guam		None

(CHAMORRO ROOTS GENEALOGY PROJECT™ TRANSCRIPTION)
(BERNARD T. PUNZALAN / HTTP://WWW.CHAMORROROOTS.COM)

DEPARTMENT OF COMMERCE-BUREAU OF THE CENSUS
WASHINGTON

FIFTEENTH CENSUS OF THE UNITED STATES: 1930-POPULATION

THE ISLAND OF GUAM

Sheet No. 12B

47B

District **Municipality of Agana**
Name of Place **Agana City (Part of San Antonio)**
[Proper name and, also, name of class, as city, town, village, barrio, etc]

Enumeration District No. 2
Enumerated by me on **April 10, 1930** Arthur W. Jackson, Enumerator

	PLACE OF ABODE			NAME	RELATION	PERSONAL DESCRIPTION				EDUCATION		NATIVITY		OCCUPATION
	Street, avenue, road, etc.	Number of dwelling house in order of visitation	Number of family in order of visitation	of each person whose place of abode on April 1, 1930, was in this family. Enter surname, first, then given name and middle initial. If any. Include every person living on April 1, 1930. Omit children born since April 1, 1930.	Relationship of this Person to the head of the family.	Sex	Color or race	Age at last birthday	Single, married, widowed or divorced	Attended school any time since Sept. 1, 1929	Whether able to read and write.	Place of birth of this person.	Whether able to speak English.	
	1	2	3	4	5	6	7	8	9	10	11	12	13	14
26	Dela Corte	94	110	Cruz, Mariano C	Head	M	Cha	25	M	N	Y	Guam	Y	Farmer
27		94	110	Cruz, Rosa A	Wife	F	Cha	25	M	N	Y	Guam	N	None
28		94	110	Cruz, Eugenia A	Daughter	F	Cha	2.3	S	N		Guam		None
29		94	110	Cruz, Concepcion A	Daughter	F	Cha	.7	S	N		Guam		None
30		94	110	Borja, Maria C	Mother in-law	F	Cha	45	Wd	N	Y	Guam	N	None
31		94	110	Cruz, Manuel C	Brother	M	Cha	17	S	N	Y	Guam	Y	Farm laborer
32		94	110	Cruz, Santiago C	Brother	M	Cha	14	S	N	Y	Guam	Y	None
33		95	111	San Agustin, Juana C	Head	F	Cha	63	Wd	N	N	Guam	N	None
34		95	111	San Agustin, Rosa C	Daughter	F	Cha	42	S	N	N	Guam	N	None
35		95	111	San Agustin, Jose SA	Grandson	M	Cha	15	S	Y	Y	Guam	Y	None
36		95	111	San Agustin, Carlos SA	Grandson	M	Cha	5	S	N		Guam		None
37		95	112	Martinez, Isabel SA	Head	F	Cha	34	Wd	N	Y	Guam	N	None
38		95	112	Martinez, Jesus SA	Son	M	Cha	11	S	Y	Y	Guam	Y	None
39		95	112	Martinez, Joaquin SA	Son	M	Cha	8	S	Y		Guam		None
40		95	112	Martinez, Emelia SA	Daughter	F	Cha	3.3	S	N		Guam		None
41		95	112	Martinez, Francisco SA	Son	M	Cha	1.7	S	N		Guam		None
42		96	113	Arceo, Ignacio	Head	M	Cha	32	M	N	Y	Guam	N	USN reserve
43		96	113	Arceo, Maria F	Wife	F	Cha	32	M	N	Y	Guam	Y	None
44		96	113	Arceo, Josefina F	Daughter	F	Cha	8	S	Y		Guam		None
45		96	113	Arceo, Maria F	Daughter	F	Cha	7	S	Y		Guam		None
46		96	113	Arceo, Jose F	Son	M	Cha	5	S	N		Guam		None
47		96	113	Arceo, Francisco F	Son	M	Cha	4.7	S	N		Guam		None
48		96	113	Arceo, Tomas F	Son	M	Cha	3.5	S	N		Guam		None
49		96	113	Arceo, Juan F	Son	M	Cha	1.8	S	N		Guam		None
50		97	114	Acosta, Rosa V	Head	F	Cha	79	Wd	N	Y	Guam	N	None

(CHAMORRO ROOTS GENEALOGY PROJECT™ TRANSCRIPTION)
(BERNARD T. PUNZALAN / HTTP://WWW.CHAMORROROOTS.COM)

DEPARTMENT OF COMMERCE-BUREAU OF THE CENSUS
WASHINGTON

FIFTEENTH CENSUS OF THE UNITED STATES: 1930-POPULATION

THE ISLAND OF GUAM

Sheet No. 13A

48

District Municipality of Agana
Name of Place Agana City (Part of San Antonio)
[Proper name and, also, name of class, as city, town, village, barrio, etc]

Enumeration District No. 2
Enumerated by me on April 10, 1930 Arthur W. Jackson, Enumerator

	PLACE OF ABODE: Street, avenue, road, etc.	Number of dwelling house in order of visitation	Number of family in order of visitation	NAME of each person whose place of abode on April 1, 1930, was in this family. Enter surname, first, then given name and middle initial. If any. Include every person living on April 1, 1930. Omit children born since April 1, 1930.	RELATION Relationship of this Person to the head of the family.	PERSONAL DESCRIPTION: Sex	Color or race	Age at last birthday	Single, married, widowed or divorced	EDUCATION: Attended school any time since Sept. 1, 1929	Whether able to read and write.	NATIVITY Place of birth of this person.	Whether able to speak English.	OCCUPATION
	1	2	3	4	5	6	7	8	9	10	11	12	13	14
1	Dela Corte	98	115	Bautista, Pablo C	Head	M	Cha	56	M	N	Y	Guam	N	Farmer
2		98	115	Bautista, Rosa C	Wife	F	Cha	47	M	N	Y	Guam	N	None
3		98	115	Bautista, Ignacio C	Son	M	Cha	24	S	N	Y	Guam	Y	Farmer
4		98	115	Bautista, Maria C	Daughter	F	Cha	19	S	N	Y	Guam	Y	None
5		98	115	Bautista, Isabel C	Daughter	F	Cha	16	S	N	Y	Guam	Y	None
6		98	115	Bautista, Enrique C	Son	M	Cha	15	S	N	Y	Guam		None
7		98	115	Bautista, Jose C	Son	M	Cha	13	S	Y	Y	Guam		None
8		98	115	Bautista, Rosario C	Daughter	F	Cha	6	S	Y		Guam		None
9		98	116	Duenas, Joaquin D	Head	M	Cha	26	M	N	Y	Guam	Y	Farmer
10		98	116	Duenas, Asuncion B	Wife	F	Cha	18	M	N	Y	Guam	Y	None
11		99	117	Crisostomo, Jesus A	Head	M	Cha	25	M	N	Y	Guam	Y	Messenger
12		99	117	Crisostomo, Maria B	Wife	F	Cha	19	M	N	Y	Guam	Y	None
13		99	117	Crisostomo, Francisco B	Son	M	Cha	.8	S	N		Guam		None
14		99	117	Baza, Ana C	Mother in-law	F	Cha	53	Wd	N	Y	Guam	N	None
15		100	118	Salas, Felix B	Head	M	Cha	28	M	N	Y	Guam	Y	Carpenter
16		100	118	Salas, Felista C	Wife	F	Cha	21	M	N	Y	Guam	Y	None
17		100	118	Salas, Jose C	Son	M	Cha	3.3	S	N		Guam		None
18		100	118	Salas, Jesus C	Son	M	Cha	2.3	S	N		Guam		None
19		100	118	Salas, Ana C	Daughter	F	Cha	.8	S	N		Guam		None
20		100	118	Salas, Josefa B	Mother	F	Cha	64	M	N	N	Guam	N	None
21		100	118	Santos, Juana B	Aunt	F	Cha	69	Wd	N	N	Guam	N	None
22		100	119	Salas, Javier D	Head	M	Cha	55	M	N	Y	Guam	N	Carpenter
23		101	120	Beuna, Ana T	Head	F	Cha	28	Wd	N	Y	Guam	N	None
24		101	120	Beuna, Victoria T	Daughter	F	Fil	8	S	Y		Guam		None
25		102	121	Castro, Juana M	Head	M	Cha	24	M	N	Y	Guam	Y	Farmer

(CHAMORRO ROOTS GENEALOGY PROJECT™ TRANSCRIPTION)
(BERNARD T. PUNZALAN / HTTP://WWW.CHAMORROROOTS.COM)

DEPARTMENT OF COMMERCE-BUREAU OF THE CENSUS
WASHINGTON

FIFTEENTH CENSUS OF THE UNITED STATES: 1930-POPULATION

THE ISLAND OF GUAM

Sheet No. 13B

48B

District Municipality of Agana
Name of Place Agana City (Part of San Antonio)
[Proper name and, also, name of class, as city, town, village, barrio, etc]

Enumeration District No. 2
Enumerated by me on April 11, 1930 Arthur W. Jackson
Enumerator

	PLACE OF ABODE			NAME	RELATION	PERSONAL DESCRIPTION				EDUCATION		NATIVITY		OCCUPATION
	Street, avenue, road, etc.	Number of dwelling house is order of visitation	Number of family in order of visitation	of each person whose place of abode on April 1, 1930, was in this family. Enter surname, first, then given name and middle initial. If any. Include every person living on April 1, 1930. Omit children born since April 1, 1930.	Relationship of this Person to the head of the family.	Sex	Color or race	Age at last birthday	Single, married, widowed or divorced	Attended school any time since Sept. 1, 1929	Whether able to read and write.	Place of birth of this person.	Whether able to speak English.	
	1	2	3	4	5	6	7	8	9	10	11	12	13	14
26	Dela Corte	102	121	Castro, Maria Q	Wife	F	Cha	20	M	N	Y	Guam	Y	None
27		102	121	Castro, Pedro Q	Son	M	Cha	.1	S	N		Guam		None
28		102	122	Castro, Santiago C	Head	M	Cha	53	M	N	Y	Guam	N	Farmer
29		102	122	Castro, Dolores M	Wife	F	Cha	53	M	N	Y	Guam	N	None
30		102	122	Castro, Librada M	Daughter	F	Cha	13	S	Y	Y	Guam	Y	None
31		103	123	Perez, Joaquin F	Head	M	Cha	44	M	N	Y	Guam	Y	Carpenter
32		103	123	Perez, Maria C. T	Wife	F	Cha	30	M	N	Y	Guam	Y	None
33		103	123	Perez, Gregorio T	Son	M	Cha	8	S	Y		Guam		None
34		103	123	Perez, Maria T	Daughter	F	Cha	7	S	Y		Guam		None
35		103	123	Perez, Rosa T	Daughter	F	Cha	6	S	N		Guam		None
36		103	123	Perez, Victoria T	Daughter	F	Cha	4.2	S	N		Guam		None
37		103	123	Perez, Jose T	Son	M	Cha	2.5	S	N		Guam		None
38		104	124	Iglesias, Francisco A	Head	M	Cha	55	M	N	Y	Guam	Y	Farmer
39		104	124	Iglesias, Cerefina G	Wife	F	Cha	55	M	N	N	Guam	N	None
40		104	125	San Nicolas, Joaquin I	Head	M	Cha	31	M	N	N	Guam	Y	Laborer
41		104	125	San Nicolas, Francisco I	Son	M	Cha	5	S	N		Guam		None
42		104	125	San Nicolas, Eugenio I	Son	M	Cha	4.5	S	N		Guam		None
43		104	125	San Nicolas, Silvia I	Daughter	F	Cha	2.2	S	N		Guam		None
44		105	126	Torres, Mariano T	Head	M	Cha	33	M	N	Y	Guam	Y	Pool room attendant
45		105	126	Torres, Maxima G	Wife	F	Cha	26	M	N	Y	Guam	Y	None
46		105	126	Torres, Juan G	Son	M	Cha	.1	S	N		Guam		None
47		106	127	Flores, Ignacio T	Head	M	Cha	43	M	N	Y	Guam	Y	Carpenter
48		106	127	Flores, Rita LG	Wife	F	Cha	46	M	N	Y	Guam	N	None
49		106	127	Flores, Jose LG	Son	M	Cha	17	S	N	Y	Guam	Y	None
50		106	127	Flores, Vicente LG	Son	M	Cha	16	S	Y	Y	Guam	Y	None

(CHAMORRO ROOTS GENEALOGY PROJECT™ TRANSCRIPTION)
(BERNARD T. PUNZALAN / HTTP://WWW.CHAMORROROOTS.COM)

DEPARTMENT OF COMMERCE-BUREAU OF THE CENSUS
WASHINGTON

FIFTEENTH CENSUS OF THE UNITED STATES: 1930-POPULATION

THE ISLAND OF GUAM

Sheet No. 14A

District **Municipality of Agana**
Name of Place **Agana City (Part of San Antonio)**
[Proper name and, also, name of class, as city, town, village, barrio, etc]

Enumeration District No. **2**
Enumerated by me on **April 11, 1930** Arthur W. Jackson
Enumerator

	PLACE OF ABODE			NAME	RELATION	PERSONAL DESCRIPTION				EDUCATION		NATIVITY		OCCUPATION
	Street, avenue, road, etc.	Number of dwelling house is order of visitation	Number of family in order of visitation	of each person whose place of abode on April 1, 1930, was in this family. Enter surname, first, then given name and middle initial. If any. Include every person living on April 1, 1930. Omit children born since April 1, 1930.	Relationship of this Person to the head of the family.	Sex	Color or race	Age at last birthday	Single, married, widowed or divorced	Attended school any time since Sept. 1, 1929	Whether able to read and write.	Place of birth of this person.	Whether able to speak English.	
	1	2	3	4	5	6	7	8	9	10	11	12	13	14
1	Dela Corte	106	127	Flores, Filomina T	Daughter	F	Cha	11	S	Y	Y	Guam	Y	None
2		106	127	Flores, Beatrice T	Daughter	F	Cha	8	S	Y		Guam		None
3		106	127	Flores, Pedro T	Son	M	Cha	7	S	Y		Guam		None
4		107	128	Flores, Luis T	Head	M	Cha	36	M	N	Y	Guam	Y	Farmer
5		107	128	Flores, Ana C	Wife	F	Cha	34	M	N	Y	Guam	Y	None
6		107	128	Flores, Concepcion C	Daughter	F	Cha	13	S	Y	Y	Guam	Y	None
7		107	128	Flores, Ramon C	Son	M	Cha	12	S	Y	Y	Guam	Y	None
8		107	128	Flores, Virginia C	Daughter	F	Cha	10	S	Y	Y	Guam	Y	None
9		107	128	Flores, Manuel C	Son	M	Cha	9	S	Y		Guam		None
10		107	128	Flores, Nieves C	Daughter	F	Cha	7	S	Y		Guam		None
11		107	128	Flores, Prudencio C	Son	M	Cha	6	S	N		Guam		None
12		107	128	Flores, Vicente C	Son	M	Cha	3.8	S	N		Guam		None
13		107	128	Flores, Quintina C	Daughter	F	Cha	1.5	S	N		Guam		None
14		107	128	Flores, Ana C	Daughter	F	Cha	.1	S	N		Guam		None
15		108	129	Guerrero, Antonio C	Head	M	Cha	65	Wd	N	N	Guam	N	None
16		108	129	Duenas, Juan S	Son	M	Cha	42	Wd	N	Y	Guam	Y	Carpenter
17		109	130	Ulloa, Juan LG	Head	M	Cha	62	M	N	Y	Guam	Y	Stone mason
18		109	130	Ulloa, Ana C	Wife	F	Cha	52	M	N	Y	Guam	N	None
19		109	131	Adriano, Jose G	Head	M	Cha	29	M	N	Y	Guam	Y	Laborer
20		109	131	Adriano, Maria U	Wife	F	Cha	24	M	N	Y	Guam	Y	None
21		109	131	Adriano, Roberta U	Daughter	F	Cha	4	S	N		Guam		None
22		109	131	Adriano, Jose U	Son	M	Cha	.3	S	N		Guam		None
23		110	132	Martinez, Teordora V	Head	F	Cha	66	Wd	N	Y	Guam	N	None
24		110	132	Martinez, Jose V	Son	M	Cha	36	S	N	Y	Guam	Y	Farmer
25		110	132	Martinez, Isabel V	Niece	F	Cha	19	S	N	Y	Guam	Y	None

(CHAMORRO ROOTS GENEALOGY PROJECT™ TRANSCRIPTION)
(BERNARD T. PUNZALAN / HTTP://WWW.CHAMORROROOTS.COM)

DEPARTMENT OF COMMERCE-BUREAU OF THE CENSUS
WASHINGTON

FIFTEENTH CENSUS OF THE UNITED STATES: 1930-POPULATION

THE ISLAND OF GUAM

Sheet No. 14B

District **Municipality of Agana**
Name of Place **Agana City (Part of San Antonio)**
[Proper name and, also, name of class, as city, town, village, barrio, etc]

Enumeration District No. 2
Enumerated by me on **April 11, 1930** Arthur W. Jackson, Enumerator

	PLACE OF ABODE			NAME	RELATION	PERSONAL DESCRIPTION				EDUCATION		NATIVITY		OCCUPATION
	Street, avenue, road, etc.	Number of dwelling house is order of visitation	Number of family in order of visitation	of each person whose place of abode on April 1, 1930, was in this family. Enter surname, first, then given name and middle initial. If any. Include every person living on April 1, 1930. Omit children born since April 1, 1930.	Relationship of this Person to the head of the family.	Sex	Color or race	Age at last birthday	Single, married, widowed or divorced	Attended school any time since Sept. 1, 1929	Whether able to read and write.	Place of birth of this person.	Whether able to speak English.	
	1	2	3	4	5	6	7	8	9	10	11	12	13	14
26	Dela Corte	110	132	Martinez, Francisco V	Nephew	M	Cha	12	S	Y	Y	Guam	Y	None
27		111	133	San Agustin, Maria D	Head	F	Cha	36	S	N	Y	Guam	N	Laundress
28		111	133	San Agustin, Joaquina SA	Daughter	F	Cha	14	S	Y	Y	Guam	Y	None
29		111	133	San Agustin, Rosario SA	Daughter	F	Cha	12	S	Y	Y	Guam	Y	None
30		111	133	San Agustin, Asuncion SA	Daughter	F	Cha	11	S	Y	Y	Guam	Y	None
31		111	133	San Agustin, Eduardo SA	Son	M	Cha	8	S	Y		Guam		None
32		111	133	San Agustin, Ursula SA	Daughter	F	Cha	1.7	S	N		Guam		None
33		111	133	San Agustin, Victoria SA	Daughter	F	Cha	.3	S	N		Guam		None
34		112	134	Benavente, Ignacio G	Head	M	Cha	56	M	N	Y	Guam	N	Farmer
35		112	134	Benavente, Carmen U	Wife	F	Cha	54	M	N	N	Guam	N	None
36		112	134	Benavente, Manuel U	Son	M	Cha	26	S	N	Y	Guam	Y	Farm laborer
37		112	134	Benavente, Jose U	Son	M	Cha	23	S	N	Y	Guam	Y	Farm laborer
38		112	134	Benavente, Maria U	Daughter	F	Cha	19	S	Y	Y	Guam	Y	None
39		112	134	Laptap, Martina L	Mother in-law	F	Cha	97	Wd	N	N	Guam	N	None
40		113	135	Torre, Jose C	Head	M	Cha	33	M	N	Y	Guam	Y	Farmer
41		113	135	Torre, Grabela T	Wife	F	Cha	30	M	N	Y	Guam	Y	None
42		113	135	Torre, Jose T	Son	M	Cha	5	S	N		Guam		None
43		113	135	Torre, Rosario T	Daughter	F	Cha	3.8	S	N		Guam		None
44		113	135	Santos, Jesus B	Servant	M	Cha	12	S	Y	Y	Guam		Servant
45		114	136	Sayama, Jesus SA	Head	M	Jap	38	M	N	Y	Guam	Y	Retail merchant
46		114	136	Sayama, Joaquina B	Wife	F	Cha	36	M	N	Y	Guam	Y	Sotre keeper
47		114	136	Sayama, Jesus B	Son	M	Jap	11	S	Y	Y	Guam	Y	None
48		114	136	Sayama, Maria B	Daughter	F	Jap	9	S	Y		Guam		None
49		114	136	Sayama, Rosario B	Daughter	F	Jap	7	S	Y		Guam		None
50		114	136	Sayama, Pedro B	Son	M	Jap	6	S	Y		Guam		None

(CHAMORRO ROOTS GENEALOGY PROJECT™ TRANSCRIPTION)
(BERNARD T. PUNZALAN / HTTP://WWW.CHAMORROROOTS.COM)

DEPARTMENT OF COMMERCE-BUREAU OF THE CENSUS
WASHINGTON

FIFTEENTH CENSUS OF THE UNITED STATES: 1930-POPULATION

THE ISLAND OF GUAM

Sheet No. 15A

50

District **Municipality of Agana**
Name of Place **Agana City (Part of San Antonio)**
[Proper name and, also, name of class, as city, town, village, barrio, etc]

Enumeration District No. **2**
Enumerated by me on **April 12, 1930** Arthur W. Jackson, Enumerator

	PLACE OF ABODE			NAME	RELATION	PERSONAL DESCRIPTION				EDUCATION		NATIVITY		OCCUPATION
	Street, avenue, road, etc.	Number of dwelling house is order of visitation	Number of family in order of visitation	of each person whose place of abode on April 1, 1930, was in this family. Enter surname, first, then given name and middle initial. If any. Include every person living on April 1, 1930. Omit children born since April 1, 1930.	Relationship of this Person to the head of the family.	Sex	Color or race	Age at last birthday	Single, married, widowed or divorced	Attended school any time since Sept. 1, 1929	Whether able to read and write.	Place of birth of this person.	Whether able to speak English.	
	1	2	3	4	5	6	7	8	9	10	11	12	13	14
1	Dela Corte	114	136	Sayama, Jesus B	Son	M	Jap	4.8	S	N		Guam		None
2		114	136	Sayama, Ursula B	Daughter	F	Jap	2.5	S	N		Guam		None
3		114	136	Rodrigues, Ana R	Servant	F	Cha	26	S	N	N	Guam	N	Servant
4		115	137	Rosario, Vicente Q	Head	M	Cha	54	M	N	Y	Guam	N	Farmer
5		115	137	Rosario, Vicenta C	Wife	F	Cha	60	M	N	Y	Guam	N	None
6		116	138	Quichocho, Jose Q	Head	M	Cha	50	M	N	Y	Guam	N	Farmer
7		116	138	Quichocho, Rosa P	Wife	F	Cha	51	M	N	N	Guam	N	None
8		116	138	Rosario, Maria P	Step-daughter	F	Cha	26	S	N	Y	Guam	N	None
9		117	139	Taitano, Joaquin R	Head	M	Cha	31	M	N	Y	Guam	Y	Farmer
10		117	139	Taitano, Joaquina M	Wife	F	Cha	35	M	N	Y	Guam	Y	None
11		117	139	Taitano, Vicente M	Son	M	Cha	1.5	S	N		Guam		None
12		117	139	Taitano, Maria M	Daughter	F	Cha	.4	S	N		Guam		None
13		118	140	Martinez, Ramon C	Head	M	Cha	60	M	N	Y	Guam	N	Farmer
14		118	140	Martinez, Antonia F	Wife	F	Cha	61	M	N	Y	Guam	N	None
15		118	140	Martinez, Jose F	Son	M	Cha	30	S	N	Y	Guam	Y	Farm laborer
16		118	140	Martinez, Maria F	Daughter	F	Cha	28	S	N	Y	Guam	Y	None
17		119	141	Rosario, Dolores M	Head	F	Cha	36	Wd	N	Y	Guam	Y	Seamstress
18		119	141	Rosario, Rosa M	Daughter	F	Cha	15	S	Y	Y	Guam	Y	None
19		119	141	Mendiola, Filomina C	Mother	F	Cha	61	S	N	N	Guam	N	None
20		120	142	Rosario, Jose S	Head	M	Cha	65	M	N	Y	Guam	Y	Laborer
21		120	142	Rosario, Dolores A	Wife	F	Cha	71	M	N	N	Guam	N	None
22		120	142	Rosario, Consuelo A	Daughter	F	Cha	32	S	N	Y	Guam	Y	None
23		120	142	Rosario, Josefina A	Daughter	F	Cha	30	S	N	Y	Guam	Y	None
24		120	142	Rosario, Juan R	Grandson	M	Cha	5	S	N		Guam		None
25		120	142	Rosario, Jesus R	Grandson	M	Cha	1.6	S	N		Guam		None

(CHAMORRO ROOTS GENEALOGY PROJECT™ TRANSCRIPTION)
(BERNARD T. PUNZALAN / HTTP://WWW.CHAMORROROOTS.COM)

DEPARTMENT OF COMMERCE-BUREAU OF THE CENSUS
WASHINGTON

FIFTEENTH CENSUS OF THE UNITED STATES: 1930-POPULATION

THE ISLAND OF GUAM

Sheet No. 15B

50B

District **Municipality of Agana**
Name of Place **Agana City (Part of San Antonio)**
[Proper name and, also, name of class, as city, town, village, barrio, etc]

Enumeration District No. 2
Enumerated by me on **April 12, 1930** Arthur W. Jackson
Enumerator

	PLACE OF ABODE			NAME	RELATION	PERSONAL DESCRIPTION				EDUCATION		NATIVITY		OCCUPATION
	Street, avenue, road, etc.	Number of dwelling house is order of visitation	Number of family in order of visitation	of each person whose place of abode on April 1, 1930, was in this family. Enter surname, first, then given name and middle initial. If any. Include every person living on April 1, 1930. Omit children born since April 1, 1930.	Relationship of this Person to the head of the family.	Sex	Color or race	Age at last birthday	Single, married, widowed or divorced	Attended school any time since Sept. 1, 1929	Whether able to read and write.	Place of birth of this person.	Whether able to speak English.	
	1	2	3	4	5	6	7	8	9	10	11	12	13	14
26	Dela Corte	120	142	Megofna, Juan A	Servant	M	Cha	17	S	N	Y	Guam	N	Servant
27		121	143	Borja, Vicente B	Head	M	Cha	47	M	N	Y	Guam	N	Farmer
28		121	143	Borja, Agustina S	Wife	F	Cha	45	M	N	N	Guam	N	None
29		121	143	Borja, Francisco S	Son	M	Cha	18	S	N	Y	Guam	Y	Servant
30		121	143	Borja, Jesus S	Son	M	Cha	17	S	N	Y	Guam	Y	Farm laborer
31		121	143	Borja, Vicente S	Son	M	Cha	15	S	Y	Y	Guam	Y	None
32		121	143	Borja, Josefa S	Daughter	F	Cha	12	S	Y	Y	Guam	Y	None
33		121	143	Borja, Maria S	Daughter	F	Cha	9	S	Y		Guam		None
34		122	144	Leon Guerrero, Vicente C	Head	M	Cha	36	M	N	Y	Guam	Y	Farmer
35		122	144	Leon Guerrero, Joaquina B	Wife	F	Cha	24	M	N	Y	Guam	Y	None
36		122	144	Leon Guerrero, Alejo B	Son	M	Cha	5	S	N		Guam		None
37		122	144	Leon Guerrero, Emelia B	Daughter	F	Cha	4.9	S	N		Guam		None
38		122	144	Leon Guerrero, Francisco B	Son	M	Cha	3.8	S	N		Guam		None
39		122	144	Leon Guerrero, Vicente B	Son	M	Cha	.3	S	N		Guam		None
40		122	145	Borja, Gregorio C	Head	M	Cha	30	S	N	Y	Guam	Y	Chauffeur
41		122	145	Borja, Juan C	Brother	M	Cha	22	S	N	Y	Guam	Y	Laborer
42		122	145	Borja, Pedro C	Brother	M	Cha	18	S	N	Y	Guam	Y	Farm laborer
43		122	145	Borja, Maria C	Sister	F	Cha	16	S	N	Y	Guam	Y	None
44		123	146	Sanchez, Ciraco	Head	M	Fil	38	M	N	N	Guam	Y	USN reserve
45		123	146	Sanchez, Ignacia S	Wife	F	Cha	27	M	N	N	Guam	Y	None
46		123	146	Sanchez, Ricardo S	Son	M	Fil	4.8	S	N	N	Guam		None
47		123	146	Sanchez, Ruperta S	Daughter	F	Fil	2.5	S	N	N	Guam		None
48		123	146	Sanchez, Candido S	Son	M	Fil	1.5	S	N	N	Guam		None
49		123	146	Sahagon, Magdalena Q	Sist-in-law	F	Cha	33	S	N	N	Guam	N	None
50		124	147	Kanagawa, Lucio H	Head	M	Jap	54	Wd	N	Y	Japan	Y	Carpenter

(CHAMORRO ROOTS GENEALOGY PROJECT™ TRANSCRIPTION)
(BERNARD T. PUNZALAN / HTTP://WWW.CHAMORROROOTS.COM)

DEPARTMENT OF COMMERCE-BUREAU OF THE CENSUS
WASHINGTON

FIFTEENTH CENSUS OF THE UNITED STATES: 1930-POPULATION

THE ISLAND OF GUAM

Sheet No. 16A

51

District **Municipality of Agana**

Name of Place **Agana City (Part of San Antonio)**
[Proper name and, also, name of class, as city, town, village, barrio, etc]

Enumeration District No. **2**

Enumerated by me on **April 12, 1930** Arthur W. Jackson
Enumerator

	PLACE OF ABODE			NAME	RELATION	PERSONAL DESCRIPTION				EDUCATION		NATIVITY		OCCUPATION
	Street, avenue, road, etc.	Number of dwelling house in order of visitation	Number of family in order of visitation	of each person whose place of abode on April 1, 1930, was in this family. Enter surname, first, then given name and middle initial. If any. Include every person living on April 1, 1930. Omit children born since April 1, 1930.	Relationship of this Person to the head of the family.	Sex	Color or race	Age at last birthday	Single, married, widowed or divorced	Attended school any time since Sept. 1, 1929	Whether able to read and write.	Place of birth of this person.	Whether able to speak English.	
	1	2	3	4	5	6	7	8	9	10	11	12	13	14
1	Dela Corte	127	147	Kanagawa, Rufina D	Daughter	F	Jap	14	S	Y	Y	Guam	Y	None
2		127	147	Kanagawa, Pedro D	Son	M	Jap	13	S	Y	Y	Guam	Y	None
3		127	147	Kanagawa, Crecencia D	Daughter	F	Jap	9	S	Y		Guam		None
4		125	148	Sanchez, Simon A	Head	M	Fil	34	M	N	Y	Guam	Y	Supervisor school
5		125	148	Sanchez, Antonia C	Wife	F	Cha	30	M	N	Y	Guam	Y	None
6		125	148	Sanchez, Julia C	Daughter	F	Fil	12	S	Y	Y	Guam	Y	None
7		125	148	Sanchez, Adriano C	Son	M	Fil	10	S	Y	Y	Guam	Y	None
8		125	148	Sanchez, Francisco C	Son	M	Fil	8	S	Y	Y	Guam		None
9		125	148	Sanchez, Juanita C	Daughter	F	Fil	6	S	Y		Guam		None
10		125	148	Sanchez, Pedro C	Son	M	Fil	4.5	S	N		Guam		None
11		125	148	Sanchez, Eulogio C	Son	M	Fil	2.8	S	N		Guam		None
12		125	148	Sanchez, Antonio C	Son	M	Fil	1.3	S	N		Guam		None
13		125	148	Cruz, Josefa S	Mother-in-law	F	Fil	68	Wd	N	N	Guam	N	None
14		125	148	Cruz, Maria S	Sist-in-law	F	Cha	27	S	N	Y	Guam	N	None
15		125	148	Cruz, Mariano C	Nephew	M	Cha	3.5	S	N		Guam		None
16		125	148	Santos, Ana S	Servant	F	Cha	15	S	N	Y	Guam	Y	Servant
17		126	149	Cruz, Pedro S	Head	M	Cha	33	M	N	Y	Guam	N	Engin tender
18		126	149	Cruz, Ana T	Wife	F	Cha	24	M	N	Y	Guam	N	None
19		126	149	Cruz, Rosa T	Daughter	F	Cha	3.6	S	N		Guam		None
20		126	149	Cruz, Ana T	Daughter	F	Cha	1.9	S	N		Guam		None
21		126	149	Cruz, Paulino G	Cousin	M	Cha	18	S	N	Y	Guam	Y	Farm laborer
22		127	150	Duenas, Dolores S	Head	F	Cha	36	Wd	N	Y	Guam	Y	Cook
23		128	151	Gomez, Jesus A	Head	M	Cha	38	M	N	N	Guam	Y	Farmer
24		128	151	Gomez, Maria C	Wife	F	Cha	40	M	N	N	Guam	N	None
25		129	152	Aguajlo, Antonia S	Head	F	Cha	57	Wd	N	N	Guam	N	None

(CHAMORRO ROOTS GENEALOGY PROJECT™ TRANSCRIPTION)
(BERNARD T. PUNZALAN / HTTP://WWW.CHAMORROROOTS.COM)

DEPARTMENT OF COMMERCE-BUREAU OF THE CENSUS
WASHINGTON

FIFTEENTH CENSUS OF THE UNITED STATES: 1930-POPULATION

THE ISLAND OF GUAM

Sheet No. 16B

51B

District Municipality of Agana
Name of Place Agana City (Part of San Antonio)
[Proper name and, also, name of class, as city, town, village, barrio, etc]

Enumeration District No. 2
Enumerated by me on April 14, 1930 Arthur W. Jackson, Enumerator

	PLACE OF ABODE			NAME	RELATION	PERSONAL DESCRIPTION				EDUCATION		NATIVITY		OCCUPATION
	Street, avenue, road, etc.	Number of dwelling house is order of visitation	Number of family in order of visitation	of each person whose place of abode on April 1, 1930, was in this family. Enter surname, first, then given name and middle initial. If any. Include every person living on April 1, 1930. Omit children born since April 1, 1930.	Relationship of this Person to the head of the family.	Sex	Color or race	Age at last birthday	Single, married, widowed or divorced	Attended school any time since Sept. 1, 1929	Whether able to read and write.	Place of birth of this person.	Whether able to speak English.	
	1	2	3	4	5	6	7	8	9	10	11	12	13	14
26	Dela Corte	129	152	Aguajlo, Ana S	Daughter	F	Cha	26	S	N	Y	Guam	Y	Laundress
27		129	152	Aguajlo, Delfina S	Grand daug	F	Cha	1	S	Y		Guam		None
28		129	152	Aguajlo, Pedro S	Grand son	M	Cha	2.3	S	N		Guam		None
29	Trafalgar	130	153	Castro, Lucas R	Head	M	Cha	26	M	N	Y	Guam	Y	Printer
30		130	153	Castro, Teresa Q	Wife	F	Cha	30	M	N	Y	Guam	Y	None
31		130	153	Castro, Angusta Q	Daughter	F	Cha	6	S	N		Guam		None
32		130	153	Castro, Juan Q	Son	M	Cha	2.8	S	N		Guam		None
33		130	153	Castro, Francisco Q	Son	M	Cha	1.5	S	N		Guam		None
34		131	154	Miner, Baldomero P	Head	M	Cha	59	M	N	Y	Guam	Y	Carpenter
35		131	154	Miner, Maria B	Wife	F	Cha	48	M	N	Y	Guam	N	None
36		131	154	Miner, Timoteo B	Son	M	Cha	6	S	N		Guam		None
37		131	155	Borja, Gravela T	Head	F	Cha	70	Wd	N	N	Guam	N	None
38		131	155	Borja, Gravela L	Grand-dau	F	Cha	20	S	N	Y	Guam	N	None
39		131	155	Borja, Ann T	Sist-in-law	F	Cha	45	S	N	Y	Guam	N	None
40		131	156	Atoigue, Eufrasia A	Head	F	Cha	22	S	N	Y	Guam	Y	None
41		131	156	Atoigue, Maria A	Daughter	F	Cha	3.8	S	N		Guam		None
42		131	156	Atoigue, Rosario A	Daughter	F	Cha	.5	S	N		Guam		None
43		132	157	San Agustin, Miguel E	Head	M	Cha	51	M	N	Y	Guam	N	Carpenter
44		132	157	San Agustin, Maria S	Wife	F	Cha	49	M	N	Y	Guam	N	None
45		132	157	San Agustin, Maria S	Daughter	F	Cha	26	S	N	Y	Guam	N	None
46		132	157	San Agustin, Rita S	Daughter	F	Cha	17	S	N	Y	Guam	Y	None
47		132	157	San Agustin, Isabel S	Daughter	F	Cha	15	S	Y	Y	Guam	Y	None
48		132	157	San Agustin, Miguel S	Son	M	Cha	10	S	Y	Y	Guam	Y	None
49		132	157	San Agustin, Pedro S	Son	M	Cha	7	S	Y		Guam		None
50		132	157	San Agustin, Juan S	Son	M	Cha	7.7	S	N		Guam		None

DEPARTMENT OF COMMERCE-BUREAU OF THE CENSUS
WASHINGTON

FIFTEENTH CENSUS OF THE UNITED STATES: 1930-POPULATION

THE ISLAND OF GUAM

Sheet No. 17A

District **Municipality of Agana**
Name of Place **Agana City (Part of San Antonio)**
[Proper name and, also, name of class, as city, town, village, barrio, etc]

Enumeration District No. 2
Enumerated by me on **April 14, 1930** Arthur W. Jackson
Enumerator

	PLACE OF ABODE			NAME	RELATION	PERSONAL DESCRIPTION				EDUCATION		NATIVITY		OCCUPATION
	Street, avenue, road, etc.	Number of dwelling house is order of visitation	Number of family in order of visitation	of each person whose place of abode on April 1, 1930, was in this family. Enter surname, first, then given name and middle initial. If any. Include every person living on April 1, 1930. Omit children born since April 1, 1930.	Relationship of this Person to the head of the family.	Sex	Color or race	Age at last birthday	Single, married, widowed or divorced	Attended school any time since Sept. 1, 1929	Whether able to read and write.	Place of birth of this person.	Whether able to speak English.	
	1	2	3	4	5	6	7	8	9	10	11	12	13	14
1	Trafalgar	132	158	Salas, Reymunda F	Head	M	Cha	60	Wd	N	N	Guam	N	None
2		132	158	Salas, Consolacion F	Daughter	F	Cha	43	S	N	N	Guam	N	Laundress
3		132	159	San Agustin, Francisco S	Head	M	Cha	29	Wd	N	Y	Guam	N	Cook
4		132	160	San Agustin, Reymunda S	Head	F	Cha	24	S	N	Y	Guam	N	Laundress
5		132	160	San Agustin, Modesta S	Daughter	F	Cha	6	S	N		Guam		None
6		132	160	San Agustin, Virginia S	Daughter	F	Cha	4.8	S	N		Guam		None
7		132	160	Salas, Maria F	Cousin	F	Cha	15	S	N	Y	Guam	Y	None
8		133	161	Acosta, Pedro A	Head	M	Cha	46	M	N	Y	Guam	N	Farmer
9		133	161	Acosta, Concepcion R	Wife	F	Cha	47	M	N	N	Guam	N	None
10		133	161	Acosta, Rosa R	Daughter	F	Cha	12	S	Y	Y	Guam	Y	None
11		134	162	Peredo, Dominga T	Head	F	Cha	57	Wd	N	N	Guam	N	None
12		134	162	Peredo, Baldomero T	Son	M	Cha	35	S	N	Y	Guam	Y	Houseboy
13		134	162	Peredo, Ana T	Daughter	F	Cha	23	S	N	Y	Guam	Y	None
14		134	162	Peredo, Jose T	Son	M	Cha	22	S	N	Y	Guam	Y	Houseboy
15		134	162	Taitinfong, Juana	Mother	F	Cha	96	Wd	N	N	Guam	N	None
16		134	162	Peredo, Beatrice P	Grand daug	F	Cha	.3	S	N		Guam		None
17		135	163	Santos, Angel B	Head	M	Cha	30	M	N	Y	Guam	Y	Laborer
18		135	163	Santos, Ana C	Wife	F	Cha	30	M	N	Y	Guam	Y	None
19		135	163	Santos, Rita C	Daughter	F	Cha	.4	S	N		Guam		None
20		135	163	Santos, Gregorio B	Brother	M	Cha	26	S	N	Y	Guam	Y	Store keeper
21		135	163	Santos, Jose B	Brother	M	Cha	35	S	N	Y	Guam	Y	Laborer
22		136	164	Bautista, Jose S	Head	M	Cha	27	S	N	Y	Guam	Y	C---boy
23		136	164	Bautista, Vicente S	Brother	M	Cha	25	S	N	Y	Guam	Y	Laborer
24		136	164	Bautista, Maria S	Sister	F	Cha	20	S	N	Y	Guam	Y	None
25		136	165	Diaz, Juan B	Head	M	Cha	31	M	N	Y	Guam	N	Farm laborer

(CHAMORRO ROOTS GENEALOGY PROJECT™ TRANSCRIPTION)
(BERNARD T. PUNZALAN / HTTP://WWW.CHAMORROROOTS.COM)

DEPARTMENT OF COMMERCE-BUREAU OF THE CENSUS
WASHINGTON

FIFTEENTH CENSUS OF THE UNITED STATES: 1930-POPULATION

THE ISLAND OF GUAM

Sheet No. 17B

52B

District **Municipality of Agana**
Name of Place **Agana City (Part of San Antonio)**
[Proper name and, also, name of class, as city, town, village, barrio, etc]

Enumeration District No. 2
Enumerated by me on **April 14, 1930** Arthur W. Jackson
Enumerator

	PLACE OF ABODE			NAME	RELATION	PERSONAL DESCRIPTION				EDUCATION		NATIVITY		OCCUPATION
	Street, avenue, road, etc.	Number of dwelling house is order of visitation	Number of family in order of visitation	of each person whose place of abode on April 1, 1930, was in this family. Enter surname, first, then given name and middle initial. If any. Include every person living on April 1, 1930. Omit children born since April 1, 1930.	Relationship of this Person to the head of the family.	Sex	Color or race	Age at last birthday	Single, married, widowed or divorced	Attended school any time since Sept. 1, 1929	Whether able to read and write.	Place of birth of this person.	Whether able to speak English.	
	1	2	3	4	5	6	7	8	9	10	11	12	13	14
26	Trafalgar	136	165	Diaz, Rosa L	Wife	F	Cha	23	M	N	Y	Guam	N	None
27		136	165	Diaz, Concepcion L	Daughter	F	Cha	6	S	N		Guam		None
28		136	165	Diaz, Francisco L	Son	M	Cha	2.3	S	N		Guam		None
29		136	165	Diaz, Veronica L	Daughter	F	Cha	.3	S	N		Guam		None
30		136	166	Bautista, Manuel S	Head	M	Cha	29	M	N	N	Guam	N	Farmer
31		136	166	Bautista, Ana A	Wife	F	Cha	26	M	N	N	Guam	N	None
32		136	166	Bautista, Juan A	Son	M	Cha	4.5	S	N		Guam		None
33		136	166	Bautista, Jose A	Son	M	Cha	2.7	S	N		Guam		None
34		136	166	Bautista, Maria A	Daughter	F	Cha	.3	S	N		Guam		None
35		137	167	Hudson, James M	Head	M	W	35	M	N	Y	Kentucky	Y	Chauffeur
36		137	167	Hudson, Gregoria A	Wife	F	Cha	29	M	N	Y	Guam	Y	None
37		137	167	Hudson, James E	Son	M	Cha	5	S	N		Guam		None
38		137	167	Hudson, Pearl E	Daughter	F	Cha	4.5	S	N		Guam		None
39		137	167	Hudson, Mary O	Daughter	F	Cha	3.8	S	N		Guam		None
40		137	167	Hudson, George E	Son	M	Cha	1.8	S	N		Guam		None
41		138	168	Flores, Benigno LG	Head	M	Cha	20	M	N	Y	Guam	Y	Cook
42		138	168	Flores, Dolores M	Wife	F	Cha	18	M	N	Y	Guam	Y	None
43		138	168	Mendiola, Nieves R	Aunt	F	Cha	56	M	N	N	Guam	N	None
44		139	169	Crisostomo, Joaquin M	Head	M	Cha	56	M	N	Y	Guam	N	Farmer
45		139	169	Crisostomo, Dolores A	Wife	F	Cha	46	M	N	Y	Guam	N	None
46		139	169	Crisostomo, Joaquin A	Son	M	Cha	18	S	N	Y	Guam	Y	Bank clerk
47		139	169	Crisostomo, Ana A	Daughter	F	Cha	15	S	Y	Y	Guam	Y	None
48		139	169	Crisostomo, Juan A	Son	M	Cha	9	S	Y		Guam		None
49		140	170	Quintanilla, Maria C	Head	F	Cha	48	Wd	N	Y	Guam	N	None
50		140	170	Quintanilla, Vicente C	Son	M	Cha	22	S	N	Y	Guam	Y	App. Carpenter

DEPARTMENT OF COMMERCE-BUREAU OF THE CENSUS
WASHINGTON

FIFTEENTH CENSUS OF THE UNITED STATES: 1930-POPULATION

THE ISLAND OF GUAM

Sheet No. 18A

District **Municipality of Agana**
Name of Place **Agana City (Part of San Antonio)**
[Proper name and, also, name of class, as city, town, village, barrio, etc]

Enumeration District No. 2
Enumerated by me on **April 15, 1930** Arthur W. Jackson, Enumerator

	PLACE OF ABODE			NAME	RELATION	PERSONAL DESCRIPTION				EDUCATION		NATIVITY		OCCUPATION
	Street, avenue, road, etc.	Number of dwelling house in order of visitation	Number of family in order of visitation	of each person whose place of abode on April 1, 1930, was in this family. Enter surname, first, then given name and middle initial. If any. Include every person living on April 1, 1930. Omit children born since April 1, 1930.	Relationship of this Person to the head of the family.	Sex	Color or race	Age at last birthday	Single, married, widowed or divorced	Attended school any time since Sept. 1, 1929	Whether able to read and write.	Place of birth of this person.	Whether able to speak English.	
	1	2	3	4	5	6	7	8	9	10	11	12	13	14
1	Trafalgar	140	170	Quintanilla, Carlos C	Son	M	Cha	18	S	N	Y	Guam	Y	Farmer
2		140	170	Quintanilla, Antonia C	Daughter	F	Cha	17	S	N	Y	Guam	Y	None
3		140	170	Quintanilla, Carmen C	Daughter	F	Cha	15	S	N	Y	Guam	Y	None
4		140	170	Quintanilla, Jose C	Son	M	Cha	13	S	Y	Y	Guam	Y	None
5		140	170	Quintanilla, Emelia C	Daughter	F	Cha	12	S	Y	Y	Guam	Y	None
6		140	170	Quintanilla, Francisca C	Daughter	F	Cha	10	S	Y	Y	Guam	Y	None
7		140	170	Quintanilla, Olimpia C	Daughter	F	Cha	5	S	N		Guam		None
8		141	171	Quintanilla, Francisco T	Head	M	Cha	36	M	N	Y	Guam	Y	Farmer
9		141	171	Quintanilla, Maria M	Wife	F	Cha	31	M	N	Y	Guam	Y	None
10		141	171	Quintanilla, Gonzalo M	Son	M	Cha	11	S	Y	Y	Guam	Y	None
11		141	171	Quintanilla, Clara M	Daughter	F	Cha	9	S	Y		Guam		None
12		142	172	Mendiola, Vicente B	Head	M	Cha	62	M	N	Y	Guam	N	None
13		142	173	Cruz, Maria B	Head	F	Cha	61	Wd	N	N	Guam	N	None
14		142	173	Cruz, Tomas B	Son	M	Cha	40	S	N	Y	Guam	N	Farmer
15		142	173	Cruz, Jose B	Grand son	M	Cha	8	S	Y		Guam		None
16		142	173	Cruz, Ana B	Grand daug	F	Cha	6	S	N		Guam		None
17		143	174	Camacho, Teresa B	Head	F	Cha	42	D	N	N	Guam	N	Cook
18		143	174	Bamba, Jose B	Nephew	M	Cha	6	S	N		Guam		None
19		144	175	Techaira, Manuel D	Head	M	Cha	37	M	N	Y	Guam	Y	Farmer
20		144	175	Techaira, Maria LG	Wife	F	Cha	33	M	N	Y	Guam	N	None
21		144	175	Techaira, Remedio LG	Daughter	F	Cha	15	S	N	Y	Guam	Y	None
22		144	175	Techaira, Maria LG	Daughter	F	Cha	13	S	Y	Y	Guam	Y	None
23		144	175	Techaira, Erminia LG	Daughter	F	Cha	11	S	Y	Y	Guam	Y	None
24		144	175	Techaira, Ramon LG	Son	M	Cha	9	S	Y		Guam		None
25		144	175	Techaira, Isabel LG	Daughter	F	Cha	6	S	N		Guam		None

DEPARTMENT OF COMMERCE-BUREAU OF THE CENSUS
WASHINGTON

FIFTEENTH CENSUS OF THE UNITED STATES: 1930-POPULATION

THE ISLAND OF GUAM

Sheet No. 18B

53B

District **Municipality of Agana**
Name of Place **Agana City (Part of San Antonio)**
[Proper name and, also, name of class, as city, town, village, barrio, etc]

Enumeration District No. 2
Enumerated by me on **April 15, 1930** Arthur W. Jackson, Enumerator

	PLACE OF ABODE: Street, avenue, road, etc.	Number of dwelling house in order of visitation	Number of family in order of visitation	NAME of each person whose place of abode on April 1, 1930, was in this family. Enter surname, first, then given name and middle initial. If any. Include every person living on April 1, 1930. Omit children born since April 1, 1930.	RELATION Relationship of this Person to the head of the family.	PERSONAL DESCRIPTION: Sex	Color or race	Age at last birthday	Single, married, widowed or divorced	EDUCATION: Attended school any time since Sept. 1, 1929	Whether able to read and write.	NATIVITY Place of birth of this person.	Whether able to speak English.	OCCUPATION
	1	2	3	4	5	6	7	8	9	10	11	12	13	14
26	Trafalgar	144	175	Techaira, Joaquina LG	Daughter	F	Cha	4.4	S	N		Guam		None
27		144	175	Techaira, Gregorio LG	Son	M	Cha	2.5	S	N		Guam		None
28		144	175	Techaira, Manuel LG	Son	M	Cha	.1	S	N		Guam		None
29		145	176	Perez, Jesus C	Head	M	Cha	37	M	N	Y	Guam	Y	Black smith
30		145	176	Perez, Maria S	Wife	F	Cha	35	M	N	Y	Guam	N	None
31		145	176	Perez, Ana S	Daughter	F	Cha	10	S	Y	Y	Guam	Y	None
32		145	176	Perez, Laura S	Daughter	F	Cha	9	S	Y		Guam		None
33		145	176	Perez, Vicente S	Son	M	Cha	8	S	Y		Guam		None
34		145	176	Perez, Jesus S	Son	M	Cha	4.8	S	N		Guam		None
35		145	176	Perez, Rita S	Daughter	F	Cha	1.8	S	N		Guam		None
36		145	176	Perez, Maria S	Daughter	F	Cha	.3	S	N		Guam		None
37	Santiago	146	177	Santos, Juan V	Head	M	Cha	41	M	N	Y	Guam	N	Farmer
38		146	177	Santos, Amparo D	Wife	F	Cha	38	M	N	N	Guam	N	
39		146	177	Santos, Leonila D	Daughter	F	Cha	12	S	Y	Y	Guam	Y	None
40		146	177	Santos, Jose D	Son	M	Cha	10	S	Y	Y	Guam	Y	None
41		146	177	Santos, Faustina D	Daughter	F	Cha	9	S	Y		Guam		None
42		146	177	Santos, Juan D	Son	M	Cha	5	S	N		Guam		None
43		146	177	Santos, Antonio D	Son	M	Cha	4.3	S	N		Guam		None
44		146	177	Santos, Jesus D	Son	M	Cha	.4	S	N		Guam		None
45		146	177	Santos, Pedro M	Father	M	Cha	68	Wd	N	Y	Guam	N	None
46		147	178	Quitugua, Vicente A	Head	M	Cha	55	M	N	Y	Guam	N	Farmer
47		147	178	Quitugua, Maria D	Wife	F	Cha	68	M	N	N	Guam	N	None
48		147	178	Techaira, Mafada C	Grandaug	F	Cha	12	S	Y	Y	Guam	Y	None
49		147	178	Techaira, Jesus C	Grandson	M	Cha	7	S	Y		Guam		None
50		147	179	Leon Guerrero, Ignacio S	Head	M	Cha	26	M	N	Y	Guam	Y	Laborer

DEPARTMENT OF COMMERCE-BUREAU OF THE CENSUS
WASHINGTON

FIFTEENTH CENSUS OF THE UNITED STATES: 1930-POPULATION

THE ISLAND OF GUAM

Sheet No. 19A

District **Municipality of Agana**
Name of Place **Agana City (Part of San Antonio)**
[Proper name and, also, name of class, as city, town, village, barrio, etc]

Enumeration District No. **2**
Enumerated by me on **April 15, 1930** Arthur W. Jackson
Enumerator

	PLACE OF ABODE			NAME	RELATION	PERSONAL DESCRIPTION				EDUCATION		NATIVITY		OCCUPATION
	Street, avenue, road, etc.	Number of dwelling house in order of visitation	Number of family in order of visitation	of each person whose place of abode on April 1, 1930, was in this family. Enter surname, first, then given name and middle initial. If any. Include every person living on April 1, 1930. Omit children born since April 1, 1930.	Relationship of this Person to the head of the family.	Sex	Color or race	Age at last birthday	Single, married, widowed or divorced	Attended school any time since Sept. 1, 1929	Whether able to read and write.	Place of birth of this person.	Whether able to speak English.	
	1	2	3	4	5	6	7	8	9	10	11	12	13	14
1	Santiago	147	179	Leon Guerrero, Josefa T	Wife	F	Cha	32	M	N	Y	Guam	N	None
2		148	180	Hernandez, Ana F	Head	F	Cha	70	Wd	N	N	Guam	N	None
3		148	180	Hernandez, Jose F	Son	M	Cha	36	S	N	N	Guam	N	Farmer
4		149	181	Benavente, Vicente A	Head	M	Cha	34	M	N	Y	Guam	Y	Laborer
5		149	181	Benavente, Asuncion R	Wife	F	Cha	31	M	N	Y	Guam	Y	None
6		149	181	Benavente, Rosa R	Daughter	F	Cha	3.5	S	N		Guam		None
7		149	181	Benavente, Joaquin R	Son	M	Cha	2.3	S	N		Guam		None
8		150	182	Tenorio, Jesus B	Head	M	Cha	29	M	N	Y	Guam	Y	Chauffeur
9		150	182	Tenorio, Ana T	Wife	F	Cha	25	M	N	Y	Guam	Y	None
10		150	182	Tenorio, Adela T	Daughter	F	Cha	6	S	N		Guam		None
11		150	182	Tenorio, Jose T	Son	M	Cha	4.3	S	N		Guam		None
12		150	182	Tenorio, Maria T	Daughter	F	Cha	.1	S	N		Guam		None
13		151	183	Toves, Jesus C	Head	M	Cha	37	M	N	Y	Guam	Y	Policeman
14		151	183	Toves, Ana B	Wife	F	Cha	38	M	N	Y	Guam	Y	None
15		151	183	Toves, Elias B	Son	M	Cha	8	S	Y		Guam		None
16		151	183	Toves, Sergio B	Son	M	Cha	5	S	N		Guam		None
17		151	183	Toves, Alejandro B	Son	M	Cha	3.8	S	N		Guam		None
18		151	183	Toves, Teodosia B	Daughter	F	Cha	1.8	S	N		Guam		None
19		151	183	Toves, Ana C	Sister	F	Cha	29	S	N	Y	Guam	Y	None
20		152	184	Migofna, Anastasio M	Head	M	Cha	50	M	N	Y	Guam	N	Shoemaker
21		152	184	Migofna, Ana A	Wife	F	Cha	46	M	N	Y	Guam	N	None
22		152	184	Migofna, Jose A	Son	M	Cha	23	S	N	Y	Guam	Y	Shoemaker
23		152	184	Migofna, Vicente A	Son	M	Cha	20	S	N	Y	Guam	Y	Laborer
24		152	184	Migofna, Ignacio A	Son	M	Cha	15	S	N	Y	Guam	Y	None
25		152	184	Fejarang, Jose M	Grandson	M	Cha	3.8	S	N		Guam		None

(CHAMORRO ROOTS GENEALOGY PROJECT™ TRANSCRIPTION)
(BERNARD T. PUNZALAN / HTTP://WWW.CHAMORROROOTS.COM)

DEPARTMENT OF COMMERCE-BUREAU OF THE CENSUS
WASHINGTON

FIFTEENTH CENSUS OF THE UNITED STATES: 1930-POPULATION

THE ISLAND OF GUAM

Sheet No. 19B

54B

District **Municipality of Agana**
Name of Place **Agana City (Part of San Antonio)**
[Proper name and, also, name of class, as city, town, village, barrio, etc]

Enumeration District No. 2
Enumerated by me on **April 15, 1930** Arthur W. Jackson, Enumerator

	PLACE OF ABODE			NAME	RELATION	PERSONAL DESCRIPTION				EDUCATION		NATIVITY		OCCUPATION
	Street, avenue, road, etc.	Number of dwelling house is order of visitation	Number of family in order of visitation	of each person whose place of abode on April 1, 1930, was in this family. Enter surname, first, then given name and middle initial. If any. Include every person living on April 1, 1930. Omit children born since April 1, 1930.	Relationship of this Person to the head of the family.	Sex	Color or race	Age at last birthday	Single, married, widowed or divorced	Attended school any time since Sept. 1, 1929	Whether able to read and write.	Place of birth of this person.	Whether able to speak English.	
	1	2	3	4	5	6	7	8	9	10	11	12	13	14
26	Santiago	152	184	Fejarang, Jesus M	Grandson	M	Cha	1.8	S	N		Guam		None
27		153	185	Manibusan, Joseph D	Head	M	Cha	31	M	N	Y	Guam	Y	Foreman
28		153	185	Manibusan, Consalasion D	Wife	F	Cha	31	M	N	Y	Guam	Y	None
29		153	185	Manibusan, John T	Son	M	Cha	8	S	Y		Guam		None
30		153	185	Manibusan, Vincent H	Son	M	Cha	7	S	Y		Guam		None
31		153	185	Manibusan, Alice D	Daughter	F	Cha	4.5	S	N		Guam		None
32		153	185	Manibusan, Albert D	Son	M	Cha	1.8	S	N		Guam		None
33		153	185	Manibusan, Mary D	Mother	F	W	61	Wd	N	Y	England	Y	None
34		154	186	Santos, Jesus V	Head	M	Cha	35	M	N	Y	Guam	Y	Blacksmith
35		154	186	Santos, Maria G	Wife	F	Cha	32	M	N	Y	Guam	Y	None
36		154	186	Santos, Juan G	Son	M	Cha	11	S	Y	Y	Guam	Y	None
37		154	186	Santos, Joaquin G	Son	M	Cha	9	S	Y		Guam		None
38		154	186	Santos, Maria G	Daughter	F	Cha	8	S	Y		Guam		None
39		154	186	Santos, Jesus G	Son	M	Cha	6	S	N		Guam		None
40		155	187	Martinez, Vicente C	Head	M	Cha	68	M	N	Y	Guam	N	Farmer
41		155	187	Martinez, Carmen V	Wife	F	Cha	50	M	N	Y	Guam	N	None
42		155	187	Martinez, Vicente V	Son	M	Cha	15	S	Y	Y	Guam	Y	Farm laborer
43		155	187	Martinez, Juan V	Son	M	Cha	10	S	Y	Y	Guam	Y	None
44		155	187	Martinez, Josefina V	Daughter	F	Cha	9	S	Y		Guam		None
45		155	188	Marrion, Geronimo B	Head	M	Cha	26	M	N	Y	Guam	Y	Chauffeur
46		155	188	Marrion, Maria M	Wife	F	Cha	25	M	N	Y	Guam	Y	None
47		155	188	Marrion, Rita M	Daughter	F	Cha	1.8	S	N		Guam		None
48		156	189	San Agustin, Joaquin C	Head	M	Cha	26	M	N	Y	Guam	Y	Laborer
49		156	189	San Agustin, Maria L	Wife	F	Cha	23	M	N	Y	Guam	Y	None
50		157	190	Cabrera, Maria T	Head	F	Cha	42	S	N	Y	Guam	N	None

(CHAMORRO ROOTS GENEALOGY PROJECT™ TRANSCRIPTION)
(BERNARD T. PUNZALAN / HTTP://WWW.CHAMORROROOTS.COM)

DEPARTMENT OF COMMERCE-BUREAU OF THE CENSUS
WASHINGTON

FIFTEENTH CENSUS OF THE UNITED STATES: 1930-POPULATION

THE ISLAND OF GUAM

Sheet No. 20A

District **Municipality of Agana**
Name of Place **Agana City (Part of San Antonio)**
[Proper name and, also, name of class, as city, town, village, barrio, etc]

Enumeration District No. **2**
Enumerated by me on **April 16, 1930** Arthur W. Jackson, Enumerator

	PLACE OF ABODE			NAME	RELATION	PERSONAL DESCRIPTION				EDUCATION		NATIVITY		OCCUPATION
	Street, avenue, road, etc.	Number of dwelling house in order of visitation	Number of family in order of visitation	of each person whose place of abode on April 1, 1930, was in this family. Enter surname, first, then given name and middle initial. If any. Include every person living on April 1, 1930. Omit children born since April 1, 1930.	Relationship of this Person to the head of the family.	Sex	Color or race	Age at last birthday	Single, married, widowed or divorced	Attended school any time since Sept. 1, 1929	Whether able to read and write.	Place of birth of this person.	Whether able to speak English.	
	1	2	3	4	5	6	7	8	9	10	11	12	13	14
1	San Victores	157	190	Cabrera, Mariano T	Son	M	Cha	24	S	N	N	Guam	Y	Tailor
2		157	190	Cabrera, Delfina T	Daughter	F	Cha	6	S	N		Guam		None
3		157	190	Cabrera, Juan T	Son	M	Cha	3.7	S	N		Guam		None
4		158	191	Leon Guerrero, Joaquin R	Head	M	Cha	51	M	N	Y	Guam	N	Farmer
5		158	191	Leon Guerrero, Maria L	Wife	F	Cha	49	M	N	N	Guam	N	None
6		158	192	Flores, Ana F	Head	F	Cha	47	M	N	N	Guam	N	None
7		158	192	Flores, Maria F	Daughter	F	Cha	23	S	N	Y	Guam	Y	None
8		158	192	Flores, Antonio F	Son	M	Cha	19	S	N	Y	Guam	Y	Farm laborer
9		158	192	Flores, Jose F	Son	M	Cha	16	S	Y	Y	Guam	Y	None
10		158	192	Flores, Joaquin F	Son	M	Cha	11	S	Y		Guam	Y	None
11		158	192	Flores, Josefina F	Daughter	F	Cha	8	S	Y		Guam		None
12		158	192	Flores, Ana F	Daughter	F	Cha	1.7	S	N		Guam		None
13		159	193	Pangelinan, Joaquin T	Head	M	Cha	69	M	N	Y	Guam	N	Farmer
14		159	193	Pangelinan, Maria U	Wife	F	Cha	61	M	N	Y	Guam	N	None
15		159	193	Pangelinan, Benancio U	Son	M	Cha	20	S	N	Y	Guam	Y	None
16		160	194	Camacho, Jose C	Head	M	Cha	36	M	N	Y	Guam	N	Laborer
17		160	194	Camacho, Rita C	Wife	F	Cha	47	M	N	N	Guam	N	None
18		160	194	Camacho, Antonio C	Son	M	Cha	12	S	Y	Y	Guam	Y	None
19		160	194	Camacho, Jose C	Son	M	Cha	7	S	Y		Guam		None
20		160	195	Benavente, Felipe C	Head	M	Cha	36	M	N	Y	Guam	Y	Farmer
21		160	195	Benavente, Josefa M	Wife	F	Cha	33	M	N	Y	Guam	N	None
22		160	195	Benavente, Ignacio M	Son	M	Cha	2.8	S	N		Guam		None
23		160	195	Benavente, Juan M	Son	M	Cha	1.8	S	N		Guam		None
24		160	195	Cruz, Elena G	Lodger	F	Cha	70	Wd	N	N	Guam	N	None
25		160	195	Camacho, Ana C	Cousin	F	Cha	50	S	N	N	Guam	N	None

DEPARTMENT OF COMMERCE-BUREAU OF THE CENSUS
WASHINGTON

FIFTEENTH CENSUS OF THE UNITED STATES: 1930-POPULATION

THE ISLAND OF GUAM

Sheet No. 20B

District Municipality of Agana
Name of Place Agana City (Part of San Antonio)
[Proper name and, also, name of class, as city, town, village, barrio, etc]

Enumeration District No. 2
Enumerated by me on April 16, 1930 Arthur W. Jackson
Enumerator

	Street, avenue, road, etc. (1)	Number of dwelling house in order of visitation (2)	Number of family in order of visitation (3)	NAME of each person whose place of abode on April 1, 1930, was in this family. Enter surname, first, then given name and middle initial. If any. Include every person living on April 1, 1930. Omit children born since April 1, 1930. (4)	RELATION Relationship of this Person to the head of the family. (5)	Sex (6)	Color or race (7)	Age at last birthday (8)	Single, married, widowed or divorced (9)	Attended school any time since Sept. 1, 1929 (10)	Whether able to read and write. (11)	NATIVITY Place of birth of this person. (12)	Whether able to speak English. (13)	OCCUPATION (14)
26	San Victores	161	196	Guerrero, Antonia R	Head	F	Cha	40	M	N	Y	Guam	N	None
27		161	196	Guerrero, Dolores R	Daughter	F	Cha	15	S	Y	Y	Guam	Y	None
28		161	196	Guerrero, Maria R	Daughter	F	Cha	13	S	Y	Y	Guam	Y	None
29		161	196	Guerrero, Concepcion R	Daughter	F	Cha	11	S	Y	Y	Guam	Y	None
30		161	196	Guerrero, Antonia R	Daughter	F	Cha	9	S	Y		Guam		None
31		161	196	Guerrero, Rosa R	Daughter	F	Cha	7	S	Y		Guam		None
32		161	196	Guerrero, Ana R	Daughter	F	Cha	6	S	N		Guam		None
33		161	196	Guerrero, Gregorio R	Son	M	Cha	1.8	S	N		Guam		None
34		162	197	Mafnas, Ana F	Head	F	Cha	67	M	N	N	Guam	N	None
35		162	197	Mafnas, Jesus F	Son	M	Cha	26	S	N	Y	Guam	Y	Farm laborer
36		162	197	Mafnas, Andres F	Son	M	Cha	14	S	N	Y	Guam	Y	None
37		163	198	Blas, Maria A	Head	F	Cha	48	S	Y	Y	Guam	N	Laundress
38		163	198	Blas, Jose A	Son	M	Cha	16	S	N	Y	Guam	Y	Servant
39		163	198	Blas, Ana A	Daughter	F	Cha	15	S	Y	Y	Guam	Y	None
40		163	198	Blas, Macarina A	Daughter	F	Cha	11	S	Y	Y	Guam	Y	None
41		163	198	Blas, Mercedes A	Daughter	F	Cha	9	S	Y		Guam		None
42		163	198	Blas, Carmen A	Daughter	F	Cha	2.8	S	N		Guam		None
43		164	199	Blas, Gregorio F	Head	M	Cha	50	M	Y	Y	Guam	Y	Farmer
44		164	199	Blas, Rosa R	Wife	F	Cha	39	M	N	Y	Guam	Y	None
45		164	199	Blas, Lagrimas R	Daughter	F	Cha	19	S	Y	Y	Guam	Y	None
46		164	199	Blas, Francsico R	Son	M	Cha	17	S	N	Y	Guam	Y	None
47		164	199	Blas, Josefa R	Daughter	F	Cha	15	S	N	Y	Guam	Y	None
48		164	199	Blas, Rosario R	Daughter	F	Cha	14	S	Y	Y	Guam	Y	None
49		164	199	Blas, Mariano R	Son	M	Cha	12	S	Y	Y	Guam	Y	None
50		164	199	Blas, Regina R	Daughter	F	Cha	11	S	Y	Y	Guam	Y	None

DEPARTMENT OF COMMERCE-BUREAU OF THE CENSUS
WASHINGTON

FIFTEENTH CENSUS OF THE UNITED STATES: 1930-POPULATION

THE ISLAND OF GUAM

Sheet No. 21A

District **Municipality of Agana**
Name of Place **Agana City (Part of San Antonio)**
[Proper name and, also, name of class, as city, town, village, barrio, etc]

Enumeration District No. 2
Enumerated by me on **April 17, 1930** Arthur W. Jackson, Enumerator

	PLACE OF ABODE			NAME	RELATION	PERSONAL DESCRIPTION				EDUCATION		NATIVITY		OCCUPATION
	Street, avenue, road, etc.	Number of dwelling house in order of visitation	Number of family in order of visitation	of each person whose place of abode on April 1, 1930, was in this family. Enter surname, first, then given name and middle initial. If any. Include every person living on April 1, 1930. Omit children born since April 1, 1930.	Relationship of this Person to the head of the family.	Sex	Color or race	Age at last birthday	Single, married, widowed or divorced	Attended school any time since Sept. 1, 1929	Whether able to read and write.	Place of birth of this person.	Whether able to speak English.	
	1	2	3	4	5	6	7	8	9	10	11	12	13	14
1	San Victores	164	199	Blas, Jesus R	Son	M	Cha	9	S	Y		Guam		None
2		164	199	Blas, Maria R	Daughter	F	Cha	7	S	Y		Guam		None
3		164	199	Blas, Rosalia R	Daughter	F	Cha	4	S	N		Guam		None
4		164	199	Blas, Antonio R	Son	M	Cha	2	S	N		Guam		None
5		164	199	Blas, Jose R	Son	M	Cha	1	S	N		Guam		None
6		165	200	Arceo, Francisco C	Head	M	Cha	27	M	N	Y	Guam	Y	Farmer
7		165	200	Arceo, Maria S	Wife	F	Cha	38	M	N	Y	Guam	Y	None
8		165	200	Arceo, Francisco S	Son	M	Cha	13	S	Y	Y	Guam	Y	None
9		165	200	Arceo, William S	Son	M	Cha	7	S	N		Guam		None
10		166	201	Aguajlo, Juan A	Head	M	Cha	30	M	N	Y	Guam	Y	Laborer
11		166	201	Aguajlo, Ana P	Wife	F	Cha	29	M	N	Y	Guam	N	None
12		167	202	Cruz, Maicala P	Head	F	Cha	57	S	N	Y	Guam	N	None
13		167	202	Cruz, Rosa C	Daughter	F	Cha	26	S	N	Y	Guam	Y	None
14		168	203	Camacho, Antonia B	Head	F	Cha	77	Wd	N	Y	Guam	N	None
15		168	203	Concepcion, Maria C	Grand daughter	F	Cha	19	S	N	Y	Guam	Y	None
16		168	203	Camacho, Jesus C	Grandson	M	Cha	16	S	N	Y	Guam	Y	None
17		169	204	Sablan, Asuncion B	Head	F	Cha	28	M	Y	Y	Guam	Y	None
18		169	204	Sablan, Harvey J	Son	M	Cha	11	S	Y	Y	Guam	Y	None
19		169	204	Sablan, Maria L	Daughter	F	Cha	10	S	Y	Y	Guam	Y	None
20		169	204	Sablan, Entropia E	Daughter	F	Cha	8	S	Y		Guam		None
21		169	204	Sablan, Pedro B	Son	M	Cha	4	S	N		Guam		None
22		169	204	Sablan, Asuncion G	Daughter	F	Cha	3	S	N		Guam		None
23		169	204	Sablan, Juan B	Son	M	Cha	1	S	N		Guam		None
24		169	204	Bamba, Francisco B	Brother	M	Cha	17	S	N	Y	Guam	Y	None
25		169	204	Bamba, Rosa B	Sister	F	Cha	34	S	N	Y	Guam	Y	Servant

(CHAMORRO ROOTS GENEALOGY PROJECT™ TRANSCRIPTION)
(BERNARD T. PUNZALAN / HTTP://WWW.CHAMORROROOTS.COM)

DEPARTMENT OF COMMERCE-BUREAU OF THE CENSUS
WASHINGTON

FIFTEENTH CENSUS OF THE UNITED STATES: 1930-POPULATION

THE ISLAND OF GUAM

Sheet No. 21B

56B

District **Municipality of Agana**
Name of Place **Agana City (Part of San Antonio)**
[Proper name and, also, name of class, as city, town, village, barrio, etc]

Enumeration District No. 2
Enumerated by me on **April 17, 1930** Arthur W. Jackson, Enumerator

	PLACE OF ABODE			NAME	RELATION	PERSONAL DESCRIPTION				EDUCATION		NATIVITY		OCCUPATION
	Street, avenue, road, etc.	Number of dwelling house in order of visitation	Number of family in order of visitation	of each person whose place of abode on April 1, 1930, was in this family. Enter surname, first, then given name and middle initial. If any. Include every person living on April 1, 1930. Omit children born since April 1, 1930.	Relationship of this Person to the head of the family.	Sex	Color or race	Age at last birthday	Single, married, widowed or divorced	Attended school any time since Sept. 1, 1929	Whether able to read and write.	Place of birth of this person.	Whether able to speak English.	
	1	2	3	4	5	6	7	8	9	10	11	12	13	14
26	San Victores	169	204	Bamba, Rosemary	Niece	F	Cha	8	S	Y		Guam		None
27		170	205	Duenas, Dolores C	Head	F	Cha	48	Wd	N	Y	Guam	N	None
28		170	205	Duenas, Maria C	Daughter	F	Cha	18	S	N	Y	Guam	Y	None
29		170	205	Duenas, Antonio C	Son	M	Cha	17	S	N	Y	Guam	Y	None
30		170	205	Duenas, Rosalia C	Daughter	F	Cha	13	S	Y	Y	Guam	Y	None
31		170	205	Duenas, Ana C	Daughter	F	Cha	6	S	N		Guam		None
32		171	206	Mendiola, Jose G	Head	M	Cha	50	M	N	Y	Guam	N	Farmer
33		171	206	Mendiola, Maria S	Wife	F	Cha	51	M	N	Y	Guam	N	None
34		171	206	Mendiola, Concepcion S	Daughter	F	Cha	16	S	N	Y	Guam	Y	None
35		171	206	Mendiola, Ignacio S	Son	M	Cha	13	S	Y	Y	Guam	Y	None
36		172	207	Salas, Ana D	Head	F	Cha	57	S	N	Y	Guam	N	None
37		172	207	Salas, Regina S	Daughter	F	Cha	19	S	N	Y	Guam	Y	None
38		173	208	Iriarte, Juan C	Head	M	Cha	54	M	N	Y	Guam	N	Farmer
39		173	208	Iriarte, Feliciana R	Wife	F	Cha	46	M	N	Y	Guam	N	None
40		173	208	Iriarte, Joaquin R	Son	M	Cha	20	S	N	Y	Guam	Y	None
41		173	208	Iriarte, Margarita R	Daughter	F	Cha	18	S	Y	Y	Guam	Y	None
42		173	208	Iriarte, Jesus R	Son	M	Cha	16	S	N	Y	Guam	Y	None
43		173	208	Iriarte, Maria R	Daughter	F	Cha	15	S	N	Y	Guam	Y	None
44		173	208	Iriarte, Ana R	Daughter	F	Cha	13	S	Y	Y	Guam	Y	None
45		173	208	Iriarte, Geronimo R	Son	M	Cha	11	S	Y	Y	Guam	Y	None
46		173	208	Iriarte, Isabel R	Daughter	F	Cha	9	S	Y		Guam		None
47		173	209	Guerrero, Pedro B	Head	M	Cha	23	M	N	Y	Guam	Y	Laborer
48		173	209	Guerrero, Francisca O	Wife	F	Cha	23	M	N	Y	Guam	Y	None
49		174	210	San Nicolas, Antonio G	Head	M	Cha	28	M	N	Y	Guam	Y	Farmer
50		174	210	San Nicolas, Joaquina C	Wife	F	Cha	20	M	N	Y	Guam	Y	None

DEPARTMENT OF COMMERCE-BUREAU OF THE CENSUS
WASHINGTON

FIFTEENTH CENSUS OF THE UNITED STATES: 1930-POPULATION

THE ISLAND OF GUAM

Sheet No. 22A

District **Municipality of Agana**
Name of Place **Agana City (Part of San Antonio)**
[Proper name and, also, name of class, as city, town, village, barrio, etc]

Enumeration District No. **2**
Enumerated by me on **April 17, 1930** Arthur W. Jackson, Enumerator

	PLACE OF ABODE			NAME	RELATION	PERSONAL DESCRIPTION				EDUCATION		NATIVITY		OCCUPATION
	Street, avenue, road, etc.	Number of dwelling house in order of visitation	Number of family in order of visitation	of each person whose place of abode on April 1, 1930, was in this family. Enter surname, first, then given name and middle initial. If any. Include every person living on April 1, 1930. Omit children born since April 1, 1930.	Relationship of this Person to the head of the family.	Sex	Color or race	Age at last birthday	Single, married, widowed or divorced	Attended school any time since Sept. 1, 1929	Whether able to read and write.	Place of birth of this person.	Whether able to speak English.	
	1	2	3	4	5	6	7	8	9	10	11	12	13	14
1	San Victores	174	210	San Nicolas, Elias C	Son	M	Cha	2.3	S	N		Guam		None
2		174	210	San Nicolas, Victoria C	Daughter	F	Cha	.3	S	N		Guam		None
3		174	211	San Nicolas, Juan S	Head	M	Cha	30	M	N	Y	Guam	Y	Laborer
4		174	211	San Nicolas, Rosa D	Wife	F	Cha	27	M	N	Y	Guam	N	None
5		174	211	San Nicolas, Maria D	Daughter	F	Cha	8	S	Y		Guam		None
6		174	211	San Nicolas, Rosario D	Daughter	F	Cha	5	S	N		Guam		None
7		174	211	San Nicolas, Pedro D	Son	M	Cha	4.5	S	N		Guam		None
8		174	211	San Nicolas, Herman D	Son	M	Cha	3.6	S	N		Guam		None
9		175	212	Quichocho, Jose Q	Head	M	Cha	32	M	N	Y	Guam	Y	Farmer
10		175	212	Quichocho, Josefa G	Wife	F	Cha	33	M	N	Y	Guam	N	None
11		175	212	Quichocho, Lourdes G	Daughter	F	Cha	12	S	Y	Y	Guam	Y	None
12		175	212	Quichocho, Jose G	Son	M	Cha	10	S	Y	Y	Guam	Y	None
13		175	212	Quichocho, Rosa G	Daughter	F	Cha	8	S	Y		Guam		None
14		176	213	Rivera, Maria SN	Head	F	Cha	42	Wd	N	N	Guam	Y	None
15		176	213	Rivera, Maria SN	Daughter	F	Cha	18	S	N	Y	Guam	Y	None
16		176	213	Rivera, Ignacio SN	Son	M	Cha	17	S	Y	Y	Guam	Y	None
17		176	213	Rivera, Miguel SN	Son	M	Cha	11	S	Y	Y	Guam	Y	None
18		176	213	Rivera, Jose SN	Son	M	Cha	10	S	Y	Y	Guam	Y	None
19		176	213	Rivera, Catalina SN	Daughter	F	Cha	7	S	Y		Guam		None
20		176	213	Yamasaki, Vicenta T	Servant	F	Jap	10	S	Y	Y	Guam	Y	Servant
21		177	214	Pangelinan, Guido B	Head	M	Cha	27	M	N	Y	Guam	Y	Carpenter
22		177	214	Pangelinan, Catalina C	Wife	F	Cha	24	M	N	Y	Guam	Y	None
23		177	214	Castro, Rosa LG	Mother-in-law	F	Cha	54	Wd	N	Y	Guam	N	None
24		177	214	San Nicolas, Benita	Lodger	F	Cha	66	S	N	Y	Guam	N	None
25		178	215	Gomabon, Jose N	Head	M	Cha	25	M	N	Y	Guam	Y	Barber

(CHAMORRO ROOTS GENEALOGY PROJECT™ TRANSCRIPTION)
(BERNARD T. PUNZALAN / HTTP://WWW.CHAMORROROOTS.COM)

DEPARTMENT OF COMMERCE-BUREAU OF THE CENSUS
WASHINGTON

FIFTEENTH CENSUS OF THE UNITED STATES: 1930-POPULATION

THE ISLAND OF GUAM

Sheet No. 22B

57B

District **Municipality of Agana**
Name of Place **Agana City (Part of San Antonio)**
[Proper name and, also, name of class, as city, town, village, barrio, etc]

Enumeration District No. **2**
Enumerated by me on **April 19, 1930** Arthur W. Jackson, Enumerator

	PLACE OF ABODE			NAME	RELATION	PERSONAL DESCRIPTION				EDUCATION		NATIVITY		OCCUPATION
	Street, avenue, road, etc.	Number of dwelling house in order of visitation	Number of family in order of visitation	of each person whose place of abode on April 1, 1930, was in this family. Enter surname, first, then given name and middle initial. If any. Include every person living on April 1, 1930. Omit children born since April 1, 1930.	Relationship of this Person to the head of the family.	Sex	Color or race	Age at last birthday	Single, married, widowed or divorced	Attended school any time since Sept. 1, 1929	Whether able to read and write.	Place of birth of this person.	Whether able to speak English.	
	1	2	3	4	5	6	7	8	9	10	11	12	13	14
26	San Victores	178	215	Gomabon, Ana B	Wife	F	Cha	27	M	N	Y	Guam	Y	None
27		178	215	Gomabon, Jose B	Son	M	Cha	4.3	S	N		Guam		None
28		178	215	Gomabon, Jesus B	Son	M	Cha	2.8	S	N		Guam		None
29		178	215	Gomabon, Juan B	Son	M	Cha	.8	S	N		Guam		None
30		178	215	Meno, Maria B	Sister-in-law	F	Cha	13	S	Y	Y	Guam	Y	None
31		178	216	Hernandez, Manuel P	Head	M	Cha	26	M	N	Y	Guam	Y	Chauffeur
32		178	216	Hernandez, Rosa B	Wife	F	Cha	19	M	N	Y	Guam	Y	None
33		178	216	Hernandez, Felix B	Son	M	Cha	2.3	S	N		Guam		None
34		178	216	Hernandez, Catalina B	Daughter	F	Cha	1.5	S	N		Guam		None
35		179	217	Sholing, Rita P	Head	F	Cha	40	Wd	N	Y	Guam	Y	Seamstress
36		179	217	Sholing, Juan P	Son	M	Chin	19	S	N	Y	Guam	Y	Farmer
37		179	217	Sholing, Magdalena P	Daughter	F	Chin	18	S	N	Y	Guam	Y	None
38		180	218	Untalan, Rosalia M	Head	F	Cha	24	M	N	Y	Guam	Y	None
39		180	218	Untalan, Roque M	Son	M	Cha	.6	S	N		Guam		None
40		181	219	Tenorio, Antonio P	Head	M	Cha	47	M	N	Y	Guam	N	Farmer
41		181	219	Tenorio, Dolores T	Wife	F	Cha	46	M	Y	Y	Guam	N	None
42		181	219	Tenorio, Maria T	Daughter	F	Cha	16	S	Y	Y	Guam	Y	None
43		181	219	Tenorio, Jesus T	Son	M	Cha	13	S	Y	Y	Guam	Y	None
44		181	219	Tenorio, Concepcion T	Daughter	F	Cha	11	S	Y	Y	Guam	Y	None
45		181	219	Tenorio, Catalina T	Daughter	F	Jap	8	S	Y		Guam		None
46		181	219	Tenorio, Dolores T	Daughter	F	Cha	5	S	N		Guam		None
47		182	220	Blaz, Juan A	Head	M	Cha	34	M	N	Y	Guam	N	Farmer
48		182	220	Blaz, Isabel G	Wife	F	Cha	39	M	N	Y	Guam	N	None
49		182	220	Blaz, Maria G	Daughter	F	Cha	9	S	Y		Guam		None
50		182	220	Blaz, Esperanza G	Daughter	F	Cha	7	S	Y		Guam		None

DEPARTMENT OF COMMERCE-BUREAU OF THE CENSUS
WASHINGTON

FIFTEENTH CENSUS OF THE UNITED STATES: 1930-POPULATION

THE ISLAND OF GUAM

Sheet No. 23A

District Municipality of Agana
Name of Place Agana City (Part of San Antonio)
[Proper name and, also, name of class, as city, town, village, barrio, etc]

Enumeration District No. 2
Enumerated by me on April 19, 1930 Arthur W. Jackson, Enumerator

	PLACE OF ABODE			NAME	RELATION	PERSONAL DESCRIPTION				EDUCATION		NATIVITY		OCCUPATION
	Street, avenue, road, etc.	Number of dwelling house is order of visitation	Number of family in order of visitation	of each person whose place of abode on April 1, 1930, was in this family. Enter surname, first, then given name and middle initial. If any. Include every person living on April 1, 1930. Omit children born since April 1, 1930.	Relationship of this Person to the head of the family.	Sex	Color or race	Age at last birthday	Single, married, widowed or divorced	Attended school any time since Sept. 1, 1929	Whether able to read and write.	Place of birth of this person.	Whether able to speak English.	
	1	2	3	4	5	6	7	8	9	10	11	12	13	14
1	San Victores	182	220	Blaz, Lourdes G	Daughter	F	Cha	5	S	N		Guam		None
2		182	220	Blaz, Isabel G	Daughter	F	Cha	4.8	S	N		Guam		None
3		182	220	Blaz, Juan G	Son	M	Cha	11	S	Y	Y	Guam	N	None
4		183	220	Lizama, Felisa M	Head	F	Cha	57	S	N	N	Guam	N	None
5		183	220	Lizama, Rosa A	Daughter	F	Cha	23	S	N	Y	Guam	Y	Servant
6		183	220	Lizama, Francisco L	Grandson	M	Cha	4.8	S	N		Guam		None
7		183	220	Lizama, Victoria L	Granddaug	F	Cha	1.5	S	N		Guam		None
8		183	220	Sy-Pingco, Virginia L	Lodger	F	Cha	8	S	Y		Guam		None
9		183	220	Sy-Pingco, Julia L	Lodger	F	Cha	2.3	S	N		Guam		None
10		184	222	Baza, Vicente U	Head	M	Cha	42	M	N	Y	Guam	Y	Carpenter
11		184	222	Baza, Maria SA	Wife	F	Cha	33	M	N	Y	Guam	N	None
12		184	222	Baza, Dolores SA	Daughter	F	Cha	8	S	Y		Guam		None
13		184	222	Baza, Maria SA	Daughter	F	Cha	7	S	N		Guam		None
14		184	222	Baza, Magdalena SA	Daughter	F	Cha	5	S	N		Guam		None
15		184	222	Baza, Francisca SA	Daughter	F	Cha	3.7	S	N		Guam		None
16		184	222	Baza, Juan SA	Son	M	Cha	1.8	S	N		Guam		None
17		184	222	Baza, Julia SA	Daughter	F	Cha	.2	S	N		Guam		None
18		185	223	Cruz, Dominga P	Head	F	Cha	59	Wd	N	N	Guam	N	None
19		185	223	Cruz, Jesus P	Son	M	Cha	23	S	N	Y	Guam	Y	Farmer
20		185	223	Cruz, Enrique P	Son	M	Cha	24	S	N	Y	Guam	Y	Farm laborer
21		185	223	Cruz, Francisco P	Son	M	Cha	16	S	N	Y	Guam	Y	Farm laborer
22		186	224	Reyes, Mariano R	Head	M	Cha	57	M	N	Y	Guam	N	Farmer
23		186	224	Reyes, Nicolasa SA	Wife	F	Cha	43	M	N	Y	Guam	N	None
24		186	224	Reyes, Jose SA	Son	M	Cha	23	S	N	Y	Guam	Y	Servant
25		186	224	Reyes, Joaquin SA	Son	M	Cha	21	S	N	Y	Guam	Y	Farm laborer

DEPARTMENT OF COMMERCE-BUREAU OF THE CENSUS
WASHINGTON

FIFTEENTH CENSUS OF THE UNITED STATES: 1930-POPULATION

THE ISLAND OF GUAM

Sheet No. 23B

District **Municipality of Agana**
Name of Place **Agana City (Part of San Antonio)**
[Proper name and, also, name of class, as city, town, village, barrio, etc]

Enumeration District No. 2
Enumerated by me on **April 19, 1930** Arthur W. Jackson, Enumerator

	PLACE OF ABODE: Street, avenue, road, etc.	Number of dwelling house is order of visitation	Number of family in order of visitation	NAME of each person whose place of abode on April 1, 1930, was in this family. Enter surname, first, then given name and middle initial. If any. Include every person living on April 1, 1930. Omit children born since April 1, 1930.	RELATION Relationship of this Person to the head of the family.	PERSONAL DESCRIPTION: Sex	Color or race	Age at last birthday	Single, married, widowed or divorced	EDUCATION: Attended school any time since Sept. 1, 1929	Whether able to read and write.	NATIVITY Place of birth of this person.	Whether able to speak English.	OCCUPATION
	1	2	3	4	5	6	7	8	9	10	11	12	13	14
26	San Victores	186	224	Reyes, Ana SA	Daughter	F	Cha	18	S	N	Y	Guam	Y	None
27		186	224	Reyes, Consuelo SA	Daughter	F	Cha	8	S	Y		Guam		None
28		186	224	Reyes, Juan SA	Son	M	Cha	4.1	S	N		Guam		None
29		187	225	Asuncion, Manuel B	Head	M	Cha	70	M	N	Y	Guam	N	None
30		187	225	Asuncion, Apolonia R	Wife	F	Cha	68	M	N	N	Guam	N	None
31		187	225	Asuncion, Natividad R	Daughter	F	Cha	40	S	N	N	Guam	N	None
32		188	226	Leon Guerrero, Francisco B	Head	M	Cha	33	M	N	Y	Guam	Y	Clerk
33		188	226	Leon Guerrero, Maria C	Wife	F	Cha	34	M	N	Y	Guam	Y	None
34		188	226	Leon Guerrero, Emelia C	Daughter	F	Cha	13	S	Y	Y	Guam	Y	None
35		188	226	Leon Guerrero, Enrique C	Son	M	Cha	12	S	Y	Y	Guam	Y	None
36		188	226	Leon Guerrero, Victoria C	Daughter	F	Cha	10	S	Y	Y	Guam	Y	None
37		188	226	Leon Guerrero, Lorenzo C	Son	M	Cha	9	S	Y		Guam		None
38		188	226	Leon Guerrero, Gloria C	Daughter	F	Cha	8	S	Y		Guam		None
39		188	226	Leon Guerrero, Vicente C	Son	M	Cha	4.5	S	N		Guam		None
40		188	226	Leon Guerrero, Ramon C	Son	M	Cha	2.8	S	N		Guam		None
41		189	227	Ulloa, Marcelo U	Head	M	Cha	40	M	N	Y	Guam	Y	Carpenter
42		189	227	Ulloa, Julia A	Wife	F	Cha	36	M	N	Y	Guam	N	None
43		189	227	Ulloa, Maria A	Daughter	F	Cha	15	S	N	Y	Guam	Y	None
44		189	227	Ulloa, Rosalia A	Daughter	F	Cha	13	S	Y	Y	Guam	Y	None
45		189	227	Ulloa, Carmen A	Daughter	F	Cha	8	S	Y		Guam		None
46		189	227	Ulloa, Ignacio A	Son	M	Cha	5	S	N		Guam		None
47		189	227	Ulloa, Jesus A	Son	M	Cha	2.8	S	N		Guam		None
48		189	227	Ulloa, Josefina A	Daughter	F	Cha	1.8	S	N		Guam		None
49		189	227	Ulloa, Tomas A	Son	M	Cha	.3	S	N		Guam		None
50		190	228	Blaz, Luis A	Head	M	Cha	36	M	N	Y	Guam	Y	Farmer

(CHAMORRO ROOTS GENEALOGY PROJECT™ TRANSCRIPTION)
(BERNARD T. PUNZALAN / HTTP://WWW.CHAMORROROOTS.COM)

DEPARTMENT OF COMMERCE-BUREAU OF THE CENSUS
WASHINGTON

FIFTEENTH CENSUS OF THE UNITED STATES: 1930-POPULATION

THE ISLAND OF GUAM

Sheet No. 24A

59

District Municipality of Agana
Name of Place Agana City (Part of San Antonio)
[Proper name and, also, name of class, as city, town, village, barrio, etc]

Enumeration District No. 2
Enumerated by me on April 21, 1930 Arthur W. Jackson
Enumerator

	PLACE OF ABODE			NAME	RELATION	PERSONAL DESCRIPTION				EDUCATION		NATIVITY		OCCUPATION
	Street, avenue, road, etc.	Number of dwelling house is order of visitation	Number of family in order of visitation	of each person whose place of abode on April 1, 1930, was in this family. Enter surname, first, then given name and middle initial. If any. Include every person living on April 1, 1930. Omit children born since April 1, 1930.	Relationship of this Person to the head of the family.	Sex	Color or race	Age at last birthday	Single, married, widowed or divorced	Attended school any time since Sept. 1, 1929	Whether able to read and write.	Place of birth of this person.	Whether able to speak English.	
	1	2	3	4	5	6	7	8	9	10	11	12	13	14
1	San Victores	190	228	Blaz, Francisca S	Wife	F	Cha	32	M	N	Y	Guam	Y	Midwife
2		190	228	Blaz, Catalina S	Daughter	F	Cha	12	S	Y	Y	Guam	Y	None
3		190	228	Blaz, Jesusa S	Daughter	F	Cha	9	S	Y		Guam		None
4		190	228	Blaz, Dolores S	Daughter	F	Cha	7	S	Y		Guam		None
5		190	228	Blaz, Francisco S	Son	M	Cha	5	S	N		Guam		None
6		190	228	Blaz, Rosa S	Daughter	F	Cha	4.8	S	N		Guam		None
7		190	228	Blaz, Rosalia S	Daughter	F	Cha	2.5	S	N		Guam		None
8		190	228	Blaz, Vicente S	Son	M	Cha	.5	S	N		Guam		None
9		191	229	Blaz, Vicente F	Head	M	Cha	62	M	N	Y	Guam	N	Farmer
10		191	229	Blaz, Ignacia A	Wife	F	Cha	57	M	N	Y	Guam	N	None
11		191	229	Blaz, Josefa A	Daughter	F	Cha	33	S	N	Y	Guam	N	None
12		191	229	Blaz, Ana A	Daughter	F	Cha	25	S	N	Y	Guam	Y	None
13		191	229	Blaz, Joaquin A	Son	M	Cha	21	S	N	Y	Guam	Y	Farm laborer
14		191	229	Blaz, Rosa A	Daughter	F	Cha	18	S	N	Y	Guam	Y	None
15		191	229	Blaz, Maria A	Daughter	F	Cha	1.8	S	N		Guam		None
16		192	230	Blaz, Jose F	Head	M	Cha	29	M	N	Y	Guam	Y	Farmer
17		192	230	Blaz, Dolores S	Wife	F	Cha	24	M	N	Y	Guam	Y	None
18		192	230	Blaz, Ignacia S	Daughter	F	Cha	3.9	S	N		Guam		None
19		192	230	Blaz, Francisco S	Son	M	Cha	2.5	S	N		Guam		None
20		192	230	Blaz, Jesus S	Son	M	Cha	1.8	S	N		Guam		None
21		192	230	Blaz, Pedro S	Son	M	Cha	.5	S	N		Guam		None
22		192	231	Pangelinan, Antonio U	Head	M	Cha	39	S	N	Y	Guam	Y	Farmer
23		192	231	Pangelinan, Vicente U	Brother	M	Cha	19	S	N	Y	Guam	Y	Farm laborer
24		193	232	Leon Guerrero, Joaquin P	Head	M	Cha	46	M	N	Y	Guam		farmer
25		193	232	Leon Guerrero, Vicenta C	Wife	F	Cha	36	M	N	Y	Guam		None

(CHAMORRO ROOTS GENEALOGY PROJECT™ TRANSCRIPTION)
(BERNARD T. PUNZALAN / HTTP://WWW.CHAMORROROOTS.COM)

DEPARTMENT OF COMMERCE-BUREAU OF THE CENSUS
WASHINGTON

FIFTEENTH CENSUS OF THE UNITED STATES: 1930-POPULATION

THE ISLAND OF GUAM

Sheet No. 24B

59B

District Municipality of Agana
Name of Place Agana City (Part of San Antonio)
[Proper name and, also, name of class, as city, town, village, barrio, etc]

Enumeration District No. 2
Enumerated by me on April 21, 1930 Arthur W. Jackson
Enumerator

	PLACE OF ABODE			NAME	RELATION	PERSONAL DESCRIPTION				EDUCATION		NATIVITY		OCCUPATION
	Street, avenue, road, etc.	Number of dwelling house is order of visitation	Number of family in order of visitation	of each person whose place of abode on April 1, 1930, was in this family. Enter surname, first, then given name and middle initial. If any. Include every person living on April 1, 1930. Omit children born since April 1, 1930.	Relationship of this Person to the head of the family.	Sex	Color or race	Age at last birthday	Single, married, widowed or divorced	Attended school any time since Sept. 1, 1929	Whether able to read and write.	Place of birth of this person.	Whether able to speak English.	
	1	2	3	4	5	6	7	8	9	10	11	12	13	14
26	San Victores	193	232	Leon Guerrero, Vicente C	Son	M	Cha	18	S	N	Y	Guam	Y	Laborer
27		193	232	Leon Guerrero, Ana C	Daughter	F	Cha	16	S	N	Y	Guam	Y	None
28		193	232	Leon Guerrero, Rosario C	Daughter	F	Cha	14	S	Y	Y	Guam	Y	None
29		193	232	Leon Guerrero, Maria C	Daughter	F	Cha	13	S	Y	Y	Guam		None
30		193	232	Leon Guerrero, Manuel C	Son	M	Cha	5	S	N		Guam		None
31		193	232	Leon Guerrero, Trinidad C	Daughter	F	Cha	3.5	S	N		Guam		None
32		193	232	Leon Guerrero, Barsalisa C	Daughter	F	Cha	.1	S	N		Guam		None
33		194	233	Leon Guerrero, Vicente P	Head	M	Cha	43	Wd	N	Y	Guam	N	Farmer
34		194	233	Leon Guerrero, Maria S	Daughter	F	Cha	17	S	N	Y	Guam	Y	None
35		194	233	Leon Guerrero, Juan S	Son	M	Cha	15	S	N	Y	Guam	Y	None
36		194	233	Leon Guerrero, Francisco S	Son	M	Cha	11	S	Y	Y	Guam	Y	None
37		194	233	Leon Guerrero, Joaquina S	Daughter	F	Cha	10	S	Y	Y	Guam	Y	None
38		194	233	Leon Guerrero, Jose S	Son	M	Cha	8	S	Y		Guam		None
39		194	233	Leon Guerrero, Florencia S	Daughter	F	Cha	3.8	S	N		Guam		None
40		194	233	Leon Guerrero, Ana P	Mother	F	Cha	68	Wd	N	N	Guam	N	None
41		195	234	Borja, Jesus T	Head	M	Cha	47	M	N	Y	Guam	Y	Blacksmith
42		195	234	Borja, Emeliana S	Wife	F	Cha	40	M	N	Y	Guam	Y	None
43		195	234	Borja, Jose L	Son	M	Cha	20	S	N	Y	Guam	Y	Printer
44		195	234	Borja, Grabela L	Daughter	F	Cha	19	S	N	Y	Guam	N	None
45		196	235	Cruz, Felipe D	Head	M	Cha	22	M	N	Y	Guam	Y	Chauffeur
46		196	235	Cruz, Dolores M	Wife	F	Cha	19	M	N	Y	Guam	Y	None
47		196	235	Cruz, Nieves M	Daughter	F	Cha	.4	S	N		Guam		None
48		196	235	Leon Guerrero, Maria P	Cousin	F	Cha	10	S	Y	Y	Guam	Y	None
49		197	236	Leon Guerrero, Jose P	Head	M	Cha	42	M	N	Y	Guam	Y	Laborer
50		197	236	Leon Guerrero, Juana C	Wife	F	Cha	42	M	N	Y	Guam	N	None

DEPARTMENT OF COMMERCE-BUREAU OF THE CENSUS
WASHINGTON

FIFTEENTH CENSUS OF THE UNITED STATES: 1930-POPULATION

THE ISLAND OF GUAM

Sheet No. 25A

District Municipality of Agana

Name of Place Agana City (Part of San Antonio)
[Proper name and, also, name of class, as city, town, village, barrio, etc]

Enumeration District No. 2

Enumerated by me on April 21, 1930 Arthur W. Jackson, Enumerator

	PLACE OF ABODE: Street, avenue, road, etc.	Number of dwelling house in order of visitation	Number of family in order of visitation	NAME of each person whose place of abode on April 1, 1930, was in this family. Enter surname, first, then given name and middle initial. If any. Include every person living on April 1, 1930. Omit children born since April 1, 1930.	RELATION Relationship of this Person to the head of the family.	PERSONAL DESCRIPTION: Sex	Color or race	Age at last birthday	Single, married, widowed or divorced	EDUCATION: Attended school any time since Sept. 1, 1929	Whether able to read and write.	NATIVITY Place of birth of this person.	Whether able to speak English.	OCCUPATION
	1	2	3	4	5	6	7	8	9	10	11	12	13	14
1	San Victores	197	236	Leon Guerrero, Jose C	Son	M	Cha	15	S	N	Y	Guam	Y	None
2		197	236	Leon Guerrero, Ana C	Daughter	F	Cha	13	S	N	Y	Guam	Y	None
3		197	236	Blas, Jesus C	Step-son	M	Cha	6	S	N		Guam		None
4		198	237	Blanco, Felipe P	Head	M	Cha	39	M	N	Y	Guam	Y	USN Reserve
5		198	237	Blanco, Joaquina F	Wife	F	Cha	38	M	N	Y	Guam	Y	None
6		198	237	Blanco, Delfina F	Daughter	F	Cha	13	S	Y	Y	Guam	Y	None
7		198	237	Blanco, Vicente F	Son	M	Cha	9	S	Y		Guam		None
8		199	238	Acosta, Joaquin C	Head	M	Cha	52	Wd	N	N	Guam	N	Farmer
9		199	238	Acosta, Isabel A	Daughter	F	Cha	17	S	N	Y	Guam	Y	None
10		199	239	Benavente, Juan C	Head	M	Cha	39	M	N	Y	Guam	Y	Farmer
11		199	239	Benavente, Maria A	Wife	F	Cha	25	M	N	Y	Guam	Y	None
12		199	239	Benavente, Eugenio A	Son	M	Cha	4.7	S	N		Guam		None
13		199	239	Benavente, Antonio A	Son	M	Cha	3.3	S	N		Guam		None
14		199	239	Benavente, Juan A	Son	M	Cha	.3	S	N		Guam		None
15		200	240	Toves, Manuela T	Head	F	Cha	54	S	N	Y	Guam	N	None
16		200	240	Toves, Jesus T	Son	M	Cha	22	S	N	Y	Guam	Y	Laborer
17		200	240	Toves, Pedro T	Son	M	Cha	20	S	N	Y	Guam	Y	Machinist
18		200	240	Garrido, Luis P	Head	M	Cha	29	M	N	Y	Guam	Y	Cable operator
19		200	240	Garrido, Maria T	Wife	F	Cha	28	M	N	Y	Guam	Y	School teacher
20		200	240	Garrido, Louise M	Daughter	F	Cha	6	S	N		Guam		None
21		200	240	Garrido, Lila P	Daughter	F	Cha	4.3	S	N		Guam		None
22		200	240	Garrido, Luis P	Son	M	Cha	1.3	S	N		Guam		None
23		200	240	Garrido, Raymond F	Son	M	Cha	.4	S	N		Guam		None
24		201	242	Morcilla, Vicente C	Head	M	Cha	46	Wd	N	Y	Guam	N	None
25		201	242	Diaz, Filomino C	Son	M	Cha	31	S	N	Y	Guam	Y	Carpenter

(CHAMORRO ROOTS GENEALOGY PROJECT™ TRANSCRIPTION)
(BERNARD T. PUNZALAN / HTTP://WWW.CHAMORROROOTS.COM)

DEPARTMENT OF COMMERCE-BUREAU OF THE CENSUS
WASHINGTON

FIFTEENTH CENSUS OF THE UNITED STATES: 1930-POPULATION

THE ISLAND OF GUAM

Sheet No. 25B

60B

District **Municipality of Agana**
Name of Place **Agana City (Part of San Antonio)**
[Proper name and, also, name of class, as city, town, village, barrio, etc]

Enumeration District No. 2
Enumerated by me on **April 22, 1930** Arthur W. Jackson
Enumerator

	PLACE OF ABODE			NAME	RELATION	PERSONAL DESCRIPTION				EDUCATION		NATIVITY		OCCUPATION
	Street, avenue, road, etc.	Number of dwelling house is order of visitation	Number of family in order of visitation	of each person whose place of abode on April 1, 1930, was in this family. Enter surname, first, then given name and middle initial. If any. Include every person living on April 1, 1930. Omit children born since April 1, 1930.	Relationship of this Person to the head of the family.	Sex	Color or race	Age at last birthday	Single, married, widowed or divorced	Attended school any time since Sept. 1, 1929	Whether able to read and write.	Place of birth of this person.	Whether able to speak English.	
	1	2	3	4	5	6	7	8	9	10	11	12	13	14
26	San Victores	202	243	Toves, Nicolas C	Head	M	Cha	23	M	N	Y	Guam	Y	Laborer
27		202	243	Toves, Maria B	Wife	F	Cha	21	M	N	Y	Guam	Y	None
28		202	243	Toves, Maria C	Daughter	F	Cha	1.8	S	N		Guam		None
29		203	244	Sablan, Vicente R	Head	M	Cha	62	M	N	Y	Guam	N	Carpenter
30		203	244	Sablan, Ana G	Wife	F	Cha	43	M	N	Y	Guam	N	None
31	Luchana	204	245	Acosta, Joaquin D	Head	M	Cha	24	M	N	Y	Guam	Y	Laborer
32		204	245	Acosta, Maria P	Wife	F	Cha	37	M	N	Y	Guam	Y	None
33		204	245	Aguigui, Luis P	Step-son	M	Cha	14	S	N	Y	Guam	Y	None
34		204	245	Aguigui, Ana P	Step-daug	F	Cha	8	S	N		Guam		None
35		205	246	Toves, Pedro T	Head	M	Cha	46	M	N	Y	Guam	Y	Laborer
36		205	246	Toves, Dolores S	Wife	F	Cha	42	M	N	Y	Guam	N	None
37		205	246	Toves, Agustin S	Son	M	Cha	19	S	N	Y	Guam	Y	None
38		205	246	Toves, Jose S	Son	M	Cha	13	S	Y	Y	Guam	Y	None
39		205	246	Toves, Jesus S	Son	M	Cha	9	S	Y		Guam		None
40		205	246	Toves, Maria S	Daughter	F	Cha	8	S	Y		Guam		None
41		205	246	Toves, Ursula S	Daughter	F	Cha	7	S	Y		Guam		None
42		205	246	Toves, Francisca S	Daughter	F	Cha	4.8	S	N		Guam		None
43		205	246	Toves, Tomas S	Son	M	Cha	2.5	S	N		Guam		None
44		206	247	Castro, Francisco R	Head	F	Cha	35	M	N	Y	Guam	N	Farmer
45		206	247	Castro, Ana LG	Wife	F	Cha	30	M	N	Y	Guam	N	None
46		206	247	Castro, Tomas LG	Son	M	Cha	15	S	N	Y	Guam	Y	None
47		206	247	Castro, Engracia LG	Daughter	F	Cha	12	S	Y	Y	Guam	Y	None
48		206	247	Castro, Gregorio LG	Son	M	Cha	10	S	Y	Y	Guam	Y	None
49		206	247	Castro, Maria LG	Daughter	F	Cha	7	S	Y		Guam		None
50		206	247	Castro, Lourdes LG	Daughter	F	Cha	5	S	Y		Guam		None

(CHAMORRO ROOTS GENEALOGY PROJECT™ TRANSCRIPTION)
(BERNARD T. PUNZALAN / HTTP://WWW.CHAMORROROOTS.COM)

DEPARTMENT OF COMMERCE-BUREAU OF THE CENSUS
WASHINGTON

FIFTEENTH CENSUS OF THE UNITED STATES: 1930-POPULATION

THE ISLAND OF GUAM

Sheet No. 26A

District **Municipality of Agana**
Name of Place **Agana City (Part of San Antonio)**
[Proper name and, also, name of class, as city, town, village, barrio, etc]

Enumeration District No. 2
Enumerated by me on **April 22, 1930** Arthur W. Jackson, Enumerator

	PLACE OF ABODE			NAME	RELATION	PERSONAL DESCRIPTION				EDUCATION		NATIVITY		OCCUPATION
	Street, avenue, road, etc.	Number of dwelling house is order of visitation	Number of family in order of visitation	of each person whose place of abode on April 1, 1930, was in this family. Enter surname, first, then given name and middle initial. If any. Include every person living on April 1, 1930. Omit children born since April 1, 1930.	Relationship of this Person to the head of the family.	Sex	Color or race	Age at last birthday	Single, married, widowed or divorced	Attended school any time since Sept. 1, 1929	Whether able to read and write.	Place of birth of this person.	Whether able to speak English.	
	1	2	3	4	5	6	7	8	9	10	11	12	13	14
1	Luchana	206	247	Castro, Margarita LG	Daughter	F	Cha	2	S	N		Guam		None
2		206	247	Castro, Julia LG	Daughter	F	Cha	.7	S	N		Guam		None
3		207	247	Castro, Juan C	Head	M	Cha	28	M	N	Y	Guam	Y	Farmer
4		207	247	Castro, Josefa G	Wife	F	Cha	26	M	N	Y	Guam	Y	None
5		208	249	Palomo, Rita LG	Head	F	Cha	67	Wd	N	Y	Guam	N	None
6		208	249	Palomo, Luis P	Grandson	M	Cha	23	S	N	Y	Guam	Y	Laborer
7		208	249	Palomo, Vicente P	Grandson	M	Cha	20	S	N	Y	Guam	Y	Farm laborer
8		208	249	Palomo, Maria P	Grandaug	F	Cha	17	S	N	Y	Guam	Y	None
9		208	249	Palomo, Clotilde P	Grandaug	F	Cha	7	S	Y		Guam		None
10		209	250	Leon Guerrero, Jose P	Head	M	Cha	37	M	N	Y	Guam	Y	Farmer
11		209	250	Leon Guerrero, Maria T	Wife	F	Cha	27	M	N	Y	Guam	N	None
12		209	250	Leon Guerrero, Clotilde T	Daughter	F	Cha	8	S	Y		Guam		None
13		209	250	Leon Guerrero, Delfina T	Daughter	F	Cha	6	S	Y		Guam		None
14		209	250	Leon Guerrero, Maria Q T	Daughter	F	Cha	5	S	N		Guam		None
15		209	250	Leon Guerrero, Concepcion T	Daughter	F	Cha	3.8	S	N		Guam		None
16		209	250	Leon Guerrero, Maria T	Daughter	F	Cha	1.9	S	N		Guam		None
17		209	251	Flores, Vicente C	Head	M	Cha	23	M	N	Y	Guam	Y	Farmer
18		209	251	Flores, Rosa S	Wife	F	Cha	28	M	N	Y	Guam	N	None
19		209	251	Flores, Joaquin S	Son	M	Cha	.7	S	N	N	Guam	N	None
20		209	251	Leon Guerrero, Magdalena P	Lodger	F	Cha	23	S	N	Y	Guam	Y	None
21		210	252	Torres, Rosa T	Head	F	Cha	65	Wd	N	Y	Guam	Y	None
22		210	252	Torres, Jesus T	Son	M	Cha	39	S	N	Y	Guam	Y	Farmer
23		210	252	Torres, Anselmo T	Son	M	Cha	35	S	N	Y	Guam	Y	Farmer
24		210	252	Torres, Juana T	Daughter	F	Cha	19	S	N	Y	Guam	Y	Storekeeper
25		210	252	Tedtaotao, Jose C	Servant	M	Cha	20	S	N	Y	Guam	Y	Servant

(CHAMORRO ROOTS GENEALOGY PROJECT™ TRANSCRIPTION)
(BERNARD T. PUNZALAN / HTTP://WWW.CHAMORROROOTS.COM)

DEPARTMENT OF COMMERCE-BUREAU OF THE CENSUS
WASHINGTON

FIFTEENTH CENSUS OF THE UNITED STATES: 1930-POPULATION

THE ISLAND OF GUAM

Sheet No. 26B

61B

District **Municipality of Agana**
Name of Place **Agana City (Part of San Antonio)**
[Proper name and, also, name of class, as city, town, village, barrio, etc]

Enumeration District No. 2
Enumerated by me on **April 22, 1930** Arthur W. Jackson, Enumerator

	PLACE OF ABODE			NAME	RELATION	PERSONAL DESCRIPTION				EDUCATION		NATIVITY		OCCUPATION
	Street, avenue, road, etc.	Number of dwelling house in order of visitation	Number of family in order of visitation	of each person whose place of abode on April 1, 1930, was in this family. Enter surname, first, then given name and middle initial. If any. Include every person living on April 1, 1930. Omit children born since April 1, 1930.	Relationship of this Person to the head of the family.	Sex	Color or race	Age at last birthday	Single, married, widowed or divorced	Attended school any time since Sept. 1, 1929	Whether able to read and write.	Place of birth of this person.	Whether able to speak English.	
	1	2	3	4	5	6	7	8	9	10	11	12	13	14
26	Luchana	211	253	Manglona, Ana F	Head	F	Cha	30	M	N	Y	Guam	Y	None
27		211	253	Manglona, Adela F	Daughter	F	Cha	7	S	Y		Guam		None
28		211	253	Manglona, Julia F	Daughter	F	Cha	4.8	S	N		Guam		None
29		211	253	Manglona, Vicente F	Son	M	Cha	3.5	S	N		Guam		None
30		211	253	Manglona, Ignacio F	Son	M	Cha	.1	S	N		Guam		None
31		211	253	Cruz, Vicenta M	Mother	F	Cha	53	Wd	N	Y	Guam	N	None
32		212	254	Castro, Jesus C	Head	M	Cha	41	M	N	Y	Guam	N	Farmer
33		212	254	Castro, Maria B	Wife	F	Cha	40	M	N	Y	Guam	N	None
34		212	254	Castro, Jose B	Son	M	Cha	15	S	Y	Y	Guam	Y	None
35		212	254	Castro, Francisco B	Son	M	Cha	13	S	Y	Y	Guam	Y	None
36		212	254	Castro, Antonia B	Daughter	F	Cha	11	S	Y	Y	Guam	Y	None
37		212	254	Castro, Juan B	Son	M	Cha	10	S	Y	Y	Guam	Y	None
38		212	254	Castro, Manuel B	Son	M	Cha	8	S	Y		Guam		None
39		212	254	Castro, Matilde B	Daughter	F	Cha	6	S	N		Guam		None
40		212	254	Castro, Maria B	Daughter	F	Cha	3.8	S	N		Guam		None
41		212	254	Castro, Jesus B	Son	M	Cha	1.8	S	N		Guam		None
42		213	255	Castro, Nieves R	Head	F	Cha	67	Wd	N	Y	Guam	N	None
43		213	255	Castro, Joaquina R	Daughter	F	Cha	39	S	N	Y	Guam	N	None
44		213	255	Castro, Maria R	Daughter	F	Cha	30	S	N	Y	Guam	N	None
45		214	256	Castro, Maria U	Head	F	Cha	42	M	N	Y	Guam	N	None
46		214	256	Rivera, Asfriro U	Son	M	Cha	20	S	N	Y	Guam	Y	None
47		214	256	Rivera, Juan U	Son	M	Cha	17	S	N	Y	Guam	Y	None
48		214	256	Rivera, Asuncion U	Daughter	F	Cha	15	S	N	Y	Guam	Y	None
49		214	256	Rivera, Leocaldo U	Son	M	Cha	13	S	Y	Y	Guam	Y	None
50		214	256	Rivera, Francisco U	Son	M	Cha	12	S	Y	Y	Guam	Y	None

DEPARTMENT OF COMMERCE-BUREAU OF THE CENSUS
WASHINGTON

FIFTEENTH CENSUS OF THE UNITED STATES: 1930-POPULATION

THE ISLAND OF GUAM

Sheet No. 27A

District **Municipality of Agana**
Name of Place **Agana City (Part of San Antonio)**
[Proper name and, also, name of class, as city, town, village, barrio, etc]

Enumeration District No. 2
Enumerated by me on **April 23, 1930** Arthur W. Jackson, Enumerator

	PLACE OF ABODE			NAME	RELATION	PERSONAL DESCRIPTION				EDUCATION		NATIVITY		OCCUPATION
	Street, avenue, road, etc.	Number of dwelling house in order of visitation	Number of family in order of visitation	of each person whose place of abode on April 1, 1930, was in this family. Enter surname, first, then given name and middle initial. If any. Include every person living on April 1, 1930. Omit children born since April 1, 1930.	Relationship of this Person to the head of the family.	Sex	Color or race	Age at last birthday	Single, married, widowed or divorced	Attended school any time since Sept. 1, 1929	Whether able to read and write.	Place of birth of this person.	Whether able to speak English.	
	1	2	3	4	5	6	7	8	9	10	11	12	13	14
1	Luchana	214	256	Rivera, Vicente U	Son	M	Cha	11	S	Y	Y	Guam	Y	None
2		214	256	Rivera, Manuela U	Daughter	F	Cha	3.6	S	N		Guam		None
3		215	257	Camacho, Luis C	Head	M	Cha	34	M	Y	Y	Guam	Y	Fireman
4		215	257	Camacho, Emelia R	Wife	F	Cha	31	M	N	Y	Guam	Y	None
5		215	257	Camacho, Rosa R	Daughter	F	Cha	6	S	N		Guam		None
6		215	257	Camacho, Remedios R	Daughter	F	Cha	4.3	S	N		Guam		None
7		215	257	Camacho, David R	Son	M	Cha	2.8	S	N		Guam		None
8		215	257	Camacho, Maria R	Daughter	F	Cha	.4	S	N		Guam		None
9	Cerinola	216	257	Sablan, Lino S	Head	M	Cha	39	M	N	Y	Guam	Y	Laborer
10		216	257	Sablan, Antonia LG	Wife	F	Cha	36	M	N	Y	Guam	Y	None
11		216	257	Sablan, Antonio LG	Son	M	Cha	17	S	Y	Y	Guam	Y	None
12		216	257	Sablan, Cristobal LG	Son	M	Cha	16	S	Y	Y	Guam	Y	None
13		216	257	Sablan, Dolores LG	Daughter	F	Cha	14	S	Y	Y	Guam	Y	None
14		216	257	Sablan, Vicenta LG	Daughter	F	Cha	11	S	Y	Y	Guam	Y	None
15		216	257	Sablan, Pedro LG	Son	M	Cha	8	S	Y		Guam		None
16		216	257	Sablan, Maria LG	Daughter	F	Cha	7	S	N		Guam		None
17		216	257	Sablan, Carmen LG	Daughter	F	Cha	2.8	S	N		Guam		None
18		217	259	Santos, Enrique S	Head	M	Cha	43	M	N	Y	Guam	Y	Laborer
19		217	259	Santos, Gertrudes T	Wife	F	Cha	40	M	N	Y	Guam	Y	None
20		217	259	Santos, Jesus T	Son	M	Cha	19	S	N	Y	Guam	Y	Farm laborer
21		217	259	Santos, Jose T	Son	M	Cha	12	S	Y	Y	Guam	Y	None
22		217	259	Santos, Ana T	Daughter	F	Cha	11	S	Y	Y	Guam	Y	None
23		217	259	Santos, Tomasa T	Daughter	F	Cha	7	S	N		Guam		None
24		217	259	Santos, Manuel T	Son	M	Cha	2.3	S	N		Guam		None
25		217	259	Santos, Tom H T	Son	M	Cha	.6	S	N		Guam		None

(CHAMORRO ROOTS GENEALOGY PROJECT™ TRANSCRIPTION)
(BERNARD T. PUNZALAN / HTTP://WWW.CHAMORROROOTS.COM)

DEPARTMENT OF COMMERCE-BUREAU OF THE CENSUS
WASHINGTON

FIFTEENTH CENSUS OF THE UNITED STATES: 1930-POPULATION

THE ISLAND OF GUAM

Sheet No. 27B

62B

District **Municipality of Agana**
Name of Place **Agana City (Part of San Antonio)**
[Proper name and, also, name of class, as city, town, village, barrio, etc]

Enumeration District No. **2**
Enumerated by me on **April 23, 1930** Arthur W. Jackson
Enumerator

	PLACE OF ABODE			NAME	RELATION	PERSONAL DESCRIPTION				EDUCATION		NATIVITY		OCCUPATION
	Street, avenue, road, etc.	Number of dwelling house in order of visitation	Number of family in order of visitation	of each person whose place of abode on April 1, 1930, was in this family. Enter surname, first, then given name and middle initial. If any. Include every person living on April 1, 1930. Omit children born since April 1, 1930.	Relationship of this Person to the head of the family.	Sex	Color or race	Age at last birthday	Single, married, widowed or divorced	Attended school any time since Sept. 1, 1929	Whether able to read and write.	Place of birth of this person.	Whether able to speak English.	
	1	2	3	4	5	6	7	8	9	10	11	12	13	14
26	Cerinola	218	260	Cruz, Jesus P	Head	M	Cha	29	M	N	Y	Guam	Y	Carpenter
27		218	260	Cruz, Maria S	Wife	F	Cha	21	M	N	Y	Guam	Y	None
28		218	260	Cruz, Julia S	Daughter	F	Cha	2.7	S	N		Guam	N	None
29		218	260	Cruz, Ana S	Daughter	F	Cha	.8	S	N		Guam	N	None
30	Padre Palomo	219	261	Pangelinan, Josefa B	Head	F	Cha	58	Wd	N	Y	Guam	Y	None
31		219	261	Pangelinan, Jose B	Son	M	Cha	39	S	N	Y	Guam	N	Farmer
32		219	261	Pangelinan, Magdalena B	Daughter	F	Cha	35	S	N	Y	Guam	Y	None
33		219	261	Pangelinan, Joaquin B	Son	M	Cha	22	S	N	Y	Guam	N	Tailor
34		219	261	Blaz, Apolonia T	Sister	F	Cha	68	S	N	Y	Guam	N	None
35		219	261	Flores, Ana T	Cousin	F	Cha	60	S	N	Y	Guam	N	None
36		220	262	Chargualaf, Josefina T	Head	F	Cha	25	M	N	Y	Guam	Y	None
37		220	262	Chargualaf, Frank T	Son	M	Cha	3.8	S	N		Guam	N	None
38		220	262	Chargualaf, Barsalisa T	Daughter	F	Cha	2.8	S	N		Guam	N	None
39		221	263	Baza, Luis M	Head	M	Cha	56	M	N	Y	Guam	Y	Farmer
40		221	263	Baza, Rosa C	Wife	F	Cha	53	M	N	Y	Guam	N	None
41		221	263	Baza, Antonio C	Son	M	Cha	22	S	N	Y	Guam	Y	Policeman
42		221	263	Baza, Felisa C	Daughter	F	Cha	19	S	N	Y	Guam	Y	None
43		221	263	Baza, Luis C	Son	M	Cha	17	S	N	Y	Guam	Y	None
44		221	263	Baza, Maria C	Daughter	F	Cha	16	S	N	Y	Guam	Y	None
45		221	263	Baza, Jose C	Son	M	Cha	13	S	Y	Y	Guam	Y	None
46		221	263	Charfauros, Margarita A	Lodger	F	Cha	3.8	S	N		Guam	N	None
47		222	264	Leon Guerrero, Joaquin B	Head	M	Cha	35	M	N	Y	Guam	Y	Policeman
48		222	264	Leon Guerrero, Maria S	Wife	F	Cha	30	M	N	Y	Guam	Y	None
49		222	264	Leon Guerrero, Jesus S	Son	M	Cha	2.8	S	N		Guam	N	None
50		222	264	Leon Guerrero, Lorenzo A	Son	M	Cha	.8	S	N		Guam	N	None

(CHAMORRO ROOTS GENEALOGY PROJECT™ TRANSCRIPTION)
(BERNARD T. PUNZALAN / HTTP://WWW.CHAMORROROOTS.COM)

DEPARTMENT OF COMMERCE-BUREAU OF THE CENSUS
WASHINGTON

FIFTEENTH CENSUS OF THE UNITED STATES: 1930-POPULATION

THE ISLAND OF GUAM

Sheet No. 28A

District **Municipality of Agana**
Name of Place **Agana City (Part of San Antonio)**
[Proper name and, also, name of class, as city, town, village, barrio, etc]

Enumeration District No. **2**
Enumerated by me on **April 23, 1930** Arthur W. Jackson
Enumerator

	PLACE OF ABODE			NAME	RELATION	PERSONAL DESCRIPTION				EDUCATION		NATIVITY		OCCUPATION
	Street, avenue, road, etc.	Number of dwelling house is order of visitation	Number of family in order of visitation	of each person whose place of abode on April 1, 1930, was in this family. Enter surname, first, then given name and middle initial. If any. Include every person living on April 1, 1930. Omit children born since April 1, 1930.	Relationship of this Person to the head of the family.	Sex	Color or race	Age at last birthday	Single, married, widowed or divorced	Attended school any time since Sept. 1, 1929	Whether able to read and write.	Place of birth of this person.	Whether able to speak English.	
	1	2	3	4	5	6	7	8	9	10	11	12	13	14
1	Padre Palomo	222	264	Leon Guerrero, Rosario B	Sister	F	Cha	31	S	N	Y	Guam	Y	Store keeper
2		222	264	Borja, Lorenzo L	Servant	M	Cha	17	S	N	Y	Guam	Y	None
3		222	264	Quichocho, Rosa L	Servant	F	Cha	50	S	N	N	Guam	N	None
4		223	265	Gogue, Enrique W	Head	M	Cha	52	M	N	Y	Guam	Y	Farmer
5		223	265	Gogue, Carmen P	Wife	F	Cha	32	M	N	Y	Guam	N	None
6		223	265	Gogue, Gregorio P	Son	M	Cha	.1	S	N		Guam		None
7		224	266	Duenas, Jose C	Head	M	Cha	23	M	N	Y	Guam	Y	Carpenter
8		224	266	Duenas, Maria G	Wife	F	Cha	17	M	N	Y	Guam	Y	None
9		225	267	White, William P	Head	M	Cha	68	M	N	Y	Guam	N	Farmer
10		225	267	White, Maria F	Wife	F	Cha	61	M	N	Y	Guam	N	None
11		225	268	Peredo, Joaquin G	Head	M	Cha	29	Wd	N	Y	Guam	Y	Carpenter
12		225	268	Peredo, Antonia G	Daughter	F	Cha	1.8	S	N		Guam		None
13		226	269	Cabrera, Rosa M	Head	F	Cha	42	Wd	N	Y	Guam	N	None
14		226	269	Cabrera, Juan M	Son	M	Cha	20	S	N	Y	Guam	Y	Cook
15		226	269	Cabrera, Maria M	Daughter	F	Cha	18	S	N	Y	Guam	Y	None
16		226	269	Cabrera, Rosario M	Daughter	F	Cha	13	S	Y	Y	Guam	Y	None
17		226	269	Cabrera, Concepcion M	Daughter	F	Cha	11	S	Y	Y	Guam	Y	None
18		226	269	Cabrera, Jose M	Son	M	Cha	1	S	N		Guam		None
19		227	270	Leon Guerrero, Francisco LG	Head	M	Cha	46	M	N	Y	Guam	Y	Electrician
20		227	270	Leon Guerrero, Isabel D	Wife	F	Cha	42	M	N	Y	Guam	Y	None
21		227	270	Leon Guerrero, Concepcion D	Daughter	F	Cha	20	S	N	Y	Guam	Y	None
22		227	270	Leon Guerrero, Juan D	Son	M	Cha	18	S	N	Y	Guam	Y	Electrician
23		227	270	Leon Guerrero, Balbino D	Son	M	Cha	15	S	Y	Y	Guam	Y	None
24		227	270	San Agustin, Lucia C	Lodger	F	Cha	3.8	S	N		Guam		None
25		228	271	Arriola, Juana A	Head	F	Cha	65	Wd	N	N	Guam	N	None

DEPARTMENT OF COMMERCE-BUREAU OF THE CENSUS
WASHINGTON

FIFTEENTH CENSUS OF THE UNITED STATES: 1930-POPULATION

THE ISLAND OF GUAM

Sheet No. 28B

63B

District **Municipality of Agana**
Name of Place **Agana City (Part of San Antonio)**
[Proper name and, also, name of class, as city, town, village, barrio, etc]

Enumeration District No. 2
Enumerated by me on **April 23, 1930** Arthur W. Jackson, Enumerator

	PLACE OF ABODE			NAME	RELATION	PERSONAL DESCRIPTION				EDUCATION		NATIVITY		OCCUPATION
	Street, avenue, road, etc.	Number of dwelling house is order of visitation	Number of family in order of visitation	of each person whose place of abode on April 1, 1930, was in this family. Enter surname, first, then given name and middle initial. If any. Include every person living on April 1, 1930. Omit children born since April 1, 1930.	Relationship of this Person to the head of the family.	Sex	Color or race	Age at last birthday	Single, married, widowed or divorced	Attended school any time since Sept. 1, 1929	Whether able to read and write.	Place of birth of this person.	Whether able to speak English.	
	1	2	3	4	5	6	7	8	9	10	11	12	13	14
26	Padre Palomo	228	271	Arriola, Jose A	Grandson	M	Cha	10	S	N	N	Guam	N	None
27		229	272	Untalan, Ana P	Head	F	Cha	60	Wd	N	N	Guam	N	None
28		229	272	Untalan, Luis P	Son	M	Cha	23	S	N	Y	Guam	Y	School teacher
29		229	273	Blaz, Joaquina U	Head	F	Cha	32	M	N	Y	Guam	Y	None
30		229	273	Blaz, Jose U	Son	M	Cha	3.8	S	N		Guam		None
31		229	273	Blaz, Fermina U	Daughter	F	Cha	1.5	S	N		Guam		None
32		230	274	Palomo, Ana C	Head	F	Cha	64	Wd	N	Y	Guam	N	None
33		230	274	Palomo, Vicente C	Son	M	Cha	23	S	N	Y	Guam	Y	Farmer
34		230	275	Ojeda, Consolacion C	Head	F	Cha	47	Wd	N	Y	Guam	N	None
35		230	275	Ojeda, Carmen C	Daughter	F	Cha	14	S	N	Y	Guam	Y	None
36		230	275	Ojeda, Maria C	Daughter	F	Cha	13	S	N	Y	Guam	Y	None
37		231	276	Duenas, Jose F	Head	M	Cha	62	M	N	Y	Guam	Y	Carpenter
38		231	276	Duenas, Antonia C	Wife	F	Cha	54	M	N	Y	Guam	N	None
39		231	276	Duenas, Francisco C	Son	M	Cha	15	S	Y	Y	Guam	Y	None
40		231	276	Duenas, Ana C	Daughter	F	Cha	13	S	N	Y	Guam	Y	None
41		232	277	Ibanez, Cayetano C	Head	M	Fil	41	M	N	Y	Phil. Island	Y	Cook
42		232	277	Ibanez, Candalera SN	Wife	F	Cha	31	M	N	Y	Guam	N	None
43		232	277	Ibanez, Pedro SN	Son	M	Fil	11	S	Y	Y	Guam	Y	None
44		232	277	Ibanez, Jesus SN	Son	M	Fil	6	S	N		Guam		None
45		232	277	Ibanez, Vicente SN	Son	M	Fil	5	S	N		Guam		None
46		232	277	Ibanez, Clotilde SN	Daughter	F	Fil	3.3	S	N		Guam		None
47		233	278	San Nicolas, Maria P	Head	F	Cha	30	M	N	Y	Guam	Y	None
48		233	278	San Nicolas, Jacinto P	Son	M	Cha	5	S	N		Guam		None
49		233	278	San Nicolas, Amelia P	Daughter	F	Cha	4.8	S	N		Guam		None
50		233	278	San Nicolas, Lourdes P	Daughter	F	Cha	2.8	S	N		Guam		None

(CHAMORRO ROOTS GENEALOGY PROJECT™ TRANSCRIPTION)
(BERNARD T. PUNZALAN / HTTP://WWW.CHAMORROROOTS.COM)

DEPARTMENT OF COMMERCE-BUREAU OF THE CENSUS
WASHINGTON

FIFTEENTH CENSUS OF THE UNITED STATES: 1930-POPULATION

THE ISLAND OF GUAM

Sheet No. 29A

District **Municipality of Agana**
Name of Place **Agana City (Part of San Antonio)**
[Proper name and, also, name of class, as city, town, village, barrio, etc]

Enumeration District No. **2**
Enumerated by me on **April 23, 1930** Arthur W. Jackson, Enumerator

	PLACE OF ABODE			NAME	RELATION	PERSONAL DESCRIPTION				EDUCATION		NATIVITY		OCCUPATION
	Street, avenue, road, etc.	Number of dwelling house in order of visitation	Number of family in order of visitation	of each person whose place of abode on April 1, 1930, was in this family. Enter surname, first, then given name and middle initial. If any. Include every person living on April 1, 1930. Omit children born since April 1, 1930.	Relationship of this Person to the head of the family.	Sex	Color or race	Age at last birthday	Single, married, widowed or divorced	Attended school any time since Sept. 1, 1929	Whether able to read and write.	Place of birth of this person.	Whether able to speak English.	
	1	2	3	4	5	6	7	8	9	10	11	12	13	14
1	Padre Palomo	233	278	San Nicolas, Felix P	Son	M	Cha	.5	S	N		Guam		None
2		233	278	San Nicolas, Ana A	Mother-in-law	F	Cha	56	Wd	N	N	Guam	N	None
3		234	279	Camacho, Vicente C	Head	M	Cha	40	M	N	Y	Guam	N	Laborer
4		234	279	Camacho, Juana Q	Wife	F	Cha	37	M	N	Y	Guam	N	None
5		234	279	Camacho, Vicente Q	Son	M	Cha	9	S	Y		Guam		None
6		234	279	Camacho, Andres Q	Son	M	Cha	7	S	Y		Guam		None
7		234	279	Camacho, Consolacion Q	Daughter	F	Cha	6	S	N		Guam		None
8		234	279	Camacho, Jose Q	Son	M	Cha	4.7	S	N		Guam		None
9		234	279	Camacho, Irene Q	Daughter	F	Cha	.1	S	N		Guam		None
10		234	280	Quitugua, Maria D	Head	F	Cha	36	S	N	Y	Guam	N	None
11		234	280	Quitugua, Josefa D	Daughter	F	Cha	6	S	N		Guam		None
12		234	280	Quitugua, Vicente D	Brother	M	Cha	33	S	N	Y	Guam	Y	Laborer
13		235	281	Wolford, Catalina C	Head	F	Fil	33	M	N	Y	Guam	Y	None
14		235	281	Wolford, Maria C	Daughter	F	Fil	13	S	Y	Y	Guam	Y	None
15		235	281	Wolford, Charlie C	Son	M	Fil	10	S	Y	Y	Guam	Y	None
16		235	281	Wolford, Alfred C	Son	M	Fil	8	S	Y		Guam		None
17		235	281	Wolford, Robert C	Son	M	Fil	2.3	S	N		Guam		None
18		235	281	Wolford, Arthur C	Son	M	Fil	1.8	S	N		Guam		None
19		235	281	Ibasco, Rita C	Sister	F	Fil	37	D	N		Guam	N	None
20		236	282	Borja, Jose L	Head	M	Cha	74	Wd	N	Y	Guam	N	None
21		236	282	Rosario, Joaquina B	Daughter	F	Cha	38	Wd	N	Y	Guam	N	None
22		237	283	Quitugua, Vicente Q	Head	M	Cha	37	M	N	Y	Guam	N	Farmer
23		237	283	Quitugua, Ana T	Wife	F	Cha	29	M	N	Y	Guam	N	None
24		237	283	Quitugua, Juan T	Son	M	Cha	10	S	Y	Y	Guam	Y	None
25		237	283	Quitugua, Felomina T	Daughter	F	Cha	4.8	S	N		Guam		None

(CHAMORRO ROOTS GENEALOGY PROJECT™ TRANSCRIPTION)
(BERNARD T. PUNZALAN / HTTP://WWW.CHAMORROROOTS.COM)

DEPARTMENT OF COMMERCE-BUREAU OF THE CENSUS
WASHINGTON

FIFTEENTH CENSUS OF THE UNITED STATES: 1930-POPULATION

THE ISLAND OF GUAM

Sheet No. 29B

64B

District **Municipality of Agana**
Name of Place **Agana City (Part of San Antonio)**
[Proper name and, also, name of class, as city, town, village, barrio, etc]

Enumeration District No. 2
Enumerated by me on **April 24, 1930** Arthur W. Jackson, Enumerator

	PLACE OF ABODE			NAME	RELATION	PERSONAL DESCRIPTION				EDUCATION		NATIVITY		OCCUPATION
	Street, avenue, road, etc.	Number of dwelling house is order of visitation	Number of family in order of visitation	of each person whose place of abode on April 1, 1930, was in this family. Enter surname, first, then given name and middle initial. If any. Include every person living on April 1, 1930. Omit children born since April 1, 1930.	Relationship of this Person to the head of the family.	Sex	Color or race	Age at last birthday	Single, married, widowed or divorced	Attended school any time since Sept. 1, 1929	Whether able to read and write.	Place of birth of this person.	Whether able to speak English.	
	1	2	3	4	5	6	7	8	9	10	11	12	13	14
26	Padre Palomo	237	283	Quitugua, Rosa T	Daughter	F	Cha	.5	S	N		Guam		None
27		238	284	Duenas, Rosa B	Head	F	Cha	36	Wd	N	N	Guam	N	None
28		238	284	Duenas, Jesus B	Son	M	Cha	15	S	N	Y	Guam	Y	None
29		238	284	Duenas, Jose B	Son	M	Cha	14	S	N	Y	Guam	Y	None
30		238	284	Duenas, Juan B	Son	M	Cha	12	S	Y	Y	Guam	Y	None
31		238	284	Duenas, Engracia B	Daughter	F	Cha	11	S	Y	Y	Guam	Y	None
32		238	284	Duenas, Francisco B	Son	M	Cha	9	S	Y		Guam		None
33		238	284	Duenas, Vicente B	Son	M	Cha	5	S	N		Guam		None
34		238	284	Duenas, Emelia B	Daughter	F	Cha	3.8	S	N		Guam		None
35		239	285	Flores, Francisco G	Head	M	Cha	46	M	N	Y	Guam	Y	Blacksmith
36		239	285	Flores, Joaquina G	Wife	F	Cha	36	M	N	Y	Guam	Y	None
37		239	285	Flores, Angel G	Son	M	Cha	19	S	N	Y	Guam	Y	School teacher
38		239	285	Flores, Aurora G	Daughter	F	Cha	18	S	N	Y	Guam	Y	None
39		239	285	Flores, Jesus G	Son	M	Cha	17	S	N	Y	Guam	Y	None
40		239	285	Flores, Nellie G	Daughter	F	Cha	15	S	N	Y	Guam	Y	None
41		239	285	Flores, Natividad G	Daughter	F	Cha	13	S	Y	Y	Guam	Y	None
42		239	285	Flores, Pedro G	Son	M	Cha	10	S	Y	Y	Guam	Y	None
43		239	285	Flores, Isidro G	Son	M	Cha	8	S	Y		Guam		None
44		239	285	Flores, Francisco G	Son	M	Cha	6	S	N		Guam		None
45		239	285	Flores, Maria G	Daughter	F	Cha	3.8	S	N		Guam		None
46		239	285	Flores, Jose G	Son	M	Cha	1.8	S	N		Guam		None
47		240	286	Manilisay, Jesus S	Head	M	Cha	27	M	N	Y	Guam	Y	Clerk
48		240	286	Manilisay, Dolores A	Wife	F	Cha	29	M	N	Y	Guam	N	None
49		240	286	Manilisay, Manuel A	Son	M	Cha	8	S	Y		Guam		None
50		240	286	Manilisay, Ana A	Daughter	F	Cha	7	S	Y		Guam		None

(CHAMORRO ROOTS GENEALOGY PROJECT™ TRANSCRIPTION)
(BERNARD T. PUNZALAN / HTTP://WWW.CHAMORROROOTS.COM)

DEPARTMENT OF COMMERCE-BUREAU OF THE CENSUS
WASHINGTON

FIFTEENTH CENSUS OF THE UNITED STATES: 1930-POPULATION

THE ISLAND OF GUAM

Sheet No. 30A

65

District Municipality of Agana
Name of Place Agana City (Part of San Antonio)
[Proper name and, also, name of class, as city, town, village, barrio, etc]

Enumeration District No. 2
Enumerated by me on April 24, 1930 Arthur W. Jackson
Enumerator

	PLACE OF ABODE			NAME	RELATION	PERSONAL DESCRIPTION				EDUCATION		NATIVITY		OCCUPATION
	Street, avenue, road, etc.	Number of dwelling house is order of visitation	Number of family in order of visitation	of each person whose place of abode on April 1, 1930, was in this family. Enter surname, first, then given name and middle initial. If any. Include every person living on April 1, 1930. Omit children born since April 1, 1930.	Relationship of this Person to the head of the family.	Sex	Color or race	Age at last birthday	Single, married, widowed or divorced	Attended school any time since Sept. 1, 1929	Whether able to read and write.	Place of birth of this person.	Whether able to speak English.	
	1	2	3	4	5	6	7	8	9	10	11	12	13	14
1	Padre Palomo	240	286	Manilisay, Maria A	Daughter	F	Cha	3.8	S	N		Guam		None
2		240	286	Manilisay, Jesus A	Son	M	Cha	2.8	S	N		Guam		None
3		241	287	Rivera, Joaquin LG	Head	M	Cha	59	M	N	Y	Guam	N	Farmer
4		241	287	Rivera, Ana R	Wife	F	Cha	53	M	N	Y	Guam	N	None
5		241	287	Rivera, Manuel R	Son	M	Cha	27	S	N	Y	Guam	Y	Farmer
6		241	287	Rivera, Jose R	Son	M	Cha	21	S	N	Y	Guam	Y	Laborer
7		241	287	Rivera, Ignacio R	Son	M	Cha	21	S	N	Y	Guam	Y	Laborer
8		241	287	Rivera, Maria R	Daughter	F	Cha	18	S	N	Y	Guam	Y	None
9		241	287	Rivera, Jesus R	Son	M	Cha	16	S	N	Y	Guam	Y	None
10		241	287	Rivera, Juan R	Son	M	Cha	11	S	Y	Y	Guam	Y	None
11		241	287	San Agustin, Magdalena R	Grandaug	F	Cha	9	S	Y		Guam		None
12		242	288	Taitinfong, Vicente De L	Head	F	Cha	66	Wd	N	Y	Guam	N	Farmer
13		242	288	Taitinfong, Jesus B	Son	M	Cha	27	S	N	Y	Guam	Y	Cable operator
14		242	288	Taitinfong, Joaquin B	Son	M	Cha	25	S	N	Y	Guam	Y	Farm laborer
15		242	288	Taitinfong, Maria B	Daughter	F	Cha	23	S	N	Y	Guam	Y	None
16		242	288	Taitinfong, Vicente B	Son	M	Cha	20	S	N	Y	Guam	Y	Farm laborer
17		242	288	Taitinfong, Ignacio B	Son	M	Cha	17	S	N	Y	Guam	Y	None
18		242	288	Taitinfong, Mariano B	Son	M	Cha	15	S	Y	Y	Guam	Y	None
19		242	288	Taitinfong, Barbara B	Daughter	F	Cha	13	S	Y	Y	Guam	Y	None
20		242	288	Taitinfong, Ana B	Daughter	F	Cha	9	S	Y		Guam		None
21		242	288	Rivera, Isabel R	Lodger	F	Cha	7	S	N		Guam		None
22		243	289	Torres, Juan LG	Head	M	Cha	44	M	N	Y	Guam	Y	Farmer
23		243	289	Torres, Dolores B	Wife	F	Cha	53	M	N	Y	Guam	N	None
24		243	289	Matanane, Ana B	Step-daug	F	Cha	19	S	N	Y	Guam	Y	None
25		243	289	Matanane, Dolores B	Step-daug	F	Cha	16	S	N	Y	Guam	Y	None

DEPARTMENT OF COMMERCE-BUREAU OF THE CENSUS
WASHINGTON

FIFTEENTH CENSUS OF THE UNITED STATES: 1930-POPULATION

THE ISLAND OF GUAM

Sheet No. 30B

District Municipality of Agana
Name of Place Agana City (Part of San Antonio)
[Proper name and, also, name of class, as city, town, village, barrio, etc]

Enumeration District No. 2
Enumerated by me on April 24, 1930 Arthur W. Jackson, Enumerator

	PLACE OF ABODE			NAME	RELATION	PERSONAL DESCRIPTION				EDUCATION		NATIVITY		OCCUPATION
	Street, avenue, road, etc.	Number of dwelling house in order of visitation	Number of family in order of visitation	of each person whose place of abode on April 1, 1930, was in this family. Enter surname, first, then given name and middle initial. If any. Include every person living on April 1, 1930. Omit children born since April 1, 1930.	Relationship of this Person to the head of the family.	Sex	Color or race	Age at last birthday	Single, married, widowed or divorced	Attended school any time since Sept. 1, 1929	Whether able to read and write.	Place of birth of this person.	Whether able to speak English.	
	1	2	3	4	5	6	7	8	9	10	11	12	13	14
26	Padre Palomo	243	289	Matanane, Eugenia B	Step-daug	F	Cha	14	S	N	Y	Guam	Y	None
27		244	290	Camacho, Vicente C	Head	M	Cha	32	M	N	Y	Guam	Y	Laborer
28		244	290	Camacho, Josefa G	Wife	F	Cha	31	M	N	Y	Guam	Y	None
29		244	290	Camacho, Maria G	Daughter	F	Cha	12	S	Y	Y	Guam	Y	None
30		244	290	Camacho, Juana G	Daughter	F	Cha	10	S	Y	Y	Guam	Y	None
31		244	290	Camacho, Ana G	Daughter	F	Cha	9	S	Y		Guam		None
32		244	290	Camacho, Felix G	Son	M	Cha	7	S	Y		Guam		None
33		244	290	Camacho, Ramona G	Daughter	F	Cha	5.6	S	N		Guam		None
34		244	290	Camacho, Jose G	Son	M	Cha	3.8	S	N		Guam		None
35		244	290	Camacho, Josefa G	Daughter	F	Cha	1.8	S	N		Guam		None
36		245	291	Mendiola, Francisco G	Head	M	Cha	46	M	N	Y	Guam	N	Laborer
37		245	291	Mendiola, Ana N	Wife	F	Cha	44	M	N	Y	Guam	N	None
38		245	291	Mendiola, Juan N	Son	M	Cha	17	S	N	Y	Guam	Y	None
39		245	291	Mendiola, Francisco N	Son	M	Cha	9	S	Y		Guam		None
40		245	291	Mendiola, Vicente N	Son	M	Cha	4.5	S	N		Guam		None
41		245	291	Mendiola, Virginia N	Daughter	F	Cha	1.8	S	N		Guam		None
42		245	291	Ninaisen, Francisca N	Mother-in-law	F	Cha	64	S	N	N	Guam	N	None
43		245	282	Lujan, Joaquin SN	Head	M	Cha	28	M	N	Y	Guam	Y	Chauffeur
44		245	282	Lujan, Maria M	Wife	F	Cha	21	M	N	Y	Guam	Y	None
45		245	282	Lujan, Oliva M	Daughter	F	Cha	.1	S	N		Guam		None
46		246	293	Lujan, Jose G	Head	M	Cha	43	M	N	Y	Guam	N	Laborer
47		246	293	Lujan, Concepcion C	Wife	F	Cha	38	M	N	Y	Guam	N	None
48		246	293	Lujan, Maria C	Daughter	F	Cha	17	S	N	Y	Guam	Y	None
49		246	293	Lujan, Concepcion C	Daughter	F	Cha	14	S	Y	Y	Guam	Y	None
50		246	293	Lujan, Florencia D	Daughter	F	Cha	13	S	Y	Y	Guam	Y	None

DEPARTMENT OF COMMERCE-BUREAU OF THE CENSUS
WASHINGTON
FIFTEENTH CENSUS OF THE UNITED STATES: 1930-POPULATION

THE ISLAND OF GUAM

Sheet No. 31A

District Municipality of Agana
Name of Place Agana City (Part of San Antonio)
[Proper name and, also, name of class, as city, town, village, barrio, etc]

Enumeration District No. 2
Enumerated by me on April 25, 1930 Arthur W. Jackson
Enumerator

	PLACE OF ABODE			NAME	RELATION	PERSONAL DESCRIPTION				EDUCATION		NATIVITY		OCCUPATION
	Street, avenue, road, etc.	Number of dwelling house is order of visitation	Number of family in order of visitation	of each person whose place of abode on April 1, 1930, was in this family. Enter surname, first, then given name and middle initial. If any. Include every person living on April 1, 1930. Omit children born since April 1, 1930.	Relationship of this Person to the head of the family.	Sex	Color or race	Age at last birthday	Single, married, widowed or divorced	Attended school any time since Sept. 1, 1929	Whether able to read and write.	Place of birth of this person.	Whether able to speak English.	
	1	2	3	4	5	6	7	8	9	10	11	12	13	14
1	Padre Palomo	246	293	Lujan, Isabel C	Daughter	F	Cha	12	S	Y	Y	Guam	Y	None
2		246	293	Lujan, Rufina C	Daughter	F	Cha	8	S	Y		Guam		None
3		246	293	Lujan, Rosario C	Daughter	F	Cha	7	S	Y		Guam		None
4		246	293	Lujan, Vicente C	Son	M	Cha	6	S	N		Guam		None
5		246	293	Lujan, Antonia C	Daughter	F	Cha	2.8	S	N		Guam		None
6		247	294	Padeson, Dolores W	Head	F	Neg?	63	Wd	N	N	Guam	N	None
7		247	294	Chiguina, Maria P	Lodger	F	Cha	34	M	N	N	Guam	Y	None
8		247	294	Pablo, Remedios P	Lodger	F	Cha	14	S	N	Y	Guam	Y	None
9		247	294	Pablo, Maria P	Lodger	F	Cha	13	S	N	Y	Guam	Y	None
10		248	295	Francisco, Juan C	Head	M	Cha	40	M	N	Y	Guam	N	Farmer
11		248	295	Francisco, Concepcion C	Wife	F	Cha	37	M	N	Y	Guam	N	None
12		248	295	Francisco, Pedro C	Son	M	Cha	10	S	Y	Y	Guam	Y	None
13		248	295	Francisco, Antonio C	Daughter	F	Cha	8	S	Y		Guam		None
14		248	295	Francisco, Jose C	Son	M	Cha	6	S	N		Guam		None
15		248	295	Francisco, Teresa C	Daughter	F	Cha	4.8	S	N		Guam		None
16		248	295	Francisco, Juana C	Son	M	Cha	.4	S	N		Guam		None
17		249	296	Duenas, Bernardino F	Head	M	Cha	57	M	N	Y	Guam	N	Farmer
18		249	296	Duenas, Antonia F	Wife	F	Cha	48	M	N	N	Guam	N	None
19		249	296	Duenas, Juan F	Son	M	Cha	23	S	N	N	Guam	Y	Farm laborer
20		249	296	Duenas, Vicente F	Son	M	Cha	16	S	N	N	Guam	Y	None
21		249	296	Duenas, Rita F	Daughter	F	Cha	9	S	Y	N	Guam		None
22		249	296	Duenas, Maria F	Daughter	F	Cha	7	S	Y	Y	Guam		None
23		250	297	Arriola, Francisco R	Head	M	Cha	56	M	N	Y	Guam	N	Printer
24		250	297	Arriola, Ramona R	Wife	F	Cha	51	M	N	Y	Guam	N	None
25		250	297	Arriola, Josefa C	Daughter	F	Cha	17	S	N	Y	Guam	Y	None

(CHAMORRO ROOTS GENEALOGY PROJECT™ TRANSCRIPTION)
(BERNARD T. PUNZALAN / HTTP://WWW.CHAMORROROOTS.COM)

DEPARTMENT OF COMMERCE-BUREAU OF THE CENSUS
WASHINGTON

FIFTEENTH CENSUS OF THE UNITED STATES: 1930-POPULATION

THE ISLAND OF GUAM

Sheet No. 31B

66B

District Municipality of Agana
Name of Place Agana City (Part of San Antonio)
[Proper name and, also, name of class, as city, town, village, barrio, etc]

Enumeration District No. 2
Enumerated by me on April 25, 1930 Arthur W. Jackson, Enumerator

	PLACE OF ABODE			NAME	RELATION	PERSONAL DESCRIPTION				EDUCATION		NATIVITY		OCCUPATION
	Street, avenue, road, etc.	Number of dwelling house in order of visitation	Number of family in order of visitation	of each person whose place of abode on April 1, 1930, was in this family. Enter surname, first, then given name and middle initial. If any. Include every person living on April 1, 1930. Omit children born since April 1, 1930.	Relationship of this Person to the head of the family.	Sex	Color or race	Age at last birthday	Single, married, widowed or divorced	Attended school any time since Sept. 1, 1929	Whether able to read and write.	Place of birth of this person.	Whether able to speak English.	
	1	2	3	4	5	6	7	8	9	10	11	12	13	14
26	Padre Palomo	250	297	Arriola, Consolacion C	Daughter	F	Cha	14	S	N	Y	Guam	Y	None
27		250	297	Arriola, Felomina C	Daughter	F	Cha	13	S	Y	Y	Guam	Y	None
28		250	297	Pangelinan, Ignacio R	Step-son	M	Cha	17	S	Y	Y	Guam	Y	None
29		250	297	Pangelinan, Maria R	Step-daug	F	Cha	14	S	Y	Y	Guam	Y	None
30		250	297	Pangelinan, Vicente R	Step-son	M	Cha	11	S	Y	Y	Guam	Y	None
31		251	298	Fernandez, Francisca C	Head	F	Cha	32	M	N	Y	Guam	Y	None
32		251	298	Fernandez, Juan C	Son	M	Cha	8	S	Y		Guam		None
33		251	298	Fernandez, Vicente C	Son	M	Cha	6	S	N		Guam		None
34		251	298	Fernandez, Ana C	Daughter	F	Cha	4.8	S	N		Guam		None
35		251	299	Pinaula, Feliciana C	Head	F	Cha	64	Wd	N	N	Guam	N	None
36		251	299	Pinaula, Antonio C	Son	M	Cha	17	S	N	Y	Guam	Y	None
37		251	299	Cruz, Jose C	Son	M	Cha	34	S	N	Y	Guam	Y	Plumber
38		251	299	Cruz, Felix C	Son	M	Cha	30	S	N	Y	Guam	Y	Farmer
39		251	299	Cruz, Joaquina C	Daughter	F	Cha	28	S	N	Y	Guam	Y	None
40		251	299	Cruz, Maria C	Daughter	F	Cha	27	S	N	Y	Guam	Y	None
41		252	300	Sgambelluri, Marcelo	Head	M	W	48	M	N	Y	Italy	Y	Retail merchant
42		252	300	Sgambelluri, Joaquina C	Wife	F	Cha	42	M	N	Y	Guam	Y	None
43		252	300	Sgambelluri, Laura C	Daughter	F	Cha	25	S	N	Y	Guam	Y	None
44		252	300	Sgambelluri, Hector C	Son	M	Cha	21	S	N	Y	Guam	Y	Chauffeur
45		252	300	Sgambelluri, Adolfo C	Son	M	Cha	16	S	N	Y	Guam	Y	None
46		252	300	Sgambelluri, Josefina C	Daughter	F	Cha	11	S	Y	Y	Guam	Y	None
47		252	300	Sgambelluri, John C	Son	M	Cha	9	S	Y		Guam		None
48		252	300	Sgambelluri, Vicenta C	Daughter	F	Cha	7	S	Y		Guam		None
49		252	300	Sgambelluri, Belta C	Daughter	F	Cha	3.3	S	N		Guam		None
50		252	300	Sgambelluri, Rafael C	Son	M	Cha	2.5	S	N		Guam		None

(CHAMORRO ROOTS GENEALOGY PROJECT™ TRANSCRIPTION)
(BERNARD T. PUNZALAN / HTTP://WWW.CHAMORROROOTS.COM)

DEPARTMENT OF COMMERCE-BUREAU OF THE CENSUS
WASHINGTON
FIFTEENTH CENSUS OF THE UNITED STATES: 1930-POPULATION

THE ISLAND OF GUAM

Sheet No. 32A

67

District **Municipality of Agana**
Name of Place **Agana City (Part of San Antonio)**
[Proper name and, also, name of class, as city, town, village, barrio, etc]

Enumeration District No. 2
Enumerated by me on **April 26, 1930** Arthur W. Jackson, Enumerator

	PLACE OF ABODE			NAME	RELATION	PERSONAL DESCRIPTION				EDUCATION		NATIVITY		OCCUPATION
	Street, avenue, road, etc.	Number of dwelling house is order of visitation	Number of family in order of visitation	of each person whose place of abode on April 1, 1930, was in this family. Enter surname, first, then given name and middle initial. If any. Include every person living on April 1, 1930. Omit children born since April 1, 1930.	Relationship of this Person to the head of the family.	Sex	Color or race	Age at last birthday	Single, married, widowed or divorced	Attended school any time since Sept. 1, 1929	Whether able to read and write.	Place of birth of this person.	Whether able to speak English.	
	1	2	3	4	5	6	7	8	9	10	11	12	13	14
1	Padre Palomo	253	301	Martinez, Jesus M	Head	M	Cha	22	M	N	Y	Guam	Y	Laborer
2		253	301	Martinez, Concepcion F	Wife	F	Cha	24	M	N	Y	Guam	Y	None
3		253	301	Martinez, Jesus F	Son	M	Cha	2.7	S	N		Guam		None
4		253	301	Martinez, Maria F	Daughter	F	Cha	.3	S	N		Guam		None
5		254	302	Martinez, Ignacio C	Head	M	Cha	56	M	N	Y	Guam	N	Farmer
6		254	302	Martinez, Francisca M	Wife	F	Cha	65	M	N	Y	Guam	N	None
7		254	302	Guerrero, Joaquin M	Step-son	M	Cha	31	S	N	Y	Guam	Y	Laborer
8		254	302	Guerrero, Concepcion M	Step-daug	F	Cha	35	S	N	Y	Guam	Y	Midwife
9		254	302	Flores, Jose G	Grandson	M	Cha	8	S	Y		Guam		None
10		255	303	Toves, Juan B	Head	M	Cha	56	M	N	N	Guam	N	Farmer
11		255	303	Toves, Ana N	Wife	F	Cha	60	M	N	N	Guam	N	None
12		255	303	Aguero, Jose A	Nephew	M	Cha	21	S	N	Y	Guam	Y	Farmer
13		255	303	Hernandez, Jose H	Nephew	M	Cha	28	S	N	Y	Guam	Y	Farmer
14		255	303	Hernandez, Maria T	Sist-in-law	F	Cha	55	S	N	N	Guam	N	None
15		255	303	Toves, Josefa H	Sist-in-law	F	Cha	55	M	N	N	Guam	N	None
16		255	303	Toves, Jose B	Brother	M	Cha	60	M	N	N	Guam	N	None
17		255	303	Toves, Candaleria H	Niece	F	Cha	15	S	N	Y	Guam	Y	None
18		256	304	Alvarez, Juan SA	Head	M	Cha	32	M	N	Y	Guam	Y	Chauffeur
19		256	304	Alvarez, Maria C	Wife	F	Cha	21	M	N	Y	Guam	Y	None
20		256	304	Alvarez, Agripina C	Daughter	F	Cha	.8	S	N		Guam		None
21		256	304	Alvarez, Rufina SA	Sister	F	Cha	27	S	N	Y	Guam	Y	None
22		257	305	Guzman, Jose P	Head	M	Cha	25	M	N	Y	Guam	Y	Garage owner
23		257	305	Guzman, Isabel P	Wife	F	Cha	25	M	N	Y	Guam	Y	None
24		257	305	Guzman, Edward P	Son	M	Cha	3.3	S	N		Guam		None
25		257	305	Guzman, Silvia P	Daughter	F	Cha	.5	S	N		Guam		None

DEPARTMENT OF COMMERCE-BUREAU OF THE CENSUS
WASHINGTON

FIFTEENTH CENSUS OF THE UNITED STATES: 1930-POPULATION

THE ISLAND OF GUAM

Sheet No. 32B

67B

District **Municipality of Agana**
Name of Place **Agana City (Part of San Antonio)**
[Proper name and, also, name of class, as city, town, village, barrio, etc]

Enumeration District No. **2**
Enumerated by me on **April 26, 1930** Arthur W. Jackson, Enumerator

	PLACE OF ABODE: Street, avenue, road, etc.	Number of dwelling house in order of visitation	Number of family in order of visitation	NAME of each person whose place of abode on April 1, 1930, was in this family. Enter surname, first, then given name and middle initial. If any. Include every person living on April 1, 1930. Omit children born since April 1, 1930.	RELATION Relationship of this Person to the head of the family.	PERSONAL DESCRIPTION: Sex	Color or race	Age at last birthday	Single, married, widowed or divorced	EDUCATION: Attended school any time since Sept. 1, 1929	Whether able to read and write.	NATIVITY Place of birth of this person.	Whether able to speak English.	OCCUPATION
	1	2	3	4	5	6	7	8	9	10	11	12	13	14
26	Padre Palomo	258	306	Aguon, Rosauro M	Head	M	Cha	53	M	N	Y	Guam	N	Farmer
27		258	306	Aguon, Andrea S	Wife	F	Cha	53	M	N	Y	Guam	N	None
28		258	306	Aguon, Ana S	Daughter	F	Cha	23	S	N	Y	Guam	N	None
29		258	306	Aguon, Joaquin S	Son	M	Cha	22	S	N	Y	Guam	Y	Laborer
30		258	306	Aguon, Rosa S	Daughter	F	Cha	19	S	N	Y	Guam	Y	None
31		258	306	Aguon, Francisco S	Son	M	Cha	17	S	N	Y	Guam	Y	None
32		258	306	Aguon, Jesus S	Son	M	Cha	16	S	Y	Y	Guam	Y	None
33		258	306	Aguon, Blandina S	Daughter	F	Cha	11	S	Y	Y	Guam	Y	None
34		258	306	Aguon, Pedro S	Son	M	Cha	9	S	Y		Guam		None
35		259	307	Aguon, Concepcion V	Head	F	Cha	22	M	N	Y	Guam	Y	None
36		259	307	Aguon, Jose V	Son	M	Cha	4.8	S	N		Guam		None
37		259	307	Aguon, Roman V	Son	M	Cha	3.5	S	N		Guam		None
38		259	307	Aguon, Felipe V	Son	M	Cha	.1	S	N		Guam		None
39		206	308	Sablan, Joaquin R	Head	M	Cha	59	M	N	Y	Guam	N	Farmer
40		206	308	Sablan, Maria C	Wife	F	Cha	50	M	N	Y	Guam	N	None
41		206	308	Sablan, Maria C	Daughter	F	Cha	25	S	N	Y	Guam	Y	Seamstress
42		206	308	Sablan, Natividad C	Daughter	F	Cha	19	S	N	Y	Guam	Y	None
43		206	308	Sablan, Mariano C	Son	M	Cha	17	S	N	Y	Guam	Y	Laborer
44		206	308	Sablan, Jose C	Son	M	Cha	14	S	Y	Y	Guam	Y	None
45		206	308	Sablan, Ana C	Daughter	F	Cha	12	S	Y	Y	Guam	Y	None
46		261	309	Flores, Jose C	Head	M	Cha	63	Wd	N	Y	Guam	N	Farmer
47		261	309	Flores, Ana C	Daughter	F	Cha	29	S	N	Y	Guam	N	None
48		261	309	Flores, Jose C	Son	M	Cha	25	S	N	Y	Guam	Y	Farm laborer
49		261	309	Flores, Juan C	Son	M	Cha	22	S	N	Y	Guam	Y	None
50		261	309	Flores, Rosa C	Daughter	F	Cha	19	S	N	Y	Guam	Y	None

(CHAMORRO ROOTS GENEALOGY PROJECT™ TRANSCRIPTION)
(BERNARD T. PUNZALAN / HTTP://WWW.CHAMORROROOTS.COM)

DEPARTMENT OF COMMERCE-BUREAU OF THE CENSUS
WASHINGTON

FIFTEENTH CENSUS OF THE UNITED STATES: 1930-POPULATION

THE ISLAND OF GUAM

Sheet No. 33A

District **Municipality of Agana**
Name of Place **Agana City (Part of San Antonio)**
[Proper name and, also, name of class, as city, town, village, barrio, etc]

Enumeration District No. **2**
Enumerated by me on **April 26, 1930** Arthur W. Jackson
Enumerator

	PLACE OF ABODE			NAME	RELATION	PERSONAL DESCRIPTION				EDUCATION		NATIVITY		OCCUPATION
	Street, avenue, road, etc.	Number of dwelling house in order of visitation	Number of family in order of visitation	of each person whose place of abode on April 1, 1930, was in this family. Enter surname, first, then given name and middle initial. If any. Include every person living on April 1, 1930. Omit children born since April 1, 1930.	Relationship of this Person to the head of the family.	Sex	Color or race	Age at last birthday	Single, married, widowed or divorced	Attended school any time since Sept. 1, 1929	Whether able to read and write.	Place of birth of this person.	Whether able to speak English.	
	1	2	3	4	5	6	7	8	9	10	11	12	13	14
1	Padre Palomo	261	309	Flores, Carmen C	Daughter	F	Cha	17	S	N	Y	Guam	Y	None
2		261	310	Crisostomo, Jose D	Head	M	Cha	30	M	N	Y	Guam	Y	Laborer
3		261	310	Crisostomo, Maria F	Wife	F	Cha	32	M	N	Y	Guam	Y	None
4		261	310	Crisostomo, Dolores F	Daughter	F	Cha	7	S	N		Guam		None
5		261	310	Crisostomo, Dionisio F	Son	M	Cha	6	S	N		Guam		None
6		261	310	Crisostomo, Maria F	Daughter	F	Cha	2.3	S	N		Guam		None
7		261	310	Crisostomo, Ignacia F	Daughter	F	Cha	.5	S	N		Guam		None
8		262	311	Mendiola, Francisco P	Head	M	Cha	26	S	N	Y	Guam	Y	Laborer
9		263	312	Flores, Josefa P	Head	F	Cha	72	Wd	N	Y	Guam	N	None
10		263	312	Flores, Joaquin P	Son	M	Cha	41	S	N	Y	Guam	Y	Farmer
11		263	312	Flores, Ana P	Daughter	F	Cha	36	S	N	Y	Guam	Y	None
12		264	313	De Leon, Joaquin U	Head	M	Cha	32	M	N	Y	Guam	Y	Book keeper
13		264	313	De Leon, Mercedes F	Wife	F	Cha	30	M	N	Y	Guam	Y	None
14		264	313	De Leon, Elizabeth B	Daughter	F	Cha	2.8	S	N		Guam		None
15		264	313	De Leon, Menna M	Daughter	F	Cha	.4	S	N		Guam		None
16		264	313	Flores, Jose C	Nephew	F	Cha	13	S	Y	Y	Guam	Y	None
17		264	313	Flores, Jesus C	Nephew	M	Cha	10	S	Y	Y	Guam	Y	None
18		265	314	Palomo, Jose C	Head	M	Cha	31	M	N	Y	Guam	Y	Laborer
19		265	314	Palomo, Carmen C	Wife	F	Cha	30	M	N	Y	Guam	Y	None
20		265	314	Palomo, Ana C	Daughter	F	Cha	5	S	N		Guam		None
21		265	314	Palomo, Jose C	Son	M	Cha	3.3	S	N		Guam		None
22		265	314	Palomo, Maria C	Daughter	F	Cha	1.8	S	N		Guam		None
23		266	315	Crisostomo, Pedro C	Head	M	Cha	30	M	N	Y	Guam	Y	Laborer
24		266	315	Crisostomo, Ana C	Wife	F	Cha	28	M	N	Y	Guam	N	None
25		267	316	Castro, Mariano C	Head	M	Cha	57	M	N	Y	Guam	N	Farmer

(CHAMORRO ROOTS GENEALOGY PROJECT™ TRANSCRIPTION)
(BERNARD T. PUNZALAN / HTTP://WWW.CHAMORROROOTS.COM)

DEPARTMENT OF COMMERCE-BUREAU OF THE CENSUS
WASHINGTON

FIFTEENTH CENSUS OF THE UNITED STATES: 1930-POPULATION

THE ISLAND OF GUAM

Sheet No. 33B

68B

District **Municipality of Agana**

Name of Place **Agana City (Part of San Antonio)**
[Proper name and, also, name of class, as city, town, village, barrio, etc]

Enumeration District No. 2

Enumerated by me on **April 28, 1930** Arthur W. Jackson, Enumerator

	PLACE OF ABODE: Street, avenue, road, etc.	Number of dwelling house in order of visitation	Number of family in order of visitation	NAME of each person whose place of abode on April 1, 1930, was in this family. Enter surname, first, then given name and middle initial. If any. Include every person living on April 1, 1930. Omit children born since April 1, 1930.	RELATION Relationship of this Person to the head of the family.	PERSONAL DESCRIPTION: Sex	Color or race	Age at last birthday	Single, married, widowed or divorced	EDUCATION: Attended school any time since Sept. 1, 1929	Whether able to read and write.	NATIVITY Place of birth of this person.	Whether able to speak English.	OCCUPATION
	1	2	3	4	5	6	7	8	9	10	11	12	13	14
26	Barrigada road	267	316	Castro, Ana B	Wife	F	Cha	57	M	N	Y	Guam	N	None
27		267	316	Castro, Rita B	Daughter	F	Cha	24	S	N	Y	Guam	N	None
28		267	316	Castro, Concepcion B	Daughter	F	Cha	19	S	N	Y	Guam	Y	None
29		267	316	Castro, Jose B	Son	M	Cha	13	S	Y	Y	Guam	Y	None
30		268	317	Perez, Jose P	Head	M	Cha	43	M	N	Y	Guam	N	Farmer
31		268	317	Perez, Rita B	Wife	F	Cha	44	M	N	Y	Guam	N	None
32		268	317	Perez, Manuel B	Son	M	Cha	18	S	Y	Y	Guam	Y	None
33		268	317	Blaz, Jesus B	Bro-in-law	M	Cha	33	S	N	Y	Guam	Y	Farm laborer
34		268	317	Perez, Jesus M	Nephew	M	Cha	19	S	N	Y	Guam	Y	Farm laborer
35		268	317	Perez, Mergilda M	Niece	F	Cha	14	S	N	Y	Guam	Y	None
36		269	318	Camacho, Ana S	Head	F	Cha	60	S	N	N	Guam	N	None
37		269	318	Camacho, Jose C	Son	M	Cha	28	S	N	Y	Guam	Y	Laborer
38		269	318	Camacho, Concepcion C	Daughter	F	Cha	18	S	N	Y	Guam	Y	None
39		270	319	Manibusan, Vicente P	Head	M	Cha	30	M	N	Y	Guam	Y	Farmer
40		270	319	Manibusan, Maria E	Wife	F	Cha	25	M	N	Y	Guam	N	None
41		270	319	Manibusan, Vicente E	Son	M	Cha	5	S	N		Guam		None
42		270	319	Manibusan, Dolores E	Daughter	F	Cha	.5	S	N		Guam	N	None
43		270	319	Manibusan, Maria P	Sister	F	Cha	28	S	N	Y	Guam	N	None
44		271	320	Cruz, Rita P	Head	F	Cha	28	M	N	Y	Guam	N	None
45		271	320	Cruz, Ramon P	Son	M	Cha	8	S	Y		Guam		None
46		271	320	Cruz, Jose P	Son	M	Cha	6	S	N		Guam		None
47		271	320	Cruz, Vicente P	Son	M	Cha	4.5	S	N		Guam		None
48		272	321	Villagomez, Jose V	Head	M	Cha	37	M	N	Y	Guam	Y	Carpenter
49		272	321	Villagomez, Ana A	Wife	F	Cha	31	M	N	Y	Guam	N	None
50		272	321	Villagomez, Artemio A	Son	M	Cha	12	S	Y	Y	Guam	Y	None

DEPARTMENT OF COMMERCE-BUREAU OF THE CENSUS
WASHINGTON

FIFTEENTH CENSUS OF THE UNITED STATES: 1930-POPULATION

THE ISLAND OF GUAM

Sheet No. 34A

District **Municipality of Agana**
Name of Place **Agana City (Part of San Antonio)**
[Proper name and, also, name of class, as city, town, village, barrio, etc]

Enumeration District No. 2
Enumerated by me on **April 28, 1930** Arthur W. Jackson, Enumerator

	PLACE OF ABODE			NAME	RELATION	PERSONAL DESCRIPTION				EDUCATION		NATIVITY		OCCUPATION
	Street, avenue, road, etc.	Number of dwelling house in order of visitation	Number of family in order of visitation	of each person whose place of abode on April 1, 1930, was in this family. Enter surname, first, then given name and middle initial. If any. Include every person living on April 1, 1930. Omit children born since April 1, 1930.	Relationship of this Person to the head of the family.	Sex	Color or race	Age at last birthday	Single, married, widowed or divorced	Attended school any time since Sept. 1, 1929	Whether able to read and write.	Place of birth of this person.	Whether able to speak English.	
	1	2	3	4	5	6	7	8	9	10	11	12	13	14
1	Barrigada road	272	321	Villagomez, Ignacio A	Son	M	Cha	10	S	Y	Y	Guam	Y	None
2		272	321	Villagomez, Francisco A	Son	M	Cha	9	S	Y		Guam		None
3		272	321	Villagomez, Felix A	Son	M	Cha	7	S	Y		Guam		None
4		272	321	Villagomez, Juan A	Son	M	Cha	5	S	N		Guam		None
5		272	321	Villagomez, Delfina A	Daughter	F	Cha	3.1	S	N		Guam		None
6		272	321	Villagomez, Ruperto A	Son	M	Cha	1.8	S	N		Guam		None
7		273	322	Cruz, Francisco J	Head	M	Cha	43	M	N	Y	Guam	Y	Farmer
8		273	322	Cruz, Rosa B	Wife	F	Cha	43	M	N	Y	Guam	N	None
9		273	322	Cruz, Rita B	Daughter	F	Cha	18	D?	Y	Y	Guam	Y	None
10		273	322	Jesus, Maria H	Servant	F	Cha	23	S	Y	Y	Guam	Y	None
11		274	323	Camacho, Jose G	Head	M	Cha	34	M	N	Y	Guam	Y	Carpenter
12		274	323	Camacho, Ana M	Wife	F	Cha	32	M	N	Y	Guam	N	None
13		274	323	Camacho, Josefina M	Daughter	F	Cha	11	S	Y	Y	Guam	Y	None
14		274	323	Camacho, Isabel M	Daughter	F	Cha	9	S	Y		Guam		None
15		274	323	Camacho, Jesus M	Son	M	Cha	2.5	S	N		Guam		None
16		275	324	Ramos, Trinidad T	Head	F	Cha	27	M	N	Y	Guam	Y	None
17		275	324	Ramos, Rosa T	Daughter	F	Cha	4.8	S	N		Guam		None
18		275	324	Ramos, Alejandro T	Son	M	Cha	2.8	S	N		Guam		None
19		275	324	Ramos, Maria T	Daughter	F	Cha	.1	S	N		Guam		None
20		275	324	Borja, Ana O	Servant	F	Cha	11	S	Y	Y	Guam	Y	Servant
21		276	325	San Nicolas, Antonio SN	Head	M	Cha	36	M	N	Y	Guam	N	Laborer
22		276	325	San Nicolas, Josefa C	Wife	F	Cha	32	M	N	Y	Guam	N	None
23		276	325	San Nicolas, Enrique C	Son	M	Cha	5	S	N		Guam		None
24		276	325	San Nicolas, Fidela C	Daughter	F	Cha	3.8	S	N		Guam		None
25		276	325	San Nicolas, Delgadina C	Daughter	F	Cha	.7	S	N		Guam		None

DEPARTMENT OF COMMERCE-BUREAU OF THE CENSUS
WASHINGTON

FIFTEENTH CENSUS OF THE UNITED STATES: 1930-POPULATION

THE ISLAND OF GUAM

Sheet No. 34B

69B

District **Municipality of Agana**
Name of Place **Agana City (Part of San Antonio)**
[Proper name and, also, name of class, as city, town, village, barrio, etc]

Enumeration District No. 2
Enumerated by me on **April 28, 1930** Arthur W. Jackson
Enumerator

	PLACE OF ABODE			NAME	RELATION	PERSONAL DESCRIPTION				EDUCATION		NATIVITY		OCCUPATION
	Street, avenue, road, etc.	Number of dwelling house is order of visitation	Number of family in order of visitation	of each person whose place of abode on April 1, 1930, was in this family. Enter surname, first, then given name and middle initial. If any. Include every person living on April 1, 1930. Omit children born since April 1, 1930.	Relationship of this Person to the head of the family.	Sex	Color or race	Age at last birthday	Single, married, widowed or divorced	Attended school any time since Sept. 1, 1929	Whether able to read and write.	Place of birth of this person.	Whether able to speak English.	
	1	2	3	4	5	6	7	8	9	10	11	12	13	14
26	Barrigada road	277	326	Untalan, Jesus B	Head	M	Cha	49	M	N	Y	Guam	N	Farmer
27		277	326	Untalan, Ana F	Wife	F	Cha	40	M	N	Y	Guam	N	None
28		277	326	Untalan, Tomas F	Son	M	Cha	19	S	N	Y	Guam	Y	Chauffeur
29		277	326	Untalan, Josefina F	Daughter	F	Cha	16	S	N	Y	Guam	Y	None
30		277	326	Untalan, Carlota F	Daughter	F	Cha	15	S	N	Y	Guam	Y	None
31		277	326	Untalan, Maria F	Daughter	F	Cha	13	S	Y	Y	Guam	Y	None
32		277	326	Untalan, Beatrice F	Daughter	F	Cha	11	S	Y	Y	Guam	Y	None
33		277	326	Untalan, Bonifacio F	Son	M	Cha	8	S	Y		Guam		None
34		277	326	Untalan, Lourdes F	Daughter	F	Cha	3.8	S	N		Guam		None
35		277	326	Untalan, Grillermo F	Son	M	Cha	1.8	S	N		Guam		None
36		278	327	Perez, Ana C	Head	F	Cha	42	Wd	N	N	Guam	N	None
37		278	327	Perez, Jose C	Son	M	Cha	22	S	N	Y	Guam	Y	Farm laborer
38		278	327	Perez, Asuncion C	Daughter	F	Cha	19	S	N	Y	Guam	Y	None
39		278	327	Perez, Ana C	Daughter	F	Cha	17	S	N	Y	Guam	Y	None
40		278	327	Perez, Rosario C	Daughter	F	Cha	13	S	Y	Y	Guam		None
41		278	327	Perez, Felipe C	Son	M	Cha	9	S	Y		Guam		None
42		278	327	Perez, Ignacio C	Son	M	Cha	.1	S	N		Guam		None
43		279	328	San Nicolas, Juan SN	Head	M	Cha	42	M	N	N	Guam	N	Farmer
44		279	328	San Nicolas, Vicenta T	Wife	F	Cha	38	M	N	N	Guam	N	None
45		280	329	Camacho, Tomasa B	Head	F	Cha	61	Wd	N	N	Guam	N	None
46		280	329	Camacho, Luis P	Son	M	Cha	27	S	N	Y	Guam	N	Laborer
47		281	330	Blaz, Rita L	Head	F	Cha	31	M	Y	Y	Guam	Y	None
48		281	330	Blaz, Jose L	Son	M	Cha	9	S	Y		Guam		None
49		281	330	Blaz, Maria L	Daughter	F	Cha	7	S	Y		Guam		None
50		281	330	Blaz, Jesus L	Son	M	Cha	5	S	N		Guam		None

DEPARTMENT OF COMMERCE-BUREAU OF THE CENSUS
WASHINGTON

FIFTEENTH CENSUS OF THE UNITED STATES: 1930-POPULATION

THE ISLAND OF GUAM

Sheet No. 35A

District **Municipality of Agana**
Name of Place **Agana City (Part of San Antonio)**
[Proper name and, also, name of class, as city, town, village, barrio, etc]

Enumeration District No. 2
Enumerated by me on **April 28, 1930** Arthur W. Jackson
Enumerator

	PLACE OF ABODE			NAME	RELATION	PERSONAL DESCRIPTION				EDUCATION		NATIVITY		OCCUPATION
	Street, avenue, road, etc.	Number of dwelling house is order of visitation	Number of family in order of visitation	of each person whose place of abode on April 1, 1930, was in this family. Enter surname, first, then given name and middle initial. If any. Include every person living on April 1, 1930. Omit children born since April 1, 1930.	Relationship of this Person to the head of the family.	Sex	Color or race	Age at last birthday	Single, married, widowed or divorced	Attended school any time since Sept. 1, 1929	Whether able to read and write.	Place of birth of this person.	Whether able to speak English.	
	1	2	3	4	5	6	7	8	9	10	11	12	13	14
1	Barrigada road	281	330	Blaz, Antonio R	Son	M	Cha	3.8	S	N		Guam		None
2		281	330	Blaz, Jesusa R	Daughter	F	Cha	1.8	S	N		Guam		None
3		281	330	Benavente, Jose G	Servant	M	Cha	18	S	N	Y	Guam	Y	None
4		282	331	Benavente, Joaquin A	Head	M	Cha	39	M	N	Y	Guam	N	Farmer
5		282	331	Benavente, Ana L	Wife	F	Cha	33	M	N	Y	Guam	N	
6		282	331	Benavente, Nieves L	Daughter	F	Cha	10	S	Y	Y	Guam	Y	None
7		282	331	Benavente, Jose L	Son	M	Cha	9	S	Y		Guam		None
8		282	331	Benavente, Virginia L	Daughter	F	Cha	5	S	N		Guam		None
9		282	331	Benavente, Maria L	Daughter	F	Cha	4.7	S	N		Guam		None
10		282	331	Benavente, Alvina L	Daughter	F	Cha	2.8	S	N		Guam		None
11		283	332	Torres, Trinidad P	Head	F	Cha	54	Wd	N	N	Guam	N	None
12		284	333	White, Jose F	Head	M	Cha	39	M	N	Y	Guam	Y	Fireman
13		284	333	White, Rosa A	Wife	F	Cha	35	M	N	Y	Guam	Y	None
14		284	333	White, Pedro A	Son	M	Cha	8	S	Y		Guam		None
15		284	333	White, Emelia A	Daughter	F	Cha	6	S	N		Guam		None
16		284	333	White, Lourdes A	Daughter	F	Cha	5	S	N		Guam		None
17		284	333	White, Tomasa A	Daughter	F	Cha	3.3	S	N		Guam		None
18		284	333	White, Oliva A	Daughter	F	Cha	2.8	S	N		Guam		None
19		285	334	Perez, Jose B	Head	M	Cha	23	M	N	Y	Guam	Y	Laborer
20		285	334	Perez, Veronica SA	Wife	F	Cha	20	M	N	Y	Guam	Y	School teacher
21		285	334	Perez, Frank SA	Son	M	Cha	1.5	S	N		Guam		None
22		286	335	Champaco, Luisa A	Head	F	Cha	35	S	N	Y	Guam	Y	Housekeeper
23		286	335	Adriano, Maria C	Grandmoth	F	Cha	90	Wd	N	N	Guam	N	None
24		287	336	Pangelinan, Carment T	Head	F	Cha	60	Wd	N	N	Guam	N	None
25		287	336	Pangelinan, Rita A	Lodger	F	Cha	46	S	N	N	Guam	N	None

DEPARTMENT OF COMMERCE-BUREAU OF THE CENSUS
WASHINGTON

FIFTEENTH CENSUS OF THE UNITED STATES: 1930-POPULATION

THE ISLAND OF GUAM

Sheet No. 35B

70B

District **Municipality of Agana**

Name of Place **Agana City (Part of San Antonio)**

[Proper name and, also, name of class, as city, town, village, barrio, etc]

Enumeration District No. **2**

Enumerated by me on **April 28, 1930** Arthur W. Jackson, Enumerator

	PLACE OF ABODE			NAME	RELATION	PERSONAL DESCRIPTION				EDUCATION		NATIVITY		OCCUPATION
	Street, avenue, road, etc.	Number of dwelling house is order of visitation	Number of family in order of visitation	of each person whose place of abode on April 1, 1930, was in this family. Enter surname, first, then given name and middle initial. If any. Include every person living on April 1, 1930. Omit children born since April 1, 1930.	Relationship of this Person to the head of the family.	Sex	Color or race	Age at last birthday	Single, married, widowed or divorced	Attended school any time since Sept. 1, 1929	Whether able to read and write.	Place of birth of this person.	Whether able to speak English.	
	1	2	3	4	5	6	7	8	9	10	11	12	13	14
26	Barrigada road	287	336	Quichocho, Jose R	Lodger	M	Cha	28	S	N	Y	Guam	N	Farmer
27		288	337	Quichocho, Vicenta G	Head	F	Cha	36	S	N	Y	Guam	N	None
28		288	338	Perez, Vicente P	Head	M	Cha	44	M	N	Y	Guam	N	Farmer
29		288	338	Perez, Maria Q	Wife	F	Cha	33	M	N	Y	Guam	N	None
30		288	338	Perez, Jose M	Son	M	Cha	13	S	Y	Y	Guam	Y	None
31		288	338	Perez, Rosa Q	Daughter	F	Cha	6	S	Y		Guam		None
32		288	338	Perez, Maria Q	Daughter	F	Cha	5	S	N		Guam		None
33		288	338	Perez, Ignacia Q	Daughter	F	Cha	4.8	S	N		Guam		None
34		289	339	Rosario, Joaquina R	Head	F	Cha	48	S	N		Guam		None
35		290	340	Quichocho, Jesus Q	Head	M	Cha	29	M	N	Y	Guam	Y	Blacksmith
36		290	340	Quichocho, Maria B	Wife	F	Cha	26	M	N	Y	Guam	N	None
37		290	340	Quichocho, Nicolas B	Son	M	Cha	3.5	S	N		Guam		None
38		290	340	Quichocho, Carmen B	Daughter	F	Cha	.8	S	N		Guam		None
39		291	340	Quichocho, Jose R	Head	M	Cha	37	M	N	Y	Guam	Y	Farmer
40		291	340	Quichocho, Rufina L	Wife	F	Cha	39	M	N	Y	Guam	Y	None
41		291	340	Quichocho, Maria L	Daughter	F	Cha	15	S	Y	Y	Guam	Y	None
42		291	340	Quichocho, Jesus L	Son	M	Cha	12	S	Y	Y	Guam	Y	None
43		291	340	Quichocho, Juan L	Son	M	Cha	9	S	Y		Guam		None
44		291	340	Quichocho, Beatrice L	Daughter	F	Cha	7	S	Y		Guam		None
45		291	340	Quichocho, Isabel L	Daughter	F	Cha	4.3	S	N		Guam		None
46		292	342	Quitugua, Jose D	Head	M	Cha	31	M	N	Y	Guam	Y	Laborer
47		292	342	Quitugua, Maria P	Wife	F	Cha	29	M	N	Y	Guam	N	None
48		292	342	Quitugua, Juan P	Son	M	Cha	6	S	N		Guam		None
49		292	342	Quitugua, Jose P	Son	M	Cha	3.2	S	N		Guam		None
50		292	342	Quitugua, Maria P	Daughter	F	Cha	.1	S	N		Guam		None

(CHAMORRO ROOTS GENEALOGY PROJECT™ TRANSCRIPTION)
(BERNARD T. PUNZALAN / HTTP://WWW.CHAMORROROOTS.COM)

DEPARTMENT OF COMMERCE-BUREAU OF THE CENSUS
WASHINGTON

FIFTEENTH CENSUS OF THE UNITED STATES: 1930-POPULATION

THE ISLAND OF GUAM

Sheet No. 36A

District **Municipality of Agana**
Name of Place **Agana City (Part of San Antonio)**
[Proper name and, also, name of class, as city, town, village, barrio, etc]

Enumeration District No. 2
Enumerated by me on **April 29, 1930** Arthur W. Jackson, Enumerator

	PLACE OF ABODE			NAME	RELATION	PERSONAL DESCRIPTION				EDUCATION		NATIVITY		OCCUPATION
	Street, avenue, road, etc.	Number of dwelling house is order of visitation	Number of family in order of visitation	of each person whose place of abode on April 1, 1930, was in this family. Enter surname, first, then given name and middle initial. If any. Include every person living on April 1, 1930. Omit children born since April 1, 1930.	Relationship of this Person to the head of the family.	Sex	Color or race	Age at last birthday	Single, married, widowed or divorced	Attended school any time since Sept. 1, 1929	Whether able to read and write.	Place of birth of this person.	Whether able to speak English.	
	1	2	3	4	5	6	7	8	9	10	11	12	13	14
1	Barrigada road	293	343	Ninaisen, Dolores S	Head	F	Cha	45	S	N	N	Guam	N	None
2		293	343	Ninaisen, Antonio S	Son	M	Cha	9	S	N		Guam		None
3		293	343	Ninaisen, Maria S	Daughter	F	Cha	5	S	N		Guam		None
4		294	344	White, Jose W	Head	M	Cha	43	M	N	Y	Guam	N	Laborer
5		294	344	White, Ana LG	Wife	F	Cha	37	M	N	Y	Guam	N	None
6		294	344	White, Jesus LG	Son	M	Cha	19	S	N	Y	Guam	Y	None
7		294	344	White, Justo LG	Son	M	Cha	17	S	N	Y	Guam	Y	None
8		294	344	White, Jose LG	Son	M	Cha	12	S	Y	Y	Guam	Y	None
9		294	344	White, Joaquin LG	Son	M	Cha	10	S	Y	Y	Guam	Y	None
10		294	344	White, Ramon LG	Son	M	Cha	8	S	Y		Guam		None
11		294	344	White, Maria LG	Daughter	F	Cha	6	S	N		Guam		None
12		294	344	White, Antonio LG	Son	M	Cha	4.3	S	N		Guam		None
13		294	344	White, Eduardo LG	Son	M	Cha	2.8	S	N		Guam		None
14		295	345	White, Juan F	Head	M	Cha	45	M	N	Y	Guam	Y	Fireman
15		295	345	White, Antonia C	Wife	F	Cha	36	M	N	Y	Guam	N	None
16		295	345	White, Maria C	Daughter	F	Cha	16	S	N	Y	Guam	Y	None
17		295	345	White, Juan C	Son	M	Cha	15	S	Y	Y	Guam	Y	None
18		295	345	White, Dolores C	Daughter	F	Cha	12	S	Y	Y	Guam	Y	None
19		296	346	Torre, Joaquin B	Head	M	Cha	42	M	N	Y	Guam	Y	Carpenter
20		296	346	Torre, Felicidad U	Wife	F	Cha	37	M	N	Y	Guam	N	None
21		296	346	Torre, Jose U	Son	M	Cha	12	S	Y	Y	Guam	Y	None
22		296	346	Torre, Vicenta U	Daughter	F	Cha	10	S	Y	Y	Guam	Y	None
23		296	346	Torre, Ana U	Daughter	F	Cha	8	S	Y		Guam		None
24		296	346	Torre, Juan U	Son	M	Cha	6	S	N		Guam		None
25		296	346	Torre, Rosa U	Daughter	F	Cha	4.2	S	N		Guam		None

(CHAMORRO ROOTS GENEALOGY PROJECT™ TRANSCRIPTION)
(BERNARD T. PUNZALAN / HTTP://WWW.CHAMORROROOTS.COM)

DEPARTMENT OF COMMERCE-BUREAU OF THE CENSUS
WASHINGTON

FIFTEENTH CENSUS OF THE UNITED STATES: 1930-POPULATION

THE ISLAND OF GUAM

Sheet No. 36B

71B

District **Municipality of Agana**
Name of Place **Agana City (Part of San Antonio)**
[Proper name and, also, name of class, as city, town, village, barrio, etc]

Enumeration District No. 2
Enumerated by me on **April 29, 1930** Arthur W. Jackson
Enumerator

	PLACE OF ABODE			NAME	RELATION	PERSONAL DESCRIPTION				EDUCATION		NATIVITY		OCCUPATION
	Street, avenue, road, etc.	Number of dwelling house is order of visitation	Number of family in order of visitation	of each person whose place of abode on April 1, 1930, was in this family. Enter surname, first, then given name and middle initial. If any. Include every person living on April 1, 1930. Omit children born since April 1, 1930.	Relationship of this Person to the head of the family.	Sex	Color or race	Age at last birthday	Single, married, widowed or divorced	Attended school any time since Sept. 1, 1929	Whether able to read and write.	Place of birth of this person.	Whether able to speak English.	
	1	2	3	4	5	6	7	8	9	10	11	12	13	14
26	[illegible]	296	346	Torre, Esperanza U	Daughter	F	Cha	2.4	S	N		Guam		None
27		296	346	Torre, Isabel U	Daughter	F	Cha	1.4	S	N		Guam		None
28		296	346	Torre, Maria U	Daughter	F	Cha	.8	S	N		Guam		None
29		297	347	Torres, Jose LG	Head	M	Cha	61	Wd	N	Y	Guam	N	Carpenter
30		297	347	Torres, Ana P	Daughter	F	Cha	21	S	N	Y	Guam	N	None
31		297	347	Torres, Vicente P	Son	M	Cha	22	S	N	Y	Guam	Y	Laborer
32		298	348	Leon Guerrero, Justa B	Head	F	Cha	62	Wd	N	Y	Guam	N	None
33		298	348	Leon Guerrero, Francisco B	Son	M	Cha	32	S	N	Y	Guam	Y	Laborer
34		298	348	Leon Guerrero, Pedro B	Son	M	Cha	20	S	N	Y	Guam	N	Farmer
35		298	349	Camacho, Enrique M	Head	M	Cha	38	M	N	Y	Guam	N	Farmer
36		298	349	Camacho, Emeteria LG	Wife	F	Cha	35	M	N	Y	Guam	N	None
37		298	349	Camacho, Antonia LG	Daughter	F	Cha	14	S	Y	Y	Guam	Y	None
38		298	349	Camacho, Maria LG	Daughter	F	Cha	12	S	Y	Y	Guam	Y	None
39		298	349	Camacho, Zoilo LG	Son	M	Cha	10	S	Y	Y	Guam	Y	None
40		298	349	Camacho, Juan LG	Son	M	Cha	6.3	S	N		Guam		None
41		298	349	Camacho, Filomina LG	Daughter	F	Cha	3.8	S	N		Guam		None
42		298	349	Camacho, Josefina LG	Daughter	F	Cha	1.5	S	N		Guam		None
43		298	349	Mendiola, Maria P	Servant	F	Cha	21	S	N	Y	Guam	Y	Servant
44		299	350	Sablan, Ana P	Head	F	Cha	65	M	N	Y	Guam	N	None
45		299	350	Sablan, Juan P	Son	M	Cha	25	S	N	Y	Guam	Y	School teacher
46		299	350	Borja, Juan S	Grandson	M	Cha	11	S	Y	Y	Guam	Y	None
47		300	351	Borja, Maria B	Head	F	Cha	46	S	N	Y	Guam	N	None
48		300	351	Borja, Manuel B	Son	M	Cha	27	S	N	Y	Guam	Y	Farmer
49		300	351	Borja, Antonio B	Son	M	Cha	21	S	N	Y	Guam	Y	Laborer
50		300	351	Borja, Jose B	Son	M	Cha	18	S	N	Y	Guam	Y	Laborer

(CHAMORRO ROOTS GENEALOGY PROJECT™ TRANSCRIPTION)
(BERNARD T. PUNZALAN / HTTP://WWW.CHAMORROROOTS.COM)

DEPARTMENT OF COMMERCE-BUREAU OF THE CENSUS
WASHINGTON

FIFTEENTH CENSUS OF THE UNITED STATES: 1930-POPULATION

THE ISLAND OF GUAM

Sheet No. 37A

District **Municipality of Agana**
Name of Place **Agana City (Part of San Antonio)**
[Proper name and, also, name of class, as city, town, village, barrio, etc]

Enumeration District No. **2**
Enumerated by me on **April 30, 1930** Arthur W. Jackson
Enumerator

	PLACE OF ABODE			NAME	RELATION	PERSONAL DESCRIPTION				EDUCATION		NATIVITY		OCCUPATION
	Street, avenue, road, etc.	Number of dwelling house is order of visitation	Number of family in order of visitation	of each person whose place of abode on April 1, 1930, was in this family. Enter surname, first, then given name and middle initial. If any. Include every person living on April 1, 1930. Omit children born since April 1, 1930.	Relationship of this Person to the head of the family.	Sex	Color or race	Age at last birthday	Single, married, widowed or divorced	Attended school any time since Sept. 1, 1929	Whether able to read and write.	Place of birth of this person.	Whether able to speak English.	
	1	2	3	4	5	6	7	8	9	10	11	12	13	14
1	Mongmong	300	351	Borja, Juan B	Son	M	Cha	13	S	Y	Y	Guam	Y	None
2		300	351	Borja, Maria B	Daughter	F	Cha	11	S	Y	Y	Guam	Y	None
3		300	352	Borja, Francisco B	Head	M	Cha	27	M	N	Y	Guam	Y	Farmer
4		300	352	Borja, Ana I	Wife	F	Cha	23	M	N	Y	Guam	Y	None
5		300	352	Borja, Rosa I	Daughter	F	Cha	3.8	S	N		Guam		None
6		300	352	Borja, Pedro I	Son	M	Cha	2.8	S	N		Guam		None
7		301	353	Claveria, Juan A	Head	M	Cha	27	M	N	Y	Guam	Y	Machinist
8		301	353	Claveria, Vicenta P	Wife	F	Cha	20	M	N	Y	Guam	Y	None
9		301	353	Claveria, Francisco P	Son	M	Cha	1.4	S	N		Guam		None
10		302	354	Castro, Juan C	Head	M	Cha	39	M	N	Y	Guam	Y	Fireman
11		302	354	Castro, Maria G	Wife	F	Cha	29	M	N	Y	Guam	Y	None
12		302	354	Castro, Leonardo F	Son	M	Cha	8	S	Y		Guam		None
13		302	354	Castro, Juan F	Son	M	Cha	7	S	Y		Guam		None
14		302	354	Castro, Maria F	Daughter	F	Cha	6	S	N		Guam		None
15		302	354	Castro, Francisco F	Son	M	Cha	5	S	N		Guam		None
16		303	355	Quichocho, Jose P	Head	M	Cha	33	M	N	Y	Guam	Y	Laborer
17		303	355	Quichocho, Juana S	Wife	F	Cha	28	M	N	Y	Guam	Y	None
18		303	355	Quichocho, Emeterio S	Daughter	F	Cha	8	S	Y		Guam		None
19		303	355	Quichocho, Isabel S	Daughter	F	Cha	6	S	N		Guam		None
20		303	355	Quichocho, Joaquin S	Son	M	Cha	4.1	S	N		Guam		None
21		303	355	Quichocho, Jose S	Son	M	Cha	2.8	S	N		Guam		None
22		303	355	Quichocho, Vicente S	Son	M	Cha	.1	S	N		Guam		None
23		303	355	Siguenza, Concepcion T	Sist-in-law	F	Cha	19	S	N	Y	Guam	Y	None
24		303	355	Siguenza, Jose T	Bro-in-law	M	Cha	20	S	N	Y	Guam	Y	Laborer
25		304	356	Flores, Jose A	Head	M	Cha	64	M	N	Y	Guam	N	Farmer

DEPARTMENT OF COMMERCE-BUREAU OF THE CENSUS
WASHINGTON

FIFTEENTH CENSUS OF THE UNITED STATES: 1930-POPULATION
THE ISLAND OF GUAM

Sheet No. 37B

72B

District Municipality of Agana
Name of Place Agana City (Part of San Antonio)
[Proper name and, also, name of class, as city, town, village, barrio, etc]

Enumeration District No. 2
Enumerated by me on April 30, 1930 Arthur W. Jackson, Enumerator

	PLACE OF ABODE			NAME	RELATION	PERSONAL DESCRIPTION				EDUCATION		NATIVITY		OCCUPATION
	Street, avenue, road, etc.	Number of dwelling house is order of visitation	Number of family in order of visitation	of each person whose place of abode on April 1, 1930, was in this family. Enter surname, first, then given name and middle initial. If any. Include every person living on April 1, 1930. Omit children born since April 1, 1930.	Relationship of this Person to the head of the family.	Sex	Color or race	Age at last birthday	Single, married, widowed or divorced	Attended school any time since Sept. 1, 1929	Whether able to read and write.	Place of birth of this person.	Whether able to speak English.	
	1	2	3	4	5	6	7	8	9	10	11	12	13	14
26	Mongmong	304	356	Flores, Magdalena B	Daughter	F	Cha	18	S	N	N	Guam	Y	None
27		305	357	Duenas, Joaquin A	Head	M	Cha	25	M	N	Y	Guam	Y	Carpenter
28		305	357	Duenas, Ana F	Wife	F	Cha	24	M	N	Y	Guam	Y	None
29		305	357	Duenas, Vicente F	Son	M	Cha	2.8	S	N		Guam		None
30		306	358	Blaz, Ramon F	Head	M	Cha	30	M	N	Y	Guam	Y	Printer
31		306	358	Blaz, Maria A	Wife	F	Cha	24	M	N	Y	Guam	Y	None
32		306	358	Blaz, Juan A	Son	M	Cha	.8	S	N		Guam		None
33		306	358	Blaz, Josefa F	Mother	F	Cha	63	Wd	N	N	Guam	N	None
34		306	358	Blaz, Ana M	Niece	F	Cha	18	S	N	Y	Guam	Y	None
35		307	359	Perez, Antonio F	Head	M	Cha	24	M	N	Y	Guam	Y	Silversmith
36		307	359	Perez, Gracia A	Wife	F	Cha	22	M	N	Y	Guam	Y	None
37		307	359	Perez, Juan D	Son	M	Cha	3.8	S	N		Guam		None
38		307	359	Perez, Vicente D	Son	M	Cha	.6	S	N		Guam		None
39		307	359	Duenas, Francisco A	Bro-in-law	M	Cha	21	S	N	Y	Guam	Y	Servant
40		307	359	Quitonguico, Engracia T	Step sister	F	Cha	14	S	N	Y	Guam	Y	None
41		308	360	Flores, Joaquin	Head	M	Cha	57	M	N	Y	Guam	Y	Farmer
42		308	360	Flores, Socorro SN	Wife	F	Fil	26	M	N	Y	Guam	Y	None
43		308	360	Flores, Joaquina SN	Daughter	F	Cha	8	S	Y		Guam		None
44		309	361	Ojeda, Juan M	Head	M	Cha	30	M	N	Y	Guam	Y	Chauffeur
45		309	361	Ojeda, Rosa SN	Wife	F	Cha	25	M	N	Y	Guam	N	None
46		309	361	Ojeda, Pedro SN	Son	M	Cha	1.8	S	N		Guam		None
47		309	361	San Agustin, Dolores L	Moth-in-law	F	Cha	60	S	N	N	Guam	N	None
48		309	361	San Nicolas, Paula SN	Lodger	F	Cha	58	S	N	N	Guam	N	None
49		309	362	Quidachay, Veronica Q	Head	F	Cha	36	S	N	Y	Guam	Y	None
50		309	362	Quidachay, Timoteo Q	Son	M	Cha	6	S	N		Guam		None

(CHAMORRO ROOTS GENEALOGY PROJECT™ TRANSCRIPTION)
(BERNARD T. PUNZALAN / HTTP://WWW.CHAMORROROOTS.COM)

DEPARTMENT OF COMMERCE-BUREAU OF THE CENSUS
WASHINGTON

FIFTEENTH CENSUS OF THE UNITED STATES: 1930-POPULATION

THE ISLAND OF GUAM

Sheet No. 38A

District **Municipality of Agana**
Name of Place **Agana City (Part of San Antonio)**
[Proper name and, also, name of class, as city, town, village, barrio, etc]

Enumeration District No. 2
Enumerated by me on **April 30, 1930** Arthur W. Jackson
Enumerator

	PLACE OF ABODE			NAME	RELATION	PERSONAL DESCRIPTION				EDUCATION		NATIVITY		OCCUPATION
	Street, avenue, road, etc.	Number of dwelling house in order of visitation	Number of family in order of visitation	of each person whose place of abode on April 1, 1930, was in this family. Enter surname, first, then given name and middle initial. If any. Include every person living on April 1, 1930. Omit children born since April 1, 1930.	Relationship of this Person to the head of the family.	Sex	Color or race	Age at last birthday	Single, married, widowed or divorced	Attended school any time since Sept. 1, 1929	Whether able to read and write.	Place of birth of this person.	Whether able to speak English.	
	1	2	3	4	5	6	7	8	9	10	11	12	13	14
1	Mongmong	309	362	Quidachay, Vicenta Q	Daughter	F	Cha	3.3	S	N		Guam		None
2		309	362	Quidachay, Barsalisa Q	Daughter	F	Cha	1.8	S	N		Guam		None
3		310	363	Francisco, Domingo	Head	M	Cha	67	M	N	Y	Guam	N	None
4		310	363	Francisco, Carmen C	Wife	F	Cha	54	M	N	Y	Guam	N	None
5		310	363	Francisco, Rosa C	Daughter	F	Cha	36	S	N	Y	Guam	N	None
6		310	363	Francisco, Ignacia C	Daughter	F	Cha	34	S	N	Y	Guam	Y	None
7		310	363	Francisco, Maria J C	Daughter	F	Cha	22	S	Y	Y	Guam	Y	None
8		310	363	Francisco, Antonio C	Son	M	Cha	15	S	Y	Y	Guam	Y	None
9		310	363	Francisco, Jose C	Son	M	Cha	11	S	Y	Y	Guam	Y	None
10		310	363	Blaz, Carmen F	Grandaug	F	Cha	8	S	Y		Guam		None
11		311	364	Blaz, Juan S	Head	M	Cha	37	M	N	Y	Guam	N	Farmer
12		311	364	Blaz, Antonia F	Wife	F	Cha	35	M	N	Y	Guam	N	None
13		311	364	Blaz, Jose F	Son	M	Cha	11	S	Y	Y	Guam	Y	None
14		311	364	Blaz, Maria F	Daughter	F	Cha	10	S	Y	Y	Guam	Y	None
15		311	364	Blaz, Juana F	Daughter	F	Cha	9	S	Y		Guam		None
16		311	364	Blaz, Victoria F	Daughter	F	Cha	5	S	N		Guam		None
17		311	364	Blaz, Roman F	Son	M	Cha	4.5	S	N		Guam		None
18		311	364	Blaz, Jesusa F	Daughter	F	Cha	3.6	S	N		Guam		None
19		311	364	Blaz, Pedro F	Son	M	Cha	1.8	S	N		Guam		None
20		312	365	Cruz, Manuel C	Head	M	Cha	61	Wd	N	Y	Guam	N	Farmer
21		312	365	Cruz, Francisco C	Son	M	Cha	27	S	N	Y	Guam	Y	Farm laborer
22		312	365	Cruz, Manuel C	Son	M	Cha	24	S	N	Y	Guam	Y	Chauffeur
23		312	365	Cruz, Engracia C	Daughter	F	Cha	23	S	N	Y	Guam	Y	None
24		312	365	Cruz, Maria C	Daughter	F	Cha	22	S	N	Y	Guam	Y	None
25		313	366	Mesa, Joaquin M	Head	M	Cha	51	M	N	Y	Guam	N	Farmer

(CHAMORRO ROOTS GENEALOGY PROJECT™ TRANSCRIPTION)
(BERNARD T. PUNZALAN / HTTP://WWW.CHAMORROROOTS.COM)

DEPARTMENT OF COMMERCE-BUREAU OF THE CENSUS
WASHINGTON

FIFTEENTH CENSUS OF THE UNITED STATES: 1930-POPULATION

THE ISLAND OF GUAM

Sheet No. 38B

73B

District **Municipality of Agana**
Name of Place **Agana City (Part of San Antonio)**
[Proper name and, also, name of class, as city, town, village, barrio, etc]

Enumeration District No. 2
Enumerated by me on **May 1, 1930** Arthur W. Jackson
Enumerator

	PLACE OF ABODE			NAME	RELATION	PERSONAL DESCRIPTION				EDUCATION		NATIVITY		OCCUPATION
	Street, avenue, road, etc.	Number of dwelling house is order of visitation	Number of family in order of visitation	of each person whose place of abode on April 1, 1930, was in this family. Enter surname, first, then given name and middle initial. If any. Include every person living on April 1, 1930. Omit children born since April 1, 1930.	Relationship of this Person to the head of the family.	Sex	Color or race	Age at last birthday	Single, married, widowed or divorced	Attended school any time since Sept. 1, 1929	Whether able to read and write.	Place of birth of this person.	Whether able to speak English.	
	1	2	3	4	5	6	7	8	9	10	11	12	13	14
26	Mongmong	313	366	Mesa, Rita M	Wife	F	Cha	45	M	N	Y	Guam	N	None
27		313	366	Mesa, Tomasa M	Daughter	F	Cha	20	S	N	Y	Guam	Y	None
28		313	366	Mesa, Jose M	Son	M	Cha	15	S	N	Y	Guam	Y	None
29		313	366	Mesa, Esther M	Daughter	F	Cha	14	S	Y	Y	Guam	Y	None
30		313	366	Mesa, Margarita M	Daughter	F	Cha	6	S	Y		Guam		None
31		314	367	Hernandez, Joaquin F	Head	M	Cha	39	M	N	Y	Guam	N	Farmer
32		314	367	Hernandez, Joaquina Q	Wife	F	Cha	32	M	N	Y	Guam	N	None
33		314	367	Hernandez, Elisa Q	Daughter	F	Cha	4.3	S	N		Guam		None
34		314	367	Hernandez, Jose Q	Son	M	Cha	3.8	S	N		Guam		None
35		314	367	Hernandez, Asuncion Q	Daughter	F	Cha	1.9	S	N		Guam		None
36		314	367	Quitugua, Vicenta C	Sist-in-law	F	Cha	38	S	N	Y	Guam	N	None
37		314	367	Quitugua, Maria C	Niece	F	Cha	9	S	Y		Guam		None
38		315	368	Mateo, Pedro C	Head	M	Cha	34	M	N	Y	Guam	Y	Laborer
39		315	368	Mateo, Rosa SN	Wife	F	Cha	35	M	N	Y	Guam	Y	Midwife
40		315	368	Mateo, Maria SN	Daughter	F	Cha	9	S	Y		Guam		None
41		315	368	Mateo, Juan SN	Son	M	Cha	8	S	Y		Guam		None
42		315	368	Mateo, Rosa SN	Daughter	F	Cha	5	S	N		Guam		None
43		315	368	Mateo, Ramon SN	Son	M	Cha	3.5	S	N		Guam		None
44		315	368	Mateo, Pedro SN	Son	M	Cha	2.8	S	N		Guam		None
45		315	368	Mateo, Gregorio SN	Son	M	Cha	.1	S	N		Guam		None
46		315	368	Mesa, Maria M	Lodger	F	Cha	21	S	N	Y	Guam	Y	None
47		316	369	Flores, Ana G	Head	F	Cha	35	M	N	Y	Guam	Y	None
48		316	369	Flores, Juan G	Son	M	Cha	6	S	N		Guam		None
49		316	369	Flores, Joaquina G	Daughter	F	Cha	5	S	N		Guam		None
50		316	369	Flores, Maria G	Daughter	F	Cha	3.1	S	N		Guam		None

(CHAMORRO ROOTS GENEALOGY PROJECT™ TRANSCRIPTION)
(BERNARD T. PUNZALAN / HTTP://WWW.CHAMORROROOTS.COM)

DEPARTMENT OF COMMERCE-BUREAU OF THE CENSUS
WASHINGTON

FIFTEENTH CENSUS OF THE UNITED STATES: 1930-POPULATION

THE ISLAND OF GUAM

Sheet No. 39A

District **Municipality of Agana**
Name of Place **Agana City (Part of San Antonio)**
[Proper name and, also, name of class, as city, town, village, barrio, etc]

Enumeration District No. 2
Enumerated by me on **May 1, 1930** Arthur W. Jackson, Enumerator

	PLACE OF ABODE			NAME	RELATION	PERSONAL DESCRIPTION				EDUCATION		NATIVITY		OCCUPATION
	Street, avenue, road, etc.	Number of dwelling house is order of visitation	Number of family in order of visitation	of each person whose place of abode on April 1, 1930, was in this family. Enter surname, first, then given name and middle initial. If any. Include every person living on April 1, 1930. Omit children born since April 1, 1930.	Relationship of this Person to the head of the family.	Sex	Color or race	Age at last birthday	Single, married, widowed or divorced	Attended school any time since Sept. 1, 1929	Whether able to read and write.	Place of birth of this person.	Whether able to speak English.	
	1	2	3	4	5	6	7	8	9	10	11	12	13	14
1	Mongmong	316	369	Flores, Pedro G	Son	M	Cha	1.8	S	N		Guam		None
2		316	369	Flores, Martin G	Son	M	Cha	.5	S	N		Guam		None
3		317	370	Ada, Antonio F	Head	M	Cha	36	M	N	Y	Guam	Y	Laborer
4		317	370	Ada, Maria Q	Wife	F	Cha	31	M	N	Y	Guam	N	None
5		317	370	Ada, Margarita Q	Daughter	F	Cha	9	S	Y		Guam		None
6		317	370	Ada, Jose Q	Son	M	Cha	7	S	Y		Guam		None
7		317	370	Ada, Jesus Q	Son	M	Cha	7	S	Y		Guam		None
8		317	370	Ada, Antonio Q	Son	M	Cha	5	S	N		Guam		None
9		317	370	Ada, Rosalia Q	Daughter	F	Cha	3.3	S	N		Guam		None
10		317	370	Ada, Mariano Q	Son	M	Cha	1.9	S	N		Guam		None
11		317	370	Quichocho, Dolores F	Aunt	F	Cha	56	S	N	N	Guam	N	None
12		318	371	Leon Guerrero, Luis T	Head	M	Cha	63	M	N	Y	Guam	N	Farmer
13		318	371	Leon Guerrero, Isabel T	Wife	F	Cha	58	M	N	N	Guam	N	None
14		319	372	Untalan, Jose P	Head	M	Cha	39	M	N	Y	Guam	Y	Carpenter
15		319	372	Untalan, Trinidad R	Wife	F	Cha	34	M	N	Y	Guam	N	None
16		319	372	Untalan, Juan R	Son	M	Cha	14	S	Y	Y	Guam	Y	None
17		319	372	Untalan, Oliva R	Daughter	F	Cha	11	S	Y	Y	Guam	Y	None
18		319	372	Untalan, Jesus R	Son	M	Cha	9	S	Y		Guam		None
19		320	373	Payne, Patrick A	Head	M	Cha	27	M	N	Y	Guam	Y	Farmer
20		320	373	Payne, Ignacia S	Wife	F	Cha	35	M	N	Y	Guam	Y	None
21		320	373	Payne, Joseph S	Son	M	Cha	8	S	Y		Guam		None
22		320	373	Payne, Rosa S	Daughter	F	Cha	5	S	N		Guam		None
23		320	373	Payne, Tomas S	Son	M	Cha	3.1	S	N		Guam		None
24		320	373	Payne, Dolores S	Daughter	F	Cha	.2	S	N		Guam		None
25		320	373	Cruz, Pedro C	Servant	M	Cha	15	S	N	Y	Guam	Y	Servant

DEPARTMENT OF COMMERCE-BUREAU OF THE CENSUS
WASHINGTON

FIFTEENTH CENSUS OF THE UNITED STATES: 1930-POPULATION

THE ISLAND OF GUAM

Sheet No. 39B

74B

District Municipality of Agana
Name of Place Agana City (Part of San Antonio)
[Proper name and, also, name of class, as city, town, village, barrio, etc]

Enumeration District No. 2
Enumerated by me on May 1, 1930 Arthur W. Jackson
Enumerator

	PLACE OF ABODE			NAME	RELATION	PERSONAL DESCRIPTION				EDUCATION		NATIVITY		OCCUPATION
	Street, avenue, road, etc.	Number of dwelling house in order of visitation	Number of family in order of visitation	Name of each person whose place of abode on April 1, 1930, was in this family. Enter surname, first, then given name and middle initial. If any. Include every person living on April 1, 1930. Omit children born since April 1, 1930.	Relationship of this Person to the head of the family.	Sex	Color or race	Age at last birthday	Single, married, widowed or divorced	Attended school any time since Sept. 1, 1929	Whether able to read and write.	Place of birth of this person.	Whether able to speak English.	
	1	2	3	4	5	6	7	8	9	10	11	12	13	14
26	Mongmong	321	374	San Nicolas, Concepcion SN	Head	F	Cha	45	S	N	Y	Guam	Y	None
27		321	375	Salas, Juan S	Head	M	Cha	36	S	N	N	Guam	Y	Plumber
28		322	376	Perez, Antonio P	Head	M	Cha	47	M	N	Y	Guam	Y	Laborer
29		322	376	Perez, Rita B	Wife	F	Cha	49	M	N	Y	Guam	Y	None
30		322	376	Perez, Candaleria B	Daughter	F	Cha	16	S	Y	Y	Guam	Y	None
31		322	376	Perez, Ana B	Daughter	F	Cha	15	S	Y	Y	Guam	Y	None
32		322	376	Perez, Maxima B	Daughter	F	Cha	6	S	N		Guam		None
33		322	376	Perez, Concepcion B	Daughter	F	Cha	3.3	S	N		Guam		None
34		322	376	Marrion, Lorenzo B	Step-son	M	Cha	23	S	N	Y	Guam	Y	Farm laborer
35		323	377	Santos, Luis A	Head	M	Cha	36	M	N	Y	Guam	Y	Laborer
36		323	377	Santos, Joaquina R	Wife	F	Cha	30	M	N	Y	Guam	N	None
37		323	377	Santos, Alfonsina R	Daughter	F	Cha	9	S	Y		Guam		None
38		323	377	Santos, Jesus R	Son	M	Cha	6	S	N		Guam		None
39		323	377	Santos, Antonio R	Son	M	Cha	5	S	N		Guam		None
40		323	377	Santos, Jose R	Son	M	Cha	3.3	S	N		Guam		None
41		323	377	Santos, Vicenta R	Daughter	F	Cha	.1	S	N		Guam		None
42		324	378	Taitinfong, Francisco B	Head	M	Cha	25	M	N	Y	Guam	Y	Farmer
43		324	378	Taitinfong, Ana C	Wife	F	Cha	24	M	N	Y	Guam	Y	None
44		324	378	Taitinfong, Guadalupe C	Daughter	F	Cha	3.3	S	N		Guam		None
45		324	378	Taitinfong, Jose C	Son	M	Cha	2.4	S	N		Guam		None
46		324	378	Taitinfong, Maria C	Daughter	F	Cha	.3	S	N		Guam		None
47		324	378	Taitinfong, Jose de L	Father	M	Cha	61	Wd	N	Y	Guam	N	Farmer
48		325	379	Oroso, Ana C	Head	F	Cha	59	Wd	N	Y	Guam	N	None
49		325	380	Atoigue, Felipe M	Head	M	Cha	27	M	N	Y	Guam	Y	Laborer
50		325	380	Atoigue, Emeliana O	Wife	F	Cha	26	M	N	Y	Guam	N	None

DEPARTMENT OF COMMERCE-BUREAU OF THE CENSUS
WASHINGTON

FIFTEENTH CENSUS OF THE UNITED STATES: 1930-POPULATION

THE ISLAND OF GUAM

Sheet No. 40A

District **Municipality of Agana**
Name of Place **Agana City (Part of San Antonio)**
[Proper name and, also, name of class, as city, town, village, barrio, etc]

Enumeration District No. 2
Enumerated by me on **May 1, 1930** Arthur W. Jackson, Enumerator

	PLACE OF ABODE			NAME	RELATION	PERSONAL DESCRIPTION				EDUCATION		NATIVITY		OCCUPATION
	Street, avenue, road, etc.	Number of dwelling house is order of visitation	Number of family in order of visitation	of each person whose place of abode on April 1, 1930, was in this family. Enter surname, first, then given name and middle initial. If any. Include every person living on April 1, 1930. Omit children born since April 1, 1930.	Relationship of this Person to the head of the family.	Sex	Color or race	Age at last birthday	Single, married, widowed or divorced	Attended school any time since Sept. 1, 1929	Whether able to read and write.	Place of birth of this person.	Whether able to speak English.	
	1	2	3	4	5	6	7	8	9	10	11	12	13	14
1		325	380	Atoigue, Jesusa O	Daughter	F	Cha	6	S	N		Guam		None
2		325	380	Atoigue, Isabel O	Daughter	F	Cha	4.3	S	N		Guam		None
3		325	380	Atoigue, Maria O	Daughter	F	Cha	2.4	S	N		Guam		None
4		325	380	Atoigue, Engracia O	Daughter	F	Cha	.1	S	N		Guam		None
5		326	381	Shimizu, Joaquin T	Head	M	Cha	23	M	N	Y	Guam	Y	Book keeper
6		326	381	Shimizu, Ana S	Wife	F	Cha	27	M	N	Y	Guam	Y	None
7		326	381	Shimizu, Joseph S	Son	M	Cha	4.3	S	N		Guam		None
8		326	381	Shimizu, Concepcion S	Daughter	F	Cha	2.3	S	N		Guam		None
9		326	381	Shimizu, Jesusa S	Daughter	F	Cha	1.8	S	N		Guam		None
10		327	382	San Nicolas, Nieves C	Head	F	Cha	60	Wd	N	Y	Guam	Y	None
11		327	382	San Nicolas, Carmen L	Daughter	F	Cha	36	S	N	Y	Guam	Y	None
12		328	383	Divera, Nicolas A	Head	M	Cha	41	M	N	Y	Guam	N	Farmer
13	Mongmong	328	383	Divera, Carmen B	Wife	F	Cha	35	M	N	Y	Guam	N	None
14		328	383	Divera, Juan B	Son	M	Cha	15	S	N	Y	Guam	Y	None
15		328	383	Divera, Rogelio B	Son	M	Cha	12	S	Y	Y	Guam	Y	None
16		328	383	Divera, Francisca B	Daughter	F	Cha	10	S	Y	Y	Guam	Y	None
17		328	383	Divera, Donato B	Son	M	Cha	9	S	Y		Guam		None
18		328	383	Divera, Ana B	Daughter	F	Cha	5	S	N		Guam		None
19		329	384	Ignacio, Pedro A	Head	M	Cha	47	M	N	Y	Guam	N	Farmer
20		329	384	Ignacio, Marcela N	Wife	F	Cha	39	M	N	Y	Guam	N	None
21		329	384	Ignacio, Francisco N	Son	M	Cha	17	S	N	Y	Guam	Y	Farm laborer
22		329	384	Ignacio, Jesus N	Son	M	Cha	16	S	N	Y	Guam	Y	Farm laborer
23		329	384	Ignacio, Maria N	Daughter	F	Cha	15	S	N	Y	Guam	Y	None
24		329	384	Ignacio, Jose N	Son	M	Cha	12	S	Y	Y	Guam	Y	None
25		329	384	Ignacio, Manuel N	Son	M	Cha	7	S	Y		Guam		None

DEPARTMENT OF COMMERCE-BUREAU OF THE CENSUS
WASHINGTON

FIFTEENTH CENSUS OF THE UNITED STATES: 1930-POPULATION

THE ISLAND OF GUAM

Sheet No. 40B

75B

District Municipality of Agana
Name of Place Agana City (Part of San Antonio)
[Proper name and, also, name of class, as city, town, village, barrio, etc]

Enumeration District No. 2
Enumerated by me on May 2, 1930 Arthur W. Jackson, Enumerator

	PLACE OF ABODE			NAME	RELATION	PERSONAL DESCRIPTION				EDUCATION		NATIVITY		OCCUPATION
	Street, avenue, road, etc.	Number of dwelling house is order of visitation	Number of family in order of visitation	of each person whose place of abode on April 1, 1930, was in this family. Enter surname, first, then given name and middle initial. If any. Include every person living on April 1, 1930. Omit children born since April 1, 1930.	Relationship of this Person to the head of the family.	Sex	Color or race	Age at last birthday	Single, married, widowed or divorced	Attended school any time since Sept. 1, 1929	Whether able to read and write.	Place of birth of this person.	Whether able to speak English.	
	1	2	3	4	5	6	7	8	9	10	11	12	13	14
26	Mongmong	329	384	Ignacio, Juan N	Son	M	Cha	4.4	S	N		Guam		None
27		329	384	Ignacio, Pedro N	Son	M	Cha	2.5	S	N		Guam		None
28		330	385	Guerrero, Nicolas M	Head	M	Cha	36	M	N	N	Guam	N	Farmer
29		330	385	Guerrero, Ana I	Wife	F	Cha	35	M	N	Y	Guam	N	Cook
30		330	385	Guerrero, Howard I	Son	M	Cha	13	S	Y	Y	Guam	Y	None
31		330	385	Guerrero, Manuel I	Son	M	Cha	10	S	Y	Y	Guam	Y	None
32		330	385	Guerrero, Rosa I	Daughter	F	Cha	5	S	N		Guam		None
33		330	385	Guerrero, Santiago I	Son	M	Cha	.3	S	N		Guam		None
34		330	385	Perez, Magdalena C	Servant	F	Cha	21	S	N	Y	Guam	Y	Servant
35		331	386	Sosico, Dominga N	Head	M	Cha	54	S	N	Y	Guam	N	None
36		331	386	Sosico, Maria N	Daughter	F	Cha	25	S	N	N	Guam	N	None
37		331	386	Sosico, Jose N	Son	M	Cha	26	S	N	N	Guam	N	Farmer
38		331	386	Sosico, Jesus N	Son	M	Cha	13	S	Y	Y	Guam	N	None
39		332	387	Cruz, Jose S	Head	M	Cha	60	Wd	N	Y	Guam	N	Farmer
40		332	387	Cruz, Dolores W	Daughter	F	Cha	23	S	N	Y	Guam	Y	None
41		332	387	Cruz, Vicente W	Son	M	Cha	20	S	N	Y	Guam	Y	None
42		332	387	Cruz, Juan B	Son	M	Cha	9	S	Y		Guam		None
43		332	387	White, Ana P	Sist-in-law	F	Cha	66	S	Y	N	Guam	N	None
44		332	387	White, Rafaela P	Sist-in-law	F	Cha	59	S	N	N	Guam	N	None
45		332	387	Gogue, Vicenta W	Niece	F	Cha	42	S	N	Y	Guam	N	None
46		332	387	Mesa, Antonia P	Niece	F	Cha	18	S	N	Y	Guam	Y	None
47		333	388	Aflague, Antonia C	Head	F	Cha	73	Wd	N	N	Guam	N	None
48		333	388	Divera, Marcos A	Son	M	Cha	48	M	N	N	Guam	N	Laborer
49		334	389	Roberto, Manuel B	Head	M	Cha	27	M	N	Y	Guam	Y	Clerk
50		334	389	Roberto, Concepcion D	Wife	F	Cha	19	M	N	Y	Guam	Y	None

(CHAMORRO ROOTS GENEALOGY PROJECT™ TRANSCRIPTION)
(BERNARD T. PUNZALAN / HTTP://WWW.CHAMORROROOTS.COM)

DEPARTMENT OF COMMERCE-BUREAU OF THE CENSUS
WASHINGTON

FIFTEENTH CENSUS OF THE UNITED STATES: 1930-POPULATION

THE ISLAND OF GUAM

Sheet No. 41A

District **Municipality of Agana**
Name of Place **Agana City (Part of San Antonio)**
[Proper name and, also, name of class, as city, town, village, barrio, etc]

Enumeration District No. 2
Enumerated by me on **May 2, 1930** Arthur W. Jackson, Enumerator

	PLACE OF ABODE: Street, avenue, road, etc.	Number of dwelling house in order of visitation	Number of family in order of visitation	NAME of each person whose place of abode on April 1, 1930, was in this family. Enter surname, first, then given name and middle initial. If any. Include every person living on April 1, 1930. Omit children born since April 1, 1930.	RELATION Relationship of this Person to the head of the family.	PERSONAL DESCRIPTION: Sex	Color or race	Age at last birthday	Single, married, widowed or divorced	EDUCATION: Attended school any time since Sept. 1, 1929	Whether able to read and write.	NATIVITY Place of birth of this person.	Whether able to speak English.	OCCUPATION
	1	2	3	4	5	6	7	8	9	10	11	12	13	14
1	Mongmong	334	389	Roberto, Emelia D	Daughter	F	Cha	.8	S	N		Guam		None
2		335	390	Muna, Jose P	Head	M	Cha	40	Wd	N	Y	Guam	N	Farmer
3		335	390	Muna, Gregorio D	Son	M	Cha	17	S	N	Y	Guam	Y	None
4		335	390	Muna, Jose D	Son	M	Cha	16	S	N	Y	Guam	Y	None
5		335	390	Muna, Ignacio D	Son	M	Cha	14	S	Y	Y	Guam	Y	None
6		335	390	Muna, Francisco D	Son	M	Cha	13	S	Y	Y	Guam	Y	None
7		335	390	Muna, Felicita D	Daughter	F	Cha	11	S	Y	Y	Guam	Y	None
8		335	390	Muna, Jesus D	Son	M	Cha	7	S	Y		Guam		None
9		336	391	Castro, Juan P	Head	M	Cha	36	M	N	Y	Guam	Y	Farmer
10		336	391	Castro, Manuela D	Wife	F	Cha	30	M	N	Y	Guam	Y	None
11		336	391	Castro, Jose D	Son	M	Cha	5	S	N		Guam		None
12		336	391	Castro, Jesus D	Son	M	Cha	4.8	S	N		Guam		None
13		336	391	Castro, Juan D	Son	M	Cha	.4	S	N		Guam		None
14		337	392	Perez, Luis C	Head	M	Cha	44	M	N	Y	Guam	N	Farmer
15		337	392	Perez, Maria P	Wife	F	Cha	46	M	N	Y	Guam	N	None
16		337	392	Perez, Jose P	Son	M	Cha	14	S	Y	Y	Guam	Y	None
17		337	392	Perez, Juan P	Son	M	Cha	12	S	Y	Y	Guam	Y	None
18		337	392	Perez, Jesus P	Son	M	Cha	10	S	Y	Y	Guam	Y	None
19		338	393	Talavera, Manuel M	Head	M	Cha	60	Wd	N	Y	Guam	N	Farmer
20		338	393	Talavera, Antonio Q	Son	M	Cha	24	S	N	Y	Guam	Y	Farm laborer
21		338	394	Talavera, Jose Q	Head	M	Cha	29	M	N	Y	Guam	Y	Farmer
22		338	394	Talavera, Concepcion P	Wife	F	Cha	30	M	N	Y	Guam	Y	None
23		338	394	Talavera, Jesus P	Son	M	Cha	8	S	Y		Guam		None
24		338	394	Talavera, Maria P	Daughter	F	Cha	6	S	N		Guam		None
25		338	394	Talavera, Dolores P	Daughter	F	Cha	.9	S	N		Guam		None

DEPARTMENT OF COMMERCE-BUREAU OF THE CENSUS
WASHINGTON

FIFTEENTH CENSUS OF THE UNITED STATES: 1930-POPULATION

THE ISLAND OF GUAM

Sheet No. 41B

District **Municipality of Agana**
Name of Place **Agana City (Part of San Antonio)**
[Proper name and, also, name of class, as city, town, village, barrio, etc]

Enumeration District No. 2
Enumerated by me on **May 2, 1930** Arthur W. Jackson, Enumerator

	PLACE OF ABODE			NAME	RELATION	PERSONAL DESCRIPTION				EDUCATION		NATIVITY		OCCUPATION
	Street, avenue, road, etc.	Number of dwelling house is order of visitation	Number of family in order of visitation	of each person whose place of abode on April 1, 1930, was in this family. Enter surname, first, then given name and middle initial. If any. Include every person living on April 1, 1930. Omit children born since April 1, 1930.	Relationship of this Person to the head of the family.	Sex	Color or race	Age at last birthday	Single, married, widowed or divorced	Attended school any time since Sept. 1, 1929	Whether able to read and write.	Place of birth of this person.	Whether able to speak English.	
	1	2	3	4	5	6	7	8	9	10	11	12	13	14
26	Mongmong	339	395	Tass, Maria A	Head	F	Cha	45	Wd	N	Y	Guam	Y	None
27		339	395	Tass, John A	Son	M	Cha	27	S	N	Y	Guam	Y	Farmer
28		340	396	Duenas, Jose Q	Head	M	Cha	32	M	N	Y	Guam	Y	Farmer
29		340	396	Duenas, Mary D	Wife	F	Cha	16	M	N	Y	Guam	Y	None
30		340	396	Duenas, Mary J	Daughter	F	Cha	.9	S	N		Guam		None
31		341	397	Borja, Jesus O	Head	M	Cha	21	M	N	Y	Guam	Y	Carpenter
32		341	397	Borja, Gertrudes Q	Wife	F	Cha	19	M	N	Y	Guam	Y	None
33		342	398	Flores, Pedro G	Head	M	Cha	45	M	N	Y	Guam	Y	Farmer
34		342	398	Flores, Carmen M	Wife	F	Cha	33	M	Y	Y	Guam	Y	None
35		342	398	Flores, Gregorio M	Son	M	Cha	12	S	Y	Y	Guam	Y	None
36		342	398	Flores, Pedro M	Son	M	Cha	4.3	S	N		Guam		None
37		342	398	Flores, Jesus M	Son	M	Cha	2.3	S	N		Guam		None
38		342	398	Flores, Ana C	Lodger	F	Cha	60	M	N	Y	Guam	N	None
39		343	399	Perez, Vicente F	Head	M	Cha	38	M	N	Y	Guam	Y	Laborer
40		343	399	Perez, Josefa S	Wife	F	Cha	28	M	N	Y	Guam	Y	None
41		343	399	Perez, Luis S	Son	M	Cha	12	S	Y	Y	Guam	Y	None
42		343	399	Perez, Antonio S	Son	M	Cha	9	S	Y		Guam		None
43		343	399	Perez, Jesus S	Son	M	Cha	8	S	Y		Guam		None
44		343	399	Perez, Margarita S	Daughter	F	Cha	6	S	N		Guam		None
45		343	399	Perez, Gregorio S	Son	M	Cha	3.2	S	N		Guam		None
46		344	400	Quintanilla, Juan P	Head	M	Cha	55	Wd	N	Y	Guam	N	Farmer
47		345	401	Cruz, Paderno P	Head	M	Cha	29	M	N	Y	Guam	Y	Laborer
48		345	401	Cruz, Isabel L	Wife	F	Cha	26	M	N	Y	Guam	N	None
49		345	401	Cruz, Jose L	Son	M	Cha	3.2	S	N		Guam		None
50		345	401	Cruz, Josefa L	Daughter	F	Cha	1.7	S	N		Guam		None

DEPARTMENT OF COMMERCE-BUREAU OF THE CENSUS
WASHINGTON

FIFTEENTH CENSUS OF THE UNITED STATES: 1930-POPULATION

THE ISLAND OF GUAM

Sheet No. 42A

District **Municipality of Agana**
Name of Place **Agana City (Part of San Antonio)**
[Proper name and, also, name of class, as city, town, village, barrio, etc]

Enumeration District No. 2
Enumerated by me on **May 2, 1930** Arthur W. Jackson, Enumerator

	PLACE OF ABODE			NAME	RELATION	PERSONAL DESCRIPTION				EDUCATION		NATIVITY		OCCUPATION
	Street, avenue, road, etc.	Number of dwelling house is order of visitation	Number of family in order of visitation	of each person whose place of abode on April 1, 1930, was in this family. Enter surname, first, then given name and middle initial. If any. Include every person living on April 1, 1930. Omit children born since April 1, 1930.	Relationship of this Person to the head of the family.	Sex	Color or race	Age at last birthday	Single, married, widowed or divorced	Attended school any time since Sept. 1, 1929	Whether able to read and write.	Place of birth of this person.	Whether able to speak English.	
	1	2	3	4	5	6	7	8	9	10	11	12	13	14
1	Mongmong	345	401	Cruz, Concepcion P	Sister	F	Cha	25	S	N	Y	Guam	Y	None
2		346	402	Torre, Josefa A	Head	F	Cha	48	S	N	Y	Guam	N	None
3		347	403	Castro, Ana A	Head	F	Cha	64	S	N	N	Guam	N	None
4		348	404	Cruz, Jose G	Head	M	Cha	68	M	N	Y	Guam	N	Farmer
5		348	404	Cruz, Ana R	Wife	F	Cha	43	M	N	Y	Guam	N	None
6		348	404	Santos, Amparo S	Daughter	F	Cha	24	S	N	Y	Guam	Y	Nurse
7		348	404	Santos, Juan S	Step-son	M	Cha	19	S	N	Y	Guam	Y	Farm laborer
8		348	404	Santos, Nicolas S	Step-son	M	Cha	15	S	N	Y	Guam	Y	None
9		348	404	Santos, Francisco S	Step-son	M	Cha	12	S	Y	Y	Guam	Y	None
10		349	405	Borja, Antonio T	Head	M	Cha	26	M	N	Y	Guam	Y	Farmer
11		349	405	Borja, Soledad M	Wife	F	Cha	25	M	N	Y	Guam	Y	None
12		349	405	Borja, Maria C M	Daughter	F	Cha	4.5	S	N		Guam		None
13		349	405	Borja, Ana M	Daughter	F	Cha	3.5	S	N		Guam		None
14		349	405	Borja, Jose M	Son	M	Cha	2.3	S	N		Guam		None
15		349	405	Borja, Jesus M	Son	M	Cha	1.1	S	N		Guam		None
16					Here ends the enumeration of enumeration district No. 1 [sic] (San Antonio)									
17					[Sheet 42B/77B intentionally left blank by the enumerator.]									
18														
19														
20														
21														
22														
23														
24														
25														

District 3
Municipality of Agana

Bilibic
San Ignacio
Togae

DEPARTMENT OF COMMERCE-BUREAU OF THE CENSUS
WASHINGTON

FIFTEENTH CENSUS OF THE UNITED STATES: 1930-POPULATION

THE ISLAND OF GUAM

Sheet No. 1A

District **Municipality of Agana**
Name of Place **Agana City (Bilibic Urban)**
[Proper name and, also, name of class, as city, town, village, barrio, etc]

Enumeration District No. **3**
Enumerated by me on **April 2, 1930** Tomas A. Calvo
Enumerator

	PLACE OF ABODE			NAME	RELATION	PERSONAL DESCRIPTION				EDUCATION		NATIVITY		OCCUPATION
	Street, avenue, road, etc.	Number of dwelling house in order of visitation	Number of family in order of visitation	of each person whose place of abode on April 1, 1930, was in this family. Enter surname, first, then given name and middle initial. If any. Include every person living on April 1, 1930. Omit children born since April 1, 1930.	Relationship of this Person to the head of the family.	Sex	Color or race	Age at last birthday	Single, married, widowed or divorced	Attended school any time since Sept. 1, 1929	Whether able to read and write.	Place of birth of this person.	Whether able to speak English.	
	1	2	3	4	5	6	7	8	9	10	11	12	13	14
1	Soledad Street	1	1	Salas, Emeterio S.	Head	M	Cha	54	M	N	Y	Guam	N	Carpenter
2		1	1	Salas, Josefa M	Wife	F	Cha	57	M	N	N	Guam	N	None
3		1	1	Salas, Ignacia	Daughter	F	Cha	22	S	N	Y	Guam	Y	None
4		1	1	Salas, Jose	Son	M	Cha	19	S	N	Y	Guam	Y	Carpenter
5		1	1	Salas, Maria	Daughter	F	Cha	16	S	N	Y	Guam	Y	None
6		2	2	Santos, Manuel M	Head	M	Cha	25	M	N	Y	Guam	Y	Carpenter
7		2	2	Santos, Maria S	Wife	F	Cha	26	M	N	Y	Guam	Y	None
8		2	2	Santos, Jaime	Son	M	Cha	4	S	N	N	Guam	N	None
9		2	2	Santos, Juan	Son	M	Cha	3	S	N	N	Guam	N	None
10		2	2	Santos, Presentacion	Daughter	F	Cha	.9	S	N	N	Guam	N	None
11		3	3	Chargualaf, Jose R	Head	M	Cha	31	M	N	Y	Guam	Y	Laborer
12		3	3	Chargualaf, Magdalena I	Wife	F	Cha	24	M	N	Y	Guam	N	None
13		3	3	Chargualaf, Angel	Son	M	Cha	5	S	N	N	Guam	N	None
14		3	3	Chargualaf, Antonio	Son	M	Cha	4	S	N	N	Guam	N	None
15		3	3	Chargualaf, Maria	Daughter	F	Cha	1	S	N	N	Guam	N	None
16		4	4	Basa, Joaquin C	Head	M	Cha	40	M	N	Y	Guam	N	Farmer
17		4	4	Basa, Josefa D	Wife	F	Cha	42	M	N	Y	Guam	N	None
18		4	4	Basa, Jesus	Son	M	Cha	10	S	N	Y	Guam	Y	None
19		5	5	Rojas, Joaquin C	Head	M	Cha	42	M	N	N	Guam	Y	Farmer
20		5	5	Rojas, Maria	Wife	F	Cha	36	M	N	N	Guam	Y	None
21		5	5	Rojas, Francisco	Son	M	Cha	16	S	N	Y	Guam	Y	Farmer
22		5	5	Rojas, Margarita	Daughter	F	Cha	14	S	Y	Y	Guam	Y	None
23		5	5	Rojas, Pedro	Son	M	Cha	11	S	Y	Y	Guam	N	None
24		5	5	Rojas, Maria	Daughter	F	Cha	9	S	Y	Y	Guam	N	None
25		5	5	Rojas, Dolores	Daughter	F	Cha	5	S	N	N	Guam	N	None

DEPARTMENT OF COMMERCE-BUREAU OF THE CENSUS
WASHINGTON

FIFTEENTH CENSUS OF THE UNITED STATES: 1930-POPULATION

THE ISLAND OF GUAM

Sheet No. 1B

78B

District Municipality of Agana
Name of Place Agana City (Bilibic Urban)
[Proper name and, also, name of class, as city, town, village, barrio, etc]

Enumeration District No. 3
Enumerated by me on April 2, 1930 Tomas A. Calvo, Enumerator

	PLACE OF ABODE			NAME	RELATION	PERSONAL DESCRIPTION				EDUCATION		NATIVITY		OCCUPATION
	Street, avenue, road, etc.	Number of dwelling house is order of visitation	Number of family in order of visitation	of each person whose place of abode on April 1, 1930, was in this family. Enter surname, first, then given name and middle initial. If any. Include every person living on April 1, 1930. Omit children born since April 1, 1930.	Relationship of this Person to the head of the family.	Sex	Color or race	Age at last birthday	Single, married, widowed or divorced	Attended school any time since Sept. 1, 1929	Whether able to read and write.	Place of birth of this person.	Whether able to speak English.	
	1	2	3	4	5	6	7	8	9	10	11	12	13	14
26	Soledad Street	5	5	Rojas, Isabel	Daughter	F	Cha	4	S	N	N	Guam	N	None
27		5	5	Rojas, Carmen	Daughter	F	Cha	2	S	N	N	Guam	N	None
28		6	6	Rosario, Luisa	Head	F	Cha	70	Wd	N	N	Guam	N	Weaver
29		7	7	Salas, Francisco Q	Head	M	Cha	70	M	N	N	Guam	N	None
30		7	7	Salas, Maria C	Wife	F	Cha	59	M	N	N	Guam	N	None
31		7	7	Salas, Jose	Son	M	Cha	29	S	N	Y	Guam	Y	Laborer
32		7	7	Salas, Ana	Daughter	F	Cha	23	S	N	Y	Guam	Y	None
33		7	7	Salas, Vicente	Son	M	Cha	19	S	N	Y	Guam	Y	Farmer
34		7	7	Perez, Jesus S	Grandson	M	Cha	8	S	Y	N	Guam	N	None
35		7	7	Perez, Emiia S	Grand daughter	F	Cha	7	S	Y	N	Guam	N	None
36		7	7	Perez, Tomas S	Grandson	M	Cha	5	S	N	N	Guam	N	None
37		8	8	Rojas, Manuel C	Head	M	Cha	44	M	N	N	Guam	N	Janitor
38		8	8	Rojas, Ana I	Wife	F	Cha	57	M	N	N	Guam	N	None
39		8	8	Rojas, Jose S	Son	M	Cha	20	S	N	Y	Guam	Y	Janitor
40		8	8	Rojas, Bonita R	Daughter	F	Cha	17	S	N	Y	Guam	Y	None
41		8	8	Rojas, Maria R	Daughter	F	Cha	15	S	N	Y	Guam	Y	None
42		8	8	Rojas, Joaquin I	Son	M	Cha	8	S	Y	Y	Guam	N	None
43		9	9	Santos, Joaquin U	Head	M	Cha	61	M	N	N	Guam	N	None
44		9	9	Santos, Ana R	Wife	F	Cha	44	M	N	N	Guam	N	None
45		9	10	Cruz, Rosario R	Head	F	Cha	26	M	N	N	Guam	Y	None
46		9	10	Gogo, Rosa R	Daughter	F	Cha	6	S	N	N	Guam	N	None
47		9	10	Indelecio, Margarita R	Daughter	F	Cha	.1	S	N	N	Guam	N	None
48		10	11	Rosario, Manuel B	Head	M	Cha	44	M	N	N	Guam	N	Blacksmith
49		10	11	Rosario, Guadalupe F	Wife	F	Cha	25	M	N	Y	Guam	N	Laundress
50		10	11	Rosario, Juan C	Son	M	Cha	15	S	Y	Y	Guam	Y	None

DEPARTMENT OF COMMERCE-BUREAU OF THE CENSUS
WASHINGTON

FIFTEENTH CENSUS OF THE UNITED STATES: 1930-POPULATION

THE ISLAND OF GUAM

Sheet No. 2A

District **Municipality of Agana**
Name of Place **Agana City (Bilibic Urban)**
[Proper name and, also, name of class, as city, town, village, barrio, etc]

Enumeration District No. 3
Enumerated by me on **April 2, 1930** Tomas A. Calvo, Enumerator

	PLACE OF ABODE: Street, avenue, road, etc.	Number of dwelling house in order of visitation	Number of family in order of visitation	NAME of each person whose place of abode on April 1, 1930, was in this family. Enter surname, first, then given name and middle initial. If any. Include every person living on April 1, 1930. Omit children born since April 1, 1930.	RELATION Relationship of this Person to the head of the family.	PERSONAL DESCRIPTION: Sex	Color or race	Age at last birthday	Single, married, widowed or divorced	EDUCATION: Attended school any time since Sept. 1, 1929	Whether able to read and write.	NATIVITY Place of birth of this person.	Whether able to speak English.	OCCUPATION
	1	2	3	4	5	6	7	8	9	10	11	12	13	14
1	Soledad Street	10	11	Rosario, Jose A	Son	M	Cha	7	S	N	N	Guam	N	None
2		10	11	Rosario, Dolores A	Daughter	F	Cha	5	S	N	N	Guam	N	None
3		11	12	Aquino, Juan C	Head	M	Cha	26	M	N	Y	Guam	Y	Laborer
4		11	12	Aquino, Ana M	Wife	F	Cha	22	M	N	Y	Guam	Y	None
5		11	12	Aquino, Artemio	Son	M	Cha	1	S	N	N	Guam	N	None
6		11	12	Aquino, Roman	Son	M	Cha	.2	S	N	N	Guam	N	None
7		12	13	Matanane, Juan C	Head	M	Cha	23	M	N	Y	Guam	Y	Farmer
8		12	13	Matanane, Magdalena C	Wife	F	Cha	23	M	N	Y	Guam	Y	None
9		12	13	Matanane, Tomas	Son	M	Cha	2.1	S	N	N	Guam	N	None
10		12	13	Charsaguas, Concepcion S	Sister-in law	F	Cha	20	S	N	Y	Guam	Y	Maid
11		12	14	Pangelinan, Luisa C	Head	F	Cha	37	S	N	Y	Guam	N	None
12		12	14	Pangelinan, Antonia	Daughter	F	Cha	1	S	Y	Y	Guam	N	None
13		12	14	Quitugua, Pedro P	Nephew	M	Cha	12	S	Y	Y	Guam	N	None
14		13	15	Gumataotao, Ignacio B	Head	M	Cha	45	M	N	Y	Guam	N	Farmer
15		13	15	Gumataotao, Rita U	Wife	F	Cha	43	M	N	N	Guam	N	None
16		13	15	Gumataotao, Agustin	Son	M	Cha	14	S	Y	N	Guam	Y	None
17		13	15	Gumataotao, Francisco	Son	M	Cha	12	S	Y	Y	Guam	Y	None
18		13	15	Cabrera, Ignacio M	Head	M	Cha	32	M	N	Y	Guam	Y	Farmer
19		13	15	Cabrera, Maria C	Wife	F	Cha	36	M	N	Y	Guam	Y	None
20		13	15	Cabrera, Maria	Daughter	F	Cha	1.5	S	N	N	Guam	N	None
21		13	15	Cabrera, Vicente	Son	M	Cha	.1	S	N	N	Guam	N	None
22		14	17	San Nicolas, Rita P	Head	F	Cha	36	Wd	N	N	Guam	N	None
23		14	17	San Nicolas, Ignacio	Son	M	Cha	12	S	Y	Y	Guam	Y	None
24		14	17	San Nicolas, Francisco	Son	M	Cha	9	S	Y	Y	Guam	N	None
25		14	17	San Nicolas, Felix	Son	M	Cha	8	S	Y	N	Guam	N	None

(CHAMORRO ROOTS GENEALOGY PROJECT™ TRANSCRIPTION)
(BERNARD T. PUNZALAN / HTTP://WWW.CHAMORROROOTS.COM)

DEPARTMENT OF COMMERCE-BUREAU OF THE CENSUS
WASHINGTON

FIFTEENTH CENSUS OF THE UNITED STATES: 1930-POPULATION

THE ISLAND OF GUAM

Sheet No. 2B

79B

District **Municipality of Agana**
Name of Place **Agana City (Bilibic Urban)**
[Proper name and, also, name of class, as city, town, village, barrio, etc]

Enumeration District No. 3
Enumerated by me on **April 2, 1930** Tomas A. Calvo, Enumerator

	PLACE OF ABODE			NAME	RELATION	PERSONAL DESCRIPTION				EDUCATION		NATIVITY		OCCUPATION
	Street, avenue, road, etc.	Number of dwelling house is order of visitation	Number of family in order of visitation	of each person whose place of abode on April 1, 1930, was in this family. Enter surname, first, then given name and middle initial. If any. Include every person living on April 1, 1930. Omit children born since April 1, 1930.	Relationship of this Person to the head of the family.	Sex	Color or race	Age at last birthday	Single, married, widowed or divorced	Attended school any time since Sept. 1, 1929	Whether able to read and write.	Place of birth of this person.	Whether able to speak English.	
	1	2	3	4	5	6	7	8	9	10	11	12	13	14
26	Soledad Street	14	17	San Nicolas, Juliana	Daughter	F	Cha	1.9	S	N	N	Guam	N	None
27		14	17	Perez, Juliana F	Mother	F	Cha	64	Wd	N	N	Guam	N	None
28		15	18	Concepcion, Jose G	Head	M	Cha	68	M	N	N	Guam	N	None
29		15	18	Concepcion, Antonia M	Wife	F	Cha	60	M	N	N	Guam	N	Laundress
30		15	18	Perez, Maria C	Daughter	F	Cha	30	M	N	N	Guam	Y	Cook
31		15	18	Concepcion, Estela C	Grand daughter	F	Cha	4	S	N	N	Guam	N	None
32		16	19	Rios, Vicente LG	Head	M	Cha	30	M	N	Y	Guam	Y	Clerk
33		16	19	Rios, Tomasa S	Wife	F	Cha	30	M	N	Y	Guam	Y	None
34		16	19	Rios, Agnes	Daughter	F	Cha	8	S	Y	Y	Guam	N	None
35		16	19	Rios, Alfred	Son	M	Cha	6	S	N	N	Guam	N	None
36		16	19	Rios, Beatris	Daughter	F	Cha	5	S	N	N	Guam	N	None
37		16	19	Rios, Ermina	Daughter	F	Cha	4	S	N	N	Guam	N	None
38		16	19	Rios, Maria	Daughter	F	Cha	1.2	S	N	N	Guam	N	None
39		17	20	Quidachay, Ramona SN	Head	F	Cha	36	M	N	Y	Guam	N	None
40		17	20	Quidachay, Maria	Daughter	F	Cha	9	S	Y	Y	Guam	N	None
41		17	20	Quidachay, Carmen	Daughter	F	Cha	6	S	N	N	Guam	N	None
42		17	20	Quidachay, Juan	Son	M	Cha	5	S	N	N	Guam	N	None
43		17	21	George, Felix P	Head	M	Cha	69	Wd	N	N	Guam	Y	None
44		17	21	George, Sara M	Daughter	F	Cha	28	S	N	Y	Guam	N	None
45		17	21	George, Josefa M	Daughter	F	Cha	25	S	N	Y	Guam	N	None
46		17	21	George, Jose M	Son	M	Cha	21	S	N	Y	Guam	Y	Laborer
47		18	22	Cruz, Jose	Head	M	Cha	39	M	N	Y	Guam	Y	Clerk
48		18	22	Cruz, Josefa D	Wife	F	Cha	37	M	N	Y	Guam	Y	None
49		18	22	Cruz, Juan	Son	M	Cha	9	S	Y	Y	Guam	N	none
50		18	22	Cruz, Jose	Son	M	Cha	8	S	Y	Y	Guam	N	None

DEPARTMENT OF COMMERCE-BUREAU OF THE CENSUS
WASHINGTON

FIFTEENTH CENSUS OF THE UNITED STATES: 1930-POPULATION

THE ISLAND OF GUAM

Sheet No. 3A

District **Municipality of Agana**
Name of Place **Agana City (Bilibic Urban)**
[Proper name and, also, name of class, as city, town, village, barrio, etc]

Enumeration District No. **3**
Enumerated by me on **April 2, 1930** Tomas A. Calvo
Enumerator

	PLACE OF ABODE			NAME	RELATION	PERSONAL DESCRIPTION				EDUCATION		NATIVITY		OCCUPATION
	Street, avenue, road, etc.	Number of dwelling house is order of visitation	Number of family in order of visitation	of each person whose place of abode on April 1, 1930, was in this family. Enter surname, first, then given name and middle initial. If any. Include every person living on April 1, 1930. Omit children born since April 1, 1930.	Relationship of this Person to the head of the family.	Sex	Color or race	Age at last birthday	Single, married, widowed or divorced	Attended school any time since Sept. 1, 1929	Whether able to read and write.	Place of birth of this person.	Whether able to speak English.	
	1	2	3	4	5	6	7	8	9	10	11	12	13	14
1	Soledad Street	18	22	Cruz, Francisco	Son	M	Cha	7	S	N	N	Guam	N	None
2		18	22	Cruz, Rita	Daughter	F	Cha	5	S	N	N	Guam	N	None
3		18	22	Cruz, Maria	Daughter	F	Cha	3	S	N	N	Guam	N	None
4		19	23	Torres, Ignacio R	Head	M	Cha	36	M	N	Y	Guam	Y	Policeman
5		19	23	Torres, Dolores W	Wife	F	Cha	43	M	N	Y	Guam	Y	None
6		19	23	Torres, Felisa	Daughter	F	Cha	9	S	Y	N	Guam	N	None
7		19	24	Torres, Maria R	Head	F	Cha	61	Wd	N	N	Guam	N	None
8		20	25	Leon Guerrero, Rosa R	Head	F	Cha	32	M	N	Y	Guam	Y	None
9		20	25	Leon Guerrero, Juan	Son	M	Cha	4	S	N	N	Guam	N	None
10		20	25	Leon Guerrero, Pedro	Son	M	Cha	2	S	N	N	Guam	N	None
11		20	25	Cruz, Juan B	Servant	M	Cha	13	S	Y	Y	Guam	Y	Servant
12		21	26	Cruz, Vicente M	Head	M	Cha	37	M	N	Y	Guam	Y	Farmer
13		21	26	Cruz, Maria D	Daughter	F	Cha	11	S	Y	Y	Guam	Y	None
14		21	26	Cruz, Rosario D	Daughter	F	Cha	9	S	Y	Y	Guam	N	None
15		21	27	Duenas, Francisco C	Head	M	Cha	22	M	N	Y	Guam	N	Farmer
16		21	27	Duenas, Milagros A	Wife	F	Cha	22	M	N	Y	Guam	N	None
17		21	27	Duenas, Francisca	Daughter	F	Cha	.8	S	N	N	Guam	N	None
18		22	28	Lizama, Vicente A	Head	M	Cha	26	M	N	Y	Guam	Y	Farmer
19		22	28	Lizama, Magdalena C	Wife	F	Cha	23	M	N	N	Guam	N	None
20		23	29	Leon Guerrero, Jose C	Head	M	Cha	38	M	N	N	Guam	Y	Farmer
21		23	29	Leon Guerrero, Rita P	Wife	F	Cha	25	M	N	N	Guam	Y	None
22		23	29	Leon Guerrero, Francisco	Son	M	Cha	9	S	Y	Y	Guam	N	None
23		23	29	Leon Guerrero, Matias	Son	M	Cha	5	S	N	N	Guam	N	None
24		23	29	Leon Guerrero, Rosa	Daughter	F	Cha	3	S	N	N	Guam	N	None
25		23	29	Leon Guerrero, Maria	Daughter	F	Cha	1.4	S	N	N	Guam	N	None

(CHAMORRO ROOTS GENEALOGY PROJECT™ TRANSCRIPTION)
(BERNARD T. PUNZALAN / HTTP://WWW.CHAMORROROOTS.COM)

DEPARTMENT OF COMMERCE-BUREAU OF THE CENSUS
WASHINGTON

FIFTEENTH CENSUS OF THE UNITED STATES: 1930-POPULATION

THE ISLAND OF GUAM

Sheet No. 3B

80B

District Municipality of Agana
Name of Place Agana City (Bilibic Urban)
[Proper name and, also, name of class, as city, town, village, barrio, etc]

Enumeration District No. 3
Enumerated by me on April 3, 1930 Tomas A. Calvo, Enumerator

	PLACE OF ABODE			NAME	RELATION	PERSONAL DESCRIPTION				EDUCATION		NATIVITY		OCCUPATION
	Street, avenue, road, etc.	Number of dwelling house is order of visitation	Number of family in order of visitation	of each person whose place of abode on April 1, 1930, was in this family. Enter surname, first, then given name and middle initial. If any. Include every person living on April 1, 1930. Omit children born since April 1, 1930.	Relationship of this Person to the head of the family.	Sex	Color or race	Age at last birthday	Single, married, widowed or divorced	Attended school any time since Sept. 1, 1929	Whether able to read and write.	Place of birth of this person.	Whether able to speak English.	
	1	2	3	4	5	6	7	8	9	10	11	12	13	14
26	Soledad Street	23	29	Pangelinan, Jose A	Brother-in-law	M	Cha	27	S	N	Y	Guam	Y	Laborer
27		23	29	Pangelinan, Juan A	Brother-in-law	M	Cha	21	S	N	Y	Guam	Y	Laborer
28		24	30	Cruz, Jesus C	Head	M	Cha	36	M	N	Y	Guam	Y	Laborer
29		24	30	Cruz, Maria A	Wife	F	Cha	33	M	N	Y	Guam	Y	None
30		24	30	Cruz, Felix	Son	M	Cha	13	S	Y	Y	Guam	Y	None
31		24	30	Cruz, Ana	Daughter	F	Cha	12	S	Y	Y	Guam	N	None
32		24	30	Cruz, Vicente	Son	M	Cha	11	S	N	N	Guam	N	None
33		24	30	Cruz, Ramon	Son	M	Cha	2	S	N	N	Guam	N	None
34		24	30	Cruz, Francisco	Son	M	Cha	.2	S	N	N	Guam	N	None
35		25	31	Concepcion, Jose M	Head	M	Cha	27	M	N	Y	Guam	N	Laborer
36		25	31	Concepcion, Ana C	Wife	F	Cha	27	M	N	Y	Guam	N	None
37		25	31	Concepcion, Felipe	Son	M	Cha	1.2	S	N	N	Guam	N	None
38		26	32	Duenas, Vicente M	Head	M	Cha	31	M	N	Y	Guam	Y	Laborer
39		26	32	Duenas, Rosa C	Wife	F	Cha	30	M	N	N	Guam	N	None
40		26	32	Duenas, Jesus	Son	M	Cha	8	S	Y	Y	Guam	N	None
41		26	32	Duenas, Maria	Daughter	F	Cha	6	S	N	N	Guam	N	None
42		26	32	Duenas, Jose	Son	M	Cha	4	S	N	N	Guam	N	None
43		26	32	Duenas, Felisa M	Mother	F	Cha	56	Wd	N	N	Guam	N	None
44		27	33	Blas, Maria B	Head	F	Cha	31	M	N	Y	Guam	Y	None
45		27	33	Blas, Felicita	Daughter	F	Cha	8	S	Y	Y	Guam	N	None
46		27	33	Blas, Josefina	Daughter	F	Cha	4	S	N	N	Guam	N	None
47		27	33	Blas, Jose	Son	M	Cha	1.9	S	N	N	Guam	N	None
48		27	33	Blas, Francisco C	Step-son	M	Cha	23	S	N	Y	Guam	Y	Carpenter
49		27	33	Blas, Josefa C	Step-daughter	F	Cha	18	S	N	Y	Guam	Y	None
50		27	33	Blas, Lourdes C	Step-daughter	F	Cha	14	S	N	Y	Guam	Y	None

(CHAMORRO ROOTS GENEALOGY PROJECT™ TRANSCRIPTION)
(BERNARD T. PUNZALAN / HTTP://WWW.CHAMORROROOTS.COM)

DEPARTMENT OF COMMERCE-BUREAU OF THE CENSUS
WASHINGTON
FIFTEENTH CENSUS OF THE UNITED STATES: 1930-POPULATION

THE ISLAND OF GUAM

Sheet No. 4A

District **Municipality of Agana**
Name of Place **Agana City (Bilibic Urban)**
[Proper name and, also, name of class, as city, town, village, barrio, etc]

Enumeration District No. 3
Enumerated by me on **April 3, 1930** Tomas A. Calvo, Enumerator

	PLACE OF ABODE			NAME	RELATION	PERSONAL DESCRIPTION				EDUCATION		NATIVITY		OCCUPATION
	Street, avenue, road, etc.	Number of dwelling house is order of visitation	Number of family in order of visitation	of each person whose place of abode on April 1, 1930, was in this family. Enter surname, first, then given name and middle initial. If any. Include every person living on April 1, 1930. Omit children born since April 1, 1930.	Relationship of this Person to the head of the family.	Sex	Color or race	Age at last birthday	Single, married, widowed or divorced	Attended school any time since Sept. 1, 1929	Whether able to read and write.	Place of birth of this person.	Whether able to speak English.	
	1	2	3	4	5	6	7	8	9	10	11	12	13	14
1	Soledad Street	27	33	Blas, Domingo C	Step-son	M	Cha	11	S	Y	Y	Guam	Y	None
2		27	33	Blas, Miguel C	Step-son	M	Cha	9	S	Y	Y	Guam	Y	None
3		27	33	Blas, Matias P	Father in law	M	Cha	65	Wd	N	Y	Guam	N	None
4		28	34	Cruz, Jose M	Head	M	Cha	42	M	N	Y	Guam	N	Farmer
5		28	34	Cruz, Ana C	Wife	F	Cha	41	M	N	N	Guam	N	None
6		28	34	Cruz, Ana	Daughter	F	Cha	19	S	N	Y	Guam	Y	None
7		28	34	Cruz, Emeterio	Son	M	Cha	15	S	Y	Y	Guam	Y	None
8		28	34	Cruz, Oscar	Son	M	Cha	10	S	Y	Y	Guam	Y	None
9		28	34	Cruz, Enrique	Son	M	Cha	7	S	Y	Y	Guam	N	None
10		28	34	Cruz, Eduardo	Son	M	Cha	5	S	N	N	Guam	N	None
11		28	34	Cruz, Maria	Daughter	F	Cha	3	S	N	N	Guam	N	None
12		28	34	Cruz, Jesus	Son	M	Cha	.2	S	N	N	Guam	N	None
13		28	34	Cruz, Ramon M	Father	M	Cha	70	Wd	N	Y	Guam	N	None
14		29	35	Fejarang, Joaquin C	Head	M	Cha	41	M	N	Y	Guam	N	Farmer
15		29	35	Fejarang, Mercedes C	Wife	F	Cha	35	M	N	Y	Guam	Y	None
16		29	35	Fejarang, Gregorio	Son	M	Cha	17	S	Y	Y	Guam	Y	None
17		29	35	Fejarang, Ana	Daughter	F	Cha	15	S	N	Y	Guam	Y	None
18		29	35	Fejarang, Jose	Son	M	Cha	13	S	Y	N	Guam	Y	None
19		29	35	Fejarang, Precila	Daughter	F	Cha	6	S	N	N	Guam	N	None
20		29	35	Fejarang, Anicia	Daughter	F	Cha	1.2	S	N	N	Guam	N	None
21		29	35	Fejarang, Rosa C	Sister	F	Cha	36	S	N	Y	Guam	N	Laundress
22		30	36	Castro, Vicente C	Head	M	Cha	43	M	N	Y	Guam	Y	Carpenter
23		30	36	Castro, Rosa B	Wife	F	Cha	34	M	N	Y	Guam	Y	None
24		30	36	Castro, Regina	Daughter	F	Cha	13	S	Y	Y	Guam	Y	None
25		30	36	Castro, Trinidat	Daughter	F	Cha	11	S	Y	Y	Guam	N	None

DEPARTMENT OF COMMERCE-BUREAU OF THE CENSUS
WASHINGTON

FIFTEENTH CENSUS OF THE UNITED STATES: 1930-POPULATION

THE ISLAND OF GUAM

Sheet No. 4B

81B

District Municipality of Agana
Name of Place Agana City (Bilibic Urban)
[Proper name and, also, name of class, as city, town, village, barrio, etc]

Enumeration District No. 3
Enumerated by me on April 3, 1930 Tomas A. Calvo
Enumerator

	PLACE OF ABODE			NAME	RELATION	PERSONAL DESCRIPTION				EDUCATION		NATIVITY		OCCUPATION
	Street, avenue, road, etc.	Number of dwelling house is order of visitation	Number of family in order of visitation	of each person whose place of abode on April 1, 1930, was in this family. Enter surname, first, then given name and middle initial. If any. Include every person living on April 1, 1930. Omit children born since April 1, 1930.	Relationship of this Person to the head of the family.	Sex	Color or race	Age at last birthday	Single, married, widowed or divorced	Attended school any time since Sept. 1, 1929	Whether able to read and write.	Place of birth of this person.	Whether able to speak English.	
	1	2	3	4	5	6	7	8	9	10	11	12	13	14
26	Soledad Street	30	36	Castro, Julita	Daughter	F	Cha	9	S	Y	Y	Guam	N	None
27		30	36	Castro, Honedina	Daughter	F	Cha	1.8	S	N	N	Guam	N	None
28		31	37	Santos, Josefa B	Head	F	Cha	64	Wd	N	Y	Guam	N	None
29		31	37	Santos, Vicente	Son	M	Cha	22	S	N	Y	Guam	Y	Farmer
30		31	37	Santos, Maria	Daughter	F	Cha	18	S	N	Y	Guam	Y	None
31		31	38	Santos, Mercedes G	Head	F	Cha	20	M	N	Y	Guam	Y	None
32		31	38	Santos, Rafael	Son	M	Cha	3.5	S	N	N	Guam	N	None
33		31	38	Santos, Josefina	Daughter	F	Cha	1.5	S	N	N	Guam	N	None
34		32	39	Cruz, Angelina LG	Head	F	Cha	25	M	N	Y	Guam	N	None
35		32	39	Cruz, Olimpia	Daughter	F	Cha	5	S	N	N	Guam	N	None
36		32	39	Cruz, Isabel	Daughter	F	Cha	4	S	N	N	Guam	N	None
37		32	39	Cruz, Cecilia	Daughter	F	Cha	1.5	S	N	N	Guam	N	None
38		33	40	Castro, Maria C	Head	F	Cha	41	S	N	Y	Guam	N	Laundress
39		33	40	Castro, Jose	Son	M	Cha	15	S	Y	Y	Guam	Y	None
40		33	40	Castro, Amalia	Daughter	F	Cha	12	S	Y	Y	Guam	Y	None
41		34	41	Taijeron, Jesus P	Head	M	Cha	38	M	N	Y	Guam	N	Laborer
42		34	41	Taijeron, Antonia C	Wife	F	Cha	34	M	N	Y	Guam	N	None
43		34	41	Taijeron, Juan	Son	M	Cha	12	S	Y	Y	Guam	N	None
44		34	41	Taijeron, Carlos	Son	M	Cha	8	S	Y	Y	Guam	N	None
45		34	41	Taijeron, Ramona	Daughter	F	Cha	2.4	S	N	N	Guam	N	None
46		35	42	Taijeron, Joaquin P	Head	M	Cha	43	M	N	Y	Guam	Y	Cook
47		35	42	Taijeron, Maria S	Wife	F	Cha	43	M	N	N	Guam	N	None
48		35	42	Taijeron, Francisco	Son	M	Cha	20	S	N	Y	Guam	Y	Farmer
49		35	42	Taijeron, Vicente	Son	M	Cha	19	S	N	Y	Guam	Y	Laborer
50		35	42	Taijeron, Juan	Son	M	Cha	18	S	N	Y	Guam	Y	Laborer

(CHAMORRO ROOTS GENEALOGY PROJECT™ TRANSCRIPTION)
(BERNARD T. PUNZALAN / HTTP://WWW.CHAMORROROOTS.COM)

DEPARTMENT OF COMMERCE-BUREAU OF THE CENSUS
WASHINGTON

FIFTEENTH CENSUS OF THE UNITED STATES: 1930-POPULATION

THE ISLAND OF GUAM

Sheet No. 5A

District **Municipality of Agana**
Name of Place **Agana City (Bilibic Urban)**
[Proper name and, also, name of class, as city, town, village, barrio, etc]

Enumeration District No. **3**
Enumerated by me on **April 3, 1930** Tomas A. Calvo
Enumerator

	PLACE OF ABODE			NAME	RELATION	PERSONAL DESCRIPTION				EDUCATION		NATIVITY		OCCUPATION
	Street, avenue, road, etc.	Number of dwelling house is order of visitation	Number of family in order of visitation	of each person whose place of abode on April 1, 1930, was in this family. Enter surname, first, then given name and middle initial. If any. Include every person living on April 1, 1930. Omit children born since April 1, 1930.	Relationship of this Person to the head of the family.	Sex	Color or race	Age at last birthday	Single, married, widowed or divorced	Attended school any time since Sept. 1, 1929	Whether able to read and write.	Place of birth of this person.	Whether able to speak English.	
	1	2	3	4	5	6	7	8	9	10	11	12	13	14
1	Soledad Street	35	42	Taijeron, Maria	Daughter	F	Cha	14	S	Y	Y	Guam	Y	None
2		35	42	Taijeron, Henry	Son	M	Cha	13	S	Y	Y	Guam	N	None
3		35	42	Taijeron, Pedro	Son	M	Cha	3	S	N	N	Guam	N	None
4		36	43	Taijeron, Vicente P	Head	M	Cha	41	M	N	Y	Guam	Y	Laborer
5		36	43	Taijeron, Carmen M	Wife	F	Cha	31	M	N	Y	Guam	Y	None
6		36	43	Taijeron, Bernardino C	Son	M	Cha	15	S	N	Y	Guam	Y	Laborer
7		36	43	Taijeron, Asuncion	Daughter	F	Cha	14	S	N	Y	Guam	Y	None
8		36	43	Taijeron, Victoria	Daughter	F	Cha	12	S	Y	Y	Guam	N	None
9		37	44	Cruz, Dolores B	Head	F	Cha	66	Wd	N	N	Guam	N	None
10		37	44	Leon Guerrero, Consolacion	Daughter	F	Cha	38	Wd	N	Y	Guam	N	Laundress
11		37	44	Cruz, Saturnina B	Daughter	F	Cha	35	S	N	Y	Guam	Y	None
12		37	44	Leon Guerrero, Dolores B	Grand daughter	F	Cha	12	S	Y	Y	Guam	Y	None
13		37	44	Cruz, Ana B	Grand daughter	F	Cha	4	S	N	N	Guam	N	None
14		37	45	Cruz, Teordoro B	Head	M	Cha	24	M	N	Y	Guam	Y	Farmer
15		37	45	Cruz, Trinidad M	Wife	F	Cha	22	M	N	Y	Guam	Y	None
16		37	45	Cruz, Jose	Son	M	Cha	2.8	S	N	N	Guam	N	None
17		37	45	Cruz, Dolores	Daughter	F	Cha	1.5	S	N	N	Guam	N	None
18		37	45	Cruz, Macario	Son	M	Cha	.9	S	N	N	Guam	N	None
19		38	46	Rojas, Juan C	Head	M	Cha	40	M	N	N	Guam	N	Farmer
20		38	46	Rojas, Juana	Wife	F	Cha	41	M	N	N	Guam	N	None
21		38	46	Rojas, Concepcion	Daughter	F	Cha	15	S	N	Y	Guam	Y	None
22		38	46	Rojas, Delores	Daughter	F	Cha	10	S	Y	Y	Guam	N	None
23		38	46	Rojas, Candelaria	Daughter	F	Cha	8	S	Y	N	Guam	N	None
24		38	46	Rojas, Isabel	Daughter	F	Cha	3.2	S	N	N	Guam	N	None
25		38	47	Crisostomo, Rosa C	Head	F	Cha	30	S	N	N	Guam	N	None

(CHAMORRO ROOTS GENEALOGY PROJECT™ TRANSCRIPTION)
(BERNARD T. PUNZALAN / HTTP://WWW.CHAMORROROOTS.COM)

DEPARTMENT OF COMMERCE-BUREAU OF THE CENSUS
WASHINGTON

FIFTEENTH CENSUS OF THE UNITED STATES: 1930-POPULATION

THE ISLAND OF GUAM

Sheet No. 5B

82B

District **Municipality of Agana**
Name of Place **Agana City (Bilibic Urban)**
[Proper name and, also, name of class, as city, town, village, barrio, etc]

Enumeration District No. **3**
Enumerated by me on **April 4, 1930** Tomas A. Calvo
Enumerator

	PLACE OF ABODE			NAME	RELATION	PERSONAL DESCRIPTION				EDUCATION		NATIVITY		OCCUPATION
	Street, avenue, road, etc.	Number of dwelling house is order of visitation	Number of family in order of visitation	of each person whose place of abode on April 1, 1930, was in this family. Enter surname, first, then given name and middle initial. If any. Include every person living on April 1, 1930. Omit children born since April 1, 1930.	Relationship of this Person to the head of the family.	Sex	Color or race	Age at last birthday	Single, married, widowed or divorced	Attended school any time since Sept. 1, 1929	Whether able to read and write.	Place of birth of this person.	Whether able to speak English.	
	1	2	3	4	5	6	7	8	9	10	11	12	13	14
26	Soledad Street	38	47	Crisostomo, Juan	Son	M	Cha	2.8	S	N	N	Guam	N	None
27		39	48	Cruz, Juan G	Head	M	Cha	48	M	N	Y	Guam	Y	Carpenter
28		39	48	Cruz, Isabel	Wife	F	Cha	47	M	N	Y	Guam	Y	None
29		39	48	Cruz, Jose	Son	M	Cha	23	S	N	Y	Guam	Y	Clerk
30		39	48	Cruz, Maria	Daughter	F	Cha	21	S	N	Y	Guam	Y	None
31		39	48	Cruz, Jesus	Son	M	Cha	20	S	N	Y	Guam	Y	Machinist
32		39	48	Cruz, Juan	Son	M	Cha	19	S	N	Y	Guam	Y	Farmer
33		39	48	Cruz, Ana	Daughter	F	Cha	17	S	Y	Y	Guam	Y	None
34		39	48	Cruz, Concepcion	Daughter	F	Cha	14	S	Y	Y	Guam	Y	None
35		39	48	Cruz, Francisco	Son	M	Cha	12	S	Y	Y	Guam	Y	None
36		39	48	Cruz, Magdalena	Daughter	F	Cha	9	S	Y	Y	Guam	Y	None
37		39	48	Cruz, Clotilde	Daughter	F	Cha	7	S	Y	Y	Guam	N	None
38		39	48	Cruz, Rosa	Daughter	F	Cha	4	S	N	N	Guam	N	None
39		39	48	Cruz, Maria Jr.?	Niece	F	Cha	14	S	Y	Y	Guam	Y	None
40		40	49	Cruz, Jose	Head	M	Cha	37	M	N	Y	Guam	Y	Fireman
41		40	49	Cruz, Maria A	Wife	F	Cha	34	M	N	Y	Guam	Y	None
42		40	49	Cruz, Concepcion	Daughter	F	Cha	9	S	Y	Y	Guam	N	None
43		40	49	Cruz, Rosario	Daughter	F	Cha	7	S	Y	N	Guam	N	None
44		40	49	Cruz, Vicente	Son	M	Cha	3.6	S	N	N	Guam	N	None
45		40	49	Cruz, Maria	Daughter	F	Cha	1.2	S	N	N	Guam	N	None
46		40	49	Cruz, Josefina	Daughter	F	Cha	.4	S	N	N	Guam	N	None
47		41	50	Quinata, Lucia T	Head	F	Cha	38	M	N	Y	Guam	Y	None
48		41	50	Quinata, Pamsy	Daughter	F	Cha	7	S	Y	N	Guam	N	None
49		41	50	Quinata, Jose	Son	M	Cha	5	S	N	N	Guam	N	None
50		41	50	Quinata, Tomas	Son	M	Cha	3.9	S	N	N	Guam	N	None

DEPARTMENT OF COMMERCE-BUREAU OF THE CENSUS
WASHINGTON

FIFTEENTH CENSUS OF THE UNITED STATES: 1930-POPULATION

THE ISLAND OF GUAM

Sheet No. 6A

District **Municipality of Agana**
Name of Place **Agana City (Bilibic Urban)**
[Proper name and, also, name of class, as city, town, village, barrio, etc]

Enumeration District No. 3
Enumerated by me on **April 4, 1930** Tomas A. Calvo, Enumerator

	PLACE OF ABODE			NAME	RELATION	PERSONAL DESCRIPTION				EDUCATION		NATIVITY		OCCUPATION
	Street, avenue, road, etc.	Number of dwelling house in order of visitation	Number of family in order of visitation	of each person whose place of abode on April 1, 1930, was in this family. Enter surname, first, then given name and middle initial. If any. Include every person living on April 1, 1930. Omit children born since April 1, 1930.	Relationship of this Person to the head of the family.	Sex	Color or race	Age at last birthday	Single, married, widowed or divorced	Attended school any time since Sept. 1, 1929	Whether able to read and write.	Place of birth of this person.	Whether able to speak English.	
	1	2	3	4	5	6	7	8	9	10	11	12	13	14
1	Soledad Street	41	50	Quinata, Daniel	Son	M	Cha	2.5	S	N	N	Guam	N	None
2		42	51	Salas, Benigno D	Head	M	Cha	54	M	N	Y	Guam	N	Carpenter
3		42	51	Salas, Ana M	Wife	F	Cha	22	M	N	Y	Guam	N	None
4		42	51	Salas, Jose	Son	M	Cha	4	S	N	N	Guam	N	None
5		42	51	Salas, Felix	Son	M	Cha	2.5	S	N	N	Guam	N	None
6		42	51	Salas, Tomas	Son	M	Cha	1.1	S	N	N	Guam	N	None
7		43	52	Ogo, Rufina T	Head	F	Cha	66	Wd	N	N	Guam	N	None
8		43	53	Borja, Maria O	Head	F	Cha	30	M	N	Y	Guam	Y	None
9		43	53	Borja, Jesus	Son	M	Cha	7	S	Y	N	Guam	N	None
10		44	54	Cruz, Ignacio M	Head	M	Cha	29	M	N	Y	Guam	Y	Clerk
11		44	54	Cruz, Rosa LG	Wife	F	Cha	27	M	N	Y	Guam	N	None
12		44	54	Cruz, Rosa	Daughter	F	Cha	3.5	S	N	N	Guam	N	None
13		44	54	Cruz, Alfonsina	Daughter	F	Cha	.4	S	N	N	Guam	N	None
14		45	55	Mesa, Vicente S	Head	M	Cha	32	M	N	Y	Guam	Y	Carpenter
15		45	55	Mesa, Dolores C	Wife	F	Cha	33	M	N	Y	Guam	N	None
16		45	55	Mesa, Maria	Daughter	F	Cha	6	S	N	N	Guam	N	None
17		45	55	Mesa, Francisco	Son	M	Cha	5	S	N	N	Guam	N	None
18		45	55	Mesa, Gloria	Daughter	F	Cha	4	S	N	N	Guam	N	None
19		46	56	San Nicolas, Eugenio V	Head	M	Cha	56	M	N	Y	Guam	Y	Plumber
20		46	56	San Nicolas, Vicenta T	Wife	F	Cha	54	M	N	N	Guam	N	None
21		46	56	San Nicolas, Francisco	Son	M	Cha	30	S	N	Y	Guam	Y	Farmer
22		46	56	San Nicolas, Olimpia	Daughter	F	Cha	24	S	N	Y	Guam	Y	None
23		46	56	San Nicolas, Eugenio	Son	M	Cha	15	S	Y	Y	Guam	Y	None
24		46	56	Salas, Luis SN	Grandson	M	Cha	13	S	Y	Y	Guam	N	None
25		46	56	Ojeda, Emilia T	Niece	F	Cha	14	S	N	Y	Guam	Y	None

DEPARTMENT OF COMMERCE-BUREAU OF THE CENSUS
WASHINGTON

FIFTEENTH CENSUS OF THE UNITED STATES: 1930-POPULATION

THE ISLAND OF GUAM

Sheet No. 6B

83B

District Municipality of Agana
Name of Place Agana City (Bilibic Urban)
[Proper name and, also, name of class, as city, town, village, barrio, etc]

Enumeration District No. 3
Enumerated by me on April 4, 1930 Tomas A. Calvo, Enumerator

	PLACE OF ABODE			NAME	RELATION	PERSONAL DESCRIPTION				EDUCATION		NATIVITY		OCCUPATION
	Street, avenue, road, etc.	Number of dwelling house in order of visitation	Number of family in order of visitation	of each person whose place of abode on April 1, 1930, was in this family. Enter surname, first, then given name and middle initial. If any. Include every person living on April 1, 1930. Omit children born since April 1, 1930.	Relationship of this Person to the head of the family.	Sex	Color or race	Age at last birthday	Single, married, widowed or divorced	Attended school any time since Sept. 1, 1929	Whether able to read and write.	Place of birth of this person.	Whether able to speak English.	
	1	2	3	4	5	6	7	8	9	10	11	12	13	14
26	Soledad Street	49	59	Ojeda, Francisco T	Nephew	M	Cha	6	S	N	N	Guam	N	None
27		47	57	Cepeda, Jose S	Head	M	Cha	48	M	N	N	Guam	N	Farmer
28		47	57	Cepeda, Maria C	Wife	F	Cha	45	M	N	N	Guam	N	None
29		47	57	Cepeda, Jose	Son	M	Cha	22	S	N	Y	Guam	Y	Tailor
30		47	57	Cepeda, Amanda	Daughter	F	Cha	20	S	N	Y	Guam	Y	None
31		47	57	Cepeda, Ignacio	Son	M	Cha	18	S	N	Y	Guam	Y	Laborer
32		47	57	Cepeda, Trinidad	Son	M	Cha	16	S	N	Y	Guam	Y	Farmer
33		47	57	Cepeda, Maria	Daughter	F	Cha	14	S	N	Y	Guam	N	None
34		47	57	Cepeda, Jesus	Son	M	Cha	12	S	Y	Y	Guam	N	None
35		47	57	Cepeda, Francisco	Son	M	Cha	10	S	Y	Y	Guam	N	None
36		47	57	Cepeda, Carmen	Daughter	F	Cha	7	S	Y	Y	Guam	N	None
37		47	57	Cepeda, Leonila	Daughter	F	Cha	5	S	N	N	Guam	N	None
38		47	57	Cepeda, Josefina	Daughter	F	Cha	1.7	S	N	N	Guam	N	None
39		48	58	Iriarte, Nicolas C	Head	M	Cha	61	M	N	Y	Guam	Y	Farmer
40		48	58	Iriarte, Agustina D	Wife	F	Cha	47	M	N	Y	Guam	N	Laundress
41		48	58	Iriarte, Juana	Daughter	F	Cha	23	S	N	Y	Guam	Y	None
42		48	58	Iriarte, Natividad	Daughter	F	Cha	22	S	N	Y	Guam	Y	Servant
43		48	58	Iriarte, Maria	Daughter	F	Cha	18	S	N	Y	Guam	Y	Servant
44		48	58	Iriarte, Tomas	Son	M	Cha	16	S	N	Y	Guam	Y	Farmer
45		48	58	Iriarte, Jesus	Son	M	Cha	13	S	Y	Y	Guam	Y	None
46		48	58	Iriarte, Dolores	Daughter	F	Cha	12	S	Y	Y	Guam	N	None
47		48	58	Iriarte, Jose	Son	M	Cha	10	S	Y	Y	Guam	N	None
48		48	58	Iriarte, Antonio	Son	M	Cha	5	S	Y	Y	Guam	N	None
49		49	59	Aguon, Felix D	Head	M	Cha	59	M	N	Y	Guam	Y	Farmer
50		49	59	Aguon, Genoveva I	Wife	F	Cha	49	M	N	N	Guam	N	Laundress

DEPARTMENT OF COMMERCE-BUREAU OF THE CENSUS
WASHINGTON

FIFTEENTH CENSUS OF THE UNITED STATES: 1930-POPULATION

THE ISLAND OF GUAM

Sheet No. 7A

District **Municipality of Agana**
Name of Place **Agana City (Bilibic Urban)**
[Proper name and, also, name of class, as city, town, village, barrio, etc]

Enumeration District No. 3
Enumerated by me on **April 4, 1930** Tomas A. Calvo
Enumerator

	PLACE OF ABODE			NAME	RELATION	PERSONAL DESCRIPTION				EDUCATION		NATIVITY		OCCUPATION
	Street, avenue, road, etc.	Number of dwelling house is order of visitation	Number of family in order of visitation	of each person whose place of abode on April 1, 1930, was in this family. Enter surname, first, then given name and middle initial. If any. Include every person living on April 1, 1930. Omit children born since April 1, 1930.	Relationship of this Person to the head of the family.	Sex	Color or race	Age at last birthday	Single, married, widowed or divorced	Attended school any time since Sept. 1, 1929	Whether able to read and write.	Place of birth of this person.	Whether able to speak English.	
	1	2	3	4	5	6	7	8	9	10	11	12	13	14
1	Soledad Street	49	59	Aguon, Pedro	Son	M	Cha	17	S	N	Y	Guam	Y	Servant
2		49	59	Aguon, Rosa	Daughter	F	Cha	15	S	N	Y	Guam	Y	None
3		49	59	Aguon, Josefa	Daughter	F	Cha	14	S	Y	Y	Guam	Y	Maid
4		49	59	Aguon, Felix	Son	M	Cha	9	S	Y	Y	Guam	N	None
5		49	59	San Nicolas, Trinidad M	Grand-niece	F	Cha	13	S	Y	Y	Guam	Y	Maid
6		50	60	Chargualaf, Francisco R	Head	M	Cha	31	M	N	Y	Guam	Y	Laborer
7		50	60	Chargualaf, Maria C	Wife	F	Cha	34	M	N	Y	Guam	Y	None
8		50	60	Chargualaf, Julia	Daughter	F	Cha	11	S	Y	Y	Guam	N	None
9		50	60	Chargualaf, Vicente	Son	M	Cha	4	S	N	N	Guam	N	None
10		50	60	Chargualaf, Carlos	Son	M	Cha	2.3	S	N	N	Guam	N	None
11		50	60	Chargualaf, Jose	Son	M	Cha	.1	S	N	N	Guam	N	None
12		51	61	Perez, Jose S	Head	M	Cha	45	M	N	Y	Guam	Y	Carpenter
13		51	61	Perez, Rita D	Wife	F	Cha	33	M	N	Y	Guam	Y	None
14		52	62	Cruz, Maria B	Head	M	Cha	76	Wd	N	N	Guam	N	None
15		52	62	Perez, Josefina	Grand-daughter	F	Cha	19	S	N	Y	Guam	Y	None
16		52	62	Perez, Jose	Grandson	M	Cha	18	S	Y	Y	Guam	Y	None
17		52	62	Perez, Eliza	Grand-daughter	F	Cha	16	S	N	Y	Guam	Y	None
18		52	62	Perez, Juan	Grandson	M	Cha	14	S	Y	Y	Guam	Y	None
19		52	62	Perez, Gregorio	Grandson	M	Cha	12	S	Y	Y	Guam	Y	None
20		52	62	Perez, Manuel	Grandson	M	Cha	11	S	Y	Y	Guam	N	None
21		52	62	Perez, Maria	Grand-daughter	F	Cha	9	S	Y	Y	Guam	N	None
22		52	62	Perez, Concepcion	Grand-daughter	F	Cha	8	S	Y	N	Guam	N	None
23		53	63	Indelecio, Pedro C	Head	M	Cha	58	M	N	Y	Guam	N	Farmer
24		53	63	Indelecio, Rufina C	Wife	F	Cha	53	M	N	N	Guam	N	None
25		53	63	Indelecio, Jose	Son	M	Cha	19	S	N	Y	Guam	Y	Electrician

DEPARTMENT OF COMMERCE-BUREAU OF THE CENSUS
WASHINGTON

FIFTEENTH CENSUS OF THE UNITED STATES: 1930-POPULATION

THE ISLAND OF GUAM

Sheet No. 7B

District Municipality of Agana
Name of Place Agana City (Bilibic Urban)
[Proper name and, also, name of class, as city, town, village, barrio, etc]

Enumeration District No. 3
Enumerated by me on April 4, 1930 Tomas A. Calvo
Enumerator

	PLACE OF ABODE			NAME	RELATION	PERSONAL DESCRIPTION				EDUCATION		NATIVITY		OCCUPATION
	Street, avenue, road, etc.	Number of dwelling house is order of visitation	Number of family in order of visitation	of each person whose place of abode on April 1, 1930, was in this family. Enter surname, first, then given name and middle initial. If any. Include every person living on April 1, 1930. Omit children born since April 1, 1930.	Relationship of this Person to the head of the family.	Sex	Color or race	Age at last birthday	Single, married, widowed or divorced	Attended school any time since Sept. 1, 1929	Whether able to read and write.	Place of birth of this person.	Whether able to speak English.	
	1	2	3	4	5	6	7	8	9	10	11	12	13	14
26	Soledad Street	53	63	Indelecio, Catalina	Daughter	F	Cha	16	S	N	Y	Guam	Y	None
27		53	63	Indelecio, Emeteria	Daughter	F	Cha	10	S	Y	Y	Guam	Y	None
28		54	64	Castro, Maria C	Head	F	Cha	49	Wd	N	N	Guam	N	None
29		54	64	Castro, Pedro	Son	M	Cha	17	S	N	Y	Guam	Y	Farmer
30		54	64	Castro, Caridad	Daughter	F	Cha	15	S	N	Y	Guam	Y	None
31		55	65	Cruz, Manuel C	Head	M	Cha	49	M	N	Y	Guam	Y	Farmer
32		55	65	Cruz, Dolores P	Wife	F	Cha	39	M	N	N	Guam	N	None
33		55	65	Cruz, Francisco	Son	M	Cha	16	S	Y	Y	Guam	Y	None
34		55	65	Cruz, Maria	Daughter	F	Cha	13	S	N	Y	Guam	Y	None
35		55	65	Cruz, Pedro	Son	M	Cha	10	S	Y	Y	Guam	Y	None
36		55	65	Cruz, Tomas	Son	M	Cha	8	S	Y	N	Guam	N	None
37		55	65	Cruz, Catalina	Daughter	F	Cha	4	S	N	N	Guam	N	None
38		55	65	Cruz, Candelaria	Daughter	F	Cha	1.8	S	N	N	Guam	N	None
39		55	65	Cruz, Encarnacion	Daughter	F	Cha	.2	S	N	N	Guam	N	None
40		56	66	Guerrero, Pedro F	Head	M	Cha	47	M	N	Y	Guam	Y	Farmer
41		56	66	Guerrero, Amparo C	Wife	F	Cha	43	M	N	Y	Guam	N	None
42		56	66	Guerrero, Maria	Daughter	F	Cha	23	S	N	Y	Guam	Y	None
43		56	66	Guerrero, Jose	Son	M	Cha	21	S	N	Y	Guam	Y	Cook
44		56	66	Guerrero, Manuel	Son	M	Cha	20	S	N	Y	Guam	Y	Farmer
45		56	66	Guerrero, Antonia	Daughter	F	Cha	15	S	N	Y	Guam	Y	None
46		56	66	Guerrero, Pedro	Son	M	Cha	11	S	Y	Y	Guam	Y	None
47		56	66	Guerrero, Jesus	Son	M	Cha	7	S	N	N	Guam	N	None
48		56	66	Guerrero, Herminia	Daughter	F	Cha	2.8	S	N	N	Guam	N	None
49		57	67	Fejarang, Juana C	Head	F	Cha	64	Wd	N	N	Guam	N	None
50		58	68	Gandeza, Aguilino A	Head	M	Fil	60	M	N	Y	Philippine Is.	Y	Mason

DEPARTMENT OF COMMERCE-BUREAU OF THE CENSUS
WASHINGTON

FIFTEENTH CENSUS OF THE UNITED STATES: 1930-POPULATION

THE ISLAND OF GUAM

Sheet No. 8A

District Municipality of Agana
Name of Place Agana City (Bilibic Urban)
[Proper name and, also, name of class, as city, town, village, barrio, etc]

Enumeration District No. 3
Enumerated by me on April 5, 1930 Tomas A. Calvo, Enumerator

	PLACE OF ABODE			NAME	RELATION	PERSONAL DESCRIPTION				EDUCATION		NATIVITY		OCCUPATION
	Street, avenue, road, etc.	Number of dwelling house in order of visitation	Number of family in order of visitation	of each person whose place of abode on April 1, 1930, was in this family. Enter surname, first, then given name and middle initial. If any. Include every person living on April 1, 1930. Omit children born since April 1, 1930.	Relationship of this Person to the head of the family.	Sex	Color or race	Age at last birthday	Single, married, widowed or divorced	Attended school any time since Sept. 1, 1929	Whether able to read and write.	Place of birth of this person.	Whether able to speak English.	
	1	2	3	4	5	6	7	8	9	10	11	12	13	14
1	Soledad Street	58	68	Gandeza, Isabel C	Wife	F	Cha	42	M	N	Y	Guam	N	None
2		58	68	Castro, Josefa C	Niece	F	Cha	12	S	Y	Y	Guam	Y	None
3		58	68	Castro, Francisco A	Father-in-law	M	Cha	69	Wd	N	Y	Guam	N	None
4		59	69	Garrido, Vicenta S	Head	F	Cha	34	M	N	Y	Guam	Y	None
5		59	69	Garrido, Dorothea	Daughter	F	Cha	15	S	Y	Y	Guam	Y	Sales lady
6		59	69	Garrido, Carmen	Daughter	F	Cha	14	S	Y	Y	Guam	Y	Sales lady
7		59	69	Garrido, Maria	Daughter	F	Cha	13	S	Y	Y	Guam	Y	None
8		59	69	Garrido, Jesus	Son	M	Cha	11	S	Y	Y	Guam	Y	None
9		59	69	Garrido, Vicente	Son	M	Cha	10	S	Y	Y	Guam	Y	None
10		59	69	Garrido, Lourdes	Daughter	F	Cha	9	S	Y	Y	Guam	N	None
11		59	69	Garrido, James	Son	M	Cha	7	S	Y	N	Guam	N	None
12		59	69	Garrido, Joseph	Son	M	Cha	4	S	N	N	Guam	N	None
13		60	70	Matanane, Maria A	Head	F	Cha	36	M	N	Y	Guam	Y	None
14		60	70	Matanane, Jose	Son	M	Cha	9	S	Y	Y	Guam	N	None
15		60	70	Matanane, Jesus	Son	M	Cha	9	S	N	N	Guam	N	None
16		60	70	Matanane, Carlos	Son	M	Cha	6	S	N	N	Guam	N	None
17		60	70	Matanane, Benedicto	Son	M	Cha	4	S	N	N	Guam	N	None
18		60	70	Matanane, Tomas	Son	M	Cha	1.5	S	N	N	Guam	N	None
19		60	70	Matanane, Francisco	Son	M	Cha	.6	S	N	N	Guam	N	None
20		60	70	Anderson, Engracia P	Sister	F	Cha	30	S	N	Y	Guam	Y	None
21		61	71	Mafnas, Jose P	Head	M	Cha	30	M	N	Y	Guam	Y	Draftsman
22		61	71	Mafnas, Carmen C	Wife	F	Cha	27	M	N	Y	Guam	Y	None
23		61	71	Mafnas, Jesus	Son	M	Cha	8	S	Y	Y	Guam	N	None
24		61	71	Mafnas, Jose	Son	M	Cha	6	S	N	N	Guam	N	None
25		61	71	Mafnas, Vicente	Son	M	Cha	4	S	N	N	Guam	N	None

DEPARTMENT OF COMMERCE-BUREAU OF THE CENSUS
WASHINGTON

FIFTEENTH CENSUS OF THE UNITED STATES: 1930-POPULATION

THE ISLAND OF GUAM

Sheet No. 8B

85B

District Municipality of Agana
Name of Place Agana City (Bilibic Urban)
[Proper name and, also, name of class, as city, town, village, barrio, etc]

Enumeration District No. 3
Enumerated by me on April 5, 1930 Tomas A. Calvo, Enumerator

	PLACE OF ABODE			NAME	RELATION	PERSONAL DESCRIPTION				EDUCATION		NATIVITY		OCCUPATION
	Street, avenue, road, etc.	Number of dwelling house is order of visitation	Number of family in order of visitation	of each person whose place of abode on April 1, 1930, was in this family. Enter surname, first, then given name and middle initial. If any. Include every person living on April 1, 1930. Omit children born since April 1, 1930.	Relationship of this Person to the head of the family.	Sex	Color or race	Age at last birthday	Single, married, widowed or divorced	Attended school any time since Sept. 1, 1929	Whether able to read and write.	Place of birth of this person.	Whether able to speak English.	
	1	2	3	4	5	6	7	8	9	10	11	12	13	14
26	Soledad Street	61	71	Mafnas, Pricila	Daughter	F	Cha	1.1	S	N	N	Guam	N	None
27		62	72	Sablan, Vicente P	Head	M	Cha	59	M	N	Y	Guam	Y	Carpenter
28		62	72	Sablan, Dolores A	Wife	F	Cha	54	M	N	N	Guam	N	None
29		62	72	Ada, Maria A	Niece	F	Cha	18	S	N	Y	Guam	Y	Dressmaker
30		62	73	Iriarte, Ignacio D	Head	M	Cha	22	M	N	Y	Guam	Y	Carpenter
31		62	73	Iriarte, Ana S	Wife	F	Cha	20	M	N	Y	Guam	Y	None
32		62	73	Iriarte, Maria	Daughter	F	Cha	1	S	N	N	Guam	N	None
33		63	74	Mendiola, Juan C	Head	M	Cha	49	M	N	Y	Guam	N	Farmer
34		63	74	Mendiola, Maria R	Wife	F	Cha	39	M	N	Y	Guam	N	None
35		63	74	Mendiola, Ignacio	Son	M	Cha	12	S	Y	Y	Guam	Y	None
36		63	74	Mendiola, Andres	Son	M	Cha	10	S	Y	Y	Guam	Y	None
37		63	74	Mendiola, Engracia	Daughter	F	Cha	8	S	Y	Y	Guam	N	None
38		63	74	Mendiola, Leonardo	Son	M	Cha	6	S	N	N	Guam	N	None
39		63	74	Mendiola, Pablo	Son	M	Cha	3	S	N	N	Guam	N	None
40		63	74	Mendiola, Francisco	Son	M	Cha	2.4	S	N	N	Guam	N	None
41		64	75	Pangelinan, Joaquin P	Head	M	Cha	51	Wd	N	Y	Guam	N	Farmer
42		64	75	Pangelinan, Joaquin	Son	M	Cha	23	S	N	Y	Guam	Y	Cook
43		64	75	Pangelinan, Rosalia	Daughter	F	Cha	20	S	N	Y	Guam	N	None
44		64	75	Pangelinan, Tomas	Son	M	Cha	17	S	N	Y	Guam	Y	Farmer
45		64	75	Pangelinan, Maria	Daughter	F	Cha	16	S	N	Y	Guam	Y	Sales lady
46		64	75	Pangelinan, Matilde	Daughter	F	Cha	12	S	Y	Y	Guam	Y	None
47		64	75	Pangelinan, Magdalena	Daughter	F	Cha	10	S	Y	Y	Guam	N	None
48		65	76	Sablan, Francisco A	Head	M	Cha	26	M	N	Y	Guam	Y	Carpenter
49		65	76	Sablan, Grabiela S	Wife	F	Cha	27	M	N	Y	Guam	Y	None
50		65	76	Sablan, Maria	Daughter	F	Cha	.8	S	N	N	Guam	N	None

DEPARTMENT OF COMMERCE-BUREAU OF THE CENSUS
WASHINGTON

FIFTEENTH CENSUS OF THE UNITED STATES: 1930-POPULATION

THE ISLAND OF GUAM

Sheet No. 9A

District **Municipality of Agana**
Name of Place **Agana City (Bilibic Urban)**
[Proper name and, also, name of class, as city, town, village, barrio, etc]

Enumeration District No. **3**
Enumerated by me on **April 7, 1930** Tomas A. Calvo, Enumerator

	PLACE OF ABODE			NAME	RELATION	PERSONAL DESCRIPTION				EDUCATION		NATIVITY		OCCUPATION
	Street, avenue, road, etc.	Number of dwelling house is order of visitation	Number of family in order of visitation	of each person whose place of abode on April 1, 1930, was in this family. Enter surname, first, then given name and middle initial. If any. Include every person living on April 1, 1930. Omit children born since April 1, 1930.	Relationship of this Person to the head of the family.	Sex	Color or race	Age at last birthday	Single, married, widowed or divorced	Attended school any time since Sept. 1, 1929	Whether able to read and write.	Place of birth of this person.	Whether able to speak English.	
	1	2	3	4	5	6	7	8	9	10	11	12	13	14
1	Soledad Street	66	77	Sablan, Lorenzo A	Head	M	Cha	42	Wd	N	Y	Guam	Y	Cook
2		66	77	Sablan, Asuncion	Daughter	F	Cha	19	S	N	Y	Guam	Y	Tel. Operator
3		66	77	Sablan, Jose	Son	M	Cha	16	S	N	Y	Guam	Y	Salesman
4		66	77	Sablan, Preciousa	Niece	F	Cha	23	S	N	Y	Guam	Y	None
5		66	77	Sablan, Potenciana	Niece	F	Cha	20	S	N	Y	Guam	Y	Maid
6		66	77	Sablan, Isabel	Niece	F	Cha	18	S	N	Y	Guam	Y	None
7		66	77	Garrido, Agustin S	Nephew	M	Cha	18	S	N	Y	Guam	Y	Servant
8		66	77	Garrido, Jesus C	Grand nephew	M	Cha	13	S	Y	Y	Guam	Y	None
9		67	78	Mendiola, Manuel P	Head	M	Cha	47	M	N	Y	Guam	N	Carpenter
10		67	78	Mendiola, Rufina P	Wife	F	Cha	35	M	N	Y	Guam	N	None
11		67	78	Mendiola, Jose	Son	M	Cha	13	S	Y	Y	Guam	Y	None
12		67	78	Mendiola, Maria	Daughter	F	Cha	10	S	Y	Y	Guam	N	None
13		67	78	Mendiola, Tomas	Son	M	Cha	8	S	Y	Y	Guam	N	None
14		67	78	Mendiola, Ana	Daughter	F	Cha	7	S	Y	N	Guam	N	None
15		67	78	Mendiola, Jesus	Son	M	Cha	5	S	N	N	Guam	N	None
16		67	78	Mendiola, Ignacio	Son	M	Cha	4	S	N	N	Guam	N	None
17		67	78	Mendiola, Vicente	Son	M	Cha	2.2	S	N	N	Guam	N	None
18		67	78	Mendiola, Cesario	Son	M	Cha	.6	S	N	N	Guam	N	None
19		67	78	Mendiola, Ana P	Mother	F	Cha	75	Wd	N	N	Guam	N	None
20		68	79	Guerrero, Lorenzo C	Head	M	Cha	48	M	N	N	Guam	N	Farmer
21		68	79	Guerrero, Maria	Wife	F	Cha	44	M	N	Y	Guam	N	None
22		68	79	Guerrero, Carmen	Daughter	F	Cha	18	S	N	Y	Guam	Y	None
23		68	79	Guerrero, Ana	Daughter	F	Cha	14	S	N	Y	Guam	Y	None
24		68	79	Leon Guerrero, Juan	Grandson	M	Cha	3	S	N	N	Guam	N	None
25		69	80	Iriarte, Jesus C	Head	M	Cha	50	M	N	Y	Guam	N	Farmer

(CHAMORRO ROOTS GENEALOGY PROJECT™ TRANSCRIPTION)
(BERNARD T. PUNZALAN / HTTP://WWW.CHAMORROROOTS.COM)

DEPARTMENT OF COMMERCE-BUREAU OF THE CENSUS
WASHINGTON

FIFTEENTH CENSUS OF THE UNITED STATES: 1930-POPULATION

THE ISLAND OF GUAM

Sheet No. 9B

86B

District Municipality of Agana
Name of Place Agana City (Bilibic Urban)
[Proper name and, also, name of class, as city, town, village, barrio, etc]

Enumeration District No. 3
Enumerated by me on April 7, 1930 Tomas A. Calvo
Enumerator

	PLACE OF ABODE			NAME	RELATION	PERSONAL DESCRIPTION				EDUCATION		NATIVITY		OCCUPATION
	Street, avenue, road, etc.	Number of dwelling house is order of visitation	Number of family in order of visitation	of each person whose place of abode on April 1, 1930, was in this family. Enter surname, first, then given name and middle initial. If any. Include every person living on April 1, 1930. Omit children born since April 1, 1930.	Relationship of this Person to the head of the family.	Sex	Color or race	Age at last birthday	Single, married, widowed or divorced	Attended school any time since Sept. 1, 1929	Whether able to read and write.	Place of birth of this person.	Whether able to speak English.	
	1	2	3	4	5	6	7	8	9	10	11	12	13	14
26	Soledad Street	69	80	Iriarte, Ignacia T	Wife	F	Cha	56	M	N	N	Guam	N	None
27		69	81	Toves, Pedro L	Head	M	Cha	30	M	N	Y	Guam	Y	Farmer
28		69	81	Toves, Juana F	Wife	F	Cha	28	M	N	N	Guam	N	None
29		69	81	Toves, Gregorio	Son	M	Cha	14	S	N	N	Guam	N	None
30		69	81	Toves, Maria	Daughter	F	Cha	2.8	S	N	N	Guam	N	None
31		69	81	Toves, Juan	Son	M	Cha	1.7	S	N	N	Guam	N	None
32		69	82	Pangelinan, Manuel P	Head	M	Cha	29	S	N	Y	Guam	Y	Carpenter
33		70	83	Borja, Lorenzo L	Head	M	Cha	53	M	N	Y	Guam	N	Farmer
34		70	83	Borja, Francisca C	Wife	F	Cha	36	M	N	N	Guam	N	None
35		70	83	Borja, Joaquin	Son	M	Cha	18	S	N	Y	Guam	Y	Farmer
36		70	83	Borja, Francisca	Son	M	Cha	12	S	Y	Y	Guam	Y	None
37		70	83	Borja, Catalina	Daughter	F	Cha	9	S	Y	Y	Guam	N	None
38		70	83	Borja, Alberto	Son	M	Cha	3	S	N	N	Guam	N	None
39		70	83	Borja, Manuel	Son	M	Cha	.4	S	N	N	Guam	N	None
40		70	84	Mendiola, Jesus C	Head	M	Cha	26	M	N	Y	Guam	Y	Farmer
41		70	84	Mendiola, Maria F	Wife	F	Cha	23	M	N	Y	Guam	Y	None
42		70	84	Mendiola, Lucia	Daughter	F	Cha	1.8	S	N	N	Guam	N	None
43		71	85	Tenorio, Jose T	Head	M	Cha	34	M	N	Y	Guam	Y	Machinist
44		71	85	Tenorio, Rosa G	Wife	F	Cha	38	M	N	Y	Guam	N	None
45		71	85	Tenorio, Gonzalo	Son	M	Cha	14	S	Y	Y	Guam	Y	None
46		71	85	Tenorio, Delfina	Daughter	F	Cha	12	S	Y	Y	Guam	N	None
47		71	85	Tenorio, Oliva	Daughter	F	Cha	9	S	Y	Y	Guam	N	None
48		71	85	Tenorio, Jose	Son	M	Cha	8	S	Y	Y	Guam	N	None
49		71	85	Tenorio, Honoria	Daughter	F	Cha	5	S	N	N	Guam	N	None
50		71	85	Tenorio, Vicente	Son	M	Cha	3	S	N	N	Guam	N	None

DEPARTMENT OF COMMERCE-BUREAU OF THE CENSUS
WASHINGTON

FIFTEENTH CENSUS OF THE UNITED STATES: 1930-POPULATION

THE ISLAND OF GUAM

Sheet No. 10A

District **Municipality of Agana**
Name of Place **Agana City (Bilibic Urban)**
[Proper name and, also, name of class, as city, town, village, barrio, etc]

Enumeration District No. 3
Enumerated by me on **April 7, 1930** Tomas A. Calvo, Enumerator

	PLACE OF ABODE			NAME	RELATION	PERSONAL DESCRIPTION				EDUCATION		NATIVITY		OCCUPATION
	Street, avenue, road, etc.	Number of dwelling house in order of visitation	Number of family in order of visitation	of each person whose place of abode on April 1, 1930, was in this family. Enter surname, first, then given name and middle initial. If any. Include every person living on April 1, 1930. Omit children born since April 1, 1930.	Relationship of this Person to the head of the family.	Sex	Color or race	Age at last birthday	Single, married, widowed or divorced	Attended school any time since Sept. 1, 1929	Whether able to read and write.	Place of birth of this person.	Whether able to speak English.	
	1	2	3	4	5	6	7	8	9	10	11	12	13	14
1	Soledad Street	71	85	Tenorio, Tomasa	Daughter	F	Cha	2.5	S	N	N	Guam	N	None
2		71	85	Tenorio, Clotilde	Daughter	F	Cha	1.4	S	N	N	Guam	N	None
3		71	85	Gumataotao, Vicente M	Nephew	M	Cha	16	S	Y	Y	Guam	Y	None
4		72	86	Taimanglo, Ana J	Head	F	Cha	49	M	N	Y	Guam	N	None
5		72	86	Taijeron, Juan	Son	M	Cha	19	S	N	Y	Guam	Y	Farmer
6		72	86	Taijeron, Jose	Son	M	Cha	18	S	N	Y	Guam	Y	Farmer
7		72	86	Taijeron, Rosario	Daughter	F	Cha	15	S	N	Y	Guam	Y	None
8		72	86	Taijeron, Jesus	Son	M	Cha	12	S	Y	Y	Guam	Y	None
9		72	86	Taijeron, Joaquin	Son	M	Cha	10	S	Y	Y	Guam	N	None
10		72	86	Iriarte, Jose	Son	M	Cha	22	S	N	Y	Guam	Y	Farmer
11		72	86	Iriarte, Juan	Son	M	Cha	20	S	N	Y	Guam	Y	Farmer
12		72	86	Iriarte, Ana	Daughter	F	Cha	15	S	N	Y	Guam	Y	None
13		72	86	Iriarte, Cristina	Daughter	F	Cha	10	S	Y	Y	Guam	Y	None
14		72	86	Iriarte, Francisco	Son	M	Cha	5	S	N	N	Guam	N	None
15		73	87	Salas, Vicente S	Head	M	Cha	69	M	N	Y	Guam	Y	Carpenter
16		73	87	Salas, Maria F	Wife	F	Cha	48	M	N	N	Guam	N	None
17		73	87	Salas, Concepcion	Daughter	F	Cha	24	S	N	Y	Guam	Y	None
18		73	87	Salas, Felix	Son	M	Cha	21	S	N	Y	Guam	Y	Carpenter
19		73	87	Salas, Vicente	Son	M	Cha	17	S	N	Y	Guam	Y	Carpenter
20		73	87	Salas, Mercedes	Daughter	F	Cha	15	S	N	Y	Guam	Y	None
21		73	87	Salas, Josefa	Daughter	F	Cha	11	S	Y	Y	Guam	Y	None
22		73	87	Salas, Trinidad	Daughter	F	Cha	5	S	N	N	Guam	N	None
23		73	87	Salas, Virginia	Daughter	F	Cha	4	S	N	N	Guam	N	None
24		74	88	Mafnas, Venancio C	Head	M	Cha	51	M	N	N	Guam	N	Farmer
25		74	88	Mafnas, Juana T	Wife	F	Cha	54	M	N	N	Guam	N	None

DEPARTMENT OF COMMERCE-BUREAU OF THE CENSUS
WASHINGTON

FIFTEENTH CENSUS OF THE UNITED STATES: 1930-POPULATION

THE ISLAND OF GUAM

Sheet No. 10B

87B

District Municipality of Agana
Name of Place Agana City (Bilibic Urban)
[Proper name and, also, name of class, as city, town, village, barrio, etc]

Enumeration District No. 3
Enumerated by me on April 7, 1930 Tomas A. Calvo
Enumerator

	PLACE OF ABODE			NAME	RELATION	PERSONAL DESCRIPTION				EDUCATION		NATIVITY		OCCUPATION
	Street, avenue, road, etc.	Number of dwelling house is order of visitation	Number of family in order of visitation	of each person whose place of abode on April 1, 1930, was in this family. Enter surname, first, then given name and middle initial. If any. Include every person living on April 1, 1930. Omit children born since April 1, 1930.	Relationship of this Person to the head of the family.	Sex	Color or race	Age at last birthday	Single, married, widowed or divorced	Attended school any time since Sept. 1, 1929	Whether able to read and write.	Place of birth of this person.	Whether able to speak English.	
	1	2	3	4	5	6	7	8	9	10	11	12	13	14
26	Soledad Street	74	89	Unpingco, Rosa M	Head	F	Cha	28	M	N	Y	Guam	Y	None
27		74	89	Unpingco, Venancio	Son	M	Cha	6	S	N	N	Guam	N	None
28		74	89	Unpingco, Pedro	Son	M	Cha	5	S	N	N	Guam	N	None
29		74	89	Unpingco, Remedios	Daughter	F	Cha	4	S	N	N	Guam	N	None
30		74	89	Unpingco, Jose	Son	M	Cha	2.1	S	N	N	Guam	N	None
31		74	89	Unpingco, Jesus	Son	M	Cha	.9	S	N	N	Guam	N	None
32		75	90	Aguon, Juan M	Head	M	Cha	34	M	N	Y	Guam	Y	Farmer
33		75	90	Aguon, Damiana C	Wife	F	Cha	32	M	N	Y	Guam	N	None
34		75	90	Aguon, Maria	Daughter	F	Cha	10	S	Y	Y	Guam	N	None
35		75	90	Aguon, Celestino	Son	M	Cha	9	S	Y	Y	Guam	N	None
36		75	90	Aguon, Pedro	Son	M	Cha	6	S	N	N	Guam	N	None
37		75	90	Aguon, Gregorio	Son	M	Cha	4	S	N	N	Guam	N	None
38		75	90	Aguon, Virginia	Daughter	F	Cha	2.5	S	N	N	Guam	N	None
39		75	90	Aguon, Ramon	Son	M	Cha	.6	S	N	N	Guam	N	None
40		75	91	Martinez, Concepcion R?	Head	F	Cha	44	S	N	N	Guam	N	Cook
41		76	92	Santos, Jose B	Head	M	Cha	62	M	N	Y	Guam	Y	Farmer
42		76	92	Santos, Ursula B	Wife	F	Cha	62	M	N	Y	Guam	N	None
43		76	92	Santos, Tomas R	Grand nephew	M	Cha	21	S	N	Y	Guam	Y	Teacher
44		76	92	Santos, Clementina R	Grand niece	F	Cha	15	S	N	Y	Guam	Y	None
45		76	92	Santos, Cristobal R	Grand nephew	M	Cha	13	S	Y	Y	Guam	Y	None
46		76	92	Santos, Raquel R	Grand niece	F	Cha	11	S	Y	Y	Guam	Y	None
47		76	92	Blaz, Maria LG	Grand niece	F	Cha	3.2	S	N	N	Guam	N	None
48		77	93	Iriarte, Vicente D	Head	M	Cha	29	M	N	Y	Guam	Y	Machinist
49		77	93	Iriarte, Maria LG	Wife	F	Cha	25	M	N	Y	Guam	Y	Midwife
50		77	93	Iriarte, Julia	Daughter	F	Cha	3.7	S	N	N	Guam	N	None

DEPARTMENT OF COMMERCE-BUREAU OF THE CENSUS
WASHINGTON

FIFTEENTH CENSUS OF THE UNITED STATES: 1930-POPULATION

THE ISLAND OF GUAM

Sheet No. 11A

District Municipality of Agana
Name of Place Agana City (Bilibic Urban)
[Proper name and, also, name of class, as city, town, village, barrio, etc]

Enumeration District No. 3
Enumerated by me on April 7, 1930 Tomas A. Calvo
Enumerator

	PLACE OF ABODE			NAME	RELATION	PERSONAL DESCRIPTION				EDUCATION		NATIVITY		OCCUPATION
	Street, avenue, road, etc.	Number of dwelling house is order of visitation	Number of family in order of visitation	of each person whose place of abode on April 1, 1930, was in this family. Enter surname, first, then given name and middle initial. If any. Include every person living on April 1, 1930. Omit children born since April 1, 1930.	Relationship of this Person to the head of the family.	Sex	Color or race	Age at last birthday	Single, married, widowed or divorced	Attended school any time since Sept. 1, 1929	Whether able to read and write.	Place of birth of this person.	Whether able to speak English.	
	1	2	3	4	5	6	7	8	9	10	11	12	13	14
1	Soledad Street	77	93	Iriarte, Rosa	Daughter	F	Cha	2.6	S	N	N	Guam	N	None
2		77	93	Iriarte, Ana	Daughter	F	Cha	1.2	S	N	N	Guam	N	None
3		77	93	Iriarte, Lorenzo	Son	M	Cha	.2	S	N	N	Guam	N	None
4		78	94	Leon Guerrero, Ana S	Head	F	Cha	36	S	N	Y	Guam	Y	Laundress
5		78	94	Leon Guerrero, Catalina	Daughter	F	Cha	11	S	Y	Y	Guam	N	None
6		78	94	Leon Guerrero, Virginia	Daughter	F	Cha	4	S	N	N	Guam	N	None
7		78	94	Leon Guerrero, James	Son	M	Cha	4	S	N	N	Guam	N	None
8		79	95	Apuron, Francisca T	Head	F	Fil	19	S	N	Y	Guam	Y	Laundress
9		79	95	Apuron, Simon T	Brother	M	Fil	17	S	N	Y	Guam	Y	Servant
10		80	96	Anderson, Joaquin M	Head	M	Cha	44	M	N	Y	Guam	Y	Farmer
11		80	96	Anderson, Tomasa LG	Wife	F	Cha	38	M	N	Y	Guam	N	Laundress
12		80	96	Anderson, Maria	Daughter	F	Cha	16	S	N	Y	Guam	Y	None
13		80	96	Anderson, Antonio	Son	M	Cha	14	S	Y	Y	Guam	Y	None
14		80	96	Anderson, Rosario	Daughter	F	Cha	13	S	Y	Y	Guam	Y	None
15		80	96	Anderson, Josefina	Daughter	F	Cha	12	S	Y	Y	Guam	N	None
16		80	96	Anderson, Jose	Son	M	Cha	8	S	Y	Y	Guam	N	None
17		80	96	Anderson, Odon	Son	M	Cha	7	S	N	N	Guam	N	None
18		80	96	Anderson, Estefania	Daughter	F	Cha	4	S	N	N	Guam	N	None
19		80	96	Anderson, Aurelia	Daughter	F	Cha	1.9	S	N	N	Guam	N	None
20		81	97	Perez, Joaquin C	Head	M	Cha	39	M	N	Y	Guam	N	Carpenter
21		81	97	Perez, Ana M	Wife	F	Cha	35	M	N	Y	Guam	N	None
22		81	97	Perez, Ignacio	Son	M	Cha	18	S	N	Y	Guam	Y	Carpenter
23		81	97	Perez, Delgadina	Daughter	F	Cha	15	S	N	Y	Guam	Y	None
24		81	97	Perez, Francisco	Son	M	Cha	14	S	Y	Y	Guam	Y	None
25		81	97	Perez, Engracia	Daughter	F	Cha	12	S	Y	Y	Guam	Y	None

DEPARTMENT OF COMMERCE-BUREAU OF THE CENSUS
WASHINGTON

FIFTEENTH CENSUS OF THE UNITED STATES: 1930-POPULATION

THE ISLAND OF GUAM

Sheet No. 11B

88B

District Municipality of Agana
Name of Place Agana City (Bilibic Urban)
[Proper name and, also, name of class, as city, town, village, barrio, etc]

Enumeration District No. 3
Enumerated by me on April 7, 1930 Tomas A. Calvo
Enumerator

	PLACE OF ABODE: Street, avenue, road, etc.	Number of dwelling house in order of visitation	Number of family in order of visitation	NAME of each person whose place of abode on April 1, 1930, was in this family. Enter surname, first, then given name and middle initial. If any. Include every person living on April 1, 1930. Omit children born since April 1, 1930.	RELATION Relationship of this Person to the head of the family.	PERSONAL DESCRIPTION: Sex	Color or race	Age at last birthday	Single, married, widowed or divorced	EDUCATION: Attended school any time since Sept. 1, 1929	Whether able to read and write.	NATIVITY Place of birth of this person.	Whether able to speak English.	OCCUPATION
	1	2	3	4	5	6	7	8	9	10	11	12	13	14
26	Soledad Street	81	97	Perez, Antonio	Son	M	Cha	11	S	Y	Y	Guam	N	None
27		81	97	Perez, Gloria	Daughter	F	Cha	9	S	Y	Y	Guam	N	None
28		81	97	Perez, Delfina	Daughter	F	Cha	7	S	Y	Y	Guam	N	None
29		81	97	Perez, Jesus	Son	M	Cha	5	S	N	N	Guam	N	None
30		81	97	Perez, Ana	Daughter	F	Cha	3.6	S	N	N	Guam	N	None
31		81	97	Perez, Magdalena	Daughter	F	Cha	1.8	S	N	N	Guam	N	None
32		82	98	Leon Guerrero, Maria A	Head	F	Cha	63	Wd	N	N	Guam	N	None
33		82	98	Leon Guerrero, Manuel	Son	M	Cha	41	Wd	N	Y	Guam	Y	Farmer
34		82	98	Leon Guerrero, Juan	Son	M	Cha	31	S	N	Y	Guam	Y	Farmer
35		82	98	Leon Guerrero, Maria	Grand daughter	F	Cha	16	S	Y	Y	Guam	Y	None
36		82	98	Leon Guerrero, Mariano	Grand son	M	Cha	12	S	Y	Y	Guam	Y	None
37		82	98	Perez, Pedro	Grand son	M	Cha	10	S	Y	Y	Guam	Y	None
38		82	98	Perez, Victoria	Grand daughter	F	Cha	9	S	Y	Y	Guam	Y	None
39		83	99	Apuron, Severino R	Head	M	Fil	64	M	N	Y	Philippines	Y	Laborer
40		83	99	Apuron, Ignacia R	Wife	F	Cha	55	M	N	N	Guam	N	None
41		83	99	Eclavea, Enrique R	Nephew	M	Fil	22	S	N	Y	Guam	Y	Farmer
42		84	100	Leon Guerrero, Jose S	Head	M	Cha	24	M	N	Y	Guam	Y	Teacher
43		84	100	Leon Guerrero, Vicenta SA	Wife	F	Cha	27	M	N	Y	Guam	Y	Teacher
44		85	101	Iriarte, Tomas D	Head	M	Cha	24	M	N	Y	Guam	Y	Farmer
45		85	101	Iriarte, Maria F	Wife	F	Cha	22	M	N	Y	Guam	N	None
46		85	101	Iriarte, Tomas	Son	M	Cha	4	S	N	N	Guam	N	None
47		85	101	Iriarte, Juan	Son	M	Cha	2.7	S	N	N	Guam	N	None
48		85	101	Iriarte, Beatris	Daughter	F	Cha	.2	S	N	N	Guam	N	None
49		85	101	Fausto, Joaquina G	Mother in law	F	Cha	43	S	N	N	Guam	N	None
50		86	102	Pablo, Ana N	Head	F	Cha	59	Wd	N	N	Guam	N	None

DEPARTMENT OF COMMERCE-BUREAU OF THE CENSUS
WASHINGTON

FIFTEENTH CENSUS OF THE UNITED STATES: 1930-POPULATION

THE ISLAND OF GUAM

Sheet No. 12A

District Municipality of Agana
Name of Place Agana City (Bilibic Urban)
[Proper name and, also, name of class, as city, town, village, barrio, etc]

Enumeration District No. 3
Enumerated by me on April 8, 1930 Tomas A. Calvo
Enumerator

	PLACE OF ABODE: Street, avenue, road, etc.	Number of dwelling house in order of visitation	Number of family in order of visitation	NAME of each person whose place of abode on April 1, 1930, was in this family. Enter surname, first, then given name and middle initial. If any. Include every person living on April 1, 1930. Omit children born since April 1, 1930.	RELATION Relationship of this Person to the head of the family.	PERSONAL DESCRIPTION: Sex	Color or race	Age at last birthday	Single, married, widowed or divorced	EDUCATION: Attended school any time since Sept. 1, 1929	Whether able to read and write.	NATIVITY Place of birth of this person.	Whether able to speak English.	OCCUPATION
	1	2	3	4	5	6	7	8	9	10	11	12	13	14
1	Soledad Street	86	102	Pablo, Maria	Daughter	F	Cha	30	S	N	Y	Guam	Y	Maid
2		86	102	Pablo, Joaquin	Son	M	Cha	19	S	N	Y	Guam	Y	Farmer
3		86	102	Villagomez, Felicita	Grand daughter	F	Cha	4	S	N	N	Guam	N	None
4		87	103	Matanane, Victorina	Head	F	Cha	31	S	N	Y	Guam	N	Laundress
5		87	103	Matanane, Ignacia	Daughter	F	Cha	12	S	Y	Y	Guam	Y	None
6		87	103	Matanane, Jesus	Son	M	Cha	10	S	Y	Y	Guam	Y	None
7		87	103	Matanane, Eduardo	Son	M	Cha	8	S	Y	Y	Guam	N	None
8		87	103	Matanane, Catalina	Daughter	F	Cha	6	S	N	N	Guam	N	None
9		87	103	Matanane, Juan	Son	M	Cha	3	S	N	N	Guam	N	None
10		88	104	Topasna, Paterno	Head	M	Cha	33	M	N	Y	Guam	Y	Farmer
11		88	104	Topasna, Ana LG	Wife	F	Cha	27	M	N	Y	Guam	Y	None
12		88	104	Topasna, Francisco	Son	M	Cha	7	S	Y	Y	Guam	N	None
13		88	104	Topasna, Rosalia	Daughter	F	Cha	5	S	N	N	Guam	N	None
14		88	104	Topasna, Antonia	Daughter	F	Cha	3.6	S	N	N	Guam	N	None
15		88	104	Topasna, Agueda	Daughter	F	Cha	2.7	S	N	N	Guam	N	None
16		89	105	Guzman, Francisco D	Head	M	Cha	64	M	N	Y	Guam	Y	Farmer
17		89	105	Guzman, Emiliana P	Wife	F	Cha	56	M	N	Y	Guam	Y	None
18		89	105	Guzman, Pilar	Daughter	F	Cha	19	S	N	Y	Guam	Y	Teacher
19		89	105	Guzman, Juan	Son	M	Cha	14	S	Y	Y	Guam	Y	None
20		90	106	Perez, Francisco M	Head	M	Cha	42	M	N	Y	Guam	Y	Farmer
21		90	106	Perez, Rosalia C	Wife	F	Cha	35	M	N	Y	Guam	Y	None
22		90	106	Perez, Honoria	Daughter	F	Cha	19	S	N	Y	Guam	Y	None
23		90	106	Perez, Maria	Daughter	F	Cha	15	S	N	Y	Guam	Y	Teacher
24		90	106	Perez, Joaquin	Son	M	Cha	13	S	Y	Y	Guam	Y	None
25		90	106	Perez, Jesus	Son	M	Cha	10	S	Y	Y	Guam	Y	None

(CHAMORRO ROOTS GENEALOGY PROJECT™ TRANSCRIPTION)
(BERNARD T. PUNZALAN / HTTP://WWW.CHAMORROROOTS.COM)

DEPARTMENT OF COMMERCE-BUREAU OF THE CENSUS
WASHINGTON

FIFTEENTH CENSUS OF THE UNITED STATES: 1930-POPULATION

THE ISLAND OF GUAM

Sheet No. 12B

89B

District **Municipality of Agana**
Name of Place **Agana City (Bilibic Urban)**
[Proper name and, also, name of class, as city, town, village, barrio, etc]

Enumeration District No. 3
Enumerated by me on **April 8, 1930** Tomas A. Calvo, Enumerator

	PLACE OF ABODE			NAME	RELATION	PERSONAL DESCRIPTION				EDUCATION		NATIVITY		OCCUPATION
	Street, avenue, road, etc.	Number of dwelling house in order of visitation	Number of family in order of visitation	of each person whose place of abode on April 1, 1930, was in this family. Enter surname, first, then given name and middle initial. If any. Include every person living on April 1, 1930. Omit children born since April 1, 1930.	Relationship of this Person to the head of the family.	Sex	Color or race	Age at last birthday	Single, married, widowed or divorced	Attended school any time since Sept. 1, 1929	Whether able to read and write.	Place of birth of this person.	Whether able to speak English.	
	1	2	3	4	5	6	7	8	9	10	11	12	13	14
26	Soledad Street	90	106	Perez, Juan	Son	M	Cha	8	S	Y	Y	Guam	N	None
27		90	106	Perez, Emiliana	Daughter	F	Cha	6	S	N	N	Guam	N	None
28		90	106	Perez, Lourdes	Daughter	F	Cha	4	S	N	N	Guam	N	None
29		90	106	Perez, Oliva	Daughter	F	Cha	1	S	N	N	Guam	N	None
30		90	106	Guzman, Juan LG	Servant	M	Cha	13	S	Y	Y	Guam	Y	Servant
31		91	107	Aflague, Concepcion LG	Head	F	Cha	30	M	N	Y	Guam	Y	None
32		91	107	Aflague, Fermin	Son	M	Cha	10	S	Y	Y	Guam	Y	None
33		92	108	Chargualaf, Jose R	Head	M	Cha	21	M	N	Y	Guam	Y	Machinist
34		92	108	Chargualaf, Dolores R	Wife	F	Cha	41	M	N	Y	Guam	Y	None
35		92	108	Chargualaf, Sergio	Son	M	Cha	6	S	N	N	Guam	N	None
36		92	108	Chargualaf, Cecilia	Daughter	F	Cha	3.1	S	N	N	Guam	N	None
37		93	109	San Nicolas, Dolores M	Head	F	Cha	46	M	N	Y	Guam	N	Laundress
38		93	109	San Nicolas, Maria	Daughter	F	Cha	23	S	N	Y	Guam	Y	Maid
39		93	109	San Nicolas, Rosalia	Daughter	F	Cha	14	S	Y	Y	Guam	Y	None
40		93	109	San Nicolas, Jesus	Son	M	Cha	10	S	Y	Y	Guam	Y	None
41		93	109	San Nicolas, Carlos	Son	M	Cha	.4	S	N	N	Guam	N	None
42		93	109	Mafnas, Maria P	Sister	F	Cha	38	S	N	N	Guam	N	None
43					Here ends the enumeration of enumeration district No 3, Bilibic, Agana urban.									
44														
45														
46														
47														
48														
49														
50														

(CHAMORRO ROOTS GENEALOGY PROJECT™ TRANSCRIPTION)
(BERNARD T. PUNZALAN / HTTP://WWW.CHAMORROROOTS.COM)

DEPARTMENT OF COMMERCE-BUREAU OF THE CENSUS
WASHINGTON

FIFTEENTH CENSUS OF THE UNITED STATES: 1930-POPULATION

THE ISLAND OF GUAM

Sheet No. 13A

District **Municipality of Agana**
Name of Place **Agana City (San Ignacio Urban)**
[Proper name and, also, name of class, as city, town, village, barrio, etc]

Enumeration District No. **3**
Enumerated by me on **April 8, 1930** Tomas A. Calvo, Enumerator

	PLACE OF ABODE			NAME	RELATION	PERSONAL DESCRIPTION				EDUCATION		NATIVITY		OCCUPATION
	Street, avenue, road, etc.	Number of dwelling house in order of visitation	Number of family in order of visitation	of each person whose place of abode on April 1, 1930, was in this family. Enter surname, first, then given name and middle initial. If any. Include every person living on April 1, 1930. Omit children born since April 1, 1930.	Relationship of this Person to the head of the family.	Sex	Color or race	Age at last birthday	Single, married, widowed or divorced	Attended school any time since Sept. 1, 1929	Whether able to read and write.	Place of birth of this person.	Whether able to speak English.	
	1	2	3	4	5	6	7	8	9	10	11	12	13	14
1	Travesia de Gomez Street	94	110	Duenas, Isabel P	Head	F	Cha	25	M	N	Y	Guam	Y	None
2		94	110	Duenas, Ana	Daughter	F	Cha	9	S	Y	Y	Guam	N	None
3		94	110	Duenas, Joaquin	Son	M	Cha	7	S	Y	Y	Guam	N	None
4		94	110	Duenas, Josefina	Daughter	F	Cha	5	S	N	N	Guam	N	None
5		94	110	Duenas, Elidia	Daughter	F	Cha	3	S	N	N	Guam	N	None
6		94	110	Duenas, Isabel	Daughter	F	Cha	1.3	S	N	N	Guam	N	None
7		94	110	Pereda, Margarita C	Sister	F	Cha	12	S	Y	Y	Guam	Y	None
8		95	111	Torres, Ana P	Head	F	Cha	49	S	N	Y	Guam	Y	Laundress
9		96	112	Castro, Jose F	Head	M	Cha	60	M	N	Y	Guam	Y	Painter
10		96	112	Castro, Angela P	Wife	F	Cha	72	M	N	N	Guam	N	None
11		96	112	Blas, Josefina M	Grandson	M	Cha	12	S	Y	Y	Guam	Y	None
12		97	113	Anderson, Arthur	Head	M	W	45	M	N	Y	Scotland	Y	Electrician
13		97	113	Anderson, Rosa C	Wife	F	Cha	41	M	N	Y	Guam	Y	None
14		97	113	Anderson, Arthur G	Son	M	Cha	18	S	N	Y	Guam	Y	Mechanic
15		97	113	Anderson, Henry	Son	M	Cha	16	S	N	Y	Guam	Y	Electrician
16		97	113	Anderson, John	Son	M	Cha	14	S	Y	Y	Guam	Y	None
17		97	113	Anderson, Lillian	Daughter	F	Cha	13	S	Y	Y	Guam	Y	None
18		97	113	Anderson, Joseph	Son	M	Cha	10	S	Y	Y	Guam	Y	None
19		97	113	Anderson, George	Son	M	Cha	7	S	Y	Y	Guam	N	None
20		98	114	Torres, Antonio M	Head	M	Cha	51	M	N	Y	Guam	Y	Merchant
21		98	114	Torres, Concepcion C	Wife	F	Cha	62	M	N	Y	Guam	N	None
22		98	114	Torres, Maria	Daughter	F	Cha	26	S	N	Y	Guam	Y	Dressmaker
23		99	115	Mesa, Geronimo R	Head	M	Cha	67	M	N	Y	Guam	N	Farmer
24		99	115	Mesa, Vicenta F	Wife	F	Cha	53	M	N	Y	Guam	N	None
25		99	115	Mesa, Maria	Daughter	F	Cha	34	S	N	Y	Guam	Y	None

DEPARTMENT OF COMMERCE-BUREAU OF THE CENSUS
WASHINGTON

FIFTEENTH CENSUS OF THE UNITED STATES: 1930-POPULATION

THE ISLAND OF GUAM

Sheet No. 13B

90B

District **Municipality of Agana**
Name of Place **Agana City (San Ignacio Urban)**
[Proper name and, also, name of class, as city, town, village, barrio, etc]

Enumeration District No. 3
Enumerated by me on **April 8, 1930** Tomas A. Calvo, Enumerator

	PLACE OF ABODE			NAME	RELATION	PERSONAL DESCRIPTION				EDUCATION		NATIVITY		OCCUPATION
	Street, avenue, road, etc.	Number of dwelling house is order of visitation	Number of family in order of visitation	of each person whose place of abode on April 1, 1930, was in this family. Enter surname, first, then given name and middle initial. If any. Include every person living on April 1, 1930. Omit children born since April 1, 1930.	Relationship of this Person to the head of the family.	Sex	Color or race	Age at last birthday	Single, married, widowed or divorced	Attended school any time since Sept. 1, 1929	Whether able to read and write.	Place of birth of this person.	Whether able to speak English.	
	1	2	3	4	5	6	7	8	9	10	11	12	13	14
26	Travesia de Gomez Street	99	115	Mesa, Soledad	Daughter	F	Cha	26	S	N	Y	Guam	Y	None
27		99	115	Mesa, Rosa	Daughter	F	Cha	22	S	N	Y	Guam	Y	Teacher
28		99	115	Mesa, Vicente	Son	M	Cha	20	S	N	Y	Guam	Y	Farmer
29		99	115	Mesa, Gloria	Daughter	F	Cha	17	S	Y	Y	Guam	Y	None
30		99	115	Mesa, Concepcion	Daughter	F	Cha	14	S	Y	Y	Guam	Y	None
31		99	115	Mesa, Francisco	Son	M	Cha	9	S	Y	Y	Guam	Y	None
32		99	115	Mesa, Jose	Son	M	Cha	31	Wd	N	Y	Guam	Y	Machinist
33		99	115	Mesa, Candelaria	Grand daughter	F	Cha	1.1	S	N	N	Guam	N	None
34		100	116	Rosario, Rosa S	Head	F	Cha	47	Wd	N	N	Guam	N	Laundress
35		100	116	Rosario, Jose	Son	M	Cha	21	S	N	Y	Guam	Y	Farmer
36		100	116	Rosario, Manuel	Son	M	Cha	19	S	N	Y	Guam	Y	Farmer
37		100	116	Rosario, Maria	Daughter	F	Cha	17	S	N	Y	Guam	Y	Maid
38		100	116	Rosario, Rosalia	Daughter	F	Cha	12	S	Y	Y	Guam	Y	None
39	Hernan Cortes Street	101	117	Martinez, Pedro	Head	M	Cha	37	M	N	Y	Guam	Y	Manufacturer
40		101	117	Martinez, Maria T	Wife	F	Cha	34	M	N	Y	Guam	Y	None
41		101	117	Martinez, Juan	Son	M	Cha	13	S	Y	Y	Guam	Y	None
42		101	117	Martinez, Ana L	Daughter	F	Cha	12	S	Y	Y	Guam	Y	None
43		101	117	Martinez, Pedro	Son	M	Cha	10	S	Y	Y	Guam	N	None
44		101	117	Martinez, Jose	Son	M	Cha	9	S	Y	Y	Guam	N	None
45		101	117	Martinez, Rosa	Daughter	F	Cha	6	S	N	N	Guam	N	None
46		101	117	Martinez, Luis	Son	M	Cha	4.1	S	N	N	Guam	N	None
47		101	117	Martinez, Maria	Daughter	F	Cha	3.2	S	N	N	Guam	N	None
48		101	117	Martinez, Josefina	Daughter	F	Cha	2.1	S	N	N	Guam	N	None
49		101	117	Martinez, Antonia	Daughter	F	Cha	.2	S	N	N	Guam	N	None
50		101	117	Torres, Josefa D	Aunt	F	Cha	62	S	N	Y	Guam	Y	None

DEPARTMENT OF COMMERCE-BUREAU OF THE CENSUS
WASHINGTON

FIFTEENTH CENSUS OF THE UNITED STATES: 1930-POPULATION

THE ISLAND OF GUAM

Sheet No. 14A

District Municipality of Agana
Name of Place Agana City (San Ignacio Urban)
[Proper name and, also, name of class, as city, town, village, barrio, etc]

Enumeration District No. 3
Enumerated by me on April 9, 1930 Tomas A. Calvo, Enumerator

	PLACE OF ABODE			NAME	RELATION	PERSONAL DESCRIPTION				EDUCATION		NATIVITY		OCCUPATION
	Street, avenue, road, etc.	Number of dwelling house in order of visitation	Number of family in order of visitation	of each person whose place of abode on April 1, 1930, was in this family. Enter surname, first, then given name and middle initial. If any. Include every person living on April 1, 1930. Omit children born since April 1, 1930.	Relationship of this Person to the head of the family.	Sex	Color or race	Age at last birthday	Single, married, widowed or divorced	Attended school any time since Sept. 1, 1929	Whether able to read and write.	Place of birth of this person.	Whether able to speak English.	
	1	2	3	4	5	6	7	8	9	10	11	12	13	14
1	Hernan Cortes Street	101	117	Torres, Carmen I	Sister in-law	F	Cha	27	S	N	Y	Guam	Y	Stenographer
2		12\02	118	Manibusan, Geronimo T	Head	M	Cha	17	S	N	Y	Guam	Y	Chauffeur
3		103	119	Shinohara, Takehama	Head	M	Jap	38	M	N	Y	Japan	Y	Merchant
4		103	119	Shinohara, Carmen T	Wife	F	Cha	25	M	N	Y	Guam	Y	None
5		103	119	Shinohara, Cecilia	Daughter	F	Jap	5	S	N	N	Guam	N	None
6		103	119	Shinohara, Gil	Son	M	Jap	1	S	N	N	Guam	N	None
7		104	120	Bordallo, Carlos P	Head	M	Cha	26	M	N	Y	Guam	Y	Grazier
8		104	120	Bordallo, Enesta P	Wife	F	Cha	22	M	N	Y	Guam	Y	None
9		104	120	Bordallo, Carlos E	Son	M	Cha	5	S	N	N	Guam	N	None
10		104	120	Bordallo, Richard C	Son	M	Cha	4	S	N	N	Guam	N	None
11		104	120	Bordallo, Erwin B	Son	F	Cha	2.9	S	N	N	Guam	N	None
12		104	120	Tenorio, Oliva Q	Servant	F	Cha	17	S	N	Y	Guam	Y	Servant
13		105	121	Terlaje, Luis A	Head	M	Cha	55	Wd	N	Y	Guam	N	Farmer
14		105	121	Terlaje, Maria	Daughter	F	Cha	26	S	N	Y	Guam	Y	None
15		105	121	Terlaje, Pedro	Son	M	Cha	19	S	N	Y	Guam	Y	Salesman
16		105	121	Terlaje, Jesus	Son	M	Cha	17	S	Y	Y	Guam	Y	None
17		105	121	Terlaje, Rosario	Daughter	F	Cha	15	S	Y	Y	Guam	Y	None
18		105	121	Terlaje, Vicente	Son	M	Cha	11	S	Y	Y	Guam	Y	None
19		105	121	Cruz, Rosario C	Pupil	F	Cha	13	S	Y	Y	Guam	Y	None
20		105	122	Terlaje, Jose F	Head	M	Cha	23	M	N	Y	Guam	Y	Chauffeur
21		105	122	Terlaje, Carmen S	Wife	F	Cha	19	M	N	Y	Guam	Y	None
22		105	122	Terlaje, Precila	Daughter	F	Cha	.4	S	N	N	Guam	N	None
23		106	123	Mendiola, Josefa C	Head	F	Cha	80	Wd	N	N	Guam	N	None
24		106	123	Mendiola, Maria	Daughter	F	Cha	55	S	N	Y	Guam	N	None
25		106	123	Mendiola, Martina	Daughter	F	Cha	52	S	N	N	Guam	N	None

DEPARTMENT OF COMMERCE-BUREAU OF THE CENSUS
WASHINGTON

FIFTEENTH CENSUS OF THE UNITED STATES: 1930-POPULATION

THE ISLAND OF GUAM

Sheet No. 14B

91B

District **Municipality of Agana**

Name of Place **Agana City (San Ignacio Urban)**
[Proper name and, also, name of class, as city, town, village, barrio, etc]

Enumeration District No. 3

Enumerated by me on **April 9, 1930** Tomas A. Calvo, Enumerator

	PLACE OF ABODE: Street, avenue, road, etc.	Number of dwelling house is order of visitation	Number of family in order of visitation	NAME of each person whose place of abode on April 1, 1930, was in this family. Enter surname, first, then given name and middle initial. If any. Include every person living on April 1, 1930. Omit children born since April 1, 1930.	RELATION Relationship of this Person to the head of the family.	PERSONAL DESCRIPTION: Sex	Color or race	Age at last birthday	Single, married, widowed or divorced	EDUCATION: Attended school any time since Sept. 1, 1929	Whether able to read and write.	NATIVITY Place of birth of this person.	Whether able to speak English.	OCCUPATION
	1	2	3	4	5	6	7	8	9	10	11	12	13	14
26	Hernan Cortes Street	106	123	Mendiola, Ana	Daughter	F	Cha	47	S	N	Y	Guam	N	None
27		106	123	Mendiola, Rosa	Daughter	F	Cha	39	S	N	Y	Guam	N	None
28		106	123	Mendiola, Rita	Daughter	F	Cha	36	S	N	Y	Guam	Y	None
29		107	124	Taitingfon, Gabriela C	Head	F	Cha	63	Wd	N	Y	Guam	N	None
30		107	124	Taitingfon, Carmen	Daughter	F	Cha	36	S	N	Y	Guam	Y	Laundress
31		107	124	Taitingfon, Ignacio	Son	M	Cha	34	S	N	Y	Guam	Y	Farmer
32		107	124	Taitingfon, Magdalena	Daughter	F	Cha	29	S	N	Y	Guam	Y	Laundress
33		107	124	Taitingfon, Rita	Daughter	F	Cha	23	S	N	Y	Guam	Y	Laundress
34		107	124	Taitingfon, Isabel	Grand daughter	F	Cha	1.9	S	N	N	Guam	N	None
35		108	125	Castro, Rita I	Head	F	Cha	57	S	N	N	Guam	N	Laundress
36		108	125	Castro, Felix	Son	M	Cha	26	S	N	Y	Guam	Y	Cook
37		108	125	Castro, Vicente I	Brother	M	Cha	45	S	N	N	Guam	N	Farmer
38		108	126	Ichida, Ana C	Head	F	Cha	43	Wd	N	N	Guam	N	Laundress
39		108	127	Untalan, Jose C	Head	M	Cha	35	M	N	Y	Guam	Y	Farmer
40		108	127	Untalan, Isabel	Wife	F	Cha	29	M	N	Y	Guam	Y	None
41		108	127	Untalan, Jesus	Son	M	Cha	3	S	N	N	Guam	N	None
42		108	127	Untalan, Maria	Daughter	F	Cha	2.1	S	N	N	Guam	N	None
43		108	127	Untalan, Josefa	Daughter	F	Cha	2.1	S	N	N	Guam	N	None
44		108	127	Untalan, Rita	Daughter	F	Cha	1	S	N	N	Guam	N	None
45		109	128	Castro, Juan C	Head	M	Cha	35	M	N	Y	Guam	Y	Farmer
46		109	128	Castro, Ana M	Wife	F	Cha	54	M	N	N	Guam	N	None
47		110	129	Leon Guerrero, Juan T	Head	M	Cha	60	Wd	N	Y	Guam	Y	Shoe maker
48		110	129	Leon Guerrero, Jose	Son	M	Cha	18	S	N	Y	Guam	Y	Clerk
49		110	129	Leon Guerrero, Pedro	Son	M	Cha	15	S	N	Y	Guam	Y	Messenger
50		110	129	Leon Guerrero, Ignacia	Daughter	F	Cha	11	S	Y	Y	Guam	Y	None

(CHAMORRO ROOTS GENEALOGY PROJECT™ TRANSCRIPTION)
(BERNARD T. PUNZALAN / HTTP://WWW.CHAMORROROOTS.COM)

DEPARTMENT OF COMMERCE-BUREAU OF THE CENSUS
WASHINGTON

FIFTEENTH CENSUS OF THE UNITED STATES: 1930-POPULATION

THE ISLAND OF GUAM

Sheet No. 15A

District **Municipality of Agana**
Name of Place **Agana City (San Ignacio Urban)**
[Proper name and, also, name of class, as city, town, village, barrio, etc]

Enumeration District No. 3
Enumerated by me on **April 9, 1930** Tomas A. Calvo, Enumerator

	PLACE OF ABODE			NAME	RELATION	PERSONAL DESCRIPTION				EDUCATION		NATIVITY		OCCUPATION
	Street, avenue, road, etc.	Number of dwelling house is order of visitation	Number of family in order of visitation	of each person whose place of abode on April 1, 1930, was in this family. Enter surname, first, then given name and middle initial. If any. Include every person living on April 1, 1930. Omit children born since April 1, 1930.	Relationship of this Person to the head of the family.	Sex	Color or race	Age at last birthday	Single, married, widowed or divorced	Attended school any time since Sept. 1, 1929	Whether able to read and write.	Place of birth of this person.	Whether able to speak English.	
	1	2	3	4	5	6	7	8	9	10	11	12	13	14
1	Hernan Cortes Street	111	130	Mesa, Jose R	Head	M	Cha	63	Wd	N	Y	Guam	Y	Farmer
2		111	130	Mesa, Nicolasa	Sister	F	Cha	70	Wd	N	Y	Guam	N	None
3		111	130	Mesa, Maria	Sister	F	Cha	64	S	N	N	Guam	N	None
4		111	130	Mesa, Carmen I	Niece	F	Cha	18	S	N	Y	Guam	Y	None
5		111	130	Mesa, Ana M	Grand niece	F	Cha	10	S	Y	Y	Guam	Y	None
6		111	131	Iwatsut, Jose	Head	M	Jap	42	M	N	N	Japan	Y	Retail merchant
7		111	131	Iwatsut, Carmen S	Wife	F	Cha	38	M	N	Y	Guam	Y	None
8		111	131	Iwatsut, Juana	Daughter	F	Jap	13	S	Y	Y	Guam	Y	None
9		111	131	Iwatsut, Tomas	Son	M	Jap	10	S	Y	Y	Guam	Y	None
10		111	131	Iwatsut, Severa	Daughter	F	Jap	5	S	N	N	Guam	N	None
11		112	132	Murphree, George M	Head	M	W	55	M	N	Y	Kansas	Y	None
12		112	132	Murphree, Carmen	Wife	F	Cha	41	M	N	Y	Guam	Y	None
13		112	132	Leon Guerrero, Bernarda C	Mother in-law	F	Fil	76	Wd	N	Y	Philippines Is.	Y	None
14		113	133	Johnston, William G	Head	M	Cha	50	M	N	Y	Guam	Y	Chief Clerk
15		113	133	Johnston, Agueda I	Wife	F	Cha	36	M	N	Y	Guam	Y	Teacher
16		113	133	Johnston, Harbert I	Son	M	Cha	15	S	Y	Y	Guam	Y	None
17		113	133	Johnston, Joseph W	Son	M	Cha	11	S	Y	Y	Guam	Y	None
18		113	133	Johnston, Marian A	Daughter	F	Cha	9	S	Y	Y	Guam	Y	None
19		113	133	Johnston, Thomas I	Son	M	Cha	8	S	Y	Y	Guam	Y	None
20		114	134	Butler, Chester C	Head	M	W	45	M	N	Y	Texas	Y	Merchant
21		114	134	Butler, Ignacia B	Wife	F	Cha	33	M	N	Y	Guam	Y	None
22		114	134	Butler, James	Son	M	Cha	13	S	Y	Y	Guam	Y	None
23		114	134	Butler, Beatrice	Daughter	F	Cha	12	S	Y	Y	Guam	Y	None
24		114	134	Butler, Clara	Daughter	F	Cha	11	S	Y	Y	Guam	Y	None
25		114	134	Butler, Benjamin	Son	M	Cha	10	S	Y	Y	Guam	Y	None

(CHAMORRO ROOTS GENEALOGY PROJECT™ TRANSCRIPTION)
(BERNARD T. PUNZALAN / HTTP://WWW.CHAMORROROOTS.COM)

DEPARTMENT OF COMMERCE-BUREAU OF THE CENSUS
WASHINGTON

FIFTEENTH CENSUS OF THE UNITED STATES: 1930-POPULATION

THE ISLAND OF GUAM

Sheet No. 15B

92B

District Municipality of Agana
Name of Place Agana City (San Ignacio Urban)
[Proper name and, also, name of class, as city, town, village, barrio, etc]

Enumeration District No. 3
Enumerated by me on April 9, 1930 Tomas A. Calvo
Enumerator

	PLACE OF ABODE			NAME	RELATION	PERSONAL DESCRIPTION				EDUCATION		NATIVITY		OCCUPATION
	Street, avenue, road, etc.	Number of dwelling house is order of visitation	Number of family in order of visitation	of each person whose place of abode on April 1, 1930, was in this family. Enter surname, first, then given name and middle initial. If any. Include every person living on April 1, 1930. Omit children born since April 1, 1930.	Relationship of this Person to the head of the family.	Sex	Color or race	Age at last birthday	Single, married, widowed or divorced	Attended school any time since Sept. 1, 1929	Whether able to read and write.	Place of birth of this person.	Whether able to speak English.	
	1	2	3	4	5	6	7	8	9	10	11	12	13	14
26	Hernan Cortes Street	114	134	Butler, Dorthy	Daughter	F	Cha	21	S	N	N	Guam	N	None
27		114	134	Butler, Berry P	Brother	M	W	43	S	N	Y	Guam	Y	Typist
28		114	134	Gutierres, Tomasa D	Maid	F	Cha	23	S	N	Y	Guam	Y	Maid
29		115	135	Mayhew, Thomas E	Head	M	W	40	M	N	Y	California	Y	Chief Clerk
30		115	135	Mayhew, Maria D	Wife	F	Cha	37	M	N	Y	Guam	Y	None
31		115	135	Mayhew, Thomas	Son	M	Cha	19	S	N	Y	Hong Kong	Y	Clerk
32		115	135	Mayhew, Harold	Son	M	Cha	18	S	N	Y	Philippine Is.	Y	Salesman
33		115	135	Mayhew, Carolyn	Daughter	F	Cha	9	S	Y	Y	Guam	Y	None
34		115	135	Mayhew, Eileen S	Daughter	F	Cha	6	S	N	N	Guam	N	None
35		115	135	Mayhew, Barbara	Daughter	F	Cha	6	S	N	N	Guam	N	None
36		115	135	Rosario, Dolores	Cook	F	Cha	48	S	N	Y	Guam	N	Cook
37		116	136	Garcia, Juan SN	Head	M	Cha	41	M	N	Y	Guam	Y	Carpenter
38		116	136	Garcia, Rosa M	Wife	F	Cha	40	M	N	Y	Guam	Y	None
39		116	136	Garcia, Francisco	Son	M	Cha	18	S	N	Y	Guam	Y	Surveyor
40		116	136	Garcia, Josefina	Daughter	F	Cha	14	S	Y	Y	Guam	Y	None
41		116	136	Garcia, Jesus	Son	M	Cha	12	S	Y	Y	Guam	Y	None
42		116	136	Garcia, Juan	Son	M	Cha	10	S	Y	Y	Guam	N	None
43		116	136	Garcia, Elizabeth	Daughter	F	Cha	9	S	Y	Y	Guam	N	None
44		116	136	Garcia, Jose	Son	M	Cha	8	S	Y	Y	Guam	N	None
45		116	136	Garcia, Edward	Son	M	Cha	3.4	S	N	N	Guam	N	None
46		116	136	Garcia, Maria	Daughter	F	Cha	1.7	S	N	N	Guam	N	None
47		117	137	Mesa, Rufina A	Head	F	Cha	67	Wd	N	Y	Guam	N	None
48		117	137	Mesa, Antonio	Son	M	Cha	33	Wd	N	Y	Guam	Y	Carpenter
49		117	137	Mesa, Ana	Daughter	F	Cha	25	S	N	Y	Guam	Y	None
50		118	138	Davis, Frank L	Head	M	W	51	M	N	Y	New York	Y	Master Joiner

(CHAMORRO ROOTS GENEALOGY PROJECT™ TRANSCRIPTION)
(BERNARD T. PUNZALAN / HTTP://WWW.CHAMORROROOTS.COM)

DEPARTMENT OF COMMERCE-BUREAU OF THE CENSUS
WASHINGTON

FIFTEENTH CENSUS OF THE UNITED STATES: 1930-POPULATION

THE ISLAND OF GUAM

Sheet No. 16A

District Municipality of Agana
Name of Place Agana City (San Ignacio Urban)
[Proper name and, also, name of class, as city, town, village, barrio, etc]

Enumeration District No. 3
Enumerated by me on April 10, 1930 Tomas A. Calvo, Enumerator

	PLACE OF ABODE			NAME	RELATION	PERSONAL DESCRIPTION				EDUCATION		NATIVITY	Whether able to speak English.	OCCUPATION
	Street, avenue, road, etc.	Number of dwelling house is order of visitation	Number of family in order of visitation	of each person whose place of abode on April 1, 1930, was in this family. Enter surname, first, then given name and middle initial. If any. Include every person living on April 1, 1930. Omit children born since April 1, 1930.	Relationship of this Person to the head of the family.	Sex	Color or race	Age at last birthday	Single, married, widowed or divorced	Attended school any time since Sept. 1, 1929	Whether able to read and write.	Place of birth of this person.		
	1	2	3	4	5	6	7	8	9	10	11	12	13	14
1	Hernan Cortes Street	118	138	Davis, Josefina C	Wife	F	Cha	48	M	N	Y	Philippine Is.	Y	None
2		119	139	Calvo, Leon P	Head	M	Cha	52	M	N	Y	Guam	Y	Retail Merchant
3		119	139	Calvo, Maria LG	Wife	F	Cha	36	M	N	Y	Guam	Y	None
4		119	139	Calvo, Jose	Son	M	Cha	18	S	N	Y	Guam	Y	Carpenter
5		120	140	Salas, Galo L	Head	M	Cha	27	M	N	Y	Guam	Y	Cashier
6		120	140	Salas, Concepcion P	Wife	F	Cha	24	M	N	N	Guam	Y	None
7		120	140	Salas, Adela	Daughter	F	Cha	4	S	N	N	Guam	N	None
8		120	140	Salas, Miguel	Son	M	Cha	2.2	S	N	N	Guam	N	None
9		120	140	Salas, Jesus	Son	M	Cha	.5	S	N	N	Guam	N	None
10		120	140	Mendiola, Ana S	Maid	F	Cha	31	S	N	N	Guam	N	Maid
11		120	140	Mendiola, Felicidad	Maid	F	Cha	10	S	Y	Y	Guam	N	Maid
12		121	141	San Agustin, Candido S	Head	M	Cha	22	M	N	Y	Guam	Y	Policeman
13		121	141	San Agustin, Maria	Wife	F	Cha	22	M	N	Y	Guam	Y	None
14		121	141	San Agustin, John	Son	M	Cha	.5	S	N	N	Guam	N	None
15		122	142	Cruz, Juan A	Head	M	Cha	56	Wd	N	Y	Guam	N	Carpenter
16		122	142	Cruz, Vicente LG	Son	M	Cha	31	S	N	Y	Guam	Y	Farmer
17		122	142	Cruz, Jesus	Son	M	Cha	26	S	N	Y	Guam	Y	Farmer
18		122	142	Cruz, Juan	Son	M	Cha	22	S	N	Y	Guam	Y	Laborer
19		122	142	Cruz, Jose	Son	M	Cha	24	S	N	Y	Guam	Y	Clerk
20		122	142	Cruz, Anparo	Daughter	F	Cha	18	S	N	Y	Guam	Y	None
21		122	142	Cruz, Mariano	Son	M	Cha	14	S	Y	Y	Guam	Y	None
22		122	142	Cruz, Maria	Daughter	F	Cha	13	S	Y	Y	Guam	Y	None
23		122	142	Cruz, Antonio	Son	M	Cha	10	S	Y	Y	Guam	N	None
24		123	143	Garcia, Jose C	Head	M	Cha	40	M	N	Y	Guam	Y	Carpenter
25		123	143	Garcia, Magdalena A	Wife	F	Cha	37	M	N	Y	Guam	Y	None

DEPARTMENT OF COMMERCE-BUREAU OF THE CENSUS
WASHINGTON

FIFTEENTH CENSUS OF THE UNITED STATES: 1930-POPULATION

THE ISLAND OF GUAM

Sheet No. 16B

93B

District Municipality of Agana
Name of Place Agana City (San Ignacio Urban)
[Proper name and, also, name of class, as city, town, village, barrio, etc]

Enumeration District No. 3
Enumerated by me on April 10, 1930 Tomas A. Calvo
Enumerator

	PLACE OF ABODE			NAME	RELATION	PERSONAL DESCRIPTION				EDUCATION		NATIVITY		OCCUPATION
	Street, avenue, road, etc.	Number of dwelling house is order of visitation	Number of family in order of visitation	of each person whose place of abode on April 1, 1930, was in this family. Enter surname, first, then given name and middle initial. If any. Include every person living on April 1, 1930. Omit children born since April 1, 1930.	Relationship of this Person to the head of the family.	Sex	Color or race	Age at last birthday	Single, married, widowed or divorced	Attended school any time since Sept. 1, 1929	Whether able to read and write.	Place of birth of this person.	Whether able to speak English.	
	1	2	3	4	5	6	7	8	9	10	11	12	13	14
26	Hernan Cortes Street	123	143	Garcia, Tomasa	Daughter	F	Cha	18	S	N	Y	Guam	Y	None
27		123	143	Garcia, Jesus	Son	M	Cha	15	S	Y	Y	Guam	Y	Carpenter
28		123	143	Garcia, Florencio	Son	M	Cha	14	S	Y	Y	Guam	Y	None
29		123	143	Garcia, Francisco	Son	M	Cha	11	S	Y	Y	Guam	Y	None
30		123	143	Garcia, Justo	Son	M	Cha	10	S	Y	Y	Guam	Y	None
31		123	143	Garcia, Gonzalo	Son	M	Cha	5	S	N	N	Guam	N	None
32		123	143	Garcia, Mariano	Son	M	Cha	3.2	S	N	N	Guam	N	None
33		123	143	Garcia, Rosa	Daughter	F	Cha	1.4	S	N	N	Guam	N	None
34		123	144	Garcia, Angela C	Head	F	Cha	61	Wd	N	Y	Guam	N	None
35		123	144	Garcia, Esperanza	Daughter	F	Cha	41	S	N	N	Guam	N	None
36		124	145	Lee, Marjorie Jean	Head	F	W	22	M	N	Y	Washington DC	Y	None
37		125	146	Taitano, Francisco	Head	M	Cha	38	M	N	Y	Guam	Y	Extension agent
38		125	146	Taitano, Dolores S	Wife	F	Cha	37	M	N	Y	Guam	Y	None
39		125	146	Taitano, Rosa	Daughter	F	Cha	19	S	N	Y	Guam	Y	None
40		125	146	Taitano, Lila B	Daughter	F	Cha	18	S	N	Y	Guam	Y	None
41		125	146	Taitano, Josefina	Daughter	F	Cha	15	S	Y	Y	Guam	Y	None
42		125	146	Taitano, Francisca	Daughter	F	Cha	13	S	Y	Y	Guam	Y	None
43		125	146	Taitano, Artemio	Son	M	Cha	12	S	Y	Y	Guam	Y	None
44		125	146	Taitano, Juana	Daughter	F	Cha	11	S	Y	Y	Guam	N	None
45		125	146	Taitano, Percy M	Son	M	Cha	9	S	Y	Y	Guam	N	None
46		125	146	Taitano, Jose I	Son	M	Cha	8	S	Y	Y	Guam	N	None
47		125	146	Taitano, Henry O	Son	M	Cha	6	S	Y	Y	Guam	N	None
48		125	146	Taitano, Rita P	Daughter	F	Cha	5	S	N	N	Guam	N	None
49		125	146	Taitano, Meary E	Daughter	F	Cha	1	S	N	N	Guam	N	None
50		125	146	Taitano, Jose M	Father	M	Cha	88	Wd	N	Y	Guam	N	None

DEPARTMENT OF COMMERCE-BUREAU OF THE CENSUS
WASHINGTON

FIFTEENTH CENSUS OF THE UNITED STATES: 1930-POPULATION

THE ISLAND OF GUAM

Sheet No. 17A

District **Municipality of Agana**
Name of Place **Agana City (San Ignacio Urban)**
[Proper name and, also, name of class, as city, town, village, barrio, etc]

Enumeration District No. 3
Enumerated by me on **April 10, 1930** Tomas A. Calvo, Enumerator

	PLACE OF ABODE: Street, avenue, road, etc.	Number of dwelling house in order of visitation	Number of family in order of visitation	NAME of each person whose place of abode on April 1, 1930, was in this family. Enter surname, first, then given name and middle initial. If any. Include every person living on April 1, 1930. Omit children born since April 1, 1930.	RELATION Relationship of this Person to the head of the family.	PERSONAL DESCRIPTION: Sex	Color or race	Age at last birthday	Single, married, widowed or divorced	EDUCATION: Attended school any time since Sept. 1, 1929	Whether able to read and write.	NATIVITY Place of birth of this person.	Whether able to speak English.	OCCUPATION
	1	2	3	4	5	6	7	8	9	10	11	12	13	14
1	Hernan Cortes Street	126	147	Perez, Rosa I	Head	F	Cha	57	S	N	Y	Guam	Y	None
2		126	147	Perez, Emilia	Sister	F	Cha	55	S	N	Y	Guam	Y	None
3		126	147	Perez, Joaquina	Sister	F	Cha	47	S	N	Y	Guam	Y	None
4		127	148	Okada, Jose S	Head	M	Jap	35	M	N	Y	Japan	Y	Machinist
5		127	148	Okada, Vicenta S	Wife	F	Cha	28	M	N	Y	Guam	Y	None
6		127	148	Okada, Juan	Son	M	Jap	14	S	Y	Y	Guam	Y	None
7		127	148	Okada, Carlos	Son	M	Jap	12	S	Y	Y	Guam	Y	None
8		127	148	Okada, Edward	Son	M	Jap	11	S	Y	Y	Guam	N	None
9		127	148	Okada, Oscar	Son	M	Jap	7	S	Y	Y	Guam	N	None
10		127	148	Okada, Gregorio	Son	M	Jap	6	S	N	N	Guam	N	None
11		127	148	Okada, Edmond	Son	M	Jap	8	S	Y	Y	Guam	N	None
12		127	148	Okada, Francisco	Son	M	Jap	4	S	N	N	Guam	N	None
13		127	148	Okada, Jesus	Son	M	Jap	9	S	Y	Y	Guam	N	None
14		128	149	Palting, Pancracio R	Head	M	Fil	54	M	N	Y	Philipine Is.	Y	Attorney at-law
15		128	149	Palting, Soledad D	Wife	F	Fil	47	M	N	Y	Guam	N	None
16		128	149	Palting, Margarito	Son	M	Fil	22	S	N	Y	Guam	Y	None
17		128	149	Palting, Florencia	Daughter	F	Fil	18	S	Y	Y	Guam	Y	None
18		128	149	Palting, Pancracio	Son	M	Fil	9	S	Y	Y	Guam	Y	None
19		128	149	Palting, Francisco	Son	M	Fil	8	S	Y	Y	Guam	N	None
20		128	149	Palting, Alejo	Son	M	Fil	6	S	Y	Y	Guam	N	None
21		128	149	Dungca, Felicita	Niece	F	Fil	29	S	N	Y	Guam	Y	None
22		128	149	Dungca, Concepcion	Niece	F	Fil	27	S	N	Y	Guam	Y	None
23		128	149	Dungca, Jose	Nephew	M	Fil	22	S	N	Y	Guam	Y	Farmer
24		128	149	Dungca, Francisco	Nephew	M	Fil	21	S	N	Y	Guam	Y	Farmer
25		128	149	Dungca, Constansia	Niece	F	Fil	17	S	Y	Y	Guam	Y	None

DEPARTMENT OF COMMERCE-BUREAU OF THE CENSUS
WASHINGTON

FIFTEENTH CENSUS OF THE UNITED STATES: 1930-POPULATION

THE ISLAND OF GUAM

Sheet No. 17B

District **Municipality of Agana**
Name of Place **Agana City (San Ignacio Urban)**
[Proper name and, also, name of class, as city, town, village, barrio, etc]

Enumeration District No. 3
Enumerated by me on **April 10, 1930** Tomas A. Calvo, Enumerator

	PLACE OF ABODE			NAME	RELATION	PERSONAL DESCRIPTION				EDUCATION		NATIVITY		OCCUPATION
	Street, avenue, road, etc.	Number of dwelling house is order of visitation	Number of family in order of visitation	of each person whose place of abode on April 1, 1930, was in this family. Enter surname, first, then given name and middle initial. If any. Include every person living on April 1, 1930. Omit children born since April 1, 1930.	Relationship of this Person to the head of the family.	Sex	Color or race	Age at last birthday	Single, married, widowed or divorced	Attended school any time since Sept. 1, 1929	Whether able to read and write.	Place of birth of this person.	Whether able to speak English.	
	1	2	3	4	5	6	7	8	9	10	11	12	13	14
26	Hernan Cortes Street	128	149	Cruz, Antonio	Servant	M	Cha	42	S	N	N	Guam	N	Servant
27		128	149	Castro, Brigida	Maid	F	Cha	13	S	Y	Y	Guam	Y	Maid
28		128	149	Perez, Concepcion	Lodger	F	Cha	14	S	Y	Y	Guam	Y	None
29	Pazos Street	129	150	Perez, Felix I	Head	M	Cha	60	M	N	Y	Guam	Y	Farmer
30		129	150	Perez, Josefa	Wife	F	Cha	48	M	N	Y	Guam	Y	None
31		129	150	Perez, Jose	Son	M	Cha	25	S	N	Y	Guam	Y	Farmer
32		129	150	Perez, Delores	Daughter	F	Cha	22	S	N	Y	Guam	Y	None
33		129	150	Perez, Josefina	Daughter	F	Cha	20	S	N	Y	Guam	Y	None
34		129	150	Perez, Amelia	Daughter	F	Cha	20	S	N	Y	Guam	Y	None
35		129	150	Perez, Pedro	Son	M	Cha	18	S	Y	Y	Guam	Y	Teacher
36		129	150	Perez, Francisca	Daughter	F	Cha	16	S	N	Y	Guam	Y	None
37		129	150	Perez, Manuel	Son	M	Cha	15	S	Y	Y	Guam	Y	None
38		129	150	Perez, Jesus	Son	M	Cha	9	S	Y	Y	Guam	N	None
39		130	151	Perez, Antonio LG	Head	M	Cha	39	M	N	Y	Guam	Y	Blacksmith
40		130	151	Perez, Nicolasa P	Wife	F	Cha	33	M	N	Y	Guam	Y	None
41		130	151	Perez, Cecilia	Daughter	F	Cha	15	S	N	Y	Guam	Y	None
42		130	151	Perez, Dorotea	Daughter	F	Cha	14	S	N	Y	Guam	Y	None
43		130	151	Perez, Clotilde	Daughter	F	Cha	12	S	Y	Y	Guam	Y	None
44		130	151	Perez, Ernesto	Son	M	Cha	11	S	Y	Y	Guam	Y	None
45		130	151	Perez, Isabel	Daughter	F	Cha	10	S	Y	Y	Guam	Y	None
46		130	151	Perez, Maria	Daughter	F	Cha	9	S	Y	Y	Guam	N	None
47		130	151	Perez, Tomas	Son	M	Cha	6	S	N	N	Guam	N	None
48		130	151	Perez, Antonio	Son	M	Cha	3	S	N	N	Guam	N	None
49		130	151	Perez, Vicente	Son	M	Cha	2.2	S	N	N	Guam	N	None
50		130	152	Perez, Jose LG	Head	M	Cha	52	Wd	N	Y	Guam	Y	Blacksmith

(CHAMORRO ROOTS GENEALOGY PROJECT™ TRANSCRIPTION)
(BERNARD T. PUNZALAN / HTTP://WWW.CHAMORROROOTS.COM)

DEPARTMENT OF COMMERCE-BUREAU OF THE CENSUS
WASHINGTON

FIFTEENTH CENSUS OF THE UNITED STATES: 1930-POPULATION

THE ISLAND OF GUAM

Sheet No. 18A

District Municipality of Agana
Name of Place Agana City (San Ignacio Urban)
[Proper name and, also, name of class, as city, town, village, barrio, etc]

Enumeration District No. 3
Enumerated by me on April 11, 1930 Tomas A. Calvo, Enumerator

	PLACE OF ABODE: Street, avenue, road, etc.	Number of dwelling house in order of visitation	Number of family in order of visitation	NAME of each person whose place of abode on April 1, 1930, was in this family. Enter surname, first, then given name and middle initial. If any. Include every person living on April 1, 1930. Omit children born since April 1, 1930.	RELATION Relationship of this Person to the head of the family.	PERSONAL DESCRIPTION: Sex	Color or race	Age at last birthday	Single, married, widowed or divorced	EDUCATION: Attended school any time since Sept. 1, 1929	Whether able to read and write.	NATIVITY Place of birth of this person.	Whether able to speak English.	OCCUPATION
	1	2	3	4	5	6	7	8	9	10	11	12	13	14
1	Pazos Street	130	152	Perez, Gregorio	Son	M	Cha	13	S	Y	Y	Guam	Y	None
2		130	152	Perez, Antonio	Son	M	Cha	12	S	Y	Y	Guam	Y	None
3		130	152	Perez, Ana LG	Sister	F	Cha	43	S	N	Y	Guam	Y	None
4		131	153	Root, Ana I	Head	F	W	29	M	N	Y	Texas	Y	None
5		131	153	Root, Doroty	Daughter	F	W	8	S	Y	Y	Texas	Y	None
6		131	153	Root, Joe	Son	M	W	5	S	N	N	Texas	N	None
7	Fragua Street	132	154	Lujan, Pedro C	Head	M	Cha	22	S	N	Y	Guam	Y	Clerk
8		132	154	Lujan, Magdalena	Sister	F	Cha	24	S	N	Y	Guam	Y	None
9		132	154	Lujan, Trinidad	Sister	F	Cha	19	S	N	Y	Guam	Y	None
10		132	154	Lujan, Perpetuo	Brother	M	Cha	17	S	N	Y	Guam	Y	Machinist
11		132	154	Lujan, Margarita	Sister	F	Cha	16	S	N	Y	Guam	Y	None
12		132	154	Lujan, Rufina	Sister	F	Cha	14	S	Y	Y	Guam	Y	Seamstress
13		132	154	Lujan, Nicolasa	Sister	F	Cha	10	S	Y	Y	Guam	Y	None
14		132	154	Lujan, Maria	Sister	F	Cha	10	S	Y	Y	Guam	Y	None
15		133	155	Lujan, Joaquin D	Head	M	Cha	68	M	N	Y	Guam	N	None
16		133	155	Lujan, Ramona C	Wife	F	Cha	62	M	N	Y	Guam	N	None
17		133	156	Crisostomo, Jesus P	Head	M	Cha	35	M	N	Y	Guam	Y	Machinist
18		133	156	Crisostomo, Soledad	Wife	F	Cha	35	M	N	Y	Guam	Y	None
19		133	156	Crisostomo, Desiderio	Son	M	Cha	9	S	Y	Y	Guam	N	None
20		133	156	Crisostomo, Maria	Daughter	F	Cha	7	S	Y	Y	Guam	N	None
21		133	156	Crisostomo, Felix	Son	M	Cha	5	S	N	N	Guam	N	None
22		133	156	Crisostomo, Brigida	Daughter	F	Cha	2.4	S	N	N	Guam	N	None
23		133	156	Crisostomo, Vicente	Son	M	Cha	.9	S	N	N	Guam	N	None
24		134	157	Taitano, Jose M	Head	M	Cha	58	M	N	Y	Guam	N	Farmer
25		134	157	Taitano, Andrea G	Wife	F	Cha	54	M	N	N	Guam	N	None

DEPARTMENT OF COMMERCE-BUREAU OF THE CENSUS
WASHINGTON

FIFTEENTH CENSUS OF THE UNITED STATES: 1930-POPULATION

THE ISLAND OF GUAM

Sheet No. 18B

District Municipality of Agana
Name of Place Agana City (San Ignacio Urban)
[Proper name and, also, name of class, as city, town, village, barrio, etc]

Enumeration District No. 3
Enumerated by me on April 11, 1930 Tomas A. Calvo
Enumerator

	PLACE OF ABODE			NAME	RELATION	PERSONAL DESCRIPTION				EDUCATION		NATIVITY		OCCUPATION
	Street, avenue, road, etc.	Number of dwelling house is order of visitation	Number of family in order of visitation	of each person whose place of abode on April 1, 1930, was in this family. Enter surname, first, then given name and middle initial. If any. Include every person living on April 1, 1930. Omit children born since April 1, 1930.	Relationship of this Person to the head of the family.	Sex	Color or race	Age at last birthday	Single, married, widowed or divorced	Attended school any time since Sept. 1, 1929	Whether able to read and write.	Place of birth of this person.	Whether able to speak English.	
	1	2	3	4	5	6	7	8	9	10	11	12	13	14
26	Fragua Street	134	157	Taitano, Liberato	Son	M	Cha	22	S	N	Y	Guam	Y	Farmer
27		134	157	Taitano, Francisco	Son	M	Cha	19	S	N	Y	Guam	Y	Farmer
28		134	157	Taitano, Emilia	Daughter	F	Cha	18	S	N	Y	Guam	Y	None
29		134	157	Taitano, Ana	Daughter	F	Cha	16	S	Y	Y	Guam	Y	None
30		134	157	Taitano, Mariano	Son	M	Cha	15	S	N	Y	Guam	Y	None
31		134	157	Taitano, Rita	Daughter	F	Cha	13	S	Y	Y	Guam	Y	None
32		135	158	Guerrero, Joaquin	Head	M	Cha	37	M	N	Y	Guam	Y	Horticulturalist
33		135	158	Guerrero, Luisa C	Wife	F	Cha	32	M	N	Y	Guam	Y	None
34		135	158	Guerrero, Joaquin	Son	M	Cha	9	S	Y	Y	Guam	Y	None
35		135	158	Guerrero, Josefina	Daughter	F	Cha	8	S	Y	Y	Guam	Y	None
36		135	158	Guerrero, Manuel	Son	M	Cha	6	S	N	N	Guam	N	None
37		135	158	Guerrero, Oliva	Daughter	F	Cha	5	S	N	N	Guam	N	None
38		135	158	Guerrero, Ramon	Son	M	Cha	3.5	S	N	N	Guam	N	None
39		135	158	Guerrero, Juan	Son	M	Cha	2.5	S	N	N	Guam	N	None
40		135	158	Castro, Mercedes L	Mother in-law	F	Cha	60	Wd	N	Y	Guam	N	None
41		135	158	Castro, Santiago	Brother	M	Cha	30	S	N	Y	Guam	Y	Laborer
42		136	159	Dungca, Felix G	Head	M	Fil	43	M	N	Y	Guam	Y	Machinist
43		136	159	Dungca, Maria C	Wife	F	Cha	39	M	N	Y	Guam	Y	None
44		136	159	Dungca, Josefina	Daughter	F	Fil	21	S	N	Y	Guam	Y	None
45		136	159	Dungca, Adela	Daughter	F	Fil	20	S	N	Y	Guam	Y	None
46		136	159	Dungca, Felix	Son	M	Fil	18	S	Y	Y	Guam	Y	Apprentice surveyor
47		136	159	Dungca, Justo	Son	M	Fil	17	S	Y	Y	Guam	Y	None
48		136	159	Dungca, Esperanza	Daughter	F	Fil	14	S	Y	Y	Guam	Y	None
49		136	159	Dungca, Felicita	Daughter	F	Fil	11	S	Y	Y	Guam	Y	None
50		136	159	Dungca, Concepcion	Daughter	F	Fil	9	S	Y	Y	Guam	Y	None

(CHAMORRO ROOTS GENEALOGY PROJECT™ TRANSCRIPTION)
(BERNARD T. PUNZALAN / HTTP://WWW.CHAMORROROOTS.COM)

DEPARTMENT OF COMMERCE-BUREAU OF THE CENSUS
WASHINGTON
FIFTEENTH CENSUS OF THE UNITED STATES: 1930-POPULATION

THE ISLAND OF GUAM

Sheet No. 19A

District **Municipality of Agana**
Name of Place **Agana City (San Ignacio Urban)**
[Proper name and, also, name of class, as city, town, village, barrio, etc]

Enumeration District No. **3**
Enumerated by me on **April 11, 1930** Tomas A. Calvo
Enumerator

	PLACE OF ABODE			NAME	RELATION	PERSONAL DESCRIPTION				EDUCATION		NATIVITY		OCCUPATION
	Street, avenue, road, etc.	Number of dwelling house is order of visitation	Number of family in order of visitation	of each person whose place of abode on April 1, 1930, was in this family. Enter surname, first, then given name and middle initial. If any. Include every person living on April 1, 1930. Omit children born since April 1, 1930.	Relationship of this Person to the head of the family.	Sex	Color or race	Age at last birthday	Single, married, widowed or divorced	Attended school any time since Sept. 1, 1929	Whether able to read and write.	Place of birth of this person.	Whether able to speak English.	
	1	2	3	4	5	6	7	8	9	10	11	12	13	14
1		136	159	Dungca, Carmen	Daughter	F	Fil	3.5	S	N	N	Guam	N	None
2		136	159	Dungca, Jose	Son	M	Fil	1.1	S	N	N	Guam	N	None
3	General Terrero Street	137	160	Tenorio, Vicente S	Head	M	Cha	23	M	N	Y	Guam	Y	Barber
4		137	160	Tenorio, Rosa T	Wife	F	Cha	27	M	N	Y	Guam	N	None
5		137	160	Tenorio, Joaquin	Son	M	Cha	.7	S	N	N	Guam	N	None
6		138	161	Torres, Juan M	Head	M	Cha	45	M	N	Y	Guam	Y	Bookkeeper
7		138	161	Torres, Concepcion C	Wife	F	Cha	42	M	N	Y	Guam	Y	None
8		138	161	Torres, Antonia	Son	M	Cha	20	S	N	Y	Guam	Y	None
9		138	161	Torres, Jose	Son	M	Cha	18	S	N	Y	Guam	Y	None
10		138	161	Torres, Lope	Son	M	Cha	17	S	N	Y	Guam	Y	Salesman
11		138	161	Torres, Ricardo	Son	M	Cha	15	S	Y	Y	Guam	Y	None
12		138	161	Torres, Juan	Son	M	Cha	13	S	Y	Y	Guam	Y	None
13		138	161	Torres, Concepcion	Daughter	F	Cha	12	S	Y	Y	Guam	Y	None
14		138	161	Torres, Pilar	Daughter	F	Cha	5	S	N	N	Guam	N	None
15		138	161	Torres, Francisco	Son	M	Cha	4	S	N	N	Guam	N	None
16		138	161	Torres, Edward	Son	M	Cha	1	S	N	N	Guam	N	None
17		138	161	Torres, Joaquina	Mother	F	Cha	68	Wd	N	Y	Guam	N	None
18		139	162	Torres, Jesus F	Head	M	Cha	26	M	N	Y	Guam	Y	Mechanic
19		139	162	Torres, Maria G	Wife	F	Cha	24	M	N	Y	Guam	Y	Saleswoman
20		139	163	Oka, Antonio T	Head	M	Jap	51	M	N	Y	Japan	Y	Farmer
21		139	164	Noda, Noaichi	Head	M	Jap	35	Wd	N	Y	Japan	Y	Cook
22	San Ignacio Street	140	165	Muna, Vicenta	Head	F	Cha	62	S	N	Y	Guam	Y	None
23		140	165	Duenas, Antonio B	Nephew	M	Cha	15	S	Y	Y	Guam	Y	None
24		140	166	Guzman, Ana M	Head	F	Cha	33	M	N	Y	Guam	Y	None
25		140	166	Guzman, Gregorio	Son	M	Cha	13	S	Y	Y	Guam	Y	None

(CHAMORRO ROOTS GENEALOGY PROJECT™ TRANSCRIPTION)
(BERNARD T. PUNZALAN / HTTP://WWW.CHAMORROROOTS.COM)

DEPARTMENT OF COMMERCE-BUREAU OF THE CENSUS
WASHINGTON

FIFTEENTH CENSUS OF THE UNITED STATES: 1930-POPULATION

THE ISLAND OF GUAM

Sheet No. 19B

96B

District Municipality of Agana
Name of Place Agana City (San Ignacio Urban)
[Proper name and, also, name of class, as city, town, village, barrio, etc]

Enumeration District No. 3
Enumerated by me on April 11, 1930 Tomas A. Calvo, Enumerator

	PLACE OF ABODE			NAME	RELATION	PERSONAL DESCRIPTION				EDUCATION		NATIVITY		OCCUPATION
	Street, avenue, road, etc.	Number of dwelling house in order of visitation	Number of family in order of visitation	of each person whose place of abode on April 1, 1930, was in this family. Enter surname, first, then given name and middle initial. If any. Include every person living on April 1, 1930. Omit children born since April 1, 1930.	Relationship of this Person to the head of the family.	Sex	Color or race	Age at last birthday	Single, married, widowed or divorced	Attended school any time since Sept. 1, 1929	Whether able to read and write.	Place of birth of this person.	Whether able to speak English.	
	1	2	3	4	5	6	7	8	9	10	11	12	13	14
26	San Ignacio Street	140	166	Guzman, Jesus	Son	M	Cha	12	S	Y	Y	Guam	Y	None
27		140	166	Guzman, Antonina	Daughter	F	Cha	11	S	Y	Y	Guam	Y	None
28		140	166	Guzman, Edward	Son	M	Cha	9	S	Y	Y	Guam	N	None
29		140	166	Guzman, Jose	Son	M	Cha	7	S	Y	Y	Guam	N	None
30		140	166	Guzman, Josefina	Daughter	F	Cha	3.9	S	N	N	Guam	N	None
31		141	167	Pangelinan, Ignacio D	Head	M	Cha	55	M	N	Y	Guam	Y	Farmer
32		141	167	Pangelinan, Maria	Wife	F	Cha	56	M	N	N	Guam	N	None
33		141	167	Pangelinan, Rita	Daughter	F	Cha	24	S	N	Y	Guam	Y	None
34		141	167	Pangelinan, Jose	Son	M	Cha	23	S	N	Y	Guam	Y	Farmer
35		141	167	Pangelinan, Ana	Daughter	F	Cha	20	S	N	Y	Guam	Y	None
36		141	167	Pangelinan, Joaquin	Son	M	Cha	18	S	N	N	Guam	N	None
37		141	167	Pangelinan, Vicente	Son	M	Cha	16	S	N	Y	Guam	Y	Farmer
38		141	167	Pangelinan, Magdalena	Daughter	F	Cha	14	S	N	Y	Guam	Y	None
39		142	168	Guzman, Dolores C	Head	F	Cha	60	Wd	N	Y	Guam	N	None
40		142	168	Guzman, Natividad	Daughter	F	Cha	27	S	N	Y	Guam	Y	None
41		142	168	Guzman, Vicente	Son	M	Cha	23	S	N	Y	Guam	Y	Painter
42		142	168	Guzman, Juan	Son	M	Cha	22	S	N	Y	Guam	Y	Farmer
43		142	168	Perez, Mariano C	Son	M	Cha	31	S	N	Y	Guam	Y	Farmer
44		143	169	Flores, Vicente S	Head	M	Cha	71	M	N	Y	Guam	Y	None
45		143	169	Flores, Maria C	Wife	F	Cha	63	M	N	N	Guam	N	None
46		143	169	Flores, Felix	Son	M	Cha	19	S	N	Y	Guam	Y	Carpenter
47		143	169	Cruz, Regina	Grand daughter	F	Cha	21	S	N	Y	Guam	Y	None
48		143	169	Cruz, Jose	Grand son	M	Cha	20	S	N	Y	Guam	Y	Carpenter
49		143	169	Cruz, Vicente	Grand son	M	Cha	18	S	N	Y	Guam	Y	Laborer
50		143	169	Cruz, Rosario	Grand daughter	F	Cha	15	S	N	Y	Guam	Y	None

DEPARTMENT OF COMMERCE-BUREAU OF THE CENSUS
WASHINGTON

FIFTEENTH CENSUS OF THE UNITED STATES: 1930-POPULATION

THE ISLAND OF GUAM

Sheet No. 20A

District **Municipality of Agana**
Name of Place **Agana City (San Ignacio Urban)**
[Proper name and, also, name of class, as city, town, village, barrio, etc]

Enumeration District No. 3
Enumerated by me on **April 12, 1930** Tomas A. Calvo, Enumerator

	PLACE OF ABODE: Street, avenue, road, etc.	Number of dwelling house in order of visitation	Number of family in order of visitation	NAME of each person whose place of abode on April 1, 1930, was in this family. Enter surname, first, then given name and middle initial. If any. Include every person living on April 1, 1930. Omit children born since April 1, 1930.	RELATION Relationship of this Person to the head of the family.	PERSONAL DESCRIPTION: Sex	Color or race	Age at last birthday	Single, married, widowed or divorced	EDUCATION: Attended school any time since Sept. 1, 1929	Whether able to read and write.	NATIVITY Place of birth of this person.	Whether able to speak English.	OCCUPATION
	1	2	3	4	5	6	7	8	9	10	11	12	13	14
1	San Ignacio Street	143	169	Cruz, Eugenio	Grand son	M	Cha	13	S	Y	Y	Guam	Y	None
2		143	169	Salas, Jesus F	Grand son	M	Cha	2.9	S	N	N	Guam	N	None
3		144	170	Mendiola, Juan L	Head	M	Cha	47	M	N	Y	Guam	Y	Farmer
4		144	170	Mendiola, Usurla A	Wife	F	Cha	48	M	N	Y	Guam	Y	None
5		144	170	Mendiola, Gonzalo	Son	M	Cha	17	S	N	Y	Guam	Y	Farmer
6		144	170	Mendiola, Juan	Son	M	Cha	16	S	Y	Y	Guam	Y	None
7		144	170	Mendiola, Maria	Daughter	F	Cha	13	S	N	Y	Guam	Y	None
8		144	170	Mendiola, Ana	Daughter	F	Cha	11	S	Y	Y	Guam	Y	None
9		144	170	Mendiola, Francisco	Son	M	Cha	9	S	Y	Y	Guam	N	None
10		144	171	Mendiola, Jesus A	Head	M	Cha	21	M	N	Y	Guam	Y	Laborer
11		144	171	Mendiola, Maria C	Wife	F	Cha	19	M	N	Y	Guam	Y	None
12		144	171	Mendiola, Juan	Son	M	Cha	.5	S	N	N	Guam	N	None
13		145	172	Cruz, Pedro P	Head	M	Cha	28	M	N	Y	Guam	Y	Carpenter
14		145	172	Cruz, Maria B	Wife	F	Cha	23	M	N	Y	Guam	Y	None
15		145	172	Cruz, Jose	Son	M	Cha	3.5	S	N	N	Guam	N	None
16		145	172	Cruz, Maria	Daughter	F	Cha	1.9	S	N	N	Guam	N	None
17		145	172	Oroso, Juan	Brother in-law	M	Cha	17	S	N	Y	Guam	Y	Farmer
18		145	172	Oroso, Vicente	Brother in-law	M	Cha	10	S	Y	Y	Guam	N	None
19		145	172	Oroso, George	Brother in-law	M	Cha	6	S	N	N	Guam	N	None
20		145	172	Oroso, Delfina	Sister in-law	F	Cha	5	S	N	N	Guam	N	None
21		146	173	Cruz, Jose P	Head	M	Cha	46	M	N	Y	Guam	Y	Chief Clerk
22		146	173	Cruz, Cecilia D	Wife	F	Cha	32	M	N	Y	Guam	Y	None
23		146	173	Cruz, Joseph	Son	M	Cha	1.7	S	N	N	Guam	N	None
24		146	173	Arceo, Felicita S	Maid	F	Cha	12	S	Y	Y	Guam	Y	Maid
25		147	174	Castro, Consalacion R	Head	F	Cha	54	Wd	N	Y	Guam	Y	None

DEPARTMENT OF COMMERCE-BUREAU OF THE CENSUS
WASHINGTON

FIFTEENTH CENSUS OF THE UNITED STATES: 1930-POPULATION

THE ISLAND OF GUAM

Sheet No. 20B

97B

District Municipality of Agana
Name of Place Agana City (San Ignacio Urban)
[Proper name and, also, name of class, as city, town, village, barrio, etc]

Enumeration District No. 3
Enumerated by me on April 12, 1930 Tomas A. Calvo
Enumerator

	PLACE OF ABODE			NAME	RELATION	PERSONAL DESCRIPTION				EDUCATION		NATIVITY		OCCUPATION
	Street, avenue, road, etc.	Number of dwelling house is order of visitation	Number of family in order of visitation	of each person whose place of abode on April 1, 1930, was in this family. Enter surname, first, then given name and middle initial. If any. Include every person living on April 1, 1930. Omit children born since April 1, 1930.	Relationship of this Person to the head of the family.	Sex	Color or race	Age at last birthday	Single, married, widowed or divorced	Attended school any time since Sept. 1, 1929	Whether able to read and write.	Place of birth of this person.	Whether able to speak English.	
	1	2	3	4	5	6	7	8	9	10	11	12	13	14
26	San Ignacio Street	147	174	Castro, Enrique	Son	M	Cha	25	S	N	Y	Guam	Y	Farmer
27		147	174	Castro, Emilia	Daughter	F	Cha	24	S	N	Y	Guam	Y	Dressmaker
28		147	174	Castro, Josefina	Daughter	F	Cha	21	S	N	Y	Guam	Y	Cook
29		147	174	Castro, Jose	Son	M	Cha	17	S	N	Y	Guam	Y	Farmer
30		147	174	Castro, Joaquina	Daughter	F	Cha	16	S	Y	Y	Guam	Y	None
31		147	174	Castro, Felix	Son	M	Cha	13	S	Y	Y	Guam	Y	None
32		148	175	Mendiola, Mariano C	Head	M	Cha	55	Wd	N	Y	Guam	Y	Farmer
33		148	175	Mendiola, Jose C	Son	M	Cha	22	S	N	Y	Guam	Y	Farmer
34		148	175	Mendiola, Mariano	Son	M	Cha	20	S	N	Y	Guam	Y	Farmer
35		148	175	Mendiola, Jesus	Son	M	Cha	18	S	N	Y	Guam	Y	Farmer
36		148	175	Mendiola, Carmen	Daughter	F	Cha	15	S	N	Y	Guam	Y	None
37		148	175	Mendiola, Enrique	Son	M	Cha	14	S	Y	Y	Guam	Y	None
38		148	175	Mendiola, Veronica	Daughter	F	Cha	12	S	Y	Y	Guam	Y	None
39		148	175	Mendiola, Joaquina	Daughter	F	Cha	10	S	Y	Y	Guam	Y	None
40		148	175	Mendiola, Julia	Daughter	F	Cha	8	S	Y	Y	Guam	Y	None
41		148	175	Mendiola, Joaquin	Son	M	Cha	2.5	S	N	N	Guam	N	None
42		148	176	Rivera, Manuel G	Head	M	Cha	35	M	N	Y	Guam	Y	Barber
43		148	176	Rivera, Maria M	Wife	F	Cha	24	M	N	Y	Guam	Y	None
44	Santa Cruz Street	149	177	Dejima, T	Head	M	Jap	46	M	N	Y	Japan	Y	Merchant
45		150	178	Arceo, Maria C	Head	F	Cha	65	Wd	N	N	Guam	N	None
46		150	178	Arceo, Nicolasa	Daughter	F	Cha	41	S	N	N	Guam	Y	Laundress
47		150	178	Arceo, Rosario	Grand daughter	F	Cha	14	S	Y	Y	Guam	Y	None
48		150	178	Santos, Ana A	Grand daughter	F	Cha	15	S	N	Y	Guam	Y	Maid
49		150	179	Cruz, Antonio C	Head	M	Cha	27	M	N	Y	Guam	Y	Farmer
50		150	179	Cruz, Carmen A	Wife	F	Cha	31	M	N	Y	Guam	Y	None

(CHAMORRO ROOTS GENEALOGY PROJECT™ TRANSCRIPTION)
(BERNARD T. PUNZALAN / HTTP://WWW.CHAMORROROOTS.COM)

DEPARTMENT OF COMMERCE-BUREAU OF THE CENSUS
WASHINGTON

FIFTEENTH CENSUS OF THE UNITED STATES: 1930-POPULATION

THE ISLAND OF GUAM

Sheet No. 21A

District **Municipality of Agana**
Name of Place **Agana City (San Ignacio Urban)**
[Proper name and, also, name of class, as city, town, village, barrio, etc]

Enumeration District No. 3
Enumerated by me on **April 12, 1930** Tomas A. Calvo, Enumerator

	PLACE OF ABODE			NAME	RELATION	PERSONAL DESCRIPTION				EDUCATION		NATIVITY		OCCUPATION
	Street, avenue, road, etc.	Number of dwelling house is order of visitation	Number of family in order of visitation	of each person whose place of abode on April 1, 1930, was in this family. Enter surname, first, then given name and middle initial. If any. Include every person living on April 1, 1930. Omit children born since April 1, 1930.	Relationship of this Person to the head of the family.	Sex	Color or race	Age at last birthday	Single, married, widowed or divorced	Attended school any time since Sept. 1, 1929	Whether able to read and write.	Place of birth of this person.	Whether able to speak English.	
	1	2	3	4	5	6	7	8	9	10	11	12	13	14
1	Santa Cruz Street	150	179	Cruz, Juan	Son	M	Cha	13	S	Y	Y	Guam	Y	None
2		150	179	Cruz, Segundo	Son	M	Cha	11	S	Y	Y	Guam	Y	None
3		150	179	Cruz, Catalina	Daughter	F	Cha	8	S	Y	Y	Guam	N	None
4		150	179	Cruz, Rosalia	Daughter	F	Cha	4.8	S	N	N	Guam	N	None
5		150	179	Cruz, Maria	Daughter	F	Cha	2.2	S	N	N	Guam	N	None
6		150	179	Cruz, Jose	Son	M	Cha	0	S	N	N	Guam	N	None
7		151	180	Cabrera, Ana D	Head	F	Cha	53	Wd	N	N	Guam	N	None
8		151	180	Cabrera, Maria	Daughter	F	Cha	22	S	N	Y	Guam	N	None
9		151	180	Cabrera, Soledad	Daughter	F	Cha	18	S	N	Y	Guam	Y	Maid
10		151	180	Cabrera, Benita	Daughter	F	Cha	16	S	Y	Y	Guam	Y	None
11		151	180	Cabrera, Isabel	Daughter	F	Cha	15	S	Y	Y	Guam	Y	None
12		151	180	Cabrera, Jesus	Son	M	Cha	9	S	Y	Y	Guam	N	None
13		152	181	Arceo, Josefa S	Head	F	Cha	36	Wd	N	Y	Guam	Y	Laundress
14		152	181	Arceo, Rosa	Daughter	F	Cha	18	S	N	Y	Guam	Y	None
15		152	181	Arceo, Antonia	Daughter	F	Cha	14	S	Y	Y	Guam	Y	None
16		152	181	Arceo, Lucia	Daughter	F	Cha	13	S	Y	Y	Guam	Y	None
17		152	181	Arceo, Felicita	Daughter	F	Cha	12	S	Y	Y	Guam	Y	None
18		152	181	Arceo, Maria	Daughter	F	Cha	11	S	Y	Y	Guam	Y	None
19		152	181	Arceo, Remedio	Daughter	F	Cha	9	S	Y	Y	Guam	N	None
20		152	181	Arceo, Brigida	Daughter	F	Cha	2.5	S	N	N	Guam	N	None
21		152	181	Arceo, Henry	Son	M	Cha	1.9	S	N	N	Guam	N	None
22		152	182	Suzuki, Sngekichi	Head	M	Jap	58	M	N	Y	Japan	Y	Gardener
23		153	183	Gutierrez, Tomas C	Head	M	Cha	52	M	N	Y	Guam	Y	Farmer
24		153	183	Gutierrez, Maria T	Wife	F	Cha	53	M	N	Y	Guam	Y	None
25		153	183	Gutierrez, Agueda	Daughter	F	Cha	30	S	N	Y	Guam	Y	Teacher

(CHAMORRO ROOTS GENEALOGY PROJECT™ TRANSCRIPTION)
(BERNARD T. PUNZALAN / HTTP://WWW.CHAMORROROOTS.COM)

DEPARTMENT OF COMMERCE-BUREAU OF THE CENSUS
WASHINGTON
FIFTEENTH CENSUS OF THE UNITED STATES: 1930-POPULATION

THE ISLAND OF GUAM

Sheet No. 21B

98B

District **Municipality of Agana**
Name of Place **Agana City (San Ignacio Urban)**
[Proper name and, also, name of class, as city, town, village, barrio, etc]

Enumeration District No. 3
Enumerated by me on **April 12, 1930** Tomas A. Calvo
Enumerator

	PLACE OF ABODE			NAME	RELATION	PERSONAL DESCRIPTION				EDUCATION		NATIVITY		OCCUPATION
	Street, avenue, road, etc.	Number of dwelling house is order of visitation	Number of family in order of visitation	of each person whose place of abode on April 1, 1930, was in this family. Enter surname, first, then given name and middle initial. If any. Include every person living on April 1, 1930. Omit children born since April 1, 1930.	Relationship of this Person to the head of the family.	Sex	Color or race	Age at last birthday	Single, married, widowed or divorced	Attended school any time since Sept. 1, 1929	Whether able to read and write.	Place of birth of this person.	Whether able to speak English.	
	1	2	3	4	5	6	7	8	9	10	11	12	13	14
26	Santa Cruz Street	153	183	Gutierrez, Maria	Daughter	F	Cha	28	S	N	Y	Guam	Y	Teacher
27		153	183	Gutierrez, Jane	Daughter	F	Cha	26	S	N	Y	Guam	Y	Teacher
28		153	183	Gutierrez, Federico	Son	M	Cha	22	S	N	Y	Guam	Y	Teacher
29		153	183	Gutierrez, Julia	Daughter	F	Cha	20	S	N	Y	Guam	Y	Teacher
30		153	183	Gutierrez, Jose	Son	M	Cha	19	S	N	Y	Guam	Y	Farmer
31		153	183	Gutierrez, Atonia	Daughter	F	Cha	18	S	N	Y	Guam	Y	Saleswoman
32		153	183	Gutierrez, Tomas	Son	M	Cha	17	S	Y	Y	Guam	Y	None
33		153	183	Gutierrez, Angustia	Daughter	F	Cha	15	S	N	Y	Guam	Y	None
34		153	183	Gutierrez, Augusto	Son	M	Cha	14	S	Y	Y	Guam	Y	None
35		153	183	Gutierrez, Carlos	Son	M	Cha	13	S	Y	Y	Guam	Y	None
36		153	183	Gutierrez, Roland	Son	M	Cha	10	S	Y	Y	Guam	Y	None
37		153	184	Thompson, Alvin L	Head	M	W	28	M	N	Y	Maine	Y	Mechanic
38		153	184	Thompson, Rosa G	Wife	F	Cha	25	M	N	Y	Guam	Y	None
39		153	184	Thompson, Ralph C	Son	M	Cha	2.1	S	N	N	Guam	N	None
40		153	184	Thompson, Alvin L	Son	M	Cha	1.1	S	N	N	Guam	N	None
41		154	185	Garcia, Antonio SN	Head	M	Cha	34	M	N	Y	Guam	Y	Carpenter
42		154	185	Garcia, Ana F	Wife	F	Cha	30	M	N	Y	Guam	N	None
43		154	185	Garcia, Francisco	Son	M	Cha	13	S	Y	Y	Guam	Y	None
44		154	185	Garcia, Maria	Daughter	F	Cha	11	S	Y	Y	Guam	Y	None
45		154	185	Garcia, Jesus	Son	M	Cha	10	S	Y	Y	Guam	N	None
46		154	185	Garcia, Demetrio	Son	M	Cha	8	S	Y	Y	Guam	N	None
47		154	185	Garcia, Isabel	Daughter	F	Cha	6	S	N	Y	Guam	N	None
48		154	185	Garcia, Nicolas	Son	M	Cha	4.6	S	N	N	Guam	N	None
49		154	185	Garcia, Jose	Son	M	Cha	2.7	S	N	N	Guam	N	None
50		154	185	Garcia, Juan	Son	M	Cha	1.2	S	N	N	Guam	N	None

DEPARTMENT OF COMMERCE-BUREAU OF THE CENSUS
WASHINGTON

FIFTEENTH CENSUS OF THE UNITED STATES: 1930-POPULATION

THE ISLAND OF GUAM

Sheet No. 22A

District **Municipality of Agana**
Name of Place **Agana City (San Ignacio Urban)**
[Proper name and, also, name of class, as city, town, village, barrio, etc]

Enumeration District No. 3
Enumerated by me on **April 14, 1930** Tomas A. Calvo, Enumerator

	PLACE OF ABODE			NAME	RELATION	PERSONAL DESCRIPTION				EDUCATION		NATIVITY		OCCUPATION
	Street, avenue, road, etc.	Number of dwelling house in order of visitation	Number of family in order of visitation	of each person whose place of abode on April 1, 1930, was in this family. Enter surname, first, then given name and middle initial. If any. Include every person living on April 1, 1930. Omit children born since April 1, 1930.	Relationship of this Person to the head of the family.	Sex	Color or race	Age at last birthday	Single, married, widowed or divorced	Attended school any time since Sept. 1, 1929	Whether able to read and write.	Place of birth of this person.	Whether able to speak English.	
	1	2	3	4	5	6	7	8	9	10	11	12	13	14
1	Santa Cruz Street	155	186	Soriano, Enrique S	Head	M	Cha	38	M	N	Y	Guam	Y	Carpenter
2		155	186	Soriano, Rita G	Wife	F	Cha	39	M	N	Y	Guam	Y	None
3		155	186	Soriano, Lucia	Daughter	F	Cha	15	S	N	Y	Guam	Y	None
4		155	186	Soriano, Jose	Son	M	Cha	12	S	Y	Y	Guam	Y	None
5		155	186	Soriano, Jesus	Son	M	Cha	5	S	N	N	Guam	N	None
6		156	187	Reyes, Dolores G	Head	F	Cha	50	M	N	N	Guam	Y	Laundress
7		156	187	Indelecio, Jose I	Nephew	M	Cha	25	S	N	Y	Guam	Y	Laborer
8		156	187	Indelecio, Rita	Niece	F	Cha	16	S	N	Y	Guam	Y	None
9		156	187	Indelecio, Belen M	Grand niece	F	Cha	.4	S	N	N	Guam	N	None
10		157	188	Wong-Pat, Ignacio	Head	M	Chin	57	D	N	Y	Guam	Y	Cook
11		158	189	Spicer, Dorothy M	Head	F	W	27	M	N	Y	Illinois	Y	None
12		159	190	Leon Guerrero, Vicente P	Head	M	Cha	52	S	N	Y	Guam	Y	Plumber
13		159	190	Leon Guerrero, Maria	Sister	F	Cha	38	S	N	Y	Guam	Y	Music Teacher
14		159	190	Leon Guerrero, Jose	Brother	M	Cha	34	S	N	Y	Guam	Y	Plumber
15		160	191	Ulloa, Rosa N	Head	F	Cha	79	Wd	N	N	Guam	N	None
16		160	191	Acosta, Juan M	Grand-son	M	Cha	11	S	Y	Y	Guam	Y	None
17		161	192	Gunn, Lititia M	Head	F	W	25	M	N	Y	Guam	Y	None
18		161	192	Gunn, Grace T	Daughter	F	W	6	S	N	N	Guam	Y	None
19		161	192	Gunn, Max C	Son	M	W	5	S	N	N	Guam	Y	None
20		161	192	Gunn, Gloria L	Daughter	F	W	2.5	S	N	N	Guam	N	None
21		161	192	Gunn, Patricia A	Daughter	F	W	.1	S	N	N	Guam	N	None
22		162	193	Townsend, Nietta	Head	F	W	30	M	N	Y	Michigan	Y	None
23		162	193	Townsend, Jack T	Son	M	W	4	S	N	N	California	Y	None
24		163	194	Peterson, Rufina C	Head	F	Cha	40	M	N	Y	Guam		Tel. Operator
25		163	194	Peterson, Meabel	Son	M	Cha	17	S	Y	Y	Guam		None

DEPARTMENT OF COMMERCE-BUREAU OF THE CENSUS
WASHINGTON

FIFTEENTH CENSUS OF THE UNITED STATES: 1930-POPULATION

THE ISLAND OF GUAM

Sheet No. 22B

99B

District Municipality of Agana
Name of Place Agana City (San Ignacio Urban)
[Proper name and, also, name of class, as city, town, village, barrio, etc]

Enumeration District No. 3
Enumerated by me on April 14, 1930 Tomas A. Calvo, Enumerator

	PLACE OF ABODE			NAME	RELATION	PERSONAL DESCRIPTION				EDUCATION		NATIVITY		OCCUPATION
	Street, avenue, road, etc.	Number of dwelling house is order of visitation	Number of family in order of visitation	of each person whose place of abode on April 1, 1930, was in this family. Enter surname, first, then given name and middle initial. If any. Include every person living on April 1, 1930. Omit children born since April 1, 1930.	Relationship of this Person to the head of the family.	Sex	Color or race	Age at last birthday	Single, married, widowed or divorced	Attended school any time since Sept. 1, 1929	Whether able to read and write.	Place of birth of this person.	Whether able to speak English.	
	1	2	3	4	5	6	7	8	9	10	11	12	13	14
26		163	194	Peterson, Annie	Daughter	F	Cha	15	S	Y	Y	Guam	Y	Tel. Operator
27		163	194	Wilson, Maria	Mother	F	Cha	83	Wd	N	Y	Guam	Y	None
28		164	195	Schell, Pearl I	Head	F	W	32	M	N	Y	Maine	Y	None
29	Dr. Hessler Street	165	196	Sherman, Joseph	Head	M	W	38	M	N	Y	New York	Y	Surveyor
30		165	196	Sherman, Jessi M	Wife	F	W	38	M	N	Y	Pennsylvania	Y	None
31		165	196	Sherman, Peter W	Son	M	W	3	S	N	N	New Jersey	N	None
32		166	197	Fall, Fred W	Head	M	W	42	M	N	Y	Washington	Y	Gral. Manager AK Co
33		166	197	Fall, Caroline W	Wife	F	W	21	M	N	Y	California	Y	None
34		167	198	Notley, William H	Head	M	W	51	M	N	Y	Rhode Island	Y	Foreman machinist
35		167	198	Notley, Emilia M	Wife	F	Cha	48	M	N	Y	Guam	Y	Merchant
36		167	198	Notley, Grace T	Daughter	F	Cha	7	S	Y	Y	Guam	Y	None
37		167	199	Millinchamp, Rita A	Head	F	Cha	57	Wd	N	Y	Guam	Y	Saleswoman
38		167	199	Millinchamp, Julia M	Daughter	F	Cha	26	S	N	Y	Guam	Y	Saleswoman
39		168	200	Calvo, Ramon P	Head	M	Cha	39	M	N	Y	Guam	Y	Plumber
40		168	200	Calvo, Isabel S	Wife	F	Cha	36	M	N	Y	Guam	Y	None
41		168	200	Calvo, Pilar	Daughter	F	Cha	11	S	Y	Y	Guam	Y	None
42		168	200	Calvo, Eluterio	Son	M	Cha	10	S	Y	Y	Guam	Y	None
43		168	200	Calvo, Rufo	Son	M	Cha	5	S	N	N	Guam	N	None
44		168	200	Calvo, Felix	Son	M	Cha	3.2	S	N	N	Guam	N	None
45		168	200	Calvo, Juana	Daughter	F	Cha	1.3	S	N	N	Guam	N	None
46		169	201	Javier, Dolores A	Head	F	Cha	50	Wd	N	Y	Guam	Y	Laundress
47		169	201	Javier, Maria	Daughter	F	Cha	19	S	N	Y	Guam	Y	Maid
48		169	201	Javier, Isabel	Daughter	F	Cha	14	S	N	Y	Guam	Y	None
49		170	202	Rosario, Carlina F	Head	F	Cha	33	M	N	Y	Guam	Y	None
50		170	202	Rosario, Sara	Daughter	F	Cha	6	S	Y	Y	Guam	N	None

DEPARTMENT OF COMMERCE-BUREAU OF THE CENSUS
WASHINGTON

FIFTEENTH CENSUS OF THE UNITED STATES: 1930-POPULATION

THE ISLAND OF GUAM

Sheet No. 23A

District **Municipality of Agana**
Name of Place **Agana City (San Ignacio Urban)**
[Proper name and, also, name of class, as city, town, village, barrio, etc]

Enumeration District No. 3
Enumerated by me on **April 14, 1930** Tomas A. Calvo, Enumerator

	PLACE OF ABODE			NAME	RELATION	PERSONAL DESCRIPTION				EDUCATION		NATIVITY		OCCUPATION
	Street, avenue, road, etc.	Number of dwelling house in order of visitation	Number of family in order of visitation	of each person whose place of abode on April 1, 1930, was in this family. Enter surname, first, then given name and middle initial. If any. Include every person living on April 1, 1930. Omit children born since April 1, 1930.	Relationship of this Person to the head of the family.	Sex	Color or race	Age at last birthday	Single, married, widowed or divorced	Attended school any time since Sept. 1, 1929	Whether able to read and write.	Place of birth of this person.	Whether able to speak English.	
	1	2	3	4	5	6	7	8	9	10	11	12	13	14
1	Dr. Hessler Street	170	202	Rosario, Dolores	Daughter	F	Cha	5	S	N	N	Guam	N	None
2		170	202	Rosario, Lourdes	Daughter	F	Cha	4.1	S	N	N	Guam	N	None
3		170	202	Rosario, Elizabeth	Daughter	F	Cha	2.7	S	N	N	Maine	N	None
4		170	202	Rosario, Rosaline	Daughter	F	Cha	1.5	S	N	N	Guam	N	None
5		170	202	Indelecio, Dolores	Maid	F	Cha	20	S	N	Y	Guam	Y	Maid
6		171	203	Vazques, Jesus	Head	M	W	63	M	N	Y	Costa Rica	Y	Navy reserve
7		171	203	Vazques, Aina	Wife	F	W	57	M	N	Y	Finland	Y	Merchant
8		171	203	Vazques, Loreta	Daughter	F	W	15	S	N	Y	Guam	Y	None
9		172	204	Cruz, Jose M	Head	M	Cha	50	M	N		Guam	Y	Painter
10		172	204	Cruz, Carmen C	Wife	F	Cha	29	M	N	Y	Guam	Y	None
11		172	204	Cruz, Jose	Son	M	Cha	11	S	Y	Y	Guam	Y	None
12		172	204	Cruz, Aurelia	Daughter	F	Cha	9	S	Y	Y	Guam	N	None
13		172	204	Cruz, Constantino	Son	M	Cha	6	S	N	Y	Guam	N	None
14		172	204	Cruz, Cecilia	Daughter	F	Cha	3.3	S	N	N	Guam	N	None
15		172	204	Cruz, Antonio	Son	M	Cha	.7	S	N	N	Guam	N	None
16		172	205	Tenison, Dale	Head	M	W	25	S	N	Y	Indiana	Y	Missionary
17		174	206	Fujikawa, Antonio M	Head	M	Jap	42	M	N	Y	Japan	Y	Shoemaker
18		174	206	Fujikawa, Maria SN	Wife	F	Cha	29	M	N	Y	Guam	Y	None
19		174	206	Fujikawa, Ana	Daughter	F	Jap	8	S	Y	Y	Guam	N	None
20		174	206	Fujikawa, Dolores	Daughter	F	Jap	6	S	N	N	Guam	N	None
21		174	206	Fujikawa, Antonio	Son	M	Jap	5	S	N	N	Guam	N	None
22		174	206	Fujikawa, Marcela	Daughter	F	Jap	2.3	S	N	N	Guam	N	None
23		174	206	Naputi, Elerio F	Brother in-law	M	Cha	32	S	N	N	Guam	N	Shoemaker
24		175	207	Cruz, Teresa M	Head	M	Cha	52	S	N	Y	Guam	N	None
25		176	208	Torres, Vicente M	Head	F	Cha	55	M	N	Y	Guam	Y	Silversmith

(CHAMORRO ROOTS GENEALOGY PROJECT™ TRANSCRIPTION)
(BERNARD T. PUNZALAN / HTTP://WWW.CHAMORROROOTS.COM)

DEPARTMENT OF COMMERCE-BUREAU OF THE CENSUS
WASHINGTON

FIFTEENTH CENSUS OF THE UNITED STATES: 1930-POPULATION

THE ISLAND OF GUAM

Sheet No. 23B

100B

District Municipality of Agana
Name of Place Agana City (San Ignacio Urban)
[Proper name and, also, name of class, as city, town, village, barrio, etc]

Enumeration District No. 3
Enumerated by me on April 14, 1930 Tomas A. Calvo
Enumerator

	PLACE OF ABODE			NAME	RELATION	PERSONAL DESCRIPTION				EDUCATION		NATIVITY		OCCUPATION
	Street, avenue, road, etc.	Number of dwelling house is order of visitation	Number of family in order of visitation	of each person whose place of abode on April 1, 1930, was in this family. Enter surname, first, then given name and middle initial. If any. Include every person living on April 1, 1930. Omit children born since April 1, 1930.	Relationship of this Person to the head of the family.	Sex	Color or race	Age at last birthday	Single, married, widowed or divorced	Attended school any time since Sept. 1, 1929	Whether able to read and write.	Place of birth of this person.	Whether able to speak English.	
	1	2	3	4	5	6	7	8	9	10	11	12	13	14
26	Dr. Hessler Street	176	208	Torres, Tomasa C	Wife	F	Cha	50	M	N	Y	Guam	Y	None
27		176	208	Calvo, Eduardo T	Nephew	M	Cha	21	S	N	Y	Guam	Y	Teller
28		176	208	Blaz, Maria O	Niece	F	Cha	12	S	Y	Y	Guam	Y	None
29		176	208	Achaigua, Esperanza A	Maid	F	Cha	25	S	N	Y	Guam	Y	Maid
30		177	209	Richison, Catherin F	Head	F	W	35	M	N	Y	Indiana	Y	None
31		177	209	Richison, Earl F	Son	M	W	12	S	Y	Y	Indiana	Y	None
32		177	209	Richison, Warren C	Son	M	W	9	S	Y	Y	Indiana	Y	None
33		177	209	Campos, Joaquina A	Maid	F	Jap	14	S	N	Y	Guam	Y	Maid
34		178	210	Torres, Luis C	Head	M	Cha	62	S	N	Y	Guam	Y	Farmer
35		178	210	Torres, Vicente C	Brother	M	Cha	58	S	N	Y	Guam	N	Farmer
36		178	210	Torres, Caridad C	Sister	F	Cha	54	S	N	Y	Guam	N	None
37		178	210	Torres, Concepcion C	Sister	F	Cha	52	S	N	Y	Guam	N	None
38		178	211	Torres, Antonio C	Head	M	Cha	44	M	N	Y	Guam	Y	Farmer
39		178	211	Torres, Josefa C	Wife	F	Cha	44	M	N	Y	Guam	Y	None
40		179	212	Shimizu, Jose K	Head	M	Jap	57	Wd	N	Y	Japan	Y	Merchant
41		179	212	Shimizu, Carmen T	Daughter	F	Jap	24	S	N	Y	Indiana	Y	Bookkeeper
42		179	212	Shimizu, Jesus	Son	M	Jap	23	S	N	Y	Japan	Y	Engineer
43		179	212	Shimizu, Joaquin	Son	M	Jap	22	M	N	Y	Guam	Y	Engineer
44		179	212	Yamanaka, Josefina M	Maid	F	Jap	14	S	N	Y	Guam	Y	Maid
45		180	213	Hasen, Margaret T	Head	F	W	42	M	N	Y	Rhode Island	Y	None
46		180	213	Hasen, Margaret M	Daughter	F	W	17	S	N	Y	Rhode Island	Y	None
47		180	213	Hasen, Robert I	Son	M	W	14	S	N	Y	Rhode Island	Y	None
48		180	213	Hasen, Owen P	Son	M	W	11	S	N	Y	Rhode Island	Y	None
49		181	214	Kurokaw, Genro	Head	M	Jap	48	S	N	Y	Japan	Y	Tailor
50		182	215	Fernandez, Jesus L	Head	M	Cha	32	S	N	Y	Guam	Y	Cook

(CHAMORRO ROOTS GENEALOGY PROJECT™ TRANSCRIPTION)
(BERNARD T. PUNZALAN / HTTP://WWW.CHAMORROROOTS.COM)

DEPARTMENT OF COMMERCE-BUREAU OF THE CENSUS
WASHINGTON

FIFTEENTH CENSUS OF THE UNITED STATES: 1930-POPULATION

THE ISLAND OF GUAM

Sheet No. 24A

101

District **Municipality of Agana**
Name of Place **Agana City (San Ignacio Urban)**
[Proper name and, also, name of class, as city, town, village, barrio, etc]

Enumeration District No. **3**
Enumerated by me on **April 14, 1930** Tomas A. Calvo, Enumerator

	PLACE OF ABODE: Street, avenue, road, etc.	Number of dwelling house in order of visitation	Number of family in order of visitation	NAME of each person whose place of abode on April 1, 1930, was in this family. Enter surname, first, then given name and middle initial. If any. Include every person living on April 1, 1930. Omit children born since April 1, 1930.	RELATION Relationship of this Person to the head of the family.	PERSONAL DESCRIPTION: Sex	Color or race	Age at last birthday	Single, married, widowed or divorced	EDUCATION: Attended school any time since Sept. 1, 1929	Whether able to read and write.	NATIVITY Place of birth of this person.	Whether able to speak English.	OCCUPATION
	1	2	3	4	5	6	7	8	9	10	11	12	13	14
1	Numancia Street	182	215	Fernandez, Maria S	Sister	F	Cha	20	S	N	Y	Guam	Y	None
2		182	215	Fernandez, Soledad S	Sister	F	Cha	18	S	N	Y	Guam	Y	None
3		183	216	San Nicolas, Dominga A	Head	F	Cha	48	Wd	N	N	Guam	N	None
4		183	216	San Nicolas, Jose	Son	M	Cha	28	Wd	N	Y	Guam	Y	Laborer
5		183	216	San Nicolas, Rita	Daughter	F	Cha	25	S	N	N	Guam	Y	Laundress
6		183	216	San Nicolas, Ana	Daughter	F	Cha	20	S	N	Y	Guam	Y	Laundress
7		183	216	San Nicolas, Jesus	Son	M	Cha	18	S	N	Y	Guam	Y	Farmer
8		183	216	San Nicolas, Joaquin	Son	M	Cha	16	S	N	Y	Guam	Y	Silversmith
9		183	216	San Nicolas, Dolores	Daughter	F	Cha	13	S	Y	Y	Guam	Y	None
10		183	216	San Nicolas, Juana	Daughter	F	Cha	11	S	Y	Y	Guam	Y	None
11		183	216	San Nicolas, Soledad	Daughter	F	Cha	9	S	Y	Y	Guam	N	None
12		184	217	Indelecio, Rosa	Head	F	Cha	47	S	N	Y	Guam	N	None
13		184	217	Indelecio, Jose	Son	M	Cha	22	S	N	Y	Guam	Y	Teacher
14		184	217	Indelecio, Ana	Daughter	F	Cha	20	S	N	Y	Guam	Y	Teacher
15		184	217	Indelecio, Dolores	Daughter	F	Cha	17	S	N	Y	Guam	Y	Teacher
16		184	217	Indelecio, Carmen	Daughter	F	Cha	14	S	Y	Y	Guam	Y	None
17		184	217	Duenas, Antonio M	Nephew	M	Cha	38	S	N	Y	Guam	Y	Cook
18		185	218	Cepeda, Maria B	Head	F	Cha	30	M	N	Y	Guam	Y	None
19		185	218	Cepeda, Maria	Daughter	F	Cha	9	S	Y	Y	Guam	Y	None
20		185	218	Cepeda, Gloria	Daughter	F	Cha	5	S	N	N	Guam	N	None
21		185	218	Cepeda, Evelia	Daughter	F	Cha	2.8	S	N	N	Guam	N	None
22		185	218	Cepeda, Dolores	Daughter	F	Cha	.8	S	N	N	Guam	N	None
23		186	219	Duenas, Jose A	Head	M	Cha	51	M	N	Y	Guam	Y	Carpenter
24		186	219	Duenas, Maria SN	Wife	F	Cha	54	M	N	Y	Guam	Y	None
25		186	219	Duenas, Eugenia	Daughter	F	Cha	20	S	N	Y	Guam	Y	Teacher

(CHAMORRO ROOTS GENEALOGY PROJECT™ TRANSCRIPTION)
(BERNARD T. PUNZALAN / HTTP://WWW.CHAMORROROOTS.COM)

DEPARTMENT OF COMMERCE-BUREAU OF THE CENSUS
WASHINGTON

FIFTEENTH CENSUS OF THE UNITED STATES: 1930-POPULATION

THE ISLAND OF GUAM

Sheet No. 24B

101B

District Municipality of Agana
Name of Place Agana City (San Ignacio Urban)
[Proper name and, also, name of class, as city, town, village, barrio, etc]

Enumeration District No. 3
Enumerated by me on April 15, 1930 Tomas A. Calvo, Enumerator

	PLACE OF ABODE			NAME	RELATION	PERSONAL DESCRIPTION				EDUCATION		NATIVITY		OCCUPATION
	Street, avenue, road, etc.	Number of dwelling house in order of visitation	Number of family in order of visitation	of each person whose place of abode on April 1, 1930, was in this family. Enter surname, first, then given name and middle initial. If any. Include every person living on April 1, 1930. Omit children born since April 1, 1930.	Relationship of this Person to the head of the family.	Sex	Color or race	Age at last birthday	Single, married, widowed or divorced	Attended school any time since Sept. 1, 1929	Whether able to read and write.	Place of birth of this person.	Whether able to speak English.	
	1	2	3	4	5	6	7	8	9	10	11	12	13	14
26		186	219	Duenas, Agustin	Son	M	Cha	18	S	N	Y	Guam	Y	Teacher
27		186	219	Duenas, Antonio	Son	M	Cha	16	S	Y	Y	Guam	Y	Clerk
28		186	219	Duenas, Vicente	Son	M	Cha	14	S	Y	Y	Guam	Y	None
29	Zaragosa Street	187	220	Borja, Luis G	Head	M	Cha	54	M	N	Y	Guam	N	Farmer
30		187	220	Borja, Paz C	Wife	F	Cha	55	M	N	Y	Guam	N	None
31		187	220	Borja, Paz	Daughter	F	Cha	8	S	Y	Y	Guam	Y	None
32		187	220	Cruz, Francisca P	Niece	F	Cha	24	S	N	Y	Guam	Y	None
33		188	221	Blaz, Jose B	Head	M	Cha	38	M	N	Y	Guam	Y	Farmer
34		188	221	Blaz, Nicolasa O	Wife	F	Cha	34	M	N	Y	Guam	Y	None
35		188	221	Blaz, Brigida	Daughter	F	Cha	14	S	Y	Y	Guam	Y	None
36		188	221	Blaz, Ememterio	Son	M	Cha	10	S	Y	Y	Guam	Y	None
37		188	221	Blaz, Fidela	Daughter	F	Cha	7	S	Y	Y	Guam	N	None
38		188	221	Blaz, Efigenia	Daughter	F	Cha	3.7	S	N	N	Guam	N	None
39		189	222	Babauta, Juan SN	Head	M	Cha	25	M	N	Y	Guam	Y	Carpenter
40		189	222	Babauta, Concepcion C	Wife	F	Cha	24	M	N	Y	Guam	Y	None
41		189	222	Okiyama, Jesus	Nephew	M	Cha	16	S	N	Y	Guam	Y	Carpenter
42		189	222	Okiyama, Maria	Niece	F	Cha	3	S	N	N	Guam	N	None
43		190	223	Aflague, Dolores C	Head	F	Cha	78	Wd	N	N	Guam	N	None
44		190	223	Isidro, Ursula A	Daughter	F	Cha	44	S	N	Y	Guam	Y	Laundress
45		191	224	Santos, Jose V	Head	M	Cha	29	M	N	Y	Guam	Y	Electrician
46		191	224	Santos, Rosa M	Wife	F	Cha	25	M	N	Y	Guam	N	None
47		191	224	Santos, Estela	Daughter	F	Cha	5	S	N	N	Guam	N	None
48		191	224	Santos, Idelfonso	Son	M	Cha	2.1	S	N	N	Guam	N	None
49		191	224	Santos, Glafira	Daughter	F	Cha	1.5	S	N	N	Guam	N	None
50		191	224	Santos, Delfin	Son	M	Cha	.7	S	N	N	Guam	N	None

DEPARTMENT OF COMMERCE-BUREAU OF THE CENSUS
WASHINGTON

FIFTEENTH CENSUS OF THE UNITED STATES: 1930-POPULATION

THE ISLAND OF GUAM

Sheet No. 25A

District **Municipality of Agana**
Name of Place **Agana City (San Ignacio Urban)**
[Proper name and, also, name of class, as city, town, village, barrio, etc]

Enumeration District No. 3
Enumerated by me on **April 15, 1930** Tomas A. Calvo, Enumerator

	PLACE OF ABODE			NAME	RELATION	PERSONAL DESCRIPTION				EDUCATION		NATIVITY		OCCUPATION
	Street, avenue, road, etc.	Number of dwelling house is order of visitation	Number of family in order of visitation	of each person whose place of abode on April 1, 1930, was in this family. Enter surname, first, then given name and middle initial. If any. Include every person living on April 1, 1930. Omit children born since April 1, 1930.	Relationship of this Person to the head of the family.	Sex	Color or race	Age at last birthday	Single, married, widowed or divorced	Attended school any time since Sept. 1, 1929	Whether able to read and write.	Place of birth of this person.	Whether able to speak English.	
	1	2	3	4	5	6	7	8	9	10	11	12	13	14
1	Zaragosa Street	192	225	Torres, Maria P	Head	F	Cha	55	S	N	Y	Guam	Y	None
2		192	225	Torres, Rita	Daughter	F	Cha	29	S	N	Y	Guam	Y	None
3		192	225	Torres, Ana	Daughter	F	Cha	24	S	N	Y	Guam	Y	Teacher
4		192	225	Torres, Pedro	Son	M	Cha	20	S	N	Y	Guam	Y	Farmer
5		192	225	Torres, Josefa	Daughter	F	Cha	18	S	Y	Y	Guam	Y	None
6		192	225	Torres, Asuncion	Daughter	F	Cha	13	S	Y	Y	Guam	Y	None
7		192	226	Limtiaco, Maria C	Head	F	Cha	30	D	N	Y	Guam	Y	Teacher
8		192	226	Limtiaco, Pedro	Son	M	Cha	7	S	Y	Y	Guam	N	None
9		192	226	Limtiaco, Rosalinda	Daughter	F	Cha	1.9	S	N	N	Guam	N	None
10	San Juan de Letran Street	193	227	Leon, Antonio C	Head	M	Cha	42	M	N	Y	Guam	Y	Farmer
11		193	227	Leon, Ana S	Wife	F	Cha	49	M	N	N	Guam	N	None
12		193	227	Achaigua, Maria L	Daughter	F	Cha	26	S	N	Y	Guam	Y	None
13		193	227	Achaigua, Pedro	Son	M	Cha	19	S	N	Y	Guam	Y	Servant
14		193	227	Achaigua, Maria	Daughter	F	Cha	16	S	N	Y	Guam	Y	None
15		193	228	Achaigua, Consolacion Q	Head	F	Cha	22	M	N	Y	Guam	Y	None
16		194	229	Peredo, Ana C	Head	F	Cha	65	Wd	N	Y	Guam	N	None
17		194	229	Peredo, Joaquina	Daughter	F	Cha	44	S	N	Y	Guam	N	None
18		194	229	Peredo, Pedro	Grand son	M	Cha	21	S	N	Y	Guam	Y	Chaufeur
19		194	229	Peredo, Maria	Grand daughter	F	Cha	19	S	N	Y	Guam	Y	Dressmaker
20		194	229	Peredo, Remedios	Grand daughter	F	Cha	17	S	Y	Y	Guam	Y	Dressmaker
21		194	229	Peredo, Carmen	Grand daughter	F	Cha	14	S	Y	Y	Guam	Y	None
22		194	229	Peredo, Antonio	Grand son	M	Cha	13	S	Y	Y	Guam	Y	None
23		194	229	Peredo, Mercedes	Grand daughter	F	Cha	11	S	Y	Y	Guam	Y	None
24		195	230	Aflague, Vicenta S	Head	F	Cha	67	Wd	N	Y	Guam	N	None
25		195	230	Aflague, Jose	Son	M	Cha	22	S	N	Y	Guam	Y	None

DEPARTMENT OF COMMERCE-BUREAU OF THE CENSUS
WASHINGTON

FIFTEENTH CENSUS OF THE UNITED STATES: 1930-POPULATION

THE ISLAND OF GUAM

Sheet No. 25B

102B

District **Municipality of Agana**

Name of Place **Agana City (San Ignacio Urban)**
[Proper name and, also, name of class, as city, town, village, barrio, etc]

Enumeration District No. 3

Enumerated by me on **April 15, 1930** Tomas A. Calvo
Enumerator

	PLACE OF ABODE			NAME	RELATION	PERSONAL DESCRIPTION				EDUCATION		NATIVITY		OCCUPATION
	Street, avenue, road, etc.	Number of dwelling house is order of visitation	Number of family in order of visitation	of each person whose place of abode on April 1, 1930, was in this family. Enter surname, first, then given name and middle initial. If any. Include every person living on April 1, 1930. Omit children born since April 1, 1930.	Relationship of this Person to the head of the family.	Sex	Color or race	Age at last birthday	Single, married, widowed or divorced	Attended school any time since Sept. 1, 1929	Whether able to read and write.	Place of birth of this person.	Whether able to speak English.	
	1	2	3	4	5	6	7	8	9	10	11	12	13	14
26	San Juan de Letran Street	196	231	Bamba, Jose B	Head	M	Cha	31	M	N	Y	Guam	Y	Stenographer
27		196	231	Bamba, Rita M	Wife	F	Cha	28	M	N	Y	Guam	Y	None
28		196	231	Bamba, Rosalia R	Daughter	F	Cha	9	S	Y	Y	Guam	Y	None
29		196	231	Bamba, Jesus M	Son	M	Cha	7	S	Y	Y	Guam	N	None
30		196	231	Bamba, Jose G	Son	M	Cha	6	S	N	N	Guam	N	None
31		196	231	Bamba, Roberto R	Son	M	Cha	3.8	S	N	N	Guam	N	None
32		196	231	Bamba, George	Son	M	Cha	1.9	S	N	N	Guam	N	None
33		196	231	Bamba, Federic	Son	M	Cha	.4	S	N	N	Guam	N	None
34		196	232	Bamba, Felisa	Head	F	Cha	54	S	N	Y	Guam	Y	None
35		196	232	Bamba, Vicente	Son	M	Cha	14	S	Y	Y	Guam	Y	None
36		197	233	Aguon, Rita U	Head	F	Cha	35	S	N	Y	Guam	Y	None
37		197	233	Aguon, Juan U	Brother	M	Cha	25	Wd	N	Y	Guam	Y	Policeman
38		197	233	Aguon, Eduardo	Nephew	M	Cha	3.4	S	N	N	Guam	N	None
39		197	233	Tertaotao, Jesus A	Servant	M	Cha	15	S	N	Y	Guam	Y	Servant
40		198	234	Munoz, Juan C	Head	M	Cha	42	M	N	Y	Guam	Y	Machinist
41		198	234	Munoz, Regina F	Wife	F	Cha	45	M	N	Y	Guam	N	None
42		198	234	Munoz, Vicente	Son	M	Cha	18	S	N	Y	Guam	Y	Farmer
43		198	234	Munoz, Adela	Daughter	F	Cha	16	S	N	Y	Guam	Y	None
44		198	234	Munoz, Jose F	Son	M	Cha	14	S	Y	Y	Guam	Y	None
45		198	234	Munoz, Jesusa	Daughter	F	Cha	10	S	Y	Y	Guam	Y	None
46		198	234	Munoz, Clotilde	Daughter	F	Cha	7	S	Y	Y	Guam	N	None
47		198	234	Munoz, Hernando	Son	M	Cha	1.4	S	N	N	Guam	N	None
48		198	234	Cruz, Juan L	Servant	M	Cha	22	S	N	Y	Guam	Y	Servant
49		199	235	Perez, Joaquin C	Head	M	Cha	70	M	N	Y	Guam	Y	Land Judge
50		199	235	Perez, Felisa S	Wife	F	Cha	56	M	N	Y	Guam	N	None

DEPARTMENT OF COMMERCE-BUREAU OF THE CENSUS
WASHINGTON

FIFTEENTH CENSUS OF THE UNITED STATES: 1930-POPULATION

THE ISLAND OF GUAM

Sheet No. 26A

District **Municipality of Agana**
Name of Place **Agana City (San Ignacio Urban)**
[Proper name and, also, name of class, as city, town, village, barrio, etc]

Enumeration District No. **3**
Enumerated by me on **April 16, 1930** Tomas A. Calvo, Enumerator

	PLACE OF ABODE			NAME	RELATION	PERSONAL DESCRIPTION				EDUCATION		NATIVITY		OCCUPATION
	Street, avenue, road, etc.	Number of dwelling house in order of visitation	Number of family in order of visitation	of each person whose place of abode on April 1, 1930, was in this family. Enter surname, first, then given name and middle initial. If any. Include every person living on April 1, 1930. Omit children born since April 1, 1930.	Relationship of this Person to the head of the family.	Sex	Color or race	Age at last birthday	Single, married, widowed or divorced	Attended school any time since Sept. 1, 1929	Whether able to read and write.	Place of birth of this person.	Whether able to speak English.	
	1	2	3	4	5	6	7	8	9	10	11	12	13	14
1	San Juan de Letran Street	199	235	Salas, Maria Y	Step daughter	F	Cha	21	S	N	Y	Guam	Y	None
2		199	235	Perez, Jose S	Son	M	Cha	13	S	Y	Y	Guam	Y	None
3		199	235	Chargualaf, Joaquin C	Lodger	M	Cha	2.2	S	N	N	Guam	N	None
4		199	235	Chargualaf, Ana	Servant	M	Cha	23	S	N	Y	Guam	Y	Servant
5		199	235	Topasna, Jesus A	Servant	M	Cha	23	S	N	Y	Guam	Y	Servant
6		200	236	Mendiola, Antonio C	Head	M	Cha	63	M	N	Y	Guam	Y	Farmer
7		200	236	Mendiola, Consolacion G	Wife	F	Cha	58	M	N	Y	Guam	Y	None
8		200	236	Mendiola, Isabel	Daughter	F	Cha	20	S	N	Y	Guam	Y	None
9		200	237	Franquez, Manuel S	Head	M	Cha	33	M	N	Y	Guam	Y	Clerk
10		200	237	Franquez, Luisa M	Wife	F	Cha	33	M	N	Y	Guam	Y	Midwife
11		201	238	Hara, Jose M	Head	M	Jap	50	M	N	Y	Japan	Y	Merchant
12		201	238	Hara, Romona C	Wife	F	Cha	42	M	N	Y	Guam	Y	Saleswoman
13		201	238	Hara, Manuel	Son	M	Jap	21	S	N	Y	Guam	Y	Salesman
14		201	238	Hara, Jose	Son	M	Jap	17	S	N	Y	Guam	Y	Laborer
15		201	238	Hara, Maria	Daughter	F	Jap	14	S	Y	Y	Guam	Y	Saleswoman
16		201	238	Hara, Jesus	Son	M	Jap	10	S	Y	Y	Guam	Y	None
17		201	238	Atoigue, Rosa	Maid	F	Cha	22	S	N	Y	Guam	Y	Maid
18		202	239	Sablan, Pedro R	Head	M	Cha	56	M	N	Y	Guam	N	Farmer
19		202	239	Sablan, Concepcion M	Wife	F	Cha	50	M	N	Y	Guam	Y	None
20		202	239	Sablan, Ramon	Son	M	Cha	28	S	N	Y	Guam	Y	Teacher
21		202	239	Perez, Rosa	Servant	F	Cha	18	S	N	Y	Guam	Y	Servant
22		203	240	Probst, Maria C	Head	F	Cha	29	M	N	Y	Guam	Y	None
23		203	240	Probst, Wesley O	Son	M	Cha	9	S	Y	Y	Guam	Y	None
24		203	240	Probst, Francis A	Son	M	Cha	8	S	Y	Y	Guam	Y	None
25		204	241	Ulloa, Manuel F	Head		Cha	37	M	N	Y	Guam	Y	Plumber

DEPARTMENT OF COMMERCE-BUREAU OF THE CENSUS
WASHINGTON

FIFTEENTH CENSUS OF THE UNITED STATES: 1930-POPULATION

THE ISLAND OF GUAM

Sheet No. 26B

103B

District **Municipality of Agana**
Name of Place **Agana City (San Ignacio Urban)**
[Proper name and, also, name of class, as city, town, village, barrio, etc]

Enumeration District No. 3
Enumerated by me on **April 16, 1930** Tomas A. Calvo, Enumerator

	PLACE OF ABODE			NAME	RELATION	PERSONAL DESCRIPTION				EDUCATION		NATIVITY		OCCUPATION
	Street, avenue, road, etc.	Number of dwelling house is order of visitation	Number of family in order of visitation	of each person whose place of abode on April 1, 1930, was in this family. Enter surname, first, then given name and middle initial. If any. Include every person living on April 1, 1930. Omit children born since April 1, 1930.	Relationship of this Person to the head of the family.	Sex	Color or race	Age at last birthday	Single, married, widowed or divorced	Attended school any time since Sept. 1, 1929	Whether able to read and write.	Place of birth of this person.	Whether able to speak English.	
	1	2	3	4	5	6	7	8	9	10	11	12	13	14
26	San Juan de Letran Street	204	241	Ulloa, Maria A	Wife	F	Cha	31	M	N	Y	Guam	Y	Teacher
27		204	241	Ulloa, Lucy	Daughter	F	Cha	11	S	Y	Y	Guam	Y	None
28		204	241	Ulloa, Paul I	Son	M	Cha	8	S	Y	Y	Guam	N	None
29		204	241	Ulloa, Evelyn R	Daughter	F	Cha	6	S	Y	Y	Guam	N	None
30		204	241	Ulloa, Elizabeth A	Daughter	F	Cha	5	S	N	N	Guam	N	None
31		204	241	Ulloa, David S	Son	M	Cha	3.8	S	N	N	Guam	N	None
32		204	241	Ulloa, Esther M	Daughter	F	Cha	1.8	S	N	N	Guam	N	None
33		204	241	Acosta, Rosario	Niece	F	Cha	15	S	N	Y	Guam	Y	None
34		204	241	Arceo, Lidia C	Sister in law	F	Cha	14	S	Y	Y	Guam	Y	None
35		205	242	Vanghan, Wallace L	Head	M	W	58	M	N	Y	Oregon	Y	Plumber
36		205	242	Vanghan, Maria D	Wife	F	Cha	59	M	N	Y	Guam	Y	None
37		205	243	Sohenberg, Netty V	Head	F	Cha	24	M	N	Y	Guam	Y	None
38		206	244	Miller, Ruth C	Head	F	W	31	M	N	Y	Colorado	Y	None
39		206	244	Miller, Elizabeth R	Daughter	F	W	7	S	Y	Y	California	Y	None
40		206	244	Miller, Loran L	Son	M	W	3	S	N	N	California	Y	None
41		207	245	Lujan, Manuel O	Head	M	Cha	42	M	N	Y	Guam	Y	Retail merchant
42		207	245	Lujan, Carmen U	Wife	F	Cha	53	M	N	Y	Guam	Y	None
43		207	245	Lujan, William	Son	M	Cha	19	S	N	Y	Guam	Y	Teacher
44		207	245	Lujan, Manuel	Son	M	Cha	18	S	N	Y	Guam	Y	Teacher
45		207	245	Lujan, Francisco	Son	M	Cha	16	S	N	Y	Guam	Y	Mechanic
46		207	245	Lujan, Antonio	Son	M	Cha	13	S	Y	Y	Guam	Y	None
47		207	245	Lujan, Enrique	Son	M	Cha	11	S	Y	Y	Guam	Y	None
48		207	245	Lujan, Maria	Daughter	F	Cha	8	S	Y	Y	Guam	Y	None
49		207	245	Ulloa, Maria F	Niece	F	Cha	12	S	Y	Y	Guam	Y	None
50		208	246	Damian, Jose B	Head	M	Fil	30	M	N	Y	Philippine Is.	Y	Clerk

(CHAMORRO ROOTS GENEALOGY PROJECT™ TRANSCRIPTION)
(BERNARD T. PUNZALAN / HTTP://WWW.CHAMORROROOTS.COM)

DEPARTMENT OF COMMERCE-BUREAU OF THE CENSUS
WASHINGTON

FIFTEENTH CENSUS OF THE UNITED STATES: 1930-POPULATION

THE ISLAND OF GUAM

Sheet No. 27A

District Municipality of Agana
Name of Place Agana City (San Ignacio Urban)
[Proper name and, also, name of class, as city, town, village, barrio, etc]

Enumeration District No. 3
Enumerated by me on April 16, 1930 Tomas A. Calvo
Enumerator

	PLACE OF ABODE			NAME	RELATION	PERSONAL DESCRIPTION				EDUCATION		NATIVITY		OCCUPATION
	Street, avenue, road, etc.	Number of dwelling house is order of visitation	Number of family in order of visitation	of each person whose place of abode on April 1, 1930, was in this family. Enter surname, first, then given name and middle initial. If any. Include every person living on April 1, 1930. Omit children born since April 1, 1930.	Relationship of this Person to the head of the family.	Sex	Color or race	Age at last birthday	Single, married, widowed or divorced	Attended school any time since Sept. 1, 1929	Whether able to read and write.	Place of birth of this person.	Whether able to speak English.	
	1	2	3	4	5	6	7	8	9	10	11	12	13	14
1	San Juan de Letran Street	208	246	Damian, Consolacion C	Wife	F	Cha	25	M	N	Y	Guam	Y	None
2		208	246	Damian, Norman	Son	M	Fil	4.8	S	N		Guam		None
3		208	246	Damian, Katharine	Daughter	F	Fil	3.9	S	N		Guam		None
4		208	246	Damian, Dorothy	Daughter	F	Fil	2	S	N		Guam		None
5		208	246	Damian, Constantine	Daughter	F	Fil	1.1	S	N		Guam		None
6		208	247	Peredo, Jose C	Head	M	Cha	42	M	N	Y	Guam	N	Farmer
7		208	247	Peredo, Antonia	Wife	F	Cha	34	M	N	Y	Guam	N	None
8		208	247	Peredo, Margarita	Daughter	F	Cha	7	S	Y		Guam		None
9		208	247	Peredo, Enrique	Son	M	Cha	6	S	N		Guam		None
10		208	247	Peredo, Emilia	Daughter	F	Cha	4.1	S	N		Guam		None
11		208	247	Peredo, Fernando	Son	M	Cha	1.1	S	N		Guam		None
12		208	247	Peredo, Genoveva	Daughter	F	Cha	.3	S	N		Guam		None
13	Mariana de Austria Street	209	248	Mendiola, Jose C	Head	M	Cha	45	M	N	Y	Guam	N	Farmer
14		209	248	Mendiola, Francisca	Wife	F	Cha	46	M	N	Y	Guam	N	None
15		209	248	Mendiola, Jose	Son	M	Cha	17	S	N	Y	Guam	Y	Farmer
16		209	248	Mendiola, Engracia	Daughter	F	Cha	16	S	N	Y	Guam	Y	None
17		209	248	Mendiola, Juan	Son	M	Cha	11	S	Y	Y	Guam	Y	None
18		209	248	Mendiola, Maria	Daughter	F	Cha	10	S	Y		Guam		None
19		209	248	Mendiola, Lourdes	Daughter	F	Cha	9	S	Y		Guam		None
20		209	248	Mendiola, Jesus	Son	M	Cha	7	S	Y		Guam		None
21		209	248	Mendiola, Catalina	Daughter	F	Cha	2	S	N		Guam		None
22		209	248	Mendiola, Jesus	Grandson	M	Cha	6	S	N		Guam		None
23		209	249	Mendiola, Rita C	Head	F	Cha	56	S	N	Y	Guam	Y	None
24		209	249	Mendiola, Maria C	Sister	F	Cha	49	S	N	Y	Guam	Y	Photographer
25		209	249	Mendiola, Juan	Nephew	M	Cha	16	S	Y	Y	Guam	Y	Painter

DEPARTMENT OF COMMERCE-BUREAU OF THE CENSUS
WASHINGTON

FIFTEENTH CENSUS OF THE UNITED STATES: 1930-POPULATION

THE ISLAND OF GUAM

Sheet No. 27B

104B

District **Municipality of Agana**
Name of Place **Agana City (San Ignacio Urban)**
[Proper name and, also, name of class, as city, town, village, barrio, etc]

Enumeration District No. 3
Enumerated by me on **April 17, 1930** Tomas A. Calvo
Enumerator

	PLACE OF ABODE			NAME	RELATION	PERSONAL DESCRIPTION				EDUCATION		NATIVITY		OCCUPATION
	Street, avenue, road, etc.	Number of dwelling house is order of visitation	Number of family in order of visitation	of each person whose place of abode on April 1, 1930, was in this family. Enter surname, first, then given name and middle initial. If any. Include every person living on April 1, 1930. Omit children born since April 1, 1930.	Relationship of this Person to the head of the family.	Sex	Color or race	Age at last birthday	Single, married, widowed or divorced	Attended school any time since Sept. 1, 1929	Whether able to read and write.	Place of birth of this person.	Whether able to speak English.	
	1	2	3	4	5	6	7	8	9	10	11	12	13	14
26	Mariana de Austria Street	210	250	Cruz, Eulalia P	Head	F	Cha	58	S	N	Y	Guam	N	Laundress
27		210	250	Cruz, Natividad	Daughter	F	Cha	20	S	N	Y	Guam	Y	Seamstress
28		210	250	Cruz, Antonio	Son	M	Cha	17	S	N	Y	Guam	Y	Messenger
29		210	250	Cruz, Pedro	Son	M	Cha	13	S	Y	Y	Guam	Y	None
30		210	250	Cruz, Juan	Son	M	Cha	9	S	Y		Guam		None
31		211	251	Cepeda, Maria C	Head	F	Cha	33	M	N	Y	Guam	Y	None
32		211	251	Cepeda, Pedro	Son	M	Cha	12	S	Y	Y	Guam	Y	None
33		211	251	Cepeda, Juan	Son	M	Cha	11	S	Y	Y	Guam	Y	None
34		211	251	Cepeda, Jesus	Son	M	Cha	9	S	Y		Guam		None
35		211	251	Cepeda, Jose	Son	M	Cha	7	S	Y		Guam		None
36		211	251	Cepeda, Virginia	Daughter	F	Cha	5	S	N		Guam		None
37		211	251	Cepeda, Esperanza	Daughter	F	Cha	3.6	S	N		Guam		None
38		211	251	Cepeda, Vicente	Son	M	Cha	1.4	S	N		Guam		None
39		211	251	Manibusan, Jesus P	Lodger	M	Cha	22	S	N	Y	Guam		Farmer
40		212	252	Castro, Jose G	Head	M	Cha	62	M	N	Y	Guam	Y	Farmer
41		212	252	Castro, Antonia LG	Wife	F	Cha	56	M	N	Y	Guam	N	None
42		212	252	Castro, Natividad	Daughter	F	Cha	24	S	N	Y	Guam	Y	None
43		212	252	Castro, Rafael	Son	M	Cha	20	S	N	Y	Guam	Y	Tailor
44		212	252	Castro, Delfina	Daughter	F	Cha	18	S	N	Y	Guam	Y	None
45		212	252	Castro, Leocadio	Son	M	Cha	16	S	Y	Y	Guam	Y	None
46		212	252	Aguon, Mariano A	Nephew	M	Cha	14	S	N	Y	Guam	Y	None
47		212	252	Eustaquio, Josefina C	Grand daughter	F	Cha	2.3	S	N		Guam		Chauffeur
48		213	253	Torres, Jose C	Head	M	Cha	64	M	N	Y	Guam	Y	Farmer
49		213	253	Torres, Ana	Wife	F	Cha	52	M	N	Y	Guam	N	None
50		213	253	Cani, Manuel C	Nephew	M	Jap	25	S	N	N	Guam	N	None

DEPARTMENT OF COMMERCE-BUREAU OF THE CENSUS
WASHINGTON

FIFTEENTH CENSUS OF THE UNITED STATES: 1930-POPULATION

THE ISLAND OF GUAM

Sheet No. 28A

District **Municipality of Agana**
Name of Place **Agana City (San Ignacio Urban)**
[Proper name and, also, name of class, as city, town, village, barrio, etc]

Enumeration District No. 3
Enumerated by me on April 17, 1930 Tomas A. Calvo, Enumerator

	PLACE OF ABODE			NAME	RELATION	PERSONAL DESCRIPTION				EDUCATION		NATIVITY		OCCUPATION
	Street, avenue, road, etc.	Number of dwelling house is order of visitation	Number of family in order of visitation	of each person whose place of abode on April 1, 1930, was in this family. Enter surname, first, then given name and middle initial. If any. Include every person living on April 1, 1930. Omit children born since April 1, 1930.	Relationship of this Person to the head of the family.	Sex	Color or race	Age at last birthday	Single, married, widowed or divorced	Attended school any time since Sept. 1, 1929	Whether able to read and write.	Place of birth of this person.	Whether able to speak English.	
	1	2	3	4	5	6	7	8	9	10	11	12	13	14
1	Mariana de Austria Street	213	523	Cani, Maria C	Niece	F	Jap	22	S	N	Y	Guam	Y	None
2		214	254	Leon Guerrero, Jose R	Head	M	Cha	52	M	N	Y	Guam	N	Farmer
3		214	254	Leon Guerrero, Maria M	Wife	F	Cha	40	M	N	Y	Guam	Y	None
4		214	254	Leon Guerrero, Rosario	Daughter	F	Cha	14	S	N	Y	Guam	Y	None
5		214	254	Leon Guerrero, Jose	Son	M	Cha	11	S	Y	Y	Guam	Y	None
6		214	254	Leon Guerrero, Maria	Daughter	F	Cha	10	S	Y	N	Guam	N	None
7		214	254	Leon Guerrero, Pedro	Son	M	Cha	7	S	Y	N	Guam	N	None
8		214	254	Leon Guerrero, Jesus	Son	M	Cha	6	S	N	N	Guam	N	None
9		214	254	Leon Guerrero, Vicente	Son	M	Cha	4.4	S	N	N	Guam	N	None
10		215	255	Anderson, Antonio Q	Head	M	Cha	68	M	N	Y	Guam	Y	Farmer
11		215	255	Anderson, Joaquina M	Wife	F	Cha	68	M	N	Y	Guam	Y	None
12		215	255	Anderson, Rita	Daughter	F	Cha	37	S	N	Y	Guam	Y	Cook
13		215	255	Anderson, Ramona	Daughter	F	Cha	31	S	N	Y	Guam	Y	Maid
14		215	255	Anderson, Juan	Son	M	Cha	27	S	N	Y	Guam	Y	Farmer
15		215	255	Anderson, Maria	Daughter	F	Cha	16	S	N	Y	Guam	Y	None
16		215	255	Anderson, Lourdes	Daughter	F	Cha	5	S	N	N	Guam	N	None
17		215	255	Anderson, Rafael	Son	M	Cha	4	S	N	N	Guam	N	None
18		215	255	Anderson, Barbara	Daughter	F	Cha	2.8	S	N	N	Guam	N	None
19		215	255	Anderson, Joaquina	Daughter	F	Cha	7	S	Y	N	Guam	N	None
20		215	255	Anderson, Magdalena	Daughter	F	Cha	5	S	N	N	Guam	N	None
21		215	255	Anderson, Margarita	Daughter	F	Cha	4	S	N	N	Guam	N	None
22		215	255	Anderson, Francisco	Son	M	Cha	.1	S	N	N	Guam	N	None
23		215	256	Anderson, Pedro M	Head	M	Cha	35	M	N	Y	Guam	Y	Farmer
24		216	257	Masterton, Amy C	Head	M	W	37	M	N	Y	California		None
25		216	257	Masterton, William B	Son	S	W	8	S	Y		Washington		None

DEPARTMENT OF COMMERCE-BUREAU OF THE CENSUS
WASHINGTON

FIFTEENTH CENSUS OF THE UNITED STATES: 1930-POPULATION

THE ISLAND OF GUAM

Sheet No. 28B

105B

District **Municipality of Agana**
Name of Place **Agana City (San Ignacio Urban)**
[Proper name and, also, name of class, as city, town, village, barrio, etc]

Enumeration District No. 3
Enumerated by me on **April 18, 1930** Tomas A. Calvo
Enumerator

	PLACE OF ABODE			NAME	RELATION	PERSONAL DESCRIPTION				EDUCATION		NATIVITY		OCCUPATION
	Street, avenue, road, etc.	Number of dwelling house is order of visitation	Number of family in order of visitation	of each person whose place of abode on April 1, 1930, was in this family. Enter surname, first, then given name and middle initial. If any. Include every person living on April 1, 1930. Omit children born since April 1, 1930.	Relationship of this Person to the head of the family.	Sex	Color or race	Age at last birthday	Single, married, widowed or divorced	Attended school any time since Sept. 1, 1929	Whether able to read and write.	Place of birth of this person.	Whether able to speak English.	
	1	2	3	4	5	6	7	8	9	10	11	12	13	14
26	Mariana de Austria Street	216	257	Masterton, Nancy	Daughter	F	W	4	S	N	N	California		None
27		217	258	Roberto, Jose	Head	M	Cha	40	M	N	Y	Guam	Y	Clerk
28		217	258	Roberto, Maria A	Wife	F	Cha	32	M	N	Y	Guam	N	None
29		217	258	Roberto, Jose	Son	M	Cha	7	S	Y	N	Guam		None
30		217	258	Roberto, Thomas J	Son	M	Cha	5	S	N	N	Guam		None
31		217	258	Roberto, Lorensa A	Niece	F	Cha	20	S	N	Y	Guam		None
32		217	258	Ada, Rosa C	Niece	F	Cha	14	S	Y	Y	Guam		None
33		218	259	Roberto, Andres A	Head	M	Cha	69	M	N	Y	Guam	Y	Farmer
34		218	259	Roberto, Dolores C	Wife	F	Cha	62	M	N	Y	Guam	N	None
35		218	260	Roberto, Ignacio T	Head	M	Cha	39	M	N	Y	Guam	Y	Machinist
36		218	260	Roberto, Margarita P	Wife	F	Cha	34	M	N	Y	Guam	Y	None
37		218	260	Roberto, William A	Son	M	Cha	11	S	Y	Y	Guam	Y	None
38		218	260	Roberto, Federica C	Daughter	F	Cha	10	S	Y	Y	Guam	N	None
39		218	260	Roberto, Matilde I	Daughter	F	Cha	9	S	Y		Guam	N	None
40		218	260	Roberto, Clara D	Daughter	F	Cha	7	S	Y		Guam	N	None
41		218	260	Roberto, Mary M	Daughter	F	Cha	4	S	N	N	Guam	N	None
42		218	260	Roberto, Ignatius I	Son	M	Cha	3	S	N	N	Guam	N	None
43		218	260	Roberto, Daniel B	Son	M	Cha	1.6	S	N	N	Guam	N	None
44		218	260	Pangelinan, Maria	Sister-in-law	F	Cha	28	S	N	Y	Guam	Y	None
45		218	260	Pangelinan, Ignacio	Brother-in-law	M	Cha	19	S	N	Y	Guam	Y	Carpenter
46		218	260	Pangelinan, Jose	Brother-in-law	M	Cha	17	S	N	Y	Guam	Y	Farmer
47		219	261	Atoigue, Joaquin C	Head	M	Cha	27	M	N	Y	Guam	Y	Chauffeur
48		219	261	Atoigue, Ana A	Wife	F	Cha	24	M	N	Y	Guam	Y	None
49		219	261	Atoigue, Maria	Daughter	F	Cha	1.9	S	N	N	Guam	N	None
50		220	262	Cruz, Maria M	Head	M	Cha	47	Wd	N	Y	Guam	N	None

DEPARTMENT OF COMMERCE-BUREAU OF THE CENSUS
WASHINGTON

FIFTEENTH CENSUS OF THE UNITED STATES: 1930-POPULATION

THE ISLAND OF GUAM

Sheet No. 29A

District **Municipality of Agana**
Name of Place **Agana City (San Ignacio Urban)**
[Proper name and, also, name of class, as city, town, village, barrio, etc]

Enumeration District No. **3**
Enumerated by me on **April 18, 1930** Tomas A. Calvo, Enumerator

	PLACE OF ABODE			NAME	RELATION	PERSONAL DESCRIPTION				EDUCATION		NATIVITY		OCCUPATION
	Street, avenue, road, etc.	Number of dwelling house in order of visitation	Number of family in order of visitation	of each person whose place of abode on April 1, 1930, was in this family. Enter surname, first, then given name and middle initial. If any. Include every person living on April 1, 1930. Omit children born since April 1, 1930.	Relationship of this Person to the head of the family.	Sex	Color or race	Age at last birthday	Single, married, widowed or divorced	Attended school any time since Sept. 1, 1929	Whether able to read and write.	Place of birth of this person.	Whether able to speak English.	
	1	2	3	4	5	6	7	8	9	10	11	12	13	14
1	Mariana de Austria Street	220	262	Zafra, Angustia E	Niece	F	Cha	33	S	N	N	Guam	Y	None
2		220	262	Sablan, Rafael C	Servant	M	Cha	18	S	N	Y	Guam	Y	Servant
3		221	263	Perez, Josefa A	Head	F	Cha	33	M	N	Y	Guam	Y	Industrial teacher
4		221	263	Perez, Maria	Daughter	F	Cha	8	S	Y	N	Guam	N	None
5		221	263	Perez, John	Son	M	Cha	7	S	Y	N	Guam	N	None
6		221	263	Perez, Frank	Son	M	Cha	5	S	N	N	Guam	N	None
7		221	263	Perez, Walter	Son	M	Cha	3.9	S	N	N	Guam	N	None
8		222	264	Joses, Maurice	Head	F	W	34	M	N	Y	California	Y	None
9		222	264	Joses, Douglas	Son	M	W	7	S	N	N	California		None
10		222	264	Joses, Robert	Son	M	W	12	S	Y	Y	California	Y	None
11		223	265	Marst, Dorothy B	Head	F	W	31	M	N	Y	Michigan	Y	None
12		223	265	Marst, John Calvin	Son	M	W	6	S	N	N	Indiana		None
13		224	266	Stockman, Winifred M	Head	F	W	28	M	N	Y	Colorado	Y	None
14		224	266	Stockman, Edith M	Daughter	F	W	7	S	Y		California		None
15		224	266	Stockman, David C	Son	M	W	5	S	N	N	California		None
16		225	267	Elliott, Hiram W	Head	M	W	50	M	N	Y	Missouri	Y	Pharmacist
17		225	267	Elliott, Concepcion M	Wife	F	Cha	37	M	N	Y	Guam	Y	None
18		225	267	Elliott, Lovie E	Daughter	F	Cha	18	S	N	Y	Guam	Y	Teacher
19		225	267	Elliott, Hiram W	Son	M	Cha	14	S	Y	Y	Guam	Y	None
20		225	267	Elliott, Joseph A	Son	M	Cha	12	S	Y	Y	Guam	Y	None
21		225	267	Elliott, Woodrow P	Son	M	Cha	11	S	Y	Y	Guam	Y	None
22		225	267	Elliott, Mary D	Daughter	F	Cha	10	S	Y		Guam		None
23		225	267	Elliott, Delia B	Daughter	F	Cha	7	S	Y		Guam		None
24		225	267	Elliott, Richard C	Son	M	Cha	1.3	S	N	N	Guam	N	None
25		226	268	Underwood, James H	Head	M	W	52	M	N	Y	North Carolina	Y	Postmaster

DEPARTMENT OF COMMERCE-BUREAU OF THE CENSUS
WASHINGTON

FIFTEENTH CENSUS OF THE UNITED STATES: 1930-POPULATION

THE ISLAND OF GUAM

Sheet No. 29B

106B

District Municipality of Agana
Name of Place Agana City (San Ignacio Urban)
[Proper name and, also, name of class, as city, town, village, barrio, etc]

Enumeration District No. 3
Enumerated by me on April 19, 1930 Tomas A. Calvo, Enumerator

	PLACE OF ABODE: Street, avenue, road, etc.	Number of dwelling house is order of visitation	Number of family in order of visitation	NAME of each person whose place of abode on April 1, 1930, was in this family. Enter surname, first, then given name and middle initial. If any. Include every person living on April 1, 1930. Omit children born since April 1, 1930.	RELATION Relationship of this Person to the head of the family.	PERSONAL DESCRIPTION: Sex	Color or race	Age at last birthday	Single, married, widowed or divorced	EDUCATION: Attended school any time since Sept. 1, 1929	Whether able to read and write.	NATIVITY Place of birth of this person.	Whether able to speak English.	OCCUPATION
	1	2	3	4	5	6	7	8	9	10	11	12	13	14
26	Mariana de Austria Street	226	268	Underwood, Ana M	Wife	F	Cha	46	M	N	Y	Guam	Y	None
27		226	268	Underwood, Rita E	Daughter	F	Cha	21	S	N	Y	Guam	Y	Book keeper
28		226	268	Underwood, John J	Son	M	Cha	18	S	N	Y	Guam	Y	Book keeper
29		226	268	Underwood, James L	Son	M	Cha	15	S	N	Y	Guam	Y	Typist
30		226	268	Underwood, Raymond F	Son	M	Cha	13	S	Y	Y	Guam	Y	None
31		226	268	Underwood, Dolores A	Daughter	F	Cha	12	S	Y	Y	Guam	Y	None
32		226	268	Underwood, Betty R	Daughter	F	Cha	11	S	Y	Y	Guam	Y	None
33	Padre Aniceto St.	226	268	Underwood, Carmen E	Daughter	F	Cha	9	S	Y		Guam		None
34		226	268	Martinez, Antonia I	Sister in-law	F	Cha	34	S	N	Y	Guam	Y	P.O. Clerk
35		227	269	Rowley, W W	Head	M	W	55	M	N	Y	Pennsylvania	Y	Master blacksmith
36		227	269	Rowley, Milagros C	Wife	F	Cha	61	M	N	Y	Guam	Y	None
37					Here ends the enumeration of enumeration district No 3									
38					San Ignacio, Agana urban									
39														
40														
41														
42														
43														
44														
45														
46														
47														
48														
49														
50														

DEPARTMENT OF COMMERCE-BUREAU OF THE CENSUS
WASHINGTON

FIFTEENTH CENSUS OF THE UNITED STATES: 1930-POPULATION

THE ISLAND OF GUAM

Sheet No. 30A

District **Municipality of Agana**
Name of Place **Agana City (Togae Agana Urban)**
[Proper name and, also, name of class, as city, town, village, barrio, etc]

Enumeration District No. 3
Enumerated by me on **April 19, 1930** Tomas A. Calvo, Enumerator

	PLACE OF ABODE			NAME	RELATION	PERSONAL DESCRIPTION				EDUCATION		NATIVITY		OCCUPATION
	Street, avenue, road, etc.	Number of dwelling house in order of visitation	Number of family in order of visitation	of each person whose place of abode on April 1, 1930, was in this family. Enter surname, first, then given name and middle initial. If any. Include every person living on April 1, 1930. Omit children born since April 1, 1930.	Relationship of this Person to the head of the family.	Sex	Color or race	Age at last birthday	Single, married, widowed or divorced	Attended school any time since Sept. 1, 1929	Whether able to read and write.	Place of birth of this person.	Whether able to speak English.	
	1	2	3	4	5	6	7	8	9	10	11	12	13	14
1	Mariana de Austria Street	228	270	Dillon, Lydia M	Head	F	W	41	M	N	Y	Missouri	Y	None
2		228	270	McCord, Pearle E	Daughter	F	W	25	Wd	N	Y	Montana	Y	None
3		228	270	McCord, Constance E	Grand daughter	F	W	4	S	N		Washington		None
4		229	271	Aflague, Ana R	Head	F	Cha	39	Wd	N	Y	Guam	N	Laundress
5		229	271	Aflague, Reguberto	Son	M	Cha	15	S	Y	Y	Guam	Y	None
6		229	271	Aflague, Simeon	Son	M	Cha	14	S	Y	Y	Guam	Y	None
7		229	271	Aflague, Rosario	Daughter	F	Cha	10	S	Y		Guam		None
8		229	271	Aflague, Felipe	Son	M	Cha	8	S	Y		Guam		None
9		229	271	Aflague, Juan	Son	M	Cha	6	S	N		Guam		None
10		229	271	Reyes, Benita G	Mother	F	Cha	64	Wd	N	N	Guam		None
11		229	271	Reyes, Jesus	Brother	M	Cha	21	S	N	Y	Guam		None
12		230	272	Aflague, Maria C	Head	F	Cha	68	S	N	N	Guam	N	Laundress
13		230	272	Aflague, Ana C	Sister	F	Cha	64	S	N	N	Guam	N	Laundress
14		230	272	Aflague, Vicenta C	Sister	F	Cha	45	S	N	N	Guam	N	Laundress
15		230	272	Manibusan, Jose A	Nephew	M	Cha	21	S	N	Y	Guam	Y	Laborer
16		231	273	Torres, Juliana P	Head	F	Cha	68	Wd	N	Y	Guam	N	None
17		231	273	Torres, Rosa P	Sister	F	Cha	64	Wd	N	Y	Guam	N	None
18		231	273	Torres, Maria P	Sister	F	Cha	63	S	N	Y	Guam	N	None
19		231	274	Ada, Jose M	Head	M	Cha	45	M	N	Y	Guam	Y	Manufacturer
20		231	274	Ada, Maria T	Wife	F	Cha	41	M	N	Y	Guam	Y	None
21		231	274	Ada, Herman	Son	M	Cha	19	S	Y	Y	Saipan	Y	Salesman
22		231	274	Ada, Herminia	Daughter	F	Cha	17	S	Y	Y	Saipan	Y	None
23		231	274	Ada, Jose	Son	M	Cha	14	S	Y	Y	Saipan	Y	None
24		231	274	Ada, Lydia	Daughter	F	Cha	12	S	Y	Y	Saipan	Y	None
25		231	274	Ada, Delia	Daughter	F	Cha	10	S	Y		Saipan		None

(CHAMORRO ROOTS GENEALOGY PROJECT™ TRANSCRIPTION)
(BERNARD T. PUNZALAN / HTTP://WWW.CHAMORROROOTS.COM)

DEPARTMENT OF COMMERCE-BUREAU OF THE CENSUS
WASHINGTON

FIFTEENTH CENSUS OF THE UNITED STATES: 1930-POPULATION

THE ISLAND OF GUAM

Sheet No. 30B

107B

District Municipality of Agana
Name of Place Agana City (Togae Agana Urban)
[Proper name and, also, name of class, as city, town, village, barrio, etc]

Enumeration District No. 3
Enumerated by me on April 19, 1930 Tomas A. Calvo
Enumerator

	PLACE OF ABODE			NAME	RELATION	PERSONAL DESCRIPTION				EDUCATION		NATIVITY		OCCUPATION
	Street, avenue, road, etc.	Number of dwelling house is order of visitation	Number of family in order of visitation	of each person whose place of abode on April 1, 1930, was in this family. Enter surname, first, then given name and middle initial. If any. Include every person living on April 1, 1930. Omit children born since April 1, 1930.	Relationship of this Person to the head of the family.	Sex	Color or race	Age at last birthday	Single, married, widowed or divorced	Attended school any time since Sept. 1, 1929	Whether able to read and write.	Place of birth of this person.	Whether able to speak English.	
	1	2	3	4	5	6	7	8	9	10	11	12	13	14
26	Mariana de Austria Street	231	274	Ada, Elvira	Daughter	F	Cha	8	S	Y		Saipan		None
27		231	274	Ada, Juan	Son	M	Cha	4	S	N		Saipan		None
28		231	274	Ada, Maria	Daughter	F	Cha	1.7	S	N		Saipan		None
29		232	275	Martin, Laura B	Head	F	W	46	M	N	Y	New Jersey	Y	Music prof.
30		233	276	Blaz, Carmen B	Head	F	Cha	46	S	N	N	Guam	Y	None
31		233	276	Blaz, Maria	Daughter	F	Cha	32	S	N	Y	Guam	Y	Cook
32		233	276	Blaz, Angustia	Daughter	F	Cha	24	S	N	Y	Guam	Y	Maid
33		233	276	Blaz, Eva	Grand daughter	F	Cha	5	S	N		Guam		None
34		233	276	Blaz, Henry	Grandson	M	Cha	14	S	N	Y	Guam	Y	Servant
35		233	276	Blaz, Alvina	Grand daughter	F	Cha	4	S	N		Guam		None
36		233	276	Blaz, Benjamin	Grandson	M	Cha	2.2	S	N		Guam		None
37		234	277	Anderson, Francisco Q	Head	M	Cha	53	M	N	Y	Guam	Y	Farmer
38		234	277	Anderson, Josefa	Wife	F	Cha	41	M	N	Y	Guam	Y	None
39		234	277	Anderson, Jose	Son	M	Cha	21	S	N	Y	Guam	Y	Farmer
40		234	277	Anderson, Ramon	Son	M	Cha	20	S	N	Y	Guam	Y	Farmer
41		234	277	Anderson, Maria	Daughter	F	Cha	18	S	Y	Y	Guam	Y	Teacher
42		234	277	Anderson, Tomas	Son	M	Cha	16	S	Y	Y	Guam	Y	None
43		234	277	Anderson, Dolores	Daughter	F	Cha	11	S	Y	Y	Guam		None
44		234	277	Anderson, Soledad	Daughter	F	Cha	9	S	Y	Y	Guam		None
45		234	277	Anderson, Josefa	Daughter	F	Cha	5	S	N		Guam		None
46		234	277	Anderson, Matilde	Daughter	F	Cha	2.1	S	N		Guam		None
47		234	277	Anderson, Joaquin	Son	M	Cha	.6	S	N		Guam		None
48		234	277	Benavente, Ana B	Mother in-law	F	Cha	67	Wd	N	Y	Guam		None
49		234	278	Anderson, Francisco B	Head	M	Cha	26	M	N	Y	Guam	Y	Farmer
50		234	278	Anderson, Josefa	Wife	F	Cha	26	M	N	Y	Guam	Y	None

(CHAMORRO ROOTS GENEALOGY PROJECT™ TRANSCRIPTION)
(BERNARD T. PUNZALAN / HTTP://WWW.CHAMORROROOTS.COM)

DEPARTMENT OF COMMERCE-BUREAU OF THE CENSUS
WASHINGTON

FIFTEENTH CENSUS OF THE UNITED STATES: 1930-POPULATION

THE ISLAND OF GUAM

Sheet No. 31A

108

District **Municipality of Agana**

Name of Place **Agana City (Togae Agana Urban)**
[Proper name and, also, name of class, as city, town, village, barrio, etc]

Enumeration District No. **3**

Enumerated by me on **April 21, 1930** Tomas A. Calvo
Enumerator

	PLACE OF ABODE			NAME	RELATION	PERSONAL DESCRIPTION				EDUCATION		NATIVITY		OCCUPATION
	Street, avenue, road, etc.	Number of dwelling house in order of visitation	Number of family in order of visitation	of each person whose place of abode on April 1, 1930, was in this family. Enter surname, first, then given name and middle initial. If any. Include every person living on April 1, 1930. Omit children born since April 1, 1930.	Relationship of this Person to the head of the family.	Sex	Color or race	Age at last birthday	Single, married, widowed or divorced	Attended school any time since Sept. 1, 1929	Whether able to read and write.	Place of birth of this person.	Whether able to speak English.	
	1	2	3	4	5	6	7	8	9	10	11	12	13	14
1	Mariana de Austria Street	234	278	Anderson, Juan	Son	M	Cha	3.4	S	N		Guam		None
2		234	278	Anderson, Beatrice	Daughter	F	Cha	.9	S	N		Guam		None
3		235	279	Quichocho, Maria P	Head	F	Cha	45	Wd	N	N	Guam	N	None
4		235	279	Quichocho, Patrocinio	Daughter	F	Cha	18	S	N	Y	Guam	Y	None
5		235	279	Quichocho, Jose	Son	M	Cha	15	S	Y	Y	Guam	Y	Servant
6		235	279	Quichocho, Ana	Daughter	F	Cha	12	S	Y	Y	Guam	Y	None
7		235	279	Borja, Juana C	Mother	F	Cha	78	Wd	N	Y	Guam	N	None
8		236	280	Salas, Susana C	Head	F	Cha	57	Wd	N	Y	Guam	N	Laundress
9		236	280	Salas, Juan	Son	M	Cha	22	S	N	Y	Guam	Y	Clerk
10		236	280	Salas, Rosario	Daughter	F	Cha	19	S	N	Y	Guam	Y	None
11		236	280	Salas, William	Grand-son	M	Cha	9	S	Y		Guam		None
12		236	280	Salas, Antonio	Grand-son	M	Cha	6	S	N		Guam		None
13		236	281	Salas, Joaquin Q	Head	M	Cha	24	M	N	Y	Guam		Farmer
14		236	281	Salas, Soledad C	Wife	F	Cha	18	M	N	Y	Guam		None
15	Pavia Street	237	282	Munoz, Jose C	Head	M	Cha	52	M	N	Y	Guam	Y	Machinist
16		237	282	Munoz, Rosa I	Wife	F	Cha	48	M	N	N	Guam	N	None
17		237	282	Munoz, Rosa	Daughter	F	Cha	26	S	N	Y	Guam	Y	None
18		237	282	Munoz, Jesus	Son	M	Cha	23	S	N	Y	Guam	Y	Farmer
19		237	282	Munoz, Antonio	Son	M	Cha	20	S	N	Y	Guam	Y	Farmer
20		237	282	Munoz, Joaquina	Daughter	F	Cha	17	S	Y	Y	Guam	Y	None
21		237	282	Munoz, Ramon	Son	M	Cha	15	S	Y	Y	Guam	Y	None
22		237	282	Munoz, Isabel	Daughter	F	Cha	13	S	N	N	Guam	N	None
23		237	282	Munoz, Juan	Son	M	Cha	12	S	Y	Y	Guam	N	None
24		238	283	Munoz, Vicente C	Head	M	Cha	36	M	N	Y	Guam	Y	Cook
25		238	283	Munoz, Maria C	Wife	F	Cha	34	M	N	Y	Guam	Y	None

DEPARTMENT OF COMMERCE-BUREAU OF THE CENSUS
WASHINGTON

FIFTEENTH CENSUS OF THE UNITED STATES: 1930-POPULATION
THE ISLAND OF GUAM

Sheet No. 31B

108B

District Municipality of Agana
Name of Place Agana City (Togae Agana Urban)
[Proper name and, also, name of class, as city, town, village, barrio, etc]

Enumeration District No. 3
Enumerated by me on April 22, 1930 Tomas A. Calvo
Enumerator

	PLACE OF ABODE			NAME	RELATION	PERSONAL DESCRIPTION				EDUCATION		NATIVITY		OCCUPATION
	Street, avenue, road, etc.	Number of dwelling house in order of visitation	Number of family in order of visitation	of each person whose place of abode on April 1, 1930, was in this family. Enter surname, first, then given name and middle initial. If any. Include every person living on April 1, 1930. Omit children born since April 1, 1930.	Relationship of this Person to the head of the family.	Sex	Color or race	Age at last birthday	Single, married, widowed or divorced	Attended school any time since Sept. 1, 1929	Whether able to read and write.	Place of birth of this person.	Whether able to speak English.	
	1	2	3	4	5	6	7	8	9	10	11	12	13	14
26	Pavia Street	238	283	Munoz, Francisco	Son	M	Cha	2.3	S	N		Guam		None
27		238	283	Cruz, Jose B	Brother in-law	M	Cha	20	S	N	Y	Guam	Y	Farmer
28		238	283	Cruz, Rosario	Sister in-law	F	Cha	18	S	N	Y	Guam	Y	None
29		238	284	Charfauros, Maria L	Head	F	Cha	90	Wd	N	N	Guam	N	None
30		238	284	Babauta, Ramona C	Daughter	F	Cha	50	Wd	N	N	Guam	N	Laundress
31		238	284	Charfauros, Regina C	Grand daughter	F	Cha	22	S	N	Y	Guam	Y	Laundress
32		239	285	Salas, Jose D	Head	M	Cha	34	M	N	Y	Guam	Y	Upholsterer
33		239	285	Salas, Josefa F	Wife	F	Cha	53	M	N	Y	Guam	Y	None
34		239	285	Salas, Jose	Son	M	Cha	7	S	Y		Guam		None
35		239	285	Salas, Catalina	Daughter	F	Cha	6	S	N		Guam		None
36		239	285	Salas, Maria	Daughter	F	Cha	4.8	S	N		Guam		None
37		239	285	Salas, Joaquin	Son	M	Cha	2.9	S	N		Guam		None
38		240	286	Ronguillo, Maicela M	Head	F	Cha	64	Wd	N	N	Guam	N	None
39		241	287	Atoigue, Dolores B	Head	F	Cha	59	Wd	N	N	Guam	N	None
40		241	287	Atoigue, Jose	Son	M	Cha	27	S	N	Y	Guam	Y	Laborer
41		241	287	Atoigue, Juan	Son	M	Cha	26	S	N	Y	Guam	Y	Farmer
42		241	287	Munoz, Isabel	Grand daughter	F	Cha	7	S	Y		Guam		None
43		241	287	Munoz, Joaquin	Grandson	M	Cha	6	S	N		Guam		None
44		242	288	Munoz, Jose C	Head	M	Cha	35	M	N	Y	Guam	Y	Policeman
45		242	288	Munoz, Candelaria C	Wife	F	Cha	29	M	N	Y	Guam	Y	None
46		243	289	Camacho, Mariana P	Head	F	Cha	59	Wd	N	Y	Guam	N	Laundress
47		243	289	Camacho, Felicidad	Daughter	F	Cha	25	S	N	Y	Guam	Y	Laundress
48		243	289	Camacho, Joaquin	Son	M	Cha	21	S	N	Y	Guam	Y	Carpenter
49		243	289	Agulto, Consuelo C	Grand daughter	F	Cha	2.3	S	N		Guam		None
50		244	290	Dungca, Teordoro G	Head	M	Fil	45	M	N	Y	Guam	Y	Machinist

DEPARTMENT OF COMMERCE-BUREAU OF THE CENSUS
WASHINGTON

FIFTEENTH CENSUS OF THE UNITED STATES: 1930-POPULATION

THE ISLAND OF GUAM

Sheet No. 32A

District **Municipality of Agana**
Name of Place **Agana City (Togae Agana Urban)**
[Proper name and, also, name of class, as city, town, village, barrio, etc]

Enumeration District No. 3
Enumerated by me on **April 22, 1930** Tomas A. Calvo, Enumerator

	PLACE OF ABODE			NAME	RELATION	PERSONAL DESCRIPTION				EDUCATION		NATIVITY		OCCUPATION
	Street, avenue, road, etc.	Number of dwelling house in order of visitation	Number of family in order of visitation	of each person whose place of abode on April 1, 1930, was in this family. Enter surname, first, then given name and middle initial. If any. Include every person living on April 1, 1930. Omit children born since April 1, 1930.	Relationship of this Person to the head of the family.	Sex	Color or race	Age at last birthday	Single, married, widowed or divorced	Attended school any time since Sept. 1, 1929	Whether able to read and write.	Place of birth of this person.	Whether able to speak English.	
	1	2	3	4	5	6	7	8	9	10	11	12	13	14
1	Pavia Street	244	290	Dungca, Emilia Q	Wife	F	Cha	30	M	N	Y	Guam	Y	None
2		244	290	Dungca, Juan	Son	M	Fil	9	S	Y		Guam		None
3		244	290	Dungca, Antonia	Daughter	F	Fil	7	S	Y		Guam		None
4		244	290	Dungca, Justo	Son	M	Fil	5	S	N		Guam		None
5		244	290	Dungca, Felisberto	Son	M	Fil	11	S	N		Guam		None
6		244	290	Dungca, Vicenta	Daughter	F	Fil	.9	S	N		Guam		None
7		244	290	Quichocho, Manuel P	Brother in-law	M	Cha	24	S	N	Y	Guam	Y	Laborer
8		245	291	Guerrero, Ignacio LG	Head	M	Cha	64	M	N	Y	Guam	Y	Farmer
9		245	291	Guerrero, Rosa T	Wife	F	Cha	53	M	N	Y	Guam	Y	Laundres
10		245	291	Guerrero, Rita	Daughter	F	Cha	28	S	N	Y	Guam	Y	Seamstress
11		245	291	Guerrero, Dolores	Daughter	F	Cha	24	S	N	Y	Guam	Y	Maid
12		245	291	Guerrero, Ignacio	Son	M	Cha	22	S	N	N	Guam	N	None
13		245	291	Guerrero, Joaquin	Son	M	Cha	21	S	N	Y	Guam	Y	Farmer
14		245	291	Guerrero, Santiago	Son	M	Cha	19	S	N	Y	Guam	Y	Messenger
15		245	291	Guerrero, Emperatris	Daughter	F	Cha	18	S	N	Y	Guam	Y	Maid
16		245	291	Guerrero, Regina	Daughter	F	Cha	16	S	N	Y	Guam	Y	None
17		245	291	Guerrero, Virginia	Daughter	F	Cha	15	S	N	Y	Guam	Y	None
18		245	291	Guerrero, Jesus	Son	M	Cha	12	S	Y	Y	Guam	Y	None
19		245	291	Guerrero, Jose	Son	M	Cha	.4	S	N		Guam		None
20		246	292	Aguon, Vicente S	Head	M	Cha	44	M	N	Y	Guam	Y	Carpenter
21		246	292	Aguon, Remedios S	Wife	F	Cha	43	M	N	Y	Guam	Y	Midwife
22		246	292	Aguon, Manuel	Son	M	Cha	18	S	Y	Y	Guam	Y	None
23		246	292	Aguon, Maria	Daughter	F	Cha	16	S	N	Y	Guam	Y	None
24		246	292	Aguon, Francisco	Son	M	Cha	14	S	Y	Y	Guam	Y	None
25		247	293	Cruz, Juan C	Head	M	Cha	35	M	N	Y	Guam	Y	Laborer

DEPARTMENT OF COMMERCE-BUREAU OF THE CENSUS
WASHINGTON

FIFTEENTH CENSUS OF THE UNITED STATES: 1930-POPULATION

THE ISLAND OF GUAM

Sheet No. 32B

109B

District **Municipality of Agana**
Name of Place **Agana City (Togae Agana Urban)**
[Proper name and, also, name of class, as city, town, village, barrio, etc]

Enumeration District No. **3**
Enumerated by me on **April 22, 1930** Tomas A. Calvo
Enumerator

	PLACE OF ABODE			NAME	RELATION	PERSONAL DESCRIPTION				EDUCATION		NATIVITY		OCCUPATION
	Street, avenue, road, etc.	Number of dwelling house is order of visitation	Number of family in order of visitation	of each person whose place of abode on April 1, 1930, was in this family. Enter surname, first, then given name and middle initial. If any. Include every person living on April 1, 1930. Omit children born since April 1, 1930.	Relationship of this Person to the head of the family.	Sex	Color or race	Age at last birthday	Single, married, widowed or divorced	Attended school any time since Sept. 1, 1929	Whether able to read and write.	Place of birth of this person.	Whether able to speak English.	
	1	2	3	4	5	6	7	8	9	10	11	12	13	14
26	Pavia Street	247	293	Cruz, Asuncion T	Wife	F	Cha	39	M	N	Y	Guam	Y	None
27		247	293	Cruz, Juan	Son	M	Cha	11	S	Y	Y	Guam	N	None
28		247	293	Cruz, Ana	Daughter	F	Cha	9	S	Y		Guam		None
29		247	293	Cruz, Engracia	Daughter	F	Cha	7	S	N		Guam		None
30		247	293	Cruz, Maria	Daughter	F	Cha	8	S	Y		Guam		None
31		247	293	Cruz, Antonio	Son	M	Cha	6	S	N		Guam		None
32		247	293	Cruz, Jesus	Son	M	Cha	4.8	S	N		Guam		None
33		247	293	Cruz, German	Son	M	Cha	3	S	N		Guam		None
34		247	293	Cruz, Gloria	Daughter	F	Cha	1	S	N		Guam		None
35	Colosa Street	248	294	Garcia, Maria E	Head	F	Cha	40	M	N	Y	Guam	Y	None
36		248	294	Garcia, Juan	Son	M	Cha	6	S	N		Guam		None
37		248	294	Garcia, Jose	Son	M	Cha	5	S	N		Guam		None
38		248	294	Garcia, Lucia	Daughter	F	Cha	3	S	N		Guam		None
39		248	294	Garcia, Adela	Daughter	F	Cha	1.1	S	N		Guam		None
40		248	294	Salas, Clotilde	Daughter	F	Cha	17	S	N	Y	Guam	Y	None
41		248	294	Salas, Ricardo	Son	M	Cha	15	S	Y	Y	Guam	Y	None
42		248	294	Eustaquio, Reducinda G	Mother	F	Cha	70	Wd	N	Y	Guam	N	None
43		249	295	Salas, Jose Q	Head	M	Cha	57	M	N	Y	Guam	N	Farmer
44		249	295	Salas, Ramona LG	Wife	F	Cha	52	M	N	Y	Guam	N	None
45		249	295	Salas, Miguel	Son	M	Cha	33	S	N	Y	Guam	Y	Teacher
46		249	295	Salas, Jose	Son	M	Cha	29	S	N	Y	Guam	Y	Farmer
47		249	295	Salas, Jesus	Son	M	Cha	25	S	N	Y	Guam	Y	Laborer
48		249	295	Salas, Maria	Daughter	F	Cha	22	S	N	Y	Guam	Y	None
49		249	295	Salas, Tomasa	Daughter	F	Cha	21	S	N	Y	Guam	Y	None
50		249	295	Salas, Dionicio	Son	M	Cha	18	S	Y	Y	Guam	Y	None

DEPARTMENT OF COMMERCE-BUREAU OF THE CENSUS
WASHINGTON

FIFTEENTH CENSUS OF THE UNITED STATES: 1930-POPULATION

THE ISLAND OF GUAM

Sheet No. 33A

District **Municipality of Agana**
Name of Place **Agana City (Togae Agana Urban)**
[Proper name and, also, name of class, as city, town, village, barrio, etc]

Enumeration District No. **3**
Enumerated by me on **April 23, 1930** Tomas A. Calvo
Enumerator

	PLACE OF ABODE			NAME	RELATION	PERSONAL DESCRIPTION				EDUCATION		NATIVITY		OCCUPATION
	Street, avenue, road, etc.	Number of dwelling house is order of visitation	Number of family in order of visitation	of each person whose place of abode on April 1, 1930, was in this family. Enter surname, first, then given name and middle initial. If any. Include every person living on April 1, 1930. Omit children born since April 1, 1930.	Relationship of this Person to the head of the family.	Sex	Color or race	Age at last birthday	Single, married, widowed or divorced	Attended school any time since Sept. 1, 1929	Whether able to read and write.	Place of birth of this person.	Whether able to speak English.	
	1	2	3	4	5	6	7	8	9	10	11	12	13	14
1	Colosa St.	249	295	Salas, Joaquin	Son	M	Cha	13	S	Y	Y	Guam	Y	None
2		249	295	Salas, Atanacio	Son	M	Cha	12	S	Y	Y	Guam		None
3		249	295	Diaz, Ana C	Aunt	F	Cha	48	Wd	N	Y	Guam	N	None
4	Lepanto Street	250	296	Haniu, Atanacio B	Head	M	Jap	20	M	N	Y	Guam	Y	Machinist
5		250	296	Haniu, Concepcion C	Wife	F	Cha	21	M	N	Y	Guam	Y	None
6		250	296	Haniu, Francisco	Son	M	Jap	.4	S	N		Guam		None
7		251	297	Untalan, Jose L	Head	M	Cha	32	M	N	Y	Guam	Y	Book keeper
8		251	297	Untalan, Josefina H	Wife	F	Jap	26	M	N	Y	Guam	Y	None
9		251	297	Untalan, Juan	Son	M	Cha	7	S	Y		Guam		None
10		251	297	Untalan, Gil	Son	M	Cha	5	S	N		Guam		None
11		251	297	Untalan, Dolores	Daughter	F	Cha	4	S	N		Guam		None
12		251	297	Untalan, Pedro	Son	M	Cha	.8	S	N		Guam		None
13		251	297	Untalan, Jose	Son	M	Cha	3	S	N		Guam		None
14		252	298	De Leon, Joaquin I	Head	M	Cha	66	Wd	N	Y	Guam	Y	Farmer
15		252	298	De Leon, Maria	Daughter	F	Cha	34	S	N	Y	Guam	Y	None
16		252	298	De Leon, Julia	Daughter	F	Cha	22	S	N	Y	Guam	Y	Teacher
17		252	298	De Leon, Elisa	Daughter	F	Cha	20	S	N	Y	Guam	Y	Teacher
18		252	298	De Leon, Adela	Daughter	F	Cha	17	S	N	Y	Guam	Y	Teacher
19		253	299	Salas, Jesus L	Head	M	Cha	29	M	N	Y	Guam	Y	Clerk
20		253	299	Salas, Dolores M	Wife	F	Cha	24	M	N	Y	Guam	Y	None
21		253	299	Salas, Eufrosina	Daughter	F	Cha	3.9	S	N		Guam		None
22		253	299	Salas, Simplicia	Daughter	F	Cha	2.8	S	N		Guam		None
23		253	300	Lujan, Luisa P	Head	F	Cha	69	Wd	N	Y	Guam	N	None
24		253	300	Salas, Pilar S	Grand daughter	F	Cha	30	S	N	Y	Guam	Y	Teacher
25		253	300	Salas, Felix	Grandson	M	Cha	26	S	N	Y	Guam	Y	Farmer

DEPARTMENT OF COMMERCE-BUREAU OF THE CENSUS
WASHINGTON

FIFTEENTH CENSUS OF THE UNITED STATES: 1930-POPULATION

THE ISLAND OF GUAM

Sheet No. 33B

110B

District **Municipality of Agana**
Name of Place **Agana City (Togae Agana Urban)**
[Proper name and, also, name of class, as city, town, village, barrio, etc]

Enumeration District No. **3**
Enumerated by me on **April 24, 1930** Tomas A. Calvo
Enumerator

	PLACE OF ABODE			NAME	RELATION	PERSONAL DESCRIPTION				EDUCATION		NATIVITY		OCCUPATION
	Street, avenue, road, etc.	Number of dwelling house is order of visitation	Number of family in order of visitation	of each person whose place of abode on April 1, 1930, was in this family. Enter surname, first, then given name and middle initial. If any. Include every person living on April 1, 1930. Omit children born since April 1, 1930.	Relationship of this Person to the head of the family.	Sex	Color or race	Age at last birthday	Single, married, widowed or divorced	Attended school any time since Sept. 1, 1929	Whether able to read and write.	Place of birth of this person.	Whether able to speak English.	
	1	2	3	4	5	6	7	8	9	10	11	12	13	14
26	Lepanto Street	253	300	Salas, Jose S	Grandson	M	Cha	24	S	N	Y	Guam	Y	Printer
27		253	300	Salas, Simplicia	Grand daughter	F	Cha	22	S	N	Y	Guam	Y	None
28		253	300	Salas, Matilde	Grand daughter	F	Cha	21	S	N	Y	Guam	Y	Dress maker
29		253	300	Salas, Carlos	Grandson	M	Cha	18	S	N	Y	Guam	Y	Farmer
30		253	300	Salas, Rafaela	Grand daughter	F	Cha	16	S	Y	Y	Guam	Y	None
31		253	300	Salas, Albina	Grand daughter	F	Cha	14	S	Y	Y	Guam	Y	None
32		253	300	Salas, Salvador	Grandson	M	Cha	13	S	Y	Y	Guam	Y	None
33		253	300	Salas, Providenia	Grand daughter	F	Cha	11	S	Y	Y	Guam	N	None
34		254	301	Salas, Cecilio S	Head	M	Cha	40	M	N	Y	Guam	Y	Carpenter
35		254	301	Salas, Luisa S	Wife	F	Cha	37	M	N	Y	Guam	Y	None
36		255	302	Sternberg, Carmen G	Head	F	Cha	60	Wd	N	N	Guam	N	None
37		255	302	Sternberg, John	Son	M	Cha	19	S	N	Y	Guam	Y	Chauffeur
38		255	302	Sternberg, George	Son	M	Cha	13	S	Y	Y	Guam	Y	None
39		255	302	Sternberg, Jesus	Son	M	Cha	8	S	Y	Y	Guam		None
40		255	302	Garrido, Salomon	Son	M	Cha	24	S	N	Y	Guam	Y	Chauffeur
41		255	302	Quidachay, Jesus A	Servant	M	Cha	17	S	N	Y	Guam	Y	Servant
42		256	303	Terlaje, Francisco J	Head	M	Cha	30	M	N	Y	Guam	Y	[illegible]
43		256	303	Terlaje, Maria S	Wife	F	Cha	30	M	N	Y	Guam	Y	None
44		256	303	Terlaje, Josefina	Daughter	F	Cha	9	S	Y		Guam		None
45		256	303	Terlaje, Augusto	Son	M	Cha	8	S	Y		Guam		None
46		256	303	Terlaje, Maria	Daughter	F	Cha	6	S	N		Guam		None
47		256	303	Terlaje, Carmen	Daughter	F	Cha	5	S	N		Guam		None
48		256	303	Terlaje, Antonia	Daughter	F	Cha	4	S	N		Guam		None
49		256	303	Terlaje, Tomas	Son	M	Cha	3	S	N		Guam		None
50		256	303	Terlaje, Pedro	Son	M	Cha	.2	S	N		Guam		None

DEPARTMENT OF COMMERCE-BUREAU OF THE CENSUS
WASHINGTON

FIFTEENTH CENSUS OF THE UNITED STATES: 1930-POPULATION

THE ISLAND OF GUAM

Sheet No. 34A

District **Municipality of Agana**
Name of Place **Agana City (Togae Agana Urban)**
[Proper name and, also, name of class, as city, town, village, barrio, etc]

Enumeration District No. 3
Enumerated by me on April 24, 1930 Tomas A. Calvo, Enumerator

	PLACE OF ABODE: Street, avenue, road, etc.	Number of dwelling house in order of visitation	Number of family in order of visitation	NAME of each person whose place of abode on April 1, 1930, was in this family. Enter surname, first, then given name and middle initial. If any. Include every person living on April 1, 1930. Omit children born since April 1, 1930.	RELATION Relationship of this Person to the head of the family.	PERSONAL DESCRIPTION: Sex	Color or race	Age at last birthday	Single, married, widowed or divorced	EDUCATION: Attended school any time since Sept. 1, 1929	Whether able to read and write.	NATIVITY Place of birth of this person.	Whether able to speak English.	OCCUPATION
	1	2	3	4	5	6	7	8	9	10	11	12	13	14
1	Lepanto Street	256	303	Salas, Genoveva F	Mother in-law	F	Cha	52	S	N	Y	Guam	N	None
2		257	304	Ojeda, Rosalia J	Head	F	Cha	37	Wd	N	Y	Guam	Y	None
3		257	304	Ojeda, Carmen	Daughter	F	Cha	21	S	N	Y	Guam	Y	Teacher
4		257	304	Ojeda, Felicidad	Daughter	F	Cha	20	S	N	Y	Guam	Y	None
5		257	304	Ojeda, Antonia	Daughter	F	Cha	18	S	Y	Y	Guam	Y	None
6		257	304	Ojeda, Eugenia	Daughter	F	Cha	15	S	Y	Y	Guam	Y	None
7		257	304	Ojeda, Maria	Daughter	F	Cha	14	S	Y	Y	Guam	Y	None
8		257	304	Ojeda, Elias	Son	M	Cha	11	S	Y	Y	Guam		None
9		257	304	Ojeda, Felicita	Daughter	F	Cha	9	S	Y	Y	Guam		None
10		257	304	Ojeda, Vicente	Son	M	Cha	7	S	Y		Guam		None
11		257	304	Ojeda, Tressie	Daughter	F	Cha	5	S	N		Guam		None
12		258	305	Aflague, Rosa A	Head	F	Cha	70	Wd	N	Y	Guam	N	None
13		258	305	Aflague, Rita	Daughter	F	Cha	28	S	N	Y	Guam	Y	Laundress
14		259	306	Sablan, Jose A	Head	M	Cha	32	M	N	Y	Guam	Y	Carpenter
15		259	306	Sablan, Maria C	Wife	F	Cha	26	M	N	Y	Guam	Y	None
16		259	306	Sablan, Jesus	Son	M	Cha	4	S	N		Guam		None
17		259	306	Campos, Dominga G	Mother in-law	F	Cha	54	Wd	N	Y	Guam	N	None
18		260	307	Eustaquio, Jose G	Head	M	Cha	48	M	N	Y	Guam	Y	Baker
19		260	307	Eustaquio, Ana C	Wife	F	Cha	32	M	N	Y	Guam	Y	None
20		260	307	Eustaquio, Gregorio B	Son	M	Cha	25	S	N	Y	Guam	Y	Baker
21		260	307	Eustaquio, Antonio B	Son	M	Cha	22	S	N	Y	Guam	Y	Carpenter
22		260	307	Eustaquio, Angel B	Son	M	Cha	20	S	N	Y	Guam	Y	Baker
23		260	307	Eustaquio, Jose B	Son	M	Cha	18	S	Y	Y	Guam	Y	None
24		260	307	Eustaquio, Felix B	Son	M	Cha	16	S	Y	Y	Guam	Y	None
25		260	307	Eustaquio, Elena B	Daughter	F	Cha	14	S	Y	Y	Guam	Y	None

DEPARTMENT OF COMMERCE-BUREAU OF THE CENSUS
WASHINGTON

FIFTEENTH CENSUS OF THE UNITED STATES: 1930-POPULATION

THE ISLAND OF GUAM

Sheet No. 34B

111B

District **Municipality of Agana**
Name of Place **Agana City (Togae Agana Urban)**
[Proper name and, also, name of class, as city, town, village, barrio, etc]

Enumeration District No. **3**
Enumerated by me on **April 25, 1930** Tomas A. Calvo
Enumerator

	PLACE OF ABODE			NAME	RELATION	PERSONAL DESCRIPTION				EDUCATION		NATIVITY		OCCUPATION
	Street, avenue, road, etc.	Number of dwelling house is order of visitation	Number of family in order of visitation	of each person whose place of abode on April 1, 1930, was in this family. Enter surname, first, then given name and middle initial. If any. Include every person living on April 1, 1930. Omit children born since April 1, 1930.	Relationship of this Person to the head of the family.	Sex	Color or race	Age at last birthday	Single, married, widowed or divorced	Attended school any time since Sept. 1, 1929	Whether able to read and write.	Place of birth of this person.	Whether able to speak English.	
	1	2	3	4	5	6	7	8	9	10	11	12	13	14
26	Lepanto Street	260	307	Eustaquio, Florencia B	Daughter	F	Cha	11	S	Y	Y	Guam		None
27		260	307	Eustaquio, Francisco C	Son	M	Cha	10	S	Y	Y	Guam		None
28		260	307	Eustaquio, Eduardo	Son	M	Cha	9	S	Y		Guam		None
29		260	307	Eustaquio, Augusto	Son	M	Cha	6	S	N		Guam		None
30		260	307	Eustaquio, Carlos	Son	M	Cha	5	S	N		Guam		None
31		260	307	Eustaquio, Virginia	Daughter	F	Cha	3.9	S	N		Guam		None
32		260	307	Eustaquio, Rosalia	Daughter	F	Cha	.7	S	N		Guam		None
33		261	308	Santos, Luisa G	Head	F	Cha	61	Wd	N	Y	Guam	N	None
34		261	308	Santos, Angelina	Daughter	F	Cha	21	S	N	Y	Guam	Y	Tel. operator
35		262	309	Cruz, Jose M	Head	M	Cha	53	M	N	Y	Guam	N	Farmer
36		262	309	Cruz, Ana C	Wife	F	Cha	48	M	N	Y	Guam	N	None
37		262	309	Cruz, Francisco	Son	M	Cha	23	S	N	Y	Guam	Y	Farmer
38		262	309	Cruz, Rosalia	Daughter	F	Cha	19	S	N	Y	Guam	Y	Seamstress
39		262	309	Cruz, Miguel	Son	M	Cha	17	S	N	Y	Guam	Y	Servant
40		262	309	Cruz, Agustin	Son	M	Cha	14	S	Y	Y	Guam	Y	None
41		262	310	Cruz, Jose M jr.	Head	M	Cha	26	M	N	Y	Guam	Y	Farmer
42		262	310	Cruz, Ignacia C	Wife	F	Cha	31	M	N	Y	Guam	Y	Teacher
43		262	310	Reyes, Jose	Step son	M	Cha	13	S	Y	Y	Guam		None
44		262	310	Reyes, Carmelo	Step son	M	Cha	10	S	Y		Guam		None
45		262	310	Reyes, Geronmio	Step son	M	Cha	6	S	N		Guam		None
46		262	310	Reyes, Rufina	Step daughter	F	Cha	4	S	N		Guam		None
47	San Quintin St.	263	311	Cruz, Vicente M	Head	M	Cha	45	M	N	Y	Guam	Y	Machinist
48		263	311	Cruz, Dolores C	Wife	F	Cha	39	M	N	N	Guam	N	None
49		263	311	Cruz, Vicente	Son	M	Cha	19	S	N	Y	Guam	Y	Musician
50		263	311	Cruz, Justo	Son	M	Cha	15	S	Y	Y	Guam	Y	None

DEPARTMENT OF COMMERCE-BUREAU OF THE CENSUS
WASHINGTON
FIFTEENTH CENSUS OF THE UNITED STATES: 1930-POPULATION

THE ISLAND OF GUAM

Sheet No. 35A

District **Municipality of Agana**
Name of Place **Agana City (Togae Agana Urban)**
[Proper name and, also, name of class, as city, town, village, barrio, etc]

Enumeration District No. **3**
Enumerated by me on **April 25, 1930** Tomas A. Calvo
Enumerator

	PLACE OF ABODE			NAME	RELATION	PERSONAL DESCRIPTION				EDUCATION		NATIVITY		OCCUPATION
	Street, avenue, road, etc.	Number of dwelling house is order of visitation	Number of family in order of visitation	of each person whose place of abode on April 1, 1930, was in this family. Enter surname, first, then given name and middle initial. If any. Include every person living on April 1, 1930. Omit children born since April 1, 1930.	Relationship of this Person to the head of the family.	Sex	Color or race	Age at last birthday	Single, married, widowed or divorced	Attended school any time since Sept. 1, 1929	Whether able to read and write.	Place of birth of this person.	Whether able to speak English.	
	1	2	3	4	5	6	7	8	9	10	11	12	13	14
1	San Quintin Street	263	311	Cruz, Jose	Son	M	Cha	13	S	Y	Y	Guam	Y	None
2		264	312	Sablan, Maria C	Head	F	Cha	56	Wd	N	N	Guam	N	None
3		264	312	Sablan, Carmen	Daughter	F	Cha	31	S	N	Y	Guam	Y	None
4		264	312	Sablan, Jose G	Grand son	M	Cha	7	S	Y		Guam		None
5		265	313	Farrell, Maria A	Head	F	Cha	45	M	N	Y	Guam		None
6		265	313	Farrell, Filomena	Daughter	F	Cha	26	S	N	Y	Guam	Y	Cook
7		265	313	Farrell, Antonia	Daughter	F	Cha	12	S	Y	Y	Guam	Y	None
8		265	313	Farrell, Joaquin	Son	M	Cha	5	S	N		Guam		None
9		266	314	Salas, Antonio Q	Head	M	Cha	44	M	N	Y	Guam	N	Farmer
10		266	314	Salas, Manuela C	Wife	F	Cha	44	M	N	Y	Guam	N	Laundress
11		266	314	Salas, Rosario	Daughter	F	Cha	21	S	N	Y	Guam	Y	None
12		266	314	Salas, Remedios	Daughter	F	Cha	19	S	N	Y	Guam	Y	Saleswoman
13		266	314	Salas, Regina	Daughter	F	Cha	17	S	N	Y	Guam	Y	Saleswoman
14		266	314	Salas, Joaquin	Son	M	Cha	14	S	Y	Y	Guam	Y	None
15		266	314	Salas, Engracia	Daughter	F	Cha	12	S	Y	Y	Guam	Y	None
16		266	314	Salas, Magdalena	Daughter	F	Cha	9	S	Y		Guam		None
17		266	315	Delgado, Pedro M	Head	M	Cha	25	M	N	Y	Guam	Y	Servant
18		266	315	Delgado, Ana S	Wife	F	Cha	23	M	N	Y	Guam	Y	None
19		266	315	Delgado, Antonio	Son	M	Cha	5	S	N		Guam		None
20		266	315	Delgado, Dorotea	Daughter	F	Cha	3.4	S	N		Guam		None
21		266	315	Delgado, Juan	Son	M	Cha	.3	S	N		Guam		None
22		266	316	Cruz, Vicenta M	Head	M	Cha	54	S	N	Y	Guam	N	None
23		266	316	Cruz, Jesus	Son	M	Cha	18	S	N	Y	Guam	Y	Cook
24		266	316	Cruz, Vicente	Son	M	Cha	10	S	Y		Guam		None
25		267	317	Mariano, Ana Q	Head	F	Cha	63	Wd	N	N	Guam	N	None

DEPARTMENT OF COMMERCE-BUREAU OF THE CENSUS
WASHINGTON

FIFTEENTH CENSUS OF THE UNITED STATES: 1930-POPULATION

THE ISLAND OF GUAM

Sheet No. 35B

112B

District Municipality of Agana
Name of Place Agana City (Togae Agana Urban)
[Proper name and, also, name of class, as city, town, village, barrio, etc]

Enumeration District No. 3
Enumerated by me on April 26, 1930 Tomas A. Calvo, Enumerator

	PLACE OF ABODE			NAME	RELATION	PERSONAL DESCRIPTION				EDUCATION		NATIVITY		OCCUPATION
	Street, avenue, road, etc.	Number of dwelling house is order of visitation	Number of family in order of visitation	of each person whose place of abode on April 1, 1930, was in this family. Enter surname, first, then given name and middle initial. If any. Include every person living on April 1, 1930. Omit children born since April 1, 1930.	Relationship of this Person to the head of the family.	Sex	Color or race	Age at last birthday	Single, married, widowed or divorced	Attended school any time since Sept. 1, 1929	Whether able to read and write.	Place of birth of this person.	Whether able to speak English.	
	1	2	3	4	5	6	7	8	9	10	11	12	13	14
26	San Quintin Street	267	318	San Nicolas, Maria M	Head	F	Cha	27	M	N	Y	Guam	Y	Clerk
27		267	318	San Nicolas, Vicenta	Daughter	F	Cha	7	S	Y		Guam		None
28		267	318	San Nicolas, Luis	Son	M	Cha	5	S	N		Guam		None
29		267	318	San Nicolas, Jose R	Son	M	Cha	3	S	N		Guam		None
30		267	319	Mariano, Juan Q	Head	M	Cha	41	M	N	Y	Guam	Y	Farmer
31		267	319	Mariano, Candelaria F	Wife	F	Cha	40	M	N	Y	Guam	N	None
32		267	319	Mariano, Ana	Daughter	F	Cha	22	S	N	Y	Guam	Y	Sales woman
33		267	319	Mariano, Vicente	Son	M	Cha	20	S	N	Y	Guam	Y	Carpenter
34		267	319	Mariano, Amalia	Daughter	F	Cha	18	S	N	Y	Guam	Y	None
35		267	319	Mariano, Nicolas	Son	M	Cha	16	S	Y	Y	Guam	Y	None
36		267	319	Mariano, Antonio	Son	M	Cha	10	S	Y		Guam		None
37		267	319	Mariano, Jose	Son	M	Cha	8	S	Y		Guam		None
38		267	319	Mariano, Jesus	Son	M	Cha	5	S	N		Guam		None
39		267	319	Mariano, Maria	Daughter	F	Cha	5	S	N		Guam		None
40		267	319	Mariano, Juan	Son	M	Cha	3.3	S	N		Guam		None
41		268	320	Santos, Francisco F	Head	M	Fil	52	Wd	N	Y	Philippine Is.	Y	Carpenter
42		268	320	Santos, Carlos	Son	M	Fil	24	S	N	Y	Guam	Y	Farmer
43		268	320	Santos, Francisco	Son	M	Fil	19	S	N	Y	Guam	Y	Carpenter
44		268	320	Santos, Fructuoso	Son	M	Fil	18	S	N	Y	Guam	Y	Carpenter
45		268	320	Santos, Leonida	Daughter	F	Fil	15	S	Y	Y	Guam	Y	None
46		268	320	Santos, Ignacio	Son	M	Fil	13	S	Y	Y	Guam	Y	None
47		268	320	Santos, Jesus	Son	M	Fil	11	S	Y	Y	Guam		None
48		268	320	Santos, Wenseslao	Son	M	Fil	9	S	Y		Guam		None
49		268	320	Santos, Ignacia	Daughter	F	Fil	7	S	Y		Guam		None
50		268	320	Santos, Nicolas F	Brother	M	Fil	30	S	N	N	Philippine Is.	N	None

DEPARTMENT OF COMMERCE-BUREAU OF THE CENSUS
WASHINGTON

FIFTEENTH CENSUS OF THE UNITED STATES: 1930-POPULATION

THE ISLAND OF GUAM

Sheet No. 36A

District Municipality of Agana
Name of Place Agana City (Togae Agana Urban)
[Proper name and, also, name of class, as city, town, village, barrio, etc]

Enumeration District No. 3
Enumerated by me on April 26, 1930 Tomas A. Calvo, Enumerator

	PLACE OF ABODE			NAME	RELATION	PERSONAL DESCRIPTION				EDUCATION		NATIVITY		OCCUPATION
	Street, avenue, road, etc.	Number of dwelling house is order of visitation	Number of family in order of visitation	of each person whose place of abode on April 1, 1930, was in this family. Enter surname, first, then given name and middle initial. If any. Include every person living on April 1, 1930. Omit children born since April 1, 1930.	Relationship of this Person to the head of the family.	Sex	Color or race	Age at last birthday	Single, married, widowed or divorced	Attended school any time since Sept. 1, 1929	Whether able to read and write.	Place of birth of this person.	Whether able to speak English.	
	1	2	3	4	5	6	7	8	9	10	11	12	13	14
1	San Quintin Street	269	321	Johnson, Ignacia P	Head	F	Cha	41	M	N	Y	Guam	Y	Laundress
2		269	321	Johnson, Andrew	Son	M	Cha	21	S	N	Y	Guam	Y	Servant
3		269	321	Johnson, Patrick	Son	M	Cha	20	S	N	Y	Guam	Y	Laborer
4		269	321	Johnson, Olga	Daughter	F	Cha	18	S	N	Y	Guam	Y	None
5		269	321	Johnson, Juan	Son	M	Cha	16	S	Y	Y	Guam	Y	None
6		269	321	Johnson, Leonisa	Daughter	F	Cha	14	S	Y	Y	Guam	Y	None
7		269	321	Johnson, Jesus	Son	M	Cha	7	S	N		Guam		None
8		269	321	Johnson, Francis	Son	M	Cha	6	S	N		Guam		None
9		270	322	Camacho, Victoriano P	Head	M	Cha	38	M	N	Y	Guam	Y	Carpenter
10		270	322	Camacho, Concepcion C	Wife	F	Cha	37	M	N	Y	Guam	Y	None
11		270	322	Camacho, Rosalia	Daughter	F	Cha	16	S	N	Y	Guam	Y	None
12		270	322	Camacho, Maria	Daughter	F	Cha	12	S	Y	Y	Guam		None
13		270	322	Camacho, Pedro	Son	M	Cha	11	S	Y	Y	Guam		None
14		270	322	Camacho, Jesus	Son	M	Cha	8	S	Y		Guam		None
15		270	322	Camacho, Jose	Son	M	Cha	7	S	Y		Guam		None
16		270	322	Camacho, Olfa	Daughter	F	Cha	5	S	N		Guam		None
17		270	322	Camacho, Pilar	Daughter	F	Cha	4	S	N		Guam		None
18		270	322	Camacho, Guadalupe	Daughter	F	Cha	2	S	N		Guam		None
19		270	322	Camacho, Remedio	Daughter	F	Cha	.3	S	N		Guam		None
20		271	323	Campos, Antonio	Head	M	Cha	54	M	N	Y	Guam	N	Farmer
21		271	323	Campos, Antonia R	Wife	F	Cha	52	M	N	N	Guam	N	None
22		271	323	Campos, Ramon	Son	M	Cha	22	S	N	Y	Guam	Y	Farmer
23		271	323	Campos, Jose	Son	M	Cha	20	S	N	Y	Guam	Y	Farmer
24		271	323	Campos, Juan	Son	M	Cha	18	S	N	Y	Guam	Y	Farmer
25		271	323	Campos, Elisa	Daughter	F	Cha	16	S	Y	Y	Guam	Y	None

(CHAMORRO ROOTS GENEALOGY PROJECT™ TRANSCRIPTION)
(BERNARD T. PUNZALAN / HTTP://WWW.CHAMORROROOTS.COM)

DEPARTMENT OF COMMERCE-BUREAU OF THE CENSUS
WASHINGTON

FIFTEENTH CENSUS OF THE UNITED STATES: 1930-POPULATION

THE ISLAND OF GUAM

Sheet No. 36B

113B

District **Municipality of Agana**
Name of Place **Agana City (Togae Agana Urban)**
[Proper name and, also, name of class, as city, town, village, barrio, etc]

Enumeration District No. **3**
Enumerated by me on **April 26, 1930** Tomas A. Calvo
Enumerator

	PLACE OF ABODE			NAME	RELATION	PERSONAL DESCRIPTION				EDUCATION		NATIVITY		OCCUPATION
	Street, avenue, road, etc.	Number of dwelling house is order of visitation	Number of family in order of visitation	of each person whose place of abode on April 1, 1930, was in this family. Enter surname, first, then given name and middle initial. If any. Include every person living on April 1, 1930. Omit children born since April 1, 1930.	Relationship of this Person to the head of the family.	Sex	Color or race	Age at last birthday	Single, married, widowed or divorced	Attended school any time since Sept. 1, 1929	Whether able to read and write.	Place of birth of this person.	Whether able to speak English.	
	1	2	3	4	5	6	7	8	9	10	11	12	13	14
26	San Quintin Street	271	323	Campos, Maria	Daughter	F	Cha	9	S	Y		Guam		None
27		272	324	Quichocho, Ana Q	Head	F	Cha	39	S	N	N	Guam	N	Laundress
28		272	324	Quichocho, Rita	Daughter	F	Cha	21	S	N	Y	Guam	Y	Laundress
29		272	324	Quichocho, Jose	Son	M	Cha	15	S	Y	Y	Guam	Y	None
30		272	324	Quichocho, Juan	Son	M	Cha	11	S	Y	Y	Guam		None
31		272	324	Quichocho, Esperansa	Daughter	F	Cha	7	S	Y		Guam		None
32		272	324	Quichocho, Antonia	Daughter	F	Cha	2.9	S	N		Guam		None
33		272	324	Quichocho, Lorenzo	Son	M	Cha	0.2	S	N		Guam		None
34		273	325	Bell, Ana J	Head	F	Cha	52	Wd	N	Y	Guam	Y	None
35		273	325	Bell, Henry	Son	M	Cha	20	S	N	Y	Guam	Y	Machinist
36		273	325	Javier, Julia P	Niece	F	Cha	12	S	Y	Y	Guam		None
37	Togae	274	326	Best, Hazel B	Head	F	W	34	M	N	Y	Vermont	Y	None
38		275	327	McCormick, Margaret M	Head	F	W	39	M	N	Y	Massachusetts	Y	None
39		275	327	McCormick, Betty G	Daughter	F	W	12	S		Y	Massachusetts	Y	None
40		275	327	McCormick, Joana A	Daughter	F	W	8	S			Colorado		None
41		276	328	McDonald, John F	Head	M	W	54	M	N	Y	Massachusetts		[blank]
42		276	328	McDonald, Dolores M	Wife	F	Cha	37	M	N	Y	Guam		None
43		276	328	McDonald, Francis	Son	M	Cha	19	S	Y	Y	Guam		None
44		276	328	McDonald, Veronica	Daughter	F	Cha	16	S	Y	Y	Guam		None
45		276	328	McDonald, Mary I	Daughter	F	Cha	14	S	Y	Y	Guam		None
46		276	328	McDonald, Elizabeth A	Daughter	F	Cha	12	S	Y	Y	Guam		None
47		276	328	McDonald, James B	Son	M	Cha	7	S	Y		Guam		None
48		276	328	McDonald, Charles H	Son	M	Cha	5	S	N		Guam		None
49		276	328	McDonald, Josephine F	Daughter	F	Cha	2.3	S	N		Guam		None
50		276	328	McDonald, Catherine C	Daughter	F	Cha	.3	S	N		Guam		None

DEPARTMENT OF COMMERCE-BUREAU OF THE CENSUS
WASHINGTON

FIFTEENTH CENSUS OF THE UNITED STATES: 1930-POPULATION

THE ISLAND OF GUAM

Sheet No. 37A

District Municipality of Agana
Name of Place Agana City (Togae Agana Urban)
[Proper name and, also, name of class, as city, town, village, barrio, etc]

Enumeration District No. 3
Enumerated by me on April 28, 1930 Tomas A. Calvo, Enumerator

	PLACE OF ABODE			NAME	RELATION	PERSONAL DESCRIPTION				EDUCATION		NATIVITY		OCCUPATION
	Street, avenue, road, etc.	Number of dwelling house in order of visitation	Number of family in order of visitation	of each person whose place of abode on April 1, 1930, was in this family. Enter surname, first, then given name and middle initial. If any. Include every person living on April 1, 1930. Omit children born since April 1, 1930.	Relationship of this Person to the head of the family.	Sex	Color or race	Age at last birthday	Single, married, widowed or divorced	Attended school any time since Sept. 1, 1929	Whether able to read and write.	Place of birth of this person.	Whether able to speak English.	
	1	2	3	4	5	6	7	8	9	10	11	12	13	14
1	Togae	276	328	Santos, Juan M	Nephew	M	Cha	34	S	N	Y	Guam	Y	Laborer
2		277	329	Garrison, Andrew	Head	M	W	60	M	N	Y	Indiana	Y	Laborer
3		277	329	Garrison, Francisca J	Wife	F	Cha	56	M	N	N	Guam	N	None
4		277	329	Garrison, Maria	Daughter	F	Cha	27	S	N	N	Guam	N	None
5		277	329	Garrison, Manuel	Son	M	Cha	26	S	N	Y	Guam	Y	Laborer
6		277	329	Garrison, Jose	Son	M	Cha	18	S	N	Y	Guam	Y	Farmer
7		277	329	Garrison, Tomas	Son	M	Cha	17	S	N	Y	Guam	Y	Farmer
8		277	329	Garrison, Delila	Daughter	F	Cha	15	S	Y	Y	Guam	Y	None
9		278	330	Camacho, Jesus P	Head	M	Cha	28	M	N	Y	Guam	Y	Carpenter
10		278	330	Camacho, Maria	Wife	F	Cha	28	M	N	Y	Guam	Y	None
11		278	330	Camacho, Jose	Son	M	Cha	8	S	Y		Guam		None
12		278	330	Camacho, Pedro	Son	M	Cha	7	S	Y		Guam		None
13		278	330	Camacho, Antonio	Son	M	Cha	5	S	N		Guam		None
14		278	330	Camacho, Jesus	Son	M	Cha	4	S	N		Guam		None
15		278	330	Camacho, Higinio	Son	M	Cha	2.8	S	N		Guam		None
16		278	330	Camacho, Ignacio	Son	M	Cha	.4	S	N		Guam		None
17		279	331	Fejarang, Jose P	Head	M	Cha	36	M	N	Y	Guam	Y	Carpenter
18		279	331	Fejarang, Maria	Wife	F	Cha	26	M	N	Y	Guam	Y	None
19		279	331	Fejarang, Jesus	Son	M	Cha	8	S	Y		Guam		None
20		279	331	Fejarang, Laura	Daughter	F	Cha	6	S	N		Guam		None
21		279	331	Fejarang, Maria	Daughter	F	Cha	5	S	N		Guam		None
22		279	331	Fejarang, Angelina	Daughter	F	Cha	1.9	S	N		Guam		None
23		279	331	Fejarang, Jose	Son	M	Cha	.3	S	N		Guam		None
24		280	332	San Nicolas, Jose C	Head	M	Cha	50	M	N	Y	Guam	N	Farmer
25		280	332	San Nicolas, Carmen R	Wife	F	Cha	48	M	N	Y	Guam	N	None

DEPARTMENT OF COMMERCE-BUREAU OF THE CENSUS
WASHINGTON

FIFTEENTH CENSUS OF THE UNITED STATES: 1930-POPULATION

THE ISLAND OF GUAM

Sheet No. 37B

District **Municipality of Agana**
Name of Place **Agana City (Togae Agana Urban)**
[Proper name and, also, name of class, as city, town, village, barrio, etc]

Enumeration District No. 3
Enumerated by me on **April 28, 1930** Tomas A. Calvo
Enumerator

	PLACE OF ABODE			NAME	RELATION	PERSONAL DESCRIPTION				EDUCATION		NATIVITY		OCCUPATION
	Street, avenue, road, etc.	Number of dwelling house is order of visitation	Number of family in order of visitation	of each person whose place of abode on April 1, 1930, was in this family. Enter surname, first, then given name and middle initial. If any. Include every person living on April 1, 1930. Omit children born since April 1, 1930.	Relationship of this Person to the head of the family.	Sex	Color or race	Age at last birthday	Single, married, widowed or divorced	Attended school any time since Sept. 1, 1929	Whether able to read and write.	Place of birth of this person.	Whether able to speak English.	
	1	2	3	4	5	6	7	8	9	10	11	12	13	14
26	Togae	280	332	San Nicolas, Magdalena	Daughter	F	Cha	24	S	N	Y	Guam	Y	None
27		280	332	San Nicolas, Joaquina	Daughter	F	Cha	23	S	N	Y	Guam	Y	None
28		280	332	San Nicolas, Pedro	Son	M	Cha	22	S	N	Y	Guam	Y	Farmer
29		280	332	San Nicolas, Olimpia	Daughter	F	Cha	19	S	N	Y	Guam	Y	None
30		280	332	San Nicolas, Juan	Son	M	Cha	17	S	Y	Y	Guam	Y	Chauffeur
31		280	332	San Nicolas, Francisco	Son	M	Cha	14	S	Y	Y	Guam	Y	None
32		280	332	San Nicolas, Rosa	Daughter	F	Cha	13	S	Y	Y	Guam	Y	None
33		280	332	San Nicolas, Maria	Daughter	F	Cha	9	S	Y		Guam		None
34		280	332	San Nicolas, Emilia	Daughter	F	Cha	5	S	N		Guam		None
35		280	332	Concepcion, Tomas A	Nephew	M	Cha	10	S	Y		Guam		None
36		281	333	Hong Yee, Vicente A	Head	M	Chin	23	M	N	Y	Guam	Y	Cook
37		281	333	Hong Yee, Jose	Son	M	Chin	2.9	S	N		Guam		None
38		281	333	Hong Yee, Rosa	Daughter	F	Chin	0.3	S	N		Guam		None
39		282	334	Mendiola, Joaquin P	T.B.Hospital	M	Cha	35	S	N	Y	Guam	Y	Farmer
40		282	334	Salas, Juan S	T.B.Hospital	M	Cha	29	S	N	Y	Guam	N	None
41		282	334	Leon Guerrero, Jesus G	T.B.Hospital	M	Cha	25	M	N	Y	Guam	Y	Laborer
42		282	334	Quichocho, Jesus P	T.B.Hospital	M	Cha	20	S	N	Y	Guam	Y	Farmer
43		282	334	Zamora, Doroteo C	T.B.Hospital	M	Fil	21	S	N	Y	Guam	Y	None
44		282	334	Peredo, Ignacio M	T.B.Hospital	M	Fil	8	S	Y		Guam		None
45		283	335	Garrido, Maria C	T.B.Hospital	F	Cha	28	D	N	Y	Guam	Y	None
46		283	335	Mendiola, Maria A	T.B.Hospital	F	Cha	27	M	N	Y	Guam	Y	None
47		283	335	Quinata, Ana C	T.B.Hospital	F	Cha	20	S	N		Guam		None
48		284	336	Cruz, Antonio I	Head	M	Cha	24	M	N	Y	Guam	Y	Scientific Aide
49		284	336	Cruz, Maria A	Wife	F	W	23	M	N	Y	Hawaii Territory	Y	None
50					Here ends the enumeration of enumeration district No 3, Toagae, Agana.									

District 4
Municipality of Agana

Anigua
Julale
Santa Cruz

DEPARTMENT OF COMMERCE-BUREAU OF THE CENSUS
WASHINGTON

FIFTEENTH CENSUS OF THE UNITED STATES: 1930-POPULATION

THE ISLAND OF GUAM

Sheet No. 1A

District Municipality of Agana

Name of Place Agana City (Anigua)
[Proper name and, also, name of class, as city, town, village, barrio, etc]

Enumeration District No. 4

Enumerated by me on April 2, 1930 Vicente Tydingco, Enumerator

	PLACE OF ABODE			NAME	RELATION	PERSONAL DESCRIPTION				EDUCATION		NATIVITY		OCCUPATION
	Street, avenue, road, etc.	Number of dwelling house in order of visitation	Number of family in order of visitation	of each person whose place of abode on April 1, 1930, was in this family. Enter surname, first, then given name and middle initial. If any. Include every person living on April 1, 1930. Omit children born since April 1, 1930.	Relationship of this Person to the head of the family.	Sex	Color or race	Age at last birthday	Single, married, widowed or divorced	Attended school any time since Sept. 1, 1929	Whether able to read and write.	Place of birth of this person.	Whether able to speak English.	
	1	2	3	4	5	6	7	8	9	10	11	12	13	14
1	Agana Piti Road	1	1	Palomo, Gertrudes T	Head	F	Cha	57	Wd	N	N	Guam	N	None
2		1	1	Palomo, Ignacio T	Son	M	Cha	25	M	N	Y	Guam	Y	Laborer
3		1	1	Palomo, Vicenta S	Daughter in law	F	Cha	26	M	N	Y	Guam	N	None
4		2	2	Palomo, Jose T	Head	M	Cha	26	M	N	Y	Guam	Y	Rigger
5		2	2	Palomo, Estofonia C	Wife	F	Cha	25	M	N	Y	Guam	Y	Laundress
6		2	2	Palomo, Maria C	Daughter	F	Cha	5	S	N		Guam		None
7		2	2	Palomo, Pedro C	Son	M	Cha	4.5	S	N		Guam		None
8		2	2	Palomo, Cecilia C	Daughter	F	Cha	2.7	S	N		Guam		None
9		2	2	Palomo, Francisco C	Son	M	Cha	.2	S	N		Guam		None
10		3	3	Cruz, Dominga P	Head	F	Cha	29	M	N	Y	Guam	Y	None
11		3	3	Cruz, Jesus P	Son	M	Cha	7	S	Y		Guam		None
12		3	3	Cruz, Jose P	Son	M	Cha	6	S	N		Guam		None
13		3	3	Cruz, Juan P	Son	M	Cha	4.4	S	N		Guam		None
14		3	3	Cruz, Carlos P	Son	M	Cha	1.5	S	N		Guam		None
15		4	4	Nauta, Antonio T	Head	M	Cha	26	M	N	Y	Guam	N	Rigger
16		4	4	Nauta, Felicidad C	Wife	F	Cha	18	M	N	Y	Guam	Y	None
17		4	4	Nauta, Antonia C	Daughter	F	Cha	.8	S	N		Guam		None
18		4	4	Taimanglo, Ana O	Mother in law	F	Cha	43	D	N	N	Guam	N	None
19		5	5	Torre, Maria C	Head	F	Cha	39	M	N	N	Guam	N	None
20		5	5	Torre, Juan C	Son	M	Cha	12	S	Y	Y	Guam	Y	None
21		5	5	Torre, Dolores C	Son	F	Cha	11	S	Y	Y	Guam	Y	None
22		5	5	Torre, Benjamin C	Son	M	Cha	9	S	Y		Guam		None
23		5	5	Torre, Joaquin C	Son	M	Cha	6	S	N		Guam		None
24		5	5	Torre, Luis C	Son	M	Cha	5	S	N		Guam		None
25		5	5	Torre, Rosalia C	Daughter	F	Cha	3.3	S	N		Guam		None

(CHAMORRO ROOTS GENEALOGY PROJECT™ TRANSCRIPTION)
(BERNARD T. PUNZALAN / HTTP://WWW.CHAMORROROOTS.COM)

DEPARTMENT OF COMMERCE-BUREAU OF THE CENSUS
WASHINGTON

FIFTEENTH CENSUS OF THE UNITED STATES: 1930-POPULATION

THE ISLAND OF GUAM

Sheet No. 1B

115B

District **Municipality of Agana**
Name of Place **Agana City (Anigua)**
[Proper name and, also, name of class, as city, town, village, barrio, etc]

Enumeration District No. 4
Enumerated by me on **April 2, 1930** Vicente Tydingco
Enumerator

	PLACE OF ABODE			NAME	RELATION	PERSONAL DESCRIPTION				EDUCATION		NATIVITY		OCCUPATION
	Street, avenue, road, etc.	Number of dwelling house is order of visitation	Number of family in order of visitation	of each person whose place of abode on April 1, 1930, was in this family. Enter surname, first, then given name and middle initial. If any. Include every person living on April 1, 1930. Omit children born since April 1, 1930.	Relationship of this Person to the head of the family.	Sex	Color or race	Age at last birthday	Single, married, widowed or divorced	Attended school any time since Sept. 1, 1929	Whether able to read and write.	Place of birth of this person.	Whether able to speak English.	
	1	2	3	4	5	6	7	8	9	10	11	12	13	14
26	Agana Piti Road	5	5	Torre, Magdalena C	Daughter	F	Cha	.3	S	Y		Guam		None
27		5	5	Torre, Rosa N	Mother	F	Cha	70	Wd	N	N	Guam	N	None
28		6	6	Crisostimo, Pedro	Head	M	Cha	47	M	N	Y	Guam	N	Farmer
29		6	6	Crisostimo, Maria A	Wife	F	Cha	58	M	N	N	Guam	N	None
30		6	6	Crisostimo, Jose A	Son	M	Cha	22	S	N	Y	Guam	Y	Rigger
31		6	6	Crisostimo, Josefa A	Daughter	F	Cha	16	S	N	Y	Guam	Y	None
32		7	7	Toves, Pedro I	Head	M	Cha	37	M	N	Y	Guam	Y	Laborer
33		7	7	Toves, Ana D	Wife	F	Cha	25	M	N	Y	Guam	Y	None
34		7	7	Toves, Maria D	Daughter	F	Cha	7	S	Y		Guam		None
35		7	7	Toves, Magdalena D	Daughter	F	Cha	4.1	S	N		Guam		None
36		7	7	Toves, Jose D	Son	M	Cha	3.2	S	N		Guam		None
37		7	7	Toves, Antonio D	Son	M	Cha	1.7	S	N		Guam		None
38		7	7	Toves, Rosa D	Daughter	F	Cha	.2	S	N		Guam		None
39		8	8	Cruz, Manuel I	Head	M	Cha	22	M	N	Y	Guam	Y	Farmer
40		8	8	Cruz, Ana C	Wife	F	Cha	24	M	N	Y	Guam	Y	None
41		8	8	Cruz, Vicente C	Son	M	Cha	3.8	S	N		Guam		None
42		8	8	Cruz, Josefina C	Daughter	F	Cha	2.5	S	N		Guam		None
43		8	8	Cruz, Isabel C	Daughter	F	Cha	.8	S	N		Guam		None
44		9	9	Mendiola, Juan P	Head	M	Cha	45	M	N	Y	Guam	N	Carpenter
45		9	9	Mendiola, Teresa C	Wife	F	Cha	31	M	N	Y	Guam	Y	None
46		9	9	Mendiola, Rosa C	Daughter	F	Cha	10	S	N		Guam		None
47		9	9	Mendiola, Pilar C	Daughter	F	Cha	7	S	Y		Guam		None
48		9	9	Mendiola, Maria C	Daughter	F	Cha	5	S	N		Guam		None
49		9	9	Mendiola, Jesus C	Son	M	Cha	2.2	S	N		Guam		None
50		9	9	Mendiola, Francisco C	Son	M	Cha	.3	S	N		Guam		None

DEPARTMENT OF COMMERCE-BUREAU OF THE CENSUS
WASHINGTON

FIFTEENTH CENSUS OF THE UNITED STATES: 1930-POPULATION

THE ISLAND OF GUAM

Sheet No. 2A

District **Municipality of Agana**
Name of Place **Agana City (Anigua)**
[Proper name and, also, name of class, as city, town, village, barrio, etc]

Enumeration District No. 4
Enumerated by me on **April 2, 1930** Vicente Tydingco
Enumerator

	PLACE OF ABODE			NAME	RELATION	PERSONAL DESCRIPTION				EDUCATION		NATIVITY		OCCUPATION
	Street, avenue, road, etc.	Number of dwelling house is order of visitation	Number of family in order of visitation	of each person whose place of abode on April 1, 1930, was in this family. Enter surname, first, then given name and middle initial. If any. Include every person living on April 1, 1930. Omit children born since April 1, 1930.	Relationship of this Person to the head of the family.	Sex	Color or race	Age at last birthday	Single, married, widowed or divorced	Attended school any time since Sept. 1, 1929	Whether able to read and write.	Place of birth of this person.	Whether able to speak English.	
	1	2	3	4	5	6	7	8	9	10	11	12	13	14
1	Agana Piti Road	10	10	Ignacio, Manuel P	Head	M	Cha	48	M	N	Y	Guam	N	Farmer
2		10	10	Ignacio, Ana C	Wife	F	Cha	49	M	N	N	Guam	N	None
3		10	10	Ignacio, Barbara C	Daughter	F	Cha	20	S	N	Y	Guam	Y	None
4		10	10	Ignacio, Felipe C	Son	M	Cha	15	S	Y	Y	Guam	Y	Farm Laborer
5		10	10	Ignacio, Rafael C	Son	M	Cha	13	S	Y	Y	Guam	Y	None
6		10	10	Ignacio, Loreta C	Daughter	F	Cha	12	S	Y	Y	Guam	Y	None
7		10	10	Ignacio, Maria C	Daughter	F	Cha	7	S	Y		Guam		None
8		10	10	Ignacio, Juana C	Daughter	F	Cha	4.3	S	N		Guam		None
9		10	10	Ignacio, Rita C	Daughter	F	Cha	2.3	S	N		Guam		None
10		10	10	Ignacio, Jesus C	Son	M	Cha	1.1	S	N		Guam		None
11		11	11	Cruz, Antonio R	Head	M	Cha	60	M	N	Y	Guam	N	Farmer
12		11	11	Cruz, Asuncion C	Wife	F	Cha	22	M	N	Y	Guam	Y	None
13		11	11	Cruz, Maria I	Daughter	F	Cha	21	M	N	Y	Guam	Y	None
14		11	11	Cruz, Jose I	Son	M	Cha	15	M	Y	Y	Guam	Y	None
15		11	11	Cruz, Miguel C	Son	M	Cha	3.5	S	N		Guam		None
16		11	11	Cruz, Quintina C	Daughter	F	Cha	2.1	S	N		Guam		None
17		11	11	Cruz, Ana C	Daughter	F	Cha	1.3	S	N		Guam		None
18		11	11	Ignacio, Francisco C	Brother in law	M	Cha	45	D	N	N	Guam	N	Laborer
19		12	12	Cruz, Domingo A	Head	M	Cha	35	M	N	Y	Guam	Y	Labor Foreman
20		12	12	Cruz, Carmen N	Wife	F	Cha	36	M	N	N	Guam	N	None
21		12	12	Cruz, Jose N	Son	M	Cha	14	S	Y	Y	Guam	Y	None
22		12	12	Cruz, Juan N	Son	M	Cha	12	S	Y	Y	Guam	Y	None
23		12	12	Cruz, Enriques N	Son	M	Cha	9	S	Y		Guam		None
24		12	12	Cruz, Maria N	Daughter	F	Cha	7	S	Y		Guam		None
25		12	12	Cruz, Joaquin N	Son	M	Cha	6	S	N		Guam		None

(CHAMORRO ROOTS GENEALOGY PROJECT™ TRANSCRIPTION)
(BERNARD T. PUNZALAN / HTTP://WWW.CHAMORROROOTS.COM)

DEPARTMENT OF COMMERCE-BUREAU OF THE CENSUS
WASHINGTON

FIFTEENTH CENSUS OF THE UNITED STATES: 1930-POPULATION

THE ISLAND OF GUAM

Sheet No. 2B

116B

District Municipality of Agana
Name of Place Agana City (Anigua)
[Proper name and, also, name of class, as city, town, village, barrio, etc]

Enumeration District No. 4
Enumerated by me on April 2, 1930 Vicente Tydingco, Enumerator

	PLACE OF ABODE			NAME	RELATION	PERSONAL DESCRIPTION				EDUCATION		NATIVITY		OCCUPATION
	Street, avenue, road, etc.	Number of dwelling house in order of visitation	Number of family in order of visitation	of each person whose place of abode on April 1, 1930, was in this family. Enter surname, first, then given name and middle initial. If any. Include every person living on April 1, 1930. Omit children born since April 1, 1930.	Relationship of this Person to the head of the family.	Sex	Color or race	Age at last birthday	Single, married, widowed or divorced	Attended school any time since Sept. 1, 1929	Whether able to read and write.	Place of birth of this person.	Whether able to speak English.	
	1	2	3	4	5	6	7	8	9	10	11	12	13	14
26	Agana Piti Road	13	13	Diaz, Doroteo D	Head	M	Cha	33	M	N	Y	Guam	Y	Painter
27		13	13	Diaz, Maria T	Wife	F	Cha	30	M	N	Y	Guam	N	None
28		13	13	Diaz, Natividad T	Daughter	F	Cha	8	S	Y		Guam		None
29		13	13	Diaz, Agustin T	Son	M	Cha	6	S	N		Guam		None
30		13	13	Diaz, Vicente T	Son	M	Cha	4.5	S	N		Guam		None
31		13	13	Diaz, Cecilio T	Son	M	Cha	3.3	S	N		Guam		None
32		13	13	Diaz, Alejandro T	Son	M	Cha	2.4	S	N		Guam		None
33		13	13	Diaz, Grabiel T	Son	M	Cha	1.3	S	N		Guam		None
34		13	13	Diaz, Atanacio T	Son	M	Cha	.7	S	N		Guam		None
35		14	14	Taimanglo, Mariano T	Head	M	Cha	60	M	N	Y	Guam	N	Farmer
36		14	14	Taimanglo, Rita T	Wife	F	Cha	63	M	N	N	Guam	N	None
37		14	15	Aguon, Juan T	Head	M	Cha	36	Wd	N	Y	Guam	N	Laborer
38		14	15	Aguon, Julian LG	Son	M	Cha	12	S	Y	Y	Guam	Y	None
39		14	15	Aguon, Maria LG	Daughter	F	Cha	11	S	Y	Y	Guam	Y	None
40		14	15	Aguon, Francisco LG	Son	M	Cha	9	S	Y		Guam		None
41		14	15	Aguon, Teresa LG	Daughter	F	Cha	7	S	N		Guam		None
42		14	15	Leon Guerrero, Ana F	Cousin	F	Cha	57	Wd	N	N	Guam	N	None
43		15	16	Quitonguico, Pedro C	Head	M	Cha	55	Wd	N	N	Guam	N	Farmer
44		16	17	Terlaje, Josefa S	Head	F	Cha	68	Wd	N	Y	Guam	N	None
45		16	17	Terlaje, Jesus S	Son	M	Cha	22	S	N	Y	Guam	Y	Farmer
46		16	17	Terlaje, Rosalia S	Daughter	F	Cha	19	S	Y	Y	Guam	Y	Laundress
47		16	17	Terlaje, Juan S	Son	M	Cha	18	S	Y	Y	Guam	Y	None
48		17	18	Gumataotao, Ramona T	Head	F	Cha	56	Wd	N	N	Guam	N	None
49		17	18	Gumataotao, Isabel T	Daughter	F	Cha	26	S	N	Y	Guam	Y	None
50		17	18	Gumataotao, Atanacio T	Son	M	Cha	22	S	N	Y	Guam	Y	Typist

(CHAMORRO ROOTS GENEALOGY PROJECT™ TRANSCRIPTION)
(BERNARD T. PUNZALAN / HTTP://WWW.CHAMORROROOTS.COM)

DEPARTMENT OF COMMERCE-BUREAU OF THE CENSUS
WASHINGTON

FIFTEENTH CENSUS OF THE UNITED STATES: 1930-POPULATION

THE ISLAND OF GUAM

Sheet No. 3A

District **Municipality of Agana**
Name of Place **Agana City (Anigua)**
[Proper name and, also, name of class, as city, town, village, barrio, etc]

Enumeration District No. 4
Enumerated by me on **April 2, 1930** Vicente Tydingco
Enumerator

	PLACE OF ABODE			NAME	RELATION	PERSONAL DESCRIPTION				EDUCATION		NATIVITY		OCCUPATION
	Street, avenue, road, etc.	Number of dwelling house in order of visitation	Number of family in order of visitation	of each person whose place of abode on April 1, 1930, was in this family. Enter surname, first, then given name and middle initial. If any. Include every person living on April 1, 1930. Omit children born since April 1, 1930.	Relationship of this Person to the head of the family.	Sex	Color or race	Age at last birthday	Single, married, widowed or divorced	Attended school any time since Sept. 1, 1929	Whether able to read and write.	Place of birth of this person.	Whether able to speak English.	
	1	2	3	4	5	6	7	8	9	10	11	12	13	14
1	Agana Piti Road	17	18	Gumataotao, Juan T	Son	M	Cha	17	S	Y	Y	Guam	Y	None
2		17	18	Gumataotao, Vicente T	Son	M	Cha	14	S	Y	Y	Guam	Y	None
3		17	18	Gumataotao, Jose T	Son	M	Cha	12	S	Y	Y	Guam	Y	None
4		17	18	Gumataotao, Catalina T	Daughter	F	Cha	6	S	N		Guam		None
5		17	18	Aguon, Jose C	Servant	M	Cha	29	S	N	N	Guam	N	Farm Laborer
6		17	18	San Nicolas, Josefa S	Servant	F	Cha	33	S	N	Y	Guam	N	None
7		18	19	Mesa, Jesus C	Head	M	Cha	26	M	N	Y	Guam	Y	Rigger
8		18	19	Mesa, Consolacion M	Wife	F	Cha	30	M	N	Y	Guam	Y	None
9		18	19	Ignacio, Enrique M	Step son	M	Cha	15	S	Y	Y	Guam	Y	None
10		18	19	Ignacio, Maria M	Step daughter	F	Cha	14	S	Y	Y	Guam	Y	None
11		18	19	Ignacio, Regina M	Step daughter	F	Cha	12	S	Y	Y	Guam	Y	None
12		18	19	Mesa, Jose M	Son	M	Cha	7	S	Y		Guam		None
13		18	19	Mesa, Isabel M	Daughter	F	Cha	2.7	S	N		Guam		None
14		18	19	Misara, Rosa M	Mother in law	F	Cha	65	Wd	N	N	Guam	N	None
15		19	20	Taijeran, Jose	Head	M	Cha	48	M	N	N	Guam	Y	Farm Laborer
16		19	20	Taijeran, Ana Q	Wife	F	Cha	47	M	N	N	Guam	N	None
17		19	20	Reyes, Vicente Q	Step son	M	Cha	22	S	N	Y	Guam	Y	Servant
18		19	20	Reyes, Jose Q	Step son	M	Cha	16	S	N	N	Guam	N	Farm Laborer
19		19	20	Reyes, Jesus Q	Step son	M	Cha	14	S	Y	Y	Guam	Y	None
20		21	21	Lujan, Mariano LG	Head	M	Cha	38	M	N	Y	Guam	Y	Blacksmith
21		21	21	Lujan, Ana F	Wife	F	Cha	36	M	N	Y	Guam	N	None
22		21	21	Lujan, Joaquin F	Son	M	Cha	9	S	Y		Guam		None
23		21	21	Lujan, Maria F	Daughter	F	Cha	8	S	Y		Guam		None
24		21	21	Lujan, Roman F	Son	M	Cha	6	S	N		Guam		None
25		21	21	Lujan, Frankie F	Son	M	Cha	3.3	S	N		Guam		None

(CHAMORRO ROOTS GENEALOGY PROJECT™ TRANSCRIPTION)
(BERNARD T. PUNZALAN / HTTP://WWW.CHAMORROROOTS.COM)

DEPARTMENT OF COMMERCE-BUREAU OF THE CENSUS
WASHINGTON

FIFTEENTH CENSUS OF THE UNITED STATES: 1930-POPULATION

THE ISLAND OF GUAM

Sheet No. 3B

117B

District **Municipality of Agana**

Name of Place **Agana City (Anigua)**

[Proper name and, also, name of class, as city, town, village, barrio, etc]

Enumeration District No. 4

Enumerated by me on **April 2, 1930** Vicente Tydingco, Enumerator

	PLACE OF ABODE			NAME	RELATION	PERSONAL DESCRIPTION				EDUCATION		NATIVITY		OCCUPATION
	Street, avenue, road, etc.	Number of dwelling house in order of visitation	Number of family in order of visitation	of each person whose place of abode on April 1, 1930, was in this family. Enter surname, first, then given name and middle initial. If any. Include every person living on April 1, 1930. Omit children born since April 1, 1930.	Relationship of this Person to the head of the family.	Sex	Color or race	Age at last birthday	Single, married, widowed or divorced	Attended school any time since Sept. 1, 1929	Whether able to read and write.	Place of birth of this person.	Whether able to speak English.	
	1	2	3	4	5	6	7	8	9	10	11	12	13	14
26	Agana Piti Road	21	21	Lujan, Rosa F	Daughter	F	Cha	1.3	S	N		Guam		None
27		21	22	Flores, Ana L	Head	F	Cha	68	Wd	N	N	Guam	N	None
28		21	22	Flores, Maria L	Daughter	F	Cha	34	S	N	Y	Guam	N	Laundress
29		21	22	Flores, Jose L	Son	M	Cha	26	S	N	Y	Guam	Y	Carpenter
30		21	22	Flores, Manuel F	Grandson	M	Cha	13	S	Y	Y	Guam	Y	None
31		21	22	Flores, Juan F	Grandson	M	Cha	5	S	N		Guam		None
32		21	22	Flores, Rosario F	Grand daughter	F	Cha	3.4	S	N		Guam		None
33		21	22	Cruz, Herman F	Grandson	M	Cha	8	S	Y		Guam		None
34		21	22	Cruz, Angel F	Grandson	M	Cha	6	S	N		Guam		None
35		21	22	Cruz, Josefina F	Grand daughter	F	Cha	5	S	N		Guam		None
36		22	23	Materne, Juan M	Head	M	Cha	35	M	N	Y	Guam	N	Farmer
37		22	23	Materne, Pontinciana	Wife	F	Cha	29	M	N	Y	Guam	Y	None
38		22	23	Materne, Teresa M	Daughter	F	Cha	15	S	N	Y	Guam	N	None
39		22	23	Materne, Mercedes M	Daughter	F	Cha	13	S	Y	Y	Guam	Y	None
40		22	23	Materne, Domingo M	Son	M	Cha	10	S	Y		Guam		None
41		22	23	Materne, Inez M	Daughter	F	Cha	8	S	Y		Guam		None
42		22	23	Materne, Francisco M	Son	M	Cha	7	S	Y		Guam		None
43		22	23	Materne, Petronilla M	Daughter	F	Cha	6	S	N		Guam		None
44		22	23	Materne, Luis M	Son	M	Cha	4.2	S	Y		Guam		None
45		22	23	Materne, Margarita M	Daughter	F	Cha	2.7	S	N		Guam		None
46		22	23	Materne, Francisca M	Mother	F	Cha	70	Wd	N	N	Guam	N	None
47		22	23	Materne, Maria S	Aunt	F	Cha	60	Wd	N	N	Guam	N	None
48		23	24	Perez, Concepcion A	Head	F	Cha	28	M	N	Y	Guam	N	None
49		23	24	Perez, Rosario A	Daughter	F	Cha	7	S	Y		Guam		None
50		23	24	Angoco, Agustin C	Mother-in-law	F	Cha	47	Wd	N	Y	Guam	N	Laundress

DEPARTMENT OF COMMERCE-BUREAU OF THE CENSUS
WASHINGTON

FIFTEENTH CENSUS OF THE UNITED STATES: 1930-POPULATION

THE ISLAND OF GUAM

Sheet No. 4A

District **Municipality of Agana**
Name of Place **Agana City (Anigua)**
[Proper name and, also, name of class, as city, town, village, barrio, etc]

Enumeration District No. 4
Enumerated by me on **April 2, 1930** Vicente Tydingco
Enumerator

	PLACE OF ABODE			NAME	RELATION	PERSONAL DESCRIPTION				EDUCATION		NATIVITY		OCCUPATION
	Street, avenue, road, etc.	Number of dwelling house is order of visitation	Number of family in order of visitation	of each person whose place of abode on April 1, 1930, was in this family. Enter surname, first, then given name and middle initial. If any. Include every person living on April 1, 1930. Omit children born since April 1, 1930.	Relationship of this Person to the head of the family.	Sex	Color or race	Age at last birthday	Single, married, widowed or divorced	Attended school any time since Sept. 1, 1929	Whether able to read and write.	Place of birth of this person.	Whether able to speak English.	
	1	2	3	4	5	6	7	8	9	10	11	12	13	14
1	Agana Piti Road	23	24	Zamora, Martin A	Servant	M	Fil	42	S	N	Y	Philippine Islands	Y	Cook
2		24	25	Mendiola, Pedro M	Head	M	Cha	28	M	N	Y	Guam	Y	Engine Man
3		24	25	Mendiola, Ana C	Wife	F	Cha	28	M	N	Y	Guam	Y	None
4		24	25	Mendiola, Julian C	Son	M	Cha	8	S	Y		Guam		None
5		24	25	Mendiola, Eliza C	Daughter	F	Cha	7	S	Y		Guam		None
6		24	25	Mendiola, Enrique C	Son	M	Cha	5	S	N		Guam		None
7		24	25	Mendiola, Elias C	Son	M	Cha	4.3	S	N		Guam		None
8		24	25	Mendiola, Clotilde C	Daughter	F	Cha	1.3	S	N		Guam		None
9		24	25	Marcelo, Julian C	Grandfather	M	Fil	98	Wd	N	Y	Philippine Islands	N	None
10		24	25	Mendiola, Maria M	Sister	F	Cha	25	S	N	Y	Guam	Y	Nurse
11		25	26	Atoigue, Pedro M	Head	M	Cha	30	M	N	Y	Guam	N	Laborer
12		25	26	Atoigue, Teodora A	Wife	F	Cha	26	M	N	Y	Guam	N	None
13		25	26	Atoigue, Oliva A	Daughter	F	Cha	5	S	N		Guam		None
14		25	26	Atoigue, Nicolas A	Son	M	Cha	2.1	S	N		Guam		None
15		25	26	Atoigue, Jesus A	Son	M	Cha	.2	S	N		Guam		None
16		26	27	Lizama, Vicente L	Head	M	Cha	56	M	N	N	Guam	N	None
17		26	27	Lizama, Rita N	Wife	F	Cha	54	M	N	N	Guam	N	Laundress
18		27	28	Gonzalo, Pedro G	Head	M	Fil	34	M	N	Y	Philippine Islands	Y	Labor Foreman
19		27	28	Gonzalo, Antonia N	Wife	F	Fil	30	M	N	Y	Guam	Y	None
20		27	28	Gonzalo, Josefina N	Daughter	F	Fil	12	S	Y	Y	Guam	Y	None
21		27	28	Gonzalo, Clotilde N	Daughter	F	Fil	6	S	N		Guam		None
22		27	28	Cruz, Rosa R	Servant	F	Cha	19	S	N	Y	Guam	Y	Servant
23		28	29	Tuncap, Dolores	Head	F	Cha	36	S	N	Y	Guam	Y	Laundress
24		28	29	Tuncap, Maria	Sister	F	Fil	23	S	N	Y	Guam		Laundress
25		28	29	Tuncap, Concepcion	Sister	F	Fil	21	S	N	Y	Guam	Y	Laundress

(CHAMORRO ROOTS GENEALOGY PROJECT™ TRANSCRIPTION)
(BERNARD T. PUNZALAN / HTTP://WWW.CHAMORROROOTS.COM)

DEPARTMENT OF COMMERCE-BUREAU OF THE CENSUS
WASHINGTON

FIFTEENTH CENSUS OF THE UNITED STATES: 1930-POPULATION

THE ISLAND OF GUAM

Sheet No. 4B

118B

District Municipality of Agana
Name of Place Agana City (Anigua)
[Proper name and, also, name of class, as city, town, village, barrio, etc]

Enumeration District No. 4
Enumerated by me on April 3, 1930 Vicente Tydingco, Enumerator

	PLACE OF ABODE: Street, avenue, road, etc.	Number of dwelling house in order of visitation	Number of family in order of visitation	NAME of each person whose place of abode on April 1, 1930, was in this family. Enter surname, first, then given name and middle initial. If any. Include every person living on April 1, 1930. Omit children born since April 1, 1930.	RELATION Relationship of this Person to the head of the family.	PERSONAL DESCRIPTION: Sex	Color or race	Age at last birthday	Single, married, widowed or divorced	EDUCATION: Attended school any time since Sept. 1, 1929	Whether able to read and write.	NATIVITY Place of birth of this person.	Whether able to speak English.	OCCUPATION
	1	2	3	4	5	6	7	8	9	10	11	12	13	14
26	Agana Piti Road	28	29	Tuncap, Delfina T	Daughter	F	Fil	15	S	Y	Y	Guam	Y	None
27		28	29	Tuncap, Jesus T	Son	M	Fil	12	S	Y	Y	Guam	Y	None
28		28	29	Tuncap, Enrique T	Son	M	Fil	6	S	N		Guam		None
29		28	29	Tuncap, Florentina T	Daughter	F	Fil	4.7	S	N	N	Guam		None
30		28	29	Tuncap, Angel	Son	M	Fil	2.5	S	N		Guam		None
31		28	29	Fegurgur, Isabel T	Servant	F	Cha	17	S	N	Y	Guam	N	Cook
32		28	29	Angoco, Mariano A	Servant	M	Cha	49	S	N	Y	Guam	N	Farm Laborer
33		28	30	Tuncap, Clemente N	Head	M	Fil	28	M	N	Y	Guam	Y	Laborer
34		28	30	Tuncap, Rosa T	Wife	F	Cha	20	M	N	Y	Guam	Y	None
35		28	30	Tuncap, Celedonia T	Daughter	F	Fil	7	S	Y		Guam		None
36		28	30	Tuncap, Jesus T	Son	M	Fil	.7	S	N		Guam		None
37		28	30	Fegurgur, Francisco F	Lodger	M	Cha	15	S	Y	Y	Guam	Y	None
38		29	31	Salas, Jose I	Head	M	Cha	51	S	N	N	Guam	N	Farm Laborer
39		30	32	Celes, Jose I	Head	M	Cha	42	M	N	N	Guam	N	Farmer
40		30	32	Celes, Nieves T	Wife	F	Cha	34	M	N	Y	Guam	Y	None
41		30	32	Celes, Jose T	Son	M	Cha	11	S	Y	Y	Guam	Y	None
42		30	32	Celes, Jesus T	Son	M	Cha	10	S	Y		Guam		None
43		30	32	Celes, Brigida T	Daughter	F	Cha	7	S	Y		Guam		None
44		30	32	Celes, Guadalupe T	Daughter	F	Cha	6	S	N		Guam		None
45		30	32	Celes, Juan T	Son	M	Cha	3.7	S	N		Guam		None
46		31	33	Gutierrez, Esiquiel N	Head	M	Cha	56	M	N	Y	Guam	N	Farmer
47		31	33	Gutierrez, Maria	Wife	F	Cha	55	M	N	N	Guam	N	None
48		31	33	Taijeron, Maria T	Servant	F	Cha	12	S	N	N	Guam	N	Servant
49		31	34	Gutierrez, Jesus T	Head	M	Cha	25	M	N	Y	Guam	Y	Chauffeur
50		31	34	Gutierrez, Maria M	Wife	F	Cha	72	M	N	Y	Guam	Y	None

(CHAMORRO ROOTS GENEALOGY PROJECT™ TRANSCRIPTION)
(BERNARD T. PUNZALAN / HTTP://WWW.CHAMORROROOTS.COM)

DEPARTMENT OF COMMERCE-BUREAU OF THE CENSUS
WASHINGTON
FIFTEENTH CENSUS OF THE UNITED STATES: 1930-POPULATION

THE ISLAND OF GUAM

Sheet No. 5A

District **Municipality of Agana**
Name of Place **Agana City (Anigua)**
[Proper name and, also, name of class, as city, town, village, barrio, etc]

Enumeration District No. 4
Enumerated by me on **April 3, 1930** Vicente Tydingco
Enumerator

	PLACE OF ABODE			NAME	RELATION	PERSONAL DESCRIPTION				EDUCATION		NATIVITY		OCCUPATION
	Street, avenue, road, etc.	Number of dwelling house is order of visitation	Number of family in order of visitation	of each person whose place of abode on April 1, 1930, was in this family. Enter surname, first, then given name and middle initial. If any. Include every person living on April 1, 1930. Omit children born since April 1, 1930.	Relationship of this Person to the head of the family.	Sex	Color or race	Age at last birthday	Single, married, widowed or divorced	Attended school any time since Sept. 1, 1929	Whether able to read and write.	Place of birth of this person.	Whether able to speak English.	
	1	2	3	4	5	6	7	8	9	10	11	12	13	14
1	Agana Piti Road	31	34	Gutierrez, Domingo M	Son	M	Cha	5.3	S	N		Guam		None
2		31	34	Gutierrez, Ignacia M	Daughter	F	Cha	1.8	S	N		Guam		None
3		31	34	Gutierrez, Catalina M	Daughter	F	Cha	.1	S	N		Guam		None
4		32	35	Nauta, Jesus M	Head	M	Cha	42	M	N	Y	Guam	N	Farm Laborer
5		32	35	Nauta, Francisca T	Wife	F	Cha	46	M	N	Y	Guam	N	None
6		32	35	Nauta, Carmen T	Daughter	F	Cha	18	S	N	N	Guam	N	None
7		32	35	Nauta, Pedro T	Son	M	Cha	14	S	Y	Y	Guam	Y	None
8		32	35	Nauta, Paulina T	Daughter	F	Cha	12	S	Y	Y	Guam	Y	None
9		32	35	Nauta, Joaquin T	Son	M	Cha	11	S	Y	Y	Guam	Y	None
10		32	35	Nauta, Maria T	Daughter	F	Cha	7	S	Y		Guam		None
11		32	35	Nauta, Maria T	Daughter	F	Cha	5	S	N		Guam		None
12		32	35	Nauta, Juan T	Son	M	Cha	2.7	S	N		Guam		None
13		33	36	Salas, Soledad A	Head	F	Cha	42	M	N	Y	Guam	N	None
14		33	36	Salas, Juan A	Son	M	Cha	22	S	N	Y	Guam	Y	Farm Laborer
15		33	36	Salas, Jesus A	Son	M	Cha	19	S	N	Y	Guam	Y	Servant
16		33	36	Salas, Dolores A	Daughter	F	Cha	17	S	N	Y	Guam	Y	None
17		33	36	Salas, Enrique A	Son	M	Cha	15	S	Y	Y	Guam	Y	None
18		33	36	Salas, Vinancio A	Son	M	Cha	12	S	Y	Y	Guam	Y	None
19		33	36	Salas, Carmen A	Daughter	F	Cha	10	S	Y	Y	Guam		None
20		33	36	Salas, Guilliermo A	Son	M	Cha	7	S	Y		Guam		None
21		33	36	Salas, Magdalena A	Daughter	F	Cha	4.5	S	N		Guam		None
22		33	36	Salas, Ana A	Daughter	F	Cha	1.3	S	N		Guam		None
23		33	37	Salas, Vicente A	Head	M	Cha	23	M	N	Y	Guam	Y	Clerk
24		33	37	Salas, Maria M	Wife	F	Cha	22	M	N	Y	Guam	Y	None
25		34	38	Cruz, Joaquin M	Head	M	Cha	36	M	N	N	Guam	N	Farm Laborer

DEPARTMENT OF COMMERCE-BUREAU OF THE CENSUS
WASHINGTON

FIFTEENTH CENSUS OF THE UNITED STATES: 1930-POPULATION

THE ISLAND OF GUAM

Sheet No. 5B

119B

District **Municipality of Agana**
Name of Place **Agana City (Anigua)**
[Proper name and, also, name of class, as city, town, village, barrio, etc]

Enumeration District No. **4**
Enumerated by me on **April 3, 1930** Vicente Tydingco, Enumerator

	PLACE OF ABODE			NAME	RELATION	PERSONAL DESCRIPTION				EDUCATION		NATIVITY		OCCUPATION
	Street, avenue, road, etc.	Number of dwelling house in order of visitation	Number of family in order of visitation	of each person whose place of abode on April 1, 1930, was in this family. Enter surname, first, then given name and middle initial. If any. Include every person living on April 1, 1930. Omit children born since April 1, 1930.	Relationship of this Person to the head of the family.	Sex	Color or race	Age at last birthday	Single, married, widowed or divorced	Attended school any time since Sept. 1, 1929	Whether able to read and write.	Place of birth of this person.	Whether able to speak English.	
	1	2	3	4	5	6	7	8	9	10	11	12	13	14
26	Agana Piti Road	34	38	Cruz, Maria S	Wife	F	Cha	38	M	N	N	Guam	N	None
27		34	38	Cruz, Joaquin S	Son	M	Cha	24	S	N	Y	Guam	Y	Teamster
28		34	38	Cruz, Regina S	Daughter	F	Cha	18	S	N	Y	Guam	N	None
29		34	38	Cruz, Antonia S	Daughter	F	Cha	14	S	Y	Y	Guam	Y	None
30		34	38	Cruz, Juan S	Son	M	Cha	9	S	Y		Guam		None
31		34	38	Cruz, Manuel S	Son	M	Cha	33	S	N		Guam		None
32		34	38	Cruz, Bernadita S	Daughter	F	Cha	.3	S	N		Guam		None
33		35	39	Salas, Ignacio N	Head	M	Cha	35	M	N	Y	Guam	Y	Chauffeur
34		35	39	Salas, Rosa T	Wife	F	Cha	34	M	N	Y	Guam	N	None
35		35	39	Salas, Jesus T	Son	M	Cha	2.3	S	N		Guam		None
36		35	39	Salas, Pedro T	Son	M	Cha	.3	S	N		Guam		None
37		35	39	Terlaje, Maria G	Mother in law	F	Cha	53	Wd	N	N	Guam	N	None
38		35	39	Terlaje, Antonia T	Sister in law	F	Cha	33	S	N	Y	Guam	N	None
39		35	39	Nauta, Francisco N	Cousin	M	Cha	30	S	N	Y	Guam	N	Farm Laborer
40		35	39	Guerrero, Manuel M	Nephew	M	Cha	11	S	Y	Y	Guam	Y	None
41		36	40	Muna, Jose C	Head	M	Cha	35	M	N	Y	Guam	Y	Farmer
42		36	40	Muna, Maria G	Wife	F	Cha	28	M	N	Y	Guam	Y	None
43		36	40	Muna, Flora G	Daughter	F	Cha	5.3	S	N		Guam		None
44		36	40	Muna, Genoveva G	Daughter	F	Cha	1.2	S	N		Guam		None
45		37	41	Namauleg, Maria T	Head	F	Cha	63	Wd	N	N	Guam	N	None
46		37	42	Cruz, Vicente LG	Head	M	Cha	30	M	N	Y	Guam	N	Farmer
47		37	42	Cruz, Eufracia N	Wife	F	Cha	27	M	N	Y	Guam	Y	None
48		38	43	Diaz, Antonio SN	Head	M	Cha	48	M	N	Y	Guam	N	Farm Laborer
49		38	43	Diaz, Ana G	Wife	F	Cha	46	M	N	Y	Guam	N	None
50		38	43	Diaz, Maria G	Daughter	F	Cha	20	S	N	Y	Guam	N	None

(CHAMORRO ROOTS GENEALOGY PROJECT™ TRANSCRIPTION)
(BERNARD T. PUNZALAN / HTTP://WWW.CHAMORROROOTS.COM)

DEPARTMENT OF COMMERCE-BUREAU OF THE CENSUS
WASHINGTON

FIFTEENTH CENSUS OF THE UNITED STATES: 1930-POPULATION

THE ISLAND OF GUAM

Sheet No. 6A

120

District **Municipality of Agana**
Name of Place **Agana City (Anigua)**
[Proper name and, also, name of class, as city, town, village, barrio, etc]

Enumeration District No. **4**
Enumerated by me on **April 3, 1930** Vicente Tydingco
Enumerator

	PLACE OF ABODE			NAME	RELATION	PERSONAL DESCRIPTION				EDUCATION		NATIVITY		OCCUPATION
	Street, avenue, road, etc.	Number of dwelling house in order of visitation	Number of family in order of visitation	of each person whose place of abode on April 1, 1930, was in this family. Enter surname, first, then given name and middle initial. If any. Include every person living on April 1, 1930. Omit children born since April 1, 1930.	Relationship of this Person to the head of the family.	Sex	Color or race	Age at last birthday	Single, married, widowed or divorced	Attended school any time since Sept. 1, 1929	Whether able to read and write.	Place of birth of this person.	Whether able to speak English.	
	1	2	3	4	5	6	7	8	9	10	11	12	13	14
1	Agana Piti Road	38	43	Diaz, Julia G	Daughter	F	Cha	12	S	Y	Y	Guam	Y	None
2		38	43	Diaz, Zacarias G	Son	M	Cha	10	S	Y		Guam		None
3		39	44	Roberto, Maria B	Head	F	Cha	30	S	N	Y	Guam	Y	Laundress
4		40	45	Gutierrez, Luis N	Head	M	Cha	60	M	N	Y	Guam	N	Farm Laborer
5		40	45	Gutierrez, Filomenia D	Wife	F	Cha	47	M	N	Y	Guam	N	None
6		40	45	Gutierrez, Tomasa D	Daughter	F	Cha	24	S	N	Y	Guam	Y	Cook
7		40	45	Gutierrez, Maria D	Daughter	F	Cha	20	S	N	Y	Guam	Y	None
8		40	45	Gutierrez, Ana D	Daughter	F	Cha	15	S	Y	Y	Guam	Y	None
9		40	45	Gutierrez, Felecita D	Daughter	F	Cha	13	S	Y	Y	Guam	Y	None
10		40	45	Gutierrez, Jose D	Son	M	Cha	12	S	Y	Y	Guam	Y	None
11		40	45	Gutierrez, Carlos D	Son	M	Cha	8	S	N	Y	Guam		None
12		41	46	Bautista, Luis P	Head	M	Cha	24	M	N	Y	Guam	Y	Clerk
13		41	46	Bautista, Rosa G	Wife	F	Cha	28	M	N	Y	Guam	N	None
14		41	46	Bautista, Alfonsina	Daughter	F	Cha	2.4	S	N		Guam		None
15		42	47	Flores, Julian L	Head	M	Cha	44	M	N	Y	Guam	N	Laborer
16		42	47	Flores, Rita L	Wife	F	Cha	36	M	N	Y	Guam	N	None
17		42	47	Flores, Gregorio L	Son	M	Cha	18	S	Y	Y	Guam	Y	None
18		42	47	Flores, Maria L	Daughter	F	Cha	17	S	N	Y	Guam	Y	None
19		42	47	Flores, Jesus L	Son	M	Cha	14	S	Y	Y	Guam	Y	None
20		42	47	Flores, Jose L	Son	M	Cha	13	S	Y	Y	Guam	Y	None
21		42	47	Flores, Joaquin L	Son	M	Cha	11	S	Y	Y	Guam	Y	None
22		42	47	Flores, George L	Son	M	Cha	5	S	N		Guam		None
23		42	47	Flores, Beatris L	Daughter	F	Cha	3.2	S	N		Guam		None
24		42	47	Flores, Lorenzo L	Son	M	Cha	1.3	S	N		Guam		None
25		43	48	Tuncap, Joaquin N	Head	M	Fil	39	M	N	Y	Guam	Y	Laborer

(CHAMORRO ROOTS GENEALOGY PROJECT™ TRANSCRIPTION)
(BERNARD T. PUNZALAN / HTTP://WWW.CHAMORROROOTS.COM)

DEPARTMENT OF COMMERCE-BUREAU OF THE CENSUS
WASHINGTON

FIFTEENTH CENSUS OF THE UNITED STATES: 1930-POPULATION

THE ISLAND OF GUAM

Sheet No. 6B

120B

District **Municipality of Agana**
Name of Place **Agana City (Anigua)**
[Proper name and, also, name of class, as city, town, village, barrio, etc]

Enumeration District No. 4
Enumerated by me on **April 3, 1930** Vicente Tydingco, Enumerator

	PLACE OF ABODE			NAME	RELATION	PERSONAL DESCRIPTION				EDUCATION		NATIVITY		OCCUPATION
	Street, avenue, road, etc.	Number of dwelling house in order of visitation	Number of family in order of visitation	of each person whose place of abode on April 1, 1930, was in this family. Enter surname, first, then given name and middle initial. If any. Include every person living on April 1, 1930. Omit children born since April 1, 1930.	Relationship of this Person to the head of the family.	Sex	Color or race	Age at last birthday	Single, married, widowed or divorced	Attended school any time since Sept. 1, 1929	Whether able to read and write.	Place of birth of this person.	Whether able to speak English.	
	1	2	3	4	5	6	7	8	9	10	11	12	13	14
26	Agana Piti Road	43	48	Tuncap, Caridad P	Wife	F	Cha	42	M	N	Y	Guam	N	None
27		43	48	Tuncap, Jose P	Son	M	Fil	22	S	N	Y	Guam	Y	Teamster
28		43	48	Tuncap, Gonzalo P	Son	M	Fil	15	S	Y	Y	Guam	Y	None
29		43	48	Tuncap, Manuel P	Son	M	Fil	14	S	Y	Y	Guam	Y	None
30		43	48	Tuncap, Maria P	Daughter	F	Fil	1	S	Y		Guam		None
31		44	49	Cruz, Manuel A	Head	M	Cha	63	M	N	Y	Guam	N	Net weaver
32		44	49	Cruz, Ana M	Wife	F	Cha	65	M	N	N	Guam	N	None
33		44	49	Cruz, Maria M	Daughter	F	Cha	27	S	N	Y	Guam	N	None
34		44	49	Cruz, Jesus M	Son	M	Cha	23	S	N	Y	Guam	Y	Farm Laborer
35		45	50	Tenorio, Rosa G	Head	F	Cha	36	Wd	N	N	Guam	N	None
36		45	50	Tenorio, Amanda G	Daughter	F	Cha	24	S	N	N	Guam	N	Laundress
37		45	50	Tenorio, Rita G	Daughter	F	Cha	22	S	N	Y	Guam	Y	Laundress
38		45	50	Tenorio, Encarnacion G	Daughter	F	Cha	20	S	N	Y	Guam	Y	Laundress
39		45	50	Tenorio, Jose G	Son	M	Cha	18	S	Y	Y	Guam	Y	None
40		45	50	Tenorio, Juan G	Son	M	Cha	14	S	Y	Y	Guam	Y	None
41		45	50	Tenorio, Joaquin G	Son	M	Cha	7	S	Y		Guam		None
42		45	50	Tenorio, Enrique G	Son	M	Cha	3.3	S	N		Guam		None
43		45	50	Tenorio, Jesus T	Grandson	M	Cha	4.3	S	N		Guam		None
44		45	50	Tenorio, Francisco T	Grandson	M	Cha	2.9	S	N		Guam		None
45		45	50	Tenorio, Atanacio T	Grandson	M	Cha	.4	S	N		Guam		None
46		46	51	Lizama, Caridad L	Head	F	Cha	40	S	N	N	Guam	N	Laundress
47		46	51	Lizama, Vicente L	Son	M	Cha	27	S	N	N	Guam	Y	Farmer
48		46	51	Lizama, Emilia L	Daughter	F	Cha	15	S	N	Y	Guam	Y	Servant
49		46	51	Lizama, Maria M	Aunt	F	Cha	72	S	N	N	Guam	N	None
50		46	52	Lizama, Felix L	Head	M	Cha	40	M	N	Y	Guam	N	Rigger

DEPARTMENT OF COMMERCE-BUREAU OF THE CENSUS
WASHINGTON

FIFTEENTH CENSUS OF THE UNITED STATES: 1930-POPULATION

THE ISLAND OF GUAM

Sheet No. 7A

District Municipality of Agana
Name of Place Agana City (Anigua) [Proper name and, also, name of class, as city, town, village, barrio, etc]

Enumeration District No. 4
Enumerated by me on April 3, 1930 Vicente Tydingco, Enumerator

	PLACE OF ABODE: Street, avenue, road, etc.	Number of dwelling house in order of visitation	Number of family in order of visitation	NAME of each person whose place of abode on April 1, 1930, was in this family. Enter surname, first, then given name and middle initial. If any. Include every person living on April 1, 1930. Omit children born since April 1, 1930.	RELATION Relationship of this Person to the head of the family.	PERSONAL DESCRIPTION: Sex	Color or race	Age at last birthday	Single, married, widowed or divorced	EDUCATION: Attended school any time since Sept. 1, 1929	Whether able to read and write.	NATIVITY Place of birth of this person.	Whether able to speak English.	OCCUPATION
	1	2	3	4	5	6	7	8	9	10	11	12	13	14
1	Agana Piti Road	46	52	Lizama, Maria A	Wife	F	Cha	50	M	N	Y	Guam	N	None
2		46	52	Lizama, Jose A	Son	M	Cha	13	S	Y	Y	Guam	Y	None
3		46	52	Lizama, Francisco A	Son	M	Cha	10	S	Y	Y	Guam		None
4		46	52	Lizama, Luis A	Son	M	Cha	8	S	Y		Guam		None
5		46	52	Lizama, Juan A	Son	M	Cha	4.2	S	N		Guam		None
6		46	52	Lizama, Tomas A	Son	M	Cha	1.5	S	N		Guam		None
7		46	53	Cruz, Maria B	Head	F	Cha	25	S	N	Y	Guam	Y	Laundress
8		46	53	Cruz, Gregorio B	Brother	M	Cha	14	S	Y	Y	Guam	Y	None
9		47	54	Gutierrez, Juan D	Head	M	Cha	37	M	N	Y	Guam	Y	Laborer
10		47	54	Gutierrez, Maria P	Wife	F	Cha	27	M	N	Y	Guam		None
11		47	54	Gutierrez, Atanacio P	Son	M	Cha	.8	S	N		Guam		None
12		48	55	Gutierrez, Rosa D	Head	F	Cha	51	Wd	N	N	Guam	N	None
13		48	55	Gutierrez, Jose	Son	M	Cha	30	S	N	Y	Guam	Y	Farmer
14		48	55	Gutierrez, Soledad	Daughter	F	Cha	18	S	N	Y	Guam	Y	None
15		48	55	Gutierrez, Leonila	Daughter	F	Cha	14	S	Y	Y	Guam	Y	None
16		49	56	Sakakibara, Concepcion P	Head	F	Cha	30	D	N	Y	Guam	Y	Seamstress
17		49	56	Sakakibara, Florence P	Daughter	F	Jap	11	S	Y	Y	Tokyo, Japan	Y	None
18		49	56	Sakakibara, Frank P	Son	M	Jap	8	S	Y		Guam		None
19		49	56	Sakakibara, June P	Daughter	F	Jap	6	S	Y		Guam		None
20		49	56	Sakakibara, Carmen P	Daughter	F	Jap	5	S	N		Guam		None
21		49	56	Sakakibara, Millan P	Son	M	Jap	3.4	S	N		Guam		None
22		49	56	Sakakibara, Benjamin P	Son	M	Jap	1.9	S	N		Guam		None
23		50	57	Angoco, Pedro A	Head	M	Cha	41	M	N	Y	Guam	N	Farmer
24		50	57	Angoco, Manuela M	Wife	F	Cha	40	M	N	N	Guam	N	None
25		50	57	Angoco, Ana M	Daughter	F	Cha	6	S	N		Guam		None

DEPARTMENT OF COMMERCE-BUREAU OF THE CENSUS
WASHINGTON

FIFTEENTH CENSUS OF THE UNITED STATES: 1930-POPULATION

THE ISLAND OF GUAM

Sheet No. 7B

121B

District **Municipality of Agana**
Name of Place **Agana City (Anigua)**
[Proper name and, also, name of class, as city, town, village, barrio, etc]

Enumeration District No. 4
Enumerated by me on **April 3, 1930** Vicente Tydingco
Enumerator

	PLACE OF ABODE			NAME	RELATION	PERSONAL DESCRIPTION				EDUCATION		NATIVITY		OCCUPATION
	Street, avenue, road, etc.	Number of dwelling house is order of visitation	Number of family in order of visitation	of each person whose place of abode on April 1, 1930, was in this family. Enter surname, first, then given name and middle initial. If any. Include every person living on April 1, 1930. Omit children born since April 1, 1930.	Relationship of this Person to the head of the family.	Sex	Color or race	Age at last birthday	Single, married, widowed or divorced	Attended school any time since Sept. 1, 1929	Whether able to read and write.	Place of birth of this person.	Whether able to speak English.	
	1	2	3	4	5	6	7	8	9	10	11	12	13	14
26	Agana Piti Road	50	57	Angoco, Jose M	Son	M	Cha	4.3	S	N		Guam		None
27		50	57	Angoco, Vicente M	Son	M	Cha	2.3	S	N		Guam		None
28		51	58	San Nicolas, Pedro C	Head	M	Cha	37	M	N	Y	Guam	Y	Rigger
29		51	58	San Nicolas, Magdalena B	Wife	F	Cha	37	M	N	Y	Guam	N	None
30		52	59	Perez, Pedro LG	Head	M	Cha	44	M	N	Y	Guam	Y	Carpenter
31		52	59	Perez, Ana A	Wife	F	Cha	40	M	N	Y	Guam	N	None
32		52	59	Perez, Rosa A	Daughter	F	Cha	15	S	Y	Y	Guam	Y	None
33		52	59	Perez, Joaquin A	Son	M	Cha	14	S	Y	Y	Guam	Y	None
34		52	59	Perez, Maria A	Daughter	F	Cha	12	S	Y	Y	Guam	Y	None
35		52	59	Perez, Francisco A	Son	M	Cha	10	S	Y	Y	Guam		None
36		52	59	Perez, Emaculada A	Daughter	F	Cha	8	S	Y		Guam		None
37		52	59	Perez, Rosario A	Daughter	F	Cha	6	S	N		Guam		None
38		52	59	Perez, Pedro A	Son	M	Cha	5	S	N		Guam		None
39		52	59	Perez, Julia A	Daughter	F	Cha	3.2	S	N		Guam		None
40		52	59	Perez, Manuel A	Son	M	Cha	.5	S	N		Guam		None
41		52	59	Angoco, Ana G	Wife's sister	G	Cha	63	Wd	N	Y	Guam	N	None
42		53	60	Blas, Joaquin B	Head	M	Cha	52	M	N	Y	Guam	N	Farmer
43		53	60	Blas, Catalina A	Wife	F	Cha	50	M	N	N	Guam	N	None
44		53	60	Cruz, Antonia A	Niece	F	Cha	5	S	N		Guam		None
45		53	61	Blas, Jose A	Head	M	Cha	26	M	N	Y	Saipan	Y	Laborer
46		53	61	Blas, Rosalia A	Wife	F	Cha	29	M	N	N	Guam	Y	None
47		54	62	Blas, Jesus A	Head	M	Cha	28	M	N	Y	Guam	Y	Laborer
48		54	62	Blas, Maria M	Wife	F	Cha	20	M	N	Y	Guam	Y	None
49		55	63	Towner, William H	Head	M	W	54	M	N	Y	Cleveland, Ohio	Y	Machinist
50		55	63	Towner, Emilia L	Wife	F	Cha	48	M	N	Y	Guam	Y	None

DEPARTMENT OF COMMERCE-BUREAU OF THE CENSUS
WASHINGTON
FIFTEENTH CENSUS OF THE UNITED STATES: 1930-POPULATION

THE ISLAND OF GUAM

Sheet No. 8A

District **Municipality of Agana**
Name of Place **Agana City (Anigua)**
[Proper name and, also, name of class, as city, town, village, barrio, etc]

Enumeration District No. **4**
Enumerated by me on **April 4, 1930** Vicente Tydingco, Enumerator

	PLACE OF ABODE			NAME	RELATION	PERSONAL DESCRIPTION				EDUCATION		NATIVITY		OCCUPATION
	Street, avenue, road, etc.	Number of dwelling house is order of visitation	Number of family in order of visitation	of each person whose place of abode on April 1, 1930, was in this family. Enter surname, first, then given name and middle initial. If any. Include every person living on April 1, 1930. Omit children born since April 1, 1930.	Relationship of this Person to the head of the family.	Sex	Color or race	Age at last birthday	Single, married, widowed or divorced	Attended school any time since Sept. 1, 1929	Whether able to read and write.	Place of birth of this person.	Whether able to speak English.	
	1	2	3	4	5	6	7	8	9	10	11	12	13	14
1	Agana Piti Road	55	63	Towner, William A	Son	M	W	17	S	Y	Y	Guam	Y	Machinist
2		56	64	Nelson, Peter M	Head	M	W	50	Wd	N	Y	Brooklyn, New York	Y	Clerk
3		56	64	Nelson, Henry	Son	M	W	24	S	N	Y	Guam	Y	Farmer
4		56	64	Nelson, Peter M	Son	M	W	21	S	N	Y	Guam	Y	Machinist
5		56	64	Nelson, Catherine C	Daughter	F	W	18	S	Y	Y	Guam	Y	None
6		56	64	Nelson, Florence	Daughter	F	W	17	S	Y	Y	Guam	Y	None
7		56	64	Flores, Maria A	Wife's Aunt	F	Cha	68	S	N	Y	Guam	Y	None
8		57	65	Siguenza, Felix N	Head	M	Cha	32	M	N	Y	Guam	N	Laborer
9		57	65	Siguenza, Soledad D	Wife	F	Cha	30	M	N	Y	Guam	N	None
10		58	66	Angoco, Joaquin T	Head	M	Cha	47	M	N	Y	Guam	N	Farmer
11		58	66	Angoco, Rosa T	Wife	F	Cha	49	M	N	Y	Guam	N	None
12		58	66	Concepcion, Susana A	Niece	F	Cha	12	S	Y	Y	Guam	Y	None
13		58	66	Concepcion, Dolores A	Niece	F	Cha	10	S	Y		Guam		None
14		58	66	Chargualaf, Gregorio C	Nephew	M	Cha	9	S	Y		Guam		None
15		58	67	Angoco, Juan T	Head	M	Cha	23	M	N	Y	Guam	Y	Janitor
16		58	67	Angoco, Ana T	Wife	F	Cha	22	M	N	Y	Guam	Y	None
17		58	67	Angoco, Concepcion T	Daughter	F	Cha	3.3	S	N		Guam		None
18		58	67	Angoco, Joaquin T	Son	M	Cha	1.3	S			Guam		None
19		59	68	Angoco, Ramona D	Head	F	Cha	56	Wd	N	N	Guam	N	Laundress
20		59	68	Angoco, Dolores D	Daughter	F	Cha	22	S	N	Y	Guam	Y	Laundress
21		59	68	Angoco, Vicenta D	Daughter	F	Cha	21	S	N	Y	Guam	Y	Laundress
22		59	68	Angoco, Santiago D	Son	M	Cha	18	S	N	Y	Guam	Y	Farmer
23		59	68	Angoco, Jesus D	Son	M	Cha	15	S	Y	Y	Guam	Y	None
24		60	69	Angoco, Manuel D	Head	M	Cha	29	M	N	Y	Guam	Y	Laborer
25		60	69	Angoco, Teresa S	Wife	F	Cha	23	M	N	N	Guam	N	None

DEPARTMENT OF COMMERCE-BUREAU OF THE CENSUS
WASHINGTON

FIFTEENTH CENSUS OF THE UNITED STATES: 1930-POPULATION

THE ISLAND OF GUAM

Sheet No. 8B

122B

District **Municipality of Agana**
Name of Place **Agana City (Anigua)**
[Proper name and, also, name of class, as city, town, village, barrio, etc]

Enumeration District No. 4
Enumerated by me on **April 4, 1930** Vicente Tydingco
Enumerator

	PLACE OF ABODE			NAME	RELATION	PERSONAL DESCRIPTION				EDUCATION		NATIVITY		OCCUPATION
	Street, avenue, road, etc.	Number of dwelling house is order of visitation	Number of family in order of visitation	of each person whose place of abode on April 1, 1930, was in this family. Enter surname, first, then given name and middle initial. If any. Include every person living on April 1, 1930. Omit children born since April 1, 1930.	Relationship of this Person to the head of the family.	Sex	Color or race	Age at last birthday	Single, married, widowed or divorced	Attended school any time since Sept. 1, 1929	Whether able to read and write.	Place of birth of this person.	Whether able to speak English.	
	1	2	3	4	5	6	7	8	9	10	11	12	13	14
26	Agana Piti Road	60	69	Angoco, Librada S	Daughter	F	Cha	4.3	S	N		Guam		None
27		60	69	Angoco, Dionicia S	Daughter	F	Cha	3.3	S	N		Guam		None
28		60	69	Angoco, Felix S	Son	M	Cha	2.4	S	N		Guam		None
29		60	69	Angoco, Maria S	Daughter	F	Cha	.3	S	N		Guam		None
30		61	70	Taijeron, Silvano T	Head	M	Cha	30	D	N	Y	Guam	Y	Laborer
31		61	70	Taijeron, Rufina Q	Daughter	F	Cha	5	S	N		Guam		None
32		62	71	Cruz, Vicente A	Head	M	Cha	65	M	N	Y	Guam	Y	Farmer
33		62	71	Cruz, Josefa U	Wife	F	Cha	65	M	N	Y	Guam	N	None
34		62	71	Lazaro, Juan U	Nephew	M	Cha	24	S	N	Y	Guam	Y	Carpenter
35		62	71	Leon Guerrero, Ana C	Granddaughter	F	Cha	13	S	N	Y	Guam	N	None
36		62	71	Leon Guerrero, Remedios C	Granddaughter	F	Cha	12	S	N	Y	Guam	Y	None
37		62	72	Martinez, Remedios C	Head	F	Cha	36	Wd	N	Y	Guam	N	Laundress
38		62	72	Martinez, Angelina C	Daughter	F	Cha	13	S	N	Y	Guam	Y	None
39		62	72	Martinez, Fidel C	Son	M	Cha	6	S	N		Guam		None
40		62	72	Martinez, Jose C	Son	M	Cha	4.8	S	N		Guam		None
41		62	72	Martinez, Julia C	Daughter	F	Cha	1.2	S	N		Guam		None
42		63	73	Lujan, Jose P	Head	M	Cha	39	M	N	Y	Guam	Y	Carpenter
43		63	73	Lujan, Dolores C	Wife	F	Cha	37	M	N	Y	Guam	Y	None
44		63	73	Lujan, Salvador C	Son	M	Cha	10	S	Y		Guam		None
45		63	73	Lujan, Gregorio C	Son	M	Cha	9	S	Y		Guam		None
46		63	73	Lujan, Ana C	Daughter	F	Cha	8	S	Y		Guam		None
47		63	73	Lujan, Rosario C	Daughter	F	Cha	6	S	N		Guam		None
48		63	73	Lujan, Luisa C	Daughter	F	Cha	5	S	N		Guam		None
49		63	73	Lujan, Vicente C	Son	M	Cha	3.1	S	N		Guam		None
50		63	73	Lujan, Jose C	Son	M	Cha	1.3	S	N		Guam		None

(CHAMORRO ROOTS GENEALOGY PROJECT™ TRANSCRIPTION)
(BERNARD T. PUNZALAN / HTTP://WWW.CHAMORROROOTS.COM)

DEPARTMENT OF COMMERCE-BUREAU OF THE CENSUS
WASHINGTON

FIFTEENTH CENSUS OF THE UNITED STATES: 1930-POPULATION

THE ISLAND OF GUAM

Sheet No. 9A

District **Municipality of Agana**
Name of Place **Agana City (Anigua)**
[Proper name and, also, name of class, as city, town, village, barrio, etc]

Enumeration District No. **4**
Enumerated by me on **April 4, 1930** Vicente Tydingco, Enumerator

	PLACE OF ABODE			NAME	RELATION	PERSONAL DESCRIPTION				EDUCATION		NATIVITY		OCCUPATION
	Street, avenue, road, etc.	Number of dwelling house in order of visitation	Number of family in order of visitation	of each person whose place of abode on April 1, 1930, was in this family. Enter surname, first, then given name and middle initial. If any. Include every person living on April 1, 1930. Omit children born since April 1, 1930.	Relationship of this Person to the head of the family.	Sex	Color or race	Age at last birthday	Single, married, widowed or divorced	Attended school any time since Sept. 1, 1929	Whether able to read and write.	Place of birth of this person.	Whether able to speak English.	
	1	2	3	4	5	6	7	8	9	10	11	12	13	14
1	Agana Piti Road	64	74	Pangelinan, Francisco D	Head	M	Cha	40	M	N	Y	Guam	Y	Carpenter
2		64	74	Pangelinan, Natividad L	Wife	F	Cha	34	M	N	Y	Guam	Y	None
3		64	74	Pangelinan, Doroteo L	Son	M	Cha	9	S	Y		Guam		None
4		64	74	Pangelinan, Juan L	Son	M	Cha	8	S	Y		Guam		None
5		64	74	Pangelinan, Salvador L	Son	M	Cha	7	S	Y		Guam		None
6		64	74	Pangelinan, Serafina L	Daughter	F	Cha	4.6	S	N		Guam		None
7		64	74	Pangelinan, Maria L	Daughter	F	Cha	2.9	S	N		Guam		None
8		64	74	Pangelinan, Francisca L	Daughter	F	Cha	1.3	S	N		Guam		None
9		65	75	Cruz, Jose F	Head	M	Cha	42	M	N	Y	Guam	Y	Laborer
10		65	75	Cruz, Maria O	Wife	F	Cha	38	M	N	Y	Guam	N	None
11		65	75	Cruz, Dolores O	Daughter	F	Cha	14	S	Y	Y	Guam	Y	None
12		65	75	Cruz, Jose O	Son	M	Cha	10	S	Y		Guam		None
13		65	75	Cruz, Juan O	Son	M	Cha	7	S	Y		Guam		None
14		65	75	Cruz, Rosario O	Daughter	F	Cha	4.3	S	N		Guam		None
15		66	76	Rosa, Felipe R	Head	M	Cha	47	M	N	Y	Guam	Y	Farmer
16		66	76	Rosa, Josefa J	Wife	F	Cha	45	M	N	Y	Guam	N	None
17		66	76	Rosa, Teresa G	Niece	F	Cha	33	S	N	Y	Guam	N	None
18		66	76	Rosa, Emilio G	Nephew	M	Cha	35	S	N	Y	Guam	N	Farm Laborer
19		66	76	Rosa, Jose G	Nephew	M	Cha	7	S	Y		Guam		None
20		67	77	Fegurgur, Enrique F	Head	M	Cha	39	M	N	Y	Guam	Y	Farmer
21		67	77	Fegurgur, Rita J	Wife	F	Cha	31	M	N	Y	Guam	Y	None
22		67	77	Fegurgur, Rosalia J	Daughter	F	Cha	8	S	Y		Guam		None
23		67	77	Fegurgur, Francisco J	Son	M	Cha	.5	S	N		Guam		None
24		68	78	Gumataotao, Eulogio E	Head	M	Cha	27	M	N	Y	Guam	Y	Clerk
25		68	78	Gumataotao, Maria P	Wife	F	Cha	19	M	N	Y	Guam	Y	None

(CHAMORRO ROOTS GENEALOGY PROJECT™ TRANSCRIPTION)
(BERNARD T. PUNZALAN / HTTP://WWW.CHAMORROROOTS.COM)

DEPARTMENT OF COMMERCE-BUREAU OF THE CENSUS
WASHINGTON

FIFTEENTH CENSUS OF THE UNITED STATES: 1930-POPULATION

THE ISLAND OF GUAM

Sheet No. 9B

123B

District **Municipality of Agana**
Name of Place **Agana City (Anigua)**
[Proper name and, also, name of class, as city, town, village, barrio, etc]

Enumeration District No. 4
Enumerated by me on **April 4, 1930** Vicente Tydingco
Enumerator

	PLACE OF ABODE			NAME	RELATION	PERSONAL DESCRIPTION				EDUCATION		NATIVITY		OCCUPATION
	Street, avenue, road, etc.	Number of dwelling house in order of visitation	Number of family in order of visitation	of each person whose place of abode on April 1, 1930, was in this family. Enter surname, first, then given name and middle initial. If any. Include every person living on April 1, 1930. Omit children born since April 1, 1930.	Relationship of this Person to the head of the family.	Sex	Color or race	Age at last birthday	Single, married, widowed or divorced	Attended school any time since Sept. 1, 1929	Whether able to read and write.	Place of birth of this person.	Whether able to speak English.	
	1	2	3	4	5	6	7	8	9	10	11	12	13	14
26	Agana Piti Road	69	79	Gumataotao, Manuela G	Head	F	Cha	57	Wd	N	Y	Guam	N	None
27		69	79	Gumataotao, Teresa G	Daughter	F	Cha	30	S	N	Y	Guam	Y	None
28		69	79	Gumataotao, Fermin G	Son	M	Cha	22	S	N	Y	Guam	Y	Clerk
29		70	80	Gumataotao, Francisco G	Head	M	Cha	28	M	N	Y	Guam	Y	Typist
30		70	80	Gumataotao, Maria I	Wife	F	Cha	24	M	N	Y	Guam	Y	None
31		70	80	Gumataotao, Guadalupe I	Daughter	F	Cha	4.3	S	N		Guam		None
32		70	80	Gumataotao, Felix I	Son	M	Cha	3.2	S	N		Guam		None
33		70	80	Gumataotao, Carlos I	Son	M	Cha	1.4	S	N		Guam		None
34		70	80	Gumataotao, Dolores I	Daughter	F	Cha	.3	S	N		Guam		None
35		71	80	Gumataotao, Paciano D	Head	M	Cha	26	M	N	Y	Guam	Y	Chauffeur
36		71	80	Gumataotao, Ignacia C	Wife	F	Cha	19	M	N	Y	Saipan	Y	None
37		72	82	Torres, Vicente N	Head	M	Cha	48	M	N	Y	Guam	N	Laborer
38		72	82	Torres, Juana M	Wife	F	Cha	48	M	N	N	Guam	N	None
39		72	82	Torres, Delfina M	Daughter	F	Cha	15	S	N	Y	Guam	Y	Servant
40		72	82	Torres, Juan M	Son	M	Cha	13	S	Y	Y	Guam	Y	None
41		72	82	Torres, Jose M	Son	N	Cha	11	S	Y	Y	Guam		None
42		72	82	Torres, Francisco M	Son	M	Cha	8	S	Y		Guam		None
43		72	82	Torres, Tomas M	Son	M	Cha	6	S	Y		Guam		None
44		73	83	Parker, Nance	Head	F	W	36	M	N	Y	New Castle, England	Y	Teacher
45		73	83	Parker, Edith M	Daughter	F	W	15	S	N	Y	?, Pennsylvania	Y	None
46		73	83	Parker, Dorothy C	Daughter	F	W	6	S	Y	Y	Washington DC		None
47		73	83	Parker, Joan I	Daughter	F	W	3.9	S	N		Guam		None
48		73	83	Parker, Patricia A	Daughter	F	W	2.4	S	N		Guam		None
49		73	83	Taitano, Amparo M	Servant	F	Cha	24	S	N	Y	Guam	Y	Cook
50		74	84	Aflague, Alfonso C	Head	M	Cha	45	Wd	N	Y	Guam	N	Farmer

(CHAMORRO ROOTS GENEALOGY PROJECT™ TRANSCRIPTION)
(BERNARD T. PUNZALAN / HTTP://WWW.CHAMORROROOTS.COM)

DEPARTMENT OF COMMERCE-BUREAU OF THE CENSUS
WASHINGTON

FIFTEENTH CENSUS OF THE UNITED STATES: 1930-POPULATION

THE ISLAND OF GUAM

Sheet No. 10A

124

District **Municipality of Agana**
Name of Place **Agana City (Anigua)**
[Proper name and, also, name of class, as city, town, village, barrio, etc]

Enumeration District No. 4
Enumerated by me on April 4, 1930 Vicente Tydingco, Enumerator

	PLACE OF ABODE			NAME	RELATION	PERSONAL DESCRIPTION				EDUCATION		NATIVITY	Whether able to speak English.	OCCUPATION
	Street, avenue, road, etc.	Number of dwelling house in order of visitation	Number of family in order of visitation	of each person whose place of abode on April 1, 1930, was in this family. Enter surname, first, then given name and middle initial. If any. Include every person living on April 1, 1930. Omit children born since April 1, 1930.	Relationship of this Person to the head of the family.	Sex	Color or race	Age at last birthday	Single, married, widowed or divorced	Attended school any time since Sept. 1, 1929	Whether able to read and write.	Place of birth of this person.		
	1	2	3	4	5	6	7	8	9	10	11	12	13	14
1	Agana Piti Road	74	84	Aflague, Francisco T	Son	M	Cha	21	S	N	Y	Guam	Y	Cook
2		74	84	Taijeron, Antonia S	Servant	F	Cha	33	S	N	N	Guam	N	Cook
3		75	85	Muna, Vicente F	Head	M	Cha	29	M	N	Y	Guam	Y	Rigger
4		75	85	Muna, Maria C	Wife	F	Cha	28	M	N	Y	Guam	Y	None
5		75	85	San Nicolas, Juan C	Brother in law	M	Cha	19	S	N	Y	Guam	Y	Servant
6		75	86	San Nicolas, Vicente C	Head	M	Cha	24	M	N	Y	Guam	Y	Servant
7		75	86	San Nicolas, Maria C	Wife	F	Cha	28	M	N	Y	Guam	Y	None
8		75	86	San Nicolas, Barbara C	Daughter	F	Cha	.3	S	N		Guam		None
9		76	87	Cruz, Mariano A	Head	M	Cha	40	M	N	Y	Guam	N	Rigger
10		76	87	Cruz, Luisa T	Wife	F	Cha	34	M	N	Y	Guam	N	None
11		76	87	Cruz, Tomas T	Son	M	Cha	16	S	Y	Y	Guam	Y	Farm Laborer
12		76	87	Cruz, Ignacio T	Son	M	Cha	12	S	Y	Y	Guam	Y	None
13		76	87	Cruz, Francisco T	Son	M	Cha	8	S	Y		Guam		None
14		76	87	Cruz, Jose T	Son	M	Cha	7	S	Y		Guam		None
15		76	87	Cruz, Antonio T	Son	M	Cha	6	S	N		Guam		None
16		76	87	Cruz, Leonora T	Daughter	F	Cha	2.7	S	N		Guam		None
17		76	87	Cruz, Juan T	Son	M	Cha	.8	S	N		Guam		None
18		77	88	Leon Guerrero, Faustino C	Head	M	Cha	50	M	N	Y	Guam	N	Farmer
19		77	88	Leon Guerrero, Maria C	Wife	F	Cha	53	M	N	Y	Guam	N	None
20		77	88	Leon Guerrero, Juan C	Son	M	Cha	26	S	N	Y	Guam	Y	Lumberman
21		77	88	Leon Guerrero, Ana C	Daughter	F	Cha	19	S	N	Y	Guam	Y	Servant
22		77	88	Leon Guerrero, Vicente C	Son	M	Cha	17	S	N	Y	Guam	Y	Farm Laborer
23		77	88	Leon Guerrero, Lourdes C	Daughter	F	Cha	15	S	Y	Y	Guam	Y	None
24		77	88	Leon Guerrero, Dolores C	Daughter	F	Cha	12	S	Y	Y	Guam		None
25		77	88	Leon Guerrero, Manuel C	Son	M	Cha	9	S	Y		Guam		None

DEPARTMENT OF COMMERCE-BUREAU OF THE CENSUS
WASHINGTON

FIFTEENTH CENSUS OF THE UNITED STATES: 1930-POPULATION

THE ISLAND OF GUAM

Sheet No. 10B

124B

District **Municipality of Agana**
Name of Place **Agana City (Anigua)**
[Proper name and, also, name of class, as city, town, village, barrio, etc]

Enumeration District No. 4
Enumerated by me on **April 4, 1930** Vicente Tydingco, Enumerator

	PLACE OF ABODE			NAME	RELATION	PERSONAL DESCRIPTION				EDUCATION		NATIVITY		OCCUPATION
	Street, avenue, road, etc.	Number of dwelling house in order of visitation	Number of family in order of visitation	of each person whose place of abode on April 1, 1930, was in this family. Enter surname, first, then given name and middle initial. If any. Include every person living on April 1, 1930. Omit children born since April 1, 1930.	Relationship of this Person to the head of the family.	Sex	Color or race	Age at last birthday	Single, married, widowed or divorced	Attended school any time since Sept. 1, 1929	Whether able to read and write.	Place of birth of this person.	Whether able to speak English.	
	1	2	3	4	5	6	7	8	9	10	11	12	13	14
26	Agana Piti Road	77	88	Leon Guerrero, Ignacio C	Son	M	Cha	6	S	N		Guam		None
27		78	89	Fejeran, Ramon C	Head	M	Cha	30	M	N	Y	Guam	Y	Machinist
28		78	89	Fejeran, Remedios C	Wife	F	Cha	28	M	N	Y	Guam	N	None
29		78	89	Fejeran, Juliana C	Daughter	F	Cha	2.5	S	N		Guam		None
30		79	90	Benito, Pedro R	Head	M	Fil	37	M	N	Y	Philippine Islands	Y	Bookkeeper
31		79	90	Benito, Beatrice P	Wife	F	Cha	25	M	N	Y	Guam	Y	None
32		79	90	Benito, Margarita P	Daughter	F	Fil	7.2	S	Y		Guam		None
33		79	90	Benito, Roy P	Son	M	Fil	5	S	N		Guam		None
34		79	90	Benito, Barbara P	Daughter	F	Fil	4.1	S	N		Guam		None
35		79	90	Benito, Joseph P	Son	M	Fil	.9	S	N		Guam		None
36		80	91	Ogo, Manuel G	Head	M	Cha	29	M	N	Y	Guam	Y	Chauffeur
37		80	91	Ogo, Rosa D	Wife	F	Cha	23	M	N	Y	Guam	Y	None
38		80	91	Ogo, Ulita D	Daughter	F	Cha	6	S	N		Guam		None
39		80	91	Ogo, Vicenta D	Daughter	F	Cha	1.3	S	N		Guam		None
40		81	92	Manibusan, Juan T	Head	M	Cha	53	M	N	Y	Guam	N	Farmer
41		81	92	Manibusan, Agueda C	Wife	F	Cha	51	M	N	N	Guam	N	None
42		81	92	Manibusan, Trinidad C	Daughter	F	Cha	23	S	N	Y	Guam	Y	None
43		81	92	Ignacio, Imperatris C	Grand daughter	F	Cha	12	S	Y	Y	Guam	Y	None
44		82	93	Quitugua, Juan C	Head	M	Cha	26	M	N	Y	Guam	Y	Machinist
45		82	93	Quitugua, Ana C	Wife	F	Cha	22	M	N	Y	Guam	Y	None
46		82	93	Quitugua, Vicente C	Son	M	Cha	2.9	S	N		Guam		None
47		82	93	Quitugua, Joaquin C	Son	M	Cha	.5	S	N		Guam		None
48		83	94	Day, Petronila U	Head	F	Fil	57	Wd	N	Y	Guam	Y	None
49		83	94	Lazaro, Antonia U	Niece	F	Fil	22	S	N	Y	Guam	Y	None
50		83	94	Lazaro, Ernesto U	Nephew	M	Fil	15	S	Y	Y	Guam	Y	None

(CHAMORRO ROOTS GENEALOGY PROJECT™ TRANSCRIPTION)
(BERNARD T. PUNZALAN / HTTP://WWW.CHAMORROROOTS.COM)

DEPARTMENT OF COMMERCE-BUREAU OF THE CENSUS
WASHINGTON

FIFTEENTH CENSUS OF THE UNITED STATES: 1930-POPULATION

THE ISLAND OF GUAM

Sheet No. 11A

District Municipality of Agana
Name of Place Agana City (Anigua)
[Proper name and, also, name of class, as city, town, village, barrio, etc]

Enumeration District No. 4
Enumerated by me on April 4, 1930 Vicente Tydingco
Enumerator

	PLACE OF ABODE			NAME	RELATION	PERSONAL DESCRIPTION				EDUCATION		NATIVITY		OCCUPATION
	Street, avenue, road, etc.	Number of dwelling house in order of visitation	Number of family in order of visitation	of each person whose place of abode on April 1, 1930, was in this family. Enter surname, first, then given name and middle initial. If any. Include every person living on April 1, 1930. Omit children born since April 1, 1930.	Relationship of this Person to the head of the family.	Sex	Color or race	Age at last birthday	Single, married, widowed or divorced	Attended school any time since Sept. 1, 1929	Whether able to read and write.	Place of birth of this person.	Whether able to speak English.	
	1	2	3	4	5	6	7	8	9	10	11	12	13	14
1	Agana Piti Road	83	95	Santos, Francisco M	Head	M	Cha	29	M	N	Y	Guam	Y	Dentist
2		83	95	Santos, Josefina D	Wife	F	Cha	26	M	N	Y	Guam	Y	None
3		83	95	Cruz, Nicolasa M	Servant	F	Cha	42	S	N	N	Guam	N	Cook
4		84	96	Untalan, Pedro C	Head	M	Cha	49	M	N	Y	Guam	Y	Farmer
5		84	96	Untalan, Rita LG	Wife	F	Cha	43	M	N	Y	Guam	Y	None
6		84	96	Untalan, Serafina LG	Daughter	F	Cha	20	S	N	Y	Guam	Y	None
7		84	96	Untalan, Guadalupe LG	Daughter	F	Cha	14	S	Y	Y	Guam	Y	None
8		84	96	Untalan, Antonia LG	Daughter	F	Cha	12	S	Y	Y	Guam	Y	None
9		84	96	Untalan, Jose LG	Son	M	Cha	9	S	Y		Guam		None
10		84	96	Untalan, Pedro LG	Son	M	Cha	6	S	Y		Guam		None
11		84	96	Leon Guerrero, Jose C	Nephew	M	Cha	26	S	N	Y	Guam	Y	Farm Laborer
12		84	97	Arroyo, Olivia U	Head	F	Cha	18	M	N	Y	Guam	Y	Teacher
13		85	98	Quitugua, Vicente Q	Head	M	Cha	45	M	N	Y	Guam	N	Carpenter
14		85	98	Quitugua, Natividad C	Wife	F	Cha	53	M	N	Y	Guam	N	None
15		85	98	Quitugua, Concepcion C	Daughter	F	Cha	15	S	N	Y	Guam	Y	None
16		85	98	Quitugua, Adela C	Daughter	F	Cha	14	S	Y	Y	Guam	Y	None
17		86	99	Alarm, Carmen D	Head	F	Cha	40	Wd	N	N	Guam	N	Laundress
18		86	99	Ahlam, Leon D	Son	M	Cha	21	S	N	Y	Guam	Y	None
19		86	99	Ahlam, Pilar D	Daughter	F	Cha	11	S	Y	Y	Guam	Y	None
20		86	99	Ahlam, Josefina D	Daughter	F	Cha	8	S	Y		Guam		None
21		86	99	Ahlam, Maria D	Daughter	F	Cha	3.3	S	N		Guam		None
22		86	99	Ahlam, Francisco D	Son	M	Cha	1.3	S	N		Guam		None
23		87	100	Materne, Mariano M	Head	M	Cha	48	M	N	Y	Guam	N	Machinist
24		87	100	Materne, Mariana P	Wife	F	Cha	51	M	N	Y	Guam	N	None
25		87	100	Materne, Joaquin P	Son	M	Cha	13	S	Y	Y	Guam	Y	None

(CHAMORRO ROOTS GENEALOGY PROJECT™ TRANSCRIPTION)
(BERNARD T. PUNZALAN / HTTP://WWW.CHAMORROROOTS.COM)

DEPARTMENT OF COMMERCE-BUREAU OF THE CENSUS
WASHINGTON

FIFTEENTH CENSUS OF THE UNITED STATES: 1930-POPULATION

THE ISLAND OF GUAM

Sheet No. 11B

125B

District **Municipality of Agana**
Name of Place **Agana City (Anigua)**
[Proper name and, also, name of class, as city, town, village, barrio, etc]

Enumeration District No. 4
Enumerated by me on **April 4, 1930** Vicente Tydingco
Enumerator

	PLACE OF ABODE			NAME	RELATION	PERSONAL DESCRIPTION				EDUCATION		NATIVITY		OCCUPATION
	Street, avenue, road, etc.	Number of dwelling house is order of visitation	Number of family in order of visitation	of each person whose place of abode on April 1, 1930, was in this family. Enter surname, first, then given name and middle initial. If any. Include every person living on April 1, 1930. Omit children born since April 1, 1930.	Relationship of this Person to the head of the family.	Sex	Color or race	Age at last birthday	Single, married, widowed or divorced	Attended school any time since Sept. 1, 1929	Whether able to read and write.	Place of birth of this person.	Whether able to speak English.	
	1	2	3	4	5	6	7	8	9	10	11	12	13	14
26	Agana Piti Road	87	100	Materne, Ana P	Daughter	F	Cha	10	S	Y	Y	Guam	Y	None
27		88	101	Pablo, Jose C	Head	M	Cha	31	M	N	Y	Guam	N	Rigger
28		88	101	Pablo, Concepcion M	Wife	F	Cha	29	M	N	Y	Guam	N	None
29		88	101	Pablo, Josefina M	Daughter	F	Cha	7	S	Y		Guam		None
30		88	101	Pablo, Jose M	Son	M	Cha	5	S	N		Guam		None
31		88	101	Pablo, Angustia M	Daughter	F	Cha	.7	S	N		Guam		None
32		88	101	Taitano, Nieves S	Sister in law	F	Cha	18	S	N	Y	Guam	N	Cook
33		89	102	Pablo, Felicidad A	Head	F	Cha	36	S	N	Y	Guam	Y	Servant
34		89	102	Pablo, Dolores A	Sister	F	Cha	14	S	Y	Y	Guam	Y	None
35		90	103	Cruz, Tomas C	Head	M	Cha	54	Wd	N	Y	Guam	N	Farmer
36		90	103	Cruz, Consalacion C	Daughter	F	Cha	13	S	Y	Y	Guam	Y	None
37		90	103	Cruz, Ana C	Sister	F	Cha	60	S	N	N	Guam	N	None
38		90	103	Cruz, Jose C	Brother	M	Cha	30	S	N	Y	Guam	N	Farm Laborer
39				Here ends the enumeration of enumeration district No. 4 (Anigua)										
40														
41														
42														
43														
44														
45														
46														
47														
48														
49														
50														

DEPARTMENT OF COMMERCE-BUREAU OF THE CENSUS
WASHINGTON

FIFTEENTH CENSUS OF THE UNITED STATES: 1930-POPULATION

THE ISLAND OF GUAM

Sheet No. 12A

District Municipality of Agana
Name of Place Agana City (Julale)
[Proper name and, also, name of class, as city, town, village, barrio, etc]

Enumeration District No. 4
Enumerated by me on April 5, 1930 Vicente Tydingco, Enumerator

	PLACE OF ABODE			NAME	RELATION	PERSONAL DESCRIPTION				EDUCATION		NATIVITY		OCCUPATION
	Street, avenue, road, etc.	Number of dwelling house is order of visitation	Number of family in order of visitation	of each person whose place of abode on April 1, 1930, was in this family. Enter surname, first, then given name and middle initial. If any. Include every person living on April 1, 1930. Omit children born since April 1, 1930.	Relationship of this Person to the head of the family.	Sex	Color or race	Age at last birthday	Single, married, widowed or divorced	Attended school any time since Sept. 1, 1929	Whether able to read and write.	Place of birth of this person.	Whether able to speak English.	
	1	2	3	4	5	6	7	8	9	10	11	12	13	14
1	Cristobal Colon Street	91	104	Cruz, Rita D	Head	F	Cha	56	Wd	N	Y	Guam	Y	None
2		91	104	Cruz, Joaquin D	Son	M	Cha	20	S	N	Y	Guam	Y	Laborer
3		92	105	Pablo, Jacinto A	Head	M	Cha	58	M	N	Y	Guam	N	Foreman
4		92	105	Pablo, Agueda D	Wife	F	Cha	29	M	N	Y	Guam	Y	None
5		92	105	Pablo, Juan D	Son	M	Cha	22	S	N	Y	Guam		Laborer
6		92	105	Pablo, Soledad D	Daughter	F	Cha	6	S	N		Guam		None
7		92	106	Cruz, Amable B	Head	F	Cha	29	D	N	Y	Guam	N	Cook
8		93	107	Dimapan, Mariano D	Head	M	Cha	58	Wd	N	Y	Guam	N	Fisherman
9		93	107	Dimapan, Ignacio A	Son	M	Cha	15	S	Y	Y	Guam	Y	None
10		94	108	Haller, Fred	Head	M	W	54	M	N	Y	Flag Staff, Arizona	Y	
11		94	108	Haller, Dolores U	Wife	F	Cha	48	M	N	Y	Guam	Y	None
12		94	108	Haller, Johnny F	Son	M	Cha	9	S	Y		Guam		None
13		94	108	Acosta, Antonia A	Servant	F	Cha	14	S	N	Y	Guam	Y	Servant
14		95	109	Concepcion, Juana P	Head	F	Cha	33	M	N	Y	Guam	Y	None
15		95	109	Mafnas, Manuel P	Uncle	M	Cha	66	S	N	Y	Guam	N	Farm Laborer
16		96	110	Torres, Vicente G	Head	M	Cha	54	Wd	N	Y	Guam	N	Farmer
17		96	110	Torres, Concepcion C	Daughter	F	Cha	22	S	N	Y	Guam	Y	None
18		96	110	Torres, Vicente C	Son	M	Cha	18	S	N	Y	Saipan	Y	Cook
19		96	110	Torres, Josefina C	Daughter	F	Cha	17	S	Y	Y	Guam	Y	None
20		96	110	Torres, Francisco C	Son	M	Cha	15	S	Y	Y	Guam	Y	None
21		96	110	Torres, Ignacia C	Daughter	F	Cha	9	S	Y		Guam		None
22		96	110	Torres, Tomas C	Son	M	Cha	8	S	Y		Guam		None
23		97	111	Mesa, Joaquin M	Head	M	Cha	24	M	N	Y	Guam	Y	Farmer
24		97	111	Mesa, Maria B	Wife	F	Cha	20	M	N	Y	Guam	Y	None
25		98	112	San Nicolas, Dolores T	Head	F	Cha	30	M	N	Y	Guam	Y	None

DEPARTMENT OF COMMERCE-BUREAU OF THE CENSUS
WASHINGTON

FIFTEENTH CENSUS OF THE UNITED STATES: 1930-POPULATION

THE ISLAND OF GUAM

Sheet No. 12B

District **Municipality of Agana**
Name of Place **Agana City (Julale)**
[Proper name and, also, name of class, as city, town, village, barrio, etc]

Enumeration District No. **4**
Enumerated by me on **April 5, 1930** **Vicente Tydingco**
Enumerator

	PLACE OF ABODE			NAME	RELATION	PERSONAL DESCRIPTION				EDUCATION		NATIVITY		OCCUPATION
	Street, avenue, road, etc.	Number of dwelling house is order of visitation	Number of family in order of visitation	of each person whose place of abode on April 1, 1930, was in this family. Enter surname, first, then given name and middle initial. If any. Include every person living on April 1, 1930. Omit children born since April 1, 1930.	Relationship of this Person to the head of the family.	Sex	Color or race	Age at last birthday	Single, married, widowed or divorced	Attended school any time since Sept. 1, 1929	Whether able to read and write.	Place of birth of this person.	Whether able to speak English.	
	1	2	3	4	5	6	7	8	9	10	11	12	13	14
26	Cristobal Colon Street	98	112	San Nicolas, Jose T	Son	M	Cha	8	S	Y		Guam		None
27		99	113	Concepcion, Ana C	Head	F	Cha	50	S	N	N	Guam	N	Washerwoman
28		99	113	Concepcion, Juan C	Son	M	Cha	25	S	N	Y	Guam	Y	Laborer
29		99	114	Mesa, Ignacio M	Head	M	Cha	56	M	N	Y	Guam	Y	Farmer
30		99	114	Mesa, Rosa T	Wife	F	Cha	45	M	N	Y	Guam	N	None
31		99	114	Mesa, Jose T	Son	M	Cha	10	S	Y		Guam		None
32		101	115	Concepcion, Teresa A	Head	F	Cha	30	M	N	Y	Guam	N	None
33		101	115	Concepcion, Juan A	Son	M	Cha	12	S	Y	Y	Guam	Y	None
34		101	115	Concepcion, Atanacio A	Son	M	Cha	10	S	Y	Y	Guam	Y	None
35		101	115	Concepcion, Guadalupe A	Daughter	F	Cha	8	S	Y		Guam		None
36		101	115	Concepcion, Pedro A	Son	M	Cha	7	S	N		Guam		None
37		101	115	Concepcion, Enrique A	Son	M	Cha	6	S	N		Guam		None
38		101	115	Concepcion, Felicita A	Daughter	F	Cha	2.8	S	N		Guam		None
39		102	116	Tolentino, Maximo L	Head	M	Fil	50	Wd	N	Y	Philippine Islands	Y	Laborer
40		102	116	Crisostimo, Dolores	Mother in law	F	Cha	82	Wd	N	Y	Guam		None
41		103	117	Mafnas, Jose C	Head	M	Cha	42	M	N	Y	Guam	N	Laborer
42		103	117	Mafnas, Rosa L	Wife	F	Cha	39	M	N	Y	Guam		None
43		103	117	Mafnas, Regina L	Daughter	F	Cha	15	S	N	Y	Guam		Servant
44		103	117	Mafnas, Francisco L	Son	M	Cha	13	S	Y	Y	Guam		None
45		103	117	Mafnas, Antonio L	Son	M	Cha	11	S	Y	Y	Guam		None
46		103	117	Mafnas, Ana L	Daughter	F	Cha	9	S	Y		Guam		None
47		103	117	Mafnas, Dolores L	Daughter	F	Cha	4.3	S	N		Guam		None
48		103	117	Mafnas, Tomasa L	Daughter	F	Cha	1.3	S	N		Guam		None
49		103	117	Mafnas, Vicenta C	Mother	F	Cha	69	Wd	N	N	Guam	N	None
50		104	118	Torres, Jose C	Head	M	Cha	34	Wd	N	Y	Guam	Y	Farmer

DEPARTMENT OF COMMERCE-BUREAU OF THE CENSUS
WASHINGTON

FIFTEENTH CENSUS OF THE UNITED STATES: 1930-POPULATION

THE ISLAND OF GUAM

Sheet No. 13A

District Municipality of Agana
Name of Place Agana City (Julale)
[Proper name and, also, name of class, as city, town, village, barrio, etc]

Enumeration District No. 4
Enumerated by me on April 5, 1930 Vicente Tydingco
Enumerator

	PLACE OF ABODE			NAME	RELATION	PERSONAL DESCRIPTION				EDUCATION		NATIVITY		OCCUPATION
	Street, avenue, road, etc.	Number of dwelling house in order of visitation	Number of family in order of visitation	of each person whose place of abode on April 1, 1930, was in this family. Enter surname, first, then given name and middle initial. If any. Include every person living on April 1, 1930. Omit children born since April 1, 1930.	Relationship of this Person to the head of the family.	Sex	Color or race	Age at last birthday	Single, married, widowed or divorced	Attended school any time since Sept. 1, 1929	Whether able to read and write.	Place of birth of this person.	Whether able to speak English.	
	1	2	3	4	5	6	7	8	9	10	11	12	13	14
1	Cristobal Colon Street	104	118	Torres, Jose C	Son	M	Cha	11	S	Y	Y	Guam	Y	None
2		104	118	Torres, Rosalia C	Daughter	F	Cha	9	S	Y	Y	Guam		None
3		104	118	Torres, Juan C	Son	M	Cha	7	S	Y		Guam		None
4		104	118	Torres, Ana C	Daughter	F	Cha	4.2	S	N		Guam		None
5		104	118	Torres, Julia C	Daughter	F	Cha	3.1	S	N		Guam		None
6		104	118	Torres, Vicente C	Son	M	Cha	.9	S	N		Guam		None
7		104	119	Santos, Antonia S	Head	F	Cha	53	S	N	N	Guam	N	None
8		104	119	Santos, Jesus S	Son	M	Cha	29	S	N	Y	Guam	N	Laborer
9		104	119	Santos, Joaquin S	Son	M	Cha	24	S	N	Y	Guam	N	Laborer
10		104	119	Santos, Manuel S	Son	M	Cha	22	S	N	Y	Guam	Y	Laborer
11		104	119	Santos, Ana S	Daughter	F	Cha	18	S	N	Y	Guam	Y	Servant
12		105	120	Toves, Rita G	Head	F	Cha	52	S	N	N	Guam	N	Laundress
13		105	120	Toves, Agueda T	Daughter	F	Cha	20	S	N	Y	Guam	Y	Servant
14		105	120	Toves, Jose T	Son	M	Cha	14	S	Y	Y	Guam	Y	None
15		106	121	Fejeran, Potenciana F	Head	F	Cha	32	S	N	Y	Guam	Y	Cook
16		106	121	Fejeran, Manuel F	Son	M	Cha	12	S	Y	Y	Guam	Y	None
17		106	121	Fejeran, Ramon F	Son	M	Cha	7	S	Y		Guam		None
18		107	122	Muna, Jose C	Head	M	Cha	54	M	N	Y	Guam	N	Farmer
19		107	122	Muna, Ana G	Wife	F	Cha	49	M	N	N	Guam	N	None
20		107	122	Muna, Ana G	Daughter	F	Cha	30	S	N	Y	Guam	N	None
21		107	122	Muna, Tomasa G	Daughter	F	Cha	23	S	N	N	Guam	N	None
22		107	122	Muna, Saturnina G	Daughter	F	Cha	22	S	N	Y	Guam	Y	Laundress
23		107	122	Muna, Vicenta C	Sister	F	Cha	50	S	N	Y	Guam	N	Laundress
24		108	123	Arnold, Frank L	Head	M	W	21	S	N	Y	Moscow, Idaho	Y	Radioman
25		108	124	Button, Bruce E	Head	M	W	27	S	N	Y	Tracy, California	Y	Radioman

(CHAMORRO ROOTS GENEALOGY PROJECT™ TRANSCRIPTION)
(BERNARD T. PUNZALAN / HTTP://WWW.CHAMORROROOTS.COM)

DEPARTMENT OF COMMERCE-BUREAU OF THE CENSUS
WASHINGTON

FIFTEENTH CENSUS OF THE UNITED STATES: 1930-POPULATION

THE ISLAND OF GUAM

Sheet No. 13B

127B

District **Municipality of Agana**
Name of Place **Agana City (Julale)**
[Proper name and, also, name of class, as city, town, village, barrio, etc]

Enumeration District No. 4
Enumerated by me on **April 7, 1930** Vicente Tydingco
Enumerator

	PLACE OF ABODE			NAME	RELATION	PERSONAL DESCRIPTION				EDUCATION		NATIVITY		OCCUPATION
	Street, avenue, road, etc.	Number of dwelling house is order of visitation	Number of family in order of visitation	of each person whose place of abode on April 1, 1930, was in this family. Enter surname, first, then given name and middle initial. If any. Include every person living on April 1, 1930. Omit children born since April 1, 1930.	Relationship of this Person to the head of the family.	Sex	Color or race	Age at last birthday	Single, married, widowed or divorced	Attended school any time since Sept. 1, 1929	Whether able to read and write.	Place of birth of this person.	Whether able to speak English.	
	1	2	3	4	5	6	7	8	9	10	11	12	13	14
26	Cristobal Colon Street	109	125	Cruz, Silviestre C	Head	M	Cha	46	M	N	Y	Guam	Y	Farmer
27		109	125	Cruz, Maria L	Wife	F	Cha	45	M	N	N	Guam	N	None
28		109	125	Cruz, Mariano L	Son	M	Cha	22	S	N	N	Guam	Y	Carpenter
29		109	125	Cruz, Concepcion L	Daughter	F	Cha	18	S	N	Y	Guam	Y	None
30		109	125	Cruz, Miguel L	Son	M	Cha	13	S	N	Y	Guam	Y	Farm Laborer
31		109	125	Cruz, Dolores L	Daughter	F	Cha	11	S	Y	Y	Guam	Y	None
32		109	125	Cruz, Magdalena L	Daughter	F	Cha	9	S	Y		Guam		None
33		109	125	Cruz, Lourdes L	Daughter	F	Cha	4.8	S	N		Guam		None
34		109	125	Cruz, Bernadino L	Son	M	Cha	1.3	S	N		Guam		None
35		109	125	Cruz, Maria C	Mother	F	Cha	68	Wd	N	N	Guam	N	None
36		110	126	Ogo, Francisco A	Head	M	Cha	68	Wd	N	N	Guam	N	Farm Laborer
37		111	127	Mesa, Vicente M	Head	M	Cha	64	M	N	N	Guam	N	Farmer
38		111	127	Mesa, Antonia C	Wife	F	Cha	54	M	N	N	Guam	N	None
39		111	127	Mesa, Ignacio C	Son	M	Cha	15	S	Y	Y	Guam	Y	None
40		111	127	Mesa, Juan C	Grandson	M	Cha	9	S	Y		Guam		None
41		112	128	Lizama, Felipe C	Head	M	Cha	41	M	N	Y	Guam	Y	Farmer
42		112	128	Lizama, Saturnina A	Wife	F	Cha	42	M	N	N	Guam	N	None
43		112	128	Lizama, Cristobal A	Son	M	Cha	18	S	N	Y	Guam	Y	Cook
44		112	129	Lizama, Carmen A	Daughter	F	Cha	16	S	Y	Y	Guam	Y	None
45		112	129	Lizama, Lorenzo C	Head	M	Cha	37	M	N	N	Guam	N	Farm Laborer
46		112	129	Lizama, Gregorio P	Son	M	Cha	16	S	N	Y	Guam	Y	Farm Laborer
47		112	129	Lizama, Jose P	Son	M	Cha	14	S	Y	Y	Guam	Y	None
48		112	129	Lizama, Maria P	Daughter	F	Cha	12	S	Y	Y	Guam	Y	None
49		112	129	Lizama, Francisca P	Daughter	F	Cha	4.1	S	N		Guam		None
50		112	129	Lizama, Marcelino B	Father	M	Cha	72	Wd	N	N	Guam	N	None

(CHAMORRO ROOTS GENEALOGY PROJECT™ TRANSCRIPTION)
(BERNARD T. PUNZALAN / HTTP://WWW.CHAMORROROOTS.COM)

DEPARTMENT OF COMMERCE-BUREAU OF THE CENSUS
WASHINGTON

FIFTEENTH CENSUS OF THE UNITED STATES: 1930-POPULATION

THE ISLAND OF GUAM

Sheet No. 14A

District Municipality of Agana
Name of Place Agana City (Julale)
[Proper name and, also, name of class, as city, town, village, barrio, etc]

Enumeration District No. 4
Enumerated by me on April 7, 1930 Vicente Tydingco
Enumerator

	PLACE OF ABODE			NAME	RELATION	PERSONAL DESCRIPTION				EDUCATION		NATIVITY		OCCUPATION
	Street, avenue, road, etc.	Number of dwelling house is order of visitation	Number of family in order of visitation	of each person whose place of abode on April 1, 1930, was in this family. Enter surname, first, then given name and middle initial. If any. Include every person living on April 1, 1930. Omit children born since April 1, 1930.	Relationship of this Person to the head of the family.	Sex	Color or race	Age at last birthday	Single, married, widowed or divorced	Attended school any time since Sept. 1, 1929	Whether able to read and write.	Place of birth of this person.	Whether able to speak English.	
	1	2	3	4	5	6	7	8	9	10	11	12	13	14
1	Cristobal Colon Street	112	129	Arriola, Magdalena S	Half sister	F	Cha	18	S	N	N	Guam	N	Cook
2		113	130	Manglona, Juan S	Head	M	Cha	30	M	N	Y	Guam	Y	Farmer
3		113	130	Manglona, Dolores C	Wife	F	Cha	32	M	N	N	Guam	N	None
4		113	130	Manglona, Antonio C	Son	M	Cha	12	S	Y	Y	Guam	Y	None
5		113	130	Manglona, Francisco C	Son	M	Cha	9	S	Y		Guam		None
6		113	130	Manglona, Adriano C	Son	M	Cha	7	S	Y		Guam		None
7		113	130	Manglona, Bernadita C	Daughter	F	Cha	5	S	N		Guam		None
8		113	130	Manglona, Inocencio C	Son	M	Cha	3.2	S	N		Guam		None
9		113	130	Manglona, Rosita C	Daughter	F	Cha	.3	S	N		Guam		None
10		114	131	Maanao, Jose I	Head	M	Cha	26	M	N	Y	Guam	Y	Laborer
11		114	131	Maanao, Dolores R	Wife	F	Cha	21	M	N	Y	Guam	Y	None
12		114	131	Maanao, Antonia R	Daughter	F	Cha	1.8	S	N		Guam		None
13		114	131	Maanao, Guadalupe R	Daughter	F	Cha	.3	S	N		Guam		None
14		115	132	Camacho, Jose O	Head	M	Cha	26	M	N	Y	Guam	Y	Laborer
15		115	132	Camacho, Dolores R	Wife	F	Cha	21	M	N	Y	Guam	N	None
16		115	132	Camacho, Juan R	Son	M	Cha	4.2	S	N		Guam		None
17		115	132	Camacho, Jesus R	Son	M	Cha	2.2	S	N		Guam		None
18		116	133	Aguon, Vicente T	Head	M	Cha	44	M	N	Y	Guam	Y	Electrician
19		116	133	Aguon, Rosa M	Wife	F	Cha	43	M	N	N	Guam	N	None
20		116	133	Aguon, Vicenta M	Daughter	F	Cha	22	S	N	Y	Guam	Y	None
21		116	133	Aguon, Concepcion M	Daughter	F	Cha	16	S	Y	Y	Guam	Y	None
22		116	133	Aguon, Joaquin M	Son	M	Cha	13	S	Y	Y	Guam	Y	None
23		116	133	Aguon, Jose M	Son	M	Cha	11	S	Y	Y	Guam	Y	None
24		116	133	Aguon, Maria M	Daughter	F	Cha	9	S	Y		Guam		None
25		116	133	Aguon, Barcelisa M	Daughter	F	Cha	1.1	S	N		Guam		None

DEPARTMENT OF COMMERCE-BUREAU OF THE CENSUS
WASHINGTON

FIFTEENTH CENSUS OF THE UNITED STATES: 1930-POPULATION

THE ISLAND OF GUAM

Sheet No. 14B

128B

District **Municipality of Agana**
Name of Place **Agana City (Julale)**
[Proper name and, also, name of class, as city, town, village, barrio, etc]

Enumeration District No. **4**
Enumerated by me on **April 7, 1930** Vicente Tydingco
Enumerator

	PLACE OF ABODE			NAME	RELATION	PERSONAL DESCRIPTION				EDUCATION		NATIVITY		OCCUPATION
	Street, avenue, road, etc.	Number of dwelling house is order of visitation	Number of family in order of visitation	of each person whose place of abode on April 1, 1930, was in this family. Enter surname, first, then given name and middle initial. If any. Include every person living on April 1, 1930. Omit children born since April 1, 1930.	Relationship of this Person to the head of the family.	Sex	Color or race	Age at last birthday	Single, married, widowed or divorced	Attended school any time since Sept. 1, 1929	Whether able to read and write.	Place of birth of this person.	Whether able to speak English.	
	1	2	3	4	5	6	7	8	9	10	11	12	13	14
26	Cristobal Colon Street	117	134	Crisostimo, Juan P	Head	M	Cha	28	M	N	Y	Guam	Y	Farmer
27		117	134	Crisostimo, Dolores P	Wife	F	Cha	27	M	N	Y	Guam	N	None
28		117	134	Crisostimo, Felomenia P	Daughter	F	Cha	3.4	S	N		Guam		None
29		117	134	Crisostimo, Jose P	Son	M	Cha	.3	S	N		Guam		None
30		118	135	Pangelinan, Jesus R	Head	M	Cha	38	M	N	Y	Guam	Y	Laborer
31		118	135	Pangelinan, Rita C	Wife	F	Cha	22	M	N	Y	Guam	Y	None
32		118	135	Pangelinan, Benita C	Daughter	F	Cha	3.1	S	N		Guam		None
33		118	135	Pangelinan, Jesusa C	Daughter	F	Cha	.7	S	N		Guam		None
34		118	135	Crisostimo, Josefina V	Sister in law	F	Cha	19	S	N	Y	Guam	Y	None
35		118	135	Crisostimo, Purification V	Sister in law	F	Cha	16	S	N	Y	Guam	Y	Servant
36		118	135	Crisostimo, Francisco V	Brother in law	M	Cha	10	S	Y	Y	Guam	Y	None
37		118	135	Crisostimo, Primitiva V	Sister in law	F	Cha	6	S	N		Guam		None
38		118	135	Crisostimo, Pacita V	Niece	F	Cha	.2	S	N		Guam		None
39		119	136	Manglona, Felix C	Head	M	Cha	68	M	N	N	Guam	N	Farmer
40		119	136	Manglona, Maria S	Wife	F	Cha	64	M	N	N	Guam	N	None
41		119	136	Manglona, Susana S	Daughter	F	Cha	29	S	N	Y	Guam	Y	Laundress
42		119	136	Manglona, Tomas M	Grandson	M	Cha	4.3	S	N		Guam		None
43		120	137	Taitano, Ana M	Head	F	Cha	35	M	N	Y	Guam	Y	None
44		120	137	Taitano, Felibetto M	Son	M	Cha	6	S	N		Guam		None
45		121	138	Manglona, Vicente S	Head	M	Cha	43	M	N	Y	Guam	N	Farmer
46		121	138	Manglona, Ana L	Wife	F	Cha	48	M	N	N	Guam	N	None
47		121	138	Manglona, Carmen L	Daughter	F	Cha	26	S	N	Y	Guam	Y	Servant
48		121	138	Manglona, Gregorio L	Son	M	Cha	18	S	N	Y	Guam	Y	Farm Laborer
49		121	138	Manglona, Reymundo L	Son	M	Cha	17	S	Y	Y	Guam	Y	None
50		121	138	Manglona, Maria L	Daughter	F	Cha	16	S	N	Y	Guam	N	None

DEPARTMENT OF COMMERCE-BUREAU OF THE CENSUS
WASHINGTON

FIFTEENTH CENSUS OF THE UNITED STATES: 1930-POPULATION

THE ISLAND OF GUAM

Sheet No. 15A

District **Municipality of Agana**
Name of Place **Agana City (Julale)**
[Proper name and, also, name of class, as city, town, village, barrio, etc]

Enumeration District No. 4
Enumerated by me on **April 7, 1930** Vicente Tydingco, Enumerator

	PLACE OF ABODE			NAME	RELATION	PERSONAL DESCRIPTION				EDUCATION		NATIVITY		OCCUPATION
	Street, avenue, road, etc.	Number of dwelling house in order of visitation	Number of family in order of visitation	of each person whose place of abode on April 1, 1930, was in this family. Enter surname, first, then given name and middle initial. If any. Include every person living on April 1, 1930. Omit children born since April 1, 1930.	Relationship of this Person to the head of the family.	Sex	Color or race	Age at last birthday	Single, married, widowed or divorced	Attended school any time since Sept. 1, 1929	Whether able to read and write.	Place of birth of this person.	Whether able to speak English.	
	1	2	3	4	5	6	7	8	9	10	11	12	13	14
1	Cristobal Colon Street	121	138	Manglona, Virginia L	Daughter	F	Cha	13	S	Y	Y	Guam	Y	None
2		121	138	Manglona, Luisa L	Daughter	F	Cha	11	S	Y	Y	Guam	Y	None
3		121	138	Manglona, Jose L	Son	M	Cha	6	S	N		Guam		None
4		121	138	Manglona, Juan M	Grandson	M	Cha	1.8	S	N		Guam		None
5		121	138	Manglona, Rosario M	Granddaughter	F	Cha	.8	S	N		Guam		None
6		122	139	Jesus, Rosalia C	Head	F	Cha	57	Wd	N	N	Guam	N	None
7		122	139	Jesus, Francisco C	Son	M	Cha	20	S	N	Y	Guam	Y	Farmer
8		122	139	Jesus, Jose C	Son	M	Cha	18	S	N	Y	Guam	Y	Farm Laborer
9		122	139	Jesus, Josefa C	Daughter	F	Cha	16	S	N	Y	Guam	Y	None
10		122	139	Jesus, Vicente C	Son	M	Cha	12	S	Y	Y	Guam	Y	None
11		123	140	Jesus, Antonio C	Head	M	Cha	34	M	N	Y	Guam	Y	Farmer
12		123	140	Jesus, Josefa B	Wife	F	Cha	33	M	N	Y	Guam	Y	None
13		123	140	Jesus, Juan B	Son	M	Cha	3.4	S	N		Guam		None
14		123	140	Jesus, Guadalupe B	Daughter	F	Cha	1.3	S	N		Guam		None
15		124	141	Gay, Elmer L	Head	M	W	56	M	N	Y	Minonk, Illinois	Y	Bookkeeper
16		124	141	Gay, Ana T	Wife	F	Cha	53	M	N	Y	Guam	Y	Farm
17		124	141	Gay, Emma L	Daughter	F	Cha	18	S	N	Y	Tonika, Illinois	Y	Teacher
18		124	141	Gay, Elizabeth L	Daughter	F	Cha	17	S	N	Y	Guam	Y	Teacher
19		124	141	Gay, Emily L	Daughter	F	Cha	16	S	N	Y	Guam	Y	Clerk
20		124	141	Gay, Elmer L	Son	M	Cha	13	S	Y	Y	Guam	Y	None
21		124	141	Gay, James K	Son	M	Cha	10	S	Y	Y	Guam	Y	None
22		124	141	San Nicolas, Vicente B	Servant	F	Cha	60	S	N	N	Guam	N	Farm Laborer
23		125	142	Cruz, Vicente B	Head	M	Cha	64	M	N	Y	Guam	N	Farmer
24		125	142	Cruz, Baltazara S	Wife	F	Cha	43	M	N	N	Guam	N	None
25		125	142	Cruz, Jose S	Son	M	Cha	19	S	N	Y	Guam	Y	Farm Laborer

DEPARTMENT OF COMMERCE-BUREAU OF THE CENSUS
WASHINGTON

FIFTEENTH CENSUS OF THE UNITED STATES: 1930-POPULATION

THE ISLAND OF GUAM

Sheet No. 15B

129B

District Municipality of Agana
Name of Place Agana City (Julale)
[Proper name and, also, name of class, as city, town, village, barrio, etc]

Enumeration District No. 4
Enumerated by me on April 7, 1930 Vicente Tydingco
Enumerator

	PLACE OF ABODE			NAME	RELATION	PERSONAL DESCRIPTION				EDUCATION		NATIVITY		OCCUPATION
	Street, avenue, road, etc.	Number of dwelling house in order of visitation	Number of family in order of visitation	of each person whose place of abode on April 1, 1930, was in this family. Enter surname, first, then given name and middle initial. If any. Include every person living on April 1, 1930. Omit children born since April 1, 1930.	Relationship of this Person to the head of the family.	Sex	Color or race	Age at last birthday	Single, married, widowed or divorced	Attended school any time since Sept. 1, 1929	Whether able to read and write.	Place of birth of this person.	Whether able to speak English.	
	1	2	3	4	5	6	7	8	9	10	11	12	13	14
26	Cristobal Colon Street	125	142	Cruz, Maria S	Daughter	F	Cha	17	S	N	Y	Guam	Y	None
27		125	142	Cruz, Gregorio S	Son	M	Cha	15	S	Y	Y	Guam	Y	None
28		125	142	Cruz, Engracia S	Daughter	F	Cha	12	S	Y	Y	Guam	Y	None
29		125	142	Cruz, Josefa S	Daughter	F	Cha	10	S	Y	Y	Guam	Y	None
30		125	142	Cruz, Antonia S	Daughter	F	Cha	6	S	N		Guam		None
31		125	142	Cruz, Rita S	Daughter	F	Cha	5	S	N		Guam		None
32		126	143	Cruz, Ana S	Daughter	F	Cha	2.2	S	N		Guam		None
33		126	143	Cruz, Juan B	Head	M	Cha	40	M	N	Y	Guam	N	Farmer
34		126	143	Cruz, Maria S	Wife	F	Cha	41	M	N	N	Guam	N	None
35		126	143	Cruz, Manuel S	Son	M	Cha	20	S	N	Y	Guam	Y	Laborer
36		126	143	Cruz, Jose S	Son	M	Cha	15	S	N	Y	Guam	Y	Farm Laborer
37		126	143	Cruz, Natividad S	Daughter	F	Cha	14	S	Y	Y	Guam	Y	None
38		126	143	Cruz, Maria S	Daughter	F	Cha	12	S	Y	Y	Guam	Y	None
39		126	143	Cruz, Josefina S	Daughter	F	Cha	5	S	N		Guam		None
40		126	143	Cruz, Rosario S	Daughter	F	Cha	1.5	S	N		Guam		None
41	Legaspi Street	127	144	Bayona, Juan I	Head	M	Cha	33	M	N		Guam	Y	Farmer
42		127	144	Bayona, Fabiana M	Wife	F	Cha	36	M	N		Guam	Y	None
43		127	144	Bayona, Teodora M	Daughter	F	Cha	11	S	Y	Y	Guam	Y	None
44		127	144	Bayona, Antonio M	Son	M	Cha	7	S	Y		Guam		None
45		127	144	Bayona, Rosalia M	Daughter	F	Cha	3.2	S	N		Guam		None
46		127	144	Bayona, Candido M	Son	M	Cha	1.5	S	N		Guam		None
47		127	144	Bayona, Rosa G	Mother	F	Cha	67	Wd	N	N	Guam	N	None
48		127	144	Bayona, Catalina I	Sister	F	Cha	26	S	N	N	Guam	Y	None
49		127	144	Bayona, Jose I	Brother	M	Cha	18	S	N	Y	Guam		Farm Laborer
50		127	144	Bayona, Antonio B	Nephew	M	Cha	4.4	S	N		Guam		None

DEPARTMENT OF COMMERCE-BUREAU OF THE CENSUS
WASHINGTON

FIFTEENTH CENSUS OF THE UNITED STATES: 1930-POPULATION

THE ISLAND OF GUAM

Sheet No. 16A

District **Municipality of Agana**
Name of Place **Agana City (Julale)**
[Proper name and, also, name of class, as city, town, village, barrio, etc]

Enumeration District No. **4**
Enumerated by me on **April 7, 1930** **Vicente Tydingco**
Enumerator

	PLACE OF ABODE			NAME	RELATION	PERSONAL DESCRIPTION				EDUCATION		NATIVITY		OCCUPATION
	Street, avenue, road, etc.	Number of dwelling house is order of visitation	Number of family in order of visitation	of each person whose place of abode on April 1, 1930, was in this family. Enter surname, first, then given name and middle initial. If any. Include every person living on April 1, 1930. Omit children born since April 1, 1930.	Relationship of this Person to the head of the family.	Sex	Color or race	Age at last birthday	Single, married, widowed or divorced	Attended school any time since Sept. 1, 1929	Whether able to read and write.	Place of birth of this person.	Whether able to speak English.	
	1	2	3	4	5	6	7	8	9	10	11	12	13	14
1	Legaspi Street	127	144	Bayona, Desiderio B	Nephew	M	Cha	.9	S	N		Guam		None
2		128	145	Reyes, Ignacio C	Head	M	Cha	27	M	N	Y	Guam	Y	Carpenter
3		128	145	Reyes, Ana M	Wife	F	Cha	26	M	N	Y	Guam	Y	None
4		128	145	Reyes, Ignacio M	Son	M	Cha	7	S	Y		Guam		None
5		128	145	Reyes, Guadalupe M	Daughter	F	Cha	5	S	N		Guam		None
6		128	145	Reyes, Margarita M	Daughter	F	Cha	2.3	S	N		Guam		None
7		128	145	Cruz, Juan LG	Cousin in law	M	Cha	34	S	N		Guam	N	Farm Laborer
8		129	146	Torres, Joaquin N	Head	M	Cha	22	M	N	Y	Guam	Y	Farmer
9		129	146	Torres, Vicenta Q	Wife	F	Cha	19	M	N	Y	Guam	Y	None
10		129	146	Quitugua, Josefa C	Mother in law	F	Cha	54	Wd	N		Guam	N	None
11		129	146	Quitugua, Vicente Q	Brother in law	M	Cha	16	S	Y	Y	Guam	Y	None
12		130	147	Taitano, John	Head	M	Cha	42	M	N	Y	Guam	Y	Stockman
13		130	147	Taitano, Rosario F	Wife	F	Cha	34	M	N	Y	Guam	Y	None
14		130	147	Taitano, Rosario F	Daughter	F	Cha	23	S	N	Y	Guam	Y	Teacher
15		130	147	Taitano, Carlos F	Son	M	Cha	20	S	N	Y	Guam	Y	Moulder
16		130	147	Taitano, Esther F	Daughter	F	Cha	17	S	N	Y	Guam	Y	Teacher
17		130	147	Taitano, Catalina F	Daughter	F	Cha	15	S	Y	Y	Guam	Y	None
18		130	147	Taitano, John F	Son	M	Cha	12	S	Y	Y	Guam	Y	None
19		130	147	Taitano, Richard F	Son	M	Cha	9	S	Y		Guam		None
20		130	147	Taitano, Joseph F	Son	M	Cha	7	S	Y		Guam		None
21		130	147	Taitano, Frank F	Son	M	Cha	5	S	N		Guam		None
22		130	147	Taitano, Henry F	Son	M	Cha	3.3	S	N		Guam		None
23		131	148	Teubner, Maryane F	Head	F	W	33	M	N	Y	Monroeville, Alabama	Y	None
24		131	148	Teubner, Leysa M	Daughter	F	W	15	S	N	Y	Pensacola, Florida	Y	None
25		131	148	Teubner, Raymond	Son	M	W	13	S	Y	Y	Pensacola, Florida	Y	None

DEPARTMENT OF COMMERCE-BUREAU OF THE CENSUS
WASHINGTON

FIFTEENTH CENSUS OF THE UNITED STATES: 1930-POPULATION

THE ISLAND OF GUAM

Sheet No. 16B

130B

District Municipality of Agana
Name of Place Agana City (Julale)
[Proper name and, also, name of class, as city, town, village, barrio, etc]

Enumeration District No. 4
Enumerated by me on April 7, 1930 Vicente Tydingco
Enumerator

	PLACE OF ABODE			NAME	RELATION	PERSONAL DESCRIPTION				EDUCATION		NATIVITY		OCCUPATION
	Street, avenue, road, etc.	Number of dwelling house is order of visitation	Number of family in order of visitation	of each person whose place of abode on April 1, 1930, was in this family. Enter surname, first, then given name and middle initial. If any. Include every person living on April 1, 1930. Omit children born since April 1, 1930.	Relationship of this Person to the head of the family.	Sex	Color or race	Age at last birthday	Single, married, widowed or divorced	Attended school any time since Sept. 1, 1929	Whether able to read and write.	Place of birth of this person.	Whether able to speak English.	
	1	2	3	4	5	6	7	8	9	10	11	12	13	14
26	Legaspi Street	132	149	Sablan, Maria A	Head	F	Cha	49	Wd	N	Y	Guam	N	None
27		132	149	Sablan, Illuminada A	Daughter	F	Cha	22	S	N	Y	Guam	Y	None
28		132	149	Sablan, Marcial A	Son	M	Cha	20	S	N	Y	Guam	Y	Teacher
29		132	149	Sablan, Lourdes A	Daughter	F	Cha	17	S	N	Y	Guam	Y	Teacher
30		132	149	Sablan, Emerenciana A	Daughter	F	Cha	14	S	Y	Y	Guam	Y	None
31		132	150	Sablan, Angel A	Head	M	Cha	24	M	N	Y	Guam	Y	Chauffeur
32		132	150	Sablan, Rosario G	Wife	F	Cha	23	M	N	Y	Guam	Y	None
33		133	151	Schuam, Emilia G	Head	F	Cha	60	Wd	N	Y	Guam	Y	Laundress
34		133	151	Guerrero, Jose G	Son	M	Cha	23	S	N	Y	Guam	Y	Servant
35		134	152	Cabe, Antonio D	Head	M	Cha	61	M	N	Y	Guam	N	Shoemaker
36		134	152	Cabe, Nicolasa D	Wife	F	Cha	64	M	N	Y	Guam	N	None
37		135	153	Sablan, Jose L	Head	M	Cha	48	M	N	N	Guam	N	Farmer
38		135	153	Sablan, Maria T	Wife	F	Cha	32	M	N	Y	Guam	N	None
39		135	153	Sablan, Rosalia T	Daughter	F	Cha	16	S	Y	Y	Guam	Y	None
40		135	153	Sablan, Soledad T	Daughter	F	Cha	14	S	Y	Y	Guam	Y	None
41		135	153	Sablan, Carlos T	Son	M	Cha	12	S	Y	Y	Guam	Y	None
42		135	153	Sablan, Magdalena T	Daughter	F	Cha	9	S	Y		Guam		None
43		135	153	Sablan, Dolores T	Daughter	F	Cha	7	S	Y		Guam		None
44		135	153	Sablan, Margarita T	Daughter	F	Cha	2.2	S	N		Guam		None
45		135	153	Sablan, Eugenia T	Daughter	F	Cha	.2	S	N		Guam		None
46		136	154	Martinez, Maria R	Head	F	Cha	36	S	N	N	Guam	N	Laundress
47		136	154	Martinez, Caridad M	Daughter	F	Cha	14	S	N	Y	Guam	Y	Servant
48		136	154	Martinez, Francisco M	Son	M	Cha	5	S	N		Guam		None
49		136	154	Martinez, Margarita M	Daughter	F	Cha	3.3	S	N		Guam		None
50		136	154	Martinez, Juan M	Son	M	Cha	1.5	S	N		Guam		None

DEPARTMENT OF COMMERCE-BUREAU OF THE CENSUS
WASHINGTON

FIFTEENTH CENSUS OF THE UNITED STATES: 1930-POPULATION

THE ISLAND OF GUAM

Sheet No. 17A

District **Municipality of Agana**
Name of Place **Agana City (Julale)**
[Proper name and, also, name of class, as city, town, village, barrio, etc]

Enumeration District No. 4
Enumerated by me on **April 8, 1930** Vicente Tydingco
Enumerator

	PLACE OF ABODE			NAME	RELATION	PERSONAL DESCRIPTION				EDUCATION		NATIVITY		OCCUPATION
	Street, avenue, road, etc.	Number of dwelling house in order of visitation	Number of family in order of visitation	of each person whose place of abode on April 1, 1930, was in this family. Enter surname, first, then given name and middle initial. If any. Include every person living on April 1, 1930. Omit children born since April 1, 1930.	Relationship of this Person to the head of the family.	Sex	Color or race	Age at last birthday	Single, married, widowed or divorced	Attended school any time since Sept. 1, 1929	Whether able to read and write.	Place of birth of this person.	Whether able to speak English.	
	1	2	3	4	5	6	7	8	9	10	11	12	13	14
1	Legaspi Street	137	155	Cruz, Antonia A	Head	F	Cha	47	S	N	Y	Guam	Y	None
2		137	155	Velasco, Jose A	Nephew	M	Cha	16	S	Y	Y	Guam	Y	None
3		137	155	Toves, Magdalena A	Niece	F	Cha	16	S	Y	Y	Guam	Y	None
4		137	155	Aguon, Rosario S	Niece	F	Cha	10	S	Y	Y	Guam		None
5		138	156	Mesa, Jose T	Head	M	Cha	27	M	N	Y	Guam	Y	Farmer
6		138	156	Mesa, Rosa B	Wife	F	Cha	25	M	N	Y	Guam	Y	None
7		138	156	Mesa, Maria B	Daughter	F	Cha	3.2	S	N		Guam		None
8		138	156	Mesa, Jesus B	Son	M	Cha	1.2	S	N		Guam		None
9		139	157	Mesa, Enrique A	Head	M	Cha	23	M	N	Y	Guam	Y	Laborer
10		139	157	Mesa, Ana C	Wife	F	Cha	22	M	N	Y	Guam	Y	None
11		139	157	Mesa, Josefina C	Daughter	F	Cha	3.8	S	N		Guam		None
12		140	158	Tenorio, Maria B	Head	F	Cha	29	Wd	N	Y	Guam	Y	None
13		140	158	Tenorio, Rosario B	Daughter	F	Cha	8	S	Y		Guam		None
14		140	158	Tenorio, Julia B	Daughter	F	Cha	4.7	S	N		Guam		None
15		140	158	Tenorio, Juan B	Son	M	Cha	2.8	S	N		Guam		None
16		140	158	Tenorio, Miguel R	Boarder	M	Cha	75	S	N	Y	Guam	Y	None
17		141	159	Limtiaco, Francisco A	Head	M	Cha	28	M	N	Y	Guam	Y	Cook
18		141	159	Limtiaco, Ursula I	Wife	F	Cha	24	M	N	Y	Guam	Y	Cook
19		141	159	Limtiaco, Delfina I	Daughter	F	Cha	5.2	S	N		Guam		None
20		141	159	Limtiaco, Gregorio I	Son	M	Cha	3.1	S	N		Guam		None
21		141	159	Limtiaco, Juan I	Son	M	Cha	1.2	S	N		Guam		None
22		141	159	Ignacio, Maria C	Sister in law	F	Cha	21	S	N	Y	Guam	Y	Cook
23		142	160	Untalan, Francisco C	Head	M	Cha	58	M	N	Y	Guam	N	Road Contractor
24		142	160	Untalan, Juana C	Wife	F	Cha	45	M	N	Y	Guam	N	None
25		142	160	Untalan, Higinio C	Son	M	Cha	22	S	N	Y	Guam	Y	Farmer

(CHAMORRO ROOTS GENEALOGY PROJECT™ TRANSCRIPTION)
(BERNARD T. PUNZALAN / HTTP://WWW.CHAMORROROOTS.COM)

DEPARTMENT OF COMMERCE-BUREAU OF THE CENSUS
WASHINGTON

FIFTEENTH CENSUS OF THE UNITED STATES: 1930-POPULATION

THE ISLAND OF GUAM

Sheet No. 17B

131B

District **Municipality of Agana**
Name of Place **Agana City (Julale)**
[Proper name and, also, name of class, as city, town, village, barrio, etc]

Enumeration District No. 4
Enumerated by me on **April 8, 1930** Vicente Tydingco
Enumerator

	PLACE OF ABODE: Street, avenue, road, etc.	Number of dwelling house is order of visitation	Number of family in order of visitation	NAME of each person whose place of abode on April 1, 1930, was in this family. Enter surname, first, then given name and middle initial. If any. Include every person living on April 1, 1930. Omit children born since April 1, 1930.	RELATION Relationship of this Person to the head of the family.	PERSONAL DESCRIPTION: Sex	Color or race	Age at last birthday	Single, married, widowed or divorced	EDUCATION: Attended school any time since Sept. 1, 1929	Whether able to read and write.	NATIVITY Place of birth of this person.	Whether able to speak English.	OCCUPATION
	1	2	3	4	5	6	7	8	9	10	11	12	13	14
26	Legaspi Street	142	161	Camacho, Bidad A	Head	M	Cha	49	Wd	N	Y	Guam	N	None
27		142	161	Camacho, Vicente A	Son	M	Cha	22	S	N	Y	Guam	Y	Farm Laborer
28		142	161	Camacho, Silvestre A	Son	M	Cha	21	S	N	Y	Guam	Y	Servant
29		142	161	Camacho, Ignacia C	Daughter	f	Cha	16	S	N	Y	Guam	Y	Cook
30		142	161	Camacho, Rita C	Daughter	F	Cha	11	S	Y	Y	Guam	Y	None
31		142	162	Lecadio, Antonia U	Head	F	Cha	20	M	N	Y	Guam	Y	None
32		142	162	Lecadio, Carmilita U	Daughter	F	Cha	2.7	S	N		Guam		None
33		142	162	Lecadio, Fermetiva U	Daughter	F	Cha	1.6	S	N		Guam		None
34		143	163	Cruz, Maria G	Head	F	Cha	56	S	N	N	Guam	N	None
35		143	163	Cruz, Joaquin G	Son	M	Cha	30	S	N	Y	Guam	N	Farm Laborer
36		143	163	Cruz, Ana G	Daughter	F	Cha	28	S	N	Y	Guam	Y	Laundress
37		143	163	Cruz, Felecita C	Daughter	F	Cha	17	S	N	Y	Guam	N	None
38		143	163	Cruz, Tomas C	Grandson	M	Cha	13	S	Y	Y	Guam	Y	None
39		143	163	Cruz, Maria	Granddaughter	F	Cha	6	S	N		Guam		None
40		143	163	Cleofas, Sixto C	Lodger	M	Fil	75	M	N	Y	Philippine Islands	N	Farmer
41		144	164	Gogue, Jose C	Head	M	Cha	35	M	N	Y	Guam	Y	Laborer
42		144	164	Gogue, Antonia LG	Wife	F	Cha	27	M	N	Y	Guam	N	None
43		144	164	Gogue, Rosa LG	Daughter	F	Cha	5	S	N		Guam		None
44		144	164	Gogue, Antonio LG	Son	M	Cha	1.7	S	N		Guam		None
45		144	164	Gogue, Jesus G	Cousin	M	Cha	26	S	N	Y	Guam	Y	Farmer
46		144	165	Lizama, Juan C	Head	M	Cha	91	M	N	Y	Guam	N	None
47		144	165	Lizama, Luisa G	Wife	F	Cha	80	M	N	N	Guam	N	None
48		145	166	Mendiola, Antonia M	Head	F	Cha	38	S	N	Y	Guam	N	Laundress
49		145	166	Mendiola, Ana M	Daughter	F	Cha	11	S	Y	Y	Guam	Y	None
50		145	166	Mendiola, Rosario M	Daughter	F	Cha	6	S	N		Guam		None

DEPARTMENT OF COMMERCE-BUREAU OF THE CENSUS
WASHINGTON
FIFTEENTH CENSUS OF THE UNITED STATES: 1930-POPULATION

THE ISLAND OF GUAM

Sheet No. 18A

District **Municipality of Agana**
Name of Place **Agana City (Julale)**
[Proper name and, also, name of class, as city, town, village, barrio, etc]

Enumeration District No. 4
Enumerated by me on **April 8, 1930** Vicente Tydingco, Enumerator

	PLACE OF ABODE			NAME	RELATION	PERSONAL DESCRIPTION				EDUCATION		NATIVITY		OCCUPATION
	Street, avenue, road, etc.	Number of dwelling house is order of visitation	Number of family in order of visitation	of each person whose place of abode on April 1, 1930, was in this family. Enter surname, first, then given name and middle initial. If any. Include every person living on April 1, 1930. Omit children born since April 1, 1930.	Relationship of this Person to the head of the family.	Sex	Color or race	Age at last birthday	Single, married, widowed or divorced	Attended school any time since Sept. 1, 1929	Whether able to read and write.	Place of birth of this person.	Whether able to speak English.	
	1	2	3	4	5	6	7	8	9	10	11	12	13	14
1	Legaspi Street	145	166	Mendiola, Concepcion M	Daughter	F	Cha	5	S	N		Guam		None
2		145	166	Mendiola, Juan M	Son	M	Cha	3.7	S	N		Guam		None
3		145	166	Mendiola, Jesus M	Son	M	Cha	.8	S	N		Guam		None
4		146	167	Tuncap, Rita D	Head	F	Cha	42	M	N	N	Guam	N	Laundress
5		146	167	Tuncap, Felecita D	Daughter	F	Cha	11	S	N	N	Guam	N	Laundress
6		146	167	Diaz, Jose D	Brother	M	Cha	15	S	N	N	Guam	N	Laborer
7		147	168	Castro, Maria I	Head	F	Cha	28	M	N	Y	Guam		None
8		147	168	Castro, Leonicio I	Son	M	Cha	1	S	N		Guam		None
9		147	169	Ignacio, Leonsio C	Head	M	Cha	52	Wd	N	Y	Guam	N	Farmer
10		147	169	Ignacio, Jesus C	Son	M	Cha	20	S	N	Y	Guam	Y	Laborer
11		147	169	Ignacio, Rosa C	Daughter	F	Cha	11	S	Y	Y	Guam	Y	None
12		148	170	Namauleg, Mariano G	Head	M	Cha	60	M	N	Y	Guam	N	Farmer
13		148	170	Namauleg, Maria N	Wife	F	Cha	61	M	N	Y	Guam	N	None
14		148	170	Leon Guerrero, Jesus N	Nephew	M	Cha	17	S	N	Y	Caroline Island	Y	Farm Laborer
15		148	170	Aldan, Antonio N	Nephew	M	Cha	13	S	Y	Y	Caroline Island	Y	None
16		148	171	Sacramento, Francisca N	Head	F	Cha	23	D	N	N	Caroline Island	N	Laundress
17		148	171	Sacramento, Angel N	Son	M	Cha	2.3	S	N		Solomon Island		None
18		149	172	Pangelinan, Jose C	Head	M	Cha	53	Wd	N	N	Guam	N	Farmer
19		149	172	Pangelinan, Jose M	Son	M	Cha	19	S	N	Y	Guam	N	Farm Laborer
20		149	172	Pangelinan, Juan M	Son	M	Cha	17	S	N	Y	Guam	Y	Farm Laborer
21		149	172	Pangelinan, Margarita M	Daughter	F	Cha	16	S	N	Y	Guam	Y	None
22		149	172	Pangelinan, Rosa M	Daughter	F	Cha	14	S	N	Y	Guam	Y	None
23		149	172	Pangelinan, Vicente M	Son	M	Cha	11	S	Y	Y	Guam	Y	None
24		149	172	Pangelinan, Julia M	Daughter	F	Cha	10	S	Y	Y	Guam	Y	None
25		149	173	Pangelinan, Juan M	Head	M	Cha	23	M	N	Y	Guam	Y	Farm Laborer

DEPARTMENT OF COMMERCE-BUREAU OF THE CENSUS
WASHINGTON

FIFTEENTH CENSUS OF THE UNITED STATES: 1930-POPULATION

THE ISLAND OF GUAM

Sheet No. 18B

132B

District **Municipality of Agana**
Name of Place **Agana City (Julale)**
[Proper name and, also, name of class, as city, town, village, barrio, etc]

Enumeration District No. **4**
Enumerated by me on **April 8, 1930** Vicente Tydingco
Enumerator

	PLACE OF ABODE			NAME	RELATION	PERSONAL DESCRIPTION				EDUCATION		NATIVITY		OCCUPATION
	Street, avenue, road, etc.	Number of dwelling house is order of visitation	Number of family in order of visitation	of each person whose place of abode on April 1, 1930, was in this family. Enter surname, first, then given name and middle initial. If any. Include every person living on April 1, 1930. Omit children born since April 1, 1930.	Relationship of this Person to the head of the family.	Sex	Color or race	Age at last birthday	Single, married, widowed or divorced	Attended school any time since Sept. 1, 1929	Whether able to read and write.	Place of birth of this person.	Whether able to speak English.	
	1	2	3	4	5	6	7	8	9	10	11	12	13	14
26	Legaspi Street	149	173	Pangelinan, Carmen R	Wife	F	Cha	22	M	N	Y	Guam		None
27		149	173	Pangelinan, Jesus R	Son	M	Cha	2.3	S	N		Guam		None
28		149	173	Pangelinan, Ignacia R	Daughter	F	Cha	.6	S	N		Guam		None
29		150	174	Leon Guerrero, Pedro P	Head	M	Cha	53	M	N	N	Guam	N	Farmer
30		150	174	Leon Guerrero, Juana C	Wife	F	Cha	58	M	N	N	Guam	N	None
31		150	174	Leon Guerrero, Ana C	Daughter	F	Cha	31	S	N	Y	Guam	N	Laundress
32		150	174	Leon Guerrero, Pedro C	Son	M	Cha	18	S	N	Y	Guam	Y	Farm Laborer
33		150	174	Leon Guerrero, Eriberto C	Son	M	Cha	16	S	N	Y	Guam	Y	Farm Laborer
34		150	174	Leon Guerrero, Rosario C	Daughter	F	Cha	8	S	Y		Guam		None
35		150	174	Leon Guerrero, Nicolasa C	Daughter	F	Cha	4.1	S	N		Guam		None
36		151	175	Lucero, Maria M	Head	F	Cha	40	M	N	N	Guam	N	Laundress
37		151	175	Lucero, Vicente M	Son	M	Cha	1.3	S	N		Guam		None
38		151	175	Aguon, Jose T	Lodger	M	Cha	41	S	N	Y	Guam	N	Farmer
39		152	176	San Nicolas, Felipe U	Head	M	Cha	33	M	N	Y	Guam	N	Farmer
40		152	176	San Nicolas, Rosa M	Wife	F	Cha	32	M	N	Y	Guam	N	None
41		152	176	San Nicolas, Cecilia M	Daughter	F	Cha	8	S	Y		Guam		None
42		152	176	San Nicolas, Francisca M	Daughter	F	Cha	5	S	N		Guam		None
43		152	176	San Nicolas, Julian M	Son	M	Cha	4.1	S	N		Guam		None
44		152	176	San Nicolas, Eugenio M	Son	M	Cha	2.3	S	N		Guam		None
45		152	176	Mendiola, Juliana M	Mother in law	F	Cha	72	Wd	N	N	Guam	N	None
46		153	177	Okiyama, Jose G	Head	M	Jap	47	M	N	N	Tokyo, Japan	N	Carpenter
47		153	177	Okiyama, Jacoba G	Wife	F	Cha	37	M	N	Y	Guam	N	None
48		153	177	Okiyama, Maria G	Daughter	F	Jap	15	S	Y	Y	Guam	Y	None
49		153	177	Okiyama, Ana G	Daughter	F	Jap	14	S	Y	Y	Guam	Y	None
50		153	177	Okiyama, Carmen G	Daughter	F	Jap	13	S	Y	Y	Guam	Y	None

DEPARTMENT OF COMMERCE-BUREAU OF THE CENSUS
WASHINGTON

FIFTEENTH CENSUS OF THE UNITED STATES: 1930-POPULATION

THE ISLAND OF GUAM

Sheet No. 19A

District **Municipality of Agana**
Name of Place **Agana City (Julale)**
[Proper name and, also, name of class, as city, town, village, barrio, etc]

Enumeration District No. **4**
Enumerated by me on **April 8, 1930** Vicente Tydingco
Enumerator

	PLACE OF ABODE			NAME	RELATION	PERSONAL DESCRIPTION				EDUCATION		NATIVITY		OCCUPATION
	Street, avenue, road, etc.	Number of dwelling house is order of visitation	Number of family in order of visitation	of each person whose place of abode on April 1, 1930, was in this family. Enter surname, first, then given name and middle initial. If any. Include every person living on April 1, 1930. Omit children born since April 1, 1930.	Relationship of this Person to the head of the family.	Sex	Color or race	Age at last birthday	Single, married, widowed or divorced	Attended school any time since Sept. 1, 1929	Whether able to read and write.	Place of birth of this person.	Whether able to speak English.	
	1	2	3	4	5	6	7	8	9	10	11	12	13	14
1	Legaspi Street	153	177	Okiyama, Jose C	Son	M	Jap	10	S	Y	Y	Guam	Y	None
2		153	177	Charfauros, Francisco C	Nephew	F	Cha	22	S	N	Y	Guam	Y	Cook
3		154	178	Toves, Juan C	Head	M	Cha	42	M	N	Y	Guam	Y	Farmer
4		154	178	Toves, Maria M	Wife's mother	F	Cha	40	M	N	Y	Guam	Y	None
5		154	178	Toves, Inez M	Daughter	F	Cha	18	S	N	Y	Guam	N	None
6		154	178	Toves, Teodoro M	Son	M	Cha	15	S	Y	Y	Guam	Y	None
7		154	178	Toves, Rosario M	Daughter	F	Cha	13	S	Y	Y	Guam		None
8		154	178	Toves, Julia M	Daughter	F	Cha	11	S	Y	Y	Guam		None
9		154	178	Toves, Jose M	Son	M	Cha	9	S	Y		Guam		None
10		154	178	Toves, Maria M	Daughter	F	Cha	8	S	Y		Guam		None
11		154	178	Toves, Rosalia M	Daughter	F	Cha	6	S	N		Guam		None
12		154	178	Toves, Isabel M	Daughter	F	Cha	4.5	S	N		Guam		None
13		154	178	Toves, Ramona M	Daughter	F	Cha	1.5	S	N		Guam		None
14		154	178	Mendiola, Concepcion M	Sister in law	F	Cha	34	S	N	Y	Guam	Y	Cook
15		154	178	Mendiola, Magdalena M	Niece	M	Cha	6	S	N		Guam		None
16		155	179	Terlaje, Francisco T	Head	M	Cha	65	M	N	Y	Guam	N	Farm Laborer
17		155	179	Terlaje, Saturnina S	Wife	F	Cha	60	M	N	N	Guam	N	None
18		155	179	Terlaje, Teresa S	Daughter	F	Cha	21	S	N	Y	Guam	Y	Teacher
19		155	180	Martinez, Manuel C?	Head	M	Cha	36	M	N	Y	Guam	N	Laborer
20		155	180	Martinez, Trinidad SN	Wife	F	Cha	24	M	N	Y	Guam	Y	None
21		156	181	Guzman, Joaquin C	Head	M	Cha	45	M	N	Y	Guam	N	Farmer
22		156	181	Guzman, Ana M	Wife	F	Cha	38	M	N	Y	Guam	N	None
23		156	181	Guzman, Gonzalo M	Son	M	Cha	16	S	Y	Y	Guam	Y	None
24		156	181	Guzman, Jose M	Son	M	Cha	15	S	Y	Y	Guam	Y	None
25		156	181	Guzman, Julio M	Son	M	Cha	12	S	Y	Y	Guam	Y	None

(CHAMORRO ROOTS GENEALOGY PROJECT ™ TRANSCRIPTION)
(BERNARD T. PUNZALAN / HTTP://WWW.CHAMORROROOTS.COM)

DEPARTMENT OF COMMERCE-BUREAU OF THE CENSUS
WASHINGTON

FIFTEENTH CENSUS OF THE UNITED STATES: 1930-POPULATION

THE ISLAND OF GUAM

Sheet No. 19B

133B

District **Municipality of Agana**
Name of Place **Agana City (Julale)**
[Proper name and, also, name of class, as city, town, village, barrio, etc]

Enumeration District No. 4
Enumerated by me on **April 8, 1930** Vicente Tydingco
Enumerator

	PLACE OF ABODE			NAME	RELATION	PERSONAL DESCRIPTION				EDUCATION		NATIVITY		OCCUPATION
	Street, avenue, road, etc.	Number of dwelling house is order of visitation	Number of family in order of visitation	of each person whose place of abode on April 1, 1930, was in this family. Enter surname, first, then given name and middle initial. If any. Include every person living on April 1, 1930. Omit children born since April 1, 1930.	Relationship of this Person to the head of the family.	Sex	Color or race	Age at last birthday	Single, married, widowed or divorced	Attended school any time since Sept. 1, 1929	Whether able to read and write.	Place of birth of this person.	Whether able to speak English.	
	1	2	3	4	5	6	7	8	9	10	11	12	13	14
26	Legaspi Street	156	181	Guzman, Adela M	Daughter	F	Cha	11	S	Y	Y	Guam	Y	None
27		156	181	Guzman, Francisca M	Daughter	F	Cha	7	S	Y		Guam		None
28		156	181	Guzman, Pedro M	Son	M	Cha	6	S	N		Guam		None
29		156	181	Guzman, Norberto M	Son	M	Cha	4.3	S	N		Guam		None
30		156	181	Guzman, Ana M	Daughter	F	Cha	2.4	S	N		Guam		None
31		156	181	Oracion, Maria C	Aunt	F	Cha	70	Wd	N	Y	Guam	N	Laundress
32		157	182	Lizama, Jose B	Head	M	Cha	68	M	N	N	Guam	N	Farmer
33		157	182	Lizama, Soledad LG	Wife	F	Cha	45	M	N	N	Guam	N	None
34		157	182	Quitugua, Joaquin G	Stepson	M	Cha	28	S	N	Y	Guam	Y	Farm Laborer
35		157	182	Quitugua, Dolores G	Stepdaughter	F	Cha	30	S	N	Y	Guam	Y	Laundress
36		157	183	Quitugua, Juan G	Head	M	Cha	36	Wd	N	Y	Guam	Y	Farmer
37		157	183	Quitugua, Joaquin J	Son	M	Cha	8	S	Y		Guam		None
38		157	183	Quitugua, Rosario J	Daughter	F	Cha	5	S	N		Guam		None
39		157	184	Leon Guerrero, Manuel LG	Cousin	M	Cha	22	S	N	Y	Guam	Y	Farm Laborer
40		158	185	Quitugua, Vicente	Head	M	Cha	40	M	N	Y	Guam	Y	Farm Laborer
41		158	185	Mendiola, Antonio Q	Head	M	Cha	32	M	N	Y	Guam	Y	Chauffeur
42		158	185	Mendiola, Maria F	Wife	F	Cha	28	M	N	Y	Guam	Y	None
43		158	185	Mendiola, Juan F	Son	M	Cha	10	S	Y	Y	Guam		None
44		158	185	Mendiola, Brigida F	Daughter	F	Cha	8	S	Y		Guam		None
45		158	185	Mendiola, Margarita F	Daughter	F	Cha	6	S	N		Guam		None
46		158	185	Mendiola, Tomas F	Son	M	Cha	4.2	S	N		Guam		None
47		158	185	Mendiola, Priscilla F	Daughter	F	Cha	2.3	S	N		Guam		None
48		158	185	Mendiola, Ana F	Daughter	F	Cha	1.5	S	N		Guam		None
49		159	186	Lusk, Marjorie D	Head	F	W	26	M	N	Y	Philadelphia, Pennsylvania	Y	None
50		159	186	Lusk, Truett C	Son	M	W	2.3	S	N		Deland, Florida		None

DEPARTMENT OF COMMERCE-BUREAU OF THE CENSUS
WASHINGTON

FIFTEENTH CENSUS OF THE UNITED STATES: 1930-POPULATION

THE ISLAND OF GUAM

Sheet No. 20A

District **Municipality of Agana**
Name of Place **Agana City (Julale)**
[Proper name and, also, name of class, as city, town, village, barrio, etc]

Enumeration District No. **4**
Enumerated by me on **April 8, 1930** Vicente Tydingco
Enumerator

	PLACE OF ABODE			NAME	RELATION	PERSONAL DESCRIPTION				EDUCATION		NATIVITY		OCCUPATION
	Street, avenue, road, etc.	Number of dwelling house is order of visitation	Number of family in order of visitation	of each person whose place of abode on April 1, 1930, was in this family. Enter surname, first, then given name and middle initial. If any. Include every person living on April 1, 1930. Omit children born since April 1, 1930.	Relationship of this Person to the head of the family.	Sex	Color or race	Age at last birthday	Single, married, widowed or divorced	Attended school any time since Sept. 1, 1929	Whether able to read and write.	Place of birth of this person.	Whether able to speak English.	
	1	2	3	4	5	6	7	8	9	10	11	12	13	14
1	Santa Cruz Street	159	186	Lusk, Virginia W	Daughter	F	W	1.9	S	N		Jacksonville, Florida		None
2		160	187	Santos, Jose R	Head	M	Cha	59	M	N	N	Guam	Y	Farmer
3		160	187	Santos, Maria C	Wife	F	Cha	48	M	N	N	Guam	N	None
4		160	187	Santos, Juan C	Son	M	Cha	12	S	Y	Y	Guam	Y	None
5		160	187	Santos, Jose C	Son	M	Cha	10	S	Y	Y	Guam	Y	None
6		161	188	Untalan, Enrique LG	Head	M	Cha	22	M	N	Y	Guam	Y	Teacher
7		161	188	Untalan, Rosario DL	Wife	F	Cha	20	M	N	Y	Guam	Y	Teacher
8		162	189	Untalan, Rosa DL	Head	F	Cha	57	Wd	N	Y	Guam	Y	None
9		162	189	Untalan, Virginia DL	Daughter	F	Cha	26	S	N	Y	Guam	Y	None
10		162	189	Untalan, Antonio DL	Son	M	Cha	25	S	N	Y	Guam	Y	Draftsman
11		162	189	Untalan, Lourdes DL	Daughter	F	Cha	19	S	Y	Y	Guam	Y	None
12		162	189	Untalan, Modesta DL	Daughter	F	Cha	15	S	Y	Y	Guam	Y	None
13		162	190	Untalan, Agustin DL	Head	M	Cha	32	Wd	N	Y	Guam	Y	Carpenter
14		162	190	Untalan, Rosalia	Daughter	F	Cha	6	S	N		Guam		None
15		163	191	Bernardo, Joaquin C	Head	M	Cha	26	M	N	Y	Guam	Y	Farmer
16		163	191	Bernardo, Josefa LG	Wife	F	Cha	26	M	N	Y	Guam	Y	None
17		163	191	Bernardo, Tomas C	Son	M	Cha	1.1	S	N		Guam		None
18		164	192	Salas, Antonio LG	Head	M	Cha	32	M	N	Y	Guam	Y	Chauffeur
19		164	192	Salas, Maria B	Wife	F	Fil	29	M	N	Y	Guam	Y	None
20		164	192	Salas, Encarnacion B	Daughter	F	Cha	6	S	N		Guam		None
21		164	192	Salas, Agueda B	Daughter	F	Cha	1.2	S	N		Guam		None
22		164	192	Salas, Estella B	Daughter	F	Cha	2.1	S	N		Guam		None
23		164	192	Salas, Rosa B	Daughter	F	Cha	.4	S	N		Guam		None
24		164	192	Salas, Ramon C	Father	M	Cha	68	Wd	N	N	Guam	N	Farm Laborer
25		165	193	Baza, Pedro T	Head	M	Cha	23	M	N	Y	Guam	Y	Carpenter

DEPARTMENT OF COMMERCE-BUREAU OF THE CENSUS
WASHINGTON

FIFTEENTH CENSUS OF THE UNITED STATES: 1930-POPULATION

THE ISLAND OF GUAM

Sheet No. 20B

134B

District **Municipality of Agana**
Name of Place **Agana City (Julale)**
[Proper name and, also, name of class, as city, town, village, barrio, etc]

Enumeration District No. **4**
Enumerated by me on **April 8, 1930** Vicente Tydingco, Enumerator

	PLACE OF ABODE			NAME	RELATION	PERSONAL DESCRIPTION				EDUCATION		NATIVITY		OCCUPATION
	Street, avenue, road, etc.	Number of dwelling house in order of visitation	Number of family in order of visitation	of each person whose place of abode on April 1, 1930, was in this family. Enter surname, first, then given name and middle initial. If any. Include every person living on April 1, 1930. Omit children born since April 1, 1930.	Relationship of this Person to the head of the family.	Sex	Color or race	Age at last birthday	Single, married, widowed or divorced	Attended school any time since Sept. 1, 1929	Whether able to read and write.	Place of birth of this person.	Whether able to speak English.	
	1	2	3	4	5	6	7	8	9	10	11	12	13	14
26	Santa Cruz Street	165	193	Baza, Soledad C	Wife	F	Cha	25	M	N	Y	Guam	Y	Laundress
27		165	193	Baza, Barcelisa C	Daughter	F	Cha	2.3	S	N		Guam		None
28		165	194	Lizama, Raymundo L	Head	M	Cha	61	Wd	N	N	Guam	N	None
29		165	194	Ogo, Manuel L	Grandson	M	Cha	16	S	Y	Y	Guam	Y	None
30		166	195	Terlaje, Jose I	Head	M	Cha	37	M	N	Y	Guam	Y	Farmer
31		166	195	Terlaje, Maria C	Wife	F	Cha	37	M	N	Y	Guam	Y	None
32		166	195	Terlaje, Francisco C	Son	M	Cha	12	S	Y	Y	Guam	Y	None
33		166	195	Terlaje, Felisa C	Daughter	F	Cha	10	S	Y		Guam	Y	None
34		166	195	Terlaje, Isabel C	Daughter	F	Cha	9	S	Y		Guam		None
35		166	195	Terlaje, Jesus C	Son	M	Cha	6	S	N		Guam		None
36		166	195	Terlaje, Gregorio C	Son	M	Cha	.5	S	N		Guam		None
37		167	196	Leon Guerrero, Miguel A	Head	M	Cha	29	M	N	Y	Guam	N	Farmer
38		167	196	Leon Guerrero, Rosa S	Wife	F	Cha	27	M	N	Y	Guam	Y	None
39		167	196	Leon Guerrero, Ana S	Daughter	F	Cha	6	S	N		Guam		None
40		167	196	Leon Guerrero, Felis S	Son	M	Cha	4.3	S	N		Guam		None
41		167	196	Leon Guerrero, Dolores S	Daughter	F	Cha	.1	S	N		Guam		None
42		167	196	Leon Guerrero, Maria A	Sister	F	Cha	28	S	N	Y	Guam	N	None
43		168	197	Merfalen, Joaquin P	Head	M	Cha	40	M	N	Y	Guam	N	Farmer
44		168	197	Merfalen, Maria M	Wife	F	Cha	36	M	N	N	Guam	N	Laundress
45		168	197	Merfalen, Antonio M	Son	M	Cha	22	S	N	Y	Guam	Y	Farm Laborer
46		168	197	Merfalen, Josefina M	Daughter	F	Cha	17	S	N	Y	Guam		Laundress
47		168	197	Merfalen, Lourdes M	Daughter	F	Cha	14	S	N	Y	Guam	Y	None
48		168	197	Merfalen, Jose M	Son	M	Cha	13	S	Y	Y	Guam	Y	None
49		168	197	Merfalen, Vicente M	Son	M	Cha	6	S	N		Guam		None
50		168	197	Merfalen, Pedro M	Son	M	Cha	4.3	S	N		Guam		None

(CHAMORRO ROOTS GENEALOGY PROJECT™ TRANSCRIPTION)
(BERNARD T. PUNZALAN / HTTP://WWW.CHAMORROROOTS.COM)

DEPARTMENT OF COMMERCE-BUREAU OF THE CENSUS
WASHINGTON

FIFTEENTH CENSUS OF THE UNITED STATES: 1930-POPULATION

THE ISLAND OF GUAM

Sheet No. 21A

135

District Municipality of Agana
Name of Place Agana City (Julale)
[Proper name and, also, name of class, as city, town, village, barrio, etc]

Enumeration District No. 4
Enumerated by me on April 8, 1930 Vicente Tydingco, Enumerator

	PLACE OF ABODE: Street, avenue, road, etc.	Number of dwelling house in order of visitation	Number of family in order of visitation	NAME of each person whose place of abode on April 1, 1930, was in this family. Enter surname, first, then given name and middle initial. If any. Include every person living on April 1, 1930. Omit children born since April 1, 1930.	RELATION Relationship of this Person to the head of the family.	PERSONAL DESCRIPTION: Sex	Color or race	Age at last birthday	Single, married, widowed or divorced	EDUCATION: Attended school any time since Sept. 1, 1929	Whether able to read and write.	NATIVITY Place of birth of this person.	Whether able to speak English.	OCCUPATION
	1	2	3	4	5	6	7	8	9	10	11	12	13	14
1	Santa Cruz Street	168	197	Merfalen, Manuel M	Son	M	Cha	2.4	S	N		Guam		None
2		169	198	Yoshida, Juan A	Head	M	Jap	22	M	N	Y	Guam		Laborer
3		169	198	Yoshida, Rita H	Wife	F	Cha	24	M	N	Y	Guam		None
4		169	198	Yoshida, Rosa H	Daughter	F	Jap	3.3	S	N		Guam		None
5		170	199	Cruz, Enrique LG	Head	M	Cha	24	M	N	Y	Guam	Y	Laborer
6		170	199	Cruz, Joaquina L	Wife	F	Cha	20	M	N	Y	Guam	Y	Laundress
7		171	200	Crisostimo, Angel P	Head	M	Cha	25	M	N	Y	Guam	Y	Farmer
8		171	200	Crisostimo, Felecita A	Wife	F	Cha	27	M	N	Y	Guam	N	None
9		171	200	Crisostimo, Teresa A	Daughter	F	Cha	2.3	S	N		Guam		None
10		171	200	Crisostimo, Nicolasa A	Daughter	F	Cha	.1	S	N		Guam		None
11		172	201	Santos, Maria M	Head	F	Cha	32	Wd	N	Y	Guam	N	Laundress
12		172	201	Santos, Veronica M	Daughter	F	Cha	10	S	Y	Y	Guam	Y	None
13		172	201	Santos, Jose M	Son	M	Cha	8	S	Y		Guam		None
14		172	201	Santos, Carlos M	Son	M	Cha	4.2	S	N		Guam		None
15		172	201	Santos, Crispin M	Son	M	Cha	2.9	S	N		Guam		None
16		173	202	Cruz, Consolacion LG	Head	F	Cha	62	Wd	N	N	Guam	N	None
17		173	202	Cruz, Jose LG	Son	M	Cha	30	D	N	Y	Guam	Y	Farmer
18		173	202	Cruz, Dolores C	Granddaughter	F	Cha	14	S	Y	Y	Guam	Y	None
19		174	203	Duenas, Maria B	Head	F	Cha	49	Wd	N	N	Guam	N	None
20		174	203	Duenas, Juan B	Son	M	Cha	24	S	N	Y	Guam	Y	Chauffeur
21		174	203	Duenas, Ana B	Daughter	F	Cha	20	S	N	Y	Guam	Y	Laundress
22		174	203	Duenas, Rita B	Daughter	F	Cha	18	S	N	Y	Guam	Y	Laundress
23		174	203	Duenas, Remedios B	Daughter	F	Cha	15	S	N	Y	Guam	Y	Cook
24		174	203	Duenas, Vicente B	Son	M	Cha	9	S	Y		Guam		None
25		174	203	Duenas, Rosario B	Daughter	F	Cha	8	S	N		Guam		None

DEPARTMENT OF COMMERCE-BUREAU OF THE CENSUS
WASHINGTON

FIFTEENTH CENSUS OF THE UNITED STATES: 1930-POPULATION

THE ISLAND OF GUAM

Sheet No. 21B

135B

District **Municipality of Agana**
Name of Place **Agana City (Julale)**
[Proper name and, also, name of class, as city, town, village, barrio, etc]

Enumeration District No. **4**
Enumerated by me on **April 9, 1930** Vicente Tydingco
Enumerator

	PLACE OF ABODE			NAME	RELATION	PERSONAL DESCRIPTION				EDUCATION		NATIVITY		OCCUPATION
	Street, avenue, road, etc.	Number of dwelling house is order of visitation	Number of family in order of visitation	of each person whose place of abode on April 1, 1930, was in this family. Enter surname, first, then given name and middle initial. If any. Include every person living on April 1, 1930. Omit children born since April 1, 1930.	Relationship of this Person to the head of the family.	Sex	Color or race	Age at last birthday	Single, married, widowed or divorced	Attended school any time since Sept. 1, 1929	Whether able to read and write.	Place of birth of this person.	Whether able to speak English.	
	1	2	3	4	5	6	7	8	9	10	11	12	13	14
26	Santa Cruz Street	174	203	Duenas, Olympia B	Daughter	F	Cha	3.3	S	N		Guam		None
27		174	203	Duenas, Maria D	Granddaughter	F	Cha	3.3	S	N		Guam		None
28		175	204	Leon Guerrero, Ignacio P	Head	M	Cha	49	M	N	Y	Guam	N	Farmer
29		175	204	Leon Guerrero, Carmen P	Wife	F	Cha	54	M	N	N	Guam	N	None
30		175	204	Leon Guerrero, Rosa P	Daughter	F	Cha	24	S	N	Y	Guam	N	Laundress
31		175	204	Leon Guerrero, Regina P	Daughter	F	Cha	18	S	N	Y	Guam	N	Laundress
32		175	204	Leon Guerrero, Lourdes P	Daughter	F	Cha	16	S	N	Y	Guam	Y	Servant
33		175	204	Leon Guerrero, Juan P	Son	M	Cha	13	S	Y	Y	Guam	Y	None
34		176	205	Leon Guerrero, Luisa A	Head	F	Cha	64	Wd	N	N	Guam	N	Laundress
35		176	205	Borja, Carridad LG	Daughter	F	Cha	38	Wd	N	Y	Guam	N	Laundress
36		176	205	Borja, Ana LG	Granddaughter	F	Cha	4.1	S	N		Guam		None
37		176	205	Borja, Josefa LG	Granddaughter	F	Cha	2.1	S	N		Guam		None
38		177	206	Cruz, Jesus D	Head	M	Cha	37	M	N	Y	Guam	Y	Farmer
39		177	206	Cruz, Juliana F	Wife	F	Cha	36	M	N	Y	Guam	Y	None
40		177	206	Cruz, Robert F	Son	M	Cha	13	S	Y	Y	Guam	Y	None
41		177	206	Cruz, Albert F	Son	M	Cha	12	S	Y	Y	Guam	Y	None
42		177	206	Cruz, Teodoro F	Son	M	Cha	11	S	Y	Y	Guam	Y	None
43		177	206	Cruz, Rosaline F	Daughter	F	Cha	9	S	Y		Guam		None
44		177	206	Cruz, Peter F	Son	M	Cha	7	S	Y		Guam		None
45		177	206	Cruz, Henry F	Son	M	Cha	2.1	S	N		Guam		None
46		177	206	Cruz, Tomas F	Son	M	Cha	.8	S	N		Guam		None
47		177	206	Leon Guerrero, Ana N	Lodger	F	Cha	23	S	N	Y	Guam	Y	Cook
48		177	206	Taitague, Gregorio D	Lodger	M	Cha	19	S	Y	Y	Guam	Y	None
49		178	207	Cristobal, Adriano M	Head	M	Fil	43	M	N	Y	Philippine Islands	Y	Clerk
50		178	207	Cristobal, Carmen U	Wife	F	Fil	35	M	N	Y	Guam	Y	None

(CHAMORRO ROOTS GENEALOGY PROJECT™ TRANSCRIPTION)
(BERNARD T. PUNZALAN / HTTP://WWW.CHAMORROROOTS.COM)

DEPARTMENT OF COMMERCE-BUREAU OF THE CENSUS
WASHINGTON

FIFTEENTH CENSUS OF THE UNITED STATES: 1930-POPULATION

THE ISLAND OF GUAM

Sheet No. 22A

136

District Municipality of Agana
Name of Place Agana City (Julale)
[Proper name and, also, name of class, as city, town, village, barrio, etc]

Enumeration District No. 4
Enumerated by me on April 9, 1930 Vicente Tydingco, Enumerator

	PLACE OF ABODE: Street, avenue, road, etc.	Number of dwelling house in order of visitation	Number of family in order of visitation	NAME of each person whose place of abode on April 1, 1930, was in this family. Enter surname, first, then given name and middle initial. If any. Include every person living on April 1, 1930. Omit children born since April 1, 1930.	RELATION Relationship of this Person to the head of the family.	PERSONAL DESCRIPTION: Sex	Color or race	Age at last birthday	Single, married, widowed or divorced	EDUCATION: Attended school any time since Sept. 1, 1929	Whether able to read and write.	NATIVITY Place of birth of this person.	Whether able to speak English.	OCCUPATION
	1	2	3	4	5	6	7	8	9	10	11	12	13	14
1	Hernan Cortes Street	178	207	Cristobal, Fe U	Daughter	F	Fil	14	S	Y	Y	Guam	Y	None
2		178	207	Cristobal, George U	Son	M	Fil	11	S	Y	Y	Guam	Y	None
3		178	207	Cristobal, Adriano U	Son	M	Fil	8	S	Y		Guam		None
4		178	207	Cristobal, Eduviges U	Daughter	F	Fil	1.3	S	N		Guam		None
5		178	207	Untalan, Rosario L	Sister in law	F	Fil	24	S	N	Y	Guam	Y	Parochial Teacher
6		178	207	Untalan, Delfina L	Sister in law	F	Fil	21	S	N	Y	Guam		Parochial Teacher
7		178	207	Untalan, Antonia L	Sister in law	F	Fil	18	S	Y	Y	Guam	Y	Teacher
8		179	208	Dimapan, Vicente A	Head	M	Cha	39	M	N	Y	Guam	N	Laborer
9		179	208	Dimapan, Carmen C	Wife	F	Cha	45	M	N	N	Guam	N	None
10		179	208	Dimapan, Rosa C	Daughter	F	Cha	14	S	N	Y	Guam	Y	Servant
11		179	208	Dimapan, Jose C	Son	M	Cha	10	S	Y	Y	Guam		None
12		179	208	Dimapan, Rosario C	Daughter	F	Cha	8	S	Y		Guam		None
13		179	208	Perez, Francisca D	Aunt	F	Cha	78	Wd	N	N	Guam	N	None
14		179	208	Cruz, Anacleto D	Cousin	M	Cha	40	M	N	N	Guam		Laborer
15		180	209	Herrero, Vicente P	Head	M	Cha	46	M	N	Y	Guam	Y	Merchant
16		180	209	Herrero, Alice W	Wife	F	W	43	M	N	Y	Bonin Islands	Y	None
17		180	209	Herrero, Henry A	Son	M	Cha	22	S	N	Y	Guam	Y	Chauffeur
18		180	209	Herrero, Helen C	Daughter	F	Cha	16	S	Y	Y	Guam	Y	None
19		180	209	Herrero, Lillian J	Daughter	F	Cha	14	S	Y	Y	Guam	Y	None
20		180	209	Herrero, Ruth L	Daughter	F	Cha	13	S	Y	Y	Guam	Y	None
21		180	209	Ungacta, Felix U	Boarder	M	Cha	17	S	Y	Y	Guam	Y	None
22		181	210	Santos, Carmelo A	Head	M	Cha	53	M	N	Y	Guam	N	Farmer
23		181	210	Santos, Faustina C	Wife	F	Cha	48	M	N	N	Guam	N	None
24		182	211	Taitano, Antonio M	Head	M	Cha	45	M	N	Y	Guam	N	Farmer
25		182	211	Taitano, Manuela L	Wife	F	Cha	43	M	N	Y	Guam	N	None

(CHAMORRO ROOTS GENEALOGY PROJECT™ TRANSCRIPTION)
(BERNARD T. PUNZALAN / HTTP://WWW.CHAMORROROOTS.COM)

DEPARTMENT OF COMMERCE-BUREAU OF THE CENSUS
WASHINGTON

FIFTEENTH CENSUS OF THE UNITED STATES: 1930-POPULATION

THE ISLAND OF GUAM

Sheet No. 22B

136B

District **Municipality of Agana**
Name of Place **Agana City (Julale)**
[Proper name and, also, name of class, as city, town, village, barrio, etc]

Enumeration District No. 4
Enumerated by me on **April 9, 1930** Vicente Tydingco
Enumerator

	PLACE OF ABODE			NAME	RELATION	PERSONAL DESCRIPTION				EDUCATION		NATIVITY		OCCUPATION
	Street, avenue, road, etc.	Number of dwelling house is order of visitation	Number of family in order of visitation	of each person whose place of abode on April 1, 1930, was in this family. Enter surname, first, then given name and middle initial. If any. Include every person living on April 1, 1930. Omit children born since April 1, 1930.	Relationship of this Person to the head of the family.	Sex	Color or race	Age at last birthday	Single, married, widowed or divorced	Attended school any time since Sept. 1, 1929	Whether able to read and write.	Place of birth of this person.	Whether able to speak English.	
	1	2	3	4	5	6	7	8	9	10	11	12	13	14
26	Hernan Cortes Street	182	211	Taitano, Ana L	Daughter	F	Cha	24	S	N	Y	Guam	N	None
27	Hernan Cortes Street	182	211	Taitano, Felicita L	Daughter	F	Cha	22	S	N	Y	Guam	N	None
28	Hernan Cortes Street	182	211	Taitano, Maria L	Daughter	F	Cha	19	S	N	Y	Guam	Y	None
29	Hernan Cortes Street	182	211	Taitano, Rosario L	Daughter	F	Cha	17	S	N	Y	Guam	Y	Servant
30	Hernan Cortes Street	182	211	Taitano, Rosa L	Daughter	F	Cha	16	S	N	Y	Guam	Y	None
31	Hernan Cortes Street	182	211	Taitano, Joaquin L	Son	M	Cha	13	S	Y	Y	Guam	Y	None
32	Hernan Cortes Street	182	211	Taitano, Concepcion L	Daughter	F	Cha	11	S	Y	Y	Guam	Y	None
33	Hernan Cortes Street	182	211	Taitano, Juan L	Son	M	Cha	9	S	Y		Guam		None
34	Hernan Cortes Street	182	211	Taitano, Rita L	Daughter	F	Cha	8	S	Y		Guam		None
35	Hernan Cortes Street	182	211	Taitano, Francisco L	Son	M	Cha	5	S	N		Guam		None
36	Hernan Cortes Street	182	211	Pablo, Antonio A	Wife's nephew	M	Cha	23	S	N	Y	Guam		Farm Laborer
37	Hernan Cortes Street	183	212	Mesa, Vicente M	Head	M	Cha	49	M	N	Y	Guam		Farmer
38	Hernan Cortes Street	183	212	Mesa, Ana P	Wife	F	Cha	56	M	N	Y	Guam		None
39	Hernan Cortes Street	183	212	Mesa, Jose P	Son	M	Cha	22	S	N	Y	Guam		None
40	Hernan Cortes Street	183	212	Mesa, Felis P	Son	M	Cha	17	S	Y	Y	Guam	Y	None
41	Hernan Cortes Street	183	212	Mesa, Manuel P	Son	M	Cha	14	S	Y	Y	Guam	Y	None
42	Hernan Cortes Street	183	212	Mesa, Rafael P	Son	M	Cha	11	S	Y	Y	Guam	Y	None
43	Hernan Cortes Street	183	212	Cruz, Concepcion C	Step daughter	F	Cha	31	S	N	Y	Guam	N	None
44	Hernan Cortes Street	183	213	Salas, Maria P	Head	F	Cha	33	Wd	N	Y	Guam	Y	Seamstress
45	Hernan Cortes Street	183	213	Salas, Concepcion P	Daughter	F	Cha	8	S	Y		Guam		None
46	Hernan Cortes Street	183	213	Salas, Antonio P	Son	M	Cha	7	S	Y		Guam		None
47	Hernan Cortes Street	183	213	Salas, Juan P	Son	M	Cha	4.9	S	N		Guam		None
48	Hernan Cortes Street	183	213	Salas, Francisco P	Son	M	Cha	3.6	S	N		Guam		None
49	Hernan Cortes Street	183	213	Salas, Rosa P	Daughter	F	Cha	1.9	S	N		Guam		None
50	Hernan Cortes Street	184	214	Cruz, Francisco P	Head	M	Cha	28	M	N	Y	Guam	Y	Laborer

DEPARTMENT OF COMMERCE-BUREAU OF THE CENSUS
WASHINGTON

FIFTEENTH CENSUS OF THE UNITED STATES: 1930-POPULATION

THE ISLAND OF GUAM

Sheet No. 23A

District Municipality of Agana
Name of Place Agana City (Julale)
[Proper name and, also, name of class, as city, town, village, barrio, etc]

Enumeration District No. 4
Enumerated by me on April 9, 1930 Vicente Tydingco, Enumerator

	PLACE OF ABODE: Street, avenue, road, etc.	Number of dwelling house in order of visitation	Number of family in order of visitation	NAME of each person whose place of abode on April 1, 1930, was in this family. Enter surname, first, then given name and middle initial. If any. Include every person living on April 1, 1930. Omit children born since April 1, 1930.	RELATION Relationship of this Person to the head of the family.	PERSONAL DESCRIPTION: Sex	Color or race	Age at last birthday	Single, married, widowed or divorced	EDUCATION: Attended school any time since Sept. 1, 1929	Whether able to read and write.	NATIVITY Place of birth of this person.	Whether able to speak English.	OCCUPATION
	1	2	3	4	5	6	7	8	9	10	11	12	13	14
1	Hernan Cortes Street	184	214	Cruz, Cecilia B	Wife	F	W	17	M	N	Y	Guam	Y	None
2		184	214	Cruz, Joaquin B	Son	M	Cha	.8	S	N		Guam		None
3		185	215	Elatico, Juan A	Head	M	Fil	32	M	N	Y	Philippine Islands	Y	Machinist
4		185	215	Elatico, Tomasa M	Wife	F	Cha	26	M	N	Y	Guam	N	None
5		186	216	Taitano, Jose SN	Head	M	Cha	54	M	N	Y	Guam	Y	Farmer
6		186	216	Taitano, Dolores P	Wife	F	Cha	51	M	N	Y	Guam	N	None
7		186	216	Taitano, Juan P	Son	M	Cha	24	S	N	Y	Guam	Y	Farm Laborer
8		186	216	Taitano, Ana P	Daughter	F	Cha	20	S	N	Y	Guam	Y	None
9		186	216	Taitano, Rafael P	Son	M	Cha	16	S	Y	Y	Guam	Y	None
10		186	216	Taitano, Carlos P	Son	M	Cha	13	S	Y	Y	Guam	Y	None
11		186	216	Taitano, Joaquin P	Son	M	Cha	10	S	Y	Y	Guam	Y	None
12		186	217	Taitano, Ramon P	Head	M	Cha	26	M	N	Y	Guam	Y	Machinist
13		186	217	Taitano, Trinidad P	Wife	F	Cha	21	M	N	Y	Guam	Y	None
14		186	217	Santos, Ana L	Lodger	F	Cha	62	S	N	N	Guam	N	None
15		187	218	Leon Guerrero, Jose F	Head	M	Cha	46	M	N	Y	Guam	Y	Carpenter
16		187	218	Leon Guerrero, Ana C	Wife	F	Cha	37	M	N	Y	Guam	N	None
17		187	218	Leon Guerrero, Rita C	Daughter	F	Cha	20	S	N	Y	Guam	Y	Seamstress
18		187	218	Leon Guerrero, Justo C	Son	M	Cha	14	S	Y	Y	Guam	Y	None
19		187	218	Leon Guerrero, Ephraim C	Son	M	Cha	11	S	Y	Y	Guam	Y	None
20		187	218	Leon Guerrero, Vicente C	Son	M	Cha	9	S	Y		Guam		None
21		187	218	Leon Guerrero, Jose C	Son	M	Cha	6	S	N		Guam		None
22		187	218	Leon Guerrero, Juan C	Son	M	Cha	3.6	S	N		Guam		None
23		187	218	Leon Guerrero, Ana C	Daughter	F	Cha	.3	S	N		Guam		None
24		188	219	Salas, Rosa S	Head	M	Cha	47	Wd	N	Y	Guam	N	None
25		188	219	Salas, Ramon S	Son	M	Cha	27	S	N	Y	Guam	N	Farmer

DEPARTMENT OF COMMERCE-BUREAU OF THE CENSUS
WASHINGTON

FIFTEENTH CENSUS OF THE UNITED STATES: 1930-POPULATION

THE ISLAND OF GUAM

Sheet No. 23B

137B

District Municipality of Agana
Name of Place Agana City (Julale)
[Proper name and, also, name of class, as city, town, village, barrio, etc]

Enumeration District No. 4
Enumerated by me on April 9, 1930 Vicente Tydingco
Enumerator

	PLACE OF ABODE			NAME	RELATION	PERSONAL DESCRIPTION				EDUCATION		NATIVITY		OCCUPATION
	Street, avenue, road, etc.	Number of dwelling house is order of visitation	Number of family in order of visitation	of each person whose place of abode on April 1, 1930, was in this family. Enter surname, first, then given name and middle initial. If any. Include every person living on April 1, 1930. Omit children born since April 1, 1930.	Relationship of this Person to the head of the family.	Sex	Color or race	Age at last birthday	Single, married, widowed or divorced	Attended school any time since Sept. 1, 1929	Whether able to read and write.	Place of birth of this person.	Whether able to speak English.	
	1	2	3	4	5	6	7	8	9	10	11	12	13	14
26	Hernan Cortes Street	188	219	Salas, Enrique S	Son	M	Cha	21	S	N	Y	Guam	N	Laborer
27		188	219	Salas, Esperanza S	Daughter	F	Cha	17	S	N	Y	Guam	Y	Servant
28		188	219	Salas, Felix S	Son	M	Cha	14	S	Y	Y	Guam	Y	None
29		188	219	Salas, Patricia S	Daughter	F	Cha	12	S	Y	Y	Guam	Y	None
30		188	219	Taitingfong, Magdalena S	Daughter	F	Cha	21	Wd	N	Y	Guam	N	Cook
31		188	219	Taitingfong, Juan S	Grandson	M	Cha	2.3	S	N		Guam		None
32		188	220	Pangelinan, Tomas P	Head	M	Cha	28	M	N	Y	Guam	Y	Laborer
33		188	220	Pangelinan, Ana S	Wife	F	Cha	28	M	N	N	Guam	N	None
34		188	220	Pangelinan, Perpetua S	Daughter	F	Cha	6	S	N		Guam		None
35		188	220	Pangelinan, Juan S	Son	M	Cha	4.1	S	N		Guam		None
36		188	220	Pangelinan, Jesusa S	Daughter	F	Cha	2.1	S	N		Guam		None
37		188	220	Pangelinan, Tomas S	Son	M	Cha	.1	S	N		Guam		None
38		189	221	Diaz, Amparo LG	Head	F	Cha	59	Wd	N	Y	Guam	N	None
39		189	221	Diaz, Dolores LG	Daughter	F	Cha	20	S	N	Y	Guam	Y	Dressmaker
40		189	221	Diaz, Rosa LG	Daughter	F	Cha	17	S	Y	Y	Guam	Y	None
41		190	222	Castro, Felix P	Head	M	Cha	24	M	N	Y	Guam	Y	Machinist
42		190	222	Castro, Concepcion C	Wife	F	Cha	24	M	N	Y	Guam	Y	None
43		190	222	Castro, Ramon C	Son	M	Cha	.5	S	N		Guam		None
44		191	223	Castro, Francisco W	Head	M	Cha	61	M	N	Y	Rota Island	N	Blacksmith
45		191	223	Castro, Maria P	Wife	F	Cha	60	M	N	Y	Guam	N	None
46		191	223	Castro, Margarita P	Daughter	F	Cha	27	S	N	Y	Guam	Y	None
47		191	224	May, Luella H	Head	F	W	35	M	N	Y	Massachusetts	Y	None
48		192	225	Mafnas, Joaquin R	Head	M	Cha	43	M	N	Y	Guam	N	Farmer
49		192	225	Mafnas, Maria C	Wife	F	Cha	43	M	N	Y	Guam	N	None
50		192	225	Mafnas, Antonio C	Son	M	Cha	17	S		Y	Guam	Y	Farm Laborer

(CHAMORRO ROOTS GENEALOGY PROJECT™ TRANSCRIPTION)
(BERNARD T. PUNZALAN / HTTP://WWW.CHAMORROROOTS.COM)

DEPARTMENT OF COMMERCE-BUREAU OF THE CENSUS
WASHINGTON
FIFTEENTH CENSUS OF THE UNITED STATES: 1930-POPULATION

THE ISLAND OF GUAM

Sheet No. 24A

District Municipality of Agana
Name of Place Agana City (Julale)
[Proper name and, also, name of class, as city, town, village, barrio, etc]

Enumeration District No. 4
Enumerated by me on April 9, 1930 Vicente Tydingco, Enumerator

	PLACE OF ABODE			NAME	RELATION	PERSONAL DESCRIPTION				EDUCATION		NATIVITY		OCCUPATION
	Street, avenue, road, etc.	Number of dwelling house in order of visitation	Number of family in order of visitation	of each person whose place of abode on April 1, 1930, was in this family. Enter surname, first, then given name and middle initial. If any. Include every person living on April 1, 1930. Omit children born since April 1, 1930.	Relationship of this Person to the head of the family.	Sex	Color or race	Age at last birthday	Single, married, widowed or divorced	Attended school any time since Sept. 1, 1929	Whether able to read and write.	Place of birth of this person.	Whether able to speak English.	
	1	2	3	4	5	6	7	8	9	10	11	12	13	14
1	Hernan Cortes Street	192	225	Mafnas, Rosario C	Daughter	F	Cha	15	S	N	Y	Guam	Y	Cook
2		192	225	Mafnas, Juan C	Son	M	Cha	13	S	Y	Y	Guam	Y	None
3		192	225	Mafnas, Silvestre C	Son	M	Cha	9	S	Y		Guam		None
4		192	225	Mafnas, Trinidad C	Daughter	F	Cha	7	S	Y		Guam		None
5		192	225	Mafnas, Francisco C	Son	M	Cha	4.7	S	N		Guam		None
6		192	225	Mafnas, Jose C	Son	M	Cha	2.3	S	N		Guam		None
7		193	226	Borja, Vicente M	Head	M	Cha	48	M	N	N	Guam	N	Farmer
8		193	226	Borja, Joaquina S	Wife	F	Cha	44	M	N	N	Guam	N	Washerwoman
9		193	226	Borja, Juan S	Son	M	Cha	22	S	N	Y	Guam	Y	Farm Laborer
10		193	226	Borja, Isabel S	Daughter	F	Cha	13	S	Y	Y	Guam	Y	None
11		194	227	Rojas, Joaquin R	Head	M	Cha	58	M	N	N	Guam	N	Farmer
12		194	227	Rojas, Maria M	Wife	F	Cha	70	M	Y	N	Guam	N	Washerwoman
13		194	227	Borja, Maria S	Step niece	F	Cha	11	S	N	Y	Guam	Y	None
14		195	228	Salas, Juan S	Head	M	Cha	27	M	N	Y	Guam	Y	Clerk
15		195	228	Salas, Magdalena U	Wife	F	Cha	25	M	N	Y	Guam	Y	None
16		195	228	Salas, Silvia U	Daughter	F	Cha	2.8	S	N		Guam		None
17		195	228	Salas, Juan U	Son	M	Cha	1.9	S	N		Guam		None
18		195	228	Salas, Antonio U	Son	M	Cha	.9	S	N		Guam		None
19		195	228	San Nicolas, Maria G	Servant	F	Cha	18	S	Y	Y	Guam	Y	None
20		196	229	Taitano, Maria B	Head	F	Cha	46	Wd	N	Y	Guam	Y	None
21		196	229	Taitano, Maria B	Daughter	F	Cha	19	S	N	Y	Guam	Y	Servant
22		196	229	Taitano, Ana B	Daughter	F	Cha	17	S	N	Y	Guam	Y	Saleswoman
23		196	229	Taitano, Josefina B	Daughter	F	Cha	15	S	N	Y	Guam	Y	Cook
24		196	229	Taitano, Juan B	Son	M	Cha	13	S	N	Y	Guam	Y	Farmer
25		196	229	Taitano, Antonia B	Daughter	F	Cha	11	S	Y		Guam	Y	None

DEPARTMENT OF COMMERCE-BUREAU OF THE CENSUS
WASHINGTON

FIFTEENTH CENSUS OF THE UNITED STATES: 1930-POPULATION

THE ISLAND OF GUAM

Sheet No. 24B

138B

District **Municipality of Agana**
Name of Place **Agana City (Julale)**
[Proper name and, also, name of class, as city, town, village, barrio, etc]

Enumeration District No. **4**
Enumerated by me on **April 9, 1930** Vicente Tydingco
Enumerator

	PLACE OF ABODE			NAME	RELATION	PERSONAL DESCRIPTION				EDUCATION		NATIVITY		OCCUPATION
	Street, avenue, road, etc.	Number of dwelling house is order of visitation	Number of family in order of visitation	of each person whose place of abode on April 1, 1930, was in this family. Enter surname, first, then given name and middle initial. If any. Include every person living on April 1, 1930. Omit children born since April 1, 1930.	Relationship of this Person to the head of the family.	Sex	Color or race	Age at last birthday	Single, married, widowed or divorced	Attended school any time since Sept. 1, 1929	Whether able to read and write.	Place of birth of this person.	Whether able to speak English.	
	1	2	3	4	5	6	7	8	9	10	11	12	13	14
26	Hernan Cortes Street	196	229	Taitano, Jose B	Son	M	Cha	9	S	Y		Guam		None
27		196	229	Taitano, Magdalena B	Daughter	F	Cha	6	S	N		Guam		None
28		196	229	Taitano, Joaquin B	Son	M	Cha	4.8	S	N		Guam		None
29		196	229	Taitano, Pedro M	Brother in law	M	Cha	36	S	N	N	Guam		Laborer
30		197	230	Taitano, Joaquin F	Head	M	Cha	27	M	N	Y	Guam	Y	Policeman
31		197	230	Taitano, Luisa S	Wife	F	Cha	23	M	N	Y	Guam	N	None
32		197	230	Taitano, Agustin S	Son	M	Cha	4.5	S	N		Guam		None
33		197	230	Taitano, Juan S	Son	M	Cha	3.9	S	N		Guam		None
34		197	230	Taitano, Magdalena S	Daughter	F	Cha	2.7	S	N		Guam		None
35		198	231	Toves, Juan G	Head	M	Cha	48	M	N	Y	Guam	Y	Laborer
36		198	231	Toves, Maria A	Wife	F	Cha	46	M	N	N	Guam	N	None
37		198	231	Toves, Jose A	Son	M	Cha	29	S	N	Y	Guam	Y	Chauffeur
38		198	231	Toves, Juan A	Son	M	Cha	23	Wd	N	Y	Guam	Y	Laborer
39		198	231	Toves, Carmen A	Daughter	F	Cha	20	S	N	Y	Guam	Y	Cook
40		198	231	Toves, Ana A	Daughter	F	Cha	18	S	N	Y	Guam	Y	None
41		198	231	Toves, Francisco A	Son	M	Cha	13	S	Y	Y	Guam		None
42		198	231	Toves, Jesus A	Son	M	Cha	9	S	Y		Guam		None
43		198	231	Toves, Vicente A	Son	M	Cha	8	S	Y		Guam		None
44		199	232	Sococo, Rosa U	Head	F	Cha	36	S	N	Y	Guam	Y	Midwife
45		199	232	Sococo, Gregorio U	Son	M	Cha	12	S	Y	Y	Guam		None
46		199	232	Sococo, Peter U	Son	M	Cha	9	S	Y		Guam		None
47		199	232	Sococo, Margarita U	Daughter	F	Cha	8	S	Y		Guam		None
48		199	232	Leon Guerrero, Jesus U	Wife's nephew	m	Cha	21	S	N	Y	Guam	Y	Carpenter
49		200	233	Cruz, Mariano M	Head	M	Cha	60	M	N	N	Guam	N	Farmer
50		200	233	Cruz, Luisa C	Wife	F	Cha	59	M	N	N	Guam		None

(CHAMORRO ROOTS GENEALOGY PROJECT™ TRANSCRIPTION)
(BERNARD T. PUNZALAN / HTTP://WWW.CHAMORROROOTS.COM)

DEPARTMENT OF COMMERCE-BUREAU OF THE CENSUS
WASHINGTON

FIFTEENTH CENSUS OF THE UNITED STATES: 1930-POPULATION

THE ISLAND OF GUAM

Sheet No. 25A

District Municipality of Agana
Name of Place Agana City (Julale)
[Proper name and, also, name of class, as city, town, village, barrio, etc]

Enumeration District No. 4
Enumerated by me on April 10, 1930 Vicente Tydingco
Enumerator

	PLACE OF ABODE			NAME	RELATION	PERSONAL DESCRIPTION				EDUCATION		NATIVITY		OCCUPATION
	Street, avenue, road, etc.	Number of dwelling house in order of visitation	Number of family in order of visitation	of each person whose place of abode on April 1, 1930, was in this family. Enter surname, first, then given name and middle initial. If any. Include every person living on April 1, 1930. Omit children born since April 1, 1930.	Relationship of this Person to the head of the family.	Sex	Color or race	Age at last birthday	Single, married, widowed or divorced	Attended school any time since Sept. 1, 1929	Whether able to read and write.	Place of birth of this person.	Whether able to speak English.	
	1	2	3	4	5	6	7	8	9	10	11	12	13	14
1	Hernan Cortes Street	200	234	Cruz, Vicente C	Head	M	Cha	30	M	N	Y	Guam	Y	Farmer
2		200	234	Cruz, Maria W	Wife	F	Cha	26	M	N	Y	Guam	Y	None
3		200	234	Cruz, Rita W	Daughter	F	Cha	.7	S	N		Guam		None
4		201	235	Mafnas, Maria C	Head	F	Cha	38	Wd	N	N	Guam	N	Laundress
5		201	235	Mafnas, Ana C	Daughter	F	Cha	15	S	N	Y	Guam	Y	None
6		201	235	Mafnas, Antonia C	Daughter	F	Cha	12	S	Y	Y	Guam	Y	None
7		201	235	Mafnas, Dominga C	Daughter	F	Cha	6	S	N		Guam		None
8		201	235	Mafnas, Juan C	Son	M	Cha	3.8	S	N		Guam		None
9		202	236	Mesa, Joaquin C	Son	M	Cha	1.7	S	N		Guam		None
10		202	236	Mesa, Juan M	Head	M	Cha	54	M	N	Y	Guam	Y	Farmer
11		202	236	Mesa, Dolores A	Wife	F	Cha	58	M	N	N	Guam	N	None
12		202	236	Mesa, Sisto A	Son	M	Cha	20	S	N	Y	Guam	Y	Laborer
13		203	237	Cruz, Antonio C	Head	M	Cha	35	M	N	Y	Guam	Y	Farmer
14		203	237	Cruz, Carmen A	Wife	F	Cha	35	M	N	Y	Guam	Y	None
15		203	237	Cruz, Julia A	Daughter	F	Cha	12	S	Y	Y	Guam	Y	None
16		203	237	Cruz, Trinidad A	Daughter	F	Cha	11	S	Y		Guam	Y	None
17		203	237	Cruz, Jose A	Son	M	Cha	4.3	S	N		Guam		None
18		203	237	Cruz, Lourdes A	Daughter	F	Cha	2.3	S	N		Guam		None
19		204	238	Reyes, Juan P	Head	M	Cha	32	M	N	Y	Guam	Y	Farmer
20		204	238	Reyes, Carmen C	Wife	F	Cha	27	M	N	Y	Guam	Y	None
21		204	238	Reyes, Ruth C	Daughter	F	Cha	6	S	N		Guam		None
22		204	238	Reyes, Luis C	Son	M	Cha	3.5	S	N		Guam		None
23		204	238	Reyes, Jesus C	Son	M	Cha	.8	S	N		Guam		None
24		205	239	Cruz, Enrique C	Head	M	Cha	38	M	N	Y	Guam	Y	Farmer
25		205	239	Cruz, Josefa M	Wife	F	Cha	34	M	N	Y	Guam	N	None

DEPARTMENT OF COMMERCE-BUREAU OF THE CENSUS
WASHINGTON

FIFTEENTH CENSUS OF THE UNITED STATES: 1930-POPULATION

THE ISLAND OF GUAM

Sheet No. 25B

139B

District **Municipality of Agana**
Name of Place **Agana City (Julale)**
[Proper name and, also, name of class, as city, town, village, barrio, etc]

Enumeration District No. 4
Enumerated by me on **April 10, 1930** Vicente Tydingco
Enumerator

	PLACE OF ABODE			NAME	RELATION	PERSONAL DESCRIPTION				EDUCATION		NATIVITY		OCCUPATION
	Street, avenue, road, etc.	Number of dwelling house in order of visitation	Number of family in order of visitation	of each person whose place of abode on April 1, 1930, was in this family. Enter surname, first, then given name and middle initial. If any. Include every person living on April 1, 1930. Omit children born since April 1, 1930.	Relationship of this Person to the head of the family.	Sex	Color or race	Age at last birthday	Single, married, widowed or divorced	Attended school any time since Sept. 1, 1929	Whether able to read and write.	Place of birth of this person.	Whether able to speak English.	
	1	2	3	4	5	6	7	8	9	10	11	12	13	14
26	Hernan Cortes Street	205	239	Cruz, Simplicia M	Daughter	F	Cha	9	S	Y		Guam		None
27		205	239	Cruz, Pedro M	Son	M	Cha	7	S	Y		Guam		None
28		205	239	Cruz, Juan M	Son	M	Cha	2.5	S	N		Guam		None
29		205	239	Mafnas, Rosa R	Sister in law	F	Cha	30	S	N	Y	Guam	Y	Laundress
30		205	239	Mafnas, Jose M	Nephew	M	Cha	11	S	Y		Guam		None
31		206	240	Mafnas, Jose R	Head	M	Cha	32	M	N	Y	Guam	N	Farmer
32		206	240	Mafnas, Agueda LG	Wife	F	Cha	34	M	N	Y	Guam	N	None
33		206	240	Mafnas, Francisco LG	Son	M	Cha	8	S	Y		Guam		None
34		206	240	Mafnas, Antonia LG	Daughter	F	Cha	7	S	Y		Guam		None
35		206	240	Mafnas, Rita LG	Daughter	F	Cha	4.4	S	N		Guam		None
36		206	240	Mafnas, Carmen LG	Daughter	F	Cha	3.5	S	N		Guam		None
37		206	240	Mafnas, Ignacia LG	Daughter	F	Cha	1.2	S	N		Guam		None
38		207	241	Taitano, Francisco W	Head	M	Cha	27	M	N	Y	Guam	Y	Carpenter
39		207	241	Taitano, Tomasa M	Wife	F	Cha	34	M	N	Y	Guam	Y	Midwife
40		207	241	Taitano, Jesusa M	Daughter	F	Cha	8	S	Y		Guam		None
41		207	241	Taitano, Pedro M	Son	M	Cha	6	S	N		Guam		None
42		207	241	Taitano, Jose M	Son	M	Cha	2.7	S	N		Guam		None
43		207	241	Taitano, Rita M	Daughter	F	Cha	1.6	S	N		Guam		None
44		208	242	Blaz, de Caseda	Head	M	W	36	S	N	Y	Spain	Y	Missionary
45		208	242	Ignacio, Francisco T	Servant	M	Cha	15	S	N	Y	Guam	Y	Cook
46		209	243	Eueton, Nina C	Head	F	W	36	M	N	Y	Frederickson, Virginia	Y	None
47		210	244	Hornsong, Ralph A	Head	M	W	27	M	N	Y	San Francisco, California	Y	Dentist
48			244	Hornsong, Florence J	Wife	F	W	24	M	N	Y	Ogden,Utah	Y	None
49		211	245	Dembasher, Anna M	Head	F	W	43	M	N	Y	Lansing, Michigan	Y	None
50		212	246	Cruz, Juan M	Head	M	Cha	34	M	N	Y	Guam	N	Farmer

DEPARTMENT OF COMMERCE-BUREAU OF THE CENSUS
WASHINGTON

FIFTEENTH CENSUS OF THE UNITED STATES: 1930-POPULATION

THE ISLAND OF GUAM

Sheet No. 26A

District **Municipality of Agana**
Name of Place **Agana City (Julale)**
[Proper name and, also, name of class, as city, town, village, barrio, etc]

Enumeration District No. **4**
Enumerated by me on **April 10, 1930** Vicente Tydingco, Enumerator

	PLACE OF ABODE: Street, avenue, road, etc.	Number of dwelling house in order of visitation	Number of family in order of visitation	NAME of each person whose place of abode on April 1, 1930, was in this family. Enter surname, first, then given name and middle initial. If any. Include every person living on April 1, 1930. Omit children born since April 1, 1930.	RELATION Relationship of this Person to the head of the family.	PERSONAL DESCRIPTION: Sex	Color or race	Age at last birthday	Single, married, widowed or divorced	EDUCATION: Attended school any time since Sept. 1, 1929	Whether able to read and write.	NATIVITY Place of birth of this person.	Whether able to speak English.	OCCUPATION
	1	2	3	4	5	6	7	8	9	10	11	12	13	14
1	Hernan Cortes Street	212	246	Cruz, Maria C	Wife	F	Cha	32	M	N	Y	Guam	N	None
2		212	246	Cruz, Margarita C	Daughter	F	Cha	10	S	Y	Y	Guam	Y	None
3		212	246	Cruz, Natividad C	Daughter	F	Cha	9	S	Y		Guam		None
4		212	246	Cruz, Francisco C	Son	M	Cha	5	S	N		Guam		None
5		212	246	Cruz, Jose C	Son	M	Cha	.5	S	N		Guam		None
6		213	247	Bernardo, Pedro C	Head	M	Fil	29	M	N	Y	Guam	N	Farmer
7		213	247	Bernardo, Concepcion C	Wife	F	Cha	26	M	N	N	Guam	N	None
8		213	247	Bernardo, Guilliermo C	Son	M	Fil	4.7	S	N		Guam		None
9		213	247	Bernardo, Rosario C	Daughter	F	Fil	2.7	S	N		Guam		None
10		213	247	Cepeda, Nieves M	Mother in law	F	Cha	54	Wd	N	N	Guam	N	Laundress
11		214	248	Bernardo, Guilliermo T	Head	M	Fil	62	M	N	Y	Phillippine Island	N	Mason
12		214	248	Bernardo, Ana Q	Wife	F	Cha	38	M	N	Y	Guam	N	None
13		214	248	Bernardo, Artemeo Q	Son	M	Fil	15	S	Y	Y	Guam	Y	None
14		214	248	Bernardo, Jose Q	Son	M	Fil	10	S	Y	Y	Guam	Y	None
15		214	248	Bernardo, Maria Q	Daughter	F	Fil	4.9	S	N		Guam		None
16		214	248	Cruz, Jesus LG	Lodger	M	Cha	17	S	N	Y	Guam	N	Farm Laborer
17	Pizarro St	215	249	Leon Guerrero, Maria P	Head	F	Cha	35	S	Y	Y	Guam	N	Basket Weaver
18		215	249	Leon Guerrero, Jose P	Son	M	Cha	17	S	Y	Y	Guam	N	Farmer
19		215	249	Leon Guerrero, Pedro P	Son	M	Cha	15	S	Y	Y	Guam	Y	None
20		215	249	Leon Guerrero, Joaquin P	Son	M	Cha	10	S	Y	Y	Guam	Y	None
21		215	249	Leon Guerrero, Juan P	Son	M	Cha	4.5	S	N		Guam		None
22		215	249	Leon Guerrero, Jesusa P	Daughter	F	Cha	1.9	S	N		Guam		None
23		216	250	Castro, Francisco P	Head	M	Cha	31	M	N	Y	Guam	Y	Chauffeur
24		216	250	Castro, Joaquina P	Son	F	Cha	29	M	N	N	Guam	Y	None
25		216	250	Castro, Manuel P	Son	M	Cha	4.4	S			Guam		None

DEPARTMENT OF COMMERCE-BUREAU OF THE CENSUS
WASHINGTON

FIFTEENTH CENSUS OF THE UNITED STATES: 1930-POPULATION

THE ISLAND OF GUAM

Sheet No. 26B

140B

District **Municipality of Agana**
Name of Place **Agana City (Julale)**
[Proper name and, also, name of class, as city, town, village, barrio, etc]

Enumeration District No. 4
Enumerated by me on **April 10, 1930** Vicente Tydingco
Enumerator

	PLACE OF ABODE			NAME	RELATION	PERSONAL DESCRIPTION				EDUCATION		NATIVITY		OCCUPATION
	Street, avenue, road, etc.	Number of dwelling house in order of visitation	Number of family in order of visitation	of each person whose place of abode on April 1, 1930, was in this family. Enter surname, first, then given name and middle initial. If any. Include every person living on April 1, 1930. Omit children born since April 1, 1930.	Relationship of this Person to the head of the family.	Sex	Color or race	Age at last birthday	Single, married, widowed or divorced	Attended school any time since Sept. 1, 1929	Whether able to read and write.	Place of birth of this person.	Whether able to speak English.	
	1	2	3	4	5	6	7	8	9	10	11	12	13	14
26	Pizarro St	216	250	Castro, Felix P	Son	M	Cha	3.3	S	N		Guam		None
27		216	250	Castro, Maria P	Daughter	F	Cha	1.1	S	N		Guam		None
28		217	251	Cruz, Jose A	Head	M	Cha	56	M	N	Y	Guam	N	Farmer
29		217	251	Cruz, Candelaria T	Wife	F	Cha	58	M	N	N	Guam	N	None
30		217	251	Cruz, Maria T	Daughter	F	Cha	30	S	N	Y	Guam	Y	Laundress
31		217	251	Cruz, Beatris T	Daughter	F	Cha	17	S	N	Y	Guam	Y	Laundress
32		217	251	Cruz, Francisco T	Grandson	M	Cha	8	S	Y		Guam		None
33		218	252	Aguon, Pedro C	Head	M	Cha	40	M	N	Y	Guam	Y	Laborer
34		218	252	Aguon, Rosa S	Wife	F	Cha	38	M	N	N	Guam	N	None
35		218	252	Aguon, Remedios S	Daughter	F	Cha	14	S	N	Y	Guam	Y	None
36		218	252	Aguon, Vicente S	Son	M	Cha	8	S	Y		Guam		None
37		218	252	Aguon, Tomas S	Son	M	Cha	6	S	N		Guam		None
38		218	252	Aguon, Clotilde S	Daughter	F	Cha	4.2	S	N		Guam		None
39		218	252	Aguon, Concepcion S	Daughter	F	Cha	.9	S	N		Guam		None
40		219	253	Mafnas, Jose C	Head	M	Cha	46	M	N	N	Guam	Y	Farmer
41		219	253	Mafnas, Filomenia R	Wife	F	Cha	41	M	N	N	Guam	Y	None
42		219	253	Mafnas, Ignacia R	Daughter	F	Cha	17	S	N	N	Guam	N	Laundress
43		219	253	Mafnas, Jose R	Son	M	Cha	15	S	N	Y	Guam	Y	Farm Laborer
44		219	253	Mafnas, Maria R	Daughter	F	Cha	13	S	Y	Y	Guam	Y	None
45		219	253	Mafnas, Joaquin R	Son	M	Cha	11	S	Y	Y	Guam	Y	None
46		219	253	Mafnas, Francisco R	Son	M	Cha	9	S	Y		Guam		None
47		219	253	Mafnas, Ana R	Daughter	F	Cha	5.3	S	N		Guam		None
48		219	253	Mafnas, Ignacio R	Son	M	Cha	2.3	S	N		Guam		None
49		220	254	Indalecio, Juan I	Head	M	Cha	28	M	N	N	Guam	N	Farmer
50		220	254	Indalecio, Ignacia M	Wife	F	Cha	29	M	N	N	Guam	N	None

DEPARTMENT OF COMMERCE-BUREAU OF THE CENSUS
WASHINGTON

FIFTEENTH CENSUS OF THE UNITED STATES: 1930-POPULATION

THE ISLAND OF GUAM

Sheet No. 27A

District Municipality of Agana
Name of Place Agana City (Julale)
[Proper name and, also, name of class, as city, town, village, barrio, etc]

Enumeration District No. 4
Enumerated by me on April 11, 1930 Vicente Tydingco
Enumerator

	PLACE OF ABODE			NAME	RELATION	PERSONAL DESCRIPTION				EDUCATION		NATIVITY		OCCUPATION
	Street, avenue, road, etc.	Number of dwelling house is order of visitation	Number of family in order of visitation	of each person whose place of abode on April 1, 1930, was in this family. Enter surname, first, then given name and middle initial. If any. Include every person living on April 1, 1930. Omit children born since April 1, 1930.	Relationship of this Person to the head of the family.	Sex	Color or race	Age at last birthday	Single, married, widowed or divorced	Attended school any time since Sept. 1, 1929	Whether able to read and write.	Place of birth of this person.	Whether able to speak English.	
	1	2	3	4	5	6	7	8	9	10	11	12	13	14
1	Pizarro St	220	254	Indalecio, Antonio M	Son	M	Cha	4.9	S	N		Guam		None
2		220	254	Indalecio, Ana M	Daughter	F	Cha	2.8	S	N		Guam		None
3		220	254	Indalecio, Maria M	Daughter	F	Cha	.3	S	N		Guam		None
4		220	255	Mafnas, Antonio C	Head	M	Cha	61	M	N	N	Guam	N	Fisherman
5		220	255	Mafnas, Lucia R	Wife	F	Cha	64	M	N	N	Guam	N	None
6		220	255	Mafnas, Rosa R	Daughter	F	Cha	24	S	N	N	Guam	Y	Servant
7		220	255	Mafnas, Vicente R	Son	M	Cha	21	S	N	Y	Guam	N	Laborer
8		221	256	Acosta, Jose V	Head	M	Cha	48	M	N	Y	Guam	N	Carpenter
9		221	256	Acosta, Rosa P	Wife	F	Cha	47	M	N	N	Guam	N	None
10		221	257	Reyes, Jose M	Head	M	Cha	23	M	N	Y	Guam	N	Farm Laborer
11		221	257	Reyes, Maria A	Wife	F	Cha	22	M	N	Y	Guam	N	None
12		221	257	Reyes, Ignacia A	Daughter	F	Cha	1.9	S	N		Guam		None
13		221	257	Reyes, Angelina A	Daughter	F	Cha	.5	S	N		Guam		None
14		222	258	Mesa, Antonio T	Head	M	Cha	33	M	N	Y	Guam	Y	Farmer
15		222	258	Mesa, Juana P	Wife	F	Cha	28	M	N	Y	Guam	N	None
16		222	258	Mesa, Vicente P	Son	M	Cha	6	S	N		Guam		None
17		222	258	Mesa, Herminia P	Daughter	F	Cha	.9	S	N		Guam		None
18		222	258	Mesa, Antonio M	Father	M	Cha	59	Wd	N	N	Guam	N	Farm Laborer
19		223	259	Mafnas, Santiago C	Head	M	Cha	52	M	N	N	Guam	N	Farmer
20		223	259	Mafnas, Remedios M	Wife	F	Cha	53	M	N	N	Guam	N	Laundress
21		223	259	Mafnas, Jose M	Son	M	Cha	29	S	N	Y	Guam	Y	Laborer
22		223	259	Mafnas, Magdalena M	Daughter	F	Cha	16	S	N	Y	Guam	Y	None
23		223	259	Acosta, Felipe M	Son	M	Cha	13	S	Y	Y	Guam	Y	None
24		223	259	Mafnas, Felecita M	Daughter	F	Cha	10	S	Y	Y	Guam	Y	None
25		223	259	Gumataotao, Juana D	Mother in law	F	Cha	75	Wd	N	N	Guam	N	None

(CHAMORRO ROOTS GENEALOGY PROJECT™ TRANSCRIPTION)
(BERNARD T. PUNZALAN / HTTP://WWW.CHAMORROROOTS.COM)

DEPARTMENT OF COMMERCE-BUREAU OF THE CENSUS
WASHINGTON

FIFTEENTH CENSUS OF THE UNITED STATES: 1930-POPULATION

THE ISLAND OF GUAM

Sheet No. 27B

141B

District **Municipality of Agana**
Name of Place **Agana City (Julale)**
[Proper name and, also, name of class, as city, town, village, barrio, etc]

Enumeration District No. 4
Enumerated by me on **April 11, 1930** Vicente Tydingco, Enumerator

	PLACE OF ABODE: Street, avenue, road, etc.	Number of dwelling house in order of visitation	Number of family in order of visitation	NAME of each person whose place of abode on April 1, 1930, was in this family. Enter surname, first, then given name and middle initial. If any. Include every person living on April 1, 1930. Omit children born since April 1, 1930.	RELATION Relationship of this Person to the head of the family.	PERSONAL DESCRIPTION: Sex	Color or race	Age at last birthday	Single, married, widowed or divorced	EDUCATION: Attended school any time since Sept. 1, 1929	Whether able to read and write.	NATIVITY Place of birth of this person.	Whether able to speak English.	OCCUPATION
	1	2	3	4	5	6	7	8	9	10	11	12	13	14
26	Pizarro St	223	259	Materne, Andres D	Brother in law	M	Cha	43	S	N	N	Guam	N	Laborer
27		224	260	Borja, Juan M	Head	M	Cha	43	M	N	Y	Guam	N	Farmer
28		224	260	Borja, Ignacia R	Wife	F	Cha	32	M	N	Y	Guam	N	None
29		224	260	Borja, Maria R	Daughter	F	Cha	12	S	Y	Y	Guam	Y	None
30		224	260	Borja, Jose R	Son	M	Cha	11	S	Y	Y	Guam	Y	None
31		224	260	Guerrero, Joaquina R	Wife's aunt	F	Cha	50	Wd	N	N	Guam	N	None
32		224	260	Pangelinan, Antonio N	Nephew	M	Cha	5	S	N		Guam		None
33		225	261	Cruz, Jose SN	Head	M	Cha	46	M	N	Y	Guam	N	Farmer
34		225	261	Cruz, Vicenta R	Wife	F	Cha	46	M	N	Y	Guam	N	None
35		225	261	Cruz, Raymondo R	Son	M	Cha	26	S	N	Y	Guam	Y	Laborer
36		225	261	Cruz, Felis R	Son	M	Cha	21	S	N	Y	Guam	Y	Laborer
37		225	261	Cruz, Dolores R	Daughter	F	Cha	17	S	N	Y	Guam	Y	None
38		225	261	Cruz, Soledad R	Daughter	F	Cha	15	S	N	Y	Guam	Y	None
39		225	261	Cruz, Maria R	Daughter	F	Cha	12	S	Y	Y	Guam	Y	None
40		225	261	Cruz, Vicente R	Son	M	Cha	9	S	Y		Guam		None
41		225	261	Cruz, Rosa R	Daughter	F	Cha	4.5	S	N		Guam		None
42		225	261	Cruz, Enrique R	Son	M	Cha	1.9	S	N		Guam		None
43		225	261	Rosa, Joaquin R	Wife's nephew	M	Cha	21	S	N	N	Guam	N	Laborer
44		226	262	Cruz, Francisco B	Head	M	Cha	37	M	N	Y	Guam	Y	Policeman
45		226	262	Cruz, Rosa D	Wife	F	Cha	33	M	N	Y	Guam	Y	None
46		226	262	Cruz, Julia D	Daughter	F	Cha	14	S	Y	Y	Guam	Y	None
47		226	262	Duenas, Manuel M	Brother in law	M	Cha	20	S	N	Y	Guam	Y	Farmer
48		226	262	Duenas, Irene M	Sister in law	F	Cha	19	S	N	Y	Guam	N	Laundress
49		227	263	Garrido, Jose C	Head	M	Cha	44	M	N	Y	Guam	Y	Farmer
50		227	263	Garrido, Dolores M	Wife	F	Cha	29	M	N	Y	Guam	Y	None

DEPARTMENT OF COMMERCE-BUREAU OF THE CENSUS
WASHINGTON

FIFTEENTH CENSUS OF THE UNITED STATES: 1930-POPULATION

THE ISLAND OF GUAM

Sheet No. 28A

District **Municipality of Agana**
Name of Place **Agana City (Julale)**
[Proper name and, also, name of class, as city, town, village, barrio, etc]

Enumeration District No. 4
Enumerated by me on **April 11, 1930** Vicente Tydingco, Enumerator

	PLACE OF ABODE: Street, avenue, road, etc.	Number of dwelling house in order of visitation	Number of family in order of visitation	NAME of each person whose place of abode on April 1, 1930, was in this family. Enter surname, first, then given name and middle initial. If any. Include every person living on April 1, 1930. Omit children born since April 1, 1930.	RELATION Relationship of this Person to the head of the family.	PERSONAL DESCRIPTION: Sex	Color or race	Age at last birthday	Single, married, widowed or divorced	EDUCATION: Attended school any time since Sept. 1, 1929	Whether able to read and write.	NATIVITY Place of birth of this person.	Whether able to speak English.	OCCUPATION
	1	2	3	4	5	6	7	8	9	10	11	12	13	14
1	Pizarro St	227	263	Garrido, Mariana M	Daughter	F	Cha	4.2	S	N		Guam		None
2		227	263	Garrido, Anselmo M	Son	M	Cha	3.5	S	N		Guam		None
3		227	263	Garrido, Joaquin M	Son	M	Cha	2.1	S	N		Guam		None
4		227	263	Garrido, Jose M	Son	M	Cha	1.1	S	N		Guam		None
5		227	264	Materne, Antonio M	Head	M	Cha	27	M	N	Y	Guam	Y	Barber
6		227	264	Materne, Dolores C	Wife	F	Cha	29	M	N	Y	Guam	Y	None
7		227	264	Materne, Clementina C	Daughter	F	Cha	9	S	Y		Guam		None
8		227	264	Materne, Dolores C	Daughter	F	Cha	6	S	N		Guam		None
9		227	264	Materne, Jose C	Son	M	Cha	3.2	S	N		Guam		None
10		227	264	Materne, Eduvigis M	Mother	F	Cha	62	S	N	N	Guam	N	Servant
11		227	264	Fejeran, Enrique F	Lodger	M	Cha	13	S	Y	Y	Guam	Y	None
12		228	265	Castro, Jose P	Head	M	Cha	28	M	N	Y	Guam	Y	Farmer
13		228	265	Castro, Rosa S	Wife	F	Cha	35	M	N	Y	Guam	Y	None
14		228	265	Castro, Enrique S	Son	M	Cha	15	S	Y	Y	Guam	Y	None
15		228	265	Castro, Jose S	Son	M	Cha	13	S	Y	Y	Guam	Y	None
16		229	266	Phillips, Dorothy M	Head	F	W	28	M	N	Y	?, New Jersey	Y	None
17		229	266	Phillips, Edward A	Son	M	W	5	S	N		Norfolk, Virginia		None
18		230	267	Mesa, Jose M	Head	M	Cha	51	M	N	Y	Guam	N	Farmer
19		230	267	Mesa, Antonia M	Wife	F	Cha	46	M	N	N	Guam	N	Laundress
20		230	267	Mesa, Jose M	Son	F	Cha	14	S	N	N	Guam		None
21		231	268	Manibusan, Jesus LG	Head	M	Cha	24	M	N	Y	Guam	Y	Cook
22		231	268	Manibusan, Engracia C	Wife	F	Cha	19	M	N	Y	Guam	Y	None
23		231	268	Manibusan, Maria C	Daughter	F	Cha	.3	S	N		Guam		None
24		231	268	Manibusan, Luisa C	Mother	F	Cha	41	Wd	N	Y	Guam	N	Laundress
25		231	268	Manibusan, Ana C	Sister	F	Cha	20	S	N	Y	Guam	Y	Servant

DEPARTMENT OF COMMERCE-BUREAU OF THE CENSUS
WASHINGTON

FIFTEENTH CENSUS OF THE UNITED STATES: 1930-POPULATION

THE ISLAND OF GUAM

Sheet No. 28B

District **Municipality of Agana**
Name of Place **Agana City (Julale)**
[Proper name and, also, name of class, as city, town, village, barrio, etc]

Enumeration District No. **4**
Enumerated by me on **April 11, 1930** Vicente Tydingco
Enumerator

	PLACE OF ABODE			NAME	RELATION	PERSONAL DESCRIPTION				EDUCATION		NATIVITY		OCCUPATION
	Street, avenue, road, etc.	Number of dwelling house in order of visitation	Number of family in order of visitation	of each person whose place of abode on April 1, 1930, was in this family. Enter surname, first, then given name and middle initial. If any. Include every person living on April 1, 1930. Omit children born since April 1, 1930.	Relationship of this Person to the head of the family.	Sex	Color or race	Age at last birthday	Single, married, widowed or divorced	Attended school any time since Sept. 1, 1929	Whether able to read and write.	Place of birth of this person.	Whether able to speak English.	
	1	2	3	4	5	6	7	8	9	10	11	12	13	14
26	Pizarro St	231	268	Manibusan, Asuncion C	Sister	F	Cha	14	S	N	Y	Guam	Y	Servant
27		231	268	Manibusan, Jose C	Brother	M	Cha	12	S	Y	Y	Guam	Y	None
28		231	268	Manibusan, Rosa C	Sister	F	Cha	10	S	Y		Guam		None
29		231	268	Manibusan, Vicente C	Brother	M	Cha	7	S	Y		Guam		None
30		232	269	Lizama, Jose P	Head	M	Cha	60	M	N	Y	Guam	N	Farmer
31		232	269	Lizama, Maria S	Wife	F	Cha	60	M	N	N	Guam	N	None
32		232	269	Lizama, Rita S	Daughter	F	Cha	30	S	N	Y	Guam	Y	Seamstress
33		232	269	Lizama, Catalina S	Daughter	F	Cha	24	S	N	Y	Guam	N	None
34		232	269	Lizama, Dolores S	Daughter	F	Cha	20	S	N	Y	Guam	Y	Servant
35		232	269	Salas, Clotilde LG	Lodger	F	Cha	7	S	Y		Guam		None
36		233	270	Velanzuela, Joaquin C	Head	M	Cha	41	M	N	Y	Guam	N	Farmer
37		233	270	Velanzuela, Antonia S	Wife	F	Cha	38	M	N	Y	Guam	N	None
38		233	270	Velanzuela, Francisco S	Son	M	Cha	14	S	Y	Y	Guam	Y	None
39		233	270	Velanzuela, Regina S	Daughter	F	Cha	12	S	Y	Y	Guam	Y	None
40		233	270	Velanzuela, Jose S	Son	M	Cha	10	S	Y	Y	Guam	Y	None
41		234	271	Respicio, Luisa C	Head	F	Cha	68	Wd	N	N	Guam	N	None
42		234	271	Fejeran, Magdalena R	Granddaughter	F	Cha	17	S	N	Y	Guam	Y	None
43		234	271	Fejeran, Pedro R	Grandson	M	Cha	14	S	Y	Y	Guam	Y	None
44		234	271	Fejeran, Joaquin R	Grandson	M	Cha	12	S	Y	Y	Guam	Y	None
45		234	271	Perez, Nieves L	Sister	F	Cha	65	S	N	N	Guam	N	None
46		235	272	Cruz, Joaquin C	Head	M	Cha	47	M	N	Y	Guam	N	Farmer
47		235	272	Cruz, Magdalena C	Wife	F	Cha	48	M	N	N	Guam	N	None
48		235	272	Cruz, Tomasa C	Daughter	F	Cha	22	S	N	Y	Guam	Y	Laundress
49		235	272	Cruz, Juan C	Son	M	Cha	19	S	N	Y	Guam	Y	Farm Laborer
50		235	272	Cruz, Vicente C	Son	M	Cha	14	S	N	Y	Guam	Y	None

DEPARTMENT OF COMMERCE-BUREAU OF THE CENSUS
WASHINGTON

FIFTEENTH CENSUS OF THE UNITED STATES: 1930-POPULATION

THE ISLAND OF GUAM

Sheet No. 29A

District Municipality of Agana
Name of Place Agana City (Julale)
[Proper name and, also, name of class, as city, town, village, barrio, etc]

Enumeration District No. 4
Enumerated by me on April 12, 1930 Vicente Tydingco, Enumerator

	PLACE OF ABODE			NAME	RELATION	PERSONAL DESCRIPTION				EDUCATION		NATIVITY		OCCUPATION
	Street, avenue, road, etc.	Number of dwelling house in order of visitation	Number of family in order of visitation	of each person whose place of abode on April 1, 1930, was in this family. Enter surname, first, then given name and middle initial. If any. Include every person living on April 1, 1930. Omit children born since April 1, 1930.	Relationship of this Person to the head of the family.	Sex	Color or race	Age at last birthday	Single, married, widowed or divorced	Attended school any time since Sept. 1, 1929	Whether able to read and write.	Place of birth of this person.	Whether able to speak English.	
	1	2	3	4	5	6	7	8	9	10	11	12	13	14
1	Pizarro St	235	272	Cruz, Adela C	Daughter	F	Cha	11	S	Y	Y	Guam	Y	None
2		235	272	Cruz, Filomenia C	Daughter	F	Cha	9	S	Y		Guam		None
3		236	273	Chargualaf, Agustin M	Head	M	Cha	40	M	N	N	Guam	N	Fisherman
4		236	273	Chargualaf, Maria C	Wife	F	Cha	34	M	N	N	Guam	N	None
5		236	273	Chargualaf, Justo C	Son	M	Cha	18	S	N	Y	Guam	Y	Farmer
6		236	273	Chargualaf, Antonia C	Daughter	F	Cha	15	S	N	Y	Guam	N	None
7		236	273	Chargualaf, Vicente C	Son	M	Cha	13	S	Y	Y	Guam		None
8		236	273	Chargualaf, Rita C	Daughter	F	Cha	10	S	Y	Y	Guam		None
9		236	273	Chargualaf, Pedro C	Son	M	Cha	3.1	S	N		Guam		None
10		236	273	Chargualaf, Bernadita C	Daughter	F	Cha	1.1	S	N		Guam		None
11		237	274	Cruz, Juan C	Head	M	Cha	24	M	N	Y	Guam	Y	Laborer
12		237	274	Cruz, Dolores P	Wife	F	Cha	23	M	N	Y	Guam	Y	None
13		237	274	Cruz, Antonio P	Son	M	Cha	4.4	S	N		Guam		None
14		237	274	Cruz, Maria P	Daughter	F	Cha	2.1	S	N		Guam		None
15		237	274	Cruz, Jose P	Son	M	Cha	0	S	N		Guam		None
16		237	274	Perez, Felipe C	Father in law	M	Cha	54	Wd	N	Y	Guam	N	Fisherman
17		237	274	Perez, Angel	Brother in law	M	Cha	18	S	N	Y	Guam	Y	Laborer
18		237	274	Perez, Manuel	Brother in law	M	Cha	13	S	Y	Y	Guam	Y	None
19		238	275	Garrido, Juan C	Head	M	Cha	58	M	N	Y	Guam	N	Laborer
20		238	275	Garrido, Ana B	Wife	F	Cha	38	M	N	Y	Guam	N	None
21		238	275	Garrido, Anselmo B	Son	M	Cha	16	S	Y	Y	Guam	Y	None
22		238	275	Garrido, Facundo B	Son	M	Cha	15	S	Y	Y	Guam	Y	None
23		238	275	Garrido, Felicia B	Daughter	F	Cha	14	S	Y	Y	Guam	Y	None
24		238	275	Garrido, Simona B	Daughter	F	Cha	13	S	Y	Y	Guam	Y	None
25		238	275	Garrido, Victoriano B	Son	M	Cha	10	S	Y	Y	Guam	Y	None

(CHAMORRO ROOTS GENEALOGY PROJECT™ TRANSCRIPTION)
(BERNARD T. PUNZALAN / HTTP://WWW.CHAMORROROOTS.COM)

DEPARTMENT OF COMMERCE-BUREAU OF THE CENSUS
WASHINGTON

FIFTEENTH CENSUS OF THE UNITED STATES: 1930-POPULATION

THE ISLAND OF GUAM

Sheet No. 29B

143B

District Municipality of Agana
Name of Place Agana City (Julale)
[Proper name and, also, name of class, as city, town, village, barrio, etc]

Enumeration District No. 4
Enumerated by me on April 12, 1930 Vicente Tydingco
Enumerator

	PLACE OF ABODE			NAME	RELATION	PERSONAL DESCRIPTION				EDUCATION		NATIVITY		OCCUPATION
	Street, avenue, road, etc.	Number of dwelling house is order of visitation	Number of family in order of visitation	of each person whose place of abode on April 1, 1930, was in this family. Enter surname, first, then given name and middle initial. If any. Include every person living on April 1, 1930. Omit children born since April 1, 1930.	Relationship of this Person to the head of the family.	Sex	Color or race	Age at last birthday	Single, married, widowed or divorced	Attended school any time since Sept. 1, 1929	Whether able to read and write.	Place of birth of this person.	Whether able to speak English.	
	1	2	3	4	5	6	7	8	9	10	11	12	13	14
26	Pizarro St	238	275	Garrido, Tomas B	Son	M	Cha	9	S	Y		Guam		None
27		238	275	Garrido, Francisco B	Son	M	Cha	5	S	N		Guam		None
28		238	275	Garrido, Luisa B	Daughter	F	Cha	3.5	S	N		Guam		None
29		238	275	Garrido, Lucia B	Daughter	F	Cha	1.1	S	N		Guam		None
30		239	276	Leon Guerrero, Jose P	Head	M	Cha	28	M	N	Y	Guam	N	Farmer
31		239	276	Leon Guerrero, Nicolasa R	Wife	F	Cha	39	M	N	N	Guam	N	Laundress
32		239	276	Leon Guerrero, Jose R	Son	M	Cha	5	S	N		Guam		None
33		239	276	Leon Guerrero, Jesus R	Son	M	Cha	2.1	S	N		Guam		None
34		239	276	Rosa, Maria R	Sister in law	F	Cha	18	S	N	N	Guam	N	None
35		240	277	Rosa, Manuel M	Head	M	Cha	30	M	N	Y	Guam		Farmer
36		240	277	Rosa, Rita LG	Wife	F	Cha	26	M	N	Y	Guam		None
37		240	277	Rosa, Oliva LG	Daughter	F	Cha	4.1	S	N		Guam		None
38		240	277	Rosa, Felisa LG	Daughter	F	Cha	.9	S	N		Guam		None
39		240	277	Rosa, Rita M	Mother	F	Cha	74	Wd	N	Y	Guam	N	None
40		241	278	Mesa, Vicente M	Head	M	Cha	21	M	N	Y	Guam	Y	Laborer
41		241	278	Mesa, Engracia S	Wife	F	Cha	19	M	N	Y	Guam	Y	None
42		241	278	Mesa, Rosario S	Daughter	F	Cha	.5	S	N		Guam		None
43		242	279	Mafnas, Vicente P	Head	M	Cha	40	M	N	N	Guam	N	Farmer
44		242	279	Mafnas, Maria B	Wife	F	Cha	35	M	N	Y	Guam	N	None
45		242	279	Mafnas, Antonio B	Son	M	Cha	13	S	Y	Y	Guam	Y	None
46		242	279	Mafnas, Ana B	Daughter	F	Cha	11	S	Y	Y	Guam	Y	None
47		242	279	Mafnas, Maria B	Daughter	F	Cha	9	S	Y		Guam		None
48		242	279	Mafnas, Vicente B	Son	M	Cha	7	S	Y		Guam		None
49		242	279	Mafnas, Jose B	Son	M	Cha	4.1	S	N		Guam		None
50		242	279	Mafnas, Asuncion B	Daughter	F	Cha	3.1	S	N		Guam		None

DEPARTMENT OF COMMERCE-BUREAU OF THE CENSUS
WASHINGTON

FIFTEENTH CENSUS OF THE UNITED STATES: 1930-POPULATION

THE ISLAND OF GUAM

Sheet No. 30A

144

District **Municipality of Agana**
Name of Place **Agana City (Julale)**
[Proper name and, also, name of class, as city, town, village, barrio, etc]

Enumeration District No. 4
Enumerated by me on **April 12, 1930** Vicente Tydingco
Enumerator

	PLACE OF ABODE			NAME	RELATION	PERSONAL DESCRIPTION				EDUCATION		NATIVITY		OCCUPATION
	Street, avenue, road, etc.	Number of dwelling house is order of visitation	Number of family in order of visitation	of each person whose place of abode on April 1, 1930, was in this family. Enter surname, first, then given name and middle initial. If any. Include every person living on April 1, 1930. Omit children born since April 1, 1930.	Relationship of this Person to the head of the family.	Sex	Color or race	Age at last birthday	Single, married, widowed or divorced	Attended school any time since Sept. 1, 1929	Whether able to read and write.	Place of birth of this person.	Whether able to speak English.	
	1	2	3	4	5	6	7	8	9	10	11	12	13	14
1	Pizarro St	243	280	Mesa, Juan F	Head	M	Cha	25	M	N	Y	Guam	Y	Carpenter
2		243	280	Mesa, Emilia P	Wife	F	Cha	25	M	N	Y	Guam	N	None
3		243	280	Mesa, Jesus P	Son	M	Cha	5	S	N		Guam		None
4		243	280	Mesa, Juan P	Son	M	Cha	1.7	S	N		Guam		None
5				Here ends the enumeration of enumeration District No 4 Julale.. [Sheet 30B/144B was intentionally left blank by the Enumerator.]										
6														
7														
8														
9														
10														
11														
12														
13														
14														
15														
16														
17														
18														
19														
20														
21														
22														
23														
24														
25														

DEPARTMENT OF COMMERCE-BUREAU OF THE CENSUS
WASHINGTON

FIFTEENTH CENSUS OF THE UNITED STATES: 1930-POPULATION

THE ISLAND OF GUAM

Sheet No. 31A

District **Municipality of Agana**
Name of Place **Agana City (Santa Cruz)**
[Proper name and, also, name of class, as city, town, village, barrio, etc]

Enumeration District No. 4
Enumerated by me on **April 12, 1930** Vicente Tydingco, Enumerator

	PLACE OF ABODE			NAME	RELATION	PERSONAL DESCRIPTION				EDUCATION		NATIVITY		OCCUPATION
	Street, avenue, road, etc.	Number of dwelling house in order of visitation	Number of family in order of visitation	of each person whose place of abode on April 1, 1930, was in this family. Enter surname, first, then given name and middle initial. If any. Include every person living on April 1, 1930. Omit children born since April 1, 1930.	Relationship of this Person to the head of the family.	Sex	Color or race	Age at last birthday	Single, married, widowed or divorced	Attended school any time since Sept. 1, 1929	Whether able to read and write.	Place of birth of this person.	Whether able to speak English.	
	1	2	3	4	5	6	7	8	9	10	11	12	13	14
1	Sagunto Street	244	281	Salas, Pedro C	Head	M	Cha	71	M	N	Y	Guam	N	Farmer
2		244	281	Salas, Rosa C	Wife	F	Cha	70	M	N	Y	Guam	N	None
3		244	282	Salas, Pedro C	Head	M	Cha	31	M	N	Y	Guam	Y	Carpenter
4		244	282	Salas, Maria Q	Wife	F	Cha	27	M	N	Y	Guam	Y	None
5		244	282	Salas, Pedro Q	Son	M	Cha	1.1	S	N		Guam		None
6		245	283	Respecio, Ana D	Head	F	Cha	30	M	N	Y	Guam	Y	Laundress
7		245	283	Respecio, Roman D	Son	M	Cha	12	S	Y	Y	Guam	Y	None
8		245	283	Respecio, Jose D	Son	M	Cha	8	S	Y		Guam		None
9		245	283	Respecio, Ambrosio D	Son	M	Cha	5	S	N		Guam		None
10		245	283	Bukikosa, Maria B	Niece	F	Cha	9	S	Y		Guam		None
11		246	284	Cruz, Jose C	Head	M	Cha	30	M	N	Y	Guam	Y	Chauffeur
12		246	284	Cruz, Maria LG	Wife	F	Cha	27	M	N	Y	Guam	Y	None
13		246	284	Cruz, Joaquin LG	Son	M	Cha	5	S	N		Guam		None
14		246	284	Cruz, Juan LG	Son	M	Cha	2.3	S	N		Guam		None
15		246	284	Cruz, Jose LG	Son	M	Cha	1.3	S	N		Guam		None
16		246	284	Cruz, Concepcion LG	Daughter	F	Cha	.3	S	N		Guam		None
17		246	285	Leon Guerrero, Juan U	Head	M	Cha	29	M	N	Y	Guam	Y	Laborer
18		246	285	Leon Guerrero, Magdalena L	Wife	F	Cha	28	M	N	Y	Guam	Y	None
19		246	285	Leon Guerrero, Ana L	Daughter	F	Cha	5	S	N		Guam		None
20		246	285	Leon Guerrero, Juan L	Son	M	Cha	1.7	S	N		Guam		None
21		247	286	Ungacta, Nocolasa S	Head	F	Cha	66	Wd	N	Y	Guam	N	Laundress
22		247	286	Borja, Hermangilda S	Granddaughter	F	Cha	13	S	N	Y	Guam	Y	Servant
23		248	287	Unpingco, Pedro S	Head	M	Cha	64	M	N	Y	Guam	N	Farmer
24		248	287	Unpingco, Maria R	Wife	F	Cha	55	M	N	N	Guam	N	None
25		248	287	Unpingco, Ana R	Daughter	F	Cha	33	S	N	Y	Guam	Y	None

DEPARTMENT OF COMMERCE-BUREAU OF THE CENSUS
WASHINGTON

FIFTEENTH CENSUS OF THE UNITED STATES: 1930-POPULATION

THE ISLAND OF GUAM

Sheet No. 31B

145B

District **Municipality of Agana**
Name of Place **Agana City (Santa Cruz)**
[Proper name and, also, name of class, as city, town, village, barrio, etc]

Enumeration District No. 4
Enumerated by me on **April 12, 1930** Vicente Tydingco, Enumerator

	PLACE OF ABODE: Street, avenue, road, etc.	Number of dwelling house in order of visitation	Number of family in order of visitation	NAME of each person whose place of abode on April 1, 1930, was in this family. Enter surname, first, then given name and middle initial. If any. Include every person living on April 1, 1930. Omit children born since April 1, 1930.	RELATION Relationship of this Person to the head of the family.	PERSONAL DESCRIPTION: Sex	Color or race	Age at last birthday	Single, married, widowed or divorced	EDUCATION: Attended school any time since Sept. 1, 1929	Whether able to read and write.	NATIVITY Place of birth of this person.	Whether able to speak English.	OCCUPATION
	1	2	3	4	5	6	7	8	9	10	11	12	13	14
26	Sagunto Street	248	287	Unpingco, Jose R	Son	M	Cha	21	S	N	Y	Guam	Y	Farm Laborer
27		248	287	Unpingco, Jesus R	Son	M	Cha	17	S	Y	Y	Guam	Y	None
28		248	287	Unpingco, Consuelo R	Daughter	F	Cha	15	S	Y	Y	Guam	Y	None
29		248	287	Unpingco, Vicente M	Grandson	M	Cha	7	S	Y		Guam		None
30		249	288	Rios, Jose LG	Head	M	Cha	31	M	N	Y	Guam	Y	Teacher
31		249	288	Rios, Antonia LG	Wife	F	Cha	25	M	N	Y	Guam	Y	None
32		249	288	Rios, Elizabeth LG	Daughter	F	Cha	4.2	S	N		Guam		None
33		249	288	Rios, Albert LG	Son	M	Cha	3.3	S	N		Guam		None
34		249	288	Rios, Joseph LG	Son	M	Cha	2.2	S	N		Guam		None
35		249	288	Rios, Helen LG	Daughter	F	Cha	.4	S	N		Guam		None
36		249	288	Tertaotao, Antonia C	Servant	F	Cha	11	S	Y	Y	Guam	Y	None
37		250	289	Perez, Jose F	Head	M	Cha	45	M	N	Y	Guam	Y	Carpenter
38		250	289	Perez, Maria L	Wife	F	Cha	38	M	N	Y	Guam	N	None
39		250	289	Perez, Rosario L	Daughter	F	Cha	15	S	Y	Y	Guam	Y	None
40		250	289	Perez, Amanda L	Daughter	F	Cha	12	S	Y	Y	Guam		None
41		250	289	Perez, Dolores L	Daughter	F	Cha	3.3	S	N		Guam		None
42		250	289	Rojas, Jose R	Lodger	M	Cha	19	S	N	N	Guam		Farmer
43		251	290	Taijeron, Ramon LG	Head	M	Cha	52	Wd	N	Y	Guam	N	None
44		251	290	Taijeron, Antonio LG	Son	M	Cha	25	S	N	Y	Guam	Y	Cook
45		251	290	Taijeron, Juliana LG	Daughter	F	Cha	22	S	N	Y	Guam	Y	Cook
46		251	290	Taijeron, Mercedes LG	Daughter	F	Cha	20	S	N	Y	Guam	Y	Cook
47		251	290	Taijeron, Jose LG	Son	M	Cha	17	S	N	Y	Guam	Y	Farmer
48		251	290	Leon Guerrero, Rosario LG	Niece	F	Cha	13	S	Y	Y	Guam	Y	None
49		252	291	Cepeda, Juan C	Head	M	Cha	27	M	N	Y	Guam	Y	Stockman
50		252	291	Cepeda, Ramona SN	Wife	F	Cha	29	M	N	Y	Guam	N	None

DEPARTMENT OF COMMERCE-BUREAU OF THE CENSUS
WASHINGTON

FIFTEENTH CENSUS OF THE UNITED STATES: 1930-POPULATION

THE ISLAND OF GUAM

Sheet No. 32A

District Municipality of Agana
Name of Place Agana City (Santa Cruz)
[Proper name and, also, name of class, as city, town, village, barrio, etc]

Enumeration District No. 4
Enumerated by me on April 14, 1930 Vicente Tydingco
Enumerator

	PLACE OF ABODE			NAME	RELATION	PERSONAL DESCRIPTION				EDUCATION		NATIVITY		OCCUPATION
	Street, avenue, road, etc.	Number of dwelling house in order of visitation	Number of family in order of visitation	of each person whose place of abode on April 1, 1930, was in this family. Enter surname, first, then given name and middle initial. If any. Include every person living on April 1, 1930. Omit children born since April 1, 1930.	Relationship of this Person to the head of the family.	Sex	Color or race	Age at last birthday	Single, married, widowed or divorced	Attended school any time since Sept. 1, 1929	Whether able to read and write.	Place of birth of this person.	Whether able to speak English.	
	1	2	3	4	5	6	7	8	9	10	11	12	13	14
1	Sagunto Street	252	291	Cepeda, Jose SN	Son	M	Cha	.3	S	N		Guam		None
2		253	292	Pangelinan, Jesus G	Head	M	Cha	44	M	N	Y	Guam	N	Farmer
3		253	292	Pangelinan, Nicolas P	Wife	F	Cha	45	M	N	Y	Guam	N	None
4		253	292	Pangelinan, Maria P	Daughter	F	Cha	18	S	N	Y	Guam	Y	None
5		253	292	Pangelinan, Pedro P	Son	M	Cha	14	S	Y	Y	Guam	Y	None
6		253	292	Pangelinan, Eufrasia P	Daughter	F	Cha	10	S	Y	Y	Guam	Y	None
7		253	292	Pangelinan, Jesusa P	Daughter	F	Cha	7	S	Y		Guam		None
8		253	292	Pangelinan, Joaquin P	Son	M	Cha	6	S	N		Guam		None
9		253	292	Pangelinan, Ana P	Daughter	F	Cha	3.3	S	N		Guam		None
10		253	292	Pangelinan, Rosalia P	Daughter	F	Cha	.7	S	N		Guam		None
11		253	292	Pangelinan, Maria G	Mother	F	Cha	64	Wd	N	Y	Guam	N	None
12		253	292	Rojas, Ignacio R	Lodger	M	Cha	18	S	N	N	Guam	N	Farm Laborer
13		254	293	Ada, Pilar H	Head	F	Cha	26	M	N	Y	Guam	Y	None
14		254	293	Ada, Severina H	Daughter	F	Cha	2.8	S	N		Guam		None
15		254	293	Ada, Winifred H	Daughter	F	Cha	.1	S	N		Guam		None
16		254	293	Ada, Carmen H	Sister	F	Cha	36	S	N	Y	Guam	Y	None
17		254	293	Ada, Candelaria C	Niece	F	Cha	25	S	N	Y	Guam	Y	None
18		254	293	Ada, Felis C	Nephew	M	Cha	11	S	Y	Y	Guam	Y	None
19		255	294	Valenzuela, Ignacio P	Head	M	Cha	63	M	N	Y	Guam	N	Farmer
20		255	294	Valenzuela, Ana LG	Wife	F	Cha	56	M	N	N	Guam	N	None
21		255	294	Valenzuela, Isabel LG	Daughter	F	Cha	22	S	N	Y	Guam	Y	Servant
22		255	294	Valenzuela, Francisco LG	Son	M	Cha	15	S	Y	Y	Guam	Y	None
23		255	295	Castro, Jose C	Head	M	Cha	33	M	N	Y	Guam	Y	Salesman
24		255	295	Castro, Consalacion V	Wife	F	Cha	27	M	N	Y	Guam	Y	None
25		255	295	Castro, Rodolfo V	Son	M	Cha	5	S	N		Guam		None

DEPARTMENT OF COMMERCE-BUREAU OF THE CENSUS
WASHINGTON

FIFTEENTH CENSUS OF THE UNITED STATES: 1930-POPULATION

THE ISLAND OF GUAM

Sheet No. 32B

District **Municipality of Agana**
Name of Place **Agana City (Santa Cruz)**
[Proper name and, also, name of class, as city, town, village, barrio, etc]

Enumeration District No. 4
Enumerated by me on **April 14, 1930** Vicente Tydingco, Enumerator

	PLACE OF ABODE: Street, avenue, road, etc.	Number of dwelling house in order of visitation	Number of family in order of visitation	NAME of each person whose place of abode on April 1, 1930, was in this family. Enter surname, first, then given name and middle initial. If any. Include every person living on April 1, 1930. Omit children born since April 1, 1930.	RELATION Relationship of this Person to the head of the family.	PERSONAL DESCRIPTION: Sex	Color or race	Age at last birthday	Single, married, widowed or divorced	EDUCATION: Attended school any time since Sept. 1, 1929	Whether able to read and write.	NATIVITY Place of birth of this person.	Whether able to speak English.	OCCUPATION
	1	2	3	4	5	6	7	8	9	10	11	12	13	14
26	Sagunto Street	255	295	Castro, Herman V	Son	M	Cha	3.5	S	N		Guam		None
27		255	295	Castro, Evelyna V	Daughter	F	Cha	2.3	S	N		Guam		None
28		256	296	Crisostimo, Dolores P	Head	F	Cha	31	Wd	N	Y	Guam	Y	None
29		256	296	Crisostimo, Felicita P	Daughter	F	Cha	13	S	Y	Y	Guam	Y	None
30		256	296	Crisostimo, Jose P	Son	M	Cha	11	S	Y	Y	Guam	Y	None
31		256	296	Crisostimo, Celestine P	Daughter	F	Cha	10	S	Y	Y	Guam	Y	None
32		256	296	Crisostimo, Mariano P	Son	M	Cha	9	S	Y		Guam		None
33		256	296	Crisostimo, Ambrosio P	Son	M	Cha	4.1	S	N		Guam		None
34		256	296	Rojas, Mariano R	Lodger	M	Cha	11	S	N		Guam		None
35		257	297	Manibusan, Jose C	Head	M	Cha	34	M	N	Y	Guam	Y	Clerk
36		257	297	Manibusan, Maria E	Wife	F	Cha	31	M	N	Y	Guam	Y	None
37		257	297	Manibusan, Jesus E	Son	M	Cha	9	S	Y		Guam		None
38		257	297	Manibusan, Joaquin E	Son	M	Cha	7	S	Y		Guam		None
39		257	297	Manibusan, Julita E	Daughter	F	Cha	8	S	Y		Guam		None
40		257	297	Manibusan, Juan E	Son	M	Cha	5	S	N		Guam		None
41		257	297	Manibusan, Justina E	Daughter	F	Cha	.9	S	N		Guam		None
42		257	297	Espinosa, Dolores B	Mother in law	F	Cha	70	Wd	N	Y	Guam	N	None
43		257	297	Perez, Oligario C	Wife's nephew	M	Cha	20	S	N	Y	Guam	Y	Surveyor
44		258	298	Castro, Manuel C	Head	M	Cha	71	M	N	Y	Guam	N	Farmer
45		258	298	Castro, Rita C	Wife	F	Cha	66	M	N	Y	Guam	N	None
46		258	298	Castro, Ana C	Daughter	F	Cha	29	S	N	Y	Guam	Y	None
47		259	299	Leon Guerrero, Francisco R	Head	M	Cha	58	M	N	Y	Guam	N	Farmer
48		259	299	Leon Guerrero, Ignacia S	Wife	F	Cha	53	M	N	N	Guam	N	None
49		259	299	Leon Guerrero, Vicente S	Son	M	Cha	23	S	N	Y	Guam	Y	Farm Laborer
50		259	299	Leon Guerrero, Jose S	Son	M	Cha	22	S	N	Y	Guam	Y	Farm Laborer

DEPARTMENT OF COMMERCE-BUREAU OF THE CENSUS
WASHINGTON

FIFTEENTH CENSUS OF THE UNITED STATES: 1930-POPULATION

THE ISLAND OF GUAM

Sheet No. 33A

District Municipality of Agana
Name of Place Agana City (Santa Cruz)
[Proper name and, also, name of class, as city, town, village, barrio, etc]

Enumeration District No. 4
Enumerated by me on April 14, 1930 Vicente Tydingco, Enumerator

	PLACE OF ABODE			NAME	RELATION	PERSONAL DESCRIPTION				EDUCATION		NATIVITY		OCCUPATION
	Street, avenue, road, etc.	Number of dwelling house is order of visitation	Number of family in order of visitation	of each person whose place of abode on April 1, 1930, was in this family. Enter surname, first, then given name and middle initial. If any. Include every person living on April 1, 1930. Omit children born since April 1, 1930.	Relationship of this Person to the head of the family.	Sex	Color or race	Age at last birthday	Single, married, widowed or divorced	Attended school any time since Sept. 1, 1929	Whether able to read and write.	Place of birth of this person.	Whether able to speak English.	
	1	2	3	4	5	6	7	8	9	10	11	12	13	14
1	Sagunto Street	259	299	Leon Guerrero, Ana S	Daughter	F	Cha	15	S	N	Y	Guam	Y	None
2		260	300	Pereda, Jesus S	Head	M	Cha	55	M	N	Y	Guam	N	Farmer
3		260	300	Pereda, Maria P	Wife	F	Cha	48	M	N	Y	Guam	N	Laundress
4		260	300	Pereda, Juan P	Son	M	Cha	22	S	N	Y	Guam	Y	Farm Laborer
5		260	300	Pereda, Jesus P	Son	M	Cha	21	S	N	Y	Guam	Y	Servant
6		260	300	Pereda, Maria P	Daughter	F	Cha	17	S	N	Y	Guam	Y	None
7		260	300	Pereda, Antonio P	Son	M	Cha	13	S	Y	Y	Guam	Y	None
8		260	300	Pereda, Asuncion P	Daughter	F	Cha	11	S	Y	Y	Guam	Y	None
9		260	300	Pereda, Vicente P	Son	M	Cha	9	S	Y		Guam		None
10		260	300	Pereda, Isabel P	Daughter	F	Cha	6	S	N		Guam		None
11		261	301	Pereda, Ignacio P	Head	M	Cha	51	M	N	Y	Guam	Y	Carpenter
12		261	301	Pereda, Ana P	Wife	F	Cha	36	M	N	Y	Guam	Y	None
13		261	301	Pereda, Jose P	Son	M	Cha	7	S	Y		Guam		None
14		261	301	Pereda, Manuel P	Son	M	Cha	6	S	N		Guam		None
15		261	301	Pereda, Maria P	Daughter	F	Cha	4.7	S	N		Guam		None
16		261	301	Pereda, Asuncion P	Daughter	F	Cha	2.6	S	N		Guam		None
17		261	301	Pereda, Juan P	Son	M	Cha	.9	S	N		Guam		None
18		261	301	Pereda, Vicente S	Father	M	Cha	63	Wd	N	N	Guam	N	Farmer
19		261	301	Pangelinan, Ana P	Sister	F	Cha	38	M	N	N	Guam	N	Laundress
20		262	302	Mesa, Juan D	Head	M	Cha	33	M	N	Y	Rota Island	N	Farmer
21		262	302	Mesa, Maria C	Wife	F	Cha	24	M	N	Y	Guam	N	None
22		262	302	Mesa, Josefa C	Daughter	F	Cha	9	S	N		Guam		None
23		262	302	Mesa, Maria C	Daughter	F	Cha	7	S	N		Guam		None
24		262	302	Mesa, Pedro C	Son	M	Cha	4.1	S	N		Guam		None
25		262	302	Mesa, Andres C	Son	M	Cha	.5	S	N		Guam		None

DEPARTMENT OF COMMERCE-BUREAU OF THE CENSUS
WASHINGTON

FIFTEENTH CENSUS OF THE UNITED STATES: 1930-POPULATION

THE ISLAND OF GUAM

Sheet No. 33B

147B

District Municipality of Agana
Name of Place Agana City (Santa Cruz)
[Proper name and, also, name of class, as city, town, village, barrio, etc]

Enumeration District No. 4
Enumerated by me on April 15, 1930 Vicente Tydingco
Enumerator

	PLACE OF ABODE			NAME	RELATION	PERSONAL DESCRIPTION				EDUCATION		NATIVITY		OCCUPATION
	Street, avenue, road, etc.	Number of dwelling house is order of visitation	Number of family in order of visitation	of each person whose place of abode on April 1, 1930, was in this family. Enter surname, first, then given name and middle initial. If any. Include every person living on April 1, 1930. Omit children born since April 1, 1930.	Relationship of this Person to the head of the family.	Sex	Color or race	Age at last birthday	Single, married, widowed or divorced	Attended school any time since Sept. 1, 1929	Whether able to read and write.	Place of birth of this person.	Whether able to speak English.	
	1	2	3	4	5	6	7	8	9	10	11	12	13	14
26	Sagunto Street	263	303	Salas, Antonio D	Head	M	Cha	38	M	N	Y	Guam	N	Carpenter
27		263	303	Salas, Ana C	Wife	F	Cha	40	M	N	N	Guam	N	None
28		263	303	Salas, Jose C	Son	M	Cha	13	S	Y	Y	Guam	Y	None
29		263	303	Salas, Rita C	Daughter	F	Cha	12	S	Y	Y	Guam	Y	None
30		263	303	Salas, Vicente C	Son	M	Cha	8	S	Y		Guam	Y	None
31		263	303	Salas, Isabel C	Daughter	F	Cha	3.7	S	N		Guam		None
32		263	303	Salas, Francisco C	Son	M	Cha	2.3	S	N		Guam		None
33		264	304	Concepcion, Juan C	Head	M	Cha	27	M	N	Y	Guam	Y	Farmer
34		264	304	Concepcion, Maria LG	Wife	F	Cha	19	M	N	Y	Guam	Y	None
35		264	304	Concepcion, Jesus LG	Son	M	Cha	.8	S	N		Guam		None
36		264	304	Concepcion, Magdalena C	Mother	F	Cha	55	Wd	N	Y	Guam	N	Laundress
37		264	304	Concepcion, Ana C	Sister	F	Cha	29	S	N	Y	Guam	Y	Laundress
38		264	304	Concepcion, Rosario C	Sister	F	Cha	18	S	N	Y	Guam	Y	Laundress
39		264	304	Concepcion, Maria C	Sister	F	Cha	14	S	Y	Y	Guam	Y	None
40		264	305	Concepcion, Joaquin C	Head	M	Cha	25	M	N	Y	Guam	Y	Carpenter
41		264	305	Concepcion, Hazel C	Wife	F	Cha	16	M	N	Y	Guam	Y	None
42		265	306	Cepeda, Juan M	Head	M	Cha	49	M	N	N	Guam	N	Farmer
43		265	306	Cepeda, Francisca Q	Wife	F	Cha	48	M	N	Y	Guam	N	None
44		265	306	Cepeda, Rita Q	Daughter	F	Cha	21	S	N	Y	Guam	Y	Laundress
45		265	306	Cepeda, Juan Q	Son	M	Cha	19	S	N	Y	Guam	Y	Servant
46		265	306	Cepeda, Trinidad Q	Daughter	F	Cha	16	S	N	Y	Guam	Y	Laundress
47		265	306	Cepeda, Joaquin Q	Son	M	Cha	15	S	N	Y	Guam	Y	Farm Laborer
48		265	306	Cepeda, Rosa Q	Daughter	F	Cha	13	S	Y	Y	Guam	Y	None
49		265	306	Cepeda, Juan C	Son	M	Cha	2.9	S	N		Guam		None
50		266	307	Nauta, Joaquin N	Head	M	Cha	45	Wd	N	Y	Guam	Y	Farmer

DEPARTMENT OF COMMERCE-BUREAU OF THE CENSUS
WASHINGTON

FIFTEENTH CENSUS OF THE UNITED STATES: 1930-POPULATION

THE ISLAND OF GUAM

Sheet No. 34A

District **Municipality of Agana**
Name of Place **Agana City (Santa Cruz)**
[Proper name and, also, name of class, as city, town, village, barrio, etc]

Enumeration District No. 4
Enumerated by me on **April 15, 1930** Vicente Tydingco, Enumerator

	PLACE OF ABODE: Street, avenue, road, etc.	Number of dwelling house in order of visitation	Number of family in order of visitation	NAME of each person whose place of abode on April 1, 1930, was in this family. Enter surname, first, then given name and middle initial. If any. Include every person living on April 1, 1930. Omit children born since April 1, 1930.	RELATION Relationship of this Person to the head of the family.	PERSONAL DESCRIPTION: Sex	Color or race	Age at last birthday	Single, married, widowed or divorced	EDUCATION: Attended school any time since Sept. 1, 1929	Whether able to read and write.	NATIVITY Place of birth of this person.	Whether able to speak English.	OCCUPATION
	1	2	3	4	5	6	7	8	9	10	11	12	13	14
1	Sagunto Street	266	307	Nauta, Juan S	Son	M	Cha	20	S	N	Y	Guam	Y	Machinist
2		266	307	Nauta, Jose S	Son	M	Cha	18	S	N	Y	Guam	Y	Farm Laborer
3		266	307	Nauta, Rosario S	Daughter	F	Cha	16	S	N	Y	Guam	Y	Laundress
4		266	307	Nauta, Emilia S	Daughter	F	Cha	14	S	Y	Y	Guam	Y	None
5		266	307	Nauta, Joaquin S	Son	M	Cha	10	S	Y	Y	Guam		None
6		266	307	Nauta, Jesus S	Son	M	Cha	9	S	Y		Guam		None
7		266	307	Nauta, Francisco S	Son	M	Cha	6	S	N		Guam		None
8		266	307	Nauta, Pedro S	Son	M	Cha	4.4	S	N		Guam		None
9		267	308	Fejeran, Jose S	Head	M	Cha	81	M	N	N	Guam	N	Farmer
10		267	308	Fejeran, Vicenta P	Wife	F	Cha	67	M	N	N	Guam	N	None
11		267	308	Fejeran, Joaquin P	Son	M	Cha	43	S	N	Y	Guam	N	Farm Laborer
12		267	309	Munoz, Joaquin I	Head	M	Cha	29	M	N	Y	Guam	Y	Electrician
13		267	309	Munoz, Josefa F	Wife	F	Cha	27	M	N	Y	Guam	N	None
14		267	309	Munoz, Jesus F	Son	M	Cha	10	S	Y	Y	Guam	Y	None
15		267	309	Munoz, Clotilde F	Daughter	F	Cha	6	S	N		Guam		None
16		267	309	Munoz, Joaquin F	Son	M	Cha	4.3	S	N		Guam		None
17		267	309	Munoz, Jose F	Son	M	Cha	.4	S	N		Guam		None
18		268	310	Fejeran, Juan P	Head	M	Cha	48	M	N	Y	Guam	N	Farmer
19		268	310	Fejeran, Francisca C	Wife	F	Cha	43	M	N	N	Guam	N	Laundress
20		268	310	Fejeran, Juan C	Son	M	Cha	21	S	N	Y	Guam	Y	Laborer
21		268	310	Fejeran, Jose C	Son	M	Cha	18	S	N	Y	Guam	Y	Laborer
22		268	310	Fejeran, Luis C	Son	M	Cha	17	S	N	Y	Guam	Y	Servant
23		268	310	Fejeran, Francisco C	Son	M	Cha	14	S	Y	Y	Guam	Y	None
24		268	310	Fejeran, Maria C	Daughter	F	Cha	12	S	Y	Y	Guam	Y	None
25		268	310	Fejeran, Joaquin C	Son	M	Cha	11	S	Y	Y	Guam	Y	None

DEPARTMENT OF COMMERCE-BUREAU OF THE CENSUS
WASHINGTON

FIFTEENTH CENSUS OF THE UNITED STATES: 1930-POPULATION

THE ISLAND OF GUAM

Sheet No. 34B

District Municipality of Agana
Name of Place Agana City (Santa Cruz)
[Proper name and, also, name of class, as city, town, village, barrio, etc]

Enumeration District No. 4
Enumerated by me on April 15, 1930 Vicente Tydingco
Enumerator

	PLACE OF ABODE			NAME	RELATION	PERSONAL DESCRIPTION				EDUCATION		NATIVITY		OCCUPATION
	Street, avenue, road, etc.	Number of dwelling house is order of visitation	Number of family in order of visitation	of each person whose place of abode on April 1, 1930, was in this family. Enter surname, first, then given name and middle initial. If any. Include every person living on April 1, 1930. Omit children born since April 1, 1930.	Relationship of this Person to the head of the family.	Sex	Color or race	Age at last birthday	Single, married, widowed or divorced	Attended school any time since Sept. 1, 1929	Whether able to read and write.	Place of birth of this person.	Whether able to speak English.	
	1	2	3	4	5	6	7	8	9	10	11	12	13	14
26	Sagunto Street	268	310	Fejeran, Antonia C	Daughter	F	Cha	6	S	N		Guam		None
27		269	311	Fejeran, Josef C	Head	M	Cha	52	Wd	N	N	Guam	N	None
28		269	311	Fejeran, Rosa C	Daughter	F	Cha	20	S	N	Y	Guam	Y	Laundress
29		269	311	Fejeran, Magdalena C	Daughter	F	Cha	18	S	N	Y	Guam	Y	Laundress
30		269	311	Fejeran, Manuel C	Son	M	Cha	16	S	Y	Y	Guam	Y	None
31		269	311	Fejeran, Rosalia C	Daughter	F	Cha	13	S	Y	Y	Guam	Y	None
32		269	312	Fejeran, Joaquin C	Head	M	Cha	36	M	N	Y	Guam	Y	Laborer
33		269	312	Fejeran, Cristina C	Wife	F	Cha	36	M	N	Y	Guam	Y	None
34		269	312	Fejeran, Geronimo C	Son	M	Cha	13	S	Y	Y	Guam	Y	None
35		269	312	Fejeran, Pedro C	Son	M	Cha	3.3	S	N		Guam		None
36		269	312	Fejeran, Benigno C	Son	M	Cha	1.2	S	N		Guam		None
37		270	313	Concepcion, Ana A	Head	F	Cha	31	M	N	N	Guam	N	Laundress
38		270	313	Concepcion, Jesus A	Son	M	Cha	8	S	Y		Guam		None
39		270	313	Concepcion, Manuel A	Son	M	Cha	7	S	Y		Guam		None
40		270	313	Concepcion, Jose A	Son	M	Cha	4.3	S	N		Guam		None
41		270	313	Concepcion, Rosario A	Daughter	F	Cha	1.5	S	N		Guam		None
42		270	313	Concepcion, Julia A	Daughter	F	Cha	.3	S	N		Guam		None
43		270	313	Concepcion, Rosa G	Mother in law	F	Cha	67	Wd	N	N	Guam	N	None
44		270	313	Concepcion, Antonia C	Niece	F	Cha	16	S	N	Y	Guam	Y	Servant
45		271	314	Cruz, Jose G	Head	M	Cha	25	M	N	Y	Guam	Y	Farmer
46		271	314	Cruz, Francisca C	Wife	F	Cha	24	M	N	Y	Guam	Y	Laundress
47		271	314	Cruz, Francisco C	Son	M	Cha	2.3	S	N		Guam		None
48		271	314	Cruz, Maria C	Daughter	F	Cha	.5	S	N		Guam		None
49		272	315	Materne, Antonio M	Head	M	Cha	43	M	N	Y	Guam	N	Barber
50		272	315	Materne, Josefa P	Wife	F	Cha	47	M	N	N	Guam	N	None

DEPARTMENT OF COMMERCE-BUREAU OF THE CENSUS
WASHINGTON

FIFTEENTH CENSUS OF THE UNITED STATES: 1930-POPULATION

THE ISLAND OF GUAM

Sheet No. 35A

District Municipality of Agana
Name of Place Agana City (Santa Cruz)
[Proper name and, also, name of class, as city, town, village, barrio, etc]

Enumeration District No. 4
Enumerated by me on April 16, 1930 Vicente Tydingco
Enumerator

	PLACE OF ABODE			NAME	RELATION	PERSONAL DESCRIPTION				EDUCATION		NATIVITY		OCCUPATION
	Street, avenue, road, etc.	Number of dwelling house in order of visitation	Number of family in order of visitation	of each person whose place of abode on April 1, 1930, was in this family. Enter surname, first, then given name and middle initial. If any. Include every person living on April 1, 1930. Omit children born since April 1, 1930.	Relationship of this Person to the head of the family.	Sex	Color or race	Age at last birthday	Single, married, widowed or divorced	Attended school any time since Sept. 1, 1929	Whether able to read and write.	Place of birth of this person.	Whether able to speak English.	
	1	2	3	4	5	6	7	8	9	10	11	12	13	14
1	Sagunto Street	272	315	Materne, Jose P	Son	M	Cha	9	S	Y		Guam		None
2		272	315	Santos, Maria P	Step daughter	F	Cha	17	S	N	Y	Guam	Y	None
3		273	316	Bitanga, Anatalio A	Head	M	Fil	70	Wd	N	N	Philippine Island	N	Farmer
4		273	316	Bitanga, Jose LG	Son	M	Fil	36	S	N	Y	Guam	Y	Deputy Land Judge
5		273	316	Bitanga, Maria C	Daughter	F	Fil	31	S	N	Y	Guam	Y	None
6		273	316	Bitanga, Vicente LG	Son	M	Fil	28	S	N	Y	Guam	Y	Farm Laborer
7		273	316	Bitanga, Inocensio LG	Son	M	Fil	25	S	N	Y	Guam	Y	Surveyor
8		273	316	Bitanga, Francisca LG	Daughter	F	Fil	21	S	N	Y	Guam	Y	None
9		273	316	Bitanga, Fermin LG	Son	M	Fil	18	S	N	Y	Guam	Y	Surveyor
10		274	317	Camacho, Pedro M	Head	M	Cha	27	M	N	Y	Guam	Y	Clerk
11		274	317	Camacho, Tomasa S	Wife	F	Cha	29	M	N	Y	Guam	Y	None
12		274	317	Camacho, Maria S	Daughter	F	Cha	7	S	Y		Guam		None
13		274	317	Camacho, Lourdes S	Daughter	F	Cha	5	S	N		Guam		None
14		274	317	Camacho, Estella S	Daughter	F	Cha	3.8	S	N		Guam		None
15		274	317	Camacho, Eliza S	Daughter	F	Cha	2.5	S	N		Guam		None
16		274	317	Camacho, Matilde S	Daughter	F	Cha	1.3	S	N		Guam		None
17		274	317	Camacho, Ireneo S	Son	M	Cha	.8	S	N		Guam		None
18		275	318	Martinez, Juan C	Head	M	Cha	53	M	N	Y	Guam	N	Shoemaker
19		275	318	Martinez, Rita P	Wife	F	Cha	54	M	N	Y	Guam	N	None
20		275	318	Martinez, Jose P	Son	M	Cha	23	S	N	Y	Guam	Y	Clerk
21		275	318	Martinez, Antonio P	Son	M	Cha	21	S	N	Y	Guam	Y	Teacher
22		275	318	Martinez, Juan P	Son	M	Cha	19	S	N	Y	Guam	Y	Surveyor
23		275	318	Martinez, Concepcion P	Daughter	F	Cha	18	S	N	Y	Guam	Y	None
24		275	318	Martinez, Eduviges P	Daughter	F	Cha	14	S	N	Y	Guam	Y	None
25		275	318	Martinez, Nieves P	Daughter	F	Cha	12	S	Y	Y	Guam	Y	None

(CHAMORRO ROOTS GENEALOGY PROJECT™ TRANSCRIPTION)
(BERNARD T. PUNZALAN / HTTP://WWW.CHAMORROROOTS.COM)

DEPARTMENT OF COMMERCE-BUREAU OF THE CENSUS
WASHINGTON

FIFTEENTH CENSUS OF THE UNITED STATES: 1930-POPULATION

THE ISLAND OF GUAM

Sheet No. 35B

149B

District Municipality of Agana
Name of Place Agana City (Santa Cruz)
[Proper name and, also, name of class, as city, town, village, barrio, etc]

Enumeration District No. 4
Enumerated by me on April 16, 1930 Vicente Tydingco
Enumerator

	PLACE OF ABODE			NAME	RELATION	PERSONAL DESCRIPTION				EDUCATION		NATIVITY		OCCUPATION
	Street, avenue, road, etc.	Number of dwelling house is order of visitation	Number of family in order of visitation	of each person whose place of abode on April 1, 1930, was in this family. Enter surname, first, then given name and middle initial. If any. Include every person living on April 1, 1930. Omit children born since April 1, 1930.	Relationship of this Person to the head of the family.	Sex	Color or race	Age at last birthday	Single, married, widowed or divorced	Attended school any time since Sept. 1, 1929	Whether able to read and write.	Place of birth of this person.	Whether able to speak English.	
	1	2	3	4	5	6	7	8	9	10	11	12	13	14
26	Sagunto Street	276	319	Borja, Jesus C	Head	M	Cha	27	M	N	Y	Guam	Y	Salesman
27		276	319	Borja, Ana Q	Wife	F	Cha	27	M	N	Y	Guam	N	None
28		276	319	Borja, Jose Q	Son	M	Cha	7	S	Y		Guam		None
29		276	319	Borja, Rosalina Q	Daughter	F	Cha	1.8	S	N		Guam		None
30		276	319	Borja, Francisco C	Brother	M	Cha	22	S	N	Y	Guam	Y	Carpenter
31		277	320	Guerrero, Vicente C	Head	M	Cha	54	Wd	N	N	Guam	N	Farmer
32		277	320	Guerrero, Venancio T	Son	M	Cha	24	S	N	Y	Guam	Y	Farm Laborer
33		277	320	Guerrero, Jesus T	Son	M	Cha	22	S	N	Y	Guam	Y	Barber
34		277	320	Guerrero, Juan T	Son	M	Cha	17	S	N	Y	Guam	Y	None
35		277	320	Guerrero, Ana T	Daughter	F	Cha	16	S	N	Y	Guam	Y	None
36		277	320	Guerrero, Rita T	Daughter	F	Cha	14	S	Y	Y	Guam	Y	None
37		277	320	Taitano, Vicente G	Brother in law	M	Cha	45	S	N	N	Guam		None
38		277	320	Taitano, Ana G	Sister in law	F	Cha	47	S	N	N	Guam	N	None
39		277	320	Taitano, Joaquin G	Brother in law	M	Cha	40	S	N	N	Guam	N	Servant
40		277	320	Salas, Joaquina T	Sister in law	F	Cha	49	Wd	N	N	Guam	N	None
41		278	321	Arceo, Jose B	Head	M	Cha	46	M	N	Y	Guam	N	Blacksmith
42		278	321	Arceo, Ana G	Wife	F	Cha	39	M	N	N	Guam	N	None
43		278	321	Arceo, Francisco G	Son	M	Cha	14	S	N	Y	Guam	Y	None
44		278	321	Arceo, Vicente G	Son	M	Cha	12	S	Y	Y	Guam	Y	None
45		278	321	Arceo, Maria G	Daughter	F	Cha	11	S	Y	Y	Guam	Y	None
46		278	321	Arceo, Jose G	Son	M	Cha	10	S	Y	Y	Guam	Y	None
47		278	321	Arceo, Rosalia G	Daughter	F	Cha	8	S	Y		Guam		None
48		278	321	Arceo, Guadalupe G	Daughter	F	Cha	6	S	N		Guam		None
49		278	321	Arceo, Jesus G	Son	M	Cha	3.4	S	N		Guam		None
50		279	322	Perez, Manuela C	Head	F	Cha	48	Wd	N	Y	Guam	N	None

(CHAMORRO ROOTS GENEALOGY PROJECT™ TRANSCRIPTION)
(BERNARD T. PUNZALAN / HTTP://WWW.CHAMORROROOTS.COM)

DEPARTMENT OF COMMERCE-BUREAU OF THE CENSUS
WASHINGTON

FIFTEENTH CENSUS OF THE UNITED STATES: 1930-POPULATION

THE ISLAND OF GUAM

Sheet No. 36A

District **Municipality of Agana**
Name of Place **Agana City (Santa Cruz)**
[Proper name and, also, name of class, as city, town, village, barrio, etc]

Enumeration District No. **4**
Enumerated by me on **April 16, 1930** Vicente Tydingco
Enumerator

	PLACE OF ABODE: Street, avenue, road, etc.	Number of dwelling house in order of visitation	Number of family in order of visitation	NAME of each person whose place of abode on April 1, 1930, was in this family. Enter surname, first, then given name and middle initial. If any. Include every person living on April 1, 1930. Omit children born since April 1, 1930.	RELATION Relationship of this Person to the head of the family.	PERSONAL DESCRIPTION: Sex	Color or race	Age at last birthday	Single, married, widowed or divorced	EDUCATION: Attended school any time since Sept. 1, 1929	Whether able to read and write.	NATIVITY Place of birth of this person.	Whether able to speak English.	OCCUPATION
	1	2	3	4	5	6	7	8	9	10	11	12	13	14
1	Sagunto Street	279	322	Perez, Ismael C	Son	M	Cha	22	S	N	Y	Guam	Y	Carpenter
2		279	322	Perez, Rosalina C	Daughter	F	Cha	15	S	N	Y	Guam	Y	None
3		279	322	Perez, Joaquin C	Son	M	Cha	14	S	Y	Y	Guam	Y	None
4		279	322	Perez, Maria C	Daughter	F	Cha	10	S	Y	Y	Guam	Y	None
5		279	322	Perez, Jose C	Son	M	Cha	4.3	S	N		Guam		None
6		279	322	Perez, Juan C	Son	M	Cha	1.5	S	N		Guam		None
7		280	323	Cruz, Jose C	Head	M	Cha	32	M	N	Y	Guam	Y	Chauffeur
8		280	323	Cruz, Andrea M	Wife	F	Cha	28	M	N	Y	Guam	Y	None
9		280	323	Cruz, Henry M	Son	M	Cha	9	S	Y		Guam		None
10		280	323	Cruz, Jose M	Son	M	Cha	8	S	Y		Guam		None
11		280	323	Cruz, Delfina M	Daughter	F	Cha	6	S	N		Guam		None
12		280	323	Cruz, Francisca M	Daughter	F	Cha	2.6	S	N		Guam		None
13		280	323	Cruz, Jesus M	Son	M	Cha	1.2	S	N		Guam		None
14		280	323	Mesa, Rosalia R	Mother in law	F	Cha	69	S	N		Guam	N	None
15		281	324	Pereda, Rosa C	Head	F	Cha	57	Wd	N	Y	Guam	N	None
16		281	324	Pereda, Francisco C	Son	M	Cha	23	S	N	Y	Guam	Y	Farmer
17		281	324	Pereda, Rosa C	Daughter	F	Cha	20	S	N	Y	Guam	Y	None
18		281	324	Pereda, Fidela C	Daughter	F	Cha	17	S	N	Y	Guam	Y	None
19		281	324	Pereda, Natividad C	Daughter	F	Cha	14	S	Y	Y	Guam	Y	None
20		281	324	Pereda, Margarita C	Daughter	F	Cha	12	S	Y	Y	Guam	Y	None
21		281	324	Pereda, Juan C	Son	M	Cha	9	S	Y		Guam		None
22		282	325	Santos, Esiquel A	Head	M	Cha	48	M	N	Y	Guam	N	Farmer
23		282	325	Santos, Rosa C	Wife	F	Cha	54	M	N	Y	Guam	N	None
24		282	325	Santos, Silvia C	Daughter	F	Cha	10	S	Y	Y	Guam	Y	None
25		282	325	Celes, Joaquin I	Wife's nephew	M	Cha	39	S	N	N	Guam	N	Farm Laborer

DEPARTMENT OF COMMERCE-BUREAU OF THE CENSUS
WASHINGTON

FIFTEENTH CENSUS OF THE UNITED STATES: 1930-POPULATION

THE ISLAND OF GUAM

Sheet No. 36B

150B

District **Municipality of Agana**
Name of Place **Agana City (Santa Cruz)**
[Proper name and, also, name of class, as city, town, village, barrio, etc]

Enumeration District No. 4
Enumerated by me on **April 17, 1930** Vicente Tydingco
Enumerator

	PLACE OF ABODE			NAME	RELATION	PERSONAL DESCRIPTION				EDUCATION		NATIVITY		OCCUPATION
	Street, avenue, road, etc.	Number of dwelling house is order of visitation	Number of family in order of visitation	of each person whose place of abode on April 1, 1930, was in this family. Enter surname, first, then given name and middle initial. If any. Include every person living on April 1, 1930. Omit children born since April 1, 1930.	Relationship of this Person to the head of the family.	Sex	Color or race	Age at last birthday	Single, married, widowed or divorced	Attended school any time since Sept. 1, 1929	Whether able to read and write.	Place of birth of this person.	Whether able to speak English.	
	1	2	3	4	5	6	7	8	9	10	11	12	13	14
26	Sagunto Street	283	326	Salas, Nicolasa L	Head	F	Cha	67	Wd	N	Y	Guam	N	None
27		283	326	Salas, Emeterio G	Grandson	M	Cha	15	S	Y	Y	Guam	Y	None
28		283	326	Salas, Auria G	Granddaughter	F	Cha	13	S	N	Y	Guam	Y	None
29		283	326	Salas, Jose G	Grandson	M	Cha	11	S	Y	Y	Guam	Y	None
30		284	327	Blaz, Jose B	Head	M	Cha	60	M	N	Y	Guam	N	Farmer
31		284	327	Blaz, Josefa I	Wife	F	Cha	59	M	N	N	Guam	N	None
32		284	327	Blaz, Ana I	Daughter	F	Cha	34	S	N	Y	Guam	Y	Laundress
33		284	327	Blaz, Felisa I	Daughter	F	Cha	25	S	N	Y	Guam	Y	Laundress
34		284	327	Blaz, Magdalena I	Daughter	F	Cha	20	S	N	Y	Guam	Y	Laundress
35		284	327	Blaz, Tomasa I	Daughter	F	Cha	18	S	N	Y	Guam	Y	Seamstress
36		284	327	Blaz, Francisco B	Grandson	M	Cha	13	S	Y	Y	Guam	Y	None
37		285	328	Borja, Felipe LG	Head	M	Cha	34	M	N	Y	Guam	Y	Printer
38		285	328	Borja, Maria C	Wife	F	Cha	29	M	N	Y	Guam	N	None
39		285	328	Borja, Juan C	Son	M	Cha	10	S	Y	Y	Guam	Y	None
40		285	328	Borja, Adriano C	Son	M	Cha	9	S	Y		Guam		None
41		285	328	Borja, Julia C	Daughter	F	Cha	8	S	Y		Guam		None
42		285	328	Borja, Celestina C	Daughter	F	Cha	6	S	N		Guam		None
43		285	328	Borja, Pedro C	Son	M	Cha	3.8	S	N		Guam		None
44		285	328	Borja, Jesus C	Son	M	Cha	1.3	S	N		Guam		None
45		285	328	Castro, Concepcion I	Mother in law	F	Cha	60	S	N	N	Guam	N	None
46		286	329	Concepcion, Manuel C	Head	M	Cha	39	M	N	Y	Guam	Y	Teamster
47		286	329	Concepcion, Consolacion H	Wife	F	Cha	23	M	N	Y	Guam	Y	None
48		286	329	Concepcion, Josefina H	Daughter	F	Cha	2.3	S	N		Guam		None
49		286	329	Concepcion, Vicente H	Son	M	Cha	.5	S	N		Guam		None
50		287	330	Cruz, Jesus I	Head	M	Cha	76	M	N	Y	Guam	Y	Machinist

DEPARTMENT OF COMMERCE-BUREAU OF THE CENSUS
WASHINGTON

FIFTEENTH CENSUS OF THE UNITED STATES: 1930-POPULATION

THE ISLAND OF GUAM

Sheet No. 37A

District **Municipality of Agana**
Name of Place **Agana City (Santa Cruz)** [Proper name and, also, name of class, as city, town, village, barrio, etc]

Enumeration District No. **4**
Enumerated by me on **April 17, 1930** Vicente Tydingco, Enumerator

	PLACE OF ABODE: Street, avenue, road, etc.	Number of dwelling house in order of visitation	Number of family in order of visitation	NAME of each person whose place of abode on April 1, 1930, was in this family. Enter surname, first, then given name and middle initial, if any. Include every person living on April 1, 1930. Omit children born since April 1, 1930.	RELATION Relationship of this Person to the head of the family.	Sex	Color or race	Age at last birthday	Single, married, widowed or divorced	Attended school any time since Sept. 1, 1929	Whether able to read and write.	NATIVITY Place of birth of this person.	Whether able to speak English.	OCCUPATION
	1	2	3	4	5	6	7	8	9	10	11	12	13	14
1	Sagunto Street	287	330	Cruz, Filomena C	Wife	F	Cha	22	M	N	Y	Guam	Y	None
2		287	330	Cruz, Josefa I	Mother	F	Cha	60	Wd	N	N	Guam	N	None
3		287	330	Cruz, Pedro I	Brother	M	Cha	36	S	N	Y	Guam	Y	Fireman
4		288	331	Blaz, Antonio I	Head	M	Cha	35	M	N	Y	Guam	Y	Plumber
5		288	331	Blaz, Maria P	Wife	F	Cha	31	M	N	Y	Guam	N	None
6		288	331	Blaz, Jesus P	Son	M	Cha	9	S	Y		Guam		None
7		288	331	Blaz, Elena P	Daughter	F	Cha	8	S	Y		Guam		None
8		288	331	Blaz, Julia P	Daughter	F	Cha	7	S	Y		Guam		None
9		288	331	Blaz, Antonio P	Son	M	Cha	5	S	N		Guam		None
10		288	331	Blaz, Josefina P	Daughter	F	Cha	2.9	S	N		Guam		None
11		288	331	Blaz, Atanacio P	Son	M	Cha	.9	S	N		Guam		None
12		289	332	Mendiola, Juan H	Head	M	Cha	37	M	N	Y	Guam	Y	Farmer
13		289	332	Mendiola, Eliza S	Wife	F	Cha	29	M	N	Y	Guam	Y	None
14		289	332	Mendiola, Tomas S	Son	M	Cha	9	S	Y		Guam		None
15		289	332	Mendiola, Jesus S	Son	M	Cha	8	S	Y		Guam		None
16		289	332	Mendiola, Rosa S	Daughter	F	Cha	5	S	N		Guam		None
17		289	332	Mendiola, Magdalena S	Daughter	F	Cha	3.8	S	N		Guam		None
18		289	332	Mendiola, Magdalena H	Mother	F	Cha	61	Wd	N	Y	Guam	N	None
19		290	333	Mendiola, Jesus P	Head	M	Cha	32	M	N	Y	Guam	Y	None
20		290	333	Mendiola, Maria M	Wife	F	Cha	36	M	N	Y	Guam	Y	Carpenter
21		290	333	Mendiola, Virginia C	Daughter	F	Cha	10	S	Y	Y	Guam	Y	None
22		290	333	Mendiola, Julia C	Daughter	F	Cha	8	S	Y		Guam		None
23		290	333	Mendiola, Juan C	Son	M	Cha	5	S	Y		Guam		None
24		290	333	Mendiola, Magdalena M	Daughter	F	Cha	2.3	S	N		Guam		None
25		291	334	Mayo, Concepcion L	Head	F	Cha	49	M	N	Y	Guam	Y	None

DEPARTMENT OF COMMERCE-BUREAU OF THE CENSUS
WASHINGTON

FIFTEENTH CENSUS OF THE UNITED STATES: 1930-POPULATION

THE ISLAND OF GUAM

Sheet No. 37B

151B

District Municipality of Agana
Name of Place Agana City (Santa Cruz)
[Proper name and, also, name of class, as city, town, village, barrio, etc]

Enumeration District No. 4
Enumerated by me on April 17, 1930 Vicente Tydingco
Enumerator

	PLACE OF ABODE			NAME	RELATION	PERSONAL DESCRIPTION				EDUCATION		NATIVITY		OCCUPATION
	Street, avenue, road, etc.	Number of dwelling house is order of visitation	Number of family in order of visitation	of each person whose place of abode on April 1, 1930, was in this family. Enter surname, first, then given name and middle initial. If any. Include every person living on April 1, 1930. Omit children born since April 1, 1930.	Relationship of this Person to the head of the family.	Sex	Color or race	Age at last birthday	Single, married, widowed or divorced	Attended school any time since Sept. 1, 1929	Whether able to read and write.	Place of birth of this person.	Whether able to speak English.	
	1	2	3	4	5	6	7	8	9	10	11	12	13	14
26	Sagunto Street	291	335	Adamos, Ana LG	Head	F	Cha	25	M	N	Y	Guam	Y	None
27		291	335	Adamos, Pablo LG	Son	M	Cha	.3	S	N		Guam		None
28		292	336	Camacho, Jose M	Head	M	Cha	55	M	N	Y	Guam	Y	Farmer
29		292	336	Camacho, Cristina C	Wife	F	Cha	30	M	N	Y	Guam	Y	None
30		292	336	Camacho, Barbara C	Daughter	F	Cha	15	S	N	Y	Guam	Y	None
31		292	336	Camacho, Maria C	Daughter	F	Cha	13	S	Y	Y	Guam	Y	None
32		292	336	Camacho, Severino C	Son	M	Cha	9	S	Y		Guam		None
33		292	336	Camacho, Buenaventuro C	Son	M	Cha	6	S	N		Guam		None
34		292	336	Camacho, Abraham C	Son	M	Cha	3.5	S	N		Guam		None
35		292	336	Camacho, Florencia C	Daughter	F	Cha	1.4	S	N		Guam		None
36		292	337	Cepeda, Jesus S	Head	M	Cha	48	M	N	Y	Guam	N	Laborer
37		292	337	Cepeda, Vicenta C	Wife	F	Cha	59	M	N	Y	Guam	N	None
38		292	337	Cepeda, Joaquin C	Son	M	Cha	36	S	N	Y	Guam	Y	Servant
39		292	337	Cepeda, Lourdes C	Daughter	F	Cha	16	S	N	Y	Guam	Y	None
40		292	338	Camacho, Francisco M	Head	M	Cha	33	Wd	N	Y	Guam	N	Farmer
41		292	338	Camacho, Francisca T	Daughter	F	Cha	6	S	N		Guam		None
42		292	338	Camacho, Rita M	Aunt	F	Cha	57	S	N	N	Guam	N	None
43		292	338	Camacho, Filomenia C	Cousin	F	Cha	23	S	N	N	Guam	N	None
44		293	339	Matanane, Jesus C	Head	M	Cha	26	M	N	Y	Guam	Y	Laborer
45		293	339	Matanane, Rosa C	Wife	F	Cha	22	M	N	Y	Guam	N	None
46		293	339	Matanane, Felisa C	Daughter	F	Cha	1.9	S	N		Guam		None
47		293	339	Matanane, Francisco C	Son	M	Cha	.5	S	N		Guam		None
48		294	340	Leon Guerrero, Dolores C	Head	F	Cha	56	Wd	N	N	Guam	N	None
49		294	340	Leon Guerrero, Maria C	Daughter	F	Cha	34	S	N	N	Guam	N	None
50		294	340	Leon Guerrero, Rosa C	Daughter	F	Cha	27	S	N	Y	Guam	Y	Seamstress

DEPARTMENT OF COMMERCE-BUREAU OF THE CENSUS
WASHINGTON

FIFTEENTH CENSUS OF THE UNITED STATES: 1930-POPULATION

THE ISLAND OF GUAM

Sheet No. 38A

District Municipality of Agana
Name of Place Agana City (Santa Cruz)
[Proper name and, also, name of class, as city, town, village, barrio, etc]

Enumeration District No. 4
Enumerated by me on April 17, 1930 Vicente Tydingco
Enumerator

	PLACE OF ABODE			NAME	RELATION	PERSONAL DESCRIPTION				EDUCATION		NATIVITY		OCCUPATION
	Street, avenue, road, etc.	Number of dwelling house is order of visitation	Number of family in order of visitation	of each person whose place of abode on April 1, 1930, was in this family. Enter surname, first, then given name and middle initial. If any. Include every person living on April 1, 1930. Omit children born since April 1, 1930.	Relationship of this Person to the head of the family.	Sex	Color or race	Age at last birthday	Single, married, widowed or divorced	Attended school any time since Sept. 1, 1929	Whether able to read and write.	Place of birth of this person.	Whether able to speak English.	
	1	2	3	4	5	6	7	8	9	10	11	12	13	14
1	Sagunto Street	294	340	Leon Guerrero, Jesus LG	Grandson	M	Cha	15	S	Y	Y	Guam	Y	None
2		294	340	Leon Guerrero, Manuel LG	Grandson	M	Cha	13	S	Y	Y	Guam	Y	None
3		294	340	Leon Guerrero, Beatris LG	Granddaughter	F	Cha	12	S	Y	Y	Guam	Y	None
4		294	340	Leon Guerrero, Ignacio LG	Grandson	M	Cha	9	S	Y		Guam		None
5		294	340	Leon Guerrero, Tomas LG	Grandson	M	Cha	8	S	Y		Guam		None
6		294	340	Leon Guerrero, Mariano LG	Grandson	M	Cha	5	S	N		Guam		None
7		294	340	Cepeda, Maria S	Sister	F	Cha	42	Wd	N	N	Guam	N	Cook
8		294	340	Cepeda, Tomas C	Nephew	M	Cha	20	S	N	Y	Guam	Y	Laborer
9		295	341	Blaz, Francisco C	Head	M	Cha	35	M	N	Y	Guam	Y	Laborer
10		295	341	Blaz, Maria P	Wife	F	Cha	19	M	N	Y	Guam	Y	None
11		296	342	Cruz, Joaquin P	Head	M	Cha	26	M	N	Y	Guam	Y	Machinist
12		296	342	Cruz, Maria SN	Wife	F	Cha	26	M	N	Y	Guam	Y	None
13		296	342	Cruz, Concepcion SN	Daughter	F	Cha	1.3	S	N		Guam		None
14		296	342	San Nicolas, Juan S	Brother in law	M	Cha	21	S	N	Y	Guam	Y	Cook
15		296	342	San Nicolas, Gregorio S	Brother in law	M	Cha	17	S	Y	Y	Guam	Y	None
16		296	342	San Nicolas, Magdalena S	Sister in law	F	Cha	14	S	Y	Y	Guam	Y	None
17		297	343	Santos, Marcos U	Head	M	Cha	42	M	N	Y	Guam	N	Farmer
18		297	343	Santos, Asuncion C	Wife	F	Cha	27	M	N	N	Guam	N	None
19		297	343	Santos, Romaldo G	Son	M	Cha	12	S	Y	Y	Guam	Y	None
20		297	343	Santos, Juan G	Son	M	Cha	10	S	Y	Y	Guam	Y	None
21		297	343	Santos, Francisco G	Son	M	Cha	9	S	Y		Guam		None
22		297	343	Santos, Clemente G	Son	M	Cha	4.5	S	N		Guam		None
23		297	343	Santos, Emilasia C	Daughter	F	Cha	3.1	S	N		Guam		None
24		297	343	Santos, Maria U	Sister	F	Cha	51	S	N	N	Guam	N	Laundress
25		298	344	Perez, Cesario B	Head	M	Cha	65	Wd	N	Y	Guam	N	Farmer

DEPARTMENT OF COMMERCE-BUREAU OF THE CENSUS
WASHINGTON

FIFTEENTH CENSUS OF THE UNITED STATES: 1930-POPULATION

THE ISLAND OF GUAM

Sheet No. 38 B

152B

District **Municipality of Agana**
Name of Place **Agana City (Santa Cruz)**
[Proper name and, also, name of class, as city, town, village, barrio, etc]

Enumeration District No. 4
Enumerated by me on **April 18, 1930** Vicente Tydingco
Enumerator

	PLACE OF ABODE			NAME	RELATION	PERSONAL DESCRIPTION				EDUCATION		NATIVITY		OCCUPATION
	Street, avenue, road, etc.	Number of dwelling house is order of visitation	Number of family in order of visitation	of each person whose place of abode on April 1, 1930, was in this family. Enter surname, first, then given name and middle initial. If any. Include every person living on April 1, 1930. Omit children born since April 1, 1930.	Relationship of this Person to the head of the family.	Sex	Color or race	Age at last birthday	Single, married, widowed or divorced	Attended school any time since Sept. 1, 1929	Whether able to read and write.	Place of birth of this person.	Whether able to speak English.	
	1	2	3	4	5	6	7	8	9	10	11	12	13	14
26		298	344	Perez, Tomasa F	Daughter	F	Cha	28	S	N	Y	Guam	N	Laundress
27	Pizarro Street	299	345	Leon Guerrero, Vicente A	Head	M	Cha	65	M	N	Y	Guam	N	Farmer
28		299	345	Leon Guerrero, Maria M	Wife	F	Cha	56	M	N	Y	Guam	N	None
29		299	345	Leon Guerrero, Ana M	Daughter	F	Cha	26	S	N	Y	Guam	Y	Seamstress
30		299	345	Leon Guerrero, Josefina M	Daughter	F	Cha	22	S	N	Y	Guam	Y	Teacher
31		299	345	Leon Guerrero, Mariana M	Daughter	F	Cha	16	S	N	Y	Guam	Y	Teacher
32		299	345	Leon Guerrero, Vicente M	Son	M	Cha	13	S	Y	Y	Guam	Y	None
33		299	345	Rojas, Jesus LG	Grandson	M	Cha	9	S	Y		Guam		None
34		300	346	Leon Guerrero, Rita C	Head	F	Cha	46	Wd	N	Y	Guam	N	None
35		300	346	Leon Guerrero, Esiquiel C	Son	M	Cha	20	S	N	Y	Guam	Y	Teacher
36		300	346	Leon Guerrero, Rosario C	Daughter	F	Cha	14	S	Y	Y	Guam	Y	None
37		300	346	Leon Guerrero, Agapito C	Son	M	Cha	12	S	Y	Y	Guam	Y	None
38		300	346	Leon Guerrero, Pedro C	Son	M	Cha	8	S	Y		Guam		None
39		300	346	Leon Guerrero, Francisco C	Son	M	Cha	6	S	N		Guam		None
40		300	346	Reyes, Antonio P	Head	M	Cha	39	M	N	Y	Guam	Y	Farmer
41		301	347	Reyes, Dolores T	Wife	F	Cha	50	M	N	Y	Guam	N	None
42		301	347	Reyes, Rosalia T	Daughter	F	Cha	13	S	N	Y	Guam	Y	None
43		301	347	Reyes, Guadalupe T	Daughter	F	Cha	10	S	Y	Y	Guam	Y	None
44		301	347	Lujan, Atanasio L	Stepson	M	Cha	19	S	N	N	Guam	N	Laborer
45		301	348	Cepeda, Jose C	Head	M	Cha	24	M	N	Y	Guam	Y	Laborer
46		301	348	Cepeda, Maria C	Wife	F	Cha	26	M	N	Y	Guam	Y	None
47		301	348	Cepeda, Lourdes C	Daughter	F	Cha	.6	S	N		Guam		None
48		301	348	Blaz, Regina T	Step daughter	F	Cha	3.1	S	N		Guam		None
49		302	349	Aflague, Inocencio S	Head	M	Cha	38	M	N	Y	Guam	Y	Machinist
50		302	349	Aflague, Eugenia J	Wife	F	Cha	29	M	N	Y	Caroline Islands	Y	None

(CHAMORRO ROOTS GENEALOGY PROJECT™ TRANSCRIPTION)
(BERNARD T. PUNZALAN / HTTP://WWW.CHAMORROROOTS.COM)

DEPARTMENT OF COMMERCE-BUREAU OF THE CENSUS
WASHINGTON

FIFTEENTH CENSUS OF THE UNITED STATES: 1930-POPULATION

THE ISLAND OF GUAM

Sheet No. 39A

153

District **Municipality of Agana**
Name of Place **Agana City (Santa Cruz)**
[Proper name and, also, name of class, as city, town, village, barrio, etc]

Enumeration District No. **4**
Enumerated by me on **April 18, 1930** **Vicente Tydingco**
Enumerator

	PLACE OF ABODE			NAME	RELATION	PERSONAL DESCRIPTION				EDUCATION		NATIVITY		OCCUPATION
	Street, avenue, road, etc.	Number of dwelling house is order of visitation	Number of family in order of visitation	of each person whose place of abode on April 1, 1930, was in this family. Enter surname, first, then given name and middle initial. If any. Include every person living on April 1, 1930. Omit children born since April 1, 1930.	Relationship of this Person to the head of the family.	Sex	Color or race	Age at last birthday	Single, married, widowed or divorced	Attended school any time since Sept. 1, 1929	Whether able to read and write.	Place of birth of this person.	Whether able to speak English.	
	1	2	3	4	5	6	7	8	9	10	11	12	13	14
1	Pizarro Street	302	349	Aflague, Wilfred J	Son	M	Cha	8	S	Y		Guam		None
2		302	349	Aflague, Helen J	Daughter	F	Cha	7	S	Y		Guam		None
3		302	349	Aflague, Alexander J	Son	M	Cha	4.8	S	N		Guam		None
4		302	349	Aflague, Lawrence J	Son	M	Cha	3.3	S	N		Guam		None
5		302	349	Aflague, Joseph J	Son	M	Cha	1.3	S	N		Guam		None
6		302	349	James, Pedro F	Brother in law	M	Cha	15	S	Y	Y	Guam	Y	None
7		302	349	Villagomez, Jose Q	Godson	M	Cha	22	S	N	N	Guam	N	Servant
8		303	350	Torres, Antonio C	Head	M	Cha	28	M	N	Y	Guam	Y	Clerk
9		303	350	Torres, Josefa B	Wife	F	Cha	26	M	N	Y	Guam	Y	None
10		303	350	Torres, Trinidad B	Daughter	F	Cha	1.1	S	N		Guam		None
11		303	350	Torres, Antonia B	Daughter	F	Cha	1.1	S	N		Guam		None
12		304	351	Cruz, Ignacio M	Head	M	Cha	45	M	N	Y	Guam	Y	Carpenter
13		304	351	Cruz, Angelina L	Wife	F	Cha	25	M	N	Y	Guam	Y	Midwife
14		304	351	Cruz, Nicolasa T	Daughter	F	Cha	1.2	S	N		Guam		None
15		304	351	Cruz, Dolores T	Daughter	F	Cha	.2	S	N		Guam		None
16		305	352	Ramirez, Jesus B	Head	M	Cha	45	M	N	Y	Guam	Y	Farmer
17		305	352	Ramirez, Maria T	Wife	F	Cha	38	M	N	N	Guam	N	None
18		305	352	Ramirez, Josefina T	Daughter	F	Cha	17	S	Y	Y	Guam	Y	None
19		305	352	Ramirez, Florencio T	Son	M	Cha	14	S	Y	Y	Guam	Y	None
20		305	352	Ramirez, Jose T	Son	M	Cha	13	S	Y	Y	Guam	Y	None
21		305	352	Ramirez, Ana T	Daughter	F	Cha	8	S	Y		Guam		None
22		305	352	Ramirez, Catalina T	Daughter	F	Cha	6	S	N		Guam		None
23		305	352	Ramirez, Maria T	Daughter	F	Cha	4.3	S	N		Guam		None
24		305	352	Ramirez, Emilia T	Daughter	F	Cha	1.9	S	N		Guam		None
25		305	352	Guzman, Antonia C	Aunt	F	Cha	85	S	N	Y	Guam	N	None

(CHAMORRO ROOTS GENEALOGY PROJECT™ TRANSCRIPTION)
(BERNARD T. PUNZALAN / HTTP://WWW.CHAMORROROOTS.COM)

DEPARTMENT OF COMMERCE-BUREAU OF THE CENSUS
WASHINGTON

FIFTEENTH CENSUS OF THE UNITED STATES: 1930-POPULATION

THE ISLAND OF GUAM

Sheet No. 39B

153B

District Municipality of Agana
Name of Place Agana City (Santa Cruz)
[Proper name and, also, name of class, as city, town, village, barrio, etc]

Enumeration District No. 4
Enumerated by me on April 18, 1930 Vicente Tydingco
Enumerator

	PLACE OF ABODE			NAME	RELATION	PERSONAL DESCRIPTION				EDUCATION		NATIVITY		OCCUPATION
	Street, avenue, road, etc.	Number of dwelling house is order of visitation	Number of family in order of visitation	of each person whose place of abode on April 1, 1930, was in this family. Enter surname, first, then given name and middle initial. If any. Include every person living on April 1, 1930. Omit children born since April 1, 1930.	Relationship of this Person to the head of the family.	Sex	Color or race	Age at last birthday	Single, married, widowed or divorced	Attended school any time since Sept. 1, 1929	Whether able to read and write.	Place of birth of this person.	Whether able to speak English.	
	1	2	3	4	5	6	7	8	9	10	11	12	13	14
26	Pizarro Street	306	353	Bukikosa, Joaquina C	Head	F	Cha	28	D	N	Y	Guam	N	None
27		306	353	Bukikosa, Jose C	Son	M	Cha	5	S	N		Guam		None
28		306	353	Bukikosa, Manuel C	Son	M	Cha	2.3	S	N		Guam		None
29		307	354	Cepeda, Francisco F	Head	M	Cha	57	M	N	Y	Guam	N	Farmer
30		307	354	Cepeda, Ana F	Wife	F	Cha	64	M	N	N	Guam	N	None
31		307	354	Cepeda, Dolores F	Daughter	F	Cha	32	S	N	Y	Guam	Y	Laundress
32		307	354	Cepeda, Pedro F	Son	M	Cha	34	Wd	N	Y	Guam	Y	Chauffeur
33		307	354	Cepeda, Isabel C	Granddaughter	F	Cha	7	S	Y		Guam		None
34		307	354	Megofna, Manuel F	Nephew	M	Cha	14	S	Y	Y	Guam	Y	None
35		307	354	Megofna, Rita F	Niece	F	Cha	11	S	Y	Y	Guam	Y	None
36		308	355	Castro, Antonio I	Head	M	Cha	45	M	N	Y	Guam	N	Farmer
37		308	355	Castro, Antonia T	Wife	F	Cha	46	M	N	N	Guam	N	Laundress
38		308	355	Castro, Josefa T	Daughter	F	Cha	22	S	N	Y	Guam	Y	None
39		308	355	Castro, Ana T	Daughter	F	Cha	14	S	Y	Y	Guam	Y	None
40		308	356	Cruz, Jose T	Son	M	Cha	9	S	Y		Guam		None
41		308	356	Cruz, Joaquin B	Head	M	Cha	31	M	N	Y	Guam	Y	Farmer
42		309	356	Cruz, Margarita C	Wife	F	Cha	18	M	N	Y	Guam	Y	None
43		309	357	Perez, Joaquin S	Head	M	Cha	43	M	N	Y	Guam	N	Carpenter
44		309	357	Perez, Juana B	Wife	F	Cha	38	M	N	Y	Guam	N	None
45		309	357	Perez, Jesus B	Son	M	Cha	21	S	N	Y	Guam	Y	Carpenter
46		309	357	Perez, Segundo B	Son	M	Cha	18	S	N	Y	Guam	Y	Teacher
47		309	357	Perez, Oliva B	Daughter	F	Cha	16	S	N	Y	Guam	Y	None
48		309	357	Perez, Ingracia B	Daughter	F	Cha	12	S	Y	Y	Guam	Y	None
49		309	357	Perez, Antonio B	Son	M	Cha	10	S	Y	Y	Guam	Y	None
50		309	357	Perez, Teresita B	Daughter	F	Cha	4.2	S	N		Guam		None

DEPARTMENT OF COMMERCE-BUREAU OF THE CENSUS
WASHINGTON

FIFTEENTH CENSUS OF THE UNITED STATES: 1930-POPULATION

THE ISLAND OF GUAM

Sheet No. 440A0a

District Municipality of Agana
Name of Place Agana City (Santa Cruz)
[Proper name and, also, name of class, as city, town, village, barrio, etc]

Enumeration District No. 4
Enumerated by me on April 18, 1930 Vicente Tydingco
Enumerator

	PLACE OF ABODE			NAME	RELATION	PERSONAL DESCRIPTION				EDUCATION		NATIVITY		OCCUPATION
	Street, avenue, road, etc.	Number of dwelling house is order of visitation	Number of family in order of visitation	of each person whose place of abode on April 1, 1930, was in this family. Enter surname, first, then given name and middle initial. If any. Include every person living on April 1, 1930. Omit children born since April 1, 1930.	Relationship of this Person to the head of the family.	Sex	Color or race	Age at last birthday	Single, married, widowed or divorced	Attended school any time since Sept. 1, 1929	Whether able to read and write.	Place of birth of this person.	Whether able to speak English.	
	1	2	3	4	5	6	7	8	9	10	11	12	13	14
1	Pizarro Street	309	357	Borja, Josefa LG	Mother in law	F	Cha	57	Wd	N	N	Guam	N	None
2		310	358	Quichocho, Ignacio T	Head	M	Cha	28	M	N	Y	Guam	Y	Farmer
3		310	358	Quichocho, Rosario T	Wife	F	Cha	23	M	N	Y	Guam	Y	None
4		310	358	Quichocho, Juan T	Son	M	Cha	5.3	S	N		Guam		None
5		310	358	Quichocho, Tomas T	Son	M	Cha	3.1	S	N		Guam		None
6		310	358	Quichocho, Engracia T	Daughter	F	Cha	2.1	S	N		Guam		None
7		310	358	Quichocho, Isabel T	Daughter	F	Cha	.3	S	N		Guam		None
8		310	358	Quichocho, Maria T	Mother in law	F	Cha	62	Wd	N	N	Guam	N	None
9		310	358	Quichocho, Jose T	Brother in law	M	Cha	36	S	N	Y	Guam	N	Farm Laborer
10		311	359	Sakai, Utaro	Head	M	Jap	45	M	N	Y	Tokyo, Japan	Y	Blacksmith
11		311	359	Sakai, Rita F	Wife	F	Cha	35	M	N	Y	Guam	N	None
12		311	359	Sakai, Ana F	Daughter	F	Jap	11	S	Y	Y	Guam	Y	None
13		311	359	Sakai, Matilde F	Daughter	F	Jap	10	S	Y	Y	Guam	Y	None
14		311	359	Sakai, Tomas F	Son	M	Jap	6	S	N		Guam		None
15		312	360	Sakai, Felix F	Son	M	Jap	4.3	S	N		Guam		None
16		313	361	Lifon, Titiana L	Head	F	W	22	M	N	Y	?, Russia		None
17		313	361	Ignacio, Ramon C	Head	M	Cha	90	M	N	N	Guam		None
18		313	361	Ignacio, Tomasa A	Wife	F	Cha	75	M	N	N	Guam	N	None
19		313	362	Aguon, Magdalena M	Head	F	Cha	72	Wd	N	N	Guam	N	None
20		313	362	Aguon, Juliana M	Daughter	F	Cha	15	S	N	Y	Caroline Islands		Servant
21		314	363	Flores, Vicenta C	Head	F	Cha	69	Wd	N	Y	Guam	N	Laundress
22		314	363	Flores, Andrea C	Daughter	F	Cha	44	S	N	N	Guam	N	Servant
23		314	363	Flores, Rita C	Daughter	F	Cha	28	S	N	Y	Guam	N	Laundress
24		314	363	Flores, Rosario C	Daughter	F	Cha	23	S	N	Y	Guam	Y	Laundress
25		314	363	Flores, Carmen C	Daughter	F	Cha	7	S	Y		Guam		None

DEPARTMENT OF COMMERCE-BUREAU OF THE CENSUS
WASHINGTON

FIFTEENTH CENSUS OF THE UNITED STATES: 1930-POPULATION

THE ISLAND OF GUAM

Sheet No. 40B

154B

District Municipality of Agana
Name of Place Agana City (Santa Cruz)
[Proper name and, also, name of class, as city, town, village, barrio, etc]

Enumeration District No. 4
Enumerated by me on April 19, 1930 Vicente Tydingco
Enumerator

	PLACE OF ABODE			NAME	RELATION	PERSONAL DESCRIPTION				EDUCATION		NATIVITY		OCCUPATION
	Street, avenue, road, etc.	Number of dwelling house in order of visitation	Number of family in order of visitation	of each person whose place of abode on April 1, 1930, was in this family. Enter surname, first, then given name and middle initial. If any. Include every person living on April 1, 1930. Omit children born since April 1, 1930.	Relationship of this Person to the head of the family.	Sex	Color or race	Age at last birthday	Single, married, widowed or divorced	Attended school any time since Sept. 1, 1929	Whether able to read and write.	Place of birth of this person.	Whether able to speak English.	
	1	2	3	4	5	6	7	8	9	10	11	12	13	14
26	Pizarro Street	314	363	Flores, Barcelisa F	Granddaughter	F	Cha	4.3	S	N		Guam		None
27		314	363	Flores, Jesus F	Grand son	M	Cha	.9	S	N		Guam		None
28		315	364	Santos, Francisco I	Head	M	Cha	45	M	N	Y	Guam	N	Farmer
29		315	364	Santos, Magdalena Q	Wife	F	Cha	36	M	N	Y	Guam	N	None
30		315	364	Santos, Francisco G	Son	M	Cha	14	S	Y	Y	Guam	Y	None
31		315	364	Santos, Joaquin G	Son	M	Cha	13	S	Y	Y	Guam	Y	None
32		315	364	Santos, Jose Q	Son	M	Cha	.9	S	N		Guam		None
33		316	365	Guerrero, Jose P	Head	M	Cha	22	M	N	Y	Guam	Y	Machinist
34		316	365	Guerrero, Dolores Q	Wife	F	Cha	23	M	N	Y	Guam	Y	None
35		316	365	Guerrero, Olimpia Q	Daughter	F	Cha	.3	S	N		Guam		None
36		317	366	Guzman, Juan A	Head	M	Fil	56	M	N	Y	Phillipine Islands	N	Barber
37		317	366	Guzman, Trinidad C	Wife	F	Cha	57	M	N	N	Guam	N	None
38		317	366	Guzman, Rita C	Daughter	F	Fil	22	S	N	Y	Guam	Y	None
39		317	366	Guzman, Esperanza C	Daughter	F	Fil	21	S	N	Y	Guam	Y	Teacher
40		317	366	Guzman, Caridad C	Daughter	F	Fil	19	S	Y	Y	Guam	Y	Saleswoman
41		317	367	Cruz, Luis A	Head	M	Cha	32	Wd	N	Y	Guam	N	Chauffeur
42		317	367	Cruz, Regina A	Sister	F	Cha	36	S	N	Y	Guam	N	None
43		317	367	Cruz, Concepcion C	Daughter	F	Cha	11	S	Y	Y	Guam	N	None
44		317	367	Cruz, Delfina C	Daughter	F	Cha	5	S	N		Guam		None
45		317	368	Reyes, Maria S	Head	F	Cha	47	M	N	N	Guam	N	Laundress
46		318	369	Santos, Josefa I	Head	F	Cha	24	M	N	Y	Guam	Y	None
47		318	369	Santos, Lourdes I	Daughter	F	Cha	7	S	Y		Guam		None
48		318	369	Santos, Maria I	Daughter	F	Cha	5.3	S	N		Guam		None
49		318	369	Santos, Tomasa I	Daughter	F	Cha	.9	S	N		Guam		None
50		318	369	Santos, Magdalena I	Daughter	F	Cha	1.1	S	N		Guam		None

DEPARTMENT OF COMMERCE-BUREAU OF THE CENSUS
WASHINGTON

FIFTEENTH CENSUS OF THE UNITED STATES: 1930-POPULATION

THE ISLAND OF GUAM

Sheet No. 41A

District **Municipality of Agana**
Name of Place **Agana City (Santa Cruz)**
[Proper name and, also, name of class, as city, town, village, barrio, etc]

Enumeration District No. **4**
Enumerated by me on **April 19, 1930** Vicente Tydingco
Enumerator

	PLACE OF ABODE			NAME	RELATION	PERSONAL DESCRIPTION				EDUCATION		NATIVITY		OCCUPATION
	Street, avenue, road, etc.	Number of dwelling house is order of visitation	Number of family in order of visitation	of each person whose place of abode on April 1, 1930, was in this family. Enter surname, first, then given name and middle initial. If any. Include every person living on April 1, 1930. Omit children born since April 1, 1930.	Relationship of this Person to the head of the family.	Sex	Color or race	Age at last birthday	Single, married, widowed or divorced	Attended school any time since Sept. 1, 1929	Whether able to read and write.	Place of birth of this person.	Whether able to speak English.	
	1	2	3	4	5	6	7	8	9	10	11	12	13	14
1	Pizarro Street	319	370	Cruz, Ignacia I	Head	F	Cha	58	S	N	N	Guam	N	Laundress
2		320	371	Aguon, Vicente T	Head	M	Cha	63	M	N	Y	Guam	N	None
3		320	371	Aguon, Sabina I	Wife	F	Cha	63	M	N	Y	Guam	N	None
4		320	371	Aguon, Antonio I	Son	M	Cha	20	S	N	Y	Guam	Y	Laborer
5		321	372	Diaz, Francisco S	Head	M	Cha	46	M	N	Y	Guam	N	Farmer
6		321	372	Diaz, Ignacia F	Wife	F	Cha	40	M	N	Y	Guam	N	None
7		321	372	Diaz, Jesus F	Son	M	Cha	18	S	N	Y	Guam	Y	Farm Laborer
8		321	372	Diaz, Joaquin F	Son	M	Cha	17	S	Y	Y	Guam	Y	None
9		321	372	Diaz, Ignacio F	Son	M	Cha	12	S	Y	Y	Guam	Y	None
10		321	372	Diaz, Antonio F	Son	M	Cha	9	S	Y		Guam		None
11		321	372	Diaz, Juan F	Son	M	Cha	7	S	N		Guam		None
12		321	372	Diaz, Maria F	Daughter	F	Cha	5	S	N		Guam		None
13		321	372	Diaz, Rita F	Daughter	F	Cha	3	S	N		Guam		None
14		321	372	Diaz, Maria S	Mother	F	Cha	68	Wd	N	N	Guam	N	None
15		322	373	Diaz, Juan S	Head	M	Cha	41	M	N	Y	Guam	Y	Farmer
16		322	373	Diaz, Maria B	Wife	F	Cha	30	M	N	Y	Guam	Y	None
17		322	373	Diaz, Ana B	Daughter	F	Cha	6	S	N		Guam		None
18		322	373	Diaz, Rosa B	Daughter	F	Cha	5	S	N		Guam		None
19		322	373	Diaz, Adela B	Daughter	F	Cha	2.3	S	N		Guam		None
20		322	373	Diaz, Consolacion B	Daughter	F	Cha	.7	S	N		Guam		None
21		323	374	Cepeda, Jose	Head	M	Cha	36	M	N	Y	Guam	Y	Farmer
22		323	374	Cepeda, Ignacia A	Wife	F	Cha	32	M	N	Y	Guam	Y	None
23		323	374	Cepeda, Barcelisa A	Daughter	F	Cha	14	S	Y	Y	Guam	Y	None
24		323	374	Cepeda, Tomas A	Son	M	Cha	8	S	Y		Guam		None
25		323	374	Cepeda, Maria A	Daughter	F	Cha	6	S	N		Guam		None

(CHAMORRO ROOTS GENEALOGY PROJECT™ TRANSCRIPTION)
(BERNARD T. PUNZALAN / HTTP://WWW.CHAMORROROOTS.COM)

DEPARTMENT OF COMMERCE-BUREAU OF THE CENSUS
WASHINGTON

FIFTEENTH CENSUS OF THE UNITED STATES: 1930-POPULATION

THE ISLAND OF GUAM

Sheet No. 41B

155B

District Municipality of Agana
Name of Place Agana City (Santa Cruz)
[Proper name and, also, name of class, as city, town, village, barrio, etc]

Enumeration District No. 4
Enumerated by me on April 19, 1930 Vicente Tydingco
Enumerator

	PLACE OF ABODE			NAME	RELATION	PERSONAL DESCRIPTION				EDUCATION		NATIVITY		OCCUPATION
	Street, avenue, road, etc.	Number of dwelling house is order of visitation	Number of family in order of visitation	of each person whose place of abode on April 1, 1930, was in this family. Enter surname, first, then given name and middle initial. If any. Include every person living on April 1, 1930. Omit children born since April 1, 1930.	Relationship of this Person to the head of the family.	Sex	Color or race	Age at last birthday	Single, married, widowed or divorced	Attended school any time since Sept. 1, 1929	Whether able to read and write.	Place of birth of this person.	Whether able to speak English.	
	1	2	3	4	5	6	7	8	9	10	11	12	13	14
26	Pizarro Street	323	374	Cepeda, Rosa A	Daughter	F	Cha	4.1	S	N		Guam		None
27		323	374	Cepeda, Ana A	Daughter	F	Cha	2.2	S	N		Guam		None
28		323	374	Aquino, Jesus C	Nephew	M	Cha	3.3	S	N		Guam		None
29		324	375	Santos, Juan P	Head	M	Cha	60	Wd	N	Y	Guam	N	Farmer
30		324	375	Santos, Ana A	Daughter	F	Cha	24	S	N	Y	Guam	Y	Laundress
31		324	375	Santos, Dolores A	Daughter	F	Cha	20	S	N	Y	Guam	Y	Servant
32		324	375	Aquino, Jose C	Nephew	M	Cha	28	S	N	Y	Guam	Y	Servant
33		325	376	Portusach, Antonia M	Head	F	Cha	54	Wd	N	Y	Guam	N	None
34		325	376	Portusach, Magdalena M	Daughter	F	Cha	19	S	N	Y	Guam	Y	Teacher
35		325	376	Portusach, Maria M	Daughter	F	Cha	15	S	N	Y	Guam	Y	Salesman
36		35	377	Long, Emilia P	Head	F	Cha	19	M	N	Y	Guam	Y	None
37		325	377	Long, Betty F	Daughter	F	Cha	1.3	S	N		Guam		None
38		326	378	Leon Guerrero, Felipe g	Head	M	Cha	43	M	N	Y	Guam	N	Farmer
39		326	378	Leon Guerrero, Soledad LG	Wife	F	Cha	44	M	N	N	Guam	N	None
40		326	378	Leon Guerrero, Tomas R	Son	M	Cha	21	S	N	Y	Guam	Y	Farm Laborer
41		326	378	Leon Guerrero, Delfina R	Daughter	F	Cha	18	S	N	Y	Guam	Y	Cook
42		326	378	Leon Guerrero, Mariana LG	Daughter	F	Cha	9	S	Y	Y	Guam		None
43		326	378	Leon Guerrero, Juan LG	Son	M	Cha	6	S	N		Guam		None
44		326	378	Leon Guerrero, Sibastian LG	Son	M	Cha	3.7	S	N		Guam		None
45		327	379	Butler, Margarita R	Head	F	Cha	32	Wd	N	Y	Guam	Y	None
46		327	379	Butler, Tomas R	Son	M	Cha	12	S	Y	Y	Guam	Y	None
47		327	379	Butler, Nellie R	Daughter	F	Cha	11	S	Y	Y	Guam	Y	None
48		327	379	Butler, Robert R	Son	M	Cha	9	S	Y		Guam		None
49		327	379	Butler, William R	Son	M	Cha	5.2	S	N		Guam		None
50		327	379	Butler, Henry R	Son	M	Cha	2.1	S	N		Guam		None

DEPARTMENT OF COMMERCE-BUREAU OF THE CENSUS
WASHINGTON

FIFTEENTH CENSUS OF THE UNITED STATES: 1930-POPULATION

THE ISLAND OF GUAM

Sheet No. 42A

District Municipality of Agana
Name of Place Agana City (Santa Cruz)
[Proper name and, also, name of class, as city, town, village, barrio, etc]

Enumeration District No. 4
Enumerated by me on April 21, 1930 Vicente Tydingco
Enumerator

	PLACE OF ABODE			NAME	RELATION	PERSONAL DESCRIPTION				EDUCATION		NATIVITY		OCCUPATION
	Street, avenue, road, etc.	Number of dwelling house is order of visitation	Number of family in order of visitation	of each person whose place of abode on April 1, 1930, was in this family. Enter surname, first, then given name and middle initial. If any. Include every person living on April 1, 1930. Omit children born since April 1, 1930.	Relationship of this Person to the head of the family.	Sex	Color or race	Age at last birthday	Single, married, widowed or divorced	Attended school any time since Sept. 1, 1929	Whether able to read and write.	Place of birth of this person.	Whether able to speak English.	
	1	2	3	4	5	6	7	8	9	10	11	12	13	14
1	Pizarro Street	328	380	Mendiola, Ignacio C	Head	M	Cha	31	M	N	N	Guam	N	Farmer
2		328	380	Mendiola, Maria C	Wife	F	Cha	23	M	N	N	Guam	N	None
3		328	380	Mendiola, Jose C	Son	M	Cha	2.9	S	N		Guam		None
4		328	380	Mendiola, Isabel C	Daughter	F	Cha	1.8	S	N		Guam		None
5		328	380	Mendiola, Antonio C	Son	M	Cha	.3	S	N		Guam		None
6		328	380	Mendiola, Juliana C	Mother	F	Cha	68	Wd	N	N	Guam	N	None
7		329	381	Cruz, Rosa D	Head	F	Cha	25	M	N	Y	Guam	Y	None
8		330	382	Lizama, Rita P	Head	F	Cha	45	S	N	Y	Guam	N	None
9		330	382	Garrido, Francisco L	Nephew	M	Cha	19	S	N	Y	Guam	Y	Laborer
10		330	382	Garrido, Vicente L	Nephew	M	Cha	17	S	Y	Y	Guam	Y	None
11		330	382	Garrido, Teodoro L	Nephew	M	Cha	8	S	Y		Guam		None
12		331	383	Lizama, Juan P	Head	M	Cha	43	M	N	Y	Guam	N	Farmer
13		331	383	Lizama, Ana S	Wife	F	Cha	46	M	N	Y	Guam	N	None
14		331	383	Lizama, Jose S	Son	M	Cha	21	S	N	Y	Guam	Y	Surveyor
15		331	383	Lizama, Rosa S	Daughter	F	Cha	18	S	N	Y	Guam	Y	Servant
16		331	383	Lizama, Juan S	Son	M	Cha	16	S	Y	Y	Guam	Y	None
17		331	383	Lizama, Carmen S	Daughter	F	Cha	14	S	Y	Y	Guam	Y	None
18		331	383	Lizama, Maria S	Daughter	F	Cha	13	S	Y	Y	Guam	Y	None
19		331	383	Lizama, Concepcion S	Daughter	F	Cha	10	S	Y	Y	Guam		None
20		331	383	Lizama, Jesus S	Son	M	Cha	1.3	S	N		Guam		None
21		332	384	Quinata, Jose V	Head	M	Cha	40	M	N	Y	Guam	N	Farmer
22		332	384	Quinata, Rosa C	Wife	F	Cha	53	M	N	Y	Guam	N	None
23		332	384	Quinata, Rita C	Daughter	F	Cha	19	S	Y	Y	Guam	Y	None
24		332	384	Quinata, Jose C	Son	M	Cha	17	S	Y	Y	Guam	Y	None
25		332	384	Quinata, Josefina C	Daughter	F	Cha	15	S	Y	Y	Guam	Y	None

DEPARTMENT OF COMMERCE-BUREAU OF THE CENSUS
WASHINGTON

FIFTEENTH CENSUS OF THE UNITED STATES: 1930-POPULATION

THE ISLAND OF GUAM

Sheet No. 42B

156B

District Municipality of Agana
Name of Place Agana City (Santa Cruz)
[Proper name and, also, name of class, as city, town, village, barrio, etc]

Enumeration District No. 4
Enumerated by me on April 21, 1930 Vicente Tydingco
Enumerator

	PLACE OF ABODE: Street, avenue, road, etc.	Number of dwelling house in order of visitation	Number of family in order of visitation	NAME of each person whose place of abode on April 1, 1930, was in this family. Enter surname, first, then given name and middle initial. If any. Include every person living on April 1, 1930. Omit children born since April 1, 1930.	RELATION Relationship of this Person to the head of the family.	PERSONAL DESCRIPTION: Sex	Color or race	Age at last birthday	Single, married, widowed or divorced	EDUCATION: Attended school any time since Sept. 1, 1929	Whether able to read and write.	NATIVITY Place of birth of this person.	Whether able to speak English.	OCCUPATION
	1	2	3	4	5	6	7	8	9	10	11	12	13	14
26	Pizarro Street	332	384	Quinata, Enrique C	Son	M	Cha	11	S	Y	Y	Guam	Y	None
27		332	384	Quinata, Asunsion C	Daughter	F	Cha	9	S	Y		Guam		None
28		332	384	Quinata, Joaquin C	Son	M	Cha	6	S	N		Guam		None
29		333	385	Camacho, Joaquin F	Head	M	Cha	60	M	N	N	Guam	N	Farmer
30		333	385	Camacho, Concepcion G	Wife	F	Cha	44	M	N	N	Guam	N	None
31		333	385	Camacho, Ignacio G	Son	M	Cha	20	S	N	Y	Guam	Y	Laborer
32		333	385	Camacho, Maria G	Daughter	F	Cha	18	S	N	Y	Guam	Y	None
33		333	385	Camacho, Felicita G	Daughter	F	Cha	16	S	N	Y	Guam	Y	None
34		333	385	Camacho, Jose G	Son	M	Cha	12	S	N	Y	Guam	Y	None
35		333	385	Camacho, Juan G	Son	M	Cha	11	S	Y	Y	Guam	Y	None
36		333	385	Camacho, Jesus G	Son	M	Cha	10	S	Y	Y	Guam	Y	None
37		333	385	Camacho, Manuel G	Son	M	Cha	5	S	N		Guam		None
38		333	385	Camacho, Ana G	Daughter	F	Cha	3.5	S	N		Guam		None
39		333	385	Camacho, Felisa G	Mother	F	Cha	70	Wd	N	N	Guam	N	None
40	Hernan Cortes Street	334	386	Camacho, Antonio M	Head	M	Cha	52	M	N	Y	Guam	N	Farmer
41		334	386	Camacho, Josefa R	Wife	F	Cha	50	M	N	N	Guam	N	None
42		334	386	Camacho, Concepcion R	Daughter	F	Cha	29	S	N	Y	Guam	Y	Teacher
43		334	386	Camacho, Carmen R	Daughter	F	Cha	24	S	N	Y	Guam	Y	Dressmaker
44		334	386	Camacho, Nicolasa R	Daughter	F	Cha	22	S	N	Y	Guam	Y	Cook
45		334	386	Camacho, Gregorio R	Son	M	Cha	21	S	N	Y	Guam	Y	Carpenter
46		334	386	Camacho, Rosa R	Daughter	F	Cha	20	S	N	Y	Guam	Y	Servant
47		334	386	Camacho, Vicente R	Son	M	Cha	15	S	Y	Y	Guam	Y	None
48		334	386	Camacho, Simeon R	Son	M	Cha	13	S	Y	Y	Guam	Y	None
49		334	386	Camacho, Atanasio R	Son	M	Cha	11	S	Y	Y	Guam	Y	None
50		334	386	Rivera, Maria G	Mother in law	F	Cha	77	Wd	N	N	Guam	N	None

DEPARTMENT OF COMMERCE-BUREAU OF THE CENSUS
WASHINGTON

FIFTEENTH CENSUS OF THE UNITED STATES: 1930-POPULATION

THE ISLAND OF GUAM

Sheet No. 43A

District Municipality of Agana
Name of Place Agana City (Santa Cruz)
[Proper name and, also, name of class, as city, town, village, barrio, etc]

Enumeration District No. 4
Enumerated by me on April 22, 1930 Vicente Tydingco
Enumerator

	PLACE OF ABODE			NAME	RELATION	PERSONAL DESCRIPTION				EDUCATION		NATIVITY		OCCUPATION
	Street, avenue, road, etc.	Number of dwelling house is order of visitation	Number of family in order of visitation	of each person whose place of abode on April 1, 1930, was in this family. Enter surname, first, then given name and middle initial. If any. Include every person living on April 1, 1930. Omit children born since April 1, 1930.	Relationship of this Person to the head of the family.	Sex	Color or race	Age at last birthday	Single, married, widowed or divorced	Attended school any time since Sept. 1, 1929	Whether able to read and write.	Place of birth of this person.	Whether able to speak English.	
	1	2	3	4	5	6	7	8	9	10	11	12	13	14
1	Hernan Cortes Street	335	387	Rosario, Jose B	Head	M	Cha	61	M	N	Y	Guam	N	Farmer
2		335	387	Rosario, Vicenta R	Wife	F	Cha	52	M	N	Y	Guam	N	None
3		335	387	Rosario, Maria R	Daughter	F	Cha	31	S	N	Y	Guam	Y	Teacher
4		335	387	Rosario, Francisco R	Son	M	Cha	27	S	N	Y	Guam	Y	None
5		335	387	Rosario, Jose R	Son	M	Cha	24	S	N	Y	Guam	Y	Farm Laborer
6		335	387	Rosario, Miguel R	Son	M	Cha	22	S	N	Y	Guam	Y	Surveyor
7		335	387	Rosario, Domingo R	Son	M	Cha	20	S	N	Y	Guam	Y	Servant
8		335	387	Rosario, Carlos R	Son	M	Cha	17	S	Y	Y	Guam	Y	None
9		335	387	Rosario, Tomas R	Son	M	Cha	13	S	Y	Y	Guam	Y	None
10		336	388	Rosario, Lucille R	Granddaughter	F	Cha	5	S	N		Guam		None
11		336	388	Limtiaco, Joaquin A	Head	M	Cha	26	M	N	Y	Guam	Y	Garage Man
12		336	388	Limtiaco, Concepcion C	Wife	F	Cha	24	M	N	Y	Guam	Y	None
13		336	388	Limtiaco, Cecilia C	Daughter	F	Cha	.3	S	N		Guam		None
14		337	389	Dooley, Florence B	Head	F	Cha	24	M	N	Y	Guam	Y	None
15		337	389	Dooley, Tevis C	Son	M	Cha	1.3	S	N		Guam		None
16		338	390	Rios, Brigido A	Head	M	Cha	64	M	N	N	Guam	N	Farmer
17		338	390	Rios, Josefa LG	Wife	F	Cha	61	M	N	Y	Guam	N	None
18		338	390	Rios, Maria LG	Daughter	F	Cha	22	S	N	Y	Guam	Y	Teacher
19		338	391	Cruz, Candelario B	Head	M	Cha	40	M	N	Y	Guam	Y	Laborer
20		338	391	Cruz, Asuncion R	Wife	F	Cha	34	M	N	Y	Guam	Y	None
21		338	391	Cruz, Juan R	Son	M	Cha	14	S	Y	Y	Guam	Y	None
22		338	391	Cruz, Estella R	Daughter	F	Cha	10	S	Y	Y	Guam		None
23		338	391	Cruz, Lourdes R	Daughter	F	Cha	8	S	Y		Guam		None
24		338	391	Cruz, Edward R	Son	M	Cha	6	S	N		Guam		None
25		338	391	Cruz, Emilia R	Daughter	F	Cha	4.7	S	N		Guam		None

(CHAMORRO ROOTS GENEALOGY PROJECT™ TRANSCRIPTION)
(BERNARD T. PUNZALAN / HTTP://WWW.CHAMORROROOTS.COM)

DEPARTMENT OF COMMERCE-BUREAU OF THE CENSUS
WASHINGTON

FIFTEENTH CENSUS OF THE UNITED STATES: 1930-POPULATION

THE ISLAND OF GUAM

Sheet No. 43B

157B

District Municipality of Agana
Name of Place Agana City (Santa Cruz)
[Proper name and, also, name of class, as city, town, village, barrio, etc]

Enumeration District No. 4
Enumerated by me on April 22, 1930 Vicente Tydingco
Enumerator

	PLACE OF ABODE			NAME	RELATION	PERSONAL DESCRIPTION				EDUCATION		NATIVITY		OCCUPATION
	Street, avenue, road, etc.	Number of dwelling house is order of visitation	Number of family in order of visitation	of each person whose place of abode on April 1, 1930, was in this family. Enter surname, first, then given name and middle initial. If any. Include every person living on April 1, 1930. Omit children born since April 1, 1930.	Relationship of this Person to the head of the family.	Sex	Color or race	Age at last birthday	Single, married, widowed or divorced	Attended school any time since Sept. 1, 1929	Whether able to read and write.	Place of birth of this person.	Whether able to speak English.	
	1	2	3	4	5	6	7	8	9	10	11	12	13	14
26	Hernan Cortes Street	338	391	Cruz, Angustia R	Daughter	F	Cha	2.3	S	N		Guam		None
27		338	391	Cruz, Julia R	Daughter	F	Cha	.7	S	N		Guam		None
28		339	392	Taitano, Maria P	Head	F	Cha	42	Wd	N	Y	Guam	Y	Laundress
29		339	392	Taitano, Marcelina P	Daughter	F	Cha	16	S	N	Y	Guam	N	None
30		339	392	Taitano, Concepcion P	Daughter	F	Cha	14	S	Y	Y	Guam	Y	None
31		339	392	Taitano, Gregorio p	Son	M	Cha	10	S	Y	Y	Guam	Y	None
32		339	392	Taitano, Magdalena P	Daughter	F	Cha	7	S	Y		Guam		None
33		339	392	Taitano, Jose P	Son	M	Cha	1.4	S	N		Guam		None
34		339	392	Taitano, Monica M	Mother	F	Cha	88	Wd	N	N	Guam	N	None
35		340	393	Leon Guerrero, Carmen T	Head	F	Cha	19	M	N	Y	Guam	Y	Laundress
36		340	393	Leon Guerrero, Joaquin T	Son	M	Cha	.9	S	N		Guam		None
37		340	394	Rosario, Domingo C	Head	M	Cha	28	M	N	Y	Guam	N	Laborer
38		340	394	Rosario, Lucia C	Wife	F	Cha	40	M	N	N	Guam	N	Laundress
39		340	394	Rosario, Brigida C	Daughter	F	Cha	13	S	Y	Y	Guam	Y	None
40		340	394	Rosario, Engracia C	Daughter	F	Cha	7	S	Y		Guam		None
41		340	394	Rosario, Jose C	Son	M	Cha	5	S	N		Guam		None
42		340	394	Rosario, Francisco C	Son	M	Cha	1.5	S	N		Guam		None
43		341	395	Osone, Fudentura	Head	M	Jap	39	S	N	Y	Tokyo, Japan	N	Merchant
44		342	396	Goodwin, Avea C	Head	F	W	22	M	N	Y	[illegible]	Y	None
45		343	397	Flores, Ignacio G	Wife	M	Cha	35	M	N	Y	Guam	Y	Farmer
46		343	397	Flores, Susana F	Son	F	Cha	33	M	N	Y	Guam	Y	Laundress
47		343	397	Flores, Joaquin F	Daughter	M	Cha	10	S	Y	Y	Guam	Y	None
48		343	397	Flores, Rosario F	Son	F	Cha	9	S	Y		Guam		None
49		343	397	Flores, Francisco F	Daughter	M	Cha	8	S	Y		Guam		None
50		343	397	Flores, Maria F	Daughter	F	Cha	6	S	N		Guam		None

DEPARTMENT OF COMMERCE-BUREAU OF THE CENSUS
WASHINGTON

FIFTEENTH CENSUS OF THE UNITED STATES: 1930-POPULATION

THE ISLAND OF GUAM

Sheet No. 44A

District **Municipality of Agana**
Name of Place **Agana City (Santa Cruz)**
[Proper name and, also, name of class, as city, town, village, barrio, etc]

Enumeration District No. 4
Enumerated by me on **April 22, 1930** Vicente Tydingco, Enumerator

	PLACE OF ABODE: Street, avenue, road, etc.	Number of dwelling house in order of visitation	Number of family in order of visitation	NAME of each person whose place of abode on April 1, 1930, was in this family. Enter surname, first, then given name and middle initial. If any. Include every person living on April 1, 1930. Omit children born since April 1, 1930.	RELATION Relationship of this Person to the head of the family.	PERSONAL DESCRIPTION: Sex	Color or race	Age at last birthday	Single, married, widowed or divorced	EDUCATION: Attended school any time since Sept. 1, 1929	Whether able to read and write.	NATIVITY Place of birth of this person.	Whether able to speak English.	OCCUPATION
	1	2	3	4	5	6	7	8	9	10	11	12	13	14
1	Hernan Cortes Street	343	397	Flores, George F	Son	M	Cha	5	S	N		Guam		None
2		343	397	Flores, Ignacio F	Son	M	Cha	3.2	S	N		Guam		None
3		343	397	Flores, Pedro F	Son	M	Cha	1.5	S	N		Guam		None
4		344	398	Reynolds, Madeline J	Head	F	W	28	M	N	Y	San Francisco, California	Y	None
5		344	398	Reynolds, Jacqueline J	Daughter	F	W	1.5	S	N		San Pedro, California		None
6		345	399	Monsier, Ogla M	Head	F	W	24	M	N	Y	Harbin, China	Y	None
7		345	399	Monsier, Irene	Daughter	F	W	3.5	S	N		Shangai, China		None
8		345	399	Demokesko, Lula M	Sister in law	F	W	18	S	N	Y	Harbin, China	Y	Typist
9		346	400	Mendiola, Carlos C	Head	M	Cha	33	M	N	Y	Guam	N	Farmer
10		346	400	Mendiola, Maria I	Wife	F	Cha	16	M	N	Y	Guam	N	None
11		346	400	Ignacio, Filomena C	Mother in law	F	Cha	50	Wd	N	N	Guam	N	Laundress
12		347	401	Rosario, Joaquin C	Head	M	Cha	38	M	N	Y	Guam	Y	Farmer
13		347	401	Rosario, Magdalena A	Wife	F	Cha	36	M	N	Y	Guam	Y	None
14		347	401	Rosario, Jose A	Son	M	Cha	12	S	Y	Y	Guam	Y	None
15		347	401	Rosario, Vicente A	Son	M	Cha	11	S	Y	Y	Guam	Y	None
16		347	401	Rosario, Delfina A	Daughter	F	Cha	9	S	Y		Guam		None
17		347	401	Rosario, Francisco A	Son	M	Cha	5	S	N		Guam		None
18		347	401	Rosario, Vicenta A	Daughter	F	Cha	3.6	S	N		Guam		None
19		347	401	Rosario, Maria A	Daughter	F	Cha	.2	S	N		Guam		None
20		348	402	Chance, Harry	Head	M	W	71	M	N	Y	Clarksville, Indiana	Y	Garage man
21		348	402	Chance, Rosario	Wife	F	Cha	34	M	N	Y	Guam	Y	None
22		348	402	Chance, Hannah	Daughter	F	Cha	13	S	Y	Y	Guam	Y	None
23		348	402	Chance, Woodrow	Son	m	Cha	12	S	Y	Y	Guam	Y	None
24		348	402	Chance, Harry P	Son	M	Cha	10	S	Y	Y	Guam	Y	None
25		348	402	Chance, Harriet C	Daughter	F	Cha	9	S	Y		Guam		None

(CHAMORRO ROOTS GENEALOGY PROJECT™ TRANSCRIPTION)
(BERNARD T. PUNZALAN / HTTP://WWW.CHAMORROROOTS.COM)

DEPARTMENT OF COMMERCE-BUREAU OF THE CENSUS
WASHINGTON

FIFTEENTH CENSUS OF THE UNITED STATES: 1930-POPULATION

THE ISLAND OF GUAM

Sheet No. 44B

158B

District **Municipality of Agana**
Name of Place **Agana City (Santa Cruz)**
[Proper name and, also, name of class, as city, town, village, barrio, etc]

Enumeration District No. 4
Enumerated by me on **April 22, 1930** Vicente Tydingco
Enumerator

	PLACE OF ABODE			NAME	RELATION	PERSONAL DESCRIPTION				EDUCATION		NATIVITY		OCCUPATION
	Street, avenue, road, etc.	Number of dwelling house is order of visitation	Number of family in order of visitation	of each person whose place of abode on April 1, 1930, was in this family. Enter surname, first, then given name and middle initial. If any. Include every person living on April 1, 1930. Omit children born since April 1, 1930.	Relationship of this Person to the head of the family.	Sex	Color or race	Age at last birthday	Single, married, widowed or divorced	Attended school any time since Sept. 1, 1929	Whether able to read and write.	Place of birth of this person.	Whether able to speak English.	
	1	2	3	4	5	6	7	8	9	10	11	12	13	14
26	Hernan Cortes Street	348	402	Chance, Martha	Daughter	F	Cha	7	S	Y		Guam		None
27		348	402	Chance, John W	Son	M	Cha	5	S	N		Guam		None
28		348	402	Chance, Rosa C	Daughter	F	Cha	3.5	S	N		Guam		None
29		348	402	Flores, Ana G	Mother in law	F	Cha	61	Wd	N	Y	Guam	N	None
30		348	402	Flores, Maria G	Sister in law	F	Cha	38	S	N	Y	Guam	Y	None
31		348	402	Flores, Ramon G	Brother in law	M	Cha	24	S	N	Y	Guam	Y	Farm Laborer
32		349	403	Camacho, Felix M	Head	M	Cha	36	M	N	Y	Guam	Y	Carpenter
33		349	403	Camacho, Antonia G	Wife	F	Cha	36	M	N	Y	Guam	Y	None
34		349	403	Camacho, Josefina G	Daughter	F	Cha	14	S	Y	Y	Guam	Y	None
35		349	403	Camacho, Juan G	Son	M	Cha	12	S	Y	Y	Guam	Y	None
36		349	403	Camacho, Carlos G	Son	M	Cha	6	S	N		Guam		None
37		349	403	Camacho, Luis G	Son	M	Cha	3.3	S	N		Guam		None
38		349	403	Camacho, Edwardo G	Son	M	Cha	1.7	S	N		Guam		None
39		350	403	Roberto, Felix S	Head	M	Cha	63	M	N	Y	Guam	N	Butcher
40		350	404	Roberto, Isabel B	Wife	F	Cha	67	M	N	Y	Guam	N	None
41		350	404	Roberto, Luisa B	Daughter	F	Cha	38	S	N	Y	Guam	N	Laundress
42		350	404	Roberto, Enrique B	Son	M	Cha	24	S	N	Y	Guam	Y	Clerk
43		350	404	Roberto, Isabel R	Granddaugher	F	Cha	7	S	Y		Guam		None
44		351	405	Ada, Pedro M	Head	F	Cha	27	M	N	Y	Guam	Y	Salesman
45		351	405	Ada, Maria P	Wife	F	Cha	27	M	N	Y	Guam	Y	Teacher
46		351	405	Ada, Agnes P	Daughter	F	Cha	2.1	S	N		Guam		None
47		351	405	Santos, Jose A	Cousin	M	Cha	24	Wd	N	Y	Guam	N	Farmer
48		351	405	Tenorio, Luis C	Servant	M	Cha	18	S	Y	Y	Guam	Y	None
49		351	405	Rivera, Ana M	Servant	F	Cha	15	S	N	Y	Guam	Y	Servant
50		351	405	Rivera, Marcelina M	Goddaughter	F	Cha	14	S	Y	Y	Guam	Y	None

(CHAMORRO ROOTS GENEALOGY PROJECT™ TRANSCRIPTION)
(BERNARD T. PUNZALAN / HTTP://WWW.CHAMORROROOTS.COM)

DEPARTMENT OF COMMERCE-BUREAU OF THE CENSUS
WASHINGTON

FIFTEENTH CENSUS OF THE UNITED STATES: 1930-POPULATION

THE ISLAND OF GUAM

Sheet No. 45A

District **Municipality of Agana**
Name of Place **Agana City (Santa Cruz)**
[Proper name and, also, name of class, as city, town, village, barrio, etc]

Enumeration District No. **4**
Enumerated by me on **April 22, 1930** Vicente Tydingco
Enumerator

	PLACE OF ABODE			NAME	RELATION	PERSONAL DESCRIPTION				EDUCATION		NATIVITY		OCCUPATION
	Street, avenue, road, etc.	Number of dwelling house in order of visitation	Number of family in order of visitation	of each person whose place of abode on April 1, 1930, was in this family. Enter surname, first, then given name and middle initial. If any. Include every person living on April 1, 1930. Omit children born since April 1, 1930.	Relationship of this Person to the head of the family.	Sex	Color or race	Age at last birthday	Single, married, widowed or divorced	Attended school any time since Sept. 1, 1929	Whether able to read and write.	Place of birth of this person.	Whether able to speak English.	
	1	2	3	4	5	6	7	8	9	10	11	12	13	14
1	Hernan Cortes Street	352	406	Martinez, Juana P	Head	F	Cha	52	Wd	N	Y	Guam	N	None
2		352	406	Martinez, Joaquin P	Son	M	Cha	27	S	N	Y	Guam	Y	Farmer
3		352	406	Martinez, Manuel P	Son	M	Cha	18	S	N	Y	Guam	Y	Chauffeur
4		352	406	Martinez, Rosa P	Daughter	F	Cha	16	S	Y	Y	Guam	Y	None
5		352	406	Martinez, Jesus P	Son	M	Cha	15	S	Y	Y	Guam	Y	None
6		352	406	Martinez, Francisca P	Daughter	F	Cha	11	S	Y	Y	Guam	Y	None
7		353	407	Flores, Maria M	Head	F	Cha	23	M	N	Y	Guam	Y	None
8		353	407	Flores, Annie M	Daughter	F	Cha	3.1	S	N		Guam		None
9		353	407	Flores, Juana M	Daughter	F	Cha	1.2	S	N		Guam		None
10		354	408	Castro, Juan H	Head	M	Cha	59	Wd	N	Y	Guam	N	Farmer
11		354	408	Castro, Enrique M	Son	M	Cha	32	D	N	Y	Guam	Y	Carpenter
12		354	408	Castro, Regina M	Daughter	F	Cha	30	S	N	Y	Guam	Y	Seamstress
13		354	408	Castro, Santiago M	Son	M	Cha	22	S	N	Y	Guam	Y	Chauffeur
14		354	408	Castro, Maria M	Daughter	F	Cha	18	S	N	Y	Guam	Y	Teacher
15		354	408	Castro, Dolores W	Sister	F	Cha	62	S	N	N	Guam	N	None
16		354	408	San Nicolas, Maria M	Niece	F	Cha	9	S	Y		Guam		None
17		355	409	Ochai, Jose B	Head	M	Jap	46	M	N	Y	Tokyo, Japan	Y	Farmer
18		355	409	Ochai, Soledad B	Wife	F	Cha	38	M	N	Y	Guam	Y	Seamstress
19		355	409	Ochai, Gonzalo B	Son	M	Jap	19	S	N	Y	Guam	Y	Farm Laborer
20		355	409	Ochai, German B	Son	M	Jap	16	S	Y	Y	Guam	Y	None
21		355	409	Ochai, Jose B	Son	M	Jap	14	S	Y	Y	Guam	Y	None
22		355	409	Ochai, Maria B	Daughter	F	Jap	13	S	Y	Y	Guam	Y	None
23		355	409	Ochai, Alfred B	Son	M	Jap	11	S	Y	Y	Guam	Y	None
24		355	409	Ochai, Artemio B	Son	M	Jap	10	S	Y	Y	Guam	Y	None
25		355	409	Ochai, Concepcion B	Daughter	F	Jap	5	S	N		Guam	Y	None

DEPARTMENT OF COMMERCE-BUREAU OF THE CENSUS
WASHINGTON

FIFTEENTH CENSUS OF THE UNITED STATES: 1930-POPULATION

THE ISLAND OF GUAM

Sheet No. 45B

159B

District Municipality of Agana
Name of Place Agana City (Santa Cruz)
[Proper name and, also, name of class, as city, town, village, barrio, etc]

Enumeration District No. 4
Enumerated by me on April 23, 1930 Vicente Tydingco
Enumerator

	PLACE OF ABODE			NAME	RELATION	PERSONAL DESCRIPTION				EDUCATION		NATIVITY		OCCUPATION
	Street, avenue, road, etc.	Number of dwelling house in order of visitation	Number of family in order of visitation	of each person whose place of abode on April 1, 1930, was in this family. Enter surname, first, then given name and middle initial. If any. Include every person living on April 1, 1930. Omit children born since April 1, 1930.	Relationship of this Person to the head of the family.	Sex	Color or race	Age at last birthday	Single, married, widowed or divorced	Attended school any time since Sept. 1, 1929	Whether able to read and write.	Place of birth of this person.	Whether able to speak English.	
	1	2	3	4	5	6	7	8	9	10	11	12	13	14
26	Hernan Cortes Street	355	409	Ochai, Francisco B	Son	M	Jap	4.2	S	N		Guam		None
27		355	409	Ochai, Juan B	Son	M	Jap	2.5	S	N		Guam		None
28		355	409	Ochai, Alfonsina B	Daughter	M	Jap	.5	S	N		Guam		None
29		355	409	Blaz, Antonio LG	Father in law	M	Cha	67	Wd	N	Y	Guam	N	None
30		356	410	Sawada, Kaneskisa	Head	M	Jap	64	M	N	Y	Yokohoma, Japan	N	Merchant
31		356	410	Sawada, Nao	Wife	F	Jap	40	M	N	Y	Yokohoma, Japan	Y	Saleswoman
32		356	410	Sawada, Akira	Son	M	Jap	10	S	Y	Y	Guam	Y	None
33		356	410	Sawada, Kazuko	Daughter	F	Jap	9	S	Y		Guam		None
34		356	410	Sawada, Taiko	Daughter	F	Jap	6	S	Y		Guam		None
35		356	410	Sawada, Isamu	Son	M	Jap	4.5	S	N		Guam		None
36		356	410	Sawada, Haruko	Daughter	F	Jap	1.3	S	N		Guam		None
37		356	410	Kei, Eikichi	Lodger	M	Jap	44	M	N	Y	Japan	N	Silversmith
38		357	411	Suzuki, Trusajo	Head	M	Jap	35	M	N	Y	Tokyo, Japan	Y	Tailor
39		357	411	Suzuki, Ana C	Wife	F	Cha	30	M	N	Y	Guam	Y	Midwife
40		357	411	Suzuki, Rosita C	Daughter	F	Jap	6	S	Y		Guam		None
41		357	411	Cepeda, Vicente LG	Brother in law	M	Cha	27	S	N	Y	Guam	Y	Tailor
42		358	412	Salas, Juan S	Head	M	Cha	63	M	N	Y	Guam	N	Carpenter
43		358	412	Salas, Dolores S	Wife	F	Cha	58	M	N	Y	Guam	N	None
44		358	412	Salas, Miguel S	Son	M	Cha	14	S	Y	Y	Guam	Y	None
45		359	413	Pangelinan, Juan P	Head	M	Cha	36	Wd	N	Y	Guam	Y	Chauffeur
46		360	414	Daleyva, Noberto	Head	M	Fil	68	Wd	N	Y	Phillippine Island	Y	Musician
47		360	414	Daleyva, Vicente L	Son	M	Fil	2.3	S	N		Guam		None
48		361	415	Matias, Leonardo P	Head	M	Fil	28	S	N	Y	Phillippine Island	Y	Barber
49		362	416	Torres, Jesus C	Head	M	Cha	31	M	N	Y	Guam	Y	Salesman
50		362	416	Torres, Maria U	Wife	F	Cha	29	M	N	Y	Guam	Y	None

DEPARTMENT OF COMMERCE-BUREAU OF THE CENSUS
WASHINGTON

FIFTEENTH CENSUS OF THE UNITED STATES: 1930-POPULATION

THE ISLAND OF GUAM

Sheet No. 46A

District Municipality of Agana
Name of Place Agana City (Santa Cruz)
[Proper name and, also, name of class, as city, town, village, barrio, etc]

Enumeration District No. 4
Enumerated by me on April 23, 1930 Vicente Tydingco
Enumerator

	PLACE OF ABODE			NAME	RELATION	PERSONAL DESCRIPTION				EDUCATION		NATIVITY		OCCUPATION
	Street, avenue, road, etc.	Number of dwelling house is order of visitation	Number of family in order of visitation	of each person whose place of abode on April 1, 1930, was in this family. Enter surname, first, then given name and middle initial. If any. Include every person living on April 1, 1930. Omit children born since April 1, 1930.	Relationship of this Person to the head of the family.	Sex	Color or race	Age at last birthday	Single, married, widowed or divorced	Attended school any time since Sept. 1, 1929	Whether able to read and write.	Place of birth of this person.	Whether able to speak English.	
	1	2	3	4	5	6	7	8	9	10	11	12	13	14
1	Hernan Cortes Street	362	416	Torres, Helen U	Daughter	F	Cha	6	S	N		Guam		None
2		362	416	Torres, Juan U	Son	M	Cha	4.4	S	N		Guam		None
3		362	416	Torres, Antonio U	Son	M	Cha	2.3	S	N		Guam		None
4		362	416	Torres, Guadalupe U	Daughter	F	Cha	.3	S	N		Guam		None
5		363	417	Bordallo, Baltazar J	Head	M	Cha	29	M	N	Y	Guam	Y	Merchant
6		363	417	Bordallo, Josefina P	Wife	F	Cha	26	M	N	Y	Guam	Y	None
7		363	417	Bordallo, Irene D	Daughter	F	Cha	6	S	N		Guam		None
8		363	417	Bordallo, Sylvia L	Daughter	F	Cha	5	S	N		Guam		None
9		363	417	Bordallo, Ricardo J	Son	M	Cha	2.5	S	N		Guam		None
10		363	417	Bordallo, Barbara L	Daughter	F	Cha	1.2	S	N		Guam		None
11	San Ignacio St	364	418	Atoigue, Jose U	Head	M	Cha	29	M	N	Y	Guam	Y	Engineman
12		364	418	Atoigue, Maria M	Wife	F	Cha	29	M	N	Y	Guam	Y	None
13		364	418	Atoigue, Alejandrina M	Daughter	F	Cha	10	S	Y	Y	Guam	Y	None
14		364	418	Atoigue, Flora M	Daughter	F	Cha	9	S	Y		Guam		None
15		365	419	Mesa, Francisco G	Head	M	Cha	46	M	N	Y	Guam	N	None
16		365	419	Mesa, Rosario C	Wife	F	Cha	46	M	N	Y	Guam	N	Laundress
17		365	419	Mesa, Edwardo C	Son	M	Cha	21	S	N	Y	Guam	Y	Salesman
18		365	419	Mesa, Vicente C	Son	M	Cha	19	S	N	Y	Guam	Y	Salesman
19		366	420	Lujan, Maria T	Head	F	Cha	72	Wd	N	Y	Guam	N	None
20		366	420	Lujan, Luis G	Son	M	Cha	50	S	N	Y	Guam	Y	Farm Laborer
21		367	421	Cruz, Engranacion P	Head	F	Cha	52	Wd	N	Y	Guam	N	None
22		367	421	Cruz, Regina P	Daughter	F	Cha	18	S	N	Y	Guam	Y	None
23		367	421	Cruz, Candelaria P	Daughter	F	Cha	16	S	Y	Y	Guam	Y	Teacher
24		367	421	Cruz, Alejandro P	Son	M	Cha	14	S	Y	Y	Guam	Y	None
25		368	422	Perez, Juan D	Head	M	Cha	28	M	N	Y	Guam	Y	Cable Operator

(CHAMORRO ROOTS GENEALOGY PROJECT™ TRANSCRIPTION)
(BERNARD T. PUNZALAN / HTTP://WWW.CHAMORROROOTS.COM)

DEPARTMENT OF COMMERCE-BUREAU OF THE CENSUS
WASHINGTON

FIFTEENTH CENSUS OF THE UNITED STATES: 1930-POPULATION

THE ISLAND OF GUAM

Sheet No. 46B

160B

District Municipality of Agana
Name of Place Agana City (Santa Cruz)
[Proper name and, also, name of class, as city, town, village, barrio, etc]

Enumeration District No. 4
Enumerated by me on April 23, 1930 Vicente Tydingco, Enumerator

	PLACE OF ABODE			NAME	RELATION	PERSONAL DESCRIPTION				EDUCATION		NATIVITY		OCCUPATION
	Street, avenue, road, etc.	Number of dwelling house in order of visitation	Number of family in order of visitation	of each person whose place of abode on April 1, 1930, was in this family. Enter surname, first, then given name and middle initial. If any. Include every person living on April 1, 1930. Omit children born since April 1, 1930.	Relationship of this Person to the head of the family.	Sex	Color or race	Age at last birthday	Single, married, widowed or divorced	Attended school any time since Sept. 1, 1929	Whether able to read and write.	Place of birth of this person.	Whether able to speak English.	
	1	2	3	4	5	6	7	8	9	10	11	12	13	14
26	San Ignacio St	368	422	Perez, Remedios LG	Wife	F	Cha	28	M	N	Y	Guam	Y	Teacher
27		368	422	Perez, Teresita LG	Daughter	F	Cha	3.5	S	N		Guam		None
28		368	422	Perez, Francisco LG	Son	M	Cha	1.5	S	N		Guam		None
29		369	423	Pellecani, Ana R	Head	F	Cha	55	M	N	Y	Guam	Y	None
30		369	423	Pellecani, Rafael R	Son	M	Cha	27	S	N	Y	Guam	Y	Chauffeur
31		369	423	Pellecani, Romulo R	Son	M	Cha	18	S	N	Y	Guam	Y	Surveyor
32		370	424	Camacho, Jose M	Head	M	Cha	42	M	N	Y	Guam	Y	Judge
33		370	424	Camacho, Catalina E	Wife	F	Cha	34	M	N	Y	Guam	Y	Teacher
34		370	424	Camacho, Raimundo D	Son	M	Cha	17	S	Y	Y	Guam	Y	Messenger
35		370	424	Camacho, Pedro D	Son	M	Cha	15	S	Y	Y	Guam	Y	None
36		370	424	Camacho, Vicente D	Son	M	Cha	13	S	Y	Y	Guam	Y	None
37		370	424	Camacho, Sigena D	Daughter	F	Cha	12	S	Y	Y	Guam	Y	None
38		370	424	Camacho, Roman E	Son	M	Cha	10	S	Y	Y	Guam	Y	None
39		370	424	Camacho, Isidora E	Daughter	F	Cha	9	S	Y		Guam		None
40		370	424	Camacho, Nuncia E	Daughter	F	Cha	7	S	Y		Guam		None
41		370	424	Camacho, Crispina E	Daughter	F	Cha	6	S	Y		Guam		None
42		370	424	Camacho, Hediliza E	Daughter	F	Cha	5	S	N		Guam		None
43		370	424	Camacho, Columbina E	Daughter	F	Cha	1.1	S	N		Guam		None
44		370	424	Camacho, Carlos E	Son	M	Cha	.2	S	N		Guam		None
45		371	425	Aguero, Juan SN	Head	M	Cha	30	M	N	Y	Guam	Y	Farmer
46		371	425	Aguero, Maria T	Wife	F	Cha	26	M	N	Y	Guam	Y	None
47		371	425	Aguero, Juan T	Son	M	Cha	3.8	S	N		Guam		None
48		371	425	Aguero, Francisco T	Son	M	Cha	1.8	S	N		Guam		None
49		372	426	Cruz, Joaquin G	Head	M	Cha	55	M	N	Y	Guam	Y	Farmer
50		372	426	Cruz, Rita G	Wife	F	Cha	45	M	N	N	Guam	N	None

(CHAMORRO ROOTS GENEALOGY PROJECT™ TRANSCRIPTION)
(BERNARD T. PUNZALAN / HTTP://WWW.CHAMORROROOTS.COM)

DEPARTMENT OF COMMERCE-BUREAU OF THE CENSUS
WASHINGTON

FIFTEENTH CENSUS OF THE UNITED STATES: 1930-POPULATION

THE ISLAND OF GUAM

Sheet No. 47A

District **Municipality of Agana**
Name of Place **Agana City (Santa Cruz)**
[Proper name and, also, name of class, as city, town, village, barrio, etc]

Enumeration District No. 4
Enumerated by me on **April 24, 1930** Vicente Tydingco
Enumerator

	PLACE OF ABODE			NAME	RELATION	PERSONAL DESCRIPTION				EDUCATION		NATIVITY		OCCUPATION
	Street, avenue, road, etc.	Number of dwelling house is order of visitation	Number of family in order of visitation	of each person whose place of abode on April 1, 1930, was in this family. Enter surname, first, then given name and middle initial. If any. Include every person living on April 1, 1930. Omit children born since April 1, 1930.	Relationship of this Person to the head of the family.	Sex	Color or race	Age at last birthday	Single, married, widowed or divorced	Attended school any time since Sept. 1, 1929	Whether able to read and write.	Place of birth of this person.	Whether able to speak English.	
	1	2	3	4	5	6	7	8	9	10	11	12	13	14
1	San Ignacio St	372	426	Cruz, Rita G	Daughter	F	Cha	20	S	N	Y	Guam	Y	Laundress
2		372	426	Cruz, Jesus G	Son	M	Cha	18	S	N	Y	Guam	Y	Farm Laborer
3		372	426	Cruz, Pedro G	Son	M	Cha	15	S	Y	Y	Guam	Y	None
4		372	426	Cruz, Tomasa G	Daughter	F	Cha	13	S	Y	Y	Guam	Y	None
5		372	426	Cruz, Juan G	Son	M	Cha	10	S	Y	Y	Guam	Y	None
6		372	426	Cruz, Dolores G	Daughter	F	Cha	8	S	Y		Guam		None
7		372	426	Cruz, Francisco G	Son	M	Cha	5	S	N		Guam		None
8		372	426	Cruz, Manuel G	Son	M	Cha	2.8	S	N		Guam		None
9		373	427	Mendiola, Venancio P	Head	M	Cha	51	M	N	Y	Guam	N	Farmer
10		373	427	Mendiola, Vicenta B	Wife	F	Cha	42	M	N	Y	Guam	N	None
11		373	427	Mendiola, Jose B	Son	M	Cha	22	S	N	Y	Guam	Y	Farm Laborer
12		373	427	Mendiola, Juan B	Son	M	Cha	21	S	N	Y	Guam	Y	Farm Laborer
13		373	427	Mendiola, Maria B	Daughter	F	Cha	19	S	N	Y	Guam	Y	Seamstress
14		373	427	Mendiola, Jesus B	Son	M	Cha	18	S	Y	Y	Guam	Y	None
15		374	428	Atoigue, Maria U	Head	F	Cha	57	Wd	N	Y	Guam	N	None
16		374	428	Atoigue, Josefa U	Daughter	F	Cha	32	S	N	Y	Guam	Y	None
17		374	429	Atoigue, Brigida F	Head	F	W	19	M	N	Y	Phillippine Island	Y	None
18		375	430	Camacho, Joaquin M	Head	M	Cha	42	Wd	N	Y	Guam	N	Carpenter
19		375	430	Camacho, Pilar M	Daughter	F	Cha	19	S	N	Y	Guam	Y	None
20		375	430	Camacho, Concepcion M	Daughter	F	Cha	18	S	N	Y	Guam	Y	None
21		375	430	Camacho, Manuel M	Son	M	Cha	15	S	Y	Y	Guam	Y	None
22		375	430	Camacho, Ignacio M	Son	M	Cha	10	S	Y	Y	Guam	Y	None
23		375	430	Camacho, Jose M	Son	M	Cha	8	S	Y		Guam		None
24		375	430	Camacho, Rosario M	Daughter	F	Cha	6	S	N		Guam		None
25		376	431	Camacho, Ignacio L	Head	M	Cha	67	M	N	Y	Guam	N	Farmer

(CHAMORRO ROOTS GENEALOGY PROJECT™ TRANSCRIPTION)
(BERNARD T. PUNZALAN / HTTP://WWW.CHAMORROROOTS.COM)

DEPARTMENT OF COMMERCE-BUREAU OF THE CENSUS
WASHINGTON

FIFTEENTH CENSUS OF THE UNITED STATES: 1930-POPULATION

THE ISLAND OF GUAM

Sheet No. 47B

161B

District **Municipality of Agana**
Name of Place **Agana City (Santa Cruz)**
[Proper name and, also, name of class, as city, town, village, barrio, etc]

Enumeration District No. **4**
Enumerated by me on **April 24, 1930** Vicente Tydingco, Enumerator

	PLACE OF ABODE			NAME	RELATION	PERSONAL DESCRIPTION				EDUCATION		NATIVITY		OCCUPATION
	Street, avenue, road, etc.	Number of dwelling house is order of visitation	Number of family in order of visitation	of each person whose place of abode on April 1, 1930, was in this family. Enter surname, first, then given name and middle initial. If any. Include every person living on April 1, 1930. Omit children born since April 1, 1930.	Relationship of this Person to the head of the family.	Sex	Color or race	Age at last birthday	Single, married, widowed or divorced	Attended school any time since Sept. 1, 1929	Whether able to read and write.	Place of birth of this person.	Whether able to speak English.	
	1	2	3	4	5	6	7	8	9	10	11	12	13	14
26	Santa Cruz St	376	431	Camacho, Maria M	Wife	F	Cha	62	M	N	Y	Guam	N	None
27		376	431	Camacho, Jesus M	Son	M	Cha	24	S	N	Y	Guam	Y	Clerk
28		376	431	Camacho, Francisco M	Son	M	Cha	22	S	N	Y	Guam	Y	Farm Laborer
29		376	431	Camacho, Carlos M	Son	M	Cha	20	S	N	Y	Guam	Y	Carpenter
30		376	432	Flores, Leon L	Head	M	Fil	55	M	N	Y	Phillippine Island	Y	Attorney at law
31		376	432	Flores, Ana B	Wife	F	Cha	32	M	N	Y	Guam	Y	None
32		376	432	Flores, Leon D	Son	M	Fil	21	S	Y	Y	Guam	Y	None
33		376	432	Flores, Sergio D	Son	M	Fil	18	S	Y	Y	Guam	Y	None
34		376	432	Flores, Felisberto C	Son	M	Fil	9	S	Y		Guam		None
35		376	432	Flores, Ricardo C	Son	M	Fil	8	S	Y		Guam		None
36		377	433	Roberto, Mercedes B	Head	F	Cha	33	S	N	Y	Guam	N	Midwife
37		377	433	Roberto, Emma S	Daughter	F	Cha	14	S	N	Y	Guam	Y	None
38		377	433	Roberto, Hazel M	Daughter	G	Cha	12	S	Y	Y	Guam	Y	None
39		377	433	Roberto, Wallace H	Son	M	Cha	10	S	Y	Y	Guam	Y	None
40		377	433	Roberto, Bernice M	Daughter	F	Cha	7	S	Y		Guam		None
41		378	434	Garrido, Maria G	Head	F	Cha	46	Wd	N	Y	Guam	N	None
42		378	434	Garrido, Isabel G	Daughter	F	Cha	22	S	N	Y	Guam	Y	None
43		378	434	Garrido, Jose G	Son	M	Cha	21	S	N	Y	Guam	Y	Servant
44		378	434	Garrido, Maria G	Daughter	F	Cha	19	S	N	Y	Guam	Y	Teacher
45		378	435	Garcia, Demetrio LG	Head	M	Cha	70	Wd	N	Y	Guam	N	None
46		378	435	Garcia, Trinidad LG	Daughter	F	Cha	32	S	N	Y	Guam	N	Seamstress
47		378	436	Borja, Concepcion G	Head	F	Cha	36	Wd	N	Y	Guam	N	None
48		378	436	Borja, Beatrice G	Daughter	F	Cha	14	S	Y	Y	Guam	Y	None
49		378	436	Borja, Manuel G	Son	M	Cha	13	S	Y	Y	Guam	Y	None
50		378	436	Borja, Josefina G	Daughter	F	Cha	11	S	Y	Y	Guam	Y	None

(CHAMORRO ROOTS GENEALOGY PROJECT™ TRANSCRIPTION)
(BERNARD T. PUNZALAN / HTTP://WWW.CHAMORROROOTS.COM)

DEPARTMENT OF COMMERCE-BUREAU OF THE CENSUS
WASHINGTON

FIFTEENTH CENSUS OF THE UNITED STATES: 1930-POPULATION

THE ISLAND OF GUAM

Sheet No. 48A

District Municipality of Agana
Name of Place Agana City (Santa Cruz)
[Proper name and, also, name of class, as city, town, village, barrio, etc]

Enumeration District No. 4
Enumerated by me on April 24, 1930 Vicente Tydingco, Enumerator

	PLACE OF ABODE			NAME	RELATION	PERSONAL DESCRIPTION				EDUCATION		NATIVITY		OCCUPATION
	Street, avenue, road, etc.	Number of dwelling house in order of visitation	Number of family in order of visitation	of each person whose place of abode on April 1, 1930, was in this family. Enter surname, first, then given name and middle initial. If any. Include every person living on April 1, 1930. Omit children born since April 1, 1930.	Relationship of this Person to the head of the family.	Sex	Color or race	Age at last birthday	Single, married, widowed or divorced	Attended school any time since Sept. 1, 1929	Whether able to read and write.	Place of birth of this person.	Whether able to speak English.	
	1	2	3	4	5	6	7	8	9	10	11	12	13	14
1	San Ignacio St	378	436	Borja, Jesusa G	Daughter	F	Cha	9	S	Y		Guam		None
2		378	436	Borja, Demetrio G	Son	M	Cha	1.2	S	N		Guam		None
3		379	437	Duenas, Antonia L	Head	F	Cha	52	Wd	N	Y	Guam	N	None
4		379	437	Duenas, Maria L	Daughter	F	Cha	25	S	N	Y	Guam	N	None
5		379	437	Duenas, Rufina L	Daughter	F	Cha	17	S	N	Y	Guam	Y	None
6		379	437	Duenas, Julia E	Granddaughter	F	Cha	.9	S	N		Guam	N	None
7		380	438	Aguon, Jesus B	Head	M	Cha	42	Wd	N	Y	Guam	N	Farmer
8		380	438	Aguon, Josefa L	Daughter	F	Cha	19	S	N	Y	Guam	Y	None
9		380	438	Aguon, Vicente L	Son	M	Cha	15	S	Y	Y	Guam	Y	None
10		380	438	Aguon, Juan L	Son	M	Cha	14	S	Y	Y	Guam	Y	None
11		380	438	Aguon, Maria L	Daughter	F	Cha	12	S	Y	Y	Guam	Y	None
12		380	438	Aguon, Dolores L	Daughter	F	Cha	7	S	Y		Guam		None
13		381	439	Ada, Ignacio F	Head	M	Cha	46	Wd	N	Y	Guam	N	Farmer
14		381	439	Ada, Joaquin S	Son	M	Cha	17	S	Y	Y	Guam	Y	None
15		381	439	Ada, Antonio S	Son	M	Cha	15	S	Y	Y	Guam	Y	None
16		381	439	Aguon, Maria C	Mother in law	F	Cha	66	Wd	N	N	Guam	N	None
17		382	440	Ignacio, Manuel C	Head	M	Cha	23	M	N	Y	Guam	Y	Chauffeur
18		382	440	Ignacio, Maria S	Wife	F	Cha	21	M	N	Y	Guam	N	None
19		382	440	Ignacio, Engracia S	Daughter	F	Cha	1.2	S	N		Guam		None
20		382	440	Ignacio, Enriqueta S	Daughter	F	Cha	.8	S	N		Guam		None
21		383	441	Cann, Dorothy B	Head	F	W	26	M	N	Y	San Francisco, Ca	Y	None
22		383	441	Cann, George R	Son	M	W	.9	S	N		San Diego, Ca		None
23		384	442	Cruz, Francisco C	Head	M	Cha	31	M	N	Y	Guam	Y	Plumber
24		384	442	Cruz, Felicidad T	Wife	F	Cha	31	M	N	Y	Guam	Y	None
25		384	442	Cruz, Ignacio T	Son	M	Cha	4.7	S	N		Guam		None

(CHAMORRO ROOTS GENEALOGY PROJECT™ TRANSCRIPTION)
(BERNARD T. PUNZALAN / HTTP://WWW.CHAMORROROOTS.COM)

DEPARTMENT OF COMMERCE-BUREAU OF THE CENSUS
WASHINGTON

FIFTEENTH CENSUS OF THE UNITED STATES: 1930-POPULATION

THE ISLAND OF GUAM

Sheet No. 48B

162B

District Municipality of Agana
Name of Place Agana City (Santa Cruz)
[Proper name and, also, name of class, as city, town, village, barrio, etc]

Enumeration District No. 4
Enumerated by me on April 24, 1930 Vicente Tydingco, Enumerator

	PLACE OF ABODE: Street, avenue, road, etc.	Number of dwelling house in order of visitation	Number of family in order of visitation	NAME of each person whose place of abode on April 1, 1930, was in this family. Enter surname, first, then given name and middle initial. If any. Include every person living on April 1, 1930. Omit children born since April 1, 1930.	RELATION Relationship of this Person to the head of the family.	Sex	Color or race	Age at last birthday	Single, married, widowed or divorced	Attended school any time since Sept. 1, 1929	Whether able to read and write.	NATIVITY Place of birth of this person.	Whether able to speak English.	OCCUPATION
	1	2	3	4	5	6	7	8	9	10	11	12	13	14
26	San Ignacio St	384	442	Cruz, Rufina T	Daughter	F	Cha	2.2	S	N		Guam		None
27		384	442	Toves, Ana S	Mother in law	F	Cha	57	Wd	N	N	Guam	N	None
28		385	443	Ungacta, Domingo P	Head	M	Cha	58	M	N	Y	Guam	N	Mason
29		385	443	Ungacta, Maria C	Wife	F	Cha	52	M	N	N	Guam	N	None
30		385	443	Ungacta, Antonio C	Son	M	Cha	22	S	N	Y	Guam	Y	Farmer
31		385	443	Ungacta, Juan C	Son	M	Cha	20	S	N	Y	Guam	Y	Farm Laborer
32		385	443	Ungacta, Maria C	Daughter	F	Cha	18	S	N	Y	Guam	Y	None
33		385	443	Ungacta, Servino C	Son	M	Cha	16	S	Y	Y	Guam	Y	None
34		385	443	Ungacta, Ana C	Daughter	F	Cha	14	S	Y	Y	Guam	Y	None
35		385	443	Ungacta, Miguel C	Son	M	Cha	8	S	Y		Guam		None
36		386	444	Salas, Jose SN	Head	M	Cha	26	M	N	Y	Guam	Y	Farmer
37		386	444	Salas, Vicenta A	Wife	F	Cha	24	M	N	Y	Guam	Y	None
38		386	444	Salas, Rita A	Daughter	F	Cha	1.5	S	N		Guam		None
39		386	445	Manibusan, Antonia M	Head	F	Cha	62	Wd	N	N	Guam	N	None
40		386	445	Manibusan, Maria M	Daughter	F	Cha	37	S	N	N	Guam	N	Laundress
41		387	446	Martinez, Juan P	Head	M	Cha	30	M	N	Y	Guam	Y	Carpenter
42		387	446	Martinez, Dolores LG	Wife	F	Cha	29	M	N	Y	Guam	N	None
43		387	446	Martinez, Rita LG	Daughter	F	Cha	10	S	Y	Y	Guam	Y	None
44		387	446	Martinez, Jose LG	Son	M	Cha	7	S	Y		Guam		None
45		387	446	Martinez, Maria LG	Daughter	F	Cha	6	S	N		Guam		None
46		387	446	Martinez, Juana LG	Daughter	F	Cha	3.2	S	N		Guam		None
47		387	446	Martinez, Vicente LG	Son	M	Cha	.4	S	N		Guam		None
48		388	447	Pangelinan, Joaquin C	Head	M	Cha	58	M	N	Y	Guam	N	Farmer
49		388	447	Pangelinan, Maria T	Wife	F	Cha	54	M	N	Y	Guam	N	None
50		388	447	Pangelinan, Lino T	Son	M	Cha	19	S	N	Y	Guam	Y	?

D-4-96

(CHAMORRO ROOTS GENEALOGY PROJECT™ TRANSCRIPTION)
(BERNARD T. PUNZALAN / HTTP://WWW.CHAMORROROOTS.COM)

DEPARTMENT OF COMMERCE-BUREAU OF THE CENSUS
WASHINGTON

FIFTEENTH CENSUS OF THE UNITED STATES: 1930-POPULATION
THE ISLAND OF GUAM

Sheet No. 49A

163

District **Municipality of Agana**
Name of Place **Agana City (Santa Cruz)**
[Proper name and, also, name of class, as city, town, village, barrio, etc]

Enumeration District No. 4
Enumerated by me on April 25, 1930 Vicente Tydingco, Enumerator

	PLACE OF ABODE			NAME	RELATION	PERSONAL DESCRIPTION				EDUCATION		NATIVITY		OCCUPATION
	Street, avenue, road, etc.	Number of dwelling house is order of visitation	Number of family in order of visitation	of each person whose place of abode on April 1, 1930, was in this family. Enter surname, first, then given name and middle initial. If any. Include every person living on April 1, 1930. Omit children born since April 1, 1930.	Relationship of this Person to the head of the family.	Sex	Color or race	Age at last birthday	Single, married, widowed or divorced	Attended school any time since Sept. 1, 1929	Whether able to read and write.	Place of birth of this person.	Whether able to speak English.	
	1	2	3	4	5	6	7	8	9	10	11	12	13	14
1	San Ignacio St	388	447	Pangelinan, Antonio T	Son	M	Cha	19	S	N	Y	Guam	Y	Surveyor
2		389	448	Taison, Ana T	Head	F	Cha	55	Wd	N	N	Guam	N	None
3		389	448	Taison, Sococo T	Daughter	F	Cha	32	S	N	Y	Guam	Y	Laundress
4		389	448	Taison, Antonio T	Son	M	Cha	20	S	N	Y	Guam	Y	Farmer
5		389	448	Taison, Maria T	Daughter	F	Cha	13	S	Y	Y	Guam	Y	None
6		389	448	Taison, Roman T	Grandson	M	Cha	11	S	Y	Y	Guam	Y	None
7		389	448	Taison, Rosalia T	Granddaughter	F	Cha	7	S	Y		Guam		None
8		389	448	Taison, Ana T	Granddaughter	F	Cha	4.2	S	N		Guam		None
9		390	449	Manibusan, Jose R	Head	M	Cha	70	M	N	N	Guam	N	Farm Laborer
10		390	449	Manibusan, Juana G	Wife	F	Cha	72	M	N	N	Guam	N	None
11		390	450	Manibusan, Pedro F	Head	M	Cha	27	M	N	Y	Guam	Y	Laborer
12		390	450	Manibusan, Martina M	Wife	F	Cha	19	M	N	Y	Guam	Y	None
13		391	451	Chandler, Frederick N	Head	M	W	30	M	N	Y	Princeton, Indiana	Y	Bookkeeper
14		391	451	Chandler, Isabel O	Wife	F	Cha	26	M	N	Y	Guam	Y	None
15		391	451	Chandler, Frederick O	Son	M	Cha	6	S	N		Guam		None
16		391	451	Chandler, Harriet O	Daughter	F	Cha	3.6	S	N		Guam		None
17		391	451	Chandler, Evedine J	Daughter	F	Cha	.1	S	N		Guam		None
18		391	451	Oconner, Antonia C	Mother in law	F	Cha	49	Wd	N	Y	Guam	Y	None
19		392	452	Borja, Ignacio T	Head	M	Cha	40	M	N	Y	Guam	Y	Chauffeur
20		392	452	Borja, Vicenta S	Wife	F	Cha	41	M	N	Y	Guam	Y	None
21		392	452	Borja, Juan S	Son	M	Cha	15	S	Y	Y	Guam	Y	None
22		392	452	Borja, Bernadita S	Daughter	F	Cha	14	S	Y	Y	Guam	Y	None
23		392	452	Borja, Dolores S	Daughter	F	Cha	13	S	Y	Y	Guam	Y	None
24		392	452	Borja, Juan S	Son	M	Cha	11	S	Y	Y	Guam	Y	None
25		392	452	Borja, Francisco S	Son	M	Cha	9	S	Y		Guam		None

DEPARTMENT OF COMMERCE-BUREAU OF THE CENSUS
WASHINGTON

FIFTEENTH CENSUS OF THE UNITED STATES: 1930-POPULATION

THE ISLAND OF GUAM

Sheet No. 49B

163B

District Municipality of Agana
Name of Place Agana City (Santa Cruz)
[Proper name and, also, name of class, as city, town, village, barrio, etc]

Enumeration District No. 4
Enumerated by me on April 25, 1930 Vicente Tydingco
Enumerator

	PLACE OF ABODE			NAME	RELATION	PERSONAL DESCRIPTION				EDUCATION		NATIVITY		OCCUPATION
	Street, avenue, road, etc.	Number of dwelling house in order of visitation	Number of family in order of visitation	of each person whose place of abode on April 1, 1930, was in this family. Enter surname, first, then given name and middle initial. If any. Include every person living on April 1, 1930. Omit children born since April 1, 1930.	Relationship of this Person to the head of the family.	Sex	Color or race	Age at last birthday	Single, married, widowed or divorced	Attended school any time since Sept. 1, 1929	Whether able to read and write.	Place of birth of this person.	Whether able to speak English.	
	1	2	3	4	5	6	7	8	9	10	11	12	13	14
26		392	452	Borja, Jose S	Son	M	Cha	7	S	Y		Guam		None
27		392	452	Borja, Rosa S	Daughter	F	Cha	3.9	S	N		Guam		None
28	Santa Cruz St	393	453	Borja, Joaquin T	Head	M	Cha	31	M	N	Y	Guam	Y	Salesman
29		393	453	Borja, Rosa B	Wife	F	Cha	34	M	N	Y	Guam	Y	None
30		393	453	Borja, Felix B	Son	M	Cha	.1	S	N		Guam		None
31		393	454	Lizama, Ignacio T	Head	M	Cha	32	M	N	Y	Guam	Y	Painter
32		393	454	Lizama, Maria B	Wife	F	Cha	27	M	N	Y	Guam	N	None
33		393	454	Lizama, Jose B	Son	M	Cha	7	S	Y		Guam		None
34		393	454	Lizama, Concepcion B	Daughter	F	Cha	5	S	N		Guam		None
35		393	454	Lizama, Lucia B	Daughter	F	Cha	3.3	S	N		Guam		None
36		393	454	Lizama, Jesus B	Son	M	Cha	.2	S	N		Guam		None
37		393	455	Borja, Ana M	Head	F	Cha	56	Wd	N	N	Guam	N	None
38		393	455	Borja, Joaquin M	Son	M	Cha	29	S	N	Y	Guam	Y	Farmer
39		393	455	Borja, Pedro M	Son	M	Cha	20	S	N	Y	Guam	Y	Farm Laborer
40		394	456	Fejeran, Jose C	Head	M	Cha	67	S	N	N	Guam	N	Cook
41		394	456	Cruz, Tomas L	Lodger	M	Cha	46	S	N	Y	Guam	N	Tailor
42		394	456	Mendiola, Juan S	Lodger	M	Cha	32	S	N	Y	Guam	Y	Cook
43		395	457	Blaz, Jose P	Head	M	Cha	32	M	N	Y	Guam	Y	Chauffeur
44		395	457	Blaz, Dominga O	Wife	F	Cha	31	M	N	Y	Guam	Y	Midwife
45		395	457	Blaz, Jose O	Son	M	Cha	6	S	N		Guam		None
46		395	457	Blaz, Maria O	Daughter	F	Cha	4.2	S	N		Guam		None
47		395	457	Blaz, Matilde O	Daughter	F	Cha	2.1	S	N		Guam		None
48		395	457	Blaz, Antonio O	Son	M	Cha	.2	S	N		Guam		None
49		395	457	Ogo, Ramona O	Mother in law	F	Cha	52	Wd	N	Y	Guam	N	None
50		395	457	Ogo, Juan O	Nephew	M	Cha	18	S	N	Y	Guam	Y	Laborer

(CHAMORRO ROOTS GENEALOGY PROJECT™ TRANSCRIPTION)
(BERNARD T. PUNZALAN / HTTP://WWW.CHAMORROROOTS.COM)

DEPARTMENT OF COMMERCE-BUREAU OF THE CENSUS
WASHINGTON

FIFTEENTH CENSUS OF THE UNITED STATES: 1930-POPULATION

THE ISLAND OF GUAM

Sheet No. 50A

District Municipality of Agana
Name of Place Agana City (Santa Cruz)
[Proper name and, also, name of class, as city, town, village, barrio, etc]

Enumeration District No. 4
Enumerated by me on April 25, 1930 Vicente Tydingco
Enumerator

	PLACE OF ABODE			NAME	RELATION	PERSONAL DESCRIPTION				EDUCATION		NATIVITY		OCCUPATION
	Street, avenue, road, etc.	Number of dwelling house in order of visitation	Number of family in order of visitation	of each person whose place of abode on April 1, 1930, was in this family. Enter surname, first, then given name and middle initial. If any. Include every person living on April 1, 1930. Omit children born since April 1, 1930.	Relationship of this Person to the head of the family.	Sex	Color or race	Age at last birthday	Single, married, widowed or divorced	Attended school any time since Sept. 1, 1929	Whether able to read and write.	Place of birth of this person.	Whether able to speak English.	
	1	2	3	4	5	6	7	8	9	10	11	12	13	14
1	Santa Cruz St	395	457	Ogo, Juan O	Nephew	M	Cha	?	S	Y	Y	Guam	Y	None
2		396	458	Higaka, Tokichi	Head	M	Jap	68	S	N	Y	Kobe, Japan	N	Carpenter
3		397	459	Baza, Jesus C	Head	M	Cha	38	M	N	Y	Guam	N	Carpenter
4		397	459	Baza, Maria P	Wife	F	Cha	21	M	N	Y	Guam	N	None
5		397	459	Pablo, Antonio P	Nephew	M	Cha	4.8	S	N		Guam		None
6		397	460	Baza, Maria C	Head	F	Cha	61	Wd	N	N	Guam	N	None
7		397	460	Baza, Ana C	Daughter	F	Cha	26	S	N	Y	Guam	N	None
8		397	460	Baza, Juan C	Son	M	Cha	23	S	N	Y	Guam	Y	Farmer
9		397	460	Baza, Vicente C	Son	M	Cha	22	S	N	Y	Guam	Y	Farm Laborer
10		398	461	Cruz, Soledad T	Head	F	Cha	60	Wd	N	Y	Guam	N	None
11		398	461	Cruz, Francisco T	Son	M	Cha	26	S	N	Y	Guam	Y	Farmer
12		399	462	Camacho, Juan F	Head	M	Cha	44	M	N	Y	Guam	N	Farmer
13		399	462	Camacho, Ana M	Wife	F	Cha	46	M	N	N	Guam	N	None
14		399	462	Camacho, Cecilio M	Son	M	Cha	18	S	N	Y	Guam	Y	Servant
15		399	462	Camacho, Joaquin M	Son	M	Cha	14	S	Y	Y	Guam	Y	None
16		399	462	Camacho, Maria M	Daughter	F	Cha	12	S	Y	Y	Guam	Y	None
17		399	462	Camacho, Matilde M	Daughter	F	Cha	10	S	Y	Y	Guam	Y	None
18		399	462	Camacho, Pedro M	Son	M	Cha	8	S	Y		Guam		None
19		399	462	Camacho, Edward M	Son	M	Cha	5	S	N		Guam		None
20		400	463	Manibusan, Juan M	Head	M	Cha	38	M	N	Y	Guam	Y	Farmer
21		400	463	Manibusan, Soledad B	Wife	F	Cha	35	M	N	Y	Guam	N	None
22		400	463	Manibusan, Francisco B	Son	M	Cha	12	S	Y	Y	Guam	Y	None
23		400	463	Manibusan, Isabel B	Daughter	F	Cha	5	S	N		Guam		None
24		400	463	Manibusan, Maria B	Daughter	F	Cha	3.8	S	N		Guam		None
25		400	463	Manibusan, Jose B	Son	M	Cha	0	S	N		Guam		None

DEPARTMENT OF COMMERCE-BUREAU OF THE CENSUS
WASHINGTON

FIFTEENTH CENSUS OF THE UNITED STATES: 1930-POPULATION

THE ISLAND OF GUAM

Sheet No. 50B

164B

District Municipality of Agana
Name of Place Agana City (Santa Cruz)
[Proper name and, also, name of class, as city, town, village, barrio, etc]

Enumeration District No. 4
Enumerated by me on April 25, 1930 Vicente Tydingco, Enumerator

	PLACE OF ABODE: Street, avenue, road, etc.	Number of dwelling house in order of visitation	Number of family in order of visitation	NAME of each person whose place of abode on April 1, 1930, was in this family. Enter surname, first, then given name and middle initial. If any. Include every person living on April 1, 1930. Omit children born since April 1, 1930.	RELATION Relationship of this Person to the head of the family.	PERSONAL DESCRIPTION: Sex	Color or race	Age at last birthday	Single, married, widowed or divorced	EDUCATION: Attended school any time since Sept. 1, 1929	Whether able to read and write.	NATIVITY Place of birth of this person.	Whether able to speak English.	OCCUPATION
	1	2	3	4	5	6	7	8	9	10	11	12	13	14
26	Santa Cruz St	401	464	Guzman, Jose M	Head	M	Cha	35	M	N	Y	Guam	Y	Fireman
27		401	464	Guzman, Ana P	Wife	F	Cha	26	M	N	Y	Guam	Y	None
28		401	465	Reyes, Jesus P	Head	M	Cha	30	Wd	N	Y	Guam	Y	Farmer
29		401	465	Reyes, Maria S	Daughter	F	Cha	1.1	S	N		Guam		None
30		402	466	Cruz, Hermanigildo G	Head	M	Cha	52	M	N	Y	Guam	N	Farmer
31		402	466	Cruz, Ana A	Wife	F	Cha	44	M	N	N	Guam	N	None
32		402	466	Cruz, Vicente A	Son	M	Cha	24	S	N	Y	Guam	Y	Laborer
33		402	466	Cruz, Maria A	Daughter	F	Cha	14	S	N	Y	Guam	Y	None
34		402	466	Cruz, Jose A	Son	M	Cha	12	S	Y	Y	Guam	Y	None
35		402	466	Cruz, Rosalia A	Daughter	F	Cha	8	S	Y		Guam		None
36		402	466	Cruz, Delfina A	Daughter	F	Cha	6	S	N		Guam		None
37		402	466	Cruz, Ignacio A	Son	M	Cha	1.7	S	N		Guam		None
38		403	467	Leon, Juan M	Head	M	Cha	36	M	N	Y	Guam	N	Laborer
39		403	467	Leon, Asuncion C	Wife	F	Cha	40	M	N	Y	Guam	N	None
40		403	467	Leon, Francisco C	Son	M	Cha	6	S	N		Guam		None
41		403	467	Leon, Juan C	Son	M	Cha	4.4	S	N		Guam		None
42		403	467	Leon, Asuncion C	Daughter	F	Cha	1	S	N		Guam		None
43		404	468	Aguon, Jose V	Head	M	Cha	37	M	N	Y	Guam	Y	Farmer
44		404	468	Aguon, Antonia C	Wife	F	Cha	37	M	N	Y	Guam	Y	None
45		404	468	Aguon, Vicente C	Son	M	Cha	14	S	Y	Y	Guam	Y	None
46		404	468	Aguon, Dolores C	Daughter	F	Cha	12	S	Y	Y	Guam	Y	None
47		404	468	Aguon, Maria C	Daughter	F	Cha	10	S	Y	Y	Guam	Y	None
48		404	468	Aguon, Jose C	Son	M	Cha	8	S	Y		Guam		None
49		404	469	Aguon, Vicente C	Head	M	Cha	70	M	N	Y	Guam	N	None
50		404	469	Aguon, Rosa V	Wife	F	Cha	66	M	N	Y	Guam	N	None

(CHAMORRO ROOTS GENEALOGY PROJECT™ TRANSCRIPTION)
(BERNARD T. PUNZALAN / HTTP://WWW.CHAMORROROOTS.COM)

DEPARTMENT OF COMMERCE-BUREAU OF THE CENSUS
WASHINGTON

FIFTEENTH CENSUS OF THE UNITED STATES: 1930-POPULATION

THE ISLAND OF GUAM

Sheet No. 51A

District **Municipality of Agana**
Name of Place **Agana City (Santa Cruz)**
[Proper name and, also, name of class, as city, town, village, barrio, etc]

Enumeration District No. **4**
Enumerated by me on **April 25, 1930** Vicente Tydingco
Enumerator

	PLACE OF ABODE			NAME	RELATION	PERSONAL DESCRIPTION				EDUCATION		NATIVITY		OCCUPATION
	Street, avenue, road, etc.	Number of dwelling house in order of visitation	Number of family in order of visitation	of each person whose place of abode on April 1, 1930, was in this family. Enter surname, first, then given name and middle initial. If any. Include every person living on April 1, 1930. Omit children born since April 1, 1930.	Relationship of this Person to the head of the family.	Sex	Color or race	Age at last birthday	Single, married, widowed or divorced	Attended school any time since Sept. 1, 1929	Whether able to read and write.	Place of birth of this person.	Whether able to speak English.	
	1	2	3	4	5	6	7	8	9	10	11	12	13	14
1	Santa Cruz St	405	470	Flores, Antonio M	Head	M	Cha	42	M	N	Y	Guam	N	Farmer
2		405	470	Flores, Maria LG	Wife	F	Cha	46	M	N	N	Guam	N	None
3		405	470	Flores, Juana M	Sister	F	Cha	39	S	N	Y	Guam	N	Servant
4		405	470	Salas, Ursula S	Niece	F	Cha	5	S	N		Guam		None
5		406	471	Flores, Jose M	Head	M	Cha	34	M	N	Y	Guam	Y	Merchant
6		406	471	Flores, Remedios A	Wife	F	Cha	24	M	N	Y	Guam	Y	Saleswoman
7		406	471	Aguon, Tomasa A	Sister in law	F	Cha	15	S	N	Y	Guam	Y	Saleswoman
8		406	471	Ocampo, Dolores G	Lodger	F	Cha	49	Wd	N	Y	Guam	N	Saleswoman
9		407	472	Perez, Vicente M	Head	M	Cha	38	M	N	Y	Guam	Y	Storekeeper
10		407	472	Perez, Soledad R	Wife	F	Cha	36	M	N	Y	Saipan	N	None
11		407	472	Perez, Emiliana R	Daughter	F	Cha	16	S	N	Y	Saipan	Y	None
12		407	472	Perez, Rosa R	Daughter	F	Cha	14	S	Y	Y	Saipan	Y	None
13		407	472	Perez, Jose R	Son	M	Cha	11	S	Y	Y	Guam	Y	None
14		407	472	Perez, Juan R	Son	M	Cha	2.3	S	N		Guam		None
15		408	473	Manibusan, Nicolas C	Head	M	Cha	65	M	N	Y	Guam	N	Carpenter
16		408	473	Manibusan, Maria M	Wife	F	Cha	65	M	N	N	Guam	N	None
17		408	473	Manibusan, Magdalena M	Daughter	F	Cha	30	S	N	Y	Guam	N	None
18		408	473	Manibusan, Jose M	Son	M	Cha	28	S	N	Y	Guam	Y	Carpenter
19		409	474	Santos, Felix S	Head	M	Cha	73	Wd	N	N	Guam	N	Weaver
20		409	474	Santos, Felecita G	Daughter	F	Cha	34	S	N	Y	Guam	Y	None
21		409	474	Santos, Felicidad G	Daughter	F	Cha	32	S	N	Y	Guam	Y	None
22		409	475	Santos, Jesus G	Head	M	Cha	30	M	N	Y	Guam	Y	Carpenter
23		409	475	Santos, Maria C	Wife	F	Cha	28	M	N	Y	Guam	Y	None
24		409	475	Santos, Evergista C	Daughter	F	Cha	9	S	Y		Guam		None
25		409	475	Santos, Gil C	Son	M	Cha	6	S	N		Guam		None

DEPARTMENT OF COMMERCE-BUREAU OF THE CENSUS
WASHINGTON

FIFTEENTH CENSUS OF THE UNITED STATES: 1930-POPULATION

THE ISLAND OF GUAM

Sheet No. 51B

165B

District **Municipality of Agana**
Name of Place **Agana City (Santa Cruz)**
[Proper name and, also, name of class, as city, town, village, barrio, etc]

Enumeration District No. 4
Enumerated by me on **April 25, 1930** Vicente Tydingco
Enumerator

	PLACE OF ABODE			NAME	RELATION	PERSONAL DESCRIPTION				EDUCATION		NATIVITY		OCCUPATION
	Street, avenue, road, etc.	Number of dwelling house is order of visitation	Number of family in order of visitation	of each person whose place of abode on April 1, 1930, was in this family. Enter surname, first, then given name and middle initial. If any. Include every person living on April 1, 1930. Omit children born since April 1, 1930.	Relationship of this Person to the head of the family.	Sex	Color or race	Age at last birthday	Single, married, widowed or divorced	Attended school any time since Sept. 1, 1929	Whether able to read and write.	Place of birth of this person.	Whether able to speak English.	
	1	2	3	4	5	6	7	8	9	10	11	12	13	14
26	Santa Cruz St	409	475	Santos, Felix C	Son	M	Cha	3.3	S	N		Guam		None
27		409	475	Santos, Maria C	Daughter	F	Cha	.2	S	N		Guam		None
28		410	476	Cruz, Jose M	Head	M	Cha	68	M	N	N	Guam	N	Farmer
29		410	476	Cruz, Rita LG	Wife	F	Cha	49	M	N	N	Guam	N	None
30		410	476	Cruz, Antonio LG	Son	M	Cha	22	S	N	Y	Guam	Y	Farm Laborer
31		410	476	Cruz, Maria LG	Daughter	F	Cha	9	S	Y		Guam		None
32		411	477	Cepeda, Juan M	Head	M	Cha	32	M	N	Y	Guam	Y	Engineman
33		411	477	Cepeda, Josefina R	Wife	F	Cha	26	M	N	Y	Guam	Y	None
34		411	477	Cepeda, Rosa R	Daughter	F	Cha	1.2	S	N		Guam		None
35		412	478	Mesa, Vicente R	Head	M	Cha	60	M	N	Y	Guam	N	Farmer
36		412	478	Mesa, Dolores R	Wife	F	Cha	64	M	N	N	Guam	N	None
37		412	478	Mesa, Benigno R	Son	M	Cha	21	S	N	Y	Guam	Y	Farm Laborer
38		412	478	Pangelinan, Rosa R	Granddaughter	F	Cha	3.9	S	N		Guam		None
39		412	478	Pangelinan, Irene R	Granddaughter	F	Cha	2.8	S	N		Guam		None
40		412	479	Mesa, Tomas R	Head	M	Cha	22	M	N	Y	Guam	Y	Teacher
41		412	479	Mesa, Maria L	Wife	F	Fil	23	M	N	Y	Phillippine Island	Y	Teacher
42		412	479	Mesa, Paciencia L	Daughter	F	Cha	1.9	S	N		Guam		None
43		412	479	Mesa, Vicente L	Son	M	Cha	.2	S	N		Guam		None
44		413	480	Garrido, Juan M	Head	M	Cha	66	M	N	N	Guam	N	Farmer
45		413	480	Garrido, Dolores M	Wife	F	Cha	61	M	N	N	Guam	N	None
46		413	480	Garrido, Jesus M	Son	M	Cha	36	S	N	Y	Guam	Y	Farm Laborer
47		413	480	Garrido, Joaquin M	Son	M	Cha	32	S	N	Y	Guam	N	Carpenter
48		413	481	Tenorio, Jesus N	Head	M	Cha	25	M	N	Y	Guam	Y	Farmer
49		413	481	Tenorio, Maria G	Wife	F	Cha	31	M	N	Y	Guam	Y	None
50		413	481	Tenorio, Juan G	Son	M	Cha	1.3	S	N		Guam		None

DEPARTMENT OF COMMERCE-BUREAU OF THE CENSUS
WASHINGTON

FIFTEENTH CENSUS OF THE UNITED STATES: 1930-POPULATION

THE ISLAND OF GUAM

Sheet No. 52A

District **Municipality of Agana**
Name of Place **Agana City (Santa Cruz)**
[Proper name and, also, name of class, as city, town, village, barrio, etc]

Enumeration District No. **4**
Enumerated by me on **April 26, 1930** Vicente Tydingco
Enumerator

	PLACE OF ABODE			NAME	RELATION	PERSONAL DESCRIPTION				EDUCATION		NATIVITY		OCCUPATION
	Street, avenue, road, etc.	Number of dwelling house in order of visitation	Number of family in order of visitation	of each person whose place of abode on April 1, 1930, was in this family. Enter surname, first, then given name and middle initial. If any. Include every person living on April 1, 1930. Omit children born since April 1, 1930.	Relationship of this Person to the head of the family.	Sex	Color or race	Age at last birthday	Single, married, widowed or divorced	Attended school any time since Sept. 1, 1929	Whether able to read and write.	Place of birth of this person.	Whether able to speak English.	
	1	2	3	4	5	6	7	8	9	10	11	12	13	14
1	Santa Cruz St	414	482	Chargualaf, Gertrudes C	Head	F	Cha	66	Wd	N	N	Guam	N	Weaver
2		414	482	Chargualaf, Elias C	Grandson	M	Cha	12	S	Y	Y	Guam	Y	None
3		415	483	Unpingco, Francisco R	Head	M	Cha	34	M	N	Y	Guam	Y	Carpenter
4		415	483	Unpingco, Rita M	Wife	F	Cha	31	M	N	Y	Guam	Y	None
5		415	483	Unpingco, Juan M	Son	M	Cha	5	S	N		Guam		None
6		415	483	Unpingco, Ricardo M	Son	M	Cha	3.7	S	N		Guam		None
7		415	483	Unpingco, Joseph M	Son	M	Cha	2.1	S	N		Guam		None
8		416	484	Flores, Nieves M	Head	F	Fil	39	Wd	N	Y	Phillippines Island	Y	Teacher
9		416	484	Flores, Nieves AC	Son	M	Fil	12	S	Y	Y	Guam	Y	None
10		416	484	Flores, Sabino C	Son	M	Fil	10	S	Y	Y	Guam	Y	None
11		417	485	Lizama, Maria N	Head	F	Cha	56	Wd	N	Y	Guam	Y	None
12		417	485	Lizama, Juan N	Son	M	Cha	18	S	N	Y	Guam	Y	Farmer
13		417	485	Lizama, Simon N	Son	M	Cha	15	S	Y	Y	Guam	Y	None
14		417	486	Cepeda, Francisco C	Head	M	Cha	27	M	N	Y	Guam	Y	Farmer
15		417	486	Cepeda, Ana L	Wife	F	Cha	28	M	N	Y	Guam	Y	None
16		417	486	Cepeda, Maria L	Daughter	F	Cha	.3	S	N		Guam		None
17		418	487	Cruz, Felix A	Head	M	Cha	43	M	N	Y	Guam	N	Farmer
18		418	487	Cruz, Amparo T	Wife	F	Cha	45	M	N	Y	Guam	N	Laundress
19		418	487	Cruz, Antonio T	Son	M	Cha	15	S	Y	Y	Guam	Y	None
20		418	487	Cruz, Ana T	Daughter	F	Cha	12	S	Y	Y	Guam	Y	None
21		418	487	Cruz, Jesus T	Son	M	Cha	10	S	Y	Y	Guam	Y	None
22		418	487	Cruz, Matias T	Son	M	Cha	6	S	N		Guam		None
23		418	487	Cruz, Felix T	Son	M	Cha	1.9	S	N		Guam		None
24		419	488	Unchangco, Pedro L	Head	M	Cha	28	M	N	Y	Guam	N	Farmer
25		419	488	Unchangco, Carmen L	Wife	F	Cha	26	M	N	Y	Guam	N	None

DEPARTMENT OF COMMERCE-BUREAU OF THE CENSUS
WASHINGTON

FIFTEENTH CENSUS OF THE UNITED STATES: 1930-POPULATION

THE ISLAND OF GUAM

Sheet No. 52B

District **Municipality of Agana**
Name of Place **Agana City (Santa Cruz)**
[Proper name and, also, name of class, as city, town, village, barrio, etc]

Enumeration District No. **4**
Enumerated by me on **April 26, 1930** Vicente Tydingco, Enumerator

	PLACE OF ABODE			NAME	RELATION	PERSONAL DESCRIPTION				EDUCATION		NATIVITY		OCCUPATION
	Street, avenue, road, etc.	Number of dwelling house in order of visitation	Number of family in order of visitation	of each person whose place of abode on April 1, 1930, was in this family. Enter surname, first, then given name and middle initial. If any. Include every person living on April 1, 1930. Omit children born since April 1, 1930.	Relationship of this Person to the head of the family.	Sex	Color or race	Age at last birthday	Single, married, widowed or divorced	Attended school any time since Sept. 1, 1929	Whether able to read and write.	Place of birth of this person.	Whether able to speak English.	
	1	2	3	4	5	6	7	8	9	10	11	12	13	14
26	Santa Cruz St	419	488	Unchangco, Jose M	Son	M	Cha	3.7	S	N		Guam		None
27		419	488	Unchangco, Rosa M	Daughter	F	Cha	1.7	S	N		Guam		None
28		419	489	Unchangco, Vicente P	Head	M	Cha	64	M	N	Y	Guam	N	Farmer
29		419	489	Unchangco, Rosa L	Wife	F	Cha	68	M	N	Y	Guam	N	None
30		419	489	Taijeto, Celestina B	Niece	F	Cha	13	S	Y	Y	Guam	Y	None
31		419	489	Taijeto, Maria B	Niece	F	Cha	12	S	Y	Y	Guam	Y	None
32		419	489	Taijeto, Jesus B	Nephew	M	Cha	10	S	Y	Y	Guam		None
33		420	490	Concepcion, Jesus R	Head	M	Cha	28	M	N	Y	Guam	Y	Fireman
34		420	490	Concepcion, Maria U	Wife	F	Cha	26	M	N	Y	Guam	N	None
35		420	490	Concepcion, Vicente U	Son	M	Cha	6	S	N		Guam		None
36		420	490	Concepcion, Vicente R	Brother	M	Cha	19	S	N	Y	Guam	Y	Farmer
37		421	491	Cruz, Maria A	Head	F	Cha	57	S	N	Y	Guam	N	Seamstress
38		421	491	Cruz, Rosa A	Sister	F	Cha	50	S	N	Y	Guam	N	Laundress
39		421	491	Cruz, Jose A	Brother	M	Cha	47	S	N	Y	Guam	N	Carpenter
40		421	491	Borja, Francisco C	Nephew	M	Cha	15	S	Y	Y	Guam	Y	None
41		421	492	Santos, Maria S	Head	F	Cha	33	S	N	Y	Guam	Y	Laundress
42		421	492	Santos, Jesus S	Son	M	Cha	2.5	S	N		Guam		None
43		422	493	Maanao, Dolores I	Head	F	Cha	57	Wd	N	N	Guam	N	None
44		422	493	Maanao, Maria I	Daughter	F	Cha	19	S	N	Y	Guam	Y	Laundress
45		422	493	Perez, Rosalina I	Daughter	F	Cha	15	S	N	Y	Guam	Y	Servant
46		422	494	Maanao, Gregorio I	Head	M	Cha	22	M	N	Y	Guam	Y	Machinist
47		422	494	Maanao, Ana M	Wife	F	Cha	23	M	N	Y	Guam	N	None
48		423	495	Mendiola, Juan C	Head	M	Cha	51	M	N	Y	Guam	Y	Lumberman
49		423	495	Mendiola, Rosa M	Wife	F	Cha	30	M	N	Y	Guam	Y	None
50		423	495	Mendiola, Jesus M	Son	M	Cha	9	S	Y		Guam		None

(CHAMORRO ROOTS GENEALOGY PROJECT™ TRANSCRIPTION)
(BERNARD T. PUNZALAN / HTTP://WWW.CHAMORROROOTS.COM)

DEPARTMENT OF COMMERCE-BUREAU OF THE CENSUS
WASHINGTON

FIFTEENTH CENSUS OF THE UNITED STATES: 1930-POPULATION

THE ISLAND OF GUAM

Sheet No. 53A

167

District **Municipality of Agana**
Name of Place **Agana City (Santa Cruz)**
[Proper name and, also, name of class, as city, town, village, barrio, etc]

Enumeration District No. 4
Enumerated by me on **April 26, 1930** Vicente Tydingco
Enumerator

	PLACE OF ABODE			NAME	RELATION	PERSONAL DESCRIPTION				EDUCATION		NATIVITY		OCCUPATION
	Street, avenue, road, etc.	Number of dwelling house is order of visitation	Number of family in order of visitation	of each person whose place of abode on April 1, 1930, was in this family. Enter surname, first, then given name and middle initial. If any. Include every person living on April 1, 1930. Omit children born since April 1, 1930.	Relationship of this Person to the head of the family.	Sex	Color or race	Age at last birthday	Single, married, widowed or divorced	Attended school any time since Sept. 1, 1929	Whether able to read and write.	Place of birth of this person.	Whether able to speak English.	
	1	2	3	4	5	6	7	8	9	10	11	12	13	14
1	Santa Cruz St	423	495	Mendiola, Sergio M	Son	M	Cha	6	S	N		Guam		None
2		423	495	Mendiola, Juan M	Son	M	Cha	3	S	N		Guam		None
3		423	495	Mendiola, Rosa M	Daughter	F	Cha	2.1	S	N		Guam		None
4		424	496	Charfauros, Baldobino D	Head	M	Cha	65	M	N	Y	Guam	N	Mason
5		424	496	Charfauros, Rita S	Wife	F	Cha	23	M	N	Y	Guam	N	None
6		425	497	Taitano, Juan W	Head	M	Cha	41	M	N	Y	Guam	Y	Shoemaker
7		425	497	Taitano, Maria T	Wife	F	Cha	38	M	N	N	Guam	N	None
8		425	497	Taitano, Julita T	Daughter	F	Cha	19	S	N	Y	Guam	Y	Laundress
9		425	497	Taitano, Rosario T	Daughter	F	Cha	16	S	N	Y	Guam	Y	None
10		425	497	Taitano, Guilliermo T	Son	M	Cha	12	S	Y	Y	Guam	Y	None
11		425	497	Taitano, Sixta T	Daughter	F	Cha	10	S	Y	Y	Guam	Y	None
12		425	497	Taitano, Rita T	Daughter	F	Cha	7	S	Y		Guam		None
13		425	497	Taitano, Dolores T	Daughter	F	Cha	5	S	N		Guam		None
14		425	497	Tenorio, Lourdes L	Niece	F	Cha	4	S	N		Guam	N	None
15		426	498	Iriarte, Antonio G	Head	M	Cha	48	M	N	N	Guam	Y	Farmer
16		426	498	Iriarte, Ana T	Wife	F	Cha	37	M	N	Y	Guam	N	Laundress
17		427	499	Leon Guerrero, Maria P	Head	F	Cha	43	Wd	N	Y	Guam	Y	None
18		427	499	Leon Guerrero, Ana P	Daughter	F	Cha	20	S	N	Y	Guam	Y	Saleswoman
19		427	499	Leon Guerrero, Jose P	Son	M	Cha	18	S	N	Y	Guam	Y	Laborer
20		427	499	Leon Guerrero, Gertrudes P	Daughter	F	Cha	14	S	Y	Y	Guam	Y	None
21		427	499	Leon Guerrero, Dolores P	Daughter	F	Cha	13	S	Y	Y	Guam	Y	None
22		427	499	Leon Guerrero, Joaquin P	Son	M	Cha	11	S	Y	Y	Guam	Y	None
23		427	499	Perez, Concepcion P	Sister	F	Cha	37	S	N	Y	Guam	N	Laundress
24		427	499	Rupley, Juan SA	Head	M	Cha	26	M	N	Y	Guam	Y	Farmer
25		428	500	Rupley, Maria S	Wife	F	Cha	22	M	N	Y	Guam	Y	Laundress

D-4-105

DEPARTMENT OF COMMERCE-BUREAU OF THE CENSUS
WASHINGTON

FIFTEENTH CENSUS OF THE UNITED STATES: 1930-POPULATION

THE ISLAND OF GUAM

Sheet No. 53B

167B

District **Municipality of Agana**
Name of Place **Agana City (Santa Cruz)**
[Proper name and, also, name of class, as city, town, village, barrio, etc]

Enumeration District No. **4**
Enumerated by me on **April 28, 1930** Vicente Tydingco
Enumerator

	PLACE OF ABODE			NAME	RELATION	PERSONAL DESCRIPTION				EDUCATION		NATIVITY		OCCUPATION
	Street, avenue, road, etc.	Number of dwelling house is order of visitation	Number of family in order of visitation	of each person whose place of abode on April 1, 1930, was in this family. Enter surname, first, then given name and middle initial. If any. Include every person living on April 1, 1930. Omit children born since April 1, 1930.	Relationship of this Person to the head of the family.	Sex	Color or race	Age at last birthday	Single, married, widowed or divorced	Attended school any time since Sept. 1, 1929	Whether able to read and write.	Place of birth of this person.	Whether able to speak English.	
	1	2	3	4	5	6	7	8	9	10	11	12	13	14
26	Santa Cruz St	428	500	Rupley, Prisciliana S	Daughter	F	Cha	3.3	S	N		Guam		None
27		428	500	Rupley, Carmen S	Daughter	F	Cha	.3	S	N		Guam		None
28		428	500	Rupley, Magdalena A	Mother	F	Cha	44	M	N	Y	Guam	Y	Landress
29		428	500	Rupley, Santiago I	Brother	M	Cha	15	S	N		Guam		None
30		429	501	Borja, Jose B	Head	M	Cha	47	M	N	Y	Guam	N	Farmer
31		429	501	Borja, Consuelo M	Wife	F	Cha	44	M	N	N	Guam	N	None
32		430	502	Reyes, Jose E	Head	M	Cha	27	M	N	Y	Guam	Y	Machinist
33		430	502	Reyes, Ana M	Wife	F	Cha	28	M	N	Y	Guam	Y	None
34		430	502	Reyes, Maria M	Daughter	F	Cha	7	S	Y		Guam		None
35		430	502	Reyes, Helena M	Daughter	F	Cha	5	S	N		Guam		None
36		430	502	Reyes, Jose M	Son	M	Cha	4.8	S	N		Guam		None
37		430	502	Reyes, Lorenza M	Daughter	F	Cha	3.6	S	N		Guam		None
38		430	502	Reyes, Concepcion M	Daughter	F	Cha	.3	S	N		Guam		None
39		431	503	Roberto, Juan R	Head	M	Cha	59	M	N	N	Guam	Y	Farmer
40		431	503	Roberto, Maria D	Wife	F	Cha	56	M	N	Y	Guam	N	None
41		431	503	Roberto, Luis D	Son	M	Cha	24	S	N	Y	Guam	Y	Farm laborer
42		431	503	Roberto, Simona D	Daughter	F	Cha	23	S	N	Y	Guam	Y	None
43		431	503	Roberto, Anastacia D	Daughter	F	Cha	19	S	N	Y	Guam	N	Landress
44		431	503	Roberto, Sixta D	Daughter	F	Cha	17	S	Y	Y	Guam	Y	None
45		431	503	Roberto, Maria D	Daughter	F	Cha	14	S	Y	Y	Guam	Y	None
46		431	503	Roberto, Ana D	Daughter	F	Cha	12	S	Y	Y	Guam	Y	None
47		431	503	Roberto, Mercedes D	Daughter	F	Cha	11	S	Y	Y	Guam	Y	None
48		431	503	Roberto, Jesus R	Grandson	M	Cha	1.6	S	N		Guam		None
49		432	504	Garrido, Enrique M	Head	M	Cha	31	M	N	Y	Guam	Y	Blacksmith
50		432	504	Garrido, Trinidad LG	Wife	F	Cha	33	M	N	Y	Guam	Y	None

DEPARTMENT OF COMMERCE-BUREAU OF THE CENSUS
WASHINGTON

FIFTEENTH CENSUS OF THE UNITED STATES: 1930-POPULATION

THE ISLAND OF GUAM

Sheet No. 54A

District Municipality of Agana
Name of Place Agana City (Santa Cruz)
[Proper name and, also, name of class, as city, town, village, barrio, etc]

Enumeration District No. 4
Enumerated by me on April 28, 1930 Vicente Tydingco
Enumerator

	PLACE OF ABODE			NAME	RELATION	PERSONAL DESCRIPTION				EDUCATION		NATIVITY		OCCUPATION
	Street, avenue, road, etc.	Number of dwelling house is order of visitation	Number of family in order of visitation	of each person whose place of abode on April 1, 1930, was in this family. Enter surname, first, then given name and middle initial. If any. Include every person living on April 1, 1930. Omit children born since April 1, 1930.	Relationship of this Person to the head of the family.	Sex	Color or race	Age at last birthday	Single, married, widowed or divorced	Attended school any time since Sept. 1, 1929	Whether able to read and write.	Place of birth of this person.	Whether able to speak English.	
	1	2	3	4	5	6	7	8	9	10	11	12	13	14
1	Legaspi Street	432	504	Garrido, Maria LG	Daughter	F	Cha	6	S	N		Guam		None
2		432	504	Garrido, Roman LG	Son	M	Cha	4.8	S	N		Guam		None
3		432	504	Garrido, Beatris LG	Daughter	F	Cha	2.7	S	N		Guam		None
4		432	504	Garrido, Francisco LG	Son	M	Cha	1.1	S	N		Guam		None
5		432	504	Leon Guerrero, Carmen B	Mother in law	F	Cha	65	Wd	N	N	Guam	N	None
6		433	505	Untalan, Maria B	Head	F	Cha	29	S	N	Y	Guam	Y	Teacher
7		433	505	Untalan, Rosa B	Sister	F	Cha	26	S	N	Y	Guam	Y	Saleswoman
8		434	506	Santos, Geronimo P	Head	M	Fil	39	M	N	Y	Phillippine Island	Y	Barber
9		434	506	Santos, Rita T	Wife	F	Cha	33	M	N	Y	Guam	N	None
10		434	506	Santos, Felisiano T	Son	M	Fil	13	S	Y	Y	Guam	Y	None
11		434	506	Santos, Dolores T	Daughter	F	Fil	12	S	Y	Y	Phillippine Island	Y	None
12		434	506	Santos, Roque T	Son	M	Fil	11	S	Y	Y	Guam	Y	None
13		434	506	Santos, Paz T	Daughter	F	Fil	9	S	Y		Guam		None
14		434	506	Santos, Jesus T	Son	M	Fil	7	S	Y		Guam		None
15		434	506	Santos, Eugenio T	Son	M	Fil	5	S	N		Guam		None
16		434	506	Santos, Agapita T	Daughter	F	Fil	2.2	S	N		Guam		None
17		434	506	Santos, Samson T	Brother	M	Fil	25	S	N	Y	Phillippine Island	Y	Electrician
18		435	507	Macias, Enrique H	Head	M	Cha	36	M	N	Y	Guam	Y	Chauffeur
19		435	507	Macias, Adela C	Wife	F	Cha	27	M	N	Y	Guam	Y	None
20		435	507	Macias, Carmen C	Daughter	F	Cha	3.2	S	N		Guam		None
21		435	507	Macias, Jose C	Son	M	Cha	2.7	S	N		Guam		None
22		435	507	Macias, Magdalena C	Daughter	F	Cha	1.1	S	N		Guam		None
23		435	507	Herrero, Caridad C	Mother	F	Cha	63	S	N	Y	Guam	N	None
24		436	508	Leon Guerrero, Francisco B	Head	M	Cha	56	M	N	Y	Guam	N	Farmer
25		436	508	Leon Guerrero, Mariana P	Wife	F	Cha	57	M	N	Y	Guam	N	None

DEPARTMENT OF COMMERCE-BUREAU OF THE CENSUS
WASHINGTON

FIFTEENTH CENSUS OF THE UNITED STATES: 1930-POPULATION

THE ISLAND OF GUAM

Sheet No. 54B

168B

District **Municipality of Agana**
Name of Place **Agana City (Santa Cruz)**
[Proper name and, also, name of class, as city, town, village, barrio, etc]

Enumeration District No. **4**
Enumerated by me on **April 28, 1930** Vicente Tydingco
Enumerator

	PLACE OF ABODE			NAME	RELATION	PERSONAL DESCRIPTION				EDUCATION		NATIVITY		OCCUPATION
	Street, avenue, road, etc.	Number of dwelling house is order of visitation	Number of family in order of visitation	of each person whose place of abode on April 1, 1930, was in this family. Enter surname, first, then given name and middle initial. If any. Include every person living on April 1, 1930. Omit children born since April 1, 1930.	Relationship of this Person to the head of the family.	Sex	Color or race	Age at last birthday	Single, married, widowed or divorced	Attended school any time since Sept. 1, 1929	Whether able to read and write.	Place of birth of this person.	Whether able to speak English.	
	1	2	3	4	5	6	7	8	9	10	11	12	13	14
26	Legaspi Street	436	508	Leon Guerrero, Maria P	Daughter	F	Cha	29	S	N	Y	Guam	Y	Teacher
27		436	508	Leon Guerrero, Concepcion p	Daughter	F	Cha	26	S	N	Y	Guam	Y	Teacher
28		436	508	Leon Guerrero, Eliza P	Daughter	F	Cha	24	S	N	Y	Guam	Y	Seamstress
29		436	508	Leon Guerrero, Tomasa P	Daughter	F	Cha	21	S	Y	Y	Guam	Y	None
30		436	508	Leon Guerrero, Lagrimas P	Daughter	F	Cha	19	S	N	Y	Guam	Y	Teacher
31		436	508	Shimizu, Ambrosio T	Lodger	M	Jap	24	S	N	Y	Guam	Y	Salesman
32		436	508	Chargualaf, Maria L	Lodger	F	Cha	11	S	Y	Y	Guam	Y	Servant
33		437	509	Carrol, Anna S	Head	F	W	24	M	N	Y	Philadelphia, Pennsylvania	Y	None
34		437	509	Carrol, John J	Son	M	W	14	S	Y	Y	Philadelphia, Pennsylvania	Y	None
35		437	509	Carrol, Thomas	Son	M	W	12	S	Y	Y	Philadelphia, Pennsylvania	Y	None
36		437	509	Carrol, Anna M	Daughter	F	W	9	S	Y		Philadelphia, Pennsylvania		None
37		438	510	Santos, Jose G	Head	M	Cha	39	M	N	Y	Guam	Y	Farmer
38		438	510	Santos, Felicidad B	Wife	F	Cha	24	M	N	Y	Guam	N	None
39		438	510	Santos, Rita B	Daughter	F	Cha	6	S	N		Guam		None
40		438	510	Santos, Jose B	Son	M	Cha	3.9	S	N		Guam		None
41		438	510	Santos, Juana B	Daughter	F	Cha	2.2	S	N		Guam		None
42		438	510	Santos, Felix B	Son	M	Cha	.9	S	N		Guam		None
43		438	510	Camacho, Rita M	Aunt	F	Cha	48	S	N	N	Guam	N	Seamstress
44		439	511	Blaz, Manuel A	Head	M	Cha	67	M	N	Y	Guam	N	Farmer
45		439	511	Blaz, Nicolasa S	Wife	F	Cha	64	M	N	N	Guam	N	None
46		439	511	Leddy, Daniel B	Grandson	M	Cha	18	S	N	Y	Guam	Y	Servant
47		439	511	Leddy, Elsie B	Granddaughter	F	Cha	12	S	Y	Y	Guam	Y	None
48		439	512	Untalan, Vicente P	Head	M	Cha	24	M	N	Y	Guam	Y	Farmer
49		439	512	Untalan, Rosa B	Wife	F	Cha	28	M	Y	Y	Guam	Y	None
50		439	512	Untalan, Estella B	Daughter	F	Cha	6.7	S	N		Guam		None

DEPARTMENT OF COMMERCE-BUREAU OF THE CENSUS
WASHINGTON

FIFTEENTH CENSUS OF THE UNITED STATES: 1930-POPULATION

THE ISLAND OF GUAM

Sheet No. 55A

District Municipality of Agana
Name of Place Agana City (Santa Cruz)
[Proper name and, also, name of class, as city, town, village, barrio, etc]

Enumeration District No. 4
Enumerated by me on April 29, 1930 Vicente Tydingco, Enumerator

	PLACE OF ABODE			NAME	RELATION	PERSONAL DESCRIPTION				EDUCATION		NATIVITY		OCCUPATION
	Street, avenue, road, etc.	Number of dwelling house is order of visitation	Number of family in order of visitation	of each person whose place of abode on April 1, 1930, was in this family. Enter surname, first, then given name and middle initial. If any. Include every person living on April 1, 1930. Omit children born since April 1, 1930.	Relationship of this Person to the head of the family.	Sex	Color or race	Age at last birthday	Single, married, widowed or divorced	Attended school any time since Sept. 1, 1929	Whether able to read and write.	Place of birth of this person.	Whether able to speak English.	
	1	2	3	4	5	6	7	8	9	10	11	12	13	14
1	Legaspi Street	439	512	Untalan, Leonisa B	Daughter	F	Cha	3.2	S	N		Guam		None
2		439	513	Santos, Maria S	Head	F	Cha	40	S	N	N	Guam	N	Laundress
3		439	513	Santos, Jose S	Son	M	Cha	15	S	Y	Y	Guam	Y	None
4		439	513	Santos, Rosa S	Daughter	F	Cha	13	S	Y	Y	Guam	Y	None
5		440	514	Aguon, Juan C	Head	M	Cha	42	M	N	Y	Guam	N	Farmer
6		440	514	Aguon, Isabel C	Wife	F	Cha	41	M	N	Y	Guam	N	None
7		440	514	Aguon, Eufracia C	Daughter	F	Cha	15	S	Y	Y	Guam	Y	None
8		440	514	Aguon, Joaquin C	Son	M	Cha	14	S	Y	Y	Guam	Y	None
9		440	514	Aguon, Martina C	Daughter	F	Cha	12	S	Y	Y	Guam	Y	None
10		440	514	Aguon, Isabel C	Daughter	F	Cha	9	S	Y		Guam		None
11		440	514	Aguon, Josefa C	Daughter	F	Cha	8	S	Y		Guam		None
12		440	514	Aguon, Segundo C	Son	M	Cha	5	S	N		Guam		None
13		440	514	Aguon, Juan C	Son	M	Cha	3.8	S	N		Guam		None
14		440	514	Aguon, Jesus C	Son	M	Cha	.8	S	N		Guam		None
15		441	515	Blaz, Ramon T	Head	M	Cha	66	M	N	Y	Guam	N	Farmer
16		441	515	Blaz, Rosa B	Wife	F	Cha	67	M	N	N	Guam	N	None
17		441	515	Blaz, Trinidad B	Daughter	F	Cha	39	D	N	Y	Guam	Y	Seamstress
18		441	515	Blaz, Francisco C	Brother	M	Cha	83	Wd	N	N	Guam	N	None
19		441	515	Palacios, Rosa B	Granddaughter	F	Cha	16	S	Y	Y	Guam	Y	None
20		441	515	Palacios, Carlos B	Grandson	M	Cha	14	S	Y	Y	Guam	Y	None
21		442	516	Calvo, Tomas A	Head	M	W	48	M	N	Y	Philippines Islands		Attorney at Law
22		442	516	Calvo, Regina T	Wife	F	Cha	46	M	N	Y	Guam	Y	None
23		442	516	Calvo, Ismael T	Son	M	Cha	25	S	N	Y	Guam	Y	Machinist
24		442	516	Calvo, Trinidad T	Son	M	Cha	23	S	N	Y	Guam	Y	Carpenter
25		442	516	Calvo, Herminia T	Daughter	F	Cha	22	S	N	Y	Guam	Y	None

(CHAMORRO ROOTS GENEALOGY PROJECT™ TRANSCRIPTION)
(BERNARD T. PUNZALAN / HTTP://WWW.CHAMORROROOTS.COM)

DEPARTMENT OF COMMERCE-BUREAU OF THE CENSUS
WASHINGTON

FIFTEENTH CENSUS OF THE UNITED STATES: 1930-POPULATION

THE ISLAND OF GUAM

Sheet No. 55B

169B

District **Municipality of Agana**
Name of Place **Agana City (Santa Cruz)**
[Proper name and, also, name of class, as city, town, village, barrio, etc]

Enumeration District No. 4
Enumerated by me on **April 29, 1930** Vicente Tydingco
Enumerator

	PLACE OF ABODE			NAME	RELATION	PERSONAL DESCRIPTION				EDUCATION		NATIVITY		OCCUPATION
	Street, avenue, road, etc.	Number of dwelling house in order of visitation	Number of family in order of visitation	of each person whose place of abode on April 1, 1930, was in this family. Enter surname, first, then given name and middle initial. If any. Include every person living on April 1, 1930. Omit children born since April 1, 1930.	Relationship of this Person to the head of the family.	Sex	Color or race	Age at last birthday	Single, married, widowed or divorced	Attended school any time since Sept. 1, 1929	Whether able to read and write.	Place of birth of this person.	Whether able to speak English.	
	1	2	3	4	5	6	7	8	9	10	11	12	13	14
26	Legaspi Street	442	516	Calvo, Clotilde T	Daughter	F	Cha	19	S	N	Y	Guam	Y	None
27		442	516	Calvo, Flora T	Daughter	F	Cha	17	S	N	Y	Guam	Y	None
28		442	516	Calvo, Ricardo T	Son	M	Cha	14	S	Y	Y	Guam	Y	Salesman
29		442	516	Calvo, Carlos T	Son	M	Cha	11	s	Y	Y	Guam	Y	None
30		442	516	Calvo, Angelina T	Daughter	F	Cha	6	S	Y		Guam		None
31		442	516	Calvo, Ana A	Mother	F	Cha	80	Wd	N	Y	Guam	N	None
32		442	516	Calvo, Jacinto A	Brother	M	Cha	56	S	N	N	Phillippine Island	N	None
33		443	517	Roberto, Juan A	Head	M	Cha	33	M	N	Y	Guam	Y	Policeman
34		443	517	Roberto, Maria B	Wife	F	Cha	38	M	N	Y	Guam	Y	None
35		443	517	Roberto, Eulalia B	Daughter	F	Cha	8	S	Y		Guam		None
36		443	517	Wongpat, Francisco B	Stepson	M	Cha	10	S	Y	Y	Guam		None
37		444	518	Santos, Enrique S	Lodger	M	Cha	26	S	N	Y	Guam	Y	Farmer
38		444	518	Torres, Gregorio M	Head	M	Cha	46	M	N	Y	Guam	Y	Fisherman
39		444	519	Torres, Josefa A	Wife	F	Cha	55	M	N	Y	Guam	N	None
40		444	519	Roberto, Dolores A	Head	F	Cha	29	S	N	Y	Guam	Y	None
41		444	519	Roberto, Concepcion R	Daughter	F	Cha	13	S	Y	Y	Guam	Y	None
42		444	519	Roberto, Josefina R	Daughter	F	Cha	9	S	Y		Guam		None
43		444	519	Roberto, Jesus R	Son	M	Cha	7	S	Y		Guam		None
44		444	519	Roberto, Francisco R	Son	M	Cha	.8	S	N		Guam		None
45		444	520	Barcinas, Pilar T	Head	F	Cha	21	M	N	Y	Guam	Y	None
46		444	520	Barcinas, Amelia V	Daughter	F	Cha	6	S	N		Guam		None
47		445	521	Mesa, Carmen M	Head	F	Cha	49	M	N	Y	Guam	N	None
48		445	521	Mesa, Rosalia M	Daughter	F	Cha	10	S	Y	Y	Guam	Y	None
49		445	521	Mesa, Margarita M	Daughter	F	Cha	9	S	Y		Guam		None
50		445	521	San Nicolas, Beatris M	Niece	F	Cha	6	S	N		Guam		None

DEPARTMENT OF COMMERCE-BUREAU OF THE CENSUS
WASHINGTON

FIFTEENTH CENSUS OF THE UNITED STATES: 1930-POPULATION

THE ISLAND OF GUAM

Sheet No. 56A

District Municipality of Agana

Name of Place Agana City (Santa Cruz)

[Proper name and, also, name of class, as city, town, village, barrio, etc]

Enumeration District No. 4

Enumerated by me on April 30, 1930 Vicente Tydingco, Enumerator

	PLACE OF ABODE			NAME	RELATION	PERSONAL DESCRIPTION				EDUCATION		NATIVITY		OCCUPATION
	Street, avenue, road, etc.	Number of dwelling house in order of visitation	Number of family in order of visitation	of each person whose place of abode on April 1, 1930, was in this family. Enter surname, first, then given name and middle initial. If any. Include every person living on April 1, 1930. Omit children born since April 1, 1930.	Relationship of this Person to the head of the family.	Sex	Color or race	Age at last birthday	Single, married, widowed or divorced	Attended school any time since Sept. 1, 1929	Whether able to read and write.	Place of birth of this person.	Whether able to speak English.	
	1	2	3	4	5	6	7	8	9	10	11	12	13	14
1	Legaspi Street	446	522	Muna, Juan	Head	M	Cha	31	M	N	Y	Guam	Y	Clerk
2		446	522	Muna, Pilar P	Wife	F	Cha	30	M	N	Y	Guam	Y	None
3		446	522	Muna, Antonia P	Daughter	F	Cha	6	S	N		Guam		None
4		446	522	Muna, Norberto P	Son	M	Cha	3.8	S	N		Guam		None
5		446	522	Muna, Tomas P	Son	M	Cha	2.8	S	N		Guam		None
6		446	522	Muna, Evelyna P	Daughter	F	Cha	.5	S	N		Guam		None
7		446	523	Peraira, Manuel S	Head	M	Cha	55	Wd	N	Y	Guam	N	Farmer
8		446	523	Peraira, Rita C	Daughter	F	Cha	23	S	N	Y	Guam	N	None
9		446	523	Peraira, Bernadita C	Daughter	F	Cha	12	S	Y	Y	Guam	Y	None
10		446	523	Peraira, Jesus C	Son	M	Cha	10	S	Y	Y	Guam	Y	None
11		446	524	Peraira, Ignacio C	Head	M	Cha	29	M	N	Y	Guam	Y	Farmer
12		446	524	Peraira, Genoveva P	Wife	F	Cha	21	M	N	Y	Guam	N	None
13		446	524	Cruz, Jose	Lodger	M	Cha	39	S	N	Y	Guam	Y	Servant
14		447	525	Cruz, Maria M	Head	F	Cha	24	M	N		Guam	Y	Seamstress
15		447	525	Cruz, Josefina M	Daughter	F	Cha	3.1	S	N		Guam		None
16		447	525	Cruz, David M	Son	M	Cha	2.2	S	N		Guam		None
17		447	525	Cruz, Francisco M	Son	M	Cha	.6	S	N		Guam		None
18		448	526	Duenas, Juan F	Head	M	Cha	57	M	N	Y	Guam	N	Farmer
19		448	526	Duenas, Ignacia LG	Wife	F	Cha	52	M	N	Y	Guam	N	None
20		448	526	Duenas, Pedro LG	Son	M	Cha	30	S	N	N	Guam	N	None
21		448	526	Duenas, Maria LG	Daughter	F	Cha	27	S	N	Y	Guam	Y	Farm Laborer
22		448	526	Duenas, Jose LG	Son	M	Cha	22	S	N	N	Guam	N	None
23		448	526	Duenas, Isabel LG	Daughter	F	Cha	19	S	N	N	Guam	N	None
24		448	526	Duenas, Guadalupe LG	Daughter	F	Cha	17	S	N	Y	Guam	Y	Saleswoman
25		448	526	Duenas, Catalina LG	Daughter	F	Cha	15	S	N	Y	Guam	Y	None

DEPARTMENT OF COMMERCE-BUREAU OF THE CENSUS
WASHINGTON

FIFTEENTH CENSUS OF THE UNITED STATES: 1930-POPULATION

THE ISLAND OF GUAM

Sheet No. 56B

170B

District **Municipality of Agana**
Name of Place **Agana City (Santa Cruz)**
[Proper name and, also, name of class, as city, town, village, barrio, etc]

Enumeration District No. **4**
Enumerated by me on **April 30, 1930** Vicente Tydingco
Enumerator

	PLACE OF ABODE			NAME	RELATION	PERSONAL DESCRIPTION				EDUCATION		NATIVITY		OCCUPATION
	Street, avenue, road, etc.	Number of dwelling house is order of visitation	Number of family in order of visitation	of each person whose place of abode on April 1, 1930, was in this family. Enter surname, first, then given name and middle initial. If any. Include every person living on April 1, 1930. Omit children born since April 1, 1930.	Relationship of this Person to the head of the family.	Sex	Color or race	Age at last birthday	Single, married, widowed or divorced	Attended school any time since Sept. 1, 1929	Whether able to read and write.	Place of birth of this person.	Whether able to speak English.	
	1	2	3	4	5	6	7	8	9	10	11	12	13	14
26	Legaspi Street	448	526	Duenas, Dolores LG	Daughter	F	Cha	10	S	Y	Y	Guam	Y	None
27		449	527	Reyes, Francisco L	Head	M	Cha	53	M	N	N	Guam	N	Farmer
28		449	527	Reyes, Josefa M	Wife	F	Cha	79	M	N	N	Guam	N	None
29		449	527	Reyes, Ignacio M	Son	M	Cha	21	S	N	Y	Guam	Y	Farm Laborer
30		449	527	Reyes, Nicolasa M	Daughter	F	Cha	18	S	N	Y	Guam	Y	None
31		449	528	Reyes, Manuel M	Head	M	Cha	23	M	N	Y	Guam	Y	Farmer
32		449	528	Reyes, Catalina Q	Wife	F	Cha	26	M	N	N	Guam	N	None
33		449	528	Reyes, Barcelisa Q	Daughter	F	Cha	2.4	S	N		Guam		None
34		449	528	Reyes, Francisco Q	Son	M	Cha	.5	S	N		Guam		None
35		450	529	Leon Guerrero, Jesus I	Head	M	Cha	29	M	N	Y	Guam	Y	Policeman
36		450	529	Leon Guerrero, Amparo C	Wife	F	Cha	30	M	N	Y	Guam	Y	None
37		450	529	Leon Guerrero, Dolores C	Daughter	F	Cha	6	S	N		Guam		None
38		450	529	Leon Guerrero, Joaquin C	Son	M	Cha	4.5	S	N		Guam		None
39		450	529	Leon Guerrero, Maria C	Daughter	F	Cha	2.2	S	N		Guam		None
40		450	529	Leon Guerrero, Dolores I	Mother	F	Cha	49	Wd	N	N	Guam	N	None
41		450	529	Leon Guerrero, Concepcion I	Sister	F	Cha	23	S	N	Y	Guam	Y	Saleswoman
42		450	529	Leon Guerrero, Suzana I	Sister	F	Cha	17	S	Y	Y	Guam	Y	None
43		450	529	Leon Guerrero, Jose I	Brother	M	Cha	14	S	Y	Y	Guam	Y	None
44		450	529	Leon Guerrero, Joaquin I	Brother	M	Cha	12	S	Y	Y	Guam	Y	None
45		451	530	Mendiola, Jose L	Head	M	Cha	41	M	N	N	Guam	N	Farmer
46		451	530	Mendiola, Rita Q	Wife	F	Cha	44	M	N	N	Guam	N	None
47		451	530	Mendiola, Paula L	Mother	F	Cha	75	Wd	N	N	Guam	N	None
48		451	530	Mendiola, Vicente L	Brother	M	Cha	37	S	N	N	Guam	N	Farmer
49		452	531	Cruz, Simeon B	Head	M	Cha	37	M	N	Y	Guam	Y	Laborer
50		452	531	Cruz, Isabel M	Wife	F	Cha	26	M	N	Y	Guam	N	None

DEPARTMENT OF COMMERCE-BUREAU OF THE CENSUS
WASHINGTON

FIFTEENTH CENSUS OF THE UNITED STATES: 1930-POPULATION

THE ISLAND OF GUAM

Sheet No. 57A

District **Municipality of Agana**
Name of Place **Agana City (Santa Cruz)**
[Proper name and, also, name of class, as city, town, village, barrio, etc]

Enumeration District No. **4**
Enumerated by me on **April 30, 1930** Vicente Tydingco
Enumerator

	PLACE OF ABODE			NAME	RELATION	PERSONAL DESCRIPTION				EDUCATION		NATIVITY		OCCUPATION
	Street, avenue, road, etc.	Number of dwelling house is order of visitation	Number of family in order of visitation	of each person whose place of abode on April 1, 1930, was in this family. Enter surname, first, then given name and middle initial. If any. Include every person living on April 1, 1930. Omit children born since April 1, 1930.	Relationship of this Person to the head of the family.	Sex	Color or race	Age at last birthday	Single, married, widowed or divorced	Attended school any time since Sept. 1, 1929	Whether able to read and write.	Place of birth of this person.	Whether able to speak English.	
	1	2	3	4	5	6	7	8	9	10	11	12	13	14
1	Legaspi Street	452	531	Cruz, Jose M	Son	M	Cha	7	S	Y		Guam		None
2		452	531	Cruz, Joaquin M	Son	M	Cha	2.3	S	N		Guam		None
3		452	531	Cruz, Rosa M	Daughter	F	Cha	.7	S	N		Guam		None
4		452	531	Mendiola, Jose S	Brother in law	M	Cha	30	S	N	Y	Guam	Y	Farmer
5		453	532	Quitugua, Joaquin R	Head	M	Cha	26	M	N	Y	Guam	Y	Laborer
6		453	532	Quitugua, Dolores M	Wife	F	Cha	20	M	N	Y	Guam	Y	None
7		453	532	Quitugua, Rita M	Daughter	F	Cha	.7	S	N		Guam		None
8		454	533	Taisague, Felisa C	Head	F	Cha	56	S	N	N	Guam	Y	Laundress
9		454	533	Taisague, Rosalia T	Daughter	F	Cha	17	S	Y	Y	Guam	Y	None
10		455	534	Laguana, Jose P	Head	M	Cha	29	M	N	Y	Guam	Y	Farmer
11		455	534	Laguana, Rita C	Wife	F	Cha	29	M	N	Y	Guam	Y	None
12		455	534	Laguana, Carlos C	Son	M	Cha	4.7	S	N		Guam		None
13		455	534	Laguana, Jose C	Son	M	Cha	2.7	S	N		Guam		None
14		455	534	Laguana, Jesus C	Son	M	Cha	1.7	S	N		Guam		None
15		455	534	Laguana, Joaquina P	Mother	F	Cha	72	Wd	N	N	Guam	N	None
16		455	534	Laguana, Rosa P	Sister	F	Cha	46	S	N	Y	Guam	N	None
17		455	534	Laguana, Ignacia P	Sister	F	Cha	42	S	N	Y	Guam	N	None
18		455	534	Laguana, Soledad P	Sister	F	Cha	38	S	N	Y	Guam	N	None
19		455	534	Laguana, Felicidad P	Sister	F	Cha	32	S	N	Y	Guam	Y	None
20		456	565	Sablan, Ramon D	Head	M	Cha	43	M	N	Y	Guam	Y	Farmer
21		456	565	Sablan, Dolores T	Wife	F	Cha	46	M	N	Y	Guam	Y	None
22		456	565	Sablan, Emma T	Daughter	F	Cha	20	S	N	Y	Guam	Y	None
23		456	565	Sablan, Maria T	Daughter	F	Cha	19	S	N	Y	Guam	Y	Servant
24		456	565	Sablan, Santiago T	Son	M	Cha	18	S	Y	Y	Guam	Y	None
25		456	565	Sablan, Juanita T	Daughter	F	Cha	15	S	Y	Y	Guam	Y	None

DEPARTMENT OF COMMERCE-BUREAU OF THE CENSUS
WASHINGTON

FIFTEENTH CENSUS OF THE UNITED STATES: 1930-POPULATION

THE ISLAND OF GUAM

Sheet No. 57B

171B

District Municipality of Agana
Name of Place Agana City (Santa Cruz)
[Proper name and, also, name of class, as city, town, village, barrio, etc]

Enumeration District No. 4
Enumerated by me on April 30, 1930 Vicente Tydingco
Enumerator

	PLACE OF ABODE			NAME	RELATION	PERSONAL DESCRIPTION				EDUCATION		NATIVITY		OCCUPATION
	Street, avenue, road, etc.	Number of dwelling house in order of visitation	Number of family in order of visitation	of each person whose place of abode on April 1, 1930, was in this family. Enter surname, first, then given name and middle initial. If any. Include every person living on April 1, 1930. Omit children born since April 1, 1930.	Relationship of this Person to the head of the family.	Sex	Color or race	Age at last birthday	Single, married, widowed or divorced	Attended school any time since Sept. 1, 1929	Whether able to read and write.	Place of birth of this person.	Whether able to speak English.	
	1	2	3	4	5	6	7	8	9	10	11	12	13	14
26	Legaspi Street	456	535	Sablan, Jose T	Son	M	Cha	13	S	Y	Y	Guam	Y	None
27		456	535	Sablan, Francisco T	Son	M	Cha	10	S	Y	Y	Guam	Y	None
28		456	535	Sablan, Ramon T	Son	M	Cha	8	S	Y		Guam		None
29		456	535	Sablan, Peter T	Son	M	Cha	6	S	N		Guam		None
30		456	535	Sablan, John S	Grandson	M	Cha	.9	S	N		Guam		None
31		457	536	Calvo, Antonio B	Head	M	Cha	56	Wd	N	Y	Guam	Y	Merchant
32		457	536	Calvo, Felix V	Son	M	Cha	29	S	N	Y	Guam		Clerk
33		457	537	Velardi, Simon	Head	M	Fil	30	M	N	Y	Phillippine Island		Salesman
34		457	537	Velardi, Pilar C	Wife	F	Cha	26	M	N	Y	Guam		None
35		457	537	Velardi, Ruth C	Daughter	F	Fil	6	S	N		Guam		None
36		457	537	Velardi, Rafaela C	Daughter	F	Fil	3.4	S	N		Guam		None
37		457	537	Velardi, Concepcion C	Daughter	F	Fil	2.5	S	N		Guam		None
38		458	538	Martinez, Vicente B	Head	M	Cha	43	M	N	Y	Guam	Y	Merchant
39		458	538	Martinez, Rita C	Wife	F	Cha	45	M	N	Y	Guam	N	None
40		458	538	Martinez, Grace J	Daughter	F	Cha	16	S	N	Y	Guam	Y	None
41		458	538	Martinez, Lucy R	Daughter	F	Cha	15	S	Y	Y	Guam	Y	None
42		458	538	Martinez, May R	Daughter	F	Cha	12	S	Y	Y	Guam	Y	None
43		458	538	Martinez, Carrie M	Daughter	F	Cha	9	S	Y		Guam		None
44		458	538	Martinez, Melchor V	Son	M	Cha	7	S	Y		Guam		None
45		458	538	Calvo, Gregorio P	Brother in law	M	Cha	48	S	N	Y	Guam	N	Laborer
46		458	538	Calvo, Vicente	Brother in law	M	Cha	31	Wd	N	Y	Guam	Y	Bookkeeper
47		459	539	Sablan, Guilliermo D	Head	M	Cha	60	Wd	N	Y	Guam	N	Farmer
48		459	539	Sablan, Enrique C	Son	M	Cha	22	Wd	N	Y	Guam	Y	Chauffeur
49		459	539	Sablan, Antonio C	Son	M	Cha	20	S	N	Y	Guam	Y	Farm Laborer
50		459	539	Sablan, Carmen C	Daughter	F	Cha	16	S	N	Y	Guam	Y	None

DEPARTMENT OF COMMERCE-BUREAU OF THE CENSUS
WASHINGTON

FIFTEENTH CENSUS OF THE UNITED STATES: 1930-POPULATION

THE ISLAND OF GUAM

Sheet No. 58A

District Municipality of Agana
Name of Place Agana City (Santa Cruz)
[Proper name and, also, name of class, as city, town, village, barrio, etc]

Enumeration District No. 4
Enumerated by me on May 1, 1930 Vicente Tydingco
Enumerator

	PLACE OF ABODE			NAME	RELATION	PERSONAL DESCRIPTION				EDUCATION		NATIVITY		OCCUPATION
	Street, avenue, road, etc.	Number of dwelling house is order of visitation	Number of family in order of visitation	of each person whose place of abode on April 1, 1930, was in this family. Enter surname, first, then given name and middle initial. If any. Include every person living on April 1, 1930. Omit children born since April 1, 1930.	Relationship of this Person to the head of the family.	Sex	Color or race	Age at last birthday	Single, married, widowed or divorced	Attended school any time since Sept. 1, 1929	Whether able to read and write.	Place of birth of this person.	Whether able to speak English.	
	1	2	3	4	5	6	7	8	9	10	11	12	13	14
1	Legaspi Street	459	539	Sablan, Candelaria C	Daughter	F	Cha	13	S	Y	Y	Guam	Y	None
2		459	539	Sablan, Emilia C	Daughter	F	Cha	11	S	Y	Y	Guam	Y	None
3		460	540	Cabo, Jose D	Head	M	Cha	56	M	N	Y	Guam	N	Farmer
4		460	540	Cabo, Dolores T	Wife	F	Cha	42	M	N	Y	Guam	N	None
5		460	540	Cabo, Manuela D	Mother	F	Cha	91	Wd	N	N	Guam	N	None
6		460	540	Cabo, Angel D	Brother	M	Cha	49	S	N	N	Guam	N	Lumberman
7		460	541	Reyes, Maria C	Head	F	Cha	52	Wd	N	N	Guam	N	None
8		460	541	Reyes, Francisco C	Son	M	Cha	22	S	N	Y	Guam	Y	Farmer
9		461	542	Fejeran, Vicente C	Head	M	Cha	47	M	N	Y	Guam	N	Farmer
10		461	542	Fejeran, Francisca C	Wife	F	Cha	40	M	N	Y	Guam	N	None
11		461	542	Fejeran, Jose C	Son	M	Cha	10	S	Y	Y	Guam	Y	None
12		461	542	Fejeran, Maria C	Daughter	F	Cha	8	S	Y		Guam		None
13		461	542	Fejeran, Jesus C	Son	M	Cha	5	S	N		Guam		None
14		461	542	Cruz, Bruno F	Father in law	M	Cha	80	Wd	N	N	Guam	N	None
15		462	543	Duenas, Ignacio T	Head	M	Cha	34	M	N	Y	Guam	Y	Farmer
16		462	543	Duenas, Nicolasa P	Wife	F	Cha	31	M	N	Y	Guam	Y	None
17		462	543	Duenas, Roman P	Son	M	Cha	3.1	S	N		Guam		None
18		462	543	Duenas, Asuncion P	Daughter	F	Cha	.7	S	N		Guam		None
19		462	543	Duenas, Juana T	Mother	F	Cha	66	Wd	N	N	Guam	N	None
20		462	543	Duenas, Antonia T	Sister	F	Cha	48	S	N	N	Guam	N	None
21		462	543	Pablo, Jose A	Father in law	M	Cha	70	M	N	N	Guam	N	None
22		462	543	Pablo, Rosa G	Mother in law	F	Cha	64	M	N	N	Guam	N	None
23		462	543	Pablo, Alfonso G	Brother in law	M	Cha	28	S	N	Y	Guam	N	Laborer
24		462	543	Pablo, Ignacio P	Nephew	M	Cha	12	S	Y	Y	Guam	Y	None
25		463	544	Haniu, Maria B	Head	F	Cha	50	Wd	N	Y	Guam	N	None

DEPARTMENT OF COMMERCE-BUREAU OF THE CENSUS
WASHINGTON

FIFTEENTH CENSUS OF THE UNITED STATES: 1930-POPULATION

THE ISLAND OF GUAM

Sheet No. 58B

172B

District Municipality of Agana
Name of Place Agana City (Santa Cruz)
[Proper name and, also, name of class, as city, town, village, barrio, etc]

Enumeration District No. 4
Enumerated by me on May 1, 1930 Vicente Tydingco, Enumerator

	PLACE OF ABODE			NAME	RELATION	PERSONAL DESCRIPTION				EDUCATION		NATIVITY		OCCUPATION
	Street, avenue, road, etc.	Number of dwelling house in order of visitation	Number of family in order of visitation	of each person whose place of abode on April 1, 1930, was in this family. Enter surname, first, then given name and middle initial. If any. Include every person living on April 1, 1930. Omit children born since April 1, 1930.	Relationship of this Person to the head of the family.	Sex	Color or race	Age at last birthday	Single, married, widowed or divorced	Attended school any time since Sept. 1, 1929	Whether able to read and write.	Place of birth of this person.	Whether able to speak English.	
	1	2	3	4	5	6	7	8	9	10	11	12	13	14
26	Legaspi Street	463	544	Haniu, Jesus B	Son	M	Cha	23	S	N	Y	Guam	Y	Clerk
27		463	544	Haniu, Asuncion B	Daughter	F	Cha	22	S	N	Y	Guam	Y	Teacher
28		463	544	Haniu, Jose B	Son	M	Cha	16	S	N	Y	Guam	Y	Clerk
29		463	544	Haniu, Juan B	Son	M	Cha	14	S	Y	Y	Guam	Y	None
30		463	544	Haniu, Fidela B	Daughter	F	Cha	11	S	Y	Y	Guam	Y	None
31		463	544	Haniu, Tidela B	Daughter	F	Cha	7	S	Y		Guam		None
32		463	544	Desa, Nieves L	Mother	F	Cha	77	Wd	N	N	Guam	N	None
33		464	545	Cruz, Francisco LG	Head	M	Cha	50	M	N	Y	Guam	N	Clerk
34		464	545	Cruz, Rosario LG	Wife	F	Cha	46	M	N	Y	Guam	N	None
35		464	545	Leon Guerrero, Antonia A	Sister in law	F	Cha	48	S	N	Y	Guam	N	None
36		465	546	Manibusan, Felix M	Head	M	Cha	52	Wd	N	Y	Guam	N	Farmer
37		465	546	Manibusan, Ana L	Daughter	F	Cha	31	S	N	Y	Guam	N	None
38		465	546	Manibusan, Joaquin L	Son	M	Cha	29	S	N	Y	Guam	Y	Laborer
39		465	546	Manibusan, Rosario L	Daughter	F	Cha	17	S	N	Y	Guam	Y	None
40		465	546	Manibusan, Regina L	Daughter	F	Cha	15	S	N	Y	Guam	Y	None
41		466	547	Feld, Ferne E	Head	F	Cha	27	M	N	Y	Horton, Kansas	Y	Teacher
42		467	548	Leon, Juan M	Head	M	Cha	23	S	N	Y	Guam	Y	Farmer
43		467	548	Leon, Enrique M	Brother	M	Cha	21	S	N	Y	Guam	Y	Farm Laborer
44		467	548	Leon, Lourdes M	Sister	F	Cha	15	S	Y	Y	Guam	Y	None
45	Cristobal Colon St.	468	549	George, Vicente	Head	M	Cha	50	M	N	Y	Guam	Y	Policeman
46		468	549	George, Luisa L	Wife	F	Cha	40	M	N	N	Guam	N	None
47		468	549	George, Pilar L	Daughter	F	Cha	26	S	N	Y	Guam	N	None
48		468	549	George, Rosario L	Daughter	F	Cha	20	S	N	Y	Guam	N	None
49		468	549	George, Rosa L	Daughter	F	Cha	17	S	N	Y	Guam	Y	None
50		468	549	George, Regina L	Daughter	F	Cha	14	S	Y	Y	Guam	Y	None

DEPARTMENT OF COMMERCE-BUREAU OF THE CENSUS
WASHINGTON

FIFTEENTH CENSUS OF THE UNITED STATES: 1930-POPULATION

THE ISLAND OF GUAM

Sheet No. 59A

District Municipality of Agana
Name of Place Agana City (Santa Cruz)
[Proper name and, also, name of class, as city, town, village, barrio, etc]

Enumeration District No. 4
Enumerated by me on May 1, 1930 Vicente Tydingco
Enumerator

	PLACE OF ABODE			NAME	RELATION	PERSONAL DESCRIPTION				EDUCATION		NATIVITY		OCCUPATION
	Street, avenue, road, etc.	Number of dwelling house is order of visitation	Number of family in order of visitation	of each person whose place of abode on April 1, 1930, was in this family. Enter surname, first, then given name and middle initial. If any. Include every person living on April 1, 1930. Omit children born since April 1, 1930.	Relationship of this Person to the head of the family.	Sex	Color or race	Age at last birthday	Single, married, widowed or divorced	Attended school any time since Sept. 1, 1929	Whether able to read and write.	Place of birth of this person.	Whether able to speak English.	
	1	2	3	4	5	6	7	8	9	10	11	12	13	14
1	Cristobal Colon St.	469	550	Santos, Jose A	Head	M	Cha	36	M	N	Y	Guam	Y	Electrician
2		469	550	Santos, Maria LG	Wife	F	Cha	38	M	N	Y	Guam	N	None
3		469	550	Leon Guerrero, Maria R	Step daughter	F	Cha	16	S	Y	Y	Guam	Y	None
4		469	550	Fejeran, Rita LG	Mother in law	F	Cha	67	Wd	N	N	Guam	N	None
5		470	551	Santos, Gervasio I	Head	M	Cha	49	M	N	N	Guam	N	Farmer
6		470	551	Santos, Dolores C	Wife	F	Cha	53	M	N	N	Guam	N	None
7		470	551	Santos, Ana C	Daughter	F	Cha	33	S	N	N	Guam	N	None
8		470	551	Santos, Pedro C	Son	M	Cha	20	S	N	Y	Guam	N	Farm Laborer
9		470	551	Santos, Rosario C	Daughter	F	Cha	16	S	N	Y	Guam	Y	None
10		470	551	Santos, Manuel C	Son	M	Cha	14	S	Y	Y	Guam	Y	None
11		470	551	Santos, Francisco C	Son	M	Cha	9	S	Y		Guam		None
12		471	552	Leon Guerrero, Juan P	Head	M	Cha	16	S	N	Y	Guam	Y	Clerk
13		471	552	Leon Guerrero, Margarita P	Sister	F	Cha	14	S	N	Y	Guam	Y	None
14		471	552	Leon Guerrero, Jose P	Brother	M	Cha	11	S	Y	Y	Guam	Y	None
15		471	552	Leon Guerrero, Felis P	Brother	M	Cha	9	S	Y		Guam		None
16		471	552	Leon Guerrero, Magno P	Brother	M	Cha	6	S	N		Guam		None
17		472	553	Cruz, Maria B	Head	F	Cha	43	Wd	N	Y	Guam	N	None
18		472	553	Cruz, Antonia B	Wife	F	Cha	18	S	Y	Y	Guam	Y	None
19		472	553	Cruz, Maria B	Daughter	F	Cha	16	S	Y	Y	Guam	Y	None
20		472	553	Cruz, Jose B	Son	M	Cha	14	S	Y	Y	Guam	Y	None
21		472	553	Cruz, Jesus B	Son	M	Cha	8	S	Y		Guam		None
22		472	553	Cruz, Rosario B	Daughter	F	Cha	7	S	Y		Guam		None
23		472	554	Manibusan, Francisca B	Head	F	Cha	20	M	N	Y	Guam	Y	Teacher
24		473	555	Leddy, John B	Head	M	W	24	M	N	Y	Guam	Y	Painter
25		473	555	Leddy, Maria S	Wife	F	Cha	20	M	N	Y	Guam	Y	None

DEPARTMENT OF COMMERCE-BUREAU OF THE CENSUS
WASHINGTON

FIFTEENTH CENSUS OF THE UNITED STATES: 1930-POPULATION

THE ISLAND OF GUAM

Sheet No. 59B

173B

District Municipality of Agana
Name of Place Agana City (Santa Cruz)
[Proper name and, also, name of class, as city, town, village, barrio, etc]

Enumeration District No. 4
Enumerated by me on May 2, 1930 Vicente Tydingco
Enumerator

	PLACE OF ABODE			NAME	RELATION	PERSONAL DESCRIPTION				EDUCATION		NATIVITY		OCCUPATION
	Street, avenue, road, etc.	Number of dwelling house is order of visitation	Number of family in order of visitation	of each person whose place of abode on April 1, 1930, was in this family. Enter surname, first, then given name and middle initial. If any. Include every person living on April 1, 1930. Omit children born since April 1, 1930.	Relationship of this Person to the head of the family.	Sex	Color or race	Age at last birthday	Single, married, widowed or divorced	Attended school any time since Sept. 1, 1929	Whether able to read and write.	Place of birth of this person.	Whether able to speak English.	
	1	2	3	4	5	6	7	8	9	10	11	12	13	14
26	Cristobal Colon St.	473	555	Leddy, Henry S	Son	M	Cha	.3	S	N		Guam		None
27		474	556	Morcillas, Jesus D	Head	M	Cha	28	M	N	Y	Guam	Y	Carpenter
28		474	556	Morcillas, Maria P	Wife	F	Cha	29	M	N	Y	Guam	N	None
29		474	556	Morcillas, Dorotea P	Daughter	F	Cha	2.3	S	N		Guam		None
30		474	556	Morcillas, Jose P	Son	M	Cha	.1	S	N		Guam		None
31		474	556	Lujan, Ana L	Niece	F	Cha	3.1	S	N		Guam		None
32		475	557	Borja, Manuel L	Head	M	Cha	33	M	N	Y	Guam	Y	Farmer
33		475	557	Borja, Maria M	Wife	F	Cha	40	M	N	Y	Guam	N	None
34		475	557	Borja, Maria M	Daughter	F	Cha	12	S	Y	Y	Guam	Y	None
35		475	557	Borja, Vicente M	Son	M	Cha	8	S	Y		Guam		None
36		475	557	Borja, Josefina M	Daughter	F	Cha	6	S	N		Guam		None
37		475	557	Borja, Trinidad M	Daughter	F	Cha	5	S	N		Guam		None
38		475	557	Borja, Rosario M	Daughter	F	Cha	2.5	S	N		Guam		None
39		475	557	Borja, Carlos M	Son	M	Cha	1.3	S	N		Guam		None
40		475	557	Borja, Maria L	Mother	F	Cha	69	Wd	N		Guam		None
41		476	558	Lizama, Concepcion C	Head	F	Cha	53	M	N	N	Guam	N	None
42		476	558	Lizama, Remedios C	Daughter	F	Cha	26	S	N	Y	Guam	N	Laundress
43		476	558	Lizama, Florencia C	Daughter	F	Cha	19	S	N	Y	Guam	Y	Servant
44		476	558	Lizama, Juan C	Son	M	Cha	18	S	N	Y	Guam	Y	Farmer
45		476	558	Lizama, Jose C	Son	M	Cha	15	S	Y	Y	Guam	Y	None
46		476	558	Lizama, Joaquina C	Daughter	F	Cha	13	S	Y	Y	Guam	Y	None
47		476	558	Lizama, Bernadita C	Granddaughter	F	Cha	6	S	N		Guam		None
48		478	559	Crisostimo, Dolores C	Sister	F	Cha	51	S	N	N	Guam	N	Basket Weaver
49		478	559	Crisostimo, Vicenta P	Head	F	Cha	57	Wd	N	N	Guam	N	None
50		478	559	Crisostimo, Juan P	Son	M	Cha	23	S	N	Y	Guam	Y	Laborer

DEPARTMENT OF COMMERCE-BUREAU OF THE CENSUS
WASHINGTON

FIFTEENTH CENSUS OF THE UNITED STATES: 1930-POPULATION

THE ISLAND OF GUAM

Sheet No. 60A

174

District Municipality of Agana
Name of Place Agana City (Santa Cruz)
[Proper name and, also, name of class, as city, town, village, barrio, etc]

Enumeration District No. 4
Enumerated by me on May 2, 1930 Vicente Tydingco
Enumerator

	PLACE OF ABODE: Street, avenue, road, etc.	Number of dwelling house in order of visitation	Number of family in order of visitation	NAME of each person whose place of abode on April 1, 1930, was in this family. Enter surname, first, then given name and middle initial. If any. Include every person living on April 1, 1930. Omit children born since April 1, 1930.	RELATION Relationship of this Person to the head of the family.	PERSONAL DESCRIPTION: Sex	Color or race	Age at last birthday	Single, married, widowed or divorced	EDUCATION: Attended school any time since Sept. 1, 1929	Whether able to read and write.	NATIVITY Place of birth of this person.	Whether able to speak English.	OCCUPATION
	1	2	3	4	5	6	7	8	9	10	11	12	13	14
1	Cristobal Colon St.	478	559	Crisostimo, Antonio P	Son	M	Cha	20	S	N	Y	Guam	Y	Teacher
2		478	559	Cruz, Maria R	Aunt	F	Cha	88	Wd	N	N	Guam	N	None
3		479	560	Mesa, Juan C	Head	M	Cha	33	M	N	Y	Guam	N	Farmer
4		479	560	Mesa, Candelaria F	Wife	F	Cha	32	M	N	Y	Guam	N	None
5		479	560	Mesa, Eloterio F	Son	M	Cha	3.2	S	N		Guam		None
6		479	560	Mesa, Marcial F	Son	M	Cha	3.2	S	N		Guam		None
7		479	560	Mesa, Crisostimo F	Son	M	Cha	1.1	S	N		Guam		None
8		480	561	Balajadia, Jose G	Head	M	Cha	22	M	N	Y	Guam		Laborer
9		480	561	Balajadia, Maria R	Wife	F	Cha	19	M	N	Y	Guam		None
10		480	561	Balajadia, Agapito R	Son	M	Cha	.3	S	N		Guam		None
11		481	562	Crisostimo, Jose T	Head	M	Cha	62	Wd	N	Y	Guam	N	Farmer
12		481	562	Crisostimo, Joaquin P	Son	M	Cha	30	S	N	Y	Guam	Y	Carpenter
13		481	562	Crisostimo, Concepcion P	Daughter	F	Cha	22	S	N	Y	Guam	Y	None
14		481	562	Crisostimo, Maria T	Sister	F	Cha	65	S	N	Y	Guam	N	None
15		482	563	Crisostimo, Faustino C	Head	M	Cha	32	M	N	Y	Guam	Y	Farmer
16		482	563	Crisostimo, Maria R	Wife	F	Cha	34	M	N	Y	Guam		None
17		482	563	Crisostimo, Jesus R	Son	M	Cha	2.5	S	N		Guam		None
18		482	563	Crisostimo, Concepcion R	Daughter	F	Cha	1.4	S	N		Guam		None
19		483	564	San Nicolas, Vicente T	Head	M	Cha	32	M	N	Y	Guam	Y	Plumber
20		483	564	San Nicolas, Consalacion C	Wife	F	Cha	28	M	N	Y	Guam	Y	None
21		483	564	San Nicolas, Consalacion C	Daughter	F	Cha	9	S	Y		Guam		None
22		483	564	San Nicolas, Isabel C	Daughter	F	Cha	8	S	Y		Guam		None
23		483	564	San Nicolas, Rosa C	Daughter	F	Cha	6	S	N		Guam		None
24		483	564	San Nicolas, Beatris C	Daughter	F	Cha	5	S	N		Guam		None
25		483	564	San Nicolas, Carmen C	Daughter	F	Cha	3.1	S	N		Guam		None

DEPARTMENT OF COMMERCE-BUREAU OF THE CENSUS
WASHINGTON

FIFTEENTH CENSUS OF THE UNITED STATES: 1930-POPULATION

THE ISLAND OF GUAM

Sheet No. 60B

174B

District **Municipality of Agana**
Name of Place **Agana City (Santa Cruz)**
[Proper name and, also, name of class, as city, town, village, barrio, etc]

Enumeration District No. 4
Enumerated by me on **May 2, 1930** Vicente Tydingco, Enumerator

	PLACE OF ABODE			NAME	RELATION	PERSONAL DESCRIPTION				EDUCATION		NATIVITY		OCCUPATION
	Street, avenue, road, etc.	Number of dwelling house is order of visitation	Number of family in order of visitation	of each person whose place of abode on April 1, 1930, was in this family. Enter surname, first, then given name and middle initial. If any. Include every person living on April 1, 1930. Omit children born since April 1, 1930.	Relationship of this Person to the head of the family.	Sex	Color or race	Age at last birthday	Single, married, widowed or divorced	Attended school any time since Sept. 1, 1929	Whether able to read and write.	Place of birth of this person.	Whether able to speak English.	
	1	2	3	4	5	6	7	8	9	10	11	12	13	14
26	Cristobal Colon St.	483	564	San Nicolas, Josefina C	Daughter	F	Cha	1.1	S	N		Guam		None
27		484	565	Flores, Joaquin D	Head	M	Cha	61	M	N	Y	Guam	N	Farmer
28		484	565	Flores, Maria C	Wife	F	Cha	58	M	N	N	Guam	N	None
29		484	565	Flores, Joaquin C	Son	M	Cha	30	S	N	Y	Guam	Y	Chauffeur
30		484	565	Flores, Dolores C	Daughter	F	Cha	18	S	N	Y	Guam	Y	None
31		484	565	Flores, Engracia C	Daughter	F	Cha	14	S	Y	Y	Guam	Y	None
32		484	566	Flores, Juan C	Head	M	Cha	22	M	N	Y	Guam	Y	Chauffeur
33		484	566	Flores, Antonia N	Wife	F	Cha	20	M	N	Y	Guam	N	None
34		484	566	Flores, Francisco N	Son	M	Cha	.5	S	N		Guam		None
35		485	567	Herrero, Vicente R	Head	M	Cha	72	M	N	Y	Guam	Y	None
36		485	567	Herrero, Rosa SN	Wife	F	Cha	32	M	N	Y	Guam	Y	None
37		485	567	Herrero, Regina SN	Daughter	F	Cha	7	S	Y		Guam		None
38		485	567	Herrero, Beatris SN	Daughter	F	Cha	6	S	N		Guam		None
39		485	567	Herrero, Margarita SN	Daughter	F	Cha	2.5	S	N		Guam		None
40		486	568	Cruz, Jose C	Head	M	Cha	60	Wd	N	Y	Guam	N	Farmer
41		486	568	Cruz, Jose Q	Son	M	Cha	22	S	N	Y	Guam	Y	Farm Laborer
42		486	568	Cruz, Josefa Q	Daughter	F	Cha	20	S	N	Y	Guam	Y	None
43		487	569	Fejeran, Vicente C	Head	M	Cha	27	M	N	Y	Guam	Y	Farmer
44		487	569	Fejeran, Remedios C	Wife	F	Cha	23	M	N	Y	Guam	Y	None
45		487	569	Fejeran, Maria C	Daughter	F	Cha	2.1	S	N		Guam		None
46		487	569	Crisostimo, Marcelo C	Brother in law	M	Cha	18	S	N	Y	Guam	Y	Laborer
47		488	570	Blaz, Antonio B	Head	M	Cha	34	M	N	Y	Guam	Y	Farmer
48		488	570	Blaz, Maria F	Wife	F	Cha	31	M	N	Y	Guam	Y	None
49		488	570	Blaz, Julia F	Daughter	F	Cha	13	S	Y	Y	Guam	Y	None
50		488	570	Blaz, Francisco F	Son	M	Cha	11	S	Y	Y	Guam	Y	None

DEPARTMENT OF COMMERCE-BUREAU OF THE CENSUS
WASHINGTON

FIFTEENTH CENSUS OF THE UNITED STATES: 1930-POPULATION

THE ISLAND OF GUAM

Sheet No. 61A

District **Municipality of Agana**
Name of Place **Agana City (Santa Cruz)**
[Proper name and, also, name of class, as city, town, village, barrio, etc]

Enumeration District No. **4**
Enumerated by me on **May 3, 1930** Vicente Tydingco, Enumerator

	PLACE OF ABODE			NAME	RELATION	PERSONAL DESCRIPTION				EDUCATION		NATIVITY		OCCUPATION
	Street, avenue, road, etc.	Number of dwelling house in order of visitation	Number of family in order of visitation	of each person whose place of abode on April 1, 1930, was in this family. Enter surname, first, then given name and middle initial. If any. Include every person living on April 1, 1930. Omit children born since April 1, 1930.	Relationship of this Person to the head of the family.	Sex	Color or race	Age at last birthday	Single, married, widowed or divorced	Attended school any time since Sept. 1, 1929	Whether able to read and write.	Place of birth of this person.	Whether able to speak English.	
	1	2	3	4	5	6	7	8	9	10	11	12	13	14
1	Cristobal Colon St.	488	570	Blaz, Jesus F	Son	M	Cha	6	S	N		Guam		None
2		488	570	Blaz, Ignacio F	Son	M	Cha	5	S	N		Guam		None
3		489	571	Crisostimo, Josefa P	Head	F	Cha	43	S	N	Y	Guam	N	Seamstress
4		489	571	Crisostimo, Maria P	Sister	F	Cha	41	S	N	Y	Guam	N	None
5		489	571	Crisostimo, Ana P	Sister	F	Cha	28	S	N	Y	Guam	Y	None
6		490	572	Blas, Jesus S	Head	M	Cha	42	M	N	Y	Guam	Y	Labor Foreman
7		490	572	Blas, Rosa C	Wife	F	Cha	39	M	N	Y	Guam	N	None
8		490	572	Blas, Adam C	Son	M	Cha	17	S	N	Y	Guam	Y	Farmer
9		490	572	Blas, Trinidad C	Daughter	F	Cha	15	S	Y	Y	Guam	Y	None
10		490	572	Blas, Manuel C	Son	M	Cha	13	S	Y	Y	Guam	Y	None
11		490	572	Blas, Tomas C	Son	M	Cha	11	S	Y	Y	Guam	Y	None
12		490	572	Blas, Ramona C	Daughter	F	Cha	10	S	Y	Y	Guam	Y	None
13		490	572	Blas, Jesusa C	Daughter	F	Cha	7	S	Y		Guam		None
14		491	573	Pangelinan, Ana P	Head	F	Cha	66	Wd	N	Y	Guam	N	None
15		491	573	Pangelinan, Maria P	Daughter	F	Cha	42	S	N	Y	Guam	N	None
16		491	573	Pangelinan, Francisco P	Son	M	Cha	38	S	N	Y	Guam	Y	Farmer
17		491	573	Pangelinan, Emeterio P	Grandson	M	Cha	10	S	Y	Y	Guam	Y	None
18		492	574	Herrero, Carlos P	Head	M	Cha	30	M	N	Y	Guam	Y	Machinist
19		492	574	Herrero, Lillian J	Wife	F	W	20	M	N	Y	Guam	Y	None
20		493	575	Leon Guerrero, Segundo P	Head	M	Cha	25	M	N	Y	Guam	Y	Machinist
21		493	575	Leon Guerrero, Maria F	Wife	F	Cha	26	M	N	Y	Guam	Y	None
22		493	575	San Agustin, Ana C	Lodger	F	Cha	10	S	Y	Y	Guam	Y	None
23		493	575	San Agustin, Juan C	Lodger	M	Cha	9	S	Y		Guam		None
24		494	576	Uncangco, Baldomero C	Head	M	Cha	69	M	N	N	Guam	N	None
25		494	576	Uncangco, Ana S	Wife	F	Cha	67	M	N	N	Guam	N	None

DEPARTMENT OF COMMERCE-BUREAU OF THE CENSUS
WASHINGTON

FIFTEENTH CENSUS OF THE UNITED STATES: 1930-POPULATION

THE ISLAND OF GUAM

Sheet No. 61B

175B

District Municipality of Agana
Name of Place Agana City (Santa Cruz)
[Proper name and, also, name of class, as city, town, village, barrio, etc]

Enumeration District No. 4
Enumerated by me on May 5, 1930 Vicente Tydingco
Enumerator

	PLACE OF ABODE: Street, avenue, road, etc.	Number of dwelling house in order of visitation	Number of family in order of visitation	NAME of each person whose place of abode on April 1, 1930, was in this family. Enter surname, first, then given name and middle initial. If any. Include every person living on April 1, 1930. Omit children born since April 1, 1930.	RELATION Relationship of this Person to the head of the family.	PERSONAL DESCRIPTION: Sex	Color or race	Age at last birthday	Single, married, widowed or divorced	EDUCATION: Attended school any time since Sept. 1, 1929	Whether able to read and write.	NATIVITY Place of birth of this person.	Whether able to speak English.	OCCUPATION
	1	2	3	4	5	6	7	8	9	10	11	12	13	14
26	Cristobal Colon St.	494	577	Uncangco, Jose S	Head	M	Cha	38	M	N	Y	Guam	N	Farmer
27		494	577	Uncangco, Magdalena S	Wife	F	Cha	28	M	N	Y	Guam	Y	None
28		494	577	Uncangco, Concepcion S	Daughter	F	Cha	17	S	Y	Y	Guam	Y	None
29		494	577	Uncangco, Maria S	Daughter	F	Cha	3.7	S	N		Guam		None
30		494	577	Uncangco, Jesus S	Son	M	Cha	1.4	S	N		Guam		None
31		494	578	Uncangco, Eduardo S	Head	M	Cha	33	M	N	Y	Guam	Y	Laborer
32		494	578	Uncangco, Maria Q	Wife	F	Cha	25	M	N	Y	Guam	N	None
33		494	578	Uncangco, Jesus Q	Son	M	Cha	2.4	S	N		Guam		None
34		494	578	Uncangco, Jose Q	Son	M	Cha	.1	S	N		Guam		None
35		494	578	Montales, Eduardo	Lodger	Fil	Cha	97	Wd	N	N	Phillippine Island	N	None
36		495	579	Sablan, Ana A	Head	F	Cha	72	Wd	N	N	Guam	N	None
37		495	579	Sablan, Jose A	Son	M	Cha	30	S	N	Y	Guam	Y	Farmer
38		496	580	Sablan, Juan A	Head	M	Cha	44	M	N	Y	Guam	N	Farmer
39		496	580	Sablan, Isabel C	Wife	F	Cha	38	M	N	N	Guam	N	None
40		496	580	Sablan, Regina C	Daughter	F	Cha	20	S	N	N	Guam	N	None
41		496	580	Sablan, Jose C	Son	M	Cha	16	S	N	Y	Guam	Y	Farm Laborer
42		496	580	Sablan, Pedro C	Son	M	Cha	14	S	Y	Y	Guam	Y	None
43		496	580	Sablan, Vicente C	Son	M	Cha	13	S	Y	Y	Guam	Y	None
44		496	580	Sablan, Natividad C	Daughter	F	Cha	12	S	Y	Y	Guam	Y	None
45		496	580	Sablan, Francisco C	Son	M	Cha	11	S	Y	Y	Guam	Y	None
46		496	580	Sablan, Rosa C	Daughter	F	Cha	5	S	N		Guam		None
47		496	580	Sablan, Maria C	Daughter	F	Cha	3.3	S	N		Guam		None
48		496	580	Sablan, Rita C	Daughter	F	Cha	1.6	S	N		Guam		None
49		496	580	Sablan, Manuel C	Son	M	Cha	.2	S	N		Guam		None
50		497	581	Pangelinan, Maria C	Head	F	Cha	89	Wd	N	N	Guam	N	None

(CHAMORRO ROOTS GENEALOGY PROJECT™ TRANSCRIPTION)
(BERNARD T. PUNZALAN / HTTP://WWW.CHAMORROROOTS.COM)

DEPARTMENT OF COMMERCE-BUREAU OF THE CENSUS
WASHINGTON

FIFTEENTH CENSUS OF THE UNITED STATES: 1930-POPULATION

THE ISLAND OF GUAM

Sheet No. 62A

District Municipality of Agana
Name of Place Agana City (Santa Cruz)
[Proper name and, also, name of class, as city, town, village, barrio, etc]

Enumeration District No. 4
Enumerated by me on May 5, 1930 Vicente Tydingco
Enumerator

	PLACE OF ABODE			NAME	RELATION	PERSONAL DESCRIPTION				EDUCATION		NATIVITY		OCCUPATION
	Street, avenue, road, etc.	Number of dwelling house in order of visitation	Number of family in order of visitation	of each person whose place of abode on April 1, 1930, was in this family. Enter surname, first, then given name and middle initial. If any. Include every person living on April 1, 1930. Omit children born since April 1, 1930.	Relationship of this Person to the head of the family.	Sex	Color or race	Age at last birthday	Single, married, widowed or divorced	Attended school any time since Sept. 1, 1929	Whether able to read and write.	Place of birth of this person.	Whether able to speak English.	
	1	2	3	4	5	6	7	8	9	10	11	12	13	14
1	Cristobal Colon St.	497	581	Pangelinan, Maria C	Daughter	F	Cha	45	S	N	Y	Guam	N	Laundress
2		497	581	Pangelinan, Maria T	Granddaughter	F	Cha	23	S	N	Y	Guam	Y	Laundress
3		497	581	Mesa, Rita P	Head	F	Cha	62	Wd	N	Y	Guam	N	None
4		498	582	Mesa, Maria P	Daughter	F	Cha	36	S	N	Y	Guam	N	Servant
5		498	582	Mesa, Ana P	Daughter	F	Cha	24	S	N	Y	Guam	N	Cook
6		498	582	Mesa, Remedios P	Daughter	F	Cha	22	S	N	Y	Guam	N	Servant
7		498	582	Uncango, Francisco G	Head	M	Cha	37	M	N	Y	Guam	N	Servant
8		499	583	Uncango, Maria G	Wife	F	Cha	30	M	N	Y	Guam	N	None
9		499	583	Uncango, Maria G	Daughter	F	Cha	4.2	S	N		Guam		None
10		499	583	Uncango, Guadalupe G	Daughter	F	Cha	2.1	S	N		Guam		None
11		499	583	Uncango, Vicenta G	Daughter	F	Cha	1.2	S	N		Guam		None
12		499	583	Uncango, Vicente G	Brother	M	Cha	23	S	N	Y	Guam	N	Laborer
13		500	584	Leon Guerrero, Luisa U	Head	F	Cha	40	Wd	N	Y	Guam	N	Laundress
14		500	584	Leon Guerrero, Dolores U	Daughter	F	Cha	16	S	N	Y	Guam	Y	None
15		500	584	Leon Guerrero, Maria U	Daughter	F	Cha	12	S	Y	Y	Guam	Y	None
16		500	584	Leon Guerrero, Rosa U	Daughter	F	Cha	8	S	Y		Guam		None
17		501	585	Salas, Antonio Q	Head	M	Cha	30	M	N	Y	Guam	Y	Plumber
18		501	585	Salas, Nieves A	Wife	F	Cha	23	M	N	Y	Guam	Y	None
19		501	585	Salas, Juan A	Son	M	Cha	4.5	S	N		Guam		None
20		502	586	Crisostimo, Antonio P	Head	M	Cha	33	M	N	Y	Guam	Y	Farmer
21		502	586	Crisostimo, Maria C	Wife	F	Cha	32	M	N	Y	Guam	N	None
22		502	586	Crisostimo, Pedro C	Son	M	Cha	9	S	Y		Guam		None
23		502	586	Crisostimo, Estoquia C	Daughter	F	Cha	3.5	S	N		Guam		None
24		502	586	Crisostimo, Ramona C	Daughter	F	Cha	1.5	S	N		Guam		None
25		503	587	Gumataotao, Francisco G	Head	M	Cha	73	Wd	N	Y	Guam	N	None

DEPARTMENT OF COMMERCE-BUREAU OF THE CENSUS
WASHINGTON

FIFTEENTH CENSUS OF THE UNITED STATES: 1930-POPULATION

THE ISLAND OF GUAM

Sheet No. 62B

176B

District Municipality of Agana
Name of Place Agana City (Santa Cruz)
[Proper name and, also, name of class, as city, town, village, barrio, etc]

Enumeration District No. 4
Enumerated by me on May 6, 1930 Vicente Tydingco, Enumerator

	PLACE OF ABODE: Street, avenue, road, etc.	Number of dwelling house in order of visitation	Number of family in order of visitation	NAME of each person whose place of abode on April 1, 1930, was in this family. Enter surname, first, then given name and middle initial. If any. Include every person living on April 1, 1930. Omit children born since April 1, 1930.	RELATION Relationship of this Person to the head of the family.	PERSONAL DESCRIPTION: Sex	Color or race	Age at last birthday	Single, married, widowed or divorced	EDUCATION: Attended school any time since Sept. 1, 1929	Whether able to read and write.	NATIVITY Place of birth of this person.	Whether able to speak English.	OCCUPATION
	1	2	3	4	5	6	7	8	9	10	11	12	13	14
26	Cristobal Colon St.	503	587	Gumataotao, Soledad S	Daughter	F	Cha	30	S	N	Y	Guam	N	Laundress
27		504	588	Aguon, Ignacio I	Head	M	Cha	32	M	N	Y	Guam	Y	Servant
28		504	588	Aguon, Maria G	Wife	F	Cha	42	M	N	Y	Guam	Y	None
29		504	588	Aguon, Guadalupe G	Daughter	F	Cha	3.9	S	N		Guam	Y	None
30		504	588	Gumataotao, Antonio S	Step son	M	Cha	21	S	N	Y	Guam	Y	Servant
31	Bailen Street	505	589	Aguon, Juan S	Head	M	Cha	27	M	N	Y	Guam	Y	Clerk
32		505	589	Aguon, Ana P	Wife	F	Cha	26	M	N	Y	Guam	Y	None
33		505	589	Aguon, Ramon P	Son	M	Cha	1.7	S	N		Guam		None
34		505	589	Aguon, Jose P	Son	M	Cha	.2	S	N		Guam		None
35		506	590	Peraira, Juan C	Head	M	Cha	27	M	N	Y	Guam	Y	Plumber
36		506	590	Peraira, Juana P	Wife	F	Cha	27	M	N	Y	Guam	Y	None
37		506	590	Peraira, Maria P	Daughter	F	Cha	.4	S	N		Guam		None
38		507	591	Balajadia, Rosa G	Head	F	Cha	52	Wd	N	Y	Guam	N	None
39		507	591	Balajadia, Jesus G	Son	M	Cha	22	S	N	Y	Guam	Y	Farmer
40		507	591	Balajadia, Olivia G	Daughter	F	Cha	16	S	N	Y	Guam	Y	None
41		507	591	Balajadia, Joaquin G	Son	M	Cha	13	S	Y	Y	Guam	Y	None
42		507	591	Balajadia, Felicita G	Daughter	F	Cha	11	S	Y	Y	Guam	Y	None
43		508	592	Balajadia, Juan G	Head	M	Cha	26	M	N	Y	Guam	Y	Laborer
44		508	592	Balajadia, Anunciacion Q	Wife	F	Cha	22	M	N	Y	Guam	N	None
45		508	592	Balajadia, Priscilla Q	Daughter	F	Cha	.7	S	N		Guam		None
46		509	593	Pangelinan, Jose C	Head	M	Cha	50	M	N	N	Guam	N	Farmer
47		509	593	Pangelinan, Rita L	Wife	F	Cha	57	M	N	N	Guam	N	None
48		509	593	Pangelinan, Valeria L	Daughter	F	Cha	24	S	N	Y	Guam	N	None
49		509	593	Pangelinan, Concepcion L	Daughter	F	Cha	21	S	N	Y	Guam	Y	None
50		509	593	Pangelinan, Lorenzo L	Son	M	Cha	19	S	N	Y	Guam	Y	Farm Laborer

DEPARTMENT OF COMMERCE-BUREAU OF THE CENSUS
WASHINGTON

FIFTEENTH CENSUS OF THE UNITED STATES: 1930-POPULATION

THE ISLAND OF GUAM

Sheet No. 63A

District Municipality of Agana
Name of Place Agana City (Santa Cruz)
[Proper name and, also, name of class, as city, town, village, barrio, etc]

Enumeration District No. 4
Enumerated by me on May 6, 1930 Vicente Tydingco
Enumerator

	PLACE OF ABODE			NAME	RELATION	PERSONAL DESCRIPTION				EDUCATION		NATIVITY		OCCUPATION
	Street, avenue, road, etc.	Number of dwelling house in order of visitation	Number of family in order of visitation	of each person whose place of abode on April 1, 1930, was in this family. Enter surname, first, then given name and middle initial. If any. Include every person living on April 1, 1930. Omit children born since April 1, 1930.	Relationship of this Person to the head of the family.	Sex	Color or race	Age at last birthday	Single, married, widowed or divorced	Attended school any time since Sept. 1, 1929	Whether able to read and write.	Place of birth of this person.	Whether able to speak English.	
	1	2	3	4	5	6	7	8	9	10	11	12	13	14
1	Bailen Street	509	593	Pangelinan, Luisa L	Daughter	F	Cha	15	S	Y	Y	Guam	Y	None
2		509	593	Pangelinan, Rosario L	Daughter	F	Cha	13	S	Y	Y	Guam	Y	None
3		509	593	Pangelinan, Rosalia L	Daughter	F	Cha	12	S	Y	Y	Guam	Y	None
4		509	593	Pangelinan, Francisca L	Daughter	F	Cha	10	S	Y	Y	Guam	Y	None
5		509	593	Pangelinan, Jesus L	Son	M	Cha	8	S	Y		Guam		None
6		510	594	Pangelinan, Francisco C	Head	M	Cha	46	M	N	Y	Guam	N	Farmer
7		510	594	Pangelinan, Maria D	Wife	F	Cha	50	M	N	N	Guam	N	None
8		510	594	Dimapan, Mercedes S	Niece	F	Cha	12	S	Y	Y	Guam	Y	None
9		511	595	Mesa, Adriano C	Head	M	Cha	39	M	N	Y	Guam	Y	Merchant
10		511	595	Mesa, Susana B	Wife	F	Cha	35	M	N	Y	Guam	Y	Saleswoman
11		512	596	Pangelinan, Josefa C	Head	F	Cha	67	Wd	N	N	Guam	N	Laundress
12		513	597	Balajadia, Luis LG	Head	M	Cha	75	Wd	N	N	Guam	N	None
13		514	598	Cruz, Manuel B	Head	M	Cha	24	M	N	Y	Guam	Y	Machinist
14		514	598	Cruz, Misaericordia S	Wife	F	Cha	19	M	N	Y	Guam	Y	None
15		515	599	Bamba, Jesus B	Head	M	Cha	36	M	N	Y	Guam	Y	Farmer
16		515	599	Bamba, Magdalena S	Wife	F	Cha	29	M	N	Y	Guam	N	None
17		515	599	Bamba, Magdalena S	Daughter	F	Cha	8	S	Y		Guam		None
18		515	599	Bamba, Antonio S	Son	M	Cha	5	S	N		Guam		None
19		515	599	Bamba, Ana S	Daughter	F	Cha	3.5	S	N		Guam		None
20		515	599	Bamba, Concepcion S	Daughter	F	Cha	.8	S	N		Guam		None
21		515	599	Bamba, Maria B	Mother	F	Cha	88	S	N	N	Guam	N	None
22		516	600	Sablan, Manuel L	Head	M	Cha	32	S	N	Y	Guam	Y	Laborer
23		516	600	Sablan, Nivest L	Mother	F	Cha	65	Wd	N	Y	Guam	N	None
24		517	601	Sablan, Jesus L	Head	M	Cha	29	M	N	Y	Guam	N	Farmer
25		517	601	Sablan, Ana P	Wife	F	Cha	27	M	N	Y	Guam	N	None

DEPARTMENT OF COMMERCE-BUREAU OF THE CENSUS
WASHINGTON

FIFTEENTH CENSUS OF THE UNITED STATES: 1930-POPULATION

THE ISLAND OF GUAM

Sheet No. 63B

177B

District **Municipality of Agana**
Name of Place **Agana City (Santa Cruz)**
[Proper name and, also, name of class, as city, town, village, barrio, etc]

Enumeration District No. 4
Enumerated by me on May 7, 1930 Vicente Tydingco
Enumerator

	PLACE OF ABODE			NAME	RELATION	PERSONAL DESCRIPTION				EDUCATION		NATIVITY		OCCUPATION
	Street, avenue, road, etc.	Number of dwelling house is order of visitation	Number of family in order of visitation	of each person whose place of abode on April 1, 1930, was in this family. Enter surname, first, then given name and middle initial. If any. Include every person living on April 1, 1930. Omit children born since April 1, 1930.	Relationship of this Person to the head of the family.	Sex	Color or race	Age at last birthday	Single, married, widowed or divorced	Attended school any time since Sept. 1, 1929	Whether able to read and write.	Place of birth of this person.	Whether able to speak English.	
	1	2	3	4	5	6	7	8	9	10	11	12	13	14
26	Bailen Street	517	601	Sablan, Jose P	Son	M	Cha	8	S	Y		Guam		None
27		517	601	Sablan, Dolores P	Daughter	F	Cha	6	S	N		Guam		None
28		517	601	Sablan, Jesus P	Son	M	Cha	4.1	S	N		Guam		None
29		517	601	Sablan, Joaquin P	Son	M	Cha	2.5	S	N		Guam		None
30		518	602	Perez, Vicente B	Head	M	Cha	22	M	N	Y	Guam	Y	Carpenter
31		518	602	Perez, Maria P	Wife	F	Cha	21	M	N	Y	Guam	Y	None
32		518	602	Perez, Norberto P	Son	M	Cha	3.1	S	N		Guam		None
33		518	602	Perez, Elizabeth P	Daughter	F	Cha	1.3	S	N		Guam		None
34		519	603	Camacho, Joaquina	Head	F	Cha	64	S	N	N	Guam	N	Laundress
35		520	604	Cruz, Ignacio M	Head	M	Cha	62	M	N	N	Guam	N	Farmer
36		520	604	Cruz, Ana P	Wife	F	Cha	61	M	N	N	Guam	N	None
37		520	604	Cruz, Jose P	Son	M	Cha	35	S	N	Y	Guam	Y	Rigger
38		520	604	Cruz, Vicente P	Son	M	Cha	30	S	N	Y	Guam	Y	Farm Laborer
39		520	604	Cruz, Juan P	Son	M	Cha	21	S	N	Y	Guam	Y	None
40		520	605	Lizama, Jose F	Head	M	Cha	35	M	N	Y	Guam	Y	Rigger
41		520	605	Lizama, Dolores P	Wife	F	Cha	33	M	N	Y	Guam	N	None
42		520	605	Lizama, Petronila P	Daughter	F	Cha	5	S	N		Guam		None
43		520	605	Lizama, Marta P	Daughter	F	Cha	3.3	S	N		Guam		None
44		520	605	Lizama, Juan P	Son	M	Cha	.5	S	N		Guam		None
45		521	606	Lazaro, Manuel R	Head	M	Cha	32	S	N	Y	Guam	Y	Salesman
46		522	607	Leon Guerrero, Jose D	Head	M	Cha	18	S	N	Y	Guam	Y	Messenger
47		522	607	Leon Guerrero, Vicente D	Brother	M	Cha	17	S	N	Y	Guam	Y	Messenger
48				Here ends the enumeration of enumeration district No. 4 Santa Cruz										
49														
50														

District 5
Municipality of Agana

Barrigada Barrio
Dededo Barrio
Machanaonao Barrio
Sinajana Barrio
Tutujan Barrio
Yigo Barrio

DEPARTMENT OF COMMERCE-BUREAU OF THE CENSUS
WASHINGTON

FIFTEENTH CENSUS OF THE UNITED STATES: 1930-POPULATION

THE ISLAND OF GUAM

Sheet No. 1A

District **Municipality of Agana**
Name of Place **Barrigada Barrio**
[Proper name and, also, name of class, as city, town, village, barrio, etc]

Enumeration District No. **5**
Enumerated by me on **April 2, 1930** Jose Kamminga
Enumerator

	PLACE OF ABODE: Street, avenue, road, etc.	Number of dwelling house in order of visitation	Number of family in order of visitation	NAME of each person whose place of abode on April 1, 1930, was in this family. Enter surname, first, then given name and middle initial. If any. Include every person living on April 1, 1930. Omit children born since April 1, 1930.	RELATION Relationship of this Person to the head of the family.	PERSONAL DESCRIPTION: Sex	Color or race	Age at last birthday	Single, married, widowed or divorced	EDUCATION: Attended school any time since Sept. 1, 1929	Whether able to read and write.	NATIVITY Place of birth of this person.	Whether able to speak English.	OCCUPATION
	1	2	3	4	5	6	7	8	9	10	11	12	13	14
1	Barrigada Barrio	1	1	San Nicolas, Vicente U	Head	M	Cha	48	M	N	N	Guam	N	Carpenter
2		1	1	San Nicolas, Ignacia A	Wife	F	Cha	42	M	N	N	Guam	N	None
3		1	1	San Nicolas, Luis A	Son	M	Cha	17	S	N	Y	Guam	Y	Laborer
4		1	1	San Nicolas, Amali A	Daughter	F	Cha	9	S	Y		Guam		None
5		1	1	San Nicolas, Candido A	Son	M	Cha	6	S	N		Guam		None
6		1	1	San Nicolas, Redusindo A	Son	M	Cha	1.1	S	N		Guam		None
7		1	1	San Nicolas, Ana A	Daughter	F	Cha	.1	S	N		Guam		None
8		2	2	Santos, Mariano C	Head	M	Cha	39	M	N	Y	Guam	N	Farmer
9		2	2	Santos, Teodora B	Wife	F	Cha	36	M	N	Y	Guam	N	None
10		2	2	Santos, Josefa B	Daughter	F	Cha	11	S	Y	Y	Guam	Y	None
11		2	2	Santos, Jesus B	Son	M	Cha	7	S	Y		Guam		None
12		2	2	Santos, Maria B	Daughter	F	Cha	4.1	S	N		Guam		None
13		2	2	Santos, Isabel B	Daughter	F	Cha	.8	S	N		Guam		None
14		3	3	Cruz, Vicente M	Head	M	Cha	69	M	N	Y	Guam	N	Farmer
15		3	3	Cruz, Josefa P	Wife	F	Cha	63	M	N	Y	Guam	N	None
16		3	3	Cruz, Manuel C	Nephew	M	Cha	13	S	N	Y	Guam	Y	None
17		3	3	Cruz, Josefa C	Nephew	M	Cha	11	S	Y	Y	Guam	Y	None
18		3	4	Perez, Manuel T	Head	M	Cha	49	Wd	N	N	Guam	N	Farmer
19		4	5	Reyes, Vicente C	Head	M	Cha	59	M	N	Y	Guam	N	Farmer
20		4	5	Reyes, Ana D	Wife	F	Cha	58	M	N	N	Guam	N	None
21		5	6	Blas, Jose A	Head	M	Cha	78	M	N	Y	Guam	Y	Farmer
22		5	6	Blas, Dolores C	Wife	F	Cha	70	M	N	Y	Guam	Y	None
23		5	6	Cruz, Julia M	Servant	F	Cha	9	S	Y		Guam		None
24		6	7	Blas, Antonio L	Head	M	Cha	55	M	N	Y	Guam	N	Farmer
25		6	7	Blas, Tomasa E	Wife	F	Cha	62	M	N	Y	Guam	N	None

DEPARTMENT OF COMMERCE-BUREAU OF THE CENSUS
WASHINGTON

FIFTEENTH CENSUS OF THE UNITED STATES: 1930-POPULATION

THE ISLAND OF GUAM

Sheet No. 1B

178B

District Municipality of Agana
Name of Place Barrigada Barrio
[Proper name and, also, name of class, as city, town, village, barrio, etc]

Enumeration District No. 5
Enumerated by me on April 2, 1930 Jose Kamminga, Enumerator

	PLACE OF ABODE: Street, avenue, road, etc.	Number of dwelling house in order of visitation	Number of family in order of visitation	NAME of each person whose place of abode on April 1, 1930, was in this family. Enter surname, first, then given name and middle initial. If any. Include every person living on April 1, 1930. Omit children born since April 1, 1930.	RELATION Relationship of this Person to the head of the family.	PERSONAL DESCRIPTION: Sex	Color or race	Age at last birthday	Single, married, widowed or divorced	EDUCATION: Attended school any time since Sept. 1, 1929	Whether able to read and write.	NATIVITY Place of birth of this person.	Whether able to speak English.	OCCUPATION
	1	2	3	4	5	6	7	8	9	10	11	12	13	14
26	Barrigada Barrio	7	8	Borja, Ignacio S	Head	M	Cha	34	S	N	Y	Guam	Y	Farmer
27		7	9	Manibusan, Nicolasa P	Head	F	Cha	29	S	N	Y	Guam	Y	None
28		7	9	Manibusan, Rosa P	Daughter	M	Cha	7	S	Y		Guam		None
29		7	9	Manibusan, Francisco P	Son	M	Cha	4.7	S	N		Guam		None
30		7	9	Manibusan, Doroteo P	Son	M	Cha	4.7	S	N		Guam		None
31		7	9	Manibusan, Segundo P	Son	M	Cha	1.8	S	N		Guam		None
32		7	9	Manibusan, Tomasa P	Daughter	F	Cha	.1	S	N		Guam		None
33		8	10	Flores, Ana G	Head	F	Cha	50	S	N	Y	Guam	N	Farmer
34		8	10	Quidachay, Timoteo Q	Servant	M	Cha	5	S	N		Guam		None
35		9	11	Perez, Juan P	Head	M	Cha	54	M	N	Y	Guam	N	Farmer
36		10	12	Munoz, Manuel C	Head	M	Cha	32	M	N	Y	Guam	Y	Farmer
37		10	12	Munoz, Maria T	Wife	F	Cha	26	M	N	Y	Guam	Y	None
38		10	12	Munoz, Isabel T	Daughter	F	Cha	3.2	S	N		Guam		None
39		10	12	Munoz, Ana T	Daughter	F	Cha	1.9	S	N		Guam		None
40		10	12	Munoz, Maria T	Daughter	F	Cha	.6	S	N		Guam		None
41		11	13	Tenorio, Jose M	Head	M	Cha	64	S	N	Y	Guam	Y	Farmer
42		12	14	Manibusan, Jose T	Head	M	Cha	45	M	N	Y	Guam	N	Farmer
43		12	14	Manibusan, Dolores B	Wife	F	Cha	53	M	N	N	Guam	N	None
44		13	15	Palacios, Juan T	Head	M	Cha	47	D	N	Y	Guam	N	Farmer
45		14	16	Camacho, Joaquin O	Head	M	Cha	27	S	N	Y	Guam	Y	Farmer
46		15	17	Santos, Ana M	Head	F	Cha	57	Wd	N	Y	Guam	N	None
47		15	17	Santos, Pedro M	Son	M	Cha	18	S	N	Y	Guam	Y	Farm laborer
48		15	17	Santos, Rosa M	Daughter	F	Cha	16	S	N	Y	Guam	Y	Laundress
49		15	17	Santos, Juana M	Daughter	F	Cha	13	S	Y	Y	Guam	Y	None
50		15	17	Santos, Juan M	Son	M	Cha	11	S	Y	Y	Guam	Y	None

DEPARTMENT OF COMMERCE-BUREAU OF THE CENSUS
WASHINGTON

FIFTEENTH CENSUS OF THE UNITED STATES: 1930-POPULATION

THE ISLAND OF GUAM

Sheet No. 2A

District **Municipality of Agana**
Name of Place **Barrigada Barrio**
[Proper name and, also, name of class, as city, town, village, barrio, etc]

Enumeration District No. 5
Enumerated by me on **April 2, 1930** Jose Kamminga, Enumerator

	PLACE OF ABODE			NAME	RELATION	PERSONAL DESCRIPTION				EDUCATION		NATIVITY		OCCUPATION
	Street, avenue, road, etc.	Number of dwelling house is order of visitation	Number of family in order of visitation	of each person whose place of abode on April 1, 1930, was in this family. Enter surname, first, then given name and middle initial. If any. Include every person living on April 1, 1930. Omit children born since April 1, 1930.	Relationship of this Person to the head of the family.	Sex	Color or race	Age at last birthday	Single, married, widowed or divorced	Attended school any time since Sept. 1, 1929	Whether able to read and write.	Place of birth of this person.	Whether able to speak English.	
	1	2	3	4	5	6	7	8	9	10	11	12	13	14
1	Barrigada Barrio	16	18	Crisostomo, Mariano B	Head	M	Cha	50	M	N	Y	Guam	N	Farmer
2		16	18	Crisostomo, Juana S	Wife	F	Cha	53	M	N	N	Guam	N	None
3		16	18	Crisostomo, Juana S	Daughter	F	Cha	17	S	N	N	Guam	N	Farm laborer
4		16	18	Crisostomo, Lourdes S	Daughter	F	Cha	15	S	N	N	Guam	N	None
5		16	18	Crisostomo, Vicente S	Son	M	Cha	9	S	Y		Guam		None
6		17	19	Baza, Agustin U	Head	M	Cha	47	Wd	N	Y	Guam	N	Farmer
7		18	20	Manibusan, Jose P	Head	M	Cha	32	M	N	N	Guam	N	Farmer
8		18	20	Manibusan, Ignacia A	Wife	F	Cha	32	M	N	Y	Guam	N	None
9		18	20	Manibusan, Filomena A	Daughter	F	Cha	13	S	Y	Y	Guam	N	None
10		18	20	Manibusan, Juan A	Son	M	Cha	6	S	N		Guam		None
11		18	20	Manibusan, Isabel A	Daughter	F	Cha	4.3	S	N		Guam		None
12		18	20	Manibusan, Jose A	Son	M	Cha	3.8	S	N		Guam		None
13		18	20	Manibusan, Ana A	Daughter	F	Cha	.9	S	N		Guam		None
14		19	21	Cruz, Dolores M	Head	F	Cha	57	M	N	N	Guam	N	None
15		19	21	Pangelinan, Jose M	Son	M	Cha	18	S	N	N	Guam	N	Farm laborer
16		20	22	Rabon, Joaquin C	Head	M	Cha	31	M	N	N	Guam	N	Farmer
17		20	22	Rabon, Luisa LG	Wife	F	Cha	45	M	N	Y	Guam	N	None
18		20	22	Rabon, Jesus LG	Son	M	Cha	9	S	Y		Guam		None
19		20	22	Rabon, Jose LG	Son	M	Cha	5.7	S	N		Guam		None
20		21	23	Ogo, Jose T	Head	M	Cha	33	M	N	Y	Guam	Y	Farmer
21		21	23	Ogo, Maria M	Wife	F	Cha	25	M	N	Y	Guam	N	None
22		21	23	Ogo, Pedro M	Son	M	Cha	4.3	S	N		Guam		None
23		21	23	Ogo, Antonia M	Daughter	F	Cha	3.9	S	N		Guam		None
24		22	24	Manibusan, Antonio S	Head	M	Cha	45	M	N	N	Guam	N	Farmer
25		22	24	Manibusan, Ignaica M	Wife	F	Cha	52	M	N	N	Guam	N	None

DEPARTMENT OF COMMERCE-BUREAU OF THE CENSUS
WASHINGTON

FIFTEENTH CENSUS OF THE UNITED STATES: 1930-POPULATION

THE ISLAND OF GUAM

Sheet No. 2B

179B

District **Municipality of Agana**
Name of Place **Barrigada Barrio**
[Proper name and, also, name of class, as city, town, village, barrio, etc]

Enumeration District No. 5
Enumerated by me on **April 3, 1930** Jose Kamminga
Enumerator

	PLACE OF ABODE			NAME	RELATION	PERSONAL DESCRIPTION				EDUCATION		NATIVITY		OCCUPATION
	Street, avenue, road, etc.	Number of dwelling house is order of visitation	Number of family in order of visitation	of each person whose place of abode on April 1, 1930, was in this family. Enter surname, first, then given name and middle initial. If any. Include every person living on April 1, 1930. Omit children born since April 1, 1930.	Relationship of this Person to the head of the family.	Sex	Color or race	Age at last birthday	Single, married, widowed or divorced	Attended school any time since Sept. 1, 1929	Whether able to read and write.	Place of birth of this person.	Whether able to speak English.	
	1	2	3	4	5	6	7	8	9	10	11	12	13	14
26	Barrigada Barrio	23	25	Villagomez, Juan C	Head	M	Cha	42	M	N	Y	Guam	N	Farmer
27		23	25	Villagomez, Josefa T	Wife	F	Cha	34	M	N	Y	Guam	N	None
28		23	25	Villagomez, Rosabella T	Daughter	F	Cha	15	S	N	Y	Guam	Y	None
29		23	25	Villagomez, Francisco T	Son	M	Cha	13	S	Y	Y	Guam	Y	None
30		23	25	Villagomez, Gregorio T	Son	M	Cha	11	S	Y	Y	Guam	Y	None
31		23	25	Villagomez, Maria T	Son	M	Cha	9	S	Y		Guam		None
32		23	25	Villagomez, Concepcion T	Daughter	F	Cha	5.3	S	N		Guam		None
33		23	25	Villagomez, Jose T	Son	M	Cha	3.2	S	N		Guam		None
34		23	25	Villagomez, Juan T	Son	M	Cha	.3	S	N		Guam		None
35		24	26	Pangelinan, Silvino D	Head	M	Cha	54	M	N	Y	Guam	Y	Farmer
36		24	26	Pangelinan, Maria P	Wife	F	Cha	53	M	N	Y	Guam	N	None
37		25	27	Rabon, Jose C	Head	M	Cha	35	M	N	Y	Guam	Y	Farmer
38		25	27	Rabon, Antonia B	Wife	F	Cha	29	M	N	Y	Guam	Y	None
39		25	27	Rabon, Jesus B	Son	M	Cha	7	S	Y		Guam		None
40		26	28	Munoz, Jose I	Head	M	Cha	25	M	N	Y	Guam	Y	Farmer
41		26	28	Munoz, Elena G	Wife	F	Cha	26	M	N	Y	Guam	Y	None
42		27	29	Santos, Soledad S	Head	F	Cha	52	S	N	Y	Guam	N	None
43		27	30	Blas, Jose C	Head	M	Cha	30	M	N	Y	Guam	N	Farmer
44		27	30	Blas, Soledad M	Wife	F	Cha	23	M	N	Y	Guam	N	None
45		27	30	Blas, Juan M	Son	M	Cha	5.4	S	N		Guam		None
46		27	30	Blas, Maria M	Daughter	F	Cha	4.3	S	N		Guam		None
47		27	30	Blas, Vicenta M	Daughter	F	Cha	2.8	S	N		Guam		None
48		28	31	Garrido, Jose M	Head	M	Cha	36	M	N	Y	Guam	N	Farmer
49		28	31	Garrido, Maria B	Wife	F	Cha	35	M	N	Y	Guam	N	None
50		28	31	Garrido, Enrique B	Son	M	Cha	13	S	Y	Y	Guam	Y	None

(CHAMORRO ROOTS GENEALOGY PROJECT™ TRANSCRIPTION)
(BERNARD T. PUNZALAN / HTTP://WWW.CHAMORROROOTS.COM)

DEPARTMENT OF COMMERCE-BUREAU OF THE CENSUS
WASHINGTON

FIFTEENTH CENSUS OF THE UNITED STATES: 1930-POPULATION

THE ISLAND OF GUAM

Sheet No. 3A

180

District **Municipality of Agana**
Name of Place **Barrigada Barrio**
[Proper name and, also, name of class, as city, town, village, barrio, etc]

Enumeration District No. 5
Enumerated by me on **April 3, 1930** Jose Kamminga
Enumerator

	PLACE OF ABODE: Street, avenue, road, etc.	Number of dwelling house in order of visitation	Number of family in order of visitation	NAME of each person whose place of abode on April 1, 1930, was in this family. Enter surname, first, then given name and middle initial. If any. Include every person living on April 1, 1930. Omit children born since April 1, 1930.	RELATION Relationship of this Person to the head of the family.	PERSONAL DESCRIPTION: Sex	Color or race	Age at last birthday	Single, married, widowed or divorced	EDUCATION: Attended school any time since Sept. 1, 1929	Whether able to read and write.	NATIVITY Place of birth of this person.	Whether able to speak English.	OCCUPATION
	1	2	3	4	5	6	7	8	9	10	11	12	13	14
1	Barrigada Barrio	28	31	Garrido, Jesus B	Son	M	Cha	12	S	Y	Y	Guam	Y	None
2		28	31	Garrido, Antonia B	Daughter	F	Cha	11	S	Y	Y	Guam	Y	None
3		28	31	Garrido, Jose B	Son	M	Cha	8	S	Y		Guam		None
4		28	31	Garrido, Manuel B	Son	M	Cha	4.4	S	N		Guam		None
5		28	31	Garrido, Prudencio B	Son	M	Cha	3	S	N		Guam		None
6		28	31	Garrido, Margarita B	Daughter	F	Cha	1.3	S	N		Guam		None
7		29	32	Bontugan, Antonio C	Head	M	Cha	39	M	N	Y	Guam	Y	Farmer
8		29	32	Bontugan, Francisca F	Wife	F	Cha	31	M	N	Y	Guam	Y	None
9		30	33	Santos, Joaquin B	Head	M	Cha	54	M	N	Y	Guam	N	Farmer
10		30	33	Santos, Ana SN	Wife	F	Cha	64	M	N	N	Guam	N	None
11		30	33	Benavente, Maria SN	Step-daughter	F	Cha	32	S	N	Y	Guam	Y	None
12		31	34	Salas, Mariano SN	Head	M	Cha	29	M	N	Y	Guam	Y	Farmer
13		31	34	Salas, Maria M	Wife	F	Cha	28	M	N	Y	Guam	Y	None
14		31	34	Salas, Manuela M	Daughter	F	Cha	4.7	S	N		Guam		None
15		31	34	Salas, Jose M	Son	M	Cha	2.9	S	N		Guam		None
16		31	34	Salas, Juan M	Son	M	Cha	1.8	S	N		Guam		None
17		31	34	Salas, Jesus M	Son	M	Cha	.6	S	N		Guam		None
18		32	35	Pangelinan, Matias M	Head	M	Cha	25	M	N	Y	Guam	Y	Farmer
19		32	35	Pangelinan, Josefa Q	Wife	F	Cha	23	M	N	Y	Guam	N	None
20		33	36	Cruz, Juan F	Head	M	Cha	35	S	N	Y	Guam	Y	Farmer
21		33	37	Atao, Ana M	Head	F	Cha	41	S	N	N	Guam	N	None
22		33	37	Atao, Dolores A	Daughter	F	Cha	17	S	N	Y	Guam	Y	Servant
23		33	37	Atao, Juan A	Son	M	Cha	15	S	N	Y	Guam	Y	Farm laborer
24		34	38	Pangelinan, Juana B	Head	F	Cha	31	M	N	N	Guam	N	Laundress
25		34	38	Pangelinan, Maria B	Daughter	F	Cha	14	S	N	Y	Guam	Y	Servant

DEPARTMENT OF COMMERCE-BUREAU OF THE CENSUS
WASHINGTON

FIFTEENTH CENSUS OF THE UNITED STATES: 1930-POPULATION

THE ISLAND OF GUAM

Sheet No. 3B

180B

District Municipality of Agana
Name of Place Barrigada Barrio
[Proper name and, also, name of class, as city, town, village, barrio, etc]

Enumeration District No. 5
Enumerated by me on April 4, 1930 Jose Kamminga
Enumerator

	PLACE OF ABODE: Street, avenue, road, etc.	Number of dwelling house is order of visitation	Number of family in order of visitation	NAME of each person whose place of abode on April 1, 1930, was in this family. Enter surname, first, then given name and middle initial. If any. Include every person living on April 1, 1930. Omit children born since April 1, 1930.	RELATION Relationship of this Person to the head of the family.	PERSONAL DESCRIPTION: Sex	Color or race	Age at last birthday	Single, married, widowed or divorced	EDUCATION: Attended school any time since Sept. 1, 1929	Whether able to read and write.	NATIVITY Place of birth of this person.	Whether able to speak English.	OCCUPATION
	1	2	3	4	5	6	7	8	9	10	11	12	13	14
26	Barrigada Barrio	34	38	Pangelinan, Barcelisa B	Daughter	F	Cha	12	S	Y	Y	Guam	Y	None
27		34	38	Pangelinan, Joaquin B	Son	M	Cha	9	S	Y		Guam		None
28		34	38	Pangelinan, Jose B	Son	M	Cha	7	S	Y		Guam		None
29		35	39	Pereda, Juan S	Head	M	Cha	49	M	N	N	Guam	N	Farmer
30		35	39	Pereda, Josefa B	Wife	F	Cha	50	M	N	N	Guam	N	None
31		35	39	Pereda, Josefa B	Daughter	F	Cha	19	S	N	Y	Guam	Y	None
32		35	39	Pereda, Jose B	Son	M	Cha	16	S	N	Y	Guam	Y	Farm laborer
33		36	40	Cepeda, Vicente S	Head	M	Cha	55	M	N	N	Guam	N	Farmer
34		36	40	Cepeda, Joaquina B	Wife	F	Cha	61	M	N	N	Guam	N	None
35		37	41	Mendiola, Mariano	Head	M	Cha	34	M	N	Y	Guam	Y	Farmer
36		37	41	Mendiola, Antonia P	Wife	F	Cha	46	M	N	Y	Guam	Y	None
37		37	41	Mendiola, Maria P	Daughter	F	Cha	7	S	Y		Guam		None
38		37	41	Mendiola, Francisco P	Son	M	Cha	6	S	N		Guam		None
39		37	41	Mendiola, Juan P	Son	M	Cha	5.4	S	N		Guam		None
40		37	41	Mendiola, Serafina P	Daughter	F	Cha	3.7	S	N		Guam		None
41		37	41	Mendiola, Precilia P	Daughter	F	Cha	2.2	S	N		Guam		None
42		37	41	Mendiola, Antonia P	Daughter	F	Cha	.8	S	N		Guam		None
43		38	47	Camacho, Vicente R	Head	M	Cha	30	M	N	Y	Guam	Y	Farmer
44		38	47	Camacho, Dolores C	Wife	F	Cha	26	M	N	Y	Guam	Y	None
45		38	47	Camacho, Jose C	Son	M	Cha	5.4	S	N		Guam		None
46		38	47	Camacho, Maria C	Daughter	F	Cha	9.8	S	N		Guam		None
47		38	47	Camacho, Felicita C	Daughter	F	Cha	3.1	S	N		Guam		None
48		39	48	Blas, Jose T	Head	M	Cha	67	Wd	N	N	Guam	N	Farmer
49		39	48	Blas, Guido F	Son	M	Cha	35	S	N	N	Guam	N	Farm laborer
50		39	48	Blas, Jose F	Son	M	Cha	23	S	N	Y	Guam	Y	Farm laborer

(CHAMORRO ROOTS GENEALOGY PROJECT™ TRANSCRIPTION)
(BERNARD T. PUNZALAN / HTTP://WWW.CHAMORROROOTS.COM)

DEPARTMENT OF COMMERCE-BUREAU OF THE CENSUS
WASHINGTON

FIFTEENTH CENSUS OF THE UNITED STATES: 1930-POPULATION

THE ISLAND OF GUAM

Sheet No. 4A

District Municipality of Agana
Name of Place Barrigada Barrio
[Proper name and, also, name of class, as city, town, village, barrio, etc]

Enumeration District No. 5
Enumerated by me on April 4, 1930 Jose Kamminga
Enumerator

	PLACE OF ABODE			NAME	RELATION	PERSONAL DESCRIPTION				EDUCATION		NATIVITY		OCCUPATION
	Street, avenue, road, etc.	Number of dwelling house is order of visitation	Number of family in order of visitation	of each person whose place of abode on April 1, 1930, was in this family. Enter surname, first, then given name and middle initial. If any. Include every person living on April 1, 1930. Omit children born since April 1, 1930.	Relationship of this Person to the head of the family.	Sex	Color or race	Age at last birthday	Single, married, widowed or divorced	Attended school any time since Sept. 1, 1929	Whether able to read and write.	Place of birth of this person.	Whether able to speak English.	
	1	2	3	4	5	6	7	8	9	10	11	12	13	14
1	Barrigada Barrio	40	44	Perez, Antonio F	Head	M	Cha	39	M	N	N	Guam	N	Farmer
2		40	44	Perez, Ramona P	Wife	F	Cha	36	M	N	Y	Guam	Y	None
3		40	44	Perez, Maria P	Daughter	F	Cha	10	S	Y	Y	Guam	Y	None
4		40	44	Perez, Carmen P	Daughter	F	Cha	8	S	Y		Guam		None
5		40	44	Perez, Pilar P	Daughter	F	Cha	6	S	N		Guam		None
6		40	44	Perez, Concepcion P	Daughter	F	Cha	5.5	S	N		Guam		None
7		40	44	Perez, Jose P	Son	M	Cha	3.9	S	N		Guam		None
8		41	45	Pablo, Manuel C	Head	M	Cha	38	M	N	N	Guam	Y	Farmer
9		41	45	Pablo, Concepcion C	Wife	F	Cha	27	M	N	Y	Guam	Y	None
10		41	45	Pablo, Jose C	Son	M	Cha	7	S	Y		Guam		None
11		41	45	Pablo, Manuela C	Daughter	F	Cha	6	S	N		Guam		None
12		41	45	Pablo, Juan C	Son	M	Cha	4.7	S	N		Guam		None
13		41	45	Pablo, Vicente C	Son	M	Cha	2.5	S	N		Guam		None
14		41	45	Pablo, Angelina C	Daughter	F	Cha	1.3	S	N		Guam		None
15		42	46	Pablo, Lorenzo D	Head	M	Cha	80	Wd	N	Y	Guam	N	None
16		43	47	Cruz, Ingacio M	Head	M	Cha	60	Wd	N	N	Guam	N	Farmer
17		43	47	Cruz, Jose F	Son	M	Cha	31	S	N	Y	Guam	Y	Farm laborer
18		44	48	Cruz, Joaquin T	Head	M	Cha	34	M	N	Y	Guam	Y	Farmer
19		44	48	Cruz, Ignacia C	Wife	F	Cha	42	M	N	N	Guam	N	None
20		44	48	Cruz, Estella C	Daughter	F	Cha	6.9	S	N		Guam		None
21		44	48	Cruz, Adela C	Daughter	F	Cha	2.6	S	N		Guam		None
22		44	48	Cruz, Andesina C	Daughter	F	Cha	.5	S	N		Guam		None
23		44	48	Cruz, Jose F	Step son	M	Cha	15	S	N	Y	Guam	Y	Farm laborer
24		44	48	Cruz, Jesus F	Step son	M	Cha	12	S	N	Y	Guam	N	None
25		44	48	Cruz, Maria F	Step daughter	F	Cha	9	S	Y		Guam		None

DEPARTMENT OF COMMERCE-BUREAU OF THE CENSUS
WASHINGTON

FIFTEENTH CENSUS OF THE UNITED STATES: 1930-POPULATION

THE ISLAND OF GUAM

Sheet No. 4B

181B

District **Municipality of Agana**
Name of Place **Barrigada Barrio**
[Proper name and, also, name of class, as city, town, village, barrio, etc]

Enumeration District No. **5**
Enumerated by me on **April 4, 1930** Jose Kamminga
Enumerator

	PLACE OF ABODE			NAME	RELATION	PERSONAL DESCRIPTION				EDUCATION		NATIVITY		OCCUPATION
	Street, avenue, road, etc.	Number of dwelling house is order of visitation	Number of family in order of visitation	of each person whose place of abode on April 1, 1930, was in this family. Enter surname, first, then given name and middle initial. If any. Include every person living on April 1, 1930. Omit children born since April 1, 1930.	Relationship of this Person to the head of the family.	Sex	Color or race	Age at last birthday	Single, married, widowed or divorced	Attended school any time since Sept. 1, 1929	Whether able to read and write.	Place of birth of this person.	Whether able to speak English.	
	1	2	3	4	5	6	7	8	9	10	11	12	13	14
26	Barrigada Barrio	45	49	Cepeda, Ana C	Head	M	Cha	37	S	N	Y	Guam	N	Laundress
27		45	49	Cepeda, Francisco C	Son	F	Cha	15	S	N	Y	Guam	Y	Laborer
28		45	49	Cepeda, Nicolasa C	Daughter	F	Cha	11	S	Y	Y	Guam	Y	None
29		45	49	Cepeda, Rosa C	Daughter	F	Cha	6	S	N		Guam		None
30		45	49	Cepeda, Julia C	Daughter	F	Cha	3.8	S	N		Guam		None
31		45	49	Rabon, Nicolasa C	Mother	F	Cha	73	Wd	N	Y	Guam	N	None
32		45	49	Cepeda, Jesus M	Uncle	M	Cha	76	Wd	N	Y	Guam	N	None
33		46	50	Jesus, Luis SN	Head	M	Cha	39	M	N	N	Guam	N	Farmer
34		47	51	Pereda, Grabiel P	Head	M	Cha	39	M	N	Y	Guam	N	Farmer
35		47	51	Pereda, Rosa C	Wife	F	Cha	36	M	N	Y	Guam	N	Farm laborer
36		47	51	Pereda, Juan C	Son	M	Cha	15	S	N	Y	Guam	Y	None
37		47	51	Pereda, Ana C	Daughter	F	Cha	14	S	N	Y	Guam	Y	Farm laborer
38		47	51	Pereda, Catalina C	Daughter	F	Cha	12	S	Y	Y	Guam	Y	None
39		47	51	Pereda, Pedro C	Son	M	Cha	10	S	Y	Y	Guam	Y	None
40		47	51	Pereda, Gertrudes C	Daughter	F	Cha	5.4	S	N		Guam		None
41		47	51	Pereda, Felicita C	Daughter	F	Cha	3.8	S	N		Guam		None
42		47	51	Pereda, Rosa C	Daughter	F	Cha	2.2	S	N		Guam		None
43		47	51	Concepcion, Jesus A	Nephew	M	Cha	8	S	Y		Guam		None
44		47	51	Concepcion, Manuel A	Nephew	M	Cha	7	S	Y		Guam		None
45		47	51	Concepcion, Jose A	Nephew	M	Cha	6	S	N		Guam		None
46		48	52	Cepeda, Jose M	Head	M	Cha	23	M	N	Y	Guam	Y	Farmer
47		48	52	Cepeda, Agnes G	Wife	F	Cha	23	M	N	Y	Guam	Y	None
48		48	52	Cepeda, Emeliana G	Daughter	F	Cha	3.6	S	N		Guam		None
49		48	52	Cepeda, Natividad G	Daughter	F	Cha	1.8	S	N		Guam		None
50		48	52	Cepeda, Juana G	Daughter	F	Cha	.3	S	N		Guam		None

(CHAMORRO ROOTS GENEALOGY PROJECT™ TRANSCRIPTION)
(BERNARD T. PUNZALAN / HTTP://WWW.CHAMORROROOTS.COM)

DEPARTMENT OF COMMERCE-BUREAU OF THE CENSUS
WASHINGTON

FIFTEENTH CENSUS OF THE UNITED STATES: 1930-POPULATION

THE ISLAND OF GUAM

Sheet No. 5A

District **Municipality of Agana**
Name of Place **Barrigada Barrio**
[Proper name and, also, name of class, as city, town, village, barrio, etc]

Enumeration District No. **5**
Enumerated by me on **April 4, 1930** Jose Kamminga
Enumerator

	PLACE OF ABODE			NAME	RELATION	PERSONAL DESCRIPTION				EDUCATION		NATIVITY		OCCUPATION
	Street, avenue, road, etc.	Number of dwelling house is order of visitation	Number of family in order of visitation	of each person whose place of abode on April 1, 1930, was in this family. Enter surname, first, then given name and middle initial. If any. Include every person living on April 1, 1930. Omit children born since April 1, 1930.	Relationship of this Person to the head of the family.	Sex	Color or race	Age at last birthday	Single, married, widowed or divorced	Attended school any time since Sept. 1, 1929	Whether able to read and write.	Place of birth of this person.	Whether able to speak English.	
	1	2	3	4	5	6	7	8	9	10	11	12	13	14
1	Barrigada Barrio	49	53	Manibusan, Jose C	Head	M	Cha	71	M	N	N	Guam	N	Farmer
2		49	53	Manibusan, Maria P	Wife	F	Cha	56	M	N	N	Guam	N	None
3		49	53	Manibusan, Ramon P	Son	M	Cha	39	S	N	N	Guam	N	Farm laborer
4		49	53	Manibusan, Jesus P	Son	M	Cha	24	S	N	N	Guam	N	Farm laborer
5		49	53	Manibusan, Vicente P	Son	M	Cha	20	S	N	N	Guam	N	Farm laborer
6		49	53	Manibusan, Matias P	Son	M	Cha	18	S	N	N	Guam	N	Farm laborer
7		49	53	Manibusan, Antonio P	Son	M	Cha	16	S	N	Y	Guam	Y	Farm laborer
8		50	54	Manibusan, Juan P	Head	M	Cha	36	M	N	N	Guam	N	Farmer
9		50	54	Manibusan, Juana M	Wife	F	Cha	35	M	N	Y	Guam	N	None
10		50	54	Manibusan, Rosario M	Daughter	F	Cha	9	S	Y		Guam		None
11		50	54	Manibusan, Maria M	Daughter	F	Cha	8	S	Y		Guam		None
12		50	54	Manibusan, Ana M	Daughter	F	Cha	6	S	N		Guam		None
13		50	54	Manibusan, Jose M	Son	M	Cha	4.3	S	N		Guam		None
14		50	54	Manibusan, Francisco M	Son	M	Cha	2.1	S	N		Guam		None
15		50	54	Manibusan, Agustin M	Son	M	Cha	.5	S	N		Guam		None
16		50	54	Materne, Francisca M	Mother-in-law	F	Cha	64	S	N	N	Guam	N	None
17		51	55	Aguon, Ignacio T	Head	M	Cha	59	S	N	Y	Guam	N	Farmer
18		52	56	De La Rosa, Mariano R	Head	M	Cha	46	M	N	N	Guam	N	Farmer
19		52	56	De La Rosa, Antonia T	Wife	F	Cha	38	M	N	Y	Guam	N	Laundress
20		52	56	De La Rosa, Agueda T	Daughter	F	Cha	16	S	N	Y	Guam	Y	Laundress
21		52	56	De La Rosa, Francisco T	Son	M	Cha	12	S	Y	Y	Guam	Y	None
22		52	56	De La Rosa, Ignacia T	Daughter	F	Cha	10	S	Y	Y	Guam	Y	None
23		52	56	De La Rosa, Felisita T	Daughter	F	Cha	5	S	N		Guam		None
24		52	56	De La Rosa, Carmen T	Daughter	F	Cha	.8	S	N		Guam		None
25		53	57	Lizama, Juan SN	Head	M	Cha	26	M	N	Y	Guam	Y	Farmer

(CHAMORRO ROOTS GENEALOGY PROJECT™ TRANSCRIPTION)
(BERNARD T. PUNZALAN / HTTP://WWW.CHAMORROROOTS.COM)

DEPARTMENT OF COMMERCE-BUREAU OF THE CENSUS
WASHINGTON

FIFTEENTH CENSUS OF THE UNITED STATES: 1930-POPULATION

THE ISLAND OF GUAM

Sheet No. 5B

182B

District **Municipality of Agana**
Name of Place **Barrigada Barrio**
[Proper name and, also, name of class, as city, town, village, barrio, etc]

Enumeration District No. 5
Enumerated by me on **April 5, 1930** Jose Kamminga
Enumerator

	PLACE OF ABODE			NAME	RELATION	PERSONAL DESCRIPTION				EDUCATION		NATIVITY		OCCUPATION
	Street, avenue, road, etc.	Number of dwelling house in order of visitation	Number of family in order of visitation	of each person whose place of abode on April 1, 1930, was in this family. Enter surname, first, then given name and middle initial. If any. Include every person living on April 1, 1930. Omit children born since April 1, 1930.	Relationship of this Person to the head of the family.	Sex	Color or race	Age at last birthday	Single, married, widowed or divorced	Attended school any time since Sept. 1, 1929	Whether able to read and write.	Place of birth of this person.	Whether able to speak English.	
	1	2	3	4	5	6	7	8	9	10	11	12	13	14
26	Barrigada Barrio	53	57	Lizama, Vicenta A	Wife	F	Cha	33	M	N	Y	Guam	Y	Laundress
27		54	58	McCann, Frank	Head	M	W	52	M	N	Y	Pennsylvania	Y	Farmer
28		54	58	McCann, Rita A	Wife	F	Cha	48	M	N	Y	Guam	Y	None
29		54	58	McCann, Marvel F	Son	M	Cha	10	S	Y	Y	Guam	Y	None
30		55	59	Lujan, Jesus G	Head	M	Cha	46	M	N	Y	Guam	N	Farmer
31		55	59	Lujan, Isabel L	Wife	F	Cha	36	M	N	Y	Guam	N	None
32		55	59	Lujan, Carmen G	Daughter	F	Cha	.8	S	N		Guam		None
33		56	60	Flores, Vicente M	Head	M	Cha	39	M	N	Y	Guam	Y	Farmer
34		56	60	Flores, Ana U	Wife	F	Cha	40	M	N	Y	Guam	Y	None
35		56	60	Flores, Felix U	Son	M	Cha	.6	S	N		Guam		None
36		57	61	Borja, Manuel S	Head	M	Cha	45	M	N	Y	Guam	N	Farmer
37		57	61	Borja, Dolores F	Wife	F	Cha	43	M	N	N	Guam	N	None
38		57	61	Borja, Jose F	Son	M	Cha	10	S	Y	Y	Guam	Y	None
39		57	61	Borja, Ramon F	Son	M	Cha	8	S	Y		Guam		None
40		57	61	Borja, Vicenta F	Daughter	F	Cha	6	S	N		Guam		None
41		57	61	Borja, Maria F	Daughter	F	Cha	3.3	S	N		Guam		None
42		58	62	Pangelinan, Juan SN	Head	M	Cha	58	M	N	N	Guam	N	Farmer
43		58	62	Pangelinan, Maria M	Wife	F	Cha	49	M	N	N	Guam	N	None
44		58	62	Pangelinan, Pedro M	Son	M	Cha	16	S	N	Y	Guam	Y	Farm laborer
45		58	62	Pangelinan, Concepcion M	Daughter	F	Cha	14	S	N	Y	Guam	Y	Laundress
46		58	62	Pangelinan, Francisco M	Son	M	Cha	12	S	Y	Y	Guam	Y	None
47		58	62	Pangelinan, Juan M	Son	M	Cha	11	S	Y	Y	Guam	Y	None
48		59	63	Arceo, Jose I	Head	M	Cha	46	S	N	N	Guam	N	Farmer
49		59	64	Leon Guerrero, Jesus P	Head	M	Cha	42	M	N	N	Guam	N	Farmer
50		59	64	Leon Guerrero, Asuncion A	Wife	F	Cha	51	M	N	N	Guam	N	None

DEPARTMENT OF COMMERCE-BUREAU OF THE CENSUS
WASHINGTON

FIFTEENTH CENSUS OF THE UNITED STATES: 1930-POPULATION

THE ISLAND OF GUAM

Sheet No. 6A

District **Municipality of Agana**
Name of Place **Barrigada Barrio**
[Proper name and, also, name of class, as city, town, village, barrio, etc]

Enumeration District No. 5
Enumerated by me on **April 5, 1930** Jose Kamminga, Enumerator

	PLACE OF ABODE: Street, avenue, road, etc.	Number of dwelling house in order of visitation	Number of family in order of visitation	NAME of each person whose place of abode on April 1, 1930, was in this family. Enter surname, first, then given name and middle initial. If any. Include every person living on April 1, 1930. Omit children born since April 1, 1930.	RELATION Relationship of this Person to the head of the family.	Sex	Color or race	Age at last birthday	Single, married, widowed or divorced	Attended school any time since Sept. 1, 1929	Whether able to read and write.	NATIVITY Place of birth of this person.	Whether able to speak English.	OCCUPATION
	1	2	3	4	5	6	7	8	9	10	11	12	13	14
1	Barrigada Barrio	59	64	Leon Guerrero, Mariano A	Son	M	Cha	17	S	N	Y	Guam	Y	Laborer
2		59	64	Leon Guerrero, Joaquina A	Daughter	F	Cha	15	S	N	Y	Guam	Y	Laundress
3		59	64	Leon Guerrero, Maria A	Daughter	F	Cha	13	S	N	Y	Guam	Y	None
4		59	64	Leon Guerrero, Eulelia A	Daughter	F	Cha	10	S	Y	Y	Guam	Y	None
5		60	65	Flores, Jose M	Head	M	Cha	31	M	N	Y	Guam	Y	Farmer
6		60	65	Flores, Carmen I	Wife	F	Cha	19	M	N	Y	Guam	N	None
7		60	65	Flores, Julia I	Daughter	F	Cha	.7	S	N		Guam		None
8		61	66	Flores, Francisco M	Head	M	Cha	24	M	N	Y	Guam	Y	Farmer
9		61	66	Flores, Guillerma C	Wife	F	Cha	29	M	N	Y	Guam	Y	None
10		61	66	Flores, Francisco C	Son	M	Cha	5.7	S	N		Guam		None
11		61	66	Flores, Rosario C	Daughter	F	Cha	4.4	S	N		Guam		None
12		61	66	Flores, Rita C	Daughter	F	Cha	1.9	S	N		Guam		None
13		61	66	Flores, Julia C	Daughter	F	Cha	.9	S	N		Guam		None
14		62	67	Muna, Felix G	Head	M	Cha	27	M	N	Y	Guam	Y	Farmer
15		62	67	Muna, Ana M	Wife	F	Cha	30	M	N	Y	Guam	Y	None
16		62	67	Muna, Ignacia M	Daughter	F	Cha	3.6	S	N		Guam		None
17		62	67	Muna, Jesus M	Son	M	Cha	1.3	S	N		Guam		None
18		62	67	Muna, Maria M	Daughter	F	Cha	.5	S	N		Guam		None
19		63	68	Borja, Joaquin S	Head	M	Cha	36	M	N	Y	Guam	Y	Farmer
20		63	68	Borja, Maria D	Wife	F	Cha	39	M	N	Y	Guam	N	None
21		63	68	Borja, Joaquin D	Son	M	Cha	9	S	N		Guam		None
22		63	68	Borja, Nieves D	Daughter	F	Cha	6	S	N		Guam		None
23		63	68	Borja, Vicente D	Son	M	Cha	5.5	S	N		Guam		None
24		63	68	Borja, Rosario D	Daughter	F	Cha	4.8	S	N		Guam		None
25		63	68	Borja, Jose D	Son	M	Cha	.8	S	N		Guam		None

DEPARTMENT OF COMMERCE-BUREAU OF THE CENSUS
WASHINGTON

FIFTEENTH CENSUS OF THE UNITED STATES: 1930-POPULATION

THE ISLAND OF GUAM

Sheet No. 6B

183B

District **Municipality of Agana**
Name of Place **Barrigada Barrio**
[Proper name and, also, name of class, as city, town, village, barrio, etc]

Enumeration District No. **5**
Enumerated by me on **April 5, 1930** Jose Kamminga
Enumerator

	PLACE OF ABODE			NAME	RELATION	PERSONAL DESCRIPTION				EDUCATION		NATIVITY		OCCUPATION
	Street, avenue, road, etc.	Number of dwelling house is order of visitation	Number of family in order of visitation	of each person whose place of abode on April 1, 1930, was in this family. Enter surname, first, then given name and middle initial. If any. Include every person living on April 1, 1930. Omit children born since April 1, 1930.	Relationship of this Person to the head of the family.	Sex	Color or race	Age at last birthday	Single, married, widowed or divorced	Attended school any time since Sept. 1, 1929	Whether able to read and write.	Place of birth of this person.	Whether able to speak English.	
	1	2	3	4	5	6	7	8	9	10	11	12	13	14
26	Barrigada Barrio	64	69	Mafnas, Vicente M	Head	M	Cha	35	M	N	Y	Guam	N	Farmer
27		64	69	Mafnas, Ana A	Wife	F	Cha	39	M	N	N	Guam	N	None
28		64	69	Mafnas, Concepcion A	Daughter	F	Cha	14	S	N	Y	Guam	Y	Laundress
29		64	69	Mafnas, Antonio A	Son	M	Cha	13	S	Y	Y	Guam	Y	None
30		64	69	Mafnas, Antonia A	Daughter	F	Cha	11	S	Y	Y	Guam	Y	None
31		64	69	Mafnas, Rosa A	Daughter	F	Cha	9	S	Y		Guam		None
32		64	69	Mafnas, Jose A	Son	M	Cha	7	S	Y		Guam		None
33		64	69	Mafnas, Josefa A	Daughter	F	Cha	3	S	N		Guam		None
34		64	69	Mafnas, Vicenta A	Daughter	F	Cha	1.3	S	N		Guam		None
35		65	70	Flores, Jose B	Head	M	Cha	29	M	N	Y	Guam	Y	Farmer
36		65	70	Flores, Maria B	Wife	F	Cha	26	M	N	Y	Guam	Y	None
37		65	70	Flores, Rosa B	Daughter	F	Cha	5.6	S	N		Guam		None
38		65	70	Flores, Maria B	Daughter	F	Cha	5.6	S	N		Guam		None
39		65	70	Flores, Pedro B	Son	M	Cha	3.8	S	N		Guam		None
40		65	70	Flores, Magdalena B	Daughter	F	Cha	1.8	S	N		Guam		None
41		66	71	Castro, Luis P	Head	M	Cha	42	M	N	N	Guam	N	Farmer
42		66	71	Castro, Concepcion B	Wife	F	Cha	41	M	N	N	Guam	N	None
43		66	71	Castro, Jesus B	Son	M	Cha	16	S	Y	Y	Guam	Y	None
44		66	71	Castro, Ana B	Daughter	F	Cha	13	S	Y	Y	Guam	Y	None
45		66	71	Castro, Maria B	Daughter	F	Cha	12	S	Y	Y	Guam	Y	None
46		66	71	Castro, Jose B	Son	M	Cha	10	S	Y	Y	Guam	Y	None
47		66	71	Castro, Julita B	Daughter	F	Cha	5.3	S	N		Guam		None
48		66	71	Castro, Vicenta B	Daughter	F	Cha	4	S	N		Guam		None
49		66	71	Castro, Juan B	Son	M	Cha	1.4	S	N		Guam		None
50		67	72	Aguon, Juan P	Head	M	Cha	32	M	N	Y	Guam	Y	Farmer

DEPARTMENT OF COMMERCE-BUREAU OF THE CENSUS
WASHINGTON

FIFTEENTH CENSUS OF THE UNITED STATES: 1930-POPULATION

THE ISLAND OF GUAM

Sheet No. 7A

District **Municipality of Agana**
Name of Place **Barrigada Barrio** [Proper name and, also, name of class, as city, town, village, barrio, etc]

Enumeration District No. 5
Enumerated by me on **April 7, 1930** Jose Kamminga, Enumerator

	PLACE OF ABODE			NAME	RELATION	PERSONAL DESCRIPTION				EDUCATION		NATIVITY		OCCUPATION
	Street, avenue, road, etc.	Number of dwelling house in order of visitation	Number of family in order of visitation	of each person whose place of abode on April 1, 1930, was in this family. Enter surname, first, then given name and middle initial. If any. Include every person living on April 1, 1930. Omit children born since April 1, 1930.	Relationship of this Person to the head of the family.	Sex	Color or race	Age at last birthday	Single, married, widowed or divorced	Attended school any time since Sept. 1, 1929	Whether able to read and write.	Place of birth of this person.	Whether able to speak English.	
	1	2	3	4	5	6	7	8	9	10	11	12	13	14
1	Barrigada Barrio	67	72	Aguon, Dolores L	Wife	F	Cha	20	M	N	Y	Guam	Y	None
2		67	72	Aguon, Candelaria L	Daughter	F	Cha	.4	S	N		Guam		None
3		68	73	Aguon, Jose P	Head	M	Cha	37	M	N	Y	Guam	Y	Farmer
4		68	73	Aguon, Catalina C	Wife	F	Cha	30	M	N	Y	Guam	Y	None
5		68	73	Aguon, Luisa C	Daughter	F	Cha	14	S	N	Y	Guam	Y	Laundress
6		68	73	Aguon, Vicente C	Son	M	Cha	11	S	Y	Y	Guam	Y	None
7		68	73	Aguon, Felix C	Son	M	Cha	9	S	Y		Guam		None
8		68	73	Aguon, Carmen C	Daughter	F	Cha	7	S	Y		Guam		None
9		68	73	Aguon, Francisco C	Son	M	Cha	5.7	S	N		Guam		None
10		68	73	Aguon, Maria C	Daughter	F	Cha	4.3	S	N		Guam		None
11		68	73	Aguon, Marcela C	Daughter	F	Cha	2.3	S	N		Guam		None
12		68	73	Aguon, Jose C	Son	M	Cha	.6	S	N		Guam		None
13		69	74	Muna, Antonio C	Head	M	Cha	55	M	N	N	Guam	N	Farmer
14		70	75	Salas, Joaquin C	Head	M	Cha	35	M	N	Y	Guam	N	Farmer
15		70	75	Salas, Magdalena Q	Wife	F	Cha	34	M	N	N	Guam	N	None
16		70	75	Quidachay, Juan Q	Step son	M	Cha	18	S	N	Y	Guam	Y	Farm laborer
17		71	76	Lizama, Justo P	Head	M	Cha	53	M	N	Y	Guam	N	Farmer
18		71	76	Lizama, Juliana P	Wife	F	Cha	40	M	N	Y	Guam	N	None
19		71	76	Lizama, Catalina P	Daughter	F	Cha	12	S	Y	Y	Guam	Y	None
20		71	76	Lizama, Hipolito P	Son	M	Cha	9	S	Y		Guam		None
21		71	76	Lizama, Marcelina P	Daughter	F	Cha	6	S	Y		Guam		None
22		71	76	Lizama, Bernado P	Son	M	Cha	3.8	S	N		Guam		None
23		71	76	Lizama, Dolores P	Daughter	F	Cha	1.9	S	N		Guam		None
24		71	76	Lizama, Benita P	Daughter	F	Cha	.3	S	N		Guam		None
25		71	76	Pablo, Maria P	Niece	F	Cha	15	S	N	Y	Guam	N	Laundress

DEPARTMENT OF COMMERCE-BUREAU OF THE CENSUS
WASHINGTON

FIFTEENTH CENSUS OF THE UNITED STATES: 1930-POPULATION

THE ISLAND OF GUAM

Sheet No. 7B

184B

District **Municipality of Agana**
Name of Place **Barrigada Barrio**
[Proper name and, also, name of class, as city, town, village, barrio, etc]

Enumeration District No. 5
Enumerated by me on **April 7, 1930** Jose Kamminga, Enumerator

	PLACE OF ABODE			NAME	RELATION	PERSONAL DESCRIPTION				EDUCATION		NATIVITY		OCCUPATION
	Street, avenue, road, etc.	Number of dwelling house in order of visitation	Number of family in order of visitation	of each person whose place of abode on April 1, 1930, was in this family. Enter surname, first, then given name and middle initial. If any. Include every person living on April 1, 1930. Omit children born since April 1, 1930.	Relationship of this Person to the head of the family.	Sex	Color or race	Age at last birthday	Single, married, widowed or divorced	Attended school any time since Sept. 1, 1929	Whether able to read and write.	Place of birth of this person.	Whether able to speak English.	
	1	2	3	4	5	6	7	8	9	10	11	12	13	14
26	Barrigada Barrio	71	76	Pablo, Jesus P	Nephew	M	Cha	11	S	Y	Y	Guam	Y	None
27		72	77	Borja, Ramon S	Head	M	Cha	55	M	N	Y	Guam	N	Farmer
28		72	77	Borja, Isabel L	Wife	F	Cha	59	M	N	Y	Guam	N	None
29		72	77	Borja, Maria R	Daughter	F	Cha	41	S	N	Y	Guam	N	Farm laborer
30		72	77	Nego, Jose R	Nephew	M	Cha	24	S	N	Y	Guam	Y	Farm laborer
31		72	77	Nego, Rosa R	Niece	F	Cha	20	S	N	Y	Guam	N	Laundress
32		72	77	Nego, Vicente R	Nephew	M	Cha	17	S	N	Y	Guam	Y	None
33		72	77	Nego, Maria R	Niece	F	Cha	13	S	Y	Y	Guam	Y	None
34		72	77	Guerrero, Vicente R	Cousin	M	Cha	47	Wd	N	Y	Guam	N	Farm laborer
35		73	78	Rivera, Jose G	Head	M	Cha	41	M	N	N	Guam	N	Farmer
36		73	78	Rivera, Candelaria T	Wife	F	Cha	30	M	N	N	Guam	N	None
37		73	78	Rivera, Francisca T	Daughter	F	Cha	15	S	N	Y	Guam	Y	Laundress
38		73	78	Rivera, Dolores T	Daughter	F	Cha	12	S	Y	Y	Guam	Y	None
39		73	78	Rivera, Jose T	Son	M	Cha	11	S	Y	Y	Guam	Y	None
40		73	78	Rivera, Ana T	Daughter	F	Cha	9	S	Y		Guam		None
41		73	78	Rivera, Juan T	Son	M	Cha	6	S	N		Guam		None
42		73	78	Rivera, Antonia T	Daughter	F	Cha	4.2	S	N		Guam		None
43		73	78	Rivera, Maria T	Daughter	F	Cha	.3	S	N		Guam		None
44		74	79	Pereira, Ramon C	Head	M	Cha	27	M	N	Y	Guam	Y	Farmer
45		74	79	Pereira, Amalia D	Wife	F	Cha	33	M	N	Y	Guam	Y	None
46		74	79	Pereira, Jose D	Son	M	Cha	6	S	N		Guam		None
47		74	79	Pereira, Lucia D	Daughter	F	Cha	4.4	S	N		Guam		None
48		74	79	Pereira, Ignacio D	Son	M	Cha	2.9	S	N		Guam		None
49		74	79	Pereira, Dolores D	Daughter	F	Cha	.5	S	N		Guam		None
50		75	80	Tenorio, Joaquin S	Head	M	Cha	59	M	N	Y	Guam	N	Farmer

DEPARTMENT OF COMMERCE-BUREAU OF THE CENSUS
WASHINGTON

FIFTEENTH CENSUS OF THE UNITED STATES: 1930-POPULATION

THE ISLAND OF GUAM

Sheet No. 8A

District **Municipality of Agana**
Name of Place **Barrigada Barrio**
[Proper name and, also, name of class, as city, town, village, barrio, etc]

Enumeration District No. 5
Enumerated by me on April 7, 1930 Jose Kamminga, Enumerator

	PLACE OF ABODE			NAME	RELATION	PERSONAL DESCRIPTION				EDUCATION		NATIVITY		OCCUPATION
	Street, avenue, road, etc.	Number of dwelling house is order of visitation	Number of family in order of visitation	of each person whose place of abode on April 1, 1930, was in this family. Enter surname, first, then given name and middle initial. If any. Include every person living on April 1, 1930. Omit children born since April 1, 1930.	Relationship of this Person to the head of the family.	Sex	Color or race	Age at last birthday	Single, married, widowed or divorced	Attended school any time since Sept. 1, 1929	Whether able to read and write.	Place of birth of this person.	Whether able to speak English.	
	1	2	3	4	5	6	7	8	9	10	11	12	13	14
1	Barrigada Barrio	75	80	Tenorio, Maria Q	Wife	F	Cha	47	M	N	Y	Guam	N	None
2		75	80	Tenorio, Jesus Q	Son	M	Cha	25	S	N	Y	Guam	Y	Farm laborer
3		75	80	Tenorio, Ana Q	Daughter	F	Cha	19	S	N	Y	Guam	Y	Laundress
4		75	80	Tenorio, Ramona Q	Daughter	F	Cha	15	S	N	Y	Guam	Y	None
5		75	80	Tenorio, Juan Q	Son	M	Cha	12	S	Y	Y	Guam	Y	None
6		75	80	Tenorio, Juana Q	Daughter	F	Cha	10	S	Y	Y	Guam	Y	None
7		75	80	Benavente, Josefa C	Aunt	F	Cha	75	S	N	N	Guam	N	None
8		76	81	Tenorio, Francisco R	Head	M	Cha	20	M	N	Y	Guam	Y	Farmer
9		76	81	Tenorio, Engracia T	Wife	F	Cha	19	M	N	Y	Guam	Y	None
10		77	82	Castro, Vicente P	Head	M	Cha	46	M	N	N	Guam	N	Farmer
11		77	82	Castro, Concepcion C	Wife	F	Cha	45	M	N	N	Guam	N	None
12		78	83	Sablan, Vicenta C	Head	F	Cha	68	Wd	N	Y	Guam	N	Farmer
13		78	83	Sablan, Susana P	Sister	F	Cha	72	S	N	Y	Guam	N	None
14		79	84	Bontugan, Josefa C	Head	F	Cha	62	Wd	N	N	Guam	N	None
15		79	84	Bontugan, Juan C	Son	M	Cha	25	S	N	N	Guam	Y	Farm laborer
16		79	84	Bontugan, Regina C	Daughter	F	Cha	17	S		Y	Guam	Y	Laundress
17				Here ends the enumeration of Barrigada Barrio, district 5.										
18				[Sheet 185B/8B was intentionally left blank by the enumerator.]										
19														
20														
21														
22														
23														
24														
25														

DEPARTMENT OF COMMERCE-BUREAU OF THE CENSUS
WASHINGTON

FIFTEENTH CENSUS OF THE UNITED STATES: 1930-POPULATION

THE ISLAND OF GUAM

Sheet No. 9A

District **Municipality of Agana**
Name of Place **Dededo Barrio**
[Proper name and, also, name of class, as city, town, village, barrio, etc]

Enumeration District No. 5
Enumerated by me on **April 8, 1930** Jose Kamminga, Enumerator

	PLACE OF ABODE			NAME	RELATION	PERSONAL DESCRIPTION				EDUCATION		NATIVITY		OCCUPATION
	Street, avenue, road, etc.	Number of dwelling house in order of visitation	Number of family in order of visitation	of each person whose place of abode on April 1, 1930, was in this family. Enter surname, first, then given name and middle initial. If any. Include every person living on April 1, 1930. Omit children born since April 1, 1930.	Relationship of this Person to the head of the family.	Sex	Color or race	Age at last birthday	Single, married, widowed or divorced	Attended school any time since Sept. 1, 1929	Whether able to read and write.	Place of birth of this person.	Whether able to speak English.	
	1	2	3	4	5	6	7	8	9	10	11	12	13	14
1	Dededo Barrio	80	85	Crisostomo, Juan SA	Head	M	Cha	43	M	N	Y	Guam	N	Farmer
2		80	85	Crisostomo, Concepcion SA	Wife	F	Cha	42	M	N	Y	Guam	N	None
3		80	85	Crisostomo, Vicente SA	Son	M	Cha	16	S	N	Y	Guam	Y	Farm laborer
4		80	85	Crisostomo, Doroteo SA	Son	M	Cha	15	S	Y	Y	Guam	Y	None
5		80	85	Crisostomo, Francisco SA	Son	M	Cha	11	S	Y	Y	Guam	Y	None
6		81	86	Duenas, Julian M	Head	M	Cha	67	Wd	N		Guam	N	Farmer
7		81	86	Duenas, Manuel Q	Son	M	Cha	40	S	N	N	Guam	Y	Chauffeur
8		81	86	Duenas, Juan Q	Son	M	Cha	37	S	N	Y	Guam	Y	Farm laborer
9		81	86	Duenas, Jesus Q	Son	M	Cha	28	S	N	Y	Guam	Y	Farm laborer
10		81	86	Duenas, Maria Q	Daughter	F	Cha	31	S	N	Y	Guam	Y	None
11		81	86	Duenas, Francisco Q	Son	M	Cha	22	S	N	Y	Guam	Y	Farm laborer
12		81	86	Duenas, Rosa F	Niece	F	Cha	8	S	Y		Guam		None
13		82	87	Duenas, Jose M	Head	M	Cha	72	M	N	N	Guam	N	Farmer
14		82	87	Duenas, Juana E	Wife	F	Cha	69	M	N	N	Guam	N	None
15		82	87	Duenas, Ramon C	Nephew	M	Cha	20	S	N	Y	Guam	Y	Farm laborer
16		83	88	Uson, Ramon G	Head	M	Cha	35	M	N	Y	Guam	Y	Farmer
17		83	88	Uson, Maria A	Wife	F	Cha	37	M	N	Y	Guam	Y	None
18		83	88	Uson, Jose A	Son	M	Cha	15	S	N	Y	Guam	Y	Farm laborer
19		83	88	Uson, Juan A	Son	M	Cha	11	S	Y	Y	Guam	Y	None
20		83	88	Uson, Rosalia A	Daughter	F	Cha	6	S	N		Guam		None
21		83	88	Uson, Ramon A	Son	M	Cha	3.3	S	N		Guam		None
22		83	88	Uson, Teresa A	Daughter	F	Cha	2.3	S	N		Guam		None
23		83	88	Uson, Vicente A	Son	M	Cha	1.7	S	N		Guam		None
24		84	89	Leon Guerrero, Juan	Head	M	Cha	43	M	N	Y	Guam	Y	Farmer
25		84	89	Leon Guerrero, Maria L	Wife	F	Cha	32	M	N	Y	Guam	Y	None

(CHAMORRO ROOTS GENEALOGY PROJECT™ TRANSCRIPTION)
(BERNARD T. PUNZALAN / HTTP://WWW.CHAMORROROOTS.COM)

DEPARTMENT OF COMMERCE-BUREAU OF THE CENSUS
WASHINGTON

FIFTEENTH CENSUS OF THE UNITED STATES: 1930-POPULATION

THE ISLAND OF GUAM

Sheet No. 9B

186B

District **Municipality of Agana**
Name of Place **Dededo Barrio**
[Proper name and, also, name of class, as city, town, village, barrio, etc]

Enumeration District No. 5
Enumerated by me on **April 8, 1930** Jose Kamminga, Enumerator

	PLACE OF ABODE			NAME	RELATION	PERSONAL DESCRIPTION				EDUCATION		NATIVITY		OCCUPATION
	Street, avenue, road, etc.	Number of dwelling house is order of visitation	Number of family in order of visitation	of each person whose place of abode on April 1, 1930, was in this family. Enter surname, first, then given name and middle initial. If any. Include every person living on April 1, 1930. Omit children born since April 1, 1930.	Relationship of this Person to the head of the family.	Sex	Color or race	Age at last birthday	Single, married, widowed or divorced	Attended school any time since Sept. 1, 1929	Whether able to read and write.	Place of birth of this person.	Whether able to speak English.	
	1	2	3	4	5	6	7	8	9	10	11	12	13	14
26	Dededo Barrio	84	89	Leon Guerrero, Maria C	Daughter	F	Cha	17	S	N	Y	Guam	Y	None
27		84	89	Leon Guerrero, Rosa C	Daughter	F	Cha	16	S	Y	Y	Guam	Y	None
28		84	89	Leon Guerrero, Juan C	Son	M	Cha	14	S	Y	Y	Guam	Y	None
29		84	89	Leon Guerrero, Pedro C	Son	M	Cha	12	S	Y	Y	Guam	Y	None
30		84	89	Leon Guerrero, Oliva L	Daughter	F	Cha	7	S	Y		Guam		None
31		84	89	Leon Guerrero, Dolores L	Daughter	F	Cha	4.9	S	N		Guam		None
32		84	89	Leon Guerrero, Ester B	Daughter	F	Cha	3.8	S	N		Guam		None
33		85	90	Francisco, Vicente T	Head	M	Cha	58	M	N	Y	Guam	Y	Farmer
34		85	90	Francisco, Gracia S	Wife	F	Cha	61	M	N	Y	Guam	N	None
35		85	90	Francisco, Vicente S	Son	M	Cha	24	S	N	Y	Guam	Y	Farm laborer
36		85	90	Francisco, Rosario S	Daughter	F	Cha	21	S	N	Y	Guam	Y	None
37		85	90	Francisco, Josefa S	Daughter	F	Cha	13	S	N	Y	Guam	Y	None
38		86	91	Aquino, Matias C	Head	M	Cha	52	M	N	Y	Guam	Y	Farmer
39		86	91	Aquino, Antonia C	Wife	F	Cha	37	M	N	Y	Guam	N	None
40		86	91	Aquino, Ramon C	Son	M	Cha	17	S	N	Y	Guam	Y	Farm laborer
41		86	91	Aquino, Rufina C	Daughter	F	Cha	15	S	Y	Y	Guam	Y	None
42		86	91	Aquino, Rosario C	Daughter	F	Cha	5.7	S	N		Guam		None
43		86	91	Aquino, Maria C	Daughter	F	Cha	4.3	S	N		Guam		None
44		86	91	Aquino, Jose C	Son	M	Cha	3.8	S	N		Guam		None
45		86	91	Aquino, Gregorio C	Son	M	Cha	.9	S	N		Guam		None
46		87	92	San Agustin, Jose C	Head	M	Cha	39	M	N	N	Guam	N	Farmer
47		87	92	San Agustin, Maria C	Wife	F	Cha	32	M	N	N	Guam	N	None
48		87	92	San Agustin, Manuel C	Son	M	Cha	17	S	N	Y	Guam	Y	Farm laborer
49		87	92	San Agustin, Gonzalo C	Son	M	Cha	15	S	Y	Y	Guam	Y	None
50		87	92	San Agustin, Francisco C	Son	M	Cha	13	S	Y	Y	Guam	Y	None

DEPARTMENT OF COMMERCE-BUREAU OF THE CENSUS
WASHINGTON

FIFTEENTH CENSUS OF THE UNITED STATES: 1930-POPULATION

THE ISLAND OF GUAM

Sheet No. 10A

District **Municipality of Agana**
Name of Place **Dededo Barrio**
[Proper name and, also, name of class, as city, town, village, barrio, etc]

Enumeration District No. **5**
Enumerated by me on **April 9, 1930** Jose Kamminga
Enumerator

	PLACE OF ABODE			NAME	RELATION	PERSONAL DESCRIPTION				EDUCATION		NATIVITY		OCCUPATION
	Street, avenue, road, etc.	Number of dwelling house in order of visitation	Number of family in order of visitation	of each person whose place of abode on April 1, 1930, was in this family. Enter surname, first, then given name and middle initial. If any. Include every person living on April 1, 1930. Omit children born since April 1, 1930.	Relationship of this Person to the head of the family.	Sex	Color or race	Age at last birthday	Single, married, widowed or divorced	Attended school any time since Sept. 1, 1929	Whether able to read and write.	Place of birth of this person.	Whether able to speak English.	
	1	2	3	4	5	6	7	8	9	10	11	12	13	14
1	Dededo Barrio	88	93	Santos, Joaquin C	Head	M	Cha	28	M	N	Y	Guam	Y	Farmer
2		88	93	Santos, Maria B	Wife	F	Cha	22	M	N	Y	Guam	Y	None
3		88	93	Santos, Francisco B	Son	M	Cha	4.5	S	N		Guam		None
4		88	93	Santos, Cintia B	Daughter	F	Cha	1.8	S	N		Guam		None
5		88	93	Santos, Pedro B	Son	M	Cha	.3	S	N		Guam		None
6		89	94	Santos, Luis A	Head	M	Cha	26	M	N	Y	Guam	N	Farmer
7		89	94	Santos, Trinidad S	Wife	F	Cha	22	M	N	Y	Guam	Y	None
8		89	94	Santos, Jose S	Son	M	Cha	4.5	S	N		Guam		None
9		89	94	Santos, Maria S	Daughter	F	Cha	1.3	S	N		Guam		None
10		90	95	Santos, Francisco P	Head	M	Cha	64	M	N	Y	Guam	N	Farmer
11		90	95	Santos, Rosa V	Wife	F	Cha	60	M	N	Y	Guam	N	None
12		90	95	Santos, Jose V	Son	M	Cha	29	S	N	Y	Guam	Y	Farm laborer
13		90	95	Santos, Jesus V	Son	M	Cha	27	S	N	Y	Guam	Y	Farm laborer
14		90	95	Santos, Francisco V	Son	M	Cha	24	S	N	Y	Guam	Y	Farm laborer
15		90	95	Santos, Maria V	Daughter	F	Cha	22	S	N	Y	Guam	Y	None
16		91	96	Chiguina, Marcelo M	Head	M	Cha	49	M	N	N	Guam	N	Farmer
17		91	96	Chiguina, Maria Q	Wife	F	Cha	57	M	N	N	Guam	N	None
18		91	96	Chiguina, Jose Q	Son	M	Cha	15	S	N	Y	Guam	Y	Farm laborer
19		92	97	Tenorio, Josefa B	Head	F	Cha	63	Wd	N	N	Guam	N	None
20		93	98	Blas, Tomas C	Head	M	Cha	74	S	N	Y	Guam	N	Farmer
21		94	99	Aguon, Maria P	Head	F	Cha	50	Wd	N	N	Guam	N	None
22		94	99	Aguon, Ramon P	Son	M	Cha	39	S	N	Y	Guam	Y	Farm laborer
23		94	99	Aguon, Vicente P	Son	M	Cha	32	S	N	Y	Guam	Y	Farm laborer
24		94	99	Aguon, Luis P	Son	M	Cha	26	S	N	Y	Guam	Y	Farm laborer
25		94	99	Aguon, Jesus P	Son	M	Cha	25	S	N	Y	Guam	Y	Farm laborer

(CHAMORRO ROOTS GENEALOGY PROJECT™ TRANSCRIPTION)
(BERNARD T. PUNZALAN / HTTP://WWW.CHAMORROROOTS.COM)

DEPARTMENT OF COMMERCE-BUREAU OF THE CENSUS
WASHINGTON

FIFTEENTH CENSUS OF THE UNITED STATES: 1930-POPULATION

THE ISLAND OF GUAM

Sheet No. 10B

187B

District Municipality of Agana
Name of Place Dededo Barrio
[Proper name and, also, name of class, as city, town, village, barrio, etc]

Enumeration District No. 5
Enumerated by me on April 9, 1930 Jose Kamminga
Enumerator

	Street, avenue, road, etc.	Number of dwelling house is order of visitation	Number of family in order of visitation	NAME of each person whose place of abode on April 1, 1930, was in this family. Enter surname, first, then given name and middle initial. If any. Include every person living on April 1, 1930. Omit children born since April 1, 1930.	RELATION Relationship of this Person to the head of the family.	Sex	Color or race	Age at last birthday	Single, married, widowed or divorced	Attended school any time since Sept. 1, 1929	Whether able to read and write.	NATIVITY Place of birth of this person.	Whether able to speak English.	OCCUPATION
	1	2	3	4	5	6	7	8	9	10	11	12	13	14
26	Dededo Barrio	94	99	Aguon, Jose P	Son	M	Cha	20	S	N	Y	Guam	Y	Farm laborer
27		95	100	San Nicolas, Hilario SN	Head	M	Cha	72	M	N	N	Guam	N	Farmer
28		95	100	San Nicolas, Maria G	Wife	F	Cha	66	M	N	N	Guam	N	None
29		95	100	San Nicolas, Vicente G	Son	M	Cha	39	S	N	Y	Guam	Y	Farm laborer
30		95	100	San Nicolas, Joaquin G	Son	M	Cha	36	S	N	Y	Guam	Y	Farm laborer
31		95	100	Yamashita, Remedios Q	Servant	F	Jap	15	S	N	Y	Guam	Y	Laundress
32		95	100	Yamashita, Jose Q	Servant	M	Jap	13	S	Y	Y	Guam	Y	None
33		96	101	Santos, Dolores S	Head	F	Cha	31	S	N	Y	Guam	Y	Laundress
34		96	101	Santos, Francisca S	Daughter	F	Cha	14	S	N	Y	Guam	Y	None
35		96	101	Santos, Francisco S	Son	M	Cha	11	S	Y	Y	Guam	Y	None
36		96	101	Santos, Jose S	Son	M	Cha	8	S	Y		Guam		None
37		96	101	Santos, Tomas S	Son	M	Cha	6	S	N		Guam		None
38		96	101	Santos, Vicente S	Son	M	Cha	3.8	S	N		Guam		None
39		97	102	Santos, Ramon C	Head	M	Cha	30	M	N	Y	Guam	Y	Farmer
40		97	102	Santos, Eliza Q	Wife	F	Cha	26	M	N	Y	Guam	Y	None
41		97	102	Santos, Jesus Q	Son	M	Cha	6	S	N		Guam		None
42		97	102	Santos, Julia Q	Daughter	F	Cha	4.5	S	N		Guam		None
43		97	102	Santos, Juan Q	Son	M	Cha	2.3	S	N		Guam		None
44		97	102	Santos, Jose Q	Son	M	Cha	.5	S	N		Guam		None
45		98	103	Santos, Joaquin V	Head	M	Cha	49	M	N	N	Guam	Y	Farmer
46		98	103	Santos, Joaquina T	Wife	F	Cha	53	M	N	N	Guam	N	None
47		98	103	Santos, Emilio T	Son	M	Cha	17	S	Y	Y	Guam	Y	None
48		98	103	Santos, Francisco T	Son	M	Cha	14	S	Y	Y	Guam	Y	None
49		98	103	Santos, Rita T	Daughter	F	Cha	8	S	Y		Guam		None
50		99	104	Tenorio, Jose B	Head	M	Cha	35	M	N	Y	Guam	N	Farmer

(CHAMORRO ROOTS GENEALOGY PROJECT™ TRANSCRIPTION)
(BERNARD T. PUNZALAN / HTTP://WWW.CHAMORROROOTS.COM)

DEPARTMENT OF COMMERCE-BUREAU OF THE CENSUS
WASHINGTON

FIFTEENTH CENSUS OF THE UNITED STATES: 1930-POPULATION

THE ISLAND OF GUAM

Sheet No. 11A

188

District **Municipality of Agana**
Name of Place **Dededo Barrio**
[Proper name and, also, name of class, as city, town, village, barrio, etc]

Enumeration District No. **5**
Enumerated by me on **April 10, 1930** Jose Kamminga
Enumerator

	PLACE OF ABODE			NAME	RELATION	PERSONAL DESCRIPTION				EDUCATION		NATIVITY		OCCUPATION
	Street, avenue, road, etc.	Number of dwelling house in order of visitation	Number of family in order of visitation	of each person whose place of abode on April 1, 1930, was in this family. Enter surname, first, then given name and middle initial. If any. Include every person living on April 1, 1930. Omit children born since April 1, 1930.	Relationship of this Person to the head of the family.	Sex	Color or race	Age at last birthday	Single, married, widowed or divorced	Attended school any time since Sept. 1, 1929	Whether able to read and write.	Place of birth of this person.	Whether able to speak English.	
	1	2	3	4	5	6	7	8	9	10	11	12	13	14
1	Dededo Barrio	99	104	Tenorio, Antonia S	Wife	F	Cha	33	M	N	Y	Guam	N	None
2		99	104	Tenorio, Gregorio S	Son	M	Cha	15	S	Y	Y	Guam	Y	None
3		99	104	Tenorio, Juan S	Son	M	Cha	14	S	Y	Y	Guam	Y	None
4		99	104	Tenorio, Antonio S	Son	M	Cha	11	S	Y	Y	Guam	Y	None
5		99	104	Tenorio, Andresina S	Daughter	F	Cha	9	S	Y		Guam		None
6		99	104	Tenorio, Jose A	Son	M	Cha	4.2	S	N		Guam		None
7		99	104	Tenorio, Dolores A	Daughter	F	Cha	1	S	N		Guam		None
8		100	105	Cruz, Jose G	Head	M	Cha	43	M	N	Y	Guam	Y	Farmer
9		100	105	Cruz, Maria C	Wife	F	Cha	39	M	N	N	Guam	N	None
10		100	105	Cruz, Jose C	Son	M	Cha	19	S	N	Y	Guam	Y	None
11		100	105	Cruz, Fermina C	Daughter	F	Cha	17	S	N	Y	Guam	Y	Laundress
12		100	105	Cruz, Jesus C	Son	M	Cha	15	S	Y	Y	Guam	Y	None
13		100	105	Cruz, Francisco C	Son	M	Cha	13	S	N	Y	Guam	Y	None
14		100	105	Cruz, Maria C	Daughter	F	Cha	11	S	Y	Y	Guam	Y	None
15		100	105	Cruz, Elena C	Daughter	F	Cha	10	S	Y	Y	Guam	Y	None
16		100	105	Cruz, Antonio C	Son	M	Cha	7	S	Y		Guam		None
17		100	105	Cruz, Juan C	Son	M	Cha	4.5	S	N		Guam		None
18		100	105	Cruz, Concepcion C	Daughter	F	Cha	2.8	S	N		Guam		None
19		100	105	Cruz, Manuel C	Son	M	Cha	1.5	S	N		Guam		None
20		101	106	San Nicolas, Jose G	Head	M	Cha	46	M	N	N	Guam	N	Farmer
21		101	106	San Nicolas, Francisca C	Wife	F	Cha	39	M	N	N	Guam	N	None
22		101	106	Cruz, Soledad C	Sister-in-law	F	Cha	32	S	N	N	Guam	N	Laundress
23		102	107	Fernandez, Jose L	Head	M	Cha	29	M	N	Y	Guam	Y	Farmer
24		102	107	Fernandez, Ana SA	Wife	F	Cha	28	M	N	Y	Guam	Y	None
25		102	107	Fernandez, Antonia SA	Daughter	F	Cha	6	S	N		Guam		None

(CHAMORRO ROOTS GENEALOGY PROJECT ™ TRANSCRIPTION)
(BERNARD T. PUNZALAN / HTTP://WWW.CHAMORROROOTS.COM)

DEPARTMENT OF COMMERCE-BUREAU OF THE CENSUS
WASHINGTON
FIFTEENTH CENSUS OF THE UNITED STATES: 1930-POPULATION

THE ISLAND OF GUAM

Sheet No. 11B

188B

District **Municipality of Agana**
Name of Place **Dededo Barrio**
[Proper name and, also, name of class, as city, town, village, barrio, etc]

Enumeration District No. 5
Enumerated by me on **April 10, 1930** Jose Kamminga, Enumerator

	PLACE OF ABODE			NAME	RELATION	PERSONAL DESCRIPTION				EDUCATION		NATIVITY		OCCUPATION
	Street, avenue, road, etc.	Number of dwelling house in order of visitation	Number of family in order of visitation	of each person whose place of abode on April 1, 1930, was in this family. Enter surname, first, then given name and middle initial. If any. Include every person living on April 1, 1930. Omit children born since April 1, 1930.	Relationship of this Person to the head of the family.	Sex	Color or race	Age at last birthday	Single, married, widowed or divorced	Attended school any time since Sept. 1, 1929	Whether able to read and write.	Place of birth of this person.	Whether able to speak English.	
	1	2	3	4	5	6	7	8	9	10	11	12	13	14
26	Dededo Barrio	102	107	Fernandez, Jesus SA	Son	M	Cha	4.8	S	N		Guam		None
27		102	107	Fernandez, Maria SA	Daughter	F	Cha	3.7	S	N		Guam		None
28		103	108	San Nicolas, Luis S	Head	M	Cha	23	M	N	Y	Guam	Y	Farmer
29		103	108	San Nicolas, Dolores C	Wife	F	Cha	26	M	N	Y	Guam	N	None
30		103	108	San Nicolas, Adela C	Daughter	F	Cha	7	S	Y		Guam		None
31		103	108	San Nicolas, Francisco C	Son	M	Cha	6	S	N		Guam		None
32		103	108	San Nicolas, Elizabeth C	Daughter	F	Cha	4.8	S	N		Guam		None
33		103	108	San Nicolas, Jose C	Son	M	Cha	2	S	N		Guam		None
34		103	108	San Nicolas, Atanacio C	Son	M	Cha	.3	S	N		Guam		None
35		104	109	Sahagon, Maria Q	Head	F	Cha	64	Wd	N	N	Guam	N	None
36		104	109	Sahagon, Magdalena Q	Daughter	F	Cha	34	S	N	N	Guam	N	None
37		105	110	Babauta, Fortunato J	Head	M	Cha	34	M	N	Y	Guam	Y	Farmer
38		105	110	Babauta, Ana S	Wife	F	Cha	36	M	N	N	Guam	N	None
39		105	110	Babauta, Vicente S	Son	M	Cha	10	S	Y	Y	Guam	Y	None
40		105	110	Babauta, Maria S	Daughter	F	Cha	9	S	Y		Guam		None
41		105	110	Babauta, Joaquina S	Daughter	F	Cha	5.4	S	N		Guam		None
42		105	110	Babauta, Jose S	Son	M	Cha	2.2	S	N		Guam		None
43		105	110	Babauta, Juan S	Son	M	Cha	.4	S	N		Guam		None
44		106	111	Bamba, Juan A	Head	M	Cha	34	M	N	Y	Guam	N	Farmer
45		106	111	Bamba, Maria S	Wife	F	Cha	39	M	N	Y	Guam	N	None
46		106	111	Santos, Pedro S	Step-son	M	Cha	18	S	N	Y	Guam	Y	Farm laborer
47		106	111	Santos, Juan S	Step-son	M	Cha	17	S	N	Y	Guam	Y	Farm laborer
48		106	111	Santos, Regina S	Step-daughter	F	Cha	13	S	N	Y	Guam	Y	None
49		106	111	Santos, Santiago S	Step-son	M	Cha	9	S	Y		Guam		None
50		107	112	Bamba, Vicente SA	Head	M	Cha	33	M	N	Y	Guam	Y	Farmer

DEPARTMENT OF COMMERCE-BUREAU OF THE CENSUS
WASHINGTON

FIFTEENTH CENSUS OF THE UNITED STATES: 1930-POPULATION

THE ISLAND OF GUAM

Sheet No. 12A

District **Municipality of Agana**
Name of Place **Dededo Barrio**
[Proper name and, also, name of class, as city, town, village, barrio, etc]

Enumeration District No. 5
Enumerated by me on **April 11, 1930** Jose Kamminga
Enumerator

	PLACE OF ABODE			NAME	RELATION	PERSONAL DESCRIPTION				EDUCATION		NATIVITY		OCCUPATION
	Street, avenue, road, etc.	Number of dwelling house in order of visitation	Number of family in order of visitation	of each person whose place of abode on April 1, 1930, was in this family. Enter surname, first, then given name and middle initial. If any. Include every person living on April 1, 1930. Omit children born since April 1, 1930.	Relationship of this Person to the head of the family.	Sex	Color or race	Age at last birthday	Single, married, widowed or divorced	Attended school any time since Sept. 1, 1929	Whether able to read and write.	Place of birth of this person.	Whether able to speak English.	
	1	2	3	4	5	6	7	8	9	10	11	12	13	14
1	Dededo Barrio	107	112	Bamba, Concepcion C	Wife	F	Cha	32	M	N	Y	Guam	N	None
2		107	112	Bamba, Maria C	Daughter	F	Cha	14	S	Y	Y	Guam	Y	None
3		107	112	Bamba, Amalia C	Daughter	F	Cha	12	S	Y	Y	Guam	Y	None
4		107	112	Bamba, Nicolas C	Son	M	Cha	10	S	Y	Y	Guam	Y	None
5		107	112	Bamba, Leon C	Son	M	Cha	8	S	Y		Guam		None
6		107	112	Bamba, Jorge C	Son	M	Cha	6	S	N		Guam		None
7		107	112	Bamba, Rita C	Daughter	F	Cha	2.7	S	N		Guam		None
8		108	113	Palomo, Asuncion A	Head	M	Cha	57	Wd	N	N	Guam	N	None
9		108	113	Palomo, Manuel A	Son	M	Cha	22	S	N	Y	Guam	Y	Farm laborer
10		108	113	Palomo, Gabina A	Daughter	F	Cha	19	S	N	Y	Guam	Y	None
11		109	114	Bamba, Jose B	Head	M	Cha	23	M	N	Y	Guam	Y	Farmer
12		110	115	Quitano, Juan C	Head	M	Cha	53	M	N	N	Guam	N	Farmer
13		111	116	Castro, Luis D?	Head	M	Cha	54	M	N	Y	Guam	N	Farmer
14		111	116	Castro, Remedios C	Wife	F	Cha	39	M	N	N	Guam	N	None
15		111	116	Castro, Vicente C	Son	M	Cha	8	S	N		Guam		None
16		111	116	Castro, Vicenta C	Daughter	F	Cha	6	S	N		Guam		None
17		111	116	Castro, Maria C	Daughter	F	Cha	5.7	S	N		Guam		None
18		112	117	Benavente, Joaquin M	Head	M	Cha	40	M	N	N	Guam	N	Farmer
19		112	117	Benavente, Rita S	Wife	F	Cha	40	M	N	Y	Guam	Y	None
20		112	117	Benavente, Joaquin S	Son	M	Cha	13	S	Y	Y	Guam	Y	None
21		112	117	Benavente, Agripina S	Daughter	F	Cha	12	S	Y	Y	Guam	Y	None
22		112	117	Benavente, Jose S	Son	M	Cha	11	S	Y	Y	Guam	Y	None
23		112	117	Benavente, Jesus S	Son	M	Cha	4.8	S	N		Guam		None
24		112	117	Benavente, Vicente S	Son	M	Cha	1.5	S	N		Guam		None
25		113	118	Santos?, Juana T	Head	F	Cha	70	Wd	N	N	Guam	N	None

DEPARTMENT OF COMMERCE-BUREAU OF THE CENSUS
WASHINGTON

FIFTEENTH CENSUS OF THE UNITED STATES: 1930-POPULATION

THE ISLAND OF GUAM

Sheet No. 12B

189B

District **Municipality of Agana**
Name of Place **Dededo Barrio**
[Proper name and, also, name of class, as city, town, village, barrio, etc]

Enumeration District No. 5
Enumerated by me on **April 11, 1930** Jose Kamminga
Enumerator

	PLACE OF ABODE			NAME	RELATION	PERSONAL DESCRIPTION				EDUCATION		NATIVITY		OCCUPATION
	Street, avenue, road, etc.	Number of dwelling house is order of visitation	Number of family in order of visitation	of each person whose place of abode on April 1, 1930, was in this family. Enter surname, first, then given name and middle initial. If any. Include every person living on April 1, 1930. Omit children born since April 1, 1930.	Relationship of this Person to the head of the family.	Sex	Color or race	Age at last birthday	Single, married, widowed or divorced	Attended school any time since Sept. 1, 1929	Whether able to read and write.	Place of birth of this person.	Whether able to speak English.	
	1	2	3	4	5	6	7	8	9	10	11	12	13	14
26	Dededo Barrio	113	118	Taijeron, Enrique T	Son	M	Cha	53	S	N	Y	Guam	N	Farm laborer
27		114	119	Ignacio, Jesus R	Head	M	Cha	39	M	N	Y	Guam	N	Farmer
28		114	119	Ignacio, Rosa A	Wife	F	Cha	42	M	N	N	Guam	N	None
29		115	120	Cruz, Juan A	Head	M	Cha	39	M	N	Y	Guam	N	Farmer
30		115	120	Cruz, Lydia T	Wife	F	Cha	35	M	N	N	Guam	N	None
31		115	120	Cruz, Juan T	Son	M	Cha	11	S	Y	Y	Guam	Y	None
32		115	120	Cruz, Elude T	Son	M	Cha	9	S	Y		Guam		None
33		115	120	Cruz, Joaquin T	Son	M	Cha	6	S	N		Guam		None
34		115	120	Cruz, Elizabeth T	Daughter	F	Cha	5.5	S	N		Guam		None
35		115	120	Cruz, Luisa T	Daughter	F	Cha	3.8	S	N		Guam		None
36		115	120	Cruz, Tomas T	Son	M	Cha	1.2	S	N		Guam		None
37		115	120	Cruz, Carlos T	Son	M	Cha	.3	S	N		Guam		None
38		116	121	Benavente, Maria Q	Head	F	Cha	53	Wd	N	Y	Guam	N	Farmer
39		116	121	Benavente, Cecilia Q	Daughter	F	Cha	21	S	N	Y	Guam	Y	Farm laborer
40		116	121	Benavente, Ana Q	Daughter	F	Cha	18	S	N	Y	Guam	Y	Laundress
41		116	121	Benavente, Rita Q	Daughter	F	Cha	14	S	N	Y	Guam	Y	None
42		117	122	Delgado, Juan F	Head	M	Cha	54	M	N	Y	Guam	N	Farmer
43		117	122	Delgado, Rita M	Wife	F	Cha	52	M	N	N	Guam	N	None
44		117	122	Delgado, Jesus M	Son	M	Cha	30	S	N	Y	Guam	Y	Farm laborer
45		117	122	Delgado, Ana M	Daughter	F	Cha	25	S	N	Y	Guam	Y	None
46		118	123	Leon Guerrero, Jose A	Head	M	Cha	43	M	N	N	Guam	N	Farmer
47		118	123	Leon Guerrero, Elvira D	Wife	F	Cha	28	M	N	Y	Guam	Y	None
48		118	123	Leon Guerrero, Benigno D	Son	M	Cha	5.3	S	N		Guam		None
49		118	123	Leon Guerrero, Jose D	Son	M	Cha	2.6	S	N		Guam		None
50		119	124	Pablo, Exequiel S	Head	M	Cha	48	S	N	Y	Guam	Y	Farmer

(CHAMORRO ROOTS GENEALOGY PROJECT™ TRANSCRIPTION)
(BERNARD T. PUNZALAN / HTTP://WWW.CHAMORROROOTS.COM)

DEPARTMENT OF COMMERCE-BUREAU OF THE CENSUS
WASHINGTON

FIFTEENTH CENSUS OF THE UNITED STATES: 1930-POPULATION

THE ISLAND OF GUAM

Sheet No. 13A

190

District **Municipality of Agana**
Name of Place **Dededo Barrio**
[Proper name and, also, name of class, as city, town, village, barrio, etc]

Enumeration District No. 5
Enumerated by me on **April 12, 1930** Jose Kamminga, Enumerator

	PLACE OF ABODE: Street, avenue, road, etc.	Number of dwelling house in order of visitation	Number of family in order of visitation	NAME of each person whose place of abode on April 1, 1930, was in this family. Enter surname, first, then given name and middle initial. If any. Include every person living on April 1, 1930. Omit children born since April 1, 1930.	RELATION Relationship of this Person to the head of the family.	PERSONAL DESCRIPTION: Sex	Color or race	Age at last birthday	Single, married, widowed or divorced	EDUCATION: Attended school any time since Sept. 1, 1929	Whether able to read and write.	NATIVITY Place of birth of this person.	Whether able to speak English.	OCCUPATION
	1	2	3	4	5	6	7	8	9	10	11	12	13	14
1	Dededo Barrio	120	125	Cruz, Vicente B	Head	M	Cha	26	M	N	Y	Guam	Y	Farmer
2		120	125	Cruz, Maria Q	Wife	F	Cha	33	M	N	Y	Guam	Y	None
3		120	125	Cruz, Jose Q	Son	M	Cha	1.9	S	N		Guam		None
4		120	125	Cruz, Rosario Q	Daughter	F	Cha	.8	S	N		Guam		None
5		121	126	Santos, Pedro S	Head	M	Cha	24	M	N	Y	Guam	Y	Farmer
6		121	126	Santos, Antonia C	Wife	F	Cha	22	M	N	Y	Guam	Y	None
7		122	127	Castro, Pedro D	Head	M	Cha	46	M	N	Y	Guam	N	Farmer
8		122	127	Castro, Joaquina SN	Wife	F	Cha	43	M	N	N	Guam	N	None
9		122	127	Castro, Maria SN	Daughter	F	Cha	23	S	N	Y	Guam	Y	Laundress
10		122	127	Castro, Jesus SN	Son	M	Cha	16	S	N	Y	Guam	Y	Farm laborer
11		122	127	Castro, Rufina SN	Daughter	F	Cha	14	S	N	Y	Guam	Y	None
12		122	127	Castro, Juan SN	Son	M	Cha	9	S	Y		Guam		None
13		122	127	Castro, Pedro SN	Son	M	Cha	6	S	N		Guam		None
14		123	128	Benavente, Justo B	Head	M	Cha	56	M	N	N	Guam	Y	Farmer
15		123	128	Benavente, Dolores D	Wife	F	Cha	56	M	N	N	Guam	N	None
16		123	128	Benavente, Josefa D	Daughter	F	Cha	14	S	N	Y	Guam	Y	None
17		123	128	San Agustin, Eliza D	Niece	F	Cha	4.4	S	N		Guam		None
18		124	129	Cruz, Jose P	Head	M	Cha	52	M	N	Y	Guam	N	Farmer
19		124	129	Cruz, Josefa C	Wife	F	Cha	33	M	N	Y	Guam	Y	None
20		124	129	Cruz, Jose M	Son	M	Cha	25	S	N	Y	Guam	Y	Farm laborer
21		124	129	Afaisen, Ramon A	Step-son	M	Cha	11	S	Y	Y	Guam	Y	None
22		124	129	Afaisen, Regina A	Step-daughter	F	Cha	9	S	Y		Guam		None
23		124	129	Afaisen, Jesus A	Step-son	M	Cha	5.3	S	N		Guam		None
24		125	130	San Agustin, Vicente D	Head	M	Cha	38	M	N	N	Guam	N	Farmer
25		125	130	San Agustin, Josefa M	Wife	F	Cha	34	M	N	N	Guam	N	None

(CHAMORRO ROOTS GENEALOGY PROJECT™ TRANSCRIPTION)
(BERNARD T. PUNZALAN / HTTP://WWW.CHAMORROROOTS.COM)

DEPARTMENT OF COMMERCE-BUREAU OF THE CENSUS
WASHINGTON

FIFTEENTH CENSUS OF THE UNITED STATES: 1930-POPULATION

THE ISLAND OF GUAM

Sheet No. 13B

190B

District Municipality of Agana
Name of Place Dededo Barrio
[Proper name and, also, name of class, as city, town, village, barrio, etc]

Enumeration District No. 5
Enumerated by me on April 12, 1930 Jose Kamminga
Enumerator

	PLACE OF ABODE			NAME	RELATION	PERSONAL DESCRIPTION				EDUCATION		NATIVITY		OCCUPATION
	Street, avenue, road, etc.	Number of dwelling house is order of visitation	Number of family in order of visitation	of each person whose place of abode on April 1, 1930, was in this family. Enter surname, first, then given name and middle initial. If any. Include every person living on April 1, 1930. Omit children born since April 1, 1930.	Relationship of this Person to the head of the family.	Sex	Color or race	Age at last birthday	Single, married, widowed or divorced	Attended school any time since Sept. 1, 1929	Whether able to read and write.	Place of birth of this person.	Whether able to speak English.	
	1	2	3	4	5	6	7	8	9	10	11	12	13	14
26	Dededo Barrio	125	130	San Agustin, Joaquin C	Son	M	Cha	3.7	S	N		Guam		None
27		126	131	San Agustin, Francisco C	Head	M	Cha	64	M	N	N	Guam	N	Farmer
28		126	131	San Agustin, Antonia C	Wife	F	Cha	59	M	N	N	Guam	N	None
29		126	131	San Agustin, Mariano C	Son	M	Cha	29	S	N	Y	Guam	Y	Farm laborer
30		127	132	Santos, Ignacio A	Head	M	Cha	59	M	N	N	Guam	Y	Farmer
31		127	132	Santos, Angela S	Wife	F	Cha	59	M	N	N	Guam	N	None
32		127	132	Santos, Maria S	Daughter	F	Cha	23	S	N	Y	Guam	Y	None
33		127	132	Santos, Jesus S	Son	M	Cha	19	S	N	Y	Guam	Y	Farm laborer
34		127	132	Santos, Rosario S	Daughter	F	Cha	17	S	N	Y	Guam	Y	None
35		127	132	Santos, Jane S	Grand daughter	F	Cha	.7	S	N	Y	Guam		None
36		128	133	Rosario, Jose B	Head	M	Cha	46	M	N	Y	Guam	N	Farmer
37		128	133	Rosario, Ana P	Wife	F	Cha	36	M	N	N	Guam	N	None
38		128	133	Rosario, Jesus P	Son	M	Cha	16	S	N	Y	Guam	Y	Farm laborer
39		128	133	Rosario, Lourdes P	Daughter	F	Cha	15	S	N	Y	Guam	Y	None
40		128	133	Rosario, Jose P	Son	M	Cha	13	S	Y	Y	Guam	Y	None
41		128	133	Rosario, Gregorio P	Son	M	Cha	10	S	Y	Y	Guam	Y	None
42		128	133	Rosario, Maria P	Daughter	F	Cha	9	S	Y		Guam		None
43		128	133	Rosario, Joaquin P	Son	M	Cha	4.2	S	N		Guam		None
44		129	134	Cruz, Pedro G	Head	M	Cha	50	M	N	Y	Guam	N	Farmer
45		129	134	Cruz, Maria H	Wife	F	Cha	50	M	N	Y	Guam	N	None
46		129	134	Cruz, Maria H	Daughter	F	Cha	28	S	N	Y	Guam	Y	Laundress
47		129	134	Cruz, Rosario H	Daughter	F	Cha	18	S	N	Y	Guam	Y	None
48		129	134	Cruz, Pedro H	Son	M	Cha	13	S	Y	Y	Guam	Y	None
49		129	134	Cruz, Ignacia H	Daughter	F	Cha	10	S	Y	Y	Guam	Y	None
50		129	134	Cruz, Jesus H	Son	M	Cha	7	S	Y		Guam		None

DEPARTMENT OF COMMERCE-BUREAU OF THE CENSUS
WASHINGTON

FIFTEENTH CENSUS OF THE UNITED STATES: 1930-POPULATION

THE ISLAND OF GUAM

Sheet No. 14A

District Municipality of Agana
Name of Place Dededo Barrio
[Proper name and, also, name of class, as city, town, village, barrio, etc]

Enumeration District No. 5
Enumerated by me on April 12, 1930 Jose Kamminga, Enumerator

	PLACE OF ABODE: Street, avenue, road, etc.	Number of dwelling house in order of visitation	Number of family in order of visitation	NAME of each person whose place of abode on April 1, 1930, was in this family. Enter surname, first, then given name and middle initial. If any. Include every person living on April 1, 1930. Omit children born since April 1, 1930.	RELATION Relationship of this Person to the head of the family.	PERSONAL DESCRIPTION: Sex	Color or race	Age at last birthday	Single, married, widowed or divorced	EDUCATION: Attended school any time since Sept. 1, 1929	Whether able to read and write.	NATIVITY Place of birth of this person.	Whether able to speak English.	OCCUPATION
	1	2	3	4	5	6	7	8	9	10	11	12	13	14
1	Dededo Barrio	129	135	Benavente, Jose Q	Head	M	Cha	22	M	N	Y	Guam	Y	Farmer
2		129	135	Benavente, Elena C	Wife	F	Cha	23	M	N	Y	Guam	Y	None
3		130	136	Benavente, Vicente M	Head	M	Cha	55	M	N	Y	Guam	N	Farmer
4		130	136	Benavente, Vicenta G	Wife	F	Cha	46	M	N	N	Guam	N	None
5		130	136	Benavente, Maria G	Daughter	F	Cha	16	S	N	Y	Guam	Y	Laundress
6		130	136	Benavente, Jesus G	Son	M	Cha	14	S	Y	Y	Guam	Y	None
7		130	136	Benavente, Joaquin G	Son	M	Cha	14	S	Y	Y	Guam	Y	None
8		130	136	Benavente, Ana G	Daughter	F	Cha	11	S	Y	Y	Guam	Y	None
9		130	136	Benavente, Grabiela G	Daughter	F	Cha	9	S	Y		Guam		None
10		130	136	Benavente, Rosalia G	Daughter	F	Cha	3.3	S	N		Guam		None
11		131	137	Palomo, Francisco D	Head	M	Cha	27	M	N	Y	Guam	Y	Farmer
12		131	137	Palomo, Maria C	Wife	F	Cha	37	M	N	Y	Guam	N	None
13		131	137	Palomo, Francisco C	Son	M	Cha	2.4	S	N		Guam		None
14		131	137	Palomo, Maria C	Daughter	F	Cha	.2	S	N		Guam		None
15		132	138	Borja, Mariano R	Head	M	Cha	33	M	N	Y	Guam	N	Farmer
16		132	138	Borja, Maria M	Wife	F	Cha	35	M	N	Y	Guam	N	None
17		132	138	Mesa, Rosa	Niece	F	Cha	6	S	N		Guam		None
18		133	139	Lujan, Manuel M	Head	M	Cha	31	M	N	Y	Guam	Y	Farmer
19		133	139	Lujan, Antonia LG	Wife	F	Cha	29	M	N	Y	Guam	Y	None
20		133	139	Lujan, Jose LG	Son	M	Cha	6	S	N		Guam		None
21		133	139	Lujan, David LG	Son	M	Cha	4.4	S	N		Guam		None
22		133	139	Lujan, Ignacio LG	Son	M	Cha	3	S	N		Guam		None
23		133	139	Lujan, Josefina LG	Daughter	F	Cha	1.4	S	N		Guam		None
24		134	140	Duenas, Ramon Q	Head	M	Cha	28	M	N	N	Guam	N	Farmer
25		134	140	Duenas, Nicolasa C	Wife	F	Cha	23	M	N	N	Guam	N	None

DEPARTMENT OF COMMERCE-BUREAU OF THE CENSUS
WASHINGTON

FIFTEENTH CENSUS OF THE UNITED STATES: 1930-POPULATION

THE ISLAND OF GUAM

Sheet No. 14B

191B

District **Municipality of Agana**
Name of Place **Dededo Barrio**
[Proper name and, also, name of class, as city, town, village, barrio, etc]

Enumeration District No. **5**
Enumerated by me on **April 14, 1930** Jose Kamminga, Enumerator

	PLACE OF ABODE			NAME	RELATION	PERSONAL DESCRIPTION				EDUCATION		NATIVITY		OCCUPATION
	Street, avenue, road, etc.	Number of dwelling house is order of visitation	Number of family in order of visitation	of each person whose place of abode on April 1, 1930, was in this family. Enter surname, first, then given name and middle initial. If any. Include every person living on April 1, 1930. Omit children born since April 1, 1930.	Relationship of this Person to the head of the family.	Sex	Color or race	Age at last birthday	Single, married, widowed or divorced	Attended school any time since Sept. 1, 1929	Whether able to read and write.	Place of birth of this person.	Whether able to speak English.	
	1	2	3	4	5	6	7	8	9	10	11	12	13	14
26	Dededo Barrio	134	140	Duenas, Manuel C	Son	M	Cha	5.3	S	N		Guam		None
27		134	140	Duenas, Jose C	Son	M	Cha	3.4	S	N		Guam		None
28		134	140	Duenas, Emelia C	Daughter	F	Cha	2.3	S	N		Guam		None
29		135	141	San Agustin, Jose E	Head	M	Cha	47	M	N	Y	Guam	N	Farmer
30		135	141	San Agustin, Caridad R	Wife	F	Cha	39	M	N	N	Guam	N	None
31		135	141	San Agustin, Juan R	Son	M	Cha	18	S	N	Y	Guam	Y	Farm laborer
32		135	141	San Agustin, Isabel R	Daughter	F	Cha	15	S	N	Y	Guam	Y	Laundress
33		135	141	San Agustin, Josefina R	Daughter	F	Cha	7	S	N		Guam		None
34		135	141	San Agustin, Jesus R	Son	M	Cha	5.3	S	N		Guam		None
35		135	141	San Agustin, Maria R	Daughter	F	Cha	2.2	S	N		Guam		None
36		135	141	San Agustin, Mariano R	Son	M	Cha	1.5	S	N		Guam		None
37		136	142	Lujan, Maria S	Head	F	Cha	44	S	N	Y	Guam	N	None
38		136	142	Lujan, Enrique M	Son	M	Cha	23	S	N	Y	Guam	Y	Farm laborer
39		136	142	Lujan, Paz M	Daughter	F	Cha	21	S	N	Y	Guam	Y	Laundress
40		136	142	Lujan, Joaquin M	Son	M	Cha	14	S	N	Y	Guam	Y	Farm laborer
41		136	142	Lujan, Juan M	Son	M	Cha	12	S	Y	Y	Guam	Y	None
42		137	143	Flores, Jose F	Head	M	Cha	26	M	N	Y	Guam	Y	Farmer
43		137	143	Flores, Ana LG	Wife	F	Cha	25	M	N	Y	Guam	Y	None
44		137	143	Flores, Juan LG	Son	M	Cha	6	S	N		Guam		None
45		137	143	Flores, Artemio LG	Son	M	Cha	4.3	S	N		Guam		None
46		137	143	Flores, Jose LG	Son	M	Cha	3.7	S	N		Guam		None
47		137	143	Flores, Pedro LG	Son	M	Cha	1.6	S	N		Guam		None
48		137	143	Flores, Juana LG	Daughter	F	Cha	.5	S	N		Guam		None
49		138	144	Duenas, Florencio Q	Head	M	Cha	37	M	N	Y	Guam	N	Farmer
50		138	144	Duenas, Dolores F	Wife	F	Cha	48	M	N	Y	Guam	Y	None

DEPARTMENT OF COMMERCE-BUREAU OF THE CENSUS
WASHINGTON

FIFTEENTH CENSUS OF THE UNITED STATES: 1930-POPULATION

THE ISLAND OF GUAM

Sheet No. 15A

District Municipality of Agana
Name of Place Dededo Barrio
[Proper name and, also, name of class, as city, town, village, barrio, etc]

Enumeration District No. 5
Enumerated by me on April 15, 1930 Jose Kamminga
Enumerator

	PLACE OF ABODE			NAME	RELATION	PERSONAL DESCRIPTION				EDUCATION		NATIVITY		OCCUPATION
	Street, avenue, road, etc.	Number of dwelling house in order of visitation	Number of family in order of visitation	of each person whose place of abode on April 1, 1930, was in this family. Enter surname, first, then given name and middle initial. If any. Include every person living on April 1, 1930. Omit children born since April 1, 1930.	Relationship of this Person to the head of the family.	Sex	Color or race	Age at last birthday	Single, married, widowed or divorced	Attended school any time since Sept. 1, 1929	Whether able to read and write.	Place of birth of this person.	Whether able to speak English.	
	1	2	3	4	5	6	7	8	9	10	11	12	13	14
1	Dededo Barrio	138	144	Duenas, Juanita F	Son	M	Cha	7	S	N		Guam		None
2		138	144	Duenas, Lolita F	Daughter	F	Cha	4.2	S	N		Guam		None
3		138	144	Duenas, Conchita F	Daughter	F	Cha	2.7	S	N		Guam		None
4		138	144	James, Woodrow F	Step-son	M	Cha	11	S	Y		Guam		None
5		138	144	Duenas, Manuel L	Uncle	M	Cha	63	S	N	Y	Guam	Y	None
6		139	145	Leon Guerrero, Francisco C	Head	M	Cha	31	M	N	Y	Guam	Y	Farmer
7		139	145	Leon Guerrero, Ana C	Wife	F	Cha	37	M	N	Y	Guam	N	None
8		139	145	Leon Guerrero, Jesus C	Son	M	Cha	7	S	Y		Guam		None
9		139	145	Leon Guerrero, Juan C	Son	M	Cha	5.9	S	N		Guam		None
10		139	145	Leon Guerrero, Antonio C	Son	M	Cha	2.3	S	N		Guam		None
11		139	145	Leon Guerrero, Josefina C	Daughter	F	Cha	1	S	N		Guam		None
12		139	145	Borja, Francisco C	Step-son	M	Cha	17	S	N	Y	Guam	Y	Farm laborer
13		139	145	Borja, Gregorio C	Step-son	M	Cha	15	S	N	Y	Guam	N	Farm laborer
14		139	145	Borja, Jose C	Step-son	M	Cha	14	S	Y	Y	Guam	Y	None
15		139	145	Borja, Nicolasa C	Step-daughter	F	Cha	11	S	Y	Y	Guam	Y	None
16		139	145	Borja, Vicente C	Step-son	M	Cha	10	S	Y	Y	Guam	Y	None
17		140	146	Cruz, Carlos J	Head	M	Cha	39	M	N	Y	Guam	N	Farmer
18		140	146	Cruz, Gertrudes T	Wife	F	Cha	28	M	N	Y	Guam	N	None
19		140	146	Cruz, Francisco T	Son	M	Cha	5.3	S	N		Guam		None
20		140	146	Cruz, Margarita T	Daughter	F	Cha	3.6	S	N		Guam		None
21		140	146	Cruz, Rita T	Daughter	F	Cha	.1	S	N		Guam		None
22		141	147	Olive, Euell Francis	Head	M	W	33	M	N	Y	New Mexico	Y	Farmer
23		141	147	Olive, Concepcion T	Wife	F	Cha	29	M	N	Y	Guam	Y	None
24		141	147	Olive, Franklin T	Son	M	Cha	12	S	Y	Y	Guam	Y	None
25		141	147	Olive, Euella T	Daughter	F	Cha	8	S	Y		Philippine Is.		None

DEPARTMENT OF COMMERCE-BUREAU OF THE CENSUS
WASHINGTON

FIFTEENTH CENSUS OF THE UNITED STATES: 1930-POPULATION

THE ISLAND OF GUAM

Sheet No. 15B

192B

District **Municipality of Agana**
Name of Place **Dededo Barrio**
[Proper name and, also, name of class, as city, town, village, barrio, etc]

Enumeration District No. 5
Enumerated by me on **April 16, 1930** Jose Kamminga, Enumerator

	PLACE OF ABODE			NAME	RELATION	PERSONAL DESCRIPTION				EDUCATION		NATIVITY		OCCUPATION
	Street, avenue, road, etc.	Number of dwelling house is order of visitation	Number of family in order of visitation	of each person whose place of abode on April 1, 1930, was in this family. Enter surname, first, then given name and middle initial. If any. Include every person living on April 1, 1930. Omit children born since April 1, 1930.	Relationship of this Person to the head of the family.	Sex	Color or race	Age at last birthday	Single, married, widowed or divorced	Attended school any time since Sept. 1, 1929	Whether able to read and write.	Place of birth of this person.	Whether able to speak English.	
	1	2	3	4	5	6	7	8	9	10	11	12	13	14
26	Dededo Barrio	141	147	Olive, Ruth T	Daughter	F	Cha	3.3	S	N		Guam		None
27		142	148	Garrido, Vicente B	Head	M	Cha	50	M	N	N	Guam	N	Farmer
28		142	148	Garrido, Maria C	Wife	F	Cha	49	M	N	N	Guam	N	None
29		142	148	Garrido, Maria C	Daughter	F	Cha	26	S	N	Y	Guam	Y	Laundress
30		142	148	Garrido, Jesus C	Son	M	Cha	23	S	N	Y	Guam	Y	Farm laborer
31		142	148	Martinez, Mariano C	Boarder	M	Cha	26	S	N	Y	Guam	Y	Farmer
32		143	149	Cruz, Pedro S	Head	M	Cha	40	M	N	Y	Guam	N	Farmer
33		143	149	Cruz, Maria B	Wife	F	Cha	40	M	N	Y	Guam	N	None
34		143	149	Cruz, Vicente B	Son	M	Cha	17	S	N	Y	Guam	Y	Farm laborer
35		143	149	Cruz, Nicolasa B	Daughter	F	Cha	15	S	N	Y	Guam	Y	Laundress
36		143	149	Cruz, Josefina B	Daughter	F	Cha	13	S	Y	Y	Guam	Y	None
37		143	149	Cruz, Maria B	Daughter	F	Cha	11	S	Y	Y	Guam	Y	None
38		143	149	Cruz, Jose B	Son	M	Cha	9	S	Y		Guam		None
39		143	149	Cruz, Pedro B	Son	M	Cha	5.3	S	N		Guam		None
40		143	149	Cruz, Juan B	Son	M	Cha	2.3	S	N		Guam		None
41		143	149	Cruz, Jesus B	Son	M	Cha	.9	S	N		Guam		None
42		143	149	Guerrero, Joaquin SN	Servant	M	Cha	49	S	N	N	Guam	N	Farm laborer
43		144	150	Palomo, Juan A	Head	M	Cha	48	Wd	N	Y	Guam	N	Farmer
44		144	150	Palomo, Vicente D	Son	M	Cha	20	S	N	Y	Guam	Y	Farm laborer
45		144	150	Palomo, Rita D	Daughter	F	Cha	18	S	N	Y	Guam	Y	None
46		144	150	Palomo, Juan D	Son	M	Cha	16	S	N	Y	Guam	Y	Farm laborer
47		145	151	Tenorio, Vicente B	Head	M	Cha	41	M	N	Y	Guam	N	Farmer
48		145	151	Tenorio, Tomasa SN	Wife	F	Cha	40	M	N	N	Guam	N	None
49		145	151	Tenorio, Francisco SN	Son	M	Cha	19	S	N	Y	Guam	Y	Farm laborer
50		145	151	Tenorio, Dolores SN	Daughter	F	Cha	17	S	N	Y	Guam	Y	Laundress

(CHAMORRO ROOTS GENEALOGY PROJECT™ TRANSCRIPTION)
(BERNARD T. PUNZALAN / HTTP://WWW.CHAMORROROOTS.COM)

DEPARTMENT OF COMMERCE-BUREAU OF THE CENSUS
WASHINGTON

FIFTEENTH CENSUS OF THE UNITED STATES: 1930-POPULATION

THE ISLAND OF GUAM

Sheet No. 16A

193

District **Municipality of Agana**
Name of Place **Dededo Barrio**
[Proper name and, also, name of class, as city, town, village, barrio, etc]

Enumeration District No. 5
Enumerated by me on April 17, 1930 Jose Kamminga, Enumerator

	PLACE OF ABODE			NAME	RELATION	PERSONAL DESCRIPTION				EDUCATION		NATIVITY		OCCUPATION
	Street, avenue, road, etc.	Number of dwelling house in order of visitation	Number of family in order of visitation	of each person whose place of abode on April 1, 1930, was in this family. Enter surname, first, then given name and middle initial. If any. Include every person living on April 1, 1930. Omit children born since April 1, 1930.	Relationship of this Person to the head of the family.	Sex	Color or race	Age at last birthday	Single, married, widowed or divorced	Attended school any time since Sept. 1, 1929	Whether able to read and write.	Place of birth of this person.	Whether able to speak English.	
	1	2	3	4	5	6	7	8	9	10	11	12	13	14
1	Dededo Barrio	145	151	Tenorio, Luis SN	Son	M	Cha	13	S	Y	Y	Guam	Y	None
2		145	151	Tenorio, Roberto SN	Son	M	Cha	11	S	Y	Y	Guam	Y	None
3		145	151	Tenorio, Jose SN	Son	M	Cha	9	S	Y		Guam		None
4		145	151	Tenorio, Maria SN	Daughter	F	Cha	8	S	Y		Guam		None
5		145	151	Tenorio, Sederino SN	Son	M	Cha	6	S	N		Guam		None
6		145	151	Tenorio, Juan SN	Son	M	Cha	3.9	S	N		Guam		None
7		145	151	Tenorio, Damiana SN	Daughter	F	Cha	2.5	S	N		Guam		None
8		146	152	Cruz, Antonio G	Head	M	Cha	39	M	N	Y	Guam	N	Farmer
9		146	152	Cruz, Antonio B	Son	M	Cha	17	S	N	Y	Guam	Y	Farm laborer
10		146	152	Cruz, Maria B	Daughter	F	Cha	15	S	N	Y	Guam	Y	None
11		146	152	Cruz, Jose B	Son	M	Cha	14	S	Y	Y	Guam	Y	None
12		146	152	Cruz, Jesus B	Son	M	Cha	10	S	Y	Y	Guam	Y	None
13		146	152	Cruz, Ana B	Daughter	F	Cha	9	S	Y		Guam		None
14		146	152	Cruz, Juan B	Son	M	Cha	2.3	S	N		Guam		None
15		147	153	San Agustin, Jose D	Head	M	Cha	31	M	N	Y	Guam	Y	Farmer
16		147	153	San Agustin, Susana P	Wife	F	Cha	28	M	N	N	Guam	Y	None
17		147	153	San Agustin, Maria P	Daughter	F	Cha	6	S	N		Guam		None
18		147	153	San Agustin, Ramon P	Son	M	Cha	3.9	S	N		Guam		None
19		147	153	San Agustin, Jose P	Son	M	Cha	.6	S	N		Guam		None
20		148	154	Cruz, Joaquin A	Head	M	Cha	53	M	N	Y	Guam	N	Farmer
21		149	155	Mesa, Jose M	Head	M	Cha	37	M	N	Y	Guam	Y	Farmer
22		149	155	Mesa, Maria SA	Wife	F	Cha	37	M	N	Y	Guam	Y	None
23		149	155	San Agustin, Rosa C	Step-daughter	F	Cha	13	S	N	Y	Guam	Y	None
24		150	156	San Agustin, Maria Q	Head	F	Cha	31	Wd	N	Y	Guam	Y	Servant
25		150	156	San Agustin, Arturo C	Son	M	Cha	7	S	Y		Guam		None

DEPARTMENT OF COMMERCE-BUREAU OF THE CENSUS
WASHINGTON

FIFTEENTH CENSUS OF THE UNITED STATES: 1930-POPULATION
THE ISLAND OF GUAM

Sheet No. 16B

193B

District Municipality of Agana
Name of Place Dededo Barrio
[Proper name and, also, name of class, as city, town, village, barrio, etc]

Enumeration District No. 5
Enumerated by me on April 17, 1930 Jose Kamminga
Enumerator

	PLACE OF ABODE			NAME	RELATION	PERSONAL DESCRIPTION				EDUCATION		NATIVITY		OCCUPATION
	Street, avenue, road, etc.	Number of dwelling house is order of visitation	Number of family in order of visitation	of each person whose place of abode on April 1, 1930, was in this family. Enter surname, first, then given name and middle initial. If any. Include every person living on April 1, 1930. Omit children born since April 1, 1930.	Relationship of this Person to the head of the family.	Sex	Color or race	Age at last birthday	Single, married, widowed or divorced	Attended school any time since Sept. 1, 1929	Whether able to read and write.	Place of birth of this person.	Whether able to speak English.	
	1	2	3	4	5	6	7	8	9	10	11	12	13	14
26	Dededo Barrio	150	156	San Agustin, Jesusa C	Daughter	F	Cha	1.3	S	N		Guam		None
27		151	157	Quitugua, Manuel C	Head	M	Cha	35	S	N	Y	Guam	Y	Farmer
28		152	158	Benavente, Manuel T	Head	M	Cha	47	M	N	N	Guam	N	Farmer
29		152	158	Benavente, Teresa Q	Wife	F	Cha	41	M	N	N	Guam	N	None
30		152	158	Benavente, Tomas Q	Son	M	Cha	17	S	Y	Y	Guam	Y	None
31		152	158	Benavente, Manuel Q	Son	M	Cha	14	S	Y	Y	Guam	Y	Farm laborer
32		152	158	Benavente, Eloi Q	Son	M	Cha	13	S	Y	Y	Guam	Y	None
33		152	158	Benavente, Antonia Q	Daughter	F	Cha	11	S	Y	Y	Guam	Y	None
34		152	158	Benavente, Sisto Q	Son	M	Cha	10	S	Y	Y	Guam	Y	None
35		152	158	Benavente, Ramon Q	Son	M	Cha	8	S	Y		Guam		None
36		152	158	Benavente, Juliana Q	Daughter	F	Cha	6	S	N		Guam		None
37		152	158	Benavente, Maria Q	Daughter	F	Cha	4.6	S	N		Guam		None
38		152	158	Benavente, Juan Q	Son	M	Cha	3.6	S	N		Guam		None
39		152	158	Gomez, Jose	Boarder	M	Cha	33	S	N	N	Guam	N	Farm laborer
40		153	159	Iriarte, Jose R	Head	M	Cha	63	Wd	N	N	Guam	N	Farmer
41		153	159	Quidachay, Joaquina C	Servant	F	Cha	54	M	N	N	Guam	Y	None
42		154	160	Mesa, Dolores R	Head	F	Cha	65	Wd	N	N	Guam	N	None
43		154	160	Mesa, Maria R	Daughter	F	Cha	28	S	N	N	Guam	N	None
44		154	160	Mesa, Manuel R	Son	M	Cha	23	S	N	N	Guam	N	Farm laborer
45		154	160	Mesa, Ana R	Niece	F	Cha	3.5	S	N		Guam		None
46		155	161	Fernandez, Jose Q	Head	M	Cha	55	M	N	Y	Guam	N	Farmer
47		155	161	Fernandez, Joaquina L	Wife	F	Cha	48	M	N	N	Guam	N	None
48		155	161	Fernandez, Juan L	Son	M	Cha	26	S	N	Y	Guam	Y	Laborer
49		155	161	Fernandez, Jesus L	Son	M	Cha	19	S	N	Y	Guam	Y	Cook
50		155	161	Fernandez, Maria L	Daughter	F	Cha	18	S	N	Y	Guam	Y	Servant

(CHAMORRO ROOTS GENEALOGY PROJECT™ TRANSCRIPTION)
(BERNARD T. PUNZALAN / HTTP://WWW.CHAMORROROOTS.COM)

DEPARTMENT OF COMMERCE-BUREAU OF THE CENSUS
WASHINGTON

FIFTEENTH CENSUS OF THE UNITED STATES: 1930-POPULATION

THE ISLAND OF GUAM

Sheet No. 17A

194

District Municipality of Agana
Name of Place Dededo Barrio
[Proper name and, also, name of class, as city, town, village, barrio, etc]

Enumeration District No. 5
Enumerated by me on April 18, 1930 Jose Kamminga, Enumerator

	PLACE OF ABODE			NAME	RELATION	PERSONAL DESCRIPTION				EDUCATION		NATIVITY		OCCUPATION
	Street, avenue, road, etc.	Number of dwelling house in order of visitation	Number of family in order of visitation	of each person whose place of abode on April 1, 1930, was in this family. Enter surname, first, then given name and middle initial. If any. Include every person living on April 1, 1930. Omit children born since April 1, 1930.	Relationship of this Person to the head of the family.	Sex	Color or race	Age at last birthday	Single, married, widowed or divorced	Attended school any time since Sept. 1, 1929	Whether able to read and write.	Place of birth of this person.	Whether able to speak English.	
	1	2	3	4	5	6	7	8	9	10	11	12	13	14
1	Dededo Barrio	155	161	Fernandez, Jose L	Son	M	Cha	20	S	N	Y	Guam	Y	Farm laborer
2		155	161	Fernandez, Jesus L	Son	M	Cha	19	S	N	Y	Guam	Y	Farm laborer
3		155	161	Fernandez, Soledad L	Daughter	F	Cha	18	S	N	Y	Guam	Y	None
4		155	161	Fernandez, Vicente L	Son	M	Cha	17	S	N	Y	Guam	Y	Farm laborer
5		155	161	Fernandez, Gonzalo L	Son	M	Cha	14	S	Y	Y	Guam	Y	None
6		155	161	Fernandez, Paz L	Daughter	F	Cha	13	S	Y	Y	Guam	Y	None
7		155	161	Fernandez, Consolacion L	Daughter	F	Cha	9	S	Y		Guam		None
8		155	161	Fernandez, Santiago L	Son	M	Cha	7	S	Y		Guam		None
9		155	161	Fernandez, Ana L	Daughter	F	Cha	5.9	S	N		Guam		None
10		155	161	Lujan, Paz S	Mother-in-law	F	Cha	83	S	N	N	Guam	N	None
11		156	162	Benavente, Juan D	Head	M	Cha	42	M	N	N	Guam	N	Farmer
12		156	162	Benavente, Ana Q	Wife	F	Cha	30	M	N	Y	Guam	Y	None
13		156	162	Benavente, Josefina Q	Daughter	F	Cha	5.8	S	N		Guam		None
14		156	162	Benavente, Lourdes Q	Daughter	F	Cha	4.5	S	N		Guam		None
15		156	162	Benavente, Juan Q	Son	M	Cha	3.8	S	N		Guam		None
16		156	162	Benavente, Maria Q	Daughter	F	Cha	.8	S	N		Guam		None
17		157	163	Guerrero, Jose P	Head	M	Cha	46	M	N	N	Guam	N	Farmer
18		157	163	Guerrero, Nicolasa C	Wife	F	Cha	34	M	N	N	Guam	N	None
19		157	163	Guerrero, Jose C	Son	M	Cha	2.8	S	N		Guam		None
20		157	163	Guerrero, Francisco C	Son	M	Cha	1.5	S	N		Guam		None
21		157	163	Guerrero, Cesario P	Son	M	Cha	21	S	N	Y	Guam	Y	Farm laborer
22		157	163	Guerrero, Maria P	Daughter	F	Cha	18	S	N	Y	Guam	Y	None
23		157	163	Guerrero, Jesus P	Son	M	Cha	17	S	Y	Y	Guam	Y	None
24		157	163	Guerrero, Enrique P	Son	M	Cha	15	S	Y	Y	Guam	Y	None
25		157	163	Guerrero, Josefina P	Daughter	F	Cha	13	S	Y	Y	Guam	Y	None

(CHAMORRO ROOTS GENEALOGY PROJECT™ TRANSCRIPTION)
(BERNARD T. PUNZALAN / HTTP://WWW.CHAMORROROOTS.COM)

DEPARTMENT OF COMMERCE-BUREAU OF THE CENSUS
WASHINGTON

FIFTEENTH CENSUS OF THE UNITED STATES: 1930-POPULATION

THE ISLAND OF GUAM

Sheet No. 17B

194B

District **Municipality of Agana**
Name of Place **Dededo Barrio**
[Proper name and, also, name of class, as city, town, village, barrio, etc]

Enumeration District No. 5
Enumerated by me on **April 19, 1930** Jose Kamminga
Enumerator

	PLACE OF ABODE			NAME	RELATION	PERSONAL DESCRIPTION				EDUCATION		NATIVITY		OCCUPATION
	Street, avenue, road, etc.	Number of dwelling house in order of visitation	Number of family in order of visitation	of each person whose place of abode on April 1, 1930, was in this family. Enter surname, first, then given name and middle initial. If any. Include every person living on April 1, 1930. Omit children born since April 1, 1930.	Relationship of this Person to the head of the family.	Sex	Color or race	Age at last birthday	Single, married, widowed or divorced	Attended school any time since Sept. 1, 1929	Whether able to read and write.	Place of birth of this person.	Whether able to speak English.	
	1	2	3	4	5	6	7	8	9	10	11	12	13	14
26	Dededo Barrio	158	164	Cepeda, Jesus Q	Head	M	Cha	27	M	N	Y	Guam	Y	Farmer
27		158	164	Cepeda, Milagro A	Wife	F	Cha	19	M	N	Y	Guam	Y	None
28		158	164	Cepeda, Maria A	Daughter	F	Cha	1.5	S	N		Guam		None
29		159	165	Quidachay, Jesus B	Head	M	Cha	25	S	N	Y	Guam	Y	Farmer
30		160	166	Cruz, Jose G	Head	M	Cha	29	M	N	Y	Guam	Y	Farmer
31		160	166	Cruz, Leonsia C	Wife	F	Cha	37	M	N	Y	Guam	Y	None
32		160	167	Cruz, Paula G	Head	F	Cha	60	Wd	N	N	Guam	N	None
33		160	167	Cruz, Rosa G	Daughter	F	Cha	26	S	N	N	Guam	N	None
34		160	167	Cruz, Juliana G	Grand-daughter	F	Cha	9	S	Y		Guam		None
35		160	167	Cruz, Jesus G	Grand-son	M	Cha	2.5	S	N		Guam		None
36		160	167	Cruz, Nieves G	Grand-daughter	F	Cha	.6	S	N		Guam		None
37		161	168	Taijeron, Geronimo C	Head	M	Cha	36	M	N	N	Guam	N	Farmer
38		161	168	Taijeron, Maria S	Wife	F	Cha	38	M	N	N	Guam	N	None
39		161	168	Taijeron, Isidro S	Son	M	Cha	10	S	Y	Y	Guam	Y	None
40		161	168	Taijeron, Jose S	Son	M	Cha	8	S	Y		Guam		None
41		161	168	Taijeron, Maria S	Daughter	F	Cha	7	S	Y		Guam		None
42		161	168	Taijeron, Eliza S	Daughter	F	Cha	6.5	S	N		Guam		None
43		161	168	Taijeron, Olimpia S	Daughter	F	Cha	2.3	S	N		Guam		None
44		161	168	Taijeron, Preciardo S	Son	M	Cha	.1	S	N		Guam		None
45		162	169	Cruz, Francisco S	Head	M	Cha	54	Wd	N	N	Guam	N	Farmer
46		163	170	Bautista, Francisco B	Head	M	Cha	37	Wd ?	N	N	Guam	N	Farmer
47		164	171	Benavente, Pedro M	Head	M	Cha	30	M	N	Y	Guam	Y	Farmer
48		164	171	Benavente, Josefa G	Wife	F	Cha	27	M	N	Y	Guam	Y	None
49		164	171	Benavente, Dolores G	Daughter	F	Cha	8	S	Y		Guam		None
50		164	171	Benavente, Jose G	Son	M	Cha	4.3	S	N		Guam		None

DEPARTMENT OF COMMERCE-BUREAU OF THE CENSUS
WASHINGTON

FIFTEENTH CENSUS OF THE UNITED STATES: 1930-POPULATION

THE ISLAND OF GUAM

Sheet No. 18A

District **Municipality of Agana**
Name of Place **Dededo Barrio**
[Proper name and, also, name of class, as city, town, village, barrio, etc]

Enumeration District No. 5
Enumerated by me on **April 19, 1930** Jose Kamminga, Enumerator

	PLACE OF ABODE			NAME	RELATION	PERSONAL DESCRIPTION				EDUCATION		NATIVITY		OCCUPATION
	Street, avenue, road, etc.	Number of dwelling house in order of visitation	Number of family in order of visitation	of each person whose place of abode on April 1, 1930, was in this family. Enter surname, first, then given name and middle initial. If any. Include every person living on April 1, 1930. Omit children born since April 1, 1930.	Relationship of this Person to the head of the family.	Sex	Color or race	Age at last birthday	Single, married, widowed or divorced	Attended school any time since Sept. 1, 1929	Whether able to read and write.	Place of birth of this person.	Whether able to speak English.	
	1	2	3	4	5	6	7	8	9	10	11	12	13	14
1	Dededo Barrio	164	171	Benavente, Juan G	Son	M	Cha	2.8	S	N		Guam		None
2		164	171	Benavente, Pedro G	Son	M	Cha	1.2	S	N		Guam		None
3		165	172	Quintanilla, Jesus D	Head	M	Cha	27	M	N	Y	Guam	Y	Farmer
4		165	172	Quintanilla, Lucia S	Wife	F	Cha	21	M	N	Y	Guam	Y	None
5		165	172	Quintanilla, Maria S	Daughter	F	Cha	1.7	S	N		Guam		None
6		165	172	Quintanilla, Juan S	Son	M	Cha	.3	S	N		Guam		None
7		166	173	San Agustin, Ramon S	Head	M	Cha	25	M	N	Y	Guam	Y	Farmer
8		166	173	San Agustin, Dolores M	Wife	F	Cha	26	M	N	Y	Guam	Y	Midwife
9		166	173	San Agustin, Olimpia M	Daughter	F	Cha	2.5	S	N		Guam		None
10		167	171	Palomo, Vicente A	Head	M	Cha	57	M	N	Y	Guam	N	Farmer
11		167	171	Palomo, Ana R	Wife	F	Cha	57	M	N	Y	Guam	N	None
12		167	171	Palomo, Jesus R	Son	M	Cha	21	S	N	Y	Guam	Y	Clerk
13		167	171	Palomo, Vicente R	Son	M	Cha	16	S	Y	Y	Guam	Y	None
14		168	175	Lujan, Jesus S	Head	M	Cha	52	Wd	N	Y	Guam	N	Farmer
15		168	175	Lujan, Juan S	Son	M	Cha	31	S	N	Y	Guam	Y	Farm laborer
16		168	175	Lujan, Rosa S	Daughter	F	Cha	17	S	N	Y	Guam	Y	None
17		168	175	Lujan, Joaquin S	Son	M	Cha	15	S	N	Y	Guam	Y	Farm laborer
18		168	175	Lujan, Dolores L	Grand-daughter	F	Cha	6	S	N		Guam		None
19		169	176	Benavente, Vicente B	Head	M	Cha	46	M	N	Y	Guam	N	Farmer
20		169	176	Benavente, Maria G	Wife	F	Cha	40	M	N	Y	Guam	N	None
21		169	176	Benavente, Jose G	Son	M	Cha	21	S	N	Y	Guam	Y	Farm laborer
22		169	176	Benavente, Ignacia G	Daughter	F	Cha	19	S	N	Y	Guam	Y	None
23		169	176	Benavente, Mariano G	Son	M	Cha	18	S	N	Y	Guam	Y	Farm laborer
24		169	176	Benavente, Joaquin G	Son	M	Cha	16	S	Y	Y	Guam	Y	None
25		169	176	Benavente, Manuela G	Daughter	F	Cha	15	S	N	Y	Guam	Y	None

(CHAMORRO ROOTS GENEALOGY PROJECT™ TRANSCRIPTION)
(BERNARD T. PUNZALAN / HTTP://WWW.CHAMORROROOTS.COM)

DEPARTMENT OF COMMERCE-BUREAU OF THE CENSUS
WASHINGTON

FIFTEENTH CENSUS OF THE UNITED STATES: 1930-POPULATION

THE ISLAND OF GUAM

Sheet No. 18B

195B

District **Municipality of Agana**
Name of Place **Dededo Barrio**
[Proper name and, also, name of class, as city, town, village, barrio, etc]

Enumeration District No. 5
Enumerated by me on **April 21, 1930** Jose Kamminga, Enumerator

	PLACE OF ABODE			NAME	RELATION	PERSONAL DESCRIPTION				EDUCATION		NATIVITY		OCCUPATION
	Street, avenue, road, etc.	Number of dwelling house in order of visitation	Number of family in order of visitation	of each person whose place of abode on April 1, 1930, was in this family. Enter surname, first, then given name and middle initial. If any. Include every person living on April 1, 1930. Omit children born since April 1, 1930.	Relationship of this Person to the head of the family.	Sex	Color or race	Age at last birthday	Single, married, widowed or divorced	Attended school any time since Sept. 1, 1929	Whether able to read and write.	Place of birth of this person.	Whether able to speak English.	
	1	2	3	4	5	6	7	8	9	10	11	12	13	14
26	Dededo Barrio	169	176	Benavente, Isabel G	Daughter	F	Cha	13	S	Y	Y	Guam	Y	None
27		169	176	Benavente, Rosa G	Daughter	F	Cha	11	S	Y	Y	Guam	Y	None
28		169	176	Benavente, Maria G	Daughter	F	Cha	9	S	Y		Guam		None
29		169	176	Benavente, Rita G	Daughter	F	Cha	7	S	Y		Guam		None
30		169	176	Benavente, Rufina G	Daughter	F	Cha	5.8	S	N		Guam		None
31		169	176	Benavente, Vicente G	Son	M	Cha	3.8	S	N		Guam		None
32		169	176	Benavente, Jesus G	Son	M	Cha	2.4	S	N		Guam		None
33		169	176	Benavente, Julia G	Daughter	F	Cha	.8	S	N		Guam		None
34		169	176	Guerrero, Ignacia P	Mother-in-law	F	Cha	57	S	N	N	Guam	N	None
35		170	177	Rosario, Juan B	Head	M	Cha	36	M	N	Y	Guam	N	Farmer
36		170	177	Rosario, Maria C	Wife	F	Cha	47	M	N	N	Guam	N	None
37		170	177	Rosario, Maria C	Daughter	F	Cha	14	S	Y	Y	Guam	Y	None
38		170	177	Rosario, Antonio C	Son	M	Cha	13	S	Y	Y	Guam	Y	None
39		171	178	Cruz, Vicente S	Head	M	Cha	31	M	N	Y	Guam	Y	Farmer
40		171	178	Cruz, Juliana C	Wife	F	Cha	25	M	N	N	Guam	Y	None
41		171	178	Cruz, Dolores C	Daughter	F	Cha	5.6	S	N		Guam		None
42		171	178	Cruz, Perpetua C	Daughter	F	Cha	4.3	S	N		Guam		None
43		171	178	Cruz, Jose C	Son	M	Cha	2.7	S	N		Guam		None
44		171	178	Cruz, Veronica C	Daughter	F	Cha	1.3	S	N		Guam		None
45		172	179	Santos, Jose S	Head	M	Cha	35	Wd	N	Y	Guam	Y	Farmer
46		172	179	Santos, Maria S	Daughter	F	Cha	13	S	Y	Y	Guam	Y	None
47		172	179	Santos, Angela S	Daughter	F	Cha	7	S	Y		Guam		None
48		172	179	Santos, Ana S	Daughter	F	Cha	6	S	N		Guam		None
49		173	180	Hernandez, Ramon E	Head	M	Cha	44	M	N	N	Guam	N	Farmer
50		173	180	Hernandez, Maria B	Wife	F	Cha	43	M	N	N	Guam	N	None

(CHAMORRO ROOTS GENEALOGY PROJECT™ TRANSCRIPTION)
(BERNARD T. PUNZALAN / HTTP://WWW.CHAMORROROOTS.COM)

DEPARTMENT OF COMMERCE-BUREAU OF THE CENSUS
WASHINGTON

FIFTEENTH CENSUS OF THE UNITED STATES: 1930-POPULATION

THE ISLAND OF GUAM

Sheet No. 19A

District **Municipality of Agana**
Name of Place **Dededo Barrio**
[Proper name and, also, name of class, as city, town, village, barrio, etc]

Enumeration District No. 5
Enumerated by me on **April 22, 1930** Jose Kamminga, Enumerator

	PLACE OF ABODE			NAME	RELATION	PERSONAL DESCRIPTION				EDUCATION		NATIVITY		OCCUPATION
	Street, avenue, road, etc.	Number of dwelling house is order of visitation	Number of family in order of visitation	of each person whose place of abode on April 1, 1930, was in this family. Enter surname, first, then given name and middle initial. If any. Include every person living on April 1, 1930. Omit children born since April 1, 1930.	Relationship of this Person to the head of the family.	Sex	Color or race	Age at last birthday	Single, married, widowed or divorced	Attended school any time since Sept. 1, 1929	Whether able to read and write.	Place of birth of this person.	Whether able to speak English.	
	1	2	3	4	5	6	7	8	9	10	11	12	13	14
1	Dededo Barrio	173	180	Hernandez, Juning B	Daughter	F	Cha	15	S	N	Y	Guam	Y	None
2		173	180	Hernandez, Francisco B	Son	M	Cha	13	S	Y	Y	Guam	Y	None
3		173	180	Hernandez, Rosario B	Daughter	F	Cha	7	S	Y		Guam		None
4		173	180	Hernandez, Ignacia B	Daughter	F	Cha	6	S	N		Guam		None
5		173	180	Hernandez, Maria B	Daughter	F	Cha	6	S	N		Guam		None
6		173	180	Hernandez, Joaquin B	Son	M	Cha	4.6	S	N		Guam		None
7		173	180	Benavente, Jose B	Step-son	M	Cha	22	S	N	Y	Guam	Y	None
8		173	180	Hernandez, Carmen B	Niece	F	Cha	9	S	Y		Guam		None
9		174	181	Mesa, Luis C	Head	M	Cha	43	M	N	N	Guam	N	Farmer
10		174	181	Mesa, Consolacion S	Wife	F	Cha	35	M	N	N	Guam	Y	None
11		174	181	Santos, Juan P	Step-son	M	Cha	13	S	Y	Y	Guam	Y	None
12		175	182	Mendiola, Juan B	Head	M	Cha	52	M	N	Y	Guam	N	Farmer
13		175	183	Borja, Soledad B	Head	F	Cha	34	S	N	N	Guam	N	None
14		175	183	Borja, Josefa B	Daughter	F	Cha	10	S	Y	Y	Guam	Y	None
15		175	183	Borja, Maria B	Daughter	F	Cha	6	S	N		Guam		None
16		176	184	Castro, Juan R	Head	M	Cha	58	S	N	Y	Guam	N	Farmer
17		176	185	Borja, Ignacia B	Head	F	Cha	32	S	N	N	Guam	N	None
18		176	185	Borja, Rosa B	Daughter	F	Cha	.2	S	N		Guam		None
19		177	186	Pablo, Joaquin P	Head	M	Cha	41	M	N	N	Guam	Y	Farmer
20		177	186	Pablo, Juan C	Son	M	Cha	17	S	N	Y	Guam	Y	Farm laborer
21		177	186	Pablo, Jose C	Son	M	Cha	10	S	Y	Y	Guam	Y	None
22		178	187	Rosario, Ignacio A	Head	M	Cha	44	M	N	N	Guam	N	Farmer
23		178	187	Rosario, Soledad G	Wife	F	Cha	36	M	N	N	Guam	N	None
24		178	187	Rosario, George G	Son	M	Cha	8	S	Y		Guam		None
25		178	187	Rosario, Maria G	Daughter	F	Cha	6	S	N		Guam		None

(CHAMORRO ROOTS GENEALOGY PROJECT™ TRANSCRIPTION)
(BERNARD T. PUNZALAN / HTTP://WWW.CHAMORROROOTS.COM)

DEPARTMENT OF COMMERCE-BUREAU OF THE CENSUS
WASHINGTON

FIFTEENTH CENSUS OF THE UNITED STATES: 1930-POPULATION

THE ISLAND OF GUAM

Sheet No. 19B

196B

District **Municipality of Agana**
Name of Place **Dededo Barrio**
[Proper name and, also, name of class, as city, town, village, barrio, etc]

Enumeration District No. 5
Enumerated by me on April 23, 1930 Jose Kamminga
Enumerator

	PLACE OF ABODE			NAME	RELATION	PERSONAL DESCRIPTION				EDUCATION		NATIVITY		OCCUPATION
	Street, avenue, road, etc.	Number of dwelling house in order of visitation	Number of family in order of visitation	of each person whose place of abode on April 1, 1930, was in this family. Enter surname, first, then given name and middle initial. If any. Include every person living on April 1, 1930. Omit children born since April 1, 1930.	Relationship of this Person to the head of the family.	Sex	Color or race	Age at last birthday	Single, married, widowed or divorced	Attended school any time since Sept. 1, 1929	Whether able to read and write.	Place of birth of this person.	Whether able to speak English.	
	1	2	3	4	5	6	7	8	9	10	11	12	13	14
26	Dededo Barrio	178	187	Rosario, Jose G	Son	M	Cha	3.4	S	N		Guam		None
27		178	187	Lujan, Maria G	Step-daughter	F	Cha	18	S	N	Y	Guam	Y	None
28		178	187	Lujan, Victor G	Step-son	M	Cha	17	S	Y	Y	Guam	Y	None
29		179	188	Gomez, Manuela C	Head	F	Cha	27	M	N	Y	Guam	N	None
30		179	188	Gomez, Jose C	Son	M	Cha	3.1	S	N		Guam		None
31		179	188	Gomez, Rosa C	Daughter	F	Cha	1.5	S	N		Guam		None
32		179	188	Pablo, Antonia C	Mother	F	Cha	40	M		N	Guam	N	None
33		180	189	Cruz, Felipe A	Head	M	Cha	55	M	N	N	Guam	N	None
34		180	189	Cruz, Vicenta LG	Wife	F	Cha	54	M	N	N	Guam	N	None
35		180	189	Cruz, Rosa LG	Daughter	F	Cha	16	S	N	Y	Guam	Y	None
36		180	189	Cruz, Fidela LG	Daughter	F	Cha	14	S	N	Y	Guam	Y	None
37		180	190	Gumataotao, Tomas LG	Head	M	Cha	40	M	N	Y	Guam	N	Farmer
38		180	190	Gumataotao, Antonia C	Wife	F	Cha	26	M	N	Y	Guam	N	None
39		180	190	Gumataotao, Olimpia C	Daughter	F	Cha	6	S	N		Guam		None
40		180	190	Gumataotao, Emiliana C	Daughter	F	Cha	5.3	S	N		Guam		None
41		180	190	Gumataotao, Jose C	Son	M	Cha	.4	S	N		Guam		None
42		180	191	Chargualaf, Manuel SN	Head	M	Cha	26	M	N	N	Guam	Y	Farmer
43		180	191	Chargualaf, Isabel LG	Wife	F	Cha	21	M	N	N	Guam	N	None
44		181	192	Mendosa, Ana M	Head	F	Cha	57	Wd	N	Y	Guam	Y	None
45		181	192	Millinchamp, Henry	Father	M	W	90	Wd	N	Y	Bonin Island	Y	None
46		181	193	Garrido, Joaquin G	Head	M	Cha	63	M	N	N	Guam	N	Farmer
47		182	194	San Agustin, Faustino SA	Head	M	Cha	40	M	N	Y	Guam	N	Farmer
48		182	194	San Agustin, Josefa M	Wife	F	Cha	36	M	N	Y	Guam	N	None
49		182	194	San Agustin, Victor M	Son	M	Cha	14	S	Y	Y	Guam	Y	None
50		182	194	San Agustin, Pedro M	Son	M	Cha	11	S	Y	Y	Guam	Y	None

DEPARTMENT OF COMMERCE-BUREAU OF THE CENSUS
WASHINGTON

FIFTEENTH CENSUS OF THE UNITED STATES: 1930-POPULATION

THE ISLAND OF GUAM

Sheet No. 20A

District **Municipality of Agana**
Name of Place **Dededo Barrio**
[Proper name and, also, name of class, as city, town, village, barrio, etc]

Enumeration District No. **5**
Enumerated by me on **April 23, 1930** Jose Kamminga, Enumerator

	PLACE OF ABODE			NAME	RELATION	PERSONAL DESCRIPTION				EDUCATION		NATIVITY		OCCUPATION
	Street, avenue, road, etc.	Number of dwelling house in order of visitation	Number of family in order of visitation	of each person whose place of abode on April 1, 1930, was in this family. Enter surname, first, then given name and middle initial. If any. Include every person living on April 1, 1930. Omit children born since April 1, 1930.	Relationship of this Person to the head of the family.	Sex	Color or race	Age at last birthday	Single, married, widowed or divorced	Attended school any time since Sept. 1, 1929	Whether able to read and write.	Place of birth of this person.	Whether able to speak English.	
	1	2	3	4	5	6	7	8	9	10	11	12	13	14
1	Dededo Barrio	182	194	San Agustin, Vicente M	Son	M	Cha	8	S	Y		Guam		None
2		182	194	San Agustin, Rosa M	Daughter	F	Cha	4.8	S	N		Guam		None
3		183	195	Castro, Vicente I	Head	M	Cha	52	M	N	Y	Guam	Y	Farmer
4		183	195	Castro, Maria F	Wife	F	Cha	49	M	N	N	Guam	N	None
5		183	196	Feja, Francisco F	Head	M	Cha	31	M	N	Y	Guam	Y	Painter
6		183	196	Feja, Vicenta F	Wife	F	Cha	29	M	N	Y	Guam	N	None
7		183	196	Feja, Maria F	Daughter	F	Cha	5.9	S	N		Guam		None
8		183	197	Cruz, Jose LG	Head	M	Cha	29	M	N	N	Guam	N	Farmer
9		183	197	Cruz, Soledad C	Wife	F	Cha	26	M	N	Y	Guam	Y	None
10		183	197	Cruz, Josefa C	Daughter	F	Cha	2.3	S	N		Guam		None
11		183	197	Cruz, Natividad C	Daughter	F	Cha	.2	S	N		Guam		None
12		184	198	Cruz, Juan M	Head	M	Cha	65	M	N	N	Guam	N	Farmer
13		184	199	Sablan, Ana C	Head	F	Cha	41	S	N	N	Guam	N	None
14		184	199	Sablan, Jesus C	Son	M	Cha	26	S	N	N	Guam	N	Laborer
15		184	199	Sablan, Maria C	Daughter	F	Cha	19	S	N	N	Guam	N	None
16		184	199	Sablan, Engracia C	Daughter	F	Cha	16	S	N	N	Guam	Y	None
17		184	199	Sablan, Vicente C	Son	M	Cha	6	S	N		Guam		None
18		184	199	Sablan, Francisco C	Son	M	Cha	2.7	S	N		Guam		None
19		184	199	Sablan, Francisca C	Daughter	F	Cha	1.3	S	N		Guam		None
20		184	199	Sablan, Felicita C	Daughter	F	Cha	.2	S	N		Guam		None
21		185	200	Flores, Manuel P	Head	M	Cha	40	M	N	Y	Guam	Y	Policeman
22		185	200	Flores, Trinidad A	Wife	F	Cha	40	M	N	Y	Guam	N	None
23		185	200	Flores, Virginia A	Daughter	F	Cha	12	S	Y	Y	Guam	Y	None
24		185	200	Flores, Manuel A	Son	M	Cha	10	S	Y		Guam	Y	None
25		185	200	Flores, Jose A	Son	M	Cha	6	S	N		Guam		None

(CHAMORRO ROOTS GENEALOGY PROJECT™ TRANSCRIPTION)
(BERNARD T. PUNZALAN / HTTP://WWW.CHAMORROROOTS.COM)

DEPARTMENT OF COMMERCE-BUREAU OF THE CENSUS
WASHINGTON

FIFTEENTH CENSUS OF THE UNITED STATES: 1930-POPULATION

THE ISLAND OF GUAM

Sheet No. 20B

197B

District Municipality of Agana
Name of Place Dededo Barrio
[Proper name and, also, name of class, as city, town, village, barrio, etc]

Enumeration District No. 5
Enumerated by me on April 24, 1930 Jose Kamminga, Enumerator

	PLACE OF ABODE			NAME	RELATION	PERSONAL DESCRIPTION				EDUCATION		NATIVITY		OCCUPATION
	Street, avenue, road, etc.	Number of dwelling house is order of visitation	Number of family in order of visitation	of each person whose place of abode on April 1, 1930, was in this family. Enter surname, first, then given name and middle initial. If any. Include every person living on April 1, 1930. Omit children born since April 1, 1930.	Relationship of this Person to the head of the family.	Sex	Color or race	Age at last birthday	Single, married, widowed or divorced	Attended school any time since Sept. 1, 1929	Whether able to read and write.	Place of birth of this person.	Whether able to speak English.	
	1	2	3	4	5	6	7	8	9	10	11	12	13	14
26	Dededo Barrio	185	200	Flores, Vicente A	Son	M	Cha	3.5	S	N		Guam		None
27		185	200	Flores, Dolores A	Daughter	F	Cha	1.8	S	N		Guam		None
28		186	201	Rivera, Joaquin U	Head	M	Cha	60	Wd	N	Y	Guam	N	Farmer
29		186	201	Rivera, Rosa U	Mother	F	Cha	80	Wd	N	Y	Guam	N	None
30		186	201	Ulloa, Juan U	Nephew	M	Cha	11	S	Y	Y	Guam	Y	None
31		187	202	Aguon, Rosa I	Head	F	Cha	23	M	N	Y	Guam	Y	None
32		188	203	Iriarte, Jose C	Head	M	Cha	31	S	N	Y	Guam	N	Farmer
33		189	204	Rivera, Manuel SN	Head	M	Cha	27	M	N	Y	Guam	Y	Farmer
34		189	204	Rivera, Amalia SA	Wife	F	Cha	26	M	N	Y	Guam	Y	None
35		189	204	Rivera, Jose SA	Son	M	Cha	8	S	Y		Guam		None
36		189	204	Rivera, Juan SA	Son	M	Cha	4.8	S	N		Guam		None
37		189	204	Rivera, Gonzalo SA	Son	M	Cha	1.2	S	N		Guam		None
38		190	205	Gumataotao, Antonio L	Head	M	Cha	42	M	N	Y	Guam	N	Farmer
39		190	205	Gumataotao, Rita L	Wife	F	Cha	41	M	N	Y	Guam	N	None
40		190	205	Gumataotao, Juan L	Son	M	Cha	20	S	N	Y	Guam	Y	Laborer
41		190	205	Gumataotao, Emilia L	Daughter	F	Cha	15	S	Y	Y	Guam	Y	None
42		190	205	Gumataotao, Ana L	Daughter	F	Cha	12	S	Y	Y	Guam	Y	None
43		190	205	Gumataotao, Rafael L	Son	M	Cha	10	S	Y	Y	Guam	Y	None
44		190	205	Gumataotao, Francisco L	Son	M	Cha	8	S	Y		Guam		None
45		190	205	Gumataotao, Joaquin L	Son	M	Cha	6	S	N		Guam		None
46		190	205	Gumataotao, Maria L	Daughter	F	Cha	4.5	S	N		Guam		None
47		190	205	Gumataotao, Carlos L	Son	M	Cha	2.4	S	N		Guam		None
48		190	205	Gumataotao, Jose L	Son	M	Cha	.5	S	N		Guam		None
49		191	206	Torres, Jose L	Head	M	Cha	27	M	N	Y	Guam	Y	Farmer
50		191	206	Torres, Carmen C	Wife	F	Cha	23	M	N	Y	Guam	Y	None

(CHAMORRO ROOTS GENEALOGY PROJECT™ TRANSCRIPTION)
(BERNARD T. PUNZALAN / HTTP://WWW.CHAMORROROOTS.COM)

DEPARTMENT OF COMMERCE-BUREAU OF THE CENSUS
WASHINGTON

FIFTEENTH CENSUS OF THE UNITED STATES: 1930-POPULATION

THE ISLAND OF GUAM

Sheet No. 21A | **198**

District **Municipality of Agana**
Name of Place **Dededo Barrio**
[Proper name and, also, name of class, as city, town, village, barrio, etc]

Enumeration District No. 5
Enumerated by me on **April 24, 1930** Jose Kamminga, Enumerator

	PLACE OF ABODE			NAME	RELATION	PERSONAL DESCRIPTION				EDUCATION		NATIVITY		OCCUPATION
	Street, avenue, road, etc.	Number of dwelling house in order of visitation	Number of family in order of visitation	of each person whose place of abode on April 1, 1930, was in this family. Enter surname, first, then given name and middle initial. If any. Include every person living on April 1, 1930. Omit children born since April 1, 1930.	Relationship of this Person to the head of the family.	Sex	Color or race	Age at last birthday	Single, married, widowed or divorced	Attended school any time since Sept. 1, 1929	Whether able to read and write.	Place of birth of this person.	Whether able to speak English.	
	1	2	3	4	5	6	7	8	9	10	11	12	13	14
1	Dededo Barrio	191	206	Torres, Antonio C	Son	M	Cha	4.8	S	N		Guam		None
2		191	206	Torres, Jesus C	Son	M	Cha	3.5	S	N		Guam		None
3		191	206	Torres, Dolores C	Daughter	F	Cha	1.9	S	N		Guam		None
4		192	207	Benavente, Ignacio T	Head	M	Cha	79	Wd	N	N	Guam	N	Farmer
5		192	207	Benavente, Grabiela T	Daughter	F	Cha	49	Wd	N	N	Guam	N	None
6		192	207	Ogo, Maria F	Servant	F	Cha	16	S	N	Y	Guam	Y	None
7		193	208	Torres, Jose H	Head	M	Cha	37	M	N	Y	Guam	Y	Farmer
8		193	208	Torres, Isabel A	Wife	F	Cha	28	M	N	Y	Guam	Y	None
9		193	208	Torres, Vicente A	Son	M	Cha	2.8	S	N		Guam		None
10		193	208	Torres, Jose A	Son	M	Cha	1.8	S	N		Guam		None
11		193	208	Torres, Dolores A	Daughter	F	Cha	.3	S	N		Guam		None
12		194	209	Perez, Gregorio G	Head	M	Cha	31	M	N	Y	Guam	Y	Farmer
13		194	209	Perez, Antonia SA	Wife	F	Cha	28	M	N	N	Guam	Y	None
14		194	209	Perez, Alejandra SA	Daughter	F	Cha	8	S	Y		Guam		None
15		194	209	Perez, Josefa SA	Daughter	F	Cha	5.2	S	N		Guam		None
16		194	209	Perez, Jose SA	Son	M	Cha	1.6	S	N		Guam		None
17		194	210	Camacho, Juan B	Head	M	Cha	42	S	N	Y	Guam	N	Farmer
18		195	211	Asuncion, Vicente B	Head	M	Cha	75	M	N	Y	Guam	N	Farmer
19		195	211	Asuncion, Nieves P	Wife	F	Cha	80	M	N	N	Guam	N	None
20		195	212	Chargualaf, Jose SN	Head	M	Cha	23	M	N	N	Guam	N	Farmer
21		195	212	Chargualaf, Lorenzo P	Wife	F	Cha	25	M	N	N	Guam	N	None
22		195	212	Chargualaf, Eulogio P	Son	M	Cha	2.4	S	N		Guam		None
23		195	212	Chargualaf, Juan P	Son	M	Cha	.6	S	N		Guam		None
24		196	213	Salas, Lucas S	Head	M	Cha	70	M	N	Y	Guam	N	Farmer
25		196	213	Salas, Juana	Wife	F	Cha	68	M	N	Y	Guam	N	None

(CHAMORRO ROOTS GENEALOGY PROJECT™ TRANSCRIPTION)
(BERNARD T. PUNZALAN / HTTP://WWW.CHAMORROROOTS.COM)

DEPARTMENT OF COMMERCE-BUREAU OF THE CENSUS
WASHINGTON

FIFTEENTH CENSUS OF THE UNITED STATES: 1930-POPULATION

THE ISLAND OF GUAM

Sheet No. 21B

198B

District **Municipality of Agana**
Name of Place **Dededo Barrio**
[Proper name and, also, name of class, as city, town, village, barrio, etc]

Enumeration District No. **5**
Enumerated by me on **April 25, 1930** Jose Kamminga, Enumerator

	PLACE OF ABODE			NAME	RELATION	PERSONAL DESCRIPTION				EDUCATION		NATIVITY		OCCUPATION
	Street, avenue, road, etc.	Number of dwelling house in order of visitation	Number of family in order of visitation	of each person whose place of abode on April 1, 1930, was in this family. Enter surname, first, then given name and middle initial. If any. Include every person living on April 1, 1930. Omit children born since April 1, 1930.	Relationship of this Person to the head of the family.	Sex	Color or race	Age at last birthday	Single, married, widowed or divorced	Attended school any time since Sept. 1, 1929	Whether able to read and write.	Place of birth of this person.	Whether able to speak English.	
	1	2	3	4	5	6	7	8	9	10	11	12	13	14
26	Dededo Barrio	197	214	Anderson, Leon Q	Head	M	Cha	67	M	N	Y	Guam	Y	Farmer
27		197	214	Anderson, Antonia P	Wife	F	Cha	63	M	N	Y	Guam	N	None
28		198	215	Matanane, Juan M	Head	M	Cha	45	M	N	N	Guam	N	Farmer
29		198	215	Matanane, Carmen SN	Wife	F	Cha	40	M	N	N	Guam	N	None
30		199	216	Cruz, Vidal J	Head	M	Cha	45	M	N	N	Guam	N	Farmer
31		199	216	Cruz, Rufina C	Wife	F	Cha	40	M	N	N	Guam	N	None
32		199	216	Cruz, Ana C	Daughter	F	Cha	12	S	N	Y	Guam	Y	None
33		199	216	Cruz, Juan C	Son	M	Cha	3.8	S	N		Guam		None
34		199	216	Cruz, Gregorio C	Son	M	Cha	1.7	S	N		Guam		None
35		200	217	Chargualaf, Juan R	Head	M	Cha	44	M	N	Y	Guam	Y	Farmer
36		200	217	Chargualaf, Ana R	Wife	F	Cha	40	M	N	Y	Guam	Y	None
37		200	217	Chargualaf, Juan R	Son	M	Cha	11	S	Y	Y	Guam	Y	None
38		200	217	Chargualaf, Ana R	Daughter	F	Cha	4.2	S	N		Guam		None
39		200	217	Chargualaf, Julita R	Daughter	F	Cha	.2	S	N		Guam		None
40		201	218	Ojeda, Francisco M	Head	M	Cha	45	S	N	N	Guam	Y	Farmer
41		202	219	Pablo, Ana V	Head	F	Cha	59	Wd	N	N	Guam	N	None
42		202	219	Pablo, Maria V	Daughter	F	Cha	32	S	N	Y	Guam	Y	Servant
43		202	219	Pablo, Joaquin V	Son	M	Cha	15	S	N	N	Guam	Y	Farm laborer
44		202	219	Pablo, Felicita V	Grand daughter	F	Cha	5.9	S	N		Guam		None
45		203	220	San Agustin, Ignacio C	Head	M	Cha	30	M	N	Y	Guam	Y	Farmer
46		203	220	San Agustin, Gertrudes C	Wife	F	Cha	26	M	N	N	Guam	N	None
47		203	220	San Agustin, Juan C	Son	M	Cha	7	S	Y		Guam		None
48		203	220	San Agustin, Ana C	Daughter	F	Cha	4.6	S	N		Guam		None
49		203	220	San Agustin, Gregorio C	Son	M	Cha	1.9	S	N		Guam		None
50		204	221	Duenas, Jesus E	Head	M	Cha	59	M	N	N	Guam	N	Farmer

DEPARTMENT OF COMMERCE-BUREAU OF THE CENSUS
WASHINGTON

FIFTEENTH CENSUS OF THE UNITED STATES: 1930-POPULATION

THE ISLAND OF GUAM

Sheet No. 22A

District Municipality of Agana
Name of Place Dededo Barrio
[Proper name and, also, name of class, as city, town, village, barrio, etc]

Enumeration District No. 5
Enumerated by me on April 25, 1930 Jose Kamminga, Enumerator

	PLACE OF ABODE			NAME	RELATION	PERSONAL DESCRIPTION				EDUCATION		NATIVITY		OCCUPATION
	Street, avenue, road, etc.	Number of dwelling house is order of visitation	Number of family in order of visitation	of each person whose place of abode on April 1, 1930, was in this family. Enter surname, first, then given name and middle initial. If any. Include every person living on April 1, 1930. Omit children born since April 1, 1930.	Relationship of this Person to the head of the family.	Sex	Color or race	Age at last birthday	Single, married, widowed or divorced	Attended school any time since Sept. 1, 1929	Whether able to read and write.	Place of birth of this person.	Whether able to speak English.	
	1	2	3	4	5	6	7	8	9	10	11	12	13	14
1	Dededo Barrio	204	221	Duenas, Maria S	Wife	F	Cha	43	M	N	N	Guam	N	None
2		204	221	Duenas, Esperanza S	Daughter	F	Cha	6	S	N		Guam		None
3		204	221	Duenas, Santiago S	Son	M	Cha	6.8	S	N		Guam		None
4		204	221	Duenas, Dometrio S	Son	M	Cha	6.8	S	N		Guam		None
5		204	221	Duenas, Jose S	Son	M	Cha	.8	S	N		Guam		None
6		204	221	Duenas, Jesus S	Son	M	Cha	.8	S	N		Guam		None
7		204	221	Duenas, Isabel B	Daughter	F	Cha	16	S	N	Y	Guam	Y	Servant
8		204	221	Duenas, Maria B	Daughter	F	Cha	15	S	N	Y	Guam	Y	Servant
9		204	221	Duenas, Manuel B	Son	M	Cha	14	S	N	Y	Guam	Y	Farm laborer
10		204	221	Duenas, Joaquin B	Son	M	Cha	12	S	Y	Y	Guam	Y	None
11		205	222	Babauta, Candelario C	Head	M	Cha	37	M	N	N	Guam	N	Farmer
12		205	222	Babauta, Luisa C	Wife	F	Cha	36	M	N	Y	Guam	Y	None
13		205	222	Babauta, Angelina C	Daughter	F	Cha	10	S	Y	Y	Guam	Y	None
14		205	222	Babauta, Julita C	Daughter	F	Cha	9	S	Y		Guam		None
15		205	222	Babauta, Ana C	Daughter	F	Cha	5.3	S	N		Guam		None
16		205	222	Babauta, Antonio C	Son	M	Cha	3.8	S	N		Guam		None
17		205	222	Babauta, Carlina C	Daughter	F	Cha	1.9	S	N		Guam		None
18		205	223	Gogo, Felix C	Head	M	Cha	46	M	N	Y	Guam	N	Farmer
19		205	223	Gogo, Ana C	Wife	F	Cha	44	M	N	Y	Guam	N	None
20		205	223	Gogo, Asunsion C	Daughter	F	Cha	16	S	N	Y	Guam	Y	None
21		205	223	Gogo, Jesus C	Son	M	Cha	13	S	Y	Y	Guam	Y	None
22		205	223	Gogo, Juan C	Son	M	Cha	12	S	N	Y	Guam	Y	None
23		205	223	Gogo, Fidel C	Son	M	Cha	10	S	Y	Y	Guam	Y	None
24		205	223	Gogo, Enrique C	Son	M	Cha	8	S	Y		Guam		None
25		205	223	Gogo, Joaquin C	Son	M	Cha	7	S	N		Guam		None

(CHAMORRO ROOTS GENEALOGY PROJECT™ TRANSCRIPTION)
(BERNARD T. PUNZALAN / HTTP://WWW.CHAMORROROOTS.COM)

DEPARTMENT OF COMMERCE-BUREAU OF THE CENSUS
WASHINGTON

FIFTEENTH CENSUS OF THE UNITED STATES: 1930-POPULATION

THE ISLAND OF GUAM

Sheet No. 22B

199B

District **Municipality of Agana**
Name of Place **Dededo Barrio**
[Proper name and, also, name of class, as city, town, village, barrio, etc]

Enumeration District No. 5
Enumerated by me on **April 26, 1930** Jose Kamminga
Enumerator

	PLACE OF ABODE: Street, avenue, road, etc.	Number of dwelling house is order of visitation	Number of family in order of visitation	NAME of each person whose place of abode on April 1, 1930, was in this family. Enter surname, first, then given name and middle initial. If any. Include every person living on April 1, 1930. Omit children born since April 1, 1930.	RELATION Relationship of this Person to the head of the family.	PERSONAL DESCRIPTION: Sex	Color or race	Age at last birthday	Single, married, widowed or divorced	EDUCATION: Attended school any time since Sept. 1, 1929	Whether able to read and write.	NATIVITY Place of birth of this person.	Whether able to speak English.	OCCUPATION
	1	2	3	4	5	6	7	8	9	10	11	12	13	14
26	Dededo Barrio	205	223	Gogo, Felix C	Son	M	Cha	6	S	N		Guam		None
27		206	224	Cruz, Jose A	Head	M	Cha	46	M	N	Y	Guam	Y	Farmer
28		206	224	Cruz, Elena T	Wife	F	Cha	34	M	N	N	Guam	N	None
29		206	224	Cruz, Isabel T	Daughter	F	Cha	15	S	N	N	Guam	N	None
30		206	224	Cruz, Maria T	Daughter	F	Cha	11	S	Y	Y	Guam	Y	None
31		206	224	Cruz, Rosario T	Daughter	F	Cha	9	S	Y		Guam		None
32		206	224	Cruz, Jose T	Son	M	Cha	8	S	Y		Guam		None
33		206	224	Cruz, Rosa T	Daughter	F	Cha	6	S	N		Guam		None
34		206	224	Cruz, Emmanuel T	Son	M	Cha	4.9	S	N		Guam		None
35		206	224	Cruz, David T	Son	M	Cha	.8	S	N		Guam		None
36		207	225	Rojas, Pedro R	Head	M	Cha	68	M	N	N	Guam	N	Farmer
37		207	225	Rojas, Ana M	Wife	F	Cha	69	M	N	N	Guam	N	None
38		208	226	Juan, Camilo C	Head	M	Fil	71	M	N	N	Philippine Island	N	Farmer
39		208	226	Juan, ISabel M	Wife	F	Cha	55	M	N	N	Guam	N	None
40		209	227	Benavente, Felix R	Head	M	Cha	50	M	N	N	Guam	N	Farmer
41		209	227	Benavente, Maria SA	Wife	F	Cha	46	M	N	N	Guam	N	None
42		209	227	Benavente, Pedro SA	Son	M	Cha	21	S	N	Y	Guam	Y	Farm laborer
43		209	227	Benavente, Vicente SA	Son	M	Cha	16	S	N	Y	Guam	Y	None
44		209	227	Benavente, Francisca SA	Daughter	F	Cha	12	S	Y	Y	Guam	Y	None
45		209	227	Benavente, Jesus SA	Son	M	Cha	10	S	Y	Y	Guam	Y	None
46		209	227	Benavente, Maria SA	Daughter	F	Cha	8	S	Y		Guam		None
47		209	227	Benavente, Veronica SA	Daughter	F	Cha	6	S	N		Guam		None
48		209	227	Benavente, Jose SA	Son	M	Cha	1.2	S	N		Guam		None
49		210	228	Matanane, Jose M	Head	M	Cha	53	M	N	Y	Guam	Y	Farmer
50		210	228	Matanane, Rita L	Wife	F	Cha	59	M	N	N	Guam	N	None

(CHAMORRO ROOTS GENEALOGY PROJECT™ TRANSCRIPTION)
(BERNARD T. PUNZALAN / HTTP://WWW.CHAMORROROOTS.COM)

DEPARTMENT OF COMMERCE-BUREAU OF THE CENSUS
WASHINGTON

FIFTEENTH CENSUS OF THE UNITED STATES: 1930-POPULATION

THE ISLAND OF GUAM

Sheet No. 23A

District **Municipality of Agana**
Name of Place **Dededo Barrio**
[Proper name and, also, name of class, as city, town, village, barrio, etc]

Enumeration District No. **5**
Enumerated by me on **April 26, 1930** Jose Kamminga
Enumerator

	PLACE OF ABODE			NAME	RELATION	PERSONAL DESCRIPTION				EDUCATION		NATIVITY		OCCUPATION
	Street, avenue, road, etc.	Number of dwelling house is order of visitation	Number of family in order of visitation	of each person whose place of abode on April 1, 1930, was in this family. Enter surname, first, then given name and middle initial. If any. Include every person living on April 1, 1930. Omit children born since April 1, 1930.	Relationship of this Person to the head of the family.	Sex	Color or race	Age at last birthday	Single, married, widowed or divorced	Attended school any time since Sept. 1, 1929	Whether able to read and write.	Place of birth of this person.	Whether able to speak English.	
	1	2	3	4	5	6	7	8	9	10	11	12	13	14
1	Dededo Barrio	210	229	Matanane, Jose C	Head	M	Cha	30	M	N	Y	Guam	Y	Farmer
2		210	229	Matanane, Nicolasa A	Wife	F	Cha	25	M	N	Y	Guam	Y	None
3		210	229	Matanane, Jose A	Son	M	Cha	3.8	S	N		Guam		None
4		210	229	Matanane, Vicente A	Son	M	Cha	1.8	S	N		Guam		None
5		210	229	Matanane, Carlos A	Son	M	Cha	.8	S	N		Guam		None
6		211	230	Borja, Jose B	Head	M	Cha	43	M	N	N	Guam	N	Farmer
7		211	230	Borja, Francisca D	Wife	F	Cha	21	M	N	Y	Guam	Y	None
8		211	230	Borja, Natividad D	Daughter	F	Cha	2.8	S	N		Guam		None
9		211	230	Borja, Jose D	Son	M	Cha	18	S	N	Y	Guam	Y	Farm laborer
10		212	231	Guerrero, Jose M	Head	M	Cha	43	M	N	Y	Guam	N	Farmer
11		213	232	Lujan, Jose S	Head	M	Cha	58	Wd	N	Y	Guam	Y	Commissioner
12		214	233	Santos, Juan C	Head	M	Cha	66	Wd	N	Y	Guam	N	None
13		214	233	Santos, Juliana C	Daughter	F	Cha	37	S	N	Y	Guam	N	Farm laborer
14		214	233	Santos, Mercedez C	Daughter	F	Cha	26	S	N	Y	Guam	Y	None
15		214	233	Santos, Juan C	Nephew	M	Cha	.1	S	N		Guam		None
16		214	233	Onedera, Ana S	Niece	F	Jap	13	S	Y	Y	Guam		None
17		215	234	Duenas, Juan M	Head	M	Cha	50	Wd	N	Y	Guam	N	Farmer
18		215	234	Duenas, Pedro B	Son	M	Cha	22	S	N	Y	Guam	Y	Farm laborer
19		215	234	Duenas, Ignacio B	Son	M	Cha	14	S	N	Y	Guam	Y	Farm laborer
20		215	234	Meno, Jose B	God-son	M	Cha	25	S	N	Y	Guam	Y	Farm laborer
21		216	235	Esteban, Pedro P	Head	M	Cha	48	M	N	Y	Guam	Y	Farmer
22		216	235	Esteban, Maria E	Wife	F	Cha	40	M	N	Y	Guam	N	None
23		216	235	Esteban, Jesus E	Son	M	Cha	21	S	N	Y	Guam	Y	Farm laborer
24		216	235	Esteban, Maria E	Daughter	F	Cha	18	S	N	Y	Guam	Y	None
25		216	235	Esteban, Felipe E	Son	M	Cha	16	S	N	Y	Guam	Y	Farm laborer

(CHAMORRO ROOTS GENEALOGY PROJECT™ TRANSCRIPTION)
(BERNARD T. PUNZALAN / HTTP://WWW.CHAMORROROOTS.COM)

DEPARTMENT OF COMMERCE-BUREAU OF THE CENSUS
WASHINGTON

FIFTEENTH CENSUS OF THE UNITED STATES: 1930-POPULATION
THE ISLAND OF GUAM

Sheet No. 23B

200B

District **Municipality of Agana**
Name of Place **Dededo Barrio**
[Proper name and, also, name of class, as city, town, village, barrio, etc]

Enumeration District No. 5
Enumerated by me on **April 28, 1930** Jose Kamminga, Enumerator

	PLACE OF ABODE			NAME	RELATION	PERSONAL DESCRIPTION				EDUCATION		NATIVITY		OCCUPATION
	Street, avenue, road, etc.	Number of dwelling house is order of visitation	Number of family in order of visitation	of each person whose place of abode on April 1, 1930, was in this family. Enter surname, first, then given name and middle initial. If any. Include every person living on April 1, 1930. Omit children born since April 1, 1930.	Relationship of this Person to the head of the family.	Sex	Color or race	Age at last birthday	Single, married, widowed or divorced	Attended school any time since Sept. 1, 1929	Whether able to read and write.	Place of birth of this person.	Whether able to speak English.	
	1	2	3	4	5	6	7	8	9	10	11	12	13	14
26	Dededo Barrio	216	235	Esteban, Carmen E	Daughter	F	Cha	14	S	Y	Y	Guam	N	None
27		216	235	Esteban, Lagrimas E	Daughter	F	Cha	12	S	Y	Y	Guam	Y	None
28		216	235	Esteban, Natividad E	Daughter	F	Cha	10	S	Y	Y	Guam	Y	None
29		217	236	Leon Guerrero, Vicente B	Head	M	Cha	32	M	N	Y	Guam	Y	Farmer
30		217	236	Leon Guerrero, Maria C	Wife	F	Cha	28	M	N	N	Guam	N	None
31		217	236	Leon Guerrero, Rosa C	Daughter	F	Cha	10	S	Y	Y	Guam	Y	None
32		217	236	Leon Guerrero, Carmen C	Daughter	F	Cha	6	S	N		Guam		None
33		217	236	Leon Guerrero, Jose C	Son	M	Cha	3.5	S	N		Guam		None
34		217	236	Leon Guerrero, Maria C	Daughter	F	Cha	1.7	S	N		Guam		None
35		217	236	Cruz, Redosindo A	Father-in-law	M	Cha	56	Wd	N	N	Guam		None
36		218	237	Duenas, Manuel D	Head	M	Cha	54	M	N	N	Guam	N	Farmer
37		218	237	Duenas, Magdalena S	Wife	F	Cha	51	M	N	N	Guam	N	None
38		219	238	Iriarte, Pedro C	Head	M	Cha	38	M	N	Y	Guam	N	Farmer
39		219	238	Iriarte, Natividad L	Wife	F	Cha	37	M	N	Y	Guam	N	None
40		219	238	Iriarte, Vicente L	Son	M	Cha	3.3	S	N		Guam		None
41		219	238	Iriarte, Pedro L	Son	M	Jap	1.2	S	N		Guam		None
42		220	239	Castro, Felix R	Head	M	Cha	62	S	N	Y	Guam		Farmer
43		221	240	Hernandez, Ignacio E	Head	M	Cha	48	Wd	N	N	Guam	N	Laborer
44		222	241	Lizama, Pedro De Leon	Head	M	Cha	48	M	N	Y	Guam	Y	Farm laborer
45		222	242	Taitano, Maria S	Head	F	Cha	48	M	N	N	Guam	N	None
46		222	242	Taitano, Matilde S	Daughter	F	Cha	10	S	Y	Y	Guam	Y	None
47		222	242	Taitano, Jose S	Son	M	Cha	8	S	Y		Guam		None
48		223	243	Cruz, Ana B	Head	F	Cha	36	M	N	N	Guam	N	None
49		223	243	Cruz, Maria B	Lodger	F	Cha	29	M	N	N	Guam	N	None
50		223	243	Aguon, Joaquina F	Lodger	F	Cha	34	M	N	N	Guam	N	None

(CHAMORRO ROOTS GENEALOGY PROJECT™ TRANSCRIPTION)
(BERNARD T. PUNZALAN / HTTP://WWW.CHAMORROROOTS.COM)

DEPARTMENT OF COMMERCE-BUREAU OF THE CENSUS
WASHINGTON

FIFTEENTH CENSUS OF THE UNITED STATES: 1930-POPULATION

THE ISLAND OF GUAM

Sheet No. 24A

201

District **Municipality of Agana**
Name of Place **Dededo Barrio**
[Proper name and, also, name of class, as city, town, village, barrio, etc]

Enumeration District No. 5
Enumerated by me on **April 28, 1930** Jose Kamminga
Enumerator

	PLACE OF ABODE			NAME	RELATION	PERSONAL DESCRIPTION				EDUCATION		NATIVITY		OCCUPATION
	Street, avenue, road, etc.	Number of dwelling house in order of visitation	Number of family in order of visitation	of each person whose place of abode on April 1, 1930, was in this family. Enter surname, first, then given name and middle initial. If any. Include every person living on April 1, 1930. Omit children born since April 1, 1930.	Relationship of this Person to the head of the family.	Sex	Color or race	Age at last birthday	Single, married, widowed or divorced	Attended school any time since Sept. 1, 1929	Whether able to read and write.	Place of birth of this person.	Whether able to speak English.	
	1	2	3	4	5	6	7	8	9	10	11	12	13	14
1	Dededo Barrio	223	244	Camacho, Rosa O	Head	F	Cha	23	S	N	N	Guam	N	None
2		223	244	Camacho, Rosario O	Daughter	F	Cha	4.9	S	N		Guam		None
3		223	244	Camacho, Olimpia O	Daughter	F	Cha	.3	S	N		Guam		None
4		223	244	Cruz, Francisco G	Lodger	M	Cha	18	S	N	N	Guam	N	None
5		223	244	Blas, Francisco B	Lodger	M	Cha	13	S	N	Y	Guam	Y	None
6		223	244	Roberto, Juan B	Lodger	M	Cha	14	S	N	Y	Guam	Y	None
7		224	245	Rios, Enrique LG	Head	M	Cha	27	M	N	Y	Guam	Y	Farmer
8		224	245	Rios, Francisca G	Wife	F	Cha	23	M	N	Y	Guam	Y	None
9		224	245	Rios, Ana G	Daughter	F	Cha	3	S	N		Guam		None
10		224	245	Rios, Emeliana G	Daughter	F	Cha	1.5	S	N		Guam		None
11				Here ends the enumeration of Dededo Barrio District No. 5										
12				[Sheet 201B/24B was intentionally left blank by the enumeration.]										
13														
14														
15														
16														
17														
18														
19														
20														
21														
22														
23														
24														
25														

DEPARTMENT OF COMMERCE-BUREAU OF THE CENSUS
WASHINGTON

FIFTEENTH CENSUS OF THE UNITED STATES: 1930-POPULATION

THE ISLAND OF GUAM

Sheet No. 25A

District **Municipality of Agana**
Name of Place **Yigo Barrio**
[Proper name and, also, name of class, as city, town, village, barrio, etc]

Enumeration District No. 5
Enumerated by me on **April 29, 1930** Jose Kamminga, Enumerator

	PLACE OF ABODE			NAME	RELATION	PERSONAL DESCRIPTION				EDUCATION		NATIVITY		OCCUPATION
	Street, avenue, road, etc.	Number of dwelling house is order of visitation	Number of family in order of visitation	of each person whose place of abode on April 1, 1930, was in this family. Enter surname, first, then given name and middle initial. If any. Include every person living on April 1, 1930. Omit children born since April 1, 1930.	Relationship of this Person to the head of the family.	Sex	Color or race	Age at last birthday	Single, married, widowed or divorced	Attended school any time since Sept. 1, 1929	Whether able to read and write.	Place of birth of this person.	Whether able to speak English.	
	1	2	3	4	5	6	7	8	9	10	11	12	13	14
1	Yigo Barrio	225	245	Taitano, Manuel C	Head	M	Cha	27	M	N	Y	Guam	Y	Farmer
2		225	245	Taitano, Concepcion T	Wife	F	Cha	27	M	N	N	Guam	N	None
3		225	245	Taitano, Concepcion T	Daughter	F	Cha	4.7	S	N		Guam		None
4		225	245	Taitano, Vicente T	Son	M	Cha	2.2	S	N		Guam		None
5		226	246	Wusstig, George E	Head	M	W	56	M	N	Y	California	Y	Farmer
6		226	246	Wusstig, Maria C	Wife	F	Cha	40	M	N	N	Guam	Y	None
7		226	246	Wusstig, Dolores C	Daughter	F	Cha	20	S	N	Y	Guam	Y	Farm laborer
8		226	246	Wusstig, Antonia C	Daughter	F	Cha	19	S	N	Y	Guam	Y	Farm laborer
9		226	246	Wusstig, Manuel C	Son	M	Cha	16	S	N	Y	Guam	Y	Farm laborer
10		226	246	Wusstig, Lourdes C	Daughter	F	Cha	15	S	Y	Y	Guam	Y	None
11		226	246	Wusstig, Eliza C	Daughter	F	Cha	14	S	Y	Y	Guam	Y	None
12		226	246	Wusstig, Ernesto C	Son	M	Cha	12	S	Y	Y	Guam	Y	None
13		226	246	Wusstig, Luisa C	Daughter	F	Cha	11	S	Y	Y	Guam	Y	None
14		226	246	Wusstig, Felix C	Son	M	Cha	8	S	Y		Guam		None
15		226	246	Wusstig, Gloria C	Daughter	F	Cha	6.9	S	N		Guam		None
16		226	246	Wusstig, Naomi C	Daughter	F	Cha	5	S	N		Guam		None
17		226	246	Wusstig, Juan C	Son	M	Cha	1.8	S	N		Guam		None
18		226	246	Camacho, Jose C	Brother-in-law	M	Cha	43	S	N	N	Guam	N	Farm laborer
19		226	246	Camacho, Jesus C	Nephew	M	Cha	48	S	N	Y	Guam	Y	Farm laborer
20		227	248	Pangelinan, Vicente Q	Head	M	Cha	34	M	N	Y	Guam	Y	Farmer
21		227	248	Pangelinan, Rosa C	Wife	F	Cha	33	M	N	Y	Guam	N	None
22		227	248	Pangelinan, Josefa C	Daughter	F	Cha	10	S	Y	Y	Guam	Y	None
23		227	248	Pangelinan, Jose C	Son	M	Cha	7	S	Y		Guam		None
24		227	248	Pangelinan, Maria C	Daughter	F	Cha	6	S	N		Guam		None
25		227	248	Pangelinan, Catalina C	Daughter	F	Cha	4.9	S	N		Guam		None

DEPARTMENT OF COMMERCE-BUREAU OF THE CENSUS
WASHINGTON

FIFTEENTH CENSUS OF THE UNITED STATES: 1930-POPULATION

THE ISLAND OF GUAM

Sheet No. 25B

202B

District **Municipality of Agana**
Name of Place **Yigo Barrio**
[Proper name and, also, name of class, as city, town, village, barrio, etc]

Enumeration District No. 5
Enumerated by me on **April 29, 1930** Jose Kamminga
Enumerator

	PLACE OF ABODE			NAME	RELATION	PERSONAL DESCRIPTION				EDUCATION		NATIVITY		OCCUPATION
	Street, avenue, road, etc.	Number of dwelling house in order of visitation	Number of family in order of visitation	of each person whose place of abode on April 1, 1930, was in this family. Enter surname, first, then given name and middle initial. If any. Include every person living on April 1, 1930. Omit children born since April 1, 1930.	Relationship of this Person to the head of the family.	Sex	Color or race	Age at last birthday	Single, married, widowed or divorced	Attended school any time since Sept. 1, 1929	Whether able to read and write.	Place of birth of this person.	Whether able to speak English.	
	1	2	3	4	5	6	7	8	9	10	11	12	13	14
26	Yigo Barrio	227	248	Pangelinan, Isabel C	Daughter	F	Cha	3.6	S	N		Guam		None
27		227	248	Pangelinan, Magdalena C	Daughter	F	Cha	2.2	S	N		Guam		None
28		227	248	Pangelinan, Jesus C	Son	M	Cha	.3	S	N		Guam		None
29		228	248	Pangelinan, Manuel R	Head	M	Cha	36	M	N	N	Guam	N	Farmer
30		228	248	Pangelinan, Rosalia I	Wife	F	Cha	25	M	N	Y	Guam	Y	None
31		228	248	Pangelinan, Antonio I	Son	M	Cha	6	S	N		Guam		None
32		228	248	Pangelinan, Jose I	Son	M	Cha	3.9	S	N		Guam		None
33		228	248	Pangelinan, Barbara I	Daughter	F	Cha	2.8	S	N		Guam		None
34		228	248	Pangelinan, Pedro I	Son	M	Cha	1.4	S	N		Guam		None
35		229	249	Torres, Juan D	Head	M	Cha	60	M	N	Y	Guam	Y	Farmer
36		229	249	Torres, Trinidad C	Wife	F	Cha	58	M	N	Y	Guam	N	None
37		229	249	Torres, Jose C	Son	M	Cha	21	S	N	Y	Guam	Y	Farm laborer
38		229	249	Torres, Juan C	Son	M	Cha	18	S	N	Y	Guam	Y	Farm laborer
39		230	250	Cruz, Juan M	Head	M	Cha	67	M	N	N	Guam	N	Farmer
40		230	250	Cruz, Filomena Q	Wife	F	Cha	50	M	N	N	Guam	N	None
41		230	250	Cruz, Francisca M	Daughter	F	Cha	27	S	N	Y	Guam	Y	None
42		230	250	Cruz, Vicente M	Son	M	Cha	23	S	N	Y	Guam	Y	Chauffeur
43		230	250	Cruz, Juan	Grand-son	M	Cha	.3	S	N		Guam		None
44		230	251	Rosario, Dolores T	Head	F	Cha	56	Wd	N	N	Guam	N	None
45		230	251	Rosario, Antonio T	Son	M	Cha	23	S	N	Y	Guam	N	Farm laborer
46		230	251	Rosario, Jose T	Son	M	Cha	14	S	Y	Y	Guam	Y	None
47		230	251	Rosario, Juan T	Son	M	Cha	11	S	Y	Y	Guam	Y	None
48		230	251	Rosario, Esperanza T	Daughter	F	Cha	8	S	Y		Guam		None
49		231	252	Matanane, Manuel M	Head	M	Cha	67	M	N	Y	Guam	N	Farmer
50		231	252	Matanane, Ana Q	Wife	F	Cha	46	M	N	N	Guam	N	None

DEPARTMENT OF COMMERCE-BUREAU OF THE CENSUS
WASHINGTON

FIFTEENTH CENSUS OF THE UNITED STATES: 1930-POPULATION

THE ISLAND OF GUAM

Sheet No. 26A

District **Municipality of Agana**
Name of Place **Yigo Barrio**
[Proper name and, also, name of class, as city, town, village, barrio, etc]

Enumeration District No. **5**
Enumerated by me on **April 30, 1930** Jose Kamminga
Enumerator

	PLACE OF ABODE			NAME	RELATION	PERSONAL DESCRIPTION				EDUCATION		NATIVITY		OCCUPATION
	Street, avenue, road, etc.	Number of dwelling house is order of visitation	Number of family in order of visitation	of each person whose place of abode on April 1, 1930, was in this family. Enter surname, first, then given name and middle initial. If any. Include every person living on April 1, 1930. Omit children born since April 1, 1930.	Relationship of this Person to the head of the family.	Sex	Color or race	Age at last birthday	Single, married, widowed or divorced	Attended school any time since Sept. 1, 1929	Whether able to read and write.	Place of birth of this person.	Whether able to speak English.	
	1	2	3	4	5	6	7	8	9	10	11	12	13	14
1	Yigo Barrio	231	252	Matanane, Maria Q	Daughter	F	Cha	12	S	Y	Y	Guam	Y	None
2		231	252	Matanane, Catalina Q	Daughter	F	Cha	10	S	Y	Y	Guam	Y	None
3		231	252	Matanane, Felicita Q	Daughter	F	Cha	8	S	Y		Guam		None
4		231	252	Matanane, Josefa Q	Daughter	F	Cha	5	S	N		Guam		None
5		231	252	Matanane, Vicente Q	Son	M	Cha	.2	S	N		Guam		None
6		231	252	Santiago, Francisca Q	Step-daughter	F	Cha	15	S	N	Y	Guam	Y	Laundress
7		231	252	Quintanilla, Manuel P	Nephew	M	Cha	36	S	N	Y	Guam	N	Farm laborer
8		231	252	Cepeda, Pancracio M	Nephew	M	Cha	25	S	N	Y	Guam	Y	Farm laborer
9		232	253	San Nicolas, Antonio M	Head	M	Cha	42	Wd	N	Y	Guam	N	Farmer
10		232	253	San Nicolas, Jose S	Son	M	Cha	18	S	N	Y	Guam	Y	Farm laborer
11		232	253	San Nicolas, Jesus S	Son	M	Cha	15	S	Y	Y	Guam	Y	None
12		232	253	Santos, Dolores Q	Mother-in-law	F	Cha	58	S	N	N	Guam	N	None
13		233	254	San Nicolas, Jose D	Head	M	Cha	30	S	N	Y	Guam	N	Farmer
14		234	255	Quenga, Juan SN	Head	M	Cha	24	M	N	Y	Guam	Y	Farmer
15		234	255	Quenga, Isabel S	Wife	F	Cha	22	M	N	Y	Guam	Y	None
16		234	255	Quenga, Josefina S	Daughter	F	Cha	.8	S	N		Guam		None
17		234	255	Santiago, Jose Q	Brother-in-law	M	Cha	19	S	N	Y	Guam	Y	Farm laborer
18		235	256	Pangelinan, Jose De Leon	Head	M	Cha	64	M	N	N	Guam	N	Farmer
19		235	256	Pangelinan, Dolores Q	Wife	F	Cha	63	M	N	N	Guam	N	None
20		235	256	Pangelinan, Juan Q	Son	M	Cha	31	S	N	Y	Guam	N	Farm laborer
21		236	257	Salas, Domingo C	Head	M	Cha	47	M	N	Y	Guam	N	Farmer
22		236	257	Salas, Rita P	Wife	F	Cha	22	M	N	Y	Guam	N	None
23		236	257	Salas, Jose P	Son	M	Cha	10	S	Y	Y	Guam	Y	None
24		236	257	Salas, Juan P	Son	M	Cha	.4	S	N		Guam		None
25		237	258	De Jesus, Felix S	Head	M	Cha	35	M	N	N	Guam	N	Farmer

(CHAMORRO ROOTS GENEALOGY PROJECT™ TRANSCRIPTION)
(BERNARD T. PUNZALAN / HTTP://WWW.CHAMORROROOTS.COM)

DEPARTMENT OF COMMERCE-BUREAU OF THE CENSUS
WASHINGTON

FIFTEENTH CENSUS OF THE UNITED STATES: 1930-POPULATION

THE ISLAND OF GUAM

Sheet No. 26B

203B

District **Municipality of Agana**
Name of Place **Yigo Barrio**
[Proper name and, also, name of class, as city, town, village, barrio, etc]

Enumeration District No. 5
Enumerated by me on **April 30, 1930** Jose Kamminga
Enumerator

	PLACE OF ABODE			NAME	RELATION	PERSONAL DESCRIPTION				EDUCATION		NATIVITY		OCCUPATION
	Street, avenue, road, etc.	Number of dwelling house is order of visitation	Number of family in order of visitation	of each person whose place of abode on April 1, 1930, was in this family. Enter surname, first, then given name and middle initial. If any. Include every person living on April 1, 1930. Omit children born since April 1, 1930.	Relationship of this Person to the head of the family.	Sex	Color or race	Age at last birthday	Single, married, widowed or divorced	Attended school any time since Sept. 1, 1929	Whether able to read and write.	Place of birth of this person.	Whether able to speak English.	
	1	2	3	4	5	6	7	8	9	10	11	12	13	14
26	Yigo Barrio	237	258	De Jesus, Ignacia T	Wife	F	Cha	30	M	N	N	Guam	N	None
27		237	258	De Jesus, Maria T	Daughter	F	Cha	5.2	S	N		Guam		None
28		237	258	De Jesus, Jesus T	Son	M	Cha	4	S	N		Guam		None
29		237	258	De Jesus, Gregorio T	Son	M	Cha	2	S	N		Guam		None
30		237	258	De Jesus, Antonio T	Son	M	Cha	.8	S	N		Guam		None
31		238	259	Cruz, Luis M	Head	M	Cha	39	M	N	Y	Guam	N	Farmer
32		238	259	Cruz, Ana P	Wife	F	Cha	36	M	N	Y	Guam	N	None
33		238	259	Cruz, Maria P	Daughter	F	Cha	8	S	Y		Guam		None
34		238	259	Cruz, Jose P	Son	M	Cha	6	S	N		Guam		None
35		238	259	Cruz, Juan P	Son	M	Cha	3.3	S	N		Guam		None
36		238	259	Cruz, Francisca P	Daughter	F	Cha	1.1	S	N		Guam		None
37		239	260	Calvo, Gregorio LG	Head	M	Cha	45	M	N	Y	Guam	Y	Farmer
38		239	260	Calvo, Maria A	Wife	F	Cha	44	M	N	Y	Guam	N	None
39		239	260	Calvo, Pedro A	Son	M	Cha	19	S	N	Y	Guam	Y	Farm laborer
40		239	260	Calvo, Rita A	Daughter	F	Cha	16	S	N	Y	Guam	Y	None
41		239	260	Calvo, Manuel A	Son	M	Cha	15	S	Y	Y	Guam	Y	None
42		239	260	Calvo, Maria A	Daughter	F	Cha	10	S	Y	Y	Guam	Y	None
43		239	260	Calvo, Gregorio A	Son	M	Cha	5.5	S	N		Guam		None
44		239	260	Calvo, Antonio A	Son	M	Cha	4	S	N		Guam		None
45		240	261	Pangelinan, Vicente S	Head	M	Cha	46	M	N	Y	Guam	N	Farmer
46		240	261	Pangelinan, Ana M	Wife	F	Cha	36	M	N	Y	Guam	N	None
47		240	261	Pangelinan, Antonio M	Son	M	Cha	6	S	N		Guam		None
48		240	261	Pangelinan, Alfonso M	Son	M	Cha	2.4	S	N		Guam		None
49		240	261	Pangelinan, Regina M	Daughter	F	Cha	.5	S	N		Guam		None
50		240	261	Martinez, Vicente M	Step-son	M	Cha	16	S	N	Y	Guam	Y	Farm laborer

(CHAMORRO ROOTS GENEALOGY PROJECT™ TRANSCRIPTION)
(BERNARD T. PUNZALAN / HTTP://WWW.CHAMORROROOTS.COM)

DEPARTMENT OF COMMERCE-BUREAU OF THE CENSUS
WASHINGTON

FIFTEENTH CENSUS OF THE UNITED STATES: 1930-POPULATION

THE ISLAND OF GUAM

Sheet No. 27A

District **Municipality of Agana**
Name of Place **Yigo Barrio**
[Proper name and, also, name of class, as city, town, village, barrio, etc]

Enumeration District No. 5
Enumerated by me on **May 1, 1930** Jose Kamminga, Enumerator

	PLACE OF ABODE			NAME	RELATION	PERSONAL DESCRIPTION				EDUCATION		NATIVITY		OCCUPATION
	Street, avenue, road, etc.	Number of dwelling house in order of visitation	Number of family in order of visitation	of each person whose place of abode on April 1, 1930, was in this family. Enter surname, first, then given name and middle initial. If any. Include every person living on April 1, 1930. Omit children born since April 1, 1930.	Relationship of this Person to the head of the family.	Sex	Color or race	Age at last birthday	Single, married, widowed or divorced	Attended school any time since Sept. 1, 1929	Whether able to read and write.	Place of birth of this person.	Whether able to speak English.	
	1	2	3	4	5	6	7	8	9	10	11	12	13	14
1	Yigo Barrio	240	261	Martinez, Oliva M	Step-daughter	F	Cha	10	S	N	Y	Guam	Y	None
2		240	261	Pangelinan, Juan S	Brother	M	Cha	39	S	N	N	Guam	N	None
3		241	262	De Jesus, Joaquin S	Head	M	Cha	37	S	N	Y	Guam	N	Farmer
4		241	262	Santos, Maria R	Aunt	F	Cha	60	Wd	N	N	Guam	N	None
5		242	263	Siongco, Jacinto P	Head	M	Cha	46	M	N	N	Guam	N	Farmer
6		242	263	Siongco, Ana T	Wife	F	Cha	30	M	N	Y	Guam	Y	None
7		242	263	Siongco, Jose T	Son	M	Cha	11	S	Y	Y	Guam	Y	None
8		242	263	Siongco, Jesus T	Son	M	Cha	10	S	Y	Y	Guam	Y	None
9		242	263	Siongco, Asuncion T	Daughter	F	Cha	6	S	N		Guam		None
10		242	263	Siongco, Vicente T	Son	M	Cha	3.8	S	N		Guam		None
11		242	263	Siongco, Ana T	Daughter	F	Cha	1.5	S	N		Guam		None
12		243	264	Salas, Jose C	Head	M	Cha	45	M	N	Y	Guam	N	Farmer
13		243	264	Salas, Maria B	Wife	F	Cha	40	M	N	Y	Guam	N	None
14		243	264	Salas, Felix B	Son	M	Cha	14	S	Y	Y	Guam	Y	Farm laborer
15		243	264	Salas, Rosa B	Daughter	F	Cha	12	S	Y	Y	Guam	Y	None
16		243	264	Salas, Rosario B	Daughter	F	Cha	9	S	Y		Guam		None
17		243	264	Salas, Juan B	Son	M	Cha	3.5	S	N		Guam		None
18		244	265	Hernandez, Juan H	Head	M	Cha	26	M	N	Y	Guam	Y	Farmer
19		244	265	Hernandez, Concepcion A	Wife	F	Cha	44	M	N	N	Guam	N	None
20		244	265	Arriola, Jose A	Step-son	M	Cha	13	S	Y	Y	Guam	Y	None
21		245	266	Pangelinan, Vicente De Leon	Head	M	Cha	51	M	N	Y	Guam	N	Farmer
22		245	266	Pangelinan, Manuela B	Wife	F	Cha	56	M	N	Y	Guam	N	None
23		245	266	Pangelinan, Amparo B	Daughter	F	Cha	19	S	N	Y	Guam	Y	None
24		245	266	Pangelinan, Jose B	Grand-son	M	Cha	.8	S	N		Guam		None
25		245	267	Salas, Pedro P	Head	M	Cha	25	M	N	Y	Guam	Y	Farm laborer

DEPARTMENT OF COMMERCE-BUREAU OF THE CENSUS
WASHINGTON

FIFTEENTH CENSUS OF THE UNITED STATES: 1930-POPULATION

THE ISLAND OF GUAM

Sheet No. 27B

204B

District **Municipality of Agana**

Name of Place **Yigo Barrio**

[Proper name and, also, name of class, as city, town, village, barrio, etc]

Enumeration District No. 5

Enumerated by me on **May 1, 1930** Jose Kamminga, Enumerator

	PLACE OF ABODE			NAME	RELATION	PERSONAL DESCRIPTION				EDUCATION		NATIVITY		OCCUPATION
	Street, avenue, road, etc.	Number of dwelling house in order of visitation	Number of family in order of visitation	of each person whose place of abode on April 1, 1930, was in this family. Enter surname, first, then given name and middle initial. If any. Include every person living on April 1, 1930. Omit children born since April 1, 1930.	Relationship of this Person to the head of the family.	Sex	Color or race	Age at last birthday	Single, married, widowed or divorced	Attended school any time since Sept. 1, 1929	Whether able to read and write.	Place of birth of this person.	Whether able to speak English.	
	1	2	3	4	5	6	7	8	9	10	11	12	13	14
26	Yigo Barrio	245	267	Salas, Maria P	Wife	F	Cha	23	M	N	Y	Guam	Y	None
27		245	267	Salas, Jesus P	Son	M	Cha	3.9	S	N		Guam		None
28		245	267	Salas, Juan P	Son	M	Cha	2.3	S	N		Guam		None
29		245	267	Salas, Francisco P	Son	M	Cha	.6	S	N		Guam		None
30		246	268	Iglesias, Manuel C	Head	M	Cha	25	M	N	Y	Guam	Y	Farmer
31		246	268	Iglesias, Rosario P	Wife	F	Cha	18	M	N	Y	Guam	Y	None
32		246	268	Iglesias, Maria P	Daughter	F	Cha	.1	S	N		Guam		None
33		247	269	Sablan, Antonio D	Head	M	Cha	54	M	N	Y	Guam	N	Farmer
34		247	269	Sablan, Ana B	Wife	F	Cha	44	M	N	Y	Guam	N	None
35		247	269	Sablan, Pedro B	Son	M	Cha	28	S	N	Y	Guam	Y	Farm laborer
36		247	269	Sablan, Amalia B	Daughter	F	Cha	20	S	N	Y	Guam	Y	None
37		247	269	Sablan, Nicolas B	Son	M	Cha	18	S	N	Y	Guam	Y	Farm laborer
38		247	269	Sablan, Vicente B	Son	M	Cha	15	S	Y	Y	Guam	Y	None
39		247	269	Sablan, Cristina B	Daughter	F	Cha	13	S	Y	Y	Guam	Y	None
40		247	269	Sablan, Maria B	Daughter	F	Cha	11	S	Y	Y	Guam	Y	None
41		247	269	Sablan, Manuela B	Daughter	F	Cha	8	S	Y		Guam		None
42		247	269	Sablan, Rosa B	Daughter	F	Cha	6	S	N		Guam		None
43		247	269	Sablan, Lourdes B	Daughter	F	Cha	1.3	S	N		Guam		None
44		248	270	Taitano, Manuel G	Head	M	Cha	28	M	N	Y	Guam	Y	Farmer
45		248	270	Taitano, Ana Q	Wife	F	Cha	27	M	N	Y	Guam	Y	None
46		248	270	Taitano, Manuel Q	Son	M	Cha	1.3	S	N		Guam		None
47		249	271	Santos, Manuel L	Head	M	Cha	53	Wd	N	Y	Guam	N	Farmer
48		249	271	Santos, Antonio C	Son	M	Cha	14	S	Y	Y	Guam	Y	None
49		250	272	Perez, Manuel F	Head	M	Cha	53	M	N	Y	Guam	N	Farmer
50		250	272	Perez, Ana T	Wife	F	Cha	46	M	N	Y	Guam	N	None

(CHAMORRO ROOTS GENEALOGY PROJECT™ TRANSCRIPTION)
(BERNARD T. PUNZALAN / HTTP://WWW.CHAMORROROOTS.COM)

DEPARTMENT OF COMMERCE-BUREAU OF THE CENSUS
WASHINGTON

FIFTEENTH CENSUS OF THE UNITED STATES: 1930-POPULATION

THE ISLAND OF GUAM

Sheet No. 28A

District **Municipality of Agana**
Name of Place **Yigo Barrio**
[Proper name and, also, name of class, as city, town, village, barrio, etc]

Enumeration District No. 5
Enumerated by me on **May 2, 1930** Jose Kamminga, Enumerator

	PLACE OF ABODE			NAME	RELATION	PERSONAL DESCRIPTION				EDUCATION		NATIVITY		OCCUPATION
	Street, avenue, road, etc.	Number of dwelling house in order of visitation	Number of family in order of visitation	of each person whose place of abode on April 1, 1930, was in this family. Enter surname, first, then given name and middle initial. If any. Include every person living on April 1, 1930. Omit children born since April 1, 1930.	Relationship of this Person to the head of the family.	Sex	Color or race	Age at last birthday	Single, married, widowed or divorced	Attended school any time since Sept. 1, 1929	Whether able to read and write.	Place of birth of this person.	Whether able to speak English.	
	1	2	3	4	5	6	7	8	9	10	11	12	13	14
1	Yigo Barrio	250	272	Perez, Gregorio T	Son	M	Cha	20	S	N	Y	Guam	Y	Chauffeur
2		250	272	Perez, Jose T	Son	M	Cha	19	S	N	Y	Guam	Y	School teacher
3		250	272	Perez, Clotilde T	Daughter	F	Cha	17	S	N	Y	Guam	Y	None
4		250	272	Perez, Francisco T	Son	M	Cha	16	S	Y	Y	Guam	Y	None
5		250	272	Perez, Emelia T	Daughter	F	Cha	14	S	Y	Y	Guam	Y	None
6		250	272	Perez, Vicente T	Son	M	Cha	13	S	Y	Y	Guam	Y	None
7		250	272	Perez, Juan T	Son	M	Cha	11	S	Y	Y	Guam	Y	None
8		250	272	Perez, Ana T	Daughter	F	Cha	9	S	Y		Guam		None
9		250	272	Perez, Maria T	Daughter	F	Cha	7	S	Y		Guam		None
10		250	272	Perez, Jesus T	Son	M	Cha	5.5	S	N		Guam		None
11		250	272	Perez, Felicita T	Daughter	F	Cha	3.3	S	N		Guam		None
12		250	272	Perez, Manuel T	Son	M	Cha	1.8	S	N		Guam		None
13		251	273	Torres, Manuel F	Head	M	Cha	45	M	N	Y	Guam	Y	Commissioner
14		251	273	Torres, Juana T	Wife	F	Cha	41	M	N	Y	Guam	Y	None
15		251	273	Torres, Rosalia T	Daughter	F	Cha	18	S	N	Y	Guam	Y	None
16		251	273	Torres, Beatrice	Daughter	F	Cha	16	S	N	Y	Guam	Y	None
17		251	273	Taitano, David F	Nephew	M	Cha	8	S	Y		Guam		None
18		252	274	Nelson, J E	Head	M	Cha	45	M	N	Y	Guam	Y	Farm Manager
19		252	274	Nelson, Potenciana F	Wife	F	Cha	29	M	N	Y	Guam	Y	None
20		252	274	Nelson, Rosie E	Daughter	F	Cha	7	S	Y		Guam		None
21		252	274	Nelson, May M	Daughter	F	Cha	5.8	S	N		Guam		None
22		252	274	Nelson, George E	Son	M	Cha	4	S	N		Guam		None
23		252	274	Nelson, J E Jr.	Son	M	Cha	2.5	S	N		Guam		None
24		252	274	Fernandez, Ana Q	Sister-in-law	F	Cha	20	S	N	Y	Guam	Y	Housemaid
25		253	275	Pereda, Jose B	Head	M	Cha	30	M	Y	Y	Guam	Y	Farm laborer

(CHAMORRO ROOTS GENEALOGY PROJECT™ TRANSCRIPTION)
(BERNARD T. PUNZALAN / HTTP://WWW.CHAMORROROOTS.COM)

DEPARTMENT OF COMMERCE-BUREAU OF THE CENSUS
WASHINGTON
FIFTEENTH CENSUS OF THE UNITED STATES: 1930-POPULATION

THE ISLAND OF GUAM

Sheet No. 28B

205B

District **Municipality of Agana**
Name of Place **Yigo Barrio**
[Proper name and, also, name of class, as city, town, village, barrio, etc]

Enumeration District No. 5
Enumerated by me on **May 2, 1930** Jose Kamminga
Enumerator

	PLACE OF ABODE			NAME	RELATION	PERSONAL DESCRIPTION				EDUCATION		NATIVITY		OCCUPATION
	Street, avenue, road, etc.	Number of dwelling house in order of visitation	Number of family in order of visitation	of each person whose place of abode on April 1, 1930, was in this family. Enter surname, first, then given name and middle initial. If any. Include every person living on April 1, 1930. Omit children born since April 1, 1930.	Relationship of this Person to the head of the family.	Sex	Color or race	Age at last birthday	Single, married, widowed or divorced	Attended school any time since Sept. 1, 1929	Whether able to read and write.	Place of birth of this person.	Whether able to speak English.	
	1	2	3	4	5	6	7	8	9	10	11	12	13	14
26	Yigo Barrio	253	275	Pereda, Cristina F	Wife	F	Cha	25	M	N	Y	Guam	Y	None
27		253	275	Pereda, Ignacio F	Son	M	Cha	8	S	N		Guam		None
28		253	275	Pereda, Antonia F	Daughter	F	Cha	5.6	S	N		Guam		None
29		253	275	Pereda, Diana F	Daughter	F	Cha	2.8	S	N		Guam		None
30		254	276	Aguero, Joaquin SN	Head	M	Cha	39	S	N	Y	Guam	N	Farm laborer
31		254	276 A	Babauta, Antonio B	Head	M	Cha	22	S	N	Y	Guam	Y	Farm laborer
32		255	277	Borja, Jose D	Head	M	Cha	52	M	N	Y	Guam	N	None
33		255	277	Borja, Filomena Q	Wife	F	Cha	60	M	N	N	Guam	N	None
34		255	277	Borja, Pedro Q	Son	M	Cha	23	S	N	Y	Guam	Y	Farm laborer
35		256	278	Rivera, Joaquin R	Head	M	Cha	36	M	N	N	Guam	N	Farmer
36		256	278	Rivera, Ana L	Wife	F	Cha	20	M	N	Y	Guam	Y	None
37		257	279	Taguacta, Jesus B	Head	M	Cha	34	M	N	Y	Guam	Y	Farmer
38		257	279	Taguacta, Nicolasa T	Wife	F	Cha	34	M	N	Y	Guam	Y	None
39		257	279	Taguacta, Jose T	Son	M	Cha	9	S	Y		Guam		None
40		257	279	Taguacta, Maria T	Daughter	F	Cha	8	S	Y		Guam		None
41		257	279	Taguacta, Carlina T	Daughter	F	Cha	5.2	S	N		Guam		None
42		257	279	Taguacta, Rosa T	Daughter	F	Cha	2.6	S	N		Guam		None
43		257	279	Taguacta, Manuel T	Son	M	Cha	1.9	S	N		Guam		None
44		258	280	Blas, Manuel A	Head	M	Cha	35	M	N	Y	Guam	N	Farmer
45		258	280	Blas, Trinidad A	Wife	F	Cha	22	M	N	Y	Guam	N	None
46		258	280	Blas, Maria A	Daughter	F	Cha	3	S	N		Guam		None
47		258	280	Blas, Matilde A	Daughter	F	Cha	2.4	S	N		Guam		None
48		258	280	Blas, Soledad A	Daughter	F	Cha	.9	S	N		Guam		None
49		259	281	Borja, Juan Q	Head	M	Cha	26	M	N	N	Guam	N	Farmer
50		259	281	Borja, Maria P	Wife	F	Cha	26	M	N	Y	Guam	N	None

(CHAMORRO ROOTS GENEALOGY PROJECT™ TRANSCRIPTION)
(BERNARD T. PUNZALAN / HTTP://WWW.CHAMORROROOTS.COM)

DEPARTMENT OF COMMERCE-BUREAU OF THE CENSUS
WASHINGTON

FIFTEENTH CENSUS OF THE UNITED STATES: 1930-POPULATION

THE ISLAND OF GUAM

Sheet No. 29A

District **Municipality of Agana**
Name of Place **Yigo Barrio**
[Proper name and, also, name of class, as city, town, village, barrio, etc]

Enumeration District No. **5**
Enumerated by me on **May 3, 1930** **Jose Kamminga**, Enumerator

	PLACE OF ABODE			NAME	RELATION	PERSONAL DESCRIPTION				EDUCATION		NATIVITY		OCCUPATION
	Street, avenue, road, etc.	Number of dwelling house in order of visitation	Number of family in order of visitation	of each person whose place of abode on April 1, 1930, was in this family. Enter surname, first, then given name and middle initial. If any. Include every person living on April 1, 1930. Omit children born since April 1, 1930.	Relationship of this Person to the head of the family.	Sex	Color or race	Age at last birthday	Single, married, widowed or divorced	Attended school any time since Sept. 1, 1929	Whether able to read and write.	Place of birth of this person.	Whether able to speak English.	
	1	2	3	4	5	6	7	8	9	10	11	12	13	14
1	Yigo Barrio	259	281	Borja, Juan P	Son	M	Cha	4.8	S	N		Guam		None
2		259	281	Borja, Jose P	Son	M	Cha	4.8	S	N		Guam		None
3		260	282	Rosario, Francisco A	Head	M	Cha	40	M	N	N	Guam	N	Farm laborer
4		260	282	Rosario, Dolores P	Wife	F	Cha	29	M	N	N	Guam	N	None
5		260	282	Todela, Jose P	Nephew	M	Cha	9	S	Y		Guam		None
6		261	283	Pangelinan, Manuel P	Head	M	Cha	31	M	N	Y	Guam	N	Farmer
7		261	283	Pangelinan, Maria C	Wife	F	Cha	32	M	N	Y	Guam	N	None
8		262	284	Todela, Jose P	Head	M	Cha	27	S	N	N	Guam	N	Farmer
9		263	285	Guioco, Jesus D	Head	M	Cha	35	M	N	Y	Guam	N	Farmer
10		263	285	Guioco, Antonia S	Wife	F	Cha	40	M	N	N	Guam	N	None
11		264	286	Leon Guerrero, Vicente LG	Head	M	Cha	40	M	N	N	Guam	N	Farmer
12		264	286	Leon Guerrero, Dolores F	Wife	F	Cha	42	M	N	N	Guam	N	None
13		264	286	Leon Guerrero, Maria F	Daughter	F	Cha	9	S	Y		Guam		None
14		264	286	Leon Guerrero, Antonia F	Daughter	F	Cha	7	S	Y		Guam		None
15		265	287	Chargualaf, Antonio	Head	M	Cha	27	S	N	N	Guam	Y	Farm laborer
16		265	287	Acfalle, Jose A	Lodger	M	Cha	26	S	N	N	Guam	N	Farm laborer
17		265	287	Sablan, Jose P	Lodger	M	Cha	33	S	N	Y	Guam	N	Farm laborer
18		266	288	Rivera, Mariano G	Head	M	Cha	30	M	N	Y	Guam	N	Farmer
19		266	288	Rivera, Beatice R	Wife	F	Cha	24	M	N	Y	Guam	Y	None
20		266	288	Rivera, Pilar R	Daughter	F	Cha	4.5	S	N		Guam		None
21		266	288	Rivera, Remedios R	Daughter	F	Cha	2.7	S	N		Guam		None
22		266	288	Rivera, Dolores R	Daughter	F	Cha	.2	S	N		Guam		None
23		267	289	Quitugua, Francisco B	Head	M	Cha	50	M	N	Y	Guam	Y	Farmer
24		267	289	Quitugua, Ana SN	Wife	F	Cha	33	M	N	Y	Guam	Y	None
25		267	289	Quitugua, Jose SN	Son	M	Cha	11	S	Y	Y	Guam	Y	None

DEPARTMENT OF COMMERCE-BUREAU OF THE CENSUS
WASHINGTON
FIFTEENTH CENSUS OF THE UNITED STATES: 1930-POPULATION

THE ISLAND OF GUAM

Sheet No. 29A

206B

District Municipality of Agana
Name of Place Yigo Barrio
[Proper name and, also, name of class, as city, town, village, barrio, etc]

Enumeration District No. 5
Enumerated by me on May 3, 1930 Jose Kamminga, Enumerator

	PLACE OF ABODE: Street, avenue, road, etc.	Number of dwelling house in order of visitation	Number of family in order of visitation	NAME of each person whose place of abode on April 1, 1930, was in this family. Enter surname, first, then given name and middle initial. If any. Include every person living on April 1, 1930. Omit children born since April 1, 1930.	RELATION Relationship of this Person to the head of the family.	PERSONAL DESCRIPTION: Sex	Color or race	Age at last birthday	Single, married, widowed or divorced	EDUCATION: Attended school any time since Sept. 1, 1929	Whether able to read and write.	NATIVITY Place of birth of this person.	Whether able to speak English.	OCCUPATION
	1	2	3	4	5	6	7	8	9	10	11	12	13	14
26	Yigo Barrio	267	289	Quitugua, Silvestre SN	Son	M	Cha	9	S	Y		Guam		None
27		267	289	Quitugua, Teofila SN	Daughter	F	Cha	6	S	N		Guam		None
28		268	290	Tiquiengco, Enrique B	Head	M	Cha	27	S	N	Y	Guam	Y	Barber
29				Here ends the enumeration of Yigo Barrio District No. 5										
30														
31														
32														
33														
34														
35														
36														
37														
38														
39														
40														
41														
42														
43														
44														
45														
46														
47														
48														
49														
50														

(CHAMORRO ROOTS GENEALOGY PROJECT™ TRANSCRIPTION)
(BERNARD T. PUNZALAN / HTTP://WWW.CHAMORROROOTS.COM)

DEPARTMENT OF COMMERCE-BUREAU OF THE CENSUS
WASHINGTON

FIFTEENTH CENSUS OF THE UNITED STATES: 1930-POPULATION

THE ISLAND OF GUAM

Sheet No. 30A

District Municipality of Agana
Name of Place Machananao Barrio
[Proper name and, also, name of class, as city, town, village, barrio, etc]

Enumeration District No. 5
Enumerated by me on May 3, 1930 Jose Kamminga
Enumerator

	PLACE OF ABODE			NAME	RELATION	PERSONAL DESCRIPTION				EDUCATION		NATIVITY		OCCUPATION
	Street, avenue, road, etc.	Number of dwelling house is order of visitation	Number of family in order of visitation	of each person whose place of abode on April 1, 1930, was in this family. Enter surname, first, then given name and middle initial. If any. Include every person living on April 1, 1930. Omit children born since April 1, 1930.	Relationship of this Person to the head of the family.	Sex	Color or race	Age at last birthday	Single, married, widowed or divorced	Attended school any time since Sept. 1, 1929	Whether able to read and write.	Place of birth of this person.	Whether able to speak English.	
	1	2	3	4	5	6	7	8	9	10	11	12	13	14
1	Machananao Barrio	269	291	Castro, Joaquin O	Head	M	Cha	64	M	N	Y	Guam	N	Farmer
2		269	291	Castro, Maria C	Wife	F	Cha	63	M	N	Y	Guam	N	None
3		269	291	Mendiola, Manuel B	Nephew	M	Cha	24	S	N	Y	Guam	Y	Farm laborer
4		270	292	Megofna, Antonio G	Head	M	Cha	33	S	N	Y	Guam	Y	Farmer
5		271	293	Hernandez, Joaquin N	Head	M	Cha	36	M	N	Y	Guam	Y	Farmer
6		271	293	Hernandez, Maria SN	Wife	F	Cha	35	M	N	Y	Guam	Y	None
7		272	294	Aguero, Juan A	Head	M	Cha	25	M	N	Y	Guam	Y	Farmer
8		272	294	Aguero, Amparo C	Wife	F	Cha	25	M	N	Y	Guam	Y	None
9		273	295	Mafnas, Luis C	Head	M	Cha	53	M	N	N	Guam	N	Farmer
10		273	295	Mafnas, Jose F	Son	M	Cha	24	S	N	Y	Guam	Y	Farm laborer
11		274	296	Castro, Manuel R	Head	M	Cha	27	S	N	Y	Guam	Y	Farmer
12		274	296	Taijito, Mamerto	Servant	M	Cha	40	Wd	N	Y	Guam	N	Farm laborer
13		274	296	Camacho, Enrique	Servant	M	Cha	16	S	N	N	Guam	N	Farm laborer
14		275	297	Mendiola, Jose M	Head	M	Cha	25	M	N	N	Guam	Y	Farmer
15		275	297	Mendiola, Juana P	Wife	F	Cha	20	M	N	Y	Guam	Y	None
16		275	297	Mendiola, Jesus P	Son	M	Cha	3.3	S	N		Guam		None
17		275	297	Mendiola, Maria P	Daughter	F	Cha	1.8	S	N		Guam		None
18		276	298	Perez, Pedro C	Head	M	Cha	23	M	N	Y	Guam	Y	Farmer
19		276	298	Perez, Bernadita P	Wife	F	Cha	31	M	N	Y	Guam	Y	None
20		276	298	Perez, Dolores P	Daughter	F	Cha	1.5	S	N		Guam		None
21		277	299	De Jesus, Vicente S	Head	M	Cha	38	M	N	N	Guam	N	Farmer
22		277	299	De Jesus, Maria P	Wife	F	Cha	33	M	N	N	Guam	N	None
23		277	299	De Jesus, Dolores P	Daughter	F	Cha	11	S	Y	Y	Guam	Y	None
24		277	299	De Jesus, Antonio P	Son	M	Cha	4.3	S	N		Guam		None
25		277	299	De Jesus, Magdalena P	Daughter	F	Cha	2.1	S	N		Guam		None

(CHAMORRO ROOTS GENEALOGY PROJECT™ TRANSCRIPTION)
(BERNARD T. PUNZALAN / HTTP://WWW.CHAMORROROOTS.COM)

DEPARTMENT OF COMMERCE-BUREAU OF THE CENSUS
WASHINGTON

FIFTEENTH CENSUS OF THE UNITED STATES: 1930-POPULATION

THE ISLAND OF GUAM

Sheet No. 30B

207B

District **Municipality of Agana**
Name of Place **Machananao Barrio**
[Proper name and, also, name of class, as city, town, village, barrio, etc]

Enumeration District No. 5
Enumerated by me on May 5, 1930 Jose Kamminga
Enumerator

	PLACE OF ABODE			NAME	RELATION	PERSONAL DESCRIPTION				EDUCATION		NATIVITY		OCCUPATION
	Street, avenue, road, etc.	Number of dwelling house is order of visitation	Number of family in order of visitation	of each person whose place of abode on April 1, 1930, was in this family. Enter surname, first, then given name and middle initial. If any. Include every person living on April 1, 1930. Omit children born since April 1, 1930.	Relationship of this Person to the head of the family.	Sex	Color or race	Age at last birthday	Single, married, widowed or divorced	Attended school any time since Sept. 1, 1929	Whether able to read and write.	Place of birth of this person.	Whether able to speak English.	
	1	2	3	4	5	6	7	8	9	10	11	12	13	14
26	Machananao Barrio	278	300	Manibusan, Manuel G	Head	M	Cha	40	S	N	N	Guam	N	Farmer
27		278	300	Sipingco, Ignacia L	Servant	F	Cha	46	Wd	N	N	Guam	N	Servant
28		279	301	Ada, Ramon M	Head	M	Cha	45	M	N	Y	Guam	Y	Farmer
29		279	301	Ada, Joaquina M	Wife	F	Cha	48	M	N	Y	Guam	Y	None
30		279	301	Ada, Maria M	Daughter	F	Cha	15	S	N	Y	Guam	Y	None
31		279	301	Ada, Rosa M	Daughter	F	Cha	13	S	Y	Y	Guam	Y	None
32		279	301	Ada, Jesus M	Son	M	Cha	11	S	Y	Y	Guam	Y	None
33		279	301	Ada, Jose M	Son	M	Cha	9	S	Y		Guam		None
34		279	301	Ada, Agueda M	Daughter	F	Cha	7	S	Y		Guam		None
35		279	301	Ada, Ana M	Daughter	F	Cha	3	S	N		Guam		None
36		280	302	Manibusan, Jose G	Head	M	Cha	37	M	N	N	Guam	N	Farmer
37		280	302	Manibusan, Juana L	Wife	F	Cha	39	M	N	Y	Guam	N	None
38		280	302	Manibusan, Jesus L	Son	M	Cha	10	S	Y	Y	Guam	Y	None
39		280	302	Manibusan, Nicolas L	Son	M	Cha	7	S	Y		Guam		None
40		280	302	Manibusan, Antonio L	Son	M	Cha	4.6	S	N		Guam		None
41		280	302	Manibusan, Jose L	Son	M	Cha	2.3	S	N		Guam		None
42		281	303	Dela Torre, Gregorio A	Head	M	Cha	60	M	N	Y	Guam	N	Farmer
43		281	303	Dela Torre, Francisco C	Son	M	Cha	21	S	N	Y	Guam	Y	Farm laborer
44		281	303	Benavente, Joaquin A	Servant	M	Cha	17	S	N	N	Guam	N	Farm laborer
45		282	304	Finona, Jose G	Head	M	Cha	34	M	N	Y	Guam	Y	Farmer
46		282	304	Finona, Ignacia T	Wife	F	Cha	34	M	N	Y	Guam	Y	None
47		282	304	Finona, Vicente T	Son	M	Cha	14	S	Y	Y	Guam	Y	None
48		282	304	Finona, Eliza T	Daughter	F	Cha	13	S	Y	Y	Guam	Y	None
49		282	304	Finona, Rosalia T	Daughter	F	Cha	11	S	Y	Y	Guam	Y	None
50		282	304	Finona, Victoria T	Daughter	F	Cha	6	S	N		Guam		None

DEPARTMENT OF COMMERCE-BUREAU OF THE CENSUS
WASHINGTON

FIFTEENTH CENSUS OF THE UNITED STATES: 1930-POPULATION

THE ISLAND OF GUAM

Sheet No. 31A

District **Municipality of Agana**
Name of Place **Machananao Barrio**
[Proper name and, also, name of class, as city, town, village, barrio, etc]

Enumeration District No. 5
Enumerated by me on May 5, 1930 Jose Kamminga, Enumerator

	PLACE OF ABODE: Street, avenue, road, etc.	Number of dwelling house in order of visitation	Number of family in order of visitation	NAME of each person whose place of abode on April 1, 1930, was in this family. Enter surname, first, then given name and middle initial. If any. Include every person living on April 1, 1930. Omit children born since April 1, 1930.	RELATION Relationship of this Person to the head of the family.	Sex	Color or race	Age at last birthday	Single, married, widowed or divorced	Attended school any time since Sept. 1, 1929	Whether able to read and write.	NATIVITY Place of birth of this person.	Whether able to speak English.	OCCUPATION
	1	2	3	4	5	6	7	8	9	10	11	12	13	14
1	Machananao Barrio	282	304	Finona, Vicenta T	Daughter	F	Cha	3.9	S	N		Guam		None
2		282	304	Finona, Jose T	Son	M	Cha	1.8	S	N		Guam		None
3		283	305	Leon Guerrero, Vicente P	Head	M	Cha	30	M	N	N	Guam	Y	Farmer
4		283	305	Leon Guerrero, Carmen C	Wife	F	Cha	35	M	N	Y	Guam	Y	None
5		283	305	Leon Guerrero, Isabel C	Daughter	F	Cha	4.4	S	N		Guam		None
6		283	305	Leon Guerrero, Vicente C	Son	M	Cha	2	S	N		Guam		None
7		283	305	Leon Guerrero, Maria C	Daughter	F	Cha	1	S	N		Guam		None
8		283	305	Camacho, Antonia C	Step-daughter	F	Cha	12	S	N	Y	Guam	Y	None
9		283	305	Camacho, Jose C	Step-son	M	Cha	6	S	N		Guam		None
10		284	306	De La Torre, Juan A	Head	M	Cha	71	M	N	Y	Guam	N	Farmer
11		284	306	De La Torre, Apolonia A	Wife	F	Cha	54	M	N	N	Guam	N	None
12		284	306	De La Torre, Soledad A	Daughter	F	Cha	35	S	N	Y	Guam	Y	None
13		284	306	De La Torre, Felicita A	Daughter	F	Cha	26	S	N	Y	Guam	Y	None
14		285	307	De La Torre, Juan A de	Head	M	Cha	28	M	N	Y	Guam	Y	Farmer
15		285	307	De La Torre, Francisca	Wife	F	Cha	27	M	N	Y	Guam	Y	None
16		285	307	De La Torre, Jose A	Son	M	Cha	9	S	Y		Guam		None
17		285	307	De La Torre, Julia A	Daughter	F	Cha	5.7	S	N		Guam		None
18		285	307	De La Torre, Juan A	Son	M	Cha	2.1	S	N		Guam		None
19		285	307	De La Torre, Jesus A	Son	M	Cha	1	S	N		Guam		None
20		286	308	Borja, Antonio B	Head	M	Cha	50	S	N	N	Guam	N	Farmer
21		286	309	Camacho, Vicenta C	Head	F	Cha	27	S	N	N	Guam	N	None
22		286	309	Camacho, Rosa C	Daughter	F	Cha	6	S	N		Guam		None
23		286	309	Camacho, Francisco C	Son	M	Cha	.3	S	N		Guam		None
24		287	310	Meno, Isidro M	Head	M	Cha	51	M	N	Y	Guam	N	Farmer
25		287	310	Meno, Carmen C	Wife	F	Cha	46	M	N	N	Guam	N	None

(CHAMORRO ROOTS GENEALOGY PROJECT™ TRANSCRIPTION)
(BERNARD T. PUNZALAN / HTTP://WWW.CHAMORROROOTS.COM)

DEPARTMENT OF COMMERCE-BUREAU OF THE CENSUS
WASHINGTON

FIFTEENTH CENSUS OF THE UNITED STATES: 1930-POPULATION

THE ISLAND OF GUAM

Sheet No. 31B

208B

District **Municipality of Agana**
Name of Place **Machananao Barrio**
[Proper name and, also, name of class, as city, town, village, barrio, etc]

Enumeration District No. 5
Enumerated by me on May 5, 1930 Jose Kamminga, Enumerator

	PLACE OF ABODE			NAME	RELATION	PERSONAL DESCRIPTION				EDUCATION		NATIVITY		OCCUPATION
	Street, avenue, road, etc.	Number of dwelling house is order of visitation	Number of family in order of visitation	of each person whose place of abode on April 1, 1930, was in this family. Enter surname, first, then given name and middle initial. If any. Include every person living on April 1, 1930. Omit children born since April 1, 1930.	Relationship of this Person to the head of the family.	Sex	Color or race	Age at last birthday	Single, married, widowed or divorced	Attended school any time since Sept. 1, 1929	Whether able to read and write.	Place of birth of this person.	Whether able to speak English.	
	1	2	3	4	5	6	7	8	9	10	11	12	13	14
26	Machananao Barrio	287	310	Manibusan, Francisco Q	Cousin	M	Cha	25	S	Y	Y	Guam	N	Farm laborer
27		287	311	Mendiola, Juan P	Head	M	Cha	27	M	N	Y	Guam	Y	Farmer
28		287	311	Mendiola, Ana M	Wife	F	Cha	23	M	N	Y	Guam	Y	None
29		287	311	Mendiola, Isidro M	Son	M	Cha	6	S	N		Guam		None
30		287	311	Mendiola, Carmen M	Daughter	F	Cha	4.1	S	N		Guam		None
31		287	311	Mendiola, Lorenzo M	Son	M	Cha	3	S	N		Guam		None
32		287	311	Mendiola, Rita M	Daughter	F	Cha	1.2	S	N		Guam		None
33		288	312	Iglesias, Jose G	Head	M	Cha	25	M	N	Y	Guam	Y	Farmer
34		288	312	Iglesias, Ana LG	Wife	F	Cha	17	M	N	Y	Guam	Y	None
35		289	313	Camacho, Miguel B	Head	M	Cha	55	Wd	N	N	Guam	N	Farm laborer
36		290	314	Quichocho, Joaquin N	Head	M	Cha	60	M	N	Y	Guam	N	Farmer
37		291	315	Quichocho, Mariano Q	Head	M	Cha	39	S	N	N	Guam	N	Farmer
38		292	316	Castro, Fernando A	Head	M	Cha	59	Wd	N	Y	Guam	N	Farmer
39		293	317	Villagomez, Juan V	Head	M	Cha	22	M	N	Y	Guam	Y	Farmer
40		293	317	Villagomez, Joaquina G	Wife	F	Cha	25	M	N	Y	Guam	Y	None
41		293	317	Villagomez, Manuel G	Son	M	Cha	1	S	N		Guam		None
42		294	318	Toves, Jesus B	Head	M	Cha	30	M	N	N	Guam	N	Farmer
43		294	318	Toves, Manuela Q	Wife	F	Cha	39	M	N	N	Guam	N	None
44		294	318	Toves, Maria Q	Daughter	F	Cha	14	S	N	Y	Guam	Y	None
45		294	318	Toves, Maria Q	Daughter	F	Cha	9	S	Y		Guam		None
46		294	318	Toves, Matilde Q	Daughter	F	Cha	7	S	N		Guam		None
47		294	318	Toves, Jesus Q	Son	M	Cha	1.2	S	N		Guam		None
48		295	319	Tenorio, Joaquin Q	Head	M	Cha	22	M	N	N	Guam	N	Farmer
49		295	319	Tenorio, Enrgracia C	Wife	F	Cha	20	M	N	N	Guam	N	None
50		295	319	Tenorio, Maria C	Daughter	F	Cha	3.7	S	N		Guam		None

DEPARTMENT OF COMMERCE-BUREAU OF THE CENSUS
WASHINGTON

FIFTEENTH CENSUS OF THE UNITED STATES: 1930-POPULATION

THE ISLAND OF GUAM

Sheet No. 32A

District Municipality of Agana
Name of Place Machananao Barrio
[Proper name and, also, name of class, as city, town, village, barrio, etc]

Enumeration District No. 5
Enumerated by me on May 6, 1930 Jose Kamminga
Enumerator

	PLACE OF ABODE			NAME	RELATION	PERSONAL DESCRIPTION				EDUCATION		NATIVITY		OCCUPATION
	Street, avenue, road, etc.	Number of dwelling house is order of visitation	Number of family in order of visitation	of each person whose place of abode on April 1, 1930, was in this family. Enter surname, first, then given name and middle initial. If any. Include every person living on April 1, 1930. Omit children born since April 1, 1930.	Relationship of this Person to the head of the family.	Sex	Color or race	Age at last birthday	Single, married, widowed or divorced	Attended school any time since Sept. 1, 1929	Whether able to read and write.	Place of birth of this person.	Whether able to speak English.	
	1	2	3	4	5	6	7	8	9	10	11	12	13	14
1	Machananao Barrio	295	319	Tenorio, Leonardo C	Son	M	Cha	1.2	S	N		Guam		None
2		296	320	Mendiola, Jose H	Head	M	Cha	45	M	N	Y	Guam	Y	Farmer
3		296	320	Mendiola, Ursula A	Wife	F	Cha	35	M	N	N	Guam	N	None
4		296	320	Mendiola, Jesus A	Son	M	Cha	7	S	Y		Guam		None
5		296	320	Mendiola, Antonia A	Daughter	F	Cha	2.8	S	N		Guam		None
6		296	320	Mendiola, Juan A	Son	M	Cha	.4	S	N		Guam		None
7		296	320	Mendiola, Joaquin M	Son	M	Cha	22	S	N	Y	Guam	Y	Laborer
8		296	320	Mendiola, Vicente M	Son	M	Cha	18	S	N	Y	Guam	Y	Laborer
9		297	321	Finona, Francisco G	Head	M	Cha	37	M	N	Y	Guam	N	Farmer
10		297	321	Finona, Antonia T	Wife	F	Cha	32	M	N	N	Guam	N	None
11		297	321	Finona, Jose T	Son	M	Cha	10	S	N	N	Guam	N	None
12		297	321	Finona, Fidel T	Son	M	Cha	1.6	S	N		Guam		None
13		298	322	Castro, Jose C	Head	M	Cha	33	S	N	Y	Guam	Y	Farmer
14		299	323	Pangelinan, Jose U	Head	M	Cha	37	M	N	Y	Guam	Y	Farmer
15		299	323	Pangelinan, Maria T	Wife	F	Cha	28	M	N	Y	Guam	N	None
16		299	323	Pangelinan, Jose T	Son	M	Cha	5	S	N		Guam		None
17		299	323	Pangelinan, Regina T	Daughter	F	Cha	4	S	N		Guam		None
18		299	323	Pangelinan, Delfina T	Daughter	F	Cha	3.4	S	N		Guam		None
19		299	323	Pangelinan, Jesus T	Son	M	Cha	.5	S	N		Guam		None
20		300	324	Cepeda, Juan S	Head	M	Cha	47	M	N	N	Guam	N	Farmer
21		300	324	Cepeda, Maria P	Wife	F	Cha	26	M	N	N	Guam	N	None
22		300	324	Cepeda, Isabel P	Daughter	F	Cha	3.8	S	N		Guam		None
23		300	324	Cepeda, Jose P	Son	M	Cha	2.8	S	N		Guam		None
24		300	324	Cepeda, Francisca P	Daughter	F	Cha	.3	S	N		Guam		None
25		301	325	Rivera, Andres G	Head	M	Cha	39	S	N	Y	Guam	Y	Servant

DEPARTMENT OF COMMERCE-BUREAU OF THE CENSUS
WASHINGTON

FIFTEENTH CENSUS OF THE UNITED STATES: 1930-POPULATION

THE ISLAND OF GUAM

Sheet No. 32B

209B

District Municipality of Agana
Name of Place Machananao Barrio
[Proper name and, also, name of class, as city, town, village, barrio, etc]

Enumeration District No. 5
Enumerated by me on May 7, 1930 Jose Kamminga
Enumerator

	PLACE OF ABODE: Street, avenue, road, etc.	Number of dwelling house in order of visitation	Number of family in order of visitation	NAME of each person whose place of abode on April 1, 1930, was in this family. Enter surname, first, then given name and middle initial. If any. Include every person living on April 1, 1930. Omit children born since April 1, 1930.	RELATION Relationship of this Person to the head of the family.	PERSONAL DESCRIPTION: Sex	Color or race	Age at last birthday	Single, married, widowed or divorced	EDUCATION: Attended school any time since Sept. 1, 1929	Whether able to read and write.	NATIVITY Place of birth of this person.	Whether able to speak English.	OCCUPATION
	1	2	3	4	5	6	7	8	9	10	11	12	13	14
26	Machananao Barrio	302	326	Susuico, Ignacio	Head	M	Cha	31	M	N	Y	Guam	Y	Farmer
27		302	326	Susuico, Josefa C	Wife	F	Cha	25	M	N	N	Guam	N	None
28		302	326	Susuico, Benigno C	Son	M	Cha	6	S	N		Guam		None
29		303	327	Perez, Francisco P	Head	M	Cha	40	M	N	Y	Guam	N	Farmer
30		303	327	Perez, Tomasa S	Wife	F	Cha	26	M	N	Y	Guam	N	None
31		303	327	Salas, Agapito S	Step-son	M	Cha	3.7	S	N		Guam		None
32		304	328	Rosario, Antonio T	Head	M	Cha	31	M	N	Y	Guam	Y	Farmer
33		304	328	Rosario, Soledad SA	Wife	F	Cha	30	M	N	Y	Guam	Y	None
34		304	328	Rosario, Daisy SA	Daughter	F	Cha	11	S	Y	Y	Guam	Y	None
35		304	328	Hernandez, Jose B	Servant	M	Cha	20	S	N	N	Guam	N	Farm laborer
36				Here ends the enumeration of Machanaonao Barrio District No. 5										
37														
38														
39														
40														
41														
42														
43														
44														
45														
46														
47														
48														
49														
50														

DEPARTMENT OF COMMERCE-BUREAU OF THE CENSUS
WASHINGTON

FIFTEENTH CENSUS OF THE UNITED STATES: 1930-POPULATION

THE ISLAND OF GUAM

Sheet No. 33A

District **Municipality of Agana**
Name of Place **Barrigada Barrio**
[Proper name and, also, name of class, as city, town, village, barrio, etc]

Enumeration District No. 5
Enumerated by me on **April 2, 1930** Margarito D. Palting, Enumerator

	PLACE OF ABODE			NAME	RELATION	PERSONAL DESCRIPTION				EDUCATION		NATIVITY		OCCUPATION
	Street, avenue, road, etc.	Number of dwelling house in order of visitation	Number of family in order of visitation	of each person whose place of abode on April 1, 1930, was in this family. Enter surname, first, then given name and middle initial. If any. Include every person living on April 1, 1930. Omit children born since April 1, 1930.	Relationship of this Person to the head of the family.	Sex	Color or race	Age at last birthday	Single, married, widowed or divorced	Attended school any time since Sept. 1, 1929	Whether able to read and write.	Place of birth of this person.	Whether able to speak English.	
	1	2	3	4	5	6	7	8	9	10	11	12	13	14
1	[no street name]	1	1	Tenorio, Manuel T	Head	M	Cha	67	M	N	N	Guam	N	Farmer
2		1	1	Tenorio, Natividad N	Wife	F	Cha	51	M	N	N	Guam	N	None
3		1	1	Tenorio, Remedios	Daughter	F	Cha	19	S	Y	Y	Guam	Y	None
4		1	1	Tenorio, Teresa	Daughter	F	Cha	16	S	Y	Y	Guam	Y	None
5		1	1	Tenorio, Mercedes	Daughter	F	Cha	11	S	Y	Y	Guam	Y	None
6		2	2	Aguon, Vicente T	Head	M	Cha	63	M	N	Y	Guam	N	Farmer
7		2	2	Aguon, Sabina I	Wife	F	Cha	63	M	N	Y	Guam	N	None
8		2	2	Aguon, Antonio I	Son	M	Cha	24	S	N	Y	Guam	N	Gardiner
9		3	3	Santos, Vicente M	Head	M	Cha	50	M	N	Y	Guam	N	Farmer
10		3	3	Santos, Rosa	Wife	F	Cha	48	M	N	N	Guam	N	None
11		3	3	Santos, Jose	Son	M	Cha	27	S	N	Y	Guam	N	Farm laborer
12		3	3	Santos, Jesus	Son	M	Cha	23	S	N	N	Guam	N	Farm laborer
13		3	3	Santos, Rosario	Daughter	F	Cha	21	S	N	Y	Guam	N	None
14		3	3	Santos, Juan	Son	M	Cha	16	S	N	Y	Guam	N	None
15		3	3	Santos, Dolores	Daughter	F	Cha	6	S	N		Guam		None
16		4	4	Pangelinan, Jesus S	Head	M	Cha	32	M	N	Y	Guam	Y	Farm laborer
17		4	4	Pangelinan, Carmen Q	Wife	F	Cha	34	M	N	Y	Guam	N	None
18		4	4	Pangelinan, Jesus	Son	M	Cha	3.9	S	N		Guam		None
19		4	4	Pangelinan, Jose	Son	M	Cha	2.9	S	N		Guam		None
20		4	4	Pangelinan, Francisco	Son	M	Cha	.2	S	N		Guam		None
21		5	5	Santos, Jose Q	Head	M	Cha	26	M	N	Y	Guam	Y	Farmer
22		5	5	Santos, Gertrudes C	Wife	F	Cha	29	M	N	Y	Guam	N	None
23		6	6	Rosario, Pedro C	Head	M	Cha	31	S	N	Y	Guam	N	Farmer
24		7	7	Pangelinan, Jose I	Head	M	Cha	57	M	N	Y	Guam	N	Farmer
25		7	7	Pangelinan, Rosa LG	Wife	F	Cha	56	M	N	Y	Guam	N	None

DEPARTMENT OF COMMERCE-BUREAU OF THE CENSUS
WASHINGTON

FIFTEENTH CENSUS OF THE UNITED STATES: 1930-POPULATION

THE ISLAND OF GUAM

Sheet No. 33B

210B

District Municipality of Agana
Name of Place Barrigada Barrio
[Proper name and, also, name of class, as city, town, village, barrio, etc]

Enumeration District No. 5
Enumerated by me on April 2, 1930 Margarito D. Palting, Enumerator

	PLACE OF ABODE			NAME	RELATION	PERSONAL DESCRIPTION				EDUCATION		NATIVITY		OCCUPATION
	Street, avenue, road, etc.	Number of dwelling house is order of visitation	Number of family in order of visitation	of each person whose place of abode on April 1, 1930, was in this family. Enter surname, first, then given name and middle initial. If any. Include every person living on April 1, 1930. Omit children born since April 1, 1930.	Relationship of this Person to the head of the family.	Sex	Color or race	Age at last birthday	Single, married, widowed or divorced	Attended school any time since Sept. 1, 1929	Whether able to read and write.	Place of birth of this person.	Whether able to speak English.	
	1	2	3	4	5	6	7	8	9	10	11	12	13	14
26	[no street name]	7	7	Pangelinan, Enrique LG	Son	M	Cha	22	S	N	Y	Guam	N	None
27		7	7	Pangelinan, Nieves LG	Daughter	F	Cha	12	S	Y	Y	Guam	Y	None
28		8	8	Quichocho, Nicolas G	Head	M	Cha	56	M	N	N	Guam	N	Farmer
29		8	8	Quichocho, Felicita	Wife	F	Cha	50	M	N	Y	Guam	N	None
30		8	8	Quichocho, Jose	Son	M	Cha	21	S	N	Y	Guam	N	Farm laborer
31		8	8	Quidachay, Jesus C	Grand son	M	Cha	.5	S	N		Guam		None
32		9	9	Quichocho, Nicolasa Q	Head	F	Cha	66	S	N	N	Guam	N	Farmer
33		9	9	Quichocho, Maria	Daughter	F	Cha	40	S	N	N	Guam	N	Farm laborer
34		9	9	Quichocho, Rosa	Grand daughter	F	Cha	19	S	N	N	Guam	N	None
35		9	9	Quichocho, Nicolas	Grand son	M	Cha	14	S	Y	Y	Guam	N	None
36		9	9	Quichocho, Rosario	Grand daughter	F	Cha	4.5	S	N		Guam		None
37		10	10	Tichaira, Juan D	Head	M	W part	34	M	N	Y	Guam	N	Farm laborer
38		10	10	Tichaira, Manuela G	Wife	F	Cha	31	M	N	Y	Guam	N	None
39		10	10	Tichaira, Dolores	Daughter	F	Cha	11	S	Y	N	Guam	N	None
40		10	10	Tichaira, Jose	Son	M	Cha	9	S	Y		Guam		None
41		10	10	Tichaira, Manuel	Son	M	Cha	4.2	S	N		Guam		None
42		10	10	Tichaira, Pedro	Son	M	Cha	2.5	S	N		Guam		None
43		10	10	Tichaira, Vicente	Son	M	Cha	.8	S	N		Guam		None
44		11	11	Cruz, Agustin S	Head	M	Cha	40	M	N	Y	Guam	N	Farmer
45		11	11	Cruz, Josefa Q	Wife	F	Cha	40	M	N	N	Guam	N	None
46		11	11	Quichocho, Maria	Daughter	F	Cha	15	S	Y	N	Guam	N	None
47		11	11	Quichocho, Vicente	Son	M	Cha	8	S	N		Guam		None
48		11	11	Quichocho, Rosa	Daughter	F	Cha	7	S	N		Guam		None
49		11	11	Cruz, Magdalena Q	Daughter	F	Cha	3.2	S	N		Guam		None
50		12	12	Gumataotao, Francisco M	Head	M	Cha	70	Wd	N	N	Guam	N	Farmer

(CHAMORRO ROOTS GENEALOGY PROJECT™ TRANSCRIPTION)
(BERNARD T. PUNZALAN / HTTP://WWW.CHAMORROROOTS.COM)

DEPARTMENT OF COMMERCE-BUREAU OF THE CENSUS
WASHINGTON

FIFTEENTH CENSUS OF THE UNITED STATES: 1930-POPULATION

THE ISLAND OF GUAM

Sheet No. 34A

211

District Municipality of Agana
Name of Place Barrigada Barrio
[Proper name and, also, name of class, as city, town, village, barrio, etc]

Enumeration District No. 5
Enumerated by me on April 3, 1930 Margarito D. Palting
Enumerator

	PLACE OF ABODE			NAME	RELATION	PERSONAL DESCRIPTION				EDUCATION		NATIVITY		OCCUPATION
	Street, avenue, road, etc.	Number of dwelling house is order of visitation	Number of family in order of visitation	of each person whose place of abode on April 1, 1930, was in this family. Enter surname, first, then given name and middle initial. If any. Include every person living on April 1, 1930. Omit children born since April 1, 1930.	Relationship of this Person to the head of the family.	Sex	Color or race	Age at last birthday	Single, married, widowed or divorced	Attended school any time since Sept. 1, 1929	Whether able to read and write.	Place of birth of this person.	Whether able to speak English.	
	1	2	3	4	5	6	7	8	9	10	11	12	13	14
1	[no street name]	13	13	Leon Guerrero, Joaquin P	Head	M	Cha	47	M	N	Y	Guam	N	Farmer
2		13	14	Leon Guerrero, Jose P	Head	M	Cha	41	M	N	Y	Guam	N	Farmer
3		14	15	Quichocho, Rosa G	Head	F	Cha	58	S	N	N	Guam	N	Farmer
4		14	15	Quichocho, Teodoro	Son	M	Cha	20	S	N	Y	Guam	N	Farmer
5		15	16	Quichocho, Jesus P	Head	M	Cha	25	S	N	Y	Guam	Y	Farmer
6		15	17	Quichocho, Trinidad Q	Head	F	Cha	33	S	N	N	Guam	N	None
7		15	17	Quichocho, Francisco	Son	M	Cha	6	S	N		Guam		None
8		15	17	Quichocho, Teodoro	Son	M	Cha	1.1	S	N		Guam		None
9		16	18	Meno, Juan M	Head	M	Cha	48	M	N	N	Guam	N	Farmer
10		16	18	Meno, Maria P	Wife	F	Cha	39	M	N	N	Guam	N	None
11		16	18	Meno, Francisco	Daughter	F	Cha	22	S	N	N	Guam	N	Farm laborer
12		16	18	Meno, Dolores	Daughter	F	Cha	20	S	N	Y	Guam	Y	None
13		16	18	Meno, Justa	Daughter	F	Cha	15	S	Y	Y	Guam	Y	None
14		16	18	Meno, Consolacion	Daughter	F	Cha	13	S	Y	N	Guam	Y	None
15		16	18	Meno, Antonio	Son	M	Cha	12	S	Y	N	Guam	Y	None
16		16	18	Meno, Vicente	Son	M	Cha	2.3	S	N		Guam		None
17		17	19	Quichocho, Manuel T	Head	M	Cha	26	M	N	Y	Guam	Y	Farmer
18		17	19	Quichocho, Maria Q	Wife	F	Cha	58	M	N	N	Guam	N	None
19		18	20	Quichocho, Vicente Q	Head	M	Cha	40	M	N	N	Guam	N	Farmer
20		18	20	Quichocho, Joaquina T	Wife	F	Cha	35	M	N	N	Guam	N	None
21		18	20	Quichocho, Maria	Daughter	F	Cha	14	S	Y	N	Guam	N	None
22		18	20	Quichocho, Jesus	Son	M	Cha	13	S	Y	N	Guam	N	None
23		18	20	Quichocho, Vicente	Son	M	Cha	7	S	Y		Guam		None
24		18	20	Quichocho, Rosa	Daughter	F	Cha	5	S	N		Guam		None
25		18	20	Quichocho, Rosario	Daughter	F	Cha	3	S	N		Guam		None

(CHAMORRO ROOTS GENEALOGY PROJECT™ TRANSCRIPTION)
(BERNARD T. PUNZALAN / HTTP://WWW.CHAMORROROOTS.COM)

DEPARTMENT OF COMMERCE-BUREAU OF THE CENSUS
WASHINGTON

FIFTEENTH CENSUS OF THE UNITED STATES: 1930-POPULATION

THE ISLAND OF GUAM

Sheet No. 34B

211B

District Municipality of Agana
Name of Place Barrigada Barrio
[Proper name and, also, name of class, as city, town, village, barrio, etc]

Enumeration District No. 5
Enumerated by me on April 3, 1930 Margarito D. Palting, Enumerator

	PLACE OF ABODE			NAME	RELATION	PERSONAL DESCRIPTION				EDUCATION		NATIVITY		OCCUPATION
	Street, avenue, road, etc.	Number of dwelling house in order of visitation	Number of family in order of visitation	of each person whose place of abode on April 1, 1930, was in this family. Enter surname, first, then given name and middle initial. If any. Include every person living on April 1, 1930. Omit children born since April 1, 1930.	Relationship of this Person to the head of the family.	Sex	Color or race	Age at last birthday	Single, married, widowed or divorced	Attended school any time since Sept. 1, 1929	Whether able to read and write.	Place of birth of this person.	Whether able to speak English.	
	1	2	3	4	5	6	7	8	9	10	11	12	13	14
26	[no street name]	18	20	Quichocho, Rosalia	Daughter	F	Cha	1.3	S	N		Guam		None
27		19	21	Quichocho, Miguel Q	Head	M	Cha	30	M	N	Y	Guam	Y	Farmer
28		19	21	Quichocho, Juana R	Wife	F	Cha	25	M	N	Y	Guam	N	None
29		19	21	Quichocho, Ana	Daughter	F	Cha	4.2	S	N		Guam		None
30		19	21	Quichocho, Josefa	Daughter	F	Cha	2.2	S	N		Guam		None
31		19	21	Quichocho, Francisco	Son	M	Cha	1.4	S	N		Guam		None
32		20	22	Ungacta, Domingo P	Head	M	Cha	52	M	N	Y	Guam	N	Farm laborer
33		20	22	Ungacta, Antonio	Son	M	Cha	21	S	N	N	Guam	Y	Farm laborer
34		21	23	Borja, Paulino B	Head	M	Cha	50	M	N	Y	Guam	Y	Farmer
35		21	23	Borja, Maria C	Wife	F	Cha	49	M	N	Y	Guam	N	None
36		21	23	Borja, Luisa	Daughter	F	Cha	18	S	N	Y	Guam	Y	None
37		21	23	Borja, Vicente	Son	M	Cha	15	S	Y	Y	Guam	Y	None
38		21	23	Borja, Catalina	Daughter	F	Cha	13	S	Y	Y	Guam	Y	None
39		21	23	Borja, Antonio	Son	M	Cha	9	S	Y		Guam		None
40		21	23	Borja, Maria	Daughter	F	Cha	8	S	Y		Guam		None
41		22	24	Uncango, Jose G	Head	M	Cha	42	M	N	Y	Guam	N	Farmer
42		22	24	Uncango, Isabel S	Wife	F	Cha	42	M	N	N	Guam	N	None
43		22	24	Uncango, Gregorio	Son	M	Cha	11	S	Y	Y	Guam	Y	None
44		22	24	Uncango, Prescilla	Daughter	F	Cha	10	S	Y	N	Guam	N	None
45		22	24	Uncango, Vicenta	Daughter	F	Cha	8	S	Y		Guam		None
46		22	24	Uncango, Juana	Daughter	F	Cha	7	S	Y		Guam		None
47		22	24	Uncango, Elias	Son	M	Cha	6	S	N		Guam		None
48		22	24	Uncango, Maria	Daughter	F	Cha	4.8	S	N		Guam		None
49		23	25	Borja, Jose R	Head	M	Cha	44	M	N	N	Guam	N	Farmer
50		23	25	Borja, Ana I	Wife	F	Cha	39	M	N	Y	Guam	N	None

(CHAMORRO ROOTS GENEALOGY PROJECT™ TRANSCRIPTION)
(BERNARD T. PUNZALAN / HTTP://WWW.CHAMORROROOTS.COM)

DEPARTMENT OF COMMERCE-BUREAU OF THE CENSUS
WASHINGTON

FIFTEENTH CENSUS OF THE UNITED STATES: 1930-POPULATION

THE ISLAND OF GUAM

Sheet No. 35A

District **Municipality of Agana**
Name of Place **Barrigada Barrio**
[Proper name and, also, name of class, as city, town, village, barrio, etc]

Enumeration District No. 5
Enumerated by me on **April 4, 1930** Margarito D. Palting, Enumerator

	PLACE OF ABODE: Street, avenue, road, etc.	Number of dwelling house in order of visitation	Number of family in order of visitation	NAME of each person whose place of abode on April 1, 1930, was in this family. Enter surname, first, then given name and middle initial. If any. Include every person living on April 1, 1930. Omit children born since April 1, 1930.	RELATION Relationship of this Person to the head of the family.	PERSONAL DESCRIPTION: Sex	Color or race	Age at last birthday	Single, married, widowed or divorced	EDUCATION: Attended school any time since Sept. 1, 1929	Whether able to read and write.	NATIVITY Place of birth of this person.	Whether able to speak English.	OCCUPATION
	1	2	3	4	5	6	7	8	9	10	11	12	13	14
1	[no street name]	24	26	Cruz, Miguel M	Head	M	Cha	53	Wd	N	Y	Guam	N	Farmer
2		24	26	Cruz, Juan C	Son	M	Cha	21	S	N	Y	Guam	Y	Farm laborer
3		24	26	Cruz, Carmen	Daughter	F	Cha	19	S	N	Y	Guam	Y	None
4		24	26	Cruz, Jesus	Son	M	Cha	16	S	Y	Y	Guam	Y	None
5		24	26	Cruz, Felix	Son	M	Cha	13	S	Y	Y	Guam	Y	None
6		24	26	Cruz, Ignacio	Son	M	Cha	12	S	Y	Y	Guam	Y	None
7		25	27	Taitano, Joaquin G	Head	M	Cha	42	M	Y	Y	Guam	N	Farmer
8		25	27	Taitano, Maria C	Wife	F	Cha	38	M	N	Y	Guam	N	None
9		25	27	Taitano, Juan	Son	M	Cha	14	S	Y	Y	Guam	Y	None
10		25	27	Taitano, Jose	Son	M	Cha	12	S	Y	Y	Guam	Y	None
11		25	27	Taitano, Maria	Daughter	F	Cha	11	S	Y	Y	Guam	Y	None
12		25	27	Taitano, Jesus	Son	M	Cha	8	S			Guam		None
13		25	27	Taitano, Barcelisa	Daughter	F	Cha	6	S			Guam		None
14		25	27	Cruz, Jose C	Brother-in-law	M	Cha	51	Wd	N	Y	Guam	N	Farmer
15		25	27	Cruz, Jose Q	Son-in-law	M	Cha	21	S	N	Y	Guam	N	None
16		26	28	Calvo, Felix P	Head	M	W Span	36	M	N	Y	Guam	Y	Farmer
17		26	28	Calvo, Antonia B	Wife	F	Cha	32	M	N	Y	Guam	Y	None
18		26	28	Calvo, Fidela	Daughter	F	W Span	12	S	Y	Y	Guam	Y	None
19		26	28	Calvo, Augusto	Son	M	Span	9	S	Y		Guam		None
20		26	28	Calvo, Vicente	Son	M	Span	8	S	Y		Guam		None
21		26	28	Calvo, Jacinto	Son	M	Span	6	S	Y		Guam		None
22		26	28	Calvo, Fermin	Son	M	Span	5	S	N		Guam		None
23		26	28	Calvo, Beatriz	Daughter	F	Span	4.3	S	N		Guam		None
24		26	28	Calvo, Jesus	Son	M	Span	2.5	S	N		Guam		None
25		26	28	Calvo, Antonio	Son	M	Span	1.6	S	N		Guam		None

(CHAMORRO ROOTS GENEALOGY PROJECT™ TRANSCRIPTION)
(BERNARD T. PUNZALAN / HTTP://WWW.CHAMORROROOTS.COM)

DEPARTMENT OF COMMERCE-BUREAU OF THE CENSUS
WASHINGTON

FIFTEENTH CENSUS OF THE UNITED STATES: 1930-POPULATION

THE ISLAND OF GUAM

Sheet No. 35B

212B

District Municipality of Agana
Name of Place Barrigada Barrio
[Proper name and, also, name of class, as city, town, village, barrio, etc]

Enumeration District No. 5
Enumerated by me on April 4, 1930 Margarito D. Palting, Enumerator

	PLACE OF ABODE: Street, avenue, road, etc.	Number of dwelling house in order of visitation	Number of family in order of visitation	NAME of each person whose place of abode on April 1, 1930, was in this family. Enter surname, first, then given name and middle initial. If any. Include every person living on April 1, 1930. Omit children born since April 1, 1930.	RELATION Relationship of this Person to the head of the family.	PERSONAL DESCRIPTION: Sex	Color or race	Age at last birthday	Single, married, widowed or divorced	EDUCATION: Attended school any time since Sept. 1, 1929	Whether able to read and write.	NATIVITY Place of birth of this person.	Whether able to speak English.	OCCUPATION
	1	2	3	4	5	6	7	8	9	10	11	12	13	14
26	[no street name]	27	29	Yamasaki, Ignacio B	Head	M	Jap	45	M	N	N	Japan	N	Farmer
27		28	30	Perez, Juan C	Head	M	Cha	34	M	N	Y	Guam	N	Blacksmith
28		28	30	Perez, Carmen L	Wife	F	Cha	40	M	N	Y	Guam	N	None
29		28	30	Perez, Ignacio	Son	M	Cha	15	S	Y	Y	Guam	Y	None
30		28	30	Perez, Juan	Son	M	Cha	13	S	Y	Y	Guam	Y	None
31		28	30	Perez, Maria	Daughter	F	Cha	11	S	Y	Y	Guam	N	None
32		28	30	Perez, Concepcion	Daughter	F	Cha	9	S	Y		Guam		None
33		28	30	Perez, Emilia	Daughter	F	Cha	7	S	Y		Guam		None
34		28	30	Perez, Jose	Son	M	Cha	2.8	S	N		Guam		None
35		29	31	Palomo, Ramon C	Head	M	Cha	39	M	N	Y	Guam	N	Farmer
36		29	31	Palomo, Teresa N	Wife	F	Cha	35	M	N	Y	Guam	N	None
37		29	31	Palomo, Jesus	Son	M	Cha	13	S	Y	Y	Guam	Y	None
38		29	31	Palomo, Jose	Son	M	Cha	11	S	Y	N	Guam	N	None
39		29	31	Palomo, Consolacion	Daughter	F	Cha	6	S	Y		Guam		None
40		29	31	Palomo, Vicente	Son	M	Cha	2.1	S	N		Guam		None
41		30	32	San Miguel, Manuel Q	Head	M	Cha	29	Wd	N	Y	Guam	Y	Enginman 2c
42		30	32	San Miguel, Felipe	Son	M	Cha	8	S	Y		Guam		None
43		30	32	San Miguel, Delfina	Daughter	F	Cha	7	S	Y		Guam		None
44		30	32	San Miguel, Fidela	Daughter	F	Cha	6	S	N		Guam		None
45		30	33	Duenas, Ana M	Head	F	Cha	40	M	N	Y	Guam	Y	Seamstress
46		31	34	Palomo, Ignacio C	Head	M	Cha	34	M	N		Guam	Y	Farmer
47		31	34	Palomo, Maria SM	Wife	F	Cha	30	M	N	Y	Guam	N	None
48		31	34	Palomo, Juan	Son	M	Cha	10	S	Y	Y	Guam	N	None
49		31	34	Palomo, Ana	Daughter	F	Cha	9	S	Y	N	Guam		None
50		31	34	Palomo, Jose	Son	M	Cha	4.1	S	N		Guam		None

DEPARTMENT OF COMMERCE-BUREAU OF THE CENSUS
WASHINGTON

FIFTEENTH CENSUS OF THE UNITED STATES: 1930-POPULATION

THE ISLAND OF GUAM

Sheet No. 36A

District **Municipality of Agana**
Name of Place **Barrigada Barrio**
[Proper name and, also, name of class, as city, town, village, barrio, etc]

Enumeration District No. 5
Enumerated by me on **April 4, 1930** Margarito D. Palting
Enumerator

	PLACE OF ABODE			NAME	RELATION	PERSONAL DESCRIPTION				EDUCATION		NATIVITY		OCCUPATION
	Street, avenue, road, etc.	Number of dwelling house is order of visitation	Number of family in order of visitation	of each person whose place of abode on April 1, 1930, was in this family. Enter surname, first, then given name and middle initial. If any. Include every person living on April 1, 1930. Omit children born since April 1, 1930.	Relationship of this Person to the head of the family.	Sex	Color or race	Age at last birthday	Single, married, widowed or divorced	Attended school any time since Sept. 1, 1929	Whether able to read and write.	Place of birth of this person.	Whether able to speak English.	
	1	2	3	4	5	6	7	8	9	10	11	12	13	14
1	[no street name]	31	34	Palomo, Oliva	Daughter	F	Cha	2.8	S	N		Guam		None
2		31	34	Palomo, Roman	Son	M	Cha	.4	S	N		Guam		None
3		31	34	San Miguel, Ana Q	Sister-in-law	F	Cha	25	S	N	N	Guam	N	None
4		31	34	San Miguel, Trinidad	Sister-in-law	F	Cha	18	S	N	Y	Guam	N	None
5		32	35	Manibusan, Jose G	Head	M	Cha	38	S	N	N	Guam	N	Farmer
6		33	36	Flores, Lorenzo A	Head	M	Cha	60	S	N	Y	Guam	N	Farmer
7		33	37	Lizama, Trinidad DR	Head	F	Cha	38	S	N	N	Guam	N	Farmer
8		33	37	Lizama, Maria	Daughter	F	Cha	10	S	Y	N	Guam	N	None
9		33	37	Lizama, Francisco	Son	M	Cha	8	S	Y		Guam		None
10		33	37	Lizama, Ana	Daughter	F	Cha	7	S	Y		Guam		None
11		33	37	Lizama, Ignacia	Daughter	F	Cha	6	S	N		Guam		None
12		33	37	Lizama, Jose	Son	M	Cha	2.3	S	N		Guam		None
13		33	37	Lizama, Rosa	Daughter	F	Cha	.6	S	N		Guam		None
14		33	38	Toves, Francisco Q	Head	M	Cha	29	S	N	Y	Guam	Y	Farmer
15		33	39	Santos, Rosa V	Head	F	Cha	36	D	N	Y	Guam	N	None
16		33	40	Flores, Candelaria C	Head	F	Cha	22	M	N	Y	Guam	Y	None
17		33	40	Flores, Tomasa C	Daughter	F	Cha	.3	S	N		Guam		None
18		34	41	Fejeran, Luis A	Head	M	Cha	29	M	N	Y	Guam	Y	Farmer
19		34	41	Fejeran, Felicidad M	Wife	F	Cha	22	M	N	Y	Guam	N	None
20		35	42	Flores, Vicente A	Head	M	Cha	62	M	N	Y	Guam	N	Farmer
21		35	42	Flores, Maria T	Wife	F	Cha	31	M	N	Y	Guam	N	None
22		35	42	Flores, Magarita	Daughter	F	Cha	1.1	S	N		Guam		None
23		35	42	Taitano, Alfred J	Grandson	M	Cha	20	S	N	Y	Guam	Y	Farm laborer
24		35	42	Taitano, Robert	Grandson	M	Cha	18	S	N	Y	Guam	Y	Farm laborer
25		35	42	Taitano, George	Grandson	M	Cha	16	S	N	Y	Guam	Y	Farm laborer

DEPARTMENT OF COMMERCE-BUREAU OF THE CENSUS
WASHINGTON

FIFTEENTH CENSUS OF THE UNITED STATES: 1930-POPULATION

THE ISLAND OF GUAM

Sheet No. 36B

213B

District **Municipality of Agana**
Name of Place **Barrigada Barrio**
[Proper name and, also, name of class, as city, town, village, barrio, etc]

Enumeration District No. 5
Enumerated by me on **April 5, 1930** Margarito D. Palting, Enumerator

	PLACE OF ABODE			NAME	RELATION	PERSONAL DESCRIPTION				EDUCATION		NATIVITY		OCCUPATION
	Street, avenue, road, etc.	Number of dwelling house is order of visitation	Number of family in order of visitation	of each person whose place of abode on April 1, 1930, was in this family. Enter surname, first, then given name and middle initial. If any. Include every person living on April 1, 1930. Omit children born since April 1, 1930.	Relationship of this Person to the head of the family.	Sex	Color or race	Age at last birthday	Single, married, widowed or divorced	Attended school any time since Sept. 1, 1929	Whether able to read and write.	Place of birth of this person.	Whether able to speak English.	
	1	2	3	4	5	6	7	8	9	10	11	12	13	14
26	[no street name]	35	42	Taitano, Herminia	Granddaughter	F	Cha	16	S	Y	N	Guam	Y	None
27		35	42	Taitano, Teddy	Grandson	M	Cha	9	S	Y		Guam		None
28		35	42	Flores, Vicente A	Grandson	M	Cha	14	S	Y	N	Guam	Y	None
29		35	42	Flores, Manuel A	Grandson	M	Cha	12	S	Y	N	Guam	Y	None
30		36	43	Cruz, Manuel C	Head	M	Cha	54	Wd	N	N	Guam	N	Farmer
31		36	43	Cruz, Francisco	Son	M	Cha	21	S	N	N	Guam	Y	Photographer
32		36	43	Cruz, Trinidad	Daughter	F	Cha	20	S	N	Y	Guam	Y	None
33		36	43	Cruz, Antonio	Son	M	Cha	10	S	Y	N	Guam	Y	None
34		37	44	Tenorio, Jose Q	Head	M	Cha	29	M	N	Y	Guam	N	Farmer
35		37	44	Tenorio, Maria Q	Wife	F	Cha	30	M	N	Y	Guam	N	None
36		37	44	Tenorio, Rosa	Daughter	F	Cha	6	S	N		Guam		None
37		37	44	Tenorio, Tomas	Son	M	Cha	5	S	N		Guam		None
38		37	44	Tenorio, Jesusa	Daughter	F	Cha	2.1	S	N		Guam		None
39		38	45	Anderson, Antonio Q	Head	M	Cha	67	M	N	N	Guam	N	Farmer
40		38	45	Anderson, Joaquina M	Wife	F	Cha	67	M	N	N	Guam	N	None
41		38	45	Anderson, Rita	Daughter	F	Cha	31	S	N	N	Guam	Y	Cook
42		38	45	Anderson, Ramona	Daughter	F	Cha	31	S	N	N	Guam	Y	Cook
43		38	45	Anderson, Juan	Son	M	Cha	27	S	N	N	Guam	Y	Farm laborer
44		38	46	Anderson, Pedro M	Head	M	Cha	26	M	N	N	Guam	N	Farm laborer
45		39	47	San Nicolas, Jose SN	Head	M	Cha	35	M	N	N	Guam	N	Farm laborer
46		40	49	Tenorio, Juana S	Head	F	Cha	61	Wd	N	N	Guam	N	Weaver
47		40	49	Tenorio, Antonia D	Daughter	F	Cha	48	S	N	N	Guam	N	Weaver
48		41	49	Rojas, Pedro A	Head	M	Cha	38	M	N	Y	Guam	Y	Farmer
49		41	49	Rojas, Nieves C	Wife	F	Cha	36	M	N	N	Guam	N	None
50		41	49	Rojas, Concepcion C	Daughter	F	Cha	17	S	N	Y	Guam	Y	Teacher

DEPARTMENT OF COMMERCE-BUREAU OF THE CENSUS
WASHINGTON

FIFTEENTH CENSUS OF THE UNITED STATES: 1930-POPULATION

THE ISLAND OF GUAM

Sheet No. 37A

District **Municipality of Agana**
Name of Place **Barrigada Barrio**
[Proper name and, also, name of class, as city, town, village, barrio, etc]

Enumeration District No. **5**
Enumerated by me on **April 5, 1930** Margarito D. Palting, Enumerator

	PLACE OF ABODE			NAME	RELATION	PERSONAL DESCRIPTION				EDUCATION		NATIVITY		OCCUPATION
	Street, avenue, road, etc.	Number of dwelling house is order of visitation	Number of family in order of visitation	of each person whose place of abode on April 1, 1930, was in this family. Enter surname, first, then given name and middle initial. If any. Include every person living on April 1, 1930. Omit children born since April 1, 1930.	Relationship of this Person to the head of the family.	Sex	Color or race	Age at last birthday	Single, married, widowed or divorced	Attended school any time since Sept. 1, 1929	Whether able to read and write.	Place of birth of this person.	Whether able to speak English.	
	1	2	3	4	5	6	7	8	9	10	11	12	13	14
1	[no street name]	41	49	Rojas, Maria	Daughter	F	Cha	10	S	Y	N	Guam	N	None
2		41	49	Rojas, Jose	Son	M	Cha	8	S	Y		Guam		None
3		41	49	Rojas, Enrique	Son	M	Cha	4.4	S	N		Guam		None
4		41	49	Rojas, Rosa	Daughter	F	Cha	1.8	S	N		Guam		None
5		42	50	Villagomez, Jose C	Head	M	Cha	51	M	N	Y	Guam	Y	Farmer
6		42	51	Taitingfong, Manuel T	Head	M	Cha	43	Wd	N	Y	Guam	N	Farm laborer
7		43	52	Francisco, Nicolas P	Head	M	Cha	66	M	N	N	Guam	N	Farmer
8		43	52	Francisco, Ignacia C	Wife	F	Cha	56	M	N	N	Guam	N	None
9		43	52	Francisco, Vicente	Son	M	Cha	33	S	N	Y	Guam	Y	Farm laborer
10		43	52	Francisco, Maria	Daughter	F	Cha	28	S	N	N	Guam	N	None
11		43	52	Francisco, Carmen	Daughter	F	Cha	20	S	N	N	Guam	Y	None
12		43	52	Francisco, Juan	Son	M	Cha	19	S	N	Y	Guam	Y	Farm laborer
13		43	52	Francisco, Dolores	Daughter	F	Cha	18	S	N	Y	Guam	N	None
14		43	52	Francisco, Antonio	Son	M	Cha	15	S	Y	Y	Guam	Y	None
15		43	52	Tenorio, Jesus F	Grandson	M	Cha	7	S	Y		Guam		None
16		43	52	Francisco, Efigenia C	Granddaughter	F	Cha	9	S	Y		Guam		None
17		43	53	Francisco, Jose C	Head	M	Cha	30	M	N	Y	Guam	Y	Farm laborer
18		43	53	Francisco, Maria C	Wife	F	Cha	31	M	N	N	Guam	Y	None
19		44	54	Francisco, Joaquin S	Head	M	Cha	24	M	N	Y	Guam	Y	Farm laborer
20		44	54	Francisco, Angustia C	Wife	F	Cha	21	M	N	Y	Guam	Y	None
21		44	54	Francisco, Ignacio	Son	M	Cha	.4	S	N		Guam		None
22		45	55	Francisco, Pedro C	Head	M	Cha	26	M	N	Y	Guam	Y	Farm laborer
23		45	55	Francisco, Ana L	Wife	F	Cha	35	M	N	Y	Guam	Y	None
24		45	55	Francisco, Natividad	Daughter	F	Cha	1.3	S	N		Guam		None
25		46	56	Taisague, Joaquin C	Head	M	Cha	53	Wd	N	Y	Guam	N	Farmer

DEPARTMENT OF COMMERCE-BUREAU OF THE CENSUS
WASHINGTON

FIFTEENTH CENSUS OF THE UNITED STATES: 1930-POPULATION

THE ISLAND OF GUAM

Sheet No. 37B

214B

District **Municipality of Agana**
Name of Place **Barrigada Barrio**
[Proper name and, also, name of class, as city, town, village, barrio, etc]

Enumeration District No. 5
Enumerated by me on **April 5, 1930** Margarito D. Palting
Enumerator

	PLACE OF ABODE			NAME	RELATION	PERSONAL DESCRIPTION				EDUCATION		NATIVITY		OCCUPATION
	Street, avenue, road, etc.	Number of dwelling house is order of visitation	Number of family in order of visitation	of each person whose place of abode on April 1, 1930, was in this family. Enter surname, first, then given name and middle initial. If any. Include every person living on April 1, 1930. Omit children born since April 1, 1930.	Relationship of this Person to the head of the family.	Sex	Color or race	Age at last birthday	Single, married, widowed or divorced	Attended school any time since Sept. 1, 1929	Whether able to read and write.	Place of birth of this person.	Whether able to speak English.	
	1	2	3	4	5	6	7	8	9	10	11	12	13	14
26	[no street name]	46	56	Taisague, Vicente S	Son	M	Cha	25	S	N	N	Guam	N	Farm laborer
27		46	56	Taisague, Antonia S	Daughter	F	Cha	20	S	N	Y	Guam	Y	None
28		46	56	Taisague, Isabel S	Daughter	F	Cha	17	S	N	Y	Guam	Y	None
29		46	56	Taisague, Rosa S	Daughter	F	Cha	14	S	Y	Y	Guam	Y	None
30		47	57	Taisague, Juan S	Head	M	Cha	22	M	N	Y	Guam	Y	Farmer
31		47	57	Taisague, Maria O	Wife	F	Cha	26	M	N	N	Guam	N	None
32		47	57	Taisague, Manuela O	Daughter	F	Cha	1.7	S	N		Guam		None
33		47	57	Taisague, Maria O	Daughter	F	Cha	.3	S	N		Guam		None
34		48	58	Quichocho, Antonio C	Head	M	Cha	56	M	N	N	Guam	N	Farmer
35		48	58	Quichocho, Concepcion S	Wife	F	Cha	42	M	N	N	Guam	N	None
36		48	58	Quichocho, Jesus S	Son	M	Cha	14	S	Y	N	Guam	N	None
37		48	58	Quichocho, Maria S	Daughter	F	Cha	12	S	Y	N	Guam	N	None
38		48	58	Quichocho, Juan S	Son	M	Cha	10	S	Y	N	Guam	N	None
39		48	58	Quichocho, Josefa S	Daughter	F	Cha	6	S	N		Guam		None
40		48	58	Salas, Jose S	Step-son	M	Cha	16	S	N	N	Guam	N	None
41		49	59	Santos, Nicolas S	Head	M	Cha	78	Wd	N	N	Guam	N	Farmer
42		50	60	Salas, Juan S	Head	M	Cha	68	Wd	N	Y	Guam	N	Farmer
43		51	61	Peredo, Francisco P	Head	M	Cha	63	Wd	N	N	Guam	N	Farmer
44		52	62	Quichocho, Felipe A	Head	M	Cha	27	M	N	Y	Guam	N	Farmer
45		52	62	Quichocho, Maria C	Wife	F	Cha	30	M	N	Y	Guam	Y	None
46		52	62	Quichocho, Pedro	Son	M	Cha	6	S	N		Guam		None
47		52	62	Quichocho, Carmen	Daughter	F	Cha	3.9	S	N		Guam		None
48		52	62	Quichocho, Manuel	Son	M	Cha	2.3	S	N		Guam		None
49		52	62	Quichocho, Jose	Son	M	Cha	.2	S	N		Guam		None
50		53	63	Salas, Pedro C	Head	M	Cha	67	M	N	Y	Guam	N	Farmer

DEPARTMENT OF COMMERCE-BUREAU OF THE CENSUS
WASHINGTON

FIFTEENTH CENSUS OF THE UNITED STATES: 1930-POPULATION

THE ISLAND OF GUAM

Sheet No. 38A

District **Municipality of Agana**
Name of Place **Barrigada Barrio**
[Proper name and, also, name of class, as city, town, village, barrio, etc]

Enumeration District No. 5
Enumerated by me on **April 7, 1930** Margarito D. Palting, Enumerator

	PLACE OF ABODE: Street, avenue, road, etc.	Number of dwelling house in order of visitation	Number of family in order of visitation	NAME of each person whose place of abode on April 1, 1930, was in this family. Enter surname, first, then given name and middle initial. If any. Include every person living on April 1, 1930. Omit children born since April 1, 1930.	RELATION Relationship of this Person to the head of the family.	PERSONAL DESCRIPTION: Sex	Color or race	Age at last birthday	Single, married, widowed or divorced	EDUCATION: Attended school any time since Sept. 1, 1929	Whether able to read and write.	NATIVITY Place of birth of this person.	Whether able to speak English.	OCCUPATION
	1	2	3	4	5	6	7	8	9	10	11	12	13	14
1	[no street name]	53	63	Salas, Rosa C	Wife	F	Cha	66	M	N	Y	Guam	N	None
2		53	64	Salas, Ramon C	Head	M	Cha	63	Wd	N	N	Guam	N	Farmer
3		54	65	Ibao, Fabian C	Head	M	Fil	75	Wd	N	N	Philippine Is.	N	Farmer
4		54	65	Fejeran, Jose R	Grandson	M	Cha	18	S	N	Y	Guam	Y	None
5		55	66	Guerrero, Francisco C	Head	M	Cha	33	M	N	Y	Guam	N	Farmer
6		55	66	Guerrero, Ana C	Wife	F	Cha	26	M	N	N	Guam	N	None
7		55	66	Guerrero, Isabel	Daughter	F	Cha	12	S	Y	Y	Guam	Y	None
8		55	66	Guerrero, Maria	Daughter	F	Cha	10	S	Y	Y	Guam	Y	None
9		55	66	Guerrero, Jose	Son	M	Cha	7	S	Y		Guam		None
10		55	66	Guerrero, Francisca	Daughter	F	Cha	4.4	S	N		Guam		None
11		55	66	Guerrero, Jesus	Son	M	Cha	3.4	S	N		Guam		None
12		55	66	Guerrero, Joaquin	Son	M	Cha	1.5	S	N		Guam		None
13		56	67	Mesa, Ramon M	Head	M	Cha	64	S	N	Y	Guam	Y	Farmer
14		57	68	Taitano, Juan M	Head	M	Cha	70	Wd	N	N	Guam	N	Farmer
15		58	69	Borja, Juan O	Head	M	Cha	17	S	N	Y	Guam	Y	Farmer
16		58	69	Borja, Vicente O	Brother	M	Cha	10	S	Y	N	Guam	N	None
17		59	70	Duenas, Clemente C	Head	M	Cha	25	M	N	Y	Guam	N	Farmer
18		59	70	Duenas, Josefa B	Wife	F	Cha	19	M	N	Y	Guam	Y	None
19		60	71	Duenas, Ramon C	Head	M	Cha	27	M	N	Y	Guam	N	Farmer
20		60	71	Duenas, Carmen LG	Wife	F	Cha	20	M	N	Y	Guam	N	None
21		60	71	Duenas, Juan	Son	M	Cha	7	S	Y		Guam		None
22		60	71	Duenas, Ana	Daughter	F	Cha	5	S	N		Guam		None
23		60	71	Duenas, Maria	Daughter	F	Cha	2.1	S	N		Guam		None
24		60	71	Duenas, Clemente	Son	M	Cha	.1	S	N		Guam		None
25		60	71	Quitugua, Maria S	Aunt	F	Cha	29	S	N		Guam		None

DEPARTMENT OF COMMERCE-BUREAU OF THE CENSUS
WASHINGTON

FIFTEENTH CENSUS OF THE UNITED STATES: 1930-POPULATION

THE ISLAND OF GUAM

Sheet No. 38B

215B

District **Municipality of Agana**
Name of Place **Barrigada Barrio** [Proper name and, also, name of class, as city, town, village, barrio, etc]

Enumeration District No. 5
Enumerated by me on **April 7, 1930** Margarito D. Palting, Enumerator

	PLACE OF ABODE			NAME	RELATION	PERSONAL DESCRIPTION				EDUCATION		NATIVITY		OCCUPATION
	Street, avenue, road, etc.	Number of dwelling house in order of visitation	Number of family in order of visitation	of each person whose place of abode on April 1, 1930, was in this family. Enter surname, first, then given name and middle initial. If any. Include every person living on April 1, 1930. Omit children born since April 1, 1930.	Relationship of this Person to the head of the family.	Sex	Color or race	Age at last birthday	Single, married, widowed or divorced	Attended school any time since Sept. 1, 1929	Whether able to read and write.	Place of birth of this person.	Whether able to speak English.	
	1	2	3	4	5	6	7	8	9	10	11	12	13	14
26	[no street name]	61	72	Martinez, Marino C	Head	M	Cha	55	S	N	Y	Guam	N	Farm laborer
27		62	73	Crisostomo, Juan B	Head	M	Cha	67	M	N	N	Guam	N	Farm laborer
28		62	73	Crisostomo, Maria C	Wife	F	Cha	73	M	N	N	Guam	N	None
29		62	73	San Agustin, Lourdes C	Grand daughter	F	Cha	7	S	N		Guam		None
30		62	73	Aquino, Maria C	Grand daughter	F	Cha	.6	S	N		Guam		None
31		63	74	Ruth, James W	Head	M	W	57	Wd	N	Y	Michigan	Y	Superintendant Pineapple Plantation
32		63	74	Flores, Antonia G	Servant	F	Cha	37	S	N	Y	Guam	Y	Cook
33		63	74	Flores, Pedro G	Lodger	M	Cha	10	S	Y	Y	Guam	Y	None
34		63	74	Flores, Alfred G	Lodger	M	Cha	7	S	Y		Guam		None
35		64	75	Manibusan, Ignacio Q	Head	M	Cha	25	M	N	N	Guam	N	Farmer
36		64	75	Manibusan, Carmen	Wife	F	Cha	24	M	N	N	Guam	N	None
37		64	75	Manibusan, Jose	Son	M	Cha	5	S	N		Guam		None
38		64	75	Manibusan, Maria	Daughter	F	Cha	4.1	S	N		Guam		None
39		65	76	Santos, Lorenzo C	Head	M	Cha	74	S	N	N	Guam	N	Farm laborer
40		66	77	Materne, Pedro D	Head	M	Cha	57	Wd	N	N	Guam	N	Farmer
41		66	77	Materne, Manuel D	Son	M	Cha	21	S	N	N	Guam	N	Farm laborer
42		67	78	Crisostomo, Jesus D	Head	M	Cha	34	M	N	N	Guam	N	Farmer
43		67	78	Crisostomo, Maria C	Wife	F	Cha	37	M	N	N	Guam	N	None
44		67	78	Crisostomo, Pilar	Daughter	F	Cha	4.3	S	N		Guam		None
45		67	78	Crisostomo, Francisco	Son	M	Cha	3.8	S	N		Guam		None
46		67	78	Crisostomo, Mariano	Son	M	Cha	1.1	S	N		Guam		None
47		67	78	Flores, Jesus F	Step-son	M	Cha	12	S	Y	Y	Guam	Y	None
48		38	79	Blas, Jesus F	Head	M	Cha	40	M	N	N	Guam	N	Farmer
49		38	79	Blas, Trinidad M	Wife	F	Cha	30	M	N	N	Guam	N	None
50		38	79	Blas, Ana	Daughter	F	Cha	17	S	N	Y	Guam	Y	None

DEPARTMENT OF COMMERCE-BUREAU OF THE CENSUS
WASHINGTON

FIFTEENTH CENSUS OF THE UNITED STATES: 1930-POPULATION

THE ISLAND OF GUAM

Sheet No. 39A

District **Municipality of Agana**
Name of Place **Barrigada Barrio**
[Proper name and, also, name of class, as city, town, village, barrio, etc]

Enumeration District No. 5
Enumerated by me on **April 7, 1930** Margarito D. Palting, Enumerator

	PLACE OF ABODE			NAME	RELATION	PERSONAL DESCRIPTION				EDUCATION		NATIVITY		OCCUPATION
	Street, avenue, road, etc.	Number of dwelling house in order of visitation	Number of family in order of visitation	of each person whose place of abode on April 1, 1930, was in this family. Enter surname, first, then given name and middle initial, if any. Include every person living on April 1, 1930. Omit children born since April 1, 1930.	Relationship of this Person to the head of the family.	Sex	Color or race	Age at last birthday	Single, married, widowed or divorced	Attended school any time since Sept. 1, 1929	Whether able to read and write.	Place of birth of this person.	Whether able to speak English.	
	1	2	3	4	5	6	7	8	9	10	11	12	13	14
1	[no street name]	38	79	Blas, Juan	Son	M	Cha	15	S	N	Y	Guam	Y	None
2		38	79	Blas, Mariano	Son	M	Cha	14	S	N	Y	Guam	Y	None
3		38	79	Blas, Jose	Son	M	Cha	12	S	Y	Y	Guam	Y	None
4		38	79	Blas, Carmen	Daughter	F	Cha	10	S	Y	N	Guam	Y	None
5		38	79	Blas, Francisco	Son	M	Cha	8	S	Y		Guam		None
6		38	79	Blas, Ramon	Son	M	Cha	5	S	N		Guam		None
7		38	79	Blas, Teresa	Daughter	F	Cha	2.5	S	N		Guam		None
8		69	80	Pablo, Juan P	Head	M	Cha	38	M	N		Guam	N	Farmer
9		69	80	Pablo, Dolores F	Wife	F	Cha	25	M	N		Guam	N	None
10		69	80	Pablo, Isabel	Daughter	F	Cha	5	S	N		Guam		None
11		69	80	Pablo, Lorenzo	Son	M	Cha	2.9	S	N		Guam		None
12		69	80	Pablo, Antonia	Daughter	F	Cha	1.1	S	N		Guam		None
13		69	80	Pablo, Francisco	Son	M	Cha	.5	S	N		Guam		None
14		70	81	Borja, Vicente I	Head	M	Cha	57	M	N	Y	Guam	N	Farmer
15		70	81	Borja, Maria C	Wife	F	Cha	32	M	N	N	Guam	N	None
16		70	81	Borja, Francisco	Son	M	Cha	6	S	N		Guam		None
17		70	81	Fejeran, Concepcion	Daughter-in-law	F	Cha	27	M	N	Y	Guam	Y	Laundress
18		71	82	Cruz, Antonia M	Head	F	Cha	59	S	N	N	Guam	N	None
19		71	82	Mafnas, Vicente M	Son	M	Cha	23	M	N	Y	Guam	N	Farmer
20		71	82	Mafnas, Rosario M	Daughter	F	Cha	23	M	N	N	Guam	N	None
21		72	83	Guerrero, Mariano C	Head	M	Cha	64	M	N	N	Guam	N	Farmer
22		72	83	Guerrero, Maria C	Wife	F	Cha	56	M	N	N	Guam	N	None
23		72	83	Guerrero, Ana	Daughter	F	Cha	24	S	N	Y	Guam	N	None
24		72	83	Guerrero, Vicente	Son	M	Cha	20	S	N	N	Guam	N	Farm laborer
25		73	84	Rosario, Juan A	Head	M	Cha	60	M	N	N	Guam	N	Farmer

DEPARTMENT OF COMMERCE-BUREAU OF THE CENSUS
WASHINGTON

FIFTEENTH CENSUS OF THE UNITED STATES: 1930-POPULATION

THE ISLAND OF GUAM

Sheet No. 39B

216B

District **Municipality of Agana**
Name of Place **Barrigada Barrio**
[Proper name and, also, name of class, as city, town, village, barrio, etc]

Enumeration District No. 5
Enumerated by me on **April 7, 1930** Margarito D. Palting, Enumerator

	PLACE OF ABODE: Street, avenue, road, etc.	Number of dwelling house is order of visitation	Number of family in order of visitation	NAME of each person whose place of abode on April 1, 1930, was in this family. Enter surname, first, then given name and middle initial. If any. Include every person living on April 1, 1930. Omit children born since April 1, 1930.	RELATION Relationship of this Person to the head of the family.	PERSONAL DESCRIPTION: Sex	Color or race	Age at last birthday	Single, married, widowed or divorced	EDUCATION: Attended school any time since Sept. 1, 1929	Whether able to read and write.	NATIVITY Place of birth of this person.	Whether able to speak English.	OCCUPATION
	1	2	3	4	5	6	7	8	9	10	11	12	13	14
26	[no street name]	73	84	Rosario, Maria T	Wife	F	Cha	53	M	N	N	Guam	N	None
27		74	85	Perez, Ana B	Head	F	Cha	65	Wd	N	N	Guam	N	None
28		74	85	Perez, Vicente B	Son	M	Cha	23	S	N	Y	Guam	Y	Farm laborer
29		74	86	Manibusan, Aniceto Q	Head	M	Cha	24	M	N	Y	Guam	N	Farmer
30		74	86	Manibusan, Rita P	Wife	F	Cha	28	M	N	Y	Guam	N	None
31		74	86	Manibusan, Felix	Son	M	Cha	5	S	N		Guam		None
32		74	86	Manibusan, Ana	Daughter	F	Cha	2.4	S	N		Guam		None
33		74	86	Manibusan, Modesta	Daughter	F	Cha	1.5	S	N		Guam		None
34		75	87	Pangelinan, Vicente T	Head	M	Cha	66	M	N	Y	Guam	N	Farmer
35		76	88	Guerrero, Pedro B	Head	M	Cha	285	S	N	Y	Guam	Y	Farmer
36				Here ends the enumeration of enumeration district No. 5 Barrigada										
37														
38														
39														
40														
41														
42														
43														
44														
45														
46														
47														
48														
49														
50														

DEPARTMENT OF COMMERCE-BUREAU OF THE CENSUS
WASHINGTON

FIFTEENTH CENSUS OF THE UNITED STATES: 1930-POPULATION

THE ISLAND OF GUAM

Sheet No. 40A

217

District **Municipality of Agana**
Name of Place **Sinajana Barrio**
[Proper name and, also, name of class, as city, town, village, barrio, etc]

Enumeration District No. 5
Enumerated by me on **April 8, 1930** Margarito D. Palting
Enumerator

	PLACE OF ABODE			NAME	RELATION	PERSONAL DESCRIPTION				EDUCATION		NATIVITY		OCCUPATION
	Street, avenue, road, etc.	Number of dwelling house in order of visitation	Number of family in order of visitation	of each person whose place of abode on April 1, 1930, was in this family. Enter surname, first, then given name and middle initial. If any. Include every person living on April 1, 1930. Omit children born since April 1, 1930.	Relationship of this Person to the head of the family.	Sex	Color or race	Age at last birthday	Single, married, widowed or divorced	Attended school any time since Sept. 1, 1929	Whether able to read and write.	Place of birth of this person.	Whether able to speak English.	
	1	2	3	4	5	6	7	8	9	10	11	12	13	14
1	[no street name]	77	89	Gogo, Jose G	Head	M	Cha	34	M	N	N	Guam	N	Farmer
2		77	89	Gogo, Felicita	Wife	F	Cha	33	M	N	N	Guam	N	None
3		78	90	Gogue, Juan A	Head	M	Cha	33	M	N	Y	Guam	Y	Farmer
4		78	90	Gogue, Ana Q	Wife	F	Cha	36	M	N	Y	Guam	Y	None
5		78	90	Gogue, Juan Q	Son	M	Cha	12	S	Y	Y	Guam	Y	None
6		78	90	Gogue, Jose Q	Son	M	Cha	11	S	Y	N	Guam	Y	None
7		78	90	Gogue, Pedro Q	Son	M	Cha	9	S	Y		Guam		None
8		78	90	Gogue, Jesus Q	Son	M	Cha	5	S	N		Guam		None
9		78	90	Gogue, Vicente Q	Son	M	Cha	2.5	S	N		Guam		None
10		78	90	Gogue, Antonio	Son	M	Cha	.5	S	N		Guam		None
11		79	91	Taisague, Vicenta G	Head	F	Cha	36	S	N	N	Guam	N	Washerwoman
12		79	91	Taisague, Maria	Daughter	F	Cha	4.9	S	N		Guam		None
13		80	92	Gogue, Maria A	Head	F	Cha	74	Wd	N	N	Guam	N	Farmer
14		80	92	Gogue, Rita A	Daughter	F	Cha	32	S	N	Y	Guam	Y	Midwife
15		80	93	Gogue, Vicenta A	Head	F	Cha	45	D	N	N	Guam	N	Farmer
16		80	93	Gogue, Ramon	Son	M	Cha	14	S	Y	Y	Guam	N	Farm laborer
17		80	93	Gogue, Clotilde	Daughter	F	Cha	12	S	Y	Y	Guam	Y	None
18		81	94	Iglesias, Juan T	Head	M	Cha	48	M	N	Y	Guam	Y	Chauffeur
19		81	94	Iglesias, Consolacion G	Wife	F	Cha	36	M	N	Y	Guam	Y	Saleswoman
20		81	94	Iglesias, Jose	Son	M	Cha	12	S	N	Y	Guam	N	None
21		81	94	Iglesias, Juan	Son	M	Cha	10	S	Y	N	Guam	Y	None
22		81	94	Iglesias, Consolacion	Daughter	F	Cha	35	S	N		Guam		None
23		81	94	Iglesias, Carmen	Daughter	F	Cha	3.1	S	N		Guam		None
24		81	94	Iglesias, Rosa	Daughter	F	Cha	1.2	S	N		Guam		None
25		82	95	Atoigue, Ana Q	Head	F	Cha	50	Wd	N	N	Guam		None

DEPARTMENT OF COMMERCE-BUREAU OF THE CENSUS
WASHINGTON

FIFTEENTH CENSUS OF THE UNITED STATES: 1930-POPULATION

THE ISLAND OF GUAM

Sheet No. 40B

217B

District **Municipality of Agana**
Name of Place **Sinajana Barrio**
[Proper name and, also, name of class, as city, town, village, barrio, etc]

Enumeration District No. 5
Enumerated by me on **April 8, 1930** Margarito D. Palting, Enumerator

	PLACE OF ABODE			NAME	RELATION	PERSONAL DESCRIPTION				EDUCATION		NATIVITY		OCCUPATION
	Street, avenue, road, etc.	Number of dwelling house is order of visitation	Number of family in order of visitation	of each person whose place of abode on April 1, 1930, was in this family. Enter surname, first, then given name and middle initial. If any. Include every person living on April 1, 1930. Omit children born since April 1, 1930.	Relationship of this Person to the head of the family.	Sex	Color or race	Age at last birthday	Single, married, widowed or divorced	Attended school any time since Sept. 1, 1929	Whether able to read and write.	Place of birth of this person.	Whether able to speak English.	
	1	2	3	4	5	6	7	8	9	10	11	12	13	14
26	[no street name]	82	95	Gogo, Jesus Q	Son	M	Cha	25	S	N	Y	Guam	Y	Farm laborer
27		82	95	Atoigue, Francisco Q	Son	M	Cha	17	S	Y	Y	Guam	Y	Farm laborer
28		82	95	Atoigue, Vicente	Son	M	Cha	15	S	Y	Y	Guam	Y	None
29		83	96	Toves, Ramon S	Head	M	Cha	34	M	N	Y	Guam	Y	Laborer
30		83	96	Toves, Isabel G	Wife	F	Cha	33	M	N	Y	Guam	N	None
31		83	96	Toves, Jose G	Son	M	Cha	8	S	Y		Guam		None
32		83	96	Toves, Ana S	Sister	F	Cha	33	S	N	Y	Guam		Laundres
33		84	97	Aguajlo, Emilia C	Head	F	Cha	59	M	N	N	Guam	N	None
34		84	97	Gogo, Jose C	Son	M	Cha	33	Wd	N	Y	Guam	N	Farmer
35		84	97	Gogo, Isabel	Grand daughter	F	Cha	10	S	Y	N	Guam		None
36		84	97	Gogo, Jesus	Grandson	M	Cha	8	S	Y		Guam		None
37		85	98	Arceo, Ignacio C	Head	M	Cha	25	M	N	Y	Guam	Y	Farmer
38		85	98	Arceo, Regina C	Wife	F	Cha	26	M	N	N	Guam	N	None
39		85	98	Arceo, Dolores	Daughter	F	Cha	7	S	N		Guam		None
40		85	98	Arceo, Jose	Son	M	Cha	5	S	N		Guam		None
41		86	99	Palomo, Gregorio P	Head	M	Cha	31	M	N	Y	Guam	N	Laborer
42		86	99	Palomo, Isabel T	Wife	F	Cha	29	M	N	Y	Guam	N	None
43		86	99	Palomo, Maria	Daughter	F	Cha	7	S	Y		Guam		None
44		86	99	Palomo, Antonia	Daughter	F	Cha	5	S	N		Guam		None
45		86	99	Palomo, Jose	Son	M	Cha	1.4	S	N		Guam		None
46		87	100	Crisostomo, Felix C	Head	M	Cha	36	M	N	Y	Guam	Y	Laborer
47		87	100	Crisostomo, Ana SN	Wife	F	Cha	32	M	N	Y	Guam	Y	None
48		87	100	Crisostomo, Delfina	Daughter	F	Cha	13	S	Y	Y	Guam	Y	None
49		87	100	Crisostomo, Teodoro	Son	M	Cha	12	S	Y	Y	Guam	Y	None
50		87	100	Crisostomo, Felipe	Son	M	Cha	10	S	Y	N	Guam	N	None

DEPARTMENT OF COMMERCE-BUREAU OF THE CENSUS
WASHINGTON

FIFTEENTH CENSUS OF THE UNITED STATES: 1930-POPULATION

THE ISLAND OF GUAM

Sheet No. 41A

District **Municipality of Agana**
Name of Place **Sinajana Barrio**
[Proper name and, also, name of class, as city, town, village, barrio, etc]

Enumeration District No. 5
Enumerated by me on **April 8, 1930** Margarito D. Palting, Enumerator

	PLACE OF ABODE: Street, avenue, road, etc.	Number of dwelling house in order of visitation	Number of family in order of visitation	NAME of each person whose place of abode on April 1, 1930, was in this family. Enter surname, first, then given name and middle initial. If any. Include every person living on April 1, 1930. Omit children born since April 1, 1930.	RELATION Relationship of this Person to the head of the family.	PERSONAL DESCRIPTION: Sex	Color or race	Age at last birthday	Single, married, widowed or divorced	EDUCATION: Attended school any time since Sept. 1, 1929	Whether able to read and write.	NATIVITY Place of birth of this person.	Whether able to speak English.	OCCUPATION
	1	2	3	4	5	6	7	8	9	10	11	12	13	14
1	[no street name]	87	100	Crisostomo, Rosalia	Daughter	F	Cha	8	S	Y		Guam		None
2		87	100	Crisostomo, Nicolasa	Daughter	F	Cha	5	S	N		Guam		None
3		87	100	Crisostomo, Jose	Son	M	Cha	2.8	S	N		Guam		None
4		87	100	Crisostomo, Jesus	Son	M	Cha	1.3	S	N		Guam		None
5		88	101	Cruz, Antonio Q	Head	M	Cha	36	M	N	Y	Guam	N	Farmer
6		88	101	Cruz, Ana G	Wife	F	Cha	33	M	N	Y	Guam	N	None
7		88	101	Cruz, Pedro	Son	M	Cha	12	S	Y	Y	Guam	N	None
8		88	101	Cruz, Rosa	Daughter	F	Cha	10	S	Y	Y	Guam	Y	None
9		88	101	Cruz, Jose	Son	M	Cha	8	S	Y		Guam		None
10		88	101	Cruz, Ana	Daughter	F	Cha	6	S	N		Guam		None
11		88	101	Cruz, Antonio	Son	M	Cha	4	S	N		Guam		None
12		88	101	Cruz, Barcilisa	Daughter	F	Cha	1.9	S	N		Guam		None
13		89	102	Gogo, Ramon G	Head	M	Cha	30	M	N	N	Guam	N	Farmer
14		89	102	Gogo, Joaquina C	Wife	F	Cha	44	M	N	N	Guam	N	None
15		89	102	Gogo, Margarita	Daughter	F	Cha	7	S	Y		Guam		None
16		89	102	Gogo, Eugneia	Son	M	Cha	5	S	N		Guam		None
17		89	102	Gogo, Juan	Son	M	Cha	3	S	N		Guam		None
18		89	102	Aguajlo, Jose C	Step-son	M	Cha	22	S	N	Y	Guam		None
19		89	102	Aguajlo, Pedro C	Step-son	M	Cha	20	S	N	N	Guam		None
20		90	103	Gogue, Jose G	Head	M	Cha	43	M	N	N	Guam	N	Farmer
21		90	103	Gogue, Joaquina G	Wife	F	Cha	41	M	N	N	Guam	N	None
22		90	103	Gogue, Juan	Son	M	Cha	15	S	Y	Y	Guam	N	None
23		90	103	Gogue, Ana	Daughter	F	Cha	9	S	Y		Guam		None
24		90	103	Gogue, Jose	Son	M	Cha	4	S	N		Guam		None
25		90	103	Gogue, Pedro	Son	M	Cha	2	S	N		Guam		None

(CHAMORRO ROOTS GENEALOGY PROJECT™ TRANSCRIPTION)
(BERNARD T. PUNZALAN / HTTP://WWW.CHAMORROROOTS.COM)

DEPARTMENT OF COMMERCE-BUREAU OF THE CENSUS
WASHINGTON

FIFTEENTH CENSUS OF THE UNITED STATES: 1930-POPULATION

THE ISLAND OF GUAM

Sheet No. 41B

218B

District **Municipality of Agana**
Name of Place **Sinajana Barrio**
[Proper name and, also, name of class, as city, town, village, barrio, etc]

Enumeration District No. 5
Enumerated by me on **April 9, 1930** Margarito D. Palting
Enumerator

	PLACE OF ABODE			NAME	RELATION	PERSONAL DESCRIPTION				EDUCATION		NATIVITY		OCCUPATION
	Street, avenue, road, etc.	Number of dwelling house is order of visitation	Number of family in order of visitation	of each person whose place of abode on April 1, 1930, was in this family. Enter surname, first, then given name and middle initial. If any. Include every person living on April 1, 1930. Omit children born since April 1, 1930.	Relationship of this Person to the head of the family.	Sex	Color or race	Age at last birthday	Single, married, widowed or divorced	Attended school any time since Sept. 1, 1929	Whether able to read and write.	Place of birth of this person.	Whether able to speak English.	
	1	2	3	4	5	6	7	8	9	10	11	12	13	14
26	[no street name]	90	103	Gogue, Rita	Daughter	F	Cha	.8	S	N		Guam		None
27		91	104	Aguajlo, Rita M	Head	F	Cha	59	S	N	N	Guam	N	None
28		91	104	Aguajlo, Carmen A	Daughter	F	Cha	31	S	N	N	Guam	Y	Laundress
29		91	104	Aguajlo, Vicente A	Son	M	Cha	26	S	N	N	Guam	N	Farm laborer
30		91	104	Aguajlo, Maria	Grand daughter	F	Cha	6	S	N		Guam		None
31		91	104	Tedtaotao, Marcelina T	Niece	F	Cha	38	S	N	N	Guam	N	None
32		91	104	Aguajlo, Miguel M	Brother	M	Cha	53	M	N	N	Guam	N	Farmer
33		91	104	Tedtaotao, Rita T	Grand daughter	F	Cha	5	S	N		Guam		None
34		92	105	Navarro, Lucas M	Head	M	Cha	46	M	N	Y	Guam	N	Farmer
35		92	105	Navarro, Angela T	Wife	F	Cha	46	M	N	N	Guam	N	None
36		92	105	Navarro, Vicenta	Daughter	F	Cha	16	S	N	Y	Guam	Y	None
37		92	105	Navarro, Agnes	Daughter	F	Cha	12	S	Y	Y	Guam	Y	None
38		92	105	Navarro, Isabel	Daughter	F	Cha	10	S	Y	Y	Guam	Y	None
39		92	105	Navarro, Francisca	Daughter	F	Cha	9	S	Y		Guam		None
40		92	105	Navarro, Pedro	Son	M	Cha	5	S	N		Guam		None
41		93	106	Sablan, Telesforo S	Head	M	Cha	39	M	N	Y	Guam	N	Farmer
42		93	106	Sablan, Carolina G	Wife	F	Cha	40	M	N	N	Guam	N	None
43		93	106	Sablan, Juan	Son	M	Cha	17	S	Y	Y	Guam	Y	Farm laborer
44		93	106	Sablan, Manuel	Son	M	Cha	13	S	Y	Y	Guam	Y	None
45		93	106	Sablan, Maria	Daughter	F	Cha	8	S	Y		Guam		None
46		93	106	Sablan, Jesus	Son	M	Cha	2.3	S	N		Guam		None
47		93	106	Sablan, Florentina	Daughter	F	Cha	1.2	S	N		Guam		None
48		94	107	Tenorio, Vicente G	Head	M	Cha	27	M	N	Y	Guam	Y	Farmer
49		94	107	Tenorio, Maria A	Wife	F	Cha	22	M	N	Y	Guam	Y	None
50		94	107	Tenorio, Ana	Daughter	F	Cha	1.1	S	N		Guam		None

DEPARTMENT OF COMMERCE-BUREAU OF THE CENSUS
WASHINGTON

FIFTEENTH CENSUS OF THE UNITED STATES: 1930-POPULATION

THE ISLAND OF GUAM

Sheet No. 42A

District **Municipality of Agana**
Name of Place **Sinajana Barrio**
[Proper name and, also, name of class, as city, town, village, barrio, etc]

Enumeration District No. **5**
Enumerated by me on **April 9, 1930** Margarito D. Palting
Enumerator

	PLACE OF ABODE			NAME	RELATION	PERSONAL DESCRIPTION				EDUCATION		NATIVITY		OCCUPATION
	Street, avenue, road, etc.	Number of dwelling house in order of visitation	Number of family in order of visitation	of each person whose place of abode on April 1, 1930, was in this family. Enter surname, first, then given name and middle initial. If any. Include every person living on April 1, 1930. Omit children born since April 1, 1930.	Relationship of this Person to the head of the family.	Sex	Color or race	Age at last birthday	Single, married, widowed or divorced	Attended school any time since Sept. 1, 1929	Whether able to read and write.	Place of birth of this person.	Whether able to speak English.	
	1	2	3	4	5	6	7	8	9	10	11	12	13	14
1	[no street name]	95	108	Delgado, Pedro M	Head	M	Cha	51	M	N	Y	Guam	N	Farmer
2		95	108	Delgado, Crispina M	Wife	F	Cha	30	M	N	Y	Guam	N	None
3		95	109	Navarro, Dionisio M	Head	M	Cha	39	M	N	Y	Guam	N	Laborer
4		95	109	Navarro, Manuela Q	Wife	F	Cha	20	M	N	N	Guam	N	None
5		96	110	Gogo, Juan G	Head	M	Cha	58	M	N	N	Guam	N	Farmer
6		96	110	Gogo, Filomena A	Wife	F	Cha	51	M	N	N	Guam	N	None
7		96	110	Atoigue, Juan SN	Brother-in-law	M	Cha	37	M	N	N	Guam	N	Farm laborer
8		97	111	Taimanglo, Bartola A	Head	F	Cha	50	Wd	N	N	Guam	N	Farmer
9		97	111	Taimanglo, Pedro A	Son	M	Cha	15	S	Y	Y	Guam	Y	None
10		98	112	Taimanglo, Jose DLR	Head	M	Cha	62	M	N	Y	Guam	N	Carpenter
11		98	112	Taimanglo, Guadalupe C	Wife	F	Cha	52	M	N	N	Guam	N	None
12		98	112	Taimanglo, Jose T	God-son	M	Cha	23	S	N	Y	Guam	N	Farmer
13		99	113	Atoigue, Juan M	Head	M	Cha	40	M	N	Y	Guam	N	Farmer
14		99	113	Atoigue, Carmen T	Wife	F	Cha	39	M	N	Y	Guam	N	None
15		99	113	Atoigue, Magdalena	Daughter	F	Cha	15	S	N	N	Guam	N	None
16		99	113	Atoigue, Jose	Son	M	Cha	11	S	Y	Y	Guam	Y	None
17		99	113	Atoigue, Joaquin A	Nephew	M	Cha	12	S	Y	Y	Guam	Y	None
18		100	114	Gogo, Juan G	Head	M	Cha	38	M	N	N	Guam	N	Farmer
19		100	114	Gogo, Ana C	Wife	F	Cha	45	M	N	N	Guam	N	Laundress
20		100	114	Gogo, Pedro	Son	M	Cha	15	S	Y	Y	Guam	Y	Farm laborer
21		100	114	Crisostomo, Maria C	Step daughter	F	Cha	24	S	N	N	Guam	N	None
22		100	114	Gogo, Veronica	Daughter	F	Cha	8	S	Y		Guam		None
23		101	115	Achaigua, Dolores C	Head	F	Cha	85	Wd	N	N	Guam	N	None
24		101	115	Crisostomo, Jose C	Son	M	Cha	23	S	N	Y	Guam	Y	Laborer
25		101	115	Crisostomo, Mariano	Son	M	Cha	13	S	Y	Y	Guam	Y	None

DEPARTMENT OF COMMERCE-BUREAU OF THE CENSUS
WASHINGTON

FIFTEENTH CENSUS OF THE UNITED STATES: 1930-POPULATION

THE ISLAND OF GUAM

Sheet No. 42B

219B

District **Municipality of Agana**
Name of Place **Sinajana Barrio**
[Proper name and, also, name of class, as city, town, village, barrio, etc]

Enumeration District No. 5
Enumerated by me on April 9, 1930 Margarito D. Palting, Enumerator

	PLACE OF ABODE: Street, avenue, road, etc.	Number of dwelling house in order of visitation	Number of family in order of visitation	NAME of each person whose place of abode on April 1, 1930, was in this family. Enter surname, first, then given name and middle initial. If any. Include every person living on April 1, 1930. Omit children born since April 1, 1930.	RELATION Relationship of this Person to the head of the family.	PERSONAL DESCRIPTION: Sex	Color or race	Age at last birthday	Single, married, widowed or divorced	EDUCATION: Attended school any time since Sept. 1, 1929	Whether able to read and write.	NATIVITY Place of birth of this person.	Whether able to speak English.	OCCUPATION
	1	2	3	4	5	6	7	8	9	10	11	12	13	14
26	[no street name]	103	116	Quidachay, Ana V	Head	F	Cha	55	Wd	N	N	Guam	N	Laundress
27		103	116	Navarro, Maria Q	Grand daughter	F	Cha	4.4	S	N		Guam		None
28		103	117	Gogue, Juana T	Head	F	Cha	64	Wd	N	N	Guam		Laundress
29		103	117	Taimanglo, Joaquin C	Nephew	M	Cha	12	S	Y	Y	Guam	Y	None
30		104	118	Perez, Jose G	Head	M	Cha	33	M	N	Y	Guam	Y	Farmer
31		104	118	Perez, Maria A	Wife	F	Cha	22	M	N	Y	Guam	Y	None
32		104	118	Perez, Clotilde	Daughter	F	Cha	6	S	N		Guam		None
33		104	118	Perez, Vicente	Son	M	Cha	2.5	S	N		Guam		None
34		104	118	Perez, Jesus	Son	M	Cha	.2	S	N		Guam		None
35		104	119	Perez, Josefa G	Head	F	Cha	66	Wd	N	N	Guam		None
36		104	120	Crisostomo, Angel C	Head	M	Cha	28	M	N	N	Guam	N	Farmer
37		104	120	Crisostomo, Joaquina P	Wife	F	Cha	29	M	N	Y	Guam	Y	None
38		104	120	Crisostomo, Jose	Son	M	Cha	8	S	N		Guam		None
39		104	120	Crisostomo, Gregorio	Son	M	Cha	5	S	N		Guam		None
40		104	120	Crisostomo, Francisco	Son	M	Cha	.9	S	N		Guam		None
41		105	121	Gogo, Carmela Q	Head	F	Cha	76	S	N	N	Guam	N	None
42		105	121	Gogo, Teodora G	Daughter	F	Cha	43	S	N	N	Guam	N	Laundress
43		105	121	Gogo, Felicita	Daughter	F	Cha	16	S	N	N	Guam	Y	Laundress
44		105	121	Gogo, Jose	Son	M	Cha	15	S	N	Y	Guam	Y	None
45		105	121	Gogo, Josefa	Daughter	F	Cha	4.5	s	N		Guam		None
46		106	122	Bautista, Antonio C	Head	M	Cha	49	M	N	N	Guam	N	Farmer
47		106	122	Bautista, Rosa L	Wife	F	Cha	36	M	N	Y	Guam	N	None
48		106	122	Bautista, Matias	Son	M	Cha	19	S	N	Y	Guam	Y	Farm laborer
49		106	122	Bautista, Antonio	Son	M	Cha	17	S	N	Y	Guam	Y	Farm laborer
50		106	122	Bautista, Jesus	Son	M	Cha	15	S	Y	Y	Guam	Y	None

(CHAMORRO ROOTS GENEALOGY PROJECT™ TRANSCRIPTION)
(BERNARD T. PUNZALAN / HTTP://WWW.CHAMORROROOTS.COM)

DEPARTMENT OF COMMERCE-BUREAU OF THE CENSUS
WASHINGTON

FIFTEENTH CENSUS OF THE UNITED STATES: 1930-POPULATION

THE ISLAND OF GUAM

Sheet No. 43A

District **Municipality of Agana**
Name of Place **Sinajana Barrio**
[Proper name and, also, name of class, as city, town, village, barrio, etc]

Enumeration District No. 5
Enumerated by me on **April 10, 1930** Margarito D. Palting, Enumerator

	PLACE OF ABODE: Street, avenue, road, etc.	Number of dwelling house in order of visitation	Number of family in order of visitation	NAME of each person whose place of abode on April 1, 1930, was in this family. Enter surname, first, then given name and middle initial. If any. Include every person living on April 1, 1930. Omit children born since April 1, 1930.	RELATION Relationship of this Person to the head of the family.	PERSONAL DESCRIPTION: Sex	Color or race	Age at last birthday	Single, married, widowed or divorced	EDUCATION: Attended school any time since Sept. 1, 1929	Whether able to read and write.	NATIVITY Place of birth of this person.	Whether able to speak English.	OCCUPATION
	1	2	3	4	5	6	7	8	9	10	11	12	13	14
1	[no street name]	106	123	Bautista, Pedro L	Head	M	Cha	23	M	N	Y	Guam	N	Farm laborer
2		106	123	Bautista, Ana L	Wife	F	Cha	24	M	N	Y	Guam	Y	None
3		107	124	Tenorio, Jose M	Head	M	Cha	31	Wd	N	Y	Guam	N	Farmer
4		107	124	Tenorio, Maria B	Daughter	F	Cha	7	S	Y		Guam		None
5		107	124	Tenorio, Rosario	Daughter	F	Cha	4.6	S	N		Guam		None
6		107	124	Tenorio, Regina	Daughter	F	Cha	3.9	S	N		Guam		None
7		107	124	Tenorio, Dolores	Daughter	F	Cha	1.7	S	N		Guam		None
8		107	125	Tenorio, Maria G	Head	F	Cha	32	S	N	Y	Guam	N	None
9		107	125	Tenorio, Gregorio G	Son	M	Cha	15	S	N	N	Guam	N	None
10		107	125	Tenorio, Delfina	Daughter	F	Cha	12	S	Y	Y	Guam	Y	None
11		107	125	Tenorio, Rosario	Daughter	F	Cha	9	S	Y		Guam		None
12		107	125	Tenorio, Ricardo	Son	M	Cha	1.2	S	N		Guam		None
13		108	126	Tenorio, Enrique G	Head	M	Cha	29	M	N	Y	Guam	N	Farmer
14		108	126	Tenorio, Natividad C	Wife	F	Cha	25	M	N	N	Guam	N	None
15		108	126	Tenorio, Francisco	Son	M	Cha	5	S	N		Guam		None
16		108	126	Tenorio, Maria	Daughter	F	Cha	4.2	S	N		Guam		None
17		108	127	Atoigue, Joaquina E	Head	F	Cha	14	Wd	N	N	Guam		None
18		109	128	Garcia, Antonio LG	Head	M	Cha	62	M	N	Y	Guam	N	Farmer
19		109	128	Garcia, Gertrudes C	Wife	F	Cha	52	M	N	N	Guam	N	None
20		109	128	Blas, Domingo C	Nephew	M	Cha	12	S	N	N	Guam	Y	None
21		109	129	Garcia, Juan C	Head	M	Cha	27	M	N	N	Guam	N	Farmer
22		109	129	Garcia, Teresa T	Wife	F	Cha	23	M	N	N	Guam	N	None
23		109	129	Garcia, Antonina	Daughter	F	Cha	4.2	S	N		Guam		None
24		109	129	Garcia, Mercedes	Daughter	F	Cha	3.4	S	N		Guam		None
25		109	129	Garcia, Juan	Son	M	Cha	1.5	S	N		Guam		None

(CHAMORRO ROOTS GENEALOGY PROJECT™ TRANSCRIPTION)
(BERNARD T. PUNZALAN / HTTP://WWW.CHAMORROROOTS.COM)

DEPARTMENT OF COMMERCE-BUREAU OF THE CENSUS
WASHINGTON

FIFTEENTH CENSUS OF THE UNITED STATES: 1930-POPULATION

THE ISLAND OF GUAM

Sheet No. 43B

220B

District **Municipality of Agana**
Name of Place **Sinajana Barrio**
[Proper name and, also, name of class, as city, town, village, barrio, etc]

Enumeration District No. 5
Enumerated by me on **April 10, 1930** Margarito D. Palting
Enumerator

	PLACE OF ABODE			NAME	RELATION	PERSONAL DESCRIPTION				EDUCATION		NATIVITY		OCCUPATION
	Street, avenue, road, etc.	Number of dwelling house in order of visitation	Number of family in order of visitation	of each person whose place of abode on April 1, 1930, was in this family. Enter surname, first, then given name and middle initial. If any. Include every person living on April 1, 1930. Omit children born since April 1, 1930.	Relationship of this Person to the head of the family.	Sex	Color or race	Age at last birthday	Single, married, widowed or divorced	Attended school any time since Sept. 1, 1929	Whether able to read and write.	Place of birth of this person.	Whether able to speak English.	
	1	2	3	4	5	6	7	8	9	10	11	12	13	14
26	[no street name]	110	130	Tenorio, Francisco I	Head	M	Cha	49	M	N	N	Guam	N	Farmer
27		110	130	Tenorio, Emliana T	Wife	F	Cha	48	M	N	N	Guam	N	None
28		110	130	Atoigue, Antonio A	Nephew	M	Cha	17	S	N	Y	Guam	Y	Farm laborer
29		111	131	Imaizumi, Jose S	Head	M	Jap	44	M	N	N	Japan	N	Farm laborer
30		111	131	Imaizumi, Maria D	Wife	F	Cha	31	M	N	Y	Guam	N	None
31		111	131	Imaizumi, Francisco	Son	M	Jap	14	S	Y	Y	Guam	Y	None
32		111	131	Imaizumi, Jose	Son	M	Jap	8	S	Y		Guam		None
33		111	131	Imaizumi, Pedro	Son	M	Jap	5	S	N		Guam		None
34		112	132	San Miguel, Jose C	Head	M	Cha	33	M	N	N	Guam	N	Farm laborer
35		112	132	San Miguel, Antonia C	Wife	F	Cha	31	M	N	Y	Guam	N	None
36		112	132	San Miguel, Rosario	Daughter	F	Cha	12	S	N	N	Guam	Y	None
37		112	132	San Miguel, Angustia	Daughter	F	Cha	7	S	Y		Guam		None
38		112	132	San Miguel, Concepcion	Daughter	F	Cha	6.1	S	N		Guam		None
39		112	132	San Miguel, Juan	Son	M	Cha	3.1	S	N		Guam		None
40		112	132	San Miguel, Maria	Daughter	F	Cha	.5	S	N		Guam		None
41		113	133	Mafnas, Manuel P	Head	M	Cha	33	S	N	N	Guam	N	Farmer
42		113	0	Siguenza, Jose T	Head	M	Cha	27	M	N	Y	Guam	Y	Farmer
43		113	0	Siguenza, Carmen G	Wife	F	Cha	24	M	N	Y	Guam	Y	None
44		113	0	Siguenza, Ana	Daughter	F	Cha	5	S	N		Guam		None
45		113	0	Siguenza, Ofemia	Daughter	F	Cha	2.5	S	N		Guam		None
46		114	134	San Nicolas, Ignacio A	Head	M	Cha	35	M	N	Y	Guam	Y	Farmer
47		114	134	San Nicolas, Dolores M	Wife	F	Cha	34	M	N	Y	Guam	N	None
48		114	134	San Nicolas, Jose	Son	M	Cha	12	S	Y	Y	Guam	Y	None
49		114	134	San Nicolas, Vicente	Son	M	Cha	11	S	Y	Y	Guam	Y	None
50		114	134	San Nicolas, Maria	Daughter	F	Cha	6	S	N		Guam		None

DEPARTMENT OF COMMERCE-BUREAU OF THE CENSUS
WASHINGTON

FIFTEENTH CENSUS OF THE UNITED STATES: 1930-POPULATION

THE ISLAND OF GUAM

Sheet No. 44A

221

District Municipality of Agana
Name of Place Sinajana Barrio
[Proper name and, also, name of class, as city, town, village, barrio, etc]

Enumeration District No. 5
Enumerated by me on April 11, 1930 Margarito D. Palting, Enumerator

	PLACE OF ABODE			NAME	RELATION	PERSONAL DESCRIPTION				EDUCATION		NATIVITY		OCCUPATION
	Street, avenue, road, etc.	Number of dwelling house is order of visitation	Number of family in order of visitation	of each person whose place of abode on April 1, 1930, was in this family. Enter surname, first, then given name and middle initial. If any. Include every person living on April 1, 1930. Omit children born since April 1, 1930.	Relationship of this Person to the head of the family.	Sex	Color or race	Age at last birthday	Single, married, widowed or divorced	Attended school any time since Sept. 1, 1929	Whether able to read and write.	Place of birth of this person.	Whether able to speak English.	
	1	2	3	4	5	6	7	8	9	10	11	12	13	14
1	[no street name]	114	134	San Nicolas, Pedro	Son	M	Cha	4.3	S	N		Guam		None
2		114	134	San Nicolas, Consolacion	Daughter	F	Cha	2.3	S	N		Guam		None
3		114	134	Navarro, Mariano M	Brother-in-law	M	Cha	38	S	N	Y	Guam	N	Farm laborer
4		114	135	Castro, Ignacio J	Head	M	Cha	43	Wd	N	N	Guam	N	Farm laborer
5		115	136	Tedtaotao, Manuel T	Head	M	Cha	42	M	N	N	Guam	N	Farmer
6		115	136	Tedtaotao, Rosalina M	Wife	F	Cha	26	M	N	Y	Guam	N	None
7		115	136	Afaisen, Susana T	Sister	F	Cha	54	S	N	N	Guam	N	None
8		116	137	Baza, Ramon C	Head	M	Cha	28	M	N	Y	Guam	N	Farm laborer
9		116	137	Baza, Dolores G	Wife	F	Cha	23	M	N	Y	Guam	N	None
10		117	138	Quidachay, Juan SN	Head	M	Cha	33	M	N	N	Guam	N	Farmer
11		117	138	Quidachay, Feliciana SN	Wife	F	Cha	23	M	N	N	Guam	N	None
12		118	139	Tedtaotao, Salvador	Head	M	Cha	50	M	N	Y	Guam	N	Farmer
13		118	139	Tedtaotao, Rosa A	Wife	F	Cha	49	M	N	N	Guam	N	None
14		118	139	Tedtaotao, Lucas	Son	M	Cha	22	S	N	Y	Guam	Y	Farm laborer
15		118	139	Tedtaotao, Jesus	Son	M	Cha	14	S	Y	Y	Guam	Y	None
16		118	139	Tedtaotao, Antonio	Son	M	Cha	13	S	Y	Y	Guam	Y	None
17		119	140	Tedtaotao, Gregorio T	Head	M	Cha	57	Wd	N	Y	Guam	N	Farmer
18		119	140	Quidachay, Luisa SN	Head	F	Cha	60	Wd	N	N	Guam	N	None
19		119	140	Quidachay, Vicente	Son	M	Cha	40	S	N	N	Guam	N	Farmer
20		119	140	Quidachay, Jose	Son	M	Cha	38	S	N	N	Guam	N	Farm laborer
21		120	141	Taitano, Manuel B	Head	M	Cha	52	Wd	N	Y	Guam	N	Farmer
22		120	141	Taitano, Concepcion R	Daughter	F	Cha	20	S	N	Y	Guam	Y	None
23		120	141	Taitano, Jose	Son	M	Cha	18	S	N	Y	Guam	Y	Laborer
24		120	141	Taitano, Antonio	Son	M	Cha	14	S	Y	N	Guam	Y	None
25		120	141	Taitano, Ramon	Son	M	Cha	12	S	Y	N	Guam	N	None

(CHAMORRO ROOTS GENEALOGY PROJECT™ TRANSCRIPTION)
(BERNARD T. PUNZALAN / HTTP://WWW.CHAMORROROOTS.COM)

DEPARTMENT OF COMMERCE-BUREAU OF THE CENSUS
WASHINGTON

FIFTEENTH CENSUS OF THE UNITED STATES: 1930-POPULATION

THE ISLAND OF GUAM

Sheet No. 44B

221B

District **Municipality of Agana**
Name of Place **Sinajana Barrio**
[Proper name and, also, name of class, as city, town, village, barrio, etc]

Enumeration District No. 5
Enumerated by me on **April 11, 1930** Margarito D. Palting, Enumerator

	PLACE OF ABODE: Street, avenue, road, etc.	Number of dwelling house in order of visitation	Number of family in order of visitation	NAME of each person whose place of abode on April 1, 1930, was in this family. Enter surname, first, then given name and middle initial. If any. Include every person living on April 1, 1930. Omit children born since April 1, 1930.	RELATION Relationship of this Person to the head of the family.	PERSONAL DESCRIPTION: Sex	Color or race	Age at last birthday	Single, married, widowed or divorced	EDUCATION: Attended school any time since Sept. 1, 1929	Whether able to read and write.	NATIVITY Place of birth of this person.	Whether able to speak English.	OCCUPATION
	1	2	3	4	5	6	7	8	9	10	11	12	13	14
26	[no street name]	120	171	Taitano, Leonicio	Son	M	Cha	10	S	Y	N	Guam	N	None
27		121	142	Mateo, Antonio C	Head	M	Cha	30	M	N	Y	Guam	Y	Farmer
28		121	142	Mateo, Maria R	Wife	F	Cha	36	M	N	N	Guam	N	Laundress
29		121	142	Mateo, Maria	Daughter	F	Cha	5	S	N		Guam		None
30		121	142	Mateo, Miguel	Son	M	Cha	3.1	S	N		Guam		None
31		121	142	Rivera, Beatriz R	Step daughter	F	Cha	17	S	N	Y	Guam		None
32		121	142	Rivera, Maria R	Step daughter	F	Cha	12	S	Y	Y	Guam		None
33		121	142	Duenas, Dolores R	Mother-in-law	F	Cha	73	S	N	N	Guam		None
34		122	143	Mateo, Jose C	Head	M	Cha	43	S	N	Y	Guam	N	Farmer
35		122	144	Lujan, Marcela C	Head	F	Cha	46	Wd	N	N	Guam	Y	Farm laborer
36		122	144	Crisostomo, Romana A	Grand daughter	F	Cha	4.5	S	N		Guam		None
37		122	144	Crisostomo, German	Grandson	M	Cha	2.4	S	N		Guam		None
38		122	144	Crisostomo, Lourdes	Grand daughter	F	Cha	1.1	S	N		Guam		None
39		122	145	Crisostomo, Ana G	Head	F	Cha	46	S	N	N	Guam		Farm laborer
40		122	145	Crisostomo, Luisa G	Daughter	F	Cha	1	S	Y	Y	Guam		None
41		126	146	Quitugua, Juan S	Head	M	Cha	34	M	N	Y	Guam	Y	Farmer
42		126	146	Quitugua, Ignacia C	Wife	F	Cha	40	M	N	N	Guam	N	None
43		126	146	Quitugua, Francisca	Daughter	F	Cha	4.3	S	N		Guam		None
44		126	146	Quitugua, Rufino	Son	M	Cha	1.9	S	N	Y	Guam		None
45		126	146	Espinosa, Francisco C	Stepson	M	Cha	15	S	N	Y	Guam	Y	None
46		124	147	Castro, Miguel S	Head	M	Cha	30	M	N	Y	Guam	N	Farmer
47		124	147	Castro, Rita M	Wife	F	Cha	30	M	N	Y	Guam	N	None
48		124	147	Castro, Maria	Daughter	F	Cha	11	S	Y	N	Guam	N	None
49		124	147	Castro, Ramona	Daughter	F	Cha	10	S	Y	N	Guam	N	None
50		124	147	Castro, Dolores	Daughter	F	Cha	9	S	Y		Guam		None

(CHAMORRO ROOTS GENEALOGY PROJECT™ TRANSCRIPTION)
(BERNARD T. PUNZALAN / HTTP://WWW.CHAMORROROOTS.COM)

DEPARTMENT OF COMMERCE-BUREAU OF THE CENSUS
WASHINGTON

FIFTEENTH CENSUS OF THE UNITED STATES: 1930-POPULATION

THE ISLAND OF GUAM

Sheet No. 45A

222

District Municipality of Agana
Name of Place Sinajana Barrio
[Proper name and, also, name of class, as city, town, village, barrio, etc]

Enumeration District No. 5
Enumerated by me on April 12, 1930 Margarito D. Palting, Enumerator

	PLACE OF ABODE			NAME	RELATION	PERSONAL DESCRIPTION				EDUCATION		NATIVITY		OCCUPATION
	Street, avenue, road, etc.	Number of dwelling house is order of visitation	Number of family in order of visitation	of each person whose place of abode on April 1, 1930, was in this family. Enter surname, first, then given name and middle initial. If any. Include every person living on April 1, 1930. Omit children born since April 1, 1930.	Relationship of this Person to the head of the family.	Sex	Color or race	Age at last birthday	Single, married, widowed or divorced	Attended school any time since Sept. 1, 1929	Whether able to read and write.	Place of birth of this person.	Whether able to speak English.	
	1	2	3	4	5	6	7	8	9	10	11	12	13	14
1	[no street name]	124	147	Castro, Isabel	Daughter	F	Cha	5	S	N		Guam		None
2		124	147	Castro, Jesus	Son	M	Cha	3.1	S	N		Guam		None
3		125	148	Castro, Jesus M	Head	M	Cha	34	S	N	Y	Guam	N	Farmer
4		126	149	Rojas, Vicente T	Head	M	Cha	41	M	N	N	Guam	N	Farmer
5		126	149	Rojas, Francisca C	Wife	F	Cha	68	M	N	N	Guam	N	None
6		126	149	Rojas, Jose C	Son	M	Cha	23	S	N	N	Guam	Y	Farm laborer
7		126	150	Santos, Ines P	Head	F	Cha	44	S	N	N	Guam	N	Farm laborer
8		126	150	Santos, Juan S	Son	M	Cha	21	S	N	N	Guam	N	Farmer
9		127	151	Manibusan, Joaquin R	Head	M	Cha	62	M	N	N	Guam	N	Farmer
10		127	151	Manibusan, Dolores S	Wife	F	Cha	44	M	N	N	Guam	N	None
11		127	151	Manibusan, Mercedes	Daughter	F	Cha	11	S	Y	N	Guam	N	None
12		127	151	Manibusan, Rosario	Daughter	F	Cha	11	S	Y	N	Guam	N	None
13		128	152	Borja, Francisco S	Head	M	Cha	61	M	N	Y	Guam	Y	Farmer
14		128	152	Borja, Nicolasa S	Wife	F	Cha	59	M	N	N	Guam	N	None
15		128	152	Ibasco, Agnes S	Niece	F	Cha	21	S	N	N	Guam	N	None
16		129	153	Siguenza, Felipe T	Head	M	Cha	23	M	N	N	Guam	N	Farmer
17		129	153	Siguenza, Nicolasa SN	Wife	F	Cha	23	M	N	Y	Guam	N	None
18		129	153	Siguenza, Jose	Son	M	Cha	1.5	S	N		Guam		
19		129	153	Siguenza, Maria	Daughter	F	Cha	.2	S	N		Guam		
20		130	154	Taitingfong, Vicente S	Head	M	Cha	31	S	N	Y	Guam	N	Farmer
21		130	154	Taitingfong, Juan C	Brother	M	Cha	17	S	N	Y	Guam	N	Farm laborer
22		131	155	Arceo, Jose C	Head	M	Cha	19	M	N	N	Guam	N	Farmer
23		131	155	Arceo, Amalia G	Wife	F	Cha	18	M	N	Y	Guam	N	None
24		132	156	Castro, Nicolas M	Head	M	Cha	46	M	N	Y	Guam		Farmer
25		132	156	Castro, Vicenta S	Wife	F	Cha	42	M	N	Y	Guam		None

D-5-88

DEPARTMENT OF COMMERCE-BUREAU OF THE CENSUS
WASHINGTON

FIFTEENTH CENSUS OF THE UNITED STATES: 1930-POPULATION

THE ISLAND OF GUAM

Sheet No. 45B

222B

District **Municipality of Agana**
Name of Place **Sinajana Barrio**
[Proper name and, also, name of class, as city, town, village, barrio, etc]

Enumeration District No. **5**
Enumerated by me on **April 12, 1930** Margarito D. Palting, Enumerator

	PLACE OF ABODE			NAME	RELATION	PERSONAL DESCRIPTION				EDUCATION		NATIVITY		OCCUPATION
	Street, avenue, road, etc.	Number of dwelling house in order of visitation	Number of family in order of visitation	of each person whose place of abode on April 1, 1930, was in this family. Enter surname, first, then given name and middle initial. If any. Include every person living on April 1, 1930. Omit children born since April 1, 1930.	Relationship of this Person to the head of the family.	Sex	Color or race	Age at last birthday	Single, married, widowed or divorced	Attended school any time since Sept. 1, 1929	Whether able to read and write.	Place of birth of this person.	Whether able to speak English.	
	1	2	3	4	5	6	7	8	9	10	11	12	13	14
26	[no street name]	132	156	Pangelinan, Dolores G	Niece	F	Cha	12	S	Y	Y	Guam	N	None
27		132	156	Pangelinan, Juliana G	Niece	F	Cha	7	S	Y		Guam		None
28		132	156	Pangelinan, Vicente G	Nephew	M	Cha	6	S	N		Guam		None
29		133	157	Pangelinan, Vicente P	Head	M	Cha	41	Wd	N	N	Guam	N	Farmer
30		134	158	Gogo, Vicente G	Head	M	Cha	37	M	N	Y	Guam	Y	Farmer
31		134	158	Gogo, Amparo A	Wife	F	Cha	32	M	N	Y	Guam	Y	None
32		134	158	Gogo, Ignacio A	Son	M	Cha	13	S	Y	Y	Guam	Y	None
33		134	158	Gogo, Ana	Daughter	F	Cha	8	S	Y		Guam		None
34		134	158	Gogo, Vicente	Son	M	Cha	6	S	N		Guam		None
35		134	158	Gogo, Catalina	Daughter	F	Cha	2.7	S	N		Guam		None
36		134	158	Gogo, Pedro	Son	M	Cha	1.1	S	N		Guam		None
37		134	158	Gogo, Daniel G	Brother	M	Cha	45	S	N	N	Guam	N	Farm laborer
38		135	159	Toves, Felix U	Head	M	Cha	65	Wd	N	N	Guam	N	Farmer
39		135	160	San Nicolas, Nicolasa SN	Head	F	Cha	56	S	N	N	Guam	N	Laundress
40		136	161	Cruz, Vicente M	Head	M	Cha	60	Wd	N	Y	Guam	N	Farmer
41		137	162	Castro, Jose M	Head	M	Cha	59	M	N	Y	Guam	N	Farmer
42		137	162	Castro, Josefa S	Wife	F	Cha	65	M	N	N	Guam	N	None
43		137	162	Castro, Vicente S	Son	M	Cha	30	S	N	N	Guam	N	Farm laborer
44		137	162	Castro, Ana S	Daughter	F	Cha	22	S	N	N	Guam	N	None
45		137	162	Sanchez, Manuel S	Brother-in-law	M	Cha	47	S	N	N	Guam	N	Farmer
46		138	163	Bautista, Vicente C	Head	M	Cha	58	M	N	N	Guam	N	Farmer
47		138	163	Bautista, Manuela P	Wife	F	Cha	56	M	N	N	Guam	N	None
48		139	164	Guevarra, Vicente C	Head	M	Cha	50	M	N	Y	Guam	N	Tanner
49		139	164	Guevarra, Maria A	Wife	F	Cha	46	M	N	Y	Guam	N	Farm laborer
50		139	164	Guevarra, Jose	Son	M	Cha	15	S	Y	Y	Guam	N	None

DEPARTMENT OF COMMERCE-BUREAU OF THE CENSUS
WASHINGTON

FIFTEENTH CENSUS OF THE UNITED STATES: 1930-POPULATION

THE ISLAND OF GUAM

Sheet No. 46A

District Municipality of Agana

Name of Place Sinajana Barrio
[Proper name and, also, name of class, as city, town, village, barrio, etc]

Enumeration District No. 5

Enumerated by me on April 12, 1930 Margarito D. Palting, Enumerator

	PLACE OF ABODE			NAME	RELATION	PERSONAL DESCRIPTION				EDUCATION		NATIVITY		OCCUPATION
	Street, avenue, road, etc.	Number of dwelling house in order of visitation	Number of family in order of visitation	of each person whose place of abode on April 1, 1930, was in this family. Enter surname, first, then given name and middle initial. If any. Include every person living on April 1, 1930. Omit children born since April 1, 1930.	Relationship of this Person to the head of the family.	Sex	Color or race	Age at last birthday	Single, married, widowed or divorced	Attended school any time since Sept. 1, 1929	Whether able to read and write.	Place of birth of this person.	Whether able to speak English.	
	1	2	3	4	5	6	7	8	9	10	11	12	13	14
1	[no street name]	140	165	Guevarra, Antonio C	Head	M	Fil	52	M	N	Y	Guam	N	Farmer
2		140	165	Guevarra, Maria D	Wife	F	Cha	48	M	N	N	Guam	N	None
3		140	165	Guevarra, Froilan	Son	M	Fil	22	S	N	Y	Guam	Y	Teacher
4		140	165	Guevarra, Mariano	Son	M	Fil	21	S	N	Y	Guam	Y	Farm laborer
5		140	165	Guevarra, Eulalia	Daughter	F	Fil	14	S	Y	Y	Guam	Y	None
6		141	166	Bautista, Manuel S	Head	M	Cha	29	M	N	Y	Guam	N	Farmer
7		141	166	Bautista, Ana A	Wife	F	Cha	26	M	N	N	Guam	N	None
8		141	166	Bautista, Juan	Son	M	Cha	4.5	S	N		Guam		None
9		141	166	Bautista, Jose	Son	M	Cha	2.3	S	N		Guam		None
10		141	166	Bautista, Maria	Daughter	F	Cha	.4	S	N		Guam		None
11		142	167	Diaz, Juan B	Head	M	Cha	31	M	N	Y	Guam	N	Farmer
12		142	167	Diaz, Rosa L	Wife	F	Cha	23	M	N	Y	Guam	N	None
13		142	167	Diaz, Concepcion	Daughter	F	Cha	5	S	N		Guam		None
14		142	167	Diaz, Francisco	Son	M	Cha	2.3	S	N		Guam		None
15		142	167	Diaz, Veronica	Daughter	F	Cha	.3	S	N		Guam		None
16		143	168	Crisostomo, Jesus C	Head	M	Cha	26	M	N	Y	Guam	N	Farm laborer
17		143	168	Crisostomo, Encarnacion	Wife	F	Cha	27	M	N	Y	Guam	N	None
18		143	168	Crisostomo, Rosalina	Daughter	F	Cha	3.5	S	N		Guam		None
19		143	168	Crisostomo, Jesus	Son	M	Cha	.3	S	N		Guam		None
20		144	169	Fegurgur, Jose F	Head	M	Cha	26	M	N	N	Guam	N	Farmer
21		144	169	Fegurgur, Dolores D	Wife	F	Cha	26	M	N	N	Guam	N	None
22		145	170	Toves, Maria S	Head	F	Cha	67	Wd	N	N	Guam	N	None
23		146	171	Blaz, Antonia B	Head	F	Cha	20	S	N	Y	Guam	Y	Farm laborer
24		146	171	Blaz, Mabel	Daughter	F	Cha	2.5	S	N		Guam		None
25		146	171	Blaz, Blanche	Daughter	F	Cha	1.5	S	N		Guam		None

DEPARTMENT OF COMMERCE-BUREAU OF THE CENSUS
WASHINGTON

FIFTEENTH CENSUS OF THE UNITED STATES: 1930-POPULATION

THE ISLAND OF GUAM

Sheet No. 46A

223B

District **Municipality of Agana**
Name of Place **Sinajana Barrio**
[Proper name and, also, name of class, as city, town, village, barrio, etc]

Enumeration District No. 5
Enumerated by me on **April 14, 1930** Margarito D. Palting
Enumerator

	PLACE OF ABODE			NAME	RELATION	PERSONAL DESCRIPTION				EDUCATION		NATIVITY		OCCUPATION
	Street, avenue, road, etc.	Number of dwelling house is order of visitation	Number of family in order of visitation	of each person whose place of abode on April 1, 1930, was in this family. Enter surname, first, then given name and middle initial. If any. Include every person living on April 1, 1930. Omit children born since April 1, 1930.	Relationship of this Person to the head of the family.	Sex	Color or race	Age at last birthday	Single, married, widowed or divorced	Attended school any time since Sept. 1, 1929	Whether able to read and write.	Place of birth of this person.	Whether able to speak English.	
	1	2	3	4	5	6	7	8	9	10	11	12	13	14
26	[no street name]	147	172	Perez, Gregorio F	Head	M	Cha	42	M	N	Y	Guam	Y	Farm Manager
27		147	172	Perez, Rosario E	Wife	F	Fil	38	M	N	Y	Guam	Y	None
28		147	172	Perez, Edward	Son	M	Cha	16	S	Y	Y	Guam	Y	Messenger
29		147	172	Perez, Tomas	Son	M	Cha	14	S	Y	Y	Guam	Y	Apprentice tailor
30		147	172	Perez, Albert	Son	M	Cha	13	S	Y	Y	Guam	Y	None
31		147	172	Perez, Rosa	Daughter	F	Cha	11	S	Y	Y	Guam	Y	None
32		147	172	Perez, Gregorio	Son	M	Cha	9	S	Y		Guam		None
33		147	172	Perez, Rosario	Daughter	F	Cha	8	S	Y		Guam		None
34		147	172	Perez, Sergio	Son	M	Cha	6	S	N		Guam		None
35		147	172	Perez, Jose	Son	M	Cha	4.8	S	N		Guam		None
36		147	172	Perez, Maira	Daughter	F	Cha	1.3	S	N		Guam		None
37		147	172	Perez, Tomasa	Daughter	F	Cha	.6	S	N		Guam		None
38		147	172	Perez, Juan	Son	M	Cha	.1	S	N		Guam		None
39		147	172	Manalisay, Juana A	Servant	F	Cha	14	S	Y	Y	Guam	Y	Cook
40		148	173	Guevarra, Gregorio D	Head	M	Fil	23	M	N	Y	Guam	Y	Farmer
41		148	173	Guevarra, Elena F	Wife	F	Cha	23	M	N	Y	Guam	Y	None
42		148	173	Guevarra, Rita	Daughter	F	Fil	4.1	S	N		Guam		None
43		148	173	Guevarra, Maria	Daughter	F	Fil	.9	S	N		Guam		None
44		148	173	Fejeran, Joaquin T	Brother-in-law	M	Cha	14	S	Y	Y	Guam	Y	None
45		150	174	Mafnas, Joaqun F	Head	M	Cha	65	M	N	N	Guam	N	Farmer
46		150	174	Mafnas, Elena A	Wife	F	Cha	63	M	N	N	Guam	N	None
47		150	174	Atoigue, Pablo A	Nephew	M	Cha	38	S	N	N	Guam	N	None
48		151	175	Borja, Joaquin L	Head	M	Cha	30	M	N	Y	Guam	Y	Farmer
49		151	175	Borja, Rosa D	Wife	F	Cha	30	M	N	Y	Guam	Y	None
50		151	175	Borja, Jorge	Son	M	Cha	7	S	Y		Guam		None

DEPARTMENT OF COMMERCE-BUREAU OF THE CENSUS
WASHINGTON

FIFTEENTH CENSUS OF THE UNITED STATES: 1930-POPULATION

THE ISLAND OF GUAM

Sheet No. 47A

District Municipality of Agana
Name of Place Sinajana Barrio
[Proper name and, also, name of class, as city, town, village, barrio, etc]

Enumeration District No. 5
Enumerated by me on April 14, 1930 Margarito D. Palting
Enumerator

	PLACE OF ABODE			NAME	RELATION	PERSONAL DESCRIPTION				EDUCATION		NATIVITY		OCCUPATION
	Street, avenue, road, etc.	Number of dwelling house is order of visitation	Number of family in order of visitation	of each person whose place of abode on April 1, 1930, was in this family. Enter surname, first, then given name and middle initial. If any. Include every person living on April 1, 1930. Omit children born since April 1, 1930.	Relationship of this Person to the head of the family.	Sex	Color or race	Age at last birthday	Single, married, widowed or divorced	Attended school any time since Sept. 1, 1929	Whether able to read and write.	Place of birth of this person.	Whether able to speak English.	
	1	2	3	4	5	6	7	8	9	10	11	12	13	14
1	[no street name]	151	175	Borja, Toribia	Daughter	F	Cha	5	S	N		Guam		None
2		151	175	Borja, Rufina	Daughter	F	Cha	4.1	S	N		Guam		None
3		151	175	Borja, Carlo	Son	M	Cha	3.1	S	N		Guam		None
4		151	175	Borja, Trinidad	Daughter	F	Cha	2.2	S	N		Guam		None
5		151	175	Borja, Maria	Daughter	F	Cha	1.1	S	N		Guam		None
6		152	175	Quidachay, Baldovino A	Head	M	Cha	25	M	N	N	Guam	N	Farmer
7		152	175	Quidachay, Maria A	Wife	F	Cha	33	M	N	N	Guam	N	None
8		152	175	Quidachay, Pilar	Daughter	F	Cha	10	S	Y	N	Guam	Y	None
9		152	175	Quidachay, Jesus	Son	M	Cha	3.1	S	N		Guam		None
10		152	175	Quidachay, Barcelisa	Daughter	F	Cha	1.2	S	N		Guam		None
11		153	176	Atoigue, Joaquin C	Head	M	Cha	22	S	N	Y	Guam	Y	Farmer
12		153	176	Atoigue, Jesus L	Brother	M	Cha	27	S	N	Y	Guam	Y	Farm laborer
13		153	176	Atoigue, Vicente L	Brother	M	Cha	30	S	N	Y	Guam	Y	None
14		154	177	Santos, Felix	Head	M	Cha	35	M	N	Y	Guam	Y	Farmer
15		154	177	Santos, Carmen P	Wife	F	Cha	26	M	N	N	Guam	N	None
16		154	177	Santos, Juan	Son	M	Cha	10	S	Y	N	Guam	N	None
17		154	177	Santos, Guadalupe	Daughter	F	Cha	8	S	Y		Guam		None
18		155	178	Santos, Juan N	Head	M	Cha	56	Wd	N	N	Guam	N	None
19		155	178	Santos, Soledad SN	Daughter	F	Cha	24	S	N	Y	Guam	Y	None
20		155	178	Santos, Herbert	Grandson	M	Cha	3.2	S	N		Guam		None
21		155	178	Santos, Juan	Grandson	M	Cha	1.3	S	N		Guam		None
22		156	179	Santos, Justo N	Head	M	Cha	48	M	N	N	Guam	N	Farmer
23		156	179	Santos, Magdalena J	Wife	F	Cha	54	M	N	Y	Guam	N	None
24		157	180	Mendiola, Antonia B	Head	F	Cha	64	M	N	N	Guam	N	Farmer
25		157	180	Mendiola, Maria B	Daughter	F	Cha	31	S	N	Y	Guam	Y	Laundress

(CHAMORRO ROOTS GENEALOGY PROJECT™ TRANSCRIPTION)
(BERNARD T. PUNZALAN / HTTP://WWW.CHAMORROROOTS.COM)

DEPARTMENT OF COMMERCE-BUREAU OF THE CENSUS
WASHINGTON

FIFTEENTH CENSUS OF THE UNITED STATES: 1930-POPULATION

THE ISLAND OF GUAM

Sheet No. 47B

224B

District **Municipality of Agana**
Name of Place **Sinajana Barrio**
[Proper name and, also, name of class, as city, town, village, barrio, etc]

Enumeration District No. 5
Enumerated by me on **April 14, 1930** Margarito D. Palting
Enumerator

	PLACE OF ABODE			NAME	RELATION	PERSONAL DESCRIPTION				EDUCATION		NATIVITY		OCCUPATION
	Street, avenue, road, etc.	Number of dwelling house is order of visitation	Number of family in order of visitation	of each person whose place of abode on April 1, 1930, was in this family. Enter surname, first, then given name and middle initial. If any. Include every person living on April 1, 1930. Omit children born since April 1, 1930.	Relationship of this Person to the head of the family.	Sex	Color or race	Age at last birthday	Single, married, widowed or divorced	Attended school any time since Sept. 1, 1929	Whether able to read and write.	Place of birth of this person.	Whether able to speak English.	
	1	2	3	4	5	6	7	8	9	10	11	12	13	14
26	[no street name]	157	180	Borja, Magdalena M	Daughter	F	Cha	26	S	N	Y	Guam	Y	Laundress
27		157	180	Borja, Ignacio M	Son	M	Cha	20	S	N	Y	Guam	Y	Bookkeeper
28		157	180	Borja, Saturnina M	Daughter	F	Cha	17	S	N	Y	Guam	Y	Laundress
29		157	180	Borja, Candelaria M	Daughter	F	Cha	10	S	Y	Y	Guam	Y	None
30		158	181	Manibusan, Luis P	Head	M	Cha	35	M	N	N	Guam	N	None
31				Here ends the enumeration of enumeration District No. 5 Sinajana										
32														
33														
34														
35														
36														
37														
38														
39														
40														
41														
42														
43														
44														
45														
46														
47														
48														
49														
50														

DEPARTMENT OF COMMERCE-BUREAU OF THE CENSUS
WASHINGTON

FIFTEENTH CENSUS OF THE UNITED STATES: 1930-POPULATION

THE ISLAND OF GUAM

Sheet No. 48A

District Municipality of Agana
Name of Place Tutujan Barrio
[Proper name and, also, name of class, as city, town, village, barrio, etc]

Enumeration District No. 5
Enumerated by me on April 15, 1930 Margarito D. Palting
Enumerator

	PLACE OF ABODE			NAME	RELATION	PERSONAL DESCRIPTION				EDUCATION		NATIVITY		OCCUPATION
	Street, avenue, road, etc.	Number of dwelling house is order of visitation	Number of family in order of visitation	of each person whose place of abode on April 1, 1930, was in this family. Enter surname, first, then given name and middle initial. If any. Include every person living on April 1, 1930. Omit children born since April 1, 1930.	Relationship of this Person to the head of the family.	Sex	Color or race	Age at last birthday	Single, married, widowed or divorced	Attended school any time since Sept. 1, 1929	Whether able to read and write.	Place of birth of this person.	Whether able to speak English.	
	1	2	3	4	5	6	7	8	9	10	11	12	13	14
1	[no street name]	159	182	Acosta, Miguel C	Head	M	Cha	58	M	N	N	Guam	N	Farmer
2		159	182	Acosta, Vicenta S	Wife	F	Cha	60	M	N	N	Guam	N	None
3		159	182	Acosta, Joaquina	Daughter	F	Cha	37	S	N	N	Guam	N	None
4		159	182	Acosta, Felisa	Daughter	F	Cha	31	S	N	Y	Guam	Y	None
5		159	182	Acosta, Felix	Son	M	Cha	29	S	N	N	Guam	N	Farm laborer
6		159	182	Acosta, Dolores	Daughter	F	Cha	24	S	N	Y	Guam	Y	None
7		159	182	Acosta, Manuel	Son	M	Cha	20	S	N	Y	Guam	Y	Farm laborer
8		159	182	Acosta, Concepcion	Daughter	F	Cha	18	S	N	Y	Guam	Y	None
9		159	182	Acosta, Juan S	Grandson	M	Cha	10	S	Y	N	Guam	Y	None
10		159	182	Acosta, Mariano S	Grandson	M	Cha	2.3	S	N		Guam		None
11		159	182	Acosta, Manuel S	Grandson	M	Cha	.5	S	N		Guam		None
12		159	183	Acosta, Ramon S	Head	M	Cha	34	M	N	N	Guam	N	Carpenter
13		159	183	Acosta, Ana H	Wife	F	Cha	31	M	N	Y	Guam	N	Laundress
14		159	183	Acosta, Maria	Daughter	F	Cha	6	S	N		Guam		None
15		159	183	Acosta, Jose	Son	M	Cha	1.5	S	N		Guam		None
16		160	184	Pangelinan, Emilio P	Head	M	Cha	42	M	N	N	Guam	N	Farmer
17		160	184	Pangelinan, Maria A	Wife	F	Cha	43	M	N	N	Guam	N	None
18		160	184	Pangelinan, Juan	Son	M	Cha	14	S	N	Y	Guam	N	None
19		160	184	Pangelinan, Bartola	Daughter	F	Cha	13	S	N	Y	Guam	N	None
20		160	184	Pangelinan, Maria	Daughter	F	Cha	6	S	N		Guam		None
21		161	165	Kaminga, John R	Head	M	Cha	39	M	N	N	Guam	Y	Farmer
22		161	165	Kaminga, Catalina S	Wife	F	Cha	28	M	N	Y	Guam	Y	None
23		162	186	Ulloa, Joaquin U	Head	M	Cha	49	Wd	N	Y	Guam	N	Farmer
24		162	186	Ulloa, Joaquin I	Son	M	Cha	17	S	Y	Y	Guam	Y	None
25		163	187	Cruz, Gregorio Q	Head	M	Cha	40	M	N	Y	Guam	N	Farmer

(CHAMORRO ROOTS GENEALOGY PROJECT™ TRANSCRIPTION)
(BERNARD T. PUNZALAN / HTTP://WWW.CHAMORROROOTS.COM)

DEPARTMENT OF COMMERCE-BUREAU OF THE CENSUS
WASHINGTON

FIFTEENTH CENSUS OF THE UNITED STATES: 1930-POPULATION

THE ISLAND OF GUAM

Sheet No. 48B

225B

District **Municipality of Agana**
Name of Place **Tutujan Barrio**
[Proper name and, also, name of class, as city, town, village, barrio, etc]

Enumeration District No. 5
Enumerated by me on **April 16, 1930** Margarito D. Palting, Enumerator

	PLACE OF ABODE: Street, avenue, road, etc.	Number of dwelling house in order of visitation	Number of family in order of visitation	NAME of each person whose place of abode on April 1, 1930, was in this family. Enter surname, first, then given name and middle initial. If any. Include every person living on April 1, 1930. Omit children born since April 1, 1930.	RELATION Relationship of this Person to the head of the family.	PERSONAL DESCRIPTION: Sex	Color or race	Age at last birthday	Single, married, widowed or divorced	EDUCATION: Attended school any time since Sept. 1, 1929	Whether able to read and write.	NATIVITY Place of birth of this person.	Whether able to speak English.	OCCUPATION
	1	2	3	4	5	6	7	8	9	10	11	12	13	14
26	[no street name]	163	187	Cruz, Marcela T	Wife	F	Cha	50	M	N	N	Guam	N	None
27		164	188	Manley, Albert P	Head	M	W	51	M	N	Y	New York	Y	Farmer
28		164	188	Manley, Asuncion R	Wife	F	W	39	M	N	Y	Philippine Is.	Y	None
29		164	188	Manley, Vicenta	Daughter	F	W	12	S	Y	Y	Guam	Y	None
30		164	188	Manley, Vicente	Son	M	W	10	S	Y	Y	Guam	Y	None
31		164	188	Manley, Lilian	Daughter	F	W	3.7	S	N		Guam		None
32		165	189	Cruz, Felix C	Head	M	Cha	61	M	N	N	Guam	N	Farmer
33		165	189	Cruz, Juana C	Wife	F	Cha	47	M	N	N	Guam	N	None
34		165	189	Cruz, Vicente C	Son	M	Cha	30	Wd	N	N	Guam	N	Farm laborer
35		165	189	Cruz, Maria C	Daughter	F	Cha	24	S	N	N	Guam	N	None
36		165	189	Rosario, Jesus C	Grandson	M	Cha	19	S	N	Y	Guam	Y	Farm laborer
37		165	189	Rosario, Maria C	Grand daughter	F	Cha	18	S	N	N	Guam	N	None
38		165	189	Cruz, Jose C	Grandson	M	Cha	1.1	S	N		Guam		None
39		166	190	Gogue, Agustin SL	Head	M	Cha	34	M	N	Y	Guam	Y	Fireman 2c
40		166	190	Gogue, Antonia S	Wife	F	Cha	34	M	N	Y	Guam	N	None
41		166	190	Gogue, Jose	Son	M	Cha	14	S	Y	Y	Guam	Y	None
42		166	190	Gogue, Tomas	Son	M	Cha	13	S	Y	N	Guam	N	None
43		166	190	Gogue, Maria	Daughter	F	Cha	11	S	Y	N	Guam	Y	None
44		166	190	Gogue, Jesus	Son	M	Cha	7	S	Y		Guam		None
45		166	190	Gogue, Delfina	Daughter	F	Cha	6	S	N		Guam		None
46		166	190	Gogue, Magdalena	Daughter	F	Cha	2.1	S	N		Guam		None
47		166	190	Gogue, Vicente	Brother	M	Cha	39	Wd	N	N	Guam	N	None
48		166	190	Gogue, Josefina	Niece	F	Cha	14	S	Y	Y	Guam	Y	None
49		166	190	Gogue, Vicente	Nephew	M	Cha	7	S	Y		Guam		None
50		166	190	San Luis, Maria A	Sister	F	Cha	19	S	Y	N	Guam	N	None

(CHAMORRO ROOTS GENEALOGY PROJECT™ TRANSCRIPTION)
(BERNARD T. PUNZALAN / HTTP://WWW.CHAMORROROOTS.COM)

DEPARTMENT OF COMMERCE-BUREAU OF THE CENSUS
WASHINGTON

FIFTEENTH CENSUS OF THE UNITED STATES: 1930-POPULATION

THE ISLAND OF GUAM

Sheet No. 49A

District **Municipality of Agana**
Name of Place **Tutujan Barrio**
[Proper name and, also, name of class, as city, town, village, barrio, etc]

Enumeration District No. 5
Enumerated by me on **April 16, 1930** Margarito D. Palting, Enumerator

	PLACE OF ABODE: Street, avenue, road, etc.	Number of dwelling house in order of visitation	Number of family in order of visitation	NAME of each person whose place of abode on April 1, 1930, was in this family. Enter surname, first, then given name and middle initial. If any. Include every person living on April 1, 1930. Omit children born since April 1, 1930.	RELATION Relationship of this Person to the head of the family.	PERSONAL DESCRIPTION: Sex	Color or race	Age at last birthday	Single, married, widowed or divorced	EDUCATION: Attended school any time since Sept. 1, 1929	Whether able to read and write.	NATIVITY Place of birth of this person.	Whether able to speak English.	OCCUPATION
	1	2	3	4	5	6	7	8	9	10	11	12	13	14
1	[no street name]	167	191	Rodriguez, Lucas S	Head	M	Cha	40	M	N	Y	Guam	N	Laborer
2		167	191	Rodriguez, Dolores B	Wife	F	Cha	35	M	N	Y	Guam	N	None
3		167	191	Rodriguez, Jesus	Son	M	Cha	15	S	Y	Y	Guam	Y	None
4		167	191	Rodriguez, Maria	Daughter	F	Cha	14	S	Y	Y	Guam	Y	None
5		167	191	Rodriguez, Jose	Son	M	Cha	13	S	Y	Y	Guam	Y	None
6		167	191	Rodriguez, Ana	Daughter	F	Cha	5	S	N		Guam		None
7		167	191	Rodriguez, Ramon	Son	M	Cha	2.3	S	N		Guam		None
8		167	191	Rodriguez, Vicente	Son	M	Cha	.4	S	N		Guam		None
9		167	191	Rodriguez, Antonia R	Niece	F	Cha	26	S	N	Y	Guam	N	None
10		168	192	Salas, Juan J	Head	M	Cha	38	M	N	N	Guam	N	Laborer
11		168	192	Salas, Celestina T	Wife	F	Cha	39	M	N	N	Guam	N	None
12		168	192	Salas, Jose	Son	M	Cha	10	S	Y	N	Guam	Y	None
13		169	193	Pangelinan, Alfonso C	Head	M	Cha	60	M	N	N	Guam	N	Farmer
14		169	193	Pangelinan, Maria C	Wife	F	Cha	56	M	N	N	Guam	N	None
15		169	193	Pangelinan, Ana	Daughter	F	Cha	23	S	N	N	Guam	N	None
16		169	193	Pangelinan, Candelaria	Daughter	F	Cha	20	S	N	Y	Guam	Y	None
17		169	193	Pangelinan, Rosario	Daughter	F	Cha	13	S	Y	Y	Guam	Y	None
18		169	193	Pangelinan, Vicente	Son	M	Cha	12	S	Y	N	Guam	Y	None
19		169	194	Pangelinan, Antonio C	Head	M	Cha	26	M	N	N	Guam	N	Farmer
20		169	194	Pangelinan, Rufina G	Wife	F	Cha	16	M	N	Y	Guam	N	None
21		169	194	Pangelinan, Jose G	Son	M	Cha	1.5	S	N		Guam		None
22		169	194	Pangelinan, Maria G	Daughter	F	Cha	.1	S	N		Guam		None
23		170	195	Cruz, Lorenzo G	Head	M	Cha	40	M	N	Y	Guam	N	Laborer
24		170	195	Cruz, Natividad	Wife	F	Cha	35	M	N	Y	Guam	N	None
25		170	195	Cruz, Juan	Son	M	Cha	17	S	Y	Y	Guam	Y	Machinist

(CHAMORRO ROOTS GENEALOGY PROJECT™ TRANSCRIPTION)
(BERNARD T. PUNZALAN / HTTP://WWW.CHAMORROROOTS.COM)

DEPARTMENT OF COMMERCE-BUREAU OF THE CENSUS
WASHINGTON

FIFTEENTH CENSUS OF THE UNITED STATES: 1930-POPULATION

THE ISLAND OF GUAM

Sheet No. 49B

226B

District **Municipality of Agana**
Name of Place **Tutujan Barrio**
[Proper name and, also, name of class, as city, town, village, barrio, etc]

Enumeration District No. **5**
Enumerated by me on **April 17, 1930** Margarito D. Palting, Enumerator

	PLACE OF ABODE: Street, avenue, road, etc.	Number of dwelling house in order of visitation	Number of family in order of visitation	NAME of each person whose place of abode on April 1, 1930, was in this family. Enter surname, first, then given name and middle initial. If any. Include every person living on April 1, 1930. Omit children born since April 1, 1930.	RELATION Relationship of this Person to the head of the family.	PERSONAL DESCRIPTION: Sex	Color or race	Age at last birthday	Single, married, widowed or divorced	EDUCATION: Attended school any time since Sept. 1, 1929	Whether able to read and write.	NATIVITY Place of birth of this person.	Whether able to speak English.	OCCUPATION
	1	2	3	4	5	6	7	8	9	10	11	12	13	14
26	[no street name]	170	195	Cruz, Jose	Son	M	Cha	15	S	Y	Y	Guam	Y	None
27		170	195	Cruz, Pedro	Son	M	Cha	14	S	Y	Y	Guam	Y	None
28		170	195	Cruz, Matilde	Daughter	F	Cha	12	S	Y	Y	Guam	Y	None
29		170	195	Cruz, Natividad	Daughter	F	Cha	10	S	Y	N	Guam	N	None
30		170	195	Cruz, Lorenzo	Son	M	Cha	7	S	Y		Guam		None
31		170	195	Cruz, Dolores	Daughter	F	Cha	5	S	Y		Guam		None
32		170	195	Cruz, Consolacion	Daughter	F	Cha	2.1	S	N		Guam		None
33		170	195	Cruz, Lourdes	Daughter	F	Cha	.9	S	N		Guam		None
34		171	196	Garrido, Joaquina I	Head	F	Cha	50	S	N	Y	Guam	N	Cook
35		172	197	Javier, Rosa P	Head	F	Cha	49	Wd	N	Y	Guam	N	Laundress
36		172	197	Javier, Jose P	Son	M	Cha	15	S	Y	N	Guam	Y	None
37		172	198	Pangelinan, Enrique P	Head	M	Cha	23	M	N	Y	Guam	Y	Farmer
38		172	198	Pangelinan, Josefa	Wife	F	Cha	19	M	N	Y	Guam	Y	None
39		172	198	Pangelinan, Delfin	Son	M	Cha	1.3	S	N		Guam		None
40		172	198	Pangelinan, Alvina	Daughter	F	Cha	.2	S	N		Guam		None
41		172	198	Javier, Mariquita	Niece	F	Cha	10	S	Y	N	Guam	Y	None
42		173	199	Toves, Jose U	Head	M	Cha	52	M	N	N	Guam	N	Farmer
43		173	199	Toves, Maria C	Wife	F	Cha	59	M	N	N	Guam	N	None
44		173	199	Toves, Felix	Son	M	Cha	16	S	N	Y	Guam	Y	Farm laborer
45		174	200	Evaristo, Jose E	Head	M	Cha	35	M	N	N	Guam	N	Farm laborer
46		174	200	Evaristo, Maria L	Wife	F	Cha	26	M	N	N	Guam	N	None
47		174	200	Evaristo, Pedro	Son	M	Cha	9	S	Y		Guam		None
48		174	200	Evaristo, Joaquin	Son	M	Cha	8	S	Y		Guam		None
49		174	200	Evaristo, Margarito	Son	M	Cha	6	S	N		Guam		None
50		174	200	Evaristo, Francisco	Son	M	Cha	4.7	S	N		Guam		none

DEPARTMENT OF COMMERCE-BUREAU OF THE CENSUS
WASHINGTON

FIFTEENTH CENSUS OF THE UNITED STATES: 1930-POPULATION

THE ISLAND OF GUAM

Sheet No. 50A

District **Municipality of Agana**
Name of Place **Tutujan Barrio**
[Proper name and, also, name of class, as city, town, village, barrio, etc]

Enumeration District No. **5**
Enumerated by me on **April 19, 1930** Margarito D. Palting
Enumerator

	PLACE OF ABODE			NAME	RELATION	PERSONAL DESCRIPTION				EDUCATION		NATIVITY		OCCUPATION
	Street, avenue, road, etc.	Number of dwelling house in order of visitation	Number of family in order of visitation	of each person whose place of abode on April 1, 1930, was in this family. Enter surname, first, then given name and middle initial. If any. Include every person living on April 1, 1930. Omit children born since April 1, 1930.	Relationship of this Person to the head of the family.	Sex	Color or race	Age at last birthday	Single, married, widowed or divorced	Attended school any time since Sept. 1, 1929	Whether able to read and write.	Place of birth of this person.	Whether able to speak English.	
	1	2	3	4	5	6	7	8	9	10	11	12	13	14
1	[no street name]	174	200	Evaristo, Jesus L	Son	M	Cha	2.2	S	N		Guam		None
2		175	201	Flores, Jose G	Head	M	Cha	42	M	N	Y	Guam	Y	Plumber
3		175	201	Flores, Rita T	Wife	F	Cha	51	M	N	Y	Guam	N	None
4		175	201	Flores, Enrique	Son	M	Cha	24	S	N	Y	Guam	Y	Farm laborer
5		175	201	Flores, Emilia	Daughter	F	Cha	20	S	N	Y	Guam	Y	None
6		175	201	Flores, Virgina	Daughter	F	Cha	16	S	N	Y	Guam	Y	None
7		175	201	Flores, Joseph	Son	M	Cha	13	S	Y	Y	Guam	Y	None
8		175	201	Flores, Grace	Daughter	F	Cha	9	S	Y		Guam		None
9		175	201	Flores, Edward	Son	M	Cha	7	S	Y		Guam		None
10		175	201	Flores, George	Son	M	Cha	7	S	Y		Guam		None
11		176	202	Atoigue, Ana L	Head	F	Cha	20	S	N	Y	Guam		Laundress
12		176	202	Atoigue, Jesus	Son	M	Cha	2.1	S	N		Guam		None
13		176	203	Crisostomo, Maria A	Head	F	Cha	25	Wd	N	Y	Guam	N	Laundress
14		177	204	Rosendo, Manuel H	Head	M	Cha	42	S	N	Y	Guam	Y	Farmer
15		177	205	Gumataotao, Ana S	Head	F	Cha	30	S	N	Y	Guam	N	Laundress
16		178	206	Lusongco, Antonio D	Head	M	Chin	19	M	N	Y	Guam	Y	Farmer
17		178	206	Lusongco, Maria T	Wife	F	Cha	17	M	N	Y	Guam	Y	None
18		179	207	Lusongco, Antonio M	Head	M	Chin	61	M	N	Y	Guam	N	Farmer
19		179	207	Lusongco, Rosa D	Wife	F	Cha	59	M	N	N	Guam	N	None
20		179	207	Lusongco, Joaquin	Son	M	Chin	23	S	N	N	Guam	Y	Farm laborer
21		179	207	Lusongco, Ana	Daughter	F	Chin	14	S	Y	Y	Guam	Y	None
22		179	207	Lusongco, Dolores	Daughter	F	Chin	13	S	Y	N	Guam	Y	None
23		179	207	Lusongco, Luis	Son	M	Chin	11	S	Y	N	Guam	N	None
24		179	207	Dumapan, Pedro D	Nephew	M	Cha	25	S	N	Y	Guam	Y	Farm laborer
25		180	208	Ulloa, Amanda R	Head	F	Cha	20	M	N	Y	Guam	Y	None

DEPARTMENT OF COMMERCE-BUREAU OF THE CENSUS
WASHINGTON

FIFTEENTH CENSUS OF THE UNITED STATES: 1930-POPULATION

THE ISLAND OF GUAM

Sheet No. 50B

227B

District **Municipality of Agana**
Name of Place **Tutujan Barrio**
[Proper name and, also, name of class, as city, town, village, barrio, etc]

Enumeration District No. 5
Enumerated by me on **April 22, 1930** Margarito D. Palting, Enumerator

	PLACE OF ABODE: Street, avenue, road, etc.	Number of dwelling house in order of visitation	Number of family in order of visitation	NAME of each person whose place of abode on April 1, 1930, was in this family. Enter surname, first, then given name and middle initial. If any. Include every person living on April 1, 1930. Omit children born since April 1, 1930.	RELATION Relationship of this Person to the head of the family.	PERSONAL DESCRIPTION: Sex	Color or race	Age at last birthday	Single, married, widowed or divorced	EDUCATION: Attended school any time since Sept. 1, 1929	Whether able to read and write.	NATIVITY Place of birth of this person.	Whether able to speak English.	OCCUPATION
	1	2	3	4	5	6	7	8	9	10	11	12	13	14
26	[no street name]	181	209	Cruz, Ana U	Head	F	Cha	46	Wd	N	Y	Guam	Y	Seamstress
27		182	210	Roberto, Cristina B	Head	F	Cha	35	S	N	Y	Guam	Y	Laundress
28		182	210	Roberto, Vicente	Son	M	Cha	16	S	N	Y	Guam	Y	Farm laborer
29		182	210	Roberto, Juan	Son	M	Cha	12	S	Y	Y	Guam	Y	None
30		182	210	Roberto, Felipe	Son	M	Cha	10	S	Y	N	Guam	N	None
31		182	210	Roberto, Jose	Son	M	Cha	6	S	N		Guam		None
32		182	210	Roberto, Ana	Daughter	F	Cha	2.3	S	N		Guam		None
33		182	210	Roberto, Agustin	Son	M	Cha	.1	S	N		Guam		None
34		183	211	Quinata, Jacinto Q	Head	M	Cha	23	S	N	Y	Guam	Y	None
35		183	212	Yamasaki, Pilar T	Head	F	Cha	34	M	N	Y	Guam	N	Laundress
36		183	212	Yamasaki, Vicenta	Daughter	F	Jap	12	S	Y	Y	Guam	Y	None
37		183	212	Yamasaki, Ignacio	Son	M	Jap	10	S	Y	N	Guam	N	None
38		183	212	Yamasaki, Antonio	Son	M	Jap	9	S	Y		Guam		None
39		184	213	Mendiola, Juan C	Head	M	Cha	27	M	N	Y	Guam	Y	Carpenter
40		184	213	Mendiola, Maria E	Wife	F	Cha	27	M	N	Y	Guam	Y	None
41		184	213	Mendiola, Rosa	Daughter	F	Cha	3.1	S	N		Guam		None
42		184	213	Mendiola, Jesusa	Daughter	F	Cha	2.1	S	N		Guam		None
43		184	213	Mendiola, Francisca	Daughter	F	Cha	.9	S	N		Guam		None
44		185	214	Asuncion, Vicente M	Head	M	Cha	64	Wd	N	N	Guam	N	Farmer
45		185	215	Asuncion, Andres SL	Head	M	Cha	20	M	N	N	Guam	N	Farmer
46		185	215	Asuncion, Baltazara M	Wife	F	Cha	18	M	N	N	Guam	N	None
47		185	215	Asuncion, Maria	Daughter	F	Cha	.1	S	N		Guam		None
48		186	216	Borja, Ana P	Head	F	Cha	63	Wd	N	N	Guam	N	None
49				Here ends the enumeration of enumeration district No. 5 - Tutujan										
50														

District 6
Municipality of Agat

Agat Town

Chandia Barrio

Fena Barrio

Inaso Barrio

Omo Barrio

Opagat Barrio

Pasqual Barrio

Sagua Barrio

Salinas Barrio

Tumat

DEPARTMENT OF COMMERCE-BUREAU OF THE CENSUS
WASHINGTON

FIFTEENTH CENSUS OF THE UNITED STATES: 1930-POPULATION

THE ISLAND OF GUAM

Sheet No. 1A

228

District **Municipality of Agat**
Name of Place **Agat town**
[Proper name and, also, name of class, as city, town, village, barrio, etc]

Enumeration District No. **6**
Enumerated by me on **April 2, 1930** Pedro C Charfauros
Enumerator

	PLACE OF ABODE			NAME	RELATION	PERSONAL DESCRIPTION				EDUCATION		NATIVITY		OCCUPATION
	Street, avenue, road, etc.	Number of dwelling house is order of visitation	Number of family in order of visitation	of each person whose place of abode on April 1, 1930, was in this family. Enter surname, first, then given name and middle initial. If any. Include every person living on April 1, 1930. Omit children born since April 1, 1930.	Relationship of this Person to the head of the family.	Sex	Color or race	Age at last birthday	Single, married, widowed or divorced	Attended school any time since Sept. 1, 1929	Whether able to read and write.	Place of birth of this person.	Whether able to speak English.	
	1	2	3	4	5	6	7	8	9	10	11	12	13	14
1	Cerain Street	1	1	Taianao, Ignacia M	Head	F	Cha	56	Wd	N	N	Guam	N	Laundress
2		1	1	Taianao, Concepcion M	Daughter	F	Cha	17	S	N	Y	Guam	Y	Laundress
3		2	2	Ulloa, Gaspat U	Head	M	Cha	37	M	N	Y	Guam	Y	Farmer
4		2	2	Ulloa, Genoveba J	Wife	F	Cha	50	M	N	N	Guam	N	None
5		2	2	Ulloa, Francisco J	Son	M	Cha	11	S	Y	N	Guam	N	None
6		2	2	Jesus, Jose J	Stepson	M	Cha	22	S	N	Y	Guam	N	None
7		2	2	Jesus, Felix J	Stepson	M	Cha	20	S	N	Y	Guam	Y	Farm laborer
8		3	3	Castro, Ana R	Head	F	Cha	28	Wd	N	Y	Guam	Y	Farm laborer
9		3	3	Castro, Juan R	Son	M	Cha	5	S	N		Guam	Y	Laundress
10		3	3	Castro, Tomas R	Son	M	Cha	4	S	N		Guam	N	None
11		3	3	Castro, Dolores C	Mother	F	Cha	64	Wd	N	N	Guam	N	None
12		4	4	Sablan, Rosalia C	Head	F	Cha	28	M	N	Y	Guam	Y	None
13		4	4	Sablan, Alfred C	Son	M	Cha	11	S	Y	Y	Guam	Y	None
14		4	4	Sablan, Artemio C	Son	M	Cha	10	S	Y	Y	Guam	Y	None
15		4	4	Sablan, Virginia C	Daughter	F	Cha	7	S	N		Guam		None
16		4	4	Sablan, Enrique C	Son	M	Cha	2	S	N		Guam		None
17		5	5	Terlaji, Maria R	Head	F	Cha	39	M	N	Y	Guam	N	None
18		5	5	Terlaji, Francisco R	Son	M	Cha	7	S	Y		Guam		None
19		5	5	Terlaji, Juan R	Son	M	Cha	6	S	N		Guam		None
20		5	5	Terlaji, Vicente R	Son	M	Cha	1.7	S	N		Guam		None
21		5	5	Terlaji, Antonio R	Son	M	Cha	2.6	S	N		Guam		None
22		5	5	Terlaji, Joaquin R	Son	M	Cha	1.3	S	N		Guam		None
23		5	5	Reyes, Jose A	Stepfather	M	Cha	70	Wd	N	N	Guam	N	None
24		5	5	Reyes, Maria S	Niece	F	Cha	32	S	N	Y	Guam	Y	Laundress
25		6	6	Bordallo, Baltazar B	Head	M	Cha	71	M	N	Y	Spain	N	None

DEPARTMENT OF COMMERCE-BUREAU OF THE CENSUS
WASHINGTON

FIFTEENTH CENSUS OF THE UNITED STATES: 1930-POPULATION

THE ISLAND OF GUAM

Sheet No. 1B

228B

District **Municipality of Agat**
Name of Place **Agat town**
[Proper name and, also, name of class, as city, town, village, barrio, etc]

Enumeration District No. **6**
Enumerated by me on **April 2, 1930** Pedro C Charfauros
Enumerator

	PLACE OF ABODE			NAME	RELATION	PERSONAL DESCRIPTION				EDUCATION		NATIVITY		OCCUPATION
	Street, avenue, road, etc.	Number of dwelling house is order of visitation	Number of family in order of visitation	of each person whose place of abode on April 1, 1930, was in this family. Enter surname, first, then given name and middle initial. If any. Include every person living on April 1, 1930. Omit children born since April 1, 1930.	Relationship of this Person to the head of the family.	Sex	Color or race	Age at last birthday	Single, married, widowed or divorced	Attended school any time since Sept. 1, 1929	Whether able to read and write.	Place of birth of this person.	Whether able to speak English.	
	1	2	3	4	5	6	7	8	9	10	11	12	13	14
26	Cerain Street	6	6	Bordallo, Rita P	Wife	F	Cha	65	M	N	Y	Guam	N	None
27		7	7	Aquiningoc, Jose B	Head	M	Cha	39	M	N	Y	Guam	N	Farmer
28		7	7	Aquiningoc, Antonia C	Wife	F	Cha	42	M	N	N	Guam	N	None
29		7	7	Aquiningoc, Isabel C	Daughter	F	Cha	7	S	Y		Guam		None
30		7	7	Aquiningoc, Dormitila C	Daughter	F	Cha	5	S	N		Guam		Farmer
31		7	7	Aquiningoc, Julia C	Daughter	F	Cha	3.2	S	N		Guam		None
32		7	7	Aquiningoc, Lydia C	Daughter	F	Cha	2.6	S	N		Guam		None
33		7	7	San Nicolas, Carmen C	Step daughter	F	Cha	22	S	N	Y	Guam	Y	Laundress
34		7	7	San Nicolas, Juan C	Stepson	M	Cha	20	S	N	Y	Guam	Y	Farm laborer
35		7	7	San Nicolas, Enrique C	Stepson	M	Cha	18	S	N	N	Guam	N	Farm laborer
36		7	7	San Nicolas, Carmelo C	Stepson	M	Cha	17	S	N	Y	Guam	N	Farm laborer
37		7	7	San Nicolas, Felipe C	Stepson	M	Cha	11	S	Y	N	Guam	N	None
38		8	8	Sablan, Josefa C	Head	F	Cha	29	M	N	Y	Guam	Y	None
39		8	8	Sablan, Rowley C	Son	M	Cha	6	S	N		Guam		None
40		8	8	Sablan, Rosita C	Daughter	F	Cha	4.5	S	N		Guam		None
41		8	8	Sablan, Vicente D	Father	M	Cha	68	Wd	N	Y	Guam	N	None
42		9	9	Legaria, Eugenio de	Head	M	W	30	S	N	Y	Spain	Y	Missionary
43		10	10	Rivera, Antonio D	Head	M	Cha	47	M	N	Y	Guam	Y	Farmer
44		10	10	Rivera, Ana B	Wife	F	Cha	49	M	N	Y	Guam	N	None
45		10	10	Rivera, Vicente B	Son	M	Cha	22	S	N	Y	Guam	Y	Barber
46		10	10	Rivera, Martin B	Son	M	Cha	18	S	Y	Y	Guam	Y	None
47		10	10	Rivera, Guadalupe B	Daughter	F	Cha	8	S	Y		Guam		None
48		11	11	Carbullido, Jose B	Head	M	Cha	65	M	N	N	Guam	N	Farmer
49		11	11	Carbullido, Ana M	Wife	F	Cha	58	M	N	Y	Guam	N	None
50		11	11	Carbullido, Ignacio M	Son	M	Cha	21	S	N	Y	Guam	Y	Farm laborer

DEPARTMENT OF COMMERCE-BUREAU OF THE CENSUS
WASHINGTON

FIFTEENTH CENSUS OF THE UNITED STATES: 1930-POPULATION

THE ISLAND OF GUAM

Sheet No. 2A

District **Municipality of Agat**
Name of Place **Agat town**
[Proper name and, also, name of class, as city, town, village, barrio, etc]

Enumeration District No. 6
Enumerated by me on **April 2, 1930** Pedro C Charfauros
Enumerator

	PLACE OF ABODE			NAME	RELATION	PERSONAL DESCRIPTION				EDUCATION		NATIVITY		OCCUPATION
	Street, avenue, road, etc.	Number of dwelling house is order of visitation	Number of family in order of visitation	of each person whose place of abode on April 1, 1930, was in this family. Enter surname, first, then given name and middle initial. If any. Include every person living on April 1, 1930. Omit children born since April 1, 1930.	Relationship of this Person to the head of the family.	Sex	Color or race	Age at last birthday	Single, married, widowed or divorced	Attended school any time since Sept. 1, 1929	Whether able to read and write.	Place of birth of this person.	Whether able to speak English.	
	1	2	3	4	5	6	7	8	9	10	11	12	13	14
1	Cerain Street	11	11	Carbullido, Rita M	Daughter	F	Cha	15	S	N	Y	Guam	Y	Laundress
2		11	11	Carbullido, Jesus C	Grandson	M	Cha	9	S	Y		Guam		None
3		11	11	Carbullido, Josefa C	Grand daughter	F	Cha	5	S	N		Guam		None
4		12	12	Aguigui, Joaquin SN	Head	F	Cha	35	M	N	Y	Guam	Y	Farmer
5		12	12	Aguigui, Joaquina T	Wife	F	Cha	35	M	N	Y	Guam	Y	None
6		12	12	Aguigui, Isabel T	Daughter	F	Cha	10	S	Y	Y	Guam	Y	None
7		12	12	Aguigui, Juan T	Son	M	Cha	8	S	Y		Guam		None
8		12	12	Aguigui, Maria T	Daughter	F	Cha	5	S	N		Guam		None
9		12	12	Aguigui, Beatrise T	Daughter	F	Cha	2.6	S	N		Guam		None
10		12	12	Aguigui, Rosalia T	Daughter	F	Cha	0.2	S	N		Guam		None
11		13	13	Mendiola, Ignacio R	Head	M	Cha	32	M	N	Y	Guam	Y	Farmer
12		13	13	Mendiola, Rosalia C	Wife	F	Cha	30	M	N	Y	Guam	Y	None
13		13	13	Mendiola, Lina C	Daughter	F	Cha	7	S	N		Guam		None
14		13	13	Mendiola, Augusto C	Son	M	Cha	2.6	S	N		Guam		None
15		14	14	Mendiola, Gabriel S	Head	M	Cha	42	M	N	Y	Guam	N	Farmer
16		14	14	Mendiola, Maria G	Wife	F	Cha	44	M	N	N	Guam	N	None
17		14	14	Mendiola, Joaquina G	Daughter	F	Cha	16	S	Y	Y	Guam	Y	None
18		14	14	Mendiola, Maria G	Daughter	F	Cha	15	S	Y	Y	Guam	Y	None
19		14	14	Mendiola, Laura G	Daughter	F	Cha	13	S	Y	Y	Guam	Y	None
20		14	14	Mendiola, Ignacio G	Son	M	Cha	12	S	Y	N	Guam	N	None
21		14	14	Mendiola, Ignacia G	Daughter	F	Cha	6	S	N		Guam		None
22		15	15	Babauta, Jose R	Head	M	Cha	33	M	N	Y	Guam	N	Farmer
23		15	15	Babauta, Amable M	Wife	F	Cha	26	M	N	Y	Guam	N	None
24		15	15	Babauta, Gregorio M	Son	M	Cha	5	S	N		Guam		None
25		15	15	Babauta, Juan M	Son	M	Cha	3.1	S	N		Guam		None

(CHAMORRO ROOTS GENEALOGY PROJECT™ TRANSCRIPTION)
(BERNARD T. PUNZALAN / HTTP://WWW.CHAMORROROOTS.COM)

DEPARTMENT OF COMMERCE-BUREAU OF THE CENSUS
WASHINGTON

FIFTEENTH CENSUS OF THE UNITED STATES: 1930-POPULATION

THE ISLAND OF GUAM

Sheet No. 2B

229B

District **Municipality of Agat**
Name of Place **Agat town**
[Proper name and, also, name of class, as city, town, village, barrio, etc]

Enumeration District No. 6
Enumerated by me on **April 3, 1930** Pedro C Charfauros
Enumerator

	PLACE OF ABODE			NAME	RELATION	PERSONAL DESCRIPTION				EDUCATION		NATIVITY		OCCUPATION
	Street, avenue, road, etc.	Number of dwelling house is order of visitation	Number of family in order of visitation	of each person whose place of abode on April 1, 1930, was in this family. Enter surname, first, then given name and middle initial. If any. Include every person living on April 1, 1930. Omit children born since April 1, 1930.	Relationship of this Person to the head of the family.	Sex	Color or race	Age at last birthday	Single, married, widowed or divorced	Attended school any time since Sept. 1, 1929	Whether able to read and write.	Place of birth of this person.	Whether able to speak English.	
	1	2	3	4	5	6	7	8	9	10	11	12	13	14
26	Cerain Street	15	15	Babauta, Antonio M	Son	M	Cha	1.2	S	N		Guam		None
27		15	15	Aguigui, Josefa R	Mother in law	F	Cha	45	Wd	N	N	Guam	N	Laundress
28		15	15	Aguigui, Jose R	Brother in law	M	Cha	17	S	Y	Y	Guam	Y	None
29		15	15	Mendiola, Geronimo R	Brother in law	M	Cha	29	S	N	N	Guam	N	Farm laborer
30		16	16	Barcinas, Juan D	Head	M	Cha	36	M	N	N	Guam	N	Farmer
31		16	16	Barcinas, Rita A	Wife	F	Cha	36	M	N	Y	Guam	N	None
32		16	16	Barcinas, Jose A	Son	M	Cha	12	S	Y	N	Guam	N	None
33		16	16	Barcinas, Joaquin A	Son	M	Cha	7	S	Y		Guam		None
34		16	16	Barcinas, Francisco A	Son	M	Cha	5	S	N		Guam		None
35		16	16	Barcinas, Juan A	Son	M	Cha	0.1	S	N		Guam		None
36		17	17	Okiyama, Francisco K	Head	M	Jap	51	Wd	N	Y	Japan		Retail merchant
37		17	17	Okiyama, Jesus C	Son	M	Jap	17	S	N	Y	Guam	Y	Laborer
38		17	17	Okiyama, Maria C	Daughter	F	Jap	2.8	S	N		Guam	Y	None
39		18	18	Carbullido, Jesus B	Head	M	Cha	59	M	N	Y	Guam		Farmer
40		18	18	Carbullido, Magdalena S	Wife	F	Cha	58	M	N	N	Guam	N	Laundress
41		18	18	Jesus, Ana S	Step daughter	F	Cha	24	S	Y	Y	Guam	N	Laundress
42		18	18	Jesus, Delfina S	Step daughter	F	Cha	21	S	N	Y	Guam	N	Laundress
43		18	18	Jesus, Maria S	Step daughter	F	Cha	3.2	S	N		Guam		None
44		19	19	Carbullido, Antonio P	Head	M	Cha	35	M	N	Y	Guam	Y	Laundryman
45		19	19	Carbullido, Maria T	Wife	F	Cha	36	M	N	Y	Guam	N	None
46		19	19	Carbullido, Enriqueta T	Daughter	F	Cha	14	S	Y	Y	Guam	Y	None
47		19	19	Carbullido, Felix T	Son	M	Cha	13	S	Y	Y	Guam	Y	None
48		19	19	Carbullido, Albert Edw T	Son	M	Cha	11	S	Y	Y	Guam	Y	None
49		19	19	Carbullido, Hilda T	Daughter	F	Cha	3.1	S	N		Guam		None
50		19	19	Carbullido, Evelyn T	Daughter	F	Cha	2	S	N		Guam		None

DEPARTMENT OF COMMERCE-BUREAU OF THE CENSUS
WASHINGTON

FIFTEENTH CENSUS OF THE UNITED STATES: 1930-POPULATION

THE ISLAND OF GUAM

Sheet No. 3A

District **Municipality of Agat**
Name of Place **Agat Town**
[Proper name and, also, name of class, as city, town, village, barrio, etc]

Enumeration District No. 6
Enumerated by me on **April 3, 1930** Pedro C Charfauros
Enumerator

	PLACE OF ABODE			NAME	RELATION	PERSONAL DESCRIPTION				EDUCATION		NATIVITY		OCCUPATION
	Street, avenue, road, etc.	Number of dwelling house is order of visitation	Number of family in order of visitation	of each person whose place of abode on April 1, 1930, was in this family. Enter surname, first, then given name and middle initial. If any. Include every person living on April 1, 1930. Omit children born since April 1, 1930.	Relationship of this Person to the head of the family.	Sex	Color or race	Age at last birthday	Single, married, widowed or divorced	Attended school any time since Sept. 1, 1929	Whether able to read and write.	Place of birth of this person.	Whether able to speak English.	
	1	2	3	4	5	6	7	8	9	10	11	12	13	14
1	Cerain Street	19	19	Chargualaf, Ignacio C	Servant	M	Cha	22	S	N	Y	Guam	Y	Cook
2		20	20	Fairly, Marian B	Head	F	W	18	M	N	Y	Washington	Y	None
3		21	21	Torres, Francisco P	Head	M	Cha	27	M	N	Y	Guam	Y	Laborer
4		21	21	Torres, Natividad C	Wife	F	Cha	26	M	N	Y	Guam	Y	None
5		22	22	Babauta, Jose B	Head	M	Cha	47	M	N	Y	Guam	Y	Farmer
6		22	22	Babauta, Juana A	Wife	F	Cha	64	M	N	N	Guam	N	None
7		22	22	Babauta, Antonio A	Stepson	M	Cha	41	S	N	N	Guam	N	Farm laborer
8		22	22	Babauta, Maria A	Stepdaughter	F	Cha	26	S	N	Y	Guam	Y	Laundress
9		22	22	Babauta, Rosa A	Step granddaughter	F	Cha	5	S	N		Guam		None
10		22	22	Babauta, Manuel A	Step grandson	M	Cha	3	S	N		Guam		None
11		22	22	Babauta, Juan A	Stepgrandson	M	Cha	12	S	N		Guam	N	None
12		23	23	Charfauros, Mariano F	Head	M	Cha	50	M	N	Y	Guam	N	Farmer
13		23	23	Charfauros, Ignasia N	Wife	F	Cha	47	M	N	N	Guam	Y	None
14		23	23	Charfauros, Joaquin N	Son	M	Cha	20	S	N	Y	Guam	Y	Teacher
15		23	23	Charfauros, Francisco N	Son	M	Cha	18	S	N	Y	Guam	Y	Teacher
16		23	23	Charfauros, Jose N	Son	M	Cha	13	S	Y	Y	Guam	Y	None
17		23	23	Charfauros, Ignasio N	Son	M	Cha	11	S	Y	Y	Guam	Y	None
18		23	23	Chargualaf, Vicente C	Servant	M	Cha	16	S	N	Y	Guam	Y	Cook
19		24	24	Alcantara, Francisco B	Head	M	Cha	31	M	N	Y	Guam	Y	C.P.C. Employee
20		24	24	Alcantara, Maria I	Wife	F	Cha	26	M	N	Y	Guam	Y	None
21		24	24	Alcantara, Benita I	Son	M	Cha	5	S	N		Guam		None
22		24	24	Alcantara, Eugenia I	Daughter	F	Cha	3	S	N		Guam		None
23		24	24	Alcantara, Francisco I	Son	M	Cha	1	S	N		Guam		None
24		24	24	Alcantara, Antonia B	Mother	F	Cha	66	Wd	N	N	Guam	N	None
25		25	25	Sablan, Diego S	Head	M	Cha	34	M	N	Y	Guam	Y	Farmer

DEPARTMENT OF COMMERCE-BUREAU OF THE CENSUS
WASHINGTON

FIFTEENTH CENSUS OF THE UNITED STATES: 1930-POPULATION

THE ISLAND OF GUAM

Sheet No. 3B

230B

District **Municipality of Agat**
Name of Place **Agat Town**
[Proper name and, also, name of class, as city, town, village, barrio, etc]

Enumeration District No. **6**
Enumerated by me on **April 4, 1930** Pedro C Charfauros
Enumerator

	PLACE OF ABODE			NAME	RELATION	PERSONAL DESCRIPTION				EDUCATION		NATIVITY		OCCUPATION
	Street, avenue, road, etc.	Number of dwelling house is order of visitation	Number of family in order of visitation	of each person whose place of abode on April 1, 1930, was in this family. Enter surname, first, then given name and middle initial. If any. Include every person living on April 1, 1930. Omit children born since April 1, 1930.	Relationship of this Person to the head of the family.	Sex	Color or race	Age at last birthday	Single, married, widowed or divorced	Attended school any time since Sept. 1, 1929	Whether able to read and write.	Place of birth of this person.	Whether able to speak English.	
	1	2	3	4	5	6	7	8	9	10	11	12	13	14
26	Cerain Street	25	25	Sablan, Guadalupi B	Wife	F	Cha	28	M	N	Y	Guam	Y	None
27		25	25	Sablan, Daniel B	Son	M	Cha	10	S	Y	N	Guam	N	None
28		25	25	Sablan, Francisco B	Son	M	Cha	8	S	Y		Guam		None
29		25	25	Sablan, Maria B	Daughter	F	Cha	5	S	N		Guam		None
30		25	25	Sablan, Aliandro B	Son	M	Cha	4.5	S	N		Guam		None
31		26	26	Salas, Joaquin S	Head	M	Cha	45	M	N	Y	Guam	Y	Farmer
32		26	26	Salas, Antonia R	Wife	F	Cha	24	M	N	Y	Guam	Y	None
33		26	26	Salas, Antonio R	Son	M	Cha	1.3	S	N		Guam		None
34		26	26	Salas, Vicente C	Son	M	Cha	22	S	N	Y	Guam	Y	Farm laborer
35		27	27	Leon Guerrero, Leon C	Head	M	Cha	39	M	N	Y	Guam	N	Farmer
36		27	27	Leon Guerrero, Encarnacion B	Wife	F	Cha	39	M	N	Y	Guam	N	None
37		27	27	Leon Guerrero, Ana B	Daughter	F	Cha	20	S	N	Y	Guam	Y	Laundress
38		27	27	Leon Guerrero, Ignacia B	Daughter	F	Cha	19	S	N	Y	Guam	Y	Laundress
39		27	27	Leon Guerrero, Baltazaar B	Son	M	Cha	15	S	Y	Y	Guam	Y	None
40		27	27	Leon Guerrero, Felix B	Son	M	Cha	10	S	Y	N	Guam	N	None
41		27	27	Leon Guerrero, Jesus B	Son	M	Cha	5	S	N		Guam		None
42		27	27	Leon Guerrero, Rosa B	Daughter	F	Cha	4.4	S	N		Guam		None
43		27	27	Leon Guerrero, Efraim B	Son	M	Cha	2.1	S	N		Guam		None
44		27	27	Babauta, Soledad C	Mother in law	F	Cha	56	Wd	N	N	Guam	N	None
45		27	27	Babauta, Antonio C	Brother in law	M	Cha	34	S	N	N	Guam	N	Farm laborer
46		28	28	Aguigui, Benidicto SN	Head	F	Cha	51	M	N	Y	Guam	N	Farmer
47		28	28	Aguigui, Maria C	Wife	F	Cha	45	M	N	N	Guam	N	None
48		28	28	Aguigui, Antonio C	Son	M	Cha	21	S	N	Y	Guam	Y	Farm laborer
49		28	28	Aguigui, Milagro C	Daughter	F	Cha	24	Wd	N	Y	Guam	Y	Laundress
50		28	28	Aguigui, Juana C	Daughter	F	Cha	20	S	N	N	Guam	N	Laundress

DEPARTMENT OF COMMERCE-BUREAU OF THE CENSUS
WASHINGTON

FIFTEENTH CENSUS OF THE UNITED STATES: 1930-POPULATION

THE ISLAND OF GUAM

Sheet No. 4A

District Municipality of Agat
Name of Place Agat Town
[Proper name and, also, name of class, as city, town, village, barrio, etc]

Enumeration District No. 6
Enumerated by me on April 4, 1930 Pedro C Charfauros, Enumerator

	PLACE OF ABODE			NAME	RELATION	PERSONAL DESCRIPTION				EDUCATION		NATIVITY		OCCUPATION
	Street, avenue, road, etc.	Number of dwelling house is order of visitation	Number of family in order of visitation	of each person whose place of abode on April 1, 1930, was in this family. Enter surname, first, then given name and middle initial. If any. Include every person living on April 1, 1930. Omit children born since April 1, 1930.	Relationship of this Person to the head of the family.	Sex	Color or race	Age at last birthday	Single, married, widowed or divorced	Attended school any time since Sept. 1, 1929	Whether able to read and write.	Place of birth of this person.	Whether able to speak English.	
	1	2	3	4	5	6	7	8	9	10	11	12	13	14
1	Cerain Street	28	28	Aguigui, Luisa C	Daughter	F	Cha	14	S	Y	Y	Guam	Y	None
2		28	28	Aguigui, Dionicio C	Son	M	Cha	12	S	Y	Y	Guam	Y	None
3		28	28	Aguigui, Vicente C	Grandson	M	Cha	5	S	N		Guam		None
4		28	28	Charfauros, Jose A	Grandson	M	Cha	1.4	S	N		Guam		None
5		28	28	Cruz, Carmen D	Sister in law	F	Cha	42	S	N	N	Guam	N	Laundress
6		28	28	Cruz, Juan D	Nephew	M	Cha	11	S	Y	N	Guam	N	None
7		29	29	Chaco, Asuncion S	Head	F	Cha	22	M	N	Y	Guam	Y	None
8		29	29	Chaco, Jesus S	Son	M	Cha	2	S	N		Guam		None
9		29	29	Chaco, Sylvia S	Daughter	F	Cha	.4	S	N		Guam		None
10		30	30	Babauta, Pedro C	Head	M	Cha	36	M	N	Y	Guam	Y	Farmer
11		30	30	Babauta, Delores S	Wife	F	Cha	34	M	N	Y	Guam	Y	None
12		30	30	Babauta, Mariano S	Daughter	F	Cha	11	S	Y	N	Guam	N	None
13		30	30	Babauta, Rosalia S	Daughter	F	Cha	9	S	Y		Guam		None
14		30	30	Babauta, Natividad S	Daughter	F	Cha	8	S	Y		Guam		None
15		30	30	Babauta, Jose S	Son	M	Cha	3.5	S	N		Guam		None
16		30	30	Babauta, Serafin S	Son	M	Cha	2	S	N		Guam		None
17		31	31	Cruz, Mariano S	Head	M	Cha	42	M	N	N	Guam	N	Farmer
18		31	31	Cruz, Candelaria T	Wife	F	Cha	35	M	N	N	Guam	N	None
19		31	31	Cruz, Lagrimas N	Daughter	F	Cha	14	S	Y	Y	Guam	Y	None
20		31	31	Cruz, Ana T	Daughter	F	Cha	8	S	Y		Guam		None
21		31	31	Cruz, Rosalia T	Daughter	F	Cha	7	S	N		Guam		None
22		31	31	Cruz, Rita T	Daughter	F	Cha	4	S	N		Guam		None
23		31	31	Cruz, Vicente T	Son	M	Cha	1.5	S	N		Guam		None
24		32	32	Carbullido, Luisa M	Head	F	Cha	50	Wd	N	N	Guam	N	None
25		32	32	Carbullido, Remedios M	Daughter	F	Cha	25	S	N	N	Guam	N	Laundress

(CHAMORRO ROOTS GENEALOGY PROJECT™ TRANSCRIPTION)
(BERNARD T. PUNZALAN / HTTP://WWW.CHAMORROROOTS.COM)

DEPARTMENT OF COMMERCE-BUREAU OF THE CENSUS
WASHINGTON

FIFTEENTH CENSUS OF THE UNITED STATES: 1930-POPULATION

THE ISLAND OF GUAM

Sheet No. 4B

231B

District **Municipality of Agat**
Name of Place **Agat Town**
[Proper name and, also, name of class, as city, town, village, barrio, etc]

Enumeration District No. 6
Enumerated by me on **April 5, 1930** Pedro C Charfauros
Enumerator

	PLACE OF ABODE			NAME	RELATION	PERSONAL DESCRIPTION				EDUCATION		NATIVITY		OCCUPATION
	Street, avenue, road, etc.	Number of dwelling house is order of visitation	Number of family in order of visitation	of each person whose place of abode on April 1, 1930, was in this family. Enter surname, first, then given name and middle initial. If any. Include every person living on April 1, 1930. Omit children born since April 1, 1930.	Relationship of this Person to the head of the family.	Sex	Color or race	Age at last birthday	Single, married, widowed or divorced	Attended school any time since Sept. 1, 1929	Whether able to read and write.	Place of birth of this person.	Whether able to speak English.	
	1	2	3	4	5	6	7	8	9	10	11	12	13	14
26	Cerain Street	32	32	Carbullido, Maria M	Daughter	F	Cha	21	S	N	Y	Guam	Y	Laundress
27		32	32	Carbullido, Jose M	Son	M	Cha	18	S	N	Y	Guam	Y	Farmer
28		32	32	Carbullido, Francisco M	Son	M	Cha	12	S	Y	Y	Guam	N	None
29		32	32	Carbullido, Soledad M	Daughter	F	Cha	8	S	Y		Guam		None
30		33	33	Babauta, Francisco R	Head	M	Cha	39	M	N	N	Guam	N	Farmer
31		33	33	Babauta, Ignacia B	Wife	F	Cha	42	M	N	N	Guam	N	None
32		33	33	Babauta, Joaquin B	Son	M	Cha	6	S	N		Guam		None
33		33	33	Babauta, Vicente B	Son	M	Cha	5	S	N		Guam		None
34		33	33	Babauta, Joaquina B	Daughter	F	Cha	3	S	N		Guam		None
35		33	33	Babauta, Manuel S	Stepson	M	Cha	19	S	N	Y	Guam	Y	Laborer
36		33	33	Babauta, Francisco S	Stepson	M	Cha	16	S	N	Y	Guam	Y	Farm laborer
37		34	34	Salas, Francisco C	Head	M	Cha	27	M	N	N	Guam	N	Farmer
38		34	34	Salas, Joaquina A	Wife	F	Cha	30	M	N	Y	Guam	Y	None
39		34	34	Salas, Rosa A	Daughter	F	Cha	4.7	S	N		Guam		None
40		34	34	Salas, Jose A	Son	M	Cha	.1	S	N		Guam		None
41		35	35	Aguigui, Luis SN	Head	M	Cha	42	M	N	N	Guam	N	Farmer
42		35	35	Aguigui, Trinidad C	Wife	F	Cha	41	M	N	N	Guam	N	None
43		35	35	Aguigui, Enrique C	Son	M	Cha	24	S	N	Y	Guam	Y	Cook
44		35	35	Aguigui, Antonia C	Daughter	F	Cha	19	S	N	Y	Guam	Y	Laundress
45		35	35	Aguigui, Josefa C	Daughter	F	Cha	17	S	N	Y	Guam	Y	Laundress
46		35	35	Aguigui, Maria C	Daughter	F	Cha	10	S	Y	N	Guam	N	None
47		36	36	Chaco, Antonio Q	Head	M	Cha	61	M	N	N	Guam	N	Farmer
48		36	36	Chaco, Milagro R	Wife	F	Cha	45	M	N	Y	Guam	N	None
49		36	36	Chaco, Jose R	Son	M	Cha	23	S	N	Y	Guam	Y	Cook
50		36	36	Chaco, Vicente R	Son	M	Cha	21	S	N	Y	Guam	Y	Laborer

DEPARTMENT OF COMMERCE-BUREAU OF THE CENSUS
WASHINGTON

FIFTEENTH CENSUS OF THE UNITED STATES: 1930-POPULATION

THE ISLAND OF GUAM

Sheet No. 5A

District **Municipality of Agat**
Name of Place **Agat Town**
[Proper name and, also, name of class, as city, town, village, barrio, etc]

Enumeration District No. 6
Enumerated by me on **April 5, 1930** Pedro C Charfauros
Enumerator

	PLACE OF ABODE			NAME	RELATION	PERSONAL DESCRIPTION				EDUCATION		NATIVITY		OCCUPATION
	Street, avenue, road, etc.	Number of dwelling house in order of visitation	Number of family in order of visitation	of each person whose place of abode on April 1, 1930, was in this family. Enter surname, first, then given name and middle initial. If any. Include every person living on April 1, 1930. Omit children born since April 1, 1930.	Relationship of this Person to the head of the family.	Sex	Color or race	Age at last birthday	Single, married, widowed or divorced	Attended school any time since Sept. 1, 1929	Whether able to read and write.	Place of birth of this person.	Whether able to speak English.	
	1	2	3	4	5	6	7	8	9	10	11	12	13	14
1	Cerain Street	36	36	Chaco, Regina R	Daughter	F	Cha	19	S	N	Y	Guam	Y	Laundress
2		36	36	Chaco, Soledad R	Daughter	F	Cha	17	S	N	Y	Guam	Y	Laundress
3		36	36	Chaco, Jesus R	Son	M	Cha	12	S	Y	Y	Guam	Y	None
4		36	36	Chaco, Maria R	Daughter	F	Cha	11	S	Y	N	Guam	N	None
5		36	36	Chaco, Beatrice R	Daughter	F	Cha	3.1	S	N		Guam		None
6		37	37	Chaco, Manuel Q	Head	M	Cha	60	M	N	N	Guam	N	None
7		37	37	Chaco, Ana C	Wife	F	Cha	61	M	N	N	Guam	N	None
8		37	37	Chaco, Francisco C	Son	M	Cha	18	S	N	Y	Guam	Y	Farmer
9		37	37	Chaco, Jesus C	Son	M	Cha	12	S	Y	Y	Guam	Y	None
10		38	38	Babauta, Benjamin T	Head	M	Cha	62	M	N	N	Guam	N	None
11		38	38	Babauta, Dolores T	Wife	F	Cha	60	M	N	N	Guam	N	None
12		38	38	Babauta, Rosario T	Daughter	F	Cha	26	S	N	N	Guam	N	Laundress
13		38	38	Babauta, Vicente T	Son	M	Cha	23	S	N	Y	Guam	Y	Laborer
14		38	38	Babauta, Ignacia T	Daughter	F	Cha	15	S	N	Y	Guam	Y	None
15		39	39	Sablan, Cecilio S	Head	M	Cha	39	M	N	Y	Guam	Y	Farmer
16		39	39	Sablan, Dolores Q	Wife	F	Cha	38	M	N	Y	Guam	Y	None
17		39	39	Sablan, Antoino Q	Son	M	Cha	11	S	Y	Y	Guam	Y	None
18		39	39	Sablan, Nicolas Q	Son	M	Cha	5	S	N		Guam		None
19		39	39	Sablan, Brigida Q	Daughter	F	Cha	3.3	S	N		Guam		None
20		39	39	Sablan, Jaime Q	Son	M	Cha	1.4	S	N		Guam		None
21		40	40	Carbullido, Luis B	Head	M	Cha	70	S	N	Y	Guam	N	Farmer
22		40	40	Carbullido, Felominia B	Wife	F	Cha	56	M	N	Y	Guam	N	None
23		40	41	Quitano, Tomas C	Head	M	Cha	31	M	N	Y	Guam	N	Farmer
24		40	41	Quitano, Maria C	Wife	F	Cha	35	M	N	Y	Guam	Y	None
25		41	42	Carbullido, Joaquin P	Head	M	Cha	25	M	N	Y	Guam	Y	Barber

(CHAMORRO ROOTS GENEALOGY PROJECT™ TRANSCRIPTION)
(BERNARD T. PUNZALAN / HTTP://WWW.CHAMORROROOTS.COM)

DEPARTMENT OF COMMERCE-BUREAU OF THE CENSUS
WASHINGTON

FIFTEENTH CENSUS OF THE UNITED STATES: 1930-POPULATION

THE ISLAND OF GUAM

Sheet No. 5B

232B

District **Municipality of Agat**
Name of Place **Agat Town**
[Proper name and, also, name of class, as city, town, village, barrio, etc]

Enumeration District No. 6
Enumerated by me on April 7, 1930 Pedro C Charfauros, Enumerator

	PLACE OF ABODE			NAME	RELATION	PERSONAL DESCRIPTION				EDUCATION		NATIVITY		OCCUPATION
	Street, avenue, road, etc.	Number of dwelling house in order of visitation	Number of family in order of visitation	of each person whose place of abode on April 1, 1930, was in this family. Enter surname, first, then given name and middle initial. If any. Include every person living on April 1, 1930. Omit children born since April 1, 1930.	Relationship of this Person to the head of the family.	Sex	Color or race	Age at last birthday	Single, married, widowed or divorced	Attended school any time since Sept. 1, 1929	Whether able to read and write.	Place of birth of this person.	Whether able to speak English.	
	1	2	3	4	5	6	7	8	9	10	11	12	13	14
26	Cerain Street	41	42	Carbuillido, Rosa R	Wife	F	Cha	23	M	N	Y	Guam	Y	None
27		41	42	Carbuillido, Catherine R	Daughter	F	Cha	3.3	S	N		Guam		None
28		41	42	Carbuillido, Benjamin R	Son	M	Cha	2.1	S	N		Guam		None
29		41	42	Carbuillido, Elmer R	Daughter	F	Cha	1.4	S	N		Guam		None
30		42	43	Sablan, Juan R	Head	M	Cha	66	M	N	Y	Guam	N	Farmer
31		42	43	Sablan, Ana P	Wife	F	Cha	64	M	N	N	Guam	N	None
32		42	43	Sablan, Rosa P	Daughter	F	Cha	37	S	Y	Y	Guam	Y	Laundress
33		42	43	Sablan, Juan P	Son	M	Cha	26	S	Y	Y	Guam	Y	Teacher
34		43	44	Quitano, Emilia S	Head	F	Cha	69	Wd	N	N	Guam	N	None
35		43	44	Quitano, Juana S	Daughter	F	Cha	43	Wd	N	N	Guam	N	Laundress
36		43	44	Quitano, Ramon S	Son	M	Cha	31	S	N	Y	Guam	Y	Farmer
37		43	44	Cruz, Jose Q	Grandson	M	Cha	17	S	N	Y	Guam	Y	Farm laborer
38		43	44	Cruz, Jesus Q	Grandson	M	Cha	16	S	N	Y	Guam	Y	Farm laborer
39		43	44	Cruz, Maria Q	Granddaughter	F	Cha	14	S	Y	Y	Guam	Y	None
40		43	44	Cruz, Joaquin Q	Grandson	M	Cha	10	S	Y	N	Guam	N	None
41		44	45	Charfauros, Jesus B	Head	M	Cha	42	S	N	Y	Guam	Y	Farmer
42		44	45	Charfauros, Vinancio B	Brother	M	Cha	35	S	N	Y	Guam	Y	Farm laborer
43		44	45	Charfauros, Carmen B	Sister	F	Cha	32	S	N	Y	Guam	N	Laundress
44		44	45	Charfauros, Ana B	Sister	F	Cha	30	S	N	Y	Guam	Y	None
45		44	45	Charfauros, Felix B	Nephew	M	Cha	3.2	S	N		Guam	Y	None
46		44	45	Charfauros, Juan B	Nephew	M	Cha	3.1	S	N		Guam		None
47		44	46	Babauta, Jose P	Head	M	Cha	50	M	N	Y	Guam	N	Farmer
48		44	46	Babauta, Teodora SN	Wife	F	Cha	51	M	N	Y	Guam	N	None
49		44	46	Babauta, Francisco SN	Son	M	Cha	23	S	N	Y	Guam	Y	Laborer
50		44	46	Babauta, Felix SN	Son	M	Cha	21	S	N	Y	Guam	Y	Cook

DEPARTMENT OF COMMERCE-BUREAU OF THE CENSUS
WASHINGTON

FIFTEENTH CENSUS OF THE UNITED STATES: 1930-POPULATION

THE ISLAND OF GUAM

Sheet No. 6A

District **Municipality of Agat**
Name of Place **Agat Town** [Proper name and, also, name of class, as city, town, village, barrio, etc]

Enumeration District No. **6**
Enumerated by me on **April 7, 1930** Pedro C Charfauros, Enumerator

	PLACE OF ABODE			NAME	RELATION	PERSONAL DESCRIPTION				EDUCATION		NATIVITY		OCCUPATION
	Street, avenue, road, etc.	Number of dwelling house in order of visitation	Number of family in order of visitation	of each person whose place of abode on April 1, 1930, was in this family. Enter surname, first, then given name and middle initial. If any. Include every person living on April 1, 1930. Omit children born since April 1, 1930.	Relationship of this Person to the head of the family.	Sex	Color or race	Age at last birthday	Single, married, widowed or divorced	Attended school any time since Sept. 1, 1929	Whether able to read and write.	Place of birth of this person.	Whether able to speak English.	
	1	2	3	4	5	6	7	8	9	10	11	12	13	14
1	Cerain Street	44	46	Babauta, Joaquina SN	Daughter	F	Cha	16	S	N	Y	Guam	Y	Laundress
2		45	47	Nededoc, Juan P	Head	M	Cha	35	M	N	Y	Guam	Y	Laborer
3		45	47	Nededoc, Dolores T	Wife	F	Cha	26	M	N	Y	Guam	N	None
4		45	47	Nededoc, Rita T	Daughter	F	Cha	6	S	N		Guam		None
5		45	47	Nededoc, Juan T	Son	M	Cha	4.3	S	N		Guam		None
6		46	48	Chaco, Ana B	Head	F	Cha	19	M	N	Y	Guam	Y	None
7		47	49	Chaco, Francisco R	Head	M	Cha	31	M	N	Y	Guam	Y	Farmer
8		47	49	Chaco, Dolores C	Wife	F	Cha	32	M	N	Y	Guam	Y	None
9		47	49	Chaco, Graciosa C	Daughter	F	Cha	5	S	N		Guam		None
10		47	49	Chaco, Cary C	Daughter	F	Cha	4.1	S	N		Guam		None
11		47	49	Chaco, Frank C	Son	M	Cha	3.2	S	N		Guam		None
12		47	49	Chaco, Slate C	Daughter	F	Cha	1	S	N		Guam		None
13		48	50	Chaco, Felipe Q	Head	M	Cha	65	Wd	N	Y	Guam	N	None
14		49	51	Charfauros, Pedro C	Head	M	Cha	27	M	N	Y	Guam	Y	Farmer
15		49	51	Charfauros, Virginia B	Wife	F	Cha	25	M	N	Y	Guam	Y	None
16		49	51	Charfauros, Lydia B	Daughter	F	Cha	1.4	S	N		Guam		None
17		50	52	Chaco, Juan C	Head	M	Cha	32	M	N	N	Guam	N	Farmer
18		50	52	Chaco, Victoriana LG	Wife	F	Cha	38	M	N	N	Guam	N	None
19		50	52	Leon Guerrero, Juan LG	Stepson	M	Cha	14	S	Y	Y	Guam	Y	None
20		50	53	Babauta, Dionisio C	Head	M	Cha	32	Wd	N	N	Guam	N	Farmer
21		50	53	Babauta, Pedro C	Son	M	Cha	11	S	Y	Y	Guam	Y	None
22		50	53	Babauta, Jose C	Son	M	Cha	9	S	Y		Guam		None
23		51	54	Taitague, Domingo C	Head	M	Cha	57	M	N	Y	Guam	N	Farmer
24		51	54	Taitague, Ana C	Wife	F	Cha	67	M	N	N	Guam	N	None
25		51	55	Carbullido, Consolasion C	Head	F	Cha	30	M	N	Y	Guam	N	None

DEPARTMENT OF COMMERCE-BUREAU OF THE CENSUS
WASHINGTON

FIFTEENTH CENSUS OF THE UNITED STATES: 1930-POPULATION

THE ISLAND OF GUAM

Sheet No. 6B

233B

District Municipality of Agat
Name of Place Agat Town
[Proper name and, also, name of class, as city, town, village, barrio, etc]

Enumeration District No. 6
Enumerated by me on April 8, 1930 Pedro C Charfauros
Enumerator

	PLACE OF ABODE			NAME	RELATION	PERSONAL DESCRIPTION				EDUCATION		NATIVITY		OCCUPATION
	Street, avenue, road, etc.	Number of dwelling house in order of visitation	Number of family in order of visitation	of each person whose place of abode on April 1, 1930, was in this family. Enter surname, first, then given name and middle initial. If any. Include every person living on April 1, 1930. Omit children born since April 1, 1930.	Relationship of this Person to the head of the family.	Sex	Color or race	Age at last birthday	Single, married, widowed or divorced	Attended school any time since Sept. 1, 1929	Whether able to read and write.	Place of birth of this person.	Whether able to speak English.	
	1	2	3	4	5	6	7	8	9	10	11	12	13	14
26	Cerain Street	51	55	Carbullido, Clotilde C	Daughter	F	Cha	8	S	Y		Guam		None
27		51	55	Carbullido, Frank C	Son	M	Cha	7	S	N		Guam		None
28		51	55	Carbullido, Edward C	Son	M	Cha	5	S	N		Guam		None
29		51	55	Carbullido, Francis C	Daughter	F	Cha	3.5	S	N		Guam		None
30		51	55	Carbullido, Mildred C	Daughter	F	Cha	2	S	N		Guam		None
31		51	55	Carbullido, Junior C	Daughter	F	Cha	.2	S	N		Guam		None
32	Pareno Street	52	56	Santos, Roque S	Head	M	Cha	47	M	N	Y	Guam	N	Farmer
33		52	56	Santos, Maria C	Wife	F	Cha	43	M	N	Y	Guam	N	None
34		52	56	Santos, Juana C	Daughter	F	Cha	20	S	N	Y	Guam	Y	Laundress
35		52	56	Santos, Isabel C	Daughter	F	Cha	19	S	N	Y	Guam	Y	None
36		52	56	Santos, Amelia C	Daughter	F	Cha	15	S	Y	Y	Guam	Y	None
37		53	57	Babauta, Rosa G	Head	F	Cha	29	M	N	Y	Guam	N	Laundress
38		53	57	Babauta, Jose G	Son	M	Cha	11	S	Y	N	Guam	N	None
39		54	58	Carbullido, Joaquin C	Head	M	Cha	47	M	N	Y	Guam	N	Farmer
40		54	58	Carbullido, Trinidad C	Wife	F	Cha	41	M	N	Y	Guam	N	None
41		54	58	Carbullido, Maria C	Daughter	F	Cha	21	S	N	Y	Guam	Y	Laundress
42		54	58	Carbullido, Felicita C	Daughter	F	Cha	13	S	Y	Y	Guam	Y	None
43		54	58	Carbullido, Josefina C	Daughter	F	Cha	10	S	Y	Y	Guam	Y	None
44		54	58	Carbullido, Manuela C	Daughter	F	Cha	8	S	Y		Guam		None
45		54	58	Carbullido, Rosa C	Daughter	F	Cha	6	S	N		Guam		None
46		54	58	Carbullido, Ana C	Daughter	F	Cha	4.6	S	N		Guam		None
47		54	58	Carbullido, Concepcion C	Daughter	F	Cha	1.3	S	N		Guam		None
48		55	59	Charfauros, Maria B	Head	F	Cha	31	Wd	N	N	Guam	N	Laundress
49		55	59	Charfauros, Carmela B	Daughter	F	Cha	11	S	Y	N	Guam	N	None
50		55	59	Charfauros, Jesus B	Son	M	Cha	10	S	Y	N	Guam	N	None

(CHAMORRO ROOTS GENEALOGY PROJECT™ TRANSCRIPTION)
(BERNARD T. PUNZALAN / HTTP://WWW.CHAMORROROOTS.COM)

DEPARTMENT OF COMMERCE-BUREAU OF THE CENSUS
WASHINGTON
FIFTEENTH CENSUS OF THE UNITED STATES: 1930-POPULATION

THE ISLAND OF GUAM

Sheet No. 7A

234

District **Municipality of Agat**
Name of Place **Agat Town** [Proper name and, also, name of class, as city, town, village, barrio, etc]

Enumeration District No. **6**
Enumerated by me on **April 8, 1930** Pedro C Charfauros, Enumerator

	PLACE OF ABODE: Street, avenue, road, etc.	Number of dwelling house in order of visitation	Number of family in order of visitation	NAME of each person whose place of abode on April 1, 1930, was in this family. Enter surname, first, then given name and middle initial. If any. Include every person living on April 1, 1930. Omit children born since April 1, 1930.	RELATION Relationship of this Person to the head of the family.	PERSONAL DESCRIPTION: Sex	Color or race	Age at last birthday	Single, married, widowed or divorced	EDUCATION: Attended school any time since Sept. 1, 1929	Whether able to read and write.	NATIVITY Place of birth of this person.	Whether able to speak English.	OCCUPATION
	1	2	3	4	5	6	7	8	9	10	11	12	13	14
1	Pareno Street	55	59	Charfauros, Antonio B	Son	M	Cha	8	S	Y		Guam		None
2		55	59	Charfauros, Luis B	Son	M	Cha	3	S	N		Guam		None
3		55	59	Babauta, Jesus L	Brother	M	Cha	32	S	N	N	Guam	N	Farm laborer
4		56	60	Charfauros, Luis A	Head	M	Cha	56	M	N	Y	Guam	N	Farmer
5		56	60	Charfauros, Rosa C	Wife	F	Cha	55	M	N	N	Guam	N	None
6		56	60	Charfauros, Ignasio C	Son	M	Cha	29	S	N	Y	Guam	Y	Farm laborer
7		56	60	Charfauros, Consalasion C	Daughter	F	Cha	26	S	N	Y	Guam	N	Laundress
8		57	61	Carbullido, Vicente C	Head	M	Cha	48	Wd	N	Y	Guam	N	Farmer
9		57	61	Carbullido, Martina A	Daughter	F	Cha	19	S	N	Y	Guam	Y	None
10		57	61	Carbullido, Fransisco A	Son	M	Cha	14	S	Y	Y	Guam	Y	None
11		57	61	Carbullido, Luis A	Son	M	Cha	12	S	Y	Y	Guam	Y	None
12		58	62	Cruz, Vicente G	Head	M	Cha	65	M	N	Y	Guam	N	None
13		58	62	Cruz, Josefa SN	Wife	F	Cha	54	M	N	Y	Guam	N	None
14		59	63	Mataguly, Juan C	Head	M	Cha	30	M	N	Y	Saipan Island	Y	Farmer
15		59	63	Matagulay, Carmen S	Wife	F	Cha	24	M	N	Y	Guam	Y	Farm laborer
16		59	63	Matagulay, Ana S	Daughter	F	Cha	6	S	N		Guam		None
17		59	63	Matagulay, Flora S	Daughter	F	Cha	5.4	S	N		Guam		None
18		59	63	Matagulay, Maria S	Daughter	F	Cha	.5	S	N		Guam		None
19		60	64	Quidachay, Mariano G	Head	M	Cha	28	M	N	Y	Guam	Y	Laborer
20		60	64	Quidachay, Maria Q	Wife	F	Cha	39	M	N	Y	Guam	Y	None
21		60	64	Quidachay, Margarita Q	Daughter	F	Cha	8	S	Y		Guam		None
22		60	64	Quidachay, Sara Q	Daughter	F	Cha	5	S	N		Guam		None
23		60	64	Quidachay, Rosa Q	Daughter	F	Cha	3.7	S	N		Guam		None
24		61	65	Cruz, Mariano C	Head	M	Cha	42	M	N	N	Guam	N	Farmer
25		61	65	Cruz, Maria I	Wife	F	Cha	35	M	N	Y	Guam	N	None

DEPARTMENT OF COMMERCE-BUREAU OF THE CENSUS
WASHINGTON

FIFTEENTH CENSUS OF THE UNITED STATES: 1930-POPULATION

THE ISLAND OF GUAM

Sheet No. 7B

234B

District **Municipality of Agat**

Name of Place **Agat Town** [Proper name and, also, name of class, as city, town, village, barrio, etc]

Enumeration District No. **6**

Enumerated by me on **April 9, 1930** Pedro C Charfauros, Enumerator

	PLACE OF ABODE			NAME	RELATION	PERSONAL DESCRIPTION				EDUCATION		NATIVITY		OCCUPATION
	Street, avenue, road, etc.	Number of dwelling house in order of visitation	Number of family in order of visitation	of each person whose place of abode on April 1, 1930, was in this family. Enter surname, first, then given name and middle initial. If any. Include every person living on April 1, 1930. Omit children born since April 1, 1930.	Relationship of this Person to the head of the family.	Sex	Color or race	Age at last birthday	Single, married, widowed or divorced	Attended school any time since Sept. 1, 1929	Whether able to read and write.	Place of birth of this person.	Whether able to speak English.	
	1	2	3	4	5	6	7	8	9	10	11	12	13	14
26	Pareno Street	61	65	Cruz, Josefa J	Daughter	F	Cha	12	S	Y	Y	Guam	Y	None
27		61	65	Cruz, Miguel J	Son	M	Cha	11	S	Y	Y	Guam	N	None
28		61	65	Cruz, Delores J	Daughter	F	Cha	9	S	Y		Guam		None
29		61	65	Cruz, Maria J	Daughter	F	Cha	4	S	N		Guam		None
30		61	65	Cruz, Ana J	Daughter	F	Cha	.1	S	N		Guam		None
31		62	66	Aguigui, Ana SN	Head	F	Cha	59	Wd	N	Y	Guam	N	None
32		62	66	Aguigui, Josefina SN	Daughter	F	Cha	24	S	N	Y	Guam	Y	Housekeeper
33		62	66	Aguigui, Guadalupe SN	Daughter	F	Cha	20	S	N	Y	Guam	Y	Housekeeper
34		62	66	Aguigui, Manuel SN	Son	M	Cha	17	S	N	Y	Guam	Y	Farmer
35		62	66	Aguigui, Herbert J	Grandson	M	Cha	1.3	S	N		Guam		None
36		63	67	Nededoc, Juan S	Head	M	Cha	53	M	N	N	Guam	N	Farmer
37		63	67	Nededoc, Matea R	Wife	F	Cha	60	M	N	N	Guam	N	None
38		63	67	Nededoc, Dolores R	Daughter	F	Cha	28	S	N	N	Guam	N	Laundress
39		63	67	Nededoc, Roque N	Grandson	M	Cha	11	S	Y	Y	Guam	N	None
40		64	68	San Nicolas, Jose S	Head	M	Cha	34	M	N	Y	Guam	Y	Laborer
41		64	68	San Nicolas, Rosina G	Wife	F	Cha	27	M	N	Y	Guam	Y	None
42		64	68	San Nicolas, Tomas G	Son	M	Cha	5	S	N		Guam		None
43		64	68	San Nicolas, Maria G	Daughter	F	Cha	4	S	N		Guam		None
44		64	68	San Nicolas, Juan G	Son	M	Cha	3.5	S	N		Guam		None
45		64	68	San Nicolas, Cristina G	Daughter	F	Cha	.5	S	N		Guam		None
46		65	69	Torres, Juan P	Head	M	Cha	53	M	N	Y	Guam	N	Farmer
47		65	69	Torres, Ignasia P	Wife	F	Cha	50	M	N	Y	Guam	N	None
48		65	69	Torres, Jesus P	Son	M	Cha	25	S	N	Y	Guam	Y	Cook
49		65	69	Torres, Maria P	Daughter	F	Cha	15	S	Y	Y	Guam	Y	None
50		65	69	Torres, Antonio P	Son	M	Cha	11	S	Y	N	Guam	N	None

(CHAMORRO ROOTS GENEALOGY PROJECT™ TRANSCRIPTION)
(BERNARD T. PUNZALAN / HTTP://WWW.CHAMORROROOTS.COM)

DEPARTMENT OF COMMERCE-BUREAU OF THE CENSUS
WASHINGTON

FIFTEENTH CENSUS OF THE UNITED STATES: 1930-POPULATION

THE ISLAND OF GUAM

Sheet No. 8A

District **Municipality of Agat**
Name of Place **Agat Town**
[Proper name and, also, name of class, as city, town, village, barrio, etc]

Enumeration District No. **6**
Enumerated by me on **April 9, 1930** Pedro C Charfauros
Enumerator

	PLACE OF ABODE: Street, avenue, road, etc.	Number of dwelling house is order of visitation	Number of family in order of visitation	NAME of each person whose place of abode on April 1, 1930, was in this family. Enter surname, first, then given name and middle initial. If any. Include every person living on April 1, 1930. Omit children born since April 1, 1930.	RELATION Relationship of this Person to the head of the family.	PERSONAL DESCRIPTION: Sex	Color or race	Age at last birthday	Single, married, widowed or divorced	EDUCATION: Attended school any time since Sept. 1, 1929	Whether able to read and write.	NATIVITY Place of birth of this person.	Whether able to speak English.	OCCUPATION
	1	2	3	4	5	6	7	8	9	10	11	12	13	14
1	Pareno Street	65	59	Torres, Tomas P	Son	M	Cha	5	S	N		Guam		None
2		66	70	Chaco, Mariano Q	Head	M	Cha	52	Wd	N	N	Guam	N	Farmer
3		66	70	Chaco, Margarita L	Daughter	F	Cha	20	S	N	Y	Guam	Y	None
4		66	70	Chaco, Ignasio L	Son	M	Cha	27	M	N	Y	Guam	Y	Farm laborer
5		66	70	Chaco, Mercedes C	Daughter	F	Cha	32	M	N	Y	Guam	Y	Laundress
6		67	71	Tydingco, Antonia A	Head	F	Cha	52	Wd	N	Y	Guam	N	None
7		67	71	Herrera, Fransisco S	Nephew	M	Cha	26	M	N	Y	Guam	Y	Farmer
8		67	71	Herrera, Felicidad B	Niece in-law	F	Cha	21	M	N	Y	Guam	N	None
9		67	71	Herrera, Carmen B	Grand niece	F	Cha	1	S	N		Guam		None
10		67	71	Herrera, Jose S	Nephew	M	Cha	22	S	N	Y	Guam	Y	Farm laborer
11		67	71	Salas, Manuela S	Niece	F	Cha	15	S	N	Y	Guam	Y	None
12		68	72	Babauta, Vicente L	Head	M	Cha	46	M	N	N	Guam	N	Farmer
13		68	72	Babauta, Remedios A	Wife	F	Cha	37	M	N	N	Guam	N	None
14		68	72	Babauta, Maria A	Daughter	F	Cha	14	S	N	Y	Guam	Y	None
15		68	72	Babauta, Jose A	Son	M	Cha	12	S	N	N	Guam	N	None
16		68	72	Babauta, Josefa A	Daughter	F	Cha	2.4	S	N		Guam		None
17		68	72	Babauta, Alberto A	Son	M	Cha	.7	S	N		Guam		None
18		69	75	San Nicolas, Vicente M	Head	M	Cha	57	M	N	N	Guam	N	Farmer
19		69	75	San Nicolas, Antonia C	Wife	F	Cha	54	M	N	N	Guam	N	None
20		69	75	San Nicolas, Joaquin C	Son	M	Cha	29	M	N	Y	Guam	Y	Farm laborer
21		69	75	San Nicolas, Jose C	Son	M	Cha	23	S	N	Y	Guam	Y	Farm laborer
22		69	75	San Nicolas, Felix C	Son	M	Cha	17	S	N	Y	Guam	N	Farm laborer
23		69	75	San Nicolas, Ana C	Daughter	F	Cha	12	S	Y	Y	Guam	Y	None
24		70	74	Cruz, Vicente T	Head	M	Cha	40	M	N	Y	Guam	N	Farmer
25		70	74	Cruz, Maria S	Wife	F	Cha	40	M	N	Y	Guam	N	None

(CHAMORRO ROOTS GENEALOGY PROJECT™ TRANSCRIPTION)
(BERNARD T. PUNZALAN / HTTP://WWW.CHAMORROROOTS.COM)

DEPARTMENT OF COMMERCE-BUREAU OF THE CENSUS
WASHINGTON

FIFTEENTH CENSUS OF THE UNITED STATES: 1930-POPULATION

THE ISLAND OF GUAM

Sheet No. 8B

235B

District **Municipality of Agat**
Name of Place **Agat Town**
[Proper name and, also, name of class, as city, town, village, barrio, etc]

Enumeration District No. 6
Enumerated by me on **April 9, 1930** Pedro C Charfauros
Enumerator

	PLACE OF ABODE			NAME	RELATION	PERSONAL DESCRIPTION				EDUCATION		NATIVITY		OCCUPATION
	Street, avenue, road, etc.	Number of dwelling house is order of visitation	Number of family in order of visitation	of each person whose place of abode on April 1, 1930, was in this family. Enter surname, first, then given name and middle initial. If any. Include every person living on April 1, 1930. Omit children born since April 1, 1930.	Relationship of this Person to the head of the family.	Sex	Color or race	Age at last birthday	Single, married, widowed or divorced	Attended school any time since Sept. 1, 1929	Whether able to read and write.	Place of birth of this person.	Whether able to speak English.	
	1	2	3	4	5	6	7	8	9	10	11	12	13	14
26	Pareno Street	70	74	Cruz, Juan S	Son	M	Cha	17	S	N	Y	Guam	Y	Farm Laborer
27		70	74	Cruz, Ana S	Daughter	F	Cha	15	S	N	Y	Guam	Y	None
28		70	74	Cruz, Delores S	Daughter	F	Cha	8	S	Y		Guam		None
29		71	75	Castro, Jose C	Head	M	Cha	42	M	N	Y	Guam	N	Farmer
30		71	75	Castro, Carmen R	Wife	F	Cha	31	M	N	N	Guam	N	None
31		71	75	Castro, Maria R	Daughter	F	Cha	10	S	Y	N	Guam	N	None
32		71	75	Castro, Santiago R	Son	M	Cha	8	S	Y		Guam		None
33		71	75	Castro, Asuncion R	Daughter	F	Cha	7	S	N		Guam		None
34		71	75	Castro, Jose R	Son	M	Cha	5	S	N		Guam		None
35		71	75	Castro, Theresa R	Daughter	F	Cha	3.7	S	N		Guam		None
36		72	76	Lizama, Carmelo L	Head	M	Cha	40	M	N	Y	Guam	N	Farmer
37		72	76	Lizama, Teafela C	Wife	F	Cha	39	M	N	Y	Guam	N	None
38		72	76	Charfauros, Joaquin L	Half brother	M	Cha	23	S	N	Y	Guam	Y	Farm Laborer
39		72	76	Ignasio, Jose R	Servant	M	Cha	34	S	N	N	Guam	N	Farm Laborer
40		73	77	Reyes, Cisilo B	Head	M	Cha	29	M	N	Y	Guam	N	Farmer
41		73	77	Reyes, Carmen A	Wife	F	Cha	30	M	N	Y	Guam	N	None
42		73	77	Reyes, Tomas A	Son	M	Cha	9	S	Y		Guam		None
43		73	77	Reyes, Jesus A	Son	M	Cha	5	S	N		Guam		None
44		73	77	Reyes, May A	Daughter	F	Cha	2.3	S	N		Guam		None
45		73	77	Reyes, Rosalia A	Daughter	F	Cha	.7	S	N		Guam		None
46		74	78	Reyes, Jose SN	Head	M	Cha	33	M	N	Y	Guam	N	Farmer
47		74	78	Reyes, Magdalena C	Wife	F	Cha	23	M	N	Y	Guam	Y	None
48		75	79	San Nicolas, Vicente F	Head	M	Cha	60	M	N	N	Guam	N	None
49		75	79	San Nicolas, Concepcion M	Wife	F	Cha	53	M	N	N	Guam	N	Laundress
50		75	79	Taianao, Guadalupe M	Sister in-law	F	Cha	52	Wd	N	N	Guam	N	Laundress

(CHAMORRO ROOTS GENEALOGY PROJECT™ TRANSCRIPTION)
(BERNARD T. PUNZALAN / HTTP://WWW.CHAMORROROOTS.COM)

DEPARTMENT OF COMMERCE-BUREAU OF THE CENSUS
WASHINGTON

FIFTEENTH CENSUS OF THE UNITED STATES: 1930-POPULATION

THE ISLAND OF GUAM

Sheet No. 9A

District **Municipality of Agat**
Name of Place **Agat Town** [Proper name and, also, name of class, as city, town, village, barrio, etc]

Enumeration District No. **6**
Enumerated by me on **April 10, 1930** Pedro C Charfauros, Enumerator

	Street, avenue, road, etc. (1)	Number of dwelling house in order of visitation (2)	Number of family in order of visitation (3)	NAME of each person whose place of abode on April 1, 1930, was in this family. Enter surname, first, then given name and middle initial. If any. Include every person living on April 1, 1930. Omit children born since April 1, 1930. (4)	RELATION Relationship of this Person to the head of the family. (5)	Sex (6)	Color or race (7)	Age at last birthday (8)	Single, married, widowed or divorced (9)	Attended school any time since Sept. 1, 1929 (10)	Whether able to read and write. (11)	NATIVITY Place of birth of this person. (12)	Whether able to speak English. (13)	OCCUPATION (14)
1	Pareno Street	75	79	Taianao, Vicente M	Nephew	M	Cha	16	S	N	Y	Guam	Y	Farm laborer
2		75	79	Taianao, Joaquin M	Nephew	M	Cha	10	S	Y	Y	Guam	Y	None
3		76	80	Cruz, Bartola J	Head	F	Cha	60	S	N	N	Guam	N	None
4		77	81	Cruz, Francisco T	Head	M	Cha	37	M	N	N	Guam	N	Farmer
5		77	81	Cruz, Carmen SN	Wife	F	Cha	47	M	N	Y	Guam	N	None
6		77	81	Cruz, Carmen SN	Daughter	F	Cha	12	S	Y	Y	Guam	Y	None
7		77	81	Cruz, Felix SN	Son	M	Cha	5	S	N		Guam		None
8		78	82	Rivera, Felix D	Head	M	Cha	51	M	N	Y	Guam	N	Farmer
9		78	82	Rivera, Soledad S	Wife	F	Cha	51	M	N	Y	Guam	N	None
10		78	82	Rivera, Vicente S	Son	M	Cha	21	S	N	Y	Guam	Y	Cook
11		78	82	Rivera, Natividad S	Daughter	F	Cha	18	S	N	Y	Guam	Y	Laundress
12		78	82	Rivera, Jose S	Son	M	Cha	17	S	Y	Y	Guam	Y	None
13		78	82	Rivera, Adela S	Daughter	F	Cha	15	S	Y	Y	Guam	Y	None
14		78	82	Rivera, Ana S	Daughter	F	Cha	12	S	Y	Y	Guam	Y	None
15		79	83	Nededoc, Pedro P	Head	M	Cha	30	M	N	Y	Guam	Y	Laborer
16		79	83	Nededoc, Cristina S	Wife	F	Cha	23	M	N	Y	Guam	Y	None
17		79	83	Nededoc, Jose S	Son	M	Cha	1	S	N		Guam		None
18		80	84	Lizama, Joaquin A	Head	M	Cha	42	M	N	Y	Guam	N	Farmer
19		80	84	Lizama, Concepcion S	Wife	F	Cha	44	M	N	Y	Guam	N	None
20		80	84	Sablan, Nicolas S	Stepson	M	Cha	26	S	N	Y	Guam	Y	Cook
21		81	85	Chargualaf, Genoveba C	Head	F	Cha	62	Wd	N	N	Guam	N	None
22		81	85	Chargualaf, Juan C	Son	M	Cha	25	S	N	Y	Guam	Y	Cook
23		81	85	Chargualaf, Maria C	Daughter	F	Cha	17	S	N	Y	Guam	Y	Laundress
24		81	85	Chargualaf, Josefina C	Grand daughter	F	Cha	2.5	S	N		Guam		None
25		82	86	Lizama, Pedro L	Head	M	Cha	35	M	N	Y	Guam	Y	Farmer

DEPARTMENT OF COMMERCE-BUREAU OF THE CENSUS
WASHINGTON

FIFTEENTH CENSUS OF THE UNITED STATES: 1930-POPULATION

THE ISLAND OF GUAM

Sheet No. 9B

236B

District **Municipality of Agat**
Name of Place **Agat Town**
[Proper name and, also, name of class, as city, town, village, barrio, etc]

Enumeration District No. 6
Enumerated by me on **April 10, 1930** Pedro C Charfauros
Enumerator

	PLACE OF ABODE			NAME	RELATION	PERSONAL DESCRIPTION				EDUCATION		NATIVITY		OCCUPATION
	Street, avenue, road, etc.	Number of dwelling house is order of visitation	Number of family in order of visitation	of each person whose place of abode on April 1, 1930, was in this family. Enter surname, first, then given name and middle initial. If any. Include every person living on April 1, 1930. Omit children born since April 1, 1930.	Relationship of this Person to the head of the family.	Sex	Color or race	Age at last birthday	Single, married, widowed or divorced	Attended school any time since Sept. 1, 1929	Whether able to read and write.	Place of birth of this person.	Whether able to speak English.	
	1	2	3	4	5	6	7	8	9	10	11	12	13	14
26	Pareno Street	82	86	Lizama, Maria T	Wife	F	Cha	30	M	N	Y	Guam	N	None
27		82	86	Lizama, Gregorio T	Son	M	Cha	9	S	Y		Guam		None
28		82	86	Lizama, Jose T	Son	M	Cha	8	S	N		Guam		None
29		82	86	Lizama, Caridad T	Daughter	F	Cha	5	S	N		Guam		None
30		82	86	Lizama, Vicente T	Son	M	Cha	1.1	S	N		Guam		None
31		83	87	Borja, Antonio M	Head	M	Cha	53	M	N	Y	Guam	N	Farmer
32		83	87	Borja, Maria A	Wife	F	Cha	53	M	N	N	Guam	N	None
33		83	87	Borja, Jose A	Son	M	Cha	25	S	N	Y	Guam	Y	Farm laborer
34		83	87	Borja, Rosa A	Daughter	F	Cha	23	S	N	Y	Guam	Y	Farm laborer
35		83	87	Borja, Martina A	Daughter	F	Cha	20	S	N	Y	Guam	Y	Laundress
36		83	87	Borja, Asuncion A	Daughter	F	Cha	14	S	Y	Y	Guam	Y	None
37		83	87	Borja, Antonio A	Son	M	Cha	12	S	Y	Y	Guam	N	None
38		83	87	Borja, Mariano A	Son	M	Cha	9	S	Y		Guam		None
39		83	87	Borja, Jesus A	Grandson	M	Cha	.4	S	N		Guam		None
40		84	88	Mendiola, Juan Q	Head	M	Cha	50	M	N	N	Guam	N	Farmer
41		84	88	Mendiola, Felipa C	Wife	F	Cha	42	M	N	N	Guam	N	Laundress
42		84	88	Charfauros, Jesus A	Nephew	M	Cha	18	S	N	Y	Guam	Y	Cook
43		85	89	Quintanilla, Benabe N	Head	M	Cha	67	M	N	N	Guam	N	None
44		85	89	Quintanilla, Maria L	Wife	F	Cha	55	M	N	N	Guam	N	None
45		85	89	Quintanilla, Juan L	Son	M	Cha	37	M	N	Y	Guam	Y	Farm laborer
46		85	89	Quintanilla, Andres L	Son	M	Cha	22	S	N	Y	Guam	Y	Farmer
47		85	89	Chargualaf, Juan L	Nephew	M	Cha	18	S	N	Y	Guam	Y	Farm laborer
48		86	90	Guerrero, Carmelo G	Head	M	Cha	63	M	N	N	Guam	N	None
49		86	90	Guerrero, Maria P	Wife	F	Cha	63	M	N	N	Guam	N	None
50		86	90	Guerrero, Jesus P	Son	M	Cha	17	S	N	Y	Guam	Y	Farm laborer

DEPARTMENT OF COMMERCE-BUREAU OF THE CENSUS
WASHINGTON

FIFTEENTH CENSUS OF THE UNITED STATES: 1930-POPULATION

THE ISLAND OF GUAM

Sheet No. 10A

District **Municipality of Agat**
Name of Place **Agat Town**
[Proper name and, also, name of class, as city, town, village, barrio, etc]

Enumeration District No. **6**
Enumerated by me on **April 11, 1930** Pedro C Charfauros, Enumerator

	PLACE OF ABODE			NAME	RELATION	PERSONAL DESCRIPTION				EDUCATION		NATIVITY		OCCUPATION
	Street, avenue, road, etc.	Number of dwelling house is order of visitation	Number of family in order of visitation	of each person whose place of abode on April 1, 1930, was in this family. Enter surname, first, then given name and middle initial. If any. Include every person living on April 1, 1930. Omit children born since April 1, 1930.	Relationship of this Person to the head of the family.	Sex	Color or race	Age at last birthday	Single, married, widowed or divorced	Attended school any time since Sept. 1, 1929	Whether able to read and write.	Place of birth of this person.	Whether able to speak English.	
	1	2	3	4	5	6	7	8	9	10	11	12	13	14
1	Pareno Street	87	91	Herrera, Carmen T	Head	F	Cha	34	M	N	Y	Guam	Y	None
2		87	91	Herrera, Guadalupe T	Daughter	F	Cha	8	S	Y		Guam		None
3		87	91	Herrera, Maria T	Daughter	F	Cha	7	S	N		Guam		None
4		87	91	Herrera, Vicente T	Son	M	Cha	4	S	N		Guam		None
5		87	91	Herrera, Jose T	Son	M	Cha	2	S	N		Guam		None
6		88	92	Cruz, Jose C	Head	M	Cha	25	M	N	Y	Guam	Y	Farmer
7		88	92	Cruz, Enriqueta T	Wife	F	Cha	25	M	N	Y	Guam	Y	None
8		88	92	Cruz, Gregorio T	Son	M	Cha	8	S	Y		Guam		None
9		88	92	Cruz, Urfia T	Daughter	F	Cha	1.8	S	N		Guam		None
10		88	92	Cruz, Dolores C	Mother	F	Cha	63	Wd	N	N	Guam	N	None
11		89	93	Sablan, Jesus C	Head	M	Cha	32	M	N	Y	Guam	Y	Farmer
12		89	93	Sablan, Maria B	Wife	F	Cha	27	M	N	N	Guam	Y	None
13		89	93	Sablan, Maria B	Daughter	F	Cha	9	S	Y		Guam		None
14		89	93	Sablan, Elena B	Daughter	F	Cha	8	S	Y		Guam		None
15		89	93	Blanco, Rita M	Mother in-law	F	Cha	57	Wd	N	Y	Guam	N	None
16		89	93	Blanco, Francisco M	Brother in-law	M	Cha	17	S	N	Y	Guam	Y	Farm laborer
17		90	94	Mendiola, Vicente O	Head	M	Cha	42	M	N	Y	Guam	Y	Farmer
18		90	94	Mendiola, Barbara S	Wife	F	Cha	37	M	N	N	Guam	N	None
19		90	94	Mendiola, Regina S	Daughter	F	Cha	17	S	N	Y	Guam	Y	Laundress
20		90	94	Mendiola, Tomas S	Son	M	Cha	13	S	Y	Y	Guam	Y	None
21		91	95	Cruz, Francisco B	Head	M	Cha	42	M	N	Y	Guam	Y	Farmer
22		91	95	Cruz, Ana C	Wife	F	Cha	40	M	N	N	Guam	N	None
23		91	95	Cruz, Ramon C	Son	M	Cha	10	S	Y	N	Guam	N	None
24		91	95	Cruz, Ana C	Daughter	F	Cha	7	S	Y		Guam		None
25		91	95	Cruz, Gonzalo C	Son	M	Cha	4.2	S	N		Guam		None

DEPARTMENT OF COMMERCE-BUREAU OF THE CENSUS
WASHINGTON

FIFTEENTH CENSUS OF THE UNITED STATES: 1930-POPULATION

THE ISLAND OF GUAM

Sheet No. 10B

237B

District **Municipality of Agat**
Name of Place **Agat Town** [Proper name and, also, name of class, as city, town, village, barrio, etc]

Enumeration District No. **6**
Enumerated by me on **April 11, 1930** Pedro C Charfauros, Enumerator

	PLACE OF ABODE			NAME	RELATION	PERSONAL DESCRIPTION				EDUCATION		NATIVITY		OCCUPATION
	Street, avenue, road, etc.	Number of dwelling house in order of visitation	Number of family in order of visitation	of each person whose place of abode on April 1, 1930, was in this family. Enter surname, first, then given name and middle initial. If any. Include every person living on April 1, 1930. Omit children born since April 1, 1930.	Relationship of this Person to the head of the family.	Sex	Color or race	Age at last birthday	Single, married, widowed or divorced	Attended school any time since Sept. 1, 1929	Whether able to read and write.	Place of birth of this person.	Whether able to speak English.	
	1	2	3	4	5	6	7	8	9	10	11	12	13	14
26	Pareno Street	91	95	Cruz, Antonio C	Son	M	Cha	2	S	N		Guam		None
27		92	96	Pineda, Manuel C	Head	M	Cha	38	M	N	Y	Guam	Y	Farmer
28		92	96	Pineda, Maxine LG	Wife	F	Cha	37	M	N	N	Guam	N	None
29		92	96	Pineda, Dolores LG	Daughter	F	Cha	14	S	Y	Y	Guam	Y	None
30		92	96	Pineda, Ana LG	Daughter	F	Cha	5.1	S	N		Guam		None
31		92	96	Pineda, Juan LG	Son	M	Cha	2	S	N		Guam		None
32		92	96	Pineda, Jose C	Father	M	Cha	63	M	N	Y	Guam	N	None
33		92	96	Pineda, Dolores C	Mother	F	Cha	63	M	N	N	Guam	N	None
34		93	97	Nededoc, Emilio C	Head	M	Cha	40	M	N	Y	Guam	Y	Farmer
35		93	97	Nededoc, Carmen C	Wife	F	Cha	39	M	N	Y	Guam	N	None
36		93	97	Nededoc, Enrique C	Son	M	Cha	16	S	N	Y	Guam	Y	Cook
37		93	97	Nededoc, Francisco C	Son	M	Cha	15	S	Y	Y	Guam	Y	None
38		93	97	Nededoc, Ana C	Daughter	F	Cha	13	S	Y	Y	Guam	Y	None
39		93	97	Nededoc, Jose C	Son	M	Cha	10	S	Y	Y	Guam	Y	None
40		94	98	Babauta, Francisco L	Head	M	Cha	28	M	N	N	Guam	N	Farm Manager
41		94	98	Babauta, Carmen T	Wife	F	Cha	17	M	N	Y	Guam	Y	None
42		94	98	Babauta, Jesus T	Son	M	Cha	2.3	S	N		Guam		None
43		94	98	Babauta, Brigida T	Daughter	F	Cha	0.3	S	N		Guam		None
44		95	99	Cruz, Luis D	Head	M	Cha	46	M	N	Y	Guam	N	Farmer
45		95	99	Cruz, Simona C	Wife	F	Cha	48	M	N	Y	Guam	N	None
46		95	99	Cruz, Ignasia C	Daughter	F	Cha	24	S	N	Y	Guam	Y	Laundress
47		95	99	Cruz, Jose C	Son	M	Cha	23	S	N	Y	Guam	Y	Cook
48		95	99	Cruz, Carmen C	Daughter	F	Cha	19	S	N	Y	Guam	Y	None
49		95	99	Cruz, Remedios C	Daughter	F	Cha	11	S	Y	N	Guam	N	None
50		95	99	Laguana, Faustino C	Nephew	M	Cha	37	S	N	Y	Guam	Y	Farmer

DEPARTMENT OF COMMERCE-BUREAU OF THE CENSUS
WASHINGTON

FIFTEENTH CENSUS OF THE UNITED STATES: 1930-POPULATION

THE ISLAND OF GUAM

Sheet No. 11A

District **Municipality of Agat**
Name of Place **Agat Town**
[Proper name and, also, name of class, as city, town, village, barrio, etc]

Enumeration District No. 6
Enumerated by me on **April 12, 1930** Pedro C Charfauros, Enumerator

	PLACE OF ABODE			NAME	RELATION	PERSONAL DESCRIPTION				EDUCATION		NATIVITY		OCCUPATION
	Street, avenue, road, etc.	Number of dwelling house in order of visitation	Number of family in order of visitation	of each person whose place of abode on April 1, 1930, was in this family. Enter surname, first, then given name and middle initial. If any. Include every person living on April 1, 1930. Omit children born since April 1, 1930.	Relationship of this Person to the head of the family.	Sex	Color or race	Age at last birthday	Single, married, widowed or divorced	Attended school any time since Sept. 1, 1929	Whether able to read and write.	Place of birth of this person.	Whether able to speak English.	
	1	2	3	4	5	6	7	8	9	10	11	12	13	14
1	Pareno Street	95	99	Charfauros, Juan S	Nephew	M	Cha	21	S	N	Y	Guam	Y	Farm laborer
2		95	99	Charfauros, Manuel S	Nephew	M	Cha	20	S	N	Y	Guam	Y	Farm laborer
3		96	100	Arriola, Jose Q	Head	M	Cha	21	M	N	N	Guam	N	Laborer
4		96	100	Arriola, Isabel S	Wife	F	Cha	21	M	N	Y	Guam	Y	None
5		96	100	Arriola, Soledad S	Half sister	F	Cha	11	S	Y	N	Guam	N	None
6		96	100	Salas, Soledad S	Step daughter	F	Cha	2	S	N		Guam		None
7	Legaspi Street	97	101	Tydingco, Rosa S	Head	F	Cha	50	M	N	Y	Guam	N	None
8		97	101	Rivera, Asuncion S	Daughter	F	Cha	23	S	N	Y	Guam	Y	House keeper
9		97	101	Rivera, Maria S	Daughter	F	Cha	22	S	N	Y	Guam	Y	Teacher
10		97	101	Rivera, Francisco S	Son	M	Cha	20	S	N	Y	Guam	Y	Farmer
11		97	101	Rivera, Jose S	Son	M	Cha	18	S	Y	Y	Guam	Y	None
12		97	101	Rivera, Antonio S	Son	M	Cha	16	S	Y	Y	Guam	Y	None
13		97	101	Rivera, Remedios S	Daughter	F	Cha	15	S	Y	Y	Guam	Y	None
14		97	101	Rivera, Tomas S	Son	M	Cha	13	S	Y	Y	Guam	Y	None
15		98	102	San Nicolas, Antonio B	Head	M	Cha	41	M	N	N	Guam	N	Farmer
16		98	102	San Nicolas, Maria C	Wife	F	Cha	29	M	N	Y	Guam	N	None
17		98	102	San Nicolas, Barceliza C	Daughter	F	Cha	6	S	N		Guam		None
18		98	102	San Nicolas, Lunisia C	Daughter	F	Cha	4.2	S	N		Guam		None
19		98	102	San Nicolas, Francisco C	Son	M	Cha	0.5	S	N		Guam		None
20		99	103	Sablan, Francisco C	Head	M	Cha	36	M	N	N	Guam	N	Farmer
21		99	103	Sablan, Remedios S	Wife	F	Cha	25	M	N	Y	Guam	N	None
22		99	103	Sablan, Manuela S	Daughter	F	Cha	0.9	S	N		Guam		None
23		99	103	Salubnamnam, Juan T	Uncle	M	Cha	62	Wd	N	N	Guam	N	None
24		99	103	Salubnamnam, Faustina S	Aunt	F	Cha	63	S	N	N	Guam	N	None
25		100	104	Salas, Romeo C	Head	M	Cha	42	M	N	Y	Guam	N	Farmer

DEPARTMENT OF COMMERCE-BUREAU OF THE CENSUS
WASHINGTON

FIFTEENTH CENSUS OF THE UNITED STATES: 1930-POPULATION

THE ISLAND OF GUAM

Sheet No. 11B

238B

District Municipality of Agat
Name of Place Agat Town
[Proper name and, also, name of class, as city, town, village, barrio, etc]

Enumeration District No. 6
Enumerated by me on April 12, 1930 Pedro C Charfauros, Enumerator

	PLACE OF ABODE			NAME	RELATION	PERSONAL DESCRIPTION				EDUCATION		NATIVITY		OCCUPATION
	Street, avenue, road, etc.	Number of dwelling house is order of visitation	Number of family in order of visitation	of each person whose place of abode on April 1, 1930, was in this family. Enter surname, first, then given name and middle initial. If any. Include every person living on April 1, 1930. Omit children born since April 1, 1930.	Relationship of this Person to the head of the family.	Sex	Color or race	Age at last birthday	Single, married, widowed or divorced	Attended school any time since Sept. 1, 1929	Whether able to read and write.	Place of birth of this person.	Whether able to speak English.	
	1	2	3	4	5	6	7	8	9	10	11	12	13	14
26	Legaspi Street	100	104	Salas, Lucia M	Wife	F	Cha	39	M	N	Y	Guam	N	None
27		100	104	Salas, Vicente M	Son	M	Cha	18	S	N	Y	Guam	Y	Farm laborer
28		100	104	Salas, Juan M	Son	M	Cha	17	S	Y	Y	Guam	Y	Farm laborer
29		100	104	Salas, Soledad M	Daughter	F	Cha	12	S	Y	N	Guam	N	None
30		100	104	Salas, Jose M	Son	M	Cha	10	S	Y	N	Guam	N	None
31		100	104	Salas, Ana M	Daughter	F	Cha	7	S	Y		Guam		None
32		100	104	Salas, Antonio M	Son	M	Cha	4.1	S	N		Guam	Y	None
33		100	104	Salas, Jesus M	Son	M	Cha	3	S	N		Guam		None
34		101	105	Muna, Carmen P	Head	F	Cha	58	Wd	N	Y	Guam	N	None
35		101	105	Muna, Ana P	Daughter	F	Cha	24	S	N	Y	Guam	N	Laundress
36		102	106	Terlaji, Joaquin B	Head	M	Cha	25	M	N	Y	Guam	N	Laborer
37		102	106	Terlaji, Concepcion B	Wife	F	Cha	25	M	N	Y	Guam	N	None
38		102	106	Terlaji, Antonio B	Son	M	Cha	9	S	Y		Guam		None
39		103	107	Nededoc, Ana M	Head	F	Cha	25	M	N	Y	Guam	Y	None
40		103	107	Nededoc, Agnes M	Daughter	F	Cha	7	S	Y		Guam		None
41		103	107	Nededoc, Juan M	Son	M	Cha	5	S	N		Guam		None
42		104	108	Babauta, Vicente B	Head	M	Cha	56	M	N	Y	Guam	N	Farmer
43		104	108	Babauta, Nieves M	Wife	F	Cha	49	M	N	Y	Guam	N	None
44		104	108	Babauta, Maria M	Daughter	F	Cha	17	S	N	Y	Guam	Y	House keeper
45		104	108	Babauta, Amparo M	Daughter	F	Cha	14	S	Y	Y	Guam	Y	None
46		105	109	Nededoc, Jose N	Head	M	Cha	43	M	N	Y	Guam	Y	Farmer
47		105	109	Nededoc, Theadora C	Wife	F	Cha	33	M	N	Y	Guam	N	None
48		106	110	Terlaji, Rebustiano B	Head	M	Cha	39	M	N	Y	Guam	N	Retail Merchant
49		106	110	Terlaji, Maria C	Wife	F	Cha	39	M	N	Y	Guam	N	None
50		106	110	Terlaji, Rosalia B	Niece	F	Cha	11	S	Y	Y	Guam	Y	None

DEPARTMENT OF COMMERCE-BUREAU OF THE CENSUS
WASHINGTON

FIFTEENTH CENSUS OF THE UNITED STATES: 1930-POPULATION

THE ISLAND OF GUAM

Sheet No. 12A

District **Municipality of Agat**
Name of Place **Agat Town** [Proper name and, also, name of class, as city, town, village, barrio, etc]

Enumeration District No. **6**
Enumerated by me on **April 14, 1930** Pedro C Charfauros, Enumerator

	Street, avenue, road, etc.	Number of dwelling house in order of visitation	Number of family in order of visitation	NAME of each person whose place of abode on April 1, 1930, was in this family. Enter surname, first, then given name and middle initial. If any. Include every person living on April 1, 1930. Omit children born since April 1, 1930.	RELATION Relationship of this Person to the head of the family.	Sex	Color or race	Age at last birthday	Single, married, widowed or divorced	Attended school any time since Sept. 1, 1929	Whether able to read and write.	NATIVITY Place of birth of this person.	Whether able to speak English.	OCCUPATION
	PLACE OF ABODE					PERSONAL DESCRIPTION				EDUCATION				
	1	2	3	4	5	6	7	8	9	10	11	12	13	14
1	Legaspi Street	107	111	Nededoc, Joaquin C	Head	M	Cha	23	M	N	Y	Guam	Y	Laborer
2		107	111	Nededoc, Maria C	Wife	F	Cha	21	M	N	Y	Guam	Y	None
3		107	111	Nededoc, Tomas C	Son	M	Cha	0.4	S	N		Guam		None
4		108	112	Nededoc, Andres C	Head	M	Cha	71	M	N	N	Guam	N	None
5		108	112	Nededoc, Nicolasa C	Wife	F	Cha	65	M	N	N	Guam	N	None
6		108	112	Nededoc, Candelaria C	Daughter	F	Cha	28	S	N	Y	Guam	N	House keeper
7		108	112	Nededoc, Vicente S	Son	M	Cha	25	S	N	Y	Guam	Y	Farmer
8		109	113	Rivera, Joaquin D	Head	M	Cha	53	M	N	Y	Guam	N	Farmer
9		109	113	Rivera, Delores LG	Wife	F	Cha	47	M	N	Y	Guam	N	None
10		109	113	Rivera, Jesus LG	Son	M	Cha	16	S	Y	Y	Guam	Y	None
11		109	113	Rivera, Fransisca LG	Daughter	F	Cha	6	S	N		Guam		None
12		110	114	Salas, Carmen A	Head	F	Cha	30	M	N	N	Guam	N	None
13		110	114	Salas, Ana A	Daughter	F	Cha	11	S	Y	N	Guam	N	None
14		110	114	Salas, Juan A	Son	M	Cha	4.5	S	N		Guam		None
15		110	114	Salas, Jose S	Uncle	M	Cha	47	S	N	N	Guam	N	Farmer
16		111	115	Charfauros, Mariano A	Head	M	Cha	51	M	N	N	Guam	N	Farmer
17		111	115	Charfauros, Maria SN	Wife	F	Cha	46	M	N	N	Guam	N	None
18		111	115	Charfauros, Fransisco SN	Son	M	Cha	16	S	N	Y	Guam	Y	C.P.C. employee
19		111	115	Charfauros, Maria SN	Daughter	F	Cha	15	S	N	Y	Guam	Y	None
20		111	115	Charfauros, Juana SN	Daughter	F	Cha	13	S	Y	Y	Guam	Y	None
21		111	115	Charfauros, Carmen SN	Daughter	F	Cha	4.1	S	N		Guam		None
22		112	116	Charfauros, Tomas C	Head	M	Cha	38	M	N	Y	Guam	Y	Commissioner
23		112	116	Charfauros, Rosa B	Wife	F	Cha	34	M	N	Y	Guam	N	None
24		112	116	Charfauros, James B	Son	M	Cha	11	S	Y	Y	Guam	Y	None
25		112	116	Charfauros, Juan B	Son	M	Cha	9	S	Y		Guam		None

(CHAMORRO ROOTS GENEALOGY PROJECT™ TRANSCRIPTION)
(BERNARD T. PUNZALAN / HTTP://WWW.CHAMORROROOTS.COM)

DEPARTMENT OF COMMERCE-BUREAU OF THE CENSUS
WASHINGTON

FIFTEENTH CENSUS OF THE UNITED STATES: 1930-POPULATION

THE ISLAND OF GUAM

Sheet No. 12B

239B

District Municipality of Agat
Name of Place Agat Town
[Proper name and, also, name of class, as city, town, village, barrio, etc]

Enumeration District No. 6
Enumerated by me on April 14, 1930 Pedro C Charfauros
Enumerator

	PLACE OF ABODE			NAME	RELATION	PERSONAL DESCRIPTION				EDUCATION		NATIVITY		OCCUPATION
	Street, avenue, road, etc.	Number of dwelling house is order of visitation	Number of family in order of visitation	of each person whose place of abode on April 1, 1930, was in this family. Enter surname, first, then given name and middle initial. If any. Include every person living on April 1, 1930. Omit children born since April 1, 1930.	Relationship of this Person to the head of the family.	Sex	Color or race	Age at last birthday	Single, married, widowed or divorced	Attended school any time since Sept. 1, 1929	Whether able to read and write.	Place of birth of this person.	Whether able to speak English.	
	1	2	3	4	5	6	7	8	9	10	11	12	13	14
26	Legaspi Street	112	116	Charfauros, Angelina D	Daughter	F	Cha	5	S	N		Guam		None
27		112	116	Charfauros, Vicente B	Son	M	Cha	3.2	S	N		Guam		None
28		112	116	Charfauros, Antonio B	Son	M	Cha	2.1	S	N		Guam		None
29		113	117	Guivara, Jesus Q	Head	M	Cha	24	M	N	N	Guam	N	Farmer
30		113	117	Guivara, Antonia A	Wife	F	Cha	21	M	N	N	Guam	N	None
31		113	117	Guivara, Vicente A	Son	M	Cha	2.4	S	N		Guam		None
32		114	118	Quitano, Redibiso S	Head	M	Cha	44	M	N	N	Guam	N	Farmer
33		114	118	Quitano, Rita LG	Wife	F	Cha	53	M	N	Y	Guam	N	None
34		114	118	Quitano, Barlola LG	Daughter	F	Cha	14	S	Y	Y	Guam	Y	None
35		114	118	Quitano, Vicente LG	Son	M	Cha	12	S	Y	N	Guam	N	None
36		114	118	Quitano, Maria LG	Daughter	F	Cha	10	S	Y	N	Guam	N	None
37		114	118	Quitano, Guillelmo LG	Son	M	Cha	9	S	Y		Guam		None
38		114	118	Quitano, Hil LG	Son	M	Cha	4.7	S	N		Guam		None
39		114	118	Quitano, Ana LG	Daughter	F	Cha	3.1	S	N		Guam		None
40		115	119	Saluboramnam, Vicente T	Head	M	Cha	53	M	N	N	Guam	N	Farmer
41		115	119	Saluboramnam, Maria B	Wife	F	Cha	42	M	N	N	Guam	N	None
42		115	119	Saluboramnam, Ana B	Daughter	F	Cha	20	S	N	Y	Guam	Y	Laundress
43		115	119	Saluboramnam, Consolasion B	Daughter	F	Cha	18	S	N	Y	Guam	Y	Laundress
44		116	120	Chaco, Antonio C	Head	M	Cha	30	M	N	Y	Guam	N	Farmer
45		116	120	Chaco, Concepcion A	Wife	F	Cha	27	M	N	Y	Guam	N	None
46		116	120	Chaco, Manuel A	Son	M	Cha	8	S	Y		Guam		None
47		116	120	Chaco, Joaquin A	Son	M	Cha	5	S	N		Guam		None
48		116	120	Chaco, Guadalupe A	Daughter	F	Cha	3.5	S	N		Guam		None
49		116	120	Chaco, Soledad A	Daughter	F	Cha	0.8	S	N		Guam		None
50		111	121	Salas, Juan S	Head	M	Cha	57	M	N	N	Guam	N	Farmer

(CHAMORRO ROOTS GENEALOGY PROJECT™ TRANSCRIPTION)
(BERNARD T. PUNZALAN / HTTP://WWW.CHAMORROROOTS.COM)

DEPARTMENT OF COMMERCE-BUREAU OF THE CENSUS
WASHINGTON

FIFTEENTH CENSUS OF THE UNITED STATES: 1930-POPULATION

THE ISLAND OF GUAM

Sheet No. 13A

240

District **Municipality of Agat**
Name of Place **Agat Town**
[Proper name and, also, name of class, as city, town, village, barrio, etc]

Enumeration District No. 6
Enumerated by me on **April 15, 1930** Pedro C Charfauros
Enumerator

	PLACE OF ABODE			NAME	RELATION	PERSONAL DESCRIPTION				EDUCATION		NATIVITY		OCCUPATION
	Street, avenue, road, etc.	Number of dwelling house is order of visitation	Number of family in order of visitation	of each person whose place of abode on April 1, 1930, was in this family. Enter surname, first, then given name and middle initial. If any. Include every person living on April 1, 1930. Omit children born since April 1, 1930.	Relationship of this Person to the head of the family.	Sex	Color or race	Age at last birthday	Single, married, widowed or divorced	Attended school any time since Sept. 1, 1929	Whether able to read and write.	Place of birth of this person.	Whether able to speak English.	
	1	2	3	4	5	6	7	8	9	10	11	12	13	14
1	Legaspi Street	117	121	Salas, Rosalia S	Wife	F	Cha	58	M	N	N	Guam	N	None
2		117	121	Salas, Maria S	Daughter	F	Cha	25	S	N	Y	Guam	Y	Laundress
3		117	121	Salas, Fransisco S	Grandson	M	Cha	1.1	S	N		Guam		None
4		118	122	Castro, Ana S	Head	F	Cha	33	M	N	N	Guam	N	None
5		118	122	Castro, Margarita S	Daughter	F	Cha	10	S	Y	N	Guam	N	None
6		118	122	Castro, Veronica S	Daughter	F	Cha	5	S	N		Guam		None
7		118	122	Castro, Vicente S	Son	M	Cha	3.4	S	N		Guam		None
8		119	122	Quenga, Ana C	Head	F	Cha	23	M	N	Y	Guam	Y	Laundress
9		119	122	Quenga, Juan C	Son	M	Cha	3.6	S	N		Guam		None
10					Here ends the enumeration of Agat Town.									
11					[Sheet 240B/13B was intentional left blank by the enumerator.]									
12														
13														
14														
15														
16														
17														
18														
19														
20														
21														
22														
23														
24														
25														

DEPARTMENT OF COMMERCE-BUREAU OF THE CENSUS
WASHINGTON

FIFTEENTH CENSUS OF THE UNITED STATES: 1930-POPULATION

THE ISLAND OF GUAM

Sheet No. 14A

District **Municipality of Agat**
Name of Place **Salinas Barrio** [Proper name and, also, name of class, as city, town, village, barrio, etc]

Enumeration District No. **6**
Enumerated by me on **April 15, 1930** Pedro C Charfauros, Enumerator

	PLACE OF ABODE			NAME	RELATION	PERSONAL DESCRIPTION				EDUCATION		NATIVITY		OCCUPATION
	Street, avenue, road, etc.	Number of dwelling house in order of visitation	Number of family in order of visitation	of each person whose place of abode on April 1, 1930, was in this family. Enter surname, first, then given name and middle initial. If any. Include every person living on April 1, 1930. Omit children born since April 1, 1930.	Relationship of this Person to the head of the family.	Sex	Color or race	Age at last birthday	Single, married, widowed or divorced	Attended school any time since Sept. 1, 1929	Whether able to read and write.	Place of birth of this person.	Whether able to speak English.	
	1	2	3	4	5	6	7	8	9	10	11	12	13	14
1		120	124	Muna, Gregorio D	Head	M	Cha	58	M	N	N	Guam	N	Farmer
2		120	124	Muna, Josefa S	Wife	F	Cha	42	M	N	N	Guam	N	None
3		120	124	Muna, Pedro S	Son	M	Cha	21	S	N	N	Guam	Y	Farm laborer
4		120	124	Muna, Maria S	Daughter	F	Cha	20	S	N	Y	Guam	Y	Laundress
5		120	124	Muna, Asuncion S	Daughter	F	Cha	19	S	N	Y	Guam	Y	Laundress
6		120	124	Muna, Isabel S	Daughter	F	Cha	17	S	N	Y	Guam	Y	Laundress
7		120	124	Muna, Cesera S	Daughter	F	Cha	12	S	Y	Y	Guam	Y	None
8		120	124	Muna, Cristina S	Daughter	F	Cha	8	S	Y		Guam		None
9		120	124	Muna, Florensia S	Daughter	F	Cha	6	S	N		Guam		None
10		120	124	Pinaula, Jose P	Brother in law	M	Cha	20	S	N	N	Guam	N	Farm laborer
11		121	125	Quidachay, Jose I	Head	M	Cha	40	M	N	N	Guam	N	Farmer
12		121	125	Quidachay, Teresa B	Wife	F	Cha	50	M	N	N	Guam	N	None
13		121	125	Quidachay, Juan B	Son	M	Cha	21	S	N	Y	Guam	Y	Cook
14		121	125	Quidachay, Caridad B	Daughter	F	Cha	19	S	N	Y	Guam	Y	Chambermaid
15		121	125	Quidachay, Maria B	Daughter	F	Cha	14	S	Y	Y	Guam	Y	None
16		121	125	Quidachay, Ana B	Daughter	F	Cha	11	S	Y	N	Guam	N	None
17		121	125	Quidachay, Florensia B	Daughter	F	Cha	5	S	N		Guam		None
18		122	126	Terlaji, Jose B	Head	M	Cha	25	M	N	Y	Guam	Y	Farmer
19		122	126	Terlaji, Joaquina A	Wife	F	Cha	21	M	N	Y	Guam	Y	None
20		122	126	Terlaji, Baldovino A	Son	M	Cha	3	S	N		Guam		None
21		122	126	Terlaji, Maria A	Daughter	F	Cha	2	S	N		Guam		None
22		123	127	Jesus, Marselo B	Head	M	Cha	38	M	N	Y	Guam	N	Farmer
23		123	127	Jesus, Francisca B	Wife	F	Cha	34	M	N	Y	Guam	N	None
24		123	127	Jesus, Ernestina B	Daughter	F	Cha	12	S	Y	Y	Guam	Y	None
25		123	127	Jesus, Juan B	Son	M	Cha	9	S	Y		Guam		None

DEPARTMENT OF COMMERCE-BUREAU OF THE CENSUS
WASHINGTON

FIFTEENTH CENSUS OF THE UNITED STATES: 1930-POPULATION

THE ISLAND OF GUAM

Sheet No. 14B

241B

District **Municipality of Agat**
Name of Place **Salinas Barrio** [Proper name and, also, name of class, as city, town, village, barrio, etc]

Enumeration District No. **6**
Enumerated by me on **April 15, 1930** Pedro C Charfauros, Enumerator

	PLACE OF ABODE			NAME	RELATION	PERSONAL DESCRIPTION				EDUCATION		NATIVITY		OCCUPATION
	Street, avenue, road, etc.	Number of dwelling house in order of visitation	Number of family in order of visitation	of each person whose place of abode on April 1, 1930, was in this family. Enter surname, first, then given name and middle initial. If any. Include every person living on April 1, 1930. Omit children born since April 1, 1930.	Relationship of this Person to the head of the family.	Sex	Color or race	Age at last birthday	Single, married, widowed or divorced	Attended school any time since Sept. 1, 1929	Whether able to read and write.	Place of birth of this person.	Whether able to speak English.	
	1	2	3	4	5	6	7	8	9	10	11	12	13	14
26		123	127	Jesus, Vicente B	Son	M	Cha	7	S	Y		Guam		None
27		123	127	Jesus, Ana B	Daughter	F	Cha	5	S	N		Guam		None
28		123	127	Jesus, Joaquin B	Son	M	Cha	1.7	S	N		Guam		None
29		124	128	Jesus, Vicente B	Head	M	Cha	34	M	N	N	Guam	N	Farmer
30		124	128	Jesus, Carmen B	Wife	F	Cha	29	M	N	Y	Guam	N	None
31		124	128	Jesus, Francisco B	Son	M	Cha	9	S	Y		Guam		None
32		124	128	Jesus, Nicolasa B	Daughter	F	Cha	7	S	N		Guam		None
33		124	128	Jesus, Juana B	Daughter	F	Cha	4.7	S	N		Guam		None
34		124	128	Jesus, Jose B	Son	M	Cha	2	S	N		Guam		None
35		124	128	Jesus, Lorenzo B	Son	M	Cha	2	S	N		Guam		None
36		125	129	Nededoc, Jesus A	Head	M	Cha	27	M	N	N	Guam	N	Farmer
37		125	129	Nededoc, Carmen T	Wife	F	Cha	33	M	N	N	Guam	N	None
38		125	129	Nededoc, Juana T	Son	M	Cha	7	S	Y		Guam		None
39		125	129	Nededoc, Bastian T	Son	M	Cha	6	S	N		Guam		None
40		125	129	Nededoc, Pedro T	Son	M	Cha	2.7	S	N		Guam		None
41		125	129	Nededoc, Ana T	Daughter	F	Cha	1.7	S	N		Guam		None
42		125	129	Nededoc, Feliza C	Mother	F	Cha	64	Wd	N	N	Guam	N	None
43		126	130	Babauta, Santiago C	Head	M	Cha	39	M	N	Y	Guam	N	Farmer
44		126	130	Babauta, Carmen S	Wife	F	Cha	41	M	N	Y	Guam	N	None
45		126	130	Babauta, Joaquin S	Son	M	Cha	17	S	Y	Y	Guam	Y	None
46		127	131	Acfalle, Gregorio M	Head	M	Cha	22	M	N	Y	Guam	Y	Farmer
47		127	131	Acfalle, Rosalia Q	Wife	F	Cha	22	M	N	Y	Guam	Y	Laundress
48		127	131	Acfalle, Maria M	Mother	F	Cha	46	Wd	N	N	Guam	N	Laundress
49		127	131	Acfalle, Dolores M	Sister	F	Cha	21	S	N	Y	Guam	Y	Laundress
50		127	131	Acfalle, Rosalia M	Sister	F	Cha	15	S	N	Y	Guam	Y	Laundress

DEPARTMENT OF COMMERCE-BUREAU OF THE CENSUS
WASHINGTON

FIFTEENTH CENSUS OF THE UNITED STATES: 1930-POPULATION

THE ISLAND OF GUAM

Sheet No. 15A

District **Municipality of Agat**
Name of Place **Salinas Barrio** [Proper name and, also, name of class, as city, town, village, barrio, etc]

Enumeration District No. **6**
Enumerated by me on **April 16, 1930** Pedro C Charfauros, Enumerator

	PLACE OF ABODE			NAME	RELATION	PERSONAL DESCRIPTION				EDUCATION		NATIVITY		OCCUPATION
	Street, avenue, road, etc.	Number of dwelling house in order of visitation	Number of family in order of visitation	of each person whose place of abode on April 1, 1930, was in this family. Enter surname, first, then given name and middle initial. If any. Include every person living on April 1, 1930. Omit children born since April 1, 1930.	Relationship of this Person to the head of the family.	Sex	Color or race	Age at last birthday	Single, married, widowed or divorced	Attended school any time since Sept. 1, 1929	Whether able to read and write.	Place of birth of this person.	Whether able to speak English.	
	1	2	3	4	5	6	7	8	9	10	11	12	13	14
1		127	131	Acfalle, Rita M	Sister	F	Cha	3.2	S	N		Guam		None
2		128	132	Acfalle, Vicente B	Head	M	Cha	27	M	N	Y	Guam	Y	Laborer
3		128	132	Acfalle, Concepcion C	Wife	F	Cha	29	M	N	Y	Guam	Y	None
4		128	132	Acfalle, Francisca C	Daughter	F	Cha	2.3	S	N		Guam		None
5		128	132	Acfalle, Carmen C	Daughter	F	Cha	1.8	S	N		Guam		None
6		128	132	Acfalle, Jesus C	Son	M	Cha	0.8	S	N		Guam		None
7		128	132	Chargualaf, Jose B	Cousin	M	Cha	26	S	N	Y	Guam	Y	Farm laborer
8		129	133	Acfalle, Joaquin A	Head	M	Cha	29	S	N	Y	Guam	N	Farmer
9		130	134	Cruz, Antonio C	Head	M	Cha	40	M	N	Y	Guam	Y	Farmer
10		130	134	Cruz, Flora C	Wife	F	Cha	33	M	N	Y	Guam	N	None
11		131	135	Guerrero, Jose D	Head	M	Cha	52	M	N	Y	Guam	N	Farmer
12		131	135	Guerrero, Antonia B	Wife	F	Cha	55	M	N	N	Guam	N	None
13		131	135	Muna, Juana B	Sister in law	F	Cha	59	Wd	N	N	Guam	N	None
14		132	136	Babauta, Juan B	Head	M	Cha	30	Wd	N	Y	Guam	N	Farmer
15		132	136	Babauta, Juan C	Son	M	Cha	6	S	N		Guam		None
16		132	136	Babauta, Rosa C	Daughter	F	Cha	4.7	S	N		Guam		None
17		132	136	Babauta, Maria C	Daughter	F	Cha	3	S	N		Guam		None
18		132	136	Babauta, Rita C	Mother	F	Cha	61	Wd	N	N	Guam	N	None
19		133	137	Babauta, Jesus A	Head	M	Cha	23	M	N	Y	Guam	Y	Farmer
20		133	137	Babauta, Ana A	Wife	F	Cha	23	M	N	Y	Guam	Y	Laundress
21		134	138	Aguon, Delores C	Head	F	Cha	30	S	N	Y	Guam	N	Laundress
22		134	138	Aguon, Antonio C	Son	M	Cha	10	S	Y	N	Guam	N	None
23		134	138	Aguon, Francisco C	Son	M	Cha	7	S	Y		Guam		None
24		134	138	Aguon, Benito C	Son	M	Cha	3	S	N		Guam		None
25		134	138	Aguon, Carlos C	Son	M	Cha	0.8	S	N		Guam		None

DEPARTMENT OF COMMERCE-BUREAU OF THE CENSUS
WASHINGTON

FIFTEENTH CENSUS OF THE UNITED STATES: 1930-POPULATION

THE ISLAND OF GUAM

Sheet No. 15B

242B

District **Municipality of Agat**
Name of Place **Salinas Barrio**
[Proper name and, also, name of class, as city, town, village, barrio, etc]

Enumeration District No. **6**
Enumerated by me on **April 16, 1930** Pedro C Charfauros
Enumerator

	PLACE OF ABODE			NAME	RELATION	PERSONAL DESCRIPTION				EDUCATION		NATIVITY		OCCUPATION
	Street, avenue, road, etc.	Number of dwelling house is order of visitation	Number of family in order of visitation	of each person whose place of abode on April 1, 1930, was in this family. Enter surname, first, then given name and middle initial. If any. Include every person living on April 1, 1930. Omit children born since April 1, 1930.	Relationship of this Person to the head of the family.	Sex	Color or race	Age at last birthday	Single, married, widowed or divorced	Attended school any time since Sept. 1, 1929	Whether able to read and write.	Place of birth of this person.	Whether able to speak English.	
	1	2	3	4	5	6	7	8	9	10	11	12	13	14
26		135	139	Aguon, Jose E	Head	M	Cha	47	S	N	Y	Guam	N	Farmer
27		136	140	Rivera, Juan D	Head	M	Cha	42	M	N	N	Guam	N	Farmer
28		136	140	Rivera, Delores S	Wife	F	Cha	37	M	N	Y	Guam	N	None
29		136	140	Rivera, Maria S	Daughter	F	Cha	11	S	Y	N	Guam	N	None
30		136	140	Rivera, Jesus S	Son	M	Cha	8	S	Y		Guam		None
31		136	140	Rivera, Rosa S	Daughter	F	Cha	2.3	S	N		Guam		None
32		136	140	Rivera, Gregorio S	Son	M	Cha	0.5	S	N		Guam		None
33		137	141	Chaco, Antonio R	Head	M	Cha	21	M	N	Y	Guam	Y	None
34		137	141	Chaco, Engracia C	Wife	F	Cha	20	M	N	Y	Guam	Y	None
35		137	141	Chaco, Maria C	Daughter	F	Cha	1.3	S	N		Guam		None
36		137	141	Chaco, Jesus C	Son	M	Cha	0.2	S	N		Guam		None
37					Here ends the enumeration of Salinas Barrio.									
38														
39														
40														
41														
42														
43														
44														
45														
46														
47														
48														
49														
50														

(CHAMORRO ROOTS GENEALOGY PROJECT™ TRANSCRIPTION)
(BERNARD T. PUNZALAN / HTTP://WWW.CHAMORROROOTS.COM)

DEPARTMENT OF COMMERCE-BUREAU OF THE CENSUS
WASHINGTON

FIFTEENTH CENSUS OF THE UNITED STATES: 1930-POPULATION

THE ISLAND OF GUAM

Sheet No. 16A

District Municipality of Agat
Name of Place Pasqual Barrio
[Proper name and, also, name of class, as city, town, village, barrio, etc]

Enumeration District No. 6
Enumerated by me on April 17, 1930 Pedro C Charfauros, Enumerator

	PLACE OF ABODE			NAME	RELATION	PERSONAL DESCRIPTION				EDUCATION		NATIVITY		OCCUPATION
	Street, avenue, road, etc.	Number of dwelling house is order of visitation	Number of family in order of visitation	of each person whose place of abode on April 1, 1930, was in this family. Enter surname, first, then given name and middle initial. If any. Include every person living on April 1, 1930. Omit children born since April 1, 1930.	Relationship of this Person to the head of the family.	Sex	Color or race	Age at last birthday	Single, married, widowed or divorced	Attended school any time since Sept. 1, 1929	Whether able to read and write.	Place of birth of this person.	Whether able to speak English.	
	1	2	3	4	5	6	7	8	9	10	11	12	13	14
1		138	142	Nededoc, Vicente P	Head	M	Cha	23	M	N	Y	Guam	Y	Laborer
2		138	142	Nededoc, Maria T	Wife	F	Cha	21	M	N	Y	Guam	Y	None
3		138	142	Nededoc, Juan T	Son	M	Cha	3.3	S	Y		Guam		None
4		138	142	Nededoc, Jesus T	Son	M	Cha	1.4	S	N		Guam		None
5		139	143	San Nicolas, Francisco A	Head	M	Cha	30	M	N	Y	Guam	Y	Farmer
6		139	143	San Nicolas, Rosa T	Wife	F	Cha	31	M	N	Y	Guam	N	None
7		139	143	San Nicolas, Ana T	Daughter	F	Cha	3	S	N		Guam		None
8		139	143	Charfauros, Rita T	Step daughter	F	Cha	10	S	Y	N	Guam	N	None
9		139	143	Charfauros, Ramon T	Step son	M	Cha	5	S	N		Guam		None
10		140	144	Quintanilla, Jose R	Head	M	Cha	36	M	N	Y	Guam	Y	Farmer
11		140	144	Quintanilla, Ana C	Wife	F	Cha	28	M	N	Y	Guam	N	None
12		140	144	Quintanilla, Juan C	Son	M	Cha	9	S	Y		Guam		None
13		140	144	Quintanilla, Jesus C	Son	M	Cha	8	S	Y		Guam		None
14		140	144	Quintanilla, Carmen C	Daughter	F	Cha	6	S	N		Guam		None
15		140	144	Quintanilla, Julita C	Daughter	F	Cha	3	S	N		Guam		None
16		141	145	Charfauros, Jose L	Head	M	Cha	28	S	N	Y	Guam	Y	Laborer
17					Here ends the enumeration of Pasqual barrio.									
18					[Sheet 243B/16B was intentionally left blank by the enumerator.]									
19														
20														
21														
22														
23														
24														
25														

(CHAMORRO ROOTS GENEALOGY PROJECT™ TRANSCRIPTION)
(BERNARD T. PUNZALAN / HTTP://WWW.CHAMORROROOTS.COM)

DEPARTMENT OF COMMERCE-BUREAU OF THE CENSUS
WASHINGTON

FIFTEENTH CENSUS OF THE UNITED STATES: 1930-POPULATION

THE ISLAND OF GUAM

Sheet No. 17A

244

District **Municipality of Agat**
Name of Place **Chandia Barrio** [Proper name and, also, name of class, as city, town, village, barrio, etc]

Enumeration District No. **6**
Enumerated by me on **April 17, 1930** Pedro C Charfauros, Enumerator

	PLACE OF ABODE			NAME	RELATION	PERSONAL DESCRIPTION				EDUCATION		NATIVITY		OCCUPATION
	Street, avenue, road, etc.	Number of dwelling house in order of visitation	Number of family in order of visitation	of each person whose place of abode on April 1, 1930, was in this family. Enter surname, first, then given name and middle initial. If any. Include every person living on April 1, 1930. Omit children born since April 1, 1930.	Relationship of this Person to the head of the family.	Sex	Color or race	Age at last birthday	Single, married, widowed or divorced	Attended school any time since Sept. 1, 1929	Whether able to read and write.	Place of birth of this person.	Whether able to speak English.	
	1	2	3	4	5	6	7	8	9	10	11	12	13	14
1		142	146	Mesa, Juan M	Head	M	Cha	47	M	N	Y	Guam	N	Farmer
2		142	146	Mesa, Tomasa C	Wife	F	Cha	31	M	N	Y	Guam	N	None
3		142	146	Mesa, Rita C	Daughter	F	Cha	14	S	Y	Y	Guam	Y	None
4		142	146	Mesa, Felix C	Son	M	Cha	13	S	Y	Y	Guam	Y	None
5		142	146	Mesa, Vicente C	Son	M	Cha	7	S	Y		Guam		None
6		142	146	Mesa, Gonzales P	Son	M	Cha	20	S	N	Y	Guam	Y	Farm laborer
7		143	147	Babauta, Jose L	Head	M	Cha	47	Wd	N	N	Guam	N	Farmer
8		143	147	Babauta, Maria C	Daughter	F	Cha	14	S	Y	Y	Guam	Y	None
9		143	147	Babauta, Juan C	Son	M	Cha	12	S	Y	N	Guam	N	None
10		144	148	Cruz, Pedro G	Head	M	Cha	56	S	N	N	Guam	N	Farmer
11		145	149	Aguigui, Felix B	Head	M	Cha	38	M	N	Y	Guam	Y	Farmer
12		145	149	Aguigui, Francisca B	Wife	F	Cha	30	M	N	Y	Guam	Y	None
13		145	149	Aguigui, Maria G	Daughter	F	Cha	9	S	Y		Guam		None
14		145	149	Aguigui, Balbino G	Son	M	Cha	8	S	Y		Guam		None
15		145	149	Aguigui, Delores G	Daughter	F	Cha	0.5	S	N		Guam		None
16		146	150	Manglona, Paulino S	Head	M	Cha	44	M	N	N	Guam	N	Farmer
17		146	150	Manglona, Leoncia M	Wife	F	Cha	39	M	N	N	Guam	N	None
18		146	150	Manglona, Jesus M	Son	M	Cha	10	S	Y	N	Guam	N	None
19		146	150	Manglona, Manuel M	Son	M	Cha	9	S	Y		Guam		None
20		146	150	Manglona, Pedro M	Son	M	Cha	5	S	N		Guam		None
21		146	150	Manglona, Espreciosa M	Daughter	F	Cha	4	S	N		Guam		None
22		146	150	Manglona, Juan M	Son	M	Cha	0.1	S	N		Guam		None
23					Here ends the enumeration of Chandia Barrio									
24					[Sheet 244B/17B was intentionally left blank by the enumerator.]									
25														

(CHAMORRO ROOTS GENEALOGY PROJECT™ TRANSCRIPTION)
(BERNARD T. PUNZALAN / HTTP://WWW.CHAMORROROOTS.COM)

DEPARTMENT OF COMMERCE-BUREAU OF THE CENSUS
WASHINGTON

FIFTEENTH CENSUS OF THE UNITED STATES: 1930-POPULATION

THE ISLAND OF GUAM

Sheet No. 18A

District **Municipality of Agat**
Name of Place **Fena Barrio**
[Proper name and, also, name of class, as city, town, village, barrio, etc]

Enumeration District No. 6
Enumerated by me on **April 17, 1930** Pedro C Charfauros, Enumerator

	PLACE OF ABODE			NAME	RELATION	PERSONAL DESCRIPTION				EDUCATION		NATIVITY		OCCUPATION
	Street, avenue, road, etc.	Number of dwelling house is order of visitation	Number of family in order of visitation	of each person whose place of abode on April 1, 1930, was in this family. Enter surname, first, then given name and middle initial. If any. Include every person living on April 1, 1930. Omit children born since April 1, 1930.	Relationship of this Person to the head of the family.	Sex	Color or race	Age at last birthday	Single, married, widowed or divorced	Attended school any time since Sept. 1, 1929	Whether able to read and write.	Place of birth of this person.	Whether able to speak English.	
	1	2	3	4	5	6	7	8	9	10	11	12	13	14
1		147	151	Guivara, Antonio G	Head	M	Cha	34	M	N	Y	Guam	Y	Farmer
2		147	151	Guivara, Consolacion B	Wife	F	Cha	32	M	N	Y	Guam	N	None
3		147	151	Guivara, Jose B	Son	M	Cha	4.4	S	N		Guam		None
4		147	151	Guivara, Maria G	Mother	F	Cha	54	W D	N	N	Guam	N	None
5		148	152	Taitague, Ignacio C	Head	M	Cha	56	M	N	N	Guam	N	Farmer
6		148	152	Taitague, Susana P	Wife	F	Cha	36	M	N	N	Guam	N	None
7		148	152	Taitague, Francisco P	Son	M	Cha	7	S	Y		Guam		None
8		148	152	Taitague, Rosalia P	Daughter	F	Cha	1	S	N		Guam		None
9		148	152	Taitague, Vicente Q	Son	M	Cha	23	S	N	N	Guam	N	Farm laborer
10		148	152	Taitague, Josefa Q	Daughter	F	Cha	20	S	N	N	Guam	N	None
11		149	153	Mesa, Jose M	Head	M	Cha	55	M	N	Y	Guam	N	Farmer
12		149	153	Mesa, Ana P	Wife	F	Cha	41	M	N	N	Guam	N	None
13		149	153	Mesa, Enrique P	Son	M	Cha	19	S	N	Y	Guam	N	Farmer
14		149	153	Mesa, Francisco P	Son	M	Cha	18	S	N	Y	Guam	N	None
15		149	153	Mesa, Rosalia P	Daughter	F	Cha	17	S	N	Y	Guam	Y	Farm laborer
16		149	153	Mesa, Maria P	Daughter	F	Cha	15	S	N	N	Guam	Y	Cook
17		149	153	Mesa, Jose P	Son	M	Cha	12	S	Y	N	Guam	Y	None
18		149	153	Mesa, Alfonsina P	Daughter	F	Cha	7	S	Y		Guam	N	None
19		149	153	Mesa, Jesus P	Son	M	Cha	6	S	N		Guam	N	None
20		149	153	Mesa, Joaquin P	Son	M	Cha	4	S	N		Guam		None
21		149	153	Mesa, Tomas P	Son	M	Cha	1	S	N		Guam		None
22					Here ends the enumeration of Fena Barrio									
23					[Sheet 245B/18B was intentionally left blank by the enumerator.]									
24														
25														

DEPARTMENT OF COMMERCE-BUREAU OF THE CENSUS
WASHINGTON

FIFTEENTH CENSUS OF THE UNITED STATES: 1930-POPULATION

THE ISLAND OF GUAM

Sheet No. 19A

District **Municipality of Agat**
Name of Place **Opagat Barrio** [Proper name and, also, name of class, as city, town, village, barrio, etc]

Enumeration District No. **6**
Enumerated by me on **April 18, 1930** Pedro C Charfauros, Enumerator

	PLACE OF ABODE			NAME	RELATION	PERSONAL DESCRIPTION				EDUCATION		NATIVITY		OCCUPATION
	Street, avenue, road, etc.	Number of dwelling house is order of visitation	Number of family in order of visitation	of each person whose place of abode on April 1, 1930, was in this family. Enter surname, first, then given name and middle initial. If any. Include every person living on April 1, 1930. Omit children born since April 1, 1930.	Relationship of this Person to the head of the family.	Sex	Color or race	Age at last birthday	Single, married, widowed or divorced	Attended school any time since Sept. 1, 1929	Whether able to read and write.	Place of birth of this person.	Whether able to speak English.	
	1	2	3	4	5	6	7	8	9	10	11	12	13	14
1		150	154	Maanao, Jose A	Head	M	Cha	50	Wd	N	Y	Guam	N	Farmer
2		150	154	Maanao, Manuel	Son	M	Cha	23	S	N	Y	Guam	Y	Laborer
3		151	155	Terlaji, Vicenta A	Head	F	Cha	44	D	N	Y	Guam	N	Laundress
4		152	156	Cruz, Pedro C	Head	M	Cha	46	M	N	Y	Guam	N	Farmer
5		152	156	Cruz, Maria O	Wife	F	Cha	43	M	N	Y	Guam	N	None
6		152	156	Cruz, Dolores O	Daughter	F	Cha	21	S	N	Y	Guam	N	None
7		152	156	Cruz, Pedro O	Son	M	Cha	20	S	N	Y	Guam	Y	Farm laborer
8		152	156	Cruz, Rafael O	Son	M	Cha	17	S	N	Y	Guam	Y	Farm laborer
9		152	156	Cruz, Jesus O	Son	M	Cha	15	S	Y	Y	Guam	Y	None
10		152	156	Cruz, Juan O	Son	M	Cha	10	S	Y	N	Guam	N	None
11		152	156	Cruz, Antonia O	Daughter	F	Cha	6	S	N		Guam		None
12		152	156	Cruz, Jose O	Son	M	Cha	4.2	S	N		Guam		None
13		152	156	Cruz, Joaquin O	Son	M	Cha	2.1	S	N		Guam		None
14		152	156	Guivara, Soledad P	Step sister in law	F	Cha	33	S	N	N	Guam	N	Laundress
15		152	156	Guivara, Jose P	Step nephew	M	Cha	14	S	N	Y	Guam	Y	Farm laborer
16		153	157	Salas, Vicente S	Head	M	Cha	27	M	N	Y	Guam	Y	Farmer
17		153	157	Salas, Delfina C	Wife	F	Cha	22	M	N	Y	Guam	Y	None
18		154	158	Chargualaf, Augustin T	Head	M	Cha	59	M	N	Y	Guam	N	Farmer
19		154	158	Chargualaf, Ana A	Wife	F	Cha	61	M	N	N	Guam	N	None
20		154	158	Chargualaf, Jose A	Son	M	Cha	19	S	N	N	Guam	N	Farm laborer
21		155	159	Salas, Manuel F	Head	M	Cha	35	M	N	Y	Guam	N	Farmer
22		155	159	Salas, Caridad B	Wife	F	Cha	36	M	N	N	Guam	N	None
23		155	159	Salas, Rosario B	Daughter	F	Cha	15	S	Y	Y	Guam	Y	None
24		155	159	Salas, Guadalupe B	Daughter	F	Cha	11	S	Y	Y	Guam	Y	None
25		155	159	Salas, Francisco B	Son	M	Cha	5	S	N		Guam		None

DEPARTMENT OF COMMERCE-BUREAU OF THE CENSUS
WASHINGTON

FIFTEENTH CENSUS OF THE UNITED STATES: 1930-POPULATION

THE ISLAND OF GUAM

Sheet No. 19B

246B

District **Municipality of Agat**
Name of Place **Opagat Barrio**
[Proper name and, also, name of class, as city, town, village, barrio, etc]

Enumeration District No. 6
Enumerated by me on **April 18, 1930** Pedro C Charfauros, Enumerator

	PLACE OF ABODE			NAME	RELATION	PERSONAL DESCRIPTION				EDUCATION		NATIVITY		OCCUPATION
	Street, avenue, road, etc.	Number of dwelling house in order of visitation	Number of family in order of visitation	of each person whose place of abode on April 1, 1930, was in this family. Enter surname, first, then given name and middle initial. If any. Include every person living on April 1, 1930. Omit children born since April 1, 1930.	Relationship of this Person to the head of the family.	Sex	Color or race	Age at last birthday	Single, married, widowed or divorced	Attended school any time since Sept. 1, 1929	Whether able to read and write.	Place of birth of this person.	Whether able to speak English.	
	1	2	3	4	5	6	7	8	9	10	11	12	13	14
26		155	159	Salas, Vicente B	Son	M	Cha	4.4	S	N		Guam		None
27		155	159	Salas, Soledad B	Daughter	F	Cha	1.8	S	N		Guam		None
28		155	159	Babauta, Antonia R	Sister in law	F	Cha	39	S	N	N	Guam	N	Laundress
29		155	159	Babauta, Manuel R	Nephew	M	Cha	9	S	Y		Guam		None
30		156	160	Charfauros, Juan C	Head	M	Cha	36	M	N	Y	Guam	Y	Farmer
31		156	160	Charfauros, Victoria M	Wife	F	Cha	38	M	N	Y	Guam	N	None
32		156	160	Charfauros, Jose M	Son	M	Cha	11	S	Y	Y	Guam	Y	None
33		156	160	Charfauros, Maria M	Daughter	F	Cha	10	S	Y	Y	Guam	Y	None
34		156	160	Charfauros, Marcela M	Daughter	F	Cha	5	S	N		Guam		None
35		156	160	Charfauros, Francisco M	Son	M	Cha	2.1	S	N		Guam		None
36					Here ends the enumeration of Opagat barrio.									
37														
38														
39														
40														
41														
42														
43														
44														
45														
46														
47														
48														
49														
50														

DEPARTMENT OF COMMERCE-BUREAU OF THE CENSUS
WASHINGTON
FIFTEENTH CENSUS OF THE UNITED STATES: 1930-POPULATION

THE ISLAND OF GUAM

Sheet No. 20A

District **Municipality of Agat**
Name of Place **Tumat Barrio**
[Proper name and, also, name of class, as city, town, village, barrio, etc]

Enumeration District No. 6
Enumerated by me on **April 19, 1930** Pedro C Charfauros
Enumerator

	PLACE OF ABODE			NAME	RELATION	PERSONAL DESCRIPTION				EDUCATION		NATIVITY		OCCUPATION
	Street, avenue, road, etc.	Number of dwelling house in order of visitation	Number of family in order of visitation	of each person whose place of abode on April 1, 1930, was in this family. Enter surname, first, then given name and middle initial. If any. Include every person living on April 1, 1930. Omit children born since April 1, 1930.	Relationship of this Person to the head of the family.	Sex	Color or race	Age at last birthday	Single, married, widowed or divorced	Attended school any time since Sept. 1, 1929	Whether able to read and write.	Place of birth of this person.	Whether able to speak English.	
	1	2	3	4	5	6	7	8	9	10	11	12	13	14
1		157	161	Babauta, Pedro M	Head	M	Cha	70	W D	N	N	Guam	N	None
2		158	162	Palomo, Pedro G	Head	M	Cha	37	M	N	Y	Guam	N	Farmer
3		158	162	Palomo, Patricia C	Wife	F	Cha	40	M	N	Y	Guam	N	None
4		158	162	Palomo, Maria C	Daughter	F	Cha	11	S	Y	Y	Guam	Y	None
5		158	162	Palomo, Enrique C	Son	M	Cha	9	S	Y		Guam		None
6		158	162	Palomo, Carmen C	Daughter	F	Cha	6	S	N		Guam		None
7		158	162	Palomo, Tomas C	Son	M	Cha	3.1	S	N		Guam		None
8		158	162	Palomo, Ignacio C	Son	M	Cha	0.8	S	N		Guam		None
9		159	163	Reyes, Jose B	Head	M	Cha	40	M	N	Y	Guam	N	Farmer
10		159	163	Reyes, Consolacion C	Wife	F	Cha	35	M	N	Y	Guam	N	None
11		159	163	Reyes, Maria C	Daughter	F	Cha	12	S	Y	N	Guam	N	None
12		159	163	Reyes, Joaquin C	Son	M	Cha	8	S	Y		Guam		None
13		159	163	Reyes, Lourdes C	Daughter	F	Cha	6	S	N		Guam		None
14		159	163	Reyes, Jose C	Son	M	Cha	4	S	N		Guam		None
15		159	163	Reyes, Miguel C	Son	M	Cha	0.5	S	N		Guam		None
16		160	164	Reyes, Andres B	Head	M	Cha	42	M	N	Y	Guam	N	Farmer
17		160	164	Reyes, Maria C	Wife	F	Cha	33	M	Y	Y	Guam	N	None
18		160	164	Reyes, Enrique C	Son	M	Cha	15	S	Y	Y	Guam	Y	None
19		160	164	Reyes, Felicita C	Daughter	F	Cha	14	S	Y	Y	Guam	Y	None
20		160	164	Reyes, Ignacio C	Son	M	Cha	12	S	Y	Y	Guam	Y	None
21		160	164	Reyes, Estafania C	Daughter	F	Cha	9	S	Y		Guam		None
22		160	164	Reyes, Gonzalo C	Son	M	Cha	5	S	N		Guam		None
23		160	164	Reyes, Elvina C	Daughter	F	Cha	2	S	N		Guam		None
24					Here ends the enumeration of Tumat barrio.									
25					[Sheet 247B/20B was intentionally left blank by the enumerator.]									

(CHAMORRO ROOTS GENEALOGY PROJECT™ TRANSCRIPTION)
(BERNARD T. PUNZALAN / HTTP://WWW.CHAMORROROOTS.COM)

DEPARTMENT OF COMMERCE-BUREAU OF THE CENSUS
WASHINGTON

FIFTEENTH CENSUS OF THE UNITED STATES: 1930-POPULATION

THE ISLAND OF GUAM

Sheet No. 21A

248

District Municipality of Agat
Name of Place Sagua Barrio
[Proper name and, also, name of class, as city, town, village, barrio, etc]

Enumeration District No. 6
Enumerated by me on April 19, 1930 Pedro C Charfauros
Enumerator

	PLACE OF ABODE			NAME	RELATION	PERSONAL DESCRIPTION				EDUCATION		NATIVITY		OCCUPATION
	Street, avenue, road, etc.	Number of dwelling house is order of visitation	Number of family in order of visitation	of each person whose place of abode on April 1, 1930, was in this family. Enter surname, first, then given name and middle initial. If any. Include every person living on April 1, 1930. Omit children born since April 1, 1930.	Relationship of this Person to the head of the family.	Sex	Color or race	Age at last birthday	Single, married, widowed or divorced	Attended school any time since Sept. 1, 1929	Whether able to read and write.	Place of birth of this person.	Whether able to speak English.	
	1	2	3	4	5	6	7	8	9	10	11	12	13	14
1		161	165	Chaco, Jose Q	Head	M	Cha	60	M	N	Y	Guam	N	Farmer
2		161	165	Chaco, Joaquina R	Wife	F	Cha	55	M	N	N	Guam	N	None
3		161	165	Chaco, Carmen R	Daughter	F	Cha	28	S	N	Y	Guam	N	Laundress
4		161	165	Chaco, Tomas R	Son	M	Cha	24	S	N	Y	Guam	Y	Farm laborer
5		161	165	Acfalle, Consolacion C	Niece	F	Cha	18	S	N	Y	Guam	N	None
6		161	165	Acfalle, Ana C	Niece	F	Cha	16	S	N	Y	Guam	N	None
7		161	165	Acfalle, Margarita C	Niece	F	Cha	14	S	Y	Y	Guam	Y	None
8		162	166	Acfalle, Geronimo SN	Head	M	Cha	58	Wd	N	N	Guam	N	Farmer
9		163	167	Muna, Florentino S	Head	M	Cha	31	S	N	Y	Guam	Y	Farmer
10		164	168	Quitugua, Maria A	Head	F	Cha	36	M	N	Y	Guam	N	Laundress
11		164	168	Quitugua, Guadalupe A	Daughter	F	Cha	13	S	Y	Y	Guam	Y	None
12		164	168	Quitugua, Josefina A	Daughter	F	Cha	9	S	Y		Guam		None
13		164	168	Quitugua, Jose A	Son	M	Cha	5	S	N		Guam		None
14		164	168	Quitugua, Francisco A	Son	M	Cha	4.1	S	N		Guam		None
15		164	168	Quitugua, Maria A	Daughter	F	Cha	1	S	N		Guam		None
16		164	168	Arceo, Carmen S	Mother	F	Cha	60	Wd	N	N	Guam	N	None
17		165	169	Aguigui, Francisco A	Head	M	Cha	22	M	N	Y	Guam	Y	Farmer
18		165	169	Aguigui, Carmen G	Wife	F	Cha	21	M	N	Y	Guam	Y	None
19		165	169	Aguigui, Rosalia G	Daughter	F	Cha	0.8	S	N		Guam		None
20					Here ends the enumeration of Sagua Barrio									
21					[Sheet 248B/21B was intentionally left blank by the enumerator.]									
22														
23														
24														
25														

DEPARTMENT OF COMMERCE-BUREAU OF THE CENSUS
WASHINGTON

FIFTEENTH CENSUS OF THE UNITED STATES: 1930-POPULATION

THE ISLAND OF GUAM

Sheet No. 22A

District **Municipality of Agat**
Name of Place **Inaso Barrio**
[Proper name and, also, name of class, as city, town, village, barrio, etc]

Enumeration District No. **6**
Enumerated by me on **April 21, 1930** Pedro C Charfauros
Enumerator

	PLACE OF ABODE			NAME	RELATION	PERSONAL DESCRIPTION				EDUCATION		NATIVITY		OCCUPATION
	Street, avenue, road, etc.	Number of dwelling house is order of visitation	Number of family in order of visitation	of each person whose place of abode on April 1, 1930, was in this family. Enter surname, first, then given name and middle initial. If any. Include every person living on April 1, 1930. Omit children born since April 1, 1930.	Relationship of this Person to the head of the family.	Sex	Color or race	Age at last birthday	Single, married, widowed or divorced	Attended school any time since Sept. 1, 1929	Whether able to read and write.	Place of birth of this person.	Whether able to speak English.	
	1	2	3	4	5	6	7	8	9	10	11	12	13	14
1		166	170	Babauta, Domingo O	Head	M	Cha	49	M	N	N	Guam	N	Farm manager
2		166	170	Babauta, Maria A	Wife	F	Cha	53	M	N	N	Guam	N	None
3		166	170	Babauta, Benito A	Son	M	Cha	4	S	N		Guam		None
4		167	171	Cruz, Jose S	Head	M	Cha	45	M	N	Y	Guam	N	Farmer
5		167	171	Cruz, Maria S	Wife	F	Cha	38	M	N	N	Guam	N	None
6		167	171	Cruz, Marcela S	Daughter	F	Cha	5	S	N		Guam		None
7		167	171	Cruz, Juan S	Son	M	Cha	4	S	N		Guam		None
8		167	171	Cruz, Felix S	Son	M	Cha	1.3	S	N		Guam		None
9		168	172	Salas, Francisco S	Head	M	Cha	36	M	N	Y	Guam	Y	Farmer
10		168	172	Salas, Cecilia LG	Wife	F	Cha	35	M	N	Y	Guam	Y	None
11		168	172	Salas, Trinidad LG	Daughter	F	Cha	13	S	Y	Y	Guam	Y	None
12		168	172	Salas, Joaquin LG	Son	M	Cha	12	S	Y	N	Guam	N	None
13		168	172	Salas, Pedro LG	Son	M	Cha	9	S	Y		Guam		None
14		168	172	Salas, Dolores LG	Daughter	F	Cha	7	S	Y		Guam		None
15		168	172	Salas, Jose LG	Son	M	Cha	5	S	N		Guam		None
16		168	172	Salas, Maria LG	Daughter	F	Cha	4	S	N		Guam		None
17		169	173	San Nicolas, Jose B	Head	M	Cha	50	M	N	Y	Guam	N	Farmer
18		169	173	San Nicolas, Maria S	Wife	F	Cha	45	M	N	Y	Guam	N	None
19		169	173	San Nicolas, Maria Magdalena S	Daughter	F	Cha	9	S	Y		Guam		None
20		169	173	San Nicolas, David S	Son	M	Cha	3	S	N		Guam		None
21		169	173	San Nicolas, Jose S	Son	M	Cha	1.1	S	N		Guam		None
22		170	174	Nededoc, Joaquin P	Head	M	Cha	19	S	N	Y	Guam	Y	Laborer
23		170	175	Taitague, Inocensio C	Head	M	Cha	89	M	N	Y	Guam	Y	Farmer
24		170	175	Taitague, Candida B	Wife	F	Cha	36	M	N	Y	Guam	N	None
25		170	175	Taitague, Tomas B	Son	M	Cha	10	S	Y	N	Guam	N	None

DEPARTMENT OF COMMERCE-BUREAU OF THE CENSUS
WASHINGTON

FIFTEENTH CENSUS OF THE UNITED STATES: 1930-POPULATION

THE ISLAND OF GUAM

Sheet No. 22B

249B

District **Municipality of Agat**
Name of Place **Inaso Barrio**
[Proper name and, also, name of class, as city, town, village, barrio, etc]

Enumeration District No. **6**
Enumerated by me on **April 21, 1930** Pedro C Charfauros, Enumerator

	PLACE OF ABODE			NAME	RELATION	PERSONAL DESCRIPTION				EDUCATION		NATIVITY		OCCUPATION
	Street, avenue, road, etc.	Number of dwelling house in order of visitation	Number of family in order of visitation	of each person whose place of abode on April 1, 1930, was in this family. Enter surname, first, then given name and middle initial. If any. Include every person living on April 1, 1930. Omit children born since April 1, 1930.	Relationship of this Person to the head of the family.	Sex	Color or race	Age at last birthday	Single, married, widowed or divorced	Attended school any time since Sept. 1, 1929	Whether able to read and write.	Place of birth of this person.	Whether able to speak English.	
	1	2	3	4	5	6	7	8	9	10	11	12	13	14
26		170	175	Taitague, Ana B	Daughter	F	Cha	7	S	Y		Guam		None
27		170	175	Taitague, Delfina B	Daughter	F	Cha	3.1	S	N		Guam		None
28		170	175	Taitague, Maria B	Daughter	F	Cha	1.3	S	N		Guam		None
29		171	176	Pangelinan, Maria B	Head	F	Cha	63	S	N	Y	Guam	N	None
30		172	177	Manglona, Vicente S	Head	M	Cha	43	S	N	N	Guam	N	Farmer
31		173	178	Torres, Felisita Q	Head	F	Cha	24	S	N		Guam	Y	None
32		173	178	Torres, Beatrice Q	Daughter	F	Cha	2.1	S	N		Guam		None
33		173	178	Torres, Guadalupe Q	Daughter	F	Cha	0.3	S	N		Guam		None
34		174	179	Charfauros, Felix L	Head	M	Cha	31	S	N	Y	Guam	Y	Laborer
35					Here ends the enumeration of Inaso Barrio.									
36														
37														
38														
39														
40														
41														
42														
43														
44														
45														
46														
47														
48														
49														
50														

DEPARTMENT OF COMMERCE-BUREAU OF THE CENSUS
WASHINGTON

FIFTEENTH CENSUS OF THE UNITED STATES: 1930-POPULATION

THE ISLAND OF GUAM

Sheet No. 23A

District Municipality of Agat
Name of Place Omo Barrio
[Proper name and, also, name of class, as city, town, village, barrio, etc]

Enumeration District No. 6
Enumerated by me on April 22, 1930 Pedro C Charfauros
Enumerator

	PLACE OF ABODE			NAME	RELATION	PERSONAL DESCRIPTION				EDUCATION		NATIVITY		OCCUPATION
	Street, avenue, road, etc.	Number of dwelling house in order of visitation	Number of family in order of visitation	of each person whose place of abode on April 1, 1930, was in this family. Enter surname, first, then given name and middle initial. If any. Include every person living on April 1, 1930. Omit children born since April 1, 1930.	Relationship of this Person to the head of the family.	Sex	Color or race	Age at last birthday	Single, married, widowed or divorced	Attended school any time since Sept. 1, 1929	Whether able to read and write.	Place of birth of this person.	Whether able to speak English.	
	1	2	3	4	5	6	7	8	9	10	11	12	13	14
1		114	180	Rosario, Ana A	Head	F	Cha	48	D	N	Y	Guam	N	Laundress
2		115	181	San Nicolas, Josefa A	Head	F	Cha	51	Wd	N	N	Guam	N	Laundress
3		116	182	Terlaji, Magdalena M	Head	F	Cha	54	Wd	N	N	Guam	N	None
4		117	183	Guerrero, Joaquin P	Head	M	Cha	27	M	N	Y	Guam	Y	Laborer
5		117	183	Guerrero, Ana Q	Wife	F	Cha	33	M	N	Y	Guam	N	None
6		117	183	Guerrero, Antonina Q	Daughter	F	Cha	11	S	Y	Y	Guam	Y	None
7		117	183	Guerrero, Rosa Q	Daughter	F	Cha	9	S	Y	Y	Guam		None
8		117	183	Guerrero, Jose Q	Son	M	Cha	7	S	Y	Y	Guam		None
9		117	183	Guerrero, Maria Q	Daughter	F	Cha	5	S	N		Guam		None
10		117	183	Guerrero, Concepcion Q	Daughter	F	Cha	3.2	S	N		Guam		None
11		117	183	Guerrero, Benabe Q	Son	M	Cha	1.2	S	N		Guam		None
12		178	184	Ignacio, Vicente A	Head	M	Cha	48	M	N	Y	Guam	N	Farmer
13		178	184	Ignacio, Trinidad R	Wife	F	Cha	32	M	N	N	Guam	N	None
14		178	184	Reyes, Ramon R	Brother in law	M	Cha	22	S	N	N	Guam	N	Farm laborer
15		179	185	Babauta, Francisco R	Head	M	Cha	23	M	N	Y	Guam	Y	Farmer
16		179	185	Babauta, Ignasia S	Wife	F	Cha	20	M	N	Y	Guam	Y	None
17		179	185	Babauta, Maria S	Daughter	F	Cha	1.1	S	N		Guam		None
18		180	186	Cruz, Jose A	Head	M	Cha	29	M	N	Y	Guam	N	Farmer
19		180	186	Cruz, Ana B	Wife	F	Cha	33	M	N	N	Guam	N	None
20		180	186	Cruz, Enrique B	Son	M	Cha	6	S	N		Guam		None
21		180	186	Cruz, Antonio B	Son	M	Cha	4.5	S	N		Guam		None
22		180	186	Cruz, Joaquin B	Son	M	Cha	1.7	S	N		Guam		None
23					Here ends the enumeration of Omo Barrio.									
24														
25														

District 7
Municipality of Asan

Asan Town
Libugon

(CHAMORRO ROOTS GENEALOGY PROJECT™ TRANSCRIPTION)
(BERNARD T. PUNZALAN / HTTP://WWW.CHAMORROROOTS.COM)

DEPARTMENT OF COMMERCE-BUREAU OF THE CENSUS
WASHINGTON

FIFTEENTH CENSUS OF THE UNITED STATES: 1930-POPULATION

THE ISLAND OF GUAM

Sheet No. 1A

District **Municipality of Asan**
Name of Place **Asan Town**
[Proper name and, also, name of class, as city, town, village, barrio, etc]

Enumeration District No. 7
Enumerated by me on **April 10, 1930** Joaquin Torres, Enumerator

	PLACE OF ABODE			NAME	RELATION	PERSONAL DESCRIPTION				EDUCATION		NATIVITY		OCCUPATION
	Street, avenue, road, etc.	Number of dwelling house in order of visitation	Number of family in order of visitation	of each person whose place of abode on April 1, 1930, was in this family. Enter surname, first, then given name and middle initial. If any. Include every person living on April 1, 1930. Omit children born since April 1, 1930.	Relationship of this Person to the head of the family.	Sex	Color or race	Age at last birthday	Single, married, widowed or divorced	Attended school any time since Sept. 1, 1929	Whether able to read and write.	Place of birth of this person.	Whether able to speak English.	
	1	2	3	4	5	6	7	8	9	10	11	12	13	14
1	Agana-Piti Road	167	185	Limtiaco, Santiago A	Head	M	Chin	40	M	N	Y	Guam	Y	Commissioner
2		167	185	Limtiaco, Ana SN	Wife	F	Cha	49	M	N	Y	Guam	Y	Retail merchant
3		167	185	Limtiaco, Matilde SN	Daughter	F	Chin	19	S	N	Y	Guam	Y	None
4		167	185	Limtiaco, Josefina SN	Daughter	F	Chin	15	S	Y	Y	Guam	Y	None
5		167	185	Fejeran, Jose A	Lodger	M	Cha	33	S	N	Y	Guam	Y	Herder
6		168	186	Jesus, Joaquin L	Head	M	Cha	33	M	N	Y	Guam	Y	Herder
7		168	186	Jesus, Josefa LG	Wife	F	Cha	33	M	N	Y	Guam	N	None
8		168	186	Jesus, Ofemia LG	Daughter	F	Cha	11	S	Y	Y	Guam	Y	None
9		168	186	Jesus, Felicita LG	Daughter	F	Cha	9	S	Y		Guam		None
10		168	186	Jesus, Antonio LG	Son	M	Cha	8	S	Y		Guam		None
11		168	186	Jesus, Pedro LG	Son	M	Cha	7	S	N		Guam		None
12		168	186	Jesus, Elias LG	Son	M	Cha	5	S	N		Guam		None
13		168	186	Jesus, Fidel LG	Son	M	Cha	3.4	S	N		Guam		None
14		168	186	Jesus, Fidela LG	Daughter	F	Cha	1.2	S	N		Guam		None
15		168	186	Taijeron, Barbara J	Niece	F	Cha	20	S	N	Y	Guam		None
16		169	187	Limtiaco, Juan A	Head	M	Chin	36	M	N	Y	Guam	Y	Farmer
17		169	187	Limtiaco, Remedio T	Wife	F	Cha	26	M	N	Y	Guam	Y	None
18		169	187	Limtiaco, Dolores T	Daughter	F	Chin	4.2	S	N		Guam		None
19		169	187	Limtiaco, Maria T	Daughter	F	Chin	3.1	S	N		Guam		None
20		169	187	Limtiaco, Magdalena T	Daughter	F	Chin	1.7	S	N		Guam		None
21		170	188	Santos, Nicolas SN	Head	M	Cha	50	M	N	N	Guam	N	Farmer
22		170	188	Santos, Rosa F	Wife	F	Cha	60	M	N	N	Guam	N	None
23		171	189	Terlaje, Magdalena A	Head	F	Cha	44	S	N	N	Guam	N	None
24		171	189	Terlaje, Joaquin T	Son	M	Cha	16	S	N	Y	Guam	Y	Farm laborer
25		171	189	Terlaje, Francisco T	Son	M	Cha	12	S	Y	Y	Guam	Y	None

DEPARTMENT OF COMMERCE-BUREAU OF THE CENSUS
WASHINGTON

FIFTEENTH CENSUS OF THE UNITED STATES: 1930-POPULATION

THE ISLAND OF GUAM

Sheet No. 1B

232B

District **Municipality of Asan**
Name of Place **Asan Town**
[Proper name and, also, name of class, as city, town, village, barrio, etc]

Enumeration District No. 7
Enumerated by me on **April 11, 1930** Joaquin Torres, Enumerator

	PLACE OF ABODE			NAME	RELATION	PERSONAL DESCRIPTION				EDUCATION		NATIVITY		OCCUPATION
	Street, avenue, road, etc.	Number of dwelling house in order of visitation	Number of family in order of visitation	of each person whose place of abode on April 1, 1930, was in this family. Enter surname, first, then given name and middle initial. If any. Include every person living on April 1, 1930. Omit children born since April 1, 1930.	Relationship of this Person to the head of the family.	Sex	Color or race	Age at last birthday	Single, married, widowed or divorced	Attended school any time since Sept. 1, 1929	Whether able to read and write.	Place of birth of this person.	Whether able to speak English.	
	1	2	3	4	5	6	7	8	9	10	11	12	13	14
26	Agana-Piti Road	172	190	Fejeran, Consolacion SN	Head	F	Cha	61	Wd	N	N	Guam	N	None
27		172	190	Fejeran, Rosa SN	Daughter	F	Cha	19	S	N	Y	Guam	Y	None
28		172	190	Camacho, Luis S	Lodger	M	Cha	64	M	N	Y	Guam	N	Laborer
29		173	191	Fejeran, Jose SN	Head	M	Cha	61	Wd	N	N	Guam	N	Farmer
30		173	191	Fejeran, Amanda P	Daughter	F	Cha	23	S	N	Y	Guam	Y	Laundress
31		173	191	Fejeran, Jose P	Son	M	Cha	17	S	N	Y	Guam	Y	Laborer
32		174	192	Aflleje, Juan P	Head	M	Cha	52	M	N	Y	Guam	N	Farmer
33		174	192	Aflleje, Rita T	Wife	F	Cha	41	M	N	Y	Guam	N	None
34		174	192	Aflleje, Jose T	Son	M	Cha	22	S	N	Y	Guam	Y	Laborer
35		174	192	Aflleje, Joaquina T	Daughter	F	Cha	19	S	N	Y	Guam	Y	None
36		174	192	Aflleje, Regina T	Daughter	F	Cha	14	S	N	Y	Guam	Y	None
37		174	192	Aflleje, Ana T	Daughter	F	Cha	13	S	Y	Y	Guam	Y	None
38		174	192	Aflleje, Maria T	Daughter	F	Cha	7	S	Y		Guam		None
39		174	192	Aflleje, Antonio T	Son	M	Cha	3.7	S	N		Guam		None
40		175	193	Rojas, Juan R	Head	M	Cha	69	M	N	N	Guam	N	Farmer
41		175	193	Rojas, Ana S	Wife	F	Cha	62	M	N	N	Guam	N	None
42		175	193	Rojas, Pedro S	Son	M	Cha	23	S	N	Y	Guam	Y	Laborer
43		175	193	Rojas, Ramon S	Son	M	Cha	18	S	N	Y	Guam	Y	Farm laborer
44		175	193	Rojas, Antonia S	Daughter	F	Cha	15	S	Y	Y	Guam	Y	None
45		175	193	Rojas, Juan S	Son	M	Cha	12	S	Y	Y	Guam	Y	None
46		176	194	Mendiola, Joaquin L	Head	F	Cha	52	Wd	N	Y	Guam	Y	Farmer
47		177	195	Lorenzo, Rosa A	Head	F	Cha	44	M	N	N	Guam	N	Laundress
48		177	195	Lorenzo, Fernando A	Son	M	Cha	23	S	N	Y	Guam	Y	Chauffeur
49		177	195	Lorenzo, Matilde A	Daughter	F	Cha	20	S	N	Y	Guam	Y	None
50		178	196	Aflague, Ana S	Head	F	Cha	64	Wd	N	N	Guam	N	None

(CHAMORRO ROOTS GENEALOGY PROJECT ™ TRANSCRIPTION)
(BERNARD T. PUNZALAN / HTTP://WWW.CHAMORROROOTS.COM)

DEPARTMENT OF COMMERCE-BUREAU OF THE CENSUS
WASHINGTON

FIFTEENTH CENSUS OF THE UNITED STATES: 1930-POPULATION

THE ISLAND OF GUAM

Sheet No. 2A

District **Municipality of Asan**
Name of Place **Asan Town**
[Proper name and, also, name of class, as city, town, village, barrio, etc]

Enumeration District No. 7
Enumerated by me on **April 11, 1930** Joaquin Torres, Enumerator

	PLACE OF ABODE			NAME	RELATION	PERSONAL DESCRIPTION				EDUCATION		NATIVITY		OCCUPATION
	Street, avenue, road, etc.	Number of dwelling house is order of visitation	Number of family in order of visitation	of each person whose place of abode on April 1, 1930, was in this family. Enter surname, first, then given name and middle initial. If any. Include every person living on April 1, 1930. Omit children born since April 1, 1930.	Relationship of this Person to the head of the family.	Sex	Color or race	Age at last birthday	Single, married, widowed or divorced	Attended school any time since Sept. 1, 1929	Whether able to read and write.	Place of birth of this person.	Whether able to speak English.	
	1	2	3	4	5	6	7	8	9	10	11	12	13	14
1	Agana-Piti Road	179	197	Seimiya, Fidel T	Head	M	Jap	50	M	N	Y	Guam	Y	Retail merchant
2		179	197	Seimiya, Antonia A	Wife	F	Cha	46	M	N	Y	Guam	N	None
3		179	197	Seimiya, Juan A	Son	M	Jap	17	S	N	Y	Guam	Y	Chauffeur
4		179	197	Seimiya, Crispina A	Daughter	F	Jap	9	S	Y		Guam		None
5		179	197	Morita, Joaquin A	Step son	M	Jap	23	S	N	Y	Guam	Y	Cook
6		179	197	Morita, Jose A	Step son	M	Jap	21	S	N	Y	Guam	Y	Laborer
7		180	198	Zamora, Juana C	Head	F	Cha	59	Wd	N	N	Guam	Y	Laundress
8		180	198	Zamora, Ursula C	Daughter	F	Fil	18	S	N	Y	Guam	Y	Servant
9		180	198	Zamora, Rosita C	Daughter	F	Fil	16	S	Y	Y	Guam	Y	None
10		180	198	Zamora, Pedro C	Son	M	Fil	9	S	Y		Guam		None
11		181	199	Rapolla, Juan C	Head	M	Chin	36	M	N	Y	Guam	Y	Laborer
12		181	199	Rapolla, Vicenta T	Wife	F	Cha	38	M	N	Y	Guam	N	None
13		181	199	Rapolla, Natividad T	Daughter	F	Chin	17	S	N	Y	Guam	Y	None
14		181	199	Rapolla, Francisco T	Son	M	Chin	16	S	N	Y	Guam	Y	Farm laborer
15		181	199	Rapolla, Maria T	Daughter	F	Chin	13	S	Y	Y	Guam	Y	None
16		181	199	Rapolla, Caridad T	Daughter	F	Chin	11	S	Y	Y	Guam	Y	None
17		181	199	Rapolla, Carlos T	Son	M	Chin	9	S	Y		Guam		None
18		181	199	Rapolla, Santiago T	Son	M	Chin	5	S	N		Guam		None
19		181	199	Rapolla, Vicente T	Son	M	Chin	4.1	S	N		Guam		None
20		181	199	Rapolla, Rosalia T	Daughter	F	Chin	2.2	S	N		Guam		None
21		182	200	Santos, Juan C	Head	M	Cha	29	M	N	Y	Guam	Y	Laborer
22		182	200	Santos, Maria S	Wife	F	Cha	30	M	Y	Y	Guam	Y	None
23		182	200	Santos, Miguel S	Son	M	Cha	8	S	Y		Guam		None
24		182	200	Santos, Isabel S	Daughter	F	Cha	7	S	Y		Guam		None
25		182	200	Santos, Antonio S	Son	M	Cha	4.1	S	N		Guam		None

(CHAMORRO ROOTS GENEALOGY PROJECT™ TRANSCRIPTION)
(BERNARD T. PUNZALAN / HTTP://WWW.CHAMORROROOTS.COM)

DEPARTMENT OF COMMERCE-BUREAU OF THE CENSUS
WASHINGTON

FIFTEENTH CENSUS OF THE UNITED STATES: 1930-POPULATION

THE ISLAND OF GUAM

Sheet No. 2B

233B

District **Municipality of Asan**
Name of Place **Asan Town**
[Proper name and, also, name of class, as city, town, village, barrio, etc]

Enumeration District No. 7
Enumerated by me on **April 12, 1930** Joaquin Torres
Enumerator

	PLACE OF ABODE: Street, avenue, road, etc.	Number of dwelling house in order of visitation	Number of family in order of visitation	NAME of each person whose place of abode on April 1, 1930, was in this family. Enter surname, first, then given name and middle initial. If any. Include every person living on April 1, 1930. Omit children born since April 1, 1930.	RELATION Relationship of this Person to the head of the family.	PERSONAL DESCRIPTION: Sex	Color or race	Age at last birthday	Single, married, widowed or divorced	EDUCATION: Attended school any time since Sept. 1, 1929	Whether able to read and write.	NATIVITY Place of birth of this person.	Whether able to speak English.	OCCUPATION
	1	2	3	4	5	6	7	8	9	10	11	12	13	14
26	Agana-Piti Road	182	200	Santos, Susana S	Daughter	F	Cha	2.2	S	N		Guam		None
27		182	200	Santos, Antonia S	Daughter	F	Cha	.5	S	N		Guam		None
28		183	201	Mendiola, Antonia T	Head	F	Cha	51	M	N	Y	Guam	N	None
29		183	201	Taitano, Jose S	Nephew	M	Cha	16	S	Y	Y	Guam	Y	None
30		183	201	Taitano, Ana S	Niece	F	Cha	14	S	Y	Y	Guam	Y	None
31		183	201	Taitano, Barbina S	Niece	F	Cha	12	S	Y	Y	Guam	Y	None
32		184	202	San Nicolas, Filomeno T	Head	M	Cha	57	M	N	Y	Guam	Y	Farmer
33		184	202	San Nicolas, Vicenta C	Wife	F	Cha	44	M	N	N	Guam	N	None
34		184	202	San Nicolas, Gabriela C	Daughter	F	Cha	20	S	N	Y	Guam	Y	None
35		184	202	San Nicolas, Jose C	Son	M	Cha	17	S	N	Y	Guam	Y	Farm laborer
36		184	202	San Nicolas, Maria C	Daughter	F	Cha	15	S	Y	Y	Guam	Y	None
37		184	202	San Nicolas, Rosalia C	Daughter	F	Cha	11	S	Y	Y	Guam	Y	None
38		184	202	San Nicolas, Margarita C	Daughter	F	Cha	9	S	Y		Guam		None
39		184	202	San Nicolas, Juan C	Son	M	Cha	7	S	Y		Guam		None
40		184	202	San Nicolas, Vicente C	Son	M	Cha	1.9	S	N		Guam		None
41		185	203	San Nicolas, Vicente F	Head	M	Cha	40	M	N	Y	Guam	Y	Farmer
42		185	203	San Nicolas, Maria L	Wife	F	Cha	29	M	N	Y	Guam	Y	None
43		185	203	San Nicolas, Jose L	Son	M	Cha	4.2	S	N		Guam		None
44		185	203	San Nicolas, Antonio L	Son	M	Cha	1.7	S	N		Guam		None
45		186	204	Blas, Jose A	Head	M	Cha	45	M	N	Y	Guam	Y	Farmer
46		186	204	Blas, Joaquina L	Wife	F	Cha	38	M	N	Y	Guam	N	None
47		186	204	Blas, Lorenzo L	Son	M	Cha	13	S	Y	Y	Guam	Y	None
48		186	204	Blas, Juan L	Son	M	Cha	12	S	Y	Y	Guam	Y	None
49		186	204	Blas, Antonia L	Daughter	F	Cha	10	S	Y	Y	Guam	Y	None
50		186	204	Blas, Ana L	Daughter	F	Cha	8	S	Y		Guam		None

DEPARTMENT OF COMMERCE-BUREAU OF THE CENSUS
WASHINGTON

FIFTEENTH CENSUS OF THE UNITED STATES: 1930-POPULATION

THE ISLAND OF GUAM

Sheet No. 3A

District **Municipality of Asan**
Name of Place **Asan Town**
[Proper name and, also, name of class, as city, town, village, barrio, etc]

Enumeration District No. 7
Enumerated by me on **April 12, 1930** Joaquin Torres, Enumerator

	PLACE OF ABODE			NAME	RELATION	PERSONAL DESCRIPTION				EDUCATION		NATIVITY		OCCUPATION
	Street, avenue, road, etc.	Number of dwelling house is order of visitation	Number of family in order of visitation	of each person whose place of abode on April 1, 1930, was in this family. Enter surname, first, then given name and middle initial. If any. Include every person living on April 1, 1930. Omit children born since April 1, 1930.	Relationship of this Person to the head of the family.	Sex	Color or race	Age at last birthday	Single, married, widowed or divorced	Attended school any time since Sept. 1, 1929	Whether able to read and write.	Place of birth of this person.	Whether able to speak English.	
	1	2	3	4	5	6	7	8	9	10	11	12	13	14
1	Agana-Piti Road	186	204	Blas, Angustia L	Daughter	F	Cha	6	S	Y		Guam		None
2		187	205	Aflleje, Nicolasa P	Head	F	Cha	57	Wd	N	N	Guam	N	Laundress
3		188	206	Jesus, Joaquin F	Head	M	Cha	39	M	N	Y	Guam	Y	Laborer
4		188	206	Jesus, Vicenta C	Wife	F	Cha	33	M	N	N	Guam	N	None
5		188	206	Jesus, Francisco C	Son	M	Cha	9	S	Y		Guam		None
6		188	206	Jesus, Lucas C	Son	M	Cha	7	S	Y		Guam		None
7		188	206	Jesus, Guadalupe C	Daughter	F	Cha	3	S	N		Guam		None
8		189	207	Quitugua, Rosa A	Head	F	Cha	48	Wd	N	N	Guam	N	Laundress
9		189	207	Quitugua, Magdalena A	Daughter	F	Cha	17	S	Y	Y	Guam	Y	None
10		190	208	Santos, Manuel A	Head	M	Cha	47	M	N	Y	Guam	Y	Animal husband
11		190	208	Santos, Rtia B	Wife	F	Cha	46	M	N	N	Guam	N	None
12		190	208	Santos, Maria B	Daughter	F	Cha	24	S	N	Y	Guam	Y	None
13		190	208	Santos, Gertrudes B	Daughter	F	Cha	22	S	N	Y	Guam	Y	None
14		190	208	Santos, Enrique B	Son	M	Cha	19	S	Y	Y	Guam	Y	None
15		190	208	Santos, Beatris B	Daughter	F	Cha	16	S	Y	Y	Guam	Y	None
16		190	208	Santos, Ana B	Daughter	F	Cha	13	S	Y	Y	Guam	Y	None
17		190	208	Santos, Rosa B	Daughter	F	Cha	10	S	Y	Y	Guam	Y	None
18		190	208	Santos, Juan B	Son	M	Cha	8	S	Y		Guam		None
19		190	208	Santos, Soledad B	Daughter	F	Cha	4.7	S	N		Guam		None
20		191	209	Fejeran, Rosa Q	Head	F	Cha	34	M	N	N	Guam	N	None
21		191	209	Fejeran, Jesus Q	Son	M	Cha	10	S	Y	Y	Guam	Y	None
22		191	209	Fejeran, Joaquin Q	Son	M	Cha	8	S			Guam		None
23		191	209	Fejeran, Vicente Q	Son	M	Cha	6	S	Y		Guam		None
24		191	209	Fejeran, Maria Q	Daughter	F	Cha	3.9	S			Guam		None
25		191	209	Fejeran, Delfina Q	Daughter	M	Cha	1.1	S			Guam		None

(CHAMORRO ROOTS GENEALOGY PROJECT™ TRANSCRIPTION)
(BERNARD T. PUNZALAN / HTTP://WWW.CHAMORROROOTS.COM)

DEPARTMENT OF COMMERCE-BUREAU OF THE CENSUS
WASHINGTON
FIFTEENTH CENSUS OF THE UNITED STATES: 1930-POPULATION

THE ISLAND OF GUAM

Sheet No. 3B

234B

District **Municipality of Asan**
Name of Place **Asan Town**
[Proper name and, also, name of class, as city, town, village, barrio, etc]

Enumeration District No. 7
Enumerated by me on **April 14, 1930** Joaquin Torres
Enumerator

	PLACE OF ABODE			NAME	RELATION	PERSONAL DESCRIPTION				EDUCATION		NATIVITY		OCCUPATION
	Street, avenue, road, etc.	Number of dwelling house is order of visitation	Number of family in order of visitation	of each person whose place of abode on April 1, 1930, was in this family. Enter surname, first, then given name and middle initial. If any. Include every person living on April 1, 1930. Omit children born since April 1, 1930.	Relationship of this Person to the head of the family.	Sex	Color or race	Age at last birthday	Single, married, widowed or divorced	Attended school any time since Sept. 1, 1929	Whether able to read and write.	Place of birth of this person.	Whether able to speak English.	
	1	2	3	4	5	6	7	8	9	10	11	12	13	14
26	Agana-Piti Road	191	209	Quitugua, Pedro R	Uncle	M	Cha	54	S	N	N	Guam	N	None
27		192	210	Limtiaco, Antonio T	Head	M	Chin	62	M	N	Y	Guam	N	Farmer
28		192	210	Limtiaco, Antonia A	Wife	F	Cha	60	M	N	N	Guam	N	None
29		192	210	Limtiaco, Rosa A	Daughter	F	Chin	24	S	N	Y	Guam	Y	Laundress
30		192	210	Limtiaco, Adela A	Daughter	F	Chin	21	S	N	Y	Guam	Y	Laundress
31		192	210	Limtiaco, Ana A	Daughter	F	Chin	19	S	N	Y	Guam	Y	Laundress
32		192	210	Limtiaco, Vicente A	Son	M	Chin	16	S	N	Y	Guam	Y	Chauffeur
33		192	210	Limtiaco, Maria A	Niece	F	Cha	16	S	N	Y	Guam	Y	Laundress
34		193	211	Santos, Martin M	Head	M	Cha	68	M	N	Y	Guam	N	None
35		193	211	Santos, Maria A	Wife	F	Cha	66	M	N	N	Guam	N	None
36		193	211	Santos, Jesus A	Son	M	Cha	28	S	N	Y	Guam	Y	Chauffeur
37		193	211	Santos, Rita A	Daughter	F	Cha	26	S	N	Y	Guam	Y	None
38		194	212	Terlaje, Juan T	Head	M	Cha	25	M	N	Y	Guam	Y	Laborer
39		194	212	Terlaje, Manuela T	Wife	F	Cha	22	M	N	Y	Guam	N	None
40		194	212	Terlaje, Ignacia T	Daughter	F	Cha	.9	S	N		Guam		None
41		194	212	Taijito, Mariano T	Brother-in-law	M	Cha	32	S	N	Y	Guam	Y	Farm laborer
42		195	213	Aflleje, Jose F	Head	M	Cha	35	M	N	Y	Guam	Y	Laborer
43		195	213	Aflleje, Rosario C	Wife	F	Cha	33	M	N	N	Guam	N	None
44		195	213	Aflleje, Rosa C	Daughter	F	Cha	13	S	N	Y	Guam	Y	None
45		195	213	Aflleje, Ana C	Daughter	F	Cha	4.1	S	N		Guam		None
46		195	213	Aflleje, Magdalena C	Daughter	F	Cha	.9	S	N		Guam		None
47		196	214	Fejeran, Dolores P	Head	F	Cha	26	M	N	N	Guam	N	None
48		196	214	Fejeran, Francisco P	Son	M	Cha	7	S	Y		Guam		None
49		196	214	Fejeran, Tomas P	Son	M	Cha	5	S	N		Guam		None
50		196	214	Fejeran, Enrique P	Son	M	Cha	3.9	S	N		Guam		None

DEPARTMENT OF COMMERCE-BUREAU OF THE CENSUS
WASHINGTON

FIFTEENTH CENSUS OF THE UNITED STATES: 1930-POPULATION

THE ISLAND OF GUAM

Sheet No. 4A

District **Municipality of Asan**
Name of Place **Asan Town**
[Proper name and, also, name of class, as city, town, village, barrio, etc]

Enumeration District No. 7
Enumerated by me on **April 14, 1930** Joaquin Torres, Enumerator

	PLACE OF ABODE			NAME	RELATION	PERSONAL DESCRIPTION				EDUCATION		NATIVITY		OCCUPATION
	Street, avenue, road, etc.	Number of dwelling house is order of visitation	Number of family in order of visitation	of each person whose place of abode on April 1, 1930, was in this family. Enter surname, first, then given name and middle initial. If any. Include every person living on April 1, 1930. Omit children born since April 1, 1930.	Relationship of this Person to the head of the family.	Sex	Color or race	Age at last birthday	Single, married, widowed or divorced	Attended school any time since Sept. 1, 1929	Whether able to read and write.	Place of birth of this person.	Whether able to speak English.	
	1	2	3	4	5	6	7	8	9	10	11	12	13	14
1	Agana-Piti Road	197	215	Garcia, Jesus C	Head	M	Cha	29	M	N	Y	Guam	Y	Laborer
2		197	215	Garcia, Soledad F	Wife	F	Cha	26	M	N	Y	Guam	N	None
3		197	215	Garcia, Maria F	Daughter	F	Cha	6	S	N		Guam		None
4		197	215	Garcia, Jesus F	Son	M	Cha	4.9	S	N		Guam		None
5		197	215	Garcia, Jose F	Son	M	Cha	3.2	S	N		Guam		None
6		197	215	Garcia, Gertrudes F	Daughter	F	Cha	1.5	S	N		Guam		None
7		198	216	Fejeran, Rosa C	Head	F	Cha	22	M	N	Y	Guam	Y	None
8		198	216	Fejeran, Rosa C	Daughter	F	Cha	1.7	S	N		Guam		None
9		199	217	Santos, Vicente A	Head	M	Cha	41	M	N	Y	Guam	Y	Machinist
10		199	217	Santos, Josefa B	Wife	F	Cha	42	M	N	N	Guam	N	None
11		199	217	Santos, Dolores B	Daughter	F	Cha	21	S	N	Y	Guam	Y	None
12		199	217	Santos, Francisco B	Son	M	Cha	19	S	N	Y	Guam	Y	Chauffeur
13		199	217	Santos, Rosalia B	Daughter	F	Cha	17	S	N	Y	Guam	Y	Servant
14		199	217	Santos, Regina B	Daughter	F	Cha	14	S	N	Y	Guam	Y	None
15		199	217	Santos, Saturnina B	Daughter	F	Cha	12	S	Y	Y	Guam	Y	None
16		199	217	Santos, Santiago B	Son	M	Cha	9	S	Y		Guam		None
17		199	217	Santos, Jose B	Son	M	Cha	2.7	S	N		Guam		None
18		200	218	Santos, Juan	Head	M	Cha	46	M	N	Y	Guam	Y	Farmer
19		200	218	Santos, Maria S	Wife	F	Cha	35	M	N	Y	Guam	Y	None
20		200	218	Siguenza, Joaquin S	Stepson	M	Cha	14	S	Y	Y	Guam	Y	None
21		201	219	Chargualaf, Francisco Q	Head	M	Cha	52	M	N	Y	Guam	N	Laborer
22		201	219	Chargualaf, Dolores S	Wife	F	Cha	45	M	N	N	Guam	N	None
23		201	219	Chargualaf, Carmela S	Daughter	F	Cha	25	S	N	Y	Guam	Y	None
24		201	219	Chargualaf, Joaquina S	Daughter	F	Cha	24	S	N	Y	Guam	Y	None
25		201	219	Chargualaf, Jose S	Son	M	Cha	21	S	N	Y	Guam	Y	Laborer

DEPARTMENT OF COMMERCE-BUREAU OF THE CENSUS
WASHINGTON

FIFTEENTH CENSUS OF THE UNITED STATES: 1930-POPULATION

THE ISLAND OF GUAM

Sheet No. 4B

235B

District Municipality of Asan
Name of Place Asan Town
[Proper name and, also, name of class, as city, town, village, barrio, etc]

Enumeration District No. 7
Enumerated by me on April 15, 1930 Joaquin Torres
Enumerator

	PLACE OF ABODE			NAME	RELATION	PERSONAL DESCRIPTION				EDUCATION		NATIVITY		OCCUPATION
	Street, avenue, road, etc.	Number of dwelling house in order of visitation	Number of family in order of visitation	of each person whose place of abode on April 1, 1930, was in this family. Enter surname, first, then given name and middle initial. If any. Include every person living on April 1, 1930. Omit children born since April 1, 1930.	Relationship of this Person to the head of the family.	Sex	Color or race	Age at last birthday	Single, married, widowed or divorced	Attended school any time since Sept. 1, 1929	Whether able to read and write.	Place of birth of this person.	Whether able to speak English.	
	1	2	3	4	5	6	7	8	9	10	11	12	13	14
26	Agana-Piti Road	201	219	Chargualaf, Antonio S	Son	M	Cha	19	S	Y	Y	Guam	Y	None
27		201	219	Chargualaf, Preciosa S	Daughter	F	Cha	16	S	N	Y	Guam	Y	None
28		201	219	Chargualaf, Maria S	Daughter	F	Cha	12	S	Y	Y	Guam	Y	None
29		201	219	Chargualaf, Rosario S	Daughter	F	Cha	10	S	Y	Y	Guam	Y	None
30		201	219	Chargualaf, Francisco S	Son	M	Cha	9	S	Y		Guam		None
31		201	219	Chargualaf, Jesus	Son	M	Cha	2.9	S	N		Guam		None
32		202	220	Aflleje, Cristina N	Head	F	Cha	31	M	N	Y	Guam	N	None
33		202	220	Aflleje, Maria N	Daughter	F	Cha	10	S	Y	Y	Guam	Y	None
34		202	220	Aflleje, Francisco N	Son	M	Cha	9	S	Y		Guam		None
35		202	220	Aflleje, Beatrice N	Daughter	F	Cha	8	S	Y		Guam		None
36		202	220	Aflleje, Lourdes N	Daughter	F	Cha	7	S	N		Guam		None
37		202	220	Aflleje, Antonina N	Daughter	F	Cha	.1	S	N		Guam		None
38		203	221	Fejeran, Juan S	Head	M	Cha	59	M	N	Y	Guam	Y	Laborer
39		203	221	Fejeran, Andrea A	Wife	F	Cha	55	M	N	N	Guam	N	None
40		203	221	Fejeran, Ignacio A	Son	M	Cha	21	S	N	Y	Guam	Y	Laborer
41		204	222	Yamaguchi, Juan	Head	M	Jap	45	M	N	Y	Japan	Y	Carpenter
42		204	222	Yamaguchi, Ana A	Wife	F	Cha	39	M	N	Y	Guam	Y	None
43		204	222	Yamaguchi, Manuel A	Son	M	Jap	18	S	N	Y	Guam	Y	Carpenter
44		204	222	Yamaguchi, Visitacion A	Daughter	F	Jap	13	S	N	Y	Guam	Y	None
45		204	222	Yamaguchi, Maria A	Daughter	F	Jap	12	S	Y	Y	Guam	Y	None
46		204	222	Yamaguchi, Juan A	Son	M	Jap	8	S	Y		Guam		None
47		204	222	Yamaguchi, Trinidad A	Daughter	F	Jap	7	S	Y		Guam		None
48		204	222	Yamaguchi, Isabel A	Daughter	F	Jap	4.4	S	N		Guam		None
49		204	222	Yamaguchi, Rosalia A	Daughter	F	Jap	1.7	S	N		Guam		None
50		204	222	Yamaguchi, Melinciana A	Daughter	F	Jap	.1	S	N		Guam		None

DEPARTMENT OF COMMERCE-BUREAU OF THE CENSUS
WASHINGTON

FIFTEENTH CENSUS OF THE UNITED STATES: 1930-POPULATION

THE ISLAND OF GUAM

Sheet No. 5A

District **Municipality of Asan**
Name of Place **Asan Town**
[Proper name and, also, name of class, as city, town, village, barrio, etc]

Enumeration District No. 7
Enumerated by me on **April 16, 1930** Joaquin Torres, Enumerator

	PLACE OF ABODE: Street, avenue, road, etc.	Number of dwelling house in order of visitation	Number of family in order of visitation	NAME of each person whose place of abode on April 1, 1930, was in this family. Enter surname, first, then given name and middle initial. If any. Include every person living on April 1, 1930. Omit children born since April 1, 1930.	RELATION Relationship of this Person to the head of the family.	PERSONAL DESCRIPTION: Sex	Color or race	Age at last birthday	Single, married, widowed or divorced	EDUCATION: Attended school any time since Sept. 1, 1929	Whether able to read and write.	NATIVITY Place of birth of this person.	Whether able to speak English.	OCCUPATION
	1	2	3	4	5	6	7	8	9	10	11	12	13	14
1	Agana-Piti Road	205	223	Mendiola, Juan C	Head	M	Cha	29	M	N	Y	Guam	Y	Machinist
2		205	223	Mendiola, Carmela S	Wife	F	Cha	25	M	N	Y	Guam	N	None
3		205	223	Mendiola, Joaquin S	Son	M	Cha	2.7	S	N		Guam		None
4		206	224	Rapolla, Enrique C	Head	M	Chin	31	M	N	Y	Guam	Y	Fireman
5		206	224	Rapolla, Catlina SN	Wife	F	Cha	32	M	N	Y	Guam	Y	None
6		206	224	Rapolla, Maria SN	Daughter	F	Chin	4.8	S	N		Guam		None
7		206	224	Rapolla, Ramon SN	Son	M	Chin	2.7	S	N		Guam		None
8		206	224	Rapolla, Consolacion SN	Daughter	F	Chin	1.2	S	N		Guam		None
9		206	224	Rapolla, Francisca SN	Daughter	F	Chin	0	S	N		Guam		None
10		207	225	Quitugua, Catalina S	Head	F	Cha	31	M	N	Y	Guam		None
11		207	225	Quitugua, Juan S	Son	M	Cha	5	S	N		Guam		None
12		207	225	Quitugua, Clementina S	Daughter	F	Cha	3.3	S	N		Guam		None
13		207	225	Quitugua, Rita S	Daughter	F	Cha	1.8	S	N		Guam		None
14		207	225	Quitugua, Jose S	Son	M	Cha	0	S	N		Guam		None
15		207	225	Santos, Juana A	Mother-in-law	F	Cha	62	Wd	N	N	Guam	N	None
16		208	226	Aguon, Magdalena T	Head	F	Chin	60	Wd	N	N	Guam	N	None
17		208	226	Aguon, Mariano T	Son	M	Chin	21	S	N	Y	Guam	Y	Laborer
18		208	226	Aguon, Santiago T	Son	M	Chin	17	S	N	Y	Guam	Y	Servant
19		209	227	Tydingco, Vicente	Head	M	Chin	36	M	N	Y	Guam	Y	School teacher
20		209	227	Tydingco, Francisca L	Wife	F	Cha	34	M	N	Y	Guam	Y	None
21		209	227	Tydingco, Carlos P	Son	M	Chin	15	S	Y	Y	Guam	Y	School teacher
22		209	227	Tydingco, Helen C	Daughter	F	Chin	12	S	Y	Y	Guam	Y	None
23		209	227	Tydingco, Ruth S	Daughter	F	Chin	11	S	Y	Y	Guam	Y	None
24		209	227	Tydingco, Manuel A	Son	M	Chin	5	S	N		Guam		None
25		209	227	Tydingco, Dolores L	Daughter	F	Chin	4	S	N		Guam		None

(CHAMORRO ROOTS GENEALOGY PROJECT™ TRANSCRIPTION)
(BERNARD T. PUNZALAN / HTTP://WWW.CHAMORROROOTS.COM)

DEPARTMENT OF COMMERCE-BUREAU OF THE CENSUS
WASHINGTON

FIFTEENTH CENSUS OF THE UNITED STATES: 1930-POPULATION

THE ISLAND OF GUAM

Sheet No. 5B

236B

District **Municipality of Asan**
Name of Place **Asan Town**
[Proper name and, also, name of class, as city, town, village, barrio, etc]

Enumeration District No. 7
Enumerated by me on **April 16, 1930** Joaquin Torres, Enumerator

	PLACE OF ABODE: Street, avenue, road, etc.	Number of dwelling house in order of visitation	Number of family in order of visitation	NAME of each person whose place of abode on April 1, 1930, was in this family. Enter surname, first, then given name and middle initial. If any. Include every person living on April 1, 1930. Omit children born since April 1, 1930.	RELATION Relationship of this Person to the head of the family.	PERSONAL DESCRIPTION: Sex	Color or race	Age at last birthday	Single, married, widowed or divorced	EDUCATION: Attended school any time since Sept. 1, 1929	Whether able to read and write.	NATIVITY Place of birth of this person.	Whether able to speak English.	OCCUPATION
	1	2	3	4	5	6	7	8	9	10	11	12	13	14
26	Agana-Piti Road	209	227	Tydingco, Severa P	Daughter	F	Chin	2.1	S	N		Guam		None
27		210	228	Aflleje, Vicente	Head	M	Cha	31	M	N	Y	Guam	Y	Fisherman
28		210	228	Aflleje, Maria T	Wife	F	Chin	30	M	N	Y	Guam	Y	School teacher
29		210	228	Aflleje, Maria T	Daughter	F	Cha	8	S	Y		Guam		None
30		210	228	Aflleje, Jesus T	Son	M	Cha	6	S	Y		Guam		None
31		210	228	Aflleje, Jose T	Son	M	Cha	5	S	N		Guam		None
32		210	228	Aflleje, Jose T	Son	M	Cha	1.4	S	N		Guam		None
33		210	228	Aflleje, Carlos T	Son	M	Cha	.1	S	N		Guam		None
34		211	229	Cruz, Joaquin P	Head	M	Cha	43	Wd	N	Y	Guam	Y	Laborer
35		211	229	Cruz, Joaquin T	Son	M	Cha	17	S	N	Y	Guam	Y	Laborer
36		211	229	Cruz, Tomas T	Son	M	Cha	12	S	Y	Y	Guam	Y	None
37		211	229	Cruz, Maria T	Daughter	F	Cha	10	S	Y	Y	Guam	Y	None
38		212	230	Castro, Juan C	Head	M	Cha	45	M	N	N	Guam	N	Farmer
39		212	230	Castro, Cristina T	Wife	F	Cha	40	M	N	N	Guam	N	None
40		212	230	Castro, Ignacio T	Son	M	Cha	25	S	N	Y	Guam	Y	Laborer
41		212	230	Castro, Josefa M T	Daughter	F	Cha	21	S	N	Y	Guam	Y	None
42		212	230	Castro, Francisco T	Son	M	Cha	19	S	N	Y	Guam	Y	Laborer
43		212	230	Castro, Angelina T	Daughter	F	Cha	15	S	N	Y	Guam	Y	None
44		212	230	Castro, Jose T	Son	M	Cha	13	S	Y	Y	Guam	Y	None
45		212	230	Castro, Anunsia T	Daughter	F	Cha	10	S	Y	Y	Guam	Y	None
46		212	230	Castro, Lourdes T	Daughter	F	Cha	7	S	Y		Guam		None
47		212	231	Treltas, Antonia T	Head	F	Cha	66	M	N	N	Guam	Y	Weaver
48		213	232	Taitano, Manuel B	Head	M	Cha	35	M	N	Y	Guam	Y	Laborer
49		213	232	Taitano, Antonia F	Wife	F	Cha	38	M	N	Y	Guam	Y	None
50		213	232	Taitano, Teodoro F	Son	M	Cha	14	S	Y	Y	Guam	Y	None

DEPARTMENT OF COMMERCE-BUREAU OF THE CENSUS
WASHINGTON

FIFTEENTH CENSUS OF THE UNITED STATES: 1930-POPULATION

THE ISLAND OF GUAM

Sheet No. 6A

District **Municipality of Asan**
Name of Place **Asan Town** [Proper name and, also, name of class, as city, town, village, barrio, etc]

Enumeration District No. 7
Enumerated by me on **April 17, 1930** Joaquin Torres, Enumerator

	PLACE OF ABODE			NAME	RELATION	PERSONAL DESCRIPTION				EDUCATION		NATIVITY		OCCUPATION
	Street, avenue, road, etc.	Number of dwelling house in order of visitation	Number of family in order of visitation	of each person whose place of abode on April 1, 1930, was in this family. Enter surname, first, then given name and middle initial. If any. Include every person living on April 1, 1930. Omit children born since April 1, 1930.	Relationship of this Person to the head of the family.	Sex	Color or race	Age at last birthday	Single, married, widowed or divorced	Attended school any time since Sept. 1, 1929	Whether able to read and write.	Place of birth of this person.	Whether able to speak English.	
	1	2	3	4	5	6	7	8	9	10	11	12	13	14
1	Agana-Piti Road	213	232	Taitano, Severa F	Daughter	F	Cha	2.1	S	N		Guam		None
2		213	232	Taitano, Emilia B	Mother	F	Cha	58	S	N	N	Guam	N	None
3		214	233	Chargualaf, Eugenio C	Head	M	Cha	62	M	N	Y	Guam	N	Farmer
4		214	233	Chargualaf, Ana T	Wife	F	Cha	57	M	N	N	Guam	N	None
5		215	234	Taitano, Manuel T	Head	M	Cha	38	M	N	N	Guam	N	None
6		215	234	Taitano, Maria M	Wife	F	Cha	48	M	N	Y	Guam	N	Weaver
7		215	234	Taitano, Carmen T	Mother	F	Cha	69	Wd	N	N	Guam	N	None
8		216	235	Cruz, Joaquin S	Head	M	Cha	35	M	N	Y	Guam	Y	Farmer
9		216	235	Cruz, Cristina T	Wife	F	Cha	36	M	N	N	Guam	N	None
10		216	235	Balajadia, Rita T	Step daughter	F	Cha	14	S	Y	Y	Guam	Y	None
11		216	236	Cruz, Manuel S	Head	M	Cha	26	S	N	Y	Guam	Y	Laborer
12		217	237	Taijto, Antonio T	Head	M	Cha	58	M	N	Y	Guam	N	Farmer
13		217	237	Taijto, Maria A	Wife	F	Cha	58	M	N	N	Guam	N	None
14		218	238	Quitugua, Jose Q	Head	M	Cha	40	M	N	Y	Guam	N	Farmer
15		218	238	Quitugua, Rosa T	Wife	F	Cha	36	M	N	Y	Guam	N	None
16		218	238	Quitugua, Jesus T	Son	M	Cha	20	S	N	Y	Guam	Y	Laborer
17		218	238	Quitugua, Engracia T	Son	M	Cha	18	S	N	Y	Guam	Y	Servant
18		218	238	Quitugua, Joaquin T	Son	M	Cha	14	S	N	Y	Guam	Y	None
19		218	238	Quitugua, Miguel T	Son	M	Cha	13	S	Y	Y	Guam	Y	None
20		218	238	Quitugua, Dometrio T	Son	M	Cha	11	S	Y	Y	Guam	Y	None
21		218	238	Quitugua, Gregorio T	Son	M	Cha	7	S	Y		Guam		None
22		218	238	Quitugua, Pedro T	Son	M	Cha	4.5	S	N		Guam		None
23		218	238	Quitugua, Francisco T	Son	M	Cha	2.5	S	N		Guam		None
24		218	238	Quitugua, Roberto T	Son	M	Cha	1	S	N		Guam		None
25		219	239	Duenas, Concepcion E	Head	F	Cha	41	S	N	N	Guam	Y	Laundress

DEPARTMENT OF COMMERCE-BUREAU OF THE CENSUS
WASHINGTON

FIFTEENTH CENSUS OF THE UNITED STATES: 1930-POPULATION

THE ISLAND OF GUAM

Sheet No. 6B

237B

District **Municipality of Asan**
Name of Place **Asan Town**
[Proper name and, also, name of class, as city, town, village, barrio, etc]

Enumeration District No. 7
Enumerated by me on **April 17, 1930** Joaquin Torres
Enumerator

	PLACE OF ABODE: Street, avenue, road, etc.	Number of dwelling house in order of visitation	Number of family in order of visitation	NAME of each person whose place of abode on April 1, 1930, was in this family. Enter surname, first, then given name and middle initial. If any. Include every person living on April 1, 1930. Omit children born since April 1, 1930.	RELATION Relationship of this Person to the head of the family.	PERSONAL DESCRIPTION: Sex	Color or race	Age at last birthday	Single, married, widowed or divorced	EDUCATION: Attended school any time since Sept. 1, 1929	Whether able to read and write.	NATIVITY Place of birth of this person.	Whether able to speak English.	OCCUPATION
	1	2	3	4	5	6	7	8	9	10	11	12	13	14
26	Agana-Piti Road	220	240	Fejeran, Pedro A	Head	M	Cha	23	M	N	Y	Guam	Y	Laborer
27		220	240	Fejeran, Martina T	Wife	F	Cha	24	M	N	Y	Guam	N	None
28		220	240	Fejeran, Juan T	Son	M	Cha	4.2	S	N		Guam		None
29		220	240	Fejeran, Remedio T	Daughter	F	Cha	1.1	S	N		Guam		None
30		220	240	Fejeran, Concepcion T	Daughter	F	Cha	.1	S	N		Guam		None
31		221	241	Quichocho, Ana T	Head	F	Cha	37	Wd	N	N	Guam	N	Laundress
32		221	241	Quichocho, Juan T	Son	M	Cha	16	S	Y	Y	Guam	Y	None
33		221	241	Quichocho, Rosa T	Daughter	F	Cha	14	S	N	Y	Guam	Y	Servant
34		221	241	Quichocho, Maria T	Daughter	F	Cha	11	S	Y	Y	Guam	Y	None
35		221	241	Quichocho, Bernadita T	Daughter	F	Cha	9	S	Y		Guam		None
36		221	241	Quichocho, Rosario T	Daughter	F	Cha	7	S	Y		Guam		None
37		221	241	Quichocho, Ofracia T	Daughter	F	Cha	4.4	S	N		Guam		None
38		222	242	Treltas, Jose A	Head	M	Cha	27	M	N	Y	Guam	Y	Laborer
39		222	242	Treltas, Bartola C	Wife	F	Cha	43	M	N	N	Guam	N	None
40		222	242	Treltas, Rosalia C	Daughter	F	Cha	9	S	Y		Guam		None
41		222	242	Treltas, Vicente C	Son	M	Cha	7	S	Y		Guam		None
42		222	242	Tajalle, Andrea C	Daughter	F	Cha	16	S	N	Y	Guam	Y	Servant
43		223	243	Cruz, Vicente	Head	M	Cha	38	M	N	Y	Guam	Y	Farmer
44		223	243	Cruz, Maria M	Wife	F	Cha	43	M	N	N	Guam	N	None
45		223	243	Cruz, Pilar M	Daughter	F	Cha	3.2	S	N		Guam		None
46		223	243	Cruz, Jose M	Nephew	M	Cha	24	S	N	Y	Guam	Y	Farm laborer
47		223	243	Cruz, Nicolas M	Nephew	M	Cha	16	S	N	Y	Guam	Y	Farm laborer
48		224	244	Terlaje, Jose C	Head	M	Cha	43	M	N	Y	Guam	Y	Farmer
49		224	244	Terlaje, Josefa F	Wife	F	Cha	43	M	N	N	Guam	N	None
50		225	245	Taitano, Matias T	Head	M	Cha	49	M	N	N	Guam	N	Farmer

DEPARTMENT OF COMMERCE-BUREAU OF THE CENSUS
WASHINGTON

FIFTEENTH CENSUS OF THE UNITED STATES: 1930-POPULATION

THE ISLAND OF GUAM

Sheet No. 7A

District **Municipality of Asan**
Name of Place **Asan Town**
[Proper name and, also, name of class, as city, town, village, barrio, etc]

Enumeration District No. 7
Enumerated by me on **April 19, 1930** Joaquin Torres, Enumerator

	PLACE OF ABODE			NAME	RELATION	PERSONAL DESCRIPTION				EDUCATION		NATIVITY		OCCUPATION
	Street, avenue, road, etc.	Number of dwelling house in order of visitation	Number of family in order of visitation	of each person whose place of abode on April 1, 1930, was in this family. Enter surname, first, then given name and middle initial. If any. Include every person living on April 1, 1930. Omit children born since April 1, 1930.	Relationship of this Person to the head of the family.	Sex	Color or race	Age at last birthday	Single, married, widowed or divorced	Attended school any time since Sept. 1, 1929	Whether able to read and write.	Place of birth of this person.	Whether able to speak English.	
	1	2	3	4	5	6	7	8	9	10	11	12	13	14
1	Agana-Piti Road	225	245	Taitano, Ana G	Wife	F	Cha	39	M	N	N	Guam	N	None
2		225	245	Taitano, Justo G	Son	M	Cha	23	S	N	Y	Guam	Y	Laborer
3		225	245	Taitano, Pedro G	Son	M	Cha	20	S	N	Y	Guam	Y	Laborer
4		226	246	Munoz, Alejandro SR	Head	M	Fil	66	M	N	N	Guam	Y	Laborer
5		226	246	Munoz, Manuela C	Wife	F	Cha	37	M	N	N	Guam	N	None
6		226	246	Munoz, Rosa C	Daughter	F	Fil	5	S	N		Guam		None
7		226	246	Munoz, Vcente C	Son	M	Fil	2	S	N		Guam		None
8		227	247	Salas, Maria J	Head	F	Cha	46	M	N	N	Guam	N	Laundress
9		227	247	Salas, Catalina J	Daughter	F	Cha	21	M	N	Y	Guam	Y	Laundress
10		227	247	Salas, Nicolasa J	Daughter	F	Cha	19	S	N	Y	Guam	Y	Servant
11		227	247	Salas, Jesus J	Son	M	Cha	17	S	N	Y	Guam	Y	Farm laborer
12		227	247	Salas, Feliza J	Daughter	F	Cha	14	S	N	Y	Guam	Y	None
13		227	247	Salas, Joaquin J	Son	M	Cha	13	S	Y	Y	Guam	Y	None
14		227	247	Salas, Manuel J	Son	M	Cha	10	S	Y	Y	Guam	Y	None
15		227	247	Salas, Petronilia J	Daughter	F	Cha	9	S	Y		Guam		None
16		227	247	Salas, Angel J	Son	M	Cha	2.8	S	N		Guam		None
17		228	248	Salas, Jose J	Head	M	Cha	24	M	N	Y	Guam	Y	Chauffeur
18		228	248	Salas, Ana A	Wife	F	Cha	25	M	N	Y	Guam	Y	None
19		228	248	Salas, Brigida A	Daughter	F	Cha	5	S	N		Guam		None
20		228	248	Salas, Herman A	Son	M	Cha	3.5	S	N		Guam		None
21		228	248	Salas, Roberto A	Son	M	Cha	2.4	S	N		Guam		None
22		228	248	Salas, Frank A	Son	M	Cha	.8	S	N		Guam		None
23		228	248	Acfalle, Dominga B	Mother-in-law	F	Cha	47	S	N		Guam		None
24		228	249	Acfalle, Tomasa B	Head	F	Cha	41	S	N	Y	Guam	Y	Laundress
25		228	249	Acfalle, Carmen A	Daughter	F	Cha	13	S	Y	Y	Guam	Y	None

DEPARTMENT OF COMMERCE-BUREAU OF THE CENSUS
WASHINGTON

FIFTEENTH CENSUS OF THE UNITED STATES: 1930-POPULATION

THE ISLAND OF GUAM

Sheet No. 7B

238B

District **Municipality of Asan**
Name of Place **Asan Town**
[Proper name and, also, name of class, as city, town, village, barrio, etc]

Enumeration District No. 7
Enumerated by me on **April 19, 1930** Joaquin Torres, Enumerator

	PLACE OF ABODE: Street, avenue, road, etc.	Number of dwelling house in order of visitation	Number of family in order of visitation	NAME of each person whose place of abode on April 1, 1930, was in this family. Enter surname, first, then given name and middle initial. If any. Include every person living on April 1, 1930. Omit children born since April 1, 1930.	RELATION Relationship of this Person to the head of the family.	PERSONAL DESCRIPTION: Sex	Color or race	Age at last birthday	Single, married, widowed or divorced	EDUCATION: Attended school any time since Sept. 1, 1929	Whether able to read and write.	NATIVITY Place of birth of this person.	Whether able to speak English.	OCCUPATION
	1	2	3	4	5	6	7	8	9	10	11	12	13	14
26	Agana-Piti Road	228	249	Acfalle, Felicita A	Daughter	F	Cha	8	S	Y		Guam		None
27		228	249	Acfalle, Francisco A	Son	M	Cha	7	S	Y		Guam		None
28		228	249	Acfalle, Albert A	Son	M	Cha	5	S	N		Guam		None
29		229	250	Aflleje, Antonio T	Head	M	Cha	49	M	N	Y	Guam	N	Farmer
30		229	250	Aflleje, Dolores G	Wife	F	Cha	50	M	N	N	Guam	N	None
31		229	250	Aflleje, Natividad G	Daughter	F	Cha	28	S	N	Y	Guam	Y	Laundress
32		229	250	Aflleje, Jose G	Son	M	Cha	20	S	N	Y	Guam	Y	Cook
33		229	250	Aflleje, Teresa G	Daughter	F	Cha	11	S	Y	Y	Guam	Y	None
34		229	250	Aflleje, Marcela T	Mother	F	Cha	67	Wd	N	Y	Guam	N	None
35		229	250	Aflleje, Judit A	Grand daughter	F	Cha	5	S	N		Guam		None
36		229	250	Aflleje, Victoria A	Grand daughter	F	Cha	.2	S	N		Guam		None
37		230	251	Taitague, Jose C	Head	M	Cha	43	M	N	Y	Guam	N	Laborer
38		230	251	Taitague, Catalina C	Wife	F	Cha	36	M	N	Y	Guam	N	None
39		230	251	Taitague, Agueda C	Daughter	F	Cha	11	S	Y	Y	Guam	Y	None
40		230	251	Taitague, Maria C	Daughter	F	Cha	5	S	N		Guam		None
41		231	252	Tydingco, Jose C	Head	M	Chin	27	M	N	Y	Guam	Y	Chauffeur
42		231	252	Tydingco, Dolores A	Wife	F	Cha	26	M	N	Y	Guam	Y	None
43		231	252	Tydingco, Pedro A	Son	M	Chin	7	S	Y		Guam		None
44		231	252	Tydingco, Rufina A	Daughter	F	Chin	4.3	S	N		Guam		None
45		231	252	Tydingco, Juan A	Son	M	Chin	2.8	S	N		Guam		None
46		231	252	Tydingco, Maria A	Daughter	F	Chin	2.1	S	N		Guam		None
47		231	252	Tydingco, Jose A	Son	M	Chin	.8	S	N		Guam		None
48		232	253	Crisostomo, Juan T	Head	M	Cha	32	M	N	Y	Guam	Y	Laborer
49		232	253	Crisostomo, Antonia F	Wife	F	Cha	25	M	N	N	Guam	N	None
50		232	253	Crisostomo, Sebastian F	Son	M	Cha	4.2	S	N		Guam		None

DEPARTMENT OF COMMERCE-BUREAU OF THE CENSUS
WASHINGTON

FIFTEENTH CENSUS OF THE UNITED STATES: 1930-POPULATION

THE ISLAND OF GUAM

Sheet No. 8A

District **Municipality of Asan**
Name of Place **Asan Town**
[Proper name and, also, name of class, as city, town, village, barrio, etc]

Enumeration District No. 7
Enumerated by me on **April 21, 1930** Joaquin Torres
Enumerator

	PLACE OF ABODE			NAME	RELATION	PERSONAL DESCRIPTION				EDUCATION		NATIVITY		OCCUPATION
	Street, avenue, road, etc.	Number of dwelling house in order of visitation	Number of family in order of visitation	of each person whose place of abode on April 1, 1930, was in this family. Enter surname, first, then given name and middle initial. If any. Include every person living on April 1, 1930. Omit children born since April 1, 1930.	Relationship of this Person to the head of the family.	Sex	Color or race	Age at last birthday	Single, married, widowed or divorced	Attended school any time since Sept. 1, 1929	Whether able to read and write.	Place of birth of this person.	Whether able to speak English.	
	1	2	3	4	5	6	7	8	9	10	11	12	13	14
1	Agana-Piti Road	232	253	Crisostomo, Vicente F	Son	M	Cha	.2	S	N		Guam		None
2		233	254	Limtiaco, Jose L	Head	M	Chin	32	M	N	Y	Guam		Laborer
3		233	254	Limtiaco, Angela C	Wife	F	Cha	32	M	N	N	Guam		None
4		233	254	Limtiaco, Antonia C	Daughter	F	Chin	9	S	Y		Guam		None
5		233	254	Limtiaco, Juan C	Son	M	Chin	6	S	N		Guam		None
6		233	254	Limtiaco, Francisco C	Son	M	Chin	4.5	S	N		Guam		None
7		233	254	Limtiaco, Guillermo C	Son	M	Chin	1.1	S	N		Guam		None
8		233	254	Limtiaco, Ana T	Mother	F	Chin	53	S	N		Guam		None
9		234	255	Ignacio, Enrique R	Head	M	Cha	31	M	N	Y	Guam	Y	Laborer
10		234	255	Ignacio, Soledad J	Wife	F	Cha	35	M	N	Y	Guam	N	None
11		234	255	Ignacio, Tomas J	Son	M	Cha	9	S	Y		Guam		None
12		234	255	Ignacio, Juan J	Son	M	Cha	7	S	Y		Guam		None
13		234	255	Ignacio, Pedro J	Son	M	Cha	6	S	N		Guam		None
14		234	255	Ignacio, Anisia J	Daughter	F	Cha	5	S	N		Guam		None
15		234	255	Ignacio, Josefa J	Daughter	F	Cha	2.1	S	N		Guam		None
16		234	255	Ignacio, Celestina J	Daughter	F	Cha	.9	S	N		Guam		None
17		235	256	Limtiaco, Catlina A	Head	F	Chin	56	Wd	N	Y	Guam	N	Laundress
18		235	256	Limtiaco, Maria A	Daughter	F	Chin	24	S	N	Y	Guam	Y	Laundress
19		235	256	Limtiaco, Antonio A	Son	M	Chin	22	S	N	Y	Guam	Y	Chauffeur
20		235	256	Limtiaco, Joaquina A	Daughter	F	Chin	18	S	N	Y	Guam	Y	Laundress
21		235	257	Limtiaco, Jose A	Head	M	Chin	25	M	N	Y	Guam	Y	Storeman
22		235	257	Limtiaco, Dolores C	Wife	F	Cha	27	M	N	Y	Guam	Y	None
23		235	257	Limtiaco, Manuel C	Son	M	Chin	3.1	S	N		Guam		None
24		235	257	Limtiaco, Ana C	Daughter	F	Chin	.2	S	N		Guam		None
25		235	257	Jesus, Concepcion L	Lodger	F	Cha	64	Wd	N	N	Guam	N	None

(CHAMORRO ROOTS GENEALOGY PROJECT™ TRANSCRIPTION)
(BERNARD T. PUNZALAN / HTTP://WWW.CHAMORROROOTS.COM)

DEPARTMENT OF COMMERCE-BUREAU OF THE CENSUS
WASHINGTON

FIFTEENTH CENSUS OF THE UNITED STATES: 1930-POPULATION

THE ISLAND OF GUAM

Sheet No. 8B

239B

District **Municipality of Asan**
Name of Place **Asan Town**
[Proper name and, also, name of class, as city, town, village, barrio, etc]

Enumeration District No. 7
Enumerated by me on **April 22, 1930** Joaquin Torres
Enumerator

	PLACE OF ABODE			NAME	RELATION	PERSONAL DESCRIPTION				EDUCATION		NATIVITY		OCCUPATION
	Street, avenue, road, etc.	Number of dwelling house is order of visitation	Number of family in order of visitation	of each person whose place of abode on April 1, 1930, was in this family. Enter surname, first, then given name and middle initial. If any. Include every person living on April 1, 1930. Omit children born since April 1, 1930.	Relationship of this Person to the head of the family.	Sex	Color or race	Age at last birthday	Single, married, widowed or divorced	Attended school any time since Sept. 1, 1929	Whether able to read and write.	Place of birth of this person.	Whether able to speak English.	
	1	2	3	4	5	6	7	8	9	10	11	12	13	14
26	Agana-Piti Road	236	257	Lizama, Roduvico C	Head	M	Cha	49	M	N	Y	Guam	Y	Farmer
27		236	257	Lizama, Ana Q	Wife	F	Cha	45	M	N	Y	Guam	N	None
28		236	257	Lizama, Maria Q	Daughter	F	Cha	26	S	N	Y	Guam	Y	Laundress
29		236	257	Lizama, Milgaros Q	Daughter	F	Cha	22	S	N	Y	Guam	Y	Laundress
30		236	257	Lizama, Jose Q	Son	M	Cha	19	S	N	Y	Guam	Y	Servant
31		236	257	Lizama, Vicente Q	Son	M	Cha	14	S	Y	Y	Guam	Y	None
32		236	257	Lizama, Beatris Q	Daughter	F	Cha	12	S	Y	Y	Guam	Y	None
33		236	257	Lizama, Constancio Q	Son	M	Cha	7	S	Y		Guam		None
34		237	259	Mendiola, Jesus Q	Head	M	Cha	26	M	N	Y	Guam	Y	Farmer
35		237	259	Mendiola, Elena T	Wife	F	Cha	24	M	N	Y	Guam	Y	None
36		237	259	Mendiola, Guadalupe T	Daughter	F	Cha	5	S	N		Guam		None
37		237	259	Mendiola, Fidela T	Daughter	F	Cha	1.5	S	N		Guam		None
38		238	260	Mendiola, Jose Q	Head	M	Cha	40	M	N	Y	Guam	Y	Carpenter
39		238	260	Mendiola, Candelaria P	Wife	F	Cha	39	M	N	N	Guam	N	None
40		238	260	Mendiola, Jose P	Son	M	Cha	25	S	N	Y	Guam	Y	Carpenter
41		238	260	Mendiola, Justo D P	Son	M	Cha	18	S	N	Y	Guam	Y	Carpenter
42		238	260	Mendiola, Celia P	Daughter	F	Cha	12	S	Y	Y	Guam	Y	None
43		238	260	Mendiola, Pilar P	Daughter	F	Cha	8	S	Y		Guam		None
44		238	260	Mendiola, Pedro P	Son	M	Cha	7	S	Y		Guam		None
45		238	260	Mendiola, Joaquin P	Son	M	Cha	6	S	N		Guam		None
46		239	261	Quitugua, Juan Q	Head	M	Cha	37	M	N	Y	Guam	Y	Laborer
47		239	261	Quitugua, Maria F	Wife	F	Cha	38	M	N	Y	Guam	N	None
48		239	261	Quitugua, Eliza F	Daughter	F	Cha	18	S	N	Y	Guam	Y	None
49		239	261	Quitugua, Ana F	Daughter	F	Cha	14	S	N	Y	Guam	Y	None
50		239	261	Quitugua, Concepcion F	Daughter	F	Cha	9	S	Y		Guam		None

DEPARTMENT OF COMMERCE-BUREAU OF THE CENSUS
WASHINGTON

FIFTEENTH CENSUS OF THE UNITED STATES: 1930-POPULATION

THE ISLAND OF GUAM

Sheet No. 9A

District Municipality of Asan
Name of Place Asan Town
[Proper name and, also, name of class, as city, town, village, barrio, etc]

Enumeration District No. 7
Enumerated by me on April 22, 1930 Joaquin Torres
Enumerator

	PLACE OF ABODE			NAME	RELATION	PERSONAL DESCRIPTION				EDUCATION		NATIVITY		OCCUPATION
	Street, avenue, road, etc.	Number of dwelling house is order of visitation	Number of family in order of visitation	of each person whose place of abode on April 1, 1930, was in this family. Enter surname, first, then given name and middle initial. If any. Include every person living on April 1, 1930. Omit children born since April 1, 1930.	Relationship of this Person to the head of the family.	Sex	Color or race	Age at last birthday	Single, married, widowed or divorced	Attended school any time since Sept. 1, 1929	Whether able to read and write.	Place of birth of this person.	Whether able to speak English.	
	1	2	3	4	5	6	7	8	9	10	11	12	13	14
1	Agana-Piti Road	239	261	Quitugua, Jesus F	Son	M	Cha	7	S	N		Guam		None
2		239	261	Quitugua, Rita F	Daughter	F	Cha	5	S	N		Guam		None
3		239	261	Quitugua, Ramon F	Son	M	Cha	2.4	S	N		Guam		None
4		239	261	Quitugua, Henry F	Son	M	Cha	.2	S	N		Guam		None
5		240	262	Taijito, Jose T	Head	M	Cha	52	M	N	Y	Guam	N	Farmer
6		240	262	Taijito, Vicenta S	Wife	F	Cha	54	M	N	N	Guam	N	None
7		240	262	Taijito, Magdalena S	Daughter	F	Cha	23	S	N	Y	Guam	Y	None
8		240	262	Taijito, Francisco S	Son	M	Cha	21	S	N	Y	Guam	Y	Laborer
9		240	262	Taijito, Soledad S	Daughter	F	Cha	18	S	N	Y	Guam	Y	Servant
10		240	262	Taijito, Juan S	Son	M	Cha	16	S	N	Y	Guam	Y	Tailor
11		240	262	Taijito, Maria S	Daughter	F	Cha	11	S	Y	Y	Guam	Y	None
12		240	262	Taijito, Maristela T	Grand daughter	F	Cha	2.2	S	N		Guam		None
13		241	263	Taitano, Dolores LG	Head	F	Cha	52	Wd	N	N	Guam	N	None
14		241	263	Taitano, Felicita LG	Daughter	F	Cha	24	S	N	Y	Guam	N	Laundress
15		241	263	Taitano, Carmen LG	Daughter	F	Cha	22	S	N	Y	Guam	N	Laundress
16		241	263	Taitano, Maria LG	Daughter	F	Cha	19	S	N	Y	Guam	Y	Servant
17		241	263	Taitano, Manuela LG	Daughter	F	Cha	15	S	N	Y	Guam	Y	Servant
18		241	263	Taitano, Jesus LG	Son	M	Cha	13	S	Y	Y	Guam	Y	None
19		241	263	Taitano, Jose LG	Son	M	Cha	9	S	Y		Guam		None
20		242	264	Chargualaf, Justo Q	Head	M	Cha	46	M	N	Y	Guam	N	Farmer
21		242	264	Chargualaf, Dolores T	Wife	F	Cha	46	M	N	Y	Guam	N	None
22		242	264	Chargualaf, Maria T	Daughter	F	Cha	21	S	N	N	Guam	N	Laundress
23		242	264	Chargualaf, Encarnacion T	Daughter	F	Cha	11	S	Y	Y	Guam	Y	None
24		242	264	Chargualaf, Santiago T	Son	M	Cha	6	S	N		Guam		None
25		243	265	Salas, Isabel SN	Head	F	Cha	54	Wd	N	N	Guam	N	Farmer

DEPARTMENT OF COMMERCE-BUREAU OF THE CENSUS
WASHINGTON

FIFTEENTH CENSUS OF THE UNITED STATES: 1930-POPULATION

THE ISLAND OF GUAM

Sheet No. 9B

240B

District **Municipality of Asan**
Name of Place **Asan Town**
[Proper name and, also, name of class, as city, town, village, barrio, etc]

Enumeration District No. 7
Enumerated by me on **April 22, 1930** Joaquin Torres, Enumerator

	PLACE OF ABODE			NAME	RELATION	PERSONAL DESCRIPTION				EDUCATION		NATIVITY		OCCUPATION
	Street, avenue, road, etc.	Number of dwelling house is order of visitation	Number of family in order of visitation	of each person whose place of abode on April 1, 1930, was in this family. Enter surname, first, then given name and middle initial. If any. Include every person living on April 1, 1930. Omit children born since April 1, 1930.	Relationship of this Person to the head of the family.	Sex	Color or race	Age at last birthday	Single, married, widowed or divorced	Attended school any time since Sept. 1, 1929	Whether able to read and write.	Place of birth of this person.	Whether able to speak English.	
	1	2	3	4	5	6	7	8	9	10	11	12	13	14
26	Agana-Piti Road	243	265	Salas, Jose S	Grandson	M	Cha	16	S	N	Y	Guam	Y	Farm laborer
27		243	265	Quitugua, Juana Q	Lodger	F	Cha	60	S	N	N	Guam	N	None
28		244	266	Acfalle, Juan N	Head	M	Cha	44	Wd	N	Y	Guam	N	Farm laborer
29		245	267	Aflague, Antonio S	Head	M	Cha	41	M	N	Y	Guam	Y	Farmer
30		245	267	Aflague, Dolores T	Wife	F	Cha	29	M	N	Y	Guam	Y	None
31		245	267	Aflague, Juan T	Son	M	Cha	6	S	N		Guam		None
32		246	268	San Nicolas, Vicente T	Head	M	Cha	51	M	N	Y	Guam	Y	Teamster
33		246	268	San Nicolas, Carmen M	Wife	F	Cha	22	M	N	Y	Guam	N	None
34		246	268	San Nicolas, Francisco A	Son	M	Cha	30	S	N	Y	Guam	Y	Farm laborer
35		246	268	San Nicolas, Gregorio A	Son	M	Cha	21	S	N	Y	Guam	Y	Chauffeur
36		246	268	San Nicolas, Maria A	Daughter	F	Cha	18	S	N	Y	Guam	Y	None
37		246	268	San Nicolas, Rita A	Daughter	F	Cha	13	S	Y	Y	Guam	Y	None
38		246	268	San Nicolas, Tomasa A	Daughter	F	Cha	9	S	Y		Guam		None
39		246	268	San Nicolas, Asuncion M	Daughter	F	Cha	2.5	S	N		Guam		None
40		246	268	San Nicolas, Jesus M	Son	M	Cha	0	S	N		Guam		None
41		247	269	Aguon, Juan C	Head	M	Cha	44	M	N	Y	Guam	Y	Electrician
42		247	269	Aguon, Magdalena N	Wife	F	Cha	34	M	N	Y	Guam	Y	None
43		247	269	Aguon, Angelina M	Daughter	F	Cha	19	S	N	Y	Guam		None
44		247	269	Aguon, Juan N	Son	M	Cha	9	S	Y		Guam	Y	None
45		247	269	Aguon, Pedro N	Son	M	Cha	4.7	S	N		Guam		None
46		247	269	Aguon, Maria N	Daughter	F	Cha	2.3	S	N		Guam		None
47		247	269	Aguon, Concepcion	Daughter	F	Cha	.7	S	N		Guam		None
48		247	269	Maanao, Ramona M	Mother-in-law	F	Cha	64	Wd	N	N	Guam	N	None
49		247	269	Nauta, Maria N	Mother-in-law	F	Cha	60	S	N	N	Guam	N	None
50		248	270	Guerrero, Vicente S	Head	M	Cha	56	M	N	Y	Guam	N	Farmer

(CHAMORRO ROOTS GENEALOGY PROJECT™ TRANSCRIPTION)
(BERNARD T. PUNZALAN / HTTP://WWW.CHAMORROROOTS.COM)

DEPARTMENT OF COMMERCE-BUREAU OF THE CENSUS
WASHINGTON

FIFTEENTH CENSUS OF THE UNITED STATES: 1930-POPULATION

THE ISLAND OF GUAM

Sheet No. 10A

District **Municipality of Asan**
Name of Place **Asan Town**
[Proper name and, also, name of class, as city, town, village, barrio, etc]

Enumeration District No. 7
Enumerated by me on **April 23, 1930** Joaquin Torres, Enumerator

	PLACE OF ABODE			NAME	RELATION	PERSONAL DESCRIPTION				EDUCATION		NATIVITY		OCCUPATION
	Street, avenue, road, etc.	Number of dwelling house in order of visitation	Number of family in order of visitation	of each person whose place of abode on April 1, 1930, was in this family. Enter surname, first, then given name and middle initial. If any. Include every person living on April 1, 1930. Omit children born since April 1, 1930.	Relationship of this Person to the head of the family.	Sex	Color or race	Age at last birthday	Single, married, widowed or divorced	Attended school any time since Sept. 1, 1929	Whether able to read and write.	Place of birth of this person.	Whether able to speak English.	
	1	2	3	4	5	6	7	8	9	10	11	12	13	14
1	Agana-Piti Road	248	270	Guerrero, Caridad M	Wife	F	Cha	43	M	N	Y	Guam	N	None
2		248	270	Guerrero, Dolores M	Daughter	F	Cha	23	S	N	Y	Guam	Y	None
3		248	270	Guerrero, Jose M	Son	M	Cha	18	S	N	Y	Guam	Y	Farm laborer
4		248	270	Guerrero, Julian M	Son	M	Cha	15	S	Y	Y	Guam	Y	None
5		249	271	Guerrero, Jesus M	Head	M	Cha	22	M	N	Y	Guam	Y	Laborer
6		249	271	Guerrero, Felomena L	Wife	F	Cha	24	M	N	Y	Guam	Y	None
7		249	271	Guerrero, Jesus L	Son	M	Cha	1.1	S	N		Guam		None
8		250	272	San Nicolas, Antonio SN	Head	M	Cha	50	Wd	N	N	Guam	N	Farmer
9		250	272	San Nicolas, Rosa C	Daughter	F	Cha	16	S	N	Y	Guam	Y	None
10		250	272	San Nicolas, Maria C	Daughter	F	Cha	12	S	Y	Y	Guam	Y	None
11		250	272	San Nicolas, Beatris C	Daughter	F	Cha	10	S	Y	Y	Guam	Y	None
12		250	272	San Nicolas, Felicita C	Daughter	F	Cha	8	S	Y		Guam		None
13		251	273	Mendiola, Manuel S	Head	M	Cha	27	M	N	Y	Guam	Y	Laborer
14		251	273	Mendiola, Rosa F	Wife	F	Cha	22	M	N	Y	Guam	Y	None
15		251	273	Mendiola, Jose F	Son	M	Cha	.7	S	N		Guam		None
16		251	273	Fejeran, Jesus F	Step son	M	Cha	5	S	N		Guam		None
17		252	274	Meno, Carmen C	Head	F	Cha	45	S	N	Y	Guam	N	Weaver
18		252	274	Meno, Jose M	Son	M	Cha	24	S	N	Y	Guam	Y	Laborer
19		252	274	Meno, Sabina M	Daughter	F	Cha	19	S	N	Y	Guam	Y	Servant
20		252	274	Meno, Jesus M	Son	M	Cha	15	S	N	Y	Guam	Y	Servant
21		252	274	Meno, Francisco M	Son	M	Cha	11	S	Y	Y	Guam	Y	None
22		252	274	Meno, Vicenta M	Son	M	Cha	9	S	Y		Guam		None
23		252	274	Meno, Consolacion M	Daughter	F	Cha	3.5	S	N		Guam		None
24		253	275	Estrellas, Maria P	Head	F	Cha	61	Wd	N	N	Guam	Y	Laundress
25		254	276	Ignacio, Ana T	Head	F	Cha	45	M	N	Y	Guam	N	Laundress

DEPARTMENT OF COMMERCE-BUREAU OF THE CENSUS
WASHINGTON

FIFTEENTH CENSUS OF THE UNITED STATES: 1930-POPULATION

THE ISLAND OF GUAM

Sheet No. 10B

241B

District **Municipality of Asan**
Name of Place **Asan Town**
[Proper name and, also, name of class, as city, town, village, barrio, etc]

Enumeration District No. 7
Enumerated by me on **April 23, 1930** Joaquin Torres
Enumerator

	PLACE OF ABODE			NAME	RELATION	PERSONAL DESCRIPTION				EDUCATION		NATIVITY		OCCUPATION
	Street, avenue, road, etc.	Number of dwelling house is order of visitation	Number of family in order of visitation	of each person whose place of abode on April 1, 1930, was in this family. Enter surname, first, then given name and middle initial. If any. Include every person living on April 1, 1930. Omit children born since April 1, 1930.	Relationship of this Person to the head of the family.	Sex	Color or race	Age at last birthday	Single, married, widowed or divorced	Attended school any time since Sept. 1, 1929	Whether able to read and write.	Place of birth of this person.	Whether able to speak English.	
	1	2	3	4	5	6	7	8	9	10	11	12	13	14
26	Agana-Piti Road	254	276	Ignacio, Felix T	Son	M	Cha	19	S	N	Y	Guam	Y	Laborer
27		254	276	Ignacio, Luis T	Son	M	Cha	14	S	Y	Y	Guam	Y	None
28		254	276	Ignacio, Enrique T	Son	M	Cha	10	S	Y	Y	Guam	Y	None
29		254	276	Taitague, Antonia D	Mother	F	Cha	65	Wd	N	N	Guam	N	None
30		255	277	Blankowski, Helen K	Head	F	W	15	M	N	Y	Delaware	Y	None
31		255	277	Blankowski, Regina	Daughter	F	W	1.1	S	N		New York		None
32		256	278	Maanao, Vicente A	Head	M	Cha	26	M	N	Y	Guam	Y	Laborer
33		256	278	Maanao, Francisca T	Wife	F	Cha	22	M	N	N	Guam	N	None
34		256	278	Maanao, Ruth T	Daughter	F	Cha	5	S	N		Guam		None
35		256	278	Maanao, Rita T	Daughter	F	Cha	3.9	S	N		Guam		None
36		256	278	Maanao, Jose T	Son	M	Cha	1.2	S	N		Guam		None
37		257	279	Acfalle, Maria T	Head	F	Cha	21	M	N	Y	Guam	Y	None
38		257	279	Acfalle, Julia T	Daughter	F	Cha	4.1	S	N		Guam		None
39		258	280	Angoco, Vicente D	Head	M	Cha	28	M	N	Y	Guam	Y	Laborer
40		258	280	Angoco, Engracia A	Wife	F	Cha	23	M	N	N	Guam	N	None
41		258	280	Angoco, Tomasa A	Daughter	F	Cha	5	S	N		Guam		None
42		258	280	Angoco, Ana A	Daughter	F	Cha	3.2	S	N		Guam		None
43		258	280	Angoco, Maria A	Daughter	F	Cha	2.5	S	N		Guam		None
44		259	281	Camacho, Maria C	Head	F	Cha	20	S	N	Y	Guam	Y	Laundress
45		260	282	Lizama, Juan L	Head	M	Cha	28	M	N	Y	Guam	Y	Laborer
46		260	282	Lizama, Urfia N	Wife	F	Cha	25	M	N	Y	Guam	N	None
47		260	282	Lizama, Jesus N	Son	M	Cha	1	S	N		Guam		None
48		261	283	San Nicolas, Maria S	Head	F	Cha	57	Wd	N	N	Guam	N	None
49		261	283	San Nicolas, Consolacion S	Daughter	F	Cha	38	S	N	Y	Guam	Y	None
50		261	283	San Nicolas, Jose S	Son	M	Cha	28	S	N	Y	Guam	Y	Farm laborer

(CHAMORRO ROOTS GENEALOGY PROJECT™ TRANSCRIPTION)
(BERNARD T. PUNZALAN / HTTP://WWW.CHAMORROROOTS.COM)

DEPARTMENT OF COMMERCE-BUREAU OF THE CENSUS
WASHINGTON

FIFTEENTH CENSUS OF THE UNITED STATES: 1930-POPULATION

THE ISLAND OF GUAM

Sheet No. 11A

District **Municipality of Asan**
Name of Place **Asan Town**
[Proper name and, also, name of class, as city, town, village, barrio, etc]

Enumeration District No. 7
Enumerated by me on **April 24, 1930** Joaquin Torres
Enumerator

	PLACE OF ABODE			NAME	RELATION	PERSONAL DESCRIPTION				EDUCATION		NATIVITY		OCCUPATION
	Street, avenue, road, etc.	Number of dwelling house is order of visitation	Number of family in order of visitation	of each person whose place of abode on April 1, 1930, was in this family. Enter surname, first, then given name and middle initial. If any. Include every person living on April 1, 1930. Omit children born since April 1, 1930.	Relationship of this Person to the head of the family.	Sex	Color or race	Age at last birthday	Single, married, widowed or divorced	Attended school any time since Sept. 1, 1929	Whether able to read and write.	Place of birth of this person.	Whether able to speak English.	
	1	2	3	4	5	6	7	8	9	10	11	12	13	14
1	Agana-Piti Road	261	283	San Nicolas, Ignacia S	Daughter	F	Cha	18	S	N	Y	Guam	Y	None
2		261	283	San Nicolas, Ana S	Daughter	F	Cha	15	S	Y	Y	Guam	Y	None
3		262	284	Tydingco, Carlos M	Head	M	Cha	68	M	N	Y	Guam	Y	Farmer
4		262	284	Tydingco, Dolores C	Daughter	F	Cha	31	M	N	Y	Guam	Y	None
5		262	284	Tydingco, Antonio C	Son	M	Cha	22	S	N	Y	Guam	Y	Chauffeur
6		262	285	Rojas, Manuel S	Head	M	Cha	28	M	N	Y	Guam	Y	Salesman
7		262	285	Rojas, Antonio C	Wife	F	Cha	19	M	N	Y	Guam	Y	None
8		263	286	Cruz, Joaquin C	Head	M	Cha	46	M	N	Y	Guam	N	Farmer
9		263	286	Cruz, Rosa J	Wife	F	Cha	34	M	N	Y	Guam	N	None
10		263	286	Cruz, Maria J	Daughter	F	Cha	11	S	Y	Y	Guam	Y	None
11		263	286	Cruz, Francisco J	Son	M	Cha	8	S	Y		Guam		None
12		263	286	Cruz, Jose J	Son	M	Cha	7	S	Y		Guam		None
13		263	286	Cruz, Lourdes J	Daughter	F	Cha	6	S	N		Guam		None
14		263	286	Cruz, Roman J	Son	M	Cha	4.2	S	N		Guam		None
15		264	287	Gamboa, Vicente C	Head	M	Cha	36	M	N	Y	Guam	Y	Machinist
16		264	287	Gamboa, Isabel P	Wife	F	Cha	46	M	N	N	Guam	N	None
17		264	287	Gamboa, Lorenzo P	Son	M	Cha	19	S	N	Y	Guam	Y	Farm laborer
18		264	287	Gamboa, Julia P	Daughter	F	Cha	15	S	N	Y	Guam	Y	None
19		264	287	Gamboa, Antonio P	Son	M	Cha	13	S	Y	Y	Guam	Y	None
20		264	287	Gamboa, Vicente P	Son	M	Cha	10	S	Y	Y	Guam	Y	None
21		264	287	Gamboa, Isabel P	Daughter	F	Cha	7	S	Y		Guam		None
22		265	288	Terlaje, Felix A	Head	M	Cha	48	M	N	N	Guam	N	Farmer
23		265	288	Terlaje, Dolores S	Wife	F	Cha	51	M	N	N	Guam	N	None
24		266	289	Aflleje, Joaquin	Head	M	Cha	30	S	N	Y	Guam	Y	Farmer
25		266	289	Aflleje, Josefa P	Mother	F	Cha	70	Wd	N	N	Guam	N	None

DEPARTMENT OF COMMERCE-BUREAU OF THE CENSUS
WASHINGTON

FIFTEENTH CENSUS OF THE UNITED STATES: 1930-POPULATION

THE ISLAND OF GUAM

Sheet No. 11B

242B

District Municipality of Asan
Name of Place Asan Town
[Proper name and, also, name of class, as city, town, village, barrio, etc]

Enumeration District No. 7
Enumerated by me on April 24, 1930 Joaquin Torres
Enumerator

	PLACE OF ABODE			NAME	RELATION	PERSONAL DESCRIPTION				EDUCATION		NATIVITY		OCCUPATION
	Street, avenue, road, etc.	Number of dwelling house is order of visitation	Number of family in order of visitation	of each person whose place of abode on April 1, 1930, was in this family. Enter surname, first, then given name and middle initial. If any. Include every person living on April 1, 1930. Omit children born since April 1, 1930.	Relationship of this Person to the head of the family.	Sex	Color or race	Age at last birthday	Single, married, widowed or divorced	Attended school any time since Sept. 1, 1929	Whether able to read and write.	Place of birth of this person.	Whether able to speak English.	
	1	2	3	4	5	6	7	8	9	10	11	12	13	14
26	Agana-Piti Road	267	290	Agualo, Santiago T	Head	M	Cha	59	D	N	Y	Guam	N	Herder
27		268	291	Namauleg, Ana P	Head	F	Cha	50	Wd	N	N	Guam	N	Basket weaver
28		268	291	Namauleg, Catalina P	Daughter	F	Cha	13	S	N	Y	Guam	Y	None
29		269	292	Aguon, Jose T	Head	M	Cha	24	M	N	Y	Guam	Y	Cook
30		270	293	Mendiola, Jesus S	Head	M	Cha	20	M	N	Y	Guam	Y	Chauffeur
31		270	293	Mendiola, Severa SN	Wife	F	Cha	22	M	N	Y	Guam	Y	None
32		271	294	Bernard, Emma M	Head	F	Cha	36	M	N	Y	Guam	Y	None
33		271	294	Buckley, Harriet M	Sister-in-law	F	Cha	39	M	N	Y	Guam	Y	None
34		272	295	Meno, Pedro C	Head	M	Cha	22	M	N	Y	Guam	Y	Laborer
35		272	295	Meno, Natividad T	Wife	F	Cha	20	M	N	Y	Guam	Y	None
36		272	295	Meno, Matilda T	Daughter	F	Cha	4	S	N		Guam		None
37		272	295	Meno, Isidro T	Son	M	Cha	.7	S	N		Guam		None
38		272	295	San Agustin, Enrique Q	Lodger	M	Cha	19	S	N	N	Guam	N	Herder
39					Here ends the enumeration of Asan Town.									
40														
41														
42														
43														
44														
45														
46														
47														
48														
49														
50														

DEPARTMENT OF COMMERCE-BUREAU OF THE CENSUS
WASHINGTON

FIFTEENTH CENSUS OF THE UNITED STATES: 1930-POPULATION

THE ISLAND OF GUAM

Sheet No. 12A

District **Municipality of Asan**
Name of Place **Libugon Barrio**
[Proper name and, also, name of class, as city, town, village, barrio, etc]

Enumeration District No. 7
Enumerated by me on **April 24, 1930** Joaquin Torres, Enumerator

	PLACE OF ABODE			NAME	RELATION	PERSONAL DESCRIPTION				EDUCATION		NATIVITY		OCCUPATION
	Street, avenue, road, etc.	Number of dwelling house in order of visitation	Number of family in order of visitation	of each person whose place of abode on April 1, 1930, was in this family. Enter surname, first, then given name and middle initial. If any. Include every person living on April 1, 1930. Omit children born since April 1, 1930.	Relationship of this Person to the head of the family.	Sex	Color or race	Age at last birthday	Single, married, widowed or divorced	Attended school any time since Sept. 1, 1929	Whether able to read and write.	Place of birth of this person.	Whether able to speak English.	
	1	2	3	4	5	6	7	8	9	10	11	12	13	14
1	Radio Hill Road	273	296	Reyes, Jesus R	Head	M	Cha	41	M	N	Y	Guam	Y	Policeman
2		273	296	Reyes, Dolores M	Wife	F	Cha	38	M	N	Y	Guam	Y	None
3		273	296	Reyes, Henry M	Son	M	Cha	18	S	Y	Y	Guam	Y	None
4		273	296	Reyes, Carmen M	Daughter	F	Cha	17	S	N	Y	Guam	Y	None
5		273	296	Reyes, Jesus S M	Son	M	Cha	12	S	Y	Y	Guam	Y	None
6		273	296	Reyes, Remundo M	Son	M	Cha	9	S	Y		Guam		None
7		273	296	Reyes, Julia M	Daughter	F	Cha	7	S	N		Guam		None
8		273	296	Reyes, Roberto M	Son	M	Cha	5	S	N		Guam		None
9		273	296	Reyes, Joseph M	Son	M	Cha	3.9	S	N		Guam		None
10		273	296	Lizama, Jose L	Servant	M	Cha	16	S	N		Guam		Servant
11		274	297	Pangelinan, Joaquin A	Head	M	Cha	29	S	N	N	Guam	Y	Laborer
12		274	298	Taisipig, Jesus T	Head	M	Cha	18	S	N	Y	Guam	Y	Farmer
13		274	299	Tuncap, Juan N	Head	M	Fil	52	M	N	Y	Guam	Y	Farmer
14		274	300	Sahagun, Francisco Q	Head	M	Cha	28	S	N	Y	Guam	Y	Farmer
15		274	301	Herrera, Manuel A	Head	M	Cha	54	Wd	N	Y	Guam	N	Farmer
16		274	302	Chiguina, Enrique M	Head	M	Cha	30	M	N	Y	Guam	N	Farmer
17		274	303	Pablo, Felix P	Head	M	Cha	50	Wd	N	N	Guam	N	Farmer
18		274	304	Concepcion, Ramon G	Head	M	Cha	28	M	N	Y	Guam	Y	Farmer
19		274	305	Santos, Emilio V	Head	M	Cha	37	M	N	Y	Guam	Y	Farmer
20		274	306	Guzman, Juan C	Head	M	Cha	27	S	N	Y	Guam	Y	Laborer
21		274	307	Villagomez, Jesus U	Head	M	Cha	28	S	N	Y	Guam	Y	Laborer
22					Here ends the enumeration of the Municipality of Asan.									
23					[Sheet 243B/12B was intentionally left blank.]									
24														
25														

District 8
Municipality of Inarajan

Bubulao
Inarajan Town
Malolo Barrio
Talofofo
Talofofo Barrio

DEPARTMENT OF COMMERCE-BUREAU OF THE CENSUS
WASHINGTON

FIFTEENTH CENSUS OF THE UNITED STATES: 1930-POPULATION

THE ISLAND OF GUAM

Sheet No. 1A

District **Municipality of Agana**
Name of Place **Inarajan Town**
[Proper name and, also, name of class, as city, town, village, barrio, etc]

Enumeration District No. 8
Enumerated by me on **April 2, 1930** Francisco G. Lujan, Enumerator

	PLACE OF ABODE			NAME	RELATION	PERSONAL DESCRIPTION				EDUCATION		NATIVITY		OCCUPATION
	Street, avenue, road, etc.	Number of dwelling house is order of visitation	Number of family in order of visitation	of each person whose place of abode on April 1, 1930, was in this family. Enter surname, first, then given name and middle initial. If any. Include every person living on April 1, 1930. Omit children born since April 1, 1930.	Relationship of this Person to the head of the family.	Sex	Color or race	Age at last birthday	Single, married, widowed or divorced	Attended school any time since Sept. 1, 1929	Whether able to read and write.	Place of birth of this person.	Whether able to speak English.	
	1	2	3	4	5	6	7	8	9	10	11	12	13	14
1	[no street name]	1	1	Kamminga, Simon H	Head	M	Cha	41	M	N	Y	Guam	Y	Farmer
2		1	1	Kamminga, Felicidad T	Wife	F	Cha	43	M	N	Y	Guam	N	None
3		1	1	Torres, Jesus T	Step-son	M	Cha	17	S	N	Y	Guam	Y	School teacher
4		2	2	Paulino, Juan F	Head	M	Cha	31	M	N	Y	Guam	N	Farmer
5		2	2	Paulino, Maria SN	Wife	F	Cha	26	M	N	Y	Guam	Y	None
6		2	2	Paulino, Rosalia SN	Daughter	F	Cha	11	S	Y	Y	Guam	Y	None
7		2	2	Paulino, Josefina SN	Daughter	F	Cha	9	S	Y		Guam		None
8		2	2	Paulino, Carmen SN	Daughter	F	Cha	8	S	Y		Guam		None
9		2	2	Paulino, Jose SN	Son	M	Cha	5	S	N		Guam		None
10		2	2	Paulino, Maria SN	Daughter	F	Cha	3.5	S	N		Guam		None
11		2	2	Paulino, Trinidad SN	Daughter	F	Cha	1.5	S	N		Guam		None
12		3	3	Paulino, Jose A	Head	M	Cha	62	M	N	N	Guam	N	Farmer
13		3	3	Paulino, Felomena T	Wife	F	Cha	62	M	N	Y	Guam	N	None
14		3	3	Paulino, Ramon T	Son	M	Cha	18	S	Y	Y	Guam	Y	None
15		3	4	Paulino, Mariano T	Head	M	Cha	23	M	N	Y	Guam	Y	Farmer
16		3	4	Paulino, Maria SN	Wife	F	Cha	21	M	N	Y	Guam	Y	None
17		4	5	Paulino, Manuel A	Head	M	Cha	76	M	N	N	Guam	N	Farmer
18		4	5	Paulino, Joaquina T	Wife	F	Cha	46	M	N	N	Guam	N	None
19		4	5	Paulino, Concepcion T	Daughter	F	Cha	17	S	N	Y	Guam	Y	None
20		4	5	Paulino, Manuel T	Son	M	Cha	4.8	S	N		Guam		None
21		4	5	Taimanglo, Jose T	Grand-son	M	Cha	7	S	Y		Guam		None
22		4	5	Chiguina, Maria N	Aunt	F	Cha	60	S	N	N	Guam	N	None
23		5	6	Duenas, Juan T	Head	M	Cha	41	M	N	Y	Guam	Y	Farmer
24		5	6	Duenas, Ana M	Wife	F	Cha	31	M	N	Y	Guam	Y	None
25		5	6	Duenas, Rosalina M	Daughter	F	Cha	12	S	Y	Y	Guam	Y	None

DEPARTMENT OF COMMERCE-BUREAU OF THE CENSUS
WASHINGTON

FIFTEENTH CENSUS OF THE UNITED STATES: 1930-POPULATION

THE ISLAND OF GUAM

Sheet No. 1B

244B

District Municipality of Agana
Name of Place Inarajan Town
[Proper name and, also, name of class, as city, town, village, barrio, etc]

Enumeration District No. 8
Enumerated by me on April 2, 1930 Francisco G. Lujan
Enumerator

	PLACE OF ABODE			NAME	RELATION	PERSONAL DESCRIPTION				EDUCATION		NATIVITY		OCCUPATION
	Street, avenue, road, etc.	Number of dwelling house is order of visitation	Number of family in order of visitation	of each person whose place of abode on April 1, 1930, was in this family. Enter surname, first, then given name and middle initial. If any. Include every person living on April 1, 1930. Omit children born since April 1, 1930.	Relationship of this Person to the head of the family.	Sex	Color or race	Age at last birthday	Single, married, widowed or divorced	Attended school any time since Sept. 1, 1929	Whether able to read and write.	Place of birth of this person.	Whether able to speak English.	
	1	2	3	4	5	6	7	8	9	10	11	12	13	14
26	[no street name]	5	6	Duenas, Fredicinda M	Daughter	F	Cha	10	S	Y	Y	Guam	Y	None
27		5	6	Duenas, Dominica M	Daughter	F	Cha	8	S	Y		Guam		None
28		5	6	Duenas, Rosario M	Daughter	F	Cha	7	S	Y		Guam		None
29		5	6	Duenas, Esteban M	Son	M	Cha	3.3	S	N		Guam		None
30		6	7	Paulino, Vicente T	Head	M	Cha	25	M	N	Y	Guam	Y	Farmer
31		6	7	Paulino, Ana SN	Wife	F	Cha	24	M	N	Y	Guam	Y	None
32		6	7	Paulino, Leonardo SN	Son	M	Cha	4.1	S	N		Guam		None
33		6	7	Paulino, Tomas SN	Son	M	Cha	2.5	S	N		Guam		None
34		6	7	Paulino, Francisco SN	Son	M	Cha	.1	S	N		Guam		None
35		7	8	Lujan, Francisco G	Head	M	Cha	25	M	N	Y	Guam	Y	School teacher
36		7	8	Lujan, Gloria T	Wife	F	Jap	19	M	N	Y	Guam	Y	None
37		7	8	Tayama, Jose S	Father-in-law	M	Jap	52	Wd	N	Y	Japan	Y	Retail merchant
38		7	8	Tayama, Jose M	Brother-in-law	M	Jap	14	S	Y	Y	Guam	Y	None
39		8	9	Meno, Felipe N	Head	M	Cha	66	M	N	Y	Guam	N	Farmer
40		8	9	Meno, Soledad P	Wife	F	Cha	64	M	N	Y	Guam	N	None
41		8	9	Meno, Manuela P	Daughter	F	Cha	37	Wd	N	Y	Guam	N	Seamstress
42		8	9	Sugiyama, Josefina M	Grand daughter	F	Jap	13	S	Y	Y	Guam	Y	None
43		8	9	Sayama, Asuncion M	Grand daughter	F	Jap	16	S	Y	Y	Guam	Y	None
44		9	10	Duenas, Manuel M	Head	M	Cha	34	M	N	Y	Guam	Y	Farmer
45		9	10	Duenas, Ana P	Wife	F	Cha	23	M	N	Y	Guam	Y	None
46		9	10	Duenas, Ester P	Daughter	F	Cha	9	S	Y		Guam		None
47		9	10	Duenas, Manuel P	Son	M	Cha	3.8	S	N		Guam		None
48		9	10	Duenas, Maria P	Daughter	F	Cha	2.1	S	N		Guam		None
49		9	10	Duenas, Flora P	Daughter	F	Cha	.1	S	N		Guam		None
50		10	11	Benabente, Enrique R	Head	M	Cha	30	M	N	Y	Guam	Y	Farmer

DEPARTMENT OF COMMERCE-BUREAU OF THE CENSUS
WASHINGTON

FIFTEENTH CENSUS OF THE UNITED STATES: 1930-POPULATION

THE ISLAND OF GUAM

Sheet No. 2A

District **Municipality of Agana**
Name of Place **Inarajan Town**
[Proper name and, also, name of class, as city, town, village, barrio, etc]

Enumeration District No. **8**
Enumerated by me on **April 2, 1930** Francisco G. Lujan, Enumerator

	PLACE OF ABODE			NAME	RELATION	PERSONAL DESCRIPTION				EDUCATION		NATIVITY		OCCUPATION
	Street, avenue, road, etc.	Number of dwelling house is order of visitation	Number of family in order of visitation	of each person whose place of abode on April 1, 1930, was in this family. Enter surname, first, then given name and middle initial. If any. Include every person living on April 1, 1930. Omit children born since April 1, 1930.	Relationship of this Person to the head of the family.	Sex	Color or race	Age at last birthday	Single, married, widowed or divorced	Attended school any time since Sept. 1, 1929	Whether able to read and write.	Place of birth of this person.	Whether able to speak English.	
	1	2	3	4	5	6	7	8	9	10	11	12	13	14
1	[no street name]	10	11	Benabente, Francisca D	Wife	F	Cha	26	M	N	Y	Guam	Y	None
2		10	11	Benabente, Maria D	Daughter	F	Cha	3.4	S	N		Guam		None
3		10	11	Benabente, Carmen D	Daughter	F	Cha	1.8	S	N		Guam		None
4		10	11	Benabente, Edita D	Daughter	F	Cha	.6	S	N		Guam		None
5		11	12	Diego, Enemesio SN	Head	M	Cha	31	M	N	Y	Guam	Y	Farmer
6		11	12	Diego, Regina D	Wife	F	Cha	28	M	N	Y	Guam	Y	None
7		11	12	Diego, Florentina D	Daughter	F	Cha	11	S	Y	Y	Guam	Y	None
8		11	12	Diego, Agueda D	Daughter	F	Cha	9	S	Y		Guam		None
9		11	12	Diego, Dolores D	Daughter	F	Cha	6	S	N		Guam		None
10		11	12	Diego, Francisco D	Son	M	Cha	3.1	S	N		Guam		None
11		11	12	Diego, Maria D	Daughter	F	Cha	1.1	S	N		Guam		None
12		11	12	Diego, Vicente C	Uncle	M	Cha	55	S	N	N	Guam	N	None
13		12	13	Duenas, Francisco M	Head	M	Cha	31	M	N	Y	Guam	Y	Farmer
14		12	13	Duenas, Celedonia L	Wife	F	Cha	33	M	N	Y	Guam	Y	None
15		12	13	Duenas, Francisca L	Daughter	F	Cha	8	S	Y		Guam		None
16		12	13	Duenas, Maria L	Daughter	F	Cha	7	S	Y		Guam		None
17		12	13	Duenas, Roman L	Son	M	Cha	5	S	N		Guam		None
18		12	13	Duenas, Marta L	Daughter	F	Cha	3.4	S	N		Guam		None
19		12	13	Duenas, Laura L	Daughter	F	Cha	1.2	S	N		Guam		None
20		13	14	Paulino, Leocadio C	Head	M	Cha	32	M	N	Y	Guam	Y	Farmer
21		13	14	Paulino, Maria LG	Wife	F	Cha	26	M	N	Y	Guam	Y	None
22		13	14	Paulino, Francisco LG	Son	M	Cha	7	S	Y		Guam		None
23		13	14	Paulino, Jesus LG	Son	M	Cha	6	S	N		Guam		None
24		13	14	Paulino, Jose LG	Son	M	Cha	4.5	S	N		Guam		None
25		13	14	Paulino, Alejandro LG	Son	M	Cha	1.9	S	N		Guam		None

(CHAMORRO ROOTS GENEALOGY PROJECT™ TRANSCRIPTION)
(BERNARD T. PUNZALAN / HTTP://WWW.CHAMORROROOTS.COM)

DEPARTMENT OF COMMERCE-BUREAU OF THE CENSUS
WASHINGTON

FIFTEENTH CENSUS OF THE UNITED STATES: 1930-POPULATION

THE ISLAND OF GUAM

Sheet No. 2B

245B

District **Municipality of Agana**
Name of Place **Inarajan Town**
[Proper name and, also, name of class, as city, town, village, barrio, etc]

Enumeration District No. 8
Enumerated by me on **April 3, 1930** Francisco G. Lujan
Enumerator

	PLACE OF ABODE			NAME	RELATION	PERSONAL DESCRIPTION				EDUCATION		NATIVITY		OCCUPATION
	Street, avenue, road, etc.	Number of dwelling house in order of visitation	Number of family in order of visitation	of each person whose place of abode on April 1, 1930, was in this family. Enter surname, first, then given name and middle initial. If any. Include every person living on April 1, 1930. Omit children born since April 1, 1930.	Relationship of this Person to the head of the family.	Sex	Color or race	Age at last birthday	Single, married, widowed or divorced	Attended school any time since Sept. 1, 1929	Whether able to read and write.	Place of birth of this person.	Whether able to speak English.	
	1	2	3	4	5	6	7	8	9	10	11	12	13	14
26	[no street name]	13	14	Paulino, Ana LG	Daughter	F	Cha	3.2	S	N		Guam		None
27		14	15	Leon Guerrero, Vicente M	Head	M	Cha	63	M	N	Y	Guam	Y	Blacksmith
28		14	15	Leon Guerrero, Maria C	Wife	F	Cha	28	M	N	Y	Guam	Y	None
29		14	15	Tedtaotao, Dolores C	Servant	F	Cha	16	S	N	Y	Guam	Y	Cook
30		15	16	Meno, Jose D	Head	M	Cha	55	M	N	Y	Guam	N	Farmer
31		15	16	Meno, Genoveva N	Wife	F	Cha	53	M	N	Y	Guam	N	None
32		15	17	Meno, Antonio N	Head	M	Cha	31	M	N	Y	Guam	Y	Farmer
33		15	17	Meno, Ana C	Wife	F	Cha	30	M	N	Y	Guam	Y	None
34		15	17	Meno, Jesus C	Son	M	Cha	9	S	Y		Guam		None
35		15	17	Meno, Enriqueta C	Daughter	F	Cha	4.8	S	N		Guam		None
36		15	17	Meno, Genoveva C	Daughter	F	Cha	1.3	S	N		Guam		None
37		15	17	Meno, Eliza C	Daughter	F	Cha	.1	S	N		Guam		None
38		16	18	Afaisen, Manuel M	Head	M	Cha	29	S	N	Y	Guam	Y	Farmer
39		16	18	Afaisen, Paz M	Mother	F	Cha	62	Wd	N	Y	Guam	N	None
40		16	18	Afaisen, Dolores M	Sister	F	Cha	22	S	N	Y	Guam	Y	None
41		17	19	Tedtaotao, Pedro M	Head	M	Cha	36	M	N	N	Guam	N	Farmer
42		17	19	Tedtaotao, Angela T	Wife	F	Cha	30	M	N	N	Guam	N	None
43		17	19	Tedtaotao, Magdalena T	Daughter	F	Cha	15	S	N	Y	Guam	Y	None
44		17	19	Tedtaotao, Juan T	Son	M	Cha	12	S	Y	Y	Guam	Y	None
45		17	19	Tedtaotao, Rosario T	Daughter	F	Cha	8	S	Y		Guam		None
46		17	19	Tedtaotao, Maria T	Daughter	F	Cha	5	S	N		Guam		None
47		17	19	Tedtaotao, Rosa T	Daughter	F	Cha	.3	S	N		Guam		None
48		18	20	Delgado, Enrique SN	Head	M	Cha	24	M	N	Y	Guam	Y	Farmer
49		18	20	Delgado, Ana N	Wife	F	Cha	23	M	N	Y	Guam	Y	None
50		18	21	Naputi, Nicolasa D	Head	F	Cha	45	M	N	Y	Guam	N	None

(CHAMORRO ROOTS GENEALOGY PROJECT™ TRANSCRIPTION)
(BERNARD T. PUNZALAN / HTTP://WWW.CHAMORROROOTS.COM)

DEPARTMENT OF COMMERCE-BUREAU OF THE CENSUS
WASHINGTON

FIFTEENTH CENSUS OF THE UNITED STATES: 1930-POPULATION

THE ISLAND OF GUAM

Sheet No. 3A

246

District **Municipality of Agana**
Name of Place **Inarajan Town**
[Proper name and, also, name of class, as city, town, village, barrio, etc]

Enumeration District No. 8
Enumerated by me on **April 3, 1930** Francisco G. Lujan
Enumerator

	PLACE OF ABODE			NAME	RELATION	PERSONAL DESCRIPTION				EDUCATION		NATIVITY		OCCUPATION
	Street, avenue, road, etc.	Number of dwelling house in order of visitation	Number of family in order of visitation	of each person whose place of abode on April 1, 1930, was in this family. Enter surname, first, then given name and middle initial. If any. Include every person living on April 1, 1930. Omit children born since April 1, 1930.	Relationship of this Person to the head of the family.	Sex	Color or race	Age at last birthday	Single, married, widowed or divorced	Attended school any time since Sept. 1, 1929	Whether able to read and write.	Place of birth of this person.	Whether able to speak English.	
	1	2	3	4	5	6	7	8	9	10	11	12	13	14
1	[no street name]	18	21	Naputi, Vicente T	Husband	M	Cha	46	M	N	N	Guam	N	None
2		18	21	Naputi, Vicente D	Son	M	Cha	24	S	N	N	Guam	N	None
3		18	21	Naputi, Teresa D	Daughter	F	Cha	18	S	N	Y	Guam	Y	None
4		18	21	Naputi, Carmen D	Daughter	F	Cha	13	S	Y	Y	Guam	Y	None
5		19	22	Chargualaf, Froilan M	Head	M	Cha	55	M	N	Y	Guam	N	Farmer
6		19	22	Chargualaf, Carmen M	Wife	F	Cha	50	M	N	N	Guam	N	None
7		19	22	Chargualaf, Jose N	Grand son	M	Cha	15	S	N	Y	Guam	Y	Farm laborer
8		20	23	Meno, Francisco D	Head	M	Cha	39	M	N	Y	Guam	N	Farmer
9		20	23	Meno, Maria P	Wife	F	Cha	40	M	N	N	Guam	N	None
10		20	23	Meno, Virginia P	Daughter	F	Cha	17	S	N	Y	Guam	Y	None
11		20	23	Meno, Maria P	Daughter	F	Cha	15	S	Y	Y	Guam	Y	None
12		20	23	Meno, Ramon P	Son	M	Cha	7	S	Y		Guam		None
13		20	23	Meno, Vicente P	Daughter	F	Cha	5	S	N		Guam		None
14		20	23	Meno, Rita P	Daughter	F	Cha	2.4	S	N		Guam		None
15		20	23	Meno, Candelaria P	Daughter	F	Cha	.5	S	N		Guam		None
16		21	24	Chargualaf, Isabel D	Head	F	Cha	56	Wd	N	Y	Guam	N	Laundress
17		21	24	Delgado, Tomasa D	Daughter	F	Cha	20	S	N	Y	Guam	Y	None
18		21	24	Delgado, Jose D	Son	M	Cha	12	S	Y	Y	Guam	Y	None
19		22	25	Meno, Manuel C	Head	M	Cha	51	M	N	Y	Guam	N	Farmer
20		22	25	Meno, Concepcion L	Wife	F	Cha	44	M	N	Y	Guam	N	None
21		22	25	Meno, Jose L	Son	M	Cha	17	S	N	Y	Guam	Y	Farm laborer
22		22	25	Meno, Jesus L	Son	M	Cha	15	S	N	Y	Guam	Y	Farm laborer
23		22	25	Meno, Maria L	Daughter	F	Cha	14	S	Y	Y	Guam	Y	None
24		22	25	Meno, Ana L	Daughter	F	Cha	12	S	Y	Y	Guam	Y	None
25		22	25	Meno, Joaquin L	Son	M	Cha	10	S	Y	Y	Guam	Y	None

(CHAMORRO ROOTS GENEALOGY PROJECT™ TRANSCRIPTION)
(BERNARD T. PUNZALAN / HTTP://WWW.CHAMORROROOTS.COM)

DEPARTMENT OF COMMERCE-BUREAU OF THE CENSUS
WASHINGTON

FIFTEENTH CENSUS OF THE UNITED STATES: 1930-POPULATION

THE ISLAND OF GUAM

Sheet No. 3B

246B

District Municipality of Agana
Name of Place Inarajan Town
[Proper name and, also, name of class, as city, town, village, barrio, etc]

Enumeration District No. 8
Enumerated by me on April 3, 1930 Francisco G. Lujan, Enumerator

	PLACE OF ABODE: Street, avenue, road, etc.	Number of dwelling house is order of visitation	Number of family in order of visitation	NAME of each person whose place of abode on April 1, 1930, was in this family. Enter surname, first, then given name and middle initial. If any. Include every person living on April 1, 1930. Omit children born since April 1, 1930.	RELATION Relationship of this Person to the head of the family.	PERSONAL DESCRIPTION: Sex	Color or race	Age at last birthday	Single, married, widowed or divorced	EDUCATION: Attended school any time since Sept. 1, 1929	Whether able to read and write.	NATIVITY Place of birth of this person.	Whether able to speak English.	OCCUPATION
	1	2	3	4	5	6	7	8	9	10	11	12	13	14
26	[no street name]	22	25	Meno, Manuel L	Son	M	Cha	8	S	Y		Guam		None
27		22	25	Meno, Vicente L	Son	M	Cha	7	S	Y		Guam		None
28		22	25	Meno, Concepcion L	Daughter	F	Cha	2.1	S	N		Guam		None
29		23	26	Lujan, Andres C	Head	M	Cha	35	M	N	Y	Guam	N	Farmer
30		23	26	Lujan, Maria A	Wife	F	Cha	26	M	N	Y	Guam	N	None
31		23	26	Lujan, Jose A	Son	M	Cha	3	S	N		Guam		None
32		23	26	Lujan, Jesus A	Son	M	Cha	1.5	S	N		Guam		None
33		24	27	Flores, Jesus A	Head	M	Cha	66	M	N	Y	Guam	N	Farmer
34		24	27	Flores, Dolores D	Wife	F	Cha	62	M	N	Y	Guam	N	None
35		24	27	Flores, Prudencio D	Son	M	Cha	21	S	N	N	Guam	N	None
36		24	27	Lujan, Maria F	Grand daughter	F	Cha	16	S	N	Y	Guam	Y	None
37		24	28	Flores, Vicente D	Head	M	Cha	25	M	N	Y	Guam	Y	Farmer
38		24	28	Flores, Josefina T	Wife	F	Cha	16	M	N	Y	Guam	Y	None
39		25	29	Lujan, Jose B	Head	M	Cha	68	M	N	Y	Guam	Y	Farmer
40		25	29	Lujan, Maria C	Wife	F	Cha	70	M	N	N	Guam	N	None
41		25	29	Castro, Maria L	Grand daughter	F	Cha	13	S	Y	Y	Guam	Y	None
42		25	29	Lujan, Maria C	Grand daughter	F	Cha	12	S	Y	Y	Guam	Y	None
43		25	30	Chargualaf, Lucas M	Head	M	Cha	35	M	N	Y	Guam	Y	Farmer
44		25	30	Chargualaf, Ana L	Wife	F	Cha	43	M	N	Y	Guam	N	None
45		26	31	Duenas, Jesus T	Head	M	Cha	25	M	N	Y	Guam	Y	Farmer
46		26	31	Duenas, Maria SN	Wife	F	Cha	21	M	N	Y	Guam	Y	None
47		26	31	Duenas, Jose SN	Son	M	Cha	4.2	S	N		Guam		None
48		26	31	Duenas, Jesus SN	Son	M	Cha	3.2	S	N		Guam		None
49		26	31	Duenas, Brigida SN	Daughter	F	Cha	.8	S	N		Guam		None
50		27	32	San Nicolas, Jose C	Head	M	Cha	36	M	N	Y	Guam	N	Farmer

DEPARTMENT OF COMMERCE-BUREAU OF THE CENSUS
WASHINGTON

FIFTEENTH CENSUS OF THE UNITED STATES: 1930-POPULATION

THE ISLAND OF GUAM

Sheet No. 4A

District **Municipality of Agana**
Name of Place **Inarajan Town**
[Proper name and, also, name of class, as city, town, village, barrio, etc]

Enumeration District No. 8
Enumerated by me on April 4, 1930 Francisco G. Lujan, Enumerator

	PLACE OF ABODE			NAME	RELATION	PERSONAL DESCRIPTION				EDUCATION		NATIVITY		OCCUPATION
	Street, avenue, road, etc.	Number of dwelling house is order of visitation	Number of family in order of visitation	of each person whose place of abode on April 1, 1930, was in this family. Enter surname, first, then given name and middle initial. If any. Include every person living on April 1, 1930. Omit children born since April 1, 1930.	Relationship of this Person to the head of the family.	Sex	Color or race	Age at last birthday	Single, married, widowed or divorced	Attended school any time since Sept. 1, 1929	Whether able to read and write.	Place of birth of this person.	Whether able to speak English.	
	1	2	3	4	5	6	7	8	9	10	11	12	13	14
1	[no street name]	27	32	San Nicolas, Seferina C	Wife	F	Cha	33	M	N	N	Guam	N	None
2		27	32	San Nicolas, Rosa C	Daughter	F	Cha	13	S	Y	Y	Guam	Y	None
3		27	32	San Nicolas, Juan C	Son	M	Cha	12	S	Y	Y	Guam	Y	None
4		27	32	San Nicolas, Maria C	Daughter	F	Cha	11	S	Y	Y	Guam	Y	None
5		27	32	San Nicolas, Ana C	Daughter	F	Cha	6	S	N		Guam		None
6		27	32	San Nicolas, Pedro C	Son	M	Cha	4.1	S	N		Guam		None
7		27	32	San Nicolas, Catalina C	Daughter	F	Cha	2	S	N		Guam		None
8		28	33	Castro, Francisco C	Head	M	Cha	70	M	N	N	Guam	N	None
9		28	33	Castro, Natividad M	Wife	F	Cha	68	M	N	N	Guam	N	None
10		29	34	Delgado, Nicolas M	Head	M	Cha	32	M	N	Y	Guam	Y	Farmer
11		29	34	Delgado, Rufina F	Wife	F	Cha	25	M	N	Y	Guam	Y	None
12		29	34	Delgado, Maria F	Daughter	F	Cha	5	S	N		Guam		None
13		29	34	Delgado, Rosario F	Daughter	F	Cha	.5	S	N		Guam		None
14		30	35	Mantanona, Jesus C	Head	M	Cha	29	M	N	N	Guam	N	Farmer
15		30	35	Mantanona, Joaquina M	Wife	F	Cha	24	M	N	N	Guam	N	None
16		30	35	Mantanona, Jose M	Son	M	Cha	6	S	N		Guam		None
17		30	35	Mantanona, Jesus M	Son	M	Cha	5	S	N		Guam		None
18		30	35	Mantanona, Maria M	Daughter	F	Cha	3.5	S	N		Guam		None
19		30	35	Mantanona, Margarita M	Daughter	F	Cha	2.1	S	N		Guam		None
20		30	35	Mantanona, Baldomero C	Brother	M	Cha	23	S	N	Y	Guam	Y	Farm laborer
21		31	36	Martinez, Jose R	Head	M	Cha	32	M	N	N	Guam	N	Farmer
22		31	36	Martinez, Candelaria M	Wife	F	Cha	46	M	N	N	Guam	N	None
23		31	36	Martinez, Dolores M	Daughter	F	Cha	11	S	Y	Y	Guam	Y	None
24		31	36	Martinez, Maria M	Daughter	F	Cha	7	S	Y		Guam		None
25		31	36	Meno, Vicente C	Step son	M	Cha	19	S	N	Y	Guam	Y	Farm laborer

DEPARTMENT OF COMMERCE-BUREAU OF THE CENSUS
WASHINGTON

FIFTEENTH CENSUS OF THE UNITED STATES: 1930-POPULATION

THE ISLAND OF GUAM

Sheet No. 4B

247B

District Municipality of Agana
Name of Place Inarajan Town
[Proper name and, also, name of class, as city, town, village, barrio, etc]

Enumeration District No. 8
Enumerated by me on April 4, 1930 Francisco G. Lujan, Enumerator

	PLACE OF ABODE: Street, avenue, road, etc.	Number of dwelling house is order of visitation	Number of family in order of visitation	NAME of each person whose place of abode on April 1, 1930, was in this family. Enter surname, first, then given name and middle initial. If any. Include every person living on April 1, 1930. Omit children born since April 1, 1930.	RELATION Relationship of this Person to the head of the family.	PERSONAL DESCRIPTION: Sex	Color or race	Age at last birthday	Single, married, widowed or divorced	EDUCATION: Attended school any time since Sept. 1, 1929	Whether able to read and write.	NATIVITY Place of birth of this person.	Whether able to speak English.	OCCUPATION
	1	2	3	4	5	6	7	8	9	10	11	12	13	14
26	[no street name]	32	37	San Nicolas, Agustin M	Head	M	Cha	60	M	N	N	Guam	N	Farmer
27		32	37	San Nicolas, Martina L	Wife	F	Cha	62	M	N	N	Guam	N	None
28		32	37	San Nicolas, Lucas L	Son	M	Cha	20	S	N	Y	Guam	Y	School teacher
29		32	37	San Nicolas, Jose L	Son	M	Cha	15	S	Y	Y	Guam	Y	None
30		32	38	San Nicolas, Joaquin L	Head	M	Cha	24	Wd	N	Y	Guam	Y	Farmer
31		33	39	Mantanona, Casiano A	Head	M	Cha	58	M	N	N	Guam	N	Farmer
32		33	39	Mantanona, Rita L	Wife	F	Cha	48	M	N	N	Guam	N	None
33		33	39	Mantanona, Dolores L	Daughter	F	Cha	22	S	N	Y	Guam	Y	None
34		33	39	Mantanona, Margarita L	Daughter	F	Cha	21	S	N	Y	Guam	Y	None
35		33	39	Mantanona, Carmen L	Daughter	F	Cha	19	S	N	Y	Guam	Y	None
36		33	39	Mantanona, Jose L	Son	M	Cha	16	S	Y	Y	Guam	Y	None
37		34	40	Mantanona, Ignacio L	Head	M	Cha	30	M	N	N	Guam	N	Farmer
38		34	40	Mantanona, Genoveva T	Wife	F	Cha	20	M	N	N	Guam	N	None
39		34	40	Mantanona, Jesus T	Son	M	Cha	1.5	S	N		Guam		None
40		34	40	Mantanona, Juan T	Son	M	Cha	.3	S	N		Guam		None
41		35	41	Cruz, Francisco D	Head	M	Cha	32	M	N	Y	Guam	Y	Farmer
42		35	41	Cruz, Maria T	Wife	F	Cha	29	M	N	Y	Guam	Y	None
43		35	42	Aguon, Rosa T	Head	F	Cha	62	Wd	N	Y	Guam	N	Farmer
44		36	43	Flores, Juan D	Head	M	Cha	27	M	N	Y	Guam	Y	Farmer
45		36	43	Flores, Carmen SN	Wife	F	Cha	30	M	N	Y	Guam	Y	None
46		36	43	Flores, Consuelo SN	Daughter	F	Cha	3.1	S	N		Guam		None
47		37	44	Paulino, Manuel T	Head	M	Cha	33	M	N	Y	Guam	Y	Farmer
48		37	44	Paulino, Maria C	Wife	F	Cha	26	M	N	Y	Guam	Y	None
49		37	44	Paulino, Augusto C	Son	M	Cha	2.1	S	N		Guam		None
50		37	44	Paulino, Manuel C	Son	M	Cha	.7	S	N		Guam		None

(CHAMORRO ROOTS GENEALOGY PROJECT™ TRANSCRIPTION)
(BERNARD T. PUNZALAN / HTTP://WWW.CHAMORROROOTS.COM)

DEPARTMENT OF COMMERCE-BUREAU OF THE CENSUS
WASHINGTON

FIFTEENTH CENSUS OF THE UNITED STATES: 1930-POPULATION

THE ISLAND OF GUAM

Sheet No. 5A

248

District **Municipality of Agana**
Name of Place **Inarajan Town**
[Proper name and, also, name of class, as city, town, village, barrio, etc]

Enumeration District No. 8
Enumerated by me on **April 5, 1930** Francisco G. Lujan, Enumerator

	PLACE OF ABODE: Street, avenue, road, etc.	Number of dwelling house in order of visitation	Number of family in order of visitation	NAME of each person whose place of abode on April 1, 1930, was in this family. Enter surname, first, then given name and middle initial. If any. Include every person living on April 1, 1930. Omit children born since April 1, 1930.	RELATION Relationship of this Person to the head of the family.	PERSONAL DESCRIPTION: Sex	Color or race	Age at last birthday	Single, married, widowed or divorced	EDUCATION: Attended school any time since Sept. 1, 1929	Whether able to read and write.	NATIVITY Place of birth of this person.	Whether able to speak English.	OCCUPATION
	1	2	3	4	5	6	7	8	9	10	11	12	13	14
1	[no street name]	37	45	Cruz, Leocadio C	Head	M	Cha	63	M	N	Y	Guam	N	Farmer
2		37	45	Cruz, Luisa D	Wife	F	Cha	67	M	N	Y	Guam	N	None
3		38	46	Paulino, Juan N	Head	M	Cha	52	M	N	Y	Guam	N	Farmer
4		38	46	Paulino, Ines L	Wife	F	Cha	49	M	N	N	Guam	N	None
5		38	46	Paulino, Angela L	Daughter	F	Cha	32	S	N	Y	Guam	N	None
6		38	46	Paulino, Margarita L	Daughter	F	Cha	29	S	N	Y	Guam	N	None
7		38	46	Paulino, Concepcion L	Daughter	F	Cha	22	S	N	Y	Guam	Y	School teacher
8		38	46	Paulino, Juan L	Son	M	Cha	20	S	N	Y	Guam	Y	School teacher
9		38	46	Paulino, Lourdes P	Grand daughter	F	Cha	3.7	S	N		Guam		None
10		39	47	Crisostomo, Vicente C	Head	M	Cha	58	M	N	N	Guam	N	Farmer
11		39	47	Crisostomo, Rosa M	Wife	F	Cha	52	M	N	N	Guam	N	None
12		39	47	Crisostomo, Pedro M	Son	M	Cha	23	Wd	N	Y	Guam	Y	Farm laborer
13		39	47	Crisostomo, Elena M	Daughter	F	Cha	21	S	N	Y	Guam	N	None
14		39	47	Crisostomo, Joaquin M	Son	M	Cha	20	S	N	Y	Guam	Y	Farm laborer
15		39	47	Crisostomo, Jose M	Son	M	Cha	17	S	N	Y	Guam	Y	Farm laborer
16		39	47	Crisostomo, Jesus	Son	M	Cha	15	S	N	Y	Guam	Y	Farm laborer
17		39	47	Crisostomo, Manuel	Son	M	Cha	11	S	Y	Y	Guam	Y	None
18		39	47	Crisostomo, Ana	Daughter	F	Cha	6	S	Y		Guam		None
19		40	48	Naputi, Manuel P	Head	M	Cha	26	M	N	Y	Guam	Y	Chauffeur
20		40	48	Naputi, Magdalena SN	Wife	F	Cha	20	M	N	Y	Guam	Y	None
21		40	48	Naputi, Clotilde SN	Daughter	F	Cha	.7	S	N		Guam		None
22		40	49	Naputi, Lucas T	Head	M	Cha	52	M	N	N	Guam	N	Farmer
23		40	49	Naputi, Rosa P	Wife	F	Cha	67	M	N	N	Rota	N	None
24		40	49	Fejerang, Ignacia N	Daughter	F	Cha	28	Wd	N	Y	Guam	Y	None
25		40	49	Naputi, Herman N	Grand son	M	Cha	5	S	N		Guam		None

DEPARTMENT OF COMMERCE-BUREAU OF THE CENSUS
WASHINGTON

FIFTEENTH CENSUS OF THE UNITED STATES: 1930-POPULATION

THE ISLAND OF GUAM

Sheet No. 5B

248B

District **Municipality of Agana**
Name of Place **Inarajan Town**
[Proper name and, also, name of class, as city, town, village, barrio, etc]

Enumeration District No. 8
Enumerated by me on **April 7, 1930** Francisco G. Lujan
Enumerator

	PLACE OF ABODE			NAME	RELATION	PERSONAL DESCRIPTION				EDUCATION		NATIVITY		OCCUPATION
	Street, avenue, road, etc.	Number of dwelling house in order of visitation	Number of family in order of visitation	of each person whose place of abode on April 1, 1930, was in this family. Enter surname, first, then given name and middle initial. If any. Include every person living on April 1, 1930. Omit children born since April 1, 1930.	Relationship of this Person to the head of the family.	Sex	Color or race	Age at last birthday	Single, married, widowed or divorced	Attended school any time since Sept. 1, 1929	Whether able to read and write.	Place of birth of this person.	Whether able to speak English.	
	1	2	3	4	5	6	7	8	9	10	11	12	13	14
26	[no street name]	40	49	Naputi, Elminia N	Grand daughter	F	Cha	3.1	S	N		Guam		None
27		40	49	Naputi, Leonardo N	Grand son	M	Cha	.5	S	N		Guam		None
28		41	50	Naputi, Juan T	Head	M	Cha	49	M	N	Y	Guam	N	Farmer
29		41	50	Naputi, Maria M	Wife	F	Cha	46	M	N	N	Guam	N	None
30		41	50	Naputi, Sebastian M	Son	M	Cha	26	S	N	Y	Guam	Y	Farm laborer
31		41	50	Naputi, Remedios M	Daughter	F	Cha	17	S	N	Y	Guam	Y	None
32		41	50	Naputi, Jose M	Son	M	Cha	13	S	Y	Y	Guam	Y	None
33		41	50	Naputi, Concepcion M	Daughter	F	Cha	11	S	Y	Y	Guam	Y	None
34		41	50	Naputi, Carmen M	Daughter	F	Cha	2.7	S	N		Guam		None
35		42	51	Delgado, Silvano M	Head	M	Cha	49	M	N	N	Guam	N	Farmer
36		42	51	Delgado, Maria SN	Wife	F	Cha	43	M	N	Y	Guam	N	None
37		42	51	Delgado, Jose SN	Son	M	Cha	21	S	N	Y	Guam	Y	Farm laborer
38		42	51	Delgado, Delfina SN	Daughter	F	Cha	17	S	N	Y	Guam	Y	None
39		42	51	Delgado, Ana SN	Daughter	F	Cha	13	S	Y	Y	Guam	Y	None
40		42	51	Delgado, Consolacion SN	Daughter	F	Cha	11	S	Y	Y	Guam	Y	None
41		43	52	Cruz, Jose D	Head	M	Cha	29	M	N	Y	Guam	Y	Road laborer
42		43	52	Cruz, Maria D	Wife	F	Cha	22	M	N	Y	Guam	Y	None
43		43	52	Cruz, Ana	Daughter	F	Cha	.8	S	N		Guam		None
44		44	53	Paulino, Cleto C	Head	M	Cha	39	M	N	Y	Guam	Y	Farmer
45		44	53	Paulino, Margarita LG	Wife	F	Cha	31	M	N	Y	Guam	Y	None
46		44	53	Paulino, Julia LG	Daughter	F	Cha	9	S	Y		Guam		None
47		44	53	Paulino, Vicente LG	Son	M	Cha	8	S	Y		Guam		None
48		44	53	Paulino, Manuel LG	Son	M	Cha	5	S	N		Guam		None
49		44	53	Paulino, Pedro LG	Son	M	Cha	3.3	S	N		Guam		None
50		44	53	Paulino, Maria LG	Daughter	F	Cha	0	S	N		Guam		None

DEPARTMENT OF COMMERCE-BUREAU OF THE CENSUS
WASHINGTON

FIFTEENTH CENSUS OF THE UNITED STATES: 1930-POPULATION

THE ISLAND OF GUAM

Sheet No. 6A

District **Municipality of Agana**
Name of Place **Inarajan Town**
[Proper name and, also, name of class, as city, town, village, barrio, etc]

Enumeration District No. 8
Enumerated by me on **April 7, 1930** Francisco G. Lujan
Enumerator

	PLACE OF ABODE			NAME	RELATION	PERSONAL DESCRIPTION				EDUCATION		NATIVITY		OCCUPATION
	Street, avenue, road, etc.	Number of dwelling house is order of visitation	Number of family in order of visitation	of each person whose place of abode on April 1, 1930, was in this family. Enter surname, first, then given name and middle initial. If any. Include every person living on April 1, 1930. Omit children born since April 1, 1930.	Relationship of this Person to the head of the family.	Sex	Color or race	Age at last birthday	Single, married, widowed or divorced	Attended school any time since Sept. 1, 1929	Whether able to read and write.	Place of birth of this person.	Whether able to speak English.	
	1	2	3	4	5	6	7	8	9	10	11	12	13	14
1	[no street name]	44	53	Naputi, Maria T	Servant	F	Cha	38	S	N	N	Guam	N	Cook
2		45	54	Taimanglo, Juan C	Head	M	Cha	29	M	N	Y	Guam	N	Farmer
3		45	54	Taimanglo, Gertrudes M	Wife	F	Cha	35	M	N	Y	Guam	N	None
4		45	54	Taimanglo, Alfredo M	Son	M	Cha	9	S	Y		Guam		None
5		45	54	Taimanglo, Ignacio M	Son	M	Cha	6	S	Y		Guam		None
6		45	54	Taimanglo, Joaquin M	Son	M	Cha	1.8	S	N		Guam		None
7		45	54	Taimanglo, Jose M	Son	M	Cha	0.8	S	N		Guam		None
8		46	55	Mantanona, Jose M	Head	M	Cha	31	M	N	Y	Guam	Y	Farmer
9		46	55	Mantanona, Maria T	Wife	F	Cha	39	M	N	N	Guam	N	None
10		46	55	Mantanona, Roman T	Son	M	Cha	8	S	Y		Guam		None
11		46	55	Mantanona, Ricardo T	Son	M	Cha	5	S	N		Guam		None
12		46	55	Mantanona, Enrique T	Son	M	Cha	2.7	S	N		Guam		None
13		46	55	Mantanona, Artemio T	Son	M	Cha	.1	S	N		Guam		None
14		46	55	Borja, Juan T	Step son	M	Cha	11	S	Y	Y	Guam	Y	None
15		47	56	Leon Guerrero, Francisco S	Head	M	Cha	35	M	N	Y	Guam	N	Farmer
16		47	56	Leon Guerrero, Petra M	Wife	F	Cha	36	M	N	Y	Guam	N	None
17		47	56	Leon Guerrero, Joaquin M	Son	M	Cha	9	S	Y		Guam		None
18		47	56	Leon Guerrero, Ana M	Daughter	F	Cha	8	S	Y		Guam		None
19		47	56	Leon Guerrero, Consolacion M	Daughter	F	Cha	6	S	N		Guam		None
20		47	56	Leon Guerrero, Maria M	Daughter	F	Cha	4.3	S	N		Guam		None
21		47	56	Leon Guerrero, Jose M	Son	M	Cha	3	S	N		Guam		None
22		47	56	Leon Guerrero, Josefa M	Daughter	F	Cha	1.1	S	N		Guam		None
23		48	57	Pinaula, Vicente A	Head	M	Cha	25	M	N	Y	Guam	Y	Farmer
24		48	57	Pinaula, Natividad A	Wife	F	Cha	24	M	N	Y	Guam	Y	None
25		48	57	Pinaula, Ana	Daughter	F	Cha	4.1	S	N		Guam		None

(CHAMORRO ROOTS GENEALOGY PROJECT™ TRANSCRIPTION)
(BERNARD T. PUNZALAN / HTTP://WWW.CHAMORROROOTS.COM)

DEPARTMENT OF COMMERCE-BUREAU OF THE CENSUS
WASHINGTON

FIFTEENTH CENSUS OF THE UNITED STATES: 1930-POPULATION

THE ISLAND OF GUAM

Sheet No. 6B

249B

District **Municipality of Agana**
Name of Place **Inarajan Town**
[Proper name and, also, name of class, as city, town, village, barrio, etc]

Enumeration District No. **8**
Enumerated by me on **April 7, 1930** Francisco G. Lujan
Enumerator

	PLACE OF ABODE			NAME	RELATION	PERSONAL DESCRIPTION				EDUCATION		NATIVITY		OCCUPATION
	Street, avenue, road, etc.	Number of dwelling house in order of visitation	Number of family in order of visitation	of each person whose place of abode on April 1, 1930, was in this family. Enter surname, first, then given name and middle initial. If any. Include every person living on April 1, 1930. Omit children born since April 1, 1930.	Relationship of this Person to the head of the family.	Sex	Color or race	Age at last birthday	Single, married, widowed or divorced	Attended school any time since Sept. 1, 1929	Whether able to read and write.	Place of birth of this person.	Whether able to speak English.	
	1	2	3	4	5	6	7	8	9	10	11	12	13	14
26	[no street name]	48	57	Pinaula, Maria A	Daughter	F	Cha	1.3	S	N		Guam		None
27		48	58	Delgado, Francisco D	Head	M	Cha	34	M	N	Y	Guam	Y	Road foreman
28		48	58	Delgado, Carmen P	Wife	F	Cha	29	M	N	Y	Guam	Y	None
29		48	58	Delgado, Antonio P	Son	M	Cha	8	S	Y		Guam		None
30		48	58	Delgado, Mercedes P	Daughter	F	Cha	5	S	N		Guam		None
31		48	58	Delgado, Rosa P	Daughter	F	Cha	4	S	N		Guam		None
32		48	58	Delgado, Julia P	Daughter	F	Cha	2.8	S	N		Guam		None
33		48	58	Delgado, Beatrice	Daughter	F	Cha	.1	S	N		Guam		None
34		48	58	Chargualaf, Ramon M	Servant	M	Cha	15	S	N	Y	Guam	Y	Road laborer
35		48	58	Meno, Jose N	Servant	M	Cha	16	S	N	Y	Guam	Y	Road laborer
36		48	58	Tedpaogo, Angelina D	Servant	F	Cha	14	S	N	Y	Guam	Y	Cook
37		49	59	Taimanglo, Jose C	Head	M	Cha	41	M	N	Y	Guam	N	Farmer
38		49	59	Taimanglo, Dolores M	Wife	F	Cha	24	M	N	Y	Guam	Y	None
39		49	59	Taimanglo, Maria C	Daughter	F	Cha	14	S	N	Y	Guam	Y	None
40		49	59	Taimanglo, Jesus C	Son	M	Cha	13	S	Y	Y	Guam	Y	None
41		49	59	Taimanglo, Juan M	Son	M	Cha	.7	S	N		Guam		None
42		50	60	Leon Guerrero, Mariano R	Head	M	Cha	56	M	N	Y	Guam	Y	Copra agent
43		50	60	Leon Guerrero, Ana D	Wife	F	Cha	41	M	N	Y	Guam	N	None
44		50	60	Leon Guerrero, Carmen D	Daughter	F	Cha	22	S	N	N	Guam	N	None
45		50	60	Leon Guerrero, Mariano D	Son	M	Cha	20	S	N	Y	Guam	Y	Blacksmith
46		50	60	Leon Guerrero, Joaquin D	Son	M	Cha	15	S	Y	Y	Guam	Y	None
47		50	60	Leon Guerrero, Rosa D	Daughter	F	Cha	12	S	Y	Y	Guam	Y	None
48		50	60	Leon Guerrero, Rosario D	Daughter	F	Cha	10	S	Y	Y	Guam	Y	None
49		50	60	Leon Guerrero, Isabel D	Daughter	F	Cha	9	S	Y		Guam		None
50		50	60	Meno, Jose T	Servant	M	Cha	17	S	N	Y	Guam	Y	Blacksmith

DEPARTMENT OF COMMERCE-BUREAU OF THE CENSUS
WASHINGTON

FIFTEENTH CENSUS OF THE UNITED STATES: 1930-POPULATION

THE ISLAND OF GUAM

Sheet No. 7A

District **Municipality of Agana**
Name of Place **Inarajan Town**
[Proper name and, also, name of class, as city, town, village, barrio, etc]

Enumeration District No. **8**
Enumerated by me on **April 8, 1930** Francisco G. Lujan
Enumerator

	PLACE OF ABODE			NAME	RELATION	PERSONAL DESCRIPTION				EDUCATION		NATIVITY		OCCUPATION
	Street, avenue, road, etc.	Number of dwelling house is order of visitation	Number of family in order of visitation	of each person whose place of abode on April 1, 1930, was in this family. Enter surname, first, then given name and middle initial. If any. Include every person living on April 1, 1930. Omit children born since April 1, 1930.	Relationship of this Person to the head of the family.	Sex	Color or race	Age at last birthday	Single, married, widowed or divorced	Attended school any time since Sept. 1, 1929	Whether able to read and write.	Place of birth of this person.	Whether able to speak English.	
	1	2	3	4	5	6	7	8	9	10	11	12	13	14
1	[no street name]	51	61	Taitague, Jose D	Head	M	Cha	34	M	N	Y	Guam	Y	Farmer
2		51	61	Taitague, Antonia M	Wife	F	Cha	24	M	N	Y	Guam	Y	None
3		51	61	Taitague, Lourdes M	Daughter	F	Cha	7	S	Y		Guam		None
4		51	61	Taitague, Joseph M	Son	M	Cha	5	S	N		Guam		None
5		51	61	Taitague, Grace M	Daughter	F	Cha	3.7	S	N		Guam		None
6		51	61	Taitague, Edna M	Daughter	F	Cha	2.1	S	N		Guam		None
7		51	61	Taitague, Francisco M	Son	M	Cha	0.4	S	N		Guam		None
8		51	61	Taitague, Rosario D	Mother	F	Cha	67	Wd	N	Y	Guam	N	None
9		51	61	Taitague, Amalia D	Sister	F	Cha	44	S	N	Y	Guam	N	None
10		52	62	San Nicolas, Felipe T	Head	M	Cha	38	M	N	Y	Guam	N	Farmer
11		52	62	San Nicolas, Rosario C	Wife	F	Cha	35	M	N	Y	Guam	Y	None
12		52	62	San Nicolas, Isabel C	Daughter	F	Cha	10	S	Y	Y	Guam	Y	None
13		52	62	San Nicolas, Rosa C	Daughter	F	Cha	.1	S	N		Guam		None
14		53	63	Cruz, Jose D	Head	M	Cha	38	M	N	Y	Guam	Y	Carpenter
15		53	63	Cruz, Carmen P	Wife	F	Cha	35	M	N	Y	Guam	Y	None
16		53	63	Cruz, Francisco P	Son	M	Cha	13	S	Y	Y	Guam	Y	None
17		53	63	Cruz, Jose P	Son	M	Cha	9	S	Y		Guam		None
18		53	63	Paulino, Carmen D	Niece	F	Cha	6	S	N		Guam		None
19		54	64	Meno, Juan P	Head	M	Cha	33	M	N	Y	Guam	Y	Farmer
20		54	64	Meno, Patrona C	Wife	F	Cha	33	M	N	Y	Guam	Y	None
21		54	64	Meno, Efraim C	Son	M	Cha	12	S	Y	Y	Guam	Y	None
22		54	64	Meno, Gregorio C	Son	M	Cha	10	S	Y	Y	Guam	Y	None
23		54	64	Meno, Prudencio C	Son	M	Cha	8	S	Y		Guam		None
24		54	64	Meno, Florentina C	Daughter	F	Cha	4.1	S	N		Guam		None
25		54	64	Meno, Carmen C	Daughter	F	Cha	.7	S	N		Guam		None

DEPARTMENT OF COMMERCE-BUREAU OF THE CENSUS
WASHINGTON
FIFTEENTH CENSUS OF THE UNITED STATES: 1930-POPULATION

THE ISLAND OF GUAM

Sheet No. 7B

250B

District **Municipality of Agana**
Name of Place **Inarajan Town**
[Proper name and, also, name of class, as city, town, village, barrio, etc]

Enumeration District No. 8
Enumerated by me on **April 8, 1930** Francisco G. Lujan
Enumerator

	PLACE OF ABODE			NAME	RELATION	PERSONAL DESCRIPTION				EDUCATION		NATIVITY		OCCUPATION
	Street, avenue, road, etc.	Number of dwelling house is order of visitation	Number of family in order of visitation	of each person whose place of abode on April 1, 1930, was in this family. Enter surname, first, then given name and middle initial. If any. Include every person living on April 1, 1930. Omit children born since April 1, 1930.	Relationship of this Person to the head of the family.	Sex	Color or race	Age at last birthday	Single, married, widowed or divorced	Attended school any time since Sept. 1, 1929	Whether able to read and write.	Place of birth of this person.	Whether able to speak English.	
	1	2	3	4	5	6	7	8	9	10	11	12	13	14
26	[no street name]	55	65	Taitague, Maria N	Head	F	Cha	45	Wd	N	N	Guam	N	Farmer
27		55	65	Taitague, Josefina N	Daughter	F	Cha	19	S	N	Y	Guam	Y	None
28		55	65	Taitague, Daniel N	Son	M	Cha	14	S	Y	Y	Guam	Y	None
29		55	65	Taitague, Lorenzo N	Son	M	Cha	12	S	N	Y	Guam	Y	Farm laborer
30		55	65	Taitague, Rosalina N	Daughter	F	Cha	8	S	Y		Guam		None
31		55	65	Taitague, Jose N	Son	M	Cha	1.5	S	N		Guam		None
32		55	65	Taitague, David T	Grand son	M	Cha	0.1	S	N		Guam		None
33		56	66	San Nicolas, Mariano C	Head	M	Cha	30	M	N	Y	Guam	Y	Farmer
34		56	66	San Nicolas, Antonia F	Wife	F	Cha	27	M	N	Y	Guam	Y	None
35		56	66	San Nicolas, Maria F	Daughter	F	Cha	7	S	Y		Guam		None
36		56	66	San Nicolas, Jose F	Son	M	Cha	6	S	N		Guam		None
37		56	66	San Nicolas, Jesus F	Son	M	Cha	4.5	S	N		Guam		None
38		56	66	San Nicolas, Joaquin F	Son	M	Cha	2.2	S	N		Guam		None
39		57	67	San Nicolas, Ignacio LG	Head	M	Cha	56	M	N	N	Guam	N	Farmer
40		57	67	San Nicolas, Antonia C	Wife	F	Cha	46	M	N	N	Guam	N	None
41		57	67	Cepeda, Ana C	Step daughter	F	Cha	16	S	N	Y	Guam	Y	None
42		57	67	Cepeda, Antonia C	Step daughter	F	Cha	11	S	Y	Y	Guam	Y	None
43		57	67	Cepeda, Teresa C	Step daughter	F	Cha	9	S	Y		Guam		None
44		57	67	Cepeda, Vicente C	Step son	M	Cha	7	S	Y		Guam		None
45		58	68	Martinez, Enrique M	Head	M	Cha	22	M	N	Y	Guam	N	Farmer
46		58	68	Martinez, Rosalina C	Wife	F	Cha	18	M	N	Y	Guam	Y	None
47		59	69	San Nicolas, Manuel LG	Head	M	Cha	48	M	N	Y	Guam	Y	Farmer
48		59	69	San Nicolas, Josefa M	Wife	F	Cha	23	M	N	Y	Guam	Y	None
49		59	69	San Nicolas, Vicente C	Son	M	Cha	26	S	N	Y	Guam	Y	Farm laborer
50		59	69	San Nicolas, Vicenta C	Daughter	F	Cha	19	S	N	Y	Guam	Y	None

DEPARTMENT OF COMMERCE-BUREAU OF THE CENSUS
WASHINGTON

FIFTEENTH CENSUS OF THE UNITED STATES: 1930-POPULATION

THE ISLAND OF GUAM

Sheet No. 8A

District **Municipality of Agana**
Name of Place **Inarajan Town**
[Proper name and, also, name of class, as city, town, village, barrio, etc]

Enumeration District No. **8**
Enumerated by me on **April 8, 1930** Francisco G. Lujan, Enumerator

	PLACE OF ABODE			NAME	RELATION	PERSONAL DESCRIPTION				EDUCATION		NATIVITY		OCCUPATION
	Street, avenue, road, etc.	Number of dwelling house in order of visitation	Number of family in order of visitation	of each person whose place of abode on April 1, 1930, was in this family. Enter surname, first, then given name and middle initial. If any. Include every person living on April 1, 1930. Omit children born since April 1, 1930.	Relationship of this Person to the head of the family.	Sex	Color or race	Age at last birthday	Single, married, widowed or divorced	Attended school any time since Sept. 1, 1929	Whether able to read and write.	Place of birth of this person.	Whether able to speak English.	
	1	2	3	4	5	6	7	8	9	10	11	12	13	14
1	[no street name]	59	69	San Nicolas, Jesus C	Son	M	Cha	17	S	Y	Y	Guam	Y	Farm laborer
2		59	69	San Nicolas, Joaquina C	Daughter	F	Cha	15	S	N	Y	Guam	Y	None
3		59	69	San Nicolas, Carmen C	Daughter	F	Cha	9	S	Y		Guam		None
4		59	69	San Nicolas, Manuel C	Son	M	Cha	3.5	S	N		Guam		None
5		59	69	San Nicolas, Concepcion C	Daughter	F	Cha	2.3	S	N		Guam		None
6		59	69	San Nicolas, Rufino C	Son	M	Cha	0.5	S	N		Guam		None
7		59	69	San Nicolas, Antonia LG	Mother	F	Cha	81	Wd	N	N	Guam	N	None
8		60	70	Camacho, Ignacio R	Head	M	Cha	33	M	N	Y	Guam	Y	Farmer
9		60	70	Camacho, Teodora C	Wife	F	Cha	36	M	N	Y	Guam	N	Retail merchant
10		60	70	Kamo, Carmen C	Step daughter	F	Jap	17	S	N	Y	Guam	Y	None
11		61	71	Crisostomo, Joaquin M	Head	M	Cha	67	M	N	Y	Guam	N	Farmer
12		61	71	Crisostomo, Maria LG	Wife	F	Cha	58	M	N	N	Guam	N	None
13		61	71	Crisostomo, Pedro LG	Son	M	Cha	23	S	N	Y	Guam	Y	Salesman
14		61	71	Crisostomo, Jose LG	Son	M	Cha	21	S	N	Y	Guam	Y	Farm laborer
15		61	71	Crisostomo, Vicente LG	Son	M	Cha	19	S	N	Y	Guam	Y	Farm laborer
16		62	72	Flores, Jose D	Head	M	Cha	36	M	N	Y	Guam	Y	Farmer
17		62	72	Flores, Rafaela SN	Wife	F	Cha	34	M	N	Y	Guam	Y	None
18		62	72	Flores, Alfred SN	Son	M	Cha	13	S	Y	Y	Guam	Y	None
19		62	72	Flores, Alice SN	Daughter	F	Cha	12	S	Y	Y	Guam	Y	None
20		62	72	Flores, Ida SN	Daughter	F	Cha	11	S	Y	Y	Guam	Y	None
21		62	72	Flores, Helen SN	Daughter	F	Cha	9	S	Y		Guam		None
22		62	72	Flores, Gregorio SN	Son	M	Cha	7	S	Y		Guam		None
23		62	72	Flores, Alfonsina SN	Daughter	F	Cha	6	S	N		Guam		None
24		62	72	Flores, Jose SN	Son	M	Cha	4.4	S	N		Guam		None
25		62	72	Flores, Emma SN	Daughter	F	Cha	.5	S	N		Guam		None

D-8-16

DEPARTMENT OF COMMERCE-BUREAU OF THE CENSUS
WASHINGTON

FIFTEENTH CENSUS OF THE UNITED STATES: 1930-POPULATION

THE ISLAND OF GUAM

Sheet No. 8B

251B

District **Municipality of Agana**
Name of Place **Inarajan Town**
[Proper name and, also, name of class, as city, town, village, barrio, etc]

Enumeration District No. 8
Enumerated by me on **April 9, 1930** Francisco G. Lujan
Enumerator

	PLACE OF ABODE: Street, avenue, road, etc.	Number of dwelling house in order of visitation	Number of family in order of visitation	NAME of each person whose place of abode on April 1, 1930, was in this family. Enter surname, first, then given name and middle initial. If any. Include every person living on April 1, 1930. Omit children born since April 1, 1930.	RELATION Relationship of this Person to the head of the family.	PERSONAL DESCRIPTION: Sex	Color or race	Age at last birthday	Single, married, widowed or divorced	EDUCATION: Attended school any time since Sept. 1, 1929	Whether able to read and write.	NATIVITY Place of birth of this person.	Whether able to speak English.	OCCUPATION
	1	2	3	4	5	6	7	8	9	10	11	12	13	14
26	[no street name]	63	73	Naputi, Vicente P	Head	M	Cha	30	M	N	Y	Guam	Y	Carpenter
27		63	73	Naputi, Maria F	Wife	F	Cha	41	M	N	N	Guam	N	None
28		63	73	Naputi, Cristobal F	Son	M	Cha	15	S	Y	Y	Guam	Y	None
29		63	73	Naputi, Ana F	Daughter	F	Cha	13	S	Y	Y	Guam	Y	None
30		63	73	Naputi, Juan F	Son	M	Cha	12	S	Y	Y	Guam	Y	None
31		63	73	Naputi, Antonia F	Daughter	F	Cha	5	S	N		Guam		None
32		63	73	Naputi, Concepcion F	Daughter	F	Cha	4.8	S	N		Guam		None
33		63	73	Naputi, Francisco F	Son	M	Cha	2.1	S	N		Guam		None
34		63	73	Fejeran, Ramon G	Father in law	M	Cha	66	Wd	N	Y	Guam	N	None
35		64	74	San Nicolas, Antonio C	Head	M	Jap	32	M	N	Y	Guam	Y	Farmer
36		64	74	San Nicolas, Ignacia P	Wife	F	Cha	28	M	N	Y	Guam	Y	None
37		64	74	San Nicolas, Antonio P	Son	M	Cha	5	S	N		Guam		None
38		64	74	San Nicolas, Rafael P	Son	M	Cha	3.3	S	N		Guam		None
39		64	74	San Nicolas, Segundo P	Son	M	Cha	1.1	S	N		Guam		None
40		64	74	Camacho, Vicente C	Uncle	M	Cha	80	Wd	N	N	Guam	N	None
41		65	75	Diego, Romauldo C	Head	M	Cha	56	M	N	Y	Guam	Y	Farmer
42		65	75	Diego, Dolores SN	Wife	F	Cha	58	M	N	N	Guam	N	None
43		65	75	Diego, Vicente SN	Son	M	Cha	22	S	N	Y	Guam	Y	Chauffeur
44		65	75	Diego, Jesus SN	Son	M	Cha	20	S	N	Y	Guam	Y	Farm laborer
45		65	75	Diego, Rosa SN	Daughter	F	Cha	18	S	N	Y	Guam	Y	None
46		65	75	Diego, Joaquin SN	Son	M	Cha	15	S	Y	Y	Guam	Y	None
47		65	76	Reyes, Juan G	Head	M	Cha	31	M	N	Y	Guam	Y	School teacher
48		65	76	Reyes, Ana D	Wife	F	Cha	24	M	N	Y	Guam	N	None
49		65	76	Reyes, Edwardo D	Son	M	Cha	.1	S	N		Guam		None
50		66	77	Diego, Juan SN	Head	M	Cha	26	M	N	Y	Guam	Y	Farmer

DEPARTMENT OF COMMERCE-BUREAU OF THE CENSUS
WASHINGTON

FIFTEENTH CENSUS OF THE UNITED STATES: 1930-POPULATION

THE ISLAND OF GUAM

Sheet No. 9A

District Municipality of Agana
Name of Place Inarajan Town
[Proper name and, also, name of class, as city, town, village, barrio, etc]

Enumeration District No. 8
Enumerated by me on April 9, 1930 Francisco G. Lujan
Enumerator

	PLACE OF ABODE			NAME	RELATION	PERSONAL DESCRIPTION				EDUCATION		NATIVITY		OCCUPATION
	Street, avenue, road, etc.	Number of dwelling house is order of visitation	Number of family in order of visitation	of each person whose place of abode on April 1, 1930, was in this family. Enter surname, first, then given name and middle initial. If any. Include every person living on April 1, 1930. Omit children born since April 1, 1930.	Relationship of this Person to the head of the family.	Sex	Color or race	Age at last birthday	Single, married, widowed or divorced	Attended school any time since Sept. 1, 1929	Whether able to read and write.	Place of birth of this person.	Whether able to speak English.	
	1	2	3	4	5	6	7	8	9	10	11	12	13	14
1	[no street name]	66	77	Diego, Rosalia N	Wife	F	Cha	28	M	N	Y	Guam	N	None
2		66	77	Diego, Maria N	Daughter	F	Cha	6	S	N		Guam		None
3		66	77	Diego, Juan N	Daughter	F	Cha	2.8	S	N		Guam		None
4		66	77	Diego, Juan N	Son	M	Cha	0.4	S	N		Guam		None
5		67	78	Kirmijama, Maria M	Head	F	Cha	40	Wd	N	N	Guam	N	Farmer
6		67	78	Kirmijama, Rita M	Daughter	F	Jap	21	S	N	Y	Guam	Y	None
7		67	78	Kirmijama, Juan	Son	M	Jap	20	S	N	Y	Guam	Y	Farm laborer
8		67	78	Kirmijama, Margarita	Daughter	F	Jap	16	S	N	Y	Guam	Y	None
9		67	78	Kirmijama, Mariano	Son	M	Jap	14	S	Y	Y	Guam	Y	None
10		67	78	Ogo, Juan O	Servant	M	Cha	21	S	N	Y	Guam	Y	Farm laborer
11		68	79	Chargualaf, Jose M	Head	M	Cha	42	M	N	Y	Guam	N	Farmer
12		68	79	Chargualaf, Rosa SN	Wife	F	Cha	40	M	N	Y	Guam	N	None
13		68	79	Chargualaf, Juan N	Son	M	Cha	17	S	N	Y	Guam	Y	Farm laborer
14		68	79	Chargualaf, Adela SN	Daughter	F	Cha	7	S	Y		Guam		None
15		68	79	Chargualaf, Maria SN	Daughter	F	Cha	4.2	S	N		Guam		None
16		69	80	Taimanglo, Joaquin C	Head	M	Cha	39	M	N	N	Guam	N	Farmer
17		69	80	Taimanglo, Cornelia	Wife	F	Cha	38	M	N	N	Guam	N	None
18		69	80	Taimanglo, Beatrice	Daughter	F	Cha	18	S	N	Y	Guam	Y	None
19		69	80	Chiquina, Jesus D	Servant	M	Cha	47	Wd	N	N	Guam	N	Farm laborer
20		69	80	Meno, Engracia T	Niece	F	Cha	13	S	Y	Y	Guam	Y	None
21		70	81	Villova, Marcel D	Head	M	W	32	S	N	Y	Spain	Y	Missionary
22		70	81	Chargualaf, Luis M	Servant	M	Cha	17	S	N	Y	Guam	Y	Cook
23		71	82	Naputi, Enrique P	Head	M	Cha	41	M	N	Y	Guam	Y	Commissioner
24		71	82	Naputi, Maria M	Wife	F	Cha	30	M	N	Y	Guam	Y	None
25		71	82	Naputi, Pio C	Son	M	Cha	18	S	N	Y	Guam	Y	Carpenter

(CHAMORRO ROOTS GENEALOGY PROJECT™ TRANSCRIPTION)
(BERNARD T. PUNZALAN / HTTP://WWW.CHAMORROROOTS.COM)

DEPARTMENT OF COMMERCE-BUREAU OF THE CENSUS
WASHINGTON

FIFTEENTH CENSUS OF THE UNITED STATES: 1930-POPULATION

THE ISLAND OF GUAM

Sheet No. 9B

252B

District Municipality of Agana
Name of Place Inarajan Town
[Proper name and, also, name of class, as city, town, village, barrio, etc]

Enumeration District No. 8
Enumerated by me on April 9, 1930 Francisco G. Lujan
Enumerator

	PLACE OF ABODE			NAME	RELATION	PERSONAL DESCRIPTION				EDUCATION		NATIVITY		OCCUPATION
	Street, avenue, road, etc.	Number of dwelling house is order of visitation	Number of family in order of visitation	of each person whose place of abode on April 1, 1930, was in this family. Enter surname, first, then given name and middle initial. If any. Include every person living on April 1, 1930. Omit children born since April 1, 1930.	Relationship of this Person to the head of the family.	Sex	Color or race	Age at last birthday	Single, married, widowed or divorced	Attended school any time since Sept. 1, 1929	Whether able to read and write.	Place of birth of this person.	Whether able to speak English.	
	1	2	3	4	5	6	7	8	9	10	11	12	13	14
26	[no street name]	71	82	Naputi, Ana C	Daughter	F	Cha	16	S	N	Y	Guam	Y	None
27		71	82	Naputi, Jesus C	Son	M	Cha	13	S	Y	Y	Guam	Y	None
28		71	82	Naputi, Maria C	Daughter	F	Cha	11	S	Y	Y	Guam	Y	None
29		71	82	Naputi, Jose C	Son	M	Cha	7	S	Y		Guam		None
30		71	82	Naputi, Carmen M	Daughter	F	Cha	4	S	N		Guam		None
31		71	82	Naputi, Consolacion M	Daughter	F	Cha	1.2	S	N		Guam		None
32		72	83	Meno, Vicente M	Head	M	Cha	30	M	N	Y	Guam	Y	Farmer
33		72	83	Meno, Margarita C	Wife	F	Cha	27	M	N	Y	Guam	Y	None
34		72	83	Meno, Natividad C	Daughter	F	Cha	4.7	S	N		Guam		None
35		72	83	Meno, Enrique C	Son	M	Cha	3.7	S	N		Guam		None
36		72	83	Meno, Roman C	Son	M	Cha	2.3	S	N		Guam		None
37		73	84	Aguon, Juan T	Head	M	Cha	43	M	N	Y	Guam	N	Farmer
38		73	84	Aguon, Dolores F	Wife	F	Cha	33	M	N	Y	Guam	N	None
39		73	84	Aguon, Vicente F	Son	M	Cha	13	S	Y	Y	Guam	Y	None
40		73	84	Aguon, Concepcion F	Daughter	F	Cha	12	S	Y	Y	Guam	Y	None
41		73	84	Aguon, Rosa F	Daughter	F	Cha	10	S	Y	Y	Guam	Y	None
42		73	84	Aguon, Ana F	Daughter	F	Cha	9	S	Y		Guam		None
43		73	84	Aguon, Juan F	Son	M	Cha	7	S	Y		Guam		None
44		73	84	Aguon, Isabel F	Daughter	F	Cha	6	S	N		Guam		None
45		73	84	Aguon, Jesus F	Son	M	Cha	3.3	S	N		Guam		None
46		74	85	Meno, Felipe Q	Head	M	Cha	32	M	N	N	Guam	N	Farmer
47		74	85	Meno, Fedela C	Wife	F	Cha	31	M	N	Y	Guam	N	None
48		74	85	Meno, Rosa C	Daughter	F	Cha	7	S	Y		Guam		None
49		74	85	Meno, Esteban C	Son	M	Cha	5	S	N		Guam		None
50		74	85	Meno, Juana C	Daughter	F	Cha	4.1	S	N		Guam		None

(CHAMORRO ROOTS GENEALOGY PROJECT™ TRANSCRIPTION)
(BERNARD T. PUNZALAN / HTTP://WWW.CHAMORROROOTS.COM)

DEPARTMENT OF COMMERCE-BUREAU OF THE CENSUS
WASHINGTON

FIFTEENTH CENSUS OF THE UNITED STATES: 1930-POPULATION

THE ISLAND OF GUAM

Sheet No. 10A

253

District **Municipality of Agana**
Name of Place **Inarajan Town**
[Proper name and, also, name of class, as city, town, village, barrio, etc]

Enumeration District No. 8
Enumerated by me on **April 9, 1930** Francisco G. Lujan, Enumerator

	PLACE OF ABODE: Street, avenue, road, etc.	Number of dwelling house is order of visitation	Number of family in order of visitation	NAME of each person whose place of abode on April 1, 1930, was in this family. Enter surname, first, then given name and middle initial. If any. Include every person living on April 1, 1930. Omit children born since April 1, 1930.	RELATION Relationship of this Person to the head of the family.	PERSONAL DESCRIPTION: Sex	Color or race	Age at last birthday	Single, married, widowed or divorced	EDUCATION: Attended school any time since Sept. 1, 1929	Whether able to read and write.	NATIVITY Place of birth of this person.	Whether able to speak English.	OCCUPATION
	1	2	3	4	5	6	7	8	9	10	11	12	13	14
1	[no street name]	74	85	Meno, Carlos C	Son	M	Cha	.2	S	N		Guam		None
2		75	86	Paulino, Santiago N	Head	M	Cha	44	M	N	Y	Guam	N	Farmer
3		75	86	Paulino, Juliana D	Wife	F	Cha	33	M	N	N	Guam	N	None
4		75	86	Paulino, Jesus D	Son	M	Cha	17	S	Y	Y	Guam	Y	None
5		75	86	Paulino, Ana L	Daughter	F	Cha	8	S	Y		Guam		None
6		75	86	Paulino, Carmen L	Daughter	F	Cha	4	S	N		Guam		None
7		75	86	Paulino, Joaquin L	Son	M	Cha	1.8	S	N		Guam		None
8		75	86	Castro, Vicente L	Step-son	M	Cha	14	S	Y	Y	Guam	N	None
9		76	87	Castro, Jose D	Head	M	Cha	49	M	N	Y	Guam	N	Farmer
10		76	87	Castro, Gertrudes LG	Wife	F	Cha	48	M	N	Y	Guam	Y	None
11		76	87	Castro, Antonia LG	Daughter	F	Cha	17	S	N	Y	Guam	Y	None
12		76	87	Castro, Ana LG	Daughter	F	Cha	15	S	N	Y	Guam	Y	None
13		76	87	Castro, Joaquin LG	Son	M	Cha	14	S	Y	Y	Guam	Y	None
14		76	87	Castro, Margarita	Daughter	F	Cha	10	S	Y	Y	Guam	Y	None
15		76	88	Castro, Jose LG	Head	M	Cha	25	M	N	Y	Guam	Y	Farmer
16		76	88	Castro, Eliza A	Wife	F	Cha	23	M	N	Y	Guam	Y	None
17		76	88	Castro, Jose A	Son	M	Cha	1.7	S	N		Guam		None
18		76	88	Afaisen, Susana T	Aunt	F	Cha	59	S	N	N	Guam	N	None
19		77	89	Mesa, Jose P	Head	M	Cha	41	M	N	N	Guam	N	Farm laborer
20		77	89	Mesa, Carridad M	Wife	F	Cha	50	M	N	N	Guam	N	None
21		77	89	Mesa, Francisco M	Son	M	Cha	17	S	N	Y	Guam	Y	Farm laborer
22		77	89	Mesa, Vicente M	Son	M	Cha	10	S	Y	Y	Guam	Y	None
23		78	90	Afaisen, Joaquin SN	Head	M	Cha	36	M	N	Y	Guam	N	Farmer
24		78	90	Afaisen, Maria D	Wife	F	Cha	57	M	N	Y	Guam	N	None
25		78	90	Afaisen, Santiago	Son	M	Cha	15	S	N	Y	Guam	Y	Farm laborer

DEPARTMENT OF COMMERCE-BUREAU OF THE CENSUS
WASHINGTON

FIFTEENTH CENSUS OF THE UNITED STATES: 1930-POPULATION

THE ISLAND OF GUAM

Sheet No. 10B

253B

District **Municipality of Agana**
Name of Place **Inarajan Town**
[Proper name and, also, name of class, as city, town, village, barrio, etc]

Enumeration District No. 8
Enumerated by me on **April 9, 1930** Francisco G. Lujan, Enumerator

	PLACE OF ABODE			NAME	RELATION	PERSONAL DESCRIPTION				EDUCATION		NATIVITY		OCCUPATION
	Street, avenue, road, etc.	Number of dwelling house in order of visitation	Number of family in order of visitation	of each person whose place of abode on April 1, 1930, was in this family. Enter surname, first, then given name and middle initial, if any. Include every person living on April 1, 1930. Omit children born since April 1, 1930.	Relationship of this Person to the head of the family.	Sex	Color or race	Age at last birthday	Single, married, widowed or divorced	Attended school any time since Sept. 1, 1929	Whether able to read and write.	Place of birth of this person.	Whether able to speak English.	
	1	2	3	4	5	6	7	8	9	10	11	12	13	14
26	[no street name]	78	90	Afaisen, Cristina D	Daughter	F	Cha	13	S	Y	Y	Guam	Y	None
27		78	90	Afaisen, Juan D	Son	M	Cha	11	S	Y	Y	Guam	Y	None
28		78	90	Afaisen, Catalina D	Daughter	F	Cha	7	S	Y		Guam		None
29		78	90	Afaisen, Maria D	Daughter	F	Cha	7	S	Y		Guam		None
30		78	90	Afaisen, Jose D	Son	M	Cha	5	S	N		Guam		None
31		78	90	Afaisen, Ana D	Daughter	F	Cha	4	S	N		Guam		None
32		78	90	Afaisen, Ignacia D	Daughter	F	Cha	2.1	S	N		Guam		None
33		79	91	Rivera, Jose LG	Head	M	Cha	40	M	N		Guam	Y	Farmer
34		79	91	Rivera, Celedonia A	Wife	F	Cha	35	M	N	Y	Guam	Y	None
35		79	91	Rivera, Maria A	Daughter	F	Cha	16	S	N	Y	Guam	Y	None
36		79	91	Rivera, Pedro A	Son	M	Cha	15	S	Y	Y	Guam	Y	None
37		79	91	Rivera, Jose A	Son	M	Cha	12	S	Y	Y	Guam	Y	None
38		79	91	Rivera, Joaquin A	Son	M	Cha	8	S	Y	Y	Guam		None
39		79	91	Rivera, Francisco A	Son	M	Cha	4.7	S	N		Guam		None
40		79	91	Rivera, Carmen A	Daughter	F	Cha	2.3	S	N		Guam		None
41		79	91	Rivera, Dolores A	Daughter	F	Cha	1	S	N		Guam		None
42		79	91	Afaisen, Rita SN	Mother-in-law	F	Cha	65	Wd	N	Y	Guam	N	None
43		80	92	San Nicolas, Elias N	Head	M	Cha	48	M	N	Y	Guam	N	Farmer
44		80	92	San Nicolas, Maria M	Wife	F	Cha	42	M	N	Y	Guam	N	None
45		80	92	San Nicolas, Juan M	Son	M	Cha	21	S	N	Y	Guam	Y	Farm laborer
46		80	92	San Nicolas, Angelina M	Daughter	F	Cha	18	S	N	Y	Guam	Y	None
47		80	92	San Nicolas, Solidad M	Daughter	F	Cha	17	S	N	Y	Guam	Y	None
48		80	92	San Nicolas, Aurelia M	Daughter	F	Cha	13	S	Y	Y	Guam	Y	None
49		80	92	San Nicolas, Elizabeth M	Daughter	F	Cha	11	S	Y	Y	Guam	Y	None
50		80	92	San Nicolas, Alfredo	Son	M	Cha	7	S	Y		Guam		None

(CHAMORRO ROOTS GENEALOGY PROJECT™ TRANSCRIPTION)
(BERNARD T. PUNZALAN / HTTP://WWW.CHAMORROROOTS.COM)

DEPARTMENT OF COMMERCE-BUREAU OF THE CENSUS
WASHINGTON

FIFTEENTH CENSUS OF THE UNITED STATES: 1930-POPULATION

THE ISLAND OF GUAM

Sheet No. 11A

254

District **Municipality of Agana**
Name of Place **Inarajan Town**
[Proper name and, also, name of class, as city, town, village, barrio, etc]

Enumeration District No. **8**
Enumerated by me on **April 9, 1930** Francisco G. Lujan, Enumerator

	PLACE OF ABODE			NAME	RELATION	PERSONAL DESCRIPTION				EDUCATION		NATIVITY		OCCUPATION
	Street, avenue, road, etc.	Number of dwelling house in order of visitation	Number of family in order of visitation	of each person whose place of abode on April 1, 1930, was in this family. Enter surname, first, then given name and middle initial. If any. Include every person living on April 1, 1930. Omit children born since April 1, 1930.	Relationship of this Person to the head of the family.	Sex	Color or race	Age at last birthday	Single, married, widowed or divorced	Attended school any time since Sept. 1, 1929	Whether able to read and write.	Place of birth of this person.	Whether able to speak English.	
	1	2	3	4	5	6	7	8	9	10	11	12	13	14
1	[no street name]	80	92	San Nicolas, Jose M	Son	M	Cha	2.9	S	N		Guam		None
2		80	92	San Nicolas, Luisa M	Daughter	F	Cha	.9	S	N		Guam		None
3		80	92	Gogue, Geronimo A	Servant	M	Cha	16	S	N	Y	Guam	Y	Farm laborer
4		81	93	Quintanilla, Emeterio R	Head	M	Cha	59	M	N	Y	Guam	N	Farmer
5		81	93	Quintanilla, Manuela SN	Wife	F	Cha	56	M	N	Y	Guam	N	None
6		81	93	Quintanilla, Jose SN	Son	M	Cha	27	S	N	Y	Guam	Y	Farm laborer
7		81	93	Quintanilla, Jesus SN	Son	M	Cha	24	S	N	Y	Guam	Y	Farm laborer
8		81	93	Quintanilla, Maria SN	Daughter	F	Cha	21	S	N	Y	Guam	Y	None
9		81	93	Afaisen, Vicenta N	Cousin	F	Cha	49	S	N	N	Guam	N	None
10		81	93	San Nicolas, Dolores N	Sister-in-law	F	Cha	52	S	N	N	Guam	N	None
11		82	94	Flores, Manuel D	Head	M	Cha	39	M	N	Y	Guam	Y	Retail merchant
12		82	94	Flores, Joaquina G	Wife	F	Cha	33	M	N	Y	Guam	Y	None
13		82	94	Taitague, Henry D	Servant	M	Cha	19	S	N	Y	Guam	Y	Farm laborer
14		82	94	Taitague, Jesus N	Servant	M	Cha	25	M	N	Y	Guam	Y	Chauffeur
15		82	94	Taitague, Ignacia Q	Servant	F	Cha	19	M	N	Y	Guam	Y	Cook
16		82	94	Taitague, Jose Q	Lodger	M	Cha	.5	S	N		Guam		None
17		83	95	Meno, Sebastian N	Head	M	Cha	56	M	N	Y	Guam	N	Farmer
18		83	95	Meno, Candelaria LG	Wife	F	Cha	54	M	N	N	Guam	N	None
19		83	95	Meno, Jesus LG	Son	M	Cha	32	S	N	N	Guam	N	Farm laborer
20		83	95	Meno, Maria LG	Daughter	F	Cha	22	S	N	Y	Guam	Y	None
21		83	95	Meno, Ana LG	Daughter	F	Cha	21	S	N	Y	Guam	Y	None
22		83	95	Meno, Jose LG	Son	M	Cha	20	S	N	Y	Guam	Y	Farm laborer
23		83	95	Meno, Ramon LG	Son	M	Cha	19	S	N	Y	Guam	Y	Farm laborer
24		83	95	Meno, Justina LG	Daughter	F	Cha	17	S	N	Y	Guam	Y	None
25		83	95	Meno, Edividis LG	Daughter	F	Cha	15	S	N	Y	Guam	Y	None

DEPARTMENT OF COMMERCE-BUREAU OF THE CENSUS
WASHINGTON

FIFTEENTH CENSUS OF THE UNITED STATES: 1930-POPULATION

THE ISLAND OF GUAM

Sheet No. 11B

254B

District Municipality of Agana
Name of Place Inarajan Town
[Proper name and, also, name of class, as city, town, village, barrio, etc]

Enumeration District No. 8
Enumerated by me on April 10, 1930 Francisco G. Lujan
Enumerator

	PLACE OF ABODE			NAME	RELATION	PERSONAL DESCRIPTION				EDUCATION		NATIVITY		OCCUPATION
	Street, avenue, road, etc.	Number of dwelling house in order of visitation	Number of family in order of visitation	of each person whose place of abode on April 1, 1930, was in this family. Enter surname, first, then given name and middle initial. If any. Include every person living on April 1, 1930. Omit children born since April 1, 1930.	Relationship of this Person to the head of the family.	Sex	Color or race	Age at last birthday	Single, married, widowed or divorced	Attended school any time since Sept. 1, 1929	Whether able to read and write.	Place of birth of this person.	Whether able to speak English.	
	1	2	3	4	5	6	7	8	9	10	11	12	13	14
26	[no street name]	83	95	Meno, Juan LG	Son	M	Cha	13	S	Y	Y	Guam	Y	None
27		83	95	Meno, Concepcion M	Granddaughter	F	Cha	4.6	S	N		Guam		None
28		84	96	Meno, Joaquin LG	Head	M	Cha	29	M	N	Y	Guam	Y	Farmer
29		84	96	Meno, Antonia C	Wife	F	Cha	24	M	N	Y	Guam	Y	None
30		84	96	Meno, Maria C	Daughter	F	Cha	3.9	S	N		Guam		None
31		84	96	Meno, Jose C	Son	M	Cha	1.1	S	N		Guam		None
32		85	97	Chargualaf, Jesus M	Head	M	Cha	22	M	N	Y	Guam	Y	Farmer
33		85	97	Chargualaf, Josefa T	Wife	F	Cha	20	M	N	Y	Guam	Y	None
34		85	97	Chargualaf, Florentina T	Daughter	F	Cha	1.9	S	N		Guam		None
35		85	97	Chargualaf, Jose T	Son	M	Cha	.3	S	N		Guam		None
36		85	97	Afaisen, Antonio N	Uncle	M	Cha	56	M	N	Y	Guam	N	None
37		85	97	Afaisen, Maria C	Aunt	F	Cha	54	M	N	N	Guam	N	None
38		85	97	Chargualaf, Francisco M	Brother	M	Cha	19	S	N	Y	Guam	Y	Farm laborer
39		86	98	Meno, Vicente T	Head	M	Cha	40	M	N	Y	Guam	N	Farmer
40		86	98	Meno, Ana M	Wife	F	Cha	37	M	N	N	Guam	N	None
41		86	98	Meno, Jose M	Son	M	Cha	17	S	N	Y	Guam	Y	Farm laborer
42		86	98	Meno, Maria M	Daughter	F	Cha	15	S	N	Y	Guam	Y	None
43		86	98	Meno, Juan M	Son	M	Cha	9	S	Y		Guam		None
44		86	98	Meno, Regina M	Daughter	F	Cha	5	S	N		Guam		None
45		86	98	Meno, Felix M	Son	M	Cha	3.5	S	N		Guam		None
46		87	99	Meno, Geronimo SN	Head	M	Cha	61	M	N	Y	Guam	N	Farmer
47		87	99	Meno, Ana T	Wife	F	Cha	62	M	N	N	Guam	N	None
48		87	99	Meno, Feliza T	Daughter	F	Cha	39	S	N	Y	Guam	N	None
49		87	99	Naputi, Antonia T	Sister in law	F	Cha	73	Wd	N	N	Guam	N	None
50		88	100	Meno, Juan T	Head	M	Cha	27	M	N	Y	Guam	Y	Farmer

DEPARTMENT OF COMMERCE-BUREAU OF THE CENSUS
WASHINGTON

FIFTEENTH CENSUS OF THE UNITED STATES: 1930-POPULATION

THE ISLAND OF GUAM

Sheet No. 12A

District Municipality of Agana
Name of Place Inarajan Town
[Proper name and, also, name of class, as city, town, village, barrio, etc]

Enumeration District No. 8
Enumerated by me on April 10, 1930 Francisco G. Lujan, Enumerator

	PLACE OF ABODE			NAME	RELATION	PERSONAL DESCRIPTION				EDUCATION		NATIVITY		OCCUPATION
	Street, avenue, road, etc.	Number of dwelling house in order of visitation	Number of family in order of visitation	of each person whose place of abode on April 1, 1930, was in this family. Enter surname, first, then given name and middle initial. If any. Include every person living on April 1, 1930. Omit children born since April 1, 1930.	Relationship of this Person to the head of the family.	Sex	Color or race	Age at last birthday	Single, married, widowed or divorced	Attended school any time since Sept. 1, 1929	Whether able to read and write.	Place of birth of this person.	Whether able to speak English.	
	1	2	3	4	5	6	7	8	9	10	11	12	13	14
1	[no street name]	88	100	Meno, Maria A	Wife	F	Cha	24	M	N	Y	Guam	Y	None
2		88	100	Meno, Lourdes A	Daughter	F	Cha	5	S	N		Guam		None
3		88	100	Meno, Josefina A	Daughter	F	Cha	3.4	S	N		Guam		None
4		88	100	Meno, Juana A	Son	M	Cha	0.9	S	N		Guam		None
5		89	101	Crisostomo, Angel M	Head	M	Cha	29	M	N	N	Guam	N	Farmer
6		89	101	Crisostomo, Anunsacion P	Wife	F	Cha	25	M	N	N	Guam	N	None
7		89	101	Crisostomo, Ana P	Daughter	F	Cha	4.2	S	N		Guam		None
8		89	101	Crisostomo, Jesus P	Son	M	Cha	2.7	S	N		Guam		None
9		89	101	Crisostomo, Maria P	Daughter	F	Cha	.7	S	N		Guam		None
10		89	101	Peredo, Nicomedes C	Father in law	M	Cha	63	Wd	N	N	Guam	N	Farm laborer
11		89	101	Crisostomo, Josefina C	Brother	M	Cha	22	S	N	N	Guam	N	Farm laborer
12		90	102	Paulino, Juan C	Head	M	Cha	29	M	N	Y	Guam	Y	Farmer
13		90	102	Paulino, Rosa M	Wife	F	Cha	20	M	N	Y	Guam	Y	None
14		90	102	Paulino, Tomas M	Son	M	Cha	5	S	N		Guam		None
15		90	102	Paulino, Juan M	Son	M	Cha	4.3	S	N		Guam		None
16		90	102	Paulino, Jesus M	Son	M	Cha	3	S	N		Guam		None
17		91	103	Fejeran, Juan LG	Head	M	Cha	29	M	N	Y	Guam	Y	Carpenter
18		91	103	Fejeran, Teresa M	Wife	F	Cha	31	M	N	Y	Guam	Y	None
19		82	104	San Nicolas, Nicolasa T	Head	F	Cha	55	Wd	N	N	Guam	N	Farmer
20		82	104	San Nicolas, Jesus T	Son	M	Cha	30	S	N	N	Guam	N	Farm laborer
21		82	104	San Nicolas, Josefina T	Daughter	F	Cha	27	S	N	Y	Guam	Y	Farm laborer
22		82	104	San Nicolas, Francisco T	Son	M	Cha	23	S	N	Y	Guam	Y	Farm laborer
23		82	104	San Nicolas, Maria T	Daughter	F	Cha	18	S	N	Y	Guam	Y	None
24		82	104	San Nicolas, Ramon T	Son	M	Cha	14	S	N	Y	Guam	Y	Farm laborer
25		82	104	San Nicolas, Geronmio T	Son	M	Cha	12	S	Y	Y	Guam	Y	None

DEPARTMENT OF COMMERCE-BUREAU OF THE CENSUS
WASHINGTON

FIFTEENTH CENSUS OF THE UNITED STATES: 1930-POPULATION

THE ISLAND OF GUAM

Sheet No. 12B

255B

District **Municipality of Agana**
Name of Place **Inarajan Town**
[Proper name and, also, name of class, as city, town, village, barrio, etc]

Enumeration District No. 8
Enumerated by me on **April 10, 1930** Francisco G. Lujan, Enumerator

	PLACE OF ABODE			NAME	RELATION	PERSONAL DESCRIPTION				EDUCATION		NATIVITY		OCCUPATION
	Street, avenue, road, etc.	Number of dwelling house in order of visitation	Number of family in order of visitation	of each person whose place of abode on April 1, 1930, was in this family. Enter surname, first, then given name and middle initial. If any. Include every person living on April 1, 1930. Omit children born since April 1, 1930.	Relationship of this Person to the head of the family.	Sex	Color or race	Age at last birthday	Single, married, widowed or divorced	Attended school any time since Sept. 1, 1929	Whether able to read and write.	Place of birth of this person.	Whether able to speak English.	
	1	2	3	4	5	6	7	8	9	10	11	12	13	14
26	[no street name]	93	105	Naputi, Joaquin T	Head	M	Cha	30	S	N	Y	Guam	Y	Shoemaker
27		94	106	Naputi, Juan D	Head	M	Cha	58	M	N	Y	Guam	N	Farmer
28		94	106	Naputi, Dolores M	Wife	F	Cha	45	M	N	N	Guam	N	None
29		94	106	Naputi, Antonio C	Son	M	Cha	17	S	N	Y	Guam	Y	Farm laborer
30		94	106	Naputi, Jose C	Son	M	Cha	15	S	Y	Y	Guam	Y	Farm laborer
31		94	106	Chargualaf, Lucia M	Step daughter	F	Cha	21	S	N	Y	Guam	Y	None
32		94	107	Castro, Jesus LG	Head	M	Cha	23	M	N	Y	Guam	Y	Farmer
33		94	107	Castro, Rita N	Wife	F	Cha	21	M	N	Y	Guam	Y	None
34		94	107	Castro, Cristobal N	Son	M	Cha	3	S	N		Guam		None
35		94	107	Castro, Maria N	Daughter	F	Cha	26	S	N		Guam		None
36		94	107	Castro, Gloria N	Daughter	F	Cha	.3	S	N		Guam		None
37		94	108	Martinez, Jeus R	Head	M	Cha	30	M	N	Y	Guam	Y	Farmer
38		94	108	Martinez, Elena N	Wife	F	Cha	25	M	N	N	Guam	N	None
39		94	108	Martinez, Maria N	Daughter	F	Cha	6	S	N		Guam		None
40		94	108	Martinez, Jesus N	Son	M	Cha	4.7	S	N		Guam		None
41		94	108	Martinez, Ana N	Daughter	F	Cha	.1	S	N		Guam		None
42		95	109	Naputi, Rita D	Head	F	Cha	80	Wd	N	N	Guam	N	None
43		96	110	Martinez, Jose N	Head	M	Cha	25	M	N	Y	Guam	N	Farmer
44		96	110	Martinez, Rita M	Wife	F	Cha	29	M	N	Y	Guam	Y	None
45		96	110	Martinez, Maria M	Daughter	F	Cha	3.3	S	N		Guam		None
46		97	111	Mantanona, Luis C	Head	M	Cha	58	M	N		Guam	N	Farmer
47		97	111	Mantanona, Francisca N	Wife	F	Cha	52	M	N		Guam	N	None
48		97	111	Mantanona, Ana N	Daughter	F	Cha	8	S			Guam		None
49		97	111	Mantanona, Eliza N	Daughter	F	Cha	5	S			Guam		None
50		97	111	Mantanona, Maria N	Daughter	F	Cha	1.7	S			Guam		None

(CHAMORRO ROOTS GENEALOGY PROJECT™ TRANSCRIPTION)
(BERNARD T. PUNZALAN / HTTP://WWW.CHAMORROROOTS.COM)

DEPARTMENT OF COMMERCE-BUREAU OF THE CENSUS
WASHINGTON

FIFTEENTH CENSUS OF THE UNITED STATES: 1930-POPULATION

THE ISLAND OF GUAM

Sheet No. 13A

256

District **Municipality of Agana**
Name of Place **Inarajan Town**
[Proper name and, also, name of class, as city, town, village, barrio, etc]

Enumeration District No. 8
Enumerated by me on **April 11, 1930** Francisco G. Lujan, Enumerator

	PLACE OF ABODE			NAME	RELATION	PERSONAL DESCRIPTION				EDUCATION		NATIVITY		OCCUPATION
	Street, avenue, road, etc.	Number of dwelling house in order of visitation	Number of family in order of visitation	of each person whose place of abode on April 1, 1930, was in this family. Enter surname, first, then given name and middle initial. If any. Include every person living on April 1, 1930. Omit children born since April 1, 1930.	Relationship of this Person to the head of the family.	Sex	Color or race	Age at last birthday	Single, married, widowed or divorced	Attended school any time since Sept. 1, 1929	Whether able to read and write.	Place of birth of this person.	Whether able to speak English.	
	1	2	3	4	5	6	7	8	9	10	11	12	13	14
1	[no street name]	97	111	Meno, Ursula N	Step daughter	F	Cha	16	S	N	Y	Guam	Y	None
2		97	111	Chiguina, Monica C	Aunt	F	Cha	90	Wd	N	N	Guam	N	None
3		97	111	Chiguina, Magdalena	Cousin	F	Cha	57	S	N	N	Guam	N	None
4		98	112	Taimanglo, Jose T	Head	M	Cha	53	M	N	Y	Guam	N	Farmer
5		98	112	Taimanglo, Clara M	Wife	F	Cha	44	M	N	N	Guam	N	None
6		98	112	Taimanglo, Dolores M	Daughter	F	Cha	17	S	N	Y	Guam	Y	None
7		98	112	Taimanglo, Miguel M	Son	M	Cha	6	S	N		Guam		None
8		98	112	Taimanglo, Victurino T	Brother	M	Cha	39	S	N	Y	Guam	N	Farm laborer
9		99	113	Mantanona, Issac C	Head	M	Cha	57	M	N	Y	Guam	N	Farmer
10		99	113	Mantanona, Manuela M	Wife	F	Cha	50	M	N	N	Guam	N	None
11		99	113	Mantanona, Francisco M	Son	M	Cha	20	S	N	Y	Guam	Y	Farm laborer
12		99	113	Mantanona, Martina M	Daughter	F	Cha	17	S	N	Y	Guam	Y	None
13		100	114	Mantanona, Jose M	Head	M	Cha	22	M	N	Y	Guam	Y	Farmer
14		100	114	Mantanona, Consolacion T	Wife	F	Cha	29	M	N	N	Guam	N	None
15		100	114	Mantanona, Maria T	Daughter	F	Cha	2.4	S	N		Guam		None
16		100	114	Mantanona, Jesus T	Son	M	Cha	.1	S	N		Guam		None
17		101	115	Meno, Jesus N	Head	M	Cha	28	M	N	Y	Guam	Y	Farmer
18		101	115	Meno, Antonia C	Wife	F	Cha	20	M	N	Y	Guam	Y	None
19		101	115	Meno, Vinancio C	Son	M	Cha	0	S	N		Guam		None
20		102	116	Meno, Consolacion N	Head	F	Cha	59	Wd	N	N	Guam	N	Farmer
21		102	116	Meno, Ana N	Daughter	F	Cha	24	S	N	Y	Guam	N	Farm laborer
22		103	117	Tedtaotao, Maria C	Head	F	Cha	21	Wd	N	N	Guam	N	Laundress
23		103	117	Tedtaotao, Dolores C	Daughter	F	Cha	3.9	S	N		Guam		None
24		103	117	Tedtaotao, Robert C	Son	M	Cha	2.7	S	N		Guam		None
25		104	118	Mantanona, Silvestre N	Head	M	Cha	54	M	N	N	Guam	N	Farmer

DEPARTMENT OF COMMERCE-BUREAU OF THE CENSUS
WASHINGTON

FIFTEENTH CENSUS OF THE UNITED STATES: 1930-POPULATION

THE ISLAND OF GUAM

Sheet No. 13B

256B

District **Municipality of Agana**
Name of Place **Inarajan Town**
[Proper name and, also, name of class, as city, town, village, barrio, etc]

Enumeration District No. 8
Enumerated by me on **April 11, 1930** Francisco G. Lujan
Enumerator

	PLACE OF ABODE: Street, avenue, road, etc.	Number of dwelling house is order of visitation	Number of family in order of visitation	NAME of each person whose place of abode on April 1, 1930, was in this family. Enter surname, first, then given name and middle initial. If any. Include every person living on April 1, 1930. Omit children born since April 1, 1930.	RELATION Relationship of this Person to the head of the family.	PERSONAL DESCRIPTION: Sex	Color or race	Age at last birthday	Single, married, widowed or divorced	EDUCATION: Attended school any time since Sept. 1, 1929	Whether able to read and write.	NATIVITY Place of birth of this person.	Whether able to speak English.	OCCUPATION
	1	2	3	4	5	6	7	8	9	10	11	12	13	14
26	[no street name]	104	118	Mantanona, Ignacia M	Wife	F	Cha	53	M	N	N	Guam	N	None
27		104	118	Mantanona, Domitilia M	Daughter	F	Cha	23	S	N	Y	Guam	Y	None
28		104	118	Mantanona, Jose M	Son	M	Cha	21	S	N	Y	Guam	Y	Farm laborer
29		104	118	Mantanona, Genoveva M	Daughter	F	Cha	18	S	N	Y	Guam	Y	None
30		104	118	Mantanona, Dolores M	Daughter	F	Cha	12	S	Y	Y	Guam	Y	None
31		104	118	Mantanona, Ana M	Daughter	F	Cha	10	S	Y	Y	Guam	Y	None
32		104	119	Mantanona, Pedro M	Head	M	Cha	26	M	N	Y	Guam	Y	Deputy Commissioner
33		104	119	Mantanona, Maria N	Wife	F	Cha	19	M	N	Y	Guam	Y	None
34		104	119	Mantanona, Jesus N	Son	M	Cha	2.5	S	N		Guam		None
35		105	120	Mantanona, Jose N	Head	M	Cha	39	M	N	N	Guam	N	Farmer
36		105	120	Mantanona, Josefa M	Wife	F	Cha	60	M	N	N	Guam	N	None
37		105	120	Mantanona, Ramon M	Son	M	Cha	14	S	Y	Y	Guam	Y	None
38		105	120	Chiguina, Jesus M	Nephew	M	Cha	10	S	Y	Y	Guam	Y	None
39		105	121	Duenas, Juan T	Head	M	Cha	43	M	N	N	Guam	N	Farmer
40		105	121	Duenas, Cartina M	Wife	F	Cha	25	M	N	N	Guam	N	None
41		105	121	Duenas, Jose M	Son	M	Cha	19	S	N	Y	Guam	Y	Farm laborer
42		105	121	Duenas, Isabel M	Daughter	F	Cha	16	S	N	Y	Guam	Y	None
43		105	121	Duenas, Pedro M	Son	M	Cha	14	S	N	Y	Guam	Y	Farm laborer
44		105	121	Duenas, Jesus M	Son	M	Cha	3.3	S	N		Guam		None
45		105	121	Duenas, Vicente M	Son	M	Cha	2.1	S	N		Guam		None
46		105	121	Duenas, Enriqueta M	Daughter	F	Cha	0.7	S	N		Guam		None
47		106	122	Leon Guerrero, Joaquin S	Head	M	Cha	42	M	N	Y	Guam	N	Farmer
48		106	122	Leon Guerrero, Ana A	Wife	F	Cha	44	M	N	N	Guam	N	None
49		106	122	Leon Guerrero, Maria A	Daughter	F	Cha	17	S	N	Y	Guam	Y	None
50		106	122	Leon Guerrero, Rosario A	Daughter	F	Cha	14	S	N	Y	Guam	Y	None

DEPARTMENT OF COMMERCE-BUREAU OF THE CENSUS
WASHINGTON

FIFTEENTH CENSUS OF THE UNITED STATES: 1930-POPULATION

THE ISLAND OF GUAM

Sheet No. 14A

District **Municipality of Agana**
Name of Place **Inarajan Town**
[Proper name and, also, name of class, as city, town, village, barrio, etc]

Enumeration District No. 8
Enumerated by me on **April 11, 1930** Francisco G. Lujan
Enumerator

	PLACE OF ABODE			NAME	RELATION	PERSONAL DESCRIPTION				EDUCATION		NATIVITY		OCCUPATION
	Street, avenue, road, etc.	Number of dwelling house is order of visitation	Number of family in order of visitation	of each person whose place of abode on April 1, 1930, was in this family. Enter surname, first, then given name and middle initial. If any. Include every person living on April 1, 1930. Omit children born since April 1, 1930.	Relationship of this Person to the head of the family.	Sex	Color or race	Age at last birthday	Single, married, widowed or divorced	Attended school any time since Sept. 1, 1929	Whether able to read and write.	Place of birth of this person.	Whether able to speak English.	
	1	2	3	4	5	6	7	8	9	10	11	12	13	14
1	[no street name]	106	122	Leon Guerrero, Jesus A	Son	M	Cha	13	S	Y	Y	Guam	Y	None
2		106	122	Leon Guerrero, Dolores A	Daughter	F	Cha	10	S	Y	Y	Guam	Y	None
3		106	122	Leon Guerrero, Rosa A	Daughter	F	Cha	8	S	Y		Guam		None
4		106	122	Leon Guerrero, Dominga A	Daughter	F	Cha	6	S	N		Guam		None
5		106	122	Leon Guerrero, Ramon	Son	M	Cha	3.1	S	N		Guam		None
6		106	122	Mantanona, Jose C	Father in law	M	Cha	59	M	N	N	Guam	N	None
7		106	122	Mantanona, Rosa M	Mother in law	F	Cha	69	M	N	N	Guam	N	None
8		106	122	Mantanona, Isabel	Niece	F	Cha	7	S	Y		Guam		None
9		107	123	Fejeran, Jose LG	Head	M	Cha	38	M	N	Y	Guam	N	Farmer
10		107	123	Fejeran, Dolores A	Wife	F	Cha	33	M	N	Y	Guam	Y	None
11		107	123	Fejeran, Tomas A	Son	M	Cha	11	S	Y	Y	Guam	Y	None
12		107	123	Fejeran, Jesus A	Son	M	Cha	9	S	Y		Guam		None
13		107	123	Fejeran, Juan A	Son	M	Cha	5	S	N		Guam		None
14		108	124	Cepeda, Joaquin C	Head	M	Cha	49	M	N	Y	Guam	N	Farmer
15		108	124	Cepeda, Dolores T	Wife	F	Cha	35	M	N	N	Guam	N	None
16		108	124	Cepeda, Rosa T	Daughter	F	Cha	11	S	Y	Y	Guam	Y	None
17		108	124	Cepeda, Feleberto T	Son	M	Cha	5	S	N		Guam		None
18		108	124	Cepeda, Ester T	Daughter	F	Cha	4.1	S	N		Guam		None
19		108	124	Cepeda, Maria T	Daughter	F	Cha	2.7	S	N		Guam		None
20		108	124	Taimanglo, Guadalupe C	Mother in law	F	Cha	65	Wd	N	N	Guam	N	None
21		108	124	Chargualaf, Ramon T	Nephew	M	Cha	10	S	Y	Y	Guam	Y	None
22		109	125	Chargualaf, Ramon M	Head	M	Cha	61	M	N	Y	Guam	N	Farmer
23		109	125	Chargualaf, Estefania SN	Wife	F	Cha	50	M	N	N	Guam	N	None
24		109	125	Chargualaf, Jose SN	Son	M	Cha	24	S	N	Y	Guam	Y	Farm laborer
25		109	125	Chargualaf, Vicente SN	Son	M	Cha	20	S	N	Y	Guam	Y	Farm laborer

DEPARTMENT OF COMMERCE-BUREAU OF THE CENSUS
WASHINGTON
FIFTEENTH CENSUS OF THE UNITED STATES: 1930-POPULATION
THE ISLAND OF GUAM

Sheet No. 14B

257B

District **Municipality of Agana**
Name of Place **Inarajan Town**
[Proper name and, also, name of class, as city, town, village, barrio, etc]

Enumeration District No. 8
Enumerated by me on **April 12, 1930** Francisco G. Lujan
Enumerator

	PLACE OF ABODE			NAME	RELATION	PERSONAL DESCRIPTION				EDUCATION		NATIVITY		OCCUPATION
	Street, avenue, road, etc.	Number of dwelling house is order of visitation	Number of family in order of visitation	of each person whose place of abode on April 1, 1930, was in this family. Enter surname, first, then given name and middle initial. If any. Include every person living on April 1, 1930. Omit children born since April 1, 1930.	Relationship of this Person to the head of the family.	Sex	Color or race	Age at last birthday	Single, married, widowed or divorced	Attended school any time since Sept. 1, 1929	Whether able to read and write.	Place of birth of this person.	Whether able to speak English.	
	1	2	3	4	5	6	7	8	9	10	11	12	13	14
26	[no street name]	109	125	Chargualaf, Pedro SN	Son	M	Cha	16	S	N	Y	Guam	Y	Farm laborer
27		110	126	Taimanglo, Isidoro C	Head	M	Cha	39	M	N	N	Guam	N	Farmer
28		110	126	Taimanglo, Solidad N	Wife	F	Cha	34	M	N	Y	Guam	N	None
29		110	126	Taimanglo, Guadalupe N	Daughter	F	Cha	4.7	S	N		Guam		None
30		110	126	Taimanglo, Jose N	Son	M	Cha	3.6	S	N		Guam		None
31		110	126	Taimanglo, Manuel N	Son	M	Cha	0.1	S	N		Guam		None
32		111	127	San Nicolas, Francisco C	Head	M	Cha	38	M	N	Y	Guam	N	Farmer
33		111	127	San Nicolas, Tomasa M	Wife	F	Cha	40	M	N	Y	Guam	N	None
34		111	127	San Nicolas, Maria M	Daughter	F	Cha	16	S	N	Y	Guam	Y	None
35		111	127	San Nicolas, Quintin M	Son	M	Cha	12	S	Y	Y	Guam	Y	None
36		111	127	San Nicolas, Solidad M	Daughter	F	Cha	4.9	S	N		Guam		None
37		111	127	San Nicolas, Josefa M	Daughter	F	Cha	2.7	S	N		Guam		None
38		112	128	Quintanilla, Aniceto SN	Head	M	Cha	31	M	N	Y	Guam	Y	Farmer
39		112	128	Quintanilla, Catalina D	Wife	F	Cha	28	M	N	Y	Guam	Y	None
40		112	128	Quintanilla, Ignacia D	Daughter	F	Cha	6	S	N		Guam		None
41		112	128	Quintanilla, Alfonsina D	Daughter	F	Cha	4.2	S	N		Guam		None
42		112	128	Quintanilla, Juan D	Son	M	Cha	2.2	S	N		Guam		None
43		112	128	Quintanilla, Maria D	Son	M	Cha	.7	S	N		Guam		None
44		112	128	Diego, Ignacia LG	Mother-in-law	F	Cha	58	Wd	N	Y	Guam	N	None
45		113	129	Asanoma, Tito K	Head	M	Jap	58	M	N	Y	Japan	N	Farmer
46		113	129	Asanoma, Sabina C	Wife	F	Cha	40	M	N	N	Guam	N	None
47		113	129	Asanoma, Francisco C	Son	M	Jap	16	S	N	Y	Guam	Y	Farm laborer
48		113	129	Asanoma, Maria C	Daughter	F	Jap	14	S	Y	Y	Guam	Y	None
49		113	129	Asanoma, Jose C	Son	M	Jap	10	S	Y	Y	Guam	Y	None
50		113	129	Asanoma, Ana C	Daughter	F	Jap	5	S	N		Guam		None

(CHAMORRO ROOTS GENEALOGY PROJECT™ TRANSCRIPTION)
(BERNARD T. PUNZALAN / HTTP://WWW.CHAMORROROOTS.COM)

DEPARTMENT OF COMMERCE-BUREAU OF THE CENSUS
WASHINGTON

FIFTEENTH CENSUS OF THE UNITED STATES: 1930-POPULATION

THE ISLAND OF GUAM

Sheet No. 15A

District **Municipality of Agana**
Name of Place **Inarajan Town**
[Proper name and, also, name of class, as city, town, village, barrio, etc]

Enumeration District No. 8
Enumerated by me on **April 12, 1930** Francisco G. Lujan
Enumerator

	PLACE OF ABODE: Street, avenue, road, etc.	Number of dwelling house in order of visitation	Number of family in order of visitation	NAME of each person whose place of abode on April 1, 1930, was in this family. Enter surname, first, then given name and middle initial. If any. Include every person living on April 1, 1930. Omit children born since April 1, 1930.	RELATION Relationship of this Person to the head of the family.	PERSONAL DESCRIPTION: Sex	Color or race	Age at last birthday	Single, married, widowed or divorced	EDUCATION: Attended school any time since Sept. 1, 1929	Whether able to read and write.	NATIVITY Place of birth of this person.	Whether able to speak English.	OCCUPATION
	1	2	3	4	5	6	7	8	9	10	11	12	13	14
1	[no street name]	113	129	Asanoma, Josefa C	Daughter	F	Jap	1.1	S	N		Guam		None
2		114	130	Paulino, Nicolas C	Head	M	Cha	47	M	N	Y	Guam	N	Farmer
3		114	130	Paulino, Damiana C	Wife	F	Cha	18	M	N	Y	Guam	Y	None
4		114	130	Paulino, Vicente D	Son	M	Cha	10	S	Y	Y	Guam	Y	None
5		114	130	Paulino, Josefa D	Daughter	F	Cha	9	S	Y		Guam		None
6		114	130	Paulino, Teresa D	Daughter	F	Cha	8	S	Y		Guam		None
7		114	130	Paulino, Nicolas D	Son	M	Cha	7	S	Y		Guam		None
8		114	130	Paulino, Francisco D	Son	M	Cha	0.7	S	N		Guam		None
9		114	131	Chargualaf, Jose T	Head	M	Cha	47	M	N	N	Guam	N	Farmer
10		114	131	Chargualaf, Domitila M	Wife	F	Cha	39	M	N	N	Guam	N	None
11		114	131	Chargualaf, Maria M	Daughter	F	Cha	16	S	N	Y	Guam	Y	None
12		114	131	Chargualaf, Dolores M	Daughter	F	Cha	13	S	Y	Y	Guam	Y	None
13		114	131	Chargualaf, Francisco M	Son	M	Cha	10	S	Y	Y	Guam	Y	None
14		114	131	Chargualaf, Edivíges M	Daughter	F	Cha	4.7	S	N		Guam		None
15		114	131	Chargualaf, Jesus M	Son	M	Cha	.7	S	N		Guam		None
16		115	132	Delgado, Jose M	Head	M	Cha	63	M	N	N	Guam	N	Farmer
17		115	132	Delgado, Josefa C	Wife	F	Cha	61	M	N	N	Guam	N	None
18		115	132	San Nicolas, Luciano C	Step-son	M	Cha	35	S	N	N	Guam	N	Farm laborer
19		115	132	Delgado, Juan M	Brother	M	Cha	44	Wd	N	N	Guam	N	None
20		115	132	Delgado, Concepcion T	Niece	F	Cha	16	S	N	Y	Japan	Y	None
21		115	132	Delgado, Manuel T	Nephew	M	Cha	14	S	N	Y	Guam	Y	Farm laborer
22		115	132	Delgado, Pedro T	Nephew	M	Cha	6	S	N		Guam		None
23		116	133	Meno, Ramon M	Head	M	Cha	29	M	N	Y	Guam	Y	Farmer
24		116	133	Meno, Rosario C	Wife	F	Cha	22	M	N	Y	Guam	Y	None
25		116	133	Meno, Jose C	Son	M	Cha	1.1	S	N		Guam		None

DEPARTMENT OF COMMERCE-BUREAU OF THE CENSUS
WASHINGTON

FIFTEENTH CENSUS OF THE UNITED STATES: 1930-POPULATION

THE ISLAND OF GUAM

Sheet No. 15B

258B

District **Municipality of Agana**
Name of Place **Inarajan Town**
[Proper name and, also, name of class, as city, town, village, barrio, etc]

Enumeration District No. 8
Enumerated by me on **April 12, 1930** Francisco G. Lujan, Enumerator

	PLACE OF ABODE			NAME	RELATION	PERSONAL DESCRIPTION				EDUCATION		NATIVITY		OCCUPATION
	Street, avenue, road, etc.	Number of dwelling house is order of visitation	Number of family in order of visitation	of each person whose place of abode on April 1, 1930, was in this family. Enter surname, first, then given name and middle initial. If any. Include every person living on April 1, 1930. Omit children born since April 1, 1930.	Relationship of this Person to the head of the family.	Sex	Color or race	Age at last birthday	Single, married, widowed or divorced	Attended school any time since Sept. 1, 1929	Whether able to read and write.	Place of birth of this person.	Whether able to speak English.	
	1	2	3	4	5	6	7	8	9	10	11	12	13	14
26	[no street name]	117	134	Duenas, Teresa T	Head	F	Cha	66	Wd	N	N	Guam	N	None
27		117	134	Duenas, Joaquina T	Daughter	F	Cha	44	S	N	N	Guam	N	None
28		118	135	Quidachay, Angela T	Head	F	Cha	44	S	N	N	Guam	N	Farmer
29		118	135	Quidachay, Maria Q	Daughter	F	Cha	16	S	N	Y	Guam	Y	None
30		118	135	Quidachay, Jose Q	Son	M	Cha	12	S	Y	Y	Guam	Y	None
31		118	135	Quidachay, Jesus Q	Son	M	Cha	7	S	Y		Guam		None
32		119	136	Mantanona, Felicita P	Head	F	Cha	47	Wd	N	Y	Guam	N	Farmer
33		119	136	Mantanona, Romen P	Son	M	Cha	18	S	N	Y	Guam	Y	Farm laborer
34		119	136	Mantanona, Angelina P	Daughter	F	Cha	15	S	N	N	Guam	N	None
35		119	136	Mantanona, Sabina P	Daughter	F	Cha	14	S	N	Y	Guam	Y	None
36		119	136	Mantanona, Carmen P	Daughter	F	Cha	10	S	Y	Y	Guam	Y	None
37		120	137	Duenas, Ramon T	Head	M	Cha	42	M	N	Y	Guam	N	Farmer
38		120	137	Duenas, Catalina D	Wife	F	Cha	40	M	N	N	Guam	N	None
39		120	137	Duenas, Silvestre D	Son	M	Cha	18	S	N	Y	Guam	Y	Farm laborer
40		120	137	Duenas, Vicente D	Son	M	Cha	15	S	Y	Y	Guam	Y	None
41		120	137	Duenas, Ramon D	Son	M	Cha	14	S	Y	Y	Guam	Y	None
42		120	137	Duenas, Maria D	Daughter	F	Cha	12	S	Y	Y	Guam	Y	None
43		120	137	Duenas, Gonzalo D	Son	M	Cha	11	S	Y	Y	Guam	Y	None
44		120	137	Duenas, Gregorio D	Son	M	Cha	9	S	Y		Guam		None
45		120	137	Duenas, Jose D	Son	M	Cha	8	S	Y		Guam		None
46		120	137	Duenas, Jesus D	Son	M	Cha	5	S	N		Guam		None
47		120	137	Duenas, Juan D	Son	M	Cha	3.6	S	N		Guam		None
48		120	137	Duenas, Rita D	Daughter	F	Cha	0.7	S	N		Guam		None
49		121	138	Taimanglo, Blas T	Head	M	Cha	37	M	N	N	Guam	N	Farmer
50		121	138	Taimanglo, Ana M	Wife	F	Cha	39	M	N	N	Guam	N	None

DEPARTMENT OF COMMERCE-BUREAU OF THE CENSUS
WASHINGTON

FIFTEENTH CENSUS OF THE UNITED STATES: 1930-POPULATION

THE ISLAND OF GUAM

Sheet No. 16A

District **Municipality of Agana**
Name of Place **Inarajan Town**
[Proper name and, also, name of class, as city, town, village, barrio, etc]

Enumeration District No. 8
Enumerated by me on **April 15, 1930** Francisco G. Lujan
Enumerator

	PLACE OF ABODE			NAME	RELATION	PERSONAL DESCRIPTION				EDUCATION		NATIVITY		OCCUPATION
	Street, avenue, road, etc.	Number of dwelling house is order of visitation	Number of family in order of visitation	of each person whose place of abode on April 1, 1930, was in this family. Enter surname, first, then given name and middle initial. If any. Include every person living on April 1, 1930. Omit children born since April 1, 1930.	Relationship of this Person to the head of the family.	Sex	Color or race	Age at last birthday	Single, married, widowed or divorced	Attended school any time since Sept. 1, 1929	Whether able to read and write.	Place of birth of this person.	Whether able to speak English.	
	1	2	3	4	5	6	7	8	9	10	11	12	13	14
1	[no street name]	121	138	Taimanglo, Francisco M	Son	M	Cha	4.4	S	N		Guam		None
2		121	138	Taimanglo, Esperanza M	Daughter	F	Cha	.4	S	N		Guam		None
3		121	138	Chargualaf, Josefa M	Step daughter	F	Cha	12	S	Y	Y	Guam	Y	None
4		122	139	Lujan, Ignacio C	Head	M	Cha	46	M	N	Y	Guam	N	Guam
5		122	139	Cepeda, Andrea Q	Wife	F	Cha	32	M	N	Y	Guam	Y	Guam
6		122	139	Cepeda, Gregoria C	Step daughter	F	Cha	2	S	N		Guam		Guam
7		123	140	Paulino, Vicente N	Head	M	Cha	50	M	N	Y	Guam	N	Farmer
8		123	140	Paulino, Dolores	Wife	F	Cha	59	M	N	N	Guam	N	None
9		123	140	Meno, Maria M	Step daughter	F	Cha	15	S	N	Y	Guam	Y	None
10		124	141	Paulino, Carmen N	Wife	F	Cha	70	Wd	N	N	Guam	N	None
11		124	141	Paulino, Ana N	Daughter	F	Cha	41	S	N	N	Guam	N	None
12		125	142	Mantanona, Manuel P	Head	M	Cha	32	M	N	Y	Guam	N	Farmer
13		125	142	Mantanona, Felicita S	Head	F	Cha	27	M	N	Y	Guam	N	None
14		125	142	Mantanona, Remedios S	Daughter	F	Cha	4.2	S	N	Y	Guam		None
15		126	143	Cruz, Felix D	Head	M	Cha	35	M	N	Y	Guam	Y	Farmer
16		126	143	Duenas, Maria C	Wife	F	Cha	27	M	N	Y	Guam	Y	None
17		126	143	Duenas, Eliza C	Daughter	M	Cha	5	S	N		Guam		None
18		126	143	Duenas, Rosa C	Daughter	M	Cha	4.1	S	N		Guam		None
19		126	143	Duenas, Maria C	Daughter	M	Cha	2.7	S	N		Guam		None
20		126	143	Duenas, Jose C	Daughter	M	Cha	1.4	S	N		Guam		None
21		127	144	Leon Guerrero, Vicente S	Head	M	Cha	45	M	N	Y	Guam	N	Farmer
22		127	144	Leon Guerrero, Carlota T	Wife	F	Cha	37	M	N	Y	Guam	N	None
23		127	144	Leon Guerrero, Joaquin N	Daughter	F	Cha	16	S	N	Y	Guam	Y	None
24		127	144	Leon Guerrero, Vicenta N	Daughter	F	Cha	14	S	N		Guam		None
25		127	144	Leon Guerrero, Angustia LG	Grand daughter	F	Cha	5	S	N		Guam		None

(CHAMORRO ROOTS GENEALOGY PROJECT™ TRANSCRIPTION)
(BERNARD T. PUNZALAN / HTTP://WWW.CHAMORROROOTS.COM)

DEPARTMENT OF COMMERCE-BUREAU OF THE CENSUS
WASHINGTON

FIFTEENTH CENSUS OF THE UNITED STATES: 1930-POPULATION

THE ISLAND OF GUAM

Sheet No. 16B

259B

District **Municipality of Agana**
Name of Place **Inarajan Town**
[Proper name and, also, name of class, as city, town, village, barrio, etc]

Enumeration District No. **8**
Enumerated by me on **April 15, 1930** Francisco G. Lujan
Enumerator

	PLACE OF ABODE			NAME	RELATION	PERSONAL DESCRIPTION				EDUCATION		NATIVITY		OCCUPATION
	Street, avenue, road, etc.	Number of dwelling house is order of visitation	Number of family in order of visitation	of each person whose place of abode on April 1, 1930, was in this family. Enter surname, first, then given name and middle initial. If any. Include every person living on April 1, 1930. Omit children born since April 1, 1930.	Relationship of this Person to the head of the family.	Sex	Color or race	Age at last birthday	Single, married, widowed or divorced	Attended school any time since Sept. 1, 1929	Whether able to read and write.	Place of birth of this person.	Whether able to speak English.	
	1	2	3	4	5	6	7	8	9	10	11	12	13	14
26	[no street name]	127	144	Taitague, Gonzalo M	Servant	M	Cha	12	S	Y	Y	Guam	Y	Farm laborer
27		128	145	Flores, Joaquin D	Head	M	Cha	36	M	N	Y	Guam	Y	Farmer
28		128	145	Flores, Rita B	Wife	F	Cha	28	M	N	Y	Guam	Y	None
29		128	145	Flores, William B	Son	M	Cha	8	S	Y	Y	Guam		None
30		128	145	Flores, Amelia B	Daughter	F	Cha	5	S	N		Guam		None
31		128	145	Flores, Dolores B	Daughter	F	Cha	4.1	S	N		Guam		None
32		128	145	Flores, Delfina B	Daughter	F	Cha	2	S	N		Guam		None
33		129	146	Taitague, Juan D	Head	M	Cha	48	M	N	N	Guam	N	Farmer
34		129	146	Taitague, Saturnina M	Wife	F	Cha	32	M	N	N	Guam	N	None
35		129	146	Taitague, Baldovino M	Son	M	Cha	14	S	N	Y	Guam	Y	Farm laborer
36		129	146	Taitague, Alminla M	Daughter	F	Cha	13	S	Y	Y	Guam	Y	None
37		129	146	Taitague, Tomas M	Son	M	Cha	5	S	Y		Guam		None
38		129	146	Taitague, Edward M	Son	M	Cha	3.1	S	N		Guam		None
39		129	146	Taitague, Jose M	Son	M	Cha	1.7	S	N		Guam		None
40		130	147	Meno, Encarncion M	Head	F	Cha	50	Wd	N	N	Guam	N	None
41		131	148	Mantanona, Silvestre M	Head	M	Cha	30	M	N	Y	Guam	Y	Farmer
42		131	148	Mantanona, Potenciana T	Wife	F	Cha	44	M	N	N	Guam	N	None
43		131	148	Mantanona, Robert T	Son	M	Cha	2.7	S	N		Guam		None
44		131	148	Taitague, Ramon T	Step-son	M	Cha	16	S	N	Y	Guam	Y	Farm laborer
45		131	148	Taitague, Angelina T	Step-daughter	F	Cha	14	S	N	N	Guam	N	None
46		132	149	Meno, Regino C	Head	M	Cha	34	M	N	Y	Guam	N	Farmer
47		132	149	Meno, Cornelia C	Wife	F	Cha	36	M	N	N	Guam	N	None
48		132	149	Meno, Jesus C	Son	M	Cha	12	S	Y	Y	Guam	Y	None
49		132	149	Meno, Maria C	Daughter	F	Cha	11	S	Y	Y	Guam	Y	None
50		132	149	Meno, Margarita C	Daughter	F	Cha	9	S	Y		Guam		None

(CHAMORRO ROOTS GENEALOGY PROJECT™ TRANSCRIPTION)
(BERNARD T. PUNZALAN / HTTP://WWW.CHAMORROROOTS.COM)

DEPARTMENT OF COMMERCE-BUREAU OF THE CENSUS
WASHINGTON

FIFTEENTH CENSUS OF THE UNITED STATES: 1930-POPULATION

THE ISLAND OF GUAM

Sheet No. 17A

260

District **Municipality of Agana**
Name of Place **Inarajan Town**
[Proper name and, also, name of class, as city, town, village, barrio, etc]

Enumeration District No. 8
Enumerated by me on **April 16, 1930** Francisco G. Lujan
Enumerator

	PLACE OF ABODE			NAME	RELATION	PERSONAL DESCRIPTION				EDUCATION		NATIVITY		OCCUPATION
	Street, avenue, road, etc.	Number of dwelling house is order of visitation	Number of family in order of visitation	of each person whose place of abode on April 1, 1930, was in this family. Enter surname, first, then given name and middle initial. If any. Include every person living on April 1, 1930. Omit children born since April 1, 1930.	Relationship of this Person to the head of the family.	Sex	Color or race	Age at last birthday	Single, married, widowed or divorced	Attended school any time since Sept. 1, 1929	Whether able to read and write.	Place of birth of this person.	Whether able to speak English.	
	1	2	3	4	5	6	7	8	9	10	11	12	13	14
1	[no street name]	132	149	Meno, Asuncion C	Daughter	F	Cha	6	S	N		Guam		None
2		132	149	Meno, Jose C	Son	M	Cha	4.1	S	N		Guam		None
3		132	149	Meno, Joaquin C	Son	M	Cha	.9	S	N		Guam		None
4		133	150	Naputi, Lucas D	Head	M	Cha	39	M	N	Y	Guam	N	Farmer
5		133	150	Naputi, Remedios T	Wife	F	Cha	29	M	N	N	Guam	N	None
6		133	150	Naputi, Jose SN	Son	M	Cha	14	S	Y	Y	Guam	Y	None
7		133	150	Naputi, Marcela SN	Daughter	F	Cha	14	S	Y	Y	Guam	Y	None
8		133	150	Naputi, Antonio T	Son	M	Cha	4.7	S	N		Guam		None
9		133	150	Naputi, Juan T	Son	M	Cha	2.1	S	N		Guam		None
10		133	150	Naputi, Jesus T	Son	M	Cha	1	S	N		Guam		None
11		134	151	Taimanglo, Dolores T	Head	F	Cha	46	Wd	N	N	Guam	N	Farmer
12		134	151	Taimanglo, Jose T	Son	M	Cha	20	S	N	Y	Guam	Y	Farm laborer
13					Here ends the enumeration of Inarajan Town.									
14					[Sheet 260B/17B was intentionally left blank.]									
15														
16														
17														
18														
19														
20														
21														
22														
23														
24														
25														

DEPARTMENT OF COMMERCE-BUREAU OF THE CENSUS
WASHINGTON

FIFTEENTH CENSUS OF THE UNITED STATES: 1930-POPULATION

THE ISLAND OF GUAM

Sheet No. 18A

District **Municipality of Agana**
Name of Place **Malolo Barrio**
[Proper name and, also, name of class, as city, town, village, barrio, etc]

Enumeration District No. **8**
Enumerated by me on **April 21, 1930** Francisco G. Lujan, Enumerator

	PLACE OF ABODE			NAME	RELATION	PERSONAL DESCRIPTION				EDUCATION		NATIVITY		OCCUPATION
	Street, avenue, road, etc.	Number of dwelling house in order of visitation	Number of family in order of visitation	of each person whose place of abode on April 1, 1930, was in this family. Enter surname, first, then given name and middle initial. If any. Include every person living on April 1, 1930. Omit children born since April 1, 1930.	Relationship of this Person to the head of the family.	Sex	Color or race	Age at last birthday	Single, married, widowed or divorced	Attended school any time since Sept. 1, 1929	Whether able to read and write.	Place of birth of this person.	Whether able to speak English.	
	1	2	3	4	5	6	7	8	9	10	11	12	13	14
1	[no street name]	143	162	Mantanona, Cecilio C	Head	M	Cha	25	M	N	Y	Guam	Y	Farmer
2		143	162	Mantanona, Ana T	Wife	F	Cha	24	M	N	N	Guam	N	None
3		143	162	Mantanona, Ediviges T	Daughter	F	Cha	3.4	S	N		Guam		None
4		143	162	Mantanona, Jesus T	Son	M	Cha	0.2	S	N		Guam		None
5		143	162	Toves, Ana M	Mother-in-law	F	Cha	67	Wd	N	N	Guam	N	None
6		144	163	Chiguina, Juan M	Head	M	Cha	23	M	N	Y	Guam	Y	Farmer
7		144	163	Chiguina, Lagrimas LG	Wife	F	Cha	25	M	N	Y	Guam	Y	None
8		144	163	Chiguina, Julia LG	Daughter	F	Cha	2.4	S	N		Guam		None
9		144	163	Chiguina, Juan LG	Son	M	Cha	.1	S	N		Guam		None
10		145	164	Martinez, Manuel R	Head	M	Cha	36	M	N	Y	Guam	N	Farmer
11		145	164	Martinez, Antonia C	Wife	F	Cha	22	S	N	N	Guam	N	None
12		145	164	Martinez, Regina C	Daughter	F	Cha	5	S	N		Guam		None
13		146	165	Chargualaf, Justo T	Head	M	Cha	44	M	N	N	Guam	N	Farmer
14		146	165	Paulino, Maria Q	Wife	F	Cha	58	M	N	N	Guam	N	None
15		146	165	Quidachay, Amanda Q	Step daughter	F	Cha	12	S	Y	Y	Guam	Y	None
16		147	166	Meno, Joaquin C	Head	M	Cha	49	M	N	Y	Guam	N	Farmer
17		147	166	Meno, Rosa T	Wife	F	Cha	31	M	N	N	Guam	N	None
18		147	166	Meno, Ramon T	Son	M	Cha	12	S	Y	Y	Guam	Y	None
19		147	166	Meno, Margarita T	Daughter	F	Cha	11	S	Y	Y	Guam	Y	None
20		147	166	Meno, Joaquin T	Son	M	Cha	8	S	Y		Guam		None
21		147	166	Meno, Maria T	Daughter	F	Cha	6	S	N		Guam		None
22		147	166	Meno, Jose T	Son	M	Cha	2.2	S	N		Guam		None
23		148	167	Paulino, Jose C	Head	M	Cha	32	M	N	Y	Guam	Y	Farmer
24		148	167	Paulino, Regina M	Wife	F	Cha	20	M	N	Y	Guam	Y	None
25		148	167	Paulino, Ana M	Daughter	F	Cha	2.2	S	N		Guam		None

DEPARTMENT OF COMMERCE-BUREAU OF THE CENSUS
WASHINGTON

FIFTEENTH CENSUS OF THE UNITED STATES: 1930-POPULATION

THE ISLAND OF GUAM

Sheet No. 18B

261B

District **Municipality of Agana**
Name of Place **Malolo Barrio**
[Proper name and, also, name of class, as city, town, village, barrio, etc]

Enumeration District No. **8**
Enumerated by me on **April 21, 1930** Francisco G. Lujan
Enumerator

	PLACE OF ABODE			NAME	RELATION	PERSONAL DESCRIPTION				EDUCATION		NATIVITY		OCCUPATION
	Street, avenue, road, etc.	Number of dwelling house is order of visitation	Number of family in order of visitation	of each person whose place of abode on April 1, 1930, was in this family. Enter surname, first, then given name and middle initial. If any. Include every person living on April 1, 1930. Omit children born since April 1, 1930.	Relationship of this Person to the head of the family.	Sex	Color or race	Age at last birthday	Single, married, widowed or divorced	Attended school any time since Sept. 1, 1929	Whether able to read and write.	Place of birth of this person.	Whether able to speak English.	
	1	2	3	4	5	6	7	8	9	10	11	12	13	14
26	[no street name]	149	168	Martinez, Angel W	Head	M	Cha	43	M	N	Y	Guam	Y	Farmer
27		149	168	Martinez, Emilia K	Wife	F	Cha	40	M	N	Y	Guam	Y	None
28		149	168	Martinez, Antonio K	Son	M	Cha	12	S	Y	Y	Guam	Y	None
29		149	168	Martinez, Charlie K	Son	M	Cha	10	S	Y	Y	Guam	Y	None
30		149	168	Martinez, Inby K	Son	M	Cha	6	S	Y		Guam		None
31		149	168	Martinez, James K	Son	M	Cha	3.9	S	N		Guam		None
32					Here ends the enumeration of Malolo.									
33														
34														
35														
36														
37														
38														
39														
40														
41														
42														
43														
44														
45														
46														
47														
48														
49														
50														

DEPARTMENT OF COMMERCE-BUREAU OF THE CENSUS
WASHINGTON

FIFTEENTH CENSUS OF THE UNITED STATES: 1930-POPULATION

THE ISLAND OF GUAM

Sheet No. 19A

District **Municipality of Agana**
Name of Place **Bubulao**
[Proper name and, also, name of class, as city, town, village, barrio, etc]

Enumeration District No. 8
Enumerated by me on **April 22, 1930** Francisco G. Lujan, Enumerator

	PLACE OF ABODE			NAME	RELATION	PERSONAL DESCRIPTION				EDUCATION		NATIVITY		OCCUPATION
	Street, avenue, road, etc.	Number of dwelling house is order of visitation	Number of family in order of visitation	of each person whose place of abode on April 1, 1930, was in this family. Enter surname, first, then given name and middle initial. If any. Include every person living on April 1, 1930. Omit children born since April 1, 1930.	Relationship of this Person to the head of the family.	Sex	Color or race	Age at last birthday	Single, married, widowed or divorced	Attended school any time since Sept. 1, 1929	Whether able to read and write.	Place of birth of this person.	Whether able to speak English.	
	1	2	3	4	5	6	7	8	9	10	11	12	13	14
1	[no street name]	150	169	Barcinas, Issac R	Head	M	Cha	60	M	N	N	Guam	N	Farmer
2		150	169	Barcinas, Magdalena D	Wife	F	Cha	59	M	N	N	Guam	N	None
3		150	169	Barcinas, Mercedes D	Daughter	F	Cha	34	S	N	Y	Guam	Y	None
4		150	169	Barcinas, Jose D	Son	M	Cha	26	S	N	Y	Guam	Y	None
5		150	169	Barcinas, Maria B	Grand daughter	F	Cha	8	S	Y		Guam		Farm laborer
6		150	169	Barcinas, Andriano B	Grand son	M	Cha	2.1	S	N		Guam		None
7		150	169	Chargualaf, Cristina T	Servant	F	Cha	24	S	N	N	Guam	N	None
8		151	170	Quidachay, Jose D	Head	M	Cha	33	M	N	Y	Guam	N	Farmer
9		151	170	Quidachay, Trindad R	Wife	F	Cha	25	M	N	Y	Guam	N	None
10		151	170	Quidachay, Maria R	Daughter	F	Cha	2.1	S	N		Guam		None
11		151	170	Quidachay, Rosa R	Daughter	F	Cha	.5	S	N		Guam		None
12		151	170	Rosario, Jose R	Step-son	M	Cha	3	S	N		Guam		None
13					Here ends the enumeration of Bubulao.									
14					[Sheet 262B/19B was intentionally left blank.]									
15														
16														
17														
18														
19														
20														
21														
22														
23														
24														
25														

DEPARTMENT OF COMMERCE-BUREAU OF THE CENSUS
WASHINGTON

FIFTEENTH CENSUS OF THE UNITED STATES: 1930-POPULATION

THE ISLAND OF GUAM

Sheet No. 20A

District **Municipality of Agana**
Name of Place **Talofofo Barrio**
[Proper name and, also, name of class, as city, town, village, barrio, etc]

Enumeration District No. **8**
Enumerated by me on **April 12, 1930** Cayetano A. Quinata
Enumerator

	PLACE OF ABODE			NAME	RELATION	PERSONAL DESCRIPTION				EDUCATION		NATIVITY		OCCUPATION
	Street, avenue, road, etc.	Number of dwelling house is order of visitation	Number of family in order of visitation	of each person whose place of abode on April 1, 1930, was in this family. Enter surname, first, then given name and middle initial. If any. Include every person living on April 1, 1930. Omit children born since April 1, 1930.	Relationship of this Person to the head of the family.	Sex	Color or race	Age at last birthday	Single, married, widowed or divorced	Attended school any time since Sept. 1, 1929	Whether able to read and write.	Place of birth of this person.	Whether able to speak English.	
	1	2	3	4	5	6	7	8	9	10	11	12	13	14
1	[no street name]	1	1	Santos, Ramona D	Head	F	Cha	54	Wd	N	Y	Guam	N	None
2		1	1	Santos, Juan M	Son	M	Cha	22	S	N	Y	Guam	Y	Farmer
3		1	1	Santos, Jose M	Son	M	Cha	20	S	N	Y	Guam	Y	Farmer
4		1	1	Santos, Juana M	Daughter	F	Cha	18	S	N	Y	Guam	Y	Washer woman
5		1	1	Santos, Jesus M	Son	M	Cha	15	S	Y	Y	Guam	Y	Farm laborer
6		1	1	Santos, Adela M	Daughter	F	Cha	12	S	Y	Y	Guam	Y	None
7		1	2	Santos, Vicente U	Head	M	Cha	47	S	N	Y	Guam	N	Farmer
8		2	3	Castro, Enrique P	Head	M	Cha	26	M	N	Y	Guam	Y	Farmer
9		2	3	Castro, Ana P	Wife	F	Cha	25	M	N	Y	Guam	Y	None
10		2	3	Castro, Jesus P	Son	M	Cha	5	S	N		Guam		None
11		2	3	Castro, Virginia P	Daughter	F	Cha	3	S	N		Guam		None
12		2	3	Castro, Juan P	Son	M	Cha	1	S	N		Guam		None
13		3	4	San Nicolas, Antonio SN	Head	M	Cha	50	M	N	N	Guam	N	Farmer
14		3	4	San Nicolas, Trinidad S	Wife	F	Cha	49	M	N	N	Guam	N	None
15		3	4	San Nicolas, Enrique S	Son	M	Cha	25	S	N	Y	Guam	Y	Farm laborer
16		3	4	San Nicolas, Benancio S	Son	M	Cha	24	S	N	Y	Guam	Y	Farm laborer
17		3	4	San Nicolas, Maria S	Daughter	F	Cha	22	S	N	Y	Guam	Y	None
18		3	4	San Nicolas, Carmen S	Daughter	F	Cha	20	S	N	Y	Guam	Y	None
19		3	4	San Nicolas, Concepcion S	Daughter	F	Cha	18	S	Y	Y	Guam	Y	None
20		3	4	San Nicolas, Tomasa S	Daughter	F	Cha	16	S	Y	Y	Guam	Y	None
21		3	4	San Nicolas, Francisca S	Daughter	F	Cha	14	S	Y	Y	Guam	Y	None
22		3	4	San Nicolas, Ana S	Daughter	F	Cha	12	S	Y	Y	Guam	Y	None
23		3	4	San Nicolas, Isabel S	Daughter	F	Cha	10	S	Y	Y	Guam	Y	None
24		3	4	San Nicolas, Cristobal S	Son	M	Cha	7	S	Y		Guam		None
25		4	5	Aguigui, Santos A	Head	M	Cha	37	S	N	Y	Guam	N	Farmer

DEPARTMENT OF COMMERCE-BUREAU OF THE CENSUS
WASHINGTON

FIFTEENTH CENSUS OF THE UNITED STATES: 1930-POPULATION

THE ISLAND OF GUAM

Sheet No. 20B

263B

District **Municipality of Agana**
Name of Place **Talofofo Barrio**
[Proper name and, also, name of class, as city, town, village, barrio, etc]

Enumeration District No. 8
Enumerated by me on **April 14, 1930** Cayetano A. Quinata, Enumerator

	PLACE OF ABODE			NAME	RELATION	PERSONAL DESCRIPTION				EDUCATION		NATIVITY		OCCUPATION
	Street, avenue, road, etc.	Number of dwelling house in order of visitation	Number of family in order of visitation	of each person whose place of abode on April 1, 1930, was in this family. Enter surname, first, then given name and middle initial. If any. Include every person living on April 1, 1930. Omit children born since April 1, 1930.	Relationship of this Person to the head of the family.	Sex	Color or race	Age at last birthday	Single, married, widowed or divorced	Attended school any time since Sept. 1, 1929	Whether able to read and write.	Place of birth of this person.	Whether able to speak English.	
	1	2	3	4	5	6	7	8	9	10	11	12	13	14
26	[no street name]	5	6	Yamanaka, Diego	Head	M	Jap	42	M	N	Y	Japan	N	Farmer
27		5	6	Yamanaka, Catalina M	Wife	F	Cha	41	M	N	Y	Guam	N	None
28		5	6	Yamanaka, Josefina M	Daughter	F	Jap	15	S	Y	Y	Guam	Y	None
29		5	6	Yamanaka, Juan M	Son	M	Jap	12	S	Y	Y	Guam	Y	None
30		5	6	Yamanaka, Maria M	Daughter	F	Jap	10	S	Y	Y	Guam	Y	None
31		5	6	Yamanaka, Rosa M	Daughter	F	Jap	8	S	Y		Guam		None
32		5	6	Yamanaka, Jesus M	Son	M	Jap	6	S	N		Guam		None
33		5	6	Yamanaka, Francisco M	Son	M	Jap	1.2	S	N		Guam		None
34		6	7	Pablo, Mariano A	Head	M	Cha	59	M	N	N	Guam	N	Farmer
35		6	7	Pablo, Dolores B	Wife	F	Cha	54	M	N	Y	Guam	N	None
36		6	7	Pablo, Joaquin B	Son	M	Cha	24	S	N	Y	Guam	Y	Farm laborer
37		6	7	Pablo, Vicente B	Son	M	Cha	19	S	N	Y	Guam	Y	Farm laborer
38		6	7	Pablo, Tomas B	Son	M	Cha	14	S	Y	Y	Guam	Y	Farm laborer
39		6	7	Pablo, Gregorio B	Son	M	Cha	10	S	Y	Y	Guam	Y	None
40		6	8	Castro, Librada P	Head	F	Cha	29	D	N	Y	Guam	N	None
41		6	8	Castro, Atanacio P	Son	M	Cha	9	S	Y		Guam		None
42		6	8	Castro, Librada P	Daughter	F	Cha	7	S	Y		Guam		None
43		6	8	Castro, Roman P	Son	M	Cha	4	S	N		Guam		None
44		6	8	Pablo, Rafael P	Son	M	Cha	1.5	S	N		Guam		None
45		7	9	Pablo, Jose A	Head	M	Cha	28	M	N	Y	Guam	Y	Farmer
46		7	9	Pablo, Josefa P	Wife	F	Cha	30	M	N	Y	Guam	N	None
47		7	9	Pablo, Maria P	Daughter	F	Cha	10	S	Y	Y	Guam	Y	None
48		7	9	Pablo, Antonio P	Son	M	Cha	6	S	N		Guam		None
49		7	9	Pablo, Soledad P	Daughter	F	Cha	4	S	N		Guam		None
50		7	9	Pablo, Jose P	Son	M	Cha	2	S	N		Guam		None

DEPARTMENT OF COMMERCE-BUREAU OF THE CENSUS
WASHINGTON

FIFTEENTH CENSUS OF THE UNITED STATES: 1930-POPULATION

THE ISLAND OF GUAM

Sheet No. 21A

District **Municipality of Agana**
Name of Place **Talofofo Barrio**
[Proper name and, also, name of class, as city, town, village, barrio, etc]

Enumeration District No. 8
Enumerated by me on **April 14, 1930** Cayetano A. Quinata, Enumerator

	PLACE OF ABODE: Street, avenue, road, etc.	Number of dwelling house in order of visitation	Number of family in order of visitation	NAME of each person whose place of abode on April 1, 1930, was in this family. Enter surname, first, then given name and middle initial. If any. Include every person living on April 1, 1930. Omit children born since April 1, 1930.	RELATION Relationship of this Person to the head of the family.	PERSONAL DESCRIPTION: Sex	Color or race	Age at last birthday	Single, married, widowed or divorced	EDUCATION: Attended school any time since Sept. 1, 1929	Whether able to read and write.	NATIVITY Place of birth of this person.	Whether able to speak English.	OCCUPATION
	1	2	3	4	5	6	7	8	9	10	11	12	13	14
1	[no street name]	7	9	Pablo, Juan P	Son	M	Cha	.3	S	N		Guam		None
2		8	10	Duenas, Juan M	Head	M	Cha	44	M	N	N	Guam	N	Farmer
3		8	11	Materne, Jose S	Head	M	Cha	24	M	N	Y	Guam	Y	Farmer
4		8	11	Materne, Ana Q	Wife	F	Cha	21	M	N	Y	Guam	Y	None
5		9	12	Santos, Antonio U	Head	M	Cha	45	M	N	Y	Guam	N	Farmer
6		9	12	Santos, Maria Q	Wife	F	Cha	27	M	N	Y	Guam	Y	None
7		9	12	Santos, Maria I	Daughter	F	Cha	10	S	Y	Y	Guam	Y	None
8		9	12	Santos, Francisco I	Son	M	Cha	7	S	Y	Y	Guam		None
9		9	12	Santos, Luis Q	Son	M	Cha	4.7	S	N		Guam		None
10		9	12	Santos, Gonzalo Q	Son	M	Cha	2.4	S	N		Guam		None
11		10	13	Diego, Jose SN	Head	M	Cha	30	M	N	Y	Guam	Y	Farmer
12		10	13	Diego, Rosa S	Wife	F	Cha	32	M	N	Y	Guam	Y	None
13		10	13	Diego, Edward S	Son	M	Cha	10	S	Y	Y	Guam	Y	None
14		10	13	Diego, Juan S	Son	M	Cha	1	S	N		Guam		None
15		10	13	Diego, Tomas S	Son	M	Cha	1.1	S	N		Guam		None
16		11	14	Aguon, Joaquin C	Head	M	Cha	44	M	N	Y	Guam	N	Farmer
17		11	14	Aguon, Joaquina C	Wife	F	Cha	39	M	N	N	Guam	N	None
18		11	14	Aguon, Jose C	Son	M	Cha	17	S	Y	Y	Guam	Y	Farm laborer
19		11	14	Aguon, Teresa C	Daughter	F	Cha	16	S	N	Y	Guam	Y	None
20		11	14	Aguon, Concepcion C	Daughter	F	Cha	13	S	N	Y	Guam	Y	None
21		11	14	Aguon, Joaquin C	Son	M	Cha	11	S	Y	Y	Guam	Y	None
22		11	14	Aguon, Juan C	Son	M	Cha	8	S	Y		Guam		None
23		11	14	Aguon, Vicenta C	Daughter	F	Cha	5	S	N		Guam		None
24		11	14	Aguon, Vicente C	Son	M	Cha	3.9	S	N		Guam		None
25		11	14	Aguon, Ramon C	Son	M	Cha	2.1	S	N		Guam		None

(CHAMORRO ROOTS GENEALOGY PROJECT™ TRANSCRIPTION)
(BERNARD T. PUNZALAN / HTTP://WWW.CHAMORROROOTS.COM)

DEPARTMENT OF COMMERCE-BUREAU OF THE CENSUS
WASHINGTON

FIFTEENTH CENSUS OF THE UNITED STATES: 1930-POPULATION

THE ISLAND OF GUAM

Sheet No. 21B

264B

District **Municipality of Agana**
Name of Place **Talofofo Barrio**
[Proper name and, also, name of class, as city, town, village, barrio, etc]

Enumeration District No. 8
Enumerated by me on **April 15, 1930** Cayetano A. Quinata, Enumerator

	PLACE OF ABODE: Street, avenue, road, etc.	Number of dwelling house in order of visitation	Number of family in order of visitation	NAME of each person whose place of abode on April 1, 1930, was in this family. Enter surname, first, then given name and middle initial. If any. Include every person living on April 1, 1930. Omit children born since April 1, 1930.	RELATION Relationship of this Person to the head of the family.	PERSONAL DESCRIPTION: Sex	Color or race	Age at last birthday	Single, married, widowed or divorced	EDUCATION: Attended school any time since Sept. 1, 1929	Whether able to read and write.	NATIVITY Place of birth of this person.	Whether able to speak English.	OCCUPATION
	1	2	3	4	5	6	7	8	9	10	11	12	13	14
26	[no street name]	12	15	Quidachay, Vicente Q	Head	M	Cha	59	M	N	N	Guam	N	Farmer
27		12	15	Quidachay, Andrea R	Wife	F	Cha	64	M	N	N	Guam	N	None
28		12	15	Quidachay, Francisco R	Son	M	Cha	34	S	N	Y	Guam	Y	Farm laborer
29		12	15	Quidachay, Juan R	Son	M	Cha	15	S	N	Y	Guam	Y	Farm laborer
30		13	16	Comado, Juan P	Head	M	Cha	45	M	N	Y	Guam	N	Farmer
31		13	16	Comado, Concepcion SN	Wife	F	Cha	46	M	N	Y	Guam	N	None
32		13	16	Comado, Juan SN	Son	M	Cha	21	S	N	Y	Guam	Y	Farm laborer
33		13	16	Comado, Remedios SN	Daughter	F	Cha	15	S	N	Y	Guam	Y	None
34		13	16	Comado, Maria SN	Daughter	F	Cha	13	S	Y	Y	Guam	Y	None
35		13	16	Comado, Guardalupe SN	Daughter	F	Cha	10	S	Y	Y	Guam	Y	None
36		13	16	Comado, Prudencio SN	Son	M	Cha	9	S	Y		Guam		None
37		13	17	Afaisen, Ana SN	Head	F	Cha	52	Wd	N	N	Guam	N	None
38		14	18	Mantanona, Antonia P	Head	F	Cha	51	Wd	N	N	Guam	N	None
39		14	18	Mantanona, Manuel P	Son	M	Cha	20	S	N	Y	Guam	Y	Farmer
40		14	18	Mantanona, Juan P	Son	M	Cha	17	S	N	Y	Guam	Y	Farm laborer
41		14	18	Mantanona, Milagro P	Daughter	F	Cha	15	S	N	Y	Guam	Y	None
42		15	19	Reyes, Juan C	Head	M	Cha	56	M	N	N	Guam	N	Farmer
43		15	19	Reyes, Atelana T	Wife	F	Cha	79	M	N	N	Guam	N	None
44		16	20	Garrido, Felix SN	Head	M	Cha	32	M	N	Y	Guam	Y	Farmer
45		16	20	Garrido, Teresa M	Wife	F	Cha	24	M	N	Y	Guam	N	None
46		16	20	Garrido, Antonia M	Daughter	F	Cha	7	S	Y		Guam		None
47		16	20	Garrido, Ana M	Daughter	F	Cha	6	S	N		Guam		None
48		16	20	Garrido, Juan M	Son	M	Cha	3.2	S	N		Guam		None
49		17	21	Sahagon, Tenacio R	Head	M	Cha	34	M	N	Y	Guam	Y	Farmer
50		17	21	Sahagon, Olimpia T	Wife	F	Cha	34	M	N	N	Guam	N	None

DEPARTMENT OF COMMERCE-BUREAU OF THE CENSUS
WASHINGTON

FIFTEENTH CENSUS OF THE UNITED STATES: 1930-POPULATION

THE ISLAND OF GUAM

Sheet No. 22A

District **Municipality of Agana**
Name of Place **Talofofo Barrio**
[Proper name and, also, name of class, as city, town, village, barrio, etc]

Enumeration District No. **8**
Enumerated by me on **April 15, 1930** Cayetano A. Quinata, Enumerator

	PLACE OF ABODE			NAME	RELATION	PERSONAL DESCRIPTION				EDUCATION		NATIVITY		OCCUPATION
	Street, avenue, road, etc.	Number of dwelling house in order of visitation	Number of family in order of visitation	of each person whose place of abode on April 1, 1930, was in this family. Enter surname, first, then given name and middle initial. If any. Include every person living on April 1, 1930. Omit children born since April 1, 1930.	Relationship of this Person to the head of the family.	Sex	Color or race	Age at last birthday	Single, married, widowed or divorced	Attended school any time since Sept. 1, 1929	Whether able to read and write.	Place of birth of this person.	Whether able to speak English.	
	1	2	3	4	5	6	7	8	9	10	11	12	13	14
1	[no street name]	17	21	Taijeron, Andresinia T	Step daughter	F	Cha	6	S	N		Guam		None
2		17	22	Sahagon, Manuel C	Head	M	Cha	54	Wd	N	Y	Guam	N	None
3		17	22	Sahagon, Ana R	Daughter	F	Cha	15	S	N	Y	Guam	Y	None
4		18	23	Atoigue, Francisco T	Head	M	Cha	29	M	N	Y	Guam	Y	Farmer
5		18	23	Atoigue, Regina P	Wife	F	Cha	27	M	N	N	Guam	N	None
6		18	23	Atoigue, Jesus P	Son	M	Cha	6	S	N		Guam		None
7		18	23	Atoigue, Jose P	Son	M	Cha	4	S	N		Guam		None
8		18	23	Atoigue, Francisco P	Son	M	Cha	3	S	N		Guam		None
9		18	23	Atoigue, Dolores P	Daughter	F	Cha	.4	S	N		Guam		None
10		19	24	Meno, Vicente C	Head	M	Cha	26	M	N	Y	Guam	Y	Farmer
11		19	24	Meno, Candelaria Q	Wife	F	Cha	25	M	N	Y	Guam	Y	None
12		19	24	Meno, Lorenso Q	Son	M	Cha	2.5	S	N		Guam		None
13		19	24	Meno, Jesus Q	Daughter	F	Cha	1.1	S	N		Guam		None
14		20	25	Taimanglo, Mariano C	Head	M	Cha	26	M	N	Y	Guam	Y	Farmer
15		20	25	Taimanglo, Maria P	Wife	F	Cha	24	M	N	Y	Guam	Y	None
16		20	25	Taimanglo, Jose P	Son	M	Cha	2	S	N		Guam		None
17		21	26	Pablo, Rosa A	Head	F	Cha	21	S	N	Y	Guam	Y	None
18		21	26	Pablo, Elena A	Sister	F	Cha	19	S	N	Y	Guam	Y	None
19		21	26	Pablo, Serafin A	Brother	M	Cha	17	S	N	Y	Guam	Y	Farmer
20		21	26	Pablo, Benjamin A	Brother	M	Cha	14	S	Y	Y	Guam	Y	Farm laborer
21		21	26	Pablo, Ramon A	Brother	M	Cha	12	S	Y	Y	Guam	Y	None
22		22	27	Castro, Atanacio P	Head	M	Cha	34	D	N	Y	Guam	N	Farmer
23		23	28	Castro, Jose L	Head	M	Cha	63	M	N	Y	Guam	N	Farmer
24		23	28	Castro, Maria P	Wife	F	Cha	59	M	N	N	Guam	N	None
25		23	28	Castro, Jose C	Grandson	M	Cha	1	S	N		Guam		None

(CHAMORRO ROOTS GENEALOGY PROJECT™ TRANSCRIPTION)
(BERNARD T. PUNZALAN / HTTP://WWW.CHAMORROROOTS.COM)

DEPARTMENT OF COMMERCE-BUREAU OF THE CENSUS
WASHINGTON

FIFTEENTH CENSUS OF THE UNITED STATES: 1930-POPULATION

THE ISLAND OF GUAM

Sheet No. 22B

265B

District Municipality of Agana
Name of Place Talofofo Barrio
[Proper name and, also, name of class, as city, town, village, barrio, etc]

Enumeration District No. 8
Enumerated by me on April 16, 1930 Cayetano A. Quinata
Enumerator

	PLACE OF ABODE			NAME	RELATION	PERSONAL DESCRIPTION				EDUCATION		NATIVITY		OCCUPATION
	Street, avenue, road, etc.	Number of dwelling house is order of visitation	Number of family in order of visitation	of each person whose place of abode on April 1, 1930, was in this family. Enter surname, first, then given name and middle initial. If any. Include every person living on April 1, 1930. Omit children born since April 1, 1930.	Relationship of this Person to the head of the family.	Sex	Color or race	Age at last birthday	Single, married, widowed or divorced	Attended school any time since Sept. 1, 1929	Whether able to read and write.	Place of birth of this person.	Whether able to speak English.	
	1	2	3	4	5	6	7	8	9	10	11	12	13	14
26	[no street name]	24	29	Castro, Jose P	Head	M	Cha	20	M	N	Y	Guam	Y	Farmer
27		24	29	Castro, Amalia Q	Wife	F	Cha	19	M	N	Y	Guam	Y	None
28		25	30	Pablo, Juan SN	Head	M	Cha	54	Wd	N	N	Guam	N	Farmer
29		25	30	Pablo, Antonia T	Daughter	F	Cha	25	S	N	N	Guam	N	None
30		25	30	Pablo, Jose T	Son	M	Cha	18	S	N	Y	Guam	Y	Farm laborer
31		25	30	Pablo, Jesus T	Son	M	Cha	16	S	N	Y	Guam	Y	Farm laborer
32		25	30	Pablo, Antonio T	Son	M	Cha	14	S	Y	Y	Guam	Y	Farm laborer
33		25	30	Pablo, Engracia T	Daughter	F	Cha	12	S	Y	Y	Guam	Y	None
34		25	30	Toves, Maria T	Grand daughter	F	Cha	8	S	Y		Guam		None
35		25	30	Pablo, Jesus P	Grandson	M	Cha	4	S	N		Guam		None
36		25	30	Pablo, Jose P	Grandson	M	Cha	.1	S	N		Guam		None
37		26	31	Meno, Ramon M	Head	M	Cha	26	M	N	Y	Guam	Y	Farmer
38		26	31	Meno, Maria B	Wife	F	Cha	23	M	N	N	Guam	N	None
39		26	31	Meno, Maria B	Daughter	F	Cha	4	S	N		Guam		None
40		26	31	Meno, Ana B	Daughter	F	Cha	1.5	S	N		Guam		None
41		26	31	Meno, Jose M	Brother	M	Cha	20	S	N	N	Guam	N	Farm laborer
42		27	32	Castro, Jesus P	Head	M	Cha	23	M	N	Y	Guam	Y	Farmer
43		27	32	Castro, Dominga B	Wife	F	Cha	25	M	N	Y	Guam	N	None
44		27	32	Castro, Juan B	Son	M	Cha	.5	S	N		Guam		None
45		28	33	Babauta, Dolores Q	Head	F	Cha	48	Wd	N	N	Guam	N	None
46		28	33	Babauta, Concepcion Q	Daughter	F	Cha	20	S	N	Y	Guam	Y	None
47		28	33	Babauta, Rosalia Q	Daughter	F	Cha	18	S	N	Y	Guam	Y	None
48		28	33	Babauta, Jose Q	Son	M	Cha	16	S	Y	Y	Guam	Y	Road laborer
49		28	33	Babauta, Francisco Q	Son	M	Cha	13	S	Y	Y	Guam	Y	None
50		28	33	Babauta, Ramona P	Mother	F	Cha	71	M	N	N	Guam	N	None

DEPARTMENT OF COMMERCE-BUREAU OF THE CENSUS
WASHINGTON

FIFTEENTH CENSUS OF THE UNITED STATES: 1930-POPULATION

THE ISLAND OF GUAM

Sheet No. 23A

District **Municipality of Agana**
Name of Place **Talofofo Barrio** [Proper name and, also, name of class, as city, town, village, barrio, etc]

Enumeration District No. **8**
Enumerated by me on **April 17, 1930** Cayetano A. Quinata, Enumerator

	PLACE OF ABODE			NAME	RELATION	PERSONAL DESCRIPTION				EDUCATION		NATIVITY		OCCUPATION
	Street, avenue, road, etc.	Number of dwelling house is order of visitation	Number of family in order of visitation	of each person whose place of abode on April 1, 1930, was in this family. Enter surname, first, then given name and middle initial. If any. Include every person living on April 1, 1930. Omit children born since April 1, 1930.	Relationship of this Person to the head of the family.	Sex	Color or race	Age at last birthday	Single, married, widowed or divorced	Attended school any time since Sept. 1, 1929	Whether able to read and write.	Place of birth of this person.	Whether able to speak English.	
	1	2	3	4	5	6	7	8	9	10	11	12	13	14
1	[no street name]	29	34	Castro, Ignacio P	Head	M	Cha	29	M	N	Y	Guam	N	Farmer
2		29	34	Castro, Rita C	Wife	F	Cha	31	M	N	Y	Guam	Y	None
3		29	34	Castro, Consolacion C	Daughter	F	Cha	14	S	Y	Y	Guam	Y	None
4		29	34	Castro, Jose C	Son	M	Cha	12	S	Y	Y	Guam	Y	None
5		29	34	Castro, Joaquin C	Son	M	Cha	11	S	Y	Y	Guam	Y	None
6		29	34	Castro, Maria C	Daughter	F	Cha	9	S	Y		Guam		None
7		29	34	Castro, Ana C	Daughter	F	Cha	8	S	Y		Guam		None
8		29	34	Castro, Rita C	Daughter	F	Cha	7	S	Y		Guam		None
9		29	34	Castro, Julia C	Daughter	F	Cha	4.7	S	N		Guam		None
10		29	34	Castro, Angustia C	Daughter	F	Cha	3.6	S	N		Guam		None
11		29	34	Castro, Ignacio C	Son	M	Cha	1.9	S	N		Guam		None
12		30	35	Castro, Vicente P	Head	M	Cha	38	M	N	Y	Guam	Y	Farmer
13		30	35	Castro, Elena G	Wife	F	Cha	35	M	N	Y	Guam	Y	None
14		30	35	Castro, Concepcion G	Daughter	F	Cha	11	S	Y	Y	Guam	Y	None
15		30	35	Castro, Vicente G	Son	M	Cha	9	S	Y		Guam		None
16		30	35	Castro, Jose G	Son	M	Cha	4.8	S	N		Guam		None
17		30	35	Castro, Edward G	Son	M	Cha	3.1	S	N		Guam		None
18		30	35	Salas, Felix S	Cousin-in-law	M	Cha	14	S	Y	Y	Guam	Y	None
19		31	36	Tenorio, Leonardo C	Head	M	Cha	30	M	N	Y	Guam	Y	Farmer
20		31	36	Tenorio, Lucia C	Wife	F	Cha	26	M	N	Y	Guam	Y	None
21		31	36	Tenorio, Juan C	Son	M	Cha	3.8	S	N		Guam		None
22		31	36	Castro, Dolores C	Mother-in-law	F	Cha	60	Wd	N	Y	Guam	N	None
23		31	36	Ada, Pedro T	Nephew	M	Cha	36	S	N	Y	Guam	N	Road laborer
24		32	37	Tenorio, Pedro C	Head	M	Cha	37	M	N	Y	Guam	Y	Farmer
25		32	37	Tenorio, Ana M	Wife	F	Cha	29	M	N	Y	Guam	Y	None

(CHAMORRO ROOTS GENEALOGY PROJECT™ TRANSCRIPTION)
(BERNARD T. PUNZALAN / HTTP://WWW.CHAMORROROOTS.COM)

DEPARTMENT OF COMMERCE-BUREAU OF THE CENSUS
WASHINGTON

FIFTEENTH CENSUS OF THE UNITED STATES: 1930-POPULATION

THE ISLAND OF GUAM

Sheet No. 23B

266B

District Municipality of Agana
Name of Place Talofofo Barrio
[Proper name and, also, name of class, as city, town, village, barrio, etc]

Enumeration District No. 8
Enumerated by me on April 17, 1930 Cayetano A. Quinata, Enumerator

	PLACE OF ABODE			NAME	RELATION	PERSONAL DESCRIPTION				EDUCATION		NATIVITY		OCCUPATION
	Street, avenue, road, etc.	Number of dwelling house is order of visitation	Number of family in order of visitation	of each person whose place of abode on April 1, 1930, was in this family. Enter surname, first, then given name and middle initial. If any. Include every person living on April 1, 1930. Omit children born since April 1, 1930.	Relationship of this Person to the head of the family.	Sex	Color or race	Age at last birthday	Single, married, widowed or divorced	Attended school any time since Sept. 1, 1929	Whether able to read and write.	Place of birth of this person.	Whether able to speak English.	
	1	2	3	4	5	6	7	8	9	10	11	12	13	14
26	[no street name]	32	37	Tenorio, Maria M	Daughter	F	Cha	12	S	Y	Y	Guam	Y	None
27		32	37	Tenorio, Ana M	Daughter	F	Cha	10	S	Y	Y	Guam	Y	None
28		32	37	Tenorio, Pedro M	Son	M	Cha	7	S	Y		Guam		None
29		32	37	Tenorio, Teresa M	Daughter	F	Cha	5	S	N		Guam		None
30		33	38	Aguon, Jose Q	Head	M	Cha	27	M	N	Y	Guam	Y	Road laborer
31		33	38	Aguon, Concepcion M	Wife	F	Cha	24	M	N	N	Guam	N	None
32		33	38	Aguon, Maria M	Daughter	F	Cha	1.9	S	N		Guam		None
33		33	39	Martines, Clemente R	Head	M	Cha	49	M	N	N	Guam	N	Farmer
34		33	39	Martines, Josefa R	Wife	F	Cha	52	M	N	N	Guam	N	None
35		33	39	Martines, Carmen R	Daughter	F	Cha	20	S	N	Y	Guam		None
36		33	39	Martines, Jesus M	Grandson	M	Cha	1.9	S	N		Guam		None
37		33	39	Martines, Joaquin R	Brother	M	Cha	47	S	N	N	Guam	N	None
38		34	40	Napute, Jesus T	Head	M	Cha	32	M	N	Y	Guam	N	Farmer
39		34	40	Napute, Dolores M	Wife	F	Cha	36	M	N	Y	Guam	N	None
40		34	40	Napute, Albert M	Son	M	Cha	13	S	Y	Y	Guam	Y	None
41		34	40	Napute, Juan M	Son	M	Cha	7	S	Y		Guam		None
42		34	40	Napute, Joaquin M	Son	M	Cha	3.1	S	N		Guam		None
43		34	40	Napute, Pedro M	Son	M	Cha	.7	S	N		Guam		None
44		35	41	Ulloa, Vicente U	Head	M	Cha	59	M	N	Y	Guam	Y	Farmer
45		35	41	Ulloa, Maria R	Wife	F	Cha	46	M	N	Y	Guam	N	None
46		35	41	Ulloa, Teresa R	Daughter	F	Cha	17	S	N	Y	Guam	Y	None
47		35	41	Ulloa, Rosa R	Daughter	F	Cha	16	S	N	Y	Guam	Y	None
48		35	41	Ulloa, Soledad R	Daughter	F	Cha	12	S	Y	Y	Guam	Y	None
49		35	41	Ulloa, Elena R	Daughter	F	Cha	10	S	Y	Y	Guam	Y	None
50		35	41	Ulloa, Vicente R	Son	M	Cha	7	S	Y		Guam		None

DEPARTMENT OF COMMERCE-BUREAU OF THE CENSUS
WASHINGTON

FIFTEENTH CENSUS OF THE UNITED STATES: 1930-POPULATION

THE ISLAND OF GUAM

Sheet No. 24A

District **Municipality of Agana**
Name of Place **Talofofo Barrio**
[Proper name and, also, name of class, as city, town, village, barrio, etc]

Enumeration District No. **8**
Enumerated by me on **April 19, 1930** Cayetano A. Quinata, Enumerator

	PLACE OF ABODE: Street, avenue, road, etc.	Number of dwelling house in order of visitation	Number of family in order of visitation	NAME of each person whose place of abode on April 1, 1930, was in this family. Enter surname, first, then given name and middle initial. If any. Include every person living on April 1, 1930. Omit children born since April 1, 1930.	RELATION Relationship of this Person to the head of the family.	PERSONAL DESCRIPTION: Sex	Color or race	Age at last birthday	Single, married, widowed or divorced	EDUCATION: Attended school any time since Sept. 1, 1929	Whether able to read and write.	NATIVITY Place of birth of this person.	Whether able to speak English.	OCCUPATION
	1	2	3	4	5	6	7	8	9	10	11	12	13	14
1	[no street name]	35	41	Castro, Juana R	Mother-in-law	F	Cha	80	Wd	N	N	Guam	N	None
2		36	42	Mantanona, Juan M	Head	M	Cha	30	M	N	N	Guam	N	Farmer
3		36	42	Mantanona, Filomena A	Wife	F	Cha	41	M	N	N	Guam	N	None
4		36	42	Mantanona, Petronila A	Daughter	F	Cha	5	S	N		Guam		None
5		37	43	Flores, Jose A	Head	M	Cha	70	M	N	Y	Guam	Y	Farmer
6		37	43	Flores, Candelaria S	Wife	F	Cha	57	M	N	Y	Guam	N	None
7		37	43	Pablo, Jose P	Servant	M	Cha	78	Wd	N	N	Guam	N	Farm laborer
8		37	43	Taitano, Isabel F	Grand daughter	F	Cha	21	S	N	Y	Guam	Y	None
9		37	43	Taitano, Laura I	Great grand daughter	F	Cha	.4	S	N		Guam		None
10		38	44	Taitague, Baldobino B	Head	M	Cha	32	M	N	Y	Guam	N	Farmer
11		38	44	Taitague, Catalina T	Wife	F	Cha	45	M	N	Y	Guam	N	None
12		38	44	Duenas, Fernando T	Nephew	M	Cha	9	S	Y		Guam		None
13		39	45	Materne, Ines S	Head	F	Cha	46	M	N	N	Guam	N	None
14		40	46	Garrido, Jose S	Head	M	Cha	25	M	N	Y	Guam	Y	Farmer
15		40	46	Garrido, Joaquina P	Wife	F	Cha	23	M	N	N	Guam	N	None
16		40	46	Garrido, Juan P	Son	M	Cha	4.1	S	N		Guam		None
17		40	46	Garrido, Carmen P	Daughter	F	Cha	1.7	S	N		Guam		None
18		40	46	Garrido, Ignacio S	Brother	M	Cha	23	S	N	Y	Guam	Y	Farm laborer
19		40	46	Garrido, Maria S	Sister	F	Cha	21	S	N	Y	Guam	Y	None
20		40	46	Garrido, Enrique S	Brother	M	Cha	19	S	N	Y	Guam	Y	Road laborer
21		40	46	Garrido, Rosalia S	Sister	F	Cha	15	S	Y	Y	Guam	Y	None
22		40	46	Garrido, Concepcion S	Sister	F	Cha	12	S	Y	Y	Guam	Y	None
23		40	46	Garrido, Francisco C	Nephew	M	Cha	8	S	Y		Guam		None
24		41	47	Garrido, Vicente L	Head	M	Cha	58	M	N	N	Guam	N	Farmer
25		41	47	Garrido, Trinidad A	Wife	F	Cha	47	M	N	Y	Guam	N	None

(CHAMORRO ROOTS GENEALOGY PROJECT™ TRANSCRIPTION)
(BERNARD T. PUNZALAN / HTTP://WWW.CHAMORROROOTS.COM)

DEPARTMENT OF COMMERCE-BUREAU OF THE CENSUS
WASHINGTON

FIFTEENTH CENSUS OF THE UNITED STATES: 1930-POPULATION

THE ISLAND OF GUAM

Sheet No. 24B

267B

District Municipality of Agana
Name of Place Talofofo Barrio
[Proper name and, also, name of class, as city, town, village, barrio, etc]

Enumeration District No. 8
Enumerated by me on April 19, 1930 Cayetano A. Quinata, Enumerator

	PLACE OF ABODE			NAME	RELATION	PERSONAL DESCRIPTION				EDUCATION		NATIVITY		OCCUPATION
	Street, avenue, road, etc.	Number of dwelling house is order of visitation	Number of family in order of visitation	of each person whose place of abode on April 1, 1930, was in this family. Enter surname, first, then given name and middle initial. If any. Include every person living on April 1, 1930. Omit children born since April 1, 1930.	Relationship of this Person to the head of the family.	Sex	Color or race	Age at last birthday	Single, married, widowed or divorced	Attended school any time since Sept. 1, 1929	Whether able to read and write.	Place of birth of this person.	Whether able to speak English.	
	1	2	3	4	5	6	7	8	9	10	11	12	13	14
26	[no street name]	41	47	Garrido, Ana A	Daughter	F	Cha	9	S	Y		Guam		None
27		41	47	Garrido, Vicente A	Son	M	Cha	7	S	Y		Guam		None
28		42	48	Castro, Vicente C	Head	M	Cha	37	M	N	Y	Guam	Y	Deputy Commissioner
29		42	48	Castro, Concepcion C	Wife	F	Cha	36	M	N	Y	Guam	Y	None
30		42	48	Castro, Delfina C	Daughter	F	Cha	14	S	Y	Y	Guam	Y	None
31		42	48	Castro, Esther C	Daughter	F	Cha	12	S	N	Y	Guam	Y	None
32		42	48	Castro, Concepcion C	Daughter	F	Cha	10	S	Y	Y	Guam	Y	None
33		42	48	Castro, Rosalina C	Daughter	F	Cha	8	S	Y		Guam		None
34		42	48	Mantanona, Antonio M	Servant	M	Cha	35	S	N	Y	Guam	Y	Farm laborer
35		43	49	Quinata, Cayetano A	Head	M	Cha	30	M	N	Y	Guam	Y	School teacher
36		43	49	Quinata, Ana LG	Wife	F	Cha	29	M	N	Y	Guam	Y	None
37		43	49	Quinata, Isabel LG	Daughter	F	Cha	10	S	Y	Y	Guam	Y	None
38		43	49	Quinata, Victoria LG	Daughter	F	Cha	8	S	Y		Guam		None
39		43	49	Quinata, Francisco LG	Son	M	Cha	7	S	Y		Guam		None
40		43	49	Quinata, Aleho LG	Son	M	Cha	5	S	Y		Guam		None
41		43	49	Quinata, Mariano LG	Son	M	Cha	3.9	S	N		Guam		None
42		43	49	Quinata, Maria LG	Daughter	F	Cha	2.9	S	N		Guam		None
43		43	49	Quinata, Roman LG	Son	M	Cha	.6	S	N		Guam		None
44		44	50	Salas, Jesus S	Head	M	Cha	42	M	N	Y	Guam	Y	Farmer
45		44	50	Salas, Josefa S	Wife	F	Cha	39	M	N	Y	Guam	N	None
46		44	50	Salas, Alicia S	Daughter	F	Cha	19	S	N	Y	Guam	Y	None
47		44	50	Salas, Candelaria S	Daughter	F	Cha	18	S	N	Y	Guam	Y	None
48		44	50	Salas, Josefina S	Daughter	F	Cha	16	S	Y	Y	Guam	Y	None
49		44	50	Salas, Francisco S	Son	M	Cha	14	S	Y	Y	Guam	Y	None
50		44	50	Salas, Maria S	Daughter	F	Cha	12	S	Y	Y	Guam	Y	None

(CHAMORRO ROOTS GENEALOGY PROJECT™ TRANSCRIPTION)
(BERNARD T. PUNZALAN / HTTP://WWW.CHAMORROROOTS.COM)

DEPARTMENT OF COMMERCE-BUREAU OF THE CENSUS
WASHINGTON

FIFTEENTH CENSUS OF THE UNITED STATES: 1930-POPULATION

THE ISLAND OF GUAM

Sheet No. 25A

268

District **Municipality of Agana**
Name of Place **Talofofo Barrio**
[Proper name and, also, name of class, as city, town, village, barrio, etc]

Enumeration District No. 8
Enumerated by me on **April 21, 1930** Cayetano A. Quinata
Enumerator

	PLACE OF ABODE			NAME	RELATION	PERSONAL DESCRIPTION				EDUCATION		NATIVITY		OCCUPATION
	Street, avenue, road, etc.	Number of dwelling house is order of visitation	Number of family in order of visitation	of each person whose place of abode on April 1, 1930, was in this family. Enter surname, first, then given name and middle initial. If any. Include every person living on April 1, 1930. Omit children born since April 1, 1930.	Relationship of this Person to the head of the family.	Sex	Color or race	Age at last birthday	Single, married, widowed or divorced	Attended school any time since Sept. 1, 1929	Whether able to read and write.	Place of birth of this person.	Whether able to speak English.	
	1	2	3	4	5	6	7	8	9	10	11	12	13	14
1	[no street name]	44	50	Salas, Margarita S	Daughter	F	Cha	11	S	Y	Y	Guam	Y	None
2		44	50	Salas, Juan S	Son	M	Cha	10	S	Y	Y	Guam	Y	None
3		44	50	Salas, Guardalupe S	Daughter	F	Cha	5	S	N		Guam		None
4		44	50	Salas, Pedro S	Son	M	Cha	3.2	S	N		Guam		None
5		44	50	Salas, Jose S	Son	M	Cha	0.4	S	N		Guam		None
6		44	50	Salas, Lorenzo P	Cousin	M	Cha	29	M	N	Y	Guam	Y	Farm laborer
7		44	50	Bautista, Juan S	Servant	M	Cha	30	S	N	Y	Guam	Y	Farm laborer
8		45	51	Reyes, Jose R	Head	M	Cha	31	M	N	N	Guam	N	Farm laborer
9		45	51	Reyes, Maria P	Wife	F	Cha	32	M	N	Y	Guam	N	None
10		45	51	Reyes, Lourdes P	Daughter	F	Cha	12	S	Y	Y	Guam	Y	None
11		45	51	Reyes, Jose P	Son	M	Cha	10	S	Y	Y	Guam	Y	None
12		45	51	Reyes, Francisca P	Daughter	F	Cha	7	S	Y		Guam		None
13		45	51	Reyes, Enrique P	Son	M	Cha	6	S	N		Guam		None
14		45	51	Reyes, Juan P	Son	M	Cha	4	S	N		Guam		None
15		45	51	Reyes, Maria P	Daughter	F	Cha	1.9	S	N		Guam		None
16		45	51	Pablo, Joaquin A	Bro-in-law	M	Cha	18	S	N	Y	Guam	Y	Farm laborer
17		46	52	Sahagon, Vicente R	Head	M	Cha	25	M	N	Y	Guam	Y	Farm laborer
18		46	52	Sahagon, Esperansa P	Wife	F	Cha	25	M	N	Y	Guam	Y	None
19		47	53	Mantanona, Froilan A	Head	M	Cha	61	M	N	N	Guam	N	Farm laborer
20		47	53	Mantanona, Ascension M	Wife	F	Cha	62	M	N	N	Guam	N	None
21		48	54	Santos, Jose C	Head	M	Cha	25	S	N	Y	Guam	Y	Road laborer
22		49	55	Ignacio, Jesus C	Head	M	Cha	19	S	N	Y	Guam	Y	Road laborer
23					[Lines 23 thru 25 were left blank by the Enumerator.]									
24					[Sheet 268B/25B was left blank by the Enumerator.]									
25														

DEPARTMENT OF COMMERCE-BUREAU OF THE CENSUS
WASHINGTON

FIFTEENTH CENSUS OF THE UNITED STATES: 1930-POPULATION

THE ISLAND OF GUAM

Sheet No. 26A

District **Municipality of Agana**
Name of Place **Talofofo**
[Proper name and, also, name of class, as city, town, village, barrio, etc]

Enumeration District No. 8
Enumerated by me on **April 17, 1930** Francisco G. Lujan, Enumerator

	PLACE OF ABODE: Street, avenue, road, etc.	Number of dwelling house in order of visitation	Number of family in order of visitation	NAME of each person whose place of abode on April 1, 1930, was in this family. Enter surname, first, then given name and middle initial. If any. Include every person living on April 1, 1930. Omit children born since April 1, 1930.	RELATION Relationship of this Person to the head of the family.	Sex	Color or race	Age at last birthday	Single, married, widowed or divorced	Attended school any time since Sept. 1, 1929	Whether able to read and write.	NATIVITY Place of birth of this person.	Whether able to speak English.	OCCUPATION
	1	2	3	4	5	6	7	8	9	10	11	12	13	14
1	[no street name]	135	152	Martinez, Joaquin R	Head	M	Cha	27	M	N	N	Guam	N	Farmer
2		135	152	Martinez, Carlina T	Wife	F	Cha	28	M	N	N	Guam	N	None
3		135	152	Martinez, Jose T	Son	M	Cha	4.1	S	N		Guam		None
4		135	152	Martinez, Joaquin T	Son	M	Cha	1.1	S	N		Guam		None
5		135	152	Toves, Ramon T	Step son	M	Cha	11	S	Y	Y	Guam	Y	None
6		135	152	Toves, Ana T	Step daughter	F	Cha	7	S	Y		Guam		None
7		136	153	Taitague, Victuriano L	Head	M	Cha	61	M	N	N	Guam	N	Farmer
8		136	153	Taitague, Magdalena B	Wife	F	Cha	45	M	N	N	Guam	N	None
9		136	153	Taitague, Maria B	Daughter	F	Cha	19	S	N	Y	Guam	Y	None
10		136	154	Taitague, Felix B	Head	M	Cha	31	M	N	Y	Guam	Y	Farmer
11		136	154	Taitague, Espreciosa U	Wife	F	Cha	19	M	N	Y	Guam	Y	None
12		136	154	Taitague, Josefa U	Daughter	F	Cha	2.1	S	N		Guam		None
13		136	154	Duenas, Supiana B	Grandmother	F	Cha	79	Wd	N	N	Guam	N	None
14		136	155	Taimanglo, Silvino C	Head	M	Cha	40	M	N	Y	Guam	Y	Farmer
15		136	155	Taimanglo, Josefina T	Wife	F	Cha	27	M	N	N	Guam	N	None
16		136	155	Taimanglo, Josefa T	Daughter	F	Cha	2.1	S	N		Guam		None
17		136	155	Taimanglo, Concepcion T	Daughter	F	Cha	.9	S	N		Guam		None
18		137	156	Duenas, Antonio T	Head	M	Cha	66	Wd	N	N	Guam	N	Farmer
19		137	156	Duenas, Tomasa T	Daughter	F	Cha	37	S	N	N	Guam	N	Farm laborer
20		137	156	Duenas, Rita T	Daughter	F	Cha	33	S	N	N	Guam	N	Farm laborer
21		137	156	Duenas, Benita T	Daughter	F	Cha	30	S	N	N	Guam	N	Farm laborer
22		137	156	Toves, Maria T	Grand-daughter	F	Cha	9	S	Y		Guam		None
23		137	156	Toves, Rosario T	Grand-daughter	F	Cha	9	S	Y		Guam		None
24		137	156	Duenas, Enrique D	Grand-son	M	Cha	1.1	S	N		Guam		None
25		137	156	Ogo, Ana T	Grand-daughter	F	Cha	11	S	Y	Y	Guam	Y	None

(CHAMORRO ROOTS GENEALOGY PROJECT™ TRANSCRIPTION)
(BERNARD T. PUNZALAN / HTTP://WWW.CHAMORROROOTS.COM)

DEPARTMENT OF COMMERCE-BUREAU OF THE CENSUS
WASHINGTON

FIFTEENTH CENSUS OF THE UNITED STATES: 1930-POPULATION

THE ISLAND OF GUAM

Sheet No. 26B

269B

District **Municipality of Agana**
Name of Place **Talofofo**
[Proper name and, also, name of class, as city, town, village, barrio, etc]

Enumeration District No. 8
Enumerated by me on **April 17, 1930** Francisco G. Lujan, Enumerator

	PLACE OF ABODE			NAME	RELATION	PERSONAL DESCRIPTION				EDUCATION		NATIVITY		OCCUPATION
	Street, avenue, road, etc.	Number of dwelling house in order of visitation	Number of family in order of visitation	of each person whose place of abode on April 1, 1930, was in this family. Enter surname, first, then given name and middle initial. If any. Include every person living on April 1, 1930. Omit children born since April 1, 1930.	Relationship of this Person to the head of the family.	Sex	Color or race	Age at last birthday	Single, married, widowed or divorced	Attended school any time since Sept. 1, 1929	Whether able to read and write.	Place of birth of this person.	Whether able to speak English.	
	1	2	3	4	5	6	7	8	9	10	11	12	13	14
26	[no street name]	138	157	Alig, Jose T	Head	M	Cha	49	S	N	N	Guam	N	Farmer
27		139	159	Duenas, Ignacio T	Head	M	Cha	38	M	N	N	Guam	N	Farmer
28		139	159	Duenas, Anunsacion T	Wife	F	Cha	40	M	N	N	Guam	N	None
29		139	159	Duenas, Pedro T	Son	M	Cha	13	S	N	Y	Guam	Y	Farm laborer
30		139	159	Duenas, Vicente T	Son	M	Cha	11	S	Y	Y	Guam	Y	None
31		139	159	Duenas, Juan T	Son	M	Cha	8	S	Y		Guam		None
32		139	159	Duenas, Jose T	Son	M	Cha	6	S	Y		Guam		None
33		139	159	Duenas, Delgadina T	Daughter	F	Cha	4.1	S	N		Guam		None
34		139	159	Duenas, Carlos T	Son	M	Cha	2.7	S	N		Guam		None
35		140	159	Taijeron, Pedro T	Head	M	Cha	41	M	N	N	Guam	N	Farmer
36		140	159	Taijeron, Remedios T	Wife	F	Cha	35	M	N	N	Guam	N	None
37		140	159	Taijeron, Vicente T	Son	M	Cha	13	S	Y	Y	Guam	Y	None
38		140	159	Taijeron, Jose T	Son	M	Cha	11	S	Y	Y	Guam	Y	None
39		140	159	Taijeron, Jesus T	Son	M	Cha	8	S	Y		Guam		None
40		140	159	Taijeron, Lucia T	Daughter	F	Cha	6	S	Y		Guam		None
41		140	159	Taijeron, Maria T	Daughter	F	Cha	3	S	N		Guam		None
42		140	159	Taijeron, Felipe T	Son	M	Cha	1.2	S	N		Guam		None
43		141	160	Cabrera, Juan D	Head	M	Cha	26	M	N	Y	Guam	Y	Farmer
44		141	160	Cabrera, Josefa B	Wife	F	Cha	21	M	N	N	Guam	N	None
45		141	160	Cabrera, Enriqueta B	Daughter	F	Cha	3.7	S	N		Guam		None
46		141	160	Cabrera, Julia B	Daughter	F	Cha	1.7	S	N		Guam		None
47		141	160	Cabrera, Juan B	Son	M	Cha	.4	S	N		Guam		None
48		142	161	[blank],	Head	M	Jap	35	S	N		Japan		Farm laborer
49		142	161	Chargualaf, Jose T.	Servant	M	Cha	22	S	N	Y	Guam	Y	Cook
50					Here ends the enumeration of District # 8.									

District 9
Municipality of Merizo

Merizo Town
Umatac Barrio

DEPARTMENT OF COMMERCE-BUREAU OF THE CENSUS
WASHINGTON

FIFTEENTH CENSUS OF THE UNITED STATES: 1930-POPULATION

THE ISLAND OF GUAM

Sheet No. 1A

District **Municipality of Merizo**
Name of Place **Merizo Town**
[Proper name and, also, name of class, as city, town, village, barrio, etc]

Enumeration District No. 9
Enumerated by me on April 2, 1930 Manuel Charfauros
Enumerator

	PLACE OF ABODE			NAME	RELATION	PERSONAL DESCRIPTION				EDUCATION		NATIVITY		OCCUPATION
	Street, avenue, road, etc.	Number of dwelling house is order of visitation	Number of family in order of visitation	of each person whose place of abode on April 1, 1930, was in this family. Enter surname, first, then given name and middle initial. If any. Include every person living on April 1, 1930. Omit children born since April 1, 1930.	Relationship of this Person to the head of the family.	Sex	Color or race	Age at last birthday	Single, married, widowed or divorced	Attended school any time since Sept. 1, 1929	Whether able to read and write.	Place of birth of this person.	Whether able to speak English.	
	1	2	3	4	5	6	7	8	9	10	11	12	13	14
1	San Dimas Street	1	1	Manalisay, Gregorio C	Head	M	Cha	41	M	N	Y	Guam	N	Farmer
2		1	1	Manalisay, Maria A	Wife	F	Cha	50	M	N	N	Guam	N	None
3		1	1	Acfalle, Prudencio B	Step son	M	Cha	10	S	Y	Y	Guam	Y	None
4		1	1	Acfalle, Julia B	Step daughter	F	Cha	6	S	N	Y	Guam		None
5		2	2	Cruz, Venancio T	Head	M	Cha	43	M	N	Y	Guam	N	Farmer
6		2	2	Cruz, Maria R	Wife	F	Cha	42	M	N	Y	Guam	N	None
7		2	2	Cruz, Joaquin R	Son	M	Cha	21	S	N	Y	Guam	Y	Laborer
8		2	2	Cruz, Jose R	Son	M	Cha	17	S	N	Y	Guam	Y	Farm laborer
9		2	2	Cruz, Josefa R	Daughter	F	Cha	15	S	Y	Y	Guam	Y	None
10		2	2	Cruz, Ana R	Daughter	F	Cha	13	S	Y	Y	Guam	Y	None
11		2	2	Cruz, Manuel R	Son	M	Cha	11	S	Y	Y	Guam	Y	None
12		2	2	Cruz, Maria R	Daughter	F	Cha	9	S	Y		Guam		None
13		2	2	Cruz, Rosalia R	Daughter	F	Cha	8	S	Y		Guam		None
14		2	2	Cruz, Vicente R	Son	M	Cha	6	S	N		Guam		None
15		2	2	Cruz, Jesus R	Son	M	Cha	3.5	S	N		Guam		None
16		2	2	Cruz, Gonzalo R	Son	M	Cha	2.1	S	N		Guam		None
17		2	2	Cruz, Juan R	Son	M	Cha	0	S	N		Guam		None
18		3	3	Aguigui, Ignacio B	Head	M	Cha	37	M	N	Y	Guam	Y	Farmer
19		3	3	Aguigui, Bienvenida T	Wife	F	Cha	38	M	N	Y	Guam	N	None
20		3	3	Aguigui, Rosalia T	Daughter	F	Cha	15	S	Y	Y	Guam	Y	None
21		3	3	Aguigui, Maria T	Daughter	F	Cha	13	S	Y	Y	Guam	Y	None
22		3	3	Aguigui, Carmen T	Daughter	F	Cha	11	S	Y	Y	Guam	Y	None
23		3	3	Aguigui, Felix T	Son	M	Cha	10	S	Y	Y	Guam	Y	None
24		3	3	Aguigui, Delfina T	Daughter	F	Cha	7	S	Y		Guam		None
25		3	3	Aguigui, Isabel T	Daughter	F	Cha	5	S	N		Guam		None

DEPARTMENT OF COMMERCE-BUREAU OF THE CENSUS
WASHINGTON

FIFTEENTH CENSUS OF THE UNITED STATES: 1930-POPULATION

THE ISLAND OF GUAM

Sheet No. 1B

270B

District **Municipality of Merizo**
Name of Place **Merizo Town**
[Proper name and, also, name of class, as city, town, village, barrio, etc]

Enumeration District No. 9
Enumerated by me on **April 2, 1930** Manuel Charfauros, Enumerator

	PLACE OF ABODE: Street, avenue, road, etc.	Number of dwelling house in order of visitation	Number of family in order of visitation	NAME of each person whose place of abode on April 1, 1930, was in this family. Enter surname, first, then given name and middle initial. If any. Include every person living on April 1, 1930. Omit children born since April 1, 1930.	RELATION Relationship of this Person to the head of the family.	PERSONAL DESCRIPTION: Sex	Color or race	Age at last birthday	Single, married, widowed or divorced	EDUCATION: Attended school any time since Sept. 1, 1929	Whether able to read and write.	NATIVITY Place of birth of this person.	Whether able to speak English.	OCCUPATION
	1	2	3	4	5	6	7	8	9	10	11	12	13	14
26	San Dimas Street	3	3	Aguigui, Ana T	Daughter	F	Cha	4.6	S	N		Guam		None
27		3	3	Aguigui, Jose T	Son	M	Cha	1	S	N		Guam		None
28		3	3	Aguigui, Pedro N	Father	M	Cha	63	Wd	N	N	Guam	N	None
29		4	4	Mansapit, Felix C	Head	M	Cha	44	M	N	N	Guam		None
30		4	4	Mansapit, Felomenia M	Wife	F	Cha	45	M	N	Y	Guam	N	Farmer
31		4	4	Mansapit, Cristobal M	Son	M	Cha	18	S	N	Y	Guam	N	None
32		4	4	Mansapit, Jesus M	Son	M	Cha	14	S	Y	Y	Guam	Y	Laborer (road)
33		4	4	Mansapit, Joaquin M	Son	M	Cha	11	S	Y	Y	Guam	Y	None
34		4	4	Mansapit, Vicente M	Son	M	Cha	9	S	Y		Guam	Y	None
35		4	4	Mansapit, Gabriel M	Son	M	Cha	7	S	Y		Guam		None
36		4	4	Mansapit, Maria M	Daughter	F	Cha	3.9	S	N		Guam		None
37		5	5	Barcinas, Juan S	Head	M	Cha	37	M	N	Y	Guam		Farmer
38		5	5	Barcinas, Tomasa T	Wife	F	Cha	34	M	N	Y	Guam		None
39		5	5	Barcinas, Antonio T	Son	M	Cha	13	S	Y	Y	Guam		Farm laborer
40		5	5	Barcinas, Ignacio T	Son	M	Cha	12	S	Y	Y	Guam		None
41		5	5	Barcinas, Pedro T	Son	M	Cha	10	S	Y	Y	Guam		None
42		5	5	Barcinas, Jose T	Son	M	Cha	8	S	Y		Guam		None
43		5	5	Barcinas, Dolores T	Daughter	F	Cha	6	S	Y		Guam		None
44		5	5	Barcinas, Joaquin T	Son	M	Cha	2.9	S	N		Guam		None
45		6	6	Tedpaogo, Vicente B	Head	M	Cha	54	M	N	Y	Guam	N	Farmer
46		6	6	Tedpaogo, Jose E	Son	M	Cha	22	S	N	Y	Guam	Y	Farm laborer
47		6	7	Tyquiengco, Vicente B	Head	M	Chin	38	M	N	Y	Guam	N	Farmer
48		6	7	Tyquiengco, Petronila T	Wife	F	Cha	39	M	N	Y	Guam	N	None
49		6	7	Tyquiengco, Rosa T	Daughter	F	Chin	14	S	N	Y	Guam	Y	None
50		7	8	Pangelinan, Maria T	Head	F	Cha	38	Wd	N	Y	Guam	N	None

(CHAMORRO ROOTS GENEALOGY PROJECT™ TRANSCRIPTION)
(BERNARD T. PUNZALAN / HTTP://WWW.CHAMORROROOTS.COM)

DEPARTMENT OF COMMERCE-BUREAU OF THE CENSUS
WASHINGTON

FIFTEENTH CENSUS OF THE UNITED STATES: 1930-POPULATION

THE ISLAND OF GUAM

Sheet No. 2A

District **Municipality of Merizo** Enumeration District No. **9**
Name of Place **Merizo Town** Enumerated by me on **April 2, 1930** Manuel Charfauros, Enumerator
[Proper name and, also, name of class, as city, town, village, barrio, etc]

	PLACE OF ABODE			NAME	RELATION	PERSONAL DESCRIPTION				EDUCATION		NATIVITY		OCCUPATION
	Street, avenue, road, etc.	Number of dwelling house is order of visitation	Number of family in order of visitation	of each person whose place of abode on April 1, 1930, was in this family. Enter surname, first, then given name and middle initial. If any. Include every person living on April 1, 1930. Omit children born since April 1, 1930.	Relationship of this Person to the head of the family.	Sex	Color or race	Age at last birthday	Single, married, widowed or divorced	Attended school any time since Sept. 1, 1929	Whether able to read and write.	Place of birth of this person.	Whether able to speak English.	
	1	2	3	4	5	6	7	8	9	10	11	12	13	14
1	San Dimas Street	7	8	Tyquiengco, Antonio M	Son	M	Cha	13	S	Y	Y	Guam	Y	None
2		7	8	Pangelinan, Francisco T	Son	M	Cha	4.2	S	N		Guam		None
3		7	8	Tyquiengco, Nicolasa M	Mother	F	Cha	57	Wd	N	N	Guam	N	None
4		8	9	Mansapit, Santiago N	Head	M	Cha	22	S	N	Y	Guam	Y	Laborer (Road)
5		8	9	Mansapit, Manuel N	Brother	M	Cha	20	S	N	Y	Guam	Y	Farm laborer
6		8	9	Mansapit, Venancio N	Brother	M	Cha	16	S	Y	Y	Guam	Y	Farm laborer
7		8	9	Mansapit, Pedro N	Brother	M	Cha	13	S	Y	Y	Guam	Y	None
8		8	9	Mansapit, Clemente B	Uncle	M	Cha	62	S	N	N	Guam	N	None
9		8	9	Mansapit, Nicolasa C	Cousin	M	Cha	43	S	N	Y	Guam	N	None
10		9	10	Fegurgur, Elena B	Head	F	Cha	57	Wd	N	N	Guam	N	None
11		9	10	Babauta, Faustino B	Son	M	Cha	38	S	N	Y	Guam	N	Fisherman
12		9	10	Fegurgur, Cristina B	Daughter	F	Cha	20	S	N	Y	Guam	Y	None
13		9	10	Fegurgur, Francisco B	Son	M	Cha	16	S	Y	Y	Guam	Y	Farm laborer
14		9	10	Fegurgur, Dolores N	Sister-in-law	F	Cha	56	S	N	N	Guam	N	None
15		9	10	Fegurgur, Eugenia N	Sister-in-law	F	Cha	53	S	N	N	Guam	N	None
16		9	10	Fegurgur, Venancio N	Step nephew in law	M	Cha	23	S	N	Y	Guam	Y	Farm laborer
17		10	11	Tyquiengco, Vicente B	Head	M	Chin	59	S	N	Y	Guam	N	Farmer
18		10	11	Cruz, Nicolasa T	Sister	F	Chin	62	Wd	N	N	Guam	N	None
19		10	12	Tyquiengco, Gregorio B	Head	M	Chin	38	Wd	N	Y	Guam	N	Farmer
20		11	13	Acfalle, Juan B	Head	M	Cha	42	M	N	Y	Guam	N	Farmer
21		11	13	Acfalle, Ana M	Wife	F	Cha	43	M	N	Y	Guam	N	None
22		11	13	Acfalle, Miguel M	Son	M	Cha	13	S	Y	Y	Guam	Y	Farm laborer
23		11	13	Acfalle, Trinidad M	Daughter	F	Cha	11	S	Y	Y	Guam	Y	None
24		11	13	Acfalle, Andrea M	Daughter	F	Cha	10	S	Y	Y	Guam	N	None
25		11	13	Acfalle, Jose M	Son	M	Cha	7	S	Y		Guam		None

DEPARTMENT OF COMMERCE-BUREAU OF THE CENSUS
WASHINGTON

FIFTEENTH CENSUS OF THE UNITED STATES: 1930-POPULATION

THE ISLAND OF GUAM

Sheet No. 2B

271B

District **Municipality of Merizo**
Name of Place **Merizo Town**
[Proper name and, also, name of class, as city, town, village, barrio, etc]

Enumeration District No. **9**
Enumerated by me on **April 2, 1930** Manuel Charfauros
Enumerator

	PLACE OF ABODE			NAME	RELATION	PERSONAL DESCRIPTION				EDUCATION		NATIVITY		OCCUPATION
	Street, avenue, road, etc.	Number of dwelling house is order of visitation	Number of family in order of visitation	of each person whose place of abode on April 1, 1930, was in this family. Enter surname, first, then given name and middle initial. If any. Include every person living on April 1, 1930. Omit children born since April 1, 1930.	Relationship of this Person to the head of the family.	Sex	Color or race	Age at last birthday	Single, married, widowed or divorced	Attended school any time since Sept. 1, 1929	Whether able to read and write.	Place of birth of this person.	Whether able to speak English.	
	1	2	3	4	5	6	7	8	9	10	11	12	13	14
26	San Dimas Streeet	11	13	Acfalle, Vicente M	Son	M	Cha	4.1	S	N		Guam		None
27		12	14	Manalisay, Venancio C	Head	M	Cha	52	M	N	Y	Guam	N	Farmer
28		12	14	Manalisay, Asuncion C	Wife	F	Cha	51	M	N	N	Guam	N	None
29		12	14	Manalisay, Rita C	Daughter	F	Cha	6	S	Y		Guam		None
30		12	14	Acfalle, Jose C	Step-son	M	Cha	25	S	N	Y	Guam	Y	Farm laborer
31		12	14	Acfalle, Ana C	Step daughter	F	Cha	19	S	N	Y	Guam	Y	None
32		12	14	Acfalle, Felix C	Step-son	M	Cha	16	S	N	Y	Guam	Y	Farm laborer
33		12	14	Champaco, Jesus C	Step-son	M	Cha	8	S	Y	Y	Guam		None
34		12	15	Acfalle, Juan C	Head	M	Cha	21	M	N	Y	Guam	Y	Laborer (road)
35		12	15	Acfalle, Isabel Q	Wife	F	Cha	19	M	N	Y	Guam	Y	None
36		13	16	Charfauros, Manuel	Head	M	Cha	33	M	N	Y	Guam		School teacher
37		13	16	Charfauros, Joaquina L	Wife	F	Cha	27	M	N	Y	Guam	Y	None
38		13	16	Charfauros, Barbara L	Daughter	F	Cha	11	S	Y	Y	Guam	Y	None
39		13	16	Charfauros, William L	Son	M	Cha	8	S	Y		Guam	Y	None
40		13	16	Charfauros, Arthur L	Son	M	Cha	6	S	Y		Guam		None
41		13	16	Charfauros, George L	Son	M	Cha	4.5	S	N		Guam		None
42		13	16	Charfauros, Louise L	Daughter	F	Cha	2.4	S	N		Guam		None
43		13	16	Charfauros, Emma C L	Daughter	F	Cha	0	S	N		Guam		None
44		13	16	Barcinas, Jose C	Servant	M	Cha	16	S	Y	Y	Guam	Y	Servant
45		14	17	Reyes, Jose M	Head	M	Cha	28	M	N	Y	Guam	Y	Farmer
46		14	17	Reyes, Dolores T	Wife	F	Cha	26	M	N	Y	Guam	Y	None
47		14	17	Reyes, Maria T	Daughter	F	Cha	6	S	N		Guam		None
48		14	17	Reyes, Francisca T	Daughter	F	Cha	3	S	N		Guam		None
49		14	17	Reyes, Jose T	Son	M	Cha	1.7	S	N		Guam		None
50		15	18	Nangauta, Julian C	Head	M	Cha	55	Wd	N	Y	Guam	N	Farmer

(CHAMORRO ROOTS GENEALOGY PROJECT™ TRANSCRIPTION)
(BERNARD T. PUNZALAN / HTTP://WWW.CHAMORROROOTS.COM)

DEPARTMENT OF COMMERCE-BUREAU OF THE CENSUS
WASHINGTON

FIFTEENTH CENSUS OF THE UNITED STATES: 1930-POPULATION

THE ISLAND OF GUAM

Sheet No. 3A

District **Municipality of Merizo**
Name of Place **Merizo Town**
[Proper name and, also, name of class, as city, town, village, barrio, etc]

Enumeration District No. **9**
Enumerated by me on **April 3, 1930** Manuel Charfauros
Enumerator

	PLACE OF ABODE			NAME	RELATION	PERSONAL DESCRIPTION				EDUCATION		NATIVITY		OCCUPATION
	Street, avenue, road, etc.	Number of dwelling house in order of visitation	Number of family in order of visitation	of each person whose place of abode on April 1, 1930, was in this family. Enter surname, first, then given name and middle initial. If any. Include every person living on April 1, 1930. Omit children born since April 1, 1930.	Relationship of this Person to the head of the family.	Sex	Color or race	Age at last birthday	Single, married, widowed or divorced	Attended school any time since Sept. 1, 1929	Whether able to read and write.	Place of birth of this person.	Whether able to speak English.	
	1	2	3	4	5	6	7	8	9	10	11	12	13	14
1	San Dimas Street	15	18	Nanguata, Concepcion T	Daughter	F	Cha	28	S	N	Y	Guam	Y	None
2		15	18	Nanguata, Vicente T	Son	M	Cha	16	S	N	Y	Guam	Y	None
3		15	19	Nanguata, Joaquin T	Head	M	Cha	24	M	N	Y	Guam	Y	Farmer
4		15	19	Nanguata, Magdalena Q	Wife	F	Cha	21	M	N	Y	Guam	Y	None
5		15	19	Nanguata, Antonio Q	Son	M	Cha	1.7	S	N		Guam		None
6		16	20	Espinosa, Serafin N	Head	M	Cha	54	M	N	Y	Guam	N	Farmer
7		16	20	Espinosa, Dolores M	Wife	F	Cha	52	M	N	Y	Guam	N	None
8		16	20	Espinosa, Carmen M	Daughter	F	Cha	25	S	N	Y	Guam	Y	None
9		16	20	Espinosa, Jesus M	Son	M	Cha	17	S	N	Y	Guam	Y	Farm laborer
10		16	20	Espinosa, Ignacio M	Son	M	Cha	10	S	Y	Y	Guam	Y	None
11		16	20	Espinosa, Vicente M	Son	M	Cha	10	S	Y	Y	Guam	Y	None
12		17	21	Baza, Ramon C	Head	M	Cha	74	Wd	N	N	Guam	N	Farmer
13		17	21	Baza, Pedro T	Son	M	Cha	45	S	N	Y	Guam	N	Pedller
14		17	21	Baza, Rosa T	Daughter	F	Cha	37	S	N	Y	Guam	Y	None
15		17	21	Baza, Luisa	Grand daughter	F	Cha	7	S	Y		Guam		None
16		17	21	Baza, Maria	Grand daughter	F	Cha	3.7	S	N		Guam		None
17		17	21	San Nicolas, Jesus B	Grand son	M	Cha	16	S	N	Y	Guam	Y	Farm laborer
18		17	21	San Nicolas, Joaquin T	Grand son	M	Cha	7	S	Y		Guam		None
19		18	22	San Nicolas, Felix E	Head	M	Cha	52	M	N	Y	Guam	N	Farmer
20		18	22	San Nicolas, Concepcion C	Wife	F	Cha	47	M	N	Y	Guam	N	None
21		18	22	San Nicolas, Ana C	Daughter	F	Cha	22	S	N	Y	Guam	Y	None
22		18	22	San Nicolas, Consuelo C	Daughter	F	Cha	20	S	N	Y	Guam	Y	None
23		18	22	San Nicolas, Juan C	Son	M	Cha	17	S	N	Y	Guam	Y	Farm laborer
24		18	22	San Nicolas, Ramona C	Daughter	F	Cha	11	S	Y	Y	Guam	Y	None
25		19	23	Naputi, Lorenzo E	Head	M	Cha	60	M	N	Y	Guam	N	Farmer

(CHAMORRO ROOTS GENEALOGY PROJECT™ TRANSCRIPTION)
(BERNARD T. PUNZALAN / HTTP://WWW.CHAMORROROOTS.COM)

DEPARTMENT OF COMMERCE-BUREAU OF THE CENSUS
WASHINGTON

FIFTEENTH CENSUS OF THE UNITED STATES: 1930-POPULATION

THE ISLAND OF GUAM

Sheet No. 3B

272B

District Municipality of Merizo
Name of Place Merizo Town
[Proper name and, also, name of class, as city, town, village, barrio, etc]

Enumeration District No. 9
Enumerated by me on April 3, 1930 Manuel Charfauros
Enumerator

	PLACE OF ABODE			NAME	RELATION	PERSONAL DESCRIPTION				EDUCATION		NATIVITY		OCCUPATION
	Street, avenue, road, etc.	Number of dwelling house is order of visitation	Number of family in order of visitation	of each person whose place of abode on April 1, 1930, was in this family. Enter surname, first, then given name and middle initial. If any. Include every person living on April 1, 1930. Omit children born since April 1, 1930.	Relationship of this Person to the head of the family.	Sex	Color or race	Age at last birthday	Single, married, widowed or divorced	Attended school any time since Sept. 1, 1929	Whether able to read and write.	Place of birth of this person.	Whether able to speak English.	
	1	2	3	4	5	6	7	8	9	10	11	12	13	14
26	San Dimas Street	19	23	Naputi, Simona A	Wife	F	Cha	64	M	N	Y	Guam	N	None
27		19	23	Naputi, Jose A	Son	M	Cha	39	S	N	Y	Guam	N	Farm laborer
28		19	23	Naputi, Antonia A	Daughter	F	Cha	35	S	N	Y	Guam	N	None
29		19	23	Naputi, Narcisa A	Daughter	F	Cha	34	S	N	Y	Guam	Y	None
30		19	23	Tyquiengco, Maria N	Grand daughter	F	Chin	12	S	Y	Y	Guam	Y	None
31		19	23	Tyquiengco, Jose N	Grand son	M	Chin	10	S	Y	Y	Guam	Y	None
32		19	23	Tyquiengco, Jesus N	Grand son	M	Chin	8	S	Y		Guam		None
33		20	24	Chargualaf, Juliana T	Head	F	Cha	51	Wd	N	Y	Guam	N	None
34		20	24	Chargualaf, Jose T	Son	M	Cha	37	S	N	Y	Guam	N	Farm laborer
35		20	24	Chargualaf, Germonimo T	Son	M	Cha	35	Wd	N	Y	Guam	Y	Farm laborer
36		20	24	Chargualaf, Mariano T	Son	M	Cha	18	S	N	Y	Guam	Y	Farm laborer
37		20	25	Garrido, Rosa C	Head	F	Cha	38	Wd	N	Y	Guam	N	None
38		20	25	Garrido, Ramon C	Son	M	Cha	14	S	Y	Y	Guam	Y	None
39		20	25	Garrido, Jesus C	Son	M	Cha	12	S	Y	Y	Guam	Y	None
40		20	25	Garrido, Jose C	Son	M	Cha	10	S	Y	Y	Guam	Y	None
41		20	25	Garrido, Concepcion C	Daughter	F	Cha	7	S	N		Guam		None
42		20	25	Garrido, Miguel C	Son	M	Cha	6	S	N		Guam		None
43		20	25	Garrido, Francisco C	Son	M	Cha	5	S	N		Guam		None
44		21	26	Cruz, Juan P	Head	M	Cha	44	Wd	N	Y	Guam	N	Farmer
45		21	26	Cruz, Antonio LG	Son	M	Cha	20	S	N	Y	Guam	Y	Farm laborer
46		21	26	Cruz, Manuel LG	Son	M	Cha	15	S	Y	Y	Guam	Y	None
47		21	26	Cruz, Jose LG	Son	M	Cha	10	S	Y	Y	Guam	Y	None
48		21	26	Cruz, Jesus LG	Son	M	Cha	7	S	Y		Guam		None
49		22	27	San Nicolas, Froilan	Head	M	Cha	54	M	N	Y	Guam	N	Farmer
50		22	27	San Nicolas, Maria T	Wife	F	Cha	52	M	N	N	Guam	N	None

DEPARTMENT OF COMMERCE-BUREAU OF THE CENSUS
WASHINGTON

FIFTEENTH CENSUS OF THE UNITED STATES: 1930-POPULATION

THE ISLAND OF GUAM

Sheet No. 4A

District **Municipality of Merizo**
Name of Place **Merizo Town**
[Proper name and, also, name of class, as city, town, village, barrio, etc]

Enumeration District No. **9**
Enumerated by me on **April 3, 1930** Manuel Charfauros
Enumerator

	PLACE OF ABODE: Street, avenue, road, etc.	Number of dwelling house in order of visitation	Number of family in order of visitation	NAME of each person whose place of abode on April 1, 1930, was in this family. Enter surname, first, then given name and middle initial. If any. Include every person living on April 1, 1930. Omit children born since April 1, 1930.	RELATION Relationship of this Person to the head of the family.	PERSONAL DESCRIPTION: Sex	Color or race	Age at last birthday	Single, married, widowed or divorced	EDUCATION: Attended school any time since Sept. 1, 1929	Whether able to read and write.	NATIVITY Place of birth of this person.	Whether able to speak English.	OCCUPATION
	1	2	3	4	5	6	7	8	9	10	11	12	13	14
1	San Dimas Street	22	27	Naputi, Jesus A	Nephew	M	Cha	27	S	N	Y	Guam	Y	Farm laborer
2		23	28	San Nicolas, Maria C	Head	F	Cha	54	Wd	N	Y	Guam	N	None
3		23	28	San Nicolas, Francisco C	Son	M	Cha	27	S	N	Y	Guam	Y	Farm laborer
4		23	28	San Nicolas, Maria C	Daughter	F	Cha	20	S	N	Y	Guam	Y	None
5		23	28	San Nicolas, Ana C	Daughter	F	Cha	17	S	N	Y	Guam	Y	None
6		23	28	San Nicolas, Pedro C	Son	M	Cha	15	S	Y	Y	Guam	Y	None
7		23	28	San Nicolas, Vicente C	Son	M	Cha	11	S	Y	Y	Guam	Y	None
8		23	28	San Nicolas, Felomena E	Sister-in-law	F	Cha	52	S	N		Guam	N	None
9		23	28	Taijeron, Felisa G	Lodger	F	Cha	44	S	N		Guam	N	None
10		24	29	De Legaria, Gil	Head	M	W	35	S	N	Y	Spain	Y	Missionary
11		24	29	Cruz, Pedro LG	Servant	M	Cha	17	S	N	Y	Guam	Y	Servant
12		25	30	Naputi, Enrique A	Head	M	Cha	29	M	N	Y	Guam	Y	Farmer
13		25	30	Naputi, Rita F	Wife	F	Cha	27	M	N	Y	Guam	N	None
14		25	30	Naputi, Vicente F	Son	M	Cha	5.1	S	N		Guam		None
15		25	30	Naputi, Maria F	Daughter	F	Cha	3.1	S	N		Guam		None
16		25	30	Naputi, Juan F	Son	M	Cha	0.8	S	N		Guam		None
17		26	31	Espinosa, Pedro C	Head	M	Cha	31	M	N	Y	Guam	Y	Farmer
18		26	31	Espinosa, Josefina T	Wife	F	Chin	28	M	N	Y	Guam	Y	None
19		26	31	Espinosa, Jose T	Son	M	Cha	4.6	S	N		Guam		None
20		26	31	Espinosa, Domingo T	Son	M	Cha	3.2	S	N		Guam		None
21		26	31	Espinosa, Ana T	Daughter	F	Cha	1.4	S	N		Guam		None
22		27	32	Garrido, Asuncion N	Head	F	Cha	54	Wd	N	N	Guam	N	None
23		27	32	Garrido, Carmen N	Daughter	F	Cha	16	S	N	Y	Guam	Y	None
24		28	33	San Nicolas, Juan S	Head	M	Cha	24	M	N	Y	Guam	Y	Chauffeur
25		28	33	San Nicolas, Maria M	Wife	F	Cha	22	M	N	Y	Guam	Y	None

DEPARTMENT OF COMMERCE-BUREAU OF THE CENSUS
WASHINGTON

FIFTEENTH CENSUS OF THE UNITED STATES: 1930-POPULATION

THE ISLAND OF GUAM

Sheet No. 4B

273B

District **Municipality of Merizo**
Name of Place **Merizo Town**
[Proper name and, also, name of class, as city, town, village, barrio, etc]

Enumeration District No. 9
Enumerated by me on **April 4, 1930** Manuel Charfauros
Enumerator

	PLACE OF ABODE			NAME	RELATION	PERSONAL DESCRIPTION				EDUCATION		NATIVITY		OCCUPATION
	Street, avenue, road, etc.	Number of dwelling house is order of visitation	Number of family in order of visitation	of each person whose place of abode on April 1, 1930, was in this family. Enter surname, first, then given name and middle initial. If any. Include every person living on April 1, 1930. Omit children born since April 1, 1930.	Relationship of this Person to the head of the family.	Sex	Color or race	Age at last birthday	Single, married, widowed or divorced	Attended school any time since Sept. 1, 1929	Whether able to read and write.	Place of birth of this person.	Whether able to speak English.	
	1	2	3	4	5	6	7	8	9	10	11	12	13	14
26	San Dimas Street	29	34	Manalisay, Felix C	Head	M	Cha	51	M	N	Y	Guam	N	Carpenter
27		29	34	Manalisay, Alejandra B	Wife	F	Cha	34	M	N	Y	Guam	N	None
28		29	34	Taitajgue, Delfina B	Niece	F	Cha	2.4	S	N		Guam		None
29		29	34	Acfalle, Jesus B	Lodger	M	Cha	18	S	N	Y	Guam		Farm laborer
30		30	35	Espinosa, Enemesia N	Head	F	Cha	42	S	N	Y	Guam	N	None
31		31	36	Babauta, Elena C	Head	F	Cha	50	Wd	N	Y	Guam	N	Laundress
32		31	36	Babauta, Ana C	Daughter	F	Cha	20	S	N	Y	Guam	N	Laundress
33		31	37	Babauta, Jesus C	Head	M	Cha	24	M	N	Y	Guam	Y	Farmer
34		31	37	Babauta, Ana E	Wife	F	Cha	16	M	Y	Y	Guam	Y	None
35		32	38	Mata, Carmen M	Head	F	Cha	44	Wd	N	Y	Guam	N	Basket weaver
36		32	38	Mata, Milagro M	Daughter	F	Cha	21	S	N	Y	Guam	Y	Basket weaver
37		32	38	Mata, Jose M	Son	M	Cha	17	S	N	Y	Guam	Y	Farm laborer
38		32	38	Mata, Ignacio M	Son	M	Cha	14	S	Y	Y	Guam	Y	None
39		32	38	Mata, Martina M	Daughter	F	Cha	12	S	Y	Y	Guam	Y	None
40		32	38	Mata, Ana M	Daughter	F	Cha	11	S	Y	Y	Guam	Y	None
41		32	38	Mata, Jesus M	Son	M	Cha	9	S	Y		Guam		None
42		32	38	Mata, Joaquin M	Son	M	Cha	7	S	Y		Guam		None
43		32	38	Mata, Juan M	Son	M	Cha	6	S	N		Guam		None
44		32	38	Mata, Francisco M	Son	M	Cha	4.4	S	N		Guam		None
45		32	38	Mata, Rosa M	Daughter	F	Cha	2.7	S	N		Guam		None
46		33	39	Acfalle, Emiterio C	Head	M	Cha	32	S	N	Y	Guam	Y	Farmer
47		33	39	Acfalle, Ana C	Sister	F	Cha	24	S	N	Y	Guam	Y	None
48		34	40	Naputi, Juan A	Head	M	Cha	27	M	N	Y	Guam	Y	Farmer
49		34	40	Naputi, Maria N	Wife	F	Cha	23	M	N	Y	Guam	Y	None
50		34	40	Naputi, Lorenzo N	Son	M	Cha	2.1	S	N		Guam		None

DEPARTMENT OF COMMERCE-BUREAU OF THE CENSUS
WASHINGTON

FIFTEENTH CENSUS OF THE UNITED STATES: 1930-POPULATION

THE ISLAND OF GUAM

Sheet No. 5A

District **Municipality of Merizo**
Name of Place **Merizo Town**
[Proper name and, also, name of class, as city, town, village, barrio, etc]

Enumeration District No. **9**
Enumerated by me on **April 4, 1930** Manuel Charfauros, Enumerator

	PLACE OF ABODE: Street, avenue, road, etc.	Number of dwelling house in order of visitation	Number of family in order of visitation	NAME of each person whose place of abode on April 1, 1930, was in this family. Enter surname, first, then given name and middle initial. If any. Include every person living on April 1, 1930. Omit children born since April 1, 1930.	RELATION Relationship of this Person to the head of the family.	PERSONAL DESCRIPTION: Sex	Color or race	Age at last birthday	Single, married, widowed or divorced	EDUCATION: Attended school any time since Sept. 1, 1929	Whether able to read and write.	NATIVITY Place of birth of this person.	Whether able to speak English.	OCCUPATION
	1	2	3	4	5	6	7	8	9	10	11	12	13	14
1	Rosario Street	35	41	Cruz, Juan C	Head	M	Cha	41	M	N	Y	Guam	N	Farmer
2		35	41	Cruz, Maria A	Wife	F	Cha	47	M	N	Y	Guam	N	None
3		35	41	Cruz, Maria A	Daughter	F	Cha	16	S	N	Y	Guam	Y	None
4		35	41	Cruz, Dolores A	Daughter	F	Cha	14	S	Y	Y	Guam	Y	None
5		35	41	Cruz, Jesus A	Son	M	Cha	13	S	Y	Y	Guam	Y	None
6		35	41	Cruz, Catalina A	Daughter	F	Cha	9	S	Y		Guam		None
7		35	41	Cruz, Delfina A	Daughter	F	Cha	7	S	Y		Guam		None
8		35	41	Cruz, Juan A	Son	M	Cha	2.1	S	N		Guam		None
9		36	42	Cruz, Encarnacion C	Head	F	Cha	44	S	N	Y	Guam	N	Laundress
10		36	43	Cruz, Joaquin G	Head	M	Cha	31	M	N	Y	Guam	Y	Laborer
11		36	43	Cruz, Maria B	Wife	F	Cha	26	M	N	Y	Guam	Y	None
12		37	44	Castro, Ramon O	Head	M	Cha	41	M	N	Y	Guam	N	Farmer
13		37	44	Castro, Ana C	Wife	F	Cha	34	M	N	Y	Guam	N	None
14		37	44	Castro, Florentina C	Daughter	F	Cha	15	S	N	Y	Guam	Y	None
15		37	44	Castro, Josefa C	Daughter	F	Cha	13	S	Y	Y	Guam	Y	None
16		37	44	Castro, Jose C	Son	M	Cha	10	S	Y	Y	Guam	Y	None
17		37	44	Castro, Jesus C	Son	M	Cha	6	S	Y		Guam		None
18		37	44	Castro, David C	Son	M	Cha	4.4	S	N		Guam		None
19		37	44	Castro, Vicente C	Son	M	Cha	2.1	S	N		Guam		None
20		37	44	Castro, Maria C	Daughter	F	Cha	.1	S	N		Guam		None
21		38	45	Borja, Juan C	Head	M	Cha	26	M	N	Y	Guam	Y	Farmer
22		38	45	Borja, Antonia G	Wife	F	Cha	25	M	N	Y	Guam	Y	None
23		38	45	Borja, Vicente C	Brother	M	Cha	14	S	Y	Y	Guam	Y	None
24		39	46	Torres, Maria P	Head	F	Cha	51	Wd	N	Y	Guam	N	Retail merchant
25		39	46	Perez, Jose T	Brother	M	Cha	54	Wd	N	Y	Guam	N	Salesman

(CHAMORRO ROOTS GENEALOGY PROJECT™ TRANSCRIPTION)
(BERNARD T. PUNZALAN / HTTP://WWW.CHAMORROROOTS.COM)

DEPARTMENT OF COMMERCE-BUREAU OF THE CENSUS
WASHINGTON

FIFTEENTH CENSUS OF THE UNITED STATES: 1930-POPULATION

THE ISLAND OF GUAM

Sheet No. 5B

274B

District **Municipality of Merizo**
Name of Place **Merizo Town**
[Proper name and, also, name of class, as city, town, village, barrio, etc]

Enumeration District No. 9
Enumerated by me on **April 4, 1930** Manuel Charfauros
Enumerator

	PLACE OF ABODE			NAME	RELATION	PERSONAL DESCRIPTION				EDUCATION		NATIVITY		OCCUPATION
	Street, avenue, road, etc.	Number of dwelling house is order of visitation	Number of family in order of visitation	of each person whose place of abode on April 1, 1930, was in this family. Enter surname, first, then given name and middle initial. If any. Include every person living on April 1, 1930. Omit children born since April 1, 1930.	Relationship of this Person to the head of the family.	Sex	Color or race	Age at last birthday	Single, married, widowed or divorced	Attended school any time since Sept. 1, 1929	Whether able to read and write.	Place of birth of this person.	Whether able to speak English.	
	1	2	3	4	5	6	7	8	9	10	11	12	13	14
26	Rosario Street	39	46	Perez, Victoria T	Niece	F	Cha	5	S	N		Guam		None
27		39	46	Quinene, Ana F	Servant	F	Cha	19	S	N	Y	Guam	Y	Servant
28		40	47	Cruz, Vicente G	Head	M	Cha	40	M	N	Y	Guam	N	Farmer
29		40	47	Cruz, Dolores G	Wife	F	Cha	35	M	N	Y	Guam	N	None
30		40	47	Gogue, Carmen G	Step daughter	F	Cha	14	S	N	Y	Guam	Y	None
31		40	47	Gogue, Joaquina G	Step daughter	F	Cha	12	S	Y	Y	Guam	Y	None
32		40	47	Gogue, Maria	Step daughter	F	Cha	10	S	Y	Y	Guam	Y	None
33		40	47	Gogue, Isabel	Step daughter	F	Cha	10	S	Y	Y	Guam	Y	None
34		40	47	Gogue, Joaquin G	Step son	M	Cha	8	S	Y		Guam		None
35		40	47	Cruz, Vicente G	Son	M	Cha	5	S	N		Guam		None
36		40	47	Cruz, Josefa G	Daughter	F	Cha	3.2	S	N		Guam		None
37		40	47	Cruz, Julia G	Daughter	F	Cha	.5	S	N		Guam		None
38		41	48	Barcinas, Jesus C	Head	M	Cha	21	M	N	Y	Guam	Y	School teacher
39		41	48	Barcinas, Gertrudes T	Wife	F	Cha	22	M	N	Y	Guam	Y	School teacher
40		41	48	Cruz, Vicenta C	Servant	F	Cha	12	S	Y	Y	Guam	Y	Servant
41		42	49	Garrido, Juan R	Head	M	Cha	30	M	N	Y	Guam	Y	Farmer
42		42	49	Garrido, Ana T	Wife	F	Cha	26	M	N	Y	Guam	Y	None
43		42	49	Garrido, Soledad T	Daughter	F	Cha	8	S	Y		Guam		None
44		42	49	Garrido, Maria T	Daughter	F	Cha	7	S	Y		Guam		None
45		42	49	Garrido, Maxinimo T	Son	M	Cha	4.8	S	N		Guam		None
46		42	49	Garrido, Guadalupe T	Daughter	F	Cha	2.1	S	N		Guam		None
47		42	49	Garrido, Jose T	Son	M	Cha	.1	S	N		Guam		None
48		42	49	Garrido, Maria R	Mother	F	Cha	61	Wd	N	N	Guam	N	None
49		43	50	Cruz, Jose P	Head	M	Cha	49	M	N	Y	Guam	N	Farmer
50		43	50	Cruz, Maria C	Wife	F	Cha	45	M	N	Y	Guam	N	None

DEPARTMENT OF COMMERCE-BUREAU OF THE CENSUS
WASHINGTON

FIFTEENTH CENSUS OF THE UNITED STATES: 1930-POPULATION

THE ISLAND OF GUAM

Sheet No. 6A

District **Municipality of Merizo**
Name of Place **Merizo Town**
[Proper name and, also, name of class, as city, town, village, barrio, etc]

Enumeration District No. 9
Enumerated by me on **April 4, 1930** Manuel Charfauros, Enumerator

	PLACE OF ABODE			NAME	RELATION	PERSONAL DESCRIPTION				EDUCATION		NATIVITY		OCCUPATION
	Street, avenue, road, etc.	Number of dwelling house in order of visitation	Number of family in order of visitation	of each person whose place of abode on April 1, 1930, was in this family. Enter surname, first, then given name and middle initial. If any. Include every person living on April 1, 1930. Omit children born since April 1, 1930.	Relationship of this Person to the head of the family.	Sex	Color or race	Age at last birthday	Single, married, widowed or divorced	Attended school any time since Sept. 1, 1929	Whether able to read and write.	Place of birth of this person.	Whether able to speak English.	
	1	2	3	4	5	6	7	8	9	10	11	12	13	14
1	Rosario Street	43	50	Cruz, Maria C	Daughter	F	Cha	22	S	N	Y	Guam	N	None
2		43	50	Cruz, Isabel C	Daughter	F	Cha	16	S	N	Y	Guam	Y	None
3		43	50	Cruz, Jesus C	Son	M	Cha	13	S	Y	Y	Guam	Y	None
4		43	50	Cruz, Josefa C	Daughter	F	Cha	11	S	Y	Y	Guam	N	None
5		43	50	Cruz, Jose C	Son	M	Cha	9	S	Y		Guam		None
6		43	50	Cruz, Ana C	Daughter	F	Cha	6	S	Y		Guam		None
7		44	51	Manalisay, Juan C	Head	M	Cha	29	M	N	Y	Guam	Y	Laborer (road)
8		44	51	Manalisay, Carmen C	Wife	F	Cha	28	M	N	Y	Guam	N	None
9		44	51	Manalisay, Jesus C	Son	M	Cha	8	S	Y		Guam		None
10		44	51	Manalisay, Jose C	Son	M	Cha	7	S	Y		Guam		None
11		44	51	Manalisay, Maria C	Daughter	F	Cha	5	S	N		Guam		None
12		44	51	Manalisay, Joaquin C	Son	M	Cha	3.2	S	N		Guam		None
13		44	51	Manalisay, Manuel C	Son	M	Cha	2.9	S	N		Guam		None
14		44	51	Manalisay, Ana C	Daughter	F	Cha	1.2	S	N		Guam		None
15		44	51	Espinosa, Ignacia C	Mother-in-law	F	Cha	55	Wd	N	N	Guam	N	None
16		45	52	Lujan, Juan E	Head	M	Cha	30	M	N	Y	Guam	Y	Commissioner
17		45	52	Lujan, Rosa T	Wife	F	Cha	23	M	N	Y	Guam	Y	None
18		45	52	Tajalle, Rita T	Sister-in-law	F	Cha	15	S	N	Y	Guam	Y	None
19		45	52	Topasna, Jesus T	Nephew-in-law	M	Cha	1.2	S	N		Guam		None
20		45	52	Taijeron, Francisco T	Servant	M	Cha	12	S	Y	Y	Guam	Y	Servant
21		46	53	Cruz, Tomas E	Head	M	Cha	46	M	N	Y	Guam	N	Farmer
22		46	53	Cruz, Margarita A	Wife	F	Cha	33	M	N	Y	Guam	N	None
23		46	53	Cruz, Jesus A	Son	M	Cha	16	S	Y	Y	Guam	Y	None
24		46	53	Cruz, Maria A	Daughter	F	Cha	14	S	N	Y	Guam	Y	None
25		46	53	Cruz, Tomas A	Son	M	Cha	12	S	Y	Y	Guam	Y	None

DEPARTMENT OF COMMERCE-BUREAU OF THE CENSUS
WASHINGTON

FIFTEENTH CENSUS OF THE UNITED STATES: 1930-POPULATION

THE ISLAND OF GUAM

Sheet No. 6B

275B

District Municipality of Merizo
Name of Place Merizo Town
[Proper name and, also, name of class, as city, town, village, barrio, etc]

Enumeration District No. 9
Enumerated by me on April 5, 1930 Manuel Charfauros
Enumerator

	PLACE OF ABODE			NAME	RELATION	PERSONAL DESCRIPTION				EDUCATION		NATIVITY		OCCUPATION
	Street, avenue, road, etc.	Number of dwelling house is order of visitation	Number of family in order of visitation	of each person whose place of abode on April 1, 1930, was in this family. Enter surname, first, then given name and middle initial. If any. Include every person living on April 1, 1930. Omit children born since April 1, 1930.	Relationship of this Person to the head of the family.	Sex	Color or race	Age at last birthday	Single, married, widowed or divorced	Attended school any time since Sept. 1, 1929	Whether able to read and write.	Place of birth of this person.	Whether able to speak English.	
	1	2	3	4	5	6	7	8	9	10	11	12	13	14
26	Rosario Street	46	53	Cruz, Ana A	Daughter	F	Cha	11	S	Y	Y	Guam	Y	None
27		46	53	Cruz, Joaquin A	Son	M	Cha	8	S	Y		Guam		None
28		46	53	Cruz, Isabel A	Daughter	F	Cha	6	S	Y		Guam		None
29		46	53	Cruz, Agnes A	Daughter	F	Cha	4.8	S	N		Guam		None
30		46	53	Cruz, Dimas A	Son	M	Cha	2.9	S	N		Guam		None
31		46	53	Cruz, Jose A	Son	M	Cha	1	S	N		Guam		None
32		47	54	Lujan, Manuela E	Head	M	Cha	63	Wd	N	Y	Guam	N	None
33		47	54	Cruz, Francisca E	Daughter	F	Cha	48	S	N	Y	Guam	N	Laundress
34		47	54	Barcinas, Gabriel C	Grandson	M	Cha	14	S	Y	Y	Guam	Y	None
35		48	55	Tedpaogo, Eugenio G	Head	M	Cha	34	M	N	Y	Guam	Y	Farmer
36		48	55	Tedpaogo, Felicita C	Wife	F	Cha	28	M	N	Y	Guam	Y	None
37		48	55	Tedpaogo, Joaquin C	Son	M	Cha	10	S	Y	Y	Guam	Y	None
38		48	55	Tedpaogo, Ana C	Daughter	F	Cha	8	S	Y		Guam		None
39		48	55	Tedpaogo, Vicenta C	Daughter	F	Cha	6	S	N		Guam		None
40		48	55	Tedpaogo, Jesus C	Daughter	F	Cha	3	S	N		Guam		None
41		48	55	Tedpaogo, Jose C	Son	M	Cha	1.8	S	N		Guam		None
42		49	56	De Leon, Jose P	Head	M	Cha	34	M	N	Y	Guam	Y	Farmer
43		49	56	De Leon, Francisca T	Wife	F	Cha	23	M	N	Y	Guam	Y	None
44		50	57	Borja, Juan W	Head	M	Cha	53	M	N	Y	Guam	N	Farmer
45		50	57	Borja, Dolores C	Wife	F	Cha	47	M	N	Y	Guam	N	None
46		51	58	Lujan, Dometrio E	Head	M	Cha	39	M	N	Y	Guam	Y	Farmer
47		51	58	Lujan, Maria C	Wife	F	Cha	34	M	N	Y	Guam	N	None
48		51	58	Lujan, Juan C	Son	M	Cha	15	S	N	Y	Guam	Y	Farm laborer
49		51	58	Lujan, Jose C	Son	M	Cha	12	S	Y	Y	Guam	Y	None
50		51	58	Lujan, Rita C	Daughter	F	Cha	10	S	Y	Y	Guam	Y	None

DEPARTMENT OF COMMERCE-BUREAU OF THE CENSUS
WASHINGTON

FIFTEENTH CENSUS OF THE UNITED STATES: 1930-POPULATION

THE ISLAND OF GUAM

Sheet No. 7A

District **Municipality of Merizo**
Name of Place **Merizo Town**
[Proper name and, also, name of class, as city, town, village, barrio, etc]

Enumeration District No. 9
Enumerated by me on **April 5, 1930** Manuel Charfauros, Enumerator

	PLACE OF ABODE			NAME	RELATION	PERSONAL DESCRIPTION				EDUCATION		NATIVITY		OCCUPATION
	Street, avenue, road, etc.	Number of dwelling house in order of visitation	Number of family in order of visitation	of each person whose place of abode on April 1, 1930, was in this family. Enter surname, first, then given name and middle initial. If any. Include every person living on April 1, 1930. Omit children born since April 1, 1930.	Relationship of this Person to the head of the family.	Sex	Color or race	Age at last birthday	Single, married, widowed or divorced	Attended school any time since Sept. 1, 1929	Whether able to read and write.	Place of birth of this person.	Whether able to speak English.	
	1	2	3	4	5	6	7	8	9	10	11	12	13	14
1	Rosario Street	51	58	Concepcion, Ramon R	Brother-in-law	M	Cha	15	S	Y	Y	Guam	Y	None
2		52	59	Barcinas, Pedro B	Head	M	Cha	62	S	N	N	Guam	N	Farmer
3		52	59	Santos, Antonia B	Sister	F	Cha	58	S	N	N	Guam	N	None
4		53	60	Quidagua, Ignacio T	Head	M	Cha	50	Wd	N	Y	Guam	N	Farmer
5		53	60	Quidagua, Maria	Daughter	F	Cha	23	S	N	Y	Guam	Y	None
6		53	60	Chargualaf, Antonia Q	Sister	F	Cha	62	Wd	N	N	Guam	N	None
7		54	61	Maguadog, Moises N	Head	M	Cha	45	M	N	Y	Guam	N	Farmer
8		54	61	Maguadog, Antonia C	Wife	F	Cha	44	M	N	Y	Guam	N	None
9		55	62	Manalisay, Isidro C	Head	M	Cha	20	M	N	Y	Guam	Y	Laborer (road)
10		55	62	Manalisay, Maria B	Wife	F	Cha	22	M	N	Y	Guam	Y	None
11		55	63	Manalisay, Nieves C	Head	F	Cha	45	S	N	Y	Guam	N	Midwife
12		55	63	Manalisay, Socorro C	Daughter	F	Cha	10	S	Y	Y	Guam	Y	None
13		55	63	Manalisay, Carmen C	Sister	F	Cha	57	S	N	Y	Guam	N	None
14		55	63	Manalisay, Beatriz T	Grand niece	F	Cha	11	S	Y	Y	Guam	Y	None
15		55	63	Champaco, Maria C	Servant	F	Cha	12	S	Y	Y	Guam	Y	Servant
16		56	64	Quinene, Pedro G	Head	M	Cha	59	M	N	Y	Guam	N	Farmer
17		56	64	Quinene, Ana R	Wife	F	Cha	44	M	N	Y	Guam	N	None
18		56	64	Quinene, Silvestre R	Son	M	Cha	20	S	N	Y	Guam	Y	Farm laborer
19		56	64	Quinene, Vicente R	Son	M	Cha	14	S	N	Y	Guam	Y	Farm laborer
20		56	64	Quinene, Jesus R	Son	M	Cha	11	S	Y	Y	Guam	Y	None
21		56	64	Quinene, Jose R	Son	M	Cha	6	S	N		Guam		None
22		57	65	Acfalle, Felipe C	Head	M	Cha	40	M	N	Y	Guam	N	Farmer
23		57	65	Acfalle, Antonia R	Wife	F	Cha	52	M	N	Y	Guam	N	None
24		57	65	Acfalle, Tomasa R	Daughter	F	Cha	14	S	N	Y	Guam	Y	None
25		58	66	Chargualaf, Mariano B	Head	M	Cha	35	M		Y	Guam		Farmer

DEPARTMENT OF COMMERCE-BUREAU OF THE CENSUS
WASHINGTON

FIFTEENTH CENSUS OF THE UNITED STATES: 1930-POPULATION

THE ISLAND OF GUAM

Sheet No. 7B

276B

District **Municipality of Merizo**
Name of Place **Merizo Town**
[Proper name and, also, name of class, as city, town, village, barrio, etc]

Enumeration District No. **9**
Enumerated by me on **April 5, 1930** Manuel Charfauros
Enumerator

	PLACE OF ABODE			NAME	RELATION	PERSONAL DESCRIPTION				EDUCATION		NATIVITY		OCCUPATION
	Street, avenue, road, etc.	Number of dwelling house is order of visitation	Number of family in order of visitation	of each person whose place of abode on April 1, 1930, was in this family. Enter surname, first, then given name and middle initial. If any. Include every person living on April 1, 1930. Omit children born since April 1, 1930.	Relationship of this Person to the head of the family.	Sex	Color or race	Age at last birthday	Single, married, widowed or divorced	Attended school any time since Sept. 1, 1929	Whether able to read and write.	Place of birth of this person.	Whether able to speak English.	
	1	2	3	4	5	6	7	8	9	10	11	12	13	14
26	Rosario Street	58	66	Chargualaf, Maria C	Wife	F	Cha	37	M	N	Y	Guam	N	None
27		58	66	Chargualaf, Francisco C	Son	M	Cha	5	S	N		Guam		None
28		58	66	Chargualaf, Alice C	Daughter	F	Cha	4.1	S	N		Guam		None
29		58	66	Chargualaf, Jesusa C	Daughter	F	Cha	2.1	S	N		Guam		None
30		58	66	Chargualaf, Vicente C	Son	M	Cha	.3	S	N		Guam		None
31		59	67	Leon Guerrero, Pedro R	Head	M	Cha	46	M	N	Y	Guam	N	Farmer
32		59	67	Leon Guerrero, Estefania G	Wife	F	Cha	40	M	N	Y	Guam	N	None
33		59	67	Leon Guerrero, Maximino G	Son	M	Cha	19	S	N	Y	Guam	Y	Laborer (road)
34		59	67	Leon Guerrero, Jose G	Son	M	Cha	18	S	N	Y	Guam	Y	Farm laborer
35		59	67	Leon Guerrero, Carmen G	Daughter	F	Cha	15	S	N	Y	Guam	Y	None
36		59	67	Leon Guerrero, Jesus G	Son	M	Cha	13	S	Y	Y	Guam	Y	None
37		59	67	Leon Guerrero, Vicente G	Son	M	Cha	11	S	Y	Y	Guam	Y	None
38		59	67	Leon Guerrero, Maria G	Daughter	F	Cha	7	S	N		Guam		None
39		59	67	Leon Guerrero, Ignacio G	Son	M	Cha	.6	S	N		Guam		None
40		60	68	Reyes, Jose A	Head	M	Cha	54	M	N	N	Guam	N	Farmer
41		60	68	Reyes, Isabel S	Wife	F	Cha	47	M	N	N	Guam	N	None
42		60	68	Reyes, Maria S	Daughter	F	Cha	21	S	N	Y	Guam	Y	Laundress
43		60	68	Reyes, Rosa S	Daughter	F	Cha	20	S	N	Y	Guam	Y	None
44		60	68	Suriano, Jose S	Step-son	M	Cha	10	S	Y	Y	Guam	Y	None
45		60	68	Reyes, Rita S	Daughter	F	Cha	8	S	Y		Guam		None
46		60	68	Reyes, Ramon A	Brother	M	Cha	58	S	N	Y	Guam	N	Farm laborer
47		61	69	Quinene, Cerilo F	Head	M	Cha	41	M	N	Y	Guam	N	Farmer
48		61	69	Quinene, Ana A	Wife	F	Cha	38	M	N	N	Guam	N	None
49		61	69	Chargualaf, Maria A	Niece	F	Cha	9	S	Y		Guam		None
50		61	69	Ada, Nicolas B	Father-in-law	M	Cha	76	Wd	N	N	Guam	N	None

DEPARTMENT OF COMMERCE-BUREAU OF THE CENSUS
WASHINGTON

FIFTEENTH CENSUS OF THE UNITED STATES: 1930-POPULATION

THE ISLAND OF GUAM

Sheet No. 8A

District **Municipality of Merizo**
Name of Place **Merizo Town**
[Proper name and, also, name of class, as city, town, village, barrio, etc]

Enumeration District No. **9**
Enumerated by me on **April 5, 1930** Manuel Charfauros
Enumerator

	PLACE OF ABODE			NAME	RELATION	PERSONAL DESCRIPTION				EDUCATION		NATIVITY		OCCUPATION
	Street, avenue, road, etc.	Number of dwelling house in order of visitation	Number of family in order of visitation	of each person whose place of abode on April 1, 1930, was in this family. Enter surname, first, then given name and middle initial. If any. Include every person living on April 1, 1930. Omit children born since April 1, 1930.	Relationship of this Person to the head of the family.	Sex	Color or race	Age at last birthday	Single, married, widowed or divorced	Attended school any time since Sept. 1, 1929	Whether able to read and write.	Place of birth of this person.	Whether able to speak English.	
	1	2	3	4	5	6	7	8	9	10	11	12	13	14
1	Rosario Street	62	70	Reyes, Ignacio A	Head	M	Cha	56	M	N	Y	Guam	N	Farmer
2		62	70	Reyes, Rosa M	Wife	F	Cha	42	M	N	Y	Guam	N	Retail merchant
3		62	70	Reyes, Josefina M	Daughter	F	Cha	15	S	Y	Y	Guam	Y	None
4		62	70	Reyes, Nicolas M	Son	M	Cha	11	S	Y	Y	Guam	Y	None
5		62	70	Reyes, Jose M	Son	M	Cha	9	S	Y		Guam		None
6		62	70	Reyes, Ignacio M	Son	M	Cha	6	S	N		Guam		None
7		62	70	Nangauta, Soledad N	Servant	F	Cha	15	S	N	N	Guam	N	None
8		62	70	Taijeron, Vicente C	Servant	M	Cha	9	S	Y		Guam		None
9		63	71	Tedpaogo, Juan C	Head	M	Cha	32	M	N	Y	Guam	Y	Laborer (road)
10		63	71	Tedpaogo, Dolores C	Wife	F	Cha	23	M	N	Y	Guam	Y	None
11		63	71	Tedpaogo, Mariano C	Son	M	Cha	6	S	N		Guam		None
12		63	71	Tedpaogo, Julia C	Daughter	F	Cha	2.2	S	N		Guam		None
13		63	71	Tedpaogo, Vicente C	Son	M	Cha	1	S	N		Guam		None
14		64	72	Concepcion, Jose R	Head	M	Cha	29	M	N	Y	Guam	Y	Farmer
15		64	72	Concepcion, Carmen B	Wife	F	Cha	34	M	N	Y	Guam	N	None
16		64	72	Concepcion, Rosa B	Daughter	F	Cha	9	S	Y		Guam		None
17		64	72	Concepcion, Maria B	Daughter	F	Cha	7	S	Y		Guam		None
18		64	72	Concepcion, Tomas B	Son	M	Cha	5	S	N		Guam		None
19		64	72	Barcinas, Tomas G	Father-in-law	M	Cha	75	Wd	N	N	Guam	N	None
20		64	72	Naputi, Jose A	Lodger	M	Cha	24	S	N	Y	Guam	Y	Farm laborer
21		65	73	Manalisay, Julian C	Head	M	Cha	38	M	N	Y	Guam	Y	Carpenter
22		65	73	Manalisay, Maria SN	Wife	F	Cha	49	M	N	N	Guam	M	None
23		65	73	Tainatongo, Catlina SN	Step-daughter	F	Cha	13	S	Y	Y	Guam	M	None
24		65	73	Tainatongo, Josefa SN	Step-daughter	F	Cha	11	S	Y	Y	Guam	Y	None
25		65	74	Tainatongo, Ignacio SN	Head	M	Cha	25	M	N		Guam	Y	Farmer

(CHAMORRO ROOTS GENEALOGY PROJECT™ TRANSCRIPTION)
(BERNARD T. PUNZALAN / HTTP://WWW.CHAMORROROOTS.COM)

DEPARTMENT OF COMMERCE-BUREAU OF THE CENSUS
WASHINGTON

FIFTEENTH CENSUS OF THE UNITED STATES: 1930-POPULATION

THE ISLAND OF GUAM

Sheet No. 8B

277B

District Municipality of Merizo
Name of Place Merizo Town
[Proper name and, also, name of class, as city, town, village, barrio, etc]

Enumeration District No. 9
Enumerated by me on April 7, 1930 Manuel Charfauros, Enumerator

	PLACE OF ABODE: Street, avenue, road, etc.	Number of dwelling house in order of visitation	Number of family in order of visitation	NAME of each person whose place of abode on April 1, 1930, was in this family. Enter surname, first, then given name and middle initial. If any. Include every person living on April 1, 1930. Omit children born since April 1, 1930.	RELATION Relationship of this Person to the head of the family.	PERSONAL DESCRIPTION: Sex	Color or race	Age at last birthday	Single, married, widowed or divorced	EDUCATION: Attended school any time since Sept. 1, 1929	Whether able to read and write.	NATIVITY Place of birth of this person.	Whether able to speak English.	OCCUPATION
	1	2	3	4	5	6	7	8	9	10	11	12	13	14
26	Rosario Street	65	74	Tainatongo, Concepcion T	Wife	F	Cha	28	M	N	Y	Guam	Y	None
27		65	74	Tainatongo, Vicente T	Son	M	Cha	2.3	S	N		Guam		None
28		65	74	Tainatongo, Jesus T	Son	M	Cha	.8	S	N		Guam		None
29		65	75	Tainatongo, Greorio SN	Head	M	Cha	21	M	N	Y	Guam	Y	Farmer
30		65	75	Tainatongo, Dolores B	Wife	F	Cha	19	M	N	Y	Guam	N	None
31		65	75	Borja, Rosa C	Sister-in-law	F	Cha	16	S	N	Y	Guam	Y	None
32		66	76	Meno, Teodora C	Head	F	Cha	41	S	N	N	Guam	N	None
33		66	76	Meno, Antonio M	Son	M	Cha	14	S	N	Y	Guam	Y	Farm laborer
34		66	76	Meno, Antonia M	Daughter	F	Cha	8	S	Y		Guam		None
35		66	76	Meno, Geronimo M	Son	M	Cha	3.9	S	N		Guam		None
36		67	77	Reyes, Joaquin A	Head	M	Cha	66	M	N	N	Guam	N	Farmer
37		67	77	Reyes, Cecilia M	Wife	F	Cha	60	M	N	N	Guam	N	None
38		67	77	Reyes, Juan M	Grandson	M	Cha	22	S	N	Y	Guam	Y	Farm laborer
39		67	77	Reyes, Ignacio C	Grandson	M	Cha	12	S	Y	Y	Guam	Y	None
40		68	78	Chargualaf, Juan B	Head	M	Cha	56	M	N	Y	Guam	N	Farmer
41		68	78	Chargualaf, Manuela A	Wife	F	Cha	58	M	N	Y	Guam	N	None
42		68	78	Meno, Cevera C	Niece	F	Cha	21	S	N	Y	Guam	Y	None
43		69	79	Tedpaogo, Ignacio E	Head	M	Cha	27	M	N	Y	Guam	N	Farmer
44		69	79	Tedpaogo, Gabriela A	Wife	F	Cha	37	M	N	Y	Guam	N	None
45		69	79	Acfalle, Carmelo M	Brother-in-law	M	Cha	38	S	N	Y	Guam	N	Farmer
46		70	80	Chargualaf, Crecencio M	Head	M	Cha	37	M	N	Y	Guam	N	Farmer
47		70	80	Chargualaf, Rosalia A	Wife	F	Cha	34	M	N	Y	Guam	N	None
48		70	80	Chargualaf, Ana A	Daughter	F	Cha	15	S	N	Y	Guam	Y	Industrial teacher
49		70	80	Chargualaf, Nicolas A	Son	M	Cha	14	S	Y	Y	Guam	Y	None
50		70	80	Chargualaf, Rosa A	Daughter	F	Cha	8	S	Y		Guam		None

(CHAMORRO ROOTS GENEALOGY PROJECT™ TRANSCRIPTION)
(BERNARD T. PUNZALAN / HTTP://WWW.CHAMORROROOTS.COM)

DEPARTMENT OF COMMERCE-BUREAU OF THE CENSUS
WASHINGTON

FIFTEENTH CENSUS OF THE UNITED STATES: 1930-POPULATION

THE ISLAND OF GUAM

Sheet No. 9A

278

District Municipality of Merizo
Name of Place Merizo Town
[Proper name and, also, name of class, as city, town, village, barrio, etc]

Enumeration District No. 9
Enumerated by me on April 7, 1930 Manuel Charfauros, Enumerator

	PLACE OF ABODE			NAME	RELATION	PERSONAL DESCRIPTION				EDUCATION		NATIVITY		OCCUPATION
	Street, avenue, road, etc.	Number of dwelling house is order of visitation	Number of family in order of visitation	of each person whose place of abode on April 1, 1930, was in this family. Enter surname, first, then given name and middle initial. If any. Include every person living on April 1, 1930. Omit children born since April 1, 1930.	Relationship of this Person to the head of the family.	Sex	Color or race	Age at last birthday	Single, married, widowed or divorced	Attended school any time since Sept. 1, 1929	Whether able to read and write.	Place of birth of this person.	Whether able to speak English.	
	1	2	3	4	5	6	7	8	9	10	11	12	13	14
1	Rosario Street	70	80	Chargualaf, Vicente A	Son	M	Cha	6	S	N		Guam		None
2		70	80	Chargualaf, Lorenza A	Daughter	F	Cha	4.1	S	N		Guam		None
3		70	80	Chargualaf, Eliza A	Daughter	F	Cha	1.2	S	N		Guam		None
4		71	81	Suriano, Rosa M	Head	F	Cha	68	Wd	N	Y	Guam	N	None
5		71	81	Suriano, Joaquin M	Son	M	Cha	42	S	N	N	Guam	N	Farmer
6		71	81	Taijeron, Mariano G	Lodger	M	Cha	43	S	N	N	Guam	N	Farmer
7		71	82	Taijeron, Mariano B	Head	M	Cha	44	M	N	Y	Guam	N	None
8		71	82	Taijeron, Candelaria S	Wife	F	Cha	43	M	N	N	Guam	N	Farm laborer
9		71	82	Suriano, Juan M	Step Son	M	Cha	18	S	N	Y	Guam	N	Farm laborer
10		71	82	Taijeron, Antonio S	Step Son	M	Cha	17	S	N	Y	Guam	Y	None
11		71	82	Suriano, Vicente S	Step Son	M	Cha	15	S	Y	Y	Guam	Y	None
12		71	82	Suriano, Patricio S	Step Son	M	Cha	15	S	Y	Y	Guam	Y	None
13		71	82	Suriano, Geronmo S	Step Son	M	Cha	13	S	Y	Y	Guam	Y	None
14		71	82	Suriano, Carmen S	Step daughter	F	Cha	10	S	Y	Y	Guam	Y	None
15		71	82	Suriano, Lucia M	Step daughter	F	Cha	8	S	Y		Guam		None
16		72	83	Suriano, Ignacio M	Head	M	Cha	21	M	N	Y	Guam	Y	Farmer
17		72	83	Suriano, Dolores A	Wife	F	Cha	16	M	N	Y	Guam	Y	None
18		73	84	Candaso, Vicente T	Head	M	Cha	40	S	N	Y	Guam	Y	Farmer
19		73	84	Candaso, Jesus T	Brother	M	Cha	36	S	N	Y	Guam	N	Farmer
20		73	84	Candaso, Consolacion T	Sister	F	Cha	34	S	N	Y	Guam	N	Laundress
21		74	85	Lujan, Joaquin E	Head	M	Cha	28	M	N	Y	Guam	Y	Farmer
22		74	85	Lujan, Antonia C	Wife	F	Cha	29	M	N	Y	Guam	Y	None
23		74	85	Lujan, Jose C	Son	M	Cha	7	S	Y		Guam		None
24		74	85	Lujan, Dolores C	Daughter	F	Cha	6	S	N		Guam		None
25		74	85	Lujan, Laura C	Daughter	F	Cha	3.4	S	N		Guam		None

DEPARTMENT OF COMMERCE-BUREAU OF THE CENSUS
WASHINGTON

FIFTEENTH CENSUS OF THE UNITED STATES: 1930-POPULATION

THE ISLAND OF GUAM

Sheet No. 9B

278B

District **Municipality of Merizo**
Name of Place **Merizo Town**
[Proper name and, also, name of class, as city, town, village, barrio, etc]

Enumeration District No. 9
Enumerated by me on **April 7, 1930** Manuel Charfauros
Enumerator

	PLACE OF ABODE			NAME	RELATION	PERSONAL DESCRIPTION				EDUCATION		NATIVITY		OCCUPATION
	Street, avenue, road, etc.	Number of dwelling house in order of visitation	Number of family in order of visitation	of each person whose place of abode on April 1, 1930, was in this family. Enter surname, first, then given name and middle initial. If any. Include every person living on April 1, 1930. Omit children born since April 1, 1930.	Relationship of this Person to the head of the family.	Sex	Color or race	Age at last birthday	Single, married, widowed or divorced	Attended school any time since Sept. 1, 1929	Whether able to read and write.	Place of birth of this person.	Whether able to speak English.	
	1	2	3	4	5	6	7	8	9	10	11	12	13	14
26	Rosario Street	74	85	Lujan, Francisco C	Son	M	Cha	2.7	S	N		Guam		None
27		74	85	Lujan, Antonia C	Daughter	F	Cha	1	S	N		Guam		None
28		75	86	Barcinas, Jose S	Head	M	Cha	43	M	N	Y	Guam	N	Farmer
29		75	86	Barcinas, Ana C	Wife	F	Cha	44	M	N	Y	Guam	N	None
30		75	86	Barcinas, Tomas C	Son	M	Cha	20	S	N	Y	Guam	Y	Farm laborer
31		75	86	Barcinas, Martin C	Son	M	Cha	18	S	N	Y	Guam	Y	Farm laborer
32		75	86	Barcinas, Inigo C	Son	M	Cha	13	S	Y	Y	Guam	Y	None
33		75	86	Barcinas, Joaquin C	Son	M	Cha	10	S	Y	Y	Guam	Y	None
34		76	87	Cruz, Jose P	Head	M	Cha	37	M	N	Y	Guam	Y	Farmer
35		76	87	Cruz, Florentina C	Wife	F	Cha	33	M	N	Y	Guam	N	None
36		76	87	Cruz, Dolores C	Daughter	F	Cha	14	S	Y	Y	Guam	Y	None
37		76	87	Cruz, Josefina C	Daughter	F	Cha	10	S	Y	Y	Guam	Y	None
38		76	87	Cruz, Ignacio C	Son	M	Cha	7	S	Y		Guam		None
39		76	87	Cruz, Benita C	Daughter	F	Cha	4.3	S	N		Guam		None
40		77	88	Candaso, Jose T	Head	M	Cha	41	M	N	Y	Guam	Y	Farmer
41		77	88	Candaso, Maria D	Wife	F	Cha	34	M	N	Y	Guam	N	None
42		77	88	Candaso, Jose D	Son	M	Cha	15	S	Y	Y	Guam	Y	None
43		77	88	Candaso, Brigida D	Daughter	F	Cha	12	S	Y	Y	Guam	Y	None
44		77	88	Candaso, Carmen D	Daughter	F	Cha	11	S	Y	Y	Guam	Y	None
45		77	88	Candaso, Felix D	Son	M	Cha	8	S	Y		Guam		None
46		77	88	Candaso, Rosa D	Daughter	F	Cha	7	S	Y		Guam		None
47		77	88	Candaso, Dolores D	Daughter	F	Cha	6	S	N		Guam		None
48		77	88	Candaso, Felipe D	Son	M	Cha	5	S	N		Guam		None
49		78	89	Candaso, Antonio T	Head	M	Cha	32	M	N	Y	Guam	Y	Farmer
50		78	89	Candaso, Maria D	Wife	F	Cha	20	M	N	Y	Guam	Y	None

(CHAMORRO ROOTS GENEALOGY PROJECT™ TRANSCRIPTION)
(BERNARD T. PUNZALAN / HTTP://WWW.CHAMORROROOTS.COM)

DEPARTMENT OF COMMERCE-BUREAU OF THE CENSUS
WASHINGTON

FIFTEENTH CENSUS OF THE UNITED STATES: 1930-POPULATION

THE ISLAND OF GUAM

Sheet No. 10A

District **Municipality of Merizo**
Name of Place **Merizo Town**
[Proper name and, also, name of class, as city, town, village, barrio, etc]

Enumeration District No. **9**
Enumerated by me on **April 8, 1930** Manuel Charfauros
Enumerator

	PLACE OF ABODE			NAME	RELATION	PERSONAL DESCRIPTION				EDUCATION		NATIVITY		OCCUPATION
	Street, avenue, road, etc.	Number of dwelling house in order of visitation	Number of family in order of visitation	of each person whose place of abode on April 1, 1930, was in this family. Enter surname, first, then given name and middle initial. If any. Include every person living on April 1, 1930. Omit children born since April 1, 1930.	Relationship of this Person to the head of the family.	Sex	Color or race	Age at last birthday	Single, married, widowed or divorced	Attended school any time since Sept. 1, 1929	Whether able to read and write.	Place of birth of this person.	Whether able to speak English.	
	1	2	3	4	5	6	7	8	9	10	11	12	13	14
1	Rosario Street	78	89	Candaso, Amanda D	Daughter	F	Cha	2.1	S	N		Guam		None
2		78	89	Candaso, Vicenta D	Daughter	F	Cha	0	S	N		Guam		None
3		79	90	San Nicolas, Antonio E	Head	M	Cha	44	M	N	N	Guam	N	Farmer
4		79	90	San Nicolas, Rosaria S	Wife	F	Cha	41	M	N	N	Guam	N	None
5		79	90	San Nicolas, Juan S	Son	M	Cha	20	S	N	Y	Guam	Y	Farm laborer
6		79	90	San Nicolas, Joaquina S	Daughter	F	Cha	16	S	N	Y	Guam	Y	None
7		79	90	San Nicolas, Jose S	Son	M	Cha	14	S	Y	Y	Guam	Y	None
8		79	90	San Nicolas, Pedro S	Son	M	Cha	7	S	Y		Guam		None
9		79	90	San Nicolas, Jesus S	Son	M	Cha	6	S	N		Guam		None
10		79	90	San Nicolas, Vicente S	Son	M	Cha	0	S	N		Guam		None
11		80	91	Cruz, Miguel P	Head	M	Cha	39	M	N	Y	Guam	N	Farmer
12		80	91	Cruz, Gertrudes C	Wife	F	Cha	38	M	N	Y	Guam	N	None
13		80	91	Cruz, Antonio C	Son	M	Cha	19	S	N	Y	Guam	Y	Laborer (road)
14		80	91	Cruz, Jose C	Son	M	Cha	17	S	N	Y	Guam	Y	Farm laborer
15		80	91	Cruz, Jesus C	Son	M	Cha	10	S	Y	Y	Guam	Y	None
16		80	91	Cruz, Ignacio C	Son	M	Cha	9	S	Y		Guam		None
17		80	91	Cruz, Maria C	Daughter	F	Cha	8	S	Y		Guam		None
18		80	91	Cruz, Rosa C	Daughter	F	Cha	5	S	N		Guam		None
19		80	91	Cruz, Vicenta C	Daughter	F	Cha	3.2	S	N		Guam		None
20		80	91	Cruz, Santiago C	Son	M	Cha	1.9	S	N		Guam		None
21		81	92	Cruz, Pablo C	Head	M	Cha	39	M	N	Y	Guam	N	Farmer
22		81	92	Cruz, Dolores C	Wife	F	Cha	26	M	N	Y	Guam	N	None
23		81	92	Cruz, Luis C	Son	M	Cha	11	S	Y	Y	Guam	Y	None
24		81	92	Cruz, Carmen C	Daughter	F	Cha	9	S	Y		Guam		None
25		81	92	Cruz, Vicente C	Son	M	Cha	7	S	Y		Guam		None

DEPARTMENT OF COMMERCE-BUREAU OF THE CENSUS
WASHINGTON

FIFTEENTH CENSUS OF THE UNITED STATES: 1930-POPULATION

THE ISLAND OF GUAM

Sheet No. 10B

District **Municipality of Merizo**
Name of Place **Merizo Town**
[Proper name and, also, name of class, as city, town, village, barrio, etc]

Enumeration District No. 9
Enumerated by me on **April 8, 1930** Manuel Charfauros, Enumerator

	PLACE OF ABODE			NAME	RELATION	PERSONAL DESCRIPTION				EDUCATION		NATIVITY		OCCUPATION
	Street, avenue, road, etc.	Number of dwelling house is order of visitation	Number of family in order of visitation	of each person whose place of abode on April 1, 1930, was in this family. Enter surname, first, then given name and middle initial. If any. Include every person living on April 1, 1930. Omit children born since April 1, 1930.	Relationship of this Person to the head of the family.	Sex	Color or race	Age at last birthday	Single, married, widowed or divorced	Attended school any time since Sept. 1, 1929	Whether able to read and write.	Place of birth of this person.	Whether able to speak English.	
	1	2	3	4	5	6	7	8	9	10	11	12	13	14
26	Rosario Street	81	92	Cruz, Ana C	Daughter	F	Cha	4.1	S	N		Guam		None
27		82	93	Aguon, Santiago Q	Head	M	Cha	37	M	N	Y	Guam	N	Farmer
28		82	93	Aguon, Faustina C	Wife	F	Cha	34	M	N	N	Guam	N	None
29		82	93	Aguon, Joaquina C	Daughter	F	Cha	16	S	Y	Y	Guam	Y	None
30		82	93	Aguon, Pedro C	Son	M	Cha	13	S	Y	Y	Guam	Y	None
31		82	93	Aguon, Dolores C	Daughter	F	Cha	11	S	Y	Y	Guam	Y	None
32		82	93	Aguon, Vicente C	Son	M	Cha	9	S	Y		Guam		None
33		82	93	Aguon, Rita C	Daughter	F	Cha	4.7	S	N		Guam		None
34		82	93	Aguon, Jose C	Son	M	Cha	2.7	S	N		Guam		None
35		83	94	Acfalle, Carmelo C	Head	M	Cha	64	M	N	Y	Guam	N	Farmer
36		83	94	Acfalle, Isabel C	Wife	F	Cha	62	M	N	N	Guam	N	None
37		83	94	Acfalle, Petra C	Daughter	F	Cha	41	S	N	Y	Guam	N	None
38		83	94	Acfalle, Andrea C	Daughter	F	Cha	37	S	N	Y	Guam	N	None
39		83	94	Acfalle, Blaz C	Son	M	Cha	34	S	N	Y	Guam	Y	Farm laborer
40		83	94	Acfalle, Isabel C	Daughter	F	Cha	31	S	N		Guam		None
41		83	94	Charfauros, Lucia C	Servant	F	Cha	8	S	Y		Guam		Servant
42		84	95	Torres, Jose I	Head	M	Cha	25	M	N	Y	Guam	Y	Farmer
43		84	95	Torres, Engracia M	Wife	F	Cha	23	M	N	Y	Guam	Y	None
44		84	95	Torres, Jose M	Son	M	Cha	3.2	S	N		Guam		None
45		84	95	Torres, Maria M	Daughter	F	Cha	1.7	S	N		Guam		None
46		84	95	Torres, Beatriz M	Daughter	F	Cha	.1	S	N		Guam		None
47		84	95	Torres, Asuncion I	Mother	F	Cha	51	S	N	Y	Guam	N	None
48		85	96	Suriano, Jose M	Head	M	Cha	38	M	N	Y	Guam	N	Farmer
49		85	96	Suriano, Maria Q	Wife	F	Cha	43	M	N	N	Guam	N	None
50		85	96	Suriano, Trinidad Q	Daughter	F	Cha	5	S	N		Guam		None

(CHAMORRO ROOTS GENEALOGY PROJECT™ TRANSCRIPTION)
(BERNARD T. PUNZALAN / HTTP://WWW.CHAMORROROOTS.COM)

DEPARTMENT OF COMMERCE-BUREAU OF THE CENSUS
WASHINGTON

FIFTEENTH CENSUS OF THE UNITED STATES: 1930-POPULATION

THE ISLAND OF GUAM

Sheet No. 11A

District Municipality of Merizo
Name of Place Merizo Town
[Proper name and, also, name of class, as city, town, village, barrio, etc]

Enumeration District No. 9
Enumerated by me on April 8, 1930 Manuel Charfauros, Enumerator

	PLACE OF ABODE: Street, avenue, road, etc.	Number of dwelling house in order of visitation	Number of family in order of visitation	NAME of each person whose place of abode on April 1, 1930, was in this family. Enter surname, first, then given name and middle initial, if any. Include every person living on April 1, 1930. Omit children born since April 1, 1930.	RELATION Relationship of this Person to the head of the family.	PERSONAL DESCRIPTION: Sex	Color or race	Age at last birthday	Single, married, widowed or divorced	EDUCATION: Attended school any time since Sept. 1, 1929	Whether able to read and write.	NATIVITY Place of birth of this person.	Whether able to speak English.	OCCUPATION
	1	2	3	4	5	6	7	8	9	10	11	12	13	14
1	Rosario Street	86	97	Cruz, Juan P	Head	M	Cha	31	M	N	Y	Guam	Y	Carpenter
2		86	97	Cruz, Martina C	Wife	F	Cha	29	M	N	Y	Guam	Y	None
3		86	97	Cruz, Maria C	Daughter	F	Cha	2.2	S	N		Guam		None
4		86	97	Cruz, Juan C	Son	M	Cha	1	S	N		Guam		None
5		87	98	Tainatongo, Ramon M	Head	M	Cha	50	M	N	Y	Guam	N	Farmer
6		87	98	Tainatongo, Victorina T	Wife	F	Cha	51	M	N	Y	Guam	N	None
7		87	98	Tainatongo, Cerilo T	Son	M	Cha	17	S	Y	Y	Guam	Y	None
8		87	98	Quidachay, Vicente T	Lodger	M	Cha	17	S	N	Y	Guam	Y	Farm laborer
9		88	99	Quinene, Vicente F	Head	M	Cha	37	M	N	Y	Guam	Y	Farmer
10		88	99	Quinene, Librada C	Wife	F	Cha	32	M	N	Y	Guam	Y	None
11		88	99	Quinene, Ana C	Daughter	F	Cha	11	S	Y	Y	Guam	Y	None
12		88	99	Quinene, Jose C	Son	M	Cha	10	S	Y	Y	Guam		None
13		88	99	Quinene, Maria C	Daughter	F	Cha	8	S	Y		Guam		None
14		89	100	Garrido, Nicolas N	Head	M	Cha	40	M	N	Y	Guam	Y	Farmer
15		89	100	Garrido, Carmen C	Wife	F	Cha	30	M	N	N	Guam	N	None
16		89	100	Garrido, Jose C	Son	M	Cha	9	S	Y		Guam		None
17		89	100	Garrido, Vicente C	Son	M	Cha	7	S	Y		Guam		None
18		89	100	Garrido, Ignacio C	Son	M	Cha	5	S	N		Guam		None
19		89	100	Garrido, Maria C	Daughter	F	Cha	3.9	S	N		Guam		None
20		89	100	Garrido, Ana C	Daughter	F	Cha	2.2	S	N		Guam		None
21		89	100	Garrido, Nicolas C	Son	M	Cha	.8	S	N		Guam		None
22		89	100	Chargualaf, Angelina C	Step daughter	F	Cha	11	S	Y	Y	Guam	Y	None
23		89	100	Garrido, Ramon G	Nephew	M	Cha	18	S	N	Y	Guam	Y	Farm laborer
24		90	101	Garrido, Joaquin N	Head	M	Cha	37	M	N	Y	Guam	Y	Laborer (road)
25		90	101	Garrido, Concepcion S	Wife	F	Cha	37	M	N	Y	Guam	N	None

D-9-22

DEPARTMENT OF COMMERCE-BUREAU OF THE CENSUS
WASHINGTON

FIFTEENTH CENSUS OF THE UNITED STATES: 1930-POPULATION

THE ISLAND OF GUAM

Sheet No. 11B

280B

District **Municipality of Merizo**

Name of Place **Merizo Town** [Proper name and, also, name of class, as city, town, village, barrio, etc]

Enumeration District No. **9**

Enumerated by me on **April 9, 1930** Manuel Charfauros, Enumerator

	PLACE OF ABODE			NAME	RELATION	PERSONAL DESCRIPTION				EDUCATION		NATIVITY		OCCUPATION
	Street, avenue, road, etc.	Number of dwelling house is order of visitation	Number of family in order of visitation	of each person whose place of abode on April 1, 1930, was in this family. Enter surname, first, then given name and middle initial. If any. Include every person living on April 1, 1930. Omit children born since April 1, 1930.	Relationship of this Person to the head of the family.	Sex	Color or race	Age at last birthday	Single, married, widowed or divorced	Attended school any time since Sept. 1, 1929	Whether able to read and write.	Place of birth of this person.	Whether able to speak English.	
	1	2	3	4	5	6	7	8	9	10	11	12	13	14
26	[no street name]	90	101	Garrido, Tomas S	Nephew	M	Cha	19	S	N	Y	Guam	Y	Farm laborer
27		91	102	Naputi, Carmela T	Head	F	Cha	51	S	N	N	Guam	N	None
28		91	102	Naputi, Dolores T	Sister	F	Cha	47	S	N	Y	Guam	N	None
29		91	102	Mansapit, Jose M	Nephew	M	Cha	15	S	N	Y	Guam	Y	Farm laborer
30		92	103	Acfalle, Fausto C	Head	M	Cha	37	M	N	Y	Guam	N	Farmer
31		92	103	Acfalle, Francisca R	Wife	F	Cha	37	M	N	Y	Guam	N	None
32		92	103	Acfalle, Vicente R	Son	M	Cha	7	S	Y		Guam		None
33		92	103	Acfalle, Carmen R	Daughter	F	Cha	5.9	S	N		Guam		None
34		92	103	Acfalle, Ramon R	Son	M	Cha	4.3	S	N		Guam		None
35		92	103	Acfalle, Carmelo R	Son	M	Cha	7	S	N		Guam		None
36		93	104	Maguadog, Luis N	Head	M	Cha	33	M	N	Y	Guam	Y	Road laborer
37		93	104	Maguadog, Maria C	Wife	F	Cha	42	M	N	Y	Guam	N	None
38		93	104	Maguadog, Jesus C	Son	M	Cha	4.5	S	N		Guam		None
39		93	104	Maguadog, Maria C	Daughter	F	Cha	2.5	S	N		Guam		None
40		93	104	Baza, Jose C	Step son	M	Cha	9	S	Y		Guam		None
41		94	105	Santiago, Felipe M	Head	M	Fil	68	M	N	Y	Guam	N	Farmer
42		94	105	Santiago, Juana S	Wife	F	Cha	70	M	N	N	Guam	N	None
43		94	105	Cruz, Ana S	Daughter	F	Fil	43	Wd	N	Y	Guam	N	None
44		94	105	Cruz, Jesus S	Grandson	M	Cha	12	S	Y	Y	Guam	Y	None
45		94	105	Torres, Lourdes S	Granddaughter	F	Cha	6	S	Y		Guam		None
46		94	106	Cruz, Juan S	Head	M	Cha	20	M	N	Y	Guam	Y	Farmer
47		94	106	Cruz, Maria M	Wife	F	Cha	21	M	N	Y	Guam	Y	None
48		94	106	Cruz, Jose M	Son	M	Cha	.2	S	N		Guam		None
49		95	107	Santiago, Gregorio S	Head	M	Fil	41	M	N	Y	Guam	N	Farmer
50		95	107	Santiago, Consolacion C	Wife	F	Cha	29	M	N	Y	Guam	N	None

DEPARTMENT OF COMMERCE-BUREAU OF THE CENSUS
WASHINGTON

FIFTEENTH CENSUS OF THE UNITED STATES: 1930-POPULATION

THE ISLAND OF GUAM

Sheet No. 12A

District Municipality of Merizo
Name of Place Merizo Town
[Proper name and, also, name of class, as city, town, village, barrio, etc]

Enumeration District No. 9
Enumerated by me on April 9, 1930 Manuel Charfauros
Enumerator

	PLACE OF ABODE: Street, avenue, road, etc.	Number of dwelling house in order of visitation	Number of family in order of visitation	NAME of each person whose place of abode on April 1, 1930, was in this family. Enter surname, first, then given name and middle initial. If any. Include every person living on April 1, 1930. Omit children born since April 1, 1930.	RELATION Relationship of this Person to the head of the family.	PERSONAL DESCRIPTION: Sex	Color or race	Age at last birthday	Single, married, widowed or divorced	EDUCATION: Attended school any time since Sept. 1, 1929	Whether able to read and write.	NATIVITY Place of birth of this person.	Whether able to speak English.	OCCUPATION
	1	2	3	4	5	6	7	8	9	10	11	12	13	14
1	[no street name]	95	107	Santiago, Jose C	Son	M	Fil	9	S	Y		Guam		None
2		95	107	Santiago, Josefa C	Daughter	F	Fil	8	S	Y		Guam		None
3		95	107	Santiago, Vicente C	Son	M	Fil	5	S	N		Guam		None
4		95	107	Santiago, Juana C	Daughter	F	Fil	3.1	S	N		Guam		None
5		95	107	Santiago, Gregorio C	Son	M	Fil	2.1	S	N		Guam		None
6		96	108	Tajalle, Jose C	Head	M	Cha	27	M	N	Y	Guam	Y	Farmer
7		96	108	Tajalle, Dolores T	Wife	F	Cha	25	M	N	Y	Guam	N	None
8		96	108	Tajalle, Jose T	Son	M	Cha	.6	S	N		Guam		None
9		96	108	Santos, Ramon S	Lodger	M	Cha	5	S	N		Guam		None
10		97	109	Cruz, Ramon P	Head	M	Cha	35	M	N	Y	Guam	Y	Carpenter
11		97	109	Cruz, Justa S	Wife	F	Fil	39	M	N	Y	Guam	N	None
12		97	109	Cruz, Teodoro S	Son	M	Cha	11	S	Y	Y	Guam	Y	None
13		97	109	Cruz, Rosa S	Daughter	F	Cha	9	S	Y		Guam		None
14		97	109	Cruz, Felipe S	Son	M	Cha	6	S	N		Guam		None
15		97	109	Cruz, Vicenta S	Daughter	F	Cha	4.9	S	N		Guam		None
16		97	109	Cruz, Ignacio S	Son	M	Cha	2.8	S	N		Guam		None
17		98	110	San Nicolas, Vicente C	Head	M	Cha	48	M	N	N	Guam	N	Farmer
18		98	110	San Nicolas, Rita A	Daughter [sic]	F	Cha	49	M	N	N	Guam	N	None
19		98	110	San Nicolas, Nicolasa A	Daughter	F	Cha	19	S	N	Y	Guam	Y	Farm laborer
20		98	110	San Nicolas, Juan A	Son	M	Cha	16	S	N	Y	Guam	Y	Farm laborer
21		98	110	San Nicolas, Maria A	Daughter	F	Cha	13	S	N	Y	Guam	Y	None
22		98	110	San Nicolas, Josefina A	Daughter	F	Cha	11	S	N	Y	Guam	Y	None
23		99	111	Champaco, Dolores E	Head	F	Cha	41	S	N	N	Guam	N	None
24		99	111	Champaco, Jose E	Son	M	Cha	21	S	N	Y	Guam	Y	Farm laborer
25		99	111	Champaco, Juan C	Son	M	Cha	15	S	N	Y	Guam	Y	Farm laborer

(CHAMORRO ROOTS GENEALOGY PROJECT™ TRANSCRIPTION)
(BERNARD T. PUNZALAN / HTTP://WWW.CHAMORROROOTS.COM)

DEPARTMENT OF COMMERCE-BUREAU OF THE CENSUS
WASHINGTON

FIFTEENTH CENSUS OF THE UNITED STATES: 1930-POPULATION

THE ISLAND OF GUAM

Sheet No. 12B

281B

District Municipality of Merizo
Name of Place Merizo Town
[Proper name and, also, name of class, as city, town, village, barrio, etc]

Enumeration District No. 9
Enumerated by me on April 9, 1930 Manuel Charfauros, Enumerator

	PLACE OF ABODE			NAME	RELATION	PERSONAL DESCRIPTION				EDUCATION		NATIVITY		OCCUPATION
	Street, avenue, road, etc.	Number of dwelling house in order of visitation	Number of family in order of visitation	of each person whose place of abode on April 1, 1930, was in this family. Enter surname, first, then given name and middle initial. If any. Include every person living on April 1, 1930. Omit children born since April 1, 1930.	Relationship of this Person to the head of the family.	Sex	Color or race	Age at last birthday	Single, married, widowed or divorced	Attended school any time since Sept. 1, 1929	Whether able to read and write.	Place of birth of this person.	Whether able to speak English.	
	1	2	3	4	5	6	7	8	9	10	11	12	13	14
26	[no street name]	99	111	Champaco, Felicita C	Daughter	F	Cha	14	S	Y	Y	Guam	Y	None
27		100	112	Quidagua, Maria C	Head	F	Cha	43	Wd	N	Y	Guam	N	None
28		100	112	Quidagua, Felix C	Son	M	Cha	22	S	N	Y	Guam	Y	Farmer
29		100	112	Quidagua, Dolores C	Daughter	F	Cha	19	S	N	Y	Guam	Y	None
30		100	112	Quidagua, Pedro C	Son	M	Cha	16	S	N	Y	Guam	Y	Farm laborer
31		100	112	Quidagua, Jesus C	Son	M	Cha	11	S	Y	Y	Guam	Y	None
32		100	112	Quidagua, Vicente C	Son	M	Cha	9	S	Y		Guam		None
33		100	112	Quidagua, Jose C	Son	M	Cha	4.7	S	N		Guam		None
34		101	113	Tajalle, Gregoria C	Head	F	Cha	37	S	N	N	Guam	N	None
35		101	113	Tajalle, Dolores T	Daughter	F	Cha	12	S	Y	Y	Guam	Y	None
36		101	113	Tajalle, Regina T	Daughter	F	Cha	5	S	N		Guam		None
37		101	113	Meno, Tomas T	Grandson	M	Cha	2.1	S	N		Guam		None
38		101	113	Quidagua, Maria C	Lodger	F	Cha	85	Wd	N	N	Guam	N	None
39		102	114	San Nicolas, Juana T	Head	F	Cha	69	S	N	N	Guam	N	None
40		102	114	San Nicolas, Pilar T	Daughter	F	Cha	39	S	N	N	Guam	N	None
41		102	114	San Nicolas, Asuncion T	Daughter	F	Cha	34	S	N	N	Guam	N	None
42		102	114	San Nicolas, Antonio SN	Grandson	M	Cha	20	S	N	Y	Guam	Y	Farm laborer
43		102	114	San Nicolas, Maria SN	Granddaughter	F	Cha	13	S	N	Y	Guam	Y	None
44		103	115	Cruz, Maria C	Head	F	Cha	63	Wd	N	Y	Guam	N	None
45		103	115	Cruz, Franscico C	Son	M	Cha	32	S	N	Y	Guam	Y	Farmer
46		104	116	Chargualaf, Natividad C	Head	F	Cha	56	S	N	N	Guam	N	None
47		104	116	Chargualaf, Inigo C	Son	M	Cha	35	S	N	Y	Guam	Y	Farmer
48		105	117	Fegurgur, Joaquin N	Head	M	Cha	30	M	N	Y	Guam	Y	Farmer
49		105	117	Fegurgur, Manuela C	Wife	F	Chin	41	M	N	Y	Guam	N	None
50		105	117	Champaco, Ana E	Step-daughter	F	Cha	21	S	Y	Y	Guam	Y	None

DEPARTMENT OF COMMERCE-BUREAU OF THE CENSUS
WASHINGTON

FIFTEENTH CENSUS OF THE UNITED STATES: 1930-POPULATION

THE ISLAND OF GUAM

Sheet No. 13A

District Municipality of Merizo
Name of Place Merizo Town
[Proper name and, also, name of class, as city, town, village, barrio, etc]

Enumeration District No. 9
Enumerated by me on April 10, 1930 Manuel Charfauros, Enumerator

	PLACE OF ABODE			NAME	RELATION	PERSONAL DESCRIPTION				EDUCATION		NATIVITY		OCCUPATION
	Street, avenue, road, etc.	Number of dwelling house in order of visitation	Number of family in order of visitation	of each person whose place of abode on April 1, 1930, was in this family. Enter surname, first, then given name and middle initial. If any. Include every person living on April 1, 1930. Omit children born since April 1, 1930.	Relationship of this Person to the head of the family.	Sex	Color or race	Age at last birthday	Single, married, widowed or divorced	Attended school any time since Sept. 1, 1929	Whether able to read and write.	Place of birth of this person.	Whether able to speak English.	
	1	2	3	4	5	6	7	8	9	10	11	12	13	14
1	[no street name]	105	117	Champaco, Antonio C	Step son	M	Cha	9	S	Y		Guam		None
2		105	117	Champaco, Juan C	Step son	M	Cha	5	S	N		Guam		None
3		106	118	Fegurgur, Alejandra N	Head	F	Cha	44	Wd	N	N	Guam		None
4		106	118	Fegurgur, Ana N	Daughter	F	Cha	24	S	N	N	Guam		None
5		106	118	Fegurgur, Isidro N	Grandson	M	Cha	5	S	N		Guam		None
6		106	118	Fegurgur, Jesus N	Grandson	M	Cha	3	S	N		Guam		None
7		106	118	Fegurgur, Francisco N	Grandson	M	Cha	1.7	S	N		Guam		None
8		107	119	Nangauta, Antonia C	Head	F	Cha	50	S	N	N	Guam	N	None
9		107	119	Nangauta, Mariano C	Son	M	Cha	17	S	N	Y	Guam	Y	Farm laborer
10		107	119	Nangauta, Jose N	Son	M	Cha	11	S	Y	Y	Guam	Y	None
11		108	120	Babauta, Angel B	Head	M	Cha	64	M	N	Y	Guam	N	Farmer
12		108	120	Babauta, Vicenta N	Wife	F	Cha	58	M	N	N	Guam	N	None
13		108	120	Nangauta, Juan T	Nephew in law	M	Cha	25	S	N	Y	Guam	Y	Farm laborer
14		108	120	Nangauta, Lucia N	Niece in law	F	Cha	11	S	Y	Y	Guam	Y	None
15		109	121	Taijeron, Jose B	Head	M	Cha	49	M	N	Y	Guam	N	Farmer
16		109	121	Taijeron, Antonia A	Wife	F	Cha	50	M	N	Y	Guam	N	None
17		110	122	Taijeron, Maria B	Head	F	Cha	46	S	N	N	Guam	N	None
18		110	122	Taijeron, Jose T	Son	M	Cha	16	S	N	Y	Guam	Y	Farm laborer
19		111	123	Chargualaf, Jacobo B	Head	M	Cha	34	M	N	Y	Guam	Y	Farmer
20		111	123	Chargualaf, Candelaria N	Wife	F	Cha	44	M	N	N	Guam	N	None
21		111	123	Nangauta, Vicente N	Step-son	M	Cha	17	S	N	N	Guam	N	Farm laborer
22		111	123	Nangauta, Luis N	Step-son	M	Cha	14	S	N	N	Guam	N	Farm laborer
23		112	124	Espinosa, Vicente N	Head	M	Cha	52	M	N	Y	Guam	N	Farmer
24		112	124	Espinosa, Ignacia B	Wife	F	Cha	53	M	N	N	Guam	N	None
25		112	124	Espinosa, Joaquina B	Daughter	F	Cha	19	S	N	Y	Guam	Y	None

DEPARTMENT OF COMMERCE-BUREAU OF THE CENSUS
WASHINGTON

FIFTEENTH CENSUS OF THE UNITED STATES: 1930-POPULATION

THE ISLAND OF GUAM

Sheet No. 13B

282B

District **Municipality of Merizo**
Name of Place **Merizo Town**
[Proper name and, also, name of class, as city, town, village, barrio, etc]

Enumeration District No. **9**
Enumerated by me on **April 10, 1930** Manuel Charfauros
Enumerator

	PLACE OF ABODE			NAME	RELATION	PERSONAL DESCRIPTION				EDUCATION		NATIVITY		OCCUPATION
	Street, avenue, road, etc.	Number of dwelling house is order of visitation	Number of family in order of visitation	of each person whose place of abode on April 1, 1930, was in this family. Enter surname, first, then given name and middle initial. If any. Include every person living on April 1, 1930. Omit children born since April 1, 1930.	Relationship of this Person to the head of the family.	Sex	Color or race	Age at last birthday	Single, married, widowed or divorced	Attended school any time since Sept. 1, 1929	Whether able to read and write.	Place of birth of this person.	Whether able to speak English.	
	1	2	3	4	5	6	7	8	9	10	11	12	13	14
26	[no street name]	112	124	Espinosa, Isidro B	Son	M	Cha	17	S	N	Y	Guam	Y	Farm laborer
27		112	124	Espinosa, Francisco B	Son	M	Cha	12	S	Y	Y	Guam	Y	None
28		113	125	Tedpaogo, Manuela D	Head	F	Cha	53	Wd	N	N	Guam	N	None
29		113	125	Tedpaogo, Felipe D	Son	M	Cha	24	S	N	Y	Guam	Y	Farmer
30		113	125	Tedpaogo, Carmen D	Daughter	F	Cha	16	S	N	Y	Guam	Y	None
31		113	125	Tedpaogo, Angelina D	Daughter	F	Cha	14	S	N	Y	Guam	Y	None
32		114	125	Chargualaf, Dimas B	Head	M	Cha	63	Wd	N	N	Guam	N	Farmer
33		115	127	Tyquiengco, Rosario B	Head	M	Chin	31	M	N	Y	Guam	Y	Laborer
34		115	127	Tyquiengco, Maria A	Wife	M	Cha	16	M	N	Y	Guam	Y	None
35		116	128	Taijeron, Antonio S	Head	M	Cha	52	M	N	Y	Guam	N	Farmer
36		116	128	Taijeron, Maria D	Wife	F	Cha	50	M	N	N	Guam	N	None
37		116	128	Taijeron, Jose D	Son	M	Cha	23	S	N	Y	Guam	N	Farm laborer
38		116	128	Taijeron, Jesus D	Son	M	Cha	21	S	N	Y	Guam	Y	Farm laborer
39		117	129	Taijeron, Carmen C	Head	F	Cha	74	Wd	N	Y	Guam	N	None
40		117	129	Taijeron, Emma T	Grand daughter	F	Cha	9	S	Y		Guam		None
41		118	130	Fegurgur, Carmen F	Head	F	Cha	65	Wd	N	N	Guam	N	None
42		119	131	Babauta, Juan N	Head	M	Cha	26	M	N	Y	Guam	N	Farmer
43		119	131	Babauta, Margarita T	Wife	F	Cha	28	M	N	Y	Guam	Y	None
44		119	131	Babauta, Angelina T	Daughter	F	Cha	1.1	S	N		Guam		None
45		120	132	Meno, Angel C	Head	M	Cha	33	M	N	Y	Guam	Y	Farmer
46		120	132	Meno, Asuncion Q	Wife	F	Cha	38	M	N	N	Guam	N	None
47		120	132	Meno, Jesus Q	Son	M	Cha	8	S	Y		Guam		None
48		120	132	Meno, Dolores	Daughter	F	Cha	7	S	N		Guam		None
49		120	132	Meno, Maria	Daughter	F	Cha	3	S	N		Guam		None
50		120	132	Quinene, Jose Q	Step-son	M	Cha	14	S	Y	Y	Guam	Y	Farm laborer

(CHAMORRO ROOTS GENEALOGY PROJECT™ TRANSCRIPTION)
(BERNARD T. PUNZALAN / HTTP://WWW.CHAMORROROOTS.COM)

DEPARTMENT OF COMMERCE-BUREAU OF THE CENSUS
WASHINGTON

FIFTEENTH CENSUS OF THE UNITED STATES: 1930-POPULATION

THE ISLAND OF GUAM

Sheet No. 14A

District **Municipality of Merizo**
Name of Place **Merizo Town**
[Proper name and, also, name of class, as city, town, village, barrio, etc]

Enumeration District No. 9
Enumerated by me on **April 10, 1930** Manuel Charfauros, Enumerator

	PLACE OF ABODE			NAME	RELATION	PERSONAL DESCRIPTION				EDUCATION		NATIVITY		OCCUPATION
	Street, avenue, road, etc.	Number of dwelling house in order of visitation	Number of family in order of visitation	of each person whose place of abode on April 1, 1930, was in this family. Enter surname, first, then given name and middle initial. If any. Include every person living on April 1, 1930. Omit children born since April 1, 1930.	Relationship of this Person to the head of the family.	Sex	Color or race	Age at last birthday	Single, married, widowed or divorced	Attended school any time since Sept. 1, 1929	Whether able to read and write.	Place of birth of this person.	Whether able to speak English.	
	1	2	3	4	5	6	7	8	9	10	11	12	13	14
1	[no street name]	121	133	Nanguata, Patricio N	Head	M	Cha	41	M	N	Y	Guam	N	Farmer
2		121	133	Nanguata, Isabel Q	Wife	F	Cha	46	M	N	N	Guam	N	None
3		121	133	Quinene, Dometrio Q	Step-son	M	Cha	19	S	N	Y	Guam	Y	Farm laborer
4		121	133	Quinene, Jose Q	Step-son	M	Cha	17	S	N	N	Guam	N	None
5		122	134	Quinene, Santiago G	Head	M	Cha	34	M	N	Y	Guam	N	Farmer
6		122	134	Quinene, Josefa	Wife	F	Cha	27	M	N	Y	Guam	Y	None
7		122	134	Quinene, Lutilde	Daughter	F	Cha	3.1	S	N		Guam		None
8		122	134	Quinene, Maria	Daughter	F	Cha	1	S	N		Guam		None
9		122	134	Quinene, Josefa	Daughter	F	Cha	0	S	N		Guam		None
10		123	135	Tyquiengco, Joaquin B	Head	M	Chin	64	Wd	N	Y	Guam	N	Farmer
11		123	135	Tyquiengco, Agustina B	Daughter	F	Chin	20	S	N	Y	Guam	Y	None
12		124	136	Tainatongo, Vicente M	Head	M	Cha	52	Wd	N	Y	Guam	N	Farmer
13		125	137	Reyes, Lorenzo M	Head	M	Cha	47	M	N	Y	Guam	N	Farmer
14		125	137	Reyes, Teresa C	Wife	F	Cha	42	M	N	N	Guam	N	None
15		125	137	Reyes, Antonio C	Son	M	Cha	17	S	N	Y	Guam	Y	Laborer (road)
16		125	137	Reyes, Joaquin C	Son	M	Cha	14	S	Y	Y	Guam	Y	Farm laborer
17		125	137	Reyes, Margarita C	Daughter	F	Cha	9	S	Y		Guam		None
18		125	137	Reyes, Jose C	Son	M	Cha	8	S	Y		Guam		None
19		125	137	Reyes, Enrique C	Son	M	Cha	6	S	N		Guam		None
20		125	137	Reyes, Vicente C	Son	M	Cha	3.2	S	N		Guam		None
21		125	137	Reyes, Teresa C	Son	M	Cha	.4	S	N		Guam		None
22		126	138	Acfalle, Dimas A	Head	M	Cha	58	Wd	N	Y	Guam	N	Farmer
23		126	138	Acfalle, Nicolas A	Son	M	Cha	26	S	N	Y	Guam	Y	Farm laborer
24		126	138	Acfalle, Ana A	Daughter	F	Cha	25	S	N	Y	Guam	Y	None
25		126	138	Acfalle, Jose A	Grandson	M	Cha	1.7	S	N		Guam		None

(CHAMORRO ROOTS GENEALOGY PROJECT™ TRANSCRIPTION)
(BERNARD T. PUNZALAN / HTTP://WWW.CHAMORROROOTS.COM)

DEPARTMENT OF COMMERCE-BUREAU OF THE CENSUS
WASHINGTON

FIFTEENTH CENSUS OF THE UNITED STATES: 1930-POPULATION

THE ISLAND OF GUAM

Sheet No. 14B

283B

District **Municipality of Merizo**
Name of Place **Merizo Town**
[Proper name and, also, name of class, as city, town, village, barrio, etc]

Enumeration District No. 9
Enumerated by me on **April 11, 1930** Manuel Charfauros, Enumerator

	PLACE OF ABODE			NAME	RELATION	PERSONAL DESCRIPTION				EDUCATION		NATIVITY		OCCUPATION
	Street, avenue, road, etc.	Number of dwelling house is order of visitation	Number of family in order of visitation	of each person whose place of abode on April 1, 1930, was in this family. Enter surname, first, then given name and middle initial. If any. Include every person living on April 1, 1930. Omit children born since April 1, 1930.	Relationship of this Person to the head of the family.	Sex	Color or race	Age at last birthday	Single, married, widowed or divorced	Attended school any time since Sept. 1, 1929	Whether able to read and write.	Place of birth of this person.	Whether able to speak English.	
	1	2	3	4	5	6	7	8	9	10	11	12	13	14
26	[no street name]	127	139	Tyquiengco, Lorenzo B	Head	M	Chin	33	M	N	Y	Guam	Y	Laborer (road)
27		127	139	Tyquiengco, Rosa T	Wife	F	Cha	29	M	N	Y	Guam	Y	None
28		127	139	Tyquiengco, Milagro T	Daughter	F	Chin	6	S	N		Guam		None
29		127	139	Tyquiengco, Lourdes T	Daughter	F	Chin	1.1	S	N		Guam		None
30		128	140	Champaco, Pedro E	Head	M	Chin	53	M	N	Y	Guam	N	Farmer
31		128	140	Champaco, Ana M	Wife	F	Cha	49	M	N	Y	Guam	N	None
32		128	140	Champaco, Maria M	Daughter	F	Chin	25	S	N	Y	Guam	N	None
33		128	140	Champaco, Asuncion M	Daughter	F	Chin	22	S	N	Y	Guam	Y	None
34		128	140	Champaco, Mariano M	Son	M	Chin	21	S	N	Y	Guam	Y	Farm laborer
35		128	140	Champaco, Jose M	Son	M	Chin	15	S	Y	Y	Guam	Y	None
36		128	140	Champaco, Rosalia M	Niece	F	Chin	12	S	Y	Y	Guam	Y	None
37		129	141	Champaco, Vicente M	Head	M	Chin	25	M	N	Y	Guam	Y	Farmer
38		129	141	Champaco, Isabel T	Wife	F	Cha	17	M	N	Y	Guam	Y	None
39		130	142	Baza, Jose T	Head	M	Cha	44	M	N	Y	Guam	N	Farmer
40		130	142	Baza, Visitacion A	Wife	F	Cha	35	M	N	Y	Guam	N	None
41		130	142	Baza, Dolores A	Daughter	F	Cha	12	S	Y	Y	Guam	Y	None
42		130	142	Baza, Rosa A	Daughter	F	Cha	11	S	Y	Y	Guam	Y	None
43		130	142	Baza, Concepcion A	Daughter	F	Cha	9	S	Y		Guam		None
44		130	142	Baza, Maria A	Daughter	F	Cha	6	S	N		Guam		None
45		130	142	Baza, Jose A	Son	M	Cha	4.5	S	N		Guam		None
46		130	142	Baza, Jesus A	Son	M	Cha	.2	S	N		Guam		None
47		131	143	Garrido, Jose C	Head	M	Cha	53	M	N	Y	Guam	N	Farmer
48		131	143	Garrido, Dolores M	Wife	F	Cha	43	M	N	Y	Guam	N	None
49		131	143	Garrido, Juan M	Son	M	Cha	6	S	N		Guam		None
50		131	143	Garrido, Concepcion M	Daughter	F	Cha	4.4	S	N		Guam		None

DEPARTMENT OF COMMERCE-BUREAU OF THE CENSUS
WASHINGTON

FIFTEENTH CENSUS OF THE UNITED STATES: 1930-POPULATION

THE ISLAND OF GUAM

Sheet No. 15A

District **Municipality of Merizo**
Name of Place **Merizo Town**
[Proper name and, also, name of class, as city, town, village, barrio, etc]

Enumeration District No. 9
Enumerated by me on **April 11, 1930** Manuel Charfauros, Enumerator

	PLACE OF ABODE: Street, avenue, road, etc.	Number of dwelling house in order of visitation	Number of family in order of visitation	NAME of each person whose place of abode on April 1, 1930, was in this family. Enter surname, first, then given name and middle initial. If any. Include every person living on April 1, 1930. Omit children born since April 1, 1930.	RELATION Relationship of this Person to the head of the family.	Sex	Color or race	Age at last birthday	Single, married, widowed or divorced	Attended school any time since Sept. 1, 1929	Whether able to read and write.	NATIVITY Place of birth of this person.	Whether able to speak English.	OCCUPATION
	1	2	3	4	5	6	7	8	9	10	11	12	13	14
1	[no street name]	131	143	Garrido, Jose M	Son	M	Cha	1.1	S	N		Guam		None
2		131	143	Meno, Jose M	Step-son	M	Cha	16	S	N	Y	Guam	Y	Farm laborer
3		131	143	Meno, Joaquina M	Step-daughter	F	Cha	15	S	N	Y	Guam	Y	None
4		131	143	Meno, Felipe M	Step-son	M	Cha	12	S	Y	Y	Guam	Y	None
5		132	144	Naputi, Joaquin A	Head	M	Cha	23	M	N	Y	Guam	Y	Laborer (road)
6		132	144	Naputi, Tomasa F	Wife	F	Cha	22	M	N	Y	Guam	Y	None
7		132	144	Concepcion, Ana B	Lodger	F	Cha	3.2	S	N		Guam		None
8		133	145	Santos, Jose C	Head	M	Cha	54	M	N	N	Guam	N	Farmer
9		133	145	Santos, Dolores M	Wife	F	Cha	50	M	N	N	Guam	N	None
10		133	145	Espinosa, Vicente M	Lodger	M	Cha	27	S	N	Y	Guam	Y	Farm laborer
11					Here ends the enumeration of Merizo Town.									
12					[Sheet 284B/15B was intentionally left blank.]									
13														
14														
15														
16														
17														
18														
19														
20														
21														
22														
23														
24														
25														

DEPARTMENT OF COMMERCE-BUREAU OF THE CENSUS
WASHINGTON

FIFTEENTH CENSUS OF THE UNITED STATES: 1930-POPULATION

THE ISLAND OF GUAM

Sheet No. 16A

District **Municipality of Merizo**
Name of Place **Umatac Barrio**
[Proper name and, also, name of class, as city, town, village, barrio, etc]

Enumeration District No. 9
Enumerated by me on **April 12, 1930** Manuel Charfauros
Enumerator

	PLACE OF ABODE			NAME	RELATION	PERSONAL DESCRIPTION				EDUCATION		NATIVITY		OCCUPATION
	Street, avenue, road, etc.	Number of dwelling house is order of visitation	Number of family in order of visitation	of each person whose place of abode on April 1, 1930, was in this family. Enter surname, first, then given name and middle initial. If any. Include every person living on April 1, 1930. Omit children born since April 1, 1930.	Relationship of this Person to the head of the family.	Sex	Color or race	Age at last birthday	Single, married, widowed or divorced	Attended school any time since Sept. 1, 1929	Whether able to read and write.	Place of birth of this person.	Whether able to speak English.	
	1	2	3	4	5	6	7	8	9	10	11	12	13	14
1	San Dionisio Street	134	146	Sanchez, Manuel Q	Head	M	Cha	44	M	N	Y	Guam	N	Farmer
2		134	146	Sanchez, Teodora Q	Wife	F	Cha	49	M	N	Y	Guam	N	None
3		134	146	Sanchez, Elena Q	Daughter	F	Cha	16	S	Y	Y	Guam	Y	None
4		134	146	Sanchez, Clara Q	Daughter	F	Cha	9	S	Y		Guam		None
5		134	146	Sanchez, Pedro Q	Son	M	Cha	7	S	Y		Guam		None
6		134	146	Aguon, Jose Q	Step-son	M	Cha	31	S	N	Y	Guam	Y	None
7		135	147	Cheguina, Polocarpio A	Head	M	Cha	39	M	N	N	Guam	N	Farmer
8		135	147	Cheguina, Maxima S	Wife	F	Cha	30	M	N	N	Guam	N	None
9		135	147	Cheguina, Catalina S	Daughter	F	Cha	11	S	Y	Y	Guam	Y	None
10		135	147	Cheguina, Francisco S	Son	M	Cha	8	S	Y		Guam		None
11		135	147	Cheguina, Josefa S	Daughter	F	Cha	6	S	N		Guam		None
12		135	147	Cheguina, Regina S	Daughter	F	Cha	2.1	S	N		Guam		None
13		135	147	Cheguina, Joaquina S	Daughter	F	Cha	.1	S	N		Guam		None
14		136	146	Aquiningoc, Manuel A	Head	M	Cha	43	M	N	Y	Guam	N	Farmer
15		136	146	Aquiningoc, Ana Q	Wife	F	Cha	45	M	N	N	Guam	N	None
16		136	146	Aquiningoc, Juan Q	Son	M	Cha	20	S	N	Y	Guam	Y	None
17		136	146	Aquiningoc, Felicidad Q	Daughter	F	Cha	19	S	N	Y	Guam	Y	None
18		136	146	Aquiningoc, Maria Q	Daughter	F	Cha	17	S	N	Y	Guam	Y	None
19		136	146	Aquiningoc, Carmen Q	Daughter	F	Cha	15	S	Y	Y	Guam	Y	None
20		136	146	Aquiningoc, Jose Q	Son	M	Cha	14	S	Y	Y	Guam	Y	None
21		136	146	Aquiningoc, Dolores Q	Daughter	F	Cha	12	S	Y	Y	Guam	Y	None
22		136	146	Aquiningoc, Alice Q	Daughter	F	Cha	3	S	N		Guam		None
23		136	146	Quinata, Antonio M	Brother-in-law	M	Cha	50	S	N		Guam	Y	Farm laborer
24		137	149	Tajalle, Enrique T	Head	M	Cha	38	M	N	N	Guam	N	Farmer
25		137	149	Tajalle, Milagro A	Wife	F	Cha	27	M	N	Y	Guam	Y	None

D-9-31

DEPARTMENT OF COMMERCE-BUREAU OF THE CENSUS
WASHINGTON

FIFTEENTH CENSUS OF THE UNITED STATES: 1930-POPULATION

THE ISLAND OF GUAM

Sheet No. 16B

District **Municipality of Merizo**
Name of Place **Umatac Barrio**
[Proper name and, also, name of class, as city, town, village, barrio, etc]

Enumeration District No. 9
Enumerated by me on **April 12, 1930** Manuel Charfauros
Enumerator

	PLACE OF ABODE			NAME	RELATION	PERSONAL DESCRIPTION				EDUCATION		NATIVITY		OCCUPATION
	Street, avenue, road, etc.	Number of dwelling house is order of visitation	Number of family in order of visitation	of each person whose place of abode on April 1, 1930, was in this family. Enter surname, first, then given name and middle initial. If any. Include every person living on April 1, 1930. Omit children born since April 1, 1930.	Relationship of this Person to the head of the family.	Sex	Color or race	Age at last birthday	Single, married, widowed or divorced	Attended school any time since Sept. 1, 1929	Whether able to read and write.	Place of birth of this person.	Whether able to speak English.	
	1	2	3	4	5	6	7	8	9	10	11	12	13	14
26	San Dionisio Street	137	149	Tajalle, Jesus A	Son	M	Cha	7	S	Y		Guam		None
27		137	149	Tajalle, Antonio A	Son	M	Cha	5	S	N		Guam		None
28		137	149	Tajalle, Juan A	Son	M	Cha	2	S	N		Guam		None
29		137	149	Tajalle, Jose A	Son	M	Cha	.1	S	N		Guam		None
30		138	150	Fegurgur, Rosauro C	Head	M	Cha	54	M	N	N	Guam	N	Farmer
31		138	150	Fegurgur, Maria S	Wife	F	Cha	39	M	N	Y	Guam	N	None
32		138	150	Fegurgur, Jesus S	Son	M	Cha	17	S	N	Y	Guam	Y	Farm laborer
33		138	150	Fegurgur, Jose S	Son	M	Cha	12	S	Y	Y	Guam	Y	None
34		138	150	Fegurgur, Rita S	Son	M	Cha	10	S	Y	Y	Guam	Y	None
35		138	150	Fegurgur, Veronica S	Daughter	F	Cha	7	S	Y		Guam		None
36		139	151	Aguon, Simon C	Head	M	Cha	38	M	N	N	Guam	N	Farmer
37		139	151	Aguon, Ana A	Wife	F	Cha	39	M	N	N	Guam	N	None
38		139	151	Aguon, Vicente A	Son	M	Cha	12	S	Y	Y	Guam	Y	None
39		139	151	Aguon, Francisco A	Son	M	Cha	7	S	Y		Guam		None
40		139	151	Aguon, Rosa A	Daughter	F	Cha	4.7	S	N		Guam		None
41		139	151	Aguon, Jose A	Son	M	Cha	2.7	S	N		Guam		None
42		140	152	Aguon, Justo C	Head	M	Cha	39	M	N	Y	Guam	N	Farmer
43		140	152	Aguon, Consuelo Q	Wife	F	Cha	37	M	N	Y	Guam	N	None
44		140	152	Aguon, Ana Q	Daughter	F	Cha	12	S	Y	Y	Guam	Y	None
45		140	152	Aguon, Maria Q	Daughter	F	Cha	10	S	Y	Y	Guam	Y	None
46		140	152	Aguon, Baldovino Q	Son	M	Cha	6	S	N		Guam		None
47		140	152	Aguon, Ignacio Q	Son	M	Cha	4.4	S	N		Guam		None
48		140	152	Aguon, Joaquin Q	Son	M	Cha	2	S	N		Guam		None
49		141	153	Aguon, Juana C	Head	F	Cha	59	Wd	N	N	Guam	N	None
50		141	153	Aguon, Asuncion C	Daughter	F	Cha	30	S	N	Y	Guam	N	None

DEPARTMENT OF COMMERCE-BUREAU OF THE CENSUS
WASHINGTON

FIFTEENTH CENSUS OF THE UNITED STATES: 1930-POPULATION

THE ISLAND OF GUAM

Sheet No. 17A

District Municipality of Merizo
Name of Place Umatac Barrio
[Proper name and, also, name of class, as city, town, village, barrio, etc]

Enumeration District No. 9
Enumerated by me on April 12, 1930 Manuel Charfauros, Enumerator

	PLACE OF ABODE: Street, avenue, road, etc.	Number of dwelling house in order of visitation	Number of family in order of visitation	NAME of each person whose place of abode on April 1, 1930, was in this family. Enter surname, first, then given name and middle initial. If any. Include every person living on April 1, 1930. Omit children born since April 1, 1930.	RELATION Relationship of this Person to the head of the family.	PERSONAL DESCRIPTION: Sex	Color or race	Age at last birthday	Single, married, widowed or divorced	EDUCATION: Attended school any time since Sept. 1, 1929	Whether able to read and write.	NATIVITY Place of birth of this person.	Whether able to speak English.	OCCUPATION
	1	2	3	4	5	6	7	8	9	10	11	12	13	14
1	San Dionisio Street	141	153	Aguon, Maximo C	Son	M	Cha	29	S	N	Y	Guam	Y	Road laborer
2		141	153	Aguon, Cristina A	Grand daughter	F	Cha	15	S	N	Y	Guam	Y	None
3		141	153	Aguon, Jose A	Grand son	M	Cha	10	S	Y	Y	Guam	Y	None
4		141	153	Aguon, Agueda A	Grand son	M	Cha	6	S	Y		Guam		None
5		142	154	Quinata, Faustino M	Head	M	Cha	65	M	N	Y	Guam	N	Farmer
6		142	154	Quinata, Maria A	Wife	F	Cha	38	M	N	Y	Guam	N	None
7		142	154	Quinata, Jesus A	Son	M	Cha	20	S	N	Y	Guam	Y	School teacher
8		142	154	Quinata, Faustino A	Son	M	Cha	18	S	N	Y	Guam	Y	Farm laborer
9		143	155	Santiago, Domingo D	Head	M	Fil	39	M	N	Y	Guam	N	Farmer
10		143	155	Santiago, Petra A	Wife	F	Cha	37	M	N	N	Guam	N	None
11		143	155	Aguon, Juan A	Step-son	M	Cha	15	S	Y	Y	Guam	Y	None
12		143	155	Aguon, Isabel A	Step-daughter	F	Cha	11	S	Y	Y	Guam	Y	None
13		143	155	Santiago, Hilarion A	Son	M	Fil	7	S	Y		Guam		None
14		143	155	Santiago, Asuncion A	Daughter	F	Fil	5	S	N		Guam		None
15		143	155	Santiago, Maria A	Daughter	F	Fil	4.1	S	N		Guam		None
16		143	155	Santiago, Jose A	Son	M	Fil	2.2	S	N		Guam		None
17		144	156	Quinata, Vicente T	Head	M	Cha	31	M	N	Y	Guam	Y	Farmer
18		144	156	Quinata, Adela M	Wife	F	Cha	37	M	N	Y	Guam	N	None
19		144	156	Quinata, Vicente M	Son	M	Cha	1.2	S	N		Guam		None
20		145	157	Aguon, Lucas I	Head	M	Cha	40	M	N	Y	Guam	Y	Farmer
21		145	157	Aguon, Joaquina B	Wife	F	Cha	37	M	N	Y	Guam	N	None
22		145	157	Babauta, Jesus A	Nephew-in-law	M	Cha	13	S	Y	Y	Guam	Y	None
23		146	158	Manalisay, Jose C	Head	M	Cha	48	M	N	Y	Guam	N	Farmer
24		146	158	Manalisay, Soledad T	Wife	F	Cha	43	M	N	Y	Guam	N	None
25		147	159	Aguon, Felipe R	Head	M	Cha	37	M	N	Y	Guam	N	Farmer

DEPARTMENT OF COMMERCE-BUREAU OF THE CENSUS
WASHINGTON

FIFTEENTH CENSUS OF THE UNITED STATES: 1930-POPULATION

THE ISLAND OF GUAM

Sheet No. 17B

286B

District Municipality of Merizo
Name of Place Umatac Barrio
[Proper name and, also, name of class, as city, town, village, barrio, etc]

Enumeration District No. 9
Enumerated by me on April 14, 1930 Manuel Charfauros, Enumerator

	PLACE OF ABODE			NAME	RELATION	PERSONAL DESCRIPTION				EDUCATION		NATIVITY		OCCUPATION
	Street, avenue, road, etc.	Number of dwelling house is order of visitation	Number of family in order of visitation	of each person whose place of abode on April 1, 1930, was in this family. Enter surname, first, then given name and middle initial. If any. Include every person living on April 1, 1930. Omit children born since April 1, 1930.	Relationship of this Person to the head of the family.	Sex	Color or race	Age at last birthday	Single, married, widowed or divorced	Attended school any time since Sept. 1, 1929	Whether able to read and write.	Place of birth of this person.	Whether able to speak English.	
	1	2	3	4	5	6	7	8	9	10	11	12	13	14
26	San Dionisio Street	147	159	Aguon, Calistra T	Wife	F	Cha	33	M	N	Y	Guam		None
27		147	159	Aguon, Joaquina T	Daughter	F	Cha	12	S	Y	Y	Guam		None
28		147	159	Aguon, Delfina T	Daughter	F	Cha	9	S	Y		Guam		None
29		147	159	Aguon, Gregorio T	Son	M	Cha	4.9	S	N		Guam		None
30		147	159	Aguon, Maria T	Son	M	Cha	3.2	S	N		Guam		None
31		148	160	Quinata, Ramon A	Head	M	Cha	22	M	N	Y	Guam		Farmer
32		148	160	Quinata, Trinidad A	Wife	F	Cha	19	M	N	Y	Guam		None
33		148	160	Quinata, Jose A	Son	M	Cha	2.1	S	N		Guam		None
34		148	160	Quinata, Maria A	Daughter	F	Cha	.2	S	N		Guam		None
35		149	161	Sanchez, Inrique Q	Head	M	Cha	47	M	N	Y	Guam	N	Farmer
36		149	161	Sanchez, Trudes T	Wife	F	Cha	48	M	N	N	Guam	N	None
37		149	161	Tajalle, Felisa Q	Sister-in-law	F	Cha	49	S	N	N	Guam	N	None
38		149	161	Namauleg, Dolores Q	Niece-in-law	F	Cha	18	S	N	Y	Guam	Y	None
39		150	162	Quinata, Hermanigildo ?	Head	M	Cha	37	M	N	Y	Guam	N	Farmer
40		150	162	Quinata, Dolores A	Wife	F	Cha	47	M	N	Y	Guam	N	None
41		150	162	Quinata, Mariano A	Step-son	M	Cha	15	S	Y	Y	Guam	Y	Farm laborer
42		150	162	Quinata, Vicente A	Step-son	M	Cha	12	S	Y	Y	Guam	Y	None
43		150	162	Quinata, Ana A	Daughter	F	Cha	11	S	Y	Y	Guam	Y	None
44		150	162	Quinata, Maria A	Daughter	F	Cha	10	S	Y	N	Guam	N	None
45		150	162	Quinata, Ana A	Step-daughter	F	Cha	7	S	Y		Guam		None
46		151	163	Topasna, Jose Q	Head	M	Cha	27	M	N	Y	Guam	Y	Farmer
47		151	163	Topasna, Maria I	Wife	F	Cha	25	M	N	Y	Guam	Y	None
48		151	163	Topasna, Julian I	Son	M	Cha	7	S	Y		Guam		None
49		151	163	Topasna, Josefina I	Daughter	F	Cha	6	S	N		Guam		None
50		151	163	Topasna, Francisca I	Daughter	F	Cha	4.1	S	N		Guam		None

(CHAMORRO ROOTS GENEALOGY PROJECT™ TRANSCRIPTION)
(BERNARD T. PUNZALAN / HTTP://WWW.CHAMORROROOTS.COM)

DEPARTMENT OF COMMERCE-BUREAU OF THE CENSUS
WASHINGTON

FIFTEENTH CENSUS OF THE UNITED STATES: 1930-POPULATION

THE ISLAND OF GUAM

Sheet No. 18A

287

District **Municipality of Merizo**
Name of Place **Umatac Barrio**
[Proper name and, also, name of class, as city, town, village, barrio, etc]

Enumeration District No. 9
Enumerated by me on **April 14, 1930** Manuel Charfauros, Enumerator

	PLACE OF ABODE			NAME	RELATION	PERSONAL DESCRIPTION				EDUCATION		NATIVITY		OCCUPATION
	Street, avenue, road, etc.	Number of dwelling house in order of visitation	Number of family in order of visitation	of each person whose place of abode on April 1, 1930, was in this family. Enter surname, first, then given name and middle initial. If any. Include every person living on April 1, 1930. Omit children born since April 1, 1930.	Relationship of this Person to the head of the family.	Sex	Color or race	Age at last birthday	Single, married, widowed or divorced	Attended school any time since Sept. 1, 1929	Whether able to read and write.	Place of birth of this person.	Whether able to speak English.	
	1	2	3	4	5	6	7	8	9	10	11	12	13	14
1	San Dionisio Street	151	163	Topasna, Jose I	Son	M	Cha	2.2	S	N		Guam		None
2		151	163	Topasna, Isabel I	Daughter	F	Cha	.4	S	N		Guam		None
3		151	164	Topasna, Gregorio A	Head	M	Cha	20	M	N	Y	Guam	Y	Farmer
4		151	164	Topasna, Ana I	Wife	F	Cha	21	M	N	Y	Guam	Y	None
5		151	164	Topasna, Rita I	Daughter	F	Cha	.6	S	N		Guam		None
6		151	164	Topasna, Felipe A	Brother	M	Cha	13	S	Y	Y	Guam	Y	None
7		152	165	Topasna, Eucebio Q	Head	M	Cha	30	M	N	Y	Guam	N	Farmer
8		152	165	Topasna, Petronila A	Wife	F	Cha	33	M	N	Y	Guam	N	None
9		152	165	Topasna, Ursula A	Daughter	F	Cha	11	S	Y	Y	Guam	Y	None
10		152	165	Topasna, Jaime A	Son	M	Cha	7	S	Y		Guam		None
11		152	165	Topasna, Jose A	Son	M	Cha	5	S	N		Guam		None
12		152	165	Topasna, Francisco A	Son	M	Cha	4.5	S	N		Guam		None
13		152	165	Topasna, Roman A	Son	M	Cha	3.7	S	N		Guam		None
14		152	165	Topasna, Dolores A	Daughter	F	Cha	2.1	S	N		Guam		None
15		153	166	Topasna, Soledad Q	Head	F	Cha	57	Wd	N	N	Guam	N	Farmer
16		153	166	Topasna, Francisco Q	Son	M	Cha	17	S	N	Y	Guam	Y	Farm laborer
17		153	166	Topasna, Juan Q	Son	M	Cha	12	S	Y	Y	Guam	Y	None
18		154	167	Sanchez, Antonio A	Head	M	Cha	59	S	N	N	Guam	N	Farmer
19		154	167	Sanchez, Lucas A	Brother	M	Cha	44	S	N	N	Guam	N	Farm laborer
20		154	167	Sanchez, Emiliana C	Niece	F	Cha	35	S	N	N	Guam	N	None
21		154	167	Sanchez, Jesus S	Grand nephew	M	Cha	5	S	N		Guam		None
22		154	167	Cheguina, Jose S	Nephew	M	Cha	16	S	N	Y	Guam	Y	Farm laborer
23		154	167	Aguon, Juan A	Servant	M	Cha	7	S	Y		Guam		Servant
24		155	168	Quinata, Antonio A	Head	M	Cha	43	M	N	Y	Guam	N	Farmer
25		155	168	Quinata, Anastacia T	Wife	F	Cha	40	M	N	Y	Guam	N	None

DEPARTMENT OF COMMERCE-BUREAU OF THE CENSUS
WASHINGTON

FIFTEENTH CENSUS OF THE UNITED STATES: 1930-POPULATION

THE ISLAND OF GUAM

Sheet No. 18B

287B

District **Municipality of Merizo**
Name of Place **Umatac Barrio**
[Proper name and, also, name of class, as city, town, village, barrio, etc]

Enumeration District No. 9
Enumerated by me on **April 14, 1930** Manuel Charfauros, Enumerator

	PLACE OF ABODE			NAME	RELATION	PERSONAL DESCRIPTION				EDUCATION		NATIVITY		OCCUPATION
	Street, avenue, road, etc.	Number of dwelling house is order of visitation	Number of family in order of visitation	of each person whose place of abode on April 1, 1930, was in this family. Enter surname, first, then given name and middle initial. If any. Include every person living on April 1, 1930. Omit children born since April 1, 1930.	Relationship of this Person to the head of the family.	Sex	Color or race	Age at last birthday	Single, married, widowed or divorced	Attended school any time since Sept. 1, 1929	Whether able to read and write.	Place of birth of this person.	Whether able to speak English.	
	1	2	3	4	5	6	7	8	9	10	11	12	13	14
26		155	168	Quinata, Cevera T	Daughter	F	Cha	15	S	Y	Y	Guam	Y	None
27		155	168	Quinata, Joaquina T	Daughter	F	Cha	11	S	Y	Y	Guam	Y	None
28		155	168	Quinata, Jesus T	Son	M	Cha	7	S	Y		Guam		None
29		155	168	Quinata, Vicente T	Son	M	Cha	4.5	S	N		Guam		None
30		155	168	Quinata, Jose T	Son	M	Cha	2.1	S	N		Guam		None
31		155	168	Topasna, Rafael E	Brother-in-law	M	Cha	48	Wd	N	Y	Guam	N	Farm laborer
32		155	168	Quidachay, Enriqueta T	Niece-in-law	F	Cha	18	S	N	Y	Guam	Y	None
33		156	169	Gofigan, Jose Q	Head	M	Cha	37	M	N	Y	Guam	Y	Deputy Commissioner
34		156	169	Gofigan, Francisca A	Wife	F	Cha	33	M	N	Y	Guam	N	None
35		156	169	Aguon, Maria C	Mother-in-law	F	Cha	51	Wd	N	N	Guam	N	None
36		156	169	Aguon, Librada C	Sister-in-law	F	Cha	31	S	N	Y	Guam	Y	None
37		157	170	Santiago, Simon Q	Head	M	Fil	41	M	N	Y	Guam	N	Farmer
38		157	170	Santiago, Carmen C	Wife	F	Cha	45	M	N	Y	Guam	N	None
39		157	170	Santiago, Ana C	Daughter	F	Fil	16	S	N	Y	Guam	Y	None
40		157	170	Santiago, Dolores C	Daughter	F	Fil	13	S	Y	Y	Guam	Y	None
41		157	170	Santiago, Jose C	Son	M	Fil	11	S	Y	Y	Guam	Y	None
42		157	170	Santiago, Mariano C	Son	M	Fil	10	S	Y	Y	Guam	Y	None
43		157	170	Santiago, Joaquin C	Son	M	Fil	8	S	Y		Guam		None
44		158	171	Santiago, Marcela Q	Head	F	Cha	60	Wd	N	N	Guam	N	Farmer
45		158	171	Santiago, Teresa Q	Daughter	F	Fil	21	S	N	Y	Guam	Y	None
46		158	171	Santiago, Jose Q	Son	M	Fil	19	S	N	Y	Guam	Y	Farm laborer
47		159	172	Aguon, Vicente C	Head	M	Cha	26	M	N	Y	Guam	Y	Farmer
48		159	172	Aguon, Joaquina Q	Wife	F	Cha	24	M	N	Y	Guam	Y	None
49		159	172	Aguon, Maria Q	Daughter	F	Cha	3.4	S	N		Guam		None
50		159	172	Aguon, Brigida Q	Daughter	F	Cha	1.4	S	N		Guam		None

DEPARTMENT OF COMMERCE-BUREAU OF THE CENSUS
WASHINGTON

FIFTEENTH CENSUS OF THE UNITED STATES: 1930-POPULATION

THE ISLAND OF GUAM

Sheet No. 19A

District **Municipality of Merizo**
Name of Place **Umatac Barrio**
[Proper name and, also, name of class, as city, town, village, barrio, etc]

Enumeration District No. **9**
Enumerated by me on **April 15, 1930** Manuel Charfauros, Enumerator

	PLACE OF ABODE			NAME	RELATION	PERSONAL DESCRIPTION				EDUCATION		NATIVITY		OCCUPATION
	Street, avenue, road, etc.	Number of dwelling house in order of visitation	Number of family in order of visitation	of each person whose place of abode on April 1, 1930, was in this family. Enter surname, first, then given name and middle initial. If any. Include every person living on April 1, 1930. Omit children born since April 1, 1930.	Relationship of this Person to the head of the family.	Sex	Color or race	Age at last birthday	Single, married, widowed or divorced	Attended school any time since Sept. 1, 1929	Whether able to read and write.	Place of birth of this person.	Whether able to speak English.	
	1	2	3	4	5	6	7	8	9	10	11	12	13	14
1	San Dionisio Street	159	172	Quinata, Vicenta M	Mother in law	F	Cha	58	Wd	N	N	Guam	N	None
2		159	172	Quinata, Bardovino M	Brother in law	M	Cha	28	S	N	Y	Guam	Y	Farm laborer
3		160	173	Gofigan, Vicenta Q	Head	F	Cha	57	Wd	N	N	Guam	N	Farmer
4		160	173	Gofigan, Grabiel Q	Son	M	Cha	26	S	N	Y	Guam	Y	Farm laborer
5		160	173	Gofigan, Gregorio Q	Son	M	Cha	20	S	N	Y	Guam	Y	School teacher
6		160	173	Gofigan, Ramon Q	Son	M	Cha	13	S	Y	Y	Guam	Y	None
7		160	173	Quinata, Magdalena T	Niece	F	Cha	14	S	N	Y	Guam	Y	None
8		161	174	Gofigan, Geronimo Q	Head	M	Cha	31	M	N	Y	Guam	Y	Farmer
9		161	174	Gofigan, Ana A	Wife	F	Cha	27	M	N	Y	Guam	Y	None
10		161	174	Gofigan, Maria A	Daughter	F	Cha	5	S	N		Guam		None
11		161	174	Gofigan, Joaquina A	Daughter	F	Cha	4.2	S	N		Guam		None
12		161	174	Gofigan, Antonina A	Daughter	F	Cha	3.1	S	N		Guam		None
13		161	174	Gofigan, Oliva A	Daughter	F	Cha	.9	S	N		Guam		None
14		161	174	Cheguina, Vicente A	Uncle-in-law	M	Cha	49	S	N	N	Guam	N	None
15		162	175	Babauta, Juan G	Head	M	Cha	40	M	N	Y	Guam	N	Farmer
16		162	175	Babauta, Ana A	Wife	F	Cha	39	M	N	Y	Guam	N	None
17		162	175	Babauta, Maria A	Daughter	F	Cha	21	S	N	Y	Guam	Y	None
18		162	175	Babauta, Florencia A	Daughter	F	Cha	19	S	N	Y	Guam	Y	None
19		162	175	Babauta, Jose A	Son	M	Cha	15	S	Y	Y	Guam	Y	None
20		163	176	Babauta, Robinio G	Head	M	Cha	34	M	N	Y	Guam	N	Farmer
21		163	176	Babauta, Lagrimas A	Wife	F	Cha	28	M	N	Y	Guam	Y	None
22		163	176	Babauta, Joaquina A	Daughter	F	Cha	10	S	Y	Y	Guam	Y	None
23		163	176	Babauta, Vicente A	Son	M	Cha	8	S	Y		Guam		None
24		164	177	Quinata, Juan A	Head	M	Cha	46	M	N	Y	Guam	N	Farmer
25		164	177	Quinata, Eulogracia D	Wife	F	Cha	40	M	N	Y	Guam	Y	Basket weaver

(CHAMORRO ROOTS GENEALOGY PROJECT™ TRANSCRIPTION)
(BERNARD T. PUNZALAN / HTTP://WWW.CHAMORROROOTS.COM)

DEPARTMENT OF COMMERCE-BUREAU OF THE CENSUS
WASHINGTON

FIFTEENTH CENSUS OF THE UNITED STATES: 1930-POPULATION

THE ISLAND OF GUAM

Sheet No. 19B

288B

District Municipality of Merizo
Name of Place Umatac Barrio
[Proper name and, also, name of class, as city, town, village, barrio, etc]

Enumeration District No. 9
Enumerated by me on April 15, 1930 Manuel Charfauros, Enumerator

	PLACE OF ABODE: Street, avenue, road, etc.	Number of dwelling house in order of visitation	Number of family in order of visitation	NAME of each person whose place of abode on April 1, 1930, was in this family. Enter surname, first, then given name and middle initial. If any. Include every person living on April 1, 1930. Omit children born since April 1, 1930.	RELATION Relationship of this Person to the head of the family.	PERSONAL DESCRIPTION: Sex	Color or race	Age at last birthday	Single, married, widowed or divorced	EDUCATION: Attended school any time since Sept. 1, 1929	Whether able to read and write.	NATIVITY Place of birth of this person.	Whether able to speak English.	OCCUPATION
	1	2	3	4	5	6	7	8	9	10	11	12	13	14
26	San Dionisio Street	164	177	Quinata, Francisco D	Son	M	Cha	18	S	Y	Y	Guam	Y	Farm laborer
27		164	178	Manalisay, Francisco T	Head	M	Cha	17	M	N	Y	Guam	Y	School teacher
28		164	178	Manalisay, Guardalupe C	Wife	F	Cha	19	M	N	Y	Guam	Y	None
29		165	179	Quinata, Vicente A	Head	M	Cha	38	M	N	Y	Guam	N	Farmer
30		165	179	Quinata, Margarita S	Wife	F	Cha	34	M	N	Y	Guam	N	None
31		165	179	Quinata, Automina S	Daughter	F	Cha	17	S	N	Y	Guam	Y	None
32		165	179	Quinata, Ana S	Daughter	F	Cha	13	S	Y	Y	Guam	Y	None
33		165	179	Quinata, Lydia S	Daughter	F	Cha	10	S	Y	Y	Guam		None
34		165	179	Quinata, Jose S	Son	M	Cha	7	S	Y		Guam		None
35		165	179	Quinata, Josefina S	Daughter	F	Cha	6	S	N		Guam		None
36		165	179	Quinata, Joaquin S	Daughter	F	Cha	4.2	S	N		Guam		None
37		165	179	Quinata, Andina S	Daughter	F	Cha	2.4	S	N		Guam		None
38		165	179	Quinata, Jesus S	Son	M	Cha	.2	S	N		Guam		None
39		166	180	Quinata, Miguel A	Head	M	Cha	34	M	N	N	Guam	N	Farm laborer
40		166	180	Quinata, Teresa A	Wife	F	Cha	28	M	N	Y	Guam	Y	None
41		166	180	Quinata, Antonio A	Son	M	Cha	12	S	Y	Y	Guam	Y	None
42		166	180	Quinata, Francisco A	Son	M	Cha	10	S	Y	Y	Guam	Y	None
43		166	180	Quinata, Amparo A	Daughter	F	Cha	8	S	Y		Guam		None
44		166	180	Quinata, Grabiela A	Daughter	F	Cha	4.7	S	N		Guam		None
45		167	181	Quidachay, Ramon D	Head	M	Cha	34	M	N	Y	Guam	Y	Farmer
46		167	181	Quidachay, Maria M	Wife	F	Cha	49	M	N	N	Guam	N	None
47		167	181	Quidachay, Delgadina M	Daughter	F	Cha	4.5	S	N		Guam		None
48		167	181	Aguon, Concepcion M	Step-daughter	F	Cha	20	S	N	Y	Guam	Y	None
49		167	181	Aguon, Atanacio M	Step-son	M	Cha	14	S	Y	Y	Guam	Y	None
50		167	181	Aguon, Bernadita M	Step-daughter	F	Cha	9	S	Y		Guam		None

DEPARTMENT OF COMMERCE-BUREAU OF THE CENSUS
WASHINGTON

FIFTEENTH CENSUS OF THE UNITED STATES: 1930-POPULATION

THE ISLAND OF GUAM

Sheet No. 20A

District **Municipality of Merizo**
Name of Place **Umatac Barrio**
[Proper name and, also, name of class, as city, town, village, barrio, etc]

Enumeration District No. 9
Enumerated by me on **April 16, 1930** Manuel Charfauros
Enumerator

	PLACE OF ABODE			NAME	RELATION	PERSONAL DESCRIPTION				EDUCATION		NATIVITY		OCCUPATION
	Street, avenue, road, etc.	Number of dwelling house is order of visitation	Number of family in order of visitation	of each person whose place of abode on April 1, 1930, was in this family. Enter surname, first, then given name and middle initial. If any. Include every person living on April 1, 1930. Omit children born since April 1, 1930.	Relationship of this Person to the head of the family.	Sex	Color or race	Age at last birthday	Single, married, widowed or divorced	Attended school any time since Sept. 1, 1929	Whether able to read and write.	Place of birth of this person.	Whether able to speak English.	
	1	2	3	4	5	6	7	8	9	10	11	12	13	14
1	San Dionisio Street	167	181	Aguon, Ana M	Step-daughter	F	Cha	6	S	N		Guam		None
2		167	181	Aguon, Juan M	Step-Grandson	M	Cha	3.5	S	N		Guam		None
3		168	182	Quinata, Luis A	Head	M	Cha	38	M	N	Y	Guam	N	Farmer
4		168	182	Quinata, Antonia B	Wife	F	Cha	33	M	N	Y	Guam	N	None
5		168	182	Quinata, Jesus B	Son	M	Cha	12	S	Y	Y	Guam	Y	None
6		168	182	Quinata, Francisco B	Son	M	Cha	10	S	Y	Y	Guam	Y	None
7		168	182	Quinata, Rosabela B	Daughter	F	Cha	7	S	Y		Guam		None
8		168	182	Quinata, Jose B	Son	M	Cha	5	S	N		Guam		None
9		168	182	Quinata, Daniel B	Son	M	Cha	2.7	S	N		Guam		None
10		168	182	Quinata, Isabel B	Daughter	F	Cha	.7	S	N		Guam		None
11		169	183	Aguon, Joaquin Q	Head	M	Cha	26	M	N	Y	Guam	Y	Farmer
12		169	183	Aguon, Emilia Q	Wife	F	Cha	28	M	N	Y	Guam	Y	None
13		169	183	Aguon, Juan Q	Son	M	Cha	5	S	N		Guam		None
14		169	183	Aguon, Maria Q	Daughter	F	Cha	2.7	S	N		Guam		None
15		170	184	Topasna, Juan E	Head	M	Cha	27	M	N	Y	Guam	Y	Farmer
16		170	184	Topasna, Maria T	Wife	F	Cha	20	M	N	Y	Guam	Y	None
17		170	184	Quidachay, Francisco T	Nephew	M	Cha	13	S	Y	Y	Guam	Y	None
18		171	185	Quinata, Francisco M	Head	M	Cha	48	M	N	Y	Guam	N	Farmer
19		171	185	Quinata, Ana A	Wife	F	Cha	49	M	N	Y	Guam	N	None
20		171	185	Quidachay, Preciosa T	Niece-in-law	F	Cha	7	S	Y		Guam		None
21		172	186	Charfauros, Juan T	Head	M	Cha	47	M	N	Y	Guam	N	Farmer
22		172	186	Charfauros, Carlota C	Wife	F	Cha	37	M	N	Y	Guam	N	None
23		172	186	Charfauros, Jose C	Son	M	Cha	14	S	Y	Y	Guam	Y	None
24		172	186	Charfauros, Maria C	Daughter	F	Cha	12	S	Y	Y	Guam	Y	None
25		172	186	Charfauros, Jesus C	Son	M	Cha	11	S	Y	Y	Guam	Y	None

DEPARTMENT OF COMMERCE-BUREAU OF THE CENSUS
WASHINGTON

FIFTEENTH CENSUS OF THE UNITED STATES: 1930-POPULATION

THE ISLAND OF GUAM

Sheet No. 20B

289B

District **Municipality of Merizo**
Name of Place **Umatac Barrio**
[Proper name and, also, name of class, as city, town, village, barrio, etc]

Enumeration District No. **9**
Enumerated by me on **April 17, 1930** Manuel Charfauros
Enumerator

	PLACE OF ABODE			NAME	RELATION	PERSONAL DESCRIPTION				EDUCATION		NATIVITY		OCCUPATION
	Street, avenue, road, etc.	Number of dwelling house is order of visitation	Number of family in order of visitation	of each person whose place of abode on April 1, 1930, was in this family. Enter surname, first, then given name and middle initial. If any. Include every person living on April 1, 1930. Omit children born since April 1, 1930.	Relationship of this Person to the head of the family.	Sex	Color or race	Age at last birthday	Single, married, widowed or divorced	Attended school any time since Sept. 1, 1929	Whether able to read and write.	Place of birth of this person.	Whether able to speak English.	
	1	2	3	4	5	6	7	8	9	10	11	12	13	14
26	San Dionisio Street	172	186	Charfauros, Joaquin C	Son	M	Cha	9	S	Y		Guam		None
27		172	186	Charfauros, Antonio C	Son	M	Cha	5	S	N		Guam		None
28		172	186	Charfauros, Felix C	Son	M	Cha	3.2	S	N		Guam		None
29		172	186	Charfauros, Josefa C	Daughter	F	Cha	1.9	S	N		Guam		None
30		173	187	Sanchez, Moises Q	Head	M	Cha	35	M	N	Y	Guam	N	Farmer
31		173	187	Sanchez, Susana Q	Wife	F	Cha	34	M	N	Y	Guam	N	None
32		173	187	Sanchez, Maria Q	Daughter	F	Cha	14	S	Y	Y	Guam	Y	None
33		173	187	Sanchez, Jesus Q	Son	M	Cha	12	S	Y	Y	Guam	Y	None
34		173	187	Sanchez, Rosario Q	Son	M	Cha	9	S	Y		Guam		None
35		173	187	Sanchez, Ana Q	Daughter	F	Cha	7	S	Y		Guam		None
36		173	187	Sanchez, Jose Q	Son	M	Cha	5	S	N		Guam		None
37		173	187	Sanchez, Juan Q	Son	M	Cha	.7	S	N		Guam		None
38		174	188	Aguon, Antonio R	Head	M	Cha	30	M	N	Y	Guam	Y	Farmer
39		174	188	Aguon, Magdalena A	Wife	F	Cha	23	M	N	Y	Guam	Y	None
40		174	188	Aguon, Jose A	Son	M	Cha	3.2	S	N		Guam		None
41		174	188	Aguon, Juan A	Son	M	Cha	.9	S	N		Guam		None
42		174	188	Aguon, Sabina A	Mother	F	Cha	69	Wd	N	Y	Guam	N	None
43		175	189	Quinata, edro I	Head	M	Cha	57	M	N	Y	Guam	N	Farmer
44		175	189	Quinata, Guillerma M	Wife	F	Fil	54	M	N	N	Guam	N	None
45		175	189	Quinata, Joaquin M	Nephew	M	Cha	20	S	N	Y	Guam	Y	Farm laborer
46		175	189	Quinata, Ana M	Niece	F	Cha	16	S	N	Y	Guam	Y	None
47		175	190	Babauta, Ignacio G	Head	M	Cha	39	M	N	Y	Guam	N	Farmer
48		175	190	Babauta, Felistina Q	Wife	F	Cha	38	M	N	Y	Guam	N	None
49		176	191	Sanchez, Nicolas D	Head	M	Cha	30	Wd	N	Y	Guam	N	Farmer
50		176	192	Quinata, Jose M	Head	M	Cha	30	M	N	Y	Guam	Y	Farmer

DEPARTMENT OF COMMERCE-BUREAU OF THE CENSUS
WASHINGTON
FIFTEENTH CENSUS OF THE UNITED STATES: 1930-POPULATION
THE ISLAND OF GUAM

Sheet No. 21A

District **Municipality of Merizo**
Name of Place **Umatac Barrio**
[Proper name and, also, name of class, as city, town, village, barrio, etc]

Enumeration District No. 9
Enumerated by me on **April 18, 1930** Manuel Charfauros, Enumerator

	PLACE OF ABODE			NAME	RELATION	PERSONAL DESCRIPTION				EDUCATION		NATIVITY		OCCUPATION
	Street, avenue, road, etc.	Number of dwelling house in order of visitation	Number of family in order of visitation	of each person whose place of abode on April 1, 1930, was in this family. Enter surname, first, then given name and middle initial. If any. Include every person living on April 1, 1930. Omit children born since April 1, 1930.	Relationship of this Person to the head of the family.	Sex	Color or race	Age at last birthday	Single, married, widowed or divorced	Attended school any time since Sept. 1, 1929	Whether able to read and write.	Place of birth of this person.	Whether able to speak English.	
	1	2	3	4	5	6	7	8	9	10	11	12	13	14
1	San Dionisio Street	176	192	Quinata, Engracia A	Wife	M	Cha	25	M	N	Y	Guam	Y	None
2		176	192	Quinata, Antonia A	Daughter	F	Cha	7	S	Y		Guam		None
3		176	192	Quinata, Ignacio A	Son	M	Cha	6	S	N		Guam		None
4		176	192	Quinata, Maria A	Daughter	F	Cha	2.9	S	N		Guam		None
5		176	192	Quinata, Beatriz A	Daughter	F	Cha	.5	S	N		Guam		None
6		177	193	Quinata, Jose SN	Head	M	Cha	55	M	N	Y	Guam	N	Farmer
7		177	193	Quinata, Maria A	Wife	F	Cha	52	M	N	Y	Guam	N	None
8		177	193	Quinata, Ignacio A	Son	M	Cha	28	S	N	Y	Guam	Y	Farm laborer
9		177	193	Quinata, Josefina A	Daughter	F	Cha	22	S	N	Y	Guam	Y	None
10		177	193	Quinata, Beatriz A	Daughter	F	Cha	20	S	N	Y	Guam	Y	None
11		177	193	Quinata, Jose A	Son	M	Cha	18	S	N	Y	Guam	Y	Farm laborer
12		177	193	Quinata, Conchita A	Daughter	F	Cha	7	S	Y		Guam		None
13		177	193	Cruz, Ramon C	Lodger	M	Cha	6	S	N		Guam		None
14		177	193	Cruz, Edward C	Lodger	M	Cha	2.5	S	N		Guam		None
15		177	194	Sanchez, Joaquin Q	Head	M	Cha	24	M	N	Y	Guam	Y	Farmer
16		177	194	Sanchez, Milagro Q	Wife	F	Cha	25	M	N	Y	Guam	Y	None
17		177	194	Sanchez, Oliva Q	Daughter	F	Cha	1.1	S	N		Guam		None
18		178	195	Sanchez, Antonio S	Head	M	Cha	24	M	N	N	Guam	N	Farmer
19		178	195	Sanchez, Emilia Q	Wife	F	Cha	25	M	N	N	Guam	N	None
20		178	195	Quinata, Jesus S	Grandson	M	Cha	12	S	Y	Y	Guam	Y	None
21		178	195	Quinata, Jose S	Grandson	M	Cha	10	S	Y	Y	Guam	Y	None
22		178	196	Santiago, Vicente Q	Head	M	Fil	25	M	N	Y	Guam	Y	School teacher
23		178	196	Santiago, Maria S	Wife	F	Cha	20	M	N	Y	Guam	Y	None
24		178	196	Santiago, Francisco S	Son	M	Fil	1.1	S	N		Guam		None
25		178	197	Sanchez, Joaquin Q	Head	M	Cha	28	M	N	Y	Guam	Y	School teacher

DEPARTMENT OF COMMERCE-BUREAU OF THE CENSUS
WASHINGTON

FIFTEENTH CENSUS OF THE UNITED STATES: 1930-POPULATION

THE ISLAND OF GUAM

Sheet No. 21B

290B

District Municipality of Merizo
Name of Place Umatac Barrio
[Proper name and, also, name of class, as city, town, village, barrio, etc]

Enumeration District No. 9
Enumerated by me on April 18, 1930 Manuel Charfauros, Enumerator

	PLACE OF ABODE			NAME	RELATION	PERSONAL DESCRIPTION				EDUCATION		NATIVITY		OCCUPATION
	Street, avenue, road, etc.	Number of dwelling house is order of visitation	Number of family in order of visitation	of each person whose place of abode on April 1, 1930, was in this family. Enter surname, first, then given name and middle initial. If any. Include every person living on April 1, 1930. Omit children born since April 1, 1930.	Relationship of this Person to the head of the family.	Sex	Color or race	Age at last birthday	Single, married, widowed or divorced	Attended school any time since Sept. 1, 1929	Whether able to read and write.	Place of birth of this person.	Whether able to speak English.	
	1	2	3	4	5	6	7	8	9	10	11	12	13	14
26	San Dionisio Street	178	197	Sanchez, Antonia S	Wife	M	Cha	32	M	N	Y	Guam	Y	Midwife
27		178	197	Sanchez, Ralph S	Son	M	Cha	13	S	Y	Y	Guam	Y	None
28		178	197	Sanchez, Jose S	Son	M	Cha	8	S	Y		Guam		None
29		178	197	Sanchez, Ignacio S	Son	M	Cha	5	S	N		Guam		None
30		178	197	Sanchez, Alejo S	Son	M	Cha	4.7	S	N		Guam		None
31		178	197	Sanchez, Priscilla S	Daughter	S	Cha	.8	S	N		Guam		None
32		179	198	Isezaki, Vicente	Head	M	Jap	50	M	N	Y	Japan	N	Fisherman
33		179	198	Isezaki, Marcelina P	Wife	F	Cha	37	M	N	Y	Guam	N	None
34		179	198	Isezaki, Jose P	Daughter	F	Jap	12	S	Y	Y	Guam	Y	None
35		179	198	Isezaki, Maria P	Daughter	F	Jap	11	S	Y	Y	Guam	Y	None
36		179	198	Isezaki, Carmen P	Daughter	F	Jap	8	S	Y		Guam		None
37		179	198	Isezaki, Concepcion P	Daughter	F	Jap	5	S	N		Guam		None
38		179	198	Isezaki, Juan P	Son	M	Jap	3.7	S	N		Guam		None
39		179	198	Isezaki, William P	Son	M	Jap	2	S	N		Guam		None
40		179	198	Isezaki, Ana P	Daughter	F	Jap	1.1	S	N		Guam		None
41		179	198	Pinaula, Jesus P	Step-son	M	Cha	16	S	N	Y	Guam	Y	Farm laborer
42		179	198	Pinaula, Vicente P	Step-son	M	Cha	14	S	Y	Y	Guam	Y	None
43		180	199	Isezaki, Yokichi	Head	M	Jap	44	M	N	Y	Japan	Y	Retail merchant
44		180	199	Isezaki, Rosa M	Wife	F	Cha	48	M	N	Y	Guam	N	None
45		180	199	Isezaki, Francisco M	Son	M	Jap	10	S	Y	Y	Guam	Y	None
46		180	199	Isezaki, Josefina M	Daughter	F	Jap	8	S	Y		Guam		None
47		180	199	Isezaki, Joaquina M	Daughter	F	Jap	6	S	N		Guam		None
48		180	199	Isezaki, Lucia M	Step-daughter	F	Jap	19	S	N	Y	Guam	Y	None
49		180	199	Malijan, Rita A	Step-daughter	F	Cha	12	S	Y	Y	Guam	Y	None
50		180	199	Malijan, Luisa A	Mother-in-law	F	Cha	83	Wd	N	N	Guam	N	None

DEPARTMENT OF COMMERCE-BUREAU OF THE CENSUS
WASHINGTON

FIFTEENTH CENSUS OF THE UNITED STATES: 1930-POPULATION

THE ISLAND OF GUAM

Sheet No. 22A

District **Municipality of Merizo**
Name of Place **Umatac Barrio**
[Proper name and, also, name of class, as city, town, village, barrio, etc]

Enumeration District No. 9
Enumerated by me on **April 18, 1930** Manuel Charfauros, Enumerator

	PLACE OF ABODE			NAME	RELATION	PERSONAL DESCRIPTION				EDUCATION		NATIVITY		OCCUPATION
	Street, avenue, road, etc.	Number of dwelling house is order of visitation	Number of family in order of visitation	of each person whose place of abode on April 1, 1930, was in this family. Enter surname, first, then given name and middle initial. If any. Include every person living on April 1, 1930. Omit children born since April 1, 1930.	Relationship of this Person to the head of the family.	Sex	Color or race	Age at last birthday	Single, married, widowed or divorced	Attended school any time since Sept. 1, 1929	Whether able to read and write.	Place of birth of this person.	Whether able to speak English.	
	1	2	3	4	5	6	7	8	9	10	11	12	13	14
1	San Dionisio Street	181	200	Babauta, Jose G	Head	M	Cha	38	M	N	N	Guam	N	Farmer
2		181	200	Babauta, Ana C	Wife	F	Cha	26	M	N	Y	Guam	N	None
3		181	200	Charfauros, Maria T	Mother in law	F	Cha	65	Wd	N	Y	Guam	N	None
4	Nino Perdido Street	182	201	Santiago, Justo Q	Head	M	Fil	35	M	N	Y	Guam	N	Farmer
5		182	201	Santiago, Maria T	Wife	F	Cha	30	M	N	Y	Guam	N	None
6		182	201	Santiago, Ana T	Daughter	F	Fil	12	S	Y	Y	Guam	Y	None
7		182	201	Santiago, Juliana T	Daughter	F	Fil	9	S	Y		Guam		None
8		182	201	Santiago, Maria T	Daughter	F	Fil	7	S	N		Guam		None
9		182	201	Santiago, Rita T	Daughter	F	Fil	5	S	N		Guam		None
10		182	201	Topasna, Juan Q	Brother in law	M	Cha	16	S	N	Y	Guam	Y	Farm laborer
11		183	202	Quinata, Juan Q	Head	M	Cha	30	M	N	Y	Guam	Y	Farmer
12		183	202	Quinata, Ana Q	Wife	F	Cha	28	M	N	Y	Guam	Y	None
13		183	202	Quinata, Maria Q	Daughter	F	Cha	4.9	S	N		Guam		None
14		183	202	Quinata, Juan Q	Son	M	Cha	.1	S	N		Guam		None
15		184	203	Sanchez, Francisco Q	Head	M	Cha	30	M	N	Y	Guam	Y	School teacher
16		184	203	Sanchez, Amparo S	Wife	F	Cha	32	M	N	Y	Guam	N	None
17		184	203	Sanchez, Angelina S	Daughter	F	Cha	13	S	Y	Y	Guam	Y	None
18		185	204	Topasna, Isidoro E	Head	M	Cha	35	M	N	N	Guam	N	Farmer
19		185	204	Topasna, Resurecion Q	Wife	F	Cha	34	M	N	Y	Guam	N	None
20		185	204	Topasna, Juan Q	Son	M	Cha	13	S	Y	Y	Guam	Y	None
21		185	204	Topasna, Rosalia Q	Daughter	F	Cha	10	S	Y	Y	Guam	Y	None
22		185	204	Topasna, Antonia Q	Daughter	F	Cha	8	S	Y		Guam		None
23		185	204	Topasna, Jose Q	Son	M	Cha	3.9	S	N		Guam		None
24		185	204	Topasna, Isabel Q	Daughter	F	Cha	.9	S	N		Guam		None
25		186	205	Topasna, Pedro A	Head	M	Cha	27	M	N	Y	Guam	N	Farmer

(CHAMORRO ROOTS GENEALOGY PROJECT™ TRANSCRIPTION)
(BERNARD T. PUNZALAN / HTTP://WWW.CHAMORROROOTS.COM)

DEPARTMENT OF COMMERCE-BUREAU OF THE CENSUS
WASHINGTON

FIFTEENTH CENSUS OF THE UNITED STATES: 1930-POPULATION

THE ISLAND OF GUAM

Sheet No. 22B

291B

District Municipality of Merizo
Name of Place Umatac Barrio
[Proper name and, also, name of class, as city, town, village, barrio, etc]

Enumeration District No. 9
Enumerated by me on April 21, 1930 Manuel Charfauros, Enumerator

	PLACE OF ABODE			NAME	RELATION	PERSONAL DESCRIPTION				EDUCATION		NATIVITY		OCCUPATION
	Street, avenue, road, etc.	Number of dwelling house in order of visitation	Number of family in order of visitation	of each person whose place of abode on April 1, 1930, was in this family. Enter surname, first, then given name and middle initial. If any. Include every person living on April 1, 1930. Omit children born since April 1, 1930.	Relationship of this Person to the head of the family.	Sex	Color or race	Age at last birthday	Single, married, widowed or divorced	Attended school any time since Sept. 1, 1929	Whether able to read and write.	Place of birth of this person.	Whether able to speak English.	
	1	2	3	4	5	6	7	8	9	10	11	12	13	14
26	Nino Perdido Street	186	205	Topasna, Feliciana P	Wife	F	Cha	22	M	N	Y	Guam	N	None
27		187	206	Topasna, Amadeo A	Head	M	Cha	31	M	N	Y	Guam	N	Farmer
28		187	206	Topasna, Valentina C	Wife	F	Cha	38	M	N	Y	Guam	N	None
29		187	206	Topasna, Joaquin C	Son	M	Cha	2.1	S	N		Guam		None
30		187	206	Topasna, Dolores C	Daughter	F	Cha	.1	S	N		Guam		None
31		188	207	Aguon, Vicente R	Head	M	Cha	50	M	N	Y	Guam	N	Farmer
32		188	207	Aguon, Angela B	Wife	F	Cha	37	M	N	Y	Guam	N	None
33		188	207	Aguon, Rosa B	Daughter	F	Cha	22	S	N	Y	Guam	Y	None
34		188	207	Aguon, Manuel B	Son	M	Cha	18	S	N	Y	Guam	Y	Farm laborer
35		188	207	Aguon, Maria B	Daughter	F	Cha	13	S	Y	Y	Guam	Y	None
36		188	207	Aguon, Jose B	Son	M	Cha	11	S	Y	Y	Guam	Y	None
37		188	207	Aguon, Ana B	Daughter	F	Cha	6	S	N		Guam		None
38		188	207	Aguon, Guardalupe B	Daughter	F	Cha	4.7	S	N		Guam		None
39		189	208	Quinata, Hilarion A	Head	M	Cha	35	M	N	Y	Guam	Y	Farmer
40		189	208	Quinata, Josepha S	Wife	F	Cha	38	M	N	Y	Guam	N	None
41		189	208	Quinata, Jesus S	Son	M	Cha	14	S	Y	Y	Guam	Y	None
42		189	208	Quinata, Maria S	Daughter	F	Cha	12	S	N	Y	Guam	Y	None
43		189	208	Quinata, Jose S	Son	M	Cha	9	S	Y		Guam		None
44		189	208	Quinata, Agnes S	Daughter	F	Cha	3.2	S	N		Guam		None
45		190	209	Sanchez, Francisco Q	Head	M	Cha	29	M	N	Y	Guam	Y	Farmer
46		190	209	Sanchez, Joaquina A	Wife	F	Cha	24	M	N	Y	Guam	N	None
47		190	209	Sanchez, Juan A	Son	M	Cha	7	S	Y		Guam		None
48		190	209	Sanchez, Justo A	Son	M	Cha	5	S	N		Guam		None
49		190	209	Sanchez, Joaquin A	Son	M	Cha	3.4	S	N		Guam		None
50		190	209	Sanchez, Jose A	Son	M	Cha	1.6	S	N		Guam		None

(CHAMORRO ROOTS GENEALOGY PROJECT™ TRANSCRIPTION)
(BERNARD T. PUNZALAN / HTTP://WWW.CHAMORROROOTS.COM)

DEPARTMENT OF COMMERCE-BUREAU OF THE CENSUS
WASHINGTON

FIFTEENTH CENSUS OF THE UNITED STATES: 1930-POPULATION

THE ISLAND OF GUAM

Sheet No. 23A

District **Municipality of Merizo**
Name of Place **Umatac Barrio**
[Proper name and, also, name of class, as city, town, village, barrio, etc]

Enumeration District No. **9**
Enumerated by me on **April 21, 1930** Manuel Charfauros, Enumerator

	PLACE OF ABODE			NAME	RELATION	PERSONAL DESCRIPTION				EDUCATION		NATIVITY		OCCUPATION
	Street, avenue, road, etc.	Number of dwelling house is order of visitation	Number of family in order of visitation	of each person whose place of abode on April 1, 1930, was in this family. Enter surname, first, then given name and middle initial. If any. Include every person living on April 1, 1930. Omit children born since April 1, 1930.	Relationship of this Person to the head of the family.	Sex	Color or race	Age at last birthday	Single, married, widowed or divorced	Attended school any time since Sept. 1, 1929	Whether able to read and write.	Place of birth of this person.	Whether able to speak English.	
	1	2	3	4	5	6	7	8	9	10	11	12	13	14
1		191	210	Sanchez, Salvador A	Head	M	Cha	42	M	N	Y	Guam	N	Farmer
2		191	210	Sanchez, Virginia Q	Wife	F	Cha	43	M	N	Y	Guam	N	None
3		191	210	Sanchez, Francisco Q	Son	M	Cha	10	S	Y	N	Guam	Y	None
4		191	210	Sanchez, Vicente Q	Son	M	Cha	3	S	N		Guam		None
5		192	211	Babauta, Ignacio G	Head	M	Cha	44	M	N	Y	Guam	N	Farmer
6		192	211	Babauta, Rosa Q	Wife	F	Cha	39	M	N	Y	Guam	N	None
7		192	211	Babauta, Dolores Q	Daughter	F	Cha	13	S	Y	Y	Guam	Y	None
8		192	211	Babauta, Maria Q	Daughter	F	Cha	5	S	N		Guam		None
9		192	211	Babauta, Florentina Q	Daughter	F	Cha	2.9	S	N		Guam		None
10		193	212	Aguon, Jose Q	Head	M	Cha	37	S	N	Y	Guam	N	Farmer
11		193	212	Aguon, Ana S	Wife	F	Cha	24	S	N	Y	Guam	Y	None
12		193	212	Aguon, Maria S	Daughter	F	Cha	3.8	S	N		Guam		None
13		193	212	Sanchez, Francisco S	Step-son	M	Cha	7	S	Y		Guam		None
14		194	213	Quinata, Felicita A	Head	F	Cha	34	S	N	Y	Guam	Y	Laundress
15		194	213	Quinata, Maria Q	Daughter	F	Cha	3.8	S	N		Guam		None
16		195	214	Quinata, Antonio V	Head	M	Cha	52	M	N	Y	Guam	N	Farmer
17		195	214	Quinata, Maria Q	Wife	F	Cha	53	M	N	Y	Guam	N	None
18		195	214	Quinata, Vicente Q	Son	M	Cha	19	S	N	Y	Guam	Y	Farm laborer
19		195	214	Quinata, Eduardo Q	Son	M	Cha	16	S	N	Y	Guam	Y	Farm laborer
20		195	214	Quinata, Maria Q	Daughter	F	Cha	14	S	N	Y	Guam	Y	None
21		196	215	Santiago, Juan Q	Head	M	Cha	23	M	N	Y	Guam	N	Farmer
22		196	215	Santiago, Eduvigis A	Wife	F	Cha	22	M	N	Y	Guam	Y	None
23		196	215	Santiago, Jesus A	Son	M	Cha	1.3	S	N		Guam		None
24		196	215	Santiago, Ana A	Daughter	F	Cha	.1	S	N		Guam		None
25		196	215	Aguon, Milagro Q	Mother in-law	F	Cha	54	Wd	N	N	Guam	N	None

DEPARTMENT OF COMMERCE-BUREAU OF THE CENSUS
WASHINGTON

FIFTEENTH CENSUS OF THE UNITED STATES: 1930-POPULATION

THE ISLAND OF GUAM

Sheet No. 23B

292B

District **Municipality of Merizo**
Name of Place **Umatac Barrio**
[Proper name and, also, name of class, as city, town, village, barrio, etc]

Enumeration District No. 9
Enumerated by me on **April 22, 1930** Manuel Charfauros, Enumerator

	PLACE OF ABODE			NAME	RELATION	PERSONAL DESCRIPTION				EDUCATION		NATIVITY		OCCUPATION
	Street, avenue, road, etc.	Number of dwelling house in order of visitation	Number of family in order of visitation	of each person whose place of abode on April 1, 1930, was in this family. Enter surname, first, then given name and middle initial. If any. Include every person living on April 1, 1930. Omit children born since April 1, 1930.	Relationship of this Person to the head of the family.	Sex	Color or race	Age at last birthday	Single, married, widowed or divorced	Attended school any time since Sept. 1, 1929	Whether able to read and write.	Place of birth of this person.	Whether able to speak English.	
	1	2	3	4	5	6	7	8	9	10	11	12	13	14
26	[no street name]	197	216	Quinata, Anastacio T	Head	M	Cha	37	M	N	N	Guam	N	Farmer
27		197	216	Quinata, Nieves A	Wife	F	Cha	35	M	N	N	Guam	N	None
28		197	216	Quinata, Rita A	Daughter	F	Cha	13	S	Y	Y	Guam	Y	None
29		197	216	Quinata, Vicente A	Son	M	Cha	12	S	Y	Y	Guam	Y	None
30		197	216	Quinata, Joaquin A	Son	M	Cha	6	S	N		Guam		None
31		197	216	Quinata, Joaquina A	Daughter	F	Cha	1.1	S	N		Guam		None
32		198	217	Quidachay, Jose T	Head	M	Cha	62	M	N	N	Guam	N	Farmer
33		198	217	Quidachay, Maria I	Wife	F	Cha	69	M	N	N	Guam	N	None
34		198	217	Quidachay, Joaquin I	Son	M	Cha	36	S	N	Y	Guam	Y	Farm laborer
35		198	217	Malijan, Eliza M	Servant	F	Cha	12	S	Y	Y	Guam	Y	Servant
36		198	217	Malijan, Jose M	Servant	M	Cha	10	S	Y	Y	Guam	Y	Servant
37		199	218	Quidachay, Juan R	Head	M	Cha	38	M	N	Y	Guam	N	Farmer
38		199	218	Quidachay, Manuela S	Wife	F	Cha	42	M	N	Y	Guam	N	None
39		199	218	Quidachay, Prudencio T	Son	M	Cha	15	S	N	Y	Guam	Y	Farm laborer
40		199	218	Quidachay, Adela T	Daughter	F	Cha	11	S	Y	Y	Guam	Y	None
41		200	219	Fegurgur, Rosa A	Head	F	Cha	81	S	N	N	Guam	N	None
42					Here ends the enumeration of Merizo Municpality.									
43														
44														
45														
46														
47														
48														
49														
50														

District 10
Municipality of Piti

Piti Town
Sinengsong Barrio
Tepungan Barrio

(CHAMORRO ROOTS GENEALOGY PROJECT™ TRANSCRIPTION)
(BERNARD T. PUNZALAN / HTTP://WWW.CHAMORROROOTS.COM)

DEPARTMENT OF COMMERCE-BUREAU OF THE CENSUS
WASHINGTON

FIFTEENTH CENSUS OF THE UNITED STATES: 1930-POPULATION

THE ISLAND OF GUAM

Sheet No. 1A

293

District Municipality of Piti
Name of Place Piti Town
[Proper name and, also, name of class, as city, town, village, barrio, etc]

Enumeration District No. 10
Enumerated by me on April 2, 1930 Joaquin Torres
Enumerator

	PLACE OF ABODE			NAME	RELATION	PERSONAL DESCRIPTION				EDUCATION		NATIVITY		OCCUPATION
	Street, avenue, road, etc.	Number of dwelling house is order of visitation	Number of family in order of visitation	of each person whose place of abode on April 1, 1930, was in this family. Enter surname, first, then given name and middle initial. If any. Include every person living on April 1, 1930. Omit children born since April 1, 1930.	Relationship of this Person to the head of the family.	Sex	Color or race	Age at last birthday	Single, married, widowed or divorced	Attended school any time since Sept. 1, 1929	Whether able to read and write.	Place of birth of this person.	Whether able to speak English.	
	1	2	3	4	5	6	7	8	9	10	11	12	13	14
1	Agana-Piti Road	1	1	Santos, Jesus C	Head	M	Cha	25	M	N	Y	Guam	Y	Clerk
2		1	1	Santos, Ana D	Wife	F	Cha	24	M	N	Y	Guam	Y	None
3		2	2	Blas, Vicente	Head	M	Cha	36	M	N	Y	Guam	Y	Clerk
4		2	2	Blas, Rita G	Wife	F	Cha	32	M	N	Y	Guam	Y	None
5		2	2	Blas, Rosario G	Daughter	F	Cha	4.4	S	N		Guam		None
6		2	2	Blas, Maria G	Daughter	F	Cha	3.4	S	N		Guam		None
7		2	2	Blas, Vicente G	Son	M	Cha	2.1	S	N		Guam		None
8		2	2	Blas, Emilia G	Daughter	F	Cha	0.8	S	N		Guam		None
9		3	3	Diaz, Jose F	Head	M	Cha	28	M	N	Y	Guam	Y	Machinist
10		3	3	Diaz, Mary D M	Wife	F	Cha	28	M	N	Y	England	Y	None
11		3	3	Diaz, Elizabeth M	Daughter	F	Cha	8	S	Y		Guam		None
12		3	3	Diaz, Joaquin M	Son	M	Cha	7	S	Y		Guam		None
13		3	3	Diaz, Irene M	Daughter	F	Cha	5	S	N		Guam		None
14		3	3	Diaz, Joseph M	Son	M	Cha	3.8	S	N		Guam		None
15		3	3	Diaz, Alfred M	Son	M	Cha	2.5	S	N		Guam		None
16		3	3	Diaz, John M	Son	M	Cha	0.2	S	N		Guam		None
17		3	3	Diaz, Maria F	Sister	F	Cha	26	S	N		Guam		None
18		3	3	Diaz, Antonia F	Sister	F	Cha	22	S	N		Guam		Saleswoman
19		4	4	Cruz, Juan	Head	M	Cha	48	D	N	Y	Guam	Y	Carpenter
20		4	4	Fernandez, Engracia C	Daughter	F	Cha	25	Wd	N	N	Guam	Y	None
21		4	4	Fernandez, Agapito C	Grandson	M	Cha	3.7	S	N		Guam		None
22		4	4	Fernandez, Vicente C	Grandson	M	Cha	1.1	S	N		Guam		None
23		4	5	Chargualaf, Ana A	Head	F	Cha	42	S	N	Y	Guam	Y	Laundress
24		4	5	Chargualaf, Esperanza	Daughter	F	Cha	22	S	N	Y	Guam	Y	Laundress
25		4	5	Chargualaf, Enrique C	Son	M	Cha	19	S	N	Y	Guam	Y	Laborer

DEPARTMENT OF COMMERCE-BUREAU OF THE CENSUS
WASHINGTON

FIFTEENTH CENSUS OF THE UNITED STATES: 1930-POPULATION

THE ISLAND OF GUAM

Sheet No. 1B

293b

District **Municipality of Piti**
Name of Place **Piti Town**
[Proper name and, also, name of class, as city, town, village, barrio, etc]

Enumeration District No. **10**
Enumerated by me on **April 2, 1930** **Joaquin Torres**
Enumerator

	PLACE OF ABODE			NAME	RELATION	PERSONAL DESCRIPTION				EDUCATION		NATIVITY		OCCUPATION
	Street, avenue, road, etc.	Number of dwelling house in order of visitation	Number of family in order of visitation	of each person whose place of abode on April 1, 1930, was in this family. Enter surname, first, then given name and middle initial. If any. Include every person living on April 1, 1930. Omit children born since April 1, 1930.	Relationship of this Person to the head of the family.	Sex	Color or race	Age at last birthday	Single, married, widowed or divorced	Attended school any time since Sept. 1, 1929	Whether able to read and write.	Place of birth of this person.	Whether able to speak English.	
	1	2	3	4	5	6	7	8	9	10	11	12	13	14
26	Agana-Piti Road	4	5	Chargualaf, Consolacion C	Daughter	F	Cha	14	S	Y	Y	Guam	Y	None
27		4	5	Chargualaf, Juan C	Son	M	Cha	12	S	Y	Y	Guam	Y	None
28		4	5	Chargualaf, Margarita C	Daughter	F	Cha	9	S	Y		Guam		None
29		4	5	Chargualaf, Eduardo C	Grandson	M	Cha	3.7	S	N		Guam		None
30		5	6	Champaco, Ana T	Head	F	Cha	26	M	N	Y	Guam	Y	None
31		5	6	Champaco, Josefina T	Daughter	F	Cha	3.7	S	N		Guam		None
32		5	6	Champaco, Jose T	Son	M	Cha	2.1	S	N		Guam		None
33		5	6	Champaco, Rosa T	Daughter	F	Cha	0.5	S	N		Guam		None
34		6	7	San Nicolas, Antoino F	Head	M	Cha	52	M	N	N	Guam	Y	Farmer
35		6	7	San Nicolas, Magdalena L	Wife	F	Chin	31	M	N	N	Guam	Y	None
36		6	7	San Nicolas, Maria L	Daughter	F	Cha	8	S	Y	Y	Guam		None
37		6	7	San Nicolas, Rosa L	Daughter	F	Cha	5	S	N	N	Guam		None
38		6	7	San Nicolas, Joaquin L	Son	M	Cha	3.2	S	N	N	Guam		None
39		7	8	Shimizu, Jose I	Head	M	Jap	31	M	N	Y	Saipan	Y	Salesman
40		7	8	Shimizu, Josefina SN	Wife	F	Cha	30	M	N	Y	Guam	Y	None
41		7	8	Shimizu, Joseph SN	Son	M	Jap	4.2	S	N		Guam		None
42		7	8	Shimizu, Maria SN	Daughter	F	Jap	3.2	S	N		Guam		None
43		7	8	Shimizu, Matilde SN	Daughter	F	Jap	2.2	S	N		Guam		None
44		8	9	San Nicolas, Guillermo F	Head	M	Cha	34	M	N	Y	Guam	Y	Chauffeur
45		8	9	San Nicolas, Carmen P	Wife	F	Cha	31	M	N	Y	Guam	Y	None
46		8	9	San Nicolas, Francisco P	Son	M	Cha	13	S	Y	Y	Guam	Y	None
47		8	9	San Nicolas, Juan P	Son	M	Cha	13	S	Y	Y	Guam	Y	None
48		8	9	San Nicolas, Rufina P	Daughter	F	Cha	10	S	Y	Y	Guam	Y	None
49		8	9	San Nicolas, Adela P	Daughter	F	Cha	8	S	Y		Guam		None
50		8	9	San Nicolas, Gregorio P	Son	M	Cha	7	S	Y		Guam		None

DEPARTMENT OF COMMERCE-BUREAU OF THE CENSUS
WASHINGTON

FIFTEENTH CENSUS OF THE UNITED STATES: 1930-POPULATION

THE ISLAND OF GUAM

Sheet No. 2A

District **Municipality of Piti**
Name of Place **Piti Town**
[Proper name and, also, name of class, as city, town, village, barrio, etc]

Enumeration District No. **10**
Enumerated by me on **April 2, 1930** **Joaquin Torres**
Enumerator

	PLACE OF ABODE			NAME	RELATION	PERSONAL DESCRIPTION				EDUCATION		NATIVITY		OCCUPATION
	Street, avenue, road, etc.	Number of dwelling house is order of visitation	Number of family in order of visitation	of each person whose place of abode on April 1, 1930, was in this family. Enter surname, first, then given name and middle initial. If any. Include every person living on April 1, 1930. Omit children born since April 1, 1930.	Relationship of this Person to the head of the family.	Sex	Color or race	Age at last birthday	Single, married, widowed or divorced	Attended school any time since Sept. 1, 1929	Whether able to read and write.	Place of birth of this person.	Whether able to speak English.	
	1	2	3	4	5	6	7	8	9	10	11	12	13	14
1	Agana-Piti Road	8	9	San Nicolas, Dolores P	Daughter	F	Cha	6	S	N		Guam		None
2		8	9	San Nicolas, Manuel P	Son	M	Cha	4.6	S	N		Guam		None
3		8	9	San Nicolas, Catlina P	Daughter	F	Cha	3.1	S	N		Guam		None
4		8	9	San Nicolas, Gertrudes P	Daughter	F	Cha	0.8	S	N		Guam		None
5		9	10	Manibusan, Maria SN	Head	F	Cha	28	M	N	Y	Guam	Y	None
6		9	10	Cruz, Adelaid C	Daughter	F	Cha	18	S	N	Y	Guam	Y	None
7		9	10	Manibusan, Maria C	Daughter	F	Cha	15	S	N	Y	Guam	Y	None
8		9	10	Manibusan, Ana C	Daughter	F	Cha	13	S	Y	Y	Guam	Y	None
9		9	10	Manibusan, Rosa C	Daughter	F	Cha	9	S	Y		Guam		None
10		10	11	Manibusan, Juan SN	Head	M	Cha	48	M	N	Y	Guam	Y	Farmer
11		10	11	Manibusan, Ana F	Wife	F	Cha	56	M	N	Y	Guam	N	None
12		10	11	Cruz, Juan SN	Nephew	M	Cha	10	S	Y	Y	Guam	Y	None
13		10	11	Meno, Vicitacion C	Servant	F	Cha	19	S	N	Y	Guam	Y	Servant
14		11	12	Carbullido, Ana C	Head	F	Cha	27	M	N	Y	Guam	Y	None
15		11	12	Carbullido, Helen C	Daughter	F	Cha	3.4	S	N		Guam	Y	None
16		11	12	Carbullido, Ruth C	Daughter	F	Cha	1.2	S	N		Guam		None
17		12	13	Yamanaka, Camilo U	Head	M	Jap	39	M	N	Y	Japan	Y	Carpenter
18		12	13	Yamanaka, Paula B	Wife	F	Cha	35	M	N	N	Guam	N	None
19		12	13	Yamanaka, Maria B	Daughter	F	Jap	15	S	Y	Y	Guam	Y	None
20		12	13	Yamanaka, Alfonsina B	Daughter	F	Jap	14	S	Y	Y	Guam	Y	None
21		12	13	Yamanaka, Carmen B	Daughter	F	Jap	12	S	Y	Y	Guam	Y	None
22		12	13	Yamanaka, Concepcion B	Daughter	F	Jap	11	S	Y	Y	Guam	Y	None
23		12	13	Yamanaka, Ana B	Daughter	F	Jap	8	S	Y		Guam		None
24		12	13	Yamanaka, Jose B	Son	M	Jap	7	S	Y		Guam		None
25		12	13	Yamanaka, Rosa B	Daughter	F	Jap	3.4	S	N		Guam		None

DEPARTMENT OF COMMERCE-BUREAU OF THE CENSUS
WASHINGTON

FIFTEENTH CENSUS OF THE UNITED STATES: 1930-POPULATION

THE ISLAND OF GUAM

Sheet No. 2B

294b

District **Municipality of Piti**
Name of Place **Piti Town**
[Proper name and, also, name of class, as city, town, village, barrio, etc]

Enumeration District No. **10**
Enumerated by me on **April 2, 1930** **Joaquin Torres**
Enumerator

	PLACE OF ABODE			NAME	RELATION	PERSONAL DESCRIPTION				EDUCATION		NATIVITY		OCCUPATION
	Street, avenue, road, etc.	Number of dwelling house is order of visitation	Number of family in order of visitation	of each person whose place of abode on April 1, 1930, was in this family. Enter surname, first, then given name and middle initial. If any. Include every person living on April 1, 1930. Omit children born since April 1, 1930.	Relationship of this Person to the head of the family.	Sex	Color or race	Age at last birthday	Single, married, widowed or divorced	Attended school any time since Sept. 1, 1929	Whether able to read and write.	Place of birth of this person.	Whether able to speak English.	
	1	2	3	4	5	6	7	8	9	10	11	12	13	14
26	Agana-Piti Road	12	13	Yamanaka, Magdalena B	Daughter	F	Jap	2.1	S	N		Guam		None
27		12	13	Yamanaka, Jesus B	Son	M	Jap	1.1	S	N		Guam		None
28		13	14	Flores, Vicente A	Head	M	Cha	26	M	N	Y	Guam	Y	Farmer
29		13	14	Flores, Remedio F	Wife	F	Cha	22	M	N	Y	Guam	Y	None
30		13	14	Flores, Isabel F	Daughter	F	Cha	1.7	S	N		Guam		None
31		13	14	Flores, Jose F	Son	M	Cha	0	S	N		Guam		None
32		14	15	Brummond, Euthorpea E	Head	F	Fil	24	M	N	Y	Philippine Is.	Y	None
33		14	15	Brummond, Emily M	Daughter	F	Fil	2.4	S	N		Philippine Is.		None
34		14	15	Brummond, Alice E	Daughter	F	Fil	0.5	S	N		Philippine Is.		None
35		15	16	Concepcion, Rosa M	Head	F	Cha	41	M	N	Y	Guam	Y	None
36		16	17	San Nicolas, Antonio S	Head	M	Cha	30	M	N	Y	Guam	Y	Electrician
37		16	17	San Nicolas, Josefa C	Wife	F	Cha	28	M	N	Y	Saipan Island	Y	None
38		16	17	San Nicolas, Victorina C	Daughter	F	Cha	9	S	Y	Y	Guam		None
39		16	17	San Nicolas, Maria C	Daughter	F	Cha	5	S	N		Guam		None
40		16	17	San Nicolas, Josefina C	Daughter	F	Cha	2.6	S	N		Guam		None
41		16	17	San Nicolas, Jesus C	Son	M	Cha	1	S	N		Guam		None
42		17	18	Aflague, Lorenzo S	Head	M	Cha	28	M	N	Y	Guam	Y	Chauffeur
43		17	18	Aflague, Jesusa A	Wife	F	Cha	24	M	N	Y	Guam	Y	None
44		17	18	Aflague, Elsie A	Daughter	F	Cha	5	S	N		Guam		None
45		17	18	Aflague, Francisco A	Son	M	Cha	3.2	S	N		Guam		None
46		17	18	Aflague, Ana A	Daughter	F	Cha	1.7	S	N		Guam		None
47		18	19	Quintanilla, Manuel	Head	M	Cha	62	M	N	Y	Guam	Y	None
48		18	19	Quintanilla, Ana G	Wife	F	Cha	47	M	N	Y	Guam	N	None
49		18	19	Quintanilla, Jose G	Son	M	Cha	25	S	N	Y	Guam	Y	None
50		18	19	Quintanilla, Andrecina G	Daughter	F	Cha	23	S	N	Y	Guam	Y	None

DEPARTMENT OF COMMERCE-BUREAU OF THE CENSUS
WASHINGTON

FIFTEENTH CENSUS OF THE UNITED STATES: 1930-POPULATION

THE ISLAND OF GUAM

Sheet No. 3A

District **Municipality of Piti**
Name of Place **Piti Town**
[Proper name and, also, name of class, as city, town, village, barrio, etc]

Enumeration District No. **10**
Enumerated by me on **April 2, 1930** **Joaquin Torres**, Enumerator

	PLACE OF ABODE: Street, avenue, road, etc.	Number of dwelling house in order of visitation	Number of family in order of visitation	NAME of each person whose place of abode on April 1, 1930, was in this family. Enter surname, first, then given name and middle initial. If any. Include every person living on April 1, 1930. Omit children born since April 1, 1930.	RELATION Relationship of this Person to the head of the family.	PERSONAL DESCRIPTION: Sex	Color or race	Age at last birthday	Single, married, widowed or divorced	EDUCATION: Attended school any time since Sept. 1, 1929	Whether able to read and write.	NATIVITY Place of birth of this person.	Whether able to speak English.	OCCUPATION
	1	2	3	4	5	6	7	8	9	10	11	12	13	14
1	Agana-Piti Road	18	19	Quintanilla, Juan G	Son	M	Cha	18	S	N	Y	Guam	Y	Laborer
2		18	19	Quintanilla, Vicente G	Son	M	Cha	16	S	Y	Y	Guam	Y	None
3		19	20	Scharff, Ferdinand G E	Head	M	W	39	M	N	Y	Germany	Y	Machinist
4		19	20	Scharff, Antonia F	Wife	F	Cha	30	M	N	Y	Guam	Y	None
5		19	20	Scharff, George H	Son	M	Cha	10	S	Y		Guam	Y	None
6		19	20	Scharff, Ferdinand E	Son	M	Cha	8	S	Y		Guam		None
7		19	20	Scharff, Herman A	Son	M	Cha	7	S	Y		Guam		None
8		19	20	Scharff, Earnest	Son	M	Cha	5	S	N		Guam		None
9		19	20	Scharff, Menar	Daughter	F	Cha	4.6	S	N		Guam		None
10		19	20	Scharff, Charles E	Son	M	Cha	1.8	S	N		Guam		None
11		19	20	Scharff, Bafter	Daughter	F	Cha	0.2	S	N		Guam		None
12		20	21	Cruz, Manuel	Head	M	Cha	46	M	N	Y	Guam	Y	Farmer
13		20	21	Cruz, Maria A	Wife	F	Cha	56	M	N	Y	Guam	N	None
14		20	21	Cruz, Dolores A	Daughter	F	Cha	18	S	N	Y	Guam	Y	None
15		20	21	Cruz, Gregorio A	Son	M	Cha	16	S	N	Y	Guam	Y	Farm laborer
16		20	21	Cruz, Marcela A	Daughter	F	Cha	14	S	N	Y	Guam	Y	None
17		21	22	Camacho, Ana C	Head	F	Cha	28	M	N	Y	Guam	Y	None
18		21	22	Camacho, Brigida C	Daughter	F	Cha	5	S	N		Guam		None
19		21	22	Camacho, Clotilde C	Daughter	F	Cha	2.8	S	N		Guam		None
20		21	22	Camacho, Joaquin C	Son	M	Cha	0.8	S	N		Guam		None
21		22	23	Fejeran, Domingo SN	Head	M	Cha	52	M	N	Y	Guam	N	Farmer
22		22	23	Fejeran, Maria S	Wife	F	Cha	57	M	N	N	Guam	N	None
23		22	23	Fejeran, Jesus S	Son	M	Cha	20	S	N	Y	Guam	Y	Laborer
24		22	23	Fejeran, Juan S	Son	M	Cha	17	S	Y	Y	Guam	Y	Farm laborer
25		22	23	Fejeran, Maria S	Daughter	F	Cha	14	S	N	Y	Guam	Y	None

(CHAMORRO ROOTS GENEALOGY PROJECT™ TRANSCRIPTION)
(BERNARD T. PUNZALAN / HTTP://WWW.CHAMORROROOTS.COM)

DEPARTMENT OF COMMERCE-BUREAU OF THE CENSUS
WASHINGTON

FIFTEENTH CENSUS OF THE UNITED STATES: 1930-POPULATION

THE ISLAND OF GUAM

Sheet No. 3B

295b

District **Municipality of Piti**
Name of Place **Piti Town**
[Proper name and, also, name of class, as city, town, village, barrio, etc]

Enumeration District No. **10**
Enumerated by me on **11050** **Joaquin Torres**
Enumerator

	PLACE OF ABODE			NAME	RELATION	PERSONAL DESCRIPTION				EDUCATION		NATIVITY		OCCUPATION
	Street, avenue, road, etc.	Number of dwelling house is order of visitation	Number of family in order of visitation	of each person whose place of abode on April 1, 1930, was in this family. Enter surname, first, then given name and middle initial. If any. Include every person living on April 1, 1930. Omit children born since April 1, 1930.	Relationship of this Person to the head of the family.	Sex	Color or race	Age at last birthday	Single, married, widowed or divorced	Attended school any time since Sept. 1, 1929	Whether able to read and write.	Place of birth of this person.	Whether able to speak English.	
	1	2	3	4	5	6	7	8	9	10	11	12	13	14
26	Agana-Piti Road	22	23	Fejeran, Dolores S	Daughter	F	Cha	14	S	Y	Y	Guam	Y	None
27		22	24	Fejeran, Joaquin S	Head	M	Cha	25	M	N	Y	Guam	Y	Chauffeur
28		22	24	Fejeran, Caridad C	Wife	F	Cha	23	M	N	Y	Guam	Y	None
29		23	25	Fejeran, Ana C	Head	F	Cha	22	M	N	Y	Guam	Y	None
30		23	25	Fejeran, Maria C	Daughter	F	Cha	4.2	S	N		Guam		None
31		23	25	Fejeran, Jose C	Son	M	Cha	3.1	S	N		Guam		None
32		24	26	Fejeran, Jose S	Head	M	Cha	24	M	N	Y	Guam	Y	Laborer
33		24	26	Fejeran, Concepcion I	Wife	F	Cha	18	M	N	Y	Guam	Y	None
34		24	26	Fejeran, Jesus I	Son	M	Cha	2.1	S	N		Guam		None
35		24	26	Fejeran, Maria I	Daughter	F	Cha	0.7	S	N		Guam		None
36		25	27	Quenga, Juan B	Head	M	Chin	38	M	N	Y	Guam	Y	Carpenter
37		25	27	Quenga, Josefa C	Wife	F	Cha	25	M	N	Y	Guam	Y	None
38		25	27	Quenga, Jose S	Son	M	Chin	18	S	N	Y	Guam	Y	Farm laborer
39		25	27	Quenga, Magdalena S	Daughter	F	Chin	17	S	N	N	Guam	N	None
40		25	27	Quenga, Ana S	Daughter	F	Chin	15	S	N	Y	Guam	Y	None
41		25	27	Quenga, Maria S	Daughter	F	Chin	10	S	Y	Y	Guam	Y	None
42		25	27	Quenga, Pilar C	Daughter	F	Chin	6	S	N		Guam		None
43		25	27	Quenga, Agustin C	Son	M	Chin	4.8	S	N		Guam		None
44		25	27	Quenga, Cristobal C	Son	M	Chin	3.7	S	N		Guam		None
45		25	27	Quenga, Juana C	Daughter	F	Chin	0.2	S	N		Guam		None
46		26	28	San Nicolas, Maxima S	Head	F	Cha	31	S	N	Y	Guam	Y	Servant
47		27	29	Cruz, Vicente C	Head	M	Cha	23	M	N	Y	Guam	Y	Chauffeur
48		27	29	Cruz, Emilia D	Wife	F	Cha	19	M	N	Y	Guam	Y	None
49		28	30	Inouye, Ana S	Head	M	Cha	43	M	N	N	Guam	Y	None
50		28	30	Inouye, Joaquin S	Son	M	Jap	17	S	N	Y	Guam	Y	Laborer

DEPARTMENT OF COMMERCE-BUREAU OF THE CENSUS
WASHINGTON

FIFTEENTH CENSUS OF THE UNITED STATES: 1930-POPULATION

THE ISLAND OF GUAM

Sheet No. 4A

District **Municipality of Piti**
Name of Place **Piti Town**
[Proper name and, also, name of class, as city, town, village, barrio, etc]

Enumeration District No. **10**
Enumerated by me on **April 3, 1930** **Joaquin Torres**
Enumerator

	PLACE OF ABODE			NAME	RELATION	PERSONAL DESCRIPTION				EDUCATION		NATIVITY		OCCUPATION
	Street, avenue, road, etc.	Number of dwelling house is order of visitation	Number of family in order of visitation	of each person whose place of abode on April 1, 1930, was in this family. Enter surname, first, then given name and middle initial. If any. Include every person living on April 1, 1930. Omit children born since April 1, 1930.	Relationship of this Person to the head of the family.	Sex	Color or race	Age at last birthday	Single, married, widowed or divorced	Attended school any time since Sept. 1, 1929	Whether able to read and write.	Place of birth of this person.	Whether able to speak English.	
	1	2	3	4	5	6	7	8	9	10	11	12	13	14
1	Agana-Piti Road	28	30	Inouye, Maria S	Daughter	F	Jap	15	S	N	Y	Guam	Y	None
2		28	30	Inouye, Benedicta S	Daughter	F	Jap	11	S	Y	Y	Guam	Y	None
3		29	31	Perez, Juan	Head	M	Cha	48	M	N	Y	Guam	Y	Machinist
4		29	31	Perez, Bacilia C	Wife	F	Cha	40	M	N	Y	Guam	Y	None
5		29	31	Perez, Encarnacion C	Daughter	F	Cha	12	S	Y	Y	Guam	Y	None
6		29	31	Cruz, Joaquin C	Step-son	M	Cha	15	S	Y	Y	Guam	Y	None
7		30	32	Fejeran, Ana C	Head	F	Cha	44	M	N	Y	Guam	N	None
8		30	32	Fejeran, Jose C	Son	M	Cha	16	S	Y	Y	Guam	Y	None
9		30	32	Fejeran, Francisco C	Son	M	Cha	14	S	Y	Y	Guam	Y	None
10		30	32	Fejeran, Juan C	Son	M	Cha	10	S	Y	Y	Guam	Y	None
11		30	32	Fejeran, Dolores C	Daughter	F	Cha	8	S	Y		Guam		None
12		30	32	Fejeran, Miguel C	Son	M	Cha	7	S	N		Guam		None
13		30	32	Fejeran, Enrique C	Son	M	Cha	3.8	S	N		Guam		None
14		31	33	Blas, Domingo	Head	M	Cha	39	M	N	Y	Guam	Y	Farmer
15		31	33	Blas, Maria M	Wife	F	Cha	31	M	N	Y	Guam	Y	None
16		32	34	Quitugua, Jose C	Head	M	Cha	40	M	N	Y	Guam	Y	Laborer
17		32	34	Quitugua, Antonia C	Wife	F	Cha	36	M	N	N	Guam	N	None
18		32	34	Quitugua, Juan C	Son	M	Cha	18	S	N	Y	Guam	Y	Laborer
19		32	34	Quitugua, Dolores C	Daughter	F	Cha	15	S	N	Y	Guam	Y	None
20		32	34	Quitugua, Vicente C	Son	M	Cha	10	S	Y	Y	Guam	Y	None
21		32	34	Quitugua, Jesus C	Son	M	Cha	5	S	N		Guam		None
22		32	34	Quitugua, Jose C	Son	M	Cha	3.7	S	N		Guam		None
23		33	35	Thomas, Francis E	Head	F	W	32	M	N	Y	Illinois	Y	None
24		33	35	Thomas, Hurley K	Son	M	W	4.7	S	N		California		None
25		33	36	Gibson, Arethea V	Head	F	W	32	M	N	Y	Colorado	Y	None

DEPARTMENT OF COMMERCE-BUREAU OF THE CENSUS
WASHINGTON

FIFTEENTH CENSUS OF THE UNITED STATES: 1930-POPULATION

THE ISLAND OF GUAM

Sheet No. 4B

296b

District **Municipality of Piti**
Name of Place **Piti Town**
[Proper name and, also, name of class, as city, town, village, barrio, etc]

Enumeration District No. **10**
Enumerated by me on **April 3, 1930** **Joaquin Torres**
Enumerator

	PLACE OF ABODE			NAME	RELATION	PERSONAL DESCRIPTION				EDUCATION		NATIVITY		OCCUPATION
	Street, avenue, road, etc.	Number of dwelling house is order of visitation	Number of family in order of visitation	of each person whose place of abode on April 1, 1930, was in this family. Enter surname, first, then given name and middle initial. If any. Include every person living on April 1, 1930. Omit children born since April 1, 1930.	Relationship of this Person to the head of the family.	Sex	Color or race	Age at last birthday	Single, married, widowed or divorced	Attended school any time since Sept. 1, 1929	Whether able to read and write.	Place of birth of this person.	Whether able to speak English.	
	1	2	3	4	5	6	7	8	9	10	11	12	13	14
26	Agana-Piti Road	33	36	Gibson, Norman L	Son	M	W	3.5	S	N		Philippine Is.		None
27		34	39	Cruz, Soledad P	Head	F	Cha	25	M	N	Y	Guam	Y	None
28		34	39	Cruz, Jesus P	Son	M	Cha	6	S	N		Guam		None
29		34	39	Cruz, Maria P	Daughter	F	Cha	4.2	S	N		Guam		None
30		34	39	Cruz, Jose P	Son	M	Cha	1.7	S	N		Guam		None
31		35	38	Ignacio, Joaquin C	Head	M	Cha	60	M	N	N	Guam	N	Farmer
32		35	38	Ignacio, Juana C	Wife	F	Cha	56	M	N	N	Guam	N	None
33		35	38	Ignacio, Maria C	Daughter	F	Cha	28	S	N	Y	Guam	Y	None
34		35	38	Ignacio, Juan C	Son	M	Cha	26	S	N	Y	Guam	Y	Farm laborer
35		35	38	Ignacio, Isabel C	Daughter	F	Cha	13	S	Y	Y	Guam	Y	None
36		35	39	Ignacio, Antonio C	Head	M	Cha	36	Wd	N	Y	Guam	Y	Farmer
37		35	39	Ignacio, Aniceto C	Son	M	Cha	9	S	Y		Guam		None
38		36	40	Santos, Ignacio Q	Head	M	Cha	26	M	N	Y	Guam	Y	Laborer
39		36	40	Santos, Ana S	Wife	F	Cha	25	M	N	Y	Guam	Y	None
40		36	40	Santos, Jose S	Son	M	Cha	3.5	S	N		Guam		None
41		36	40	Santos, Jesus S	Son	M	Cha	1.8	S	N		Guam		None
42		36	40	Santos, Juan S	Son	M	Cha	0	S	N		Guam		None
43		37	41	Matsumiya, Rafael Z	Head	M	Jap	47	Wd	N	Y	Japan	Y	Carpenter
44		37	41	Matsumiya, Jesus M	Son	M	Jap	14	S	Y	Y	Guam	Y	None
45		37	41	Matsumiya, Josefina M	Daughter	F	Jap	13	S	Y	Y	Guam	Y	None
46		37	41	Matsumiya, Jose M	Son	M	Jap	12	S	Y	Y	Guam	Y	None
47		37	41	Matsumiya, Tomas M	Son	M	Jap	8	S	Y		Guam		None
48		37	41	Matsumiya, Antonio M	Son	M	Jap	4.2	S	N		Guam		None
49		37	41	Matsumiya, Joaquin M	Son	M	Jap	1.6	S	N		Guam		None
50		37	41	Mendiola, Maria M	Step daughter	F	Cha	16	S	N	Y	Guam	Y	None

DEPARTMENT OF COMMERCE-BUREAU OF THE CENSUS
WASHINGTON

FIFTEENTH CENSUS OF THE UNITED STATES: 1930-POPULATION

THE ISLAND OF GUAM

Sheet No. 5A

District **Municipality of Piti**
Name of Place **Piti Town**
[Proper name and, also, name of class, as city, town, village, barrio, etc]

Enumeration District No. **10**
Enumerated by me on **April 3, 1930** **Joaquin Torres**
Enumerator

	PLACE OF ABODE			NAME	RELATION	PERSONAL DESCRIPTION				EDUCATION		NATIVITY		OCCUPATION
	Street, avenue, road, etc.	Number of dwelling house in order of visitation	Number of family in order of visitation	of each person whose place of abode on April 1, 1930, was in this family. Enter surname, first, then given name and middle initial. If any. Include every person living on April 1, 1930. Omit children born since April 1, 1930.	Relationship of this Person to the head of the family.	Sex	Color or race	Age at last birthday	Single, married, widowed or divorced	Attended school any time since Sept. 1, 1929	Whether able to read and write.	Place of birth of this person.	Whether able to speak English.	
	1	2	3	4	5	6	7	8	9	10	11	12	13	14
1	Agana-Piti Road	38	42	Yamashita, Raymundo H	Head	M	Jap	50	M	N	Y	Japan	N	Retail merchant
2		38	42	Yamashita, Felicitas C	Wife	F	Cha	33	M	N	Y	Guam	Y	None
3		38	42	Yamashita, Luis C	Son	M	Jap	12	S	Y	Y	Guam	Y	None
4		38	42	Yamashita, Jesus C	Son	M	Jap	10	S	Y	Y	Guam	Y	None
5		38	42	Yamashita, Jose C	Son	M	Jap	9	S	Y		Guam		None
6		38	42	Yamashita, Maria C	Daughter	F	Jap	3.4	S	N		Guam		None
7		38	42	Yamashita, Concepcion C	Daughter	F	Jap	1.2	S	N		Guam		None
8		38	43	Contreras, Vicente M	Head	M	Fil	69	Wd	N	N	Philippine Is.	N	Cook
9		39	44	Torres, Barbara C	Head	F	Cha	37	M	N	Y	Guam	Y	None
10		39	44	Torres, Maria C	Daughter	F	Cha	8	S	Y		Guam		None
11		39	44	Torres, Jesus C	Son	M	Cha	5	S	N		Guam		None
12		39	44	Torres, Joaquin C	Son	M	Cha	1	S	N		Guam		None
13		40	45	Petros, Lorenzo M	Head	M	Cha	41	M	N	N	Guam	Y	Farm laborer
14		40	45	Petros, Ana C	Wife	F	Cha	42	M	N	N	Guam	N	None
15		40	45	Petros, Jose C	Son	M	Cha	16	S	N	Y	Guam	Y	None
16		40	45	Petros, Vicente C	Son	M	Cha	15	S	Y	Y	Guam	Y	None
17		40	45	Petros, Joaquin C	Son	M	Cha	14	S	Y	Y	Guam	Y	None
18		40	45	Petros, Pedro C	Son	M	Cha	13	S	Y	Y	Guam	Y	None
19		40	45	Petros, Magdalena C	Daughter	F	Cha	10	S	Y	Y	Guam	Y	None
20		40	45	Petros, Antonio C	Son	M	Cha	9	S	Y		Guam		None
21		40	45	Petros, Baltazar C	Son	M	Cha	7	S	Y		Guam		None
22		40	45	Petros, Jesus C	Son	M	Cha	6	S	N		Guam		None
23		40	45	Petros, Josefa C	Daughter	F	Cha	4	S	N		Guam		None
24		40	45	Petros, Gregorio C	Son	M	Cha	2.2	S	N		Guam		None
25		40	45	Petros, Rosa C	Daughter	F	Cha	0.2	S	N		Guam		None

DEPARTMENT OF COMMERCE-BUREAU OF THE CENSUS
WASHINGTON

FIFTEENTH CENSUS OF THE UNITED STATES: 1930-POPULATION

THE ISLAND OF GUAM

Sheet No. 5B

297b

District Municipality of Piti
Name of Place Piti Town
[Proper name and, also, name of class, as city, town, village, barrio, etc]

Enumeration District No. 10
Enumerated by me on April 3, 1930 Joaquin Torres
Enumerator

	PLACE OF ABODE			NAME	RELATION	PERSONAL DESCRIPTION				EDUCATION		NATIVITY		OCCUPATION
	Street, avenue, road, etc.	Number of dwelling house in order of visitation	Number of family in order of visitation	of each person whose place of abode on April 1, 1930, was in this family. Enter surname, first, then given name and middle initial. If any. Include every person living on April 1, 1930. Omit children born since April 1, 1930.	Relationship of this Person to the head of the family.	Sex	Color or race	Age at last birthday	Single, married, widowed or divorced	Attended school any time since Sept. 1, 1929	Whether able to read and write.	Place of birth of this person.	Whether able to speak English.	
	1	2	3	4	5	6	7	8	9	10	11	12	13	14
26	Agana-Piti Road	41	46	Castro, Rosa P	Head	F	Cha	45	M	N	Y	Guam	N	None
27		42	47	Concepcion, Tomasa P	Head	F	Cha	24	M	N	Y	Guam	Y	None
28		42	47	Concepcion, Jose P	Son	M	Cha	5	S	N		Guam		None
29		42	47	Concepcion, Asuncion P	Daughter	F	Cha	2.7	S	N		Guam		None
30		42	47	Concepcion, Jesus P	Son	M	Cha	0.2	S	N		Guam		None
31		43	48	Cruz, Jesus C	Head	M	Cha	26	M	N	Y	Guam	Y	Laborer
32		43	48	Cruz, Carmen B	Wife	F	Cha	32	M	N	Y	Guam	Y	None
33		43	48	Cruz, Ana B	Daughter	F	Cha	2.4	S	N		Guam		None
34		43	48	Cruz, Elena B	Daughter	F	Cha	0.9	S	N		Guam		None
35		43	48	Okizaki, Joaquina B	Step-daughter	F	Jap	14	S	Y	Y	Guam	Y	None
36		43	48	Okizaki, Jesus M	Step-son	M	Jap	12	S	Y	Y	Guam	Y	None
37		43	48	Okizaki, Rita M	Step-daughter	F	Jap	10	S	Y	Y	Guam	Y	None
38		43	48	Okizaki, Joaquin M	Step-son	M	Jap	8	S	Y		Guam		None
39		43	48	Martinez, Maria M	Step-daughter	F	Cha	6	S	N		Guam		None
40		44	49	Santos, Antonia M	Head	F	Cha	21	M	N	Y	Guam	Y	None
41		45	50	Hatoba, Rita M	Head	F	Cha	31	Wd	N	Y	Guam	Y	Retail merchant
42		45	50	Mesa, Juana G	Mother	F	Cha	63	Wd	N	N	Guam	N	None
43		45	50	Mesa, Maria G	Sister	F	Cha	39	S	N	Y	Guam	Y	Dressmaker
44		45	50	Mesa, Matilde M	Niece	F	Cha	18	S	N	Y	Guam	Y	Saleswoman
45		46	51	Aguon, Francisco M	Head	M	Cha	38	M	N	Y	Guam	Y	Laborer
46		46	51	Aguon, Rufina S	Wife	F	Cha	34	M	N	Y	Guam	Y	None
47		46	51	Aguon, Juan S	Son	M	Cha	6	S	N		Guam		None
48		46	51	Aguon, Vicente S	Son	M	Cha	5	S	N		Guam		None
49		46	51	Aguon, Luis S	Son	M	Cha	4.1	S	N		Guam		None
50		46	51	Aguon, Francisco S	Son	M	Cha	2.7	S	N		Guam		None

DEPARTMENT OF COMMERCE-BUREAU OF THE CENSUS
WASHINGTON

FIFTEENTH CENSUS OF THE UNITED STATES: 1930-POPULATION

THE ISLAND OF GUAM

Sheet No. 6A

District **Municipality of Piti**
Name of Place **Piti Town**
[Proper name and, also, name of class, as city, town, village, barrio, etc]

Enumeration District No. **10**
Enumerated by me on **April 3, 1930** **Joaquin Torres**, Enumerator

	PLACE OF ABODE: Street, avenue, road, etc.	Number of dwelling house in order of visitation	Number of family in order of visitation	NAME of each person whose place of abode on April 1, 1930, was in this family. Enter surname, first, then given name and middle initial. If any. Include every person living on April 1, 1930. Omit children born since April 1, 1930.	RELATION Relationship of this Person to the head of the family.	Sex	Color or race	Age at last birthday	Single, married, widowed or divorced	Attended school any time since Sept. 1, 1929	Whether able to read and write.	NATIVITY Place of birth of this person.	Whether able to speak English.	OCCUPATION
	1	2	3	4	5	6	7	8	9	10	11	12	13	14
1	Agana-Piti Road	46	51	Aguon, Dolores S	Daughter	F	Cha	1.2	S	N		Guam		None
2		46	51	Santos, Esther S	Step daughter	F	Cha	13	S	Y	Y	Guam	Y	None
3		46	52	Mendiola, Maria M	Head	F	Cha	55	Wd	N	N	Guam	N	None
4		46	52	Mendiola, Vicente M	Son	M	Cha	19	S	N	Y	Guam	Y	Farm laborer
5		46	52	Mendiola, Trinidad M	Daughter	F	Cha	16	S	N	Y	Guam	Y	None
6		46	52	Mendiola, Polonia F	Mother	F	Cha	76	S	N	N	Guam	N	None
7		47	53	Tajalle, Soledad S	Head	F	Cha	38	M	N	Y	Guam	Y	None
8		47	53	Tajalle, Juan S	Son	M	Cha	10	S	Y	Y	Guam	Y	None
9		47	53	Tajalle, Vicente S	Son	M	Cha	8	S	Y		Guam		None
10		47	53	Tajalle, Tomas S	Son	M	Cha	3.5	S	N		Guam		None
11		47	53	Tajalle, Miguel S	Son	M	Cha	1.4	S	N		Guam		None
12		47	53	Tajalle, Joaquina C	Sister	F	Cha	23	S	N		Guam		None
13		48	54	Santos, Tiburcio A	Head	M	Cha	66	Wd	N	N	Guam	N	Farmer
14		48	54	Santos, Regina C	Daughter	F	Cha	34	S	N	Y	Guam	Y	None
15		48	54	Santos, Dolores C	Daughter	F	Cha	27	S	N	Y	Guam	Y	None
16		48	54	Santos, Nicolas C	Son	M	Cha	22	S	N	Y	Guam	Y	Farm laborer
17		48	54	Santos, Natividad C	Daughter	F	Cha	21	S	N	Y	Guam	Y	None
18		48	54	Santos, Juan M	Son	M	Cha	17	S	N	Y	Guam	Y	Farm laborer
19		48	54	Santos, Maria M	Daughter	F	Cha	15	S	N	Y	Guam	N	None
20		48	54	Martinez, Susana B	Lodger	F	Cha	58	Wd	N	N	Guam	N	None
21		49	55	Santos, Jose C	Head	M	Cha	42	M	N	Y	Guam	Y	Laborer
22		49	55	Santos, Antonio S	Wife	F	Cha	40	M	N	Y	Guam	N	None
23		49	55	Santos, Martina S	Daughter	F	Cha	20	S	N	Y	Guam	Y	None
24		49	55	Santos, Virginia S	Daughter	F	Cha	17	S	N	N	Guam	N	None
25		49	55	Santos, Nicolasa S	Daughter	F	Cha	10	S	Y	Y	Guam	Y	None

DEPARTMENT OF COMMERCE-BUREAU OF THE CENSUS
WASHINGTON

FIFTEENTH CENSUS OF THE UNITED STATES: 1930-POPULATION

THE ISLAND OF GUAM

Sheet No. 6B

298b

District **Municipality of Piti**
Name of Place **Piti Town**
[Proper name and, also, name of class, as city, town, village, barrio, etc]

Enumeration District No. **10**
Enumerated by me on **April 3, 1930** **Joaquin Torres**, Enumerator

	PLACE OF ABODE			NAME	RELATION	PERSONAL DESCRIPTION				EDUCATION		NATIVITY		OCCUPATION
	Street, avenue, road, etc.	Number of dwelling house is order of visitation	Number of family in order of visitation	of each person whose place of abode on April 1, 1930, was in this family. Enter surname, first, then given name and middle initial. If any. Include every person living on April 1, 1930. Omit children born since April 1, 1930.	Relationship of this Person to the head of the family.	Sex	Color or race	Age at last birthday	Single, married, widowed or divorced	Attended school any time since Sept. 1, 1929	Whether able to read and write.	Place of birth of this person.	Whether able to speak English.	
	1	2	3	4	5	6	7	8	9	10	11	12	13	14
26	Agana-Piti Road	49	55	Santos, Enrique S	Son	M	Cha	6	S	N		Guam		None
27		49	55	Santos, Ignacio S	Son	M	Cha	5	S	N		Guam		None
28		49	55	Santos, Guadalupe S	Daughter	F	Cha	3.2	S	N		Guam		None
29		49	55	Santos, Florencia S	Daughter	F	Cha	0.7	S	N		Guam		None
30		50	56	Quenga, Antonio	Head	M	Cha	34	M	N	Y	Guam	Y	Chauffeur
31		50	56	Quenga, Maria S	Wife	F	Cha	29	M	N	Y	Guam	Y	None
32		50	56	Quenga, Isabel S	Daughter	F	Cha	7	S	Y		Guam		None
33		50	56	Quenga, Barceliza S	Daughter	F	Cha	5	S	N		Guam		None
34		51	57	Santos, Luis C	Head	M	Cha	42	M	N	N	Guam	N	Laborer
35		51	57	Santos, Magdalena C	Wife	F	Cha	43	M	N	N	Guam	N	None
36		51	57	Santos, Lorenzo C	Son	M	Cha	19	S	N	Y	Guam	Y	Farm laborer
37		51	57	Santos, Antonia C	Daughter	F	Cha	17	S	N	Y	Guam	Y	None
38		51	57	Santos, Catalina C	Daughter	F	Cha	15	S	N	Y	Guam	Y	None
39		51	57	Santos, Angelina C	Daughter	F	Cha	14	S	Y	Y	Guam	Y	None
40		51	57	Santos, Ynes C	Daughter	F	Cha	11	S	Y	Y	Guam	Y	None
41		51	57	Santos, Maria C	Daughter	F	Cha	9	S	Y		Guam		None
42		51	57	Santos, Enrique C	Son	M	Cha	7	S	Y		Guam		None
43		51	57	Santos, Dolores C	Daughter	F	Cha	5	S	N		Guam		None
44		51	57	Santos, Jose C	Son	M	Cha	2.8	S	N		Guam		None
45		52	58	San Nicolas, Manuel U	Head	M	Cha	38	M	N	Y	Guam	Y	Laborer
46		52	58	San Nicolas, Consolacion C	Wife	F	Cha	40	M	N	Y	Guam	N	None
47		52	58	San Nicolas, Jose C	Son	M	Cha	12	S	Y	Y	Guam	Y	None
48		52	58	San Nicolas, Jesus C	Son	M	Cha	10	S	Y	Y	Guam	Y	None
49		52	58	San Nicolas, Ana C	Daughter	F	Cha	8	S	Y		Guam		None
50		52	58	San Nicolas, Joaquin C	Son	M	Cha	4.2	S	N		Guam		None

DEPARTMENT OF COMMERCE-BUREAU OF THE CENSUS
WASHINGTON

FIFTEENTH CENSUS OF THE UNITED STATES: 1930-POPULATION

THE ISLAND OF GUAM

Sheet No. 7A

District **Municipality of Piti**
Name of Place **Piti Town**
[Proper name and, also, name of class, as city, town, village, barrio, etc]

Enumeration District No. **10**
Enumerated by me on **April 3, 1930** **Joaquin Torres**
Enumerator

	PLACE OF ABODE			NAME	RELATION	PERSONAL DESCRIPTION				EDUCATION		NATIVITY		OCCUPATION
	Street, avenue, road, etc.	Number of dwelling house is order of visitation	Number of family in order of visitation	of each person whose place of abode on April 1, 1930, was in this family. Enter surname, first, then given name and middle initial. If any. Include every person living on April 1, 1930. Omit children born since April 1, 1930.	Relationship of this Person to the head of the family.	Sex	Color or race	Age at last birthday	Single, married, widowed or divorced	Attended school any time since Sept. 1, 1929	Whether able to read and write.	Place of birth of this person.	Whether able to speak English.	
	1	2	3	4	5	6	7	8	9	10	11	12	13	14
1	Agana-Piti Road	52	58	San Nicolas, Tomas C	Son	M	Cha	2.7	S	N		Guam		None
2		53	59	Santos, Amparo C	Head	F	Cha	60	Wd	N	N	Guam	N	Farmer
3		53	59	Santos, Gregorio C	Son	M	Cha	16	S	Y	Y	Guam	Y	Farm laborer
4		54	60	Cruz, Lorenzo B	Head	M	Cha	69	Wd	N	Y	Guam	N	Farmer
5		54	60	Cruz, Maria B	Daughter	F	Cha	35	S	N	Y	Guam	Y	None
6		54	60	Cruz, Josefina B	Daughter	F	Cha	24	S	N	Y	Guam	Y	None
7		55	61	Cruz, Francisco S	Head	M	Cha	36	M	N	Y	Guam	Y	Farmer
8		55	61	Cruz, Romana C	Wife	F	Cha	28	M	N	Y	Guam	Y	None
9		55	61	Cruz, Manuela C	Daughter	F	Cha	5	S	N		Guam		None
10		55	61	Cruz, Juan C	Son	M	Cha	4.8	S	N		Guam		None
11		55	61	Cruz, Maria C	Daughter	F	Cha	2.9	S	N		Guam		None
12		55	61	Cruz, Lorenzo	Son	M	Cha	1.2	S	N		Guam		None
13		56	62	Fejeran, Jesus C	Head	M	Cha	19	M	N	Y	Guam	Y	Farmer
14		56	62	Fejeran, Rosa B	Wife	F	Cha	21	M	N	Y	Guam	Y	None
15		57	63	Santos, Vicente A	Head	M	Cha	69	M	N	N	Guam	N	Farmer
16		57	63	Santos, Dolores SN	Wife	F	Cha	37	M	N	Y	Guam	N	None
17		57	63	Santos, Antonio C	Son	M	Cha	31	S	N	Y	Guam	Y	Farm laborer
18		57	63	Santos, Maria SN	Daughter	F	Cha	14	S	N	Y	Guam	Y	None
19		57	63	Santos, Rosalia SN	Daughter	F	Cha	11	S	Y	Y	Guam	Y	None
20		57	63	Santos, Nicolasa SN	Daughter	F	Cha	9	S	Y		Guam		None
21		57	63	Santos, Ramon SN	Son	M	Cha	7	S	Y		Guam		None
22		57	63	Santos, Jesus SN	Son	M	Cha	5	S	N		Guam		None
23		57	63	Santos, Ana SN	Daughter	F	Cha	1.2	S	N		Guam		None
24		57	63	Santos, Rita SN	Daughter	F	Cha	0.1	S	N		Guam		None
25		58	64	Sablan, Nicolasa S	Head	F	Cha	40	M	N	Y	Guam	N	None

DEPARTMENT OF COMMERCE-BUREAU OF THE CENSUS
WASHINGTON

FIFTEENTH CENSUS OF THE UNITED STATES: 1930-POPULATION

THE ISLAND OF GUAM

Sheet No. 7B

299b

District **Municipality of Piti**

Name of Place **Piti Town**

[Proper name and, also, name of class, as city, town, village, barrio, etc]

Enumeration District No. **10**

Enumerated by me on **April 4, 1930** **Joaquin Torres**
Enumerator

	PLACE OF ABODE			NAME	RELATION	PERSONAL DESCRIPTION				EDUCATION		NATIVITY		OCCUPATION
	Street, avenue, road, etc.	Number of dwelling house is order of visitation	Number of family in order of visitation	of each person whose place of abode on April 1, 1930, was in this family. Enter surname, first, then given name and middle initial. If any. Include every person living on April 1, 1930. Omit children born since April 1, 1930.	Relationship of this Person to the head of the family.	Sex	Color or race	Age at last birthday	Single, married, widowed or divorced	Attended school any time since Sept. 1, 1929	Whether able to read and write.	Place of birth of this person.	Whether able to speak English.	
	1	2	3	4	5	6	7	8	9	10	11	12	13	14
26	Agana-Piti Road	58	64	Sablan, Martina S	Daughter	F	Cha	14	S	Y	Y	Guam	Y	None
27		58	64	Sablan, Vicente S	Son	M	Cha	13	S	Y	Y	Guam	Y	None
28		58	64	Sablan, Maria S	Daughter	F	Cha	11	S	Y	Y	Guam	Y	None
29		58	64	Sablan, Dolores S	Daughter	F	Cha	10	S	Y	Y	Guam	Y	None
30		58	64	Sablan, Jesus S	Son	M	Cha	9	S	Y		Guam		None
31		58	64	Sablan, Jose S	Son	M	Cha	6	S	N		Guam		None
32		58	64	Sablan, Joaquin S	Son	M	Cha	5	S	N		Guam		None
33		58	64	Sablan, Trinidad S	Daughter	F	Cha	3.7	S	N		Guam		None
34		58	64	Sablan, Ana S	Daughter	F	Cha	2.7	S	N		Guam		None
35		58	64	Sablan, Roque S	Son	M	Cha	0.8	S	N		Guam		None
36		59	65	Flores, Rita A	Head	F	Cha	55	S	N	Y	Guam	N	Saleswoman
37		59	65	Flores, Ramona A	Daughter	F	Cha	22	S	N	Y	Guam	Y	None
38		60	66	Quidachay, Teodosia A	Head	F	Cha	32	M	N	N	Guam	Y	None
39		60	66	Quidachay, Rosa A	Daughter	F	Cha	5	S	N		Guam		None
40		60	66	Quidachay, Andrea A	Daughter	F	Cha	4.1	S	N		Guam		None
41		60	66	Quidachay, Ana A	Daughter	F	Cha	1	S	N		Guam		None
42		61	67	Santos, Jose I	Head	M	Cha	30	M	N	Y	Guam	Y	Chauffeur
43		61	67	Santos, Maria M	Wife	F	Cha	21	M	N	Y	Guam	Y	None
44		62	68	Gusukuma, Yaisuke	Head	M	Jap	28	M	N	N	Japan	N	Fisherman
45		62	69	Uyehara, Tarusho	Head	M	Jap	34	M	N	N	Japan	N	Fisherman
46		62	70	Schira, Shokichi	Head	M	Jap	22	S	N	Y	Japan	N	Fisherman
47		62	71	Yamane, Soiyei	Head	M	Jap	22	S	N	Y	Japan	N	Fisherman
48		62	72	Naka, Shinsuke	Head	M	Jap	21	S	N	Y	Japan	N	Fisherman
49		62	73	Kina, Yoshinoku	Head	M	Jap	19	S	N	N	Japan	N	Fisherman
50		63	74	Quitugua, Francisco Q	Head	M	Cha	39	M	N	Y	Guam	N	Laborer

DEPARTMENT OF COMMERCE-BUREAU OF THE CENSUS
WASHINGTON

FIFTEENTH CENSUS OF THE UNITED STATES: 1930-POPULATION

THE ISLAND OF GUAM

Sheet No. 8A

District **Municipality of Piti**
Name of Place **Piti Town**
[Proper name and, also, name of class, as city, town, village, barrio, etc]

Enumeration District No. **10**
Enumerated by me on **April 4, 1930** **Joaquin Torres**
Enumerator

	PLACE OF ABODE			NAME	RELATION	PERSONAL DESCRIPTION				EDUCATION		NATIVITY		OCCUPATION
	Street, avenue, road, etc.	Number of dwelling house is order of visitation	Number of family in order of visitation	of each person whose place of abode on April 1, 1930, was in this family. Enter surname, first, then given name and middle initial. If any. Include every person living on April 1, 1930. Omit children born since April 1, 1930.	Relationship of this Person to the head of the family.	Sex	Color or race	Age at last birthday	Single, married, widowed or divorced	Attended school any time since Sept. 1, 1929	Whether able to read and write.	Place of birth of this person.	Whether able to speak English.	
	1	2	3	4	5	6	7	8	9	10	11	12	13	14
1	Piti-Sumay Road	63	74	Quitugua, Milagro A	Wife	F	Cha	34	M	N	N	Guam	N	None
2		63	74	Quitugua, Antonia A	Daughter	F	Cha	14	S	N	Y	Guam	Y	None
3		63	74	Quitugua, Maria A	Daughter	F	Cha	13	S	Y	Y	Guam	Y	None
4		63	74	Quitugua, Rosalia A	Daughter	F	Cha	11	S	Y	Y	Guam	Y	None
5		63	74	Quitugua, Rita A	Daughter	F	Cha	8	S	Y		Guam		None
6		63	74	Quitugua, Francisco A	Son	M	Cha	6	S	N		Guam		None
7		63	74	Quitugua, Antonio	Son	M	Cha	3.8	S	N		Guam		None
8		63	74	Quitugua, Jose	Son	M	Cha	0.9	S	N		Guam		None
9		64	75	Salas, Cecilio M	Head	M	Cha	63	M	N	N	Guam	Y	Laborer
10		64	75	Salas, Rosa F	Wife	F	Cha	37	M	N	N	Guam	N	None
11		64	75	Salas, Antonia F	Daughter	F	Cha	15	S	N	N	Guam	Y	None
12		64	75	Salas, Joaquin F	Son	M	Cha	14	S	Y	Y	Guam	Y	None
13		64	75	Salas, Ana F	Daughter	F	Cha	8	S	Y	Y	Guam		None
14		64	75	Salas, Jose F	Son	M	Cha	7	S	Y	Y	Guam		None
15		64	75	Salas, Maria F	Daughter	F	Cha	2.9	S	N	N	Guam		None
16		64	75	Salas, Jesus F	Son	M	Cha	0.5	S	N	N	Guam		None
17		64	75	Fejeran, Antonio C	Brother-in-law	M	Cha	33	S	N	N	Guam		None
18		65	76	Castro, Saturnina T	Head	F	Cha	37	M	N	Y	Guam	N	None
19		65	76	Castro, Antonio T	Son	M	Cha	14	S	Y	Y	Guam	Y	None
20		65	76	Castro, Rosa T	Daughter	F	Cha	12	S	Y	Y	Guam	Y	None
21		65	76	Castro, Jesus T	Son	M	Cha	10	S	Y	Y	Guam	Y	None
22		65	76	Castro, Jose T	Son	M	Cha	7	S	Y		Guam		None
23		65	76	Castro, Maria T	Daughter	F	Cha	5	S	N		Guam		None
24		65	76	Castro, Pedro T	Son	M	Cha	3.9	S	N		Guam		None
25		65	76	Castro, Juan T	Son	M	Cha	1.8	S	N		Guam		None

DEPARTMENT OF COMMERCE-BUREAU OF THE CENSUS
WASHINGTON

FIFTEENTH CENSUS OF THE UNITED STATES: 1930-POPULATION

THE ISLAND OF GUAM

Sheet No. 8B

300b

District Municipality of Piti
Name of Place Piti Town
[Proper name and, also, name of class, as city, town, village, barrio, etc]

Enumeration District No. 10
Enumerated by me on April 4, 1930 Joaquin Torres, Enumerator

	PLACE OF ABODE			NAME	RELATION	PERSONAL DESCRIPTION				EDUCATION		NATIVITY		OCCUPATION
	Street, avenue, road, etc.	Number of dwelling house is order of visitation	Number of family in order of visitation	of each person whose place of abode on April 1, 1930, was in this family. Enter surname, first, then given name and middle initial. If any. Include every person living on April 1, 1930. Omit children born since April 1, 1930.	Relationship of this Person to the head of the family.	Sex	Color or race	Age at last birthday	Single, married, widowed or divorced	Attended school any time since Sept. 1, 1929	Whether able to read and write.	Place of birth of this person.	Whether able to speak English.	
	1	2	3	4	5	6	7	8	9	10	11	12	13	14
26	Piti-Sumay Road	66	77	Taienao, Juan M	Head	M	Cha	20	M	N	Y	Guam	Y	Laborer
27		66	77	Taienao, Guadalupe Y	Wife	F	Jap	19	M	N	Y	Guam	Y	None
28		67	78	Santos, Antonia C	Head	F	Cha	19	S	N	Y	Guam	Y	Laundress
29		67	78	Santos, Francisca M	Daughter	F	Cha	10	S	Y		Guam	Y	None
30		67	78	Santos, Helen M	Daughter	F	Cha	7	S	Y		Guam		None
31		67	78	Santos, Julia C	Daughter	F	Cha	6	S	N		Guam		None
32		67	78	Santos, John H	Son	M	Cha	0.7	S	N		Guam		None
33		68	79	Taimanglo, Vicenta M	Head	F	Cha	56	Wd	N	N	Guam	N	None
34		68	79	Taimanglo, Ana M	Daughter	F	Cha	20	S	N	Y	Guam	Y	Laundress
35		68	79	Taimanglo, Vicente M	Son	M	Cha	16	S	Y	Y	Guam	Y	None
36		68	79	Taimanglo, Jose M	Son	M	Cha	12	S	Y	Y	Guam	Y	None
37		68	79	Taimanglo, Juan M	Son	M	Cha	11	S	Y	Y	Guam	Y	None
38					~~Here ends the enumeration of Piti Town.~~									
39														
40														
41														
42														
43														
44														
45														
46														
47														
48														
49														
50														

(CHAMORRO ROOTS GENEALOGY PROJECT™ TRANSCRIPTION)
(BERNARD T. PUNZALAN / HTTP://WWW.CHAMORROROOTS.COM)

DEPARTMENT OF COMMERCE-BUREAU OF THE CENSUS
WASHINGTON

FIFTEENTH CENSUS OF THE UNITED STATES: 1930-POPULATION

THE ISLAND OF GUAM

Sheet No. 9A

301

District **Municipality of Piti**
Name of Place **Tepungan Barrio**
[Proper name and, also, name of class, as city, town, village, barrio, etc]

Enumeration District No. **10**
Enumerated by me on **April 4, 1930** **Joaquin Torres**
Enumerator

	PLACE OF ABODE			NAME	RELATION	PERSONAL DESCRIPTION				EDUCATION		NATIVITY		OCCUPATION
	Street, avenue, road, etc.	Number of dwelling house is order of visitation	Number of family in order of visitation	of each person whose place of abode on April 1, 1930, was in this family. Enter surname, first, then given name and middle initial. If any. Include every person living on April 1, 1930. Omit children born since April 1, 1930.	Relationship of this Person to the head of the family.	Sex	Color or race	Age at last birthday	Single, married, widowed or divorced	Attended school any time since Sept. 1, 1929	Whether able to read and write.	Place of birth of this person.	Whether able to speak English.	
	1	2	3	4	5	6	7	8	9	10	11	12	13	14
1	Agana-Piti Road	69	80	Quitugua, Ramon Q	Head	M	Cha	29	M	N	Y	Guam	Y	Laborer
2		69	80	Quitugua, Ana C	Wife	F	Cha	26	M	N	Y	Guam	Y	None
3		69	80	Quitugua, Fred C	Son	M	Cha	3.1	S	N		Guam		None
4		69	80	Quitugua, Carlos C	Son	M	Cha	1.7	S	N		Guam		None
5		69	80	Quitugua, Antonia C	Daughter	F	Cha	0	S	N		Guam		None
6		70	81	Cepeda, Manuel	Head	M	Cha	46	M	N	Y	Guam	Y	Farmer
7		70	81	Cepeda, Rita S	Wife	F	Cha	47	M	N	N	Guam	Y	None
8		70	81	Cepeda, Juan S	Son	M	Cha	19	S	N	Y	Guam	Y	Chauffeur
9		70	81	Cepeda, Francisco S	Son	M	Cha	14	S	Y	Y	Guam	Y	None
10		70	81	Cepeda, Magarita S	Daughter	F	Cha	12	S	Y	Y	Guam	Y	None
11		70	81	Cepeda, Pedro S	Son	M	Cha	9	S	Y		Guam		None
12		70	81	Cepeda, Manuel S	Son	M	Cha	7	S	Y		Guam		None
13		71	82	Ocampo, Peta A	Head	F	Fil	31	M	N	Y	Philippine Is.	Y	None
14		71	83	Mafnas, Ana Q	Head	F	Cha	65	Wd	N	N	Guam	N	None
15		72	84	Babauta, Antonio D	Head	M	Cha	32	M	N	N	Guam	Y	Farmer
16		72	84	Babauta, Consolacion C	Wife	F	Cha	36	M	N	N	Guam	N	None
17		72	84	Babauta, Antonio C	Son	M	Cha	6	S	N		Guam		None
18		72	84	Babauta, Francisco C	Son	M	Cha	5	S	N		Guam		None
19		72	84	Cruz, Agustina C	Step daughter	F	Cha	12	S	Y	Y	Guam		None
20		72	84	Cruz, Jesus C	Stepson	M	Cha	10	S	Y	Y	Guam		None
21		72	84	Cruz, Ana C	Step daughter	F	Cha	8	S	Y		Guam		None
22		73	85	Quitugua, Rosa S	Head	F	Cha	36	M	N	Y	Guam	Y	None
23		73	85	Mafnas, Ynes S	Daughter	F	Cha	12	S	Y	Y	Guam	Y	None
24		73	85	Quitugua, Felicidad S	Daughter	F	Cha	9	S	Y		Guam		None
25		73	85	Quitugua, Isabel S	Daughter	F	Cha	7	S	Y		Guam		None

DEPARTMENT OF COMMERCE-BUREAU OF THE CENSUS
WASHINGTON

FIFTEENTH CENSUS OF THE UNITED STATES: 1930-POPULATION

THE ISLAND OF GUAM

Sheet No. 9B

301b

District **Municipality of Piti**
Name of Place **Tepungan Barrio**
[Proper name and, also, name of class, as city, town, village, barrio, etc]

Enumeration District No. **10**
Enumerated by me on **April 4, 1930** **Joaquin Torres**
Enumerator

	PLACE OF ABODE			NAME	RELATION	PERSONAL DESCRIPTION				EDUCATION		NATIVITY		OCCUPATION
	Street, avenue, road, etc.	Number of dwelling house is order of visitation	Number of family in order of visitation	of each person whose place of abode on April 1, 1930, was in this family. Enter surname, first, then given name and middle initial. If any. Include every person living on April 1, 1930. Omit children born since April 1, 1930.	Relationship of this Person to the head of the family.	Sex	Color or race	Age at last birthday	Single, married, widowed or divorced	Attended school any time since Sept. 1, 1929	Whether able to read and write.	Place of birth of this person.	Whether able to speak English.	
	1	2	3	4	5	6	7	8	9	10	11	12	13	14
26	Agana-Piti Road	73	85	Quitugua, Ana S	Daughter	F	Cha	5	S	N		Guam		None
27		73	85	Quitugua, Natividad S	Daughter	F	Cha	2.2	S	N		Guam		None
28		73	85	Cruz, Maria C	Niece	F	Cha	18	S	N	Y	Guam	Y	None
29		73	85	Cruz, Jose C	Nephew	M	Cha	15	S	Y	Y	Guam	Y	None
30		74	86	Aflleje, Maria L	Head	F	Cha	25	M	N	Y	Guam	Y	None
31		74	86	Aflleje, Rosa L	Daughter	F	Cha	7	S	Y		Guam	Y	None
32		74	86	Aflleje, Vicente L	Son	M	Cha	5	S	N		Guam		None
33		74	86	Aflleje, Rita L	Daughter	F	Cha	3.8	S	N		Guam		None
34		74	86	Aflleje, Maria L	Daughter	F	Cha	2.2	S	N		Guam		None
35		74	86	Aflleje, Angelina L	Daughter	F	Cha	0.7	S	N		Guam		None
36		74	87	Fejeran, Isidro S	Head	M	Cha	47	Wd	N	N	Guam	Y	Laborer
37		74	87	Fejeran, Tomas R	Son	M	Cha	11	S	Y	Y	Guam	Y	None
38		74	87	Fejeran, Jose R	Son	M	Cha	10	S	Y	Y	Guam	Y	None
39		74	87	Fejeran, Maria R	Daughter	F	Cha	8	S	Y		Guam		None
40		75	88	Fejeran, Felix S	Head	M	Cha	27	M	N	Y	Guam	Y	Farm laborer
41		75	88	Fejeran, Ana B	Wife	F	Cha	28	M	N	Y	Guam	Y	None
42		75	88	Fejeran, Vicente B	Son	M	Cha	7	S	Y		Guam		None
43		75	88	Fejeran, Maria B	Daughter	F	Cha	6	S	N		Guam		None
44		75	88	Fejeran, Barcelisa B	Daughter	F	Cha	5	S	N		Guam		None
45		75	88	Fejeran, Juan B	Son	M	Cha	2.1	S	N		Guam		None
46		75	88	Fejeran, Jesus B	Son	M	Cha	0.7	S	N		Guam		None
47		76	89	Quenga, Vicente Q	Head	M	Cha	59	Wd	N	N	Guam	N	None
48		77	90	Certeza, Gabriel A	Head	M	Fil	35	M	N	Y	Philippine Is.	Y	Machinist
49		77	90	Certeza, Maria Q	Wife	F	Chin	29	M	N	Y	Guam	Y	None
50		77	90	Certeza, Atanasio Q	Son	M	Fil	8	S	Y		Guam		None

DEPARTMENT OF COMMERCE-BUREAU OF THE CENSUS
WASHINGTON

FIFTEENTH CENSUS OF THE UNITED STATES: 1930-POPULATION

THE ISLAND OF GUAM

Sheet No. 10A

District **Municipality of Piti**
Name of Place **Tepungan Barrio**
[Proper name and, also, name of class, as city, town, village, barrio, etc]

Enumeration District No. **10**
Enumerated by me on **April 4, 1930** **Joaquin Torres**
Enumerator

	PLACE OF ABODE			NAME	RELATION	PERSONAL DESCRIPTION				EDUCATION		NATIVITY		OCCUPATION
	Street, avenue, road, etc.	Number of dwelling house is order of visitation	Number of family in order of visitation	of each person whose place of abode on April 1, 1930, was in this family. Enter surname, first, then given name and middle initial. If any. Include every person living on April 1, 1930. Omit children born since April 1, 1930.	Relationship of this Person to the head of the family.	Sex	Color or race	Age at last birthday	Single, married, widowed or divorced	Attended school any time since Sept. 1, 1929	Whether able to read and write.	Place of birth of this person.	Whether able to speak English.	
	1	2	3	4	5	6	7	8	9	10	11	12	13	14
1	Agana-Piti Road	77	90	Certeza, Delfin Q	Son	M	Fil	7	S	N		Guam		None
2		77	90	Certeza, Agapito Q	Son	M	Fil	5	S	N		Guam		None
3		77	90	Certeza, Evelino Q	Son	M	Fil	3.2	S	N		Guam		None
4		77	90	Certeza, Javier Q	Son	M	Fil	1.2	S	N		Guam		None
5		78	91	Perez, Rita S	Head	M	Cha	43	D	N	N	Guam	N	Tailoress
6		78	91	Perez, Beatriz S	Daughter	F	Cha	24	S	N	Y	Guam	Y	Laundress
7		78	91	Perez, Donna S	Daughter	F	Cha	21	S	N	Y	Guam	Y	Laundress
8		78	91	Perez, Ana S	Daughter	F	Cha	19	S	Y	Y	Guam	Y	None
9		78	91	Perez, Juan S	Son	M	Cha	14	S	Y	Y	Guam	Y	None
10		78	91	Perez, Vicente S	Son	M	Cha	12	S	Y	Y	Guam	Y	None
11		78	91	Perez, Maria S	Daughter	F	Cha	10	S	Y	Y	Guam	Y	None
12		78	91	Salas, Rita P	Daughter	F	Cha	8	S	Y		Guam		None
13		78	91	Perez, Jesus S	Grandson	M	Cha	1	S	Y		Guam		None
14		78	92	Perez, Maria C	Head	F	Cha	21	M	N	Y	Guam	N	None
15		79	93	Mendiola, Juan C	Head	M	Cha	48	M	N	Y	Guam	Y	Laborer
16		79	93	Mendiola, Carmen C	Wife	F	Cha	49	M	N	N	Guam	N	None
17		79	93	Mendiola, Ynes C	Daughter	F	Cha	16	S	N	Y	Guam	Y	None
18		79	93	Mendiola, Pedro C	Son	M	Cha	15	S	Y	Y	Guam	Y	None
19		79	93	Mendiola, Paz C	Daughter	F	Cha	12	S	Y	Y	Guam	Y	None
20		79	93	Mendiola, Precentacion C	Daughter	F	Cha	10	S	Y	Y	Guam	Y	None
21		80	94	Salas, Jose M	Head	M	Cha	44	M	N	Y	Guam	Y	Farmer
22		80	94	Salas, Dolores I	Wife	F	Cha	46	M	N	Y	Guam	N	None
23		80	94	Salas, Ana I	Daughter	F	Cha	16	S	N	N	Guam	Y	Servant
24		80	94	Salas, Maria I	Daughter	F	Cha	14	S	Y	Y	Guam	Y	None
25		80	94	Salas, Jose I	Son	M	Cha	13	S	Y	Y	Guam	Y	None

DEPARTMENT OF COMMERCE-BUREAU OF THE CENSUS
WASHINGTON

FIFTEENTH CENSUS OF THE UNITED STATES: 1930-POPULATION

THE ISLAND OF GUAM

Sheet No. 10B

302b

District **Municipality of Piti**
Name of Place **Tepungan Barrio**
[Proper name and, also, name of class, as city, town, village, barrio, etc]

Enumeration District No. **10**
Enumerated by me on **April 4, 1930** **Joaquin Torres**
Enumerator

	PLACE OF ABODE			NAME	RELATION	PERSONAL DESCRIPTION				EDUCATION		NATIVITY		OCCUPATION
	Street, avenue, road, etc.	Number of dwelling house is order of visitation	Number of family in order of visitation	of each person whose place of abode on April 1, 1930, was in this family. Enter surname, first, then given name and middle initial. If any. Include every person living on April 1, 1930. Omit children born since April 1, 1930.	Relationship of this Person to the head of the family.	Sex	Color or race	Age at last birthday	Single, married, widowed or divorced	Attended school any time since Sept. 1, 1929	Whether able to read and write.	Place of birth of this person.	Whether able to speak English.	
	1	2	3	4	5	6	7	8	9	10	11	12	13	14
26	Agana-Piti Road	80	94	Salas, Barcelisa I	Daughter	F	Cha	10	S	Y	Y	Guam	Y	None
27		80	94	Salas, Maria I	Daughter	F	Cha	8	S	Y		Guam		None
28		80	94	Santos, Manuel C	Son-in-law	M	Cha	22	M	N	Y	Guam	Y	Laborer
29		80	94	Santos, Soledad S	Daughter	F	Cha	18	M	N	Y	Guam	Y	None
30		81	95	Salas, Vicente M	Head	M	Cha	36	M	N	Y	Guam	Y	Machinist
31		81	95	Salas, Soledad B	Wife	F	Cha	34	M	N	Y	Guam	N	None
32		81	95	Salas, Juan B	Son	M	Cha	9	S	Y		Guam		None
33		81	95	Salas, Juana B	Daughter	F	Cha	6	S	N		Guam		None
34		81	95	Salas, Jose B	Son	M	Cha	3	S	N		Guam		None
35		81	95	Salas, Maria B	Daughter	F	Cha	2.8	S	N		Guam		None
36		81	95	Megofna, Ana P	Mother	F	Cha	80	Wd	N	N	Guam	N	None
37		82	96	Cruz, Josefa S	Head	M	Cha	53	Wd	N	N	Guam	N	None
38		82	96	Cruz, Rosa S	Daughter	F	Cha	34	S	N	Y	Guam	Y	Laundress
39		82	96	Cruz, Maria S	Daughter	F	Cha	32	S	N	Y	Guam	Y	Laundress
40		82	96	Cruz, Ana S	Daughter	F	Cha	22	S	N	Y	Guam	Y	Laundress
41		82	96	Cruz, Antonio S	Son	M	Cha	21	S	N	Y	Guam	Y	Laborer
42		82	96	Cruz, Jose S	Son	M	Cha	20	S	N	Y	Guam	Y	Farm laborer
43		82	96	Cruz, Vicente S	Son	M	Cha	18	S	N	Y	Guam	Y	Farm laborer
44		82	96	Cruz, Francisco S	Son	M	Cha	12	S	Y	Y	Guam	Y	None
45		82	96	Cruz, Caridad S	Daughter	F	Cha	10	S	Y	Y	Guam	Y	None
46		82	96	Cruz, Benito S	Grandson	M	Cha	6	S	N		Guam		None
47		82	96	Cruz, Clotilde S	Grand daughter	F	Cha	4.9	S	N		Guam		None
48		82	96	Cruz, Pedro S	Grandson	M	Cha	2.7	S	N		Guam		None
49		82	96	Cruz, Jesusa S	Grand daughter	F	Cha	1.2	S	N		Guam		None
50		83	97	Rios, Felipe R	Head	M	Cha	59	M	N	Y	Guam	N	Farmer

(CHAMORRO ROOTS GENEALOGY PROJECT™ TRANSCRIPTION)
(BERNARD T. PUNZALAN / HTTP://WWW.CHAMORROROOTS.COM)

DEPARTMENT OF COMMERCE-BUREAU OF THE CENSUS
WASHINGTON

FIFTEENTH CENSUS OF THE UNITED STATES: 1930-POPULATION

THE ISLAND OF GUAM

Sheet No. 11A

District **Municipality of Piti**
Name of Place **Tepungan Barrio**
[Proper name and, also, name of class, as city, town, village, barrio, etc]

Enumeration District No. **10**
Enumerated by me on **April 4, 1930** **Joaquin Torres**, Enumerator

	PLACE OF ABODE			NAME	RELATION	PERSONAL DESCRIPTION				EDUCATION		NATIVITY		OCCUPATION
	Street, avenue, road, etc.	Number of dwelling house is order of visitation	Number of family in order of visitation	of each person whose place of abode on April 1, 1930, was in this family. Enter surname, first, then given name and middle initial. If any. Include every person living on April 1, 1930. Omit children born since April 1, 1930.	Relationship of this Person to the head of the family.	Sex	Color or race	Age at last birthday	Single, married, widowed or divorced	Attended school any time since Sept. 1, 1929	Whether able to read and write.	Place of birth of this person.	Whether able to speak English.	
	1	2	3	4	5	6	7	8	9	10	11	12	13	14
1	Agana-Piti Road	83	97	Rios, Antonia S	Wife	F	Cha	50	M	N	N	Guam	N	None
2		83	97	Rios, Jesus S	Son	M	Cha	23	S	Y	Y	Guam	Y	Farm laborer
3		83	97	Rios, Jose S	Son	M	Cha	21	S	N	Y	Guam	Y	Chauffeur
4		83	97	Rios, Lagrimas S	Daughter	F	Cha	19	S	N	Y	Guam	Y	None
5		83	97	Rios, Maria S	Daughter	F	Cha	16	S	N	Y	Guam	Y	None
6		83	97	Rios, Rita S	Daughter	F	Cha	13	S	Y	Y	Guam	Y	None
7		83	97	Rios, Rosa	Daughter	F	Cha	11	S	Y	Y	Guam	Y	None
8		83	97	Rios, Juan S	Grandson	M	Cha	9	S	Y		Guam		None
9		83	97	Rios, Agueda S	Grand daughter	F	Cha	4.4	S	N		Guam		None
10		83	97	Mesa, Maria R	Grand daughter	F	Cha	9	S	Y		Guam		None
11		83	97	Taienao, Antonio R	Grandson	M	Cha	7	S	Y		Guam		None
12		84	98	Acfalle, Rosa B	Head	F	Cha	29	M	N	Y	Guam	Y	None
13		84	98	Acfalle, Maria B	Daughter	F	Cha	8	S	Y		Guam		None
14		84	98	Acfalle, Jose B	Son	M	Cha	4.8	S	N		Guam		None
15		84	98	Acfalle, Jesus B	Son	M	Cha	3.2	S	N		Guam		None
16		84	98	Acfalle, Delfina B	Daughter	F	Cha	2.6	S	N		Guam		None
17		84	98	Acfalle, Concepcion B	Daughter	F	Cha	1.2	S	N		Guam		None
18		85	99	Kamminga, Felix R	Head	M	Cha	47	M	N	Y	Guam	Y	Carpenter
19		85	99	Kamminga, Maria H	Wife	F	Cha	50	M	N	Y	Guam	N	None
20		85	99	Kamminga, Lolkje H	Daughter	F	Cha	20	S	N	Y	Guam	Y	None
21		86	100	Kamminga, Juana R	Head	F	Cha	72	Wd	N	Y	Guam	Y	None
22		87	101	Roberto, Simon K	Head	M	Cha	48	M	N	Y	Guam	Y	Farmer
23		87	101	Kamminga, Felicitas SN	Wife	F	Cha	49	M	N	Y	Guam	N	None
24		87	101	Kamminga, Juana SN	Daughter	F	Cha	16	S	N	Y	Guam	Y	None
25		87	101	Kamminga, Gretje SN	Daughter	F	Cha	14	S	N	Y	Guam	Y	None

(CHAMORRO ROOTS GENEALOGY PROJECT™ TRANSCRIPTION)
(BERNARD T. PUNZALAN / HTTP://WWW.CHAMORROROOTS.COM)

DEPARTMENT OF COMMERCE-BUREAU OF THE CENSUS
WASHINGTON

FIFTEENTH CENSUS OF THE UNITED STATES: 1930-POPULATION

THE ISLAND OF GUAM

Sheet No. 11B

303b

District **Municipality of Piti**
Name of Place **Tepungan Barrio**
[Proper name and, also, name of class, as city, town, village, barrio, etc]

Enumeration District No. **10**
Enumerated by me on **April 5, 1930** **Joaquin Torres**
Enumerator

	PLACE OF ABODE: Street, avenue, road, etc.	Number of dwelling house is order of visitation	Number of family in order of visitation	NAME of each person whose place of abode on April 1, 1930, was in this family. Enter surname, first, then given name and middle initial. If any. Include every person living on April 1, 1930. Omit children born since April 1, 1930.	RELATION Relationship of this Person to the head of the family.	PERSONAL DESCRIPTION: Sex	Color or race	Age at last birthday	Single, married, widowed or divorced	EDUCATION: Attended school any time since Sept. 1, 1929	Whether able to read and write.	NATIVITY Place of birth of this person.	Whether able to speak English.	OCCUPATION
	1	2	3	4	5	6	7	8	9	10	11	12	13	14
26	Agana-Piti Road	87	101	Kamminga, Pilar SN	Daughter	F	Cha	12	S	Y	Y	Guam	Y	None
27		87	101	Kamminga, Vicenta SN	Daughter	F	Cha	9	S	Y		Guam		None
28		88	102	Quenga, Dolores C	Head	F	Chin	43	S	N	N	Guam	N	Laundress
29		88	102	Quenga, Rufina C	Daughter	F	Chin	14	S	N	Y	Guam	Y	Saleswoman
30		88	102	Quenga, Manuel C	Son	M	Chin	10	S	Y	Y	Guam	Y	None
31		88	102	Quenga, Soledad C	Daughter	F	Chin	7	S	Y		Guam		None
32		89	103	Quenga, Enrique C	Head	M	Chin	27	M	N	Y	Guam	Y	Chauffeur
33		89	103	Quenga, Mercedes H	Wife	F	Cha	21	M	N	Y	Guam	Y	None
34		89	103	Quenga, Magdalena H	Daughter	F	Chin	3.8	S	N		Guam		None
35		89	103	Hernandez, Eugenio P	Brother-in-law	M	Cha	19	S	N	N	Guam		Farm laborer
36		90	104	Cabrera, Jose D	Head	M	Cha	29	M	N	Y	Guam	Y	Farm laborer
37		90	104	Cabrera, Maria Q	Wife	F	Chin	27	M	N	Y	Guam	Y	None
38		90	104	Cabrera, Maria Q	Daughter	F	Cha	9	S	Y		Guam		None
39		90	104	Cabrera, Pilar Q	Daughter	F	Cha	5	S	N		Guam		None
40		90	104	Cabrera, Jose Q	Son	M	Cha	3	S	N		Guam		None
41		90	104	Cabrera, Ana Q	Daughter	F	Cha	1.2	S	N		Guam		None
42		91	105	Quenga, Francisco T	Head	M	Chin	32	M	N	Y	Guam	Y	Farmer
43		91	105	Quenga, Ana M	Wife	F	Cha	29	M	N	Y	Guam	N	None
44		91	105	Quenga, Antonia M	Daughter	F	Chin	12	S	Y	Y	Guam	Y	None
45		91	105	Quenga, Matilde M	Daughter	F	Chin	11	S	Y	Y	Guam	Y	None
46		91	105	Quenga, Maria M	Daughter	F	Chin	9	S	Y		Guam		None
47		91	105	Quenga, Felix M	Son	M	Chin	7	S	Y		Guam		None
48		91	105	Quenga, Jose M	Son	M	Chin	6	S	N		Guam		None
49		91	105	Quenga, Francisca M	Daughter	F	Chin	3.4	S	N		Guam		None
50		92	106	Acfalle, Ignacio C	Head	M	Cha	36	S	N	Y	Guam	Y	Laborer

(CHAMORRO ROOTS GENEALOGY PROJECT™ TRANSCRIPTION)
(BERNARD T. PUNZALAN / HTTP://WWW.CHAMORROROOTS.COM)

DEPARTMENT OF COMMERCE-BUREAU OF THE CENSUS
WASHINGTON

FIFTEENTH CENSUS OF THE UNITED STATES: 1930-POPULATION

THE ISLAND OF GUAM

Sheet No. 12A

District **Municipality of Piti**
Name of Place **Tepungan Barrio**
[Proper name and, also, name of class, as city, town, village, barrio, etc]

Enumeration District No. **10**
Enumerated by me on **April 5, 1930** **Joaquin Torres**, Enumerator

	PLACE OF ABODE			NAME	RELATION	PERSONAL DESCRIPTION				EDUCATION		NATIVITY		OCCUPATION
	Street, avenue, road, etc.	Number of dwelling house in order of visitation	Number of family in order of visitation	of each person whose place of abode on April 1, 1930, was in this family. Enter surname, first, then given name and middle initial. If any. Include every person living on April 1, 1930. Omit children born since April 1, 1930.	Relationship of this Person to the head of the family.	Sex	Color or race	Age at last birthday	Single, married, widowed or divorced	Attended school any time since Sept. 1, 1929	Whether able to read and write.	Place of birth of this person.	Whether able to speak English.	
	1	2	3	4	5	6	7	8	9	10	11	12	13	14
1	Agana-Piti Road	92	106	Acfalle, Nieves C	Mother	F	Cha	73	Wd	N	N	Guam	N	None
2		93	107	Nauta, Jose N	Head	M	Cha	44	M	N	N	Guam	N	Farmer
3		93	107	Nauta, Felicita T	Wife	F	Cha	44	M	N	N	Guam	N	None
4		93	107	Terlaje, Amalia T	Mother-in-law	F	Cha	69	Wd	N	N	Guam	N	None
5		94	108	Manibusan, Manuel SN	Head	M	Cha	47	M	N	Y	Guam	Y	Farmer
6		94	108	Manibusan, Maria C	Wife	F	Cha	45	M	N	Y	Guam	N	None
7		94	108	Manibusan, Francisco C	Son	M	Cha	19	S	N	Y	Guam	Y	Laborer
8		94	108	Manibusan, Miguel C	Son	M	Cha	17	S	N	Y	Guam	Y	Laborer
9		94	108	Manibusan, Herminia C	Daughter	F	Cha	13	S	N	Y	Guam	Y	None
10		94	108	Manibusan, Vicente C	Son	M	Cha	11	S	Y	Y	Guam	Y	None
11		94	108	Manibusan, Juan C	Son	M	Cha	9	S	Y		Guam		None
12		94	108	Manibusan, Fidela C	Daughter	F	Cha	6	S	N		Guam		None
13		94	108	Manibusan, Ignacia C	Daughter	F	Cha	2.8	S	N		Guam		None
14		94	108	Manibusan, Victoria C	Daughter	F	Cha	0.2	S	N		Guam		None
15		95	109	Nauta, Rita M	Head	F	Cha	23	M	N	Y	Guam	Y	None
16		95	109	Nauta, Antonia M	Daughter	F	Cha	3.7	S	N		Guam		None
17		95	109	Nauta, Eulogio M	Son	M	Cha	1.7	S	N		Guam		None
18		95	109	Nauta, Carmen M	Daughter	F	Cha	0.7	S	N		Guam		None
19		95	109	Nauta, Ana M	Daughter	F	Cha	0.7	S	N		Guam		None
20		95	109	Megofna, Carmen C	Mother	F	Cha	59	Wd	N	N	Guam	N	Laundress
21		96	110	Blaz, Ignacio A	Head	M	Cha	37	M	N	Y	Guam	Y	Farm laborer
22		97	111	Concepcion, Maria C	Head	F	Cha	45	Wd	N	N	Guam	N	Laundress
23		97	111	Concepcion, Biatres C	Daughter	F	Cha	19	S	N	Y	Guam	Y	Laundress
24		97	111	Concepcion, Engracia C	Daughter	F	Cha	17	S	N	Y	Guam	Y	Laundress
25		97	111	Concepcion, Cristina C	Daughter	F	Cha	15	S	N	Y	Guam	Y	None

(CHAMORRO ROOTS GENEALOGY PROJECT™ TRANSCRIPTION)
(BERNARD T. PUNZALAN / HTTP://WWW.CHAMORROROOTS.COM)

DEPARTMENT OF COMMERCE-BUREAU OF THE CENSUS
WASHINGTON

FIFTEENTH CENSUS OF THE UNITED STATES: 1930-POPULATION

THE ISLAND OF GUAM

Sheet No. 12B

304b

District **Municipality of Piti**
Name of Place **Tepungan Barrio**
[Proper name and, also, name of class, as city, town, village, barrio, etc]

Enumeration District No. **10**
Enumerated by me on **April 5, 1930** **Joaquin Torres**, Enumerator

	PLACE OF ABODE: Street, avenue, road, etc.	Number of dwelling house in order of visitation	Number of family in order of visitation	NAME of each person whose place of abode on April 1, 1930, was in this family. Enter surname, first, then given name and middle initial. If any. Include every person living on April 1, 1930. Omit children born since April 1, 1930.	RELATION Relationship of this Person to the head of the family.	PERSONAL DESCRIPTION: Sex	Color or race	Age at last birthday	Single, married, widowed or divorced	EDUCATION: Attended school any time since Sept. 1, 1929	Whether able to read and write.	NATIVITY Place of birth of this person.	Whether able to speak English.	OCCUPATION
	1	2	3	4	5	6	7	8	9	10	11	12	13	14
26	Agana-Piti Road	97	111	Concepcion, Jesus C	Son	M	Cha	13	S	Y	Y	Guam	Y	None
27		97	111	Concepcion, Manuel C	Son	M	Cha	10	S	Y	Y	Guam	Y	None
28		98	112	Santos, Jose D L	Head	M	Cha	48	M	N	Y	Guam	Y	Farmer
29		98	112	Santos, Teresa C	Wife	F	Cha	47	M	N	Y	Guam	N	None
30		98	112	Santos, Rosa C	Daughter	F	Cha	25	S	N	Y	Guam	Y	None
31		98	112	Santos, Jose C	Son	M	Cha	17	S	Y	Y	Guam	Y	None
32		98	112	Santos, Vicente C	Son	M	Cha	15	S	Y	Y	Guam	Y	None
33		98	112	Santos, Pedro C	Son	M	Cha	20	M	N	Y	Guam	Y	Chauffeur
34		98	112	Santos, Lucy L	Daughter-in-law	F	Cha	19	M	N	Y	Guam	Y	None
35		98	112	Santos, Maria L	Grand daughter	F	Cha	1	S	N		Guam		None
36		99	113	Nauta, Mariano N	Head	M	Cha	41	M	N	Y	Guam	Y	Farmer
37		99	113	Nauta, Maria Q	Wife	F	Cha	40	M	N	N	Guam	N	None
38		99	113	Nauta, Martina Q	Daughter	F	Cha	22	S	N	Y	Guam	Y	None
39		99	113	Nauta, Lucia Q	Daughter	F	Cha	19	S	N	Y	Guam	Y	None
40		99	113	Nauta, Manuel Q	Son	M	Cha	17	S	N	Y	Guam	Y	None
41		99	113	Nauta, Pedro Q	Son	M	Cha	15	S	Y	Y	Guam	Y	None
42		99	113	Nauta, Joaquina Q	Daughter	F	Cha	14	S	Y	Y	Guam	Y	None
43		99	113	Nauta, Jesus Q	Son	M	Cha	12	S	Y	Y	Guam	Y	None
44		99	113	Nauta, Felix Q	Son	M	Cha	9	S	Y		Guam		None
45		99	113	Nauta, Maria Q	Daughter	F	Cha	8	S	Y		Guam		None
46		99	113	Nauta, Juan Q	Son	M	Cha	5	S	N		Guam		None
47		99	113	Nauta, Jose Q	Son	M	Cha	3.2	S	N		Guam		None
48		99	113	Nauta, Rita Q	Daughter	F	Cha	1.2	S	N		Guam		None
49		100	114	Rapolla, Lorenzo C	Head	M	Chin	33	M	N	Y	Guam	Y	Farmer
50		100	114	Rapolla, Antonia Q	Wife	F	Cha	26	M	N	Y	Guam	Y	None

DEPARTMENT OF COMMERCE-BUREAU OF THE CENSUS
WASHINGTON

FIFTEENTH CENSUS OF THE UNITED STATES: 1930-POPULATION

THE ISLAND OF GUAM

Sheet No. 13A

District **Municipality of Piti**
Name of Place **Tepungan Barrio**
[Proper name and, also, name of class, as city, town, village, barrio, etc]

Enumeration District No. **10**
Enumerated by me on **April 5, 1930** **Joaquin Torres**
Enumerator

	PLACE OF ABODE			NAME	RELATION	PERSONAL DESCRIPTION				EDUCATION		NATIVITY		OCCUPATION
	Street, avenue, road, etc.	Number of dwelling house in order of visitation	Number of family in order of visitation	of each person whose place of abode on April 1, 1930, was in this family. Enter surname, first, then given name and middle initial. If any. Include every person living on April 1, 1930. Omit children born since April 1, 1930.	Relationship of this Person to the head of the family.	Sex	Color or race	Age at last birthday	Single, married, widowed or divorced	Attended school any time since Sept. 1, 1929	Whether able to read and write.	Place of birth of this person.	Whether able to speak English.	
	1	2	3	4	5	6	7	8	9	10	11	12	13	14
1	Agana-Piti Road	100	114	Rapolla, Juan Q	Son	M	Chin	6	S	Y		Guam		None
2		100	114	Rapolla, Angelina Q	Daughter	F	Chin	4.2	S	N		Guam		None
3		100	114	Rapolla, Tomas Q	Son	M	Chin	3.2	S	N		Guam		None
4		100	114	Rapolla, Maria Q	Daughter	F	Chin	0.9	S	N		Guam		None
5		101	115	Rapolla, Antonio C	Head	M	Chin	36	M	N	Y	Guam	Y	Carpenter
6		101	115	Rapolla, Carmela R	Wife	F	Cha	32	M	N	Y	Guam	Y	None
7		102	116	Santos, Manuel S	Head	M	Cha	55	Wd	N	Y	Guam	Y	Farmer
8		102	116	Quichocho, Jose Q	Ward	M	Cha	3.4	S	N		Guam		None
9		103	117	Cruz, Marcela Q	Head	F	Chin	26	M	N	Y	Guam	Y	None
10		103	117	Cruz, Juan Q	Son	M	Cha	8	S	Y		Guam		None
11		103	117	Cruz, Tomas Q	Son	M	Cha	4.2	S	N		Guam		None
12		103	117	Cruz, Antonio Q	Son	M	Cha	1.6	S	N		Guam		None
13		104	118	Aflleje, Maria T	Head	F	Cha	49	S	N	N	Guam	N	Laundress
14		104	118	Aflleje, Isabel T	Daughter	F	Cha	20	S	N	Y	Guam	Y	Servant
15		104	118	Aflleje, Juana T	Daughter	F	Cha	14	S	N	Y	Guam	Y	Laundress
16		104	118	Aflleje, Catalina T	Niece	F	Cha	13	S	N	Y	Guam	Y	Laundress
17		104	118	Aflleje, Jesusa T	Grand niece	F	Cha	1.7	S	N		Guam		None
18		104	118	Quidachay, Maria T	Aunt	F	Cha	88	Wd	N	N	Guam	N	None
19		105	119	Blas, Consolacion A	Head	F	Cha	34	M	N	Y	Guam	Y	Laundress
20		105	119	Blas, Ana A	Daughter	F	Cha	14	S	N	Y	Guam	Y	Servant
21		105	119	Blas, Ignacio A	Son	M	Cha	11	S	Y	Y	Guam	Y	None
22		105	119	Blas, Francisco A	Son	M	Cha	7	S	Y		Guam		None
23		105	119	Blas, Jose A	Son	M	Cha	5	S	N		Guam		None
24		105	119	Blas, Josefa A	Daughter	F	Cha	2.9	S	N		Guam		None
25		106	120	Blas, Antonia M	Head	F	Cha	23	M	N		Guam	Y	None

(CHAMORRO ROOTS GENEALOGY PROJECT™ TRANSCRIPTION)
(BERNARD T. PUNZALAN / HTTP://WWW.CHAMORROROOTS.COM)

DEPARTMENT OF COMMERCE-BUREAU OF THE CENSUS
WASHINGTON

FIFTEENTH CENSUS OF THE UNITED STATES: 1930-POPULATION

THE ISLAND OF GUAM

Sheet No. 13B

305b

District **Municipality of Piti**
Name of Place **Tepungan Barrio**
[Proper name and, also, name of class, as city, town, village, barrio, etc]

Enumeration District No. **10**
Enumerated by me on **April 6, 1930** **Joaquin Torres**
Enumerator

	PLACE OF ABODE			NAME	RELATION	PERSONAL DESCRIPTION				EDUCATION		NATIVITY		OCCUPATION
	Street, avenue, road, etc.	Number of dwelling house is order of visitation	Number of family in order of visitation	of each person whose place of abode on April 1, 1930, was in this family. Enter surname, first, then given name and middle initial. If any. Include every person living on April 1, 1930. Omit children born since April 1, 1930.	Relationship of this Person to the head of the family.	Sex	Color or race	Age at last birthday	Single, married, widowed or divorced	Attended school any time since Sept. 1, 1929	Whether able to read and write.	Place of birth of this person.	Whether able to speak English.	
	1	2	3	4	5	6	7	8	9	10	11	12	13	14
26	Agana-Piti Road	106	120	Blas, Maria M	Daughter	F	Cha	1.9	S	N		Guam		None
27		107	121	Terlaje, Manuel C	Head	M	Cha	62	M	N	Y	Guam	N	Farmer
28		107	121	Terlaje, Gabriela A	Wife	F	Cha	58	M	N	Y	Guam	N	None
29		107	121	Terlaje, Mercedes A	Daughter	F	Cha	31	S	N	Y	Guam	Y	None
30		107	121	Terlaje, Dolores A	Daughter	F	Cha	27	S	N	Y	Guam	Y	None
31		107	121	Terlaje, Jesus A	Son	M	Cha	24	S	N	Y	Guam	Y	Farm laborer
32		107	121	Terlaje, Miguel A	Son	M	Cha	16	S	N	Y	Guam	Y	Farm laborer
33		107	122	Terlaje, Luis A	Head	M	Cha	27	M	N	Y	Guam	Y	Farmer
34		107	122	Terlaje, Carmela A	Wife	F	Cha	21	M	N	Y	Guam	Y	None
35		107	122	Terlaje, Jesus A	Son	M	Cha	1.2	S	N		Guam		None
36		107	122	Aflleje, Maria T	Grandmother	F	Cha	80	Wd	N	N	Guam	N	None
37		108	123	Salas, Antonio C	Head	M	Cha	32	M	N	Y	Guam	Y	Laborer
38		108	123	Cruz, Soledad Q	Wife	F	Chin	30	M	N	Y	Guam	Y	None
39		108	123	Cruz, Jose Q	Son	M	Cha	10	S	Y	Y	Guam	Y	None
40		108	123	Salas, Angelina Q	Daughter	F	Cha	3.7	S	N		Guam		None
41		108	123	Salas, Lucia Q	Daughter	F	Cha	2.1	S	N		Guam		None
42		109	124	Quenga, Maria B	Head	F	Cha	55	Wd	N	N	Guam	N	None
43		109	124	Quenga, Vicenta B	Daughter	F	Chin	30	S	N	Y	Guam	Y	Laundress
44		109	124	Quenga, Magdalena B	Daughter	F	Chin	23	S	N	Y	Guam	Y	Laundress
45		109	124	Quenga, Juana G	Daughter	F	Chin	18	S	N	Y	Guam	Y	Saleswoman
46		109	125	Quenga, Pedro B	Head	M	Chin	25	M	N	Y	Guam	Y	Farmer
47		109	125	Quenga, Consolacion C	Wife	F	Cha	23	M	N	Y	Guam	N	None
48		109	125	Quenga, Antonia C	Daughter	F	Chin	2.7	S	N		Guam		None
49		109	125	Quenga, Jose C	Son	M	Chin	1.6	S	N		Guam		None
50		109	125	Quenga, Joaquin	Son	M	Chin	1.4	S	N		Guam		None

(CHAMORRO ROOTS GENEALOGY PROJECT™ TRANSCRIPTION)
(BERNARD T. PUNZALAN / HTTP://WWW.CHAMORROROOTS.COM)

DEPARTMENT OF COMMERCE-BUREAU OF THE CENSUS
WASHINGTON

FIFTEENTH CENSUS OF THE UNITED STATES: 1930-POPULATION

THE ISLAND OF GUAM

Sheet No. 14A

306

District **Municipality of Piti**
Name of Place **Tepungan Barrio**
[Proper name and, also, name of class, as city, town, village, barrio, etc]

Enumeration District No. **10**
Enumerated by me on **April 7, 1930** **Joaquin Torres**
Enumerator

	PLACE OF ABODE			NAME	RELATION	PERSONAL DESCRIPTION				EDUCATION		NATIVITY		OCCUPATION
	Street, avenue, road, etc.	Number of dwelling house in order of visitation	Number of family in order of visitation	of each person whose place of abode on April 1, 1930, was in this family. Enter surname, first, then given name and middle initial. If any. Include every person living on April 1, 1930. Omit children born since April 1, 1930.	Relationship of this Person to the head of the family.	Sex	Color or race	Age at last birthday	Single, married, widowed or divorced	Attended school any time since Sept. 1, 1929	Whether able to read and write.	Place of birth of this person.	Whether able to speak English.	
	1	2	3	4	5	6	7	8	9	10	11	12	13	14
1	Agana-Piti Road	110	126	Quenga, Felix C	Head	M	Chin	57	M	N	Y	Guam	N	Farmer
2		110	126	Quenga, Maria T	Wife	F	Cha	53	M	N	N	Guam	N	None
3		110	126	Quenga, Barbara T	Daughter	F	Chin	35	S	N	Y	Guam	Y	None
4		110	126	Quenga, Maria T	Daughter	F	Chin	30	S	N	Y	Guam	Y	None
5		110	126	Quenga, Dolores T	Daughter	F	Chin	28	S	N	Y	Guam	Y	None
6		110	126	Quenga, Jose T	Son	M	Chin	22	S	N	Y	Guam	Y	Farm laborer
7		110	126	Quenga, Lorenzo T	Son	M	Chin	20	S	N	Y	Guam	Y	Farm laborer
8		110	126	Quenga, Vicenta T	Daughter	F	Chin	18	S	N	Y	Guam	Y	None
9		110	126	Quenga, Manuel T	Son	M	Chin	14	S	Y	Y	Guam	Y	None
10		110	126	Quenga, Silvino T	Son	M	Chin	12	S	Y	Y	Guam	Y	None
11		111	127	Quenga, Vicente C	Head	M	Chin	53	Wd	N	Y	Guam	N	Farmer
12		111	127	Quenga, Cevera C	Daughter	F	Chin	28	S	N	Y	Guam	Y	Laundress
13		111	127	Quenga, Josefina C	Daughter	F	Chin	26	S	N	Y	Guam	Y	Laundress
14		111	127	Quenga, Dolores C	Daughter	F	Chin	22	S	N	Y	Guam	Y	Laundress
15		111	127	Quenga, Jesus C	Son	M	Chin	17	S	N	Y	Guam	Y	Farm laborer
16		111	127	Quenga, Rosalia C	Daughter	F	Chin	15	S	Y	Y	Guam	Y	None
17		111	128	Santos, Pedro A	Head	M	Cha	34	M	N	Y	Guam	Y	Chauffeur
18		111	128	Santos, Antonia Q	Wife	F	Chin	30	M	N	Y	Guam	Y	None
19		111	128	Santos, Gabina Q	Daughter	F	Cha	2.9	S	N		Guam		None
20		111	128	Santos, Matilde Q	Daughter	F	Cha	1.1	S	N		Guam		None
21		112	129	Quenga, Sebastian C	Head	M	Chin	46	M	N	Y	Guam	N	Fisherman
22		112	129	Quenga, Milagro SN	Wife	F	Cha	48	M	N	N	Guam	N	None
23		112	129	Quenga, Vicente SN	Son	M	Chin	21	S	N	Y	Guam	Y	Farm laborer
24		112	129	Quenga, Carolina SN	Daughter	F	Chin	19	S	N	Y	Guam	Y	None
25		112	129	Quenga, Manuel SN	Son	M	Chin	16	S	Y	Y	Guam	Y	None

DEPARTMENT OF COMMERCE-BUREAU OF THE CENSUS
WASHINGTON

FIFTEENTH CENSUS OF THE UNITED STATES: 1930-POPULATION

THE ISLAND OF GUAM

Sheet No. 14B

District **Municipality of Piti**
Name of Place **Tepungan Barrio**
[Proper name and, also, name of class, as city, town, village, barrio, etc]

Enumeration District No. **10**
Enumerated by me on **April 7, 1930** **Joaquin Torres**
Enumerator

	PLACE OF ABODE			NAME	RELATION	PERSONAL DESCRIPTION				EDUCATION		NATIVITY		OCCUPATION
	Street, avenue, road, etc.	Number of dwelling house in order of visitation	Number of family in order of visitation	of each person whose place of abode on April 1, 1930, was in this family. Enter surname, first, then given name and middle initial. If any. Include every person living on April 1, 1930. Omit children born since April 1, 1930.	Relationship of this Person to the head of the family.	Sex	Color or race	Age at last birthday	Single, married, widowed or divorced	Attended school any time since Sept. 1, 1929	Whether able to read and write.	Place of birth of this person.	Whether able to speak English.	
	1	2	3	4	5	6	7	8	9	10	11	12	13	14
26	Agana-Piti Road	112	129	Quenga, Joaquina SN	Daughter	F	Chin	12	S	Y	Y	Guam	Y	None
27		112	129	Quenga, Maria SN	Daughter	F	Chin	10	S	Y	Y	Guam	Y	None
28		113	130	Quenga, Ana SN	Head	F	Cha	50	Wd	N	N	Guam	N	Laundress
29		113	130	Quenga, Angustia SN	Daughter	F	Chin	28	S	N	Y	Guam	Y	Laundress
30		113	130	Quenga, Celestina SN	Daughter	F	Chin	27	S	N	Y	Guam	Y	Laundress
31		113	130	Quenga, Manuel SN	Son	M	Chin	25	S	N	Y	Guam	Y	Farm laborer
32		114	131	Roberto, Maria A	Head	F	Cha	56	S	N	Y	Guam	Y	None
33		115	132	Quenga, Antonio C	Head	M	Chin	55	M	N	Y	Guam	N	Farmer
34		115	132	Quenga, Natividad SN	Wife	F	Cha	56	M	N	Y	Guam	N	None
35		115	132	Quenga, Vicente SN	Son	M	Chin	25	M	N	Y	Guam	Y	Chauffeur
36		115	132	Quenga, Maria SN	Daughter	F	Chin	23	S	N	Y	Guam	Y	None
37		115	132	Quenga, Teodoro SN	Son	M	Chin	19	S	N	Y	Guam	Y	Farm laborer
38		115	132	Quenga, Lourdes SN	Daughter	F	Chin	16	S	N	Y	Guam	Y	None
39		115	132	Quenga, Carlos SN	Son	M	Chin	12	S	Y	Y	Guam	Y	None
40		115	133	Santos, Manuel F	Head	M	Cha	31	M	N	Y	Guam	Y	Laborer
41		115	133	Santos, Joaquina C	Wife	F	Cha	20	M	N	Y	Guam	Y	Laborer
42		116	134	Cruz, Serafin R	Head	M	Cha	44	M	N	Y	Guam	Y	Laborer
43		116	134	Cruz, Asuncion N	Wife	F	Cha	31	M	N	Y	Guam	Y	Laundress
44		116	134	Nededog, Beatrice N	Step daughter	F	Cha	16	S	N	Y	Guam	Y	Laundress
45		117	135	San Nicolas, Rosa A	Head	F	Cha	36	Wd	N	N	Guam	N	Laundress
46		117	135	San Nicolas, Maria A	Daughter	F	Cha	13	S	Y	Y	Guam	Y	None
47		117	135	San Nicolas, Jose A	Son	M	Cha	11	S	Y	Y	Guam	Y	None
48		117	135	San Nicolas, Jesus A	Son	M	Cha	9	S	Y		Guam		None
49		117	135	San Nicolas, Juan A	Son	M	Cha	9	S	Y		Guam		None
50		118	136	Quinata, Antonio A	Head	M	Cha	28	M	N	Y	Guam	Y	Farmer

DEPARTMENT OF COMMERCE-BUREAU OF THE CENSUS
WASHINGTON

FIFTEENTH CENSUS OF THE UNITED STATES: 1930-POPULATION

THE ISLAND OF GUAM

Sheet No. 15A

District **Municipality of Piti**
Name of Place **Tepungan Barrio**
[Proper name and, also, name of class, as city, town, village, barrio, etc]

Enumeration District No. **10**
Enumerated by me on **April 7, 1930** **Joaquin Torres**
Enumerator

	PLACE OF ABODE			NAME	RELATION	PERSONAL DESCRIPTION				EDUCATION		NATIVITY		OCCUPATION
	Street, avenue, road, etc.	Number of dwelling house is order of visitation	Number of family in order of visitation	of each person whose place of abode on April 1, 1930, was in this family. Enter surname, first, then given name and middle initial. If any. Include every person living on April 1, 1930. Omit children born since April 1, 1930.	Relationship of this Person to the head of the family.	Sex	Color or race	Age at last birthday	Single, married, widowed or divorced	Attended school any time since Sept. 1, 1929	Whether able to read and write.	Place of birth of this person.	Whether able to speak English.	
	1	2	3	4	5	6	7	8	9	10	11	12	13	14
1	Agana-Piti Road	118	136	Quinata, Nicolasa M	Wife	F	Cha	33	M	N	Y	Guam	Y	None
2		118	136	Quinata, Engracia M	Daughter	F	Cha	10	S	Y	Y	Guam	Y	None
3		118	136	Quinata, Maria M	Daughter	F	Cha	6	S	N		Guam		None
4		118	136	Quinata, Jose M	Son	M	Cha	5	S	N		Guam		None
5		118	136	Quinata, Gregorio M	Son	M	Cha	0.2	S	N		Guam		None
6		119	137	Aflleje, Maximo	Head	M	Cha	44	M	N	Y	Guam	Y	Farmer
7		119	137	Aflleje, Maria C	Wife	F	Cha	39	M	N	N	Guam	N	None
8		119	137	Agualo, Alejandro C	Stepson	M	Cha	21	S	N	Y	Guam	Y	Farm laborer
9		119	137	Agualo, Jose C	Stepson	M	Cha	19	S	N	Y	Guam	Y	Farm laborer
10		119	137	Agualo, Miguel C	Stepson	M	Cha	14	S	Y	Y	Guam	Y	None
11		120	138	Torres, Joaquin	Head	M	Cha	35	M	N	Y	Guam	Y	School teacher
12		120	138	Torres, Maria U	Wife	F	Chin	34	M	N	Y	Guam	Y	None
13		120	138	Torres, Jose U	Son	M	Cha	14	S	Y	Y	Guam	Y	None
14		120	138	Torres, Maria O U	Daughter	F	Cha	13	S	Y	Y	Guam	Y	None
15		120	138	Torres, Daniel U	Son	M	Cha	10	S	Y	Y	Guam	Y	None
16		120	138	Torres, Esteban U	Son	M	Cha	9	S	Y		Guam		None
17		120	138	Torres, Ursula U	Daughter	F	Cha	2.4	S	N		Guam		None
18		120	138	Torres, Jesus U	Son	M	Cha	2.7	S	N		Guam		None
19		120	138	Torres, Francisco U	Son	M	Cha	0.8	S	N		Guam		None
20		120	138	Unpingco, Felipe A	Brother-in-law	M	Chin	19	S	N		Guam		None
21		121	139	Quichocho, Ignacio Q	Head	M	Cha	21	S	N	Y	Guam	Y	Laborer
22		122	140	Concepcion, Joaquin	Head	M	Cha	42	M	N	Y	Guam	Y	Farmer
23		122	140	Concepcion, Maria Q	Wife	F	Cha	35	M	N	Y	Guam	Y	None
24		122	140	Concepcion, Jesus Q	Son	M	Cha	16	S	N	Y	Guam	Y	Farm laborer
25		122	140	Concepcion, Jose Q	Son	M	Cha	14	S	Y	Y	Guam	Y	None

(CHAMORRO ROOTS GENEALOGY PROJECT™ TRANSCRIPTION)
(BERNARD T. PUNZALAN / HTTP://WWW.CHAMORROROOTS.COM)

DEPARTMENT OF COMMERCE-BUREAU OF THE CENSUS
WASHINGTON

FIFTEENTH CENSUS OF THE UNITED STATES: 1930-POPULATION

THE ISLAND OF GUAM

Sheet No. 15B

307b

District **Municipality of Piti**

Name of Place **Tepungan Barrio**
[Proper name and, also, name of class, as city, town, village, barrio, etc]

Enumeration District No. **10**

Enumerated by me on **April 8, 1930** **Joaquin Torres**, Enumerator

	PLACE OF ABODE			NAME	RELATION	PERSONAL DESCRIPTION				EDUCATION		NATIVITY		OCCUPATION
	Street, avenue, road, etc.	Number of dwelling house is order of visitation	Number of family in order of visitation	of each person whose place of abode on April 1, 1930, was in this family. Enter surname, first, then given name and middle initial. If any. Include every person living on April 1, 1930. Omit children born since April 1, 1930.	Relationship of this Person to the head of the family.	Sex	Color or race	Age at last birthday	Single, married, widowed or divorced	Attended school any time since Sept. 1, 1929	Whether able to read and write.	Place of birth of this person.	Whether able to speak English.	
	1	2	3	4	5	6	7	8	9	10	11	12	13	14
26		122	140	Concepcion, Ana Q	Daughter	F	Cha	12	S	N	Y	Guam	Y	None
27		122	140	Concepcion, Joaquin Q	Son	M	Cha	9	S	Y		Guam		None
28		122	140	Concepcion, Manuel Q	Son	M	Cha	7	S	Y		Guam		None
29		122	140	Concepcion, Juan Q	Son	M	Cha	4.2	S	N		Guam		None
30		122	140	Concepcion, Antonio Q	Son	M	Cha	3	S	N		Guam		None
31		122	140	Concepcion, Gregorio Q	Son	M	Cha	0.2	S	N		Guam		None
32		123	141	Fejeran, Joaquin C	Head	M	Cha	36	M	N	Y	Guam	Y	Farm laborer
33		123	141	Fejeran, Dolores S	Wife	F	Cha	30	M	N	Y	Guam	Y	None
34		123	141	Fejeran, Antonio S	Son	M	Cha	10	S	Y	Y	Guam	Y	None
35		123	141	Fejeran, Jose S	Son	M	Cha	6	S	N		Guam		None
36		123	141	Fejeran, Edward S	Son	M	Cha	4.7	S	N		Guam		None
37		123	141	Fejeran, Ignacio S	Son	M	Cha	2.7	S	N		Guam		None
38		123	141	Fejeran, Tomas S	Son	M	Cha	0.7	S	N		Guam		None
39		124	142	Camacho, Nicolasa M	Head	F	Cha	34	M	N	Y	Guam	Y	None
40		124	142	Camacho, Monica M	Daughter	F	Cha	8	S	Y		Guam		None
41		124	142	Camacho, Joaquin M	Son	M	Cha	6	S	N		Guam		None
42		124	142	Camacho, Maria M	Daughter	F	Cha	5	S	N		Guam		None
43		124	142	Camacho, Antonio M	Son	M	Cha	2.4	S	N		Guam		None
44		124	142	Camacho, Rafael M	Son	M	Cha	0.1	S	N		Guam		None
45		125	143	Quenga, Jose SN	Head	M	Chin	30	M	N	Y	Guam	Y	Chauffeur
46		125	143	Quenga, Ana S	Wife	F	Cha	31	M	N	Y	Guam	Y	None
47		125	143	Quenga, Justo S	Son	M	Chin	3.4	S	N		Guam		None
48		125	143	Quenga, William S	Son	M	Chin	2.2	S	N		Guam		None
49		125	143	Quenga, Jaime S	Son	M	Chin	1.2	S	N		Guam		None
50		125	143	Quenga, Teresita S	Daughter	F	Chin	1.2	S	N		Guam		None

DEPARTMENT OF COMMERCE-BUREAU OF THE CENSUS
WASHINGTON

FIFTEENTH CENSUS OF THE UNITED STATES: 1930-POPULATION

THE ISLAND OF GUAM

Sheet No. 16A | **308**

District **Municipality of Piti**
Name of Place **Tepungan Barrio**
[Proper name and, also, name of class, as city, town, village, barrio, etc]

Enumeration District No. **10**
Enumerated by me on **April 8, 1930** **Joaquin Torres**, Enumerator

	PLACE OF ABODE			NAME	RELATION	PERSONAL DESCRIPTION				EDUCATION		NATIVITY		OCCUPATION
	Street, avenue, road, etc.	Number of dwelling house is order of visitation	Number of family in order of visitation	of each person whose place of abode on April 1, 1930, was in this family. Enter surname, first, then given name and middle initial. If any. Include every person living on April 1, 1930. Omit children born since April 1, 1930.	Relationship of this Person to the head of the family.	Sex	Color or race	Age at last birthday	Single, married, widowed or divorced	Attended school any time since Sept. 1, 1929	Whether able to read and write.	Place of birth of this person.	Whether able to speak English.	
	1	2	3	4	5	6	7	8	9	10	11	12	13	14
1	Agana-Piti Road	125	143	Quenga, Matilde S	Daughter	F	Chin	0	S			Guam		None
2		126	144	Quenga, Jose C	Head	M	Chin	24	M	N	Y	Guam	Y	Chauffeur
3		126	144	Quenga, Regina T	Wife	F	Cha	18	M	N	Y	Guam	Y	None
4		126	144	Quenga, Jesus T	Son	M	Chin	0.7	S	N		Guam		None
5		127	145	Cruz, Jose SN	Head	M	Cha	21	S	N	Y	Guam	Y	Farm laborer
6		128	146	Vandenberg, Sidney R	Head	M	W	35	M	N	Y	Missouri	Y	Entomologist
7		129	147	Edwards, Charles W	Head	M	W	47	M	N	Y	Michigan	Y	Director Agricultural Station
8		129	147	Edwards, Francis D	Wife	F	W	36	M	N	Y	Massachusetts	Y	None
9		129	147	Edwards, Edwin F	Son	M	W	11	S	Y	Y	Guam	Y	None
10		129	147	Edwards, Richard H	Son	M	W	10	S	Y	Y	Guam	Y	None
11		130	148	Bernardo, Mariana Q	Head	F	Cha	24	Wd	N	Y	Guam	Y	Laundress
12		130	148	Quichocho, Consolacion Q	Sister	F	Cha	19	S	N	N	Guam	Y	Servant
13		130	148	Crisostomo, Jose C	Nephew	M	Cha	1.4	S	N		Guam		None
14					~~Here ends the enumeration of Tepungan Barrio.~~									
15														
16														
17														
18														
19														
20														
21														
22														
23														
24														
25					[Note: Sheet 16b / 308b was intentionally left blank.]									

DEPARTMENT OF COMMERCE-BUREAU OF THE CENSUS
WASHINGTON

FIFTEENTH CENSUS OF THE UNITED STATES: 1930-POPULATION

THE ISLAND OF GUAM

Sheet No. 17A

District **Municipality of Piti**
Name of Place **Sinengsong Barrio**
[Proper name and, also, name of class, as city, town, village, barrio, etc]

Enumeration District No. **10**
Enumerated by me on **April 8, 1930** **Joaquin Torres**
Enumerator

	PLACE OF ABODE			NAME	RELATION	PERSONAL DESCRIPTION				EDUCATION		NATIVITY		OCCUPATION
	Street, avenue, road, etc.	Number of dwelling house is order of visitation	Number of family in order of visitation	of each person whose place of abode on April 1, 1930, was in this family. Enter surname, first, then given name and middle initial. If any. Include every person living on April 1, 1930. Omit children born since April 1, 1930.	Relationship of this Person to the head of the family.	Sex	Color or race	Age at last birthday	Single, married, widowed or divorced	Attended school any time since Sept. 1, 1929	Whether able to read and write.	Place of birth of this person.	Whether able to speak English.	
	1	2	3	4	5	6	7	8	9	10	11	12	13	14
1	Piti-Sumay Road	131	149	Cruz, Juan S	Head	M	Cha	28	M	N	Y	Guam	Y	Laborer
2		131	149	Cruz, Maria H	Wife	F	Cha	22	M	N	Y	Guam	Y	None
3		131	149	Cruz, Guillermo H	Son	M	Cha	2.5	S	N		Guam		None
4		131	149	Cruz, Emilia H	Daughter	F	Cha	0.7	S	N		Guam		None
5		132	150	San Nicolas, Joaquin S	Head	M	Cha	37	M	N	Y	Guam	Y	Farmer
6		132	150	San Nicolas, Nicolasa S	Wife	F	Cha	34	M	N	Y	Guam	Y	None
7		133	151	Lizama, Vicente	Head	M	Cha	46	M	N	Y	Guam	Y	Farmer
8		133	151	Lizama, Vicenta Q	Wife	F	Cha	44	M	N	N	Guam	N	None
9		133	151	Lizama, Manuel Q	Son	M	Cha	21	S	N	Y	Guam	Y	Farm laborer
10		133	151	Lizama, Jesus Q	Son	M	Cha	18	S	N	Y	Guam	Y	Farm laborer
11		133	151	Lizama, Joaquin Q	Son	M	Cha	16	S	N	Y	Guam	Y	Farm laborer
12		133	151	Lizama, Rosa Q	Daughter	F	Cha	12	S	Y	Y	Guam	Y	None
13		133	151	Lizama, Soledad Q	Daughter	F	Cha	11	S	Y	Y	Guam	Y	None
14		133	151	Lizama, Joaquina Q	Daughter	F	Cha	5	S	N		Guam		None
15		133	151	Lizama, Ana Q	Daughter	F	Cha	3.9	S	N		Guam		None
16		133	151	Taitano, Francisco S	Nephew	M	Cha	14	S	Y	Y	Guam	Y	None
17		134	152	Iglesias, Juan	Head	M	Cha	41	S	N	Y	Guam	Y	Farmer
18		134	152	Iglesias, Magdalena	Mother	F	Cha	42	Wd	N	N	Guam	N	None
19		134	152	Iglesias, Francisco Q	Brother	M	Cha	29	S	N	Y	Guam	Y	Farm laborer
20		135	153	Iglesias, Jose Q	Head	M	Cha	20	M	N	Y	Guam	Y	Farmer
21		135	153	Iglesias, Ana M	Wife	F	Cha	18	M	N	Y	Guam	Y	None
22		136	154	Santos, Francisco A	Head	M	Cha	57	M	N	N	Guam	N	Farmer
23		136	154	Santos, Soledad S	Wife	F	Cha	54	M	N	N	Guam	N	None
24		136	154	Santos, Jose Q	Son	M	Cha	23	S	N	Y	Guam	Y	Farm laborer
25		136	154	Santos, Ana Q	Daughter	F	Cha	21	S	N	Y	Guam	Y	None

DEPARTMENT OF COMMERCE-BUREAU OF THE CENSUS
WASHINGTON

FIFTEENTH CENSUS OF THE UNITED STATES: 1930-POPULATION

THE ISLAND OF GUAM

Sheet No. 17B

309b

District **Municipality of Piti**
Name of Place **Sinengsong Barrio**
[Proper name and, also, name of class, as city, town, village, barrio, etc]

Enumeration District No. **10**
Enumerated by me on **April 8, 1930** **Joaquin Torres**
Enumerator

	PLACE OF ABODE			NAME	RELATION	PERSONAL DESCRIPTION				EDUCATION		NATIVITY		OCCUPATION
	Street, avenue, road, etc.	Number of dwelling house is order of visitation	Number of family in order of visitation	of each person whose place of abode on April 1, 1930, was in this family. Enter surname, first, then given name and middle initial. If any. Include every person living on April 1, 1930. Omit children born since April 1, 1930.	Relationship of this Person to the head of the family.	Sex	Color or race	Age at last birthday	Single, married, widowed or divorced	Attended school any time since Sept. 1, 1929	Whether able to read and write.	Place of birth of this person.	Whether able to speak English.	
	1	2	3	4	5	6	7	8	9	10	11	12	13	14
26	Piti-Sumay Road	136	154	Santos, Francisco Q	Son	M	Cha	20	S	N	Y	Guam	Y	Farm laborer
27		136	154	Santos, Antonio Q	Son	M	Cha	16	S	N	Y	Guam	Y	Farm laborer
28		136	154	Santos, Antonina Q	Daughter	F	Cha	12	S	Y	Y	Guam	Y	None
29		136	154	Quitugua, Maria Q	Mother-in-law	F	Cha	80	S	N	N	Guam	N	None
30		136	154	Quitugua, Dolores SN	Mother-in-law	F	Cha	91	Wd	N	N	Guam	N	None
31		137	155	Santos, Jose S	Head	M	Cha	60	M	N	N	Guam	N	Farmer
32		137	155	Santos, Barbara B	Wife	F	Cha	40	M	N	N	Guam	N	None
33		137	155	Santos, Joaquin S	Grandson	M	Cha	17	S	N	Y	Guam	Y	Farm laborer
34		138	156	Iglesias, Trinidad C	Head	F	Cha	29	M	N	Y	Guam	Y	None
35		138	156	Iglesias, Guadalupe C	Daughter	F	Cha	6	S	N		Philippine Is.		None
36		138	156	Iglesias, Julia C	Daughter	F	Cha	3.8	S	N		Guam		None
37		138	156	Iglesias, Jose C	Son	M	Cha	1	S	N		Guam		None
38		139	157	Duenas, Francisco SN	Head	M	Cha	36	M	N	N	Guam	N	Farmer
39		139	157	Duenas, Manuela S	Wife	F	Cha	42	M	N	N	Guam	N	None
40		139	157	Duenas, Jesus S	Son	M	Cha	11	S	Y	Y	Guam	Y	None
41		139	157	Duenas, Jose S	Son	M	Cha	9	S	Y		Guam		None
42		139	157	Duenas, Maria S	Daughter	F	Cha	7	S	Y		Guam		None
43		139	157	Duenas, Francisco S	Son	M	Cha	5	S	N		Guam		None
44		139	157	Duenas, Carlos S	Son	M	Cha	3.1	S	N		Guam		None
45		139	157	Duenas, Julian S	Son	M	Cha	1.1	S	N		Guam		None
46		139	157	Santos, Vicente S	Stepson	M	Cha	16	S	N	Y	Guam	Y	Laborer
47		140	158	Cruz, Gabriel S	Head	M	Cha	37	M	N	Y	Guam	Y	Laborer
48		140	158	Cruz, Dolores Q	Wife	F	Cha	21	M	N	Y	Guam	Y	None
49		140	158	Cruz, Juan Q	Son	M	Cha	4.7	S	N		Guam		None
50		140	158	Cruz, Miguel Q	Son	M	Cha	3.7	S	N		Guam		None

(CHAMORRO ROOTS GENEALOGY PROJECT™ TRANSCRIPTION)
(BERNARD T. PUNZALAN / HTTP://WWW.CHAMORROROOTS.COM)

DEPARTMENT OF COMMERCE-BUREAU OF THE CENSUS
WASHINGTON

FIFTEENTH CENSUS OF THE UNITED STATES: 1930-POPULATION

THE ISLAND OF GUAM

Sheet No. 18A

310

District **Municipality of Piti**
Name of Place **Sinengsong Barrio**
[Proper name and, also, name of class, as city, town, village, barrio, etc]

Enumeration District No. **10**
Enumerated by me on **April 8, 1930** **Joaquin Torres**
Enumerator

	PLACE OF ABODE			NAME	RELATION	PERSONAL DESCRIPTION				EDUCATION		NATIVITY		OCCUPATION
	Street, avenue, road, etc.	Number of dwelling house is order of visitation	Number of family in order of visitation	of each person whose place of abode on April 1, 1930, was in this family. Enter surname, first, then given name and middle initial. If any. Include every person living on April 1, 1930. Omit children born since April 1, 1930.	Relationship of this Person to the head of the family.	Sex	Color or race	Age at last birthday	Single, married, widowed or divorced	Attended school any time since Sept. 1, 1929	Whether able to read and write.	Place of birth of this person.	Whether able to speak English.	
	1	2	3	4	5	6	7	8	9	10	11	12	13	14
1	Piti-Sumay Road	140	158	Cruz, Jesus Q	Son	M	Cha	0.9	S	N		Guam		None
2		141	159	Hart, Guillermo M	Head	M	Cha	50	M	N	Y	Guam	Y	Farmer
3		141	159	Hart, Caridad Q	Wife	F	Cha	50	M	N	N	Guam	N	None
4		141	159	Hart, Jose Q	Son	M	Cha	22	S	N	Y	Guam	Y	Farm laborer
5		141	159	Hart, Vicente Q	Son	M	Cha	16	S	Y	Y	Guam	Y	Farm laborer
6		141	159	Hart, Rosa Q	Daughter	F	Cha	14	S	Y	Y	Guam	Y	None
7		141	159	Hart, Ana Q	Daughter	F	Cha	12	S	Y	Y	Guam	Y	None
8		141	159	Hart, Pedro Q	Son	M	Cha	10	S	Y	Y	Guam	Y	None
9		142	160	Salas, Antonio C	Head	M	Cha	52	M	N	Y	Guam	Y	Farmer
10		142	160	Salas, Martina C	Wife	F	Cha	50	M	N	Y	Guam	N	None
11		142	160	Salas, Maria C	Daughter	F	Cha	27	S	N	Y	Guam	Y	None
12		142	160	Salas, Josefa C	Daughter	F	Cha	23	S	N	Y	Guam	Y	None
13		142	160	Salas, Jose C	Son	M	Cha	21	S	N	Y	Guam	Y	Farm laborer
14		142	160	Salas, Ignacio C	Son	M	Cha	18	S	N	Y	Guam	Y	Farm laborer
15		142	160	Salas, Juan C	Son	M	Cha	16	S	Y	Y	Guam	Y	None
16		142	160	Salas, Marcela C	Son	M	Cha	13	S	Y	Y	Guam	Y	None
17		142	160	Salas, Magdalena C	Daughter	F	Cha	10	S	N	N	Guam	N	None
18		142	160	Salas, Teresa C	Daughter	F	Cha	9	S	Y		Guam		None
19		143	161	Salas, Jesus C	Head	M	Cha	29	M	N	Y	Guam	Y	Store keeper
20		143	161	Salas, Rosa S	Wife	F	Cha	24	M	N	Y	Guam	Y	None
21		143	161	Salas, Jose S	Son	M	Cha	4.8	S	N		Guam		None
22		143	161	Salas, Joaquin S	Son	M	Cha	3	S	N		Guam		None
23		144	162	Borja, Manuel	Head	M	Cha	36	M	N	Y	Guam	Y	Farmer
24		144	162	Borja, Maria S	Wife	F	Cha	35	M	N	Y	Guam	Y	None
25		144	162	Borja, Antonio S	Son	M	Cha	8	S	Y		Guam		None

DEPARTMENT OF COMMERCE-BUREAU OF THE CENSUS
WASHINGTON

FIFTEENTH CENSUS OF THE UNITED STATES: 1930-POPULATION

THE ISLAND OF GUAM

Sheet No. 18B

310b

District **Municipality of Piti**
Name of Place **Sinengsong Barrio**
[Proper name and, also, name of class, as city, town, village, barrio, etc]

Enumeration District No. **10**
Enumerated by me on **April 8, 1930** **Joaquin Torres**
Enumerator

	PLACE OF ABODE			NAME	RELATION	PERSONAL DESCRIPTION				EDUCATION		NATIVITY		OCCUPATION
	Street, avenue, road, etc.	Number of dwelling house in order of visitation	Number of family in order of visitation	of each person whose place of abode on April 1, 1930, was in this family. Enter surname, first, then given name and middle initial. If any. Include every person living on April 1, 1930. Omit children born since April 1, 1930.	Relationship of this Person to the head of the family.	Sex	Color or race	Age at last birthday	Single, married, widowed or divorced	Attended school any time since Sept. 1, 1929	Whether able to read and write.	Place of birth of this person.	Whether able to speak English.	
	1	2	3	4	5	6	7	8	9	10	11	12	13	14
26	Piti-Sumay Road	144	162	Borja, Manuel S	Son	M	Cha	5	S	N		Guam		None
27		144	162	Borja, Francisco S	Son	M	Cha	3.7	S	N		Guam		None
28		145	163	Santos, Ana A	Head	F	Cha	26	M	N	Y	Guam	Y	None
29		145	163	Santos, Conchita A	Daughter	F	Cha	4.2	S	N		Guam		None
30		146	164	Concepcion, Jose C	Head	M	Cha	21	M	N	Y	Guam	Y	Farm laborer
31		146	164	Concepcion, Gertrudes S	Wife	F	Cha	23	M	N	Y	Guam	Y	None
32		147	165	Cruz, Felix S	Head	M	Cha	31	M	N	Y	Guam	Y	Laborer
33		147	165	Cruz, Angela S	Wife	F	Cha	28	M	N	Y	Guam	Y	None
34		147	165	Cruz, Delgadina S	Daughter	F	Cha	1.7	S	N		Guam		None
35		148	166	Yoshida, Jose T	Head	M	Jap	50	M	N	Y	Japan	Y	Carpenter
36		148	166	Yoshida, Dolores M	Wife	F	Cha	40	M	N	N	Guam	N	None
37		148	166	Yoshida, Concepcion a	Daughter	F	Jap	17	S	N	Y	Guam	Y	None
38		148	166	Yoshida, Enrique A	Son	M	Jap	13	S	Y	Y	Guam	Y	None
39		148	166	Yoshida, Jesus M	Son	M	Jap	10	S	Y	Y	Guam		None
40		148	166	Yoshida, Manuel M	Son	M	Jap	5	S	N		Guam		None
41		148	166	Yoshida, Jose M	Son	M	Jap	3	S	N		Guam		None
42		149	167	Perez, Rita F	Head	F	Cha	22	M	N	Y	Guam	Y	None
43		149	167	Perez, Jesus F	Son	M	Cha	5	S	N		Guam		None
44		149	167	Finona, Maria SN	Aunt	F	Cha	54	S	N	N	Guam	N	None
45		149	167	Santos, Ignacio S	Lodger	M	Cha	50	S	N	N	Guam	N	Farmer
46		149	167	Duenas, Mariano D	Lodger	M	Cha	53	Wd	N	N	Guam	N	Farm laborer
47		150	168	Finona, Jose SN	Head	M	Cha	50	M	N	N	Guam	N	Farmer
48		150	168	Finona, Manuela C	Wife	F	Cha	51	M	N	N	Guam	N	None
49		150	168	Finona, Francisco C	Son	M	Cha	19	S	N	Y	Guam	Y	Laborer
50		150	168	Finona, Regina C	Daughter	F	Cha	17	S	N	Y	Guam	Y	None

(CHAMORRO ROOTS GENEALOGY PROJECT ™ TRANSCRIPTION)
(BERNARD T. PUNZALAN / HTTP://WWW.CHAMORROROOTS.COM)

DEPARTMENT OF COMMERCE-BUREAU OF THE CENSUS
WASHINGTON

FIFTEENTH CENSUS OF THE UNITED STATES: 1930-POPULATION

THE ISLAND OF GUAM

Sheet No. 19A

311

District **Municipality of Piti**
Name of Place **Sinengsong Barrio**
[Proper name and, also, name of class, as city, town, village, barrio, etc]

Enumeration District No. **10**
Enumerated by me on **April 9, 1930** **Joaquin Torres**
Enumerator

	PLACE OF ABODE			NAME	RELATION	PERSONAL DESCRIPTION				EDUCATION		NATIVITY		OCCUPATION
	Street, avenue, road, etc.	Number of dwelling house in order of visitation	Number of family in order of visitation	of each person whose place of abode on April 1, 1930, was in this family. Enter surname, first, then given name and middle initial. If any. Include every person living on April 1, 1930. Omit children born since April 1, 1930.	Relationship of this Person to the head of the family.	Sex	Color or race	Age at last birthday	Single, married, widowed or divorced	Attended school any time since Sept. 1, 1929	Whether able to read and write.	Place of birth of this person.	Whether able to speak English.	
	1	2	3	4	5	6	7	8	9	10	11	12	13	14
1	Piti-Sumay Road	150	168	Finona, Manuel C	Son	M	Cha	16	S	Y	Y	Guam	Y	None
2		150	168	Finona, Joaquin C	Son	M	Cha	13	S	Y	Y	Guam	Y	None
3		151	169	Finona, Antonio C	Head	M	Cha	21	M	N	Y	Guam	Y	Laborer
4		151	169	Finona, Teresa F	Wife	F	Cha	19	M	N	N	Guam	N	None
5		151	169	Finona, Jose F	Son	M	Cha	1.2	S	N		Guam		None
6		151	169	Finona, Antonio F	Son	M	Cha	0	S	N		Guam		None
7		152	170	Tajalle, Juan C	Head	M	Cha	40	M	N	Y	Guam	Y	Farmer
8		152	170	Tajalle, Dolores M	Wife	F	Cha	36	M	N	Y	Guam	N	None
9		152	170	Tajalle, Maria M	Daughter	F	Cha	17	S	N	Y	Guam	Y	None
10		152	170	Tajalle, Francisco M	Son	M	Cha	13	S	Y	Y	Guam	Y	None
11		152	170	Tajalle, Felix M	Son	M	Cha	11	S	Y	Y	Guam	Y	None
12		152	170	Tajalle, Rufina M	Daughter	F	Cha	8	S	Y		Guam		None
13		152	170	Tajalle, Ana M	Daughter	F	Cha	6	S	N		Guam		None
14		152	170	Tajalle, Petronilia M	Daughter	F	Cha	4.4	S	N		Guam		None
15		152	170	Tajalle, Consolacion M	Daughter	F	Cha	1.2	S	N		Guam		None
16		152	170	Tajalle, Manuel C	Son	M	Cha	19	S	N	Y	Guam	Y	Laborer
17		153	171	Fejeran, Lucas S	Head	M	Cha	64	M	N	N	Guam	N	Farmer
18		153	171	Fejeran, Encarnacion S	Wife	F	Cha	52	M	N	N	Guam	N	None
19		153	171	Fejeran, Domingo S	Son	M	Cha	23	S	N	Y	Guam	Y	Laborer
20		153	171	Fejeran, Pilar S	Daughter	F	Cha	21	S	N	Y	Guam	Y	None
21		153	171	Fejeran, Juana S	Daughter	F	Cha	16	S	N	Y	Guam	Y	None
22		153	171	Fejeran, Manuel S	Son	M	Cha	14	S	N	N	Guam	N	None
23		153	171	Fejeran, Ramona S	Daughter	F	Cha	11	S	Y	Y	Guam	Y	None
24		153	171	Naburn, Francisco S	Grandson	M	Fil	8	S	Y		Guam		None
25		154	172	Unsiog, Joaquin J	Head	M	Cha	52	S	N	Y	Guam	N	Farmer

(CHAMORRO ROOTS GENEALOGY PROJECT™ TRANSCRIPTION)
(BERNARD T. PUNZALAN / HTTP://WWW.CHAMORROROOTS.COM)

DEPARTMENT OF COMMERCE-BUREAU OF THE CENSUS
WASHINGTON

FIFTEENTH CENSUS OF THE UNITED STATES: 1930-POPULATION

THE ISLAND OF GUAM

Sheet No. 19B

311b

District Municipality of Piti
Name of Place Sinengsong Barrio
[Proper name and, also, name of class, as city, town, village, barrio, etc]

Enumeration District No. 10
Enumerated by me on April 9, 1930 Joaquin Torres, Enumerator

	PLACE OF ABODE			NAME	RELATION	PERSONAL DESCRIPTION				EDUCATION		NATIVITY		OCCUPATION
	Street, avenue, road, etc.	Number of dwelling house in order of visitation	Number of family in order of visitation	of each person whose place of abode on April 1, 1930, was in this family. Enter surname, first, then given name and middle initial. If any. Include every person living on April 1, 1930. Omit children born since April 1, 1930.	Relationship of this Person to the head of the family.	Sex	Color or race	Age at last birthday	Single, married, widowed or divorced	Attended school any time since Sept. 1, 1929	Whether able to read and write.	Place of birth of this person.	Whether able to speak English.	
	1	2	3	4	5	6	7	8	9	10	11	12	13	14
26	Piti-Sumay Road	154	172	Unsiog, Francisca J	Sister	F	Cha	36	S	N	Y	Guam	N	None
27		154	172	Unsiog, Maria U	Niece	F	Cha	8	S	Y		Guam		None
28		154	172	Unsiog, Clemente U	Nephew	M	Cha	5	S	N		Guam		None
29		155	173	Muna, Rufina C	Head	F	Cha	65	M	N	N	Guam	N	None
30		155	173	Muna, Magdalena M	Daughter	F	Cha	34	S	N	N	Guam	N	Laundress
31		155	173	Muna, Joaquin M	Grandson	M	Cha	16	S	N	Y	Guam	Y	Farm laborer
32		155	173	Muna, Manuel M	Grandson	M	Cha	14	S	Y	Y	Guam	Y	None
33		155	173	Muna, Clara M	Grand daughter	F	Cha	12	S	Y	Y	Guam	Y	None
34		155	173	Muna, Jose M	Grandson	M	Cha	10	S	Y	Y	Guam	Y	None
35		155	173	Muna, Ramon M	Grandson	M	Cha	8	S			Guam		None
36		156	174	Santos, Maria P	Head	F	Cha	28	M	N	N	Guam	N	None
37		156	174	Santos, Jose P	Son	M	Cha	5	S	N		Guam		None
38		156	174	Santos, Clotilde P	Daughter	F	Cha	2.7	S	N		Guam		None
39		156	174	Santos, Isabel P	Daughter	F	Cha	0.5	S	N		Guam		None
40		157	175	Laguana, Vicente P	Head	M	Cha	48	M	N	N	Guam	N	Farmer
41		157	175	Laguana, Rosa I	Wife	F	Cha	50	M	N	N	Guam	N	None
42		157	175	Laguana, Agustin I	Son	M	Cha	19	S	N	Y	Guam	Y	Farm laborer
43		157	175	Laguana, Jesus I	Son	M	Cha	17	S	N	Y	Guam	Y	Farm laborer
44		157	175	Laguana, Ana I	Daughter	F	Cha	14	S	N	Y	Guam	Y	None
45		157	175	Laguana, Maria I	Daughter	F	Cha	11	S	Y	Y	Guam	Y	None
46		157	175	Laguana, Ana I	Daughter	F	Cha	9	S	Y		Guam		None
47		157	175	Laguana, Ignacio I	Son	M	Cha	6	S	N		Guam		None
48		158	176	Laguana, Ramon I	Head	M	Cha	24	M	N	Y	Guam	Y	Laborer
49		158	176	Laguana, Ana S	Wife	F	Cha	24	M	N	Y	Guam	N	None
50		158	176	Laguana, Felix S	Son	M	Cha	2.7	S	N		Guam		None

(CHAMORRO ROOTS GENEALOGY PROJECT™ TRANSCRIPTION)
(BERNARD T. PUNZALAN / HTTP://WWW.CHAMORROROOTS.COM)

DEPARTMENT OF COMMERCE-BUREAU OF THE CENSUS
WASHINGTON

FIFTEENTH CENSUS OF THE UNITED STATES: 1930-POPULATION

THE ISLAND OF GUAM

Sheet No. 20A

312

District **Municipality of Piti**
Name of Place **Sinengsong Barrio**
[Proper name and, also, name of class, as city, town, village, barrio, etc]

Enumeration District No. **10**
Enumerated by me on **April 9, 1930** **Joaquin Torres**, Enumerator

	PLACE OF ABODE			NAME	RELATION	PERSONAL DESCRIPTION				EDUCATION		NATIVITY		OCCUPATION
	Street, avenue, road, etc.	Number of dwelling house in order of visitation	Number of family in order of visitation	of each person whose place of abode on April 1, 1930, was in this family. Enter surname, first, then given name and middle initial. If any. Include every person living on April 1, 1930. Omit children born since April 1, 1930.	Relationship of this Person to the head of the family.	Sex	Color or race	Age at last birthday	Single, married, widowed or divorced	Attended school any time since Sept. 1, 1929	Whether able to read and write.	Place of birth of this person.	Whether able to speak English.	
	1	2	3	4	5	6	7	8	9	10	11	12	13	14
1	Piti-Sumay Road	158	176	Laguana, Rosa S	Daughter	F	Cha	1.2	S	N		Guam		None
2		159	177	Ignacio, Jose C	Head	M	Cha	30	M	N	Y	Guam	Y	Farmer
3		159	177	Ignacio, Dolores P	Wife	F	Cha	30	M	N	Y	Guam	N	None
4		159	177	Ignacio, Francisco P	Son	M	Cha	8	S	Y		Guam		None
5		159	177	Ignacio, Regina P	Daughter	F	Cha	5	S	N		Guam		None
6		159	177	Ignacio, Juan P	Son	M	Cha	3.7	S	N		Guam		None
7		159	177	Ignacio, Josefina P	Daughter	F	Cha	0	S	N		Guam		None
8		160	178	Guerrero, Juan P	Head	M	Cha	56	M	N	Y	Guam	N	Farmer
9		160	178	Guerrero, Ana C	Wife	F	Cha	46	M	N	N	Guam	N	None
10		160	178	Guerrero, Juan M	Son	M	Cha	22	S	N	Y	Guam	Y	School teacher
11		160	178	Guerrero, Jose C	Son	M	Cha	19	S	N	Y	Guam	Y	Farm laborer
12		160	178	Guerrero, Mariano C	Son	M	Cha	17	S	N	Y	Guam	Y	Farm laborer
13		161	179	Cruz, Juan I	Head	M	Cha	65	M	N	Y	Guam	N	Farmer
14		161	179	Cruz, Maria M	Wife	F	Cha	65	M	N	Y	Guam	N	None
15		162	180	Ignacio, Manuel A	Head	M	Cha	59	M	N	N	Guam	N	Farmer
16		162	180	Ignacio, Rosa C	Wife	F	Cha	62	M	N	N	Guam	N	None
17		163	181	Sablan, Placida I	Head	F	Cha	27	M	N	Y	Guam	Y	None
18		163	181	Sablan, Ana I	Daughter	F	Cha	4.2	S	N		Guam		None
19		163	181	Sablan, Eulogio I	Son	M	Cha	2	S	N		Guam		None
20		163	181	Sablan, Manuel I	Son	M	Cha	0.2	S	N		Guam		None
21		164	182	Ignacio, Rafael P	Head	M	Cha	52	M	N	N	Guam	N	Farmer
22		164	182	Ignacio, Rita C	Wife	F	Cha	50	M	N	N	Guam	N	None
23		164	182	Santos, Juan C	Lodger	M	Fil	28	S	N	Y	Guam	Y	Fisherman
24		165	183	Santos, Juan P	Head	M	Cha	20	M	N	Y	Guam	Y	Farmer
25		165	183	Santos, Ana N	Wife	F	Cha	29	M	N	N	Guam	N	None

DEPARTMENT OF COMMERCE-BUREAU OF THE CENSUS
WASHINGTON

FIFTEENTH CENSUS OF THE UNITED STATES: 1930-POPULATION

THE ISLAND OF GUAM

Sheet No. 20B

312b

District **Municipality of Piti**
Name of Place **Sinengsong Barrio**
[Proper name and, also, name of class, as city, town, village, barrio, etc]

Enumeration District No. **10**
Enumerated by me on **April 10, 1930** **Joaquin Torres**
Enumerator

	PLACE OF ABODE			NAME	RELATION	PERSONAL DESCRIPTION				EDUCATION		NATIVITY		OCCUPATION
	Street, avenue, road, etc.	Number of dwelling house is order of visitation	Number of family in order of visitation	of each person whose place of abode on April 1, 1930, was in this family. Enter surname, first, then given name and middle initial. If any. Include every person living on April 1, 1930. Omit children born since April 1, 1930.	Relationship of this Person to the head of the family.	Sex	Color or race	Age at last birthday	Single, married, widowed or divorced	Attended school any time since Sept. 1, 1929	Whether able to read and write.	Place of birth of this person.	Whether able to speak English.	
	1	2	3	4	5	6	7	8	9	10	11	12	13	14
26	Piti-Sumay Road	165	183	Santos, Eliza N	Daughter	F	Cha	2.2	S	N		Guam		None
27		165	183	Santos, Jesusa N	Daughter	F	Cha	1.1	S	N		Guam		None
28		166	184	Ignacio, Santiago R	Head	M	Cha	41	M	N	Y	Guam	Y	Farmer
29					Here ends the enumeration of the Municipality of Piti.									
30														
31														
32														
33														
34														
35														
36														
37														
38														
39														
40														
41														
42														
43														
44														
45														
46														
47														
48														
49														
50														

District 11
Municipality of Sumay

DEPARTMENT OF COMMERCE-BUREAU OF THE CENSUS
WASHINGTON

FIFTEENTH CENSUS OF THE UNITED STATES: 1930-POPULATION

THE ISLAND OF GUAM

Sheet No. 1

District **Municipality of Sumay**
Name of Place **Sumay Town** [Proper name and, also, name of class, as city, town, village, barrio, etc]

Enumeration District No. **11**
Enumerated by me on **April 2, 1930** **Joaquin C. Cruz**, Enumerator

	PLACE OF ABODE			NAME	RELATION	PERSONAL DESCRIPTION				EDUCATION		NATIVITY		OCCUPATION
	Street, avenue, road, etc.	Number of dwelling house is order of visitation	Number of family in order of visitation	of each person whose place of abode on April 1, 1930, was in this family. Enter surname, first, then given name and middle initial. If any. Include every person living on April 1, 1930. Omit children born since April 1, 1930.	Relationship of this Person to the head of the family.	Sex	Color or race	Age at last birthday	Single, married, widowed or divorced	Attended school any time since Sept. 1, 1929	Whether able to read and write.	Place of birth of this person.	Whether able to speak English.	
	1	2	3	4	5	6	7	8	9	10	11	12	13	14
1		1	1	Santos, Maria B	Head	F	Cha	53	Wd	N	Y	Guam	Y	Cook
2		1	1	Freegord, Guadalupe B	Daughter	F	Cha	36	D	N	Y	Guam	Y	None
3		1	1	Cruz, Cristobal LG	Servant	M	Cha	18	S	N	Y	Guam	Y	Servant
4		1	1	Manley, Concepcion L	Boarder	F	Cha	7	S	Y		Guam		None
5		2	2	Cox, O.J.	Head	M	W	45	M	N	Y	Rockey, Missouri	Y	Farmer
6		2	2	Cox, Dolores B	Wife	F	Cha	34	M	N	Y	Guam	Y	None
7		3	3	Sablan, Dolores B	Head	F	Cha	70	Wd	N	Y	Guam	N	None
8		3	3	Sablan, Maria B	Daughter	F	Cha	52	S	N	Y	Guam	N	None
9		3	3	Sablan, Joaquin B	Son	M	Cha	45	S	N	N	Guam	N	Farmer
10		4	4	Anderson, Asuncion L	Head	F	Cha	21	M	N	Y	Guam	Y	None
11		4	4	Anderson, Asuncion M	Daughter	F	Cha	4.6	S			Guam		None
12		4	4	Anderson, Juan L	Son	M	Cha	3.5	S			Guam		None
13		4	4	Anderson, Jose L	Son	M	Cha	2	S			Guam		None
14		4	4	Anderson, Manuela L	Daughter	F	Cha	0.5	S			Guam		None
15		5	5	Baleto, Francisco C	Head	M	Cha	21	M	N	Y	Guam	Y	Farmer
16		5	5	Baleto, Engracia P	Wife	F	Cha	22	M	N	Y	Guam	Y	None
17		6	6	Cruz, Froilan D	Head	M	Cha	68	M	N	Y	Guam	Y	Farmer
18		6	6	Cruz, Magdalena M	Wife	F	Cha	68	M	N	N	Guam	N	Laundress
19		6	6	Anderson, Rosalina C	Grand daughter	F	Cha	14	S	Y	Y	Guam	Y	None
20		6	6	Anderson, Jose C	Grand son	M	Cha	13	S	Y	Y	Guam	Y	None
21		6	7	Hamrick, Magdalena C	Head	F	Cha	23	M	N	Y	Guam	Y	None
22		6	7	Hamrick, Edward C	Son	M	W	1.1	S			Guam		None
23		7	8	Aguigui, Dolores SN	Head	F	Cha	39	S	N	N	Guam	N	Laundress
24		7	8	Aguigui, Juan SN	Son	M	Cha	21	S	N	Y	Guam	Y	Laborer
25		7	8	Aguigui, Vicente SN	Son	M	Cha	11	S	Y	Y	Guam	Y	None

DEPARTMENT OF COMMERCE-BUREAU OF THE CENSUS
WASHINGTON

FIFTEENTH CENSUS OF THE UNITED STATES: 1930-POPULATION

THE ISLAND OF GUAM

Sheet No. 1B

251b

District **Municipality Sumay**
Name of Place **Sumay Town** [Proper name and, also, name of class, as city, town, village, barrio, etc]

Enumeration District No. **11**
Enumerated by me on **April 2, 1930** **Joaquin C. Diaz**, Enumerator

	PLACE OF ABODE: Street, avenue, road, etc.	Number of dwelling house in order of visitation	Number of family in order of visitation	NAME of each person whose place of abode on April 1, 1930, was in this family. Enter surname, first, then given name and middle initial. If any. Include every person living on April 1, 1930. Omit children born since April 1, 1930.	RELATION Relationship of this Person to the head of the family.	PERSONAL DESCRIPTION: Sex	Color or race	Age at last birthday	Single, married, widowed or divorced	EDUCATION: Attended school any time since Sept. 1, 1929	Whether able to read and write.	NATIVITY Place of birth of this person.	Whether able to speak English.	OCCUPATION
	1	2	3	4	5	6	7	8	9	10	11	12	13	14
26	Guadalupe Street	7	8	Aguigui, Elias SN	Son	M	Cha	4	S			Guam		None
27		8	9	Damian, Damazo B	Head	M	Fil	25	M	N	Y	Philippines Is.	Y	Cable operator
28		8	9	Damian, Maria R	Wife	F	Cha	20	M	N	Y	Guam	Y	None
29		8	9	Damian, Elizabeth M	Daughter	F	Fil	3.9	S			Guam		None
30		8	9	Damian, Pacita R	Daughter	F	Fil	0.9	S			Guam		None
31		8	9	Chargualaf, Joaquina F?	Servant	F	Cha	12	S			Guam		Servant
32		9	10	Santos, Jose	Head	M	Cha	63	M	N	N	Guam	Y	Farmer
33		9	10	Santos, Ana B	Wife	F	Cha	58	M	N	Y	Guam	Y	None
34		9	10	Santos, Martina L	Gran daughter	F	Cha	21	S	N	Y	Guam	Y	Laundress
35		9	10	Santos, Guadalupe L	Gran daughter	F	Cha	2.4	S			Guam		None
36		9	10	Acosta, Antonio B	Servant	M	Cha	39	S	N	N	Guam	N	Farm laborer
37		9	11	Reyes, Concepcion S	Head	F	Cha	36	Wd	N	Y	Guam	Y	Laundress
38		9	11	Reyes, Maria S	Daughter	F	Cha	15	S	N	Y	Guam	Y	None
39		9	11	Reyes, Jose S	Son	M	Cha	13	S	Y	Y	Guam	Y	None
40		9	11	Reyes, Jesus S	Son	M	Cha	12	S	Y	Y	Guam	Y	None
41		9	11	Reyes, Estefania S	Daughter	F	Cha	10	S	Y		Guam		None
42		9	11	Reyes, Ana S	Daughter	F	Cha	8	S	Y		Guam		None
43		10	12	Borja, Juan S	Head	M	Cha	42	M	N	Y	Guam	Y	Farmer
44		10	12	Borja, Dolores C	Wife	F	Cha	39	M	N	Y	Guam	N	None
45		10	12	Borja, Vicente C	Son	M	Cha	14	S	Y	Y	Guam	Y	None
46		10	12	Borja, Juan C	Son	M	Cha	12	S	Y	Y	Guam	Y	None
47		10	12	Borja, Mariano C	Son	M	Cha	7	S	Y		Guam		None
48		10	12	Borja, Maria C	Daughter	F	Cha	5	S			Guam		None
49		10	12	Borja, Andres C	Son	M	Cha	1.5	S			Guam		None
50		11	13	Babauta, Consolacion C	Head	F	Cha	57	Wd	N	Y	Guam	N	Laundress

DEPARTMENT OF COMMERCE-BUREAU OF THE CENSUS
WASHINGTON

FIFTEENTH CENSUS OF THE UNITED STATES: 1930-POPULATION

THE ISLAND OF GUAM

Sheet No. 2A

District **Municipality Sumay**
Name of Place **Sumay Town**
[Proper name and, also, name of class, as city, town, village, barrio, etc]

Enumeration District No. **11**
Enumerated by me on **April 2, 1930** **Joaquin C. Diaz**
Enumerator

	PLACE OF ABODE			NAME	RELATION	PERSONAL DESCRIPTION				EDUCATION		NATIVITY		OCCUPATION
	Street, avenue, road, etc.	Number of dwelling house in order of visitation	Number of family in order of visitation	of each person whose place of abode on April 1, 1930, was in this family. Enter surname, first, then given name and middle initial. If any. Include every person living on April 1, 1930. Omit children born since April 1, 1930.	Relationship of this Person to the head of the family.	Sex	Color or race	Age at last birthday	Single, married, widowed or divorced	Attended school any time since Sept. 1, 1929	Whether able to read and write.	Place of birth of this person.	Whether able to speak English.	
	1	2	3	4	5	6	7	8	9	10	11	12	13	14
1	Guadalupe Street	11	13	Charfauros, Rosa B	Daughter	F	Cha	30	S	N	Y	Guam	Y	Laundress
2		11	13	Charfauros, Joseph B	Son	M	Cha	5	S			Guam		None
3		11	13	Charfauros, Edward B	Son	M	Cha	3.4	S			Guam		None
4		12	14	Cruz, Joaquin B	Head	M	Cha	50	M	N	Y	Guam	Y	Farmer
5		12	14	Cruz, Guadalupe C	Wife	F	Cha	48	M	N	Y	Guam	N	None
6		12	14	Cruz, Gregorio S	Son	M	Cha	12	S	Y	Y	Guam	Y	None
7		12	14	Cruz, Julita S	Daughter	F	Cha	10	S	Y	Y	Guam	N	None
8		12	14	Cruz, Jose S	Son	M	Cha	4.4	S			Guam		None
9		12	14	Santos, Felicidad S	Servant	F	Cha	17	S	N	Y	Guam	Y	Laundress
10		13	15	Gumataotao, Maria C	Head	F	Cha	83	Wd	N	N	Guam	N	None
11		13	15	Gumataotao, Maria S	Daughter	F	Cha	44	S	N	N	Guam	N	Laundress
12		13	15	Gumataotao, George S	Grand son	M	Cha	15	S	Y	Y	Guam	Y	None
13		13	15	Gumataotao, Carmen S	Grand daughter	F	Cha	5	S			Guam		None
14		14	16	Borja, Rafael T	Head	M	Cha	70	M	N	Y	Guam	Y	Farmer
15		14	16	Borja, Carmen N	Wife	F	Cha	47	M	N	Y	Guam	Y	None
16		14	16	Borja, Francisco N	Son	M	Cha	21	S	N	Y	Guam	Y	Salesman
17		14	16	Borja, Rafael N	Son	M	Cha	16	S	N	Y	Guam	Y	Salesman
18		14	16	Won Pat, Vicente B	Grand son	M	Chin	11	S	Y	Y	Guam	Y	None
19		15	17	Santos, Miguel G	Head	M	Cha	49	M	N	Y	Guam	Y	Farmer
20		15	17	Santos, Carmen S	Wife	F	Cha	47	M	N	Y	Guam	N	None
21		15	17	Santos, Maria S	Daughter	F	Cha	25	S	N	Y	Guam	Y	Laundress
22		15	17	Santos, Vicente S	Son	M	Cha	21	S	N	Y	Guam	Y	Servant
23		15	17	Santos, Antonio S	Son	M	Cha	19	S	N	Y	Guam	Y	Farmer
24		15	17	Santos, Concepcion S	Daughter	F	Cha	14	S	Y	Y	Guam	Y	None
25		15	17	Santos, Delfina S	Daughter	F	Cha	11	S	Y	Y	Guam	Y	None

(CHAMORRO ROOTS GENEALOGY PROJECT™ TRANSCRIPTION)
(BERNARD T. PUNZALAN / HTTP://WWW.CHAMORROROOTS.COM)

DEPARTMENT OF COMMERCE-BUREAU OF THE CENSUS
WASHINGTON

FIFTEENTH CENSUS OF THE UNITED STATES: 1930-POPULATION

THE ISLAND OF GUAM

Sheet No. 2B

252b

District **Municipality Sumay**
Name of Place **Sumay Town**
[Proper name and, also, name of class, as city, town, village, barrio, etc]

Enumeration District No. **11**
Enumerated by me on **April 2, 1930** **Joaquin C. Diaz**, Enumerator

	Street, avenue, road, etc.	Number of dwelling house is order of visitation	Number of family in order of visitation	NAME of each person whose place of abode on April 1, 1930, was in this family. Enter surname, first, then given name and middle initial. If any. Include every person living on April 1, 1930. Omit children born since April 1, 1930.	RELATION Relationship of this Person to the head of the family.	Sex	Color or race	Age at last birthday	Single, married, widowed or divorced	Attended school any time since Sept. 1, 1929	Whether able to read and write.	NATIVITY Place of birth of this person.	Whether able to speak English.	OCCUPATION
	1	2	3	4	5	6	7	8	9	10	11	12	13	14
26	Guadalupe Street	15	17	Santos, Enrique S	Son	M	Cha	9	S			Guam		None
27		15	17	Santos, Guadalupe S	Daughter	F	Cha	7	S			Guam		None
28		15	17	Santos, Joseph S	Son	M	Cha	3.9	S			Guam		None
29		15	17	Santos, Rosita S	Daughter	F	Cha	2.8	S			Guam		None
30		15	18	Sablan, Luis C	Head	M	Cha	41	Wd	N	Y	Agrigan	Y	Farmer
31		16	19	Blanks, Loela E	Head	F	W	24	M	N	Y	Buckley ??	Y	None
32		16	20	Charfauros, Juan B	Head	M	Cha	34	M	N	Y	Guam	Y	Laborer
33		16	20	Charfauros, Teodora F	Wife	F	Cha	31	M	N	Y	Guam	Y	None
34		16	20	Charfauros, Jose F	Son	M	Cha	11	S	Y	Y	Guam	Y	None
35		16	20	Topasna, Rafael I	Step father	M	Cha	40	Wd	N	N	Guam	N	None
36		16	20	Topasna, Felix T	Brother-in-law	M	Cha	24	S	N	Y	Guam	Y	Laborer
37		17	21	Sablan, Thomas P	Head	M	Cha	40	M	N	Y	Guam	Y	Farmer
38		17	21	Sablan, Ana M	Wife	F	Cha	21	M	N	Y	Guam	Y	None
39		17	21	Sablan, Francisco M	Son	M	Cha	1.9	S			Guam		None
40		17	21	Sablan, Andrea M	Daughter	F	Cha	0.7	S			Guam		None
41		17	22	Manibusan, Jose D	Head	M	Cha	52	M	N	Y	Guam	Y	Farmer
42		17	22	Manibusan, Maria C	Wife	F	Fil	63	M	N	Y	Guam	N	None
43		17	23	Santos, Vidal S	Head	M	Cha	46	M	N	Y	Guam	Y	Laborer
44		17	23	Santos, Flora S	Wife	F	Cha	38	M	N	Y	Saipan	N	None
45		17	23	Santos, Maria S	Daughter	F	Cha	13	S	Y	Y	Saipan	Y	None
46		17	23	Santos, Jose S	Son	M	Cha	12	S	Y	Y	Saipan	Y	None
47		17	23	Santos, Stella S	Daughter	F	Cha	9	S			Rota		None
48		17	23	Santos, Pedro S	Son	M	Cha	3.5	S			Guam		None
49		17	23	Santos, Antonia S	Daughter	F	Cha	0.9	S			Guam		None
50		18	24	Concepcion, Enrique S	Head	M	Cha	48	M	N	Y	Guam	N	Farmer

(CHAMORRO ROOTS GENEALOGY PROJECT™ TRANSCRIPTION)
(BERNARD T. PUNZALAN / HTTP://WWW.CHAMORROROOTS.COM)

DEPARTMENT OF COMMERCE-BUREAU OF THE CENSUS
WASHINGTON

FIFTEENTH CENSUS OF THE UNITED STATES: 1930-POPULATION

THE ISLAND OF GUAM

Sheet No. 3A

253

District Municipality Sumay
Name of Place Sumay Town
[Proper name and, also, name of class, as city, town, village, barrio, etc]

Enumeration District No. 11
Enumerated by me on April 3, 1930 Joaquin C. Diaz, Enumerator

	PLACE OF ABODE: Street, avenue, road, etc.	Number of dwelling house is order of visitation	Number of family in order of visitation	NAME of each person whose place of abode on April 1, 1930, was in this family. Enter surname, first, then given name and middle initial. If any. Include every person living on April 1, 1930. Omit children born since April 1, 1930.	RELATION Relationship of this Person to the head of the family.	PERSONAL DESCRIPTION: Sex	Color or race	Age at last birthday	Single, married, widowed or divorced	EDUCATION: Attended school any time since Sept. 1, 1929	Whether able to read and write.	NATIVITY Place of birth of this person.	Whether able to speak English.	OCCUPATION
	1	2	3	4	5	6	7	8	9	10	11	12	13	14
1	Guadalupe Street	18	24	Concepcion, Juana P	Wife	F	Cha	48	M	N	Y	Guam	N	None
2		18	24	Concepcion, Enrique P	Son	M	Cha	17	S	N	Y	Guam	Y	Farmer
3		18	24	Concepcion, Catalina P	Daughter	F	Cha	15	S	N	Y	Guam	Y	None
4		18	24	Concepcion, Inocencio P	Son	M	Cha	12	S	Y	Y	Guam	Y	None
5		18	24	Concepcion, Francisco P	Son	M	Cha	9	S	Y		Guam		None
6		18	25	Cruz, Juan LG	Head	M	Cha	22	M	N	Y	Guam	Y	Carpenter
7		18	25	Cruz, Felicidad C	Wife	F	Cha	21	M	N	Y	Guam	Y	None
8		18	25	Cruz, Delores LG	Sister	F	Cha	13	S	Y	Y	Guam	Y	None
9		18	25	Cruz, Flora LG	Sister	F	Cha	5	S			Guam		None
10		19	26	Diaz, Jose C	Head	M	Cha	39	M	N	Y	Guam	Y	Farmer
11		19	26	Diaz, Rosa C	Wife	F	Cha	36	M	N	Y	Guam	Y	None
12		19	26	Diaz, Pedro C	Son	M	Cha	17	S	Y	Y	Guam	Y	None
13		19	26	Diaz, Guadalupe C	Daughter	F	Cha	15	S	N	Y	Guam	Y	None
14		19	26	Diaz, Rosa C	Daughter	F	Cha	9	S	Y		Guam		None
15		19	26	Diaz, Manuel C	Son	M	Cha	8	S	Y		Guam		None
16		19	26	Diaz, Tomasa C	Daughter	F	Cha	7	S	Y		Guam		None
17		19	26	Diaz, Engracia C	Daughter	F	Cha	4.9	S	N		Guam		None
18		19	27	Cruz, Jesus S	Head	M	Cha	36	Wd	N	Y	Guam	Y	Laborer
19		19	27	Cruz, Juan I	Son	M	Cha	12	S	Y	Y	Guam	N	None
20		19	27	Cruz, Joaquin I	Son	M	Cha	7	S	Y		Guam		None
21		19	28	Quinene, Jose B	Head	M	Cha	28	S	N	Y	Guam	Y	Laborer
22	General Prin Street	20	29	Rice, Ana D	Head	F	Cha	47	Wd	N	Y	Guam	Y	None
23		20	29	Rice, Ana M	Daughter	F	W	21	S	N	Y	Guam	Y	Tel. Operator
24		20	29	Rice, Thomas J	Son	M	W	18	S	N	Y	Guam	Y	Farmer
25		20	29	Rice, James H	Son	M	W	16	S	Y	Y	Guam	Y	None

DEPARTMENT OF COMMERCE-BUREAU OF THE CENSUS
WASHINGTON

FIFTEENTH CENSUS OF THE UNITED STATES: 1930-POPULATION

THE ISLAND OF GUAM

Sheet No. 3B

253b

District Municipality Sumay
Name of Place Sumay Town
[Proper name and, also, name of class, as city, town, village, barrio, etc]

Enumeration District No. 11
Enumerated by me on April 3, 1930 Joaquin C. Diaz
Enumerator

	PLACE OF ABODE			NAME	RELATION	PERSONAL DESCRIPTION				EDUCATION		NATIVITY		OCCUPATION
	Street, avenue, road, etc.	Number of dwelling house is order of visitation	Number of family in order of visitation	of each person whose place of abode on April 1, 1930, was in this family. Enter surname, first, then given name and middle initial. If any. Include every person living on April 1, 1930. Omit children born since April 1, 1930.	Relationship of this Person to the head of the family.	Sex	Color or race	Age at last birthday	Single, married, widowed or divorced	Attended school any time since Sept. 1, 1929	Whether able to read and write.	Place of birth of this person.	Whether able to speak English.	
	1	2	3	4	5	6	7	8	9	10	11	12	13	14
26	General PrinStreet	21	30	Mendiola, Mariano R	Head	M	Cha	57	M	N	N	Guam	N	Farmer
27		21	30	Mendiola, Maria U	Wife	F	Cha	53	M	N	N	Guam	N	None
28		21	30	Mendiola, Josefa U	Daughter	F	Cha	31	S	N	Y	Guam	Y	Laundress
29		21	30	Mendiola, Juan U	Son	M	Cha	25	S	N	Y	Guam	Y	Laborer
30		21	30	Mendiola, Concepcion U	Daughter	F	Cha	19	S	N	Y	Guam	Y	Laundress
31		21	30	Mendiola, Thomas U	Son	M	Cha	14	S	Y	Y	Guam	Y	None
32		21	31	Cruz, Cristina U	Head	F	Cha	27	M	N	Y	Guam	Y	None
33		21	31	Cruz, Maria U	Daughter	F	Cha	8	S	Y		Guam		None
34		21	31	Cruz, Joaquin U	Son	M	Cha	4.5	S			Guam		None
35		21	31	Cruz, Lourdes C	Step daughter	F	Cha	17	S			Guam	Y	None
36		21	31	Cruz, Galo U	Son	M	Cha	0.6	S			Guam		None
37		22	32	Borja, Vicente T	Head	M	Cha	62	M	N	Y	Guam	Y	Retail merchant
38		22	32	Borja, Ana S	Wife	F	Cha	53	M	N	Y	Guam	N	None
39		22	32	Borja, Maria S	Daughter	F	Cha	29	S	N	Y	Guam	Y	None
40		22	32	Borja, Gregorio S	Son	M	Cha	27	S	N	Y	Guam	Y	Salesman
41		22	32	Borja, Rita S	Daughter	F	Cha	23	S	N	Y	Guam	Y	None
42		22	32	Borja, Vicente S	Son	M	Cha	21	S	N	Y	Guam	Y	Farmer
43		22	32	Borja, Andrea S	Grand daughter	F	Cha	3.6	S			Guam		None
44		22	32	Chargualaf, Angelina	Servant	F	Cha	12	S	N	Y	Guam	Y	Servant
45		22	33	Santos, Mariano B	Head	M	Cha	25	M	N	Y	Guam	Y	Cable operator
46		22	33	Santos, Ana B	Wife	F	Cha	22	M	N	Y	Guam	Y	None
47		22	33	Santos, Florence B	Daughter	F	Cha	1.1	S			Guam		None
48		23	34	Lizama, Juan C	Head	M	Cha	28	M	N	Y	Guam	Y	Tel. operator
49		23	34	Lizama, Maria LG	Wife	F	Cha	23	M	N	Y	Guam	Y	Mid-wife
50		23	34	Lizama, Felicita C	Daughter	F	Cha	5	S			Guam		None

(CHAMORRO ROOTS GENEALOGY PROJECT™ TRANSCRIPTION)
(BERNARD T. PUNZALAN / HTTP://WWW.CHAMORROROOTS.COM)

DEPARTMENT OF COMMERCE-BUREAU OF THE CENSUS
WASHINGTON

FIFTEENTH CENSUS OF THE UNITED STATES: 1930-POPULATION

THE ISLAND OF GUAM

Sheet No. 4A

254

District **Municipality Sumay**
Name of Place **Sumay Town** [Proper name and, also, name of class, as city, town, village, barrio, etc]

Enumeration District No. **11**
Enumerated by me on **April 3, 1930** **Joaquin C. Diaz** Enumerator

	PLACE OF ABODE			NAME	RELATION	PERSONAL DESCRIPTION				EDUCATION		NATIVITY		OCCUPATION
	Street, avenue, road, etc.	Number of dwelling house in order of visitation	Number of family in order of visitation	of each person whose place of abode on April 1, 1930, was in this family. Enter surname, first, then given name and middle initial. If any. Include every person living on April 1, 1930. Omit children born since April 1, 1930.	Relationship of this Person to the head of the family.	Sex	Color or race	Age at last birthday	Single, married, widowed or divorced	Attended school any time since Sept. 1, 1929	Whether able to read and write.	Place of birth of this person.	Whether able to speak English.	
	1	2	3	4	5	6	7	8	9	10	11	12	13	14
1	General PrinStreet	23	34	Lizama, Thomas C	Son	M	Cha	4	S			Guam		None
2		23	34	Lizama, Roberto LG	Son	M	Cha	2.9	S			Guam		None
3		23	34	Lizama, Elloy LG	Son	M	Cha	1.2	S			Guam		None
4		23	34	Salas, Trinidad LG	Servant	F	Cha	12	S	Y	Y	Guam	Y	Servant
5		23	34	Ignacio, Jose T	Servant	M	Cha	16	S	N	Y	Guam	Y	Servant
6		24	35	Borja, Manuel M	Head	M	Cha	39	M	N	Y	Guam	Y	Carpenter
7		24	35	Borja, Vicenta C	Wife	F	Cha	31	M	N	Y	Guam	Y	Laundress
8		24	35	Borja, Antonio C	Son	M	Cha	12	S	Y	Y	Guam	Y	None
9		24	35	Borja, Lucas C	Son	M	Cha	10	S	Y	Y	Guam	Y	None
10		24	35	Perez, Tomasa C	Mother-in-law	F	Cha	59	Wd	N	N	Guam	N	Laundress
11		25	36	Reyes, Laurion C	Head	M	Cha	26	M	N	Y	Guam	Y	Laborer
12		25	36	Reyes, Delfina T	Wife	F	Cha	24	M	N	Y	Guam	Y	None
13		25	36	Reyes, Rosario T	Daughter	F	Cha	3.5	S			Guam		None
14		25	36	Reyes, Artemio T	Son	M	Cha	0.2	S			Guam		None
15		25	36	Reyes, Rosario C	Mother	F	Cha	57	Wd	N	N	Guam	N	None
16		26	37	Carbullido, Baltasar P	Head	M	Cha	30	M	Y	Y	Guam	Y	Principal of school
17		26	37	Carbullido, Aurelia B	Wife	F	Cha	32	M	N	Y	Guam	Y	None
18		26	37	Carbullido, Agnes B	Daughter	F	Cha	8	S	Y	Y	Guam	Y	None
19		26	37	Carbullido, Baltasar B	Son	M	Cha	6	S			Guam		None
20		26	37	Carbullido, Charles B	Son	M	Cha	4.9	S			Guam		None
21		26	37	Carbullido, Delfina B	Daughter	F	Cha	2.9	S			Guam		None
22		26	37	Carbullido, Edward B	Son	M	Cha	0.9	S			Guam		None
23		26	37	Aguigui, Enrique C	Cousin	M	Cha	24	S	N	Y	Guam	Y	Cook
24		27	38	Dumonal, Martin L	Head	M	Fil	63	Wd	N	Y	Philippine Is.	N	Poultry man
25		27	38	Dumonal, Jose G	Son	M	Fil	24	S	N	Y	Guam	Y	Laborer

D-11-8

(CHAMORRO ROOTS GENEALOGY PROJECT™ TRANSCRIPTION)
(BERNARD T. PUNZALAN / HTTP://WWW.CHAMORROROOTS.COM)

DEPARTMENT OF COMMERCE-BUREAU OF THE CENSUS
WASHINGTON

FIFTEENTH CENSUS OF THE UNITED STATES: 1930-POPULATION

THE ISLAND OF GUAM

Sheet No. 4B

254b

District **Municipality Sumay**
Name of Place **Sumay Town**
[Proper name and, also, name of class, as city, town, village, barrio, etc]

Enumeration District No. **11**
Enumerated by me on **April 3, 1930** **Joaquin C. Diaz**
Enumerator

	PLACE OF ABODE			NAME	RELATION	PERSONAL DESCRIPTION				EDUCATION		NATIVITY		OCCUPATION
	Street, avenue, road, etc.	Number of dwelling house is order of visitation	Number of family in order of visitation	of each person whose place of abode on April 1, 1930, was in this family. Enter surname, first, then given name and middle initial. If any. Include every person living on April 1, 1930. Omit children born since April 1, 1930.	Relationship of this Person to the head of the family.	Sex	Color or race	Age at last birthday	Single, married, widowed or divorced	Attended school any time since Sept. 1, 1929	Whether able to read and write.	Place of birth of this person.	Whether able to speak English.	
	1	2	3	4	5	6	7	8	9	10	11	12	13	14
26	General PrinStreet	27	38	Dumonal, Candelaria G.	Daughter	F	Fil	19	S	N	Y	Guam	Y	None
27				[line was left blank by the enumerator],										
28		28	39	Ishizaki, Francisco	Head	M	Jap	47	M	N	Y	Japan	Y	Retail merchant
29		28	39	Ishizaki, Filomena P	Wife	F	Cha	36	M	N	Y	Guam	Y	None
30		28	39	Ishizaki, Agueda P	Daughter	F	Jap	12	S	Y	Y	Guam	Y	None
31		28	39	Ishizaki, Joaquin P	Son	M	Jap	11	S	Y	Y	Guam	Y	None
32		28	39	Ishizaki, Maria P	Daughter	F	Jap	9	S	Y		Guam		None
33		28	39	Ishizaki, Dolores P	Daughter	F	Jap	7	S	Y		Guam		None
34		28	39	Ishizaki, Victoria P	Daughter	F	Jap	6	S			Guam		None
35		28	39	Ishizaki, Isabel P	Daughter	F	Jap	3	S			Guam		None
36		28	39	Ishizaki, Vicente P	Son	M	Jap	1.7	S			Guam		None
37		28	39	Ishizaki, Irene P	Daughter	F	Jap	0	S			Guam		None
38		28	39	Cruz, Enrique A	Servant	M	Cha	25	S	N	Y	Guam	Y	Chauffeur
39		28	39	Acfalle, Francisco A	Servant	M	Cha	20	S	N	Y	Guam	Y	Chauffeur
40		29	40	Perez, Ana P	Head	F	Cha	56	Wd	N	N	Guam	N	None
41		29	40	Topasna, Candido T	Servant	M	Cha	21	S	N	Y	Guam	Y	Farmer
42		30	41	Perez, Remedios B	Head	F	Cha	36	M	N	Y	Guam	Y	None
43		30	41	Perez, Alejandro B	Son	M	Cha	7	S	Y		Guam		None
44		30	41	Perez, Gregorio B	Son	M	Cha	4.9	S			Guam		None
45		30	41	Perez, Virginia B	Daughter	F	Cha	1.9	S			Guam		None
46		30	41	Baleto, Sebastian	Uncle	M	Cha	65	Wd	N	N	Guam	N	None
47		30	42	Aquiningoc, Dolores P	Head	M	Cha	62	Wd	N	N	Guam	N	None
48		30	42	Aquiningoc, Susana P	Daughter	F	Cha	27	S	N	Y	Guam	Y	Cook
49		30	42	Aquiningoc, Amparo P	Daughter	F	Cha	21	S	N	Y	Guam	Y	None
50		30	42	Aquiningoc, Grabiel P	Grandson	M	Cha	13	S	Y	Y	Guam	Y	None

DEPARTMENT OF COMMERCE-BUREAU OF THE CENSUS
WASHINGTON

FIFTEENTH CENSUS OF THE UNITED STATES: 1930-POPULATION

THE ISLAND OF GUAM

Sheet No. 5A

District **Municipality Sumay**
Name of Place **Sumay Town**
[Proper name and, also, name of class, as city, town, village, barrio, etc]

Enumeration District No. **11**
Enumerated by me on **April 3, 1930** **Joaquin C. Diaz**
Enumerator

	PLACE OF ABODE			NAME	RELATION	PERSONAL DESCRIPTION				EDUCATION		NATIVITY		OCCUPATION
	Street, avenue, road, etc.	Number of dwelling house is order of visitation	Number of family in order of visitation	of each person whose place of abode on April 1, 1930, was in this family. Enter surname, first, then given name and middle initial. If any. Include every person living on April 1, 1930. Omit children born since April 1, 1930.	Relationship of this Person to the head of the family.	Sex	Color or race	Age at last birthday	Single, married, widowed or divorced	Attended school any time since Sept. 1, 1929	Whether able to read and write.	Place of birth of this person.	Whether able to speak English.	
	1	2	3	4	5	6	7	8	9	10	11	12	13	14
1	General PrinStreet	30	42	Aquiningoc, Jose P	Grandson	M	Cha	5	S			Guam		None
2		30	42	Aquiningoc, Ruth P	Granddaughter	F	Cha	0.9	S			Guam		None
3		31	43	Eschilsman, Edna V	Head	F	W	30	M	N	Y	Valejo, California	Y	None
4		32	44	Arriola, Rosa F	Head	F	Cha	36	D	N	Y	Guam	Y	Tailoress
5		32	44	Sablan, Joaquin A	Son	M	Cha	20	S	N	Y	Guam	Y	Cable operator
6		32	44	Sablan, Vicente A	Son	M	Cha	18	S	N	Y	Guam	Y	Cable operator
7		32	44	Sablan, Sylvestre A	Son	M	Cha	15	S	N	Y	Guam	Y	None
8		32	44	James, Jose F	Servant	M	W	23	S	N	Y	Guam	Y	Servant
9		32	45	Castro, Jose R	Head	M	Cha	29	M	N	Y	Guam	Y	Cook
10		32	45	Castro, Maria S	Wife	F	Cha	26	M	N	Y	Guam	Y	None
11		32	45	Castro, Francisco S	Son	M	Cha	5	S			Guam		None
12		33	46	Baleto, Vicente B	Head	M	Cha	60	M	N	Y	Guam	N	Farmer
13		33	46	Baleto, Maria C	Wife	F	Cha	56	M	N	Y	Guam	N	None
14		33	46	Baleto, Jose C	Son	M	Cha	33	S	Y	Y	Guam	Y	None
15		33	46	Baleto, Maria C	Daughter	F	Cha	23	S	N	Y	Guam	Y	None
16		33	46	Baleto, Jesus C	Son	M	Cha	18	S	Y	Y	Guam	Y	None
17		33	46	Baleto, Vicente C	Son	M	Cha	15	S	Y	Y	Guam	Y	None
18		33	47	Cruz, Jose C	Head	M	Cha	57	Wd	N	Y	Guam	Y	Farmer
19		33	47	Cruz, Dolores C	Daughter	F	Cha	25	S	N	N	Guam	N	None
20		33	48	Babauta, Antonio B	Head	M	Cha	20	S	N	Y	Guam	Y	Laborer
21		33	49	Baleto, Maria P	Head	F	Cha	27	M	N	Y	Guam	Y	None
22		33	49	Baleto, Encarnacion P	Daughter	F	Cha	3.5	S			Guam		None
23		33	49	Baleto, Vicente P	Son	M	Cha	2.1	S			Guam		None
24		33	49	Baleto, Antonio P	Son	M	Cha	0.6	S			Guam		None
25		33	49	Mata, Vicente M	Servant	M	Cha	16	S	N	Y	Guam	Y	Servant

DEPARTMENT OF COMMERCE-BUREAU OF THE CENSUS
WASHINGTON
FIFTEENTH CENSUS OF THE UNITED STATES: 1930-POPULATION

THE ISLAND OF GUAM

Sheet No. 5B

255b

District **Municipality Sumay**
Name of Place **Sumay Town** [Proper name and, also, name of class, as city, town, village, barrio, etc]

Enumeration District No. **11**
Enumerated by me on **April 4, 1930** **Joaquin C. Diaz**, Enumerator

	PLACE OF ABODE			NAME	RELATION	PERSONAL DESCRIPTION				EDUCATION		NATIVITY		OCCUPATION
	Street, avenue, road, etc.	Number of dwelling house in order of visitation	Number of family in order of visitation	of each person whose place of abode on April 1, 1930, was in this family. Enter surname, first, then given name and middle initial. If any. Include every person living on April 1, 1930. Omit children born since April 1, 1930.	Relationship of this Person to the head of the family.	Sex	Color or race	Age at last birthday	Single, married, widowed or divorced	Attended school any time since Sept. 1, 1929	Whether able to read and write.	Place of birth of this person.	Whether able to speak English.	
	1	2	3	4	5	6	7	8	9	10	11	12	13	14
26		34	50	Duenas, Jesus	Head	M	Cha	26	M	N	Y	Guam	Y	Carpenter
27		34	50	Duenas, Maria P	Wife	F	Cha	25	M	N	Y	Guam	Y	None
28		34	50	Duenas, Lucy P	Daughter	F	Cha	5	S			Guam		None
29		34	50	Duenas, Jose P	Son	M	Cha	1.5	S			Guam		None
30		34	50	Duenas, Julia P	Daughter	F	Cha	1.1	S			Guam		None
31		34	50	Duenas, Juan P	Son	M	Cha	0.1	S			Guam		None
32		34	50	Pinaula, Miguel T	Servant	M	Cha	16	S	Y	Y	Guam	Y	Servant
33		35	51	Duenas, Santiago	Head	M	Cha	39	M	N	Y	Guam	Y	Farmer
34		35	51	Duenas, Maria Q	Wife	F	Cha	34	M	N	Y	Guam	Y	None
35		35	51	Duenas, Pedro Q	Son	M	Cha	16	S	N	Y	Guam	Y	Farmer
36		35	51	Duenas, Catalina Q	Daughter	F	Cha	14	S	Y	Y	Guam	Y	None
37		35	51	Duenas, Vicente Q	Son	M	Cha	9	S	Y		Guam		None
38		35	51	Duenas, Maria Q	Daughter	F	Cha	0.6	S			Guam		None
39		36	52	Camacho, Manuel C	Head	M	Cha	42	M	N	Y	Guam	Y	Farmer
40		36	52	Camacho, Dolores G	Wife	F	Cha	32	M	N	Y	Guam	Y	None
41		36	52	Camacho, Juan G	Son	M	Cha	8	S	Y		Guam		None
42		36	52	Camacho, Jose G	Son	M	Cha	7	S	Y		Guam		None
43		36	52	Camacho, Francisco G	Son	M	Cha	2	S			Guam		None
44		37	53	Perez, Santiago T	Head	M	Cha	51	M	N	Y	Guam	Y	Carpenter
45		37	53	Perez, Ana C	Wife	F	Cha	44	M	N	N	Guam	N	Laundress
46		37	53	Perez, Dolores C	Daughter	F	Cha	15	S	N	Y	Guam	Y	Laundress
47		37	53	Perez, Jesus C	Son	M	Cha	11	S	Y	Y	Guam	Y	None
48		37	54	Santos, Ana B	Head	F	Cha	62	S	N	N	Guam	N	None
49		37	54	Santos, Martha B	Grand niece	F	Cha	8	S	Y		Guam		None
50		37	54	Santos, Jose B	Grandson	M	Cha	6	S			Guam		None

D-11-11

DEPARTMENT OF COMMERCE-BUREAU OF THE CENSUS
WASHINGTON

FIFTEENTH CENSUS OF THE UNITED STATES: 1930-POPULATION

THE ISLAND OF GUAM

Sheet No. 6A

District **Municipality Sumay**
Name of Place **Sumay Town** [Proper name and, also, name of class, as city, town, village, barrio, etc]

Enumeration District No. **11**
Enumerated by me on **April 4, 1930** **Joaquin C. Diaz** Enumerator

	PLACE OF ABODE			NAME	RELATION	PERSONAL DESCRIPTION				EDUCATION		NATIVITY		OCCUPATION
	Street, avenue, road, etc.	Number of dwelling house in order of visitation	Number of family in order of visitation	of each person whose place of abode on April 1, 1930, was in this family. Enter surname, first, then given name and middle initial. If any. Include every person living on April 1, 1930. Omit children born since April 1, 1930.	Relationship of this Person to the head of the family.	Sex	Color or race	Age at last birthday	Single, married, widowed or divorced	Attended school any time since Sept. 1, 1929	Whether able to read and write.	Place of birth of this person.	Whether able to speak English.	
	1	2	3	4	5	6	7	8	9	10	11	12	13	14
1	General Prin Street	38	55	Quintanilla, Jose B	Head	M	Cha	42	M	N	Y	Guam	N	Farmer
2		38	55	Quintanilla, Ana Q	Wife	F	Cha	37	M	N	Y	Guam	N	None
3		39	56	Aguon, Lorenzo Q	Head	M	Cha	41	M	N	Y	Guam	N	Farmer
4		39	56	Aguon, Soledad M	Wife	F	Cha	40	M	N	Y	Guam	N	None
5		39	56	Aguon, Jose M	Son	M	Cha	15	S	N	Y	Guam	Y	Farm laborer
6		39	56	Aguon, Juan M	Son	M	Cha	12	S	Y	Y	Guam	Y	None
7		39	56	Aguon, Manuel M	Son	M	Cha	4.6	S			Guam		None
8		39	56	Aguon, Vicente M	Son	M	Cha	0.9	S			Guam		None
9		39	57	San Nicolas, Jesus	Head	M	Cha	26	S	N	Y	Guam	Y	Farmer
10		40	58	Van Meter, Consolacion C	Head	F	Cha	30	M	N	Y	Guam	Y	Farm laborer
11		40	58	Van Meter, Juan C	Son	M	Cha	11	S	Y	Y	Guam	Y	None
12		40	58	Cruz, Joseph C	Son	M	Cha	5	S			Guam		None
13		40	58	Van Meter, Brigida C	Daughter	F	Cha	2.9	S			Guam		None
14		40	58	Cruz, Isabel C	Daughter	F	Cha	1.9	S			Guam		None
15		40	58	Acfalle, Natividad M	Servant	F	Cha	15	S	Y	Y	Guam		Servant
16		40	59	Garrido, Jose R	Head	M	Cha	31	S	N	Y	Guam	Y	Cable operator
17		41	60	Mendiola, Regino Q	Head	M	Cha	45	M	N	N	Guam	Y	None
18		41	60	Mendiola, Miguela M	Wife	F	Fil	38	M	N	Y	Philippine Is.	Y	Farmer
19		42	61	Camacho, Jose C	Head	M	Cha	54	M	N	Y	Guam	Y	Farmer
20		42	61	Camacho, Josefa S	Wife	F	Cha	48	M	N	Y	Guam	N	None
21		42	61	Camacho, Julita S	Daughter	F	Cha	24	S	N	Y	Guam	Y	None
22		42	61	Camacho, Antonia S	Daughter	F	Cha	22	S	N	Y	Guam	Y	None
23		42	61	Camacho, Ana S	Daughter	F	Cha	16	S	N	Y	Guam	Y	None
24		42	61	Camacho, Pablo S	Son	M	Cha	9	S	Y	Y	Guam	Y	None
25		42	61	Camacho, Manuel	Servant	M	Cha	43	Wd	N	N	Guam	N	Farm laborer

(CHAMORRO ROOTS GENEALOGY PROJECT™ TRANSCRIPTION)
(BERNARD T. PUNZALAN / HTTP://WWW.CHAMORROROOTS.COM)

DEPARTMENT OF COMMERCE-BUREAU OF THE CENSUS
WASHINGTON

FIFTEENTH CENSUS OF THE UNITED STATES: 1930-POPULATION

THE ISLAND OF GUAM

Sheet No. 6B

256b

District **Municipality Sumay**
Name of Place **Sumay Town**
[Proper name and, also, name of class, as city, town, village, barrio, etc]

Enumeration District No. **11**
Enumerated by me on **April 4, 1930** **Joaquin C. Diaz**, Enumerator

	PLACE OF ABODE: Street, avenue, road, etc.	Number of dwelling house in order of visitation	Number of family in order of visitation	NAME of each person whose place of abode on April 1, 1930, was in this family. Enter surname, first, then given name and middle initial. If any. Include every person living on April 1, 1930. Omit children born since April 1, 1930.	RELATION Relationship of this Person to the head of the family.	PERSONAL DESCRIPTION: Sex	Color or race	Age at last birthday	Single, married, widowed or divorced	EDUCATION: Attended school any time since Sept. 1, 1929	Whether able to read and write.	NATIVITY Place of birth of this person.	Whether able to speak English.	OCCUPATION
	1	2	3	4	5	6	7	8	9	10	11	12	13	14
26	General PrinStreet	42	61	Camacho, Jesus A	Servant	M	Cha	18	S	N	Y	Guam	Y	Farm laborer
27		42	61	Camacho, Florentina A	Servant	F	Cha	15	S	N	N	Guam	N	Servant
28		42	61	Camacho, Maria A	Servant	F	Cha	12	S	Y	Y	Guam	N	Servant
29		43	62	Soriano, Jose M	Head	M	Cha	22	M	N	Y	Guam	Y	Cook
30		43	62	Soriano, Andrea SN	Wife	F	Cha	27	M	N	Y	Guam	Y	None
31		43	62	Soriano, Vicente M	Brother	M	Cha	15	S	Y	Y	Guam	Y	None
32		43	62	San Nicolas, Ramona C	Sister-in-law	F	Cha	11	S	Y	Y	Guam	Y	None
33		44	63	Sablan, Juana S	Head	F	Cha	35	Wd	N	Y	Guam	Y	None
34		44	63	Sablan, Francisco S	Son	M	Cha	3.2	S			Guam	N	None
35		44	63	Sablan, Andrea S	Daughter	F	Cha	1.2	S			Guam		None
36		44	63	Sanchez, Josefa S	Mother	F	Cha	78	S	N	N	Guam	N	None
37		44	63	Cruz, Vicente S	Nephew	M	Cha	22	S	N	Y	Guam	Y	Farmer
38		45	64	Ulloa, Vicente C	Head	M	Cha	50	S	N	Y	Guam	Y	Farmer
39		45	64	Borja, Rita C	Servant	F	Cha	38	S	N	N	Guam	N	Servant
40		45	65	Lizama, Candelaria U	Head	F	Cha	58	Wd	N	Y	Guam	Y	None
41		45	65	Lizama, Soledad C	Daughter	F	Cha	23	S	N	Y	Guam	Y	None
42		45	66	Dawson, Rosa L	Head	F	Cha	32	M	N	Y	Guam	Y	Laundress
43		45	66	Dawson, George L	Son	M	Cha	9	S	Y	Y	Guam	Y	None
44		45	66	Duenas, Francisco D	Cousin	M	Cha	10	S	Y	Y	Guam	Y	None
45		45	67	De La Cruz, Jose	Head	M	Cha	45	M	N	Y	Guam	Y	Farmer
46		45	67	De La Cruz, Nicolasa B	Wife	F	Cha	43	M	N	N	Guam	N	None
47		46	68	Duenas, Josefa S	Head	F	Cha	60	S	N	N	Guam	N	None
48		46	68	San Nicolas, Juana SN	Nephew	M	Cha	28	S	N	Y	Guam	Y	Farmer
49		46	69	Acfalle, Jose B	Head	M	Cha	27	M	N	Y	Guam	Y	Cook
50		46	69	Acfalle, Crecencia L	Wife	F	Cha	33	M	N	Y	Guam	Y	None

(CHAMORRO ROOTS GENEALOGY PROJECT™ TRANSCRIPTION)
(BERNARD T. PUNZALAN / HTTP://WWW.CHAMORROROOTS.COM)

DEPARTMENT OF COMMERCE-BUREAU OF THE CENSUS
WASHINGTON

FIFTEENTH CENSUS OF THE UNITED STATES: 1930-POPULATION

THE ISLAND OF GUAM

Sheet No. 7A

257

District **Municipality Sumay**
Name of Place **Sumay Town** [Proper name and, also, name of class, as city, town, village, barrio, etc]

Enumeration District No. **11**
Enumerated by me on **April 4, 1930** **Joaquin C. Diaz**, Enumerator

	PLACE OF ABODE: Street, avenue, road, etc.	Number of dwelling house in order of visitation	Number of family in order of visitation	NAME of each person whose place of abode on April 1, 1930, was in this family. Enter surname, first, then given name and middle initial. If any. Include every person living on April 1, 1930. Omit children born since April 1, 1930.	RELATION Relationship of this Person to the head of the family.	PERSONAL DESCRIPTION: Sex	Color or race	Age at last birthday	Single, married, widowed or divorced	EDUCATION: Attended school any time since Sept. 1, 1929	Whether able to read and write.	NATIVITY Place of birth of this person.	Whether able to speak English.	OCCUPATION
	1	2	3	4	5	6	7	8	9	10	11	12	13	14
1	General Prin Street	46	69	Acfalle, Crecencia L	Daughter	F	Cha	1.8	S			Guam		None
2		46	69	Acfalle, Estefania L	Mother	F	Cha	59	S	N	N	Guam	N	None
3		47	70	Borja, Lucas T	Head	M	Cha	58	Wd	N	Y	Guam	Y	Farmer
4		47	70	Borja, Ana M	Daughter	F	Cha	34	S	N	Y	Guam	Y	Laundress
5		47	70	Borja, Gregorio M	Son	M	Cha	24	S	N	Y	Guam	Y	Farm laborer
6		47	70	Borja, Ignacio M	Son	M	Cha	20	S	N	Y	Guam	Y	Laborer
7		47	70	Borja, Daniel M	Son	M	Cha	16	S	N	Y	Guam	Y	Farm laborer
8		47	71	James, William F	Head	M	W	26	M	N	Y	Guam	Y	Carpenter
9		47	71	James, Concepcion B	Wife	F	Cha	23	M	N	Y	Guam	Y	None
10		47	71	James, Joseph B	Son	M	W	5	S			Guam		None
11		47	71	James, Henry B	Son	M	W	4.1	S			Guam		None
12		47	71	James, Mary B	Daughter	F	W	2.9	S			Guam		None
13		47	71	James, Frank B	Son	M	W	0	S			Guam		None
14		48	72	Salas, Manuel B	Head	M	Cha	33	M	N	Y	Guam	Y	Cable operator
15		48	72	Salas, Maria B	Wife	F	Cha	30	M	N	Y	Guam	Y	None
16		48	72	Salas, Luisa B	Daughter	F	Cha	13	S	Y	Y	Guam	Y	None
17		48	72	Salas, Jose B	Son	M	Cha	9	S	Y		Guam		None
18		48	72	Salas, Julita B	Daughter	F	Cha	7	S	Y		Guam		None
19		48	72	Salas, Felicidad B	Daughter	F	Cha	5	S			Guam		None
20		48	72	Acfalle, Jose O	Servant	M	Cha	18	S	N	Y	Guam	Y	Farm laborer
21		49	73	Gumataotao, Antonio B	Head	M	Cha	60	M	N	Y	Guam	Y	Farmer
22		49	73	Gumataotao, Adela D	Wife	F	Cha	52	M	N	Y	Guam	Y	None
23		49	73	Gumataotao, Jose D	Son	M	Cha	31	S	N	Y	Guam	Y	Farmer
24		49	73	Gumataotao, Maria D	Daughter	F	Cha	29	S	N	Y	Guam	Y	Tel. operator
25		49	73	Gumataotao, Nicolas D	Son	M	Cha	21	S	N	Y	Guam	Y	Laborer

(CHAMORRO ROOTS GENEALOGY PROJECT™ TRANSCRIPTION)
(BERNARD T. PUNZALAN / HTTP://WWW.CHAMORROROOTS.COM)

DEPARTMENT OF COMMERCE-BUREAU OF THE CENSUS
WASHINGTON

FIFTEENTH CENSUS OF THE UNITED STATES: 1930-POPULATION

THE ISLAND OF GUAM

Sheet No. 7B

257b

District **Municipality Sumay**
Name of Place **Sumay Town**
[Proper name and, also, name of class, as city, town, village, barrio, etc]

Enumeration District No. **11**
Enumerated by me on **April 4, 1930** **Joaquin C. Diaz**, Enumerator

	PLACE OF ABODE: Street, avenue, road, etc.	Number of dwelling house in order of visitation	Number of family in order of visitation	NAME of each person whose place of abode on April 1, 1930, was in this family. Enter surname, first, then given name and middle initial. If any. Include every person living on April 1, 1930. Omit children born since April 1, 1930.	RELATION Relationship of this Person to the head of the family.	PERSONAL DESCRIPTION: Sex	Color or race	Age at last birthday	Single, married, widowed or divorced	EDUCATION: Attended school any time since Sept. 1, 1929	Whether able to read and write.	NATIVITY Place of birth of this person.	Whether able to speak English.	OCCUPATION
	1	2	3	4	5	6	7	8	9	10	11	12	13	14
26	General PrinStreet	49	73	Gumataotao, Oscar D	Son	M	Cha	15	S	Y	Y	Guam	Y	None
27		49	73	Gumataotao, Pedro D	Son	M	Cha	11	S	Y	Y	Guam	N	None
28		49	73	Gumataotao, Albert D	Grandson	M	Cha	3	S			Guam		None
29		49	74	Camacho, Jose Q	Head	M	Cha	30	M	N	Y	Guam	Y	Cable operator
30		49	74	Camacho, Rosa G	Wife	F	Cha	24	M	N	Y	Guam	Y	None
31		49	74	Camacho, Emma G	Daughter	F	Cha	0.75	S			Guam		None
32		50	75	Gumataotao, Leon D	Head	M	Cha	33	M	N	Y	Guam	Y	Garage owner
33		50	75	Gumataotao, Josefina D	Wife	F	Cha	23	M	N	Y	Saipan	Y	None
34		50	75	Gumataotao, Oliva D	Daughter	F	Cha	6	S	Y		Guam		None
35		50	75	Gumataotao, Adela D	Daughter	F	Cha	4.9	S			Guam		None
36		50	75	Gumataotao, Vicente D	Son	M	Cha	2.2	S			Guam		None
37		50	75	Gumataotao, Lagrimas D	Daughter	F	Cha	0.2	S			Guam		None
38		50	76	Sanchez, Carmela S	Head	F	Cha	56	Wd	N	N	Guam	N	Farmer
39		50	76	Sanchez, Estokia S	Daughter	F	Cha	35	S	N	N	Guam	N	Laundress
40		50	76	Sanchez, Jose S	Grandson	M	Cha	11	S	Y	Y	Guam	Y	None
41		50	76	Sanchez, Vicente S	Grandson	M	Cha	5	S			Guam		None
42		50	76	Sanchez, Laura A	Granddaughter	F	Cha	3	S			Guam		None
43		51	77	De Leon, Francisco P	Head	M	Cha	26	M	N	Y	Guam	Y	Cable operator
44		51	77	De Leon, Dolores C	Wife	F	Cha	19	M	N	Y	Guam	Y	None
45		51	77	De Leon, Francisco C	Son	M	Cha	0.25	S			Guam		None
46		51	78	Borja, Antonio	Head	M	Cha	20	S	N	Y	Guam	Y	Laborer
47		52	79	Ulloa, Juan D	Head	M	Cha	37	M	N	N	Guam	N	Farmer
48		52	79	Ulloa, Maria S	Wife	F	Cha	27	M	N	Y	Guam	Y	None
49		52	79	Ulloa, Vituriano S	Son	M	Cha	8	S	Y		Guam		None
50		52	79	Ulloa, Juan S	Son	M	Cha	6	S			Guam		None

DEPARTMENT OF COMMERCE-BUREAU OF THE CENSUS
WASHINGTON

FIFTEENTH CENSUS OF THE UNITED STATES: 1930-POPULATION

THE ISLAND OF GUAM

Sheet No. 8A

District Municipality Sumay
Name of Place Sumay Town
[Proper name and, also, name of class, as city, town, village, barrio, etc]

Enumeration District No. 11
Enumerated by me on April 4, 1930 Joaquin C. Diaz, Enumerator

	PLACE OF ABODE: Street, avenue, road, etc.	Number of dwelling house in order of visitation	Number of family in order of visitation	NAME of each person whose place of abode on April 1, 1930, was in this family. Enter surname, first, then given name and middle initial. If any. Include every person living on April 1, 1930. Omit children born since April 1, 1930.	RELATION Relationship of this Person to the head of the family.	PERSONAL DESCRIPTION: Sex	Color or race	Age at last birthday	Single, married, widowed or divorced	EDUCATION: Attended school any time since Sept. 1, 1929	Whether able to read and write.	NATIVITY Place of birth of this person.	Whether able to speak English.	OCCUPATION
	1	2	3	4	5	6	7	8	9	10	11	12	13	14
1	General PrinStreet	52	79	Ulloa, Ana S	Daughter	F	Cha	3.7	S			Guam		None
2		52	79	Ulloa, Gregorio S	Son	M	Cha	0.1	S			Guam		None
3		52	79	Santos, Rosalia S	Sister-in-law	F	Cha	14	S	N	Y	Guam	Y	None
4		52	79	Sanchez, Caridad A	Servant	F	Cha	19	S	N	N	Guam	N	Laundress
5		52	80	Ulloa, Vicente S	Head	M	Cha	44	S	N	N	Guam	N	Farmer
6		53	81	Sarmiento, Soledad B	Head	F	Cha	30	M	N	Y	Guam	Y	None
7		53	81	Sarmiento, Juan B	Son	M	Cha	10	S	Y	Y	Guam	Y	None
8		53	81	Sarmiento, Daniel B	Son	M	Cha	8	S	Y		Guam		None
9		53	81	Sarmiento, Luisa B	Daughter	F	Cha	6	S			Guam		None
10		53	81	Sarmiento, Maria B	Daughter	F	Cha	3.5	S			Guam		None
11		53	81	Sarmiento, Carmen B	Daughter	F	Cha	1.1	S			Guam		None
12		53	81	Sanchez, Carmen S	Servant	F	Cha	22	S	N	N	Guam		Servant
13		53	82	Perez, Maria C	Head	F	Cha	64	Wd	N	N	Guam	N	None
14		53	82	Perez, Ignacia C	Sister	F	Cha	39	S	N	N	Guam	N	None
15		53	83	Cruz, Caridad T	Head	F	Cha	35	Wd	N	N	Guam	Y	Laundress
16		54	84	Diaz, Concepcion C	Head	F	Cha	65	Wd	N	Y	Guam	N	None
17		54	85	Diaz, Joaquin C	Head	M	Cha	37	M	N	Y	Guam	Y	Commissioner
18		54	85	Diaz, Joaquina T	Wife	F	Cha	28	M	N	Y	Saipan	N	None
19		54	85	Diaz, Vicente T	Son	M	Cha	8	S	Y		Saipan		None
20		54	85	Diaz, Manuel T	Son	M	Cha	7	S	Y		Saipan		None
21		54	85	Diaz, Andresina T	Daughter	F	Cha	6	S			Guam		None
22		54	85	Diaz, Nicolas T	Son	M	Cha	2.5	S			Guam		None
23		54	86	Cruz, Ignacio B	Head	M	Cha	69	M	N	Y	Guam	N	None
24		54	86	Cruz, Carmen A	Wife	F	Cha	50	M	N	Y	Guam	N	Laundress
25		54	86	Cruz, Ignacio A	Son	M	Cha	19	S	N	Y	Guam	Y	Servant

(CHAMORRO ROOTS GENEALOGY PROJECT™ TRANSCRIPTION)
(BERNARD T. PUNZALAN / HTTP://WWW.CHAMORROROOTS.COM)

DEPARTMENT OF COMMERCE-BUREAU OF THE CENSUS
WASHINGTON

FIFTEENTH CENSUS OF THE UNITED STATES: 1930-POPULATION

THE ISLAND OF GUAM

Sheet No. 8B

258b

District **Municipality Sumay**
Name of Place **Sumay Town**
[Proper name and, also, name of class, as city, town, village, barrio, etc]

Enumeration District No. **11**
Enumerated by me on **April 5, 1930** **Joaquin C. Diaz**, Enumerator

	PLACE OF ABODE: Street, avenue, road, etc.	Number of dwelling house in order of visitation	Number of family in order of visitation	NAME of each person whose place of abode on April 1, 1930, was in this family. Enter surname, first, then given name and middle initial. If any. Include every person living on April 1, 1930. Omit children born since April 1, 1930.	RELATION Relationship of this Person to the head of the family.	PERSONAL DESCRIPTION: Sex	Color or race	Age at last birthday	Single, married, widowed or divorced	EDUCATION: Attended school any time since Sept. 1, 1929	Whether able to read and write.	NATIVITY Place of birth of this person.	Whether able to speak English.	OCCUPATION
	1	2	3	4	5	6	7	8	9	10	11	12	13	14
26	General PrinStreet	54	86	Cruz, Ana A	Daughter	F	Cha	17	S	N	Y	Guam	Y	Laundress
27		54	86	Cruz, Rosa A	Daughter	F	Cha	9	S	Y		Guam		None
28		54	87	Charfauros, Andres C	Head	M	Cha	23	M	N	Y	Guam	Y	Laborer
29		54	87	Charfauros, Maria C	Wife	F	Cha	21	M	N	Y	Guam	Y	None
30		54	87	Charfauros, Jose C	Son	M	Cha	1.1	S			Guam		None
31		54	88	Diaz, Juan C	Head	M	Cha	29	M	N	Y	Guam	Y	Farmer
32		54	88	Diaz, Magdalena F	Wife	F	Cha	28	M	N	Y	Guam	N	None
33		54	88	Diaz, Concepcion F	Daughter	F	Cha	1	S			Guam		None
34		54	88	Diaz, Justina F	Daughter	F	Cha	0.5	S			Guam		None
35		54	88	Diaz, Jose C	Nephew	M	Cha	12	S			Guam		None
36	Vicente Gomez Street	55	89	Lizama, Rosalia D	Head	F	Fil	22	M	N	Y	Guam	Y	None
37		55	89	Vinluan?, Juanita D	Daughter	F	Fil	3	S			Guam		None
38		56	90	Toves, Jose Q	Head	M	Cha	32	M	N	Y	Guam	Y	Cable operator
39		56	90	Toves, Amparo C	Wife	F	Cha	28	M	N	Y	Guam	Y	None
40		56	90	Toves, Kenneth B	Son	M	Cha	7	S	Y		Guam		None
41		56	90	Toves, Frank E	Son	M	Cha	6	S			Guam		None
42		56	90	Toves, Florence M	Daughter	F	Cha	5	S			Guam		None
43		56	90	Toves, Joseph G	Son	M	Cha	3.6	S			Guam		None
44		56	90	Toves, Authur B	Son	M	Cha	1.5	S			Guam		None
45		57	91	Duenas, Jose L	Head	M	Cha	58	M	N	Y	Guam	N	Farmer
46		57	91	Duenas, Ana S	Wife	F	Cha	51	M	N	Y	Guam	N	None
47		57	92	Duenas, Ramon S	Head	M	Cha	36	M	N	Y	Guam		Carpenter
48		57	92	Duenas, Maria SN	Wife	F	Cha	17	M	N	Y	Guam		None
49		57	92	Duenas, Jose S	Son	M	Cha	10	S	Y	Y	Guam		None
50		57	92	Duenas, Francisco S	Son	M	Cha	8	S			Guam		None

DEPARTMENT OF COMMERCE-BUREAU OF THE CENSUS
WASHINGTON

FIFTEENTH CENSUS OF THE UNITED STATES: 1930-POPULATION

THE ISLAND OF GUAM

Sheet No. 9A

259

District **Municipality Sumay**
Name of Place **Sumay Town**
[Proper name and, also, name of class, as city, town, village, barrio, etc]

Enumeration District No. **11**
Enumerated by me on **April 5, 1930** **Joaquin C. Diaz**, Enumerator

	PLACE OF ABODE			NAME	RELATION	PERSONAL DESCRIPTION				EDUCATION		NATIVITY		OCCUPATION
	Street, avenue, road, etc.	Number of dwelling house is order of visitation	Number of family in order of visitation	of each person whose place of abode on April 1, 1930, was in this family. Enter surname, first, then given name and middle initial. If any. Include every person living on April 1, 1930. Omit children born since April 1, 1930.	Relationship of this Person to the head of the family.	Sex	Color or race	Age at last birthday	Single, married, widowed or divorced	Attended school any time since Sept. 1, 1929	Whether able to read and write.	Place of birth of this person.	Whether able to speak English.	
	1	2	3	4	5	6	7	8	9	10	11	12	13	14
1	Vicente Gomez Street	57	92	Duenas, Serafina S	Daughter	F	Cha	7	S	Y		Guam		None
2		57	92	Duenas, Ana S	Daughter	F	Cha	5	S			Guam		None
3		58	93	McCullough, F	Head	F	W	39	M	Y	Y	Oregon	Y	None
4		58	93	McCullough, Florence T	Daughter	F	W	7	S	Y	Y	Virginia	Y	None
5		59	94	de Leon, Alzo Aspi	Head	M	W	40	S	Y	Y	Spain	Y	Catholic Priest
6		60	95	Alcantara, Joaquin S	Head	M	Cha	25	M	N	Y	Guam	Y	Tel. operator
7		60	95	Alcantara, Soledad T	Wife	F	Cha	22	M	N	Y	Guam	Y	None
8		60	95	Alcantara, Priscilla T	Daughter	F	Cha	2.1	S			Guam		None
9		60	95	Alcantara, John T	Son	M	Cha	0.8	S			Guam		None
10		60	95	Arriola, Margarita A	Servant	F	Cha	23	S	N	N	Guam	N	Servant
11		61	96	Sablan, Jose S	Head	M	Cha	43	M	N	Y	Guam	Y	Farmer
12		61	96	Sablan, Mecaila S	Wife	F	Cha	37	M	N	Y	Guam	Y	None
13		61	96	Sablan, Rosa S	Daughter	F	Cha	20	S	N	Y	Guam	Y	Cook
14		61	96	Sablan, Josefa S	Daughter	F	Cha	17	S	N	Y	Guam	Y	None
15		61	96	Sablan, Lourdes S	Daughter	F	Cha	14	S	Y	Y	Guam	Y	None
16		61	96	Sablan, Manuel S	Son	M	Cha	12	S	Y	Y	Guam	Y	None
17		61	96	Sablan, Francisco S	Son	M	Cha	10	S	Y		Guam		None
18		61	96	Sablan, Juan S	Son	M	Cha	7	S	Y		Guam		None
19		61	96	Sablan, Joaquin S	Son	M	Cha	5	S			Guam		None
20		61	96	Sablan, Jose S	Son	M	Cha	2.7	S			Guam		None
21		61	96	Sablan, Vicente S	Son	M	Cha	0.1	S			Guam		None
22		62	97	Agulto, Juan M	Head	M	Cha	55	M	N	Y	Guam	Y	Farmer
23		62	97	Agulto, Emilia P	Wife	F	Cha	41	M	N	Y	Guam	N	None
24		62	97	Agulto, Pedro P	Son	M	Cha	24	S	N	Y	Guam	Y	Laborer
25		62	98	Agulto, Antonio P	Head	M	Cha	39	Wd	N	Y	Guam	Y	Laborer

(CHAMORRO ROOTS GENEALOGY PROJECT™ TRANSCRIPTION)
(BERNARD T. PUNZALAN / HTTP://WWW.CHAMORROROOTS.COM)

DEPARTMENT OF COMMERCE-BUREAU OF THE CENSUS
WASHINGTON

FIFTEENTH CENSUS OF THE UNITED STATES: 1930-POPULATION

THE ISLAND OF GUAM

Sheet No. 9B

259b

District Municipality Sumay
Name of Place Sumay Town
[Proper name and, also, name of class, as city, town, village, barrio, etc]

Enumeration District No. 11
Enumerated by me on April 7, 1930 Joaquin C. Diaz, Enumerator

	PLACE OF ABODE: Street, avenue, road, etc.	Number of dwelling house in order of visitation	Number of family in order of visitation	NAME of each person whose place of abode on April 1, 1930, was in this family. Enter surname, first, then given name and middle initial. If any. Include every person living on April 1, 1930. Omit children born since April 1, 1930.	RELATION Relationship of this Person to the head of the family.	PERSONAL DESCRIPTION: Sex	Color or race	Age at last birthday	Single, married, widowed or divorced	EDUCATION: Attended school any time since Sept. 1, 1929	Whether able to read and write.	NATIVITY Place of birth of this person.	Whether able to speak English.	OCCUPATION
	1	2	3	4	5	6	7	8	9	10	11	12	13	14
26	Vicente Gomez Street	62	98	Agulto, Jesusa C	Daughter	F	Cha	7	S	Y		Guam		None
27		62	98	Agulto, Ana C	Daughter	F	Cha	5	S			Guam		None
28		62	98	Agulto, Magdalena C	Daughter	F	Cha	3.7	S			Guam		None
29		62	99	Perez, Antonio	Head	M	Cha	45	S	N	N	Guam	N	None
30		63	100	Perez, Mariano C	Head	M	Cha	27	M	N	Y	Guam	Y	Carpenter
31		63	100	Perez, Asuncion SN	Wife	F	Cha	28	M	N	Y	Guam	Y	None
32		63	100	Perez, Rosalia SN	Daughter	F	Cha	4.4	S			Guam		None
33		63	100	Perez, Santiago SN	Son	M	Cha	3	S			Guam		None
34		63	100	Perez, Patricia SN	Daughter	F	Cha	0.4	S			Guam		None
35		63	101	Meza, Dolores SN	Head	F	Cha	59	Wd	N	N	Guam	N	None
36		64	102	Sablan, Emiliana SN	Head	F	Fil	28	Wd	N	N	Philippine Is.	Y	None
37		64	102	Sablan, Maria SN	Daughter	F	Cha	7	S	N	Y	Philippine Is.		None
38		64	102	Sablan, Andres SN	Son	M	Cha	6	S	Y		Guam		None
39		64	102	Sablan, Francisco SN	Son	M	Cha	2.1	S			Guam		None
40		64	102	Sablan, Teresita SN	Daughter	F	Cha	0	S			Guam		None
41		65	103	Guzman, Juan S	Head	M	Cha	63	M	N	Y	Guam	N	None
42		65	103	Guzman, Vicenta C	Wife	F	Cha	62	M	N	N	Guam	N	None
43		66	104	Won Pat, Antonio B	Head	M	Chin	21	S	Y	Y	Guam	Y	School teacher
44		66	105	Mendiola, Manuel F	Head	M	Cha	30	S	N	Y	Guam	Y	Cook
45		66	106	Aguon, Manuel	Head	M	Cha	16	S	N	Y	Guam	Y	Servant
46		66	107	Arriola, Pedro E	Head	M	Cha	69	S	N	Y	Guam	Y	Farmer
47		67	108	Concepcion, Juan S	Head	M	Cha	59	M	N	Y	Guam	Y	Farmer
48		67	108	Concepcion, Josefa D	Wife	F	Cha	46	M	N	Y	Guam	N	None
49		67	108	Concepcion, Jose T	Son	M	Cha	25	S	N	Y	Guam		Farmer
50		67	108	Concepcion, Juan T	Son	M	Cha	21	S	N	Y	Guam	Y	Farmer

DEPARTMENT OF COMMERCE-BUREAU OF THE CENSUS
WASHINGTON

FIFTEENTH CENSUS OF THE UNITED STATES: 1930-POPULATION

THE ISLAND OF GUAM

Sheet No. 10A

District **Municipality Sumay**
Name of Place **Sumay Town**
[Proper name and, also, name of class, as city, town, village, barrio, etc]

Enumeration District No. **11**
Enumerated by me on **April 7, 1930** **Joaquin C. Diaz**, Enumerator

	PLACE OF ABODE: Street, avenue, road, etc.	Number of dwelling house in order of visitation	Number of family in order of visitation	NAME of each person whose place of abode on April 1, 1930, was in this family. Enter surname, first, then given name and middle initial. If any. Include every person living on April 1, 1930. Omit children born since April 1, 1930.	RELATION Relationship of this Person to the head of the family.	PERSONAL DESCRIPTION: Sex	Color or race	Age at last birthday	Single, married, widowed or divorced	EDUCATION: Attended school any time since Sept. 1, 1929	Whether able to read and write.	NATIVITY Place of birth of this person.	Whether able to speak English.	OCCUPATION
	1	2	3	4	5	6	7	8	9	10	11	12	13	14
1	Vicente Gomez Street	67	108	Concepcion, Enrique T	Son	M	Cha	16	S	Y	Y	Guam	Y	None
2		67	108	Concepcion, Soledad T	Daughter	F	Cha	15	S	N	Y	Guam	Y	None
3		67	108	Concepcion, Balbino T	Son	M	Cha	13	S	Y	Y	Guam	Y	None
4		68	109	Anderson, Felix LG	Head	M	Cha	49	M	N	Y	Guam	Y	Laborer
5		68	109	Anderson, Isabel A	Wife	F	Cha	44	M	N	N	Guam	Y	Laundress
6		68	109	Anderson, Jose A	Son	M	Cha	17	S	N	Y	Guam	Y	Laborer
7		68	109	Anderson, Jesus A	Son	M	Cha	12	S	Y	Y	Guam	Y	None
8		68	109	Anderson, Feliza A	Daughter	F	Cha	9	S	Y		Guam		None
9		68	109	Anderson, Felix A	Son	M	Cha	3.1	S			Guam		None
10		68	110	Anderson, Vicenta LG	Head	F	Cha	70	Wd	N	Y	Guam	N	None
11		68	111	Anderson, Mariano LG	Head	M	Cha	21	M	N	Y	Guam	Y	Farmer
12		68	111	Anderson, Ana P	Wife	F	Cha	20	M	N	Y	Guam	Y	None
13		68	111	Anderson, Thomas P	Son	M	Cha	0.4	S			Guam		None
14		69	112	Gumataotao, Juan C	Head	M	Cha	80	M	N	N	Guam	N	None
15		69	112	Gumataotao, Teresa B	Wife	F	Cha	80	M	N	N	Guam	N	None
16		69	112	Gumataotao, Juan B	Son	M	Cha	47	S	N	Y	Guam	Y	Farmer
17		69	112	Gumataotao, Andres B	Son	M	Cha	43	S	N	N	Guam	N	Farmer
18		69	112	Gumataotao, Maria B	Daughter	F	Cha	50	Wd	N	N	Guam	N	None
19		70	113	Sablan, Juan D	Head	M	Cha	64	M	N	Y	Guam	Y	Farmer
20		70	113	Sablan, Elena S	Wife	F	Cha	62	M	N	Y	Guam	Y	Laundress
21		70	114	Munoz, Francisco C	Head	M	Cha	38	M	N	Y	Guam	Y	Foreman
22		70	114	Munoz, Dolores S	Wife	F	Cha	35	M	N	Y	Guam	Y	Laundress
23		70	114	Munoz, Isabel S	Daughter	F	Cha	15	S	N	Y	Guam	Y	None
24		70	114	Munoz, Gregorio S	Son	M	Cha	10	S	Y		Guam		None
25		70	114	Taitague, Josefa Q	Servant	F	Cha	21	S	N	N	Guam	N	Servant

DEPARTMENT OF COMMERCE-BUREAU OF THE CENSUS
WASHINGTON

FIFTEENTH CENSUS OF THE UNITED STATES: 1930-POPULATION

THE ISLAND OF GUAM

Sheet No. 10B

260b

District **Municipality Sumay**
Name of Place **Sumay Town** [Proper name and, also, name of class, as city, town, village, barrio, etc]

Enumeration District No. **11**
Enumerated by me on **April 7, 1930** **Joaquin C. Diaz**, Enumerator

	PLACE OF ABODE: Street, avenue, road, etc.	Number of dwelling house in order of visitation	Number of family in order of visitation	NAME of each person whose place of abode on April 1, 1930, was in this family. Enter surname, first, then given name and middle initial. If any. Include every person living on April 1, 1930. Omit children born since April 1, 1930.	RELATION Relationship of this Person to the head of the family.	PERSONAL DESCRIPTION: Sex	Color or race	Age at last birthday	Single, married, widowed or divorced	EDUCATION: Attended school any time since Sept. 1, 1929	Whether able to read and write.	NATIVITY Place of birth of this person.	Whether able to speak English.	OCCUPATION
	1	2	3	4	5	6	7	8	9	10	11	12	13	14
26	Vicente Gomez Street	71	115	Pangelinan, Cristina S	Head	F	Cha	44	Wd	N	Y	Guam	N	Retail merchant
27		71	115	Pangelinan, Emilia S	Daughter	F	Cha	19	S	N	Y	Guam	Y	None
28		71	115	Pangelinan, Andrea S	Daughter	F	Cha	16	S	N	Y	Guam	Y	None
29		71	115	Pangelinan, Laura S	Daughter	F	Cha	14	S	Y	Y	Guam	Y	None
30		71	115	Pangelinan, Benedicto S	Son	M	Cha	12	S	Y	Y	Guam	Y	None
31		71	115	Pangelinan, Francisco S	Son	M	Cha	10	S	Y		Guam		None
32		71	115	Pangelinan, Maria S	Daughter	F	Cha	8	S	Y		Guam		None
33		71	115	Pangelinan, Serafina S	Daughter	F	Cha	5	S			Guam		None
34		71	115	Pangelinan, Jose S	Son	M	Cha	1	S			Guam		None
35		71	116	Perez, Joaquin D	Head	M	Cha	23	M	N	Y	Guam	Y	Cable operator
36		71	116	Perez, Virginia P	Wife	F	Cha	21	M	N	Y	Guam	Y	None
37		71	116	Perez, Victor P	Son	M	Cha	1.3	S			Guam		None
38		71	116	Perez, Dorothy P	Daughter	F	Cha	0.1	S			Guam		None
39		72	117	Cruz, Ignacio B	Head	M	Cha	64	M	N	Y	Guam	Y	Retail merchant
40		72	117	Cruz, Maria A	Wife	F	Cha	63	M	N	Y	Guam	N	None
41		72	117	Cruz, Ana A	Daughter	F	Cha	32	S	N	Y	Guam	Y	None
42		72	117	Cruz, Maria A	Daughter	F	Cha	26	S	N	Y	Guam	Y	None
43		72	118	Camacho, Dolores C	Head	F	Cha	33	Wd	N	Y	Guam	Y	None
44		72	118	Camacho, Gaily C	Son	M	Cha	9	S			Guam		None
45		72	118	Camacho, Dorothy C	Daughter	F	Cha	5	S			Guam		None
46		72	118	Pinaula, Enrique LG	Servant	M	Cha	16	S	N	Y	Guam	Y	Servant
47		72	119	Cruz, Ignacio A	Head	M	Cha	24	M	N	Y	Guam	Y	Machinist
48		72	119	Cruz, Oliva T	Wife	F	Cha	19	M	N	Y	Guam	Y	None
49		73	120	Guerrero, Jose B	Head	M	Cha	27	M	N	Y	Guam		Cable operator
50		73	120	Guerrero, Regina P	Wife	F	Cha	23	M	N	Y	Guam		None

DEPARTMENT OF COMMERCE-BUREAU OF THE CENSUS
WASHINGTON

FIFTEENTH CENSUS OF THE UNITED STATES: 1930-POPULATION

THE ISLAND OF GUAM

Sheet No. 11A

District **Municipality Sumay**
Name of Place **Sumay Town**
[Proper name and, also, name of class, as city, town, village, barrio, etc]

Enumeration District No. **11**
Enumerated by me on **April 8, 1930** **Joaquin C. Diaz**
Enumerator

	PLACE OF ABODE			NAME	RELATION	PERSONAL DESCRIPTION				EDUCATION		NATIVITY		OCCUPATION
	Street, avenue, road, etc.	Number of dwelling house in order of visitation	Number of family in order of visitation	of each person whose place of abode on April 1, 1930, was in this family. Enter surname, first, then given name and middle initial. If any. Include every person living on April 1, 1930. Omit children born since April 1, 1930.	Relationship of this Person to the head of the family.	Sex	Color or race	Age at last birthday	Single, married, widowed or divorced	Attended school any time since Sept. 1, 1929	Whether able to read and write.	Place of birth of this person.	Whether able to speak English.	
	1	2	3	4	5	6	7	8	9	10	11	12	13	14
1	Vicente Gomez Street	73	120	Castro, Concepcion C	Servant	F	Cha	10	S	Y	Y	Guam	N	Servant
2	Vicente Gomez Street	74	121	Santos, Luis C	Head	M	Cha	58	M	N	Y	Guam	N	Farmer
3	Vicente Gomez Street	74	121	Santos, Catalina L	Wife	F	Fil	50	M	N	N	Philippine Is.	N	None
4	Vicente Gomez Street	75	122	Perez, Antonio D	Head	M	Cha	28	M	N	Y	Guam	Y	Cable operator
5	Vicente Gomez Street	75	122	Perez, Stella P	Wife	F	Cha	22	M	N	Y	Saipan	Y	None
6	Vicente Gomez Street	75	122	Perez, Joseph P	Son	M	Cha	3.7	S			Guam		None
7	Vicente Gomez Street	75	122	Perez, Elizabeth P	Daughter	F	Cha	2.4	S			Guam		None
8	Vicente Gomez Street	75	122	Perez, Evelyn P	Daughter	F	Cha	0.7	S			Guam		None
9				[This line was left blank by the enumerator.],										
10	Velasco Street	76	123	Babauta, Juan C	Head	M	Cha	26	M	N	Y	Guam	Y	Fisherman
11	Velasco Street	76	123	Babauta, Antonia A	Wife	F	Cha	24	M	N	Y	Guam	Y	None
12	Velasco Street	76	123	Babauta, Juan S	Son	M	Cha	3.9	S			Guam		None
13	Velasco Street	76	123	Babauta, Vicente R	Servant	M	Cha	32	S	N	N	Guam	Y	Servant
14	Velasco Street	77	124	Babauta, Felix C	Head	M	Cha	31	M	N	Y	Guam	Y	Farmer
15	Velasco Street	77	124	Babauta, Rita C	Wife	F	Cha	31	M	N	Y	Guam	Y	None
16	Velasco Street	77	124	Babauta, Serafin C	Son	M	Cha	9	S	Y		Guam	Y	None
17	Velasco Street	77	124	Babauta, Justina C	Daughter	F	Cha	9	S	Y		Guam		None
18	Velasco Street	77	124	Babauta, Carmen C	Daughter	F	Cha	8	S	Y		Guam		None
19	Velasco Street	77	124	Babauta, Maria C	Daughter	F	Cha	7	S	Y		Guam		None
20	Velasco Street	77	124	Babauta, Jesus C	Son	M	Cha	6	S			Guam		None
21	Velasco Street	77	124	Babauta, Jose C	Son	M	Cha	5	S			Guam		None
22	Velasco Street	77	124	Babauta, Ana C	Daughter	F	Cha	3.9	S			Guam		None
23	Velasco Street	77	124	Babauta, Joaquin C	Son	M	Cha	1.9	S			Guam		None
24	Velasco Street	78	125	Concepcion, Antonio D	Head	M	Cha	26	M	N	Y	Guam	Y	Farmer
25	Velasco Street	78	125	Concepcion, Hinara L	Wife	F	Cha	22	M	N	Y	Guam	Y	None

DEPARTMENT OF COMMERCE-BUREAU OF THE CENSUS
WASHINGTON
FIFTEENTH CENSUS OF THE UNITED STATES: 1930-POPULATION

THE ISLAND OF GUAM

Sheet No. 11B

261b

District Municipality Sumay
Name of Place Sumay Town
[Proper name and, also, name of class, as city, town, village, barrio, etc]

Enumeration District No. 11
Enumerated by me on April 8, 1930 Joaquin C. Diaz
Enumerator

	PLACE OF ABODE			NAME	RELATION	PERSONAL DESCRIPTION				EDUCATION		NATIVITY		OCCUPATION
	Street, avenue, road, etc.	Number of dwelling house is order of visitation	Number of family in order of visitation	of each person whose place of abode on April 1, 1930, was in this family. Enter surname, first, then given name and middle initial. If any. Include every person living on April 1, 1930. Omit children born since April 1, 1930.	Relationship of this Person to the head of the family.	Sex	Color or race	Age at last birthday	Single, married, widowed or divorced	Attended school any time since Sept. 1, 1929	Whether able to read and write.	Place of birth of this person.	Whether able to speak English.	
	1	2	3	4	5	6	7	8	9	10	11	12	13	14
26	Velasco Street	78	126	Lizama, Benedicto F	Head	M	Cha	70	S	N	Y	Guam	N	Farmer
27		79	127	Aquiningoc, Francisco A	Head	M	Cha	51	M	N	Y	Guam	Y	Farmer
28		79	127	Aquiningoc, Maria C	Wife	F	Cha	49	M	N	N	Guam	N	None
29		79	127	Aquiningoc, Rosalia C	Daughter	F	Cha	26	S	N	Y	Guam	Y	None
30		79	128	Concepcion, Ana L	Head	F	Cha	47	S	N	N	Guam	N	Laundress
31		79	128	Concepcion, Juan L	Son	M	Cha	11	S	Y	Y	Guam	Y	None
32		80	129	Quan, Olin Juan	Head	M	Chin	53	M	N	Y	China	Y	Retail merchant
33		80	129	Quan, Engracia C	Wife	F	Cha	49	M	N	Y	Guam	Y	None
34		80	129	Quan, Alejandro C	Son	M	Chin	23	S	N	Y	Guam	Y	Cable operator
35		80	129	Quan, Regina C	Daughter	F	Chin	16	S	N	Y	Guam	Y	None
36		80	129	Quan, Regino C	Son	M	Chin	14	S	Y	Y	Guam	Y	None
37		80	129	Quan, Rosalia C	Daughter	F	Chin	13	S	Y	Y	Guam	Y	None
38		80	129	Quan, Delfina C	Daughter	F	Chin	11	S	Y	Y	Guam	Y	None
39		80	129	Quan, Concepcion C	Daughter	F	Chin	9	S	Y		Guam		None
40		80	129	Quan, Johnny C	Son	M	Chin	7	S	Y		Guam		None
41		80	129	Quan, Antonio C	Son	M	Chin	4.6	S			Guam		None
42		80	129	Crisostomo, Juan C	Servant	M	Cha	21	S	N		Guam		None
43		80	130	Quan, Gregorio C	Head	M	Chin	21	M	N	Y	Guam	Y	Farmer
44		80	130	Quan, Maria D	Wife	F	Cha	17	M	N	Y	Guam	Y	None
45		80	130	Duenas, Joaquin B	Servant	M	Cha	17	S	N	Y	Guam	Y	Farm laborer
46		81	131	Cruz, Guadalupe M	Head	F	Cha	55	M	N	Y	Guam	N	None
47		81	131	Cruz, Joaquin M	Son	M	Cha	22	S	N	Y	Guam	Y	Cable operator
48		81	131	Cruz, Jose M	Son	M	Cha	20	S	N	Y	Guam	Y	Cable operator
49		81	132	Cruz, Juan M	Head	M	Cha	31	M	N	Y	Guam	Y	Deputy Commissioner
50		81	132	Cruz, Maria R	Wife	F	Cha	27	M	N	Y	Guam	Y	None

DEPARTMENT OF COMMERCE-BUREAU OF THE CENSUS
WASHINGTON

FIFTEENTH CENSUS OF THE UNITED STATES: 1930-POPULATION

THE ISLAND OF GUAM

Sheet No. 12A

District **Municipality Sumay**
Name of Place **Sumay Town**
[Proper name and, also, name of class, as city, town, village, barrio, etc]

Enumeration District No. **11**
Enumerated by me on **April 8, 1930** **Joaquin C. Diaz**, Enumerator

	PLACE OF ABODE			NAME	RELATION	PERSONAL DESCRIPTION				EDUCATION		NATIVITY		OCCUPATION
	Street, avenue, road, etc.	Number of dwelling house is order of visitation	Number of family in order of visitation	of each person whose place of abode on April 1, 1930, was in this family. Enter surname, first, then given name and middle initial. If any. Include every person living on April 1, 1930. Omit children born since April 1, 1930.	Relationship of this Person to the head of the family.	Sex	Color or race	Age at last birthday	Single, married, widowed or divorced	Attended school any time since Sept. 1, 1929	Whether able to read and write.	Place of birth of this person.	Whether able to speak English.	
	1	2	3	4	5	6	7	8	9	10	11	12	13	14
1	Velasco Street	81	132	Cruz, Guadalupe R	Daughter	F	Cha	4	S			Guam		None
2		81	132	Cruz, Juan R	Son	M	Cha	2.8	S			Guam		None
3		81	132	Cruz, Joaquin R	Son	M	Cha	1.1	S			Guam		None
4		82	133	Castro, Rosa L	Head	F	Cha	36	M	N	Y	Guam	Y	None
5		83	134	Sablan, Joaquin C	Head	M	Cha	50	M	N	Y	Guam	Y	Farmer
6		83	134	Sablan, Guadalupe P	Wife	F	Cha	37	M	N	Y	Guam	Y	None
7		83	134	Sablan, Vicente P	Son	M	Cha	16	S	N	Y	Guam	Y	Laborer
8		83	134	Sablan, Enrique P	Son	M	Cha	14	S	Y	Y	Guam	Y	None
9		83	134	Sablan, Jesusa P	Daughter	F	Cha	10	S	Y	Y	Guam		None
10		83	134	Sablan, Jesus P	Son	M	Cha	3.1	S			Guam		None
11		83	134	Sablan, Francisco P	Son	M	Cha	1.9	S			Guam		None
12		83	135	San Miguel, Juan Q	Head	M	Cha	27	M	N	Y	Guam	Y	Cable operator
13		83	135	San Miguel, Tomasa S	Wife	F	Cha	20	M	N	Y	Guam	Y	None
14		83	135	San Miguel, Justa S	Daughter	F	Cha	2.6	S			Guam		None
15		83	135	San Miguel, Delfina S	Daughter	F	Cha	1.5	S			Guam		None
16		83	135	San Miguel, Sylvia S	Daughter	F	Cha	0.2	S			Guam		None
17		84	136	Quintanilla, Jose C	Head	M	Cha	84	Wd	N	N	Guam	N	None
18		84	136	Quintanilla, Carmen B	Daughter	F	Cha	50	S	N	Y	Guam	N	Laundress
19		84	137	Quintanilla, Ana B	Head	F	Cha	52	D	N	Y	Guam	Y	None
20		84	137	Quintanilla, Joaquin P	Son	M	Cha	25	S	N	Y	Guam	Y	Farmer
21		84	138	Quintanilla, Guillermo B	Head	M	Cha	54	M	N	Y	Guam	Y	Farmer
22		84	138	Quintanilla, Carmen SN	Wife	F	Cha	40	M	N	Y	Guam	N	None
23		84	138	Quintanilla, Antonio SN	Son	M	Cha	22	S	N	Y	Guam	Y	Laborer
24		84	138	Quintanilla, Jose SN	Son	M	Cha	5	S			Guam		None
25		84	138	Quintanilla, Josefina SN	Daughter	F	Cha	3.5	S			Guam		None

(CHAMORRO ROOTS GENEALOGY PROJECT™ TRANSCRIPTION)
(BERNARD T. PUNZALAN / HTTP://WWW.CHAMORROROOTS.COM)

DEPARTMENT OF COMMERCE-BUREAU OF THE CENSUS
WASHINGTON
FIFTEENTH CENSUS OF THE UNITED STATES: 1930-POPULATION

THE ISLAND OF GUAM

Sheet No. 12B

262b

District **Municipality Sumay**
Name of Place **Sumay Town** [Proper name and, also, name of class, as city, town, village, barrio, etc]

Enumeration District No. **11**
Enumerated by me on **April 8, 1930** **Joaquin C. Diaz**, Enumerator

	PLACE OF ABODE: Street, avenue, road, etc.	Number of dwelling house in order of visitation	Number of family in order of visitation	NAME of each person whose place of abode on April 1, 1930, was in this family. Enter surname, first, then given name and middle initial. If any. Include every person living on April 1, 1930. Omit children born since April 1, 1930.	RELATION Relationship of this Person to the head of the family.	PERSONAL DESCRIPTION: Sex	Color or race	Age at last birthday	Single, married, widowed or divorced	EDUCATION: Attended school any time since Sept. 1, 1929	Whether able to read and write.	NATIVITY Place of birth of this person.	Whether able to speak English.	OCCUPATION
	1	2	3	4	5	6	7	8	9	10	11	12	13	14
26	Velasco Street	84	139	San Nicolas, Mariano R	Head	M	Cha	39	M	N	N	Guam	N	Farmer
27		84	139	San Nicolas, Antonia T	Wife	F	Cha	26	M	N	Y	Guam	Y	None
28		85	140	Quintanilla, Felix B	Head	M	Cha	55	M	N	Y	Guam	N	Farmer
29		85	140	Quintanilla, Josefa T	Wife	F	Cha	23	M	N	Y	Guam	Y	Laundress
30		85	140	Quintanilla, Manuela T	Daughter	F	Cha	3.5	S			Guam		None
31		85	140	Quintanilla, Soledad T	Daughter	F	Cha	0.8	S			Guam		None
32		85	140	Quintanilla, Jose L	Son	M	Cha	12	S	Y	Y	Guam	Y	None
33		86	141	Turner, Francis M	Head	F	W	39	M	N	Y	Virginia	Y	None
34		87	142	Cruz, Vicente B	Head	M	Cha	50	S	N	Y	Guam	Y	Farmer
35		87	142	Cruz, Rita B	Sister	F	Cha	59	S	N	Y	Guam	N	Laundress
36		87	142	Cruz, Maria B	Sister	F	Cha	54	S	N	Y	Guam	N	Laundress
37		87	142	Cruz, Ana B	Sister	F	Cha	48	S	N	Y	Guam	Y	None
38		88	143	Speer, Ana M	Head	F	W	41	M	N	Y	Penneyslvania	Y	None
39		88	144	Cruz, Josefa C	Head	F	Cha	46	Wd	N	Y	Guam	Y	None
40		88	144	Cruz, Rosa C	Daughter	F	Cha	20	S	N	Y	Guam	Y	None
41		88	144	Cruz, Maria C	Daughter	F	Cha	18	S	N	Y	Guam	Y	None
42		88	144	Cruz, Juan C	Son	M	Cha	14	S	Y	Y	Guam	Y	None
43		88	144	Cruz, Enes C	Grandmother	F	Cha	79	S	N	N	Guam	Y	None
44		89	145	Camacho, Jose C	Head	M	Cha	44	M	N	N	Guam	N	Farmer
45		89	145	Camacho, Ana A	Wife	F	Cha	31	M	N	Y	Guam	N	Laundress
46		89	145	Camacho, Josefa C	Daughter	F	Cha	3.5	S			Guam		None
47		89	146	Reyes, Teresa C	Head	F	Cha	34	S	N	N	Guam	N	Laundress
48		89	146	Reyes, Thomas C	Son	M	Cha	0.5	S			Guam		None
49		90	147	Walters, Jose A	Head	M	W	25	M	N	Y	Guam	Y	Cabel operator
50		90	147	Walters, Alfonsina S	Wife	F	W	22	M	N	Y	Guam	Y	None

DEPARTMENT OF COMMERCE-BUREAU OF THE CENSUS
WASHINGTON

FIFTEENTH CENSUS OF THE UNITED STATES: 1930-POPULATION

THE ISLAND OF GUAM

Sheet No. 13A

263

District **Municipality Sumay**
Name of Place **Sumay Town** [Proper name and, also, name of class, as city, town, village, barrio, etc]

Enumeration District No. **11**
Enumerated by me on **April 9, 1930** **Joaquin C. Diaz**, Enumerator

	PLACE OF ABODE			NAME	RELATION	PERSONAL DESCRIPTION				EDUCATION		NATIVITY		OCCUPATION
	Street, avenue, road, etc.	Number of dwelling house is order of visitation	Number of family in order of visitation	of each person whose place of abode on April 1, 1930, was in this family. Enter surname, first, then given name and middle initial. If any. Include every person living on April 1, 1930. Omit children born since April 1, 1930.	Relationship of this Person to the head of the family.	Sex	Color or race	Age at last birthday	Single, married, widowed or divorced	Attended school any time since Sept. 1, 1929	Whether able to read and write.	Place of birth of this person.	Whether able to speak English.	
	1	2	3	4	5	6	7	8	9	10	11	12	13	14
1	Velasco Street	90	147	Walters, Adolfo S	Son	M	W	0.9	S			Guam		None
2		91	148	Perez, Antonio C	Head	M	Cha	23	M	N	Y	Guam	Y	Cable operator
3		91	148	Perez, Antonia M	Wife	F	Cha	21	M	N	Y	Guam	Y	None
4		91	148	Perez, Ana M	Daughter	F	Cha	3.1	S			Guam		None
5		91	148	Perez, Gregorio M	Son	M	Cha	2	S			Guam		None
6		91	148	Perez, Galo M	Son	M	Cha	0.7	S			Guam		None
7		91	148	Demapan, Manuel D	Servant	M	Cha	32	S	N	Y	Guam	Y	Servant
8		91	149	Borja, Luis A	Head	M	Cha	30	M	N	Y	Guam	Y	Laborer
9		91	149	Borja, Antonia Q	Wife	F	Cha	23	M	N	Y	Guam	Y	None
10		91	149	Borja, Jesus Q	Son	M	Cha	4.5	S			Guam		None
11		91	149	Borja, Jose Q	Son	M	Cha	3.1	S			Guam		None
12		91	149	Borja, Maria Q	Daughter	F	Cha	1.5	S			Guam		None
13		92	150	Cruz, Antonio B	Head	M	Cha	61	M	N	Y	Guam	N	Farmer
14		92	150	Cruz, Maria Q	Wife	F	Cha	59	M	N	Y	Guam	N	None
15		92	150	Cruz, Vicente Q	Son	M	Cha	21	S	N	Y	Guam	Y	Farm laborer
16		92	150	Cruz, Antonio Q	Grandson	M	Cha	2	S			Guam		None
17		93	151	Mendiola, Ana S	Head	F	Cha	63	Wd	N	Y	Guam	Y	None
18		93	151	Mendiola, Luis S	Son	M	Cha	41	S	N	Y	Guam	Y	Carpenter
19		93	151	Mendiola, Martina S	Daughter	F	Cha	38	S	N	Y	Guam	Y	None
20		93	151	Mendiola, Consolascion S	Daughter	F	Cha	29	S	N	Y	Guam	Y	None
21		93	151	Mendiola, Beatrice S	Daughter	F	Cha	24	S	Y	Y	Guam	Y	None
22		93	151	Mendiola, Ignacio S	Son	M	Cha	21	S	N	Y	Guam	Y	Farmer
23		93	151	Cruz, Manuel S	Nephew	M	Cha	27	S	N	Y	Guam	Y	Farm laborer
24		93	151	Chargualaf, Consolacion S	Servant	F	Cha	14	S	N	N	Guam	N	Servant
25		93	151	Chargualaf, Rita S	Servant	F	Cha	17	S	N	Y	Guam	Y	Servant

D-11-26

DEPARTMENT OF COMMERCE-BUREAU OF THE CENSUS
WASHINGTON

FIFTEENTH CENSUS OF THE UNITED STATES: 1930-POPULATION

THE ISLAND OF GUAM

Sheet No. 13B

263b

District **Municipality Sumay**
Name of Place **Sumay Town** [Proper name and, also, name of class, as city, town, village, barrio, etc]

Enumeration District No. **11**
Enumerated by me on **April 9, 1930** **Joaquin C. Diaz** Enumerator

	PLACE OF ABODE: Street, avenue, road, etc.	Number of dwelling house in order of visitation	Number of family in order of visitation	NAME of each person whose place of abode on April 1, 1930, was in this family. Enter surname, first, then given name and middle initial. If any. Include every person living on April 1, 1930. Omit children born since April 1, 1930.	RELATION Relationship of this Person to the head of the family.	PERSONAL DESCRIPTION: Sex	Color or race	Age at last birthday	Single, married, widowed or divorced	EDUCATION: Attended school any time since Sept. 1, 1929	Whether able to read and write.	NATIVITY Place of birth of this person.	Whether able to speak English.	OCCUPATION
	1	2	3	4	5	6	7	8	9	10	11	12	13	14
26	Velasco Street	93	151	Chargualaf, Rosa L	Boarder	F	Cha	0.1	S			Guam		None
27		94	152	Gumataotao, Joaquin D	Head	M	Cha	27	M	N	Y	Guam	Y	Cable operator
28		94	152	Gumataotao, Delores M	Wife	F	Cha	23	M	N	Y	Guam	Y	None
29		94	152	Gumataotao, Stella M	Daughter	F	Cha	0.9	S			Guam		None
30		94	152	Mendiola, Ignacio Q	Uncle-in-law	M	Cha	48	S	N	Y	Guam	Y	Farmer
31		95	153	Bugbee, Beatrice V	Head	F	W	25	M	N	Y	New York	Y	None
32		95	153	Santos, Isabel C	Servant	F	Cha	18	S	N	Y	Guam	Y	Servant
33		96	154	Pangelinan, Ana Q	Head	F	Cha	56	Wd	N	Y	Guam	N	Retail merchant
34		96	154	Pangelinan, Felix Q	Son	M	Cha	19	S	Y	Y	Guam	Y	None
35		96	154	Franquez, Rosalia P	Daughter	F	Cha	28	D	Y	Y	Guam	Y	None
36		96	154	Franquez, George P	Grandson	M	Cha	11	S	Y	Y	Guam	Y	None
37		96	154	Pangelinan, Pedro S	Servant	M	Cha	24	S	N	Y	Guam	Y	Farm laborer
38		96	154	Okada, Rosa	Servant	F	Cha	60	Wd	N	N	Guam	N	Servant
39		97	155	Guzman, Antonio S	Head	M	Cha	60	M	N	Y	Guam	N	Farmer
40		97	155	Guzman, Dolores C	Wife	F	Cha	58	M	N	Y	Guam	N	None
41		97	155	Guzman, Guadalupe C	Daughter	F	Cha	35	S	N	Y	Guam	Y	Servant
42		97	155	Guzman, Gregorio C	Grandson	M	Cha	12	S	Y	Y	Guam	Y	None
43		97	155	Guzman, Francisco C	Grandson	M	Cha	11	S	Y	Y	Guam	N	None
44		97	155	Guzman, Petronila C	Granddaughter	F	Cha	6	S	Y		Guam		None
45		97	155	Guzman, Enestina C	Granddaughter	F	Cha	10	S	Y		Guam		None
46		98	156	Lizama, Felix F	Head	M	Cha	66	M	N	N	Guam	N	None
47		98	156	Lizama, Rosa D	Wife	F	Cha	60	M	N	Y	Guam	N	None
48		98	156	Lizama, Manuel D	Son	M	Cha	39	S	N	Y	Guam	Y	None
49		98	157	Lizama, Juan D	Head	M	Cha	37	M	N	Y	Guam	Y	Farmer
50		98	157	Lizama, Agueda S	Wife	F	Cha	41	M	N	N	Guam	N	None

DEPARTMENT OF COMMERCE-BUREAU OF THE CENSUS
WASHINGTON
FIFTEENTH CENSUS OF THE UNITED STATES: 1930-POPULATION

THE ISLAND OF GUAM

Sheet No. 14A

District **Municipality Sumay**
Name of Place **Sumay Town** [Proper name and, also, name of class, as city, town, village, barrio, etc]

Enumeration District No. **11**
Enumerated by me on **April 9, 1930** **Joaquin C. Diaz**, Enumerator

	PLACE OF ABODE			NAME	RELATION	PERSONAL DESCRIPTION				EDUCATION		NATIVITY		OCCUPATION
	Street, avenue, road, etc.	Number of dwelling house is order of visitation	Number of family in order of visitation	of each person whose place of abode on April 1, 1930, was in this family. Enter surname, first, then given name and middle initial. If any. Include every person living on April 1, 1930. Omit children born since April 1, 1930.	Relationship of this Person to the head of the family.	Sex	Color or race	Age at last birthday	Single, married, widowed or divorced	Attended school any time since Sept. 1, 1929	Whether able to read and write.	Place of birth of this person.	Whether able to speak English.	
	1	2	3	4	5	6	7	8	9	10	11	12	13	14
1	Velasco Street	98	157	Fejerang, Francisco	Servant	M	Cha	35	S	N	N	Guam	Y	Farm laborer
2		99	158	Duenas, Ignacia C	Head	F	Cha	57	Wd	N	N	Guam	N	None
3		99	158	Duenas, Soledad D	Daughter	F	Cha	27	S	N	Y	Guam	Y	Laundress
4		100	159	Wisley, Ignacio T	Head	M	Cha	70	S	N	N	Guam	N	Farmer
5		100	159	Wisley, Dolores T	Sister	F	Cha	66	S	N	N	Guam	N	Laundress
6		100	160	Wisley, Jose T	Head	M	Cha	36	M	N	Y	Guam	Y	Laborer
7		100	160	Wisley, Amalia S	Wife	F	Cha	21	M	N	Y	Guam	Y	None
8		100	160	Wisley, Jose S	Son	M	Cha	1.4	S			Guam		None
9		100	160	Wisley, Juan S	Son	M	Cha	0.5	S			Guam		None
10		101	161	Perez, Antonio	Head	M	Cha	42	M	N	Y	Guam	Y	Farmer
11		101	161	Perez, Ana B	Wife	F	Cha	23	M	N	Y	Guam	Y	None
12		101	161	Perez, Antonio N	Son	M	Cha	12	S	Y	Y	Guam	Y	None
13		101	161	Perez, Juan N	Son	M	Cha	10	S	Y	Y	Guam	Y	None
14		101	161	Perez, Vicente B	Son	M	Cha	3.5	S			Guam		None
15		101	161	Perez, Ursula B	Daughter	F	Cha	1.9	S			Guam		None
16		101	161	Perez, Maria C	Mother	F	Cha	64	Wd	N	Y	Guam	N	None
17		101	161	Babauta, Catalina R	Sister-in-law	F	Cha	21	S	N	Y	Guam	Y	Servant
18		101	161	Babauta, Josefa R	Sister-in-law	F	Cha	15	S	N	Y	Guam	Y	Laundress
19		101	161	Babauta, Manuel R	Servant	M	Cha	20	S	N	N	Guam	N	Farm laborer
20		101	161	Garrido, Rosa N	Lodger	F	Cha	17	S	N	Y	Guam	Y	Servant
21	Quintero Street	101	162	Santos, Jesus S	Head	M	Cha	26	M	N	Y	Guam	Y	Farmer
22		101	162	Santos, Magdalena S	Wife	F	Cha	18	M	N	Y	Guam	Y	None
23		102	163	Quintanilla, Felix C	Head	M	Cha	53	M	N	N	Guam	N	Farmer
24		102	163	Quintanilla, Milagro C	Wife	F	Cha	44	M	N	N	Guam	N	Laundress
25		102	163	Quintanilla, Manuel C	Son	M	Cha	16	S	Y	Y	Guam	Y	Farm laborer

(CHAMORRO ROOTS GENEALOGY PROJECT™ TRANSCRIPTION)
(BERNARD T. PUNZALAN / HTTP://WWW.CHAMORROROOTS.COM)

DEPARTMENT OF COMMERCE-BUREAU OF THE CENSUS
WASHINGTON

FIFTEENTH CENSUS OF THE UNITED STATES: 1930-POPULATION

THE ISLAND OF GUAM

Sheet No. 14B

264b

District **Municipality Sumay**
Name of Place **Sumay Town** [Proper name and, also, name of class, as city, town, village, barrio, etc]

Enumeration District No. **11**
Enumerated by me on **April 10, 1930** **Joaquin C. Diaz**, Enumerator

	Street, avenue, road, etc. (PLACE OF ABODE)	Number of dwelling house in order of visitation	Number of family in order of visitation	NAME of each person whose place of abode on April 1, 1930, was in this family. Enter surname, first, then given name and middle initial. If any. Include every person living on April 1, 1930. Omit children born since April 1, 1930.	RELATION Relationship of this Person to the head of the family.	Sex (PERSONAL DESCRIPTION)	Color or race	Age at last birthday	Single, married, widowed or divorced	Attended school any time since Sept. 1, 1929 (EDUCATION)	Whether able to read and write.	NATIVITY Place of birth of this person.	Whether able to speak English.	OCCUPATION
	1	2	3	4	5	6	7	8	9	10	11	12	13	14
26	Quintero Street	102	163	Quintanilla, Ignacio C	Son	M	Cha	15	S	Y	Y	Guam	Y	None
27		102	163	Quintanilla, Maria C	Daughter	F	Cha	13	S	Y	Y	Guam	Y	None
28		102	163	Quintanilla, Jose C	Nephew	M	Cha	18	S	N	Y	Guam	Y	Farm laborer
29		103	164	Aquiningoc, Juana C	Head	F	Cha	49	M	N	N	Guam	N	None
30		103	164	Aquiningoc, Mariano C	Son	M	Cha	23	S	N	Y	Saipan	Y	Farmer
31		103	164	Aquiningoc, Nicolas C	Son	M	Cha	21	S	N	Y	Saipan	Y	Laborer
32		103	164	Aquiningoc, Maria C	Daughter	F	Cha	19	S	N	Y	Saipan	Y	Laundress
33		104	165	Reyes, Joaquin P	Head	M	Cha	29	M	N	Y	Guam	Y	Cook
34		104	165	Reyes, Soledad M	Wife	F	Cha	27	M	N	Y	Guam	Y	Laundress
35		105	166	Perez, Juan C	Head	M	Cha	37	M	N	Y	Guam	Y	Farmer
36		105	166	Perez, Ana M	Wife	F	Cha	36	M	N	Y	Guam	N	None
37		105	166	Perez, Juan M	Son	M	Cha	14	S	Y	Y	Guam	Y	None
38		105	166	Perez, Jose M	Son	M	Cha	12	S	Y	Y	Guam	Y	None
39		105	166	Perez, Gregorio M	Son	M	Cha	10	S	Y		Guam		None
40		105	166	Perez, Ignacio M	Son	M	Cha	8	S	Y		Guam		None
41		105	166	Perez, Rosa M	Daughter	F	Cha	6	S			Guam		None
42		105	166	Perez, Pedro M	Son	M	Cha	2.8	S			Guam		None
43		105	166	Mendiola, Vicente C	Brother-in-law	M	Cha	64	Wd	N	N	Guam	N	Farmer
44		105	167	Quinata, Engracia M	Head	F	Cha	23	S	N	N	Guam	Y	None
45		106	168	Sablan, Jose C	Head	M	Cha	39	Wd	N	Y	Guam	Y	Laborer
46		106	168	Sablan, Maria T	Daughter	F	Cha	15	S	N	Y	Guam	Y	None
47		106	168	Sablan, Vicente T	Son	M	Cha	13	S	Y	Y	Guam	Y	None
48		106	168	Sablan, Juan T	Son	M	Cha	11	S	Y	Y	Guam	Y	None
49		106	168	Sablan, Dolores T	Daughter	F	Cha	10	S	Y		Guam		None
50		106	168	Sablan, Jesus T	Son	M	Cha	7	S	Y		Guam		None

(CHAMORRO ROOTS GENEALOGY PROJECT™ TRANSCRIPTION)
(BERNARD T. PUNZALAN / HTTP://WWW.CHAMORROROOTS.COM)

DEPARTMENT OF COMMERCE-BUREAU OF THE CENSUS
WASHINGTON

FIFTEENTH CENSUS OF THE UNITED STATES: 1930-POPULATION

THE ISLAND OF GUAM

Sheet No. 15A

District **Municipality Sumay**
Name of Place **Sumay Town**
[Proper name and, also, name of class, as city, town, village, barrio, etc]

Enumeration District No. **11**
Enumerated by me on **April 10, 1930** **Joaquin C. Diaz**, Enumerator

	PLACE OF ABODE: Street, avenue, road, etc.	Number of dwelling house in order of visitation	Number of family in order of visitation	NAME of each person whose place of abode on April 1, 1930, was in this family. Enter surname, first, then given name and middle initial. If any. Include every person living on April 1, 1930. Omit children born since April 1, 1930.	RELATION Relationship of this Person to the head of the family.	Sex	Color or race	Age at last birthday	Single, married, widowed or divorced	Attended school any time since Sept. 1, 1929	Whether able to read and write.	NATIVITY Place of birth of this person.	Whether able to speak English.	OCCUPATION
	1	2	3	4	5	6	7	8	9	10	11	12	13	14
1	Quintero Street	107	169	Quintanilla, Juan R	Head	M	Cha	27	M	N	Y	Guam	Y	Laborer
2		107	169	Quintanilla, Catalina A	Wife	F	Cha	24	M	N	Y	Guam	N	None
3		107	169	Quintanilla, Edward A	Son	M	Cha	4.5	S			Guam		None
4		107	169	Quintanilla, Antonio A	Son	M	Cha	2.7	S			Guam		None
5		107	169	Quintanilla, Rosario A	Daughter	F	Cha	0.5	S			Guam		None
6		107	169	Quintanilla, Stella A	Daughter	F	Cha	1.1	S			Guam		None
7		107	170	Quinata, Eugenio A	Head	M	Cha	26	S	N	Y	Guam	Y	Laborer
8		108	171	Camacho, Thomas S	Head	M	Cha	69	M	N	N	Guam	N	Farmer
9		108	171	Camacho, Dolores M	Wife	F	Cha	66	M	N	N	Guam	N	None
10		108	172	Camacho, Soledad A	Head	F	Fil	27	M	N	Y	Philippine Is.	Y	None
11		108	172	Camacho, Juan D	Step-son	M	Cha	10	S	Y	Y	Guam	Y	None
12		108	173	Camacho, Fidela M	Head	F	Cha	35	M	N	Y	Guam	N	None
13		108	173	Camacho, Thomas M	Son	M	Cha	9	S	Y		Guam		None
14		108	173	Camacho, Antonio M	Son	M	Cha	8	S	Y		Guam		None
15		108	173	Camacho, Jesus M	Son	M	Cha	5	S			Guam		None
16		108	173	Camacho, Dolores M	Daughter	F	Cha	1.1	S			Guam		None
17		108	173	Fejerang, Maria M	Daughter	F	Cha	13	S	N	Y	Guam		None
18		109	174	Guerrero, Ignacio B	Head	M	Cha	42	M	N	Y	Guam	Y	Farmer
19		109	174	Guerrero, Maxima M	Wife	F	Cha	38	M	N	N	Guam	N	Laundress
20		109	174	Guerrero, Maria M	Daughter	F	Cha	12	S	Y	Y	Guam	Y	None
21		109	174	Guerrero, Rosa M	Daughter	F	Cha	9	S	Y		Guam		None
22		109	174	Guerrero, Thomas M	Son	M	Cha	8	S	Y		Guam		None
23		109	174	Guerrero, Joaquina M	Daughter	F	Cha	4.1	S			Guam		None
24		110	175	Aquiningoc, Antonio A	Head	M	Cha	59	M	N	N	Guam	N	Farmer
25		110	175	Aquiningoc, Ana D	Wife	F	Cha	45	M	N	N	Guam	N	None

D-11-30

DEPARTMENT OF COMMERCE-BUREAU OF THE CENSUS
WASHINGTON

FIFTEENTH CENSUS OF THE UNITED STATES: 1930-POPULATION

THE ISLAND OF GUAM

Sheet No. 15B

265b

District Municipality Sumay
Name of Place Sumay Town
[Proper name and, also, name of class, as city, town, village, barrio, etc]

Enumeration District No. 11
Enumerated by me on April 10, 1930 Joaquin C. Diaz, Enumerator

	PLACE OF ABODE: Street, avenue, road, etc.	Number of dwelling house is order of visitation	Number of family in order of visitation	NAME of each person whose place of abode on April 1, 1930, was in this family. Enter surname, first, then given name and middle initial. If any. Include every person living on April 1, 1930. Omit children born since April 1, 1930.	RELATION Relationship of this Person to the head of the family.	PERSONAL DESCRIPTION: Sex	Color or race	Age at last birthday	Single, married, widowed or divorced	EDUCATION: Attended school any time since Sept. 1, 1929	Whether able to read and write.	NATIVITY Place of birth of this person.	Whether able to speak English.	OCCUPATION
	1	2	3	4	5	6	7	8	9	10	11	12	13	14
26	Quintero Street	110	175	Aquiningoc, Maria C	Niece	F	Cha	8	S	Y		Guam		None
27		111	176	Mendiola, Antonio R	Head	M	Cha	66	M	N	N	Guam	N	Farmer
28		111	176	Mendiola, Ana Q	Wife	F	Cha	67	M	N	N	Guam	N	Laundress
29		111	176	Mendiola, Rosa Q	Daughter	F	Cha	43	S	N	Y	Guam	N	Servant
30		111	176	Mendiola, Juan Q	Son	M	Cha	41	S	N	Y	Guam	Y	Farmer
31		111	176	Mendiola, Saturnino Q	Son	M	Cha	38	S	N	Y	Guam	Y	Laundress
32		111	176	Mendiola, Manuel Q	Son	M	Cha	35	S	N	Y	Guam	Y	Farmer
33		111	176	Mendiola, Dolores Q	Daughter	F	Cha	29	S	N	Y	Guam	Y	Laundress
34		111	176	Mendiola, Maria Q	Daughter	F	Cha	23	S	N	Y	Guam	Y	Laundress
35		111	176	Cruz, Hinara C	Niece	F	Cha	20	S	N	Y	Guam	Y	Laundress
36		111	177	Mendiola, Ignacio Q	Head	M	Cha	26	M	N	Y	Guam	Y	Laborer
37		111	177	Mendiola, Benedicta M	Wife	F	Cha	23	M	N	Y	Guam	Y	None
38		111	177	Mendiola, Juan M	Son	M	Cha	2.9	S			Guam		None
39		111	177	Mendiola, Joaquina M	Daughter	F	Cha	1.5	S			Guam		None
40		111	177	Mendiola, Guadalupe M	Daughter	F	Cha	0.2	S			Guam		None
41		112	178	Cruz, Jesus C	Head	M	Cha	29	M	N	Y	Guam	Y	Farmer
42		112	178	Cruz, Encarnacio A	Wife	F	Cha	26	M	N	Y	Guam	Y	None
43		112	178	Cruz, Manuel A	Son	M	Cha	2.2	S			Guam		None
44		112	178	Cruz, Juan A	Son	M	Cha	1.1	S			Guam		None
45		112	178	Cruz, Jose Q	Servant	M	Cha	26	S	N	N	Guam	Y	Farm laborer
46		112	179	Tenorio, Ignacia P	Head	F	Cha	65	Wd	N	Y	Guam	N	None
47		112	179	Noda, Barcilisa P	Grand daughter	F	Jap	7	S	Y		Guam		None
48		113	180	Gogue, Vicente R	Head	M	Cha	26	M	N	Y	Guam	Y	Cable operator
49		113	180	Gogue, Gloria P	Wife	F	Cha	21	M	Y	Y	Guam	Y	School teacher
50		113	180	Gogue, Patricia P	Daughter	F	Cha	1.9	S			Guam		None

DEPARTMENT OF COMMERCE-BUREAU OF THE CENSUS
WASHINGTON

FIFTEENTH CENSUS OF THE UNITED STATES: 1930-POPULATION

THE ISLAND OF GUAM

Sheet No. 16A

District **Municipality Sumay**
Name of Place **Sumay Town**
[Proper name and, also, name of class, as city, town, village, barrio, etc]

Enumeration District No. **11**
Enumerated by me on **April 10, 1930** **Joaquin C. Diaz**, Enumerator

	PLACE OF ABODE			NAME	RELATION	PERSONAL DESCRIPTION				EDUCATION		NATIVITY		OCCUPATION
	Street, avenue, road, etc.	Number of dwelling house is order of visitation	Number of family in order of visitation	of each person whose place of abode on April 1, 1930, was in this family. Enter surname, first, then given name and middle initial. If any. Include every person living on April 1, 1930. Omit children born since April 1, 1930.	Relationship of this Person to the head of the family.	Sex	Color or race	Age at last birthday	Single, married, widowed or divorced	Attended school any time since Sept. 1, 1929	Whether able to read and write.	Place of birth of this person.	Whether able to speak English.	
	1	2	3	4	5	6	7	8	9	10	11	12	13	14
1	Quintero Street	113	180	Gogue, Roy B	Son	M	Cha	0.6	S			Guam		None
2		113	180	Gogue, Isabel R	Mother	F	Cha	62	Wd	N	Y	Guam	N	None
3		113	180	Champaco, Joaquina E	Servant	F	Cha	14	S	Y	Y	Guam	Y	Servant
4		113	181	Aquiningoc, Manuel C	Head	M	Cha	25	M	N	Y	Guam	Y	Farmer
5		113	181	Aquiningoc, Caridad M	Wife	F	Cha	19	M	N	Y	Guam	Y	None
6		113	181	Aquiningoc, Maria M	Daughter	F	Cha	4.1	S			Guam		None
7		113	181	Aquiningoc, Isabel M	Daughter	F	Cha	2.5	S			Guam		None
8		113	181	Aquiningoc, German M	Son	M	Cha	0.5	S			Guam		None
9		114	182	Kellison, Grace	Head	F	W	36	M	N	Y	California	Y	None
10		114	182	Kellison, Janet M	Daughter	F	W	16	S	N	Y	California	Y	None
11		114	182	Kellison, Edna M	Daughter	F	W	2.5	S			California		None
12		115	183	Wilson, Mabel S	Head	F	W	23	M	N	Y	Virginia	Y	None
13		115	183	Wilson, Ellen M	Daughter	F	W	1.6	S			Virginia		None
14		116	184	Sanchez, Ignacio Q	Head	M	Cha	26	M	N	Y	Guam	Y	Cable operator
15		116	184	Sanchez, Isabel G	Wife	F	Cha	23	M	N	Y	Guam	Y	None
16		116	184	Sanchez, Juan C	Son	M	Cha	3	S			Guam		None
17		116	184	Sanchez, Manuel C	Son	M	Cha	1.2	S			Guam		None
18		116	184	Borja, Pilar O	Cousin-in-law	F	Cha	13	S	Y	Y	Guam	Y	Servant
19		117	185	Santos, Manuel C	Head	M	Cha	62	M	N	N	Guam	N	Farmer
20		117	185	Santos, Maria P	Wife	F	Cha	57	M	N	N	Guam	N	None
21		118	186	Concepcion, Clara D	Head	F	Cha	77	S	N	N	Guam	N	None
22		118	186	Concepcion, Dolores C	Daughter	F	Cha	40	S	N	N	Guam	N	Laundress
23		118	187	Guzman, Francisco L	Head	M	Cha	55	M	N	N	Guam	N	Farmer
24		118	187	Guzman, Maria C	Wife	F	Cha	46	M	N	N	Guam	N	None
25		118	187	Guzman, Joaquin C	Son	M	Cha	17	S	N	Y	Guam	Y	Laborer

(CHAMORRO ROOTS GENEALOGY PROJECT™ TRANSCRIPTION)
(BERNARD T. PUNZALAN / HTTP://WWW.CHAMORROROOTS.COM)

DEPARTMENT OF COMMERCE-BUREAU OF THE CENSUS
WASHINGTON

FIFTEENTH CENSUS OF THE UNITED STATES: 1930-POPULATION

THE ISLAND OF GUAM

Sheet No. 16B

266b

District **Municipality Sumay**
Name of Place **Sumay Town**
[Proper name and, also, name of class, as city, town, village, barrio, etc]

Enumeration District No. **11**
Enumerated by me on **April 11, 1930** **Joaquin C. Diaz**, Enumerator

	PLACE OF ABODE			NAME	RELATION	PERSONAL DESCRIPTION				EDUCATION		NATIVITY		OCCUPATION
	Street, avenue, road, etc.	Number of dwelling house in order of visitation	Number of family in order of visitation	of each person whose place of abode on April 1, 1930, was in this family. Enter surname, first, then given name and middle initial. If any. Include every person living on April 1, 1930. Omit children born since April 1, 1930.	Relationship of this Person to the head of the family.	Sex	Color or race	Age at last birthday	Single, married, widowed or divorced	Attended school any time since Sept. 1, 1929	Whether able to read and write.	Place of birth of this person.	Whether able to speak English.	
	1	2	3	4	5	6	7	8	9	10	11	12	13	14
26	Quintero Street	118	187	Guzman, Jesus C	Son	M	Cha	15	S	Y	Y	Guam	Y	None
27		118	187	Guzman, Antonia C	Daughter	F	Cha	11	S	Y	Y	Guam	Y	None
28		118	188	Guzman, Jose C	Head	M	Cha	22	M	N	Y	Guam	Y	Farmer
29		118	188	Guzman, Maria C	Wife	F	Cha	21	M	N	Y	Guam	Y	None
30		119	189	Diaz, Joaquin M	Head	M	Cha	38	M	N	Y	Guam	Y	Chauffeur
31		119	189	Diaz, Concepcion L	Wife	F	Cha	31	M	N	Y	Guam	Y	None
32		119	189	Diaz, Isabel L	Daughter	F	Cha	9	S	Y		Guam		None
33		119	189	Diaz, Vicente L	Son	M	Cha	7	S	Y		Guam		None
34		119	189	Diaz, Felix L	Son	M	Cha	5	S			Guam		None
35		119	189	Diaz, Francisco L	Son	M	Cha	2.9	S			Guam		None
36		119	189	Diaz, Magdalena M	Mother	F	Cha	66	Wd	N	Y	Guam	N	None
37		120	190	Pangelinan, Luis P	Head	M	Cha	44	M	N	N	Guam	N	Farmer
38		120	190	Pangelinan, Rufina C	Wife	F	Cha	44	M	N	N	Guam	N	None
39		120	190	Pangelinan, Jose C	Son	M	Cha	20	S	N	N	Guam	N	Laborer
40		120	190	Cruz, Enrique C	Nephew	M	Cha	19	S	N	Y	Guam	Y	Laborer
41		120	190	Ignacio, Gregorio C	Nephew	M	Cha	18	S	N	Y	Guam	Y	Laborer
42		121	191	Santos, Pedro Q	Head	M	Cha	49	M	N	Y	Guam	Y	Farmer
43		121	191	Santos, Maria L	Wife	F	Cha	42	M	N	Y	Guam	N	None
44		121	191	Santos, Jose L	Son	M	Cha	19	S	N	Y	Guam	Y	Laborer
45		121	191	Santos, Concepcion L	Daughter	F	Cha	17	S	N	Y	Guam	Y	None
46		121	191	Santos, Guadalupe L	Daughter	F	Cha	7	S	Y		Guam		None
47		121	191	Santos, Alejandro L	Son	M	Cha	5	S			Guam		None
48		121	191	Santos, Jose L	Son	M	Cha	3.5	S			Guam		None
49		121	191	Santos, Rosa L	Daughter	F	Cha	1.6	S			Guam		None
50		122	192	Wisley, Mariano T	Head	M	Cha	55	Wd	N	N	Guam	N	Farmer

(CHAMORRO ROOTS GENEALOGY PROJECT™ TRANSCRIPTION)
(BERNARD T. PUNZALAN / HTTP://WWW.CHAMORROROOTS.COM)

DEPARTMENT OF COMMERCE-BUREAU OF THE CENSUS
WASHINGTON

FIFTEENTH CENSUS OF THE UNITED STATES: 1930-POPULATION

THE ISLAND OF GUAM

Sheet No. 17A

District **Municipality Sumay**
Name of Place **Sumay Town** [Proper name and, also, name of class, as city, town, village, barrio, etc]

Enumeration District No. **11**
Enumerated by me on **April 11, 1930** **Joaquin C. Diaz**, Enumerator

	PLACE OF ABODE			NAME	RELATION	PERSONAL DESCRIPTION				EDUCATION		NATIVITY		OCCUPATION
	Street, avenue, road, etc.	Number of dwelling house in order of visitation	Number of family in order of visitation	of each person whose place of abode on April 1, 1930, was in this family. Enter surname, first, then given name and middle initial. If any. Include every person living on April 1, 1930. Omit children born since April 1, 1930.	Relationship of this Person to the head of the family.	Sex	Color or race	Age at last birthday	Single, married, widowed or divorced	Attended school any time since Sept. 1, 1929	Whether able to read and write.	Place of birth of this person.	Whether able to speak English.	
	1	2	3	4	5	6	7	8	9	10	11	12	13	14
1	Quintero Street	122	192	Wisley, Vicente D	Son	M	Cha	35	S	N	Y	Guam	Y	Farmer
2		122	193	Wisley, Juan D	Head	M	Cha	29	M	N	Y	Guam	Y	Cook
3		122	193	Wisley, Feliza A	Wife	F	Cha	31	M	N	Y	Guam	Y	None
4		122	193	Wisley, Benito A	Son	M	Cha	7	S	Y		Guam		None
5		122	193	Wisley, Elias A	Son	M	Cha	4.1	S			Guam		None
6		122	193	Wisley, Rita A	Daughter	F	Cha	2.9	S			Guam		None
7		122	193	Wisley, Remedio A	Daughter	F	Cha	1	S			Guam		None
8		123	194	Aquiningoc, Magdalena W	Head	F	Cha	53	Wd	N	N	Guam	N	Laundress
9		123	194	Aquiningoc, Ana W	Daughter	F	Cha	20	S	N	Y	Guam	Y	None
10		124	195	Quintanilla, Francisco C	Head	M	Cha	25	M	N	Y	Guam	Y	Chauffeur
11		124	195	Quintanilla, Trinidad C	Wife	F	Cha	24	M	N	Y	Guam	Y	None
12		124	195	Quintanilla, Albert C	Son	M	Cha	2	S			Guam		None
13		124	195	Charguane, Maria C	Step-daughter	F	Cha	6	S			Guam		None
14		124	195	Charguane, Francisco T	Brother-in-law	M	Cha	27	S	N	Y	Guam	Y	Farm laborer
15		125	196	Saloaga, Cristina C	Head	F	Cha	37	Wd	N	Y	Guam	Y	None
16		125	196	Camacho, Juan C	Son	M	Cha	9	S	Y		Guam		None
17		125	196	Camacho, Thomas C	Son	M	Cha	8	S	Y		Guam		None
18		125	196	Camacho, Rita C	Daughter	F	Cha	7	S	Y		Guam		None
19		125	196	Camacho, Beatrice C	Daughter	F	Cha	5	S			Guam		None
20		125	196	Camacho, Ursula C	Daughter	F	Cha	2.5	S			Guam		None
21		125	196	Camacho, Rosalia C	Daughter	F	Cha	1.1	S			Guam		None
22		125	196	Quintanilla, Francisca C	Niece	F	Cha	20	S	N	Y	Guam	Y	None
23		126	197	Babauta, Antonio R	Head	M	Cha	31	M	N	Y	Guam	Y	Farmer
24		126	197	Babauta, Maria C	Wife	F	Cha	28	M	N	Y	Guam	Y	None
25		126	197	Babauta, Carmen C	Daughter	F	Cha	4.9	S			Guam		None

DEPARTMENT OF COMMERCE-BUREAU OF THE CENSUS
WASHINGTON

FIFTEENTH CENSUS OF THE UNITED STATES: 1930-POPULATION

THE ISLAND OF GUAM

Sheet No. 17B

267b

District **Municipality Sumay**
Name of Place **Sumay Town** [Proper name and, also, name of class, as city, town, village, barrio, etc]

Enumeration District No. **11**
Enumerated by me on **April 11, 1930** **Joaquin C. Diaz**, Enumerator

	PLACE OF ABODE			NAME	RELATION	PERSONAL DESCRIPTION				EDUCATION		NATIVITY		OCCUPATION
	Street, avenue, road, etc.	Number of dwelling house in order of visitation	Number of family in order of visitation	of each person whose place of abode on April 1, 1930, was in this family. Enter surname, first, then given name and middle initial. If any. Include every person living on April 1, 1930. Omit children born since April 1, 1930.	Relationship of this Person to the head of the family.	Sex	Color or race	Age at last birthday	Single, married, widowed or divorced	Attended school any time since Sept. 1, 1929	Whether able to read and write.	Place of birth of this person.	Whether able to speak English.	
	1	2	3	4	5	6	7	8	9	10	11	12	13	14
26	Quintero Street	126	197	Babauta, Florence C	Daughter	F	Cha	2.2	S			Guam		None
27		126	197	Babauta, Jesus C	Son	M	Cha	1.2	S			Guam		None
28		126	198	Quintanilla, Rosa W	Head	F	Cha	26	M	N	Y	Guam	Y	None
29		126	198	Quintanilla, Dolores W	Daughter	F	Cha	2	S			Guam		None
30		127	199	Camacho, Guillermo S	Head	M	Cha	71	M	N	Y	Guam	N	None
31		127	199	Camacho, Rita T	Wife	F	Cha	60	M	N	N	Guam	N	None
32		127	199	Camacho, Thomas T	Son	M	Cha	40	Wd	N	Y	Guam	Y	Farmer
33		127	199	Quitugua, Jose	Grandson	M	Cha	4.9	S			Guam		None
34		128	200	Santos, Jose S	Head	M	Cha	70	M	N	N	Rota	N	Farmer
35		128	200	Santos, Alejandra L	Wife	F	Cha	52	M	N	N	Guam	N	None
36		128	200	Santos, Abraham L	Son	M	Cha	12	S	Y	Y	Guam	Y	None
37		128	200	Fegurgur, Joaquin S	Nephew	M	Cha	20	S	N	Y	Guam	Y	Farm laborer
38		128	200	Fegurgur, Jesus S	Nephew	M	Cha	21	S	N	Y	Guam	Y	Farm laborer
39		128	200	Tajalle, Maria	Boarder	F	Cha	32	S	N	N	Guam	N	Laundress
40		128	200	Chargualaf, Rosalia C	Boarder	F	Cha	20	S	N	N	Guam	N	Laundress
41		129	201	Crisostomo, Ramon J	Head	M	Cha	70	M	N	Y	Guam	N	Farmer
42		129	201	Crisostomo, Ignacia M	Wife	F	Cha	69	M	N	Y	Guam	N	None
43		129	201	Crisostomo, Genaro M	Son	M	Cha	37	S	N	Y	Guam	N	Farmer
44		129	201	Crisostomo, Soledad M	Daughter	F	Cha	31	S	N	Y	Guam	Y	None
45		129	201	Crisostomo, Maria M	Daughter	F	Cha	29	S	N	Y	Guam	Y	None
46		129	202	Mendiola, Joaquina C	Head	F	Cha	41	Wd	N	Y	Guam	Y	Laundress
47		129	202	Mendiola, Geronimo C	Son	M	Cha	17	S	N	Y	Guam	Y	Farm laborer
48		129	202	Mendiola, Juan C	Son	M	Cha	15	S	Y	Y	Guam	Y	None
49		129	203	Mantanona, Andrea C	Head	F	Cha	34	Wd	N	Y	Guam	Y	Laundress
50		129	203	Mantanona, Mariana C	Daughter	F	Cha	8	S	Y		Guam		None

(CHAMORRO ROOTS GENEALOGY PROJECT™ TRANSCRIPTION)
(BERNARD T. PUNZALAN / HTTP://WWW.CHAMORROROOTS.COM)

DEPARTMENT OF COMMERCE-BUREAU OF THE CENSUS
WASHINGTON

FIFTEENTH CENSUS OF THE UNITED STATES: 1930-POPULATION

THE ISLAND OF GUAM

Sheet No. 18A

268

District **Municipality Sumay**
Name of Place **Sumay Town**
[Proper name and, also, name of class, as city, town, village, barrio, etc]

Enumeration District No. **11**
Enumerated by me on **April 11, 1930** **Joaquin C. Diaz**, Enumerator

	PLACE OF ABODE: Street, avenue, road, etc.	Number of dwelling house in order of visitation	Number of family in order of visitation	NAME of each person whose place of abode on April 1, 1930, was in this family. Enter surname, first, then given name and middle initial. If any. Include every person living on April 1, 1930. Omit children born since April 1, 1930.	RELATION Relationship of this Person to the head of the family.	PERSONAL DESCRIPTION: Sex	Color or race	Age at last birthday	Single, married, widowed or divorced	EDUCATION: Attended school any time since Sept. 1, 1929	Whether able to read and write.	NATIVITY Place of birth of this person.	Whether able to speak English.	OCCUPATION
	1	2	3	4	5	6	7	8	9	10	11	12	13	14
1	Quintero Street	130	204	Crisostomo, Francisco M	Head	M	Cha	39	M	N	Y	Guam	Y	Laborer
2		130	204	Crisostomo, Margarita M	Wife	F	Cha	46	M	N	N	Guam	N	None
3		130	204	Crisostomo, Concepcion M	Daughter	F	Cha	10	S	Y		Guam		None
4		130	204	Crisostomo, Isabel M	Daughter	F	Cha	9	S	Y		Guam		None
5		130	204	Crisostomo, Jose M	Son	M	Cha	7	S	Y		Guam		None
6		130	204	Crisostomo, Dolores M	Daughter	F	Cha	6	S			Guam		None
7		130	204	Crisostomo, Ana M	Daughter	F	Cha	1.9	S			Guam		None
8		131	205	Limtiaco, Manuela C	Head	F	Cha	32	M	N	Y	Guam	Y	None
9		131	205	Limtiaco, Ignacio M	Brother	M	Cha	39	M	N	Y	Guam	Y	Farmer
10		131	205	Limtiaco, Stanley C	Son	M	Cha	4.2	S			Guam		None
11		131	205	Limtiaco, Aurora C	Daughter	F	Cha	2	S			Guam		None
12		131	205	Limtiaco, Justina C	Daughter	F	Cha	0.5	S			Guam		None
13		131	205	Limtiaco, Dolores M	Mother	F	Cha	64	Wd	N	Y	Guam		None
14		131	205	Limtiaco, Ignacio Q	Nephew	M	Cha	9	S	Y		Guam		None
15		132	206	Mendiola, Catalino Q	Head	M	Cha	40	M	N	Y	Guam	Y	Laborer
16		132	206	Mendiola, Preciosa G	Wife	F	Cha	40	M	N	Y	Guam	N	None
17		132	206	Mendiola, Jose G	Son	M	Cha	12	S	Y	Y	Guam	Y	None
18		132	206	Mendiola, Jesus G	Son	M	Cha	11	S	Y	N	Guam	N	None
19		132	206	Mendiola, Juan G	Son	M	Cha	9	S	Y		Guam		None
20		132	206	Mendiola, Gregorio G	Son	M	Cha	7	S	Y		Guam		None
21		132	206	Mendiola, Ana G	Daughter	F	Cha	3.4	S			Guam		None
22		132	206	Mendiola, Maria G	Daughter	F	Cha	1.1	S			Guam		None
23		133	207	Quintanilla, Jose C	Head	M	Cha	29	M	N	Y	Guam	Y	Laborer
24		133	207	Quintanilla, Engracia C	Wife	F	Cha	26	M	N	Y	Guam	Y	None
25		133	207	Quintanilla, Jose C	Son	M	Cha	3.7	S			Guam		None

(CHAMORRO ROOTS GENEALOGY PROJECT™ TRANSCRIPTION)
(BERNARD T. PUNZALAN / HTTP://WWW.CHAMORROROOTS.COM)

DEPARTMENT OF COMMERCE-BUREAU OF THE CENSUS
WASHINGTON

FIFTEENTH CENSUS OF THE UNITED STATES: 1930-POPULATION

THE ISLAND OF GUAM

Sheet No. 18B

268b

District **Municipality Sumay**
Name of Place **Sumay Town**
[Proper name and, also, name of class, as city, town, village, barrio, etc]

Enumeration District No. **11**
Enumerated by me on **April 11, 1930** **Joaquin C. Diaz**
Enumerator

	PLACE OF ABODE			NAME	RELATION	PERSONAL DESCRIPTION				EDUCATION		NATIVITY		OCCUPATION
	Street, avenue, road, etc.	Number of dwelling house is order of visitation	Number of family in order of visitation	of each person whose place of abode on April 1, 1930, was in this family. Enter surname, first, then given name and middle initial. If any. Include every person living on April 1, 1930. Omit children born since April 1, 1930.	Relationship of this Person to the head of the family.	Sex	Color or race	Age at last birthday	Single, married, widowed or divorced	Attended school any time since Sept. 1, 1929	Whether able to read and write.	Place of birth of this person.	Whether able to speak English.	
	1	2	3	4	5	6	7	8	9	10	11	12	13	14
26	Quintero Street	133	207	Quintanilla, Luis C	Son	M	Cha	1.9	S			Guam		None
27		133	207	Quintanilla, Francisco C	Son	M	Cha	0.5	S			Guam		None
28		133	207	Babauta, Vicente C	Boarder	M	Cha	11	S	Y	Y	Guam	Y	None
29		134	208	Quintanilla, Joaquin R	Head	M	Cha	34	M	N	Y	Guam	Y	Farmer
30		134	208	Quintanilla, Antonia P	Wife	F	Cha	31	M	N	Y	Guam	Y	None
31		134	208	Quintanilla, Luis P	Son	M	Cha	9	S			Guam		None
32		134	208	Quintanilla, Ladislao P	Daughter	F	Cha	7	S			Guam		None
33		134	208	Quintanilla, Vicente P	Son	M	Cha	6	S			Guam		None
34		134	208	Quintanilla, Beatrice P	Daughter	F	Cha	4.9	S			Guam		None
35		134	209	Aquiningoc, Jose C	Head	M	Cha	31	M	N	Y	Guam	Y	Farmer
36		134	209	Aquiningoc, Rosario C	Wife	F	Cha	47	M	N	N	Guam	N	Laundress
37		134	209	Quintanilla, Francisca Q	Step-daughter	F	Cha	17	S	N	Y	Guam	Y	Laundress
38	Togai Street	135	210	Lizama, Jose D	Head	M	Cha	42	M	N	N	Guam	Y	Farmer
39		135	210	Lizama, Dolores C	Wife	F	Cha	38	M	N	N	Guam	N	Laundress
40		135	210	Lizama, Daniel Q	Son	M	Cha	14	S	N	Y	Guam	Y	Farm laborer
41		135	210	Lizama, Cecilia Q	Daughter	F	Cha	12	S	Y	Y	Guam	Y	None
42		135	210	Lizama, Juan Q	Son	M	Cha	5	S			Guam		None
43		135	210	Lizama, Simeon Q	Son	M	Cha	1.1	S			Guam		None
44		135	210	Quitugua, Ana Q	Step-daughter	F	Cha	17	S	N	Y	Guam	Y	Laundress
45		136	211	Sablan, Francisco S	Head	M	Cha	50	M	N	Y	Guam	Y	Farmer
46		136	211	Sablan, Maria S	Wife	F	Cha	53	M	N	N	Guam	Y	Laundress
47		136	211	Angoco, Manuel M	Servant	M	Cha	23	S	N	Y	Guam	N	Farm laborer
48		137	212	Castro, Antonio P	Head	M	Cha	44	M	N	Y	Guam	Y	Farmer
49		137	212	Castro, Soledad C	Wife	F	Cha	26	M	N	Y	Guam	Y	None
50		137	212	Matanane, Maria C	Servant	F	Cha	29	S	N	N	Guam	N	Servant

DEPARTMENT OF COMMERCE-BUREAU OF THE CENSUS
WASHINGTON

FIFTEENTH CENSUS OF THE UNITED STATES: 1930-POPULATION

THE ISLAND OF GUAM

Sheet No. 19A

District **Municipality Sumay**
Name of Place **Sumay Town**
[Proper name and, also, name of class, as city, town, village, barrio, etc]

Enumeration District No. **11**
Enumerated by me on **April 12, 1930** **Joaquin C. Diaz**, Enumerator

	PLACE OF ABODE			NAME	RELATION	PERSONAL DESCRIPTION				EDUCATION		NATIVITY		OCCUPATION
	Street, avenue, road, etc.	Number of dwelling house in order of visitation	Number of family in order of visitation	of each person whose place of abode on April 1, 1930, was in this family. Enter surname, first, then given name and middle initial. If any. Include every person living on April 1, 1930. Omit children born since April 1, 1930.	Relationship of this Person to the head of the family.	Sex	Color or race	Age at last birthday	Single, married, widowed or divorced	Attended school any time since Sept. 1, 1929	Whether able to read and write.	Place of birth of this person.	Whether able to speak English.	
	1	2	3	4	5	6	7	8	9	10	11	12	13	14
1	Togai Street	138	213	Santos, Concepcion C	Head	F	Cha	35	M	N	Y	Guam	Y	None
2		138	213	Santos, Ignacio C	Son	M	Cha	4.1	S			Guam		None
3		139	214	Dumonal, Pedro G	Head	M	Fil	34	M	N	Y	Guam	Y	Farmer
4		139	214	Dumonal, Rosalia Q	Wife	F	Cha	25	M	N	Y	Guam	Y	None
5		139	214	Dumonal, Maria Q	Daughter	F	Fil	5	S			Guam		None
6		139	214	Dumonal, Andresina Q	Daughter	F	Fil	2.2	S			Guam		None
7		139	214	Dumonal, Rosa Q	Daughter	F	Fil	0.2	S			Guam		None
8		140	215	Concepcion, Teodoro D	Head	M	Cha	44	M	N	Y	Guam	Y	Laborer
9		140	215	Concepcion, Eduviges D	Wife	F	Cha	44	M	N	Y	Guam	Y	None
10		140	215	Concepcion, Delfina D	Daughter	F	Cha	15	S	Y	Y	Guam	Y	None
11		140	215	Concepcion, Enrique D	Daughter	F	Cha	8	S	Y		Guam		None
12		140	215	Concepcion, Maria D	Son	M	Cha	7	S	Y		Guam		None
13		140	215	Concepcion, Cristobal D	Daughter	F	Cha	4.6	S			Guam		None
14		141	216	Quintanilla, Vicente C	Head	M	Cha	58	M	N	N	Guam	N	Farmer
15		141	216	Quintanilla, Gertrudes R	Wife	F	Cha	57	M	N	N	Guam	N	None
16		141	216	Quintanilla, Rita R	Daughter	F	Cha	23	S	N	Y	Guam	Y	None
17		141	216	Quintanilla, Francisco R	Son	M	Cha	17	S	N	N	Guam	N	Farm laborer
18		141	216	Quintanilla, Deonicia R	Daughter	F	Cha	10	S	Y		Guam		None
19		142	217	Mulford, James A	Lodger	M	W	0.3	S			Guam		None
20		143	218	Taitano, Carmen P	Head	F	Cha	49	M	N	N	Guam	N	None
21		143	218	Taitano, Dolores G	Step daughter	F	Cha	8	S	Y		Guam		None
22		143	218	Taitano, Jose G	Step son	M	Cha	6	S	Y		Guam		None
23		144	219	Santos, Jose S	Head	M	Cha	36	M	N	Y	Guam	Y	Laborer
24		144	219	Santos, Dolores Q	Wife	F	Cha	30	M	N	Y	Guam	Y	None
25		144	219	Santos, Benito Q	Son	M	Cha	5.9	S			Guam		None

DEPARTMENT OF COMMERCE-BUREAU OF THE CENSUS
WASHINGTON

FIFTEENTH CENSUS OF THE UNITED STATES: 1930-POPULATION

THE ISLAND OF GUAM

Sheet No. 19B

269b

District **Municipality Sumay**
Name of Place **Sumay Town** [Proper name and, also, name of class, as city, town, village, barrio, etc]

Enumeration District No. **11**
Enumerated by me on **April 12, 1930** **Joaquin C. Diaz**, Enumerator

	PLACE OF ABODE: Street, avenue, road, etc.	Number of dwelling house in order of visitation	Number of family in order of visitation	NAME of each person whose place of abode on April 1, 1930, was in this family. Enter surname, first, then given name and middle initial. If any. Include every person living on April 1, 1930. Omit children born since April 1, 1930.	RELATION Relationship of this Person to the head of the family.	PERSONAL DESCRIPTION: Sex	Color or race	Age at last birthday	Single, married, widowed or divorced	EDUCATION: Attended school any time since Sept. 1, 1929	Whether able to read and write.	NATIVITY Place of birth of this person.	Whether able to speak English.	OCCUPATION
	1	2	3	4	5	6	7	8	9	10	11	12	13	14
26	Togai Street	144	219	Santos, Leonardo T	Son	M	Cha	2.9	S			Guam		None
27		144	220	Santos, Juana S	Head	F	Cha	65	Wd	N	N	Guam	N	None
28		145	221	Espinosa, Tomasa M	Head	F	Cha	55	Wd	N	Y	Guam	N	Laundress
29		145	221	Espinosa, Joaquina M	Daughter	F	Cha	24	S	N	Y	Guam	Y	Servant
30		145	221	Espinosa, Jose M	Son	M	Cha	22	S	N	Y	Guam	Y	Laborer
31		145	221	Espinosa, Jesus M	Son	M	Cha	19	S	Y	Y	Guam	Y	Farmer
32		145	221	Espinosa, Maria M	Daughter	F	Cha	16	S	N	Y	Guam	Y	Laundress
33		145	221	Espinosa, Ana M	Daughter	F	Cha	11	S	Y	Y	Guam	Y	None
34		145	221	Espinosa, William E	Son	M	Cha	2.6	S			Guam		None
35		145	221	Espinosa, Josephine E	Grand daughter	F	Cha	0.2	S			Guam		None
36		146	222	Hansen, Martin F	Head	M	W	39	M	N	Y	Denmark	Y	Cable employee
37		146	222	Hansen, Carmen M	Wife	F	Cha	26	M	N	Y	Guam	Y	None
38		147	223	Sablan, Vicente U	Head	M	Cha	72	M	N	Y	Guam	Y	Farmer
39		147	223	Sablan, Carmen S	Wife	F	Cha	70	M	N	N	Guam	N	None
40		147	223	Sablan, Ana S	Daughter	F	Cha	42	S	N	Y	Guam	Y	Laundress
41		147	223	Sablan, Juan S	Grandson	M	Cha	13	S	Y	Y	Guam	Y	None
42		147	224	Sablan, Juan S	Head	M	Cha	41	D	N	Y	Guam	Y	Farmer
43		147	225	Sablan, Jose S	Head	M	Cha	27	M	N	Y	Guam	Y	Cook
44		147	225	Sablan, Estefania E	Wife	F	Cha	20	M	N	Y	Guam	Y	None
45		148	226	Sablan, Vicente S	Head	M	Cha	29	M	N	Y	Guam	Y	Cook
46		148	226	Sablan, Maria C	Wife	F	Cha	21	M	N	Y	Guam	Y	None
47		148	226	Sablan, Alfred C	Son	M	Cha	3	S			Guam		None
48		148	226	Sablan, Thomas C	Son	M	Cha	1.1	S			Guam		None
49		149	227	Duenas, Maria G	Head	F	Cha	61	Wd	N	N	Guam	N	None
50		149	227	Guzman, Juan G	Son	M	Cha	18	S	N	Y	Guam	Y	Farmer

DEPARTMENT OF COMMERCE-BUREAU OF THE CENSUS
WASHINGTON

FIFTEENTH CENSUS OF THE UNITED STATES: 1930-POPULATION

THE ISLAND OF GUAM

Sheet No. 20A

District **Municipality Sumay**
Name of Place **Sumay Town** [Proper name and, also, name of class, as city, town, village, barrio, etc]

Enumeration District No. **11**
Enumerated by me on **April 12, 1930** **Joaquin C. Diaz**, Enumerator

	PLACE OF ABODE			NAME	RELATION	PERSONAL DESCRIPTION				EDUCATION		NATIVITY		OCCUPATION
	Street, avenue, road, etc.	Number of dwelling house is order of visitation	Number of family in order of visitation	of each person whose place of abode on April 1, 1930, was in this family. Enter surname, first, then given name and middle initial. If any. Include every person living on April 1, 1930. Omit children born since April 1, 1930.	Relationship of this Person to the head of the family.	Sex	Color or race	Age at last birthday	Single, married, widowed or divorced	Attended school any time since Sept. 1, 1929	Whether able to read and write.	Place of birth of this person.	Whether able to speak English.	
	1	2	3	4	5	6	7	8	9	10	11	12	13	14
1	Togai Street	149	228	Cruz, Jose C	Head	M	Cha	21	M	N	Y	Guam	Y	Laborer
2		149	228	Cruz, Preciosa Q	Wife	F	Cha	23	M	N	Y	Guam	Y	None
3		149	228	Quichocho, Soledad A	Sister-in-law	F	Cha	14	S	Y	Y	Guam	Y	None
4		150	229	Mendiola, Francisco U	Head	M	Cha	25	M	N	Y	Guam	Y	Laborer
5		150	229	Mendiola, Dolores LG	Wife	F	Cha	22	M	N	Y	Guam	Y	None
6		150	229	Mendiola, Jesus LG	Son	M	Cha	0.7	S			Guam		None
7		151	230	Tolentino, Joaquin T	Head	M	Fil	39	M	N	Y	Guam	Y	Carpenter
8		151	230	Tolentino, Tomasa DG	Wife	F	Fil	33	M	N	Y	Guam	Y	None
9		151	230	Tolentino, Rosalia D	Daughter	F	Fil	13	S	Y	Y	Guam	Y	None
10		151	230	Tolentino, Matilde D	Daughter	F	Fil	10	S	Y		Guam		None
11		151	230	Tolentino, Florencia D	Daughter	F	Fil	7	S	Y		Guam		None
12		151	230	Tolentino, Maria D	Daughter	F	Fil	5	S			Guam		None
13		151	230	Tolentino, Felicita D	Daughter	F	Fil	2	S			Guam		None
14		152	231	Santos, Agustin S	Head	M	Cha	50	M	N	Y	Guam	Y	Foreman
15		152	231	Santos, Teresa M	Wife	F	Cha	45	M	N	Y	Guam	N	None
16		152	231	Santos, Rosa M	Daughter	F	Cha	19	S	N	Y	Guam	N	Laundress
17		152	231	Santos, Gil M	Son	M	Cha	12	S	Y	Y	Guam	Y	None
18		152	231	Santos, Jesus M	Son	M	Cha	6	S			Guam		None
19		152	231	Mendiola, Joaquin M	Nephew	M	Jap	1.7	S			Guam		None
20		152	232	Camacho, Jose R	Head	M	Cha	27	M	N	Y	Guam	Y	Carpenter
21		152	232	Camacho, Maria S	Wife	F	Cha	24	M	N	Y	Guam	Y	None
22		152	232	Camacho, Leonora S	Daughter	F	Cha	1.5	S			Guam		None
23		152	232	Camacho, Maria S	Daughter	F	Cha	0.2	S			Guam		None
24		153	233	Aquiningoc, Juan B	Head	M	Cha	61	Wd	N	N	Guam	N	None
25		153	233	Aquiningoc, Antonio T	Son	M	Cha	24	S	N	Y	Guam	Y	Laborer

(CHAMORRO ROOTS GENEALOGY PROJECT™ TRANSCRIPTION)
(BERNARD T. PUNZALAN / HTTP://WWW.CHAMORROROOTS.COM)

DEPARTMENT OF COMMERCE-BUREAU OF THE CENSUS
WASHINGTON

FIFTEENTH CENSUS OF THE UNITED STATES: 1930-POPULATION

THE ISLAND OF GUAM

Sheet No. 20B

270b

District **Municipality Sumay**
Name of Place **Sumay Town**
[Proper name and, also, name of class, as city, town, village, barrio, etc]

Enumeration District No. **11**
Enumerated by me on **April 14, 1930** **Joaquin C. Diaz**
Enumerator

	PLACE OF ABODE			NAME	RELATION	PERSONAL DESCRIPTION				EDUCATION		NATIVITY		OCCUPATION
	Street, avenue, road, etc.	Number of dwelling house in order of visitation	Number of family in order of visitation	of each person whose place of abode on April 1, 1930, was in this family. Enter surname, first, then given name and middle initial. If any. Include every person living on April 1, 1930. Omit children born since April 1, 1930.	Relationship of this Person to the head of the family.	Sex	Color or race	Age at last birthday	Single, married, widowed or divorced	Attended school any time since Sept. 1, 1929	Whether able to read and write.	Place of birth of this person.	Whether able to speak English.	
	1	2	3	4	5	6	7	8	9	10	11	12	13	14
26	Togai Street	153	234	Mendiola, Maria A	Head	F	Cha	29	M	N	Y	Guam	Y	None
27		153	234	Mendiola, Isabel A	Daughter	F	Cha	6	S			Guam		None
28		153	234	Mendiola, Stella A	Daughter	F	Cha	5	S			Guam		None
29		153	234	Mendiola, Francisco A	Son	M	Cha	1.5	S			Guam		None
30		153	235	Aguon, Jesus L	Head	M	Cha	23	S	N	Y	Guam	Y	Cook
31		154	236	Arceo, Jose M	Head	M	Cha	63	M	N	Y	Guam	N	Farmer
32		154	236	Arceo, Natividad N	Wife	F	Cha	62	M	N	N	Guam	N	None
33		154	236	Arceo, Guadalupe N	Daughter	F	Cha	28	S	N	Y	Guam	Y	None
34		154	237	Arceo, Maria A	Head	F	Cha	70	Wd	N	Y	Guam	N	None
35		155	238	Perez, Jose	Head	M	Cha	44	M	N	Y	Guam	Y	Farmer
36		155	238	Perez, Maria L	Wife	F	Cha	29	M	N	Y	Guam	Y	None
37		155	238	Perez, Rosario C	Daughter	F	Cha	16	S	N	Y	Guam	Y	None
38		155	238	Perez, Concepcion C	Daughter	F	Cha	10	S	Y		Guam		None
39		155	238	Perez, Vicente C	Son	M	Cha	6	S	Y		Guam		None
40		155	238	Perez, Francisco L	Son	M	Cha	3.9	S			Guam		None
41		155	238	Perez, Rosa L	Daughter	F	Cha	2.6	S			Guam		None
42		155	238	Perez, Jose L	Son	M	Cha	1.2	S			Guam		None
43		155	238	Perez, Eloy L	Son	M	Cha	0.2	S			Guam		None
44		155	238	Myers, Guadalupe S	Sister	F	Cha	67	S	N	N	Guam	N	None
45		156	239	Lizama, Vicente D	Head	M	Cha	33	M	N	Y	Guam	Y	Farmer
46		156	239	Lizama, Guadalupe C	Wife	F	Cha	32	M	N	Y	Guam	Y	None
47		156	239	Lizama, Jesus C	Son	M	Cha	3.6	S			Guam		None
48		156	239	Lizama, Maria C	Daughter	F	Cha	1.9	S			Guam		None
49		157	240	Quintanilla, Ignacio R	Head	M	Cha	31	M	N	Y	Guam	Y	Farmer
50		157	240	Quintanilla, Caridad P	Wife	F	Cha	25	M	N	Y	Guam	Y	Laundress

(CHAMORRO ROOTS GENEALOGY PROJECT™ TRANSCRIPTION)
(BERNARD T. PUNZALAN / HTTP://WWW.CHAMORROROOTS.COM)

DEPARTMENT OF COMMERCE-BUREAU OF THE CENSUS
WASHINGTON

FIFTEENTH CENSUS OF THE UNITED STATES: 1930-POPULATION

THE ISLAND OF GUAM

Sheet No. 21A

District **Municipality Sumay**
Name of Place **Sumay Town**
[Proper name and, also, name of class, as city, town, village, barrio, etc]

Enumeration District No. **11**
Enumerated by me on **April 14, 1930** **Joaquin C. Diaz**, Enumerator

	PLACE OF ABODE			NAME	RELATION	PERSONAL DESCRIPTION				EDUCATION		NATIVITY		OCCUPATION
	Street, avenue, road, etc.	Number of dwelling house in order of visitation	Number of family in order of visitation	of each person whose place of abode on April 1, 1930, was in this family. Enter surname, first, then given name and middle initial. If any. Include every person living on April 1, 1930. Omit children born since April 1, 1930.	Relationship of this Person to the head of the family.	Sex	Color or race	Age at last birthday	Single, married, widowed or divorced	Attended school any time since Sept. 1, 1929	Whether able to read and write.	Place of birth of this person.	Whether able to speak English.	
	1	2	3	4	5	6	7	8	9	10	11	12	13	14
1	Togai Street	157	240	Quintanilla, Jesusa P	Daughter	F	Cha	5	S			Guam		None
2		157	240	Quintanilla, Jesus P	Son	M	Cha	2.1	S			Guam		None
3		157	240	Quintanilla, Antonio P	Son	M	Cha	1.1	S			Guam		None
4		158	241	Mafnas, Joaquin C	Head	M	Cha	32	M	N	Y	Guam	Y	Farmer
5		158	241	Mafnas, Rosalia T	Wife	F	Cha	28	M	N	Y	Guam	Y	Laundress
6		158	241	Mafnas, Consolacion T	Daughter	F	Cha	7	S	Y		Guam		None
7		158	241	Mafnas, Jose T	Son	M	Cha	5	S			Guam		None
8		158	241	Mafnas, Juan T	Son	M	Cha	3.8	S			Guam		None
9		158	241	Mafnas, Antonio T	Son	M	Cha	0.1	S			Guam		None
10		158	242	Taitano, Maria P	Head	F	Cha	64	Wd	N	N	Guam	N	None
11		159	243	Grey, Paul	Head	M	W	64	M	N	N	Germany	Y	Farmer
12		159	243	Grey, Rosario C	Wife	F	Cha	54	M	N	Y	Guam	Y	None
13		159	243	Grey, Wilhelmina C	Daughter	F	W	32	S	Y	Y	Guam	Y	None
14		159	243	Grey, Gustav C	Son	M	W	12	S	Y	Y	Guam	Y	None
15		159	243	Grey, Nicolas C	Son	M	W	10	S	Y		Guam		None
16		159	243	Maekawa, Aurelia D	Sister-in-law	F	Jap	22	S	N	Y	Guam	Y	Sales woman
17		160	244	Reyes, Luis T	Head	M	Cha	59	M	N	Y	Guam	N	Farmer
18		160	244	Reyes, Dolores P	Wife	F	Cha	54	M	N	Y	Guam	N	None
19		160	244	Reyes, Jose P	Son	M	Cha	26	S	N	Y	Guam	Y	None
20		160	244	Reyes, Rosa P	Daughter	F	Cha	21	S	N	Y	Guam	Y	None
21		160	244	Reyes, Trinidad P	Daughter	F	Cha	17	S	N	Y	Guam	Y	None
22		160	244	Reyes, Salome P	Daughter	F	Cha	13	S	Y	Y	Guam	Y	None
23		160	244	Reyes, Concepcion P	Grand daughter	F	Cha	0.2	S			Guam		None
24		161	245	Sanchez, Teodoro S	Head	M	Cha	38	M	N	Y	Guam	Y	Farmer
25		161	245	Sanchez, Eliza S	Wife	F	Cha	32	M	N	Y	Guam	Y	None

DEPARTMENT OF COMMERCE-BUREAU OF THE CENSUS
WASHINGTON

FIFTEENTH CENSUS OF THE UNITED STATES: 1930-POPULATION

THE ISLAND OF GUAM

Sheet No. 21B

271b

District **Municipality Sumay**
Name of Place **Sumay Town**
[Proper name and, also, name of class, as city, town, village, barrio, etc]

Enumeration District No. **11**
Enumerated by me on **April 14, 1930** **Joaquin C. Diaz**, Enumerator

	PLACE OF ABODE			NAME	RELATION	PERSONAL DESCRIPTION				EDUCATION		NATIVITY		OCCUPATION
	Street, avenue, road, etc.	Number of dwelling house is order of visitation	Number of family in order of visitation	of each person whose place of abode on April 1, 1930, was in this family. Enter surname, first, then given name and middle initial. If any. Include every person living on April 1, 1930. Omit children born since April 1, 1930.	Relationship of this Person to the head of the family.	Sex	Color or race	Age at last birthday	Single, married, widowed or divorced	Attended school any time since Sept. 1, 1929	Whether able to read and write.	Place of birth of this person.	Whether able to speak English.	
	1	2	3	4	5	6	7	8	9	10	11	12	13	14
26	Togai Street	161	246	Duenas, Maria D	Head	F	Cha	63	S	N	Y	Guam	N	None
27		162	247	Santos, Luis Q	Head	M	Cha	38	S	N	Y	Guam	N	Farmer
28		162	247	Santos, Rita Q	Sister	F	Cha	40	S	N	Y	Guam	N	Laundress
29		162	247	Santos, Emiliana Q	Sister	F	Cha	43	S	N	N	Guam	N	Laundress
30		162	247	Santos, Thomas Q	Nephew	M	Cha	20	S	N	Y	Guam	Y	Servant
31		162	248	Babauta, Carmen C	Head	F	Cha	34	Wd	N	Y	Guam	N	None
32		22	32	Borja, Rita M	Grand daughter	F	Cha	9	S	Y		Guam		None
33					~~Here ends the enumeration of Sumay Town.~~									
34					[Note: lines 33 through 50 were left blank by the Enumerator.]									
35														
36														
37														
38														
39														
40														
41														
42														
43														
44														
45														
46														
47														
48														
49														
50														

DEPARTMENT OF COMMERCE-BUREAU OF THE CENSUS
WASHINGTON

FIFTEENTH CENSUS OF THE UNITED STATES: 1930-POPULATION

THE ISLAND OF GUAM

Sheet No. 22A

District **Municipality Sumay**
Name of Place **Sumay Town**
[Proper name and, also, name of class, as city, town, village, barrio, etc]

Enumeration District No. **11**
Enumerated by me on **April 15, 1930** **Joaquin C. Diaz**, Enumerator

	PLACE OF ABODE: Street, avenue, road, etc.	Number of dwelling house in order of visitation	Number of family in order of visitation	NAME of each person whose place of abode on April 1, 1930, was in this family. Enter surname, first, then given name and middle initial. If any. Include every person living on April 1, 1930. Omit children born since April 1, 1930.	RELATION Relationship of this Person to the head of the family.	PERSONAL DESCRIPTION: Sex	Color or race	Age at last birthday	Single, married, widowed or divorced	EDUCATION: Attended school any time since Sept. 1, 1929	Whether able to read and write.	NATIVITY Place of birth of this person.	Whether able to speak English.	OCCUPATION
	1	2	3	4	5	6	7	8	9	10	11	12	13	14
1	[no street listed]	163	249	Degracia, Manuel B	Head	M	Fil	35	M	N	Y	Guam	Y	Carpenter
2		163	249	Degracia, Dolores T	Wife	F	Fil	36	M	N	N	Guam	N	None
3		163	249	Degracia, Monica T	Daughter	F	Fil	10	S	Y		Guam		None
4		163	249	Degracia, Ana T	Daughter	F	Fil	10	S	Y		Guam		None
5		163	249	Degracia, Esteban T	Son	M	Fil	8	S	Y		Guam		None
6		163	249	Degracia, Elena T	Daughter	F	Fil	6	S			Guam		None
7		163	249	Degracia, Francisco T	Son	M	Fil	6	S			Guam		None
8		164	250	Cruz, Vicente C	Head	M	Cha	42	Wd	N	Y	Guam	Y	Farmer
9		164	250	Cruz, Trinidad A	Daughter	F	Cha	20	S	N	Y	Guam	Y	None
10		165	251	Anderson, Concepcion D	Head	F	Cha	30	M	N	Y	Guam	Y	None
11		165	251	Anderson, Maria D	Daughter	F	Cha	10	S	Y		Guam		None
12		165	251	Anderson, Antonio D	Son	M	Cha	7	S	Y		Guam		None
13		165	251	Anderson, Rosa D	Daughter	F	Cha	5	S			Guam		None
14		165	251	Anderson, Gertrudes D	Daughter	F	Cha	2.8	S			Guam		None
15		165	251	Anderson, Isabel D	Daughter	F	Cha	0.8	S			Guam		None
16		165	252	Duenas, Antonio S	Head	M	Cha	58	Wd	N	Y	Guam	N	Farmer
17		165	252	Duenas, Jose C	Son	M	Cha	25	S	N	Y	Guam	Y	Laborer
18		165	252	Duenas, Carmen C	Daughter	F	Cha	17	S	N	Y	Guam	Y	None
19		166	253	Diaz, Juan M	Head	M	Cha	45	M	N	Y	Guam	Y	Farmer
20		166	253	Diaz, Ana P	Wife	F	Cha	42	M	N	Y	Guam	Y	None
21		166	253	Diaz, Ana P	Daughter	F	Cha	14	S	Y	Y	Guam	Y	None
22		166	253	Diaz, Dolores P	Daughter	F	Cha	11	S	Y	Y	Guam	N	None
23		166	253	Diaz, Elpidia P	Daughter	F	Cha	9	S	Y		Guam		None
24		166	253	Diaz, Vicente P	Son	M	Cha	6	S			Guam		None
25		166	253	Diaz, Manuel P	Son	M	Cha	4.4	S			Guam		None

(CHAMORRO ROOTS GENEALOGY PROJECT™ TRANSCRIPTION)
(BERNARD T. PUNZALAN / HTTP://WWW.CHAMORROROOTS.COM)

DEPARTMENT OF COMMERCE-BUREAU OF THE CENSUS
WASHINGTON

FIFTEENTH CENSUS OF THE UNITED STATES: 1930-POPULATION

THE ISLAND OF GUAM

Sheet No. 22B

272b

District **Municipality Sumay**
Name of Place **Sumay Town**
[Proper name and, also, name of class, as city, town, village, barrio, etc]

Enumeration District No. **11**
Enumerated by me on **April 15, 1930** **Joaquin C. Diaz**
Enumerator

	PLACE OF ABODE			NAME	RELATION	PERSONAL DESCRIPTION				EDUCATION		NATIVITY		OCCUPATION
	Street, avenue, road, etc.	Number of dwelling house is order of visitation	Number of family in order of visitation	of each person whose place of abode on April 1, 1930, was in this family. Enter surname, first, then given name and middle initial. If any. Include every person living on April 1, 1930. Omit children born since April 1, 1930.	Relationship of this Person to the head of the family.	Sex	Color or race	Age at last birthday	Single, married, widowed or divorced	Attended school any time since Sept. 1, 1929	Whether able to read and write.	Place of birth of this person.	Whether able to speak English.	
	1	2	3	4	5	6	7	8	9	10	11	12	13	14
26	[no street listed]	166	253	Diaz, Regina P	Daughter	F	Cha	1.3	S			Guam		None
27		167	254	Duenas, Carmelo S	Head	M	Cha	53	M	N	Y	Guam	N	Farmer
28		167	254	Duenas, Carmen A	Wife	F	Cha	43	M	N	N	Guam	N	None
29		167	254	Duenas, Enrique A	Son	M	Cha	6	S			Guam		None
30		167	254	Duenas, Pedro A	Son	M	Cha	4.1	S			Guam		None
31		167	254	Aquiningoc, Francisco	Nephew	M	Cha	14	S	N	N	Guam	N	None
32		167	255	Aquiningoc, Jesus C	Head	M	Cha	26	M	N	Y	Guam	Y	Laborer
33		167	255	Aquiningoc, Maria R	Wife	F	Cha	26	M	N	Y	Guam	N	None
34		167	255	Aquiningoc, Jesus R	Son	M	Cha	0.2	S			Guam		None
35		168	256	Ulloa, Mariano D	Head	M	Cha	53	M	N	Y	Guam	Y	Farmer
36		168	256	Ulloa, Rosa G	Wife	F	Cha	52	M	N	N	Guam	N	None
37		168	256	Ulloa, Joaquina G	Daughter	F	Cha	16	S	N	Y	Guam	Y	Laundress
38		168	257	Sablan, Pedro P	Head	M	Cha	32	M	N	Y	Guam	Y	Farmer
39		168	257	Sablan, Maria U	Wife	F	Cha	25	M	N	Y	Guam	Y	Laundress
40		168	257	Sablan, Ramon U	Son	M	Cha	2.1	S			Guam		None
41		168	257	Sablan, Francisco U	Son	M	Cha	1.8	S			Guam		None
42		168	257	Sablan, Juan U	Son	M	Cha	0.5	S			Guam		None
43		169	258	Borja, Jose S	Head	M	Cha	43	M	N	Y	Guam	Y	Farmer
44		169	258	Borja, Soledad M	Wife	F	Cha	39	M	N	Y	Guam	N	None
45		169	258	Borja, Ana S	Daughter	F	Cha	6	S			Guam		None
46		169	258	Borja, Dolores M	Daughter	F	Cha	3.7	S			Guam		None
47		170	259	Borja, Francisco S	Head	M	Cha	37	M	N	Y	Guam	Y	Carpenter
48		170	259	Borja, Isabel M	Wife	F	Cha	30	M	N	Y	Guam	Y	None
49		170	259	Borja, Vicente M	Son	M	Cha	8	S	Y		Guam		None
50		170	259	Borja, Isabel M	Daughter	F	Cha	5	S			Guam		None

DEPARTMENT OF COMMERCE-BUREAU OF THE CENSUS
WASHINGTON

FIFTEENTH CENSUS OF THE UNITED STATES: 1930-POPULATION
THE ISLAND OF GUAM

Sheet No. 23A

District **Municipality Sumay**
Name of Place **Sumay Town** [Proper name and, also, name of class, as city, town, village, barrio, etc]

Enumeration District No. **11**
Enumerated by me on **April 16, 1930** **Joaquin C. Diaz** Enumerator

	PLACE OF ABODE			NAME	RELATION	PERSONAL DESCRIPTION				EDUCATION		NATIVITY		OCCUPATION
	Street, avenue, road, etc.	Number of dwelling house is order of visitation	Number of family in order of visitation	of each person whose place of abode on April 1, 1930, was in this family. Enter surname, first, then given name and middle initial. If any. Include every person living on April 1, 1930. Omit children born since April 1, 1930.	Relationship of this Person to the head of the family.	Sex	Color or race	Age at last birthday	Single, married, widowed or divorced	Attended school any time since Sept. 1, 1929	Whether able to read and write.	Place of birth of this person.	Whether able to speak English.	
	1	2	3	4	5	6	7	8	9	10	11	12	13	14
1	[no street listed]	170	259	Borja, Jose M	Son	M	Cha	3.1	S			Guam		None
2		170	259	Borja, Francisco M	Son	M	Cha	2.1	S			Guam		None
3		170	259	Borja, Jesus M	Son	M	Cha	0.5	S			Guam		None
4		171	260	De La Cruz, Blas	Head	M	Cha	33	M	N	Y	Guam	Y	Farmer
5		171	260	De La Cruz, Natividad R	Wife	F	Cha	35	M	N	Y	Guam	N	None
6		171	260	De La Cruz, Antonio R	Son	M	Cha	6	S			Guam		None
7		171	260	De La Cruz, Beatrice R	Daughter	F	Cha	4.1	S			Guam		None
8		171	260	De La Cruz, Jose R	Son	M	Cha	1.2	S			Guam		None
9		172	261	Cruz, Jose A	Head	M	Cha	37	M	N	Y	Guam	N	Farmer
10		172	261	Cruz, Felicita P	Wife	F	Cha	26	M	N	N	Guam	N	None
11		173	262	Rabago, Juan C	Head	M	Cha	29	M	N	Y	Guam	Y	Farmer
12		173	262	Rabago, Natividad J	Wife	F	Cha	25	M	N	Y	Guam	Y	None
13		173	262	Rabago, Jose J	Son	M	Cha	2.6	S			Guam		None
14		173	262	Rabago, Vicente J	Son	M	Cha	0.2	S			Guam		None
15		174	263	Rabago, Josefa C	Head	F	Cha	62	Wd	N	N	Guam	N	None
16		174	263	Rabago, Jose C	Son	M	Cha	34	S	N	Y	Guam	Y	Farmer
17		174	263	Rabago, Enrique C	Son	M	Cha	21	S	N	Y	Guam	Y	Farm laborer
18		175	264	Santos, Felis T	Head	M	Cha	35	M	N	Y	Guam	Y	Carpenter
19		175	264	Santos, Ana R	Wife	F	Cha	33	M	N	N	Guam	N	None
20		175	264	Santos, Jesus R	Son	M	Cha	8	S	Y		Guam		None
21		175	264	Santos, Isabel R	Daughter	F	Cha	2	S			Guam		None
22		175	264	Santos, Juan R	Son	M	Cha	1.7	S			Guam		None
23		176	265	Santos, Antonio B	Head	M	Cha	35	M	N	Y	Guam	Y	Farmer
24		176	265	Santos, Maria H	Wife	F	Cha	35	M	N	Y	Guam	Y	None
25		176	265	Santos, Isabel H	Daughter	F	Cha	14	S	N	Y	Guam	Y	None

(CHAMORRO ROOTS GENEALOGY PROJECT™ TRANSCRIPTION)
(BERNARD T. PUNZALAN / HTTP://WWW.CHAMORROROOTS.COM)

DEPARTMENT OF COMMERCE-BUREAU OF THE CENSUS
WASHINGTON

FIFTEENTH CENSUS OF THE UNITED STATES: 1930-POPULATION

THE ISLAND OF GUAM

Sheet No. 23B

273b

District **Municipality Sumay**
Name of Place **Sumay Town**
[Proper name and, also, name of class, as city, town, village, barrio, etc]

Enumeration District No. **11**
Enumerated by me on **April 16, 1930** **Joaquin C. Diaz**, Enumerator

	PLACE OF ABODE			NAME	RELATION	PERSONAL DESCRIPTION				EDUCATION		NATIVITY		OCCUPATION
	Street, avenue, road, etc.	Number of dwelling house in order of visitation	Number of family in order of visitation	of each person whose place of abode on April 1, 1930, was in this family. Enter surname, first, then given name and middle initial. If any. Include every person living on April 1, 1930. Omit children born since April 1, 1930.	Relationship of this Person to the head of the family.	Sex	Color or race	Age at last birthday	Single, married, widowed or divorced	Attended school any time since Sept. 1, 1929	Whether able to read and write.	Place of birth of this person.	Whether able to speak English.	
	1	2	3	4	5	6	7	8	9	10	11	12	13	14
26	[no street listed]	176	265	Santos, Aurelia H	Daughter	F	Cha	12	S	Y	Y	Guam	Y	None
27		176	265	Santos, Maria A	Daughter	F	Cha	0.6	S			Guam		None
28		176	265	Cruz, Antonio D	Servant	M	Cha	59	Wd	N	N	Guam	N	Farm laborer
29		176	265	Cruz, Joaquina D	Servant	F	Cha	16	S	N	Y	Guam	N	Servant
30		177	266	Nededog, Juan N	Head	M	Cha	70	M	N	Y	Guam	N	Farmer
31		177	266	Nededog, Antonia P	Wife	F	Cha	60	M	N	N	Guam	N	None
32		177	266	Nededog, Ignacio P	Son	M	Cha	27	S	N	Y	Guam	N	Farm laborer
33		177	266	Nededog, Veronica P	Daughter	F	Cha	20	S	N	Y	Guam	Y	Laundress
34		177	266	Nededog, Enrique P	Daughter	F	Cha	16	S	N	Y	Guam	N	Farm laborer
35		177	266	Nededog, Magdalena P	Grand daughter	F	Cha	13	S	Y	Y	Guam	Y	None
36		178	267	Taeanao, Carmelo M	Head	M	Cha	38	M	N	Y	Guam	N	Farmer
37		178	267	Taeanao, Joaquina C	Wife	F	Cha	33	M	N	N	Guam	N	None
38		178	267	Taeanao, Jesus C	Son	M	Cha	12	S	Y	Y	Guam	Y	None
39		178	267	Taeanao, Dolores C	Daughter	F	Cha	3.1	S			Guam		None
40		178	267	Taeanao, Francisco C	Son	M	Cha	0.1	S			Guam		None
41		179	267	Unsiok, Sisto	Head	M	Cha	38	S	N	Y	Guam	Y	Farmer
42		179	267	Baleto, Andrea	Mother	F	Cha	60	M	N	N	Guam	N	None
43		179	267	Unsiok, Carmelo N	Nephew	M	Cha	4	S			Guam		None
44		180	269	Quintanilla, Jesus L	Head	M	Cha	33	M	N	N	Guam	N	Farm laborer
45		180	269	Quintanilla, Luisa M	Wife	F	Cha	29	M	N	N	Guam	N	None
46		180	269	Quintanilla, Dolores M	Daughter	F	Cha	7	S	Y		Guam		None
47		180	269	Jesus, Felix	Border	M	Cha	21	S	N	Y	Guam	N	Farm laborer
48		181	270	Lizama, Agustin A	Head	M	Cha	35	M	N	Y	Guam	N	Farmer
49		181	270	Lizama, Dolores C	Wife	F	Cha	30	M	N	Y	Guam	N	Laundress
50		181	270	Lizama, Cristina C	Daughter	F	Cha	11	S	Y	Y	Guam	N	None

D-11-47

DEPARTMENT OF COMMERCE-BUREAU OF THE CENSUS
WASHINGTON

FIFTEENTH CENSUS OF THE UNITED STATES: 1930-POPULATION

THE ISLAND OF GUAM

Sheet No. 24A

District Municipality Sumay
Name of Place Sumay Town
[Proper name and, also, name of class, as city, town, village, barrio, etc]

Enumeration District No. 11
Enumerated by me on April 17, 1930 Joaquin C. Diaz, Enumerator

	PLACE OF ABODE			NAME	RELATION	PERSONAL DESCRIPTION				EDUCATION		NATIVITY		OCCUPATION
	Street, avenue, road, etc.	Number of dwelling house in order of visitation	Number of family in order of visitation	of each person whose place of abode on April 1, 1930, was in this family. Enter surname, first, then given name and middle initial. If any. Include every person living on April 1, 1930. Omit children born since April 1, 1930.	Relationship of this Person to the head of the family.	Sex	Color or race	Age at last birthday	Single, married, widowed or divorced	Attended school any time since Sept. 1, 1929	Whether able to read and write.	Place of birth of this person.	Whether able to speak English.	
	1	2	3	4	5	6	7	8	9	10	11	12	13	14
1	[no street listed]	181	270	Perez, Maria C	Step daughter	F	Cha	11	S	Y	Y	Guam	N	None
2		181	271	Cruz, Maria L	Head	F	Cha	60	Wd	N	N	Guam	N	None
3		182	272	Unsiok, Benefacio J	Head	M	Cha	40	M	N	Y	Guam	Y	Farmer
4		182	272	Unsiok, Maria N	Wife	F	Cha	39	M	N	N	Guam	N	None
5		182	272	Unsiok, Jose N	Son	M	Cha	11	S	Y	Y	Guam	Y	None
6		182	272	Unsiok, Ana N	Daughter	F	Cha	6	S			Guam		None
7		182	272	Unsiok, Agustin N	Son	M	Cha	3	S			Guam		None
8		182	272	Unsiok, Rosa N	Daughter	F	Cha	0.7	S			Guam		None
9		183	273	Sanchez, Lorenzo Q	Head	M	Cha	41	M	N	N	Guam	N	Farmer
10		183	273	Sanchez, Amparo G	Wife	F	Cha	47	M	N	N	Guam	N	None
11		183	273	Sanchez, Vicenta F	Cousin	F	Cha	90	S	N	N	Guam	N	None
12		183	273	Quinata, Mariano S	Nephew	M	Cha	11	S	Y	Y	Guam	Y	None
13		183	273	Quinata, Luisa S	Niece	F	Cha	6	S			Guam		None
14		183	274	Quinata, Lucio M	Head	M	Cha	33	M	N	Y	Guam	Y	Laborer
15		183	274	Quinata, Feliciana T	Wife	F	Cha	35	M	N	N	Guam	N	Laundress
16		183	274	Quinata, Lucia T	Daughter	F	Cha	3.1	S			Guam		None
17		184	274	Duenas, Vicente A	Head	M	Cha	44	S	N	Y	Guam	Y	None
18		185	275	Degracia, Rosa A	Head	F	Cha	41	Wd	N	N	Guam	N	None
19		185	275	Degracia, Lorenzo A	Son	M	Fil	18	S	N	Y	Guam	Y	Farmer
20		185	275	Degracia, Antonio A	Son	M	Fil	17	S	N	Y	Guam	Y	Laundress
21		185	275	Degracia, Clemete A	Son	M	Fil	8	S	Y		Guam		None
22		185	275	Degracia, Petronila A	Daughter	F	Fil	4.3	S			Guam		None
23		185	275	Degracia, Gregorio A	Son	M	Fil	1.5	S			Guam		None
24		186	276	Santos, Antonio M	Head	M	Cha	40	M	N	N	Guam	N	Farmer
25		186	276	Santos, Catalina D	Wife	F	Cha	29	M	N	N	Guam	N	None

DEPARTMENT OF COMMERCE-BUREAU OF THE CENSUS
WASHINGTON

FIFTEENTH CENSUS OF THE UNITED STATES: 1930-POPULATION

THE ISLAND OF GUAM

Sheet No. 24B

274b

District **Municipality Sumay**

Name of Place **Sumay Town** [Proper name and, also, name of class, as city, town, village, barrio, etc]

Enumeration District No. **11**

Enumerated by me on **April 19, 1930** **Joaquin C. Diaz**, Enumerator

	PLACE OF ABODE			NAME	RELATION	PERSONAL DESCRIPTION				EDUCATION		NATIVITY		OCCUPATION
	Street, avenue, road, etc.	Number of dwelling house in order of visitation	Number of family in order of visitation	of each person whose place of abode on April 1, 1930, was in this family. Enter surname, first, then given name and middle initial. If any. Include every person living on April 1, 1930. Omit children born since April 1, 1930.	Relationship of this Person to the head of the family.	Sex	Color or race	Age at last birthday	Single, married, widowed or divorced	Attended school any time since Sept. 1, 1929	Whether able to read and write.	Place of birth of this person.	Whether able to speak English.	
	1	2	3	4	5	6	7	8	9	10	11	12	13	14
26	[no street listed]	186	276	Santos, Ignacio D	Son	M	Cha	11	S	Y	Y	Guam	Y	None
27		186	276	Santos, Aniceto D	Son	M	Cha	7	S	Y		Guam		None
28		186	276	Santos, Cecilia D	Daughter	F	Cha	5	S			Guam		None
29		186	276	Santos, Jesus D	Son	M	Cha	2.5	S			Guam		None
30		186	276	Santos, Vicente D	Son	M	Cha	0.9	S			Guam		None
31		187	277	Reyes, Jose T	Head	M	Cha	30	S	N	N	Guam	N	Farmer
32		187	278	Duenas, Veronica Q	Head	F	Cha	23	S	N	Y	Guam	Y	Weaver
33					[Note: Lines 33 through 50 were left blank by the Enumerator.]									
34														
35														
36														
37														
38														
39														
40														
41														
42														
43														
44														
45														
46														
47														
48														
49														
50														

(CHAMORRO ROOTS GENEALOGY PROJECT™ TRANSCRIPTION)
(BERNARD T. PUNZALAN / HTTP://WWW.CHAMORROROOTS.COM)

DEPARTMENT OF COMMERCE-BUREAU OF THE CENSUS
WASHINGTON

FIFTEENTH CENSUS OF THE UNITED STATES: 1930-POPULATION

THE ISLAND OF GUAM

Sheet No. 25A

District **Municipality Sumay**
Name of Place **Sumay Town** [Proper name and, also, name of class, as city, town, village, barrio, etc]

Enumeration District No. **11**
Enumerated by me on **April 21, 1930** **Joaquin C. Diaz**, Enumerator

	PLACE OF ABODE: Street, avenue, road, etc.	Number of dwelling house in order of visitation	Number of family in order of visitation	NAME of each person whose place of abode on April 1, 1930, was in this family. Enter surname, first, then given name and middle initial. If any. Include every person living on April 1, 1930. Omit children born since April 1, 1930.	RELATION Relationship of this Person to the head of the family.	PERSONAL DESCRIPTION: Sex	Color or race	Age at last birthday	Single, married, widowed or divorced	EDUCATION: Attended school any time since Sept. 1, 1929	Whether able to read and write.	NATIVITY Place of birth of this person.	Whether able to speak English.	OCCUPATION
	1	2	3	4	5	6	7	8	9	10	11	12	13	14
1	[no street listed]	188	279	Mullahey, Thomas F	Head	M	W	45	M	N	Y	New York	Y	Superintendant Cable Station
2		188	279	Mullahey, Mary A	Wife	F	W	45	M	N	Y	California	Y	None
3		188	279	Mullahey, Thomas Jr	Son	M	W	10	S	Y	Y	California	Y	None
4		189	280	Hayes, May C	Head	F	W	28	M	N	Y	South Carolina	Y	None
5		189	281	Meza, Francisco P	Head	M	Cha	20	S	N	Y	Guam	Y	Servant
6		189	282	Harrison, N E	Head	M	W	35	M	N	Y	California	Y	Cable operator
7		189	283	Horvick, Paul I	Head	M	W	47	S	N	Y	Norway	Y	Machinist
8		190	284	Fodden, George G	Head	M	W	42	M	N	Y	Nova Scotia	Y	Submarine telegraphy
9		190	284	Fodden, Mildred J	Wife	F	W	42	M	N	Y	Nova Scotia	Y	None
10		191	285	Kuhnz, Eugene S	Head	M	W	27	M	N	Y	Hawaii	Y	Cable operator
11		191	286	Zilvach, William C	Head	M	W	34	S	N	Y	New York	Y	Cable operator
12		192	287	Torres, Jesus P	Head	M	Cha	25	S	N	Y	Guam	Y	Servant
13		193	288	Alcantara, Maria S	Head	F	Cha	47	Wd	N	Y	Guam	N	None
14		193	288	Alcantara, Luis S	Son	M	Cha	21	S	N	Y	Guam	Y	Laborer
15		193	278	Babauta, Felix SN	Head	M	Cha	21	S	N	Y	Guam	Y	Servant
16		194	290	Gumataotao, Francisco B	Head	M	Cha	45	M	N	N	Guam	N	Farmer
17		194	290	Gumataotao, Mariano P	Son	M	Cha	12	S	Y	Y	Guam	N	None
18		194	290	Gumataotao, Juan P	Son	M	Cha	8	S	Y		Guam		None
19		195	291	Cruz, Mariano M	Head	M	Cha	42	M	N	Y	Guam	Y	Farmer
20		195	291	Cruz, Maria SN	Wife	F	Cha	55	M	N	N	Guam	N	None
21		195	291	Cruz, Regina SN	Daughter	F	Cha	12	S	Y	Y	Guam	N	None
22		195	291	Cruz, Francisca SN	Daughter	F	Cha	10	S	Y		Guam		None
23		196	292	Borja, Joaquin T	Head	M	Cha	52	M	N	Y	Guam	Y	Farmer
24		196	292	Borja, Dolores A	Wife	F	Cha	42	M	N	N	Guam	N	None
25		196	292	Borja, Julian A	Son	M	Cha	16	S	N	Y	Guam	Y	Servant

(CHAMORRO ROOTS GENEALOGY PROJECT™ TRANSCRIPTION)
(BERNARD T. PUNZALAN / HTTP://WWW.CHAMORROROOTS.COM)

DEPARTMENT OF COMMERCE-BUREAU OF THE CENSUS
WASHINGTON

FIFTEENTH CENSUS OF THE UNITED STATES: 1930-POPULATION

THE ISLAND OF GUAM

Sheet No. 25B

275b

District **Municipality Sumay**
Name of Place **Sumay Town** [Proper name and, also, name of class, as city, town, village, barrio, etc]

Enumeration District No. **11**
Enumerated by me on **April 22, 1930** **Joaquin C. Diaz**, Enumerator

	PLACE OF ABODE: Street, avenue, road, etc.	Number of dwelling house in order of visitation	Number of family in order of visitation	NAME of each person whose place of abode on April 1, 1930, was in this family. Enter surname, first, then given name and middle initial. If any. Include every person living on April 1, 1930. Omit children born since April 1, 1930.	RELATION Relationship of this Person to the head of the family.	PERSONAL DESCRIPTION: Sex	Color or race	Age at last birthday	Single, married, widowed or divorced	EDUCATION: Attended school any time since Sept. 1, 1929	Whether able to read and write.	NATIVITY Place of birth of this person.	Whether able to speak English.	OCCUPATION
	1	2	3	4	5	6	7	8	9	10	11	12	13	14
26	[no street listed]	196	292	Borja, Gregorio A	Son	M	Cha	14	S	Y	Y	Guam	Y	None
27		196	292	Borja, Manuel A	Son	M	Cha	11	S	N	N	Guam	N	None
28		196	292	Borja, Antonio A	Son	M	Cha	10	S	Y		Guam		None
29		197	283	Hamamoto, I	Head	M	Jap	51	M	N	Y	Guam	N	Farmer
30		197	283	Hamamoto, Maria A	Wife	F	Cha	37	M	N	Y	Guam	Y	None
31		197	283	Hamamoto, Juanita A	Daughter	F	Jap	15	S	N	Y	Guam	Y	None
32		197	283	Hamamoto, Maria A	Daughter	F	Jap	13	S	Y	Y	Guam	Y	None
33		197	283	Hamamoto, Concepcion A	Daughter	F	Jap	11	S	Y	Y	Guam	Y	None
34		197	283	Hamamoto, Jesus A	Son	M	Jap	10	S	Y	Y	Guam	Y	None
35		197	283	Hamamoto, Francisco A	Son	M	Jap	6	S			Guam		None
36		197	283	Hamamoto, Dolores A	Daughter	F	Jap	3.2	S			Guam		None
37		197	283	Hamamoto, Jose A	Son	M	Jap	1.3	S			Guam		None
38		198	294	Toves, Juan T	Head	F	Cha	30	M	N	Y	Guam	Y	Cable operator
39		198	294	Toves, Consolacion A	Wife	F	Cha	25	M	N	Y	Guam	Y	None
40		198	294	Toves, Harry A	Son	M	Cha	5	S			Guam		None
41		198	294	Toves, John A	Son	M	Cha	3.4	S			Guam		None
42		198	295	Aguigui, Guadalupe A	Head	F	Cha	20	S	N	Y	Guam	Y	Servant
43		199	296	Charfauros, Joaquin T	Head	M	Cha	29	S	N	Y	Guam	Y	Cable operator
44		200	297	Taitano, Vicente S	Head	M	Cha	29	M	N	Y	Saipan	Y	Laborer
45		200	297	Taitano, Maria D	Wife	F	Cha	28	M	N	Y	Guam	Y	None
46		200	297	Taitano, Amanda D	Daughter	F	Cha	5	S			Guam		None
47		200	297	Taitano, Ana D	Daughter	F	Cha	4	S			Guam		None
48		200	297	Taitano, Jesus D	Son	M	Cha	3	S			Guam		None
49		200	297	Taitano, Regina D	Daughter	F	Cha	2	S			Guam		None
50					Here ends the enumeration district of the Municipality of Sumay.									

District 12
Municipality of Yona

(CHAMORRO ROOTS GENEALOGY PROJECT™ TRANSCRIPTION)
(BERNARD T. PUNZALAN / HTTP://WWW.CHAMORROROOTS.COM)

DEPARTMENT OF COMMERCE-BUREAU OF THE CENSUS
WASHINGTON

FIFTEENTH CENSUS OF THE UNITED STATES: 1930-POPULATION

THE ISLAND OF GUAM

Sheet No. 1A

District **Municipality of Yona**
Name of Place **Yona Municipality**
[Proper name and, also, name of class, as city, town, village, barrio, etc]

Enumeration District No. **12**
Enumerated by me on **April 2, 1930** **Cayetano A. Quinata**
Enumerator

	PLACE OF ABODE			NAME	RELATION	PERSONAL DESCRIPTION				EDUCATION		NATIVITY		OCCUPATION
	Street, avenue, road, etc.	Number of dwelling house is order of visitation	Number of family in order of visitation	of each person whose place of abode on April 1, 1930, was in this family. Enter surname, first, then given name and middle initial. If any. Include every person living on April 1, 1930. Omit children born since April 1, 1930.	Relationship of this Person to the head of the family.	Sex	Color or race	Age at last birthday	Single, married, widowed or divorced	Attended school any time since Sept. 1, 1929	Whether able to read and write.	Place of birth of this person.	Whether able to speak English.	
	1	2	3	4	5	6	7	8	9	10	11	12	13	14
1	[no street]	1	1	Dimapan, Vicente I	Head	M	Cha	61	M	N	Y	Guam	Y	Farmer
2		1	1	Dimapan, Antonia A	Wife	F	Cha	55	M	N	Y	Guam	N	None
3		1	1	Tenorio, Magdalena T	Niece	F	Cha	11	S	Y	Y	Guam	Y	None
4		2	2	Balajadia, Joaquin J	Head	M	Cha	38	M	N	N	Guam	N	Farmer
5		2	2	Balajadia, Susana P	Wife	F	Cha	36	M	N	Y	Guam	N	None
6		2	2	Balajadia, Vicente P	Son	M	Cha	18	S	N	Y	Guam	Y	Farm laborer
7		2	2	Balajadia, Remedios P	Daughter	F	Cha	14	S	Y	Y	Guam	Y	None
8		2	2	Balajadia, Jose P	Son	M	Cha	11	S	Y	Y	Guam	Y	None
9		2	2	Balajadia, Pedro P	Son	M	Cha	8	S	Y	Y	Guam		None
10		2	2	Balajadia, Cecilia P	Daughter	F	Cha	3.25	S	N		Guam		None
11		2	2	Balajadia, Juan P	Son	M	Cha	1.25	S	N		Guam		None
12		3	3	Ogo, Francisco M	Head	M	Cha	47	M	N	Y	Guam	N	Farmer
13		3	3	Ogo, Magdalena O	Wife	F	Cha	46	M	N	N	Guam	N	None
14		3	3	Ogo, Jesus O	Son	M	Cha	18	S	Y	Y	Guam	Y	None
15		3	3	Ogo, Esperansa O	Daughter	F	Cha	17	S	N	Y	Guam	Y	None
16		3	3	Ogo, Eseqiel O	Son	M	Cha	8	S	Y		Guam		None
17		3	3	Ogo, Isabel O	Daughter	F	Cha	7	S	Y		Guam		None
18		4	4	Cruz, Raymundo C	Head	M	Cha	40	M	N	N	Guam	N	Farmer
19		4	4	Cruz, Ana T	Wife	F	Cha	40	M	N	N	Guam	N	None
20		4	4	Cruz, Maria T	Daughter	F	Cha	17	S	N	Y	Guam	Y	None
21		4	4	Cruz, Vicente T	Son	M	Cha	12	S	Y	Y	Guam	Y	None
22		4	4	Cruz, Francisco T	Son	M	Cha	10	S	Y	Y	Guam	Y	None
23		4	4	Cruz, Gonsalo T	Son	M	Cha	7	S	Y		Guam		None
24		4	4	Cruz, Pedro T	Son	M	Cha	4	S	N		Guam		None
25		5	5	Cruz, Joaquin C	Head	M	Cha	42	M	N	N	Guam	N	Farmer

DEPARTMENT OF COMMERCE-BUREAU OF THE CENSUS
WASHINGTON

FIFTEENTH CENSUS OF THE UNITED STATES: 1930-POPULATION

THE ISLAND OF GUAM

Sheet No. 1B

276b

District Municipality of Yona
Name of Place Yona Municipality
[Proper name and, also, name of class, as city, town, village, barrio, etc]

Enumeration District No. 12
Enumerated by me on April 2, 1930 Cayetano A. Quinata
Enumerator

	PLACE OF ABODE			NAME	RELATION	PERSONAL DESCRIPTION				EDUCATION		NATIVITY		OCCUPATION
	Street, avenue, road, etc.	Number of dwelling house is order of visitation	Number of family in order of visitation	of each person whose place of abode on April 1, 1930, was in this family. Enter surname, first, then given name and middle initial. If any. Include every person living on April 1, 1930. Omit children born since April 1, 1930.	Relationship of this Person to the head of the family.	Sex	Color or race	Age at last birthday	Single, married, widowed or divorced	Attended school any time since Sept. 1, 1929	Whether able to read and write.	Place of birth of this person.	Whether able to speak English.	
	1	2	3	4	5	6	7	8	9	10	11	12	13	14
26	[no street]	5	5	Cruz, Maria O	Wife	F	Cha	32	M	N	N	Guam	N	None
27		5	5	Cruz, Concepcion R	Daughter	F	Cha	19	S	N	Y	Guam	Y	None
28		5	5	Cruz, Rosalia R	Daughter	F	Cha	17	S	N	Y	Guam	Y	None
29		5	5	Cruz, Pedro R	Son	M	Cha	14	S	Y	Y	Guam	Y	None
30		5	5	Cruz, Maria O	Daughter	F	Cha	5.25	S	N		Guam		None
31		5	5	Cruz, Rita O	Daughter	F	Cha	3.1	S	N		Guam		None
32		5	5	Cruz, Jose O	Son	M	Cha	2.2	S	N		Guam		None
33		5	5	Cruz, Joaquin O	Son	M	Cha	1.1	S	N		Guam		None
34		6	6	Cruz, Manuel B	Head	M	Cha	34	M	N	Y	Guam	Y	Farmer
35		6	6	Cruz, Dometila Q	Wife	F	Cha	29	M	N	Y	Guam	Y	None
36		6	6	Cruz, Cristobal Q	Son	M	Cha	9	S	Y		Guam		None
37		6	6	Cruz, Maria Lourdes Q	Daughter	F	Cha	1.1	S	N		Guam		None
38		6	6	Fernandez, Carmen Q	Sister-in-law	F	Cha	20	S	N	Y	Guam	Y	Cook
39		6	6	Rodrigez, Maria R	Servant	F	Cha	44	S	N	N	Guam	N	Washer woman
40		6	6	Rodrigez, Vicente M	Servant	M	Cha	22	S	N	Y	Guam	Y	Farm laborer
41		6	6	Fernandez, Obdulia Q	Niece	F	Cha	0.6	S	N		Guam		None
42		7	7	Balajadia, Vicente M	Head	M	Cha	47	M	N	Y	Guam	N	Farmer
43		7	7	Balajadia, Ana S	Wife	F	Cha	46	M	N	Y	Guam	N	None
44		7	7	Balajadia, Felix S	Son	M	Cha	17	S	Y	Y	Guam	Y	Farm laborer
45		7	7	Balajadia, Jesus S	Son	M	Cha	10	S	Y	Y	Guam	Y	None
46		7	7	Balajadia, Maria S	Daughter	F	Cha	7	S	Y		Guam		None
47		8	8	Balajadia, Jose J	Head	M	Cha	45	M	N	Y	Guam	N	Farmer
48		8	8	Balajadia, Cornelia I	Wife	F	Cha	42	M	N	Y	Guam	N	None
49		8	8	Balajadia, Manuel I	Son	M	Cha	17	S	Y	Y	Guam	Y	Farm laborer
50		8	8	Balajadia, Catalina I	Daughter	F	Cha	15	S	N	Y	Guam	Y	None

(CHAMORRO ROOTS GENEALOGY PROJECT™ TRANSCRIPTION)
(BERNARD T. PUNZALAN / HTTP://WWW.CHAMORROROOTS.COM)

DEPARTMENT OF COMMERCE-BUREAU OF THE CENSUS
WASHINGTON

FIFTEENTH CENSUS OF THE UNITED STATES: 1930-POPULATION

THE ISLAND OF GUAM

Sheet No. 2A

277

District **Municipality of Yona**
Name of Place **Yona Municipality**
[Proper name and, also, name of class, as city, town, village, barrio, etc]

Enumeration District No. **12**
Enumerated by me on **April 2, 1930** **Cayetano A. Quinata**
Enumerator

	PLACE OF ABODE			NAME	RELATION	PERSONAL DESCRIPTION				EDUCATION		NATIVITY		OCCUPATION
	Street, avenue, road, etc.	Number of dwelling house is order of visitation	Number of family in order of visitation	of each person whose place of abode on April 1, 1930, was in this family. Enter surname, first, then given name and middle initial. If any. Include every person living on April 1, 1930. Omit children born since April 1, 1930.	Relationship of this Person to the head of the family.	Sex	Color or race	Age at last birthday	Single, married, widowed or divorced	Attended school any time since Sept. 1, 1929	Whether able to read and write.	Place of birth of this person.	Whether able to speak English.	
	1	2	3	4	5	6	7	8	9	10	11	12	13	14
1	[no street]	8	8	Balajadia, Jose I	Son	M	Cha	12	S	Y	Y	Guam	Y	None
2		8	8	Balajadia, Antonio I	Son	M	Cha	10	S	Y	Y	Guam	Y	None
3		8	8	Balajadia, Roman I	Son	M	Cha	8	S	Y		Guam		None
4		8	8	Balajadia, Pilar I	Daughter	F	Cha	6	S	N		Guam		None
5		8	8	Balajadia, Jesus I	Son	M	Cha	4.2	S	N		Guam		None
6		8	8	Balajadia, Elisa I	Daughter	F	Cha	2.3	S	N		Guam		None
7		8	8	Balajadia, Romana I	Daughter	F	Cha	0.4	S	N		Guam		None
8		9	9	Baza, Ramon S	Head	M	Cha	39	M	N	Y	Guam	Y	Farmer
9		9	9	Baza, Rosa C	Wife	F	Cha	36	M	N	Y	Guam	Y	None
10		9	9	Baza, Jesus C	Son	M	Cha	9	S	Y		Guam		None
11		9	9	Baza, Enrique C	Son	M	Cha	8	S	Y		Guam		None
12		9	9	Baza, Julia C	Daughter	F	Cha	5	S	N		Guam		None
13		9	9	Rodrigez, Carmen R	God daughter	F	Cha	19	S	N	Y	Guam	Y	None
14		10	10	Quichocho, Joaquin D	Head	M	Cha	42	M	N	N	Guam	N	Farmer
15		10	10	Quichocho, Josefa C	Wife	F	Cha	51	M	N	N	Guam	N	None
16		10	10	Quichocho, Jesus C	Son	M	Cha	17	S	N	Y	Guam	Y	Farm laborer
17		10	10	Quichocho, Ignacio C	Son	M	Cha	15	S	Y	Y	Guam	Y	Farm laborer
18		11	11	Cruz, Juan LG	Head	M	Cha	51	M	N	Y	Guam	N	Farmer
19		11	11	Cruz, Victoria I	Wife	F	Cha	49	M	N	Y	Guam	Y	None
20		11	11	Cruz, Tomas I	Son	M	Cha	4.3	S	N		Guam		None
21		12	12	Baza, Vicente S	Head	M	Cha	44	M	N	N	Guam	N	Farmer
22		12	12	Baza, Teresa C	Wife	F	Cha	42	M	N	N	Guam	N	None
23		12	12	Baza, Beatris C	Daughter	F	Cha	18	S	N	Y	Guam	Y	None
24		12	12	Baza, Tito C	Son	M	Cha	15	S	Y	Y	Guam	Y	Farm laborer
25		12	12	Baza, Pilar C	Daughter	F	Cha	13	S	Y	Y	Guam	Y	None

(CHAMORRO ROOTS GENEALOGY PROJECT™ TRANSCRIPTION)
(BERNARD T. PUNZALAN / HTTP://WWW.CHAMORROROOTS.COM)

DEPARTMENT OF COMMERCE-BUREAU OF THE CENSUS
WASHINGTON

FIFTEENTH CENSUS OF THE UNITED STATES: 1930-POPULATION

THE ISLAND OF GUAM

Sheet No. 2B

277b

District **Municipality of Yona**
Name of Place **Yona Municipality**
[Proper name and, also, name of class, as city, town, village, barrio, etc]

Enumeration District No. **12**
Enumerated by me on **April 3, 1930** **Cayetano A. Quinata**
Enumerator

	PLACE OF ABODE			NAME	RELATION	PERSONAL DESCRIPTION				EDUCATION		NATIVITY		OCCUPATION
	Street, avenue, road, etc.	Number of dwelling house is order of visitation	Number of family in order of visitation	of each person whose place of abode on April 1, 1930, was in this family. Enter surname, first, then given name and middle initial. If any. Include every person living on April 1, 1930. Omit children born since April 1, 1930.	Relationship of this Person to the head of the family.	Sex	Color or race	Age at last birthday	Single, married, widowed or divorced	Attended school any time since Sept. 1, 1929	Whether able to read and write.	Place of birth of this person.	Whether able to speak English.	
	1	2	3	4	5	6	7	8	9	10	11	12	13	14
26	[no street]	12	12	Baza, Maria C	Daughter	M	Cha	12	S	Y	Y	Guam	Y	None
27		12	12	Baza, Carmen C	Daughter	F	Cha	10	S	Y	Y	Guam	Y	None
28		12	12	Baza, Virginia C	Daughter	F	Cha	8	S	Y		Guam		None
29		12	12	Baza, Jose C	Son	M	Cha	6	S	N		Guam		None
30		12	12	Baza, Juan C	Son	M	Cha	3.4	S	N		Guam		None
31		12	12	Baza, Gloria C	Daughter	F	Cha	0.3	S	N		Guam		None
32		13	13	Baza, Jose C	Head	M	Cha	39	M	N	Y	Guam	N	Farmer
33		13	13	Baza, Manuela C	Wife	F	Cha	34	M	N	Y	Guam	Y	None
34		13	13	Baza, Maria C	Daughter	F	Cha	17	S	N	Y	Guam	Y	None
35		13	13	Baza, Vicente C	Son	M	Cha	14	S	Y	Y	Guam	Y	None
36		13	13	Baza, Adela C	Daughter	F	Cha	11	S	Y	Y	Guam	Y	None
37		13	13	Baza, Juana C	Daughter	F	Cha	9	S	Y		Guam		None
38		13	13	Baza, Enrique C	Son	M	Cha	8	S	Y		Guam		None
39		13	13	Baza, Rosario C	Daughter	F	Cha	5	S	N		Guam		None
40		13	13	Baza, Gregorio C	Son	M	Cha	3.1	S	N		Guam		None
41		13	13	Baza, Telefaro C	Son	M	Cha	1.6	S	N		Guam		None
42		14	14	Quitaro, Agustin P	Head	M	Cha	39	M	N	N	Guam	N	Farmer
43		14	14	Quitaro, Soledad B	Wife	F	Cha	42	M	N	N	Guam	N	None
44		14	14	Quitaro, Jesus B	Son	M	Cha	17	S	N	Y	Guam	Y	Farm laborer
45		14	14	Quitaro, Jose B	Son	m	Cha	16	S	Y	Y	Guam	Y	None
46		14	14	Quitaro, Juan B	Son	M	Cha	11	S	Y	Y	Guam		None
47		14	14	Quitaro, Antonia B	Daughter	F	Cha	8	S	Y		Guam		None
48		14	14	Quitaro, Maria B	Daughter	F	Cha	6	S	N		Guam		None
49		14	14	Quitaro, Ramon B	Son	M	Cha	0.3	S	N		Guam		None
50		15	15	Charguiya, Rita B	Head	F	Cha	67	Wd	N	N	Guam	N	Farmer

DEPARTMENT OF COMMERCE-BUREAU OF THE CENSUS
WASHINGTON

FIFTEENTH CENSUS OF THE UNITED STATES: 1930-POPULATION

THE ISLAND OF GUAM

Sheet No. 3A

278

District **Municipality of Yona**
Name of Place **Yona Municipality**
[Proper name and, also, name of class, as city, town, village, barrio, etc]

Enumeration District No. **12**
Enumerated by me on **April 3, 1930** **Cayetano A. Quinata**
Enumerator

	PLACE OF ABODE			NAME	RELATION	PERSONAL DESCRIPTION				EDUCATION		NATIVITY		OCCUPATION
	Street, avenue, road, etc.	Number of dwelling house is order of visitation	Number of family in order of visitation	of each person whose place of abode on April 1, 1930, was in this family. Enter surname, first, then given name and middle initial. If any. Include every person living on April 1, 1930. Omit children born since April 1, 1930.	Relationship of this Person to the head of the family.	Sex	Color or race	Age at last birthday	Single, married, widowed or divorced	Attended school any time since Sept. 1, 1929	Whether able to read and write.	Place of birth of this person.	Whether able to speak English.	
	1	2	3	4	5	6	7	8	9	10	11	12	13	14
1	[no street]	15	16	Sudo, Gregorio	Head	M	Jap	47	M	N	Y	Japan	Y	Retail merchant
2		15	16	Sudo, Ana B	Wife	F	Cha	32	M	N	Y	Guam	Y	None
3		15	16	Sudo, Jose B	Son	M	Jap	13	S	Y	Y	Guam	Y	None
4		15	16	Sudo, Dolroes B	Daughter	F	Jap	12	S	Y	Y	Guam	Y	None
5		15	16	Sudo, Maria B	Daughter	F	Jap	10	S	Y	Y	Guam	Y	None
6		15	16	Sudo, Rosa B	Daughter	F	Jap	8	S	Y		Guam		None
7		15	16	Sudo, Margarita B	Daughter	F	Jap	6	S	N		Guam		None
8		15	16	Sudo, Carmen B	Daughter	F	Jap	4.6	S	N		Guam		None
9		15	16	Sudo, Felicita B	Daughter	F	Jap	3.7	S	N		Guam		None
10		15	16	Sudo, Ereni B	Daughter	F	Jap	0.8	S	N		Guam		None
11		16	17	Camacho, Francisco B	Head	M	Cha	54	M	N	N	Guam	N	Farmer
12		16	17	Camacho, Maria O	Wife	F	Cha	54	M	N	N	Guam	N	None
13		16	17	Camacho, Vicente O	Son	M	Cha	23	S	N	Y	Guam	Y	Farm laborer
14		16	17	Camacho, Pedro O	Son	M	Cha	18	S	N	Y	Guam	Y	Farm laborer
15		16	17	Camacho, Ramon O	Son	M	Cha	15	S	Y	Y	Guam	Y	Farm laborer
16		16	17	Camacho, Josefina O	Daughter	F	Cha	11	S	Y	Y	Guam	Y	None
17		16	17	Camacho, Jesusa O	Daughter	F	Cha	5	S	N		Guam		None
18		16	18	Camacho, Jose O	Head	M	Cha	42	Wd	N	N	Guam		None
19		17	19	Pocaigue, Domingo P	Head	M	Fil	46	M	N	Y	Guam	N	Farmer
20		17	19	Pocaigue, Dolores O	Wife	F	Cha	47	M	N	N	Guam	N	None
21		17	19	Pocaigue, Jose O	Son	M	Cha	20	S	N	Y	Guam	Y	Farm laborer
22		17	19	Pocaigue, Rafael O	Son	M	Cha	15	S	N	Y	Guam	Y	Farm laborer
23		17	19	Pocaigue, Maria O	Daughter	F	Cha	13	S	N	Y	Guam	Y	None
24		17	19	Pocaigue, Jesusa O	Daughter	F	Cha	11	S	Y	Y	Guam	Y	None
25		17	19	Pocaigue, Rita O	Daughter	F	Cha	6	S	Y		Guam		None

(CHAMORRO ROOTS GENEALOGY PROJECT™ TRANSCRIPTION)
(BERNARD T. PUNZALAN / HTTP://WWW.CHAMORROROOTS.COM)

DEPARTMENT OF COMMERCE-BUREAU OF THE CENSUS
WASHINGTON

FIFTEENTH CENSUS OF THE UNITED STATES: 1930-POPULATION

THE ISLAND OF GUAM

Sheet No. 3B

278b

District Municipality of Yona
Name of Place Yona Municipality
[Proper name and, also, name of class, as city, town, village, barrio, etc]

Enumeration District No. 12
Enumerated by me on April 3, 1930 Cayetano A. Quinata
Enumerator

	PLACE OF ABODE			NAME	RELATION	PERSONAL DESCRIPTION				EDUCATION		NATIVITY		OCCUPATION
	Street, avenue, road, etc.	Number of dwelling house is order of visitation	Number of family in order of visitation	of each person whose place of abode on April 1, 1930, was in this family. Enter surname, first, then given name and middle initial. If any. Include every person living on April 1, 1930. Omit children born since April 1, 1930.	Relationship of this Person to the head of the family.	Sex	Color or race	Age at last birthday	Single, married, widowed or divorced	Attended school any time since Sept. 1, 1929	Whether able to read and write.	Place of birth of this person.	Whether able to speak English.	
	1	2	3	4	5	6	7	8	9	10	11	12	13	14
26	[no street]	17	19	Pocaigue, Paz O	Daughter	F	Fil	3.8	S	N		Guam		None
27		18	20	Fernandez, Antonio O	Head	M	Cha	28	M	N	Y	Guam	Y	Farmer
28		18	20	Fernandez, Isabel P	Wife	F	Fil	25	M	N	N	Guam	N	None
29		18	20	Fernandez, Maria P	Daughter	F	Cha	6	S	N		Guam		None
30		18	20	Fernandez, Jose P	Son	M	Cha	3.2	S	N		Guam		None
31		18	20	Fernandez, Jesus P	Son	M	Cha	0.3	S	N		Guam		None
32		19	21	Fernandez, Roque O	Head	M	Cha	26	M	N	Y	Guam	Y	Farmer
33		19	21	Fernandez, Mercedes Q	Wife	F	Cha	19	M	N	Y	Guam	Y	None
34		20	22	Quidachay, Mariano P	Head	M	Cha	38	M	N	Y	Guam	Y	Farmer
35		20	22	Quidachay, Rita S	Wife	F	Cha	37	M	N	N	Guam	N	None
36		20	22	Quidachay, Delgadina S	Daughter	F	Cha	11	S	Y	Y	Guam	Y	None
37		20	22	Quidachay, Dolores S	Daughter	F	Cha	5	S	N		Guam		None
38		21	23	Taitingfong, Juan C	Head	M	Cha	28	M	N	Y	Guam	Y	Farmer
39		21	23	Taitingfong, Grabiela Q	Wife	F	Cha	40	M	N	N	Guam	N	None
40		21	23	Taitingfong, Antonia Q	Daughter	F	Cha	9	S	Y		Guam		None
41		21	23	Fernandez, Maria Q	Step daughter	F	Cha	16	S	N	Y	Guam	Y	None
42		21	23	Fernandez, Jesus Q	Step son	M	Cha	14	S	Y	Y	Guam	Y	None
43		22	24	Quidachay, Vicente P	Head	M	Cha	48	M	N	N	Guam	N	Farmer
44		22	24	Quidachay, Ana P	Wife	F	Cha	36	M	N	N	Guam	N	None
45		22	24	Quidachay, Joaquin P	Son	M	Cha	15	S	Y	Y	Guam	Y	Farm laborer
46		22	24	Quidachay, Jose P	Son	M	Cha	12	S	Y	Y	Guam	Y	None
47		22	24	Quidachay, Dolores P	Daughter	F	Cha	5	S	N		Guam		None
48		22	24	Quidachay, Ramon P	Son	M	Cha	2.1	S	N		Guam		None
49		22	24	Quidachay, Francisco P	Son	M	Cha	0.8	S	N		Guam		None
50		23	25	Mafnas, Serafin B	Head	M	Cha	40	M	N	Y	Guam	Y	Farmer

(CHAMORRO ROOTS GENEALOGY PROJECT™ TRANSCRIPTION)
(BERNARD T. PUNZALAN / HTTP://WWW.CHAMORROROOTS.COM)

DEPARTMENT OF COMMERCE-BUREAU OF THE CENSUS
WASHINGTON

FIFTEENTH CENSUS OF THE UNITED STATES: 1930-POPULATION

THE ISLAND OF GUAM

Sheet No. 4A

District **Municipality of Yona**
Name of Place **Yona Municipality**
[Proper name and, also, name of class, as city, town, village, barrio, etc]

Enumeration District No. **12**
Enumerated by me on **April 4, 1930** **Cayetano A. Quinata**
Enumerator

	PLACE OF ABODE			NAME	RELATION	PERSONAL DESCRIPTION				EDUCATION		NATIVITY		OCCUPATION
	Street, avenue, road, etc.	Number of dwelling house in order of visitation	Number of family in order of visitation	of each person whose place of abode on April 1, 1930, was in this family. Enter surname, first, then given name and middle initial. If any. Include every person living on April 1, 1930. Omit children born since April 1, 1930.	Relationship of this Person to the head of the family.	Sex	Color or race	Age at last birthday	Single, married, widowed or divorced	Attended school any time since Sept. 1, 1929	Whether able to read and write.	Place of birth of this person.	Whether able to speak English.	
	1	2	3	4	5	6	7	8	9	10	11	12	13	14
1	[no street]	23	25	Mafnas, Maria C	Wife	F	Cha	36	M	N	Y	Guam	Y	None
2		23	25	Mafnas, Maria C	Daughter	F	Cha	18	S	N	Y	Guam	Y	None
3		23	25	Mafnas, Juan C	Son	M	Cha	10	S	Y	Y	Guam	Y	None
4		23	25	Mafnas, Geronimo C	Son	M	Cha	9	S	Y		Guam		None
5		23	25	Mafnas, Vicenta C	Daughter	F	Cha	7	S	Y		Guam		None
6		23	25	Mafnas, Francisco C	Son	M	Cha	5	S	N		Guam		None
7		23	25	Mafnas, Elisa C	Daughter	F	Cha	3.8	S	N		Guam		None
8		23	25	Mafnas, Serafin C	Son	M	Cha	2.8	S	N		Guam		None
9		23	25	Mafnas, Joaquin C	Son	M	Cha	0.1	S	N		Guam		None
10		24	26	Aguero, Jose SN	Head	M	Cha	32	M	N	Y	Guam	Y	Farmer
11		24	26	Aguero, Remedios T	Wife	F	Cha	25	M	N	Y	Guam	Y	None
12		24	26	Aguero, Tomas T	Son	M	Cha	4	S	N		Guam		None
13		24	26	Aguero, Oliva T	Daughter	F	Cha	2.7	S	N		Guam		None
14		24	26	Aguero, Vicente T	Son	M	Cha	1.1	S	N		Guam		None
15		25	27	Pangelinan, Jose O	Head	M	Cha	25	M	N	Y	Guam	Y	Farmer
16		25	27	Pangelinan, Francisca B	Wife	F	Cha	18	M	N	Y	Guam	Y	None
17		25	27	Pangelinan, Juan B	Son	M	Cha	2.2	S	N		Guam		None
18		25	27	Pangelinan, Veronica B	Daughter	F	Cha	1.1	S	N		Guam		None
19		26	28	Cruz, Francisco C	Head	M	Cha	23	S	N	Y	Guam	Y	Farmer
20		26	28	Concepcion, Enriqueta C	Mother	F	Cha	49	M	N	N	Guam	N	None
21		26	28	Tenorio, Juan T	Servant	M	Cha	9	S	Y		Guam		None
22		27	29	Castro, Vicente B	Head	M	Cha	67	M	N	N	Guam	Y	Farmer
23		27	29	Castro, Maria T	Wife	F	Cha	25	M	N	N	Guam	N	None
24		27	29	Tenorio, Ignacia T	Step daughter	F	Cha	8	S	Y		Guam		None
25		28	30	Quichocho, Jesus Q	Head	M	Cha	33	M	N	N	Guam	N	Farm laborer

DEPARTMENT OF COMMERCE-BUREAU OF THE CENSUS
WASHINGTON

FIFTEENTH CENSUS OF THE UNITED STATES: 1930-POPULATION

THE ISLAND OF GUAM

Sheet No. 4B

279b

District **Municipality of Yona**
Name of Place **Yona Municipality**
[Proper name and, also, name of class, as city, town, village, barrio, etc]

Enumeration District No. **12**
Enumerated by me on **April 4, 1930** **Cayetano A. Quinata**, Enumerator

	PLACE OF ABODE			NAME	RELATION	PERSONAL DESCRIPTION				EDUCATION		NATIVITY		OCCUPATION
	Street, avenue, road, etc.	Number of dwelling house in order of visitation	Number of family in order of visitation	of each person whose place of abode on April 1, 1930, was in this family. Enter surname, first, then given name and middle initial. If any. Include every person living on April 1, 1930. Omit children born since April 1, 1930.	Relationship of this Person to the head of the family.	Sex	Color or race	Age at last birthday	Single, married, widowed or divorced	Attended school any time since Sept. 1, 1929	Whether able to read and write.	Place of birth of this person.	Whether able to speak English.	
	1	2	3	4	5	6	7	8	9	10	11	12	13	14
26	[no street]	28	30	Quichocho, Maria P	Wife	F	Cha	34	M	N	Y	Guam	N	None
27		28	30	Perez, Catalina B	Step daughter	F	Cha	9	S	Y		Guam		None
28		28	30A	Mantanona, Atanacio I	Head	M	Cha	34	Wd	N	Y	Guam	N	Cow herd
29		28	30A	Mantanona, Carmen I	Daughter	F	Cha	9	S	Y		Guam		None
30		29	31	Siguenza, Joaquin T	Head	M	Cha	32	M	N	Y	Guam	Y	Farmer
31		29	31	Siguenza, Ana B	Wife	F	Cha	30	M	N	Y	Guam	Y	None
32		29	31	Siguenza, Ejinio B	Son	M	Cha	11	S	Y	Y	Guam	Y	None
33		29	31	Siguenza, Concepcion B	Daughter	F	Cha	5	S	N		Guam		None
34		29	31	Siguenza, Ana B	Daughter	F	Cha	3.8	S	N		Guam		None
35		29	31	Siguenza, Jose B	Son	M	Cha	2.5	S	N		Guam		None
36		30	32	Delgado, Alfonso M	Head	M	Cha	37	S	N	Y	Guam	N	Farmer
37		31	32	Baza, Teleforo Q	Head	M	Cha	65	M	N	Y	Guam	N	Farmer
38		31	32	Baza, Margarita C	Wife	F	Cha	63	M	N	N	Guam	N	None
39		32	34	Baza, Vicente C	Head	M	Cha	28	M	N	Y	Guam	Y	Farmer
40		32	34	Baza, Ana M	Wife	F	Cha	23	M	N	Y	Guam	Y	None
41		32	34	Baza, Rita M	Daughter	F	Cha	5	S	N		Guam		None
42		32	34	Baza, Margarita M	Daughter	F	Cha	3.5	S	N		Guam		None
43		33	35	Baza, Jesus C	Head	M	Cha	33	M	N	Y	Guam	Y	Farmer
44		33	35	Baza, Maria G	Wife	F	Cha	35	M	N	Y	Guam	Y	None
45		33	35	Baza, Concepcion G	Daughter	F	Cha	11	S	Y	Y	Guam	Y	None
46		33	35	Baza, Ana G	Daughter	F	Cha	9	S	Y		Guam		None
47		33	35	Baza, Juan G	Son	M	Cha	5	S	N		Guam		None
48		33	35	Baza, Ramon G	Son	M	Cha	3.5	S	N		Guam		None
49		34	36	Pangelinan, Pedro C	Head	M	Cha	52	S	N	Y	Guam	N	None
50		35	37	Pangelinan, Juan B	Head	M	Cha	39	M	N	Y	Guam	N	Farmer

(CHAMORRO ROOTS GENEALOGY PROJECT™ TRANSCRIPTION)
(BERNARD T. PUNZALAN / HTTP://WWW.CHAMORROROOTS.COM)

DEPARTMENT OF COMMERCE-BUREAU OF THE CENSUS
WASHINGTON

FIFTEENTH CENSUS OF THE UNITED STATES: 1930-POPULATION

THE ISLAND OF GUAM

Sheet No. 5A

District Municipality of Yona
Name of Place Yona Municipality
[Proper name and, also, name of class, as city, town, village, barrio, etc]

Enumeration District No. 12
Enumerated by me on April 5, 1930 Cayetano A. Quinata
Enumerator

	PLACE OF ABODE			NAME	RELATION	PERSONAL DESCRIPTION				EDUCATION		NATIVITY		OCCUPATION
	Street, avenue, road, etc.	Number of dwelling house is order of visitation	Number of family in order of visitation	of each person whose place of abode on April 1, 1930, was in this family. Enter surname, first, then given name and middle initial. If any. Include every person living on April 1, 1930. Omit children born since April 1, 1930.	Relationship of this Person to the head of the family.	Sex	Color or race	Age at last birthday	Single, married, widowed or divorced	Attended school any time since Sept. 1, 1929	Whether able to read and write.	Place of birth of this person.	Whether able to speak English.	
	1	2	3	4	5	6	7	8	9	10	11	12	13	14
1	[no street]	35	37	Pangelinan, Maria B	Wife	F	Cha	37	M	N	Y	Guam	N	None
2		35	37	Pangelinan, Francisco B	Son	M	Cha	7	S	Y		Guam		None
3		35	37	Pangelinan, Antonia B	Daughter	F	Cha	6	S	N		Guam		None
4		35	37	Pangelinan, Jose B	Son	M	Cha	5	S	N		Guam		None
5		35	37	Pangelinan, Pedro B	Son	M	Cha	3.3	S	N		Guam		None
6		35	37	Pangelinan, Vicente B	Son	M	Cha	1.3	S	N		Guam		None
7		36	38	Pangelinan, Pedro R	Head	M	Cha	69	M	N	N	Guam	N	Farmer
8		36	38	Pangelinan, Nieves C	Wife	F	Cha	60	M	N	N	Guam	N	None
9		36	39	Cruz, Susana L	Head	F	Cha	63	S	N	Y	Guam	N	None
10		37	40	Peredo, Camilo J	Head	M	Cha	53	M	N	Y	Guam	N	Farmer
11		37	40	Peredo, Ana B	Wife	F	Cha	52	M	N	Y	Guam	N	None
12		37	40	Peredo, Juan B	Son	M	Cha	26	S	N	Y	Guam	Y	Farm laborer
13		37	40	Peredo, Francisco B	Son	M	Cha	22	S	N	Y	Guam	Y	Farm laborer
14		37	40	Peredo, Joaquin B	Son	M	Cha	20	S	N	Y	Guam	Y	Farm laborer
15		37	40	Peredo, Pedro B	Son	M	Cha	11	S	Y	Y	Guam	Y	Farm laborer
16		38	41	Camacho, Vicente S	Head	M	Cha	47	M	N	N	Guam	N	Farmer
17		38	41	Camacho, Josefa P	Wife	F	Cha	39	M	N	Y	Guam	N	None
18		38	41	Camacho, Lourdes P	Daughter	F	Cha	7	S	Y		Guam		None
19		38	41	Camacho, Francisca P	Daughter	F	Cha	5	S	N		Guam		None
20		38	41	Camacho, Vicente P	Son	M	Cha	0.2	S	N		Guam		None
21		38	41	Quichocho, Maria P	Step daughter	F	Cha	19	S	N	Y	Guam	Y	None
22		38	41	Quichocho, Jose P	Step son	M	Cha	18	S	N	Y	Guam	Y	Farm laborer
23		38	41	Quichocho, Soledad P	Step daughter	F	Cha	15	S	N	Y	Guam	Y	None
24		38	41	Quichocho, Rosario P	Step daughter	F	Cha	13	S	N	Y	Guam	Y	None
25		38	41	Quichocho, Ana P	Step daughter	F	Cha	11	S	Y	Y	Guam	Y	None

DEPARTMENT OF COMMERCE-BUREAU OF THE CENSUS
WASHINGTON

FIFTEENTH CENSUS OF THE UNITED STATES: 1930-POPULATION

THE ISLAND OF GUAM

Sheet No. 5B

280b

District Municipality of Yona
Name of Place Yona Municipality
[Proper name and, also, name of class, as city, town, village, barrio, etc]

Enumeration District No. 12
Enumerated by me on April 7, 1930 Cayetano A. Quinata
Enumerator

	PLACE OF ABODE			NAME	RELATION	PERSONAL DESCRIPTION				EDUCATION		NATIVITY		OCCUPATION
	Street, avenue, road, etc.	Number of dwelling house is order of visitation	Number of family in order of visitation	of each person whose place of abode on April 1, 1930, was in this family. Enter surname, first, then given name and middle initial. If any. Include every person living on April 1, 1930. Omit children born since April 1, 1930.	Relationship of this Person to the head of the family.	Sex	Color or race	Age at last birthday	Single, married, widowed or divorced	Attended school any time since Sept. 1, 1929	Whether able to read and write.	Place of birth of this person.	Whether able to speak English.	
	1	2	3	4	5	6	7	8	9	10	11	12	13	14
26	[no street]	38	42	Pocaigue, Pedro P	Head	M	Fil	97	M	N	N	Philippine Islands	N	None
27		38	42	Pocaigue, Maria P	Wife	F	Cha	65	M	N	N	Guam	N	None
28		38	42	Rosa, Teodora T	Step daughter	F	Cha	51	Wd	N	N	Guam	N	None
29		39	43	Balajadia, Pedro I	Head	M	Cha	23	M	N	Y	Guam	Y	Farmer
30		39	43	Balajadia, Rosa P	Wife	F	Cha	19	M	N	Y	Guam	Y	None
31		39	43	Balajadia, Tomas P	Son	M	Cha	1.2	S	N		Guam		None
32		39	44	Pangelinan, Elmenijildia M	Head	F	Cha	50	Wd	N	Y	Guam	N	None
33		39	44	Pangelinan, Jose M	Son	M	Cha	15	S	Y	Y	Guam	Y	None
34		39	45	Atoigue, Jose R	Head	M	Cha	49	M	N	N	Guam	N	Farmer
35		40	46	Cruz, Enrique A	Head	M	Cha	33	M	N	Y	Guam	Y	Farmer
36		40	46	Cruz, Rosario T	Wife	F	Cha	32	M	N	Y	Guam	Y	None
37		40	46	Cruz, Jose T	Son	M	Cha	8	S	Y		Guam		None
38		40	46	Cruz, Maria T	Daughter	F	Cha	6	S	N		Guam		None
39		40	46	Cruz, Enrique T	Son	M	Cha	5	S	N		Guam		None
40		40	46	Cruz, Tomas T	Son	M	Cha	4	S	N		Guam		None
41		40	46	Cruz, Orelia T	Daughter	F	Cha	2.5	S	N		Guam		None
42		40	46	Cruz, Dolores T	Daughter	F	Cha	0.1	S	N		Guam		None
43		41	47	Murray, Ida R	Head	F	Cha	21	M	N	Y	California	Y	School teacher
44		42	48	Balajadia, Rosa B	Head	F	Cha	64	S	N	N	Guam	N	Farmer
45		42	48	Balajadia, Vicenta R	Sister	F	Cha	75	S	N	N	Guam	N	None
46		42	48	Camacho, Maria B	Grand daughter	F	Cha	19	S	N	Y	Guam	Y	None
47		42	48	Camacho, Rosario B	Grand daughter	F	Cha	17	S	N	Y	Guam	Y	None
48		42	48	Camacho, Ana B	Grand daughter	F	Cha	16	S	Y	Y	Guam	Y	None
49		43	49	Taitingfong, Daniel C	Head	M	Cha	31	M	N	Y	Guam	Y	Farmer
50		43	49	Taitingfong, Rosa B	Wife	F	Cha	25	M	N	Y	Guam	Y	None

DEPARTMENT OF COMMERCE-BUREAU OF THE CENSUS
WASHINGTON

FIFTEENTH CENSUS OF THE UNITED STATES: 1930-POPULATION

THE ISLAND OF GUAM

Sheet No. 6A

District **Municipality of Yona**
Name of Place **Yona Municipality**
[Proper name and, also, name of class, as city, town, village, barrio, etc]

Enumeration District No. **12**
Enumerated by me on **April 7, 1930** **Cayetano A. Quinata**
Enumerator

	PLACE OF ABODE			NAME	RELATION	PERSONAL DESCRIPTION				EDUCATION		NATIVITY		OCCUPATION
	Street, avenue, road, etc.	Number of dwelling house is order of visitation	Number of family in order of visitation	of each person whose place of abode on April 1, 1930, was in this family. Enter surname, first, then given name and middle initial. If any. Include every person living on April 1, 1930. Omit children born since April 1, 1930.	Relationship of this Person to the head of the family.	Sex	Color or race	Age at last birthday	Single, married, widowed or divorced	Attended school any time since Sept. 1, 1929	Whether able to read and write.	Place of birth of this person.	Whether able to speak English.	
	1	2	3	4	5	6	7	8	9	10	11	12	13	14
1	[no street]	43	49	Taitingfong, Catalina B	Daughter	F	Cha	9	S	N		Guam		None
2		43	49	Taitingfong, Francisca B	Daughter	F	Cha	4.5	S	N		Guam		None
3		43	49	Taitingfong, Ramon B	Son	M	Cha	2.5	S	N		Guam		None
4		43	49	Taitingfong, Jose B	Son	M	Cha	0.2	S	N		Guam		None
5		44	50	Taitingfong, Manuel C	Head	M	Cha	34	M	N	Y	Guam	Y	Farmer
6		44	50	Taitingfong, Carmen A	Wife	F	Cha	33	M	N	Y	Guam	Y	None
7		44	50	Taitingfong, Francisco A	Son	M	Cha	9	S	Y		Guam		None
8		44	50	Taitingfong, Rosalia A	Daughter	F	Cha	8	S	Y		Guam		None
9		44	50	Taitingfong, Maria A	Daughter	F	Cha	5	S	N		Guam		None
10		44	50	Taitingfong, Angelina A	Daughter	F	Cha	4.1	S	N		Guam		None
11		44	50	Taitingfong, Concepcion A	Daughter	F	Cha	2.8	S	N		Guam		None
12		44	50	Taitingfong, Isabel A	Daughter	F	Cha	0.8	S	N		Guam		None
13		45	51	Taitingfong, Rosa C	Head	F	Cha	60	S	N	N	Guam	N	None
14		46	52	Aguero, Jesus SN	Head	M	Cha	24	M	N	Y	Guam	Y	Farmer
15		46	52	Aguero, Felisa T	Wife	F	Cha	23	M	N	Y	Guam	Y	None
16		46	52	Aguero, Pedro T	Son	M	Cha	2.7	S	N		Guam		None
17		46	52	Aguero, Soledad T	Daughter	F	Cha	1.1	S	N		Guam		None
18		46	52	Aguero, Maria SN	Mother	F	Cha	68	Wd	N	N	Guam	N	None
19		47	53	Aguero, Vicente SN	Head	M	Cha	37	D	N	Y	Guam	N	Farmer
20		47	53	Aguero, Felix Q	Son	M	Cha	15	S	N	Y	Guam	Y	Farm laborer
21		48	54	Benavente, Jesus R	Head	M	Cha	55	M	N	Y	Guam	Y	Farmer
22		48	54	Benavente, Nicolasa Q	Wife	F	Cha	56	M	N	N	Guam	N	None
23		48	54	Benavente, Ramon Q	Son	M	Cha	25	S	N	Y	Guam	Y	Farm laborer
24		48	54	Benavente, Dolores Q	Daughter	F	Cha	24	S	N	Y	Guam	Y	None
25		49	55	Pangelinan, Jose C	Head	M	Cha	63	Wd	N	Y	Guam	N	Farmer

(CHAMORRO ROOTS GENEALOGY PROJECT™ TRANSCRIPTION)
(BERNARD T. PUNZALAN / HTTP://WWW.CHAMORROROOTS.COM)

DEPARTMENT OF COMMERCE-BUREAU OF THE CENSUS
WASHINGTON

FIFTEENTH CENSUS OF THE UNITED STATES: 1930-POPULATION

THE ISLAND OF GUAM

Sheet No. 6B

281b

District **Municipality of Yona**
Name of Place **Yona Municipality**
[Proper name and, also, name of class, as city, town, village, barrio, etc]

Enumeration District No. **12**
Enumerated by me on **April 8, 1930** **Cayetano A. Quinata**
Enumerator

	PLACE OF ABODE			NAME	RELATION	PERSONAL DESCRIPTION				EDUCATION		NATIVITY		OCCUPATION
	Street, avenue, road, etc.	Number of dwelling house in order of visitation	Number of family in order of visitation	of each person whose place of abode on April 1, 1930, was in this family. Enter surname, first, then given name and middle initial. If any. Include every person living on April 1, 1930. Omit children born since April 1, 1930.	Relationship of this Person to the head of the family.	Sex	Color or race	Age at last birthday	Single, married, widowed or divorced	Attended school any time since Sept. 1, 1929	Whether able to read and write.	Place of birth of this person.	Whether able to speak English.	
	1	2	3	4	5	6	7	8	9	10	11	12	13	14
26	[no street]	50	56	Quichocho, Juan P	Head	M	Cha	51	M	N	N	Guam	N	Farmer
27		50	56	Quichocho, Maria I	Wife	F	Cha	48	M	N	Y	Guam	N	None
28		50	56	Quichocho, Trinidad I	Daughter	F	Cha	23	S	N	Y	Guam	Y	None
29		50	56	Quichocho, Manuel I	Son	M	Cha	21	S	N	Y	Guam	Y	None
30		50	56	Quichocho, Dolores I	Daughter	F	Cha	18	S	N	Y	Guam	Y	None
31		50	56	Quichocho, Juan I	Son	M	Cha	9	S	Y		Guam		None
32		50	56	Quichocho, Jesus I	Son	M	Cha	5	S	N		Guam		None
33		50	56	Quichocho, Jose I	Son	M	Cha	2.7	S	N		Guam		None
34		50	56	Quichocho, Veronica I	Grand daughter	F	Cha	3.2	S	N		Guam		None
35		50	57	Toves, Isidro F	Head	M	Cha	28	M	N	Y	Guam	Y	Farmer
36		50	57	Toves, Rosa Q	Wife	F	Cha	27	M	N	Y	Guam	Y	None
37		50	57	Toves, Olimpia Q	Daughter	F	Cha	6	S	N		Guam		None
38		50	57	Toves, Leonila Q	Daughter	F	Cha	4.2	S	N		Guam		None
39		50	57	Toves, Antonio Q	Son	M	Cha	2.8	S	N		Guam		None
40		51	58	Quifunas, Jose C	Head	M	Cha	36	M	N	Y	Guam	N	Farmer
41		51	58	Quifunas, Felicita T	Wife	F	Cha	34	M	N	Y	Guam	N	None
42		51	58	Quifunas, Maria T	Daughter	F	Cha	14	S	Y	Y	Guam	Y	None
43		51	58	Quifunas, Jose T	Son	M	Cha	12	S	Y	Y	Guam	Y	Farm laborer
44		51	58	Quifunas, Lourdes T	Daughter	F	Cha	9	S	N		Guam		None
45		51	58	Quifunas, Clotilde T	Daughter	F	Cha	7	S	N		Guam		None
46		51	58	Quifunas, Manuel T	Son	M	Cha	5	S	N		Guam		None
47		51	58	Quifunas, Pedro T	Son	M	Cha	2	S	N		Guam		None
48		51	58	Quifunas, Manuel A	Father	M	Cha	67	M	N		Guam	N	None
49		52	59	Taisipig, Gregorio M	Head	M	Cha	41	M	N	Y	Guam	N	Farmer
50		52	59	Taisipig, Ana T	Wife	F	Cha	40	M	N	N	Guam	N	None

DEPARTMENT OF COMMERCE-BUREAU OF THE CENSUS
WASHINGTON

FIFTEENTH CENSUS OF THE UNITED STATES: 1930-POPULATION

THE ISLAND OF GUAM

Sheet No. 7A

District **Municipality of Yona**
Name of Place **Yona Municipality**
[Proper name and, also, name of class, as city, town, village, barrio, etc]

Enumeration District No. **12**
Enumerated by me on **April 8, 1930** **Cayetano A. Quinata**, Enumerator

	PLACE OF ABODE			NAME	RELATION	PERSONAL DESCRIPTION				EDUCATION		NATIVITY		OCCUPATION
	Street, avenue, road, etc.	Number of dwelling house is order of visitation	Number of family in order of visitation	of each person whose place of abode on April 1, 1930, was in this family. Enter surname, first, then given name and middle initial. If any. Include every person living on April 1, 1930. Omit children born since April 1, 1930.	Relationship of this Person to the head of the family.	Sex	Color or race	Age at last birthday	Single, married, widowed or divorced	Attended school any time since Sept. 1, 1929	Whether able to read and write.	Place of birth of this person.	Whether able to speak English.	
	1	2	3	4	5	6	7	8	9	10	11	12	13	14
1	[no street]	52	59	Taisipig, Herminia T	Daughter	F	Cha	19	S	N	Y	Guam	Y	None
2		52	59	Taisipig, Antonia T	Daughter	F	Cha	15	S	N	Y	Guam	Y	None
3		52	59	Taisipig, Dolores T	Daughter	F	Cha	13	S	Y	Y	Guam	Y	None
4		52	59	Taisipig, Rosa T	Daughter	F	Cha	11	S	Y	Y	Guam	Y	None
5		52	59	Taisipig, Juan T	Son	M	Cha	9	S	Y		Guam		None
6		52	59	Taisipig, Gregorio T	Son	M	Cha	7	S	N		Guam		None
7		52	59	Taisipig, Jose T	Son	M	Cha	6	S	N		Guam		None
8		52	59	Taisipig, Balbino T	Son	M	Cha	3.5	S	N		Guam		None
9		52	59	Taisipig, Carmen T	Daughter	F	Cha	2.8	S	N		Guam		None
10		53	60	Benavente, Vicente R	Head	M	Cha	56	M	N	N	Guam	N	Farmer
11		53	60	Benavente, Dolores P	Wife	F	Cha	65	M	N	N	Guam	N	None
12		54	61	Ogo, Vicente J	Head	M	Cha	39	M	N	Y	Guam	N	Farmer
13		54	61	Ogo, Ana O	Wife	F	Cha	36	M	N	N	Guam	N	None
14		54	61	Ogo, Joaquina O	Daughter	F	Cha	14	S	N	Y	Guam	Y	None
15		54	61	Ogo, Antonia O	Daughter	F	Cha	11	S	Y	Y	Guam	Y	None
16		54	61	Ogo, Teodora O	Daughter	F	Cha	10	S	Y	Y	Guam	Y	None
17		54	61	Ogo, Pedro O	Son	M	Cha	7	S	Y		Guam		None
18		54	61	Ogo, Maria O	Daughter	F	Cha	2.5	S	N		Guam		None
19		55	62	Taitingfong, Ana T	Head	F	Cha	49	S	N	N	Guam	N	Farmer
20		56	63	Blaz, Francisco C	Head	M	Cha	26	M	N	Y	Guam	Y	Farmer
21		56	63	Blaz, Maria D	Wife	F	Cha	18	M	N	Y	Guam	Y	None
22		56	63	Blaz, Enrique D	Son	M	Cha	0	S	N		Guam		None
23		57	64	Quidachay, Juan M	Head	M	Cha	34	M	N	Y	Guam	N	Farmer
24		57	64	Quidachay, Ana T	Wife	F	Cha	25	M	N	Y	Guam	N	None
25		57	64	Quidachay, Antonio T	Son	M	Cha	3.8	S	N		Guam		None

DEPARTMENT OF COMMERCE-BUREAU OF THE CENSUS
WASHINGTON

FIFTEENTH CENSUS OF THE UNITED STATES: 1930-POPULATION

THE ISLAND OF GUAM

Sheet No. 7B

District **Municipality of Yona**
Name of Place **Yona Municipality**
[Proper name and, also, name of class, as city, town, village, barrio, etc]

Enumeration District No. **12**
Enumerated by me on **April 8, 1930** **Cayetano A. Quinata**
Enumerator

	PLACE OF ABODE			NAME	RELATION	PERSONAL DESCRIPTION				EDUCATION		NATIVITY		OCCUPATION
	Street, avenue, road, etc.	Number of dwelling house is order of visitation	Number of family in order of visitation	of each person whose place of abode on April 1, 1930, was in this family. Enter surname, first, then given name and middle initial. If any. Include every person living on April 1, 1930. Omit children born since April 1, 1930.	Relationship of this Person to the head of the family.	Sex	Color or race	Age at last birthday	Single, married, widowed or divorced	Attended school any time since Sept. 1, 1929	Whether able to read and write.	Place of birth of this person.	Whether able to speak English.	
	1	2	3	4	5	6	7	8	9	10	11	12	13	14
26	[no street]	57	64	Quidachay, Emilia T	Daughter	F	Cha	1.1	S	N		Guam		None
27		58	65	Pangilinan, Jose C	Head	M	Cha	39	M	N	Y	Guam	N	Farmer
28		58	65	Pangilinan, Magdalena F	Wife	F	Cha	30	M	N	Y	Guam	N	None
29		58	65	Pangilinan, Francisco F	Son	M	Cha	13	S	N	Y	Guam	Y	Farm laborer
30		58	65	Pangilinan, Carlos F	Son	M	Cha	2.5	S	N		Guam		None
31		58	65	Pangilinan, Ana F	Daughter	F	Cha	1.5	S	N		Guam		None
32		58	65	Pangilinan, Maria F	Daughter	F	Cha	0.1	S	N		Guam		None
33		58	65	Quichocho, Ana D	Mother-in-law	F	Cha	51	Wd	N	N	Guam	N	None
34		59	66	Balajadia, Juan I	Head	M	Cha	21	M	N	Y	Guam	Y	Farmer
35		59	66	Balajadia, Emiliana P	Wife	F	Cha	18	M	N	Y	Guam	Y	None
36		59	66	Balajadia, Fermin P	Son	M	Cha	0.8	S	N		Guam		None
37		60	67	Ogo, Rita A	Head	F	Cha	68	S	N	N	Guam	N	None
38		61	68	Atoigue, Rosa M	Head	F	Cha	44	Wd	N	N	Guam	N	Farmer
39		61	68	Atoigue, Joaquin M	Son	M	Cha	16	S	N	Y	Guam	Y	Farm laborer
40		61	68	Atoigue, Juan M	Son	M	Cha	11	S	Y	Y	Guam	Y	None
41		61	68	Atoigue, Vicente M	Son	M	Cha	6	S	N		Guam		None
42		62	69	San Nicolas, Vicente A	Head	M	Cha	40	M	N	Y	Guam	N	Farmer
43		62	69	San Nicolas, Magdalena G	Wife	F	Cha	33	M	N	Y	Guam	N	None
44		62	69	San Nicolas, Vicente G	Son	M	Cha	21	S	N	Y	Guam	Y	Farm laborer
45		62	69	San Nicolas, Soledad G	Daughter	F	Cha	18	S	N	Y	Guam	Y	None
46		62	69	San Nicolas, Ignacio G	Son	M	Cha	17	S	N	Y	Guam	Y	Farm laborer
47		62	69	San Nicolas, Jose G	Son	M	Cha	15	S	Y		Guam	Y	Farm laborer
48		62	69	San Nicolas, Maria G	Daughter	F	Cha	13	S	Y		Guam	Y	None
49		62	69	San Nicolas, Victoria G	Daughter	F	Cha	6	S	N		Guam		None
50		62	69	San Nicolas, Carmen G	Daughter	F	Cha	0.8	S	N		Guam		None

DEPARTMENT OF COMMERCE-BUREAU OF THE CENSUS
WASHINGTON

FIFTEENTH CENSUS OF THE UNITED STATES: 1930-POPULATION

THE ISLAND OF GUAM

Sheet No. 8A

District **Municipality of Yona**
Name of Place **Yona Municipality**
[Proper name and, also, name of class, as city, town, village, barrio, etc]

Enumeration District No. **12**
Enumerated by me on **April 9, 1930** **Cayetano A. Quinata**
Enumerator

	PLACE OF ABODE			NAME	RELATION	PERSONAL DESCRIPTION				EDUCATION		NATIVITY		OCCUPATION
	Street, avenue, road, etc.	Number of dwelling house is order of visitation	Number of family in order of visitation	of each person whose place of abode on April 1, 1930, was in this family. Enter surname, first, then given name and middle initial. If any. Include every person living on April 1, 1930. Omit children born since April 1, 1930.	Relationship of this Person to the head of the family.	Sex	Color or race	Age at last birthday	Single, married, widowed or divorced	Attended school any time since Sept. 1, 1929	Whether able to read and write.	Place of birth of this person.	Whether able to speak English.	
	1	2	3	4	5	6	7	8	9	10	11	12	13	14
1	[no street]	63	70	San Nicolas, Juan A	Head	M	Cha	34	M	N	Y	Guam	Y	Farmer
2		63	70	San Nicolas, Soledad M	Wife	F	Cha	35	M	N	Y	Guam	Y	None
3		63	70	San Nicolas, Jose M	Son	M	Cha	8	S	Y		Guam		None
4		63	70	San Nicolas, Maria M	Daughter	F	Cha	2.3	S	N		Guam		None
5		64	71	San Nicolas, Jesus A	Head	M	Cha	32	S	N	Y	Guam	Y	Farmer
6		64	71	San Nicolas, Maria A	Mother	F	Cha	54	Wd	N	N	Guam	N	None
7		64	71	Quidachay, Ana A	Aunt	F	Cha	64	Wd	N	N	Guam	N	None
8		64	71	San Nicolas, Joaquin A	Adopted son	M	Cha	19	S	N	Y	Guam	Y	None
9		64	71	Atoigue, Maria H	Cousin	F	Cha	16	S	N	Y	Guam	Y	None
10		65	72	Fegurgur, Enrique F	Head	M	Cha	42	M	N	Y	Guam	N	Farmer
11		65	72	Fegurgur, Maria SN	Wife	F	Cha	27	M	N	N	Guam	N	None
12		65	72	Fegurgur, Nicolas SN	Son	M	Cha	9	S	Y		Guam		None
13		65	72	Fegurgur, Felix SN	Son	M	Cha	4.9	S	N		Guam		None
14		65	72	Fegurgur, Dolores SN	Daughter	F	Cha	3.1	S	N		Guam		None
15		65	72	Fegurgur, Francisco SN	Son	M	Cha	1.1	S	N		Guam		None
16		66	73	Gogue, Vicente T	Head	M	Cha	25	M	N	Y	Guam	Y	Farmer
17		66	73	Gogue, Ana SN	Wife	F	Cha	23	M	N	Y	Guam	N	None
18		66	73	Gogue, Maria SN	Daughter	F	Cha	4.8	S	N		Guam		None
19		66	73	Gogue, Catalina SN	Daughter	F	Cha	3	S	N		Guam		None
20		66	73	Gogue, Tomas SN	Son	M	Cha	1.5	S	N		Guam		None
21		67	74	Quidachay, Jose L	Head	M	Cha	28	M	N	Y	Guam	Y	Farmer
22		67	74	Quidachay, Ana T	Wife	F	Cha	22	M	N	N	Guam	N	None
23		67	74	Quidachay, Jesus T	Son	M	Cha	1.9	S	N		Guam		None
24		67	74	Taimanglo, Soledad SN	Mother-in-law	F	Cha	50	Wd	N	N	Guam	N	None
25		67	74	Quichocho, Joaquin L	Brother	M	Cha	14	S	N	N	Guam	N	Farm laborer

DEPARTMENT OF COMMERCE-BUREAU OF THE CENSUS
WASHINGTON

FIFTEENTH CENSUS OF THE UNITED STATES: 1930-POPULATION

THE ISLAND OF GUAM

Sheet No. 8B

283b

District Municipality of Yona
Name of Place Yona Municipality
[Proper name and, also, name of class, as city, town, village, barrio, etc]

Enumeration District No. 12
Enumerated by me on April 10, 1930 Cayetano A. Quinata
Enumerator

	PLACE OF ABODE			NAME	RELATION	PERSONAL DESCRIPTION				EDUCATION		NATIVITY		OCCUPATION
	Street, avenue, road, etc.	Number of dwelling house is order of visitation	Number of family in order of visitation	of each person whose place of abode on April 1, 1930, was in this family. Enter surname, first, then given name and middle initial. If any. Include every person living on April 1, 1930. Omit children born since April 1, 1930.	Relationship of this Person to the head of the family.	Sex	Color or race	Age at last birthday	Single, married, widowed or divorced	Attended school any time since Sept. 1, 1929	Whether able to read and write.	Place of birth of this person.	Whether able to speak English.	
	1	2	3	4	5	6	7	8	9	10	11	12	13	14
26	[no street]	68	75	Cruz, Jose P	Head	M	Fil	23	S	N	Y	Guam	Y	Farm laborer
27		68	76	Cruz, Manuel S	Lodger	M	Cha	19	S	N	Y	Guam	Y	Farm laborer
28		68	77	Reyes, Manuel M	Lodger	M	Cha	28	M	N	Y	Guam	Y	Farm laborer
29		68	78	Bautista, Antonio L	Lodger	M	Cha	19	S	N	Y	Guam	Y	Farm laborer
30		68	79	Pangilinan, Jesus R	Lodger	M	Cha	39	M	N	Y	Guam	Y	Farm laborer
31		68	80	Duenas, Francisco M	Lodger	M	Cha	23	S	N	Y	Guam	Y	Farm laborer
32		68	81	Bautista, Vicente S	Lodger	M	Fil	22	S	N	Y	Guam	Y	Farm laborer
33		69	82	Onidera, Juan J	Head	M	Jap	44	M	N	Y	Japan	Y	Farmer
34		69	82	Onidera, Maria S	Wife	F	Cha	34	M	N	Y	Guam	Y	None
35		69	82	Onidera, Carmen S	Daughter	F	Jap	16	S	N	Y	Guam	Y	None
36		69	82	Onidera, Maria S	Daughter	F	Jap	15	S	Y	Y	Guam	Y	None
37		69	82	Onidera, Juan S	Son	M	Jap	12	S	Y	Y	Guam	Y	None
38		69	82	Onidera, Agueda S	Daughter	F	Jap	9	S	Y	Y	Guam		None
39		70	83	Aguon, Pedro T	Head	M	Cha	66	Wd	N	Y	Guam	N	Farmer
40		70	83	Aguon, Vicente L	Son	M	Cha	17	S	N	Y	Guam	Y	Farm laborer
41		70	83	Aguon, Francisco L	Son	M	Cha	15	S	Y	Y	Guam	Y	Farm laborer
42		71	84	Aguon, Luis L	Head	M	Cha	33	M	N	Y	Guam	Y	Farmer
43		71	84	Aguon, Catalina F	Wife	F	Cha	33	M	N	Y	Guam	Y	None
44		71	84	Aguon, Maria F	Daughter	F	Cha	12	S	Y	Y	Guam	Y	None
45		71	84	Aguon, Pedro F	Son	M	Cha	10	S	Y	Y	Guam		None
46		71	84	Aguon, Julia F	Daughter	F	Cha	8	S	Y		Guam		None
47		71	84	Aguon, Rosa F	Daughter	F	Cha	7	S	Y		Guam		None
48		71	84	Aguon, Rita F	Daughter	F	Cha	0.1	S	N		Guam		None
49		72	85	Aguon, Venancio T	Head	M	Cha	52	M	N	N	Guam	N	Farmer
50		72	85	Aguon, Tomasa O	Wife	F	Cha	46	M	N	N	Guam	N	None

DEPARTMENT OF COMMERCE-BUREAU OF THE CENSUS
WASHINGTON

FIFTEENTH CENSUS OF THE UNITED STATES: 1930-POPULATION

THE ISLAND OF GUAM

Sheet No. 9A

District **Municipality of Yona**
Name of Place **Yona Municipality**
[Proper name and, also, name of class, as city, town, village, barrio, etc]

Enumeration District No. **12**
Enumerated by me on **April 10, 1930** **Cayetano A. Quinata**, Enumerator

	PLACE OF ABODE			NAME	RELATION	PERSONAL DESCRIPTION				EDUCATION		NATIVITY		OCCUPATION
	Street, avenue, road, etc.	Number of dwelling house is order of visitation	Number of family in order of visitation	of each person whose place of abode on April 1, 1930, was in this family. Enter surname, first, then given name and middle initial. If any. Include every person living on April 1, 1930. Omit children born since April 1, 1930.	Relationship of this Person to the head of the family.	Sex	Color or race	Age at last birthday	Single, married, widowed or divorced	Attended school any time since Sept. 1, 1929	Whether able to read and write.	Place of birth of this person.	Whether able to speak English.	
	1	2	3	4	5	6	7	8	9	10	11	12	13	14
1		72	85	Aguon, Ignacio O	Son	M	Cha	23	S	N	Y	Guam	Y	Farm laborer
2		72	85	Aguon, Jose O	Son	M	Cha	14	S	Y	Y	Guam	Y	Farm laborer
3		72	85	Aguon, Maria O	Daughter	F	Cha	13	S	N	Y	Guam	Y	None
4		72	85	Aguon, Rita O	Daughter	F	Cha	5	S	N		Guam		None
5		73	86	Aguon, Jose T	Head	M	Cha	66	Wd	N	Y	Guam	N	Farmer
6		74	87	Cruz, Joaquin R	Head	M	Cha	50	M	N	Y	Guam	N	Farmer
7		74	87	Cruz, Rosa T	Wife	F	Cha	49	M	N	N	Guam	N	None
8		74	87	Cruz, Jesus T	Son	M	Cha	15	S	N	Y	Guam	Y	None
9		74	87	Cruz, Ana T	Daughter	F	Cha	9	S	Y		Guam		None
10		74	87	Cruz, Juan T	Son	M	Cha	8	S	Y		Guam		None
11		75	88	Aguon, Jose L	Head	M	Cha	19	M	N	Y	Guam	Y	Farmer
12		75	88	Aguon, Purdiria T	Wife	F	Cha	19	M	N	Y	Guam	Y	None
13		76	89	Aguon, Juan L	Head	M	Cha	28	M	N	Y	Guam	Y	Farmer
14		76	89	Aguon, Jesus G	Son	M	Cha	4.2	D	N		Guam		None
15		76	89	Aguon, Jose G	Son	M	Cha	2.2	S	N		Guam		None
16		76	89	Aguon, Bernadita G	Daughter	F	Cha	1.3	S	N		Guam		None
17		77	90	Castro, Juan S	Head	M	Cha	34	S	N	Y	Guam	Y	Farmer
18		78	91	Cruz, Jesus B	Head	M	Cha	32	M	N	Y	Guam	Y	Commissioner
19		78	91	Cruz, Rosalia A	Wife	F	Cha	28	M	N	Y	Guam	Y	None
20		78	91	Cruz, Jose A	Son	M	Cha	8	S	Y		Guam		None
21		78	91	Cruz, Jesus A	Son	M	Cha	7	S	Y		Guam		None
22		78	91	Cruz, Maria A	Daughter	F	Cha	5	S	N		Guam		None
23		78	91	Cruz, Santiago A	Son	M	Cha	4.2	S	N		Guam		None
24		78	91	Cruz, Rosa A	Daughter	F	Cha	2.3	S	N		Guam		None
25		78	91	Cruz, Amadeo Artemio A	Son	M	Cha	1.1	S	N		Guam		None

DEPARTMENT OF COMMERCE-BUREAU OF THE CENSUS
WASHINGTON

FIFTEENTH CENSUS OF THE UNITED STATES: 1930-POPULATION

THE ISLAND OF GUAM

Sheet No. 9B

284b

District Municipality of Yona
Name of Place Yona Municipality
[Proper name and, also, name of class, as city, town, village, barrio, etc]

Enumeration District No. 12
Enumerated by me on April 11, 1930 Cayetano A. Quinata, Enumerator

	PLACE OF ABODE: Street, avenue, road, etc.	Number of dwelling house in order of visitation	Number of family in order of visitation	NAME of each person whose place of abode on April 1, 1930, was in this family. Enter surname, first, then given name and middle initial. If any. Include every person living on April 1, 1930. Omit children born since April 1, 1930.	RELATION Relationship of this Person to the head of the family.	PERSONAL DESCRIPTION: Sex	Color or race	Age at last birthday	Single, married, widowed or divorced	EDUCATION: Attended school any time since Sept. 1, 1929	Whether able to read and write.	NATIVITY Place of birth of this person.	Whether able to speak English.	OCCUPATION
	1	2	3	4	5	6	7	8	9	10	11	12	13	14
26	[no street]	78	91	Arceo, Maria C	Sister-in-law	F	Cha	39	S	N	N	Guam	N	None
27		79	92	Cepeda, Juan C	Head	M	Cha	58	M	N	Y	Guam	N	Farmer
28		80	93	Torres, Luis H	Head	M	Cha	40	Wd	N	Y	Guam	Y	Farmer
29		81	94	Torres, Felix H	Head	M	Cha	31	S	N	Y	Guam	Y	Farmer
30		82	95	Toves, Vicenta G	Head	F	Cha	56	Wd	N	N	Guam	N	None
31		83	96	Toves, Juan G	Head	M	Cha	29	M	N	Y	Guam	Y	Farmer
32		83	96	Toves, Ana M	Wife	F	Cha	25	M	N	N	Guam	N	None
33		83	96	Toves, Jesus M	Son	M	Cha	11	S	Y	Y	Guam	Y	None
34		83	96	Toves, Dometro M	Son	M	Cha	10	S	Y	Y	Guam	Y	None
35		83	96	Toves, Maria M	Daughter	F	Cha	9	S	Y		Guam		None
36		83	96	Toves, Joaquin M	Son	M	Cha	5	S	Y		Guam		None
37		83	96	Toves, Pedro M	Son	M	Cha	3.2	S	N		Guam		None
38		83	96	Toves, Rita M	Daughter	F	Cha	0	S	N		Guam		None
39		84	97	Castro, Jose R	Head	M	Cha	67	Wd	N	N	Guam	N	None
40		85	98	Lizama, Ignacio C	Head	M	Cha	36	M	N	Y	Guam	Y	Farmer
41		85	98	Lizama, Regina T	Wife	F	Cha	28	M	N	Y	Guam	Y	None
42		85	98	Lizama, Pedro T	Son	M	Cha	11	S	Y	Y	Guam	Y	None
43		85	98	Lizama, Francisco T	Son	M	Cha	9	S	Y		Guam		None
44		85	98	Lizama, Maria T	Daughter	F	Cha	6	S	N		Guam		None
45		85	98	Lizama, Gregorio T	Son	M	Cha	1.9	S	N		Guam		None
46		85	98	Lizama, Jose T	Son	M	Cha	2.7	S	N		Guam		None
47		85	98	Lizama, Jesus T	Son	M	Cha	0.5	S	N		Guam		None
48		85	98	Mantanona, Benito M	God brother	M	Cha	37	Wd	N	N	Guam	N	Farm laborer
49		86	99	Meno, Jose J	Head	M	Cha	53	M	N	Y	Guam	N	Farmer
50		86	99	Meno, Rita C	Wife	F	Cha	73	M	N	N	Guam	N	None

DEPARTMENT OF COMMERCE-BUREAU OF THE CENSUS
WASHINGTON

FIFTEENTH CENSUS OF THE UNITED STATES: 1930-POPULATION

THE ISLAND OF GUAM

Sheet No. 10A

District **Municipality of Yona**
Name of Place **Yona Municipality**
[Proper name and, also, name of class, as city, town, village, barrio, etc]

Enumeration District No. **12**
Enumerated by me on **April 11, 1930** **Cayetano A. Quinata**
Enumerator

	PLACE OF ABODE			NAME	RELATION	PERSONAL DESCRIPTION				EDUCATION		NATIVITY		OCCUPATION
	Street, avenue, road, etc.	Number of dwelling house is order of visitation	Number of family in order of visitation	of each person whose place of abode on April 1, 1930, was in this family. Enter surname, first, then given name and middle initial. If any. Include every person living on April 1, 1930. Omit children born since April 1, 1930.	Relationship of this Person to the head of the family.	Sex	Color or race	Age at last birthday	Single, married, widowed or divorced	Attended school any time since Sept. 1, 1929	Whether able to read and write.	Place of birth of this person.	Whether able to speak English.	
	1	2	3	4	5	6	7	8	9	10	11	12	13	14
1	[no street]	87	100	Cruz, Vicente S	Head	M	Cha	29	M	N	Y	Guam	Y	Farmer
2		87	100	Cruz, Isabel M	Wife	F	Cha	23	M	N	Y	Guam	Y	None
3		87	100	Cruz, Jose M	Son	M	Cha	4	S	N		Guam		None
4		87	100	Cruz, Vicente M	Son	M	Cha	2.4	S	N		Guam		None
5		87	100	Cruz, Rosalia M	Daughter	F	Cha	0.9	S	N		Guam		None
6		88	101	Quichocho, Jose C	Head	M	Cha	26	M	N	Y	Guam	Y	Farmer
7		88	101	Quichocho, Natividad P	Wife	F	Cha	22	M	N	Y	Guam	Y	None
8		88	101	Quichocho, Maria P	Daughter	F	Cha	2.2	S	N		Guam		None
9		89	102	Santos, Joaquin D	Head	M	Cha	42	M	N	Y	Guam	Y	Farmer
10		89	102	Santos, Ana B	Wife	F	Cha	44	M	N	Y	Guam	N	None
11		89	102	Santos, Teresa D	Daughter	F	Cha	12	S	N	Y	Guam	Y	None
12		90	103	Pangelinan, Maria B	Head	F	Cha	35	Wd	N	N	Guam	N	None
13		91	104	Cruz, Santiago LG	Head	M	Cha	65	M	N	Y	Guam	N	Farmer
14		91	104	Cruz, Josefa B	Wife	F	Cha	54	M	N	Y	Guam	N	None
15		91	104	Cruz, Maria B	Daughter	F	Cha	24	S	N	Y	Guam	Y	None
16		91	104	Cruz, Isabel B	Daughter	F	Cha	20	S	N	Y	Guam	Y	None
17		91	104	Cruz, Luisa B	Daughter	F	Cha	17	S	N	Y	Guam	Y	None
18		91	104	Cruz, Gloria B	Daughter	F	Cha	15	S	N	Y	Guam	Y	None
19		92	105	Cruz, Juan B	Head	M	Cha	29	M	N	Y	Guam	Y	Farmer
20		92	105	Cruz, Magdalena Q	Wife	F	Cha	24	M	N	Y	Guam	Y	None
21		92	105	Cruz, Lorenzo Q	Son	M	Cha	9	S	Y		Guam		None
22		92	105	Cruz, Josefina Q	Daughter	F	Cha	5	S	N		Guam		None
23		92	105	Cruz, Jaime Q	Son	M	Cha	3.7	S	N		Guam		None
24		92	105	Cruz, Carlos Q	Son	M	Cha	2.2	S	N		Guam		None
25		93	106	Ty-Quiongco, Francisco B	Head	M	Chin	24	S	N	Y	Guam	Y	Farm laborer

DEPARTMENT OF COMMERCE-BUREAU OF THE CENSUS
WASHINGTON

FIFTEENTH CENSUS OF THE UNITED STATES: 1930-POPULATION

THE ISLAND OF GUAM

Sheet No. 10B

District Municipality of Yona
Name of Place Yona Municipality
[Proper name and, also, name of class, as city, town, village, barrio, etc]

Enumeration District No. 12
Enumerated by me on April 12, 1930 Cayetano A. Quinata
Enumerator

	PLACE OF ABODE			NAME	RELATION	PERSONAL DESCRIPTION				EDUCATION		NATIVITY		OCCUPATION
	Street, avenue, road, etc.	Number of dwelling house is order of visitation	Number of family in order of visitation	of each person whose place of abode on April 1, 1930, was in this family. Enter surname, first, then given name and middle initial. If any. Include every person living on April 1, 1930. Omit children born since April 1, 1930.	Relationship of this Person to the head of the family.	Sex	Color or race	Age at last birthday	Single, married, widowed or divorced	Attended school any time since Sept. 1, 1929	Whether able to read and write.	Place of birth of this person.	Whether able to speak English.	
	1	2	3	4	5	6	7	8	9	10	11	12	13	14
26	[no street]	93	107	Benavente, Francisco C	Head	M	Cha	18	S	N	Y	Guam	Y	Farm laborer
27		94	108	Taimanglo, Felix Q	Head	M	Cha	20	S	N	Y	Guam	Y	Farmer
28		94	108	Taimanglo, Maria Q	Mother	F	Cha	36	Wd	N	N	Guam	N	None
29		94	108	Taimanglo, Teodoro Q	Brother	M	Cha	14	S	N	Y	Guam	Y	Farm laborer
30		94	108	Taimanglo, Gregorio Q	Brother	M	Cha	13	S	Y	Y	Guam	Y	None
31		94	108	Taimanglo, Dolores Q	Sister	F	Cha	3.8	S	N		Guam		None
32		95	109	Pangelinan, Jesus Q	Head	M	Cha	12	S	N	Y	Guam	Y	Farm laborer
33		95	110	Ogo, Joaquin O	Head	M	Cha	15	S	Y	Y	Guam	Y	None
34		96	111	Aguon, Manuel T	Head	M	Cha	60	M	N	N	Guam	N	Farmer
35		96	111	Cruz, Jose A	Lodger	M	Cha	11	S	Y	Y	Guam	Y	None
36		97	112	Barbour, James	Head	M	W	56	M	N	Y	Minnesota	Y	Farmer
37		97	112	Barbour, Maria C	Wife	F	Cha	57	M	N	Y	Guam	N	None
38		98	113	Atoigue, Tomas M	Head	M	Cha	18	S	N	Y	Guam	Y	Road laborer
39		99	114	Uyeno, Unichich	Head	M	Jap	38	S	N	Y	Japan	Y	Farm laborer
40					Here ends the enumeration of enumerative district No. 12 Yona Municipality									
41														
42														
43														
44														
45														
46														
47														
48														
49														
50														

District 13
Naval Reservations and Ships

(CHAMORRO ROOTS GENEALOGY PROJECT™ TRANSCRIPTION)
(BERNARD T. PUNZALAN / HTTP://WWW.CHAMORROROOTS.COM)

DEPARTMENT OF COMMERCE-BUREAU OF THE CENSUS
WASHINGTON

FIFTEENTH CENSUS OF THE UNITED STATES: 1930-POPULATION

THE ISLAND OF GUAM

Sheet No. 1A

286

District «DistrictName»
Name of Place «NameOfPlace» [Proper name and, also, name of class, as city, town, village, barrio, etc]

Enumeration District No. «DistrictNumber»
Enumerated by me on «EnumeratedDate» «EnumeratorFName» «EnumeratorLName»
Enumerator

	PLACE OF ABODE			NAME	RELATION	PERSONAL DESCRIPTION				EDUCATION		NATIVITY		OCCUPATION
	Street, avenue, road, etc.	Number of dwelling house is order of visitation	Number of family in order of visitation	of each person whose place of abode on April 1, 1930, was in this family. Enter surname, first, then given name and middle initial. If any. Include every person living on April 1, 1930. Omit children born since April 1, 1930.	Relationship of this Person to the head of the family.	Sex	Color or race	Age at last birthday	Single, married, widowed or divorced	Attended school any time since Sept. 1, 1929	Whether able to read and write.	Place of birth of this person.	Whether able to speak English.	
	1	2	3	4	5	6	7	8	9	10	11	12	13	14
1		1	1	Hopper, Raymond E	Head	M	W	28	M	N	Y	Mississippi	Y	US Marine Corps
2		1	1	Hopper, Mildred C	Wife	F	W	29	M	N	Y	Illinois	Y	None
3		2	2	Smith, Perry R	Head	M	W	28	M	N	Y	New York	Y	US Marine Corps
4		2	2	Smith, Edit N	Wife	F	W	26	M	N	Y	Maryland	Y	None
5		2	2	Smith, Shirley A	Daughter	F	W	5	S	N		Pennsylvania		None
6		3	3	Campbell, Harold D	Head	M	W	35	M	N	Y	Vermont	y	US Marine Corps
7		3	3	Campbell, Mildred F	Wife	F	W	32	M	N	Y	Massachusetts	y	None
8		3	3	Campbell, Marilyn D	Daughter	F	W	6	S	Y		Santo Domingo		None
9		3	3	Campbell, Harold D	Son	M	W	3.9	S	N		California		None
10		3	3	Campbell, Nancy J	Daughter	F	W	0.4	S	N		Virginia		None
11		4	4	DeHarber, Louis G	Head	M	W	35	M	N	Y	Delaware	Y	US Marine Corps
12		4	4	DeHarber, Grace H	Wife	F	W	33	M	N	Y	Virginia	Y	None
13		4	4	DeHarber, Helen S	Daughter	F	W	5	S	Y		Virginia		None
14		4	4	DeHarber, Barbara D	Daughter	F	W	4.2	S	N		California		None
15		4	4	DeHarber, Pauline H	Daughter	F	W	2.9	S	N		California		None
16		5	5	Cushing, Francis C	Head	M	W	51	M	N	Y	Missouri	Y	US Marine Corps
17		5	5	Cushing, Alice R	Wife	F	W	44	M	N	Y	Virginia	Y	None
18		5	5	Cushing, Edith E	Daughter	F	W	21	S	N	Y	District of Columbia	Y	Teacher
19		5	5	Cushing, Alice R	Daughter	F	W	17	S	N	Y	District of Columbia	Y	Teacher
20		5	5	Cushing, Francis C	Son	M	W	2.7	S	N		District of Columbia		None
21		6	6	Plachta, Jacob F	Head	M	W	39	M	N	Y	Austria	Y	US Marine Corps
22		6	6	Plachta, Helen K	Wife	F	W	33	M	N	Y	Pennsylvania	Y	None
23		6	6	Plachta, Robert A	Son	M	W	7	S	Y		Haiti		None
24		7	7	Adams, Henry F	Head	M	W	46	M	N	Y	Missouri	Y	US Marine Corps
25		7	7	Adams, Sarah J	Wife	F	W	31	M	N	Y	Pennsylvania	Y	None

DEPARTMENT OF COMMERCE-BUREAU OF THE CENSUS
WASHINGTON
FIFTEENTH CENSUS OF THE UNITED STATES: 1930-POPULATION

THE ISLAND OF GUAM

Sheet No. 1B

286B

District **Municipality**
Name of Place **Naval Reservations and Ships** [Proper name and, also, name of class, as city, town, village, barrio, etc]

Enumeration District No. **13**
Enumerated by me on **April 3, 1930** **Susan W. Bradley**, Enumerator

	PLACE OF ABODE: Street, avenue, road, etc.	Number of dwelling house in order of visitation	Number of family in order of visitation	NAME of each person whose place of abode on April 1, 1930, was in this family. Enter surname, first, then given name and middle initial. If any. Include every person living on April 1, 1930. Omit children born since April 1, 1930.	RELATION Relationship of this Person to the head of the family.	PERSONAL DESCRIPTION: Sex	Color or race	Age at last birthday	Single, married, widowed or divorced	EDUCATION: Attended school any time since Sept. 1, 1929	Whether able to read and write.	NATIVITY Place of birth of this person.	Whether able to speak English.	OCCUPATION
	1	2	3	4	5	6	7	8	9	10	11	12	13	14
26	Sumay Quarters	7	7	Adams, Henry F	Son	M	W	6	S	Y		Virginia		None
27		7	7	Adams, Philip C	Son	M	W	1.1	S	N		Virginia		None
28	Rudes Hill	8	8	Hall, Francis J	Head	M	W	33	M	N	Y	Illionois	Y	US Marine Corps
29		8	8	Hall, Lorene H	Wife	F	W	31	M	N	Y	Illionois	Y	None
30		8	8	Hall, Virginia L	Daughter	F	W	7	S	Y		Illionois		None
31		8	8	Hall, Robert W	Son	M	W	6	S	Y		Illionois		None
32		8	8	Hall, Thurman F	Son	M	W	4.1	S			California		None
33		9	9	Scheid, Peter A	Head	M	W	32	M	N	Y	New York	Y	US Marine Corps
34		9	9	Scheid, Wanda C	Wife	F	W	29	M	N	Y	Texas	Y	None
35	Marine Quarters	9	9	Scheid, Robert F	Son	M	W	9	S	Y		Arkansas		None
36		10	10	Le Gette, Curtis W	Head	M	W	37	M	N	Y	South Carolina	Y	US Marine Corps
37		10	10	Le Gette, Geraldine	Wife	F	W	33	M	N	Y	Virginia	Y	None
38		11	11	Mullaly, Eugene L	Head	M	W	43	M	N	Y	New York	Y	US Marine Corps
39		11	11	Mullaly, Evelyn H	Wife	F	W	32	M	N	Y	California	Y	None
40		11	11	Mullaly, Patricia V	Daughter	F	W	11	S	Y	Y	Virginia	Y	None
41		12	12	Fenton, Francis I	Head	M	W	37	M	N	Y	Washington	Y	US Marine Corps
42		12	12	Fenton, Mary E	Wife	F	W	29	M	N	Y	California	Y	None
43		12	12	Fenton, Michael E	Son	M	W	1.1	S	N		California		None
44		12	12	Fenton, Francis I	Son	M	W	7	S	Y		California		None
45		13	13	Yaecker, Walter E	Head	M	W	38	M	N	Y	Pennsylvania	Y	US Marine Corps
46		13	13	Yaecker, Agne L	Wife	F	W	35	M	N	Y	Wisconsin	Y	None
47	Piti Quarters	14	14	Rolnicko, Walter O	Head	M	W	32	M	N	Y	Oregon	y	US Navy
48		14	14	Rolnicko, Doris R	Wife	F	W	25	M	N	Y	Washington	y	Teacher
49		14	14	Rolnicko, Walter O	Son	M	W	6	S	Y		California		None
50		14	14	Rolnicko, Janet D	Daughter	F	W	1.5	S			Guam		None

DEPARTMENT OF COMMERCE-BUREAU OF THE CENSUS
WASHINGTON

FIFTEENTH CENSUS OF THE UNITED STATES: 1930-POPULATION

THE ISLAND OF GUAM

Sheet No. 2A

District **Municipality**
Name of Place **Naval Reservations and Ships**
[Proper name and, also, name of class, as city, town, village, barrio, etc]

Enumeration District No. **13**
Enumerated by me on **April 5, 1930** **Susan W. Bradley**
Enumerator

	PLACE OF ABODE			NAME	RELATION	PERSONAL DESCRIPTION				EDUCATION		NATIVITY		OCCUPATION
	Street, avenue, road, etc.	Number of dwelling house is order of visitation	Number of family in order of visitation	of each person whose place of abode on April 1, 1930, was in this family. Enter surname, first, then given name and middle initial. If any. Include every person living on April 1, 1930. Omit children born since April 1, 1930.	Relationship of this Person to the head of the family.	Sex	Color or race	Age at last birthday	Single, married, widowed or divorced	Attended school any time since Sept. 1, 1929	Whether able to read and write.	Place of birth of this person.	Whether able to speak English.	
	1	2	3	4	5	6	7	8	9	10	11	12	13	14
1	Marine Quarters	15	15	Gravelle, Homer J	Head	M	W	34	M	N	Y	Michigan	Y	US Marine Corps
2		15	15	Gravelle, Anna O	Wife	F	W	34	M	N	Y	Illinois	Y	None
3		16	16	Swift, Edwin O	Head	M	W	44	M	N	Y	New York	Y	US Marine Corps
4		16	16	Swift, Mable A	Wife	F	W	38	M	N	Y	Iowa	Y	None
5		17	17	Caspers, Frank K	Head	M	W	44	M	N	Y	Illinois	Y	US Marine Corps
6		17	17	Caspers, Mary A	Wife	F	W	49	M	N	Y	District of Columbia	Y	None
7		18	18	Siegrist, Norman B	Head	M	W	41	M	N	Y	New York	Y	US Marine Corps
8		18	18	Siegrist, Laura M	Wife	F	W	34	M	N	Y	New York	Y	None
9		18	18	Siegrist, Mariore T	Daughter	F	W	11	S	Y	Y	South Carolina	Y	None
10		18	18	Siegrist, Warren H	Son	M	W	8	S	Y		China		None
11		18	18	Siegrist, Norma D	Daughter	F	W	5	S	Y		California		None
12		19	19	Hill, James A	Head	M	W	34	M	N	Y	Texas	Y	US Navy
13		19	19	Hill, Annette A	Wife	F	W	27	M	N	Y	Massachusetts	Y	None
14		20	20	Bird, Samuel K	Head	M	W	28	M	N	Y	Oklahoma	Y	US Marine Corps
15		20	20	Bird, Mary M	Wife	F	W	24	M	N	Y	Missouri	Y	None
16		20	20	Bird, Emily S	Daughter	F	W	0.6	S	N		California		None
17	Marine Barracks			Adams, Robert L		M	W	22	S	N	Y	North Carolina	Y	US Marine Corps
18				Anderson, Donald W		M	W	22	S	N	Y	Minnesota	Y	US Marine Corps
19				Anderson, Leo		M	W	23	S	N	Y	Indiana	Y	US Marine Corps
20				Anthony, John P		M	W	22	S	N	Y	North Carolina	Y	US Marine Corps
21				Bennett, Basil H		M	W	22	S	N	Y	Idaho	Y	US Marine Corps
22				Bicio, Pete P		M	W	20	S	N	Y	New York	Y	US Marine Corps
23				Blaire, Elmer R		M	W	21	S	N	Y	Missouri	Y	US Marine Corps
24				Boorman, Thomas T		M	W	19	S	N	Y	Colorado	Y	US Marine Corps
25				Boyle, Howard R		M	W	18	S	N	Y	Kansas	Y	US Marine Corps

DEPARTMENT OF COMMERCE-BUREAU OF THE CENSUS
WASHINGTON

FIFTEENTH CENSUS OF THE UNITED STATES: 1930-POPULATION

THE ISLAND OF GUAM

Sheet No. 2B **287B**

District **Municipality**
Name of Place **Naval Reservations and Ships**
[Proper name and, also, name of class, as city, town, village, barrio, etc]

Enumeration District No. **13**
Enumerated by me on **April 5, 1930** **Susan W. Bradley**
Enumerator

	PLACE OF ABODE			NAME	RELATION	PERSONAL DESCRIPTION				EDUCATION		NATIVITY		OCCUPATION
	Street, avenue, road, etc.	Number of dwelling house is order of visitation	Number of family in order of visitation	of each person whose place of abode on April 1, 1930, was in this family. Enter surname, first, then given name and middle initial. If any. Include every person living on April 1, 1930. Omit children born since April 1, 1930.	Relationship of this Person to the head of the family.	Sex	Color or race	Age at last birthday	Single, married, widowed or divorced	Attended school any time since Sept. 1, 1929	Whether able to read and write.	Place of birth of this person.	Whether able to speak English.	
	1	2	3	4	5	6	7	8	9	10	11	12	13	14
26	Marine Barracks			Braucher, Frances E		M	W	19	S	N	Y	Nebraska	Y	US Marine Corps
27				Brennan, Thomas P		M	W	36	S	N	Y	New York	Y	US Marine Corps
28				Brynn, William L		M	W	28	S	N	Y	Missouri	Y	US Marine Corps
29				Buckner, Walter C		M	W	18	S	N	Y	North Carolina	Y	US Marine Corps
30				Byrando, Everette J		M	W	21	S	N	Y	California	Y	US Marine Corps
31				Calls, Ora E		M	W	19	S	N	Y	Kansas	Y	US Marine Corps
32				Cayez, Maurice		M	W	30	S	N	Y	France	Y	US Marine Corps
33				Christian, Frank P		M	W	22	S	N	Y	Illinois	Y	US Marine Corps
34				Clapper, Daniel R		M	W	19	S	N	Y	North Dakota	Y	US Marine Corps
35				Clark, Alfred B		M	W	18	S	N	Y	Colorado	Y	US Marine Corps
36				Comer, Ernest M		M	W	19	S	N	Y	Mississippi	Y	US Marine Corps
37				Cook, Harvey M		M	W	23	S	N	Y	North Carolina	Y	US Marine Corps
38				Culmer, Franklin RD		M	W	23	S	N	Y	Illinois	Y	US Marine Corps
39				[Blank]										
40				Dalrymple, Jess R		M	W		S	N	Y	Oklahoma	Y	US Marine Corps
41				Davis, James E		M	W		S	N	Y	North Carolina	Y	US Marine Corps
42				Davis, William J. Jr.		M	W		S	N	Y	Montana	Y	US Marine Corps
43				Devin, Kenneth C		M	W		S	N	Y	Indiana	Y	US Marine Corps
44				Digue, Alvin A		M	W		S	N	Y	Michigan	Y	US Marine Corps
45				Dixon, Kenneth E		M	W		S	N	Y	Oregon	Y	US Marine Corps
46				Doty, Thomas W		M	W		S	N	Y	Illinois	Y	US Marine Corps
47				Duckett, Andrew J		M	W		S	N	Y	Texas	Y	US Marine Corps
48				Cokins, Ralph G		M	W		S	N	Y	Iowa	Y	US Marine Corps
49				Eastham, Walter H		M	W		S	N	Y	Texas	Y	US Marine Corps
50				Eaton, Albert L		M	W		S	N	Y	Georgia	Y	US Marine Corps

[Line 39 left blank by Enumerator.]

DEPARTMENT OF COMMERCE-BUREAU OF THE CENSUS
WASHINGTON

FIFTEENTH CENSUS OF THE UNITED STATES: 1930-POPULATION

THE ISLAND OF GUAM

Sheet No. 3A

District **Municipality**
Name of Place **Naval Reservations and Ships**
[Proper name and, also, name of class, as city, town, village, barrio, etc]

Enumeration District No. **13**
Enumerated by me on **April 5, 1930** **Susan W. Bradley**, Enumerator

	PLACE OF ABODE			NAME	RELATION	PERSONAL DESCRIPTION				EDUCATION		NATIVITY		OCCUPATION
	Street, avenue, road, etc.	Number of dwelling house is order of visitation	Number of family in order of visitation	of each person whose place of abode on April 1, 1930, was in this family. Enter surname, first, then given name and middle initial. If any. Include every person living on April 1, 1930. Omit children born since April 1, 1930.	Relationship of this Person to the head of the family.	Sex	Color or race	Age at last birthday	Single, married, widowed or divorced	Attended school any time since Sept. 1, 1929	Whether able to read and write.	Place of birth of this person.	Whether able to speak English.	
	1	2	3	4	5	6	7	8	9	10	11	12	13	14
1	Marine Barracks			Ely, Harold M		M	W	18	S	N	Y	Iowa	Y	US Marine Corps
2				Ernest, William B		M	W	21	S	N	Y	Washington	Y	US Marine Corps
3				Erb, Clifford A		M	W	19	S	N	Y	Pennsylvania	Y	US Marine Corps
4				Farmer, Cylde A		M	W	18	S	N	Y	Kentucky	Y	US Marine Corps
5				Ferguson, John C		M	W	29	S	N	Y	North Carolina	Y	US Marine Corps
6				Florence, Orion A		M	W	18	S	N	Y	Washington	Y	US Marine Corps
7				Ford, Daniel		M	W	18	S	N	Y	Washington	Y	US Marine Corps
8				Foster, Arthur B		M	W	19	S	N	Y	Florida	Y	US Marine Corps
9				Forbes, Hosea D		M	W	19	S	N	Y	Texas	Y	US Marine Corps
10				Francis, Oliver T		M	W	33	S	N	Y	Minnesota	Y	US Marine Corps
11				Garlow, Jesse J		M	W	21	S	N	Y	North Dakota	Y	US Marine Corps
12				Gilpise, Robert E		M	W	25	S	N	Y	Indianna	Y	US Marine Corps
13				Glenn, John S		M	W	26	S	N	Y	Tennessee	Y	US Marine Corps
14				Goodall, Jack W		M	W	27	S	N	Y	Austrailia	Y	US Marine Corps
15				Gray, William L		M	W	19	S	N	Y	Mississippi	Y	US Marine Corps
16				Grote, Nelis N		M	W	19	S	N	Y	Illinois	Y	US Marine Corps
17				Hair, Robert R		M	W	19	S	N	Y	Texas	Y	US Marine Corps
18				Harrison, Clifford A		M	W	22	S	N	Y	Minnesota	Y	US Marine Corps
19				Harding, Oscar L		M	W	23	S	N	Y	Maryland	Y	US Marine Corps
20				Harriet, John T. Jr.		M	W	18	S	N	Y	Hawaii	Y	US Marine Corps
21				Harrison, Yan B		M	W	26	S	N	Y	Tennessee	Y	US Marine Corps
22				Hassig, Edwin F		M	W	19	S	N	Y	North Dakota	Y	US Marine Corps
23				Naune, Ernie		M	W	19	S	N	Y	Ohio	Y	US Marine Corps
24				Heng, James L		M	W	22	S	N	Y	California	Y	US Marine Corps
25				Talehart, Claude N		M	W	18	S	N	Y	Texas	Y	US Marine Corps

(CHAMORRO ROOTS GENEALOGY PROJECT™ TRANSCRIPTION)
(BERNARD T. PUNZALAN / HTTP://WWW.CHAMORROROOTS.COM)

DEPARTMENT OF COMMERCE-BUREAU OF THE CENSUS
WASHINGTON
FIFTEENTH CENSUS OF THE UNITED STATES: 1930-POPULATION

THE ISLAND OF GUAM

Sheet No. 3B

288B

District **Municipality**
Name of Place **Naval Reservations and Ships**
[Proper name and, also, name of class, as city, town, village, barrio, etc]

Enumeration District No. **13**
Enumerated by me on **April 5, 1930** **Susan W. Bradley**
Enumerator

	PLACE OF ABODE			NAME	RELATION	PERSONAL DESCRIPTION				EDUCATION		NATIVITY		OCCUPATION
	Street, avenue, road, etc.	Number of dwelling house is order of visitation	Number of family in order of visitation	of each person whose place of abode on April 1, 1930, was in this family. Enter surname, first, then given name and middle initial. If any. Include every person living on April 1, 1930. Omit children born since April 1, 1930.	Relationship of this Person to the head of the family.	Sex	Color or race	Age at last birthday	Single, married, widowed or divorced	Attended school any time since Sept. 1, 1929	Whether able to read and write.	Place of birth of this person.	Whether able to speak English.	
	1	2	3	4	5	6	7	8	9	10	11	12	13	14
26	Marine Barracks			Narpen, Edward T A		M	W	19	S	N	Y	Minnesota	Y	US Marine Corps
27				Niny, Charles R		M	W	22	S	N	Y	Pennsylvania	Y	US Marine Corps
28				Krein, Henry		M	W	22	S	N	Y	North Dakota	Y	US Marine Corps
29				Lamb, Hughey		M	W	33	S	N	Y	Georgia	Y	US Marine Corps
30				Lauf, Lester P		M	W	21	S	N	Y	Texas	Y	US Marine Corps
31				Laughridge, George C		M	W	22	S	N	Y	Kansas	Y	US Marine Corps
32				Lebsock, Daniel R		M	W	19	S	N	Y	Colorado	Y	US Marine Corps
33				Leech, Lawrence E		M	W	23	S	N	Y	Colorado	Y	US Marine Corps
34				Leffa, George M		M	W	20	S	N	Y	California	Y	US Marine Corps
35				Ledria, Harry F		M	W	25	S	N	Y	Pennsylvania	Y	US Marine Corps
36				Lorighbaugh, Harry I		M	W	18	S	N	Y	Georgia	Y	US Marine Corps
37				Loresg, William H		M	W	20	S	N	Y	Kansas	Y	US Marine Corps
38				Ludweck, Joseph B		M	W	25	S	N	Y	Missouri	Y	US Marine Corps
39				Mapleson, Joseph		M	W	35	S	N	Y	Pennsylvania	Y	US Marine Corps
40				Mcleit, Clifford J		M	W	18	S	N	Y	Minnesota	Y	US Marine Corps
41				McDonnell, Wilbur J		M	W	19	S	N	Y	Washington	Y	US Marine Corps
42				McKinley, Rufus W		M	W	28	S	N	Y	Kentucky	Y	US Marine Corps
43				McNeil, Earnest		M	W	20	S	N	Y	Kansas	Y	US Marine Corps
44				McOdeum, Earnest D		M	W	28	S	N	Y	Massachusetts	Y	US Marine Corps
45				McWilliams, Garland L		M	W	18	S	N	Y	Texas	Y	US Marine Corps
46				Metzinger, Lawarence M		M	W	27	S	N	Y	Missouri	Y	US Marine Corps
47				Miteno, Arthur W		M	W	19	S	N	Y	Washington	Y	US Marine Corps
48				Milies, Burlie H		M	W	18	S	N	Y	Texas	Y	US Marine Corps
49				Morien, Trimmon O		M	W	17	S	N	Y	Colorado	Y	US Marine Corps
50				Morwich, John J		M	W	24	S	N	Y	Missouri	Y	US Marine Corps

DEPARTMENT OF COMMERCE-BUREAU OF THE CENSUS
WASHINGTON

FIFTEENTH CENSUS OF THE UNITED STATES: 1930-POPULATION

THE ISLAND OF GUAM

Sheet No. 4A

District **Municipality**
Name of Place **Naval Reservations and Ships**
[Proper name and, also, name of class, as city, town, village, barrio, etc]

Enumeration District No. **13**
Enumerated by me on **April 6, 1930** **Susan W. Bradley**, Enumerator

	PLACE OF ABODE: Street, avenue, road, etc.	Number of dwelling house in order of visitation	Number of family in order of visitation	NAME of each person whose place of abode on April 1, 1930, was in this family. Enter surname, first, then given name and middle initial. If any. Include every person living on April 1, 1930. Omit children born since April 1, 1930.	RELATION Relationship of this Person to the head of the family.	PERSONAL DESCRIPTION: Sex	Color or race	Age at last birthday	Single, married, widowed or divorced	EDUCATION: Attended school any time since Sept. 1, 1929	Whether able to read and write.	NATIVITY Place of birth of this person.	Whether able to speak English.	OCCUPATION
	1	2	3	4	5	6	7	8	9	10	11	12	13	14
1	Marine Barracks			Nateo, Pete M		M	W	31	S	N	Y	Pennsylvania	Y	US Marine Corps
2				Neaves, Roscol B		M	W	19	S	N	Y	Missouri	Y	US Marine Corps
3				Norris, Frank J		M	W	29	S	N	Y	Nebraska	Y	US Marine Corps
4				O'Bryant, Paul J		M	W	24	S	N	Y	New York	Y	US Marine Corps
5				Orfie, Russell J		M	W	19	S	N	Y	Pennsylvania	Y	US Marine Corps
6				Peeples, Monroe T		M	W	33	S	N	Y	North Carolina	Y	US Marine Corps
7				Pereria, Lester L		M	W	24	S	N	Y	California	Y	US Marine Corps
8				Peters, Edward T		M	W	20	S	N	Y	California	Y	US Marine Corps
9				Pollock, Verl D		M	W	19	S	N	Y	Utah	Y	US Marine Corps
10				Rathbories, Ray M		M	W	26	S	N	Y	Washington	Y	US Marine Corps
11				Rebb, Albert S		M	W	18	S	N	Y	New York	Y	US Marine Corps
12				Reid, William E		M	W	19	S	N	Y	Michigan	Y	US Marine Corps
13				Reiter, Harold W		M	W	20	S	N	Y	Minnesota	Y	US Marine Corps
14				Reiter, Henry G		M	W	22	S	N	Y	Minnesota	Y	US Marine Corps
15				Rich, Otto W		M	W	22	S	N	Y	Alabama	Y	US Marine Corps
16				Richards, William S		M	W	22	S	N	Y	West Virginia	Y	US Marine Corps
17				Risch, Harold F		M	W	21	S	N	Y	Ohio	Y	US Marine Corps
18				Roales, Troy H		M	W	22	S	N	Y	Arkansas	Y	US Marine Corps
19				Safford, Rollo		M	W	19	S	N	Y	Wisconsin	Y	US Marine Corps
20				Sergessi, Arnol		M	W	19	S	N	Y	Oklahoma	Y	US Marine Corps
21				Sartorina, Claude X		M	W	34	S	N	Y	Missouri	Y	US Marine Corps
22				Sarp, Orlan R		M	W	20	S	N	Y	Utah	Y	US Marine Corps
23				Schoenecker, Raymond J		M	W	23	S	N	Y	Minnesota	Y	US Marine Corps
24				Shedler, Glenn D		M	W	18	S	N	Y	Colorado	Y	US Marine Corps
25				Skolaski, Lawrence P		M	W	18	S	N	Y	Wisconsin	Y	US Marine Corps

DEPARTMENT OF COMMERCE-BUREAU OF THE CENSUS
WASHINGTON

FIFTEENTH CENSUS OF THE UNITED STATES: 1930-POPULATION

THE ISLAND OF GUAM

Sheet No. 4B

289B

District **Municipality**

Name of Place **Naval Reservations and Ships**
[Proper name and, also, name of class, as city, town, village, barrio, etc]

Enumeration District No. **13**

Enumerated by me on **April 6, 1930** **Susan W. Bradley**
Enumerator

	PLACE OF ABODE			NAME	RELATION	PERSONAL DESCRIPTION				EDUCATION		NATIVITY		OCCUPATION
	Street, avenue, road, etc.	Number of dwelling house is order of visitation	Number of family in order of visitation	of each person whose place of abode on April 1, 1930, was in this family. Enter surname, first, then given name and middle initial. If any. Include every person living on April 1, 1930. Omit children born since April 1, 1930.	Relationship of this Person to the head of the family.	Sex	Color or race	Age at last birthday	Single, married, widowed or divorced	Attended school any time since Sept. 1, 1929	Whether able to read and write.	Place of birth of this person.	Whether able to speak English.	
	1	2	3	4	5	6	7	8	9	10	11	12	13	14
26	Marine Barracks			Slaughter, John B		M	W	20	S	N	Y	Georgia	Y	US Marine Corps
27				Smith, Claude V		M	W	27	S	N	Y	Kansas	Y	US Marine Corps
28				Smith, Wayne W		M	W	31	S	N	Y	Nebraska	Y	US Marine Corps
29				Spice, Lloyd C		M	W	30	S	N	Y	Canada	Y	US Marine Corps
30				Stone, Carlo W		M	W	21	S	N	Y	California	Y	US Marine Corps
31				Startovant, Wlmer M		M	W	18	S	N	Y	Massachusetts	Y	US Marine Corps
32				Tackett, Clifford G		M	W	19	S	N	Y	West Virginia	Y	US Marine Corps
33				Taylor, Edgar		M	W	26	S	N	Y	Georgia	Y	US Marine Corps
34				Thomas, William A		M	W	20	S	N	Y	Missouri	Y	US Marine Corps
35				Thrower, Wiley J		M	W	26	S	N	Y	North Carolina	Y	US Marine Corps
36				Toner, Martin J		M	W	18	S	N	Y	Washington	Y	US Marine Corps
37				Townsend, John W		M	W	18	S	N	Y	Nebraska	Y	US Marine Corps
38				Tracy, Albert H		M	W	20	S	N	Y	Indianna	Y	US Marine Corps
39				Vallandingham, Howard H		M	W	21	S	N	Y	Nebraska	Y	US Marine Corps
40				Whatley, Chester		M	W	22	S	N	Y	Washington	Y	US Marine Corps
41				Wilburn, Richmond W		M	W	30	S	N	Y	Kentucky	Y	US Marine Corps
42				Wilhelm, Vincent R		M	W	23	S	N	Y	Ohio	Y	US Marine Corps
43				Wilson, Robert L		M	W	26	S	N	Y	Texas	Y	US Marine Corps
44				Wood, Laurance A		M	W	18	S	N	Y	Minnesota	Y	US Marine Corps
45				Wood, Robert W		M	W	21	S	N	Y	Virginia	Y	US Marine Corps
46				Worthington, Ralph		M	W	21	S	N	Y	California	Y	US Marine Corps
47				Wyatt, James R		M	W	18	S	N	Y	Virginia	Y	US Marine Corps
48				Abtue, Joseph W		M	W	49	S	N	Y	Virginia	Y	US Marine Corps
49				Anderson, George		M	W	47	S	N	Y	South Dakota	Y	US Marine Corps
50				Anderson, John H		M	W	22	S	N	Y	Wisconsin	Y	US Marine Corps

DEPARTMENT OF COMMERCE-BUREAU OF THE CENSUS
WASHINGTON

FIFTEENTH CENSUS OF THE UNITED STATES: 1930-POPULATION

THE ISLAND OF GUAM

Sheet No. 5A

District **Municipality**
Name of Place **Naval Reservations and Ships**
[Proper name and, also, name of class, as city, town, village, barrio, etc]

Enumeration District No. **13**
Enumerated by me on **April 7, 1930** **Susan W. Bradley**, Enumerator

	PLACE OF ABODE: Street, avenue, road, etc.	Number of dwelling house in order of visitation	Number of family in order of visitation	NAME of each person whose place of abode on April 1, 1930, was in this family. Enter surname, first, then given name and middle initial. If any. Include every person living on April 1, 1930. Omit children born since April 1, 1930.	RELATION Relationship of this Person to the head of the family.	PERSONAL DESCRIPTION: Sex	Color or race	Age at last birthday	Single, married, widowed or divorced	EDUCATION: Attended school any time since Sept. 1, 1929	Whether able to read and write.	NATIVITY Place of birth of this person.	Whether able to speak English.	OCCUPATION
	1	2	3	4	5	6	7	8	9	10	11	12	13	14
1	Marine Barracks			Baker, Clyde C		M	W	23	S	N	Y	Wisconsin	Y	US Marine Corps
2				Ballard, Albert G		M	W	21	S	N	Y	North Carolina	Y	US Marine Corps
3				Barnes, Russell M		M	W	26	S	N	Y	Indiana	Y	US Marine Corps
4				Battles, Marvin S		M	W	19	S	N	Y	Texas	Y	US Marine Corps
5				Bennette, Maurices O		M	W	20	S	N	Y	Missouri	Y	US Marine Corps
6				Bishop, Vernin E		M	W	21	S	N	Y	Florida	Y	US Marine Corps
7				Bourne, Dana H		M	W	21	S	N	Y	West Virginia	Y	US Marine Corps
8				Bowdre, Paul A		M	W	24	S	N	Y	Florida	Y	US Marine Corps
9				Brackels, Dale S		M	W	22	S	N	Y	Texas	Y	US Marine Corps
10				Brocker, Edward W		M	W	19	S	N	Y	Utah	Y	US Marine Corps
11				Brown, Charle D		M	W	21	S	N	Y	Alabama	Y	US Marine Corps
12				Browning, Lewis J		M	W	19	S	N	Y	Pennsylvania	Y	US Marine Corps
13				Burns, Florence V		M	W	22	S	N	Y	Massachusetts	Y	US Marine Corps
14				Carroll, Luis R		M	W	31	S	N	Y	Illinois	Y	US Marine Corps
15				Cobb, Lesley F		M	W	20	S	N	Y	Georgia	Y	US Marine Corps
16				Coffey, Albert R		M	W	27	S	N	Y	California	Y	US Marine Corps
17				Cox, John W		M	W	18	S	N	Y	Texas	Y	US Marine Corps
18				Cranit, John F		M	W	22	S	N	Y	New York	Y	US Marine Corps
19				Crawford, Arden V		M	W	20	S	N	Y	South Dakota	Y	US Marine Corps
20				Cruickshank, Harold E		M	W	19	S	N	Y	California	Y	US Marine Corps
21				Daily, James T		M	W	23	S	N	Y	Nebraska	Y	US Marine Corps
22				Davis, Edward R		M	W	21	S	N	Y	Oklahoma	Y	US Marine Corps
23				Dawson, John S		M	W	25	S	N	Y	Kansas	Y	US Marine Corps
24				Deal, John D		M	W	22	S	N	Y	Missouri	Y	US Marine Corps
25				Devore, David A		M	W	20	S	N	Y	California	Y	US Marine Corps

(CHAMORRO ROOTS GENEALOGY PROJECT™ TRANSCRIPTION)
(BERNARD T. PUNZALAN / HTTP://WWW.CHAMORROROOTS.COM)

DEPARTMENT OF COMMERCE-BUREAU OF THE CENSUS
WASHINGTON

FIFTEENTH CENSUS OF THE UNITED STATES: 1930-POPULATION

THE ISLAND OF GUAM

Sheet No. 5B

290B

District **Municipality**
Name of Place **Naval Reservations and Ships**
[Proper name and, also, name of class, as city, town, village, barrio, etc]

Enumeration District No. **13**
Enumerated by me on **April 7, 1930** **Susan W. Bradley**, Enumerator

	PLACE OF ABODE			NAME	RELATION	PERSONAL DESCRIPTION				EDUCATION		NATIVITY		OCCUPATION
	Street, avenue, road, etc.	Number of dwelling house is order of visitation	Number of family in order of visitation	of each person whose place of abode on April 1, 1930, was in this family. Enter surname, first, then given name and middle initial. If any. Include every person living on April 1, 1930. Omit children born since April 1, 1930.	Relationship of this Person to the head of the family.	Sex	Color or race	Age at last birthday	Single, married, widowed or divorced	Attended school any time since Sept. 1, 1929	Whether able to read and write.	Place of birth of this person.	Whether able to speak English.	
	1	2	3	4	5	6	7	8	9	10	11	12	13	14
26	Marine Barracks			Dodson, Vern		M	W	20	S	N	Y	Oklahoma	Y	US Marine Corps
27				Dorsine, Charles E		M	W	21	S	N	Y	California	Y	US Marine Corps
28				Darsey, James W		M	W	29	S	N	Y	Ohio	Y	US Marine Corps
29				Downey, Francis P		M	W	31	S	N	Y	Pennsylvania	Y	US Marine Corps
30				Ellis, Augustine J		M	W	27	S	N	Y	Kentucky	Y	US Marine Corps
31				Elliott, Marion J		M	W	20	S	N	Y	Ohio	Y	US Marine Corps
32				Eschiliman, Charles		M	W	25	M	N	Y	Colorado	Y	US Marine Corps
33				Gabriel, Reginal L		M	W	22	S	N	Y	Louisiana	Y	US Marine Corps
34				Gorsuch, Wilbur P		M	W	23	S	N	Y	Iowa	Y	US Marine Corps
35				Gourley, William J		M	W	21	S	N	Y	Pennsylvania	Y	US Marine Corps
36				Graham, Grey M		M	W	20	S	N	Y	New Mexico	Y	US Marine Corps
37				Granson, Lester M		M	W	21	S	N	Y	Nebraska	Y	US Marine Corps
38				Harrison, Paul H		M	W	23	S	N	Y	Texas	Y	US Marine Corps
39				Hemmerl, Peter		M	W	44	S	N	Y	Wisconsin	Y	US Marine Corps
40				Hess, Kenneth B		M	W	19	S	N	Y	California	Y	US Marine Corps
41				Hiddleston, Heschel D		M	W	20	S	N	Y	Kansas	Y	US Marine Corps
42				Haphayer, Raymond B		M	W	23	S	N	Y	Missouri	Y	US Marine Corps
43				Hunt, Thomas D		M	W	36	S	N	Y	Missouri	Y	US Marine Corps
44				Huntise, George C		M	W	23	S	N	Y	Minnesota	Y	US Marine Corps
45				Huntise, Warren J		M	W	20	S	N	Y	Pennsylvania	Y	US Marine Corps
46				Johnson, Joseph E		M	W	23	S	N	Y	Massachusetts	Y	US Marine Corps
47				Jones, Milburn K		M	W	19	S	N	Y	Indiana	Y	US Marine Corps
48				Kellett, Wayne D		M	W	21	S	N	Y	South Dakota	Y	US Marine Corps
49				Kelly, Kenneth P		M	W	19	S	N	Y	Colorado	Y	US Marine Corps
50				Kennedy, Paul B		M	W	28	S	N	Y	Oklahoma	Y	US Marine Corps

DEPARTMENT OF COMMERCE-BUREAU OF THE CENSUS
WASHINGTON

FIFTEENTH CENSUS OF THE UNITED STATES: 1930-POPULATION

THE ISLAND OF GUAM

Sheet No. 6A

District **Municipality**
Name of Place **Naval Reservations and Ships**
[Proper name and, also, name of class, as city, town, village, barrio, etc]

Enumeration District No. **13**
Enumerated by me on **April 7, 1930** **Susan W. Bradley**, Enumerator

	PLACE OF ABODE			NAME	RELATION	PERSONAL DESCRIPTION				EDUCATION		NATIVITY		OCCUPATION
	Street, avenue, road, etc.	Number of dwelling house is order of visitation	Number of family in order of visitation	of each person whose place of abode on April 1, 1930, was in this family. Enter surname, first, then given name and middle initial. If any. Include every person living on April 1, 1930. Omit children born since April 1, 1930.	Relationship of this Person to the head of the family.	Sex	Color or race	Age at last birthday	Single, married, widowed or divorced	Attended school any time since Sept. 1, 1929	Whether able to read and write.	Place of birth of this person.	Whether able to speak English.	
	1	2	3	4	5	6	7	8	9	10	11	12	13	14
1	Marine Barracks			Kucharski, Edmund		M	W	33	S	N	Y	Illinois	Y	US Marine Corps
2				Kusz, Joseph Q		M	W	29	S	N	Y	Germany	Y	US Marine Corps
3				Lanen, Leonard G		M	W	19	S	N	Y	Montana	Y	US Marine Corps
4				Larson, Nathan P		M	W	25	S	N	Y	South Dakota	Y	US Marine Corps
5				Lawrence, John T. Jr.		M	W	26	S	N	Y	Iowa	Y	US Marine Corps
6				Leonard, Charles H		M	W	24	S	N	Y	New Hampshire	Y	US Marine Corps
7				Lee, Charles H		M	W	22	S	N	Y	Pennsylvania	Y	US Marine Corps
8				Levi, Robert D		M	W	19	S	N	Y	Michigan	Y	US Marine Corps
9				Lewis, Daniel P		M	W	18	S	N	Y	Canada	Y	US Marine Corps
10				Lippold, John A		M	W	25	S	N	Y	Iowa	Y	US Marine Corps
11				Long, Vern		M	W	34	S	N	Y	Missouri	Y	US Marine Corps
12				Lurhinas, Charles D		M	W	39	M	N	Y	Sweden	Y	US Marine Corps
13				Mace, John W		M	W	32	S	N	Y	Missouri	Y	US Marine Corps
14				Malcom, Walter L		M	W	21	S	N	Y	Iowa	Y	US Marine Corps
15				Marguss, Feliz A		M	W	22	S	N	Y	Colorado	Y	US Marine Corps
16				Mason, Sidney E		M	W	22	S	N	Y	Kansas	Y	US Marine Corps
17				May, Harold V		M	W	22	S	N	Y	Indiana	Y	US Marine Corps
18				Mare, William H		M	W	46	M	N	Y	Pennsylvania	Y	US Marine Corps
19				McAvory, Harry M		M	W	25	S	N	Y	Texas	Y	US Marine Corps
20				Meadows, John H		M	W	18	S	N	Y	Missouri	Y	US Marine Corps
21				Medockers, Carl W		M	W	19	S	N	Y	Missouri	Y	US Marine Corps
22				Moore, David D		M	W	23	S	N	Y	Minnesota	Y	US Marine Corps
23				Moore, Linwood J		M	W	24	S	N	Y	Virginia	Y	US Marine Corps
24				Morgan, Donald E		M	W	29	S	N	Y	Canada	Y	US Marine Corps
25				Mullaby, Patrick A		M	W	20	S	N	Y	Wisconsin	Y	US Marine Corps

DEPARTMENT OF COMMERCE-BUREAU OF THE CENSUS
WASHINGTON

FIFTEENTH CENSUS OF THE UNITED STATES: 1930-POPULATION

THE ISLAND OF GUAM

Sheet No. 6B | **291B**

District **Municipality**
Name of Place **Naval Reservations and Ships**
[Proper name and, also, name of class, as city, town, village, barrio, etc]

Enumeration District No. **13**
Enumerated by me on **April 7, 1930** **Susan W. Bradley**, Enumerator

	PLACE OF ABODE			NAME	RELATION	PERSONAL DESCRIPTION				EDUCATION		NATIVITY		OCCUPATION
	Street, avenue, road, etc.	Number of dwelling house in order of visitation	Number of family in order of visitation	of each person whose place of abode on April 1, 1930, was in this family. Enter surname, first, then given name and middle initial. If any. Include every person living on April 1, 1930. Omit children born since April 1, 1930.	Relationship of this Person to the head of the family.	Sex	Color or race	Age at last birthday	Single, married, widowed or divorced	Attended school any time since Sept. 1, 1929	Whether able to read and write.	Place of birth of this person.	Whether able to speak English.	
	1	2	3	4	5	6	7	8	9	10	11	12	13	14
26	Marine Barracks			Myers, Walter R		M	W	19	S	N	Y	Indiana	Y	US Marine Corps
27				O'Leary, William C		M	W	18	S	N	Y	Mississippi	Y	US Marine Corps
28				Patnade, Frederick O		M	W	22	S	N	Y	Washington	Y	US Marine Corps
29				Patterson, Milan H		M	W	22	S	N	Y	Kansas	Y	US Marine Corps
30				Patton, Diamond		M	W	23	S	N	Y	North Carolina	Y	US Marine Corps
31				Petterson, Gorden P		M	W	23	S	N	Y	Minnesota	Y	US Marine Corps
32				Petrelli, Anthony		M	W	20	S	N	Y	Massachusetts	Y	US Marine Corps
33				Perry, William R		M	W	32	S	N	Y	Maine	Y	US Marine Corps
34				Pralt, Parnell		M	W	19	S	N	Y	Utah	Y	US Marine Corps
35				Quinlan, Mark G		M	W	29	S	N	Y	North Dakota	Y	US Marine Corps
36				Rayburn, Lloyd D		M	W	21	S	N	Y	Iowa	Y	US Marine Corps
37				Reno, Edward M		M	W	18	S	N	Y	Pennsylvania	Y	US Marine Corps
38				Rider, Ervin R		M	W	19	S	N	Y	Oklahoma	Y	US Marine Corps
39				Routridge, Shurl W		M	W	24	S	N	Y	Missouri	Y	US Marine Corps
40				Russell, Mayton		M	W	22	S	N	Y	Louisiana	Y	US Marine Corps
41				Sage, Edward V		M	W	21	S	N	Y	Colorado	Y	US Marine Corps
42				Santee, Lester H		M	W	21	S	N	Y	Minnesota	Y	US Marine Corps
43				Sealey, Armon Q		M	W	24	S	N	Y	Kansas	Y	US Marine Corps
44				Simpson, Lewis G		M	W	20	S	N	Y	Kansas	Y	US Marine Corps
45				Simpson, Millard C		M	W	18	S	N	Y	North Carolina	Y	US Marine Corps
46				Smith, Paul		M	W	22	S	N	Y	Alabama	Y	US Marine Corps
47				Sawers, John P. Jr.		M	W	19	S	N	Y	Virginia	Y	US Marine Corps
48				Stewart, Leon R		M	W	23	S	N	Y	Washington	Y	US Marine Corps
49				Stram, Henry A		M	W	27	S	N	Y	Minnesota	Y	US Marine Corps
50				Thompson, Thomas R		M	W	22	S	N	Y	Missouri	Y	US Marine Corps

(CHAMORRO ROOTS GENEALOGY PROJECT™ TRANSCRIPTION)
(BERNARD T. PUNZALAN / HTTP://WWW.CHAMORROROOTS.COM)

DEPARTMENT OF COMMERCE-BUREAU OF THE CENSUS
WASHINGTON

FIFTEENTH CENSUS OF THE UNITED STATES: 1930-POPULATION

THE ISLAND OF GUAM

Sheet No. 7A

292

District **Municipality**

Name of Place **Naval Reservations and Ships** [Proper name and, also, name of class, as city, town, village, barrio, etc]

Enumeration District No. **13**

Enumerated by me on **April 8, 1930** **Susan W. Bradley** Enumerator

	PLACE OF ABODE			NAME	RELATION	PERSONAL DESCRIPTION				EDUCATION		NATIVITY		OCCUPATION
	Street, avenue, road, etc.	Number of dwelling house is order of visitation	Number of family in order of visitation	of each person whose place of abode on April 1, 1930, was in this family. Enter surname, first, then given name and middle initial. If any. Include every person living on April 1, 1930. Omit children born since April 1, 1930.	Relationship of this Person to the head of the family.	Sex	Color or race	Age at last birthday	Single, married, widowed or divorced	Attended school any time since Sept. 1, 1929	Whether able to read and write.	Place of birth of this person.	Whether able to speak English.	
	1	2	3	4	5	6	7	8	9	10	11	12	13	14
1	Marine Barracks			Thompson, Rober Jr.		M	W	25	S	N	Y	Tennessee	Y	US Marine Corps
2				Tinkler, Harold J		M	W	20	S	N	Y	Kansas	Y	US Marine Corps
3				Tollis, James B		M	W	20	S	N	Y	Oklahoma	Y	US Marine Corps
4				Frontislan, Wiliiam L		M	W	19	S	N	Y	North Carolina	Y	US Marine Corps
5				Turner, Herschell		M	W	28	S	N	Y	Alabama	Y	US Marine Corps
6				Vulte, Nelson T		M	W	49	S	N	Y	New York	Y	US Marine Corps
7				Walker, Edmund		M	W	28	S	N	Y	Nebraska	Y	US Marine Corps
8				Warburn, James D		M	W	18	S	N	Y	Montana	Y	US Marine Corps
9				Walters, Frederick E		M	W	26	S	N	Y	Kentucky	Y	US Marine Corps
10				Weaber, Walter H		M	W	23	S	N	Y	Pennsylvania	Y	US Marine Corps
11				Whitaker, Albert L		M	W	42	S	N	Y	Utah	Y	US Marine Corps
12				White, Horace G		M	W	26	S	N	Y	England	Y	US Marine Corps
13				Whitehead, Harry A		M	W	23	S	N	Y	Kansas	Y	US Marine Corps
14				Wightman, Robert R		M	W	27	S	N	Y	Wyoming	Y	US Marine Corps
15				Wilares, Peter J		M	W	27	S	N	Y	Pennsylvania	Y	US Marine Corps
16				Williford, Elijah C		M	W	23	S	N	Y	Georgia	Y	US Marine Corps
17				Young, Francis W		M	W	18	S	N	Y	North Dakota	Y	US Marine Corps
18				Young, Otis F		M	W	22	S	N	Y	Delaware	Y	US Marine Corps
19				Cziems, Herbert L		M	W	23	S	N	Y	Nebraska	Y	US Marine Corps
20				Ylibana, Simonas		M	W	38	S	N	Y	?	Y	US Marine Corps
21				Zudick, Enor L		M	W	26	S	N	Y	Massachusetts	Y	US Marine Corps
22				Anderson, Chester E		M	W	21	S	N	Y	Indiana	Y	US Marine Corps
23				Balletti, Herbert C		M	W	30	S	N	Y	Washington	Y	US Marine Corps
24				Geer, Dave		M	W	23	S	N	Y	California	Y	US Marine Corps
25				Blasingame, Fred		M	W	26	S	N	Y	Arkansas	Y	US Marine Corps

DEPARTMENT OF COMMERCE-BUREAU OF THE CENSUS
WASHINGTON

FIFTEENTH CENSUS OF THE UNITED STATES: 1930-POPULATION

THE ISLAND OF GUAM

Sheet No. 7B

292B

District **Municipality**

Name of Place **Naval Reservations and Ships**
[Proper name and, also, name of class, as city, town, village, barrio, etc]

Enumeration District No. **13**

Enumerated by me on **April 8, 1930** **Susan W. Bradley**, Enumerator

	PLACE OF ABODE: Street, avenue, road, etc.	Number of dwelling house is order of visitation	Number of family in order of visitation	NAME of each person whose place of abode on April 1, 1930, was in this family. Enter surname, first, then given name and middle initial. If any. Include every person living on April 1, 1930. Omit children born since April 1, 1930.	RELATION Relationship of this Person to the head of the family.	PERSONAL DESCRIPTION: Sex	Color or race	Age at last birthday	Single, married, widowed or divorced	EDUCATION: Attended school any time since Sept. 1, 1929	Whether able to read and write.	NATIVITY Place of birth of this person.	Whether able to speak English.	OCCUPATION
	1	2	3	4	5	6	7	8	9	10	11	12	13	14
26	Marine Barracks			Bond, Clayton T		M	W	25	S	N	Y	Texas	Y	US Marine Corps
27				Brooke, Wayd L		M	W	22	S	N	Y	Oklahoma	Y	US Marine Corps
28				Brudere, Charles		M	W	26	S	N	Y	Switzerland	Y	US Marine Corps
29				Bumps, Arthur E		M	W	25	S	N	Y	Kansas	Y	US Marine Corps
30				Burger, Arthur W		M	W	25	S	N	Y	Iowa	Y	US Marine Corps
31				Butterfield, Willis A		M	W	25	S	N	Y	Nebraska	Y	US Marine Corps
32				Call, Donald M		M	W	28	S	N	Y	Kansas	Y	US Marine Corps
33				Charlasuro, Anthony		M	W	22	S	N	Y	Pennsylvania	Y	US Marine Corps
34				Chase, Donald W		M	W	19	S	N	Y	Colorado	Y	US Marine Corps
35				Conrad, Constant F		M	W	22	S	N	Y	Illinois	Y	US Marine Corps
36				Corbin, William O		M	W	48	M	N	Y	Ohio	Y	US Marine Corps
37				Davis, Willian H Jr.		M	W	22	S	N	Y	Washington	Y	US Marine Corps
38				Dennen, William A		M	W	19	S	N	Y	Minnesota	Y	US Marine Corps
39				Dennis, Edward D		M	W	24	S	N	Y	Missouri	Y	US Marine Corps
40				Ditlerson, Raymond E		M	W	20	S	N	Y	Minnesota	Y	US Marine Corps
41				Dooley, William		M	W	21	S	N	Y	Montana	Y	US Marine Corps
42				Dugnay, James A		M	W	46	S	N	Y	Ohio	Y	US Marine Corps
43				Derguan, Joseph O		M	W	24	S	N	Y	Maine	Y	US Marine Corps
44				Durna, William H Jr.		M	W	22	S	N	Y	Oklahoma	Y	US Marine Corps
45				Dyer, Virgil R		M	W	29	S	N	Y	Illinois	Y	US Marine Corps
46				Eintinis, Edonaldo		M	W	35	S	N	Y	Italy	Y	US Marine Corps
47				Feldman, Joseph		M	W	23	S	N	Y	Massachusetts	Y	US Marine Corps
48				Fisher, George M		M	W	20	S	N	Y	Oregon	Y	US Marine Corps
49				Foster, John C		M	W	24	S	N	Y	Texas	Y	US Marine Corps
50				Fountain, James L		M	W	20	S	N	Y	Georgia	Y	US Marine Corps

DEPARTMENT OF COMMERCE-BUREAU OF THE CENSUS
WASHINGTON

FIFTEENTH CENSUS OF THE UNITED STATES: 1930-POPULATION

THE ISLAND OF GUAM

Sheet No. 8A

District **Municipality**
Name of Place **Naval Reservations and Ships**
[Proper name and, also, name of class, as city, town, village, barrio, etc]

Enumeration District No. **13**
Enumerated by me on **April 8, 1930** **Susan W. Bradley**
Enumerator

	PLACE OF ABODE			NAME	RELATION	PERSONAL DESCRIPTION				EDUCATION		NATIVITY		OCCUPATION
	Street, avenue, road, etc.	Number of dwelling house is order of visitation	Number of family in order of visitation	of each person whose place of abode on April 1, 1930, was in this family. Enter surname, first, then given name and middle initial. If any. Include every person living on April 1, 1930. Omit children born since April 1, 1930.	Relationship of this Person to the head of the family.	Sex	Color or race	Age at last birthday	Single, married, widowed or divorced	Attended school any time since Sept. 1, 1929	Whether able to read and write.	Place of birth of this person.	Whether able to speak English.	
	1	2	3	4	5	6	7	8	9	10	11	12	13	14
1	Marine Barracks			Franklin, William J		M	W	20	S	N	Y	New Mexico	Y	US Marine Corps
2				Fritz, George J		M	W	21	S	N	Y	Montana	Y	US Marine Corps
3				Furst, David J		M	W	28	S	N	Y	Nebraska	Y	US Marine Corps
4				Gallagher, James A		M	W	33	S	N	Y	Pennsylvania	Y	US Marine Corps
5				Gibson, Charles C		M	W	19	S	N	Y	Kentucky	Y	US Marine Corps
6				Gregory, James C		M	W	29	S	N	Y	Idaho	Y	US Marine Corps
7				Gunnoc, Kenneth S		M	W	18	S	N	Y	West Virginia	Y	US Marine Corps
8				Hamilton, Byron C		M	W	28	S	N	Y	Texas	Y	US Marine Corps
9				Handley, Henry A		M	W	21	S	N	Y	Alabama	Y	US Marine Corps
10				Hangels, William R		M	W	20	S	N	Y	Nebraska	Y	US Marine Corps
11				Hebern, Charles E		M	W	18	S	N	Y	California	Y	US Marine Corps
12				Helman, Chester R		M	W	20	S	N	Y	North Carolina	Y	US Marine Corps
13				Heraling, Wayne G		M	W	20	S	N	Y	Ohio	Y	US Marine Corps
14				Inks, Richard R		M	W	27	S	N	Y	California	Y	US Marine Corps
15				Israel, Otis A		M	W	26	S	N	Y	South Carolina	Y	US Marine Corps
16				James, Gurnie		M	W	22	S	N	Y	Nebraska	Y	US Marine Corps
17				Klappholz, Henry E		M	W	30	S	N	Y	New Jersey	Y	US Marine Corps
18				Knokes, Henry L		M	W	21	S	N	Y	Washington	Y	US Marine Corps
19				Lee, Will G		M	W	33	M	N	Y	Texas	Y	US Marine Corps
20				Linville, Bert S		M	W	19	S	N	Y	Indiana	Y	US Marine Corps
21				Martel, Edward T		M	W	18	S	N	Y	Massachusetts	Y	US Marine Corps
22				Martin, Bird M		M	W	24	S	N	Y	Oklahoma	Y	US Marine Corps
23				McDugle, Hershel L		M	W	18	S	N	Y	Texas	Y	US Marine Corps
24				McCan, James H		M	W	49	M	N	Y	Alabama	Y	US Marine Corps
25				McIslen, Meret L		M	W	22	S	N	Y	Iowa	Y	US Marine Corps

(CHAMORRO ROOTS GENEALOGY PROJECT™ TRANSCRIPTION)
(BERNARD T. PUNZALAN / HTTP://WWW.CHAMORROROOTS.COM)

DEPARTMENT OF COMMERCE-BUREAU OF THE CENSUS
WASHINGTON
FIFTEENTH CENSUS OF THE UNITED STATES: 1930-POPULATION

THE ISLAND OF GUAM

Sheet No. 8B

293B

District Municipality
Name of Place Naval Reservations and Ships
[Proper name and, also, name of class, as city, town, village, barrio, etc]

Enumeration District No. 13
Enumerated by me on April 8, 1930 Susan W. Bradley
Enumerator

	PLACE OF ABODE			NAME	RELATION	PERSONAL DESCRIPTION				EDUCATION		NATIVITY		OCCUPATION
	Street, avenue, road, etc.	Number of dwelling house is order of visitation	Number of family in order of visitation	of each person whose place of abode on April 1, 1930, was in this family. Enter surname, first, then given name and middle initial. If any. Include every person living on April 1, 1930. Omit children born since April 1, 1930.	Relationship of this Person to the head of the family.	Sex	Color or race	Age at last birthday	Single, married, widowed or divorced	Attended school any time since Sept. 1, 1929	Whether able to read and write.	Place of birth of this person.	Whether able to speak English.	
	1	2	3	4	5	6	7	8	9	10	11	12	13	14
26	Marine Barracks			McNeely, Thomas W		M	W	24	S	N	Y	Washington	Y	US Marine Corps
27				McNutt, Wesley D		M	W	32	S	N	Y	Mississippi	Y	US Marine Corps
28				Meeker, Victor H		M	W	21	S	N	Y	[illegible]	Y	US Marine Corps
29				Moody, Harry W		M	W	23	S	N	Y	Minnesota	Y	US Marine Corps
30				Moore, Loyd F		M	W	21	S	N	Y	South Carolina	Y	US Marine Corps
31				Moreland, Asa H		M	W	21	S	N	Y	Minnesota	Y	US Marine Corps
32				Morrison, Ted R		M	W	19	S	N	Y	Missouri	Y	US Marine Corps
33				Morrone, Luther T		M	W	18	M	N	Y	Rhode Island	Y	US Marine Corps
34				Mullenax, William D		M	W	19	S	N	Y	Missouri	Y	US Marine Corps
35				Murray, Wallace J		M	W	39	S	N	Y	Indiana	Y	US Marine Corps
36				Neumann, Elmer G		M	W	18	S	N	Y	Illinois	Y	US Marine Corps
37				Medhamer, William R		M	W	19	S	N	Y	Ohio	Y	US Marine Corps
38				Oates, Clive		M	W	38	S	N	Y	Nebraska	Y	US Marine Corps
39				Osborn, Oscar E		M	W	23	S	N	Y	Arkansas	Y	US Marine Corps
40				Parrott, George C		M	W	47	S	N	Y	Kentucky	Y	US Marine Corps
41				Pollock, James R		M	W	24	S	N	Y	Utah	Y	US Marine Corps
42				Price, Harry C		M	W	19	S	N	Y	North Carolina	Y	US Marine Corps
43				Randolph, George H		M	W	21	S	N	Y	Oklahoma	Y	US Marine Corps
44				Rash, Orval		M	W	19	M	N	Y	Washington	Y	US Marine Corps
45				Retz, George I		M	W	25	S	N	Y	Indiana	Y	US Marine Corps
46				Revelles, Clyde E		M	W	24	S	N	Y	Missouri	Y	US Marine Corps
47				Reynolds, Jack A		M	W	29	S	N	Y	California	Y	US Marine Corps
48				Rice, Clarence R		M	W	25	S	N	Y	[illegible]	Y	US Marine Corps
49				Roberts, Carl H		M	W	19	M	N	Y	Nebraska	Y	US Marine Corps
50				Rumelhart, Leland		M	W	19	S	N	Y	Minnesota	Y	US Marine Corps

(CHAMORRO ROOTS GENEALOGY PROJECT™ TRANSCRIPTION)
(BERNARD T. PUNZALAN / HTTP://WWW.CHAMORROROOTS.COM)

DEPARTMENT OF COMMERCE-BUREAU OF THE CENSUS
WASHINGTON

FIFTEENTH CENSUS OF THE UNITED STATES: 1930-POPULATION

THE ISLAND OF GUAM

Sheet No. 9A

294

District **Municipality**
Name of Place **Naval Reservations and Ships**
[Proper name and, also, name of class, as city, town, village, barrio, etc]

Enumeration District No. **13**
Enumerated by me on **April 9, 1930** **Susan W. Bradley**
Enumerator

	PLACE OF ABODE			NAME	RELATION	PERSONAL DESCRIPTION				EDUCATION		NATIVITY		OCCUPATION
	Street, avenue, road, etc.	Number of dwelling house is order of visitation	Number of family in order of visitation	of each person whose place of abode on April 1, 1930, was in this family. Enter surname, first, then given name and middle initial. If any. Include every person living on April 1, 1930. Omit children born since April 1, 1930.	Relationship of this Person to the head of the family.	Sex	Color or race	Age at last birthday	Single, married, widowed or divorced	Attended school any time since Sept. 1, 1929	Whether able to read and write.	Place of birth of this person.	Whether able to speak English.	
	1	2	3	4	5	6	7	8	9	10	11	12	13	14
1	Marine Barracks			Salatesrio, W		M	W	31	S	N	Y	Illinois	Y	US Marine Corps
2				Schieder, Harry A		M	W	18	S	N	Y	North Dakota	Y	US Marine Corps
3				Scott, James R		M	W	45	M	N	Y	Texas	Y	US Marine Corps
4				Sridder, Clarence F		M	W	19	S	N	Y	Wisconsin	Y	US Marine Corps
5				Sides, Samuel H		M	W	20	S	N	Y	North Carolina	Y	US Marine Corps
6				Silvester, Frank P		M	W	31	S	N	Y	California	Y	US Marine Corps
7				Staskey, Orville R		M	W	20	S	N	Y	Arkansas	Y	US Marine Corps
8				Steter, Eugne F		M	W	29	S	N	Y	Minnesota	Y	US Marine Corps
9				Stuart, James A		M	W	31	M	N	Y	Washington	Y	US Marine Corps
10				Theodorsin, Orel G		M	W	25	S	N	Y	Minnesota	Y	US Marine Corps
11				Van Dewaker, Henry P		M	W	41	S	N	Y	New York	Y	US Marine Corps
12				Waddle, Howard W		M	W	19	S	N	Y	Colorado	Y	US Marine Corps
13				Waland, Robert H		M	W	21	S	N	Y	Wisconsin	Y	US Marine Corps
14				West, Garfield H		M	W	19	S	N	Y	Washington	Y	US Marine Corps
15				Wilson, Alva B		M	W	32	S	N	Y	Oklahoma	Y	US Marine Corps
16	US Naval Hospital			Porter, Frederick E		M	W	54	M	N	Y	Ohio	Y	U.S. Navy
17				Richardson, Earl		M	W	42	M	N	Y	Ohio	Y	U.S. Navy
18				Jones, Maurice		M	W	38	M	N	Y	California	Y	U.S. Navy
19				Epstein, William I		M	W	31	M	N	Y	Colorado	Y	U.S. Navy
20				Sargent, Willard S		M	W	35	M	N	Y	Utah	Y	U.S. Navy
21				Hays, James F		M	W	32	M	N	Y	West Virginia	Y	U.S. Navy
22				Miller, Jay F		M	W	34	M	N	Y	Missouri	Y	U.S. Navy
23				Cann, George A		M	W	28	M	N	Y	Nevada	Y	U.S. Navy
24				Wallen, Eugene R		M	W	40	M	N	Y	District of Columbia	Y	U.S. Navy
25				McCormack, John A		M	W	42	M	N	Y	Massachusetts	Y	U.S. Navy

(CHAMORRO ROOTS GENEALOGY PROJECT™ TRANSCRIPTION)
(BERNARD T. PUNZALAN / HTTP://WWW.CHAMORROROOTS.COM)

DEPARTMENT OF COMMERCE-BUREAU OF THE CENSUS
WASHINGTON

FIFTEENTH CENSUS OF THE UNITED STATES: 1930-POPULATION

THE ISLAND OF GUAM

Sheet No. 9B

294B

District **Municipality**
Name of Place **Naval Reservations and Ships**
[Proper name and, also, name of class, as city, town, village, barrio, etc]

Enumeration District No. 13
Enumerated by me on April 9, 1930 Susan W. Bradley, Enumerator

	PLACE OF ABODE			NAME	RELATION	PERSONAL DESCRIPTION				EDUCATION		NATIVITY		OCCUPATION
	Street, avenue, road, etc.	Number of dwelling house is order of visitation	Number of family in order of visitation	of each person whose place of abode on April 1, 1930, was in this family. Enter surname, first, then given name and middle initial. If any. Include every person living on April 1, 1930. Omit children born since April 1, 1930.	Relationship of this Person to the head of the family.	Sex	Color or race	Age at last birthday	Single, married, widowed or divorced	Attended school any time since Sept. 1, 1929	Whether able to read and write.	Place of birth of this person.	Whether able to speak English.	
	1	2	3	4	5	6	7	8	9	10	11	12	13	14
26	US Naval Hospital			Blankenhorn, Florence A		F	W	26	Wd	N	Y	Wisconsin	Y	U.S. Navy
27				Bollerud, Irene		F	W	37	Wd	N	Y	Wisconsin	Y	U.S. Navy
28				Bonistsorn, Annie E		F	W	19	Wd	N	Y	Pennsylvania	Y	U.S. Navy
29				Brostie, Ida E		F	W	45	Wd	N	Y	New York	Y	U.S. Navy
30				Furst, Mildred E		F	W	33	Wd	N	Y	Ohio	Y	U.S. Navy
31				Newala, June H		F	W	31	Wd	N	Y	Illinois	Y	U.S. Navy
32				Linderman, Florence A		F	W	34	S	N	Y	Pennsylvania	Y	U.S. Navy
33				Rotherrnel, Ella M		F	W	35	S	N	Y	Pennsylvania	Y	U.S. Navy
34				Russell, Ruby		F	W	40	S	N	Y	Massachusetts	Y	U.S. Navy
35				Auger, Thomas C		M	W	29	S	N	Y	Minnesota	Y	U.S. Navy
36				Austin, Harold N		M	W	18	S	N	Y	Ohio	Y	U.S. Navy
37				Bennett, Charles E		M	W	23	S	N	Y	Arkansas	Y	U.S. Navy
38				Bennett, Robert P		M	W	29	S	N	Y	Alabama	Y	U.S. Navy
39				Birdzell, Donald T		M	W	20	S	N	Y	Illinois	Y	U.S. Navy
40				Bixby, Robert		M	W	25	S	N	Y	Idaho	Y	U.S. Navy
41				Beaton, Frank E		M	W	19	S	N	Y	Washington	Y	U.S. Navy
42				Combs, Elmer G		M	W	25	M	N	Y	California	Y	U.S. Navy
43				Conant, Arnold M		M	W	28	M	N	Y	Massachusetts	Y	U.S. Navy
44				Condon, Clifford K		M	W	26	S	N	Y	Pennsylvania	Y	U.S. Navy
45				Cowan, Alex R		M	W	22	S	N	Y	Tennessee	Y	U.S. Navy
46				Cramton, Kenneth B		M	W	32	S	N	Y	Colorado	Y	U.S. Navy
47				Danio, Donald E		M	W	19	S	N	Y	California	Y	U.S. Navy
48				Delia, John M		M	W	23	S	N	Y	New Jersey	Y	U.S. Navy
49				Edmondson, Harold D		M	W	27	S	N	Y	Illinois	Y	U.S. Navy
50				Elson, Oscar E		M	W	19	S	N	Y	Minnesota	Y	U.S. Navy

(CHAMORRO ROOTS GENEALOGY PROJECT™ TRANSCRIPTION)
(BERNARD T. PUNZALAN / HTTP://WWW.CHAMORROROOTS.COM)

DEPARTMENT OF COMMERCE-BUREAU OF THE CENSUS
WASHINGTON
FIFTEENTH CENSUS OF THE UNITED STATES: 1930-POPULATION

THE ISLAND OF GUAM

Sheet No. 10A

295

District **Municipality**
Name of Place **Naval Reservations and Ships**
[Proper name and, also, name of class, as city, town, village, barrio, etc]

Enumeration District No. **13**
Enumerated by me on **April 9, 1930** **Susan W. Bradley**
Enumerator

	PLACE OF ABODE			NAME	RELATION	PERSONAL DESCRIPTION				EDUCATION		NATIVITY		OCCUPATION
	Street, avenue, road, etc.	Number of dwelling house in order of visitation	Number of family in order of visitation	of each person whose place of abode on April 1, 1930, was in this family. Enter surname, first, then given name and middle initial. If any. Include every person living on April 1, 1930. Omit children born since April 1, 1930.	Relationship of this Person to the head of the family.	Sex	Color or race	Age at last birthday	Single, married, widowed or divorced	Attended school any time since Sept. 1, 1929	Whether able to read and write.	Place of birth of this person.	Whether able to speak English.	
	1	2	3	4	5	6	7	8	9	10	11	12	13	14
1	US Naval Hospital			Faula, James M		M	W	39	M	N	Y	Mississippi	Y	U.S. Navy
2				Flennils, Harold C		M	W	20	S	N	Y	Alabama	Y	U.S. Navy
3				French, [illegible] F		M	W	21	S	N	Y	Kentucky	Y	U.S. Navy
4				Gove, William D		M	W	24	S	N	Y	Illinois	Y	U.S. Navy
5				[illegible], [illegible] D		M	W	33	S	N	Y	Tennessee	Y	U.S. Navy
6				Hind, Frederick S		M	W	24	S	N	Y	Tennessee	Y	U.S. Navy
7				Horwell, Richard W		M	W	23	S	N	Y	Kentucky	Y	U.S. Navy
8				Isam, Roscoe W		M	W	29	S	N	Y	Kentucky	Y	U.S. Navy
9				Jergenson, Tiels W		M	W	34	M	N	Y	Florida	Y	U.S. Navy
10				Kilroy, Lawrence C		M	W	29	S	N	Y	Alaska	Y	U.S. Navy
11				Kreiling, Howard F		M	W	21	D	N	Y	Ohio	Y	U.S. Navy
12				[illegible], Keith Q		M	W	28	S	N	Y	North Dakota	Y	U.S. Navy
13				Legg, Lawrence M		M	W	20	S	N	Y	[illegible]	Y	U.S. Navy
14				McChicken, Herbert S		M	W	19	S	N	Y	Kansas	Y	U.S. Navy
15				Nelson, Edward A		M	W	22	M	N	Y	Iowa	Y	U.S. Navy
16				Olive, Robert H B		M	W	24	S	N	Y	Missouri	Y	U.S. Navy
17				Ploke, John F		M	W	28	S	N	Y	Nebraska	Y	U.S. Navy
18				Rudbern, Stanley H B		M	W	21	S	N	Y	Indiana	Y	U.S. Navy
19				Sheridan, Bernard W		M	W	25	S	N	Y	Kansas	Y	U.S. Navy
20				Simmons, Clyde O		M	W	22	S	N	Y	Arkansas	Y	U.S. Navy
21				Simpson, [illegible]		M	W	22	M	N	Y	Texas	Y	U.S. Navy
22				Soke, John M		M	W	20	M	N	Y	California	Y	U.S. Navy
23				thomas, Luther W		M	W	28	S	N	Y	Texas	Y	U.S. Navy
24				Troy, John J		M	W	33	M	N	Y	Pennsylvania	Y	U.S. Navy
25				Van Valey, Howard A		M	W	22	S	N	Y	Illinois	Y	U.S. Navy

DEPARTMENT OF COMMERCE-BUREAU OF THE CENSUS
WASHINGTON

FIFTEENTH CENSUS OF THE UNITED STATES: 1930-POPULATION

THE ISLAND OF GUAM

Sheet No. 10B

295B

District **Municipality**
Name of Place **Naval Reservations and Ships**
[Proper name and, also, name of class, as city, town, village, barrio, etc]

Enumeration District No. **13**
Enumerated by me on **April 9, 1930** **Susan W. Bradley**
Enumerator

	PLACE OF ABODE			NAME	RELATION	PERSONAL DESCRIPTION				EDUCATION		NATIVITY		OCCUPATION
	Street, avenue, road, etc.	Number of dwelling house is order of visitation	Number of family in order of visitation	of each person whose place of abode on April 1, 1930, was in this family. Enter surname, first, then given name and middle initial. If any. Include every person living on April 1, 1930. Omit children born since April 1, 1930.	Relationship of this Person to the head of the family.	Sex	Color or race	Age at last birthday	Single, married, widowed or divorced	Attended school any time since Sept. 1, 1929	Whether able to read and write.	Place of birth of this person.	Whether able to speak English.	
	1	2	3	4	5	6	7	8	9	10	11	12	13	14
26	USS Gold Star	23		Bernard, Richard F		M	W	45	M	N	Y	Virginia	Y	U.S. Navy
27				Blaslar, Arthur F		M	W	39	M	N	Y	Kansas	Y	U.S. Navy
28				Dillon, Lloyd A		M	W	42	M	N	Y	Ohio	Y	U.S. Navy
29				Hare, Theron S		M	W	37	M	N	Y	Illinois	Y	U.S. Navy
30				Loftuard, Stepen A		M	W	45	M	N	Y	Colorado	Y	U.S. Navy
31				Matterson, Wiston C		M	W	40	M	N	Y	Minnesota	Y	U.S. Navy
32				McBride, George T		M	W	39	M	N	Y	Pennsylvania	Y	U.S. Navy
33				Root, James E Jr		M	W	38	M	N	Y	Minnesota	Y	U.S. Navy
34				Sullivan, Russell H		M	W	27	M	N	Y	Massachusetts	Y	U.S. Navy
35				Teronend, Arthur M		M	W	28	M	N	Y	Michigan	Y	U.S. Navy
36				Acfalle, Jesus C		M	Cha	39	M	N	Y	Guam	Y	U.S. Navy
37				Ada, Manuel		M	Cha	24	M	N	Y	Guam	Y	U.S. Navy
38				Aflleje, Andres		M	Cha	30	M	N	Y	Guam	Y	U.S. Navy
39				Arola, Joseph L		M	W	23	S	N	Y	Louisiana	Y	U.S. Navy
40				Allen, Harold Q		M	W	25	S	N	Y	Kansas	Y	U.S. Navy
41				Amber, Lovell H		M	W	29	S	N	Y	Illinois	Y	U.S. Navy
42				Benjamin, Alexander		M	W	31	S	N	Y	Connecticut	Y	U.S. Navy
43				Blai, Anthony C		M	W	25	S	N	Y	Minnesota	Y	U.S. Navy
44				Blouin, William		M	W	25	S	N	Y	Massachusetts	Y	U.S. Navy
45				Blonkowski, John J		M	W	27	M	N	Y	New York	Y	U.S. Navy
46				Bojra, Juan M		M	Cha	35	M	N	Y	Guam	Y	U.S. Navy
47				Broll, Isadore		M	W	24	S	N	Y	Texas	Y	U.S. Navy
48				Laingot, Luis L		M	Fil	39	S	N	Y	Philippine Island	Y	U.S. Navy
49				Calesqa, Pablo		M	Fil	23	M	N	Y	Philippine Island	Y	U.S. Navy
50				Camacho, Jose		M	Cha	35	M	N	Y	Guam	Y	U.S. Navy

(CHAMORRO ROOTS GENEALOGY PROJECT™ TRANSCRIPTION)
(BERNARD T. PUNZALAN / HTTP://WWW.CHAMORROROOTS.COM)

DEPARTMENT OF COMMERCE-BUREAU OF THE CENSUS
WASHINGTON

FIFTEENTH CENSUS OF THE UNITED STATES: 1930-POPULATION

THE ISLAND OF GUAM

Sheet No. 11A — 296

District **Municipality**
Name of Place **Naval Reservations and Ships**
[Proper name and, also, name of class, as city, town, village, barrio, etc]

Enumeration District No. **13**
Enumerated by me on **April 9, 1930** **Susan W. Bradley**, Enumerator

	PLACE OF ABODE			NAME	RELATION	PERSONAL DESCRIPTION				EDUCATION		NATIVITY		OCCUPATION
	Street, avenue, road, etc.	Number of dwelling house is order of visitation	Number of family in order of visitation	of each person whose place of abode on April 1, 1930, was in this family. Enter surname, first, then given name and middle initial. If any. Include every person living on April 1, 1930. Omit children born since April 1, 1930.	Relationship of this Person to the head of the family.	Sex	Color or race	Age at last birthday	Single, married, widowed or divorced	Attended school any time since Sept. 1, 1929	Whether able to read and write.	Place of birth of this person.	Whether able to speak English.	
	1	2	3	4	5	6	7	8	9	10	11	12	13	14
1	USS Gold Star			Cardese, William		M	W	25	S	N	Y	Wisconsin	Y	U.S. Navy
2				Cato, Paul D		M	W	29	S	N	Y	Pennsylvania	Y	U.S. Navy
3				Cepeda, Jose B		M	Cha	32	M	N	Y	Guam	Y	U.S. Navy
4				Clache, George T		M	W	32	M	N	Y	New York	Y	U.S. Navy
5				Collette, Edwin R		M	W	39	Wd	N	Y	Minnesota	Y	U.S. Navy
6				Concepcion, Juan		M	Cha	45	M	N	Y	Guam	Y	U.S. Navy
7				Cortez, Felix		M	Fil	36	S	N	Y	Philippine Island	Y	U.S. Navy
8				Crorides, Lule Q		M	W	23	S	N	Y	Washington	Y	U.S. Navy
9				Cruz, Enrique		M	Cha	48	M	N	Y	Guam	Y	U.S. Navy
10				Cruz, Jose P		M	Cha	32	M	N	Y	Guam	Y	U.S. Navy
11				Cruz, Vincente		M	Cha	31	M	N	Y	Guam	Y	U.S. Navy
12				Crullena, Clemente		M	Fil	34	M	N	Y	Philippine Island	Y	U.S. Navy
13				Cummings, Wade C		M	W	22	S	N	Y	Texas	Y	U.S. Navy
14				De Castro, Crispulo		M	Fil	20	M	N	Y	Philippine Island	Y	U.S. Navy
15				De Jesus, Rosendo		M	Fil	25	M	N	Y	Philippine Island	Y	U.S. Navy
16				De Los Santos, Guilermo		M	Cha	33	S	N	Y	Guam	Y	U.S. Navy
17				Dell, George F		M	W	35	S	N	Y	Illinois	Y	U.S. Navy
18				De Torres, Jose		M	Cha	43	M	N	Y	Guam	Y	U.S. Navy
19				Dobry, John H		M	W	23	S	N	Y	Arkansas	Y	U.S. Navy
20				Donato, Juan C		M	Fil	36	M	N	Y	Philippine Island	Y	U.S. Navy
21				Dooley, Tevin F		M	W	30	M	N	Y	Kentucky	Y	U.S. Navy
22				Borband, Elmber F		M	W	25	S	N	Y	Illinois	Y	U.S. Navy
23				Dorsey, Oscar D		M	W	31	D	N	Y	Texas	Y	U.S. Navy
24				Dorrett, David A		M	W	21	S	N	Y	Massachusetts	Y	U.S. Navy
25				Egbert, Willard E		M	W	22	S	N	Y	Washington	Y	U.S. Navy

(CHAMORRO ROOTS GENEALOGY PROJECT™ TRANSCRIPTION)
(BERNARD T. PUNZALAN / HTTP://WWW.CHAMORROROOTS.COM)

DEPARTMENT OF COMMERCE-BUREAU OF THE CENSUS
WASHINGTON
FIFTEENTH CENSUS OF THE UNITED STATES: 1930-POPULATION

THE ISLAND OF GUAM

Sheet No. 11B

296B

District **Municipality**
Name of Place **Naval Reservations and Ships**
[Proper name and, also, name of class, as city, town, village, barrio, etc]

Enumeration District No. **13**
Enumerated by me on **April 9, 1930** **Susan W. Bradley**
Enumerator

	PLACE OF ABODE			NAME	RELATION	PERSONAL DESCRIPTION				EDUCATION		NATIVITY		OCCUPATION
	Street, avenue, road, etc.	Number of dwelling house is order of visitation	Number of family in order of visitation	of each person whose place of abode on April 1, 1930, was in this family. Enter surname, first, then given name and middle initial. If any. Include every person living on April 1, 1930. Omit children born since April 1, 1930.	Relationship of this Person to the head of the family.	Sex	Color or race	Age at last birthday	Single, married, widowed or divorced	Attended school any time since Sept. 1, 1929	Whether able to read and write.	Place of birth of this person.	Whether able to speak English.	
	1	2	3	4	5	6	7	8	9	10	11	12	13	14
26	USS Gold Star			Filbins, Kenneth R		M	W	19	S	N	Y	Oregon	Y	U.S. Navy
27				Fischer, William F		M	W	24	S	N	Y	Wisconsin	Y	U.S. Navy
28				Fitzgerald, George		M	W	31	D	N	Y	Mississippi	Y	U.S. Navy
29				Ford, Thomas		M	W	45	S	N	Y	Pennsylvania	Y	U.S. Navy
30				Freeman, Thomas J		M	W	28	S	N	Y	Alabama	Y	U.S. Navy
31				Fyman, Ara L		M	W	29	S	N	Y	Oregon	Y	U.S. Navy
32				Gogo, Juan		M	Cha	35	M	N	Y	Guam	Y	U.S. Navy
33				Grand, Alex A		M	W	27	S	N	Y	California	Y	U.S. Navy
34				Grugautren, William		M	W	33	S	N	Y	New York	Y	U.S. Navy
35				Guinn, George E Jr		M	W	20	S	N	Y	California	Y	U.S. Navy
36				Hallsworth, Norman		M	W	30	S	N	Y	England	Y	U.S. Navy
37				Hartley, George W		M	W	27	S	N	Y	North Carolina	Y	U.S. Navy
38				Hefer, Roman		M	Fil	49	M	N	Y	Philippine Islands	Y	U.S. Navy
39				Hefferon, Robert L		M	W	39	S	N	Y	Missouri	Y	U.S. Navy
40				Hutchens, Frank C		M	W	19	S	N	Y	California	Y	U.S. Navy
41				Javier, Benito		M	Fil	33	M	N	Y	Philippine Islands	Y	U.S. Navy
42				Jone, George A		M	W	21	S	N	Y	North Carolina	Y	U.S. Navy
43				Kearney, James F		M	W	34	S	N	Y	Massachusetts	Y	U.S. Navy
44				Kirisay, Debert W		M	W	25	M	N	Y	Indiana	Y	U.S. Navy
45				La Crosse, Rudolph D		M	W	23	S	N	Y	Wisconsin	Y	U.S. Navy
46				Lindsey, Arthur W		M	W	21	S	N	Y	Nebraska	Y	U.S. Navy
47				Luna, Juan		M	Fil	33	M	N	Y	Philippine Islands	Y	U.S. Navy
48				Lupa, Jose		M	Fil	29	M	N	Y	Philippine Islands	Y	U.S. Navy
49				Manibusan, Ignacio DLG		M	W	46	M	N	Y	Guam	Y	U.S. Navy
50				Manibusan, Jose Q		M	Cha	32	M	N	Y	Guam	Y	U.S. Navy

DEPARTMENT OF COMMERCE-BUREAU OF THE CENSUS
WASHINGTON

FIFTEENTH CENSUS OF THE UNITED STATES: 1930-POPULATION

THE ISLAND OF GUAM

Sheet No. 12A

District **Municipality**
Name of Place **Naval Reservations and Ships**
[Proper name and, also, name of class, as city, town, village, barrio, etc]

Enumeration District No. **13**
Enumerated by me on **April 10, 1930** **Susan W. Bradley**
Enumerator

	PLACE OF ABODE: Street, avenue, road, etc.	Number of dwelling house is order of visitation	Number of family in order of visitation	NAME of each person whose place of abode on April 1, 1930, was in this family. Enter surname, first, then given name and middle initial. If any. Include every person living on April 1, 1930. Omit children born since April 1, 1930.	RELATION Relationship of this Person to the head of the family.	PERSONAL DESCRIPTION: Sex	Color or race	Age at last birthday	Single, married, widowed or divorced	EDUCATION: Attended school any time since Sept. 1, 1929	Whether able to read and write.	NATIVITY Place of birth of this person.	Whether able to speak English.	OCCUPATION
	1	2	3	4	5	6	7	8	9	10	11	12	13	14
1	USS Gold Star			Marak, Joseph		M	W	29	S	N	Y	Connecticut	Y	U.S. Navy
2				Maxwell, Walter G		M	W	29	S	N	Y	Missouri	Y	U.S. Navy
3				Mayor, Felipe		M	Fil	23	M	N	Y	Philippine Island	Y	U.S. Navy
4				McClain, John B		M	W	35	S	N	Y	Indiana	Y	U.S. Navy
5				Mensoto, Pedro		M	Fil	25	S	N	Y	Philippine Island	Y	U.S. Navy
6				Meno, Quintin		M	Cha	34	M	N	Y	Guam	Y	U.S. Navy
7				Midyette, Robert S		M	W	29	S	N	Y	North Carolina	Y	U.S. Navy
8				Monnito, Edward E		M	W	37	M	N	Y	California	Y	U.S. Navy
9				Myers, Clem Q		M	W	31	S	N	Y	Florida	Y	U.S. Navy
10				Naburn, Albert		M	Fil	36	M	N	Y	Philippine Island	Y	U.S. Navy
11				Namauleg, Pedro C		M	Cha	33	M	N	Y	Guam	Y	U.S. Navy
12				Neri, Victor		M	Fil	31	Wd	N	Y	Philippine Island	Y	U.S. Navy
13				Ocampo, Macario		M	Fil	36	M	N	Y	Philippine Island	Y	U.S. Navy
14				Oliva, Frank D		M	W	38	M	N	Y	California	Y	U.S. Navy
15				Onquit, Arcadio		M	Fil	21	M	N	Y	Philippine Island	Y	U.S. Navy
16				Paat, Fidel E		M	Fil	29	M	N	Y	Philippine Island	Y	U.S. Navy
17				Pangelinan, Juan		M	Cha	34	M	N	Y	Guam	Y	U.S. Navy
18				Pasich, Steven		M	W	19	S	N	Y	Minnesota	Y	U.S. Navy
19				Pelas, Leon		M	Fil	35	M	N	Y	Philippine Island	Y	U.S. Navy
20				Perkins, Travis T		M	W	27	S	N	Y	Georgia	Y	U.S. Navy
21				Pludre, Joseph F		M	W	24	S	N	Y	Missouri	Y	U.S. Navy
22				Poole, David L		M	W	22	Wd	N	Y	Ohio	Y	U.S. Navy
23				Price, Jimmie D		M	W	37	S	N	Y	Texas	Y	U.S. Navy
24				Ratiles, Charles W		M	W	35	S	N	Y	Texas	Y	U.S. Navy
25				Rowls, Julian		M	W	26	S	N	Y	Georgia	Y	U.S. Navy

(CHAMORRO ROOTS GENEALOGY PROJECT™ TRANSCRIPTION)
(BERNARD T. PUNZALAN / HTTP://WWW.CHAMORROROOTS.COM)

DEPARTMENT OF COMMERCE-BUREAU OF THE CENSUS
WASHINGTON

FIFTEENTH CENSUS OF THE UNITED STATES: 1930-POPULATION

THE ISLAND OF GUAM

Sheet No. 12B

297B

District Municipality

Name of Place Naval Reservations and Ships
[Proper name and, also, name of class, as city, town, village, barrio, etc]

Enumeration District No. 13

Enumerated by me on April 10, 1930 Susan W. Bradley
Enumerator

	PLACE OF ABODE			NAME	RELATION	PERSONAL DESCRIPTION				EDUCATION		NATIVITY		OCCUPATION
	Street, avenue, road, etc.	Number of dwelling house is order of visitation	Number of family in order of visitation	of each person whose place of abode on April 1, 1930, was in this family. Enter surname, first, then given name and middle initial. If any. Include every person living on April 1, 1930. Omit children born since April 1, 1930.	Relationship of this Person to the head of the family.	Sex	Color or race	Age at last birthday	Single, married, widowed or divorced	Attended school any time since Sept. 1, 1929	Whether able to read and write.	Place of birth of this person.	Whether able to speak English.	
	1	2	3	4	5	6	7	8	9	10	11	12	13	14
26	USS Gold Star			Reinnardt, Shierford M		M	W	34	D	N	Y	Arkansas	Y	U.S. Navy
27				Robert, Raymond R		M	W	35	S	N	Y	Pennsylvania	Y	U.S. Navy
28				Rual, Dorn		M	W	30	S	N	Y	Texas	Y	U.S. Navy
29				Sablan, Jose S		M	Cha	31	M	N	Y	Guam	Y	U.S. Navy
30				Salas, Facundo C		M	Cha	32	S	N	Y	Guam	Y	U.S. Navy
31				Sannils, Arturo		M	W	44	S	N	Y	Missouri	Y	U.S. Navy
32				Santos, Joaquin		M	Cha	23	S	N	Y	Guam	Y	U.S. Navy
33				Santos, Jose C		M	Cha	24	M	N	Y	Guam	Y	U.S. Navy
34				Sarmiento, Juan		M	Cha	39	M	N	Y	Guam	Y	U.S. Navy
35				Schiflerie, Elmers A		M	W	37	S	N	Y	New York	Y	U.S. Navy
36				Sneirki, Ben R		M	W	30	S	N	Y	Texas	Y	U.S. Navy
37				Socoro, Jose		M	Cha	20	M	N	Y	Guam	Y	U.S. Navy
38				Stewart, Lawrence LT		M	W	31	S	N	Y	[illegible]	Y	U.S. Navy
39				Strauch, Henry E		M	W	26	S	N	Y	Tennessee	Y	U.S. Navy
40				Gretuky, Tony		M	W	18	S	N	Y	[illegible]	Y	U.S. Navy
41				Taimanglo, Vincente T		M	Cha	41	M	N	Y	Guam	Y	U.S. Navy
42				Taitano, Joaquin		M	Cha	19	M	N	Y	Guam	Y	U.S. Navy
43				Taitano, Luis		M	Cha	38	M	N	Y	Guam	Y	U.S. Navy
44				Tajalle, Felix		M	Cha	26	M	N	Y	Guam	Y	U.S. Navy
45				Taparan, Nicomede		M	Fil	33	M	N	Y	Philippine Island	Y	U.S. Navy
46				Tenorio, Jesus		M	Cha	34	M	N	Y	Guam	Y	U.S. Navy
47				Villaflor, Lorenzo		M	Fil	29	M	N	Y	Philippine Island	Y	U.S. Navy
48				Villorin, Silvestre		M	Fil	28	M	N	Y	Philippine Island	Y	U.S. Navy
49				Walten, George D		M	W	25	S	N	Y	California	Y	U.S. Navy
50				Watson, Charles F		M	W	22	S	N	Y	Idaho	Y	U.S. Navy

(CHAMORRO ROOTS GENEALOGY PROJECT™ TRANSCRIPTION)
(BERNARD T. PUNZALAN / HTTP://WWW.CHAMORROROOTS.COM)

DEPARTMENT OF COMMERCE-BUREAU OF THE CENSUS
WASHINGTON

FIFTEENTH CENSUS OF THE UNITED STATES: 1930-POPULATION

THE ISLAND OF GUAM

Sheet No. 13A | 298

District **Municipality**
Name of Place **Naval Reservations and Ships**
[Proper name and, also, name of class, as city, town, village, barrio, etc]

Enumeration District No. **13**
Enumerated by me on **April 10, 1930** **Susan W. Bradley**
Enumerator

	PLACE OF ABODE			NAME	RELATION	PERSONAL DESCRIPTION				EDUCATION		NATIVITY		OCCUPATION
	Street, avenue, road, etc.	Number of dwelling house is order of visitation	Number of family in order of visitation	of each person whose place of abode on April 1, 1930, was in this family. Enter surname, first, then given name and middle initial. If any. Include every person living on April 1, 1930. Omit children born since April 1, 1930.	Relationship of this Person to the head of the family.	Sex	Color or race	Age at last birthday	Single, married, widowed or divorced	Attended school any time since Sept. 1, 1929	Whether able to read and write.	Place of birth of this person.	Whether able to speak English.	
	1	2	3	4	5	6	7	8	9	10	11	12	13	14
1	USS Gold Star			Winert, Josejain		M	W	29	S	N	Y	Austria	Y	U.S. Navy
2				Williams, William H		M	W	29	S	N	Y	New York	Y	U.S. Navy
3				Willson, Leo Q		M	W	25	S	N	Y	Oklahoma	Y	U.S. Navy
4				Yabot, Silvens		M	Fil	32	M	N	Y	Philippine Island	Y	U.S. Navy
5				Ybay, Tomas		M	Fil	35	M	N	Y	Philippine Island	Y	U.S. Navy
6				Cruz, Paterno M		M	Cha	22	M	N	Y	Guam	Y	U.S. Navy
7				Espinosa, Jesus		M	Cha	36	S	N	Y	Guam	Y	U.S. Navy
8				Folleon, Haskon		M	W	23	S	N	Y	Wisconsin	Y	U.S. Navy
9				Julian, Vincent V		M	W	29	M	N	Y	[illegible]	Y	U.S. Navy
10				Lason, Malcom W		M	W	29	M	N	Y	Kansas	Y	U.S. Navy
11				Matteson, Clyde Q		M	W	29	S	N	Y	Iowa	Y	U.S. Navy
12				Moore, Carl P		M	W	20	S	N	Y	West Virginia	Y	U.S. Navy
13				Parker, Chester D		M	W	44	M	N	Y	New Hampshire	Y	U.S. Navy
14				Perkins, Hugh E		M	W	24	M	N	Y	Alabama	Y	U.S. Navy
15				Vanson, Ove P O		M	W	43	M	N	Y	Denmark	Y	U.S. Navy
16				Lansdowne, Herbert S		M	W	44	M	N	Y	California	Y	U.S. Navy
17				Marsh, John A		M	W	42	M	N	Y	Indiana	Y	U.S. Navy
18				Terhune, John A		M	W	24	D	N	Y	New York	Y	U.S. Navy
19	USS R.L. Barnes			Anderson, Frank		M	Cha	22	M	N	Y	Guam	Y	U.S. Navy
20				Aquiningoc, Joaquin T		M	Cha	25	S	N	Y	Guam	Y	U.S. Navy
21				Aquiningoc, Jose		M	Cha	29	M	N	Y	Guam	Y	U.S. Navy
22				Blaz, Jose Blaz		M	Cha	30	M	N	Y	Guam	Y	U.S. Navy
23				Duenas, Juan R		M	Cha	29	M	N	Y	Guam	Y	U.S. Navy
24				Fejeran, Florencio P		M	Cha	20	M	N	Y	Guam	Y	U.S. Navy
25				Fernandez, Francisco D		M	Cha	30	M	N	Y	Guam	Y	U.S. Navy

DEPARTMENT OF COMMERCE-BUREAU OF THE CENSUS
WASHINGTON
FIFTEENTH CENSUS OF THE UNITED STATES: 1930-POPULATION

THE ISLAND OF GUAM

Sheet No. 13B

District **Municipality**
Name of Place **Naval Reservations and Ships**
[Proper name and, also, name of class, as city, town, village, barrio, etc]

Enumeration District No. **13**
Enumerated by me on **April 10, 1930** **Susan W. Bradley**, Enumerator

	PLACE OF ABODE			NAME	RELATION	PERSONAL DESCRIPTION				EDUCATION		NATIVITY		OCCUPATION
	Street, avenue, road, etc.	Number of dwelling house is order of visitation	Number of family in order of visitation	of each person whose place of abode on April 1, 1930, was in this family. Enter surname, first, then given name and middle initial. If any. Include every person living on April 1, 1930. Omit children born since April 1, 1930.	Relationship of this Person to the head of the family.	Sex	Color or race	Age at last birthday	Single, married, widowed or divorced	Attended school any time since Sept. 1, 1929	Whether able to read and write.	Place of birth of this person.	Whether able to speak English.	
	1	2	3	4	5	6	7	8	9	10	11	12	13	14
26	USS R.L. Barnes			Guevarra, Vincente A		M	Cha	30	S	N	Y	Guam	Y	U.S. Navy
27				Guisara, Vibencio		M	Fil	34	M	N	Y	Philippine Islands	Y	U.S. Navy
28				Ignacio, Luis C		M	Cha	26	S	N	Y	Guam	Y	U.S. Navy
29				Lizama, Pedro C		M	Cha	21	Wd	N	Y	Guam	Y	U.S. Navy
30				Perez, Jose A		M	Cha	34	M	N	Y	Guam	Y	U.S. Navy
31				Perez, Jose S		M	Cha	23	M	N	Y	Guam	Y	U.S. Navy
32				Quidachay, Francisco		M	Cha	29	M	N	Y	Guam	Y	U.S. Navy
33				Quidachay, Manuel Q		M	Cha	20	S	N	Y	Guam	Y	U.S. Navy
34				Salas, Agapito		M	Cha	46	M	N	Y	Guam	Y	U.S. Navy
35				Sanchez, Jose T		M	Cha	30	S	N	Y	Guam	Y	U.S. Navy
36				San Nicolas, Geronimo C		M	Cha	29	M	N	Y	Guam	Y	U.S. Navy
37				Taitano, Luis S		M	Cha	39	M	N	Y	Guam	Y	U.S. Navy
38				Taitano, Miguel C		M	Cha	29	M	N	Y	Guam	Y	U.S. Navy
39				Ulloa, Juan Q		M	Cha	21	M	N	Y	Guam	Y	U.S. Navy
40				Unpingco, Juan R		M	Cha	29	M	N	Y	Guam	Y	U.S. Navy
41	[blank]	25		Agoun, Joaquin T		M	Cha	30	M	N	Y	Guam	Y	U.S. Navy
42				Blaz, Vincente C		M	Cha	28	M	N	Y	Guam	Y	U.S. Navy
43				Cruz, Carlos P		M	Cha	30	M	N	Y	Guam	Y	U.S. Navy
44				Dydasco, Jesus T		M	Cha	39	M	N	Y	Guam	Y	U.S. Navy
45				Felt, Theodoreo M		M	W	26	M	N	Y	Colorado	Y	U.S. Navy
46				Flores, Jose		M	Cha	29	M	N	Y	Guam	Y	U.S. Navy
47				Franquez, Jesus T		M	Cha	22	S	N	Y	Guam	Y	U.S. Navy
48				Garcia, Jaime M		M	Cha	19	S	N	Y	Guam	Y	U.S. Navy
49				Garrido, Vincente		M	Cha	38	M	N	Y	Guam	Y	U.S. Navy
50				Quichocho?, Juan		M	Cha	22	S	N	Y	Guam	Y	U.S. Navy

(CHAMORRO ROOTS GENEALOGY PROJECT™ TRANSCRIPTION)
(BERNARD T. PUNZALAN / HTTP://WWW.CHAMORROROOTS.COM)

DEPARTMENT OF COMMERCE-BUREAU OF THE CENSUS
WASHINGTON

FIFTEENTH CENSUS OF THE UNITED STATES: 1930-POPULATION

THE ISLAND OF GUAM

Sheet No. 14A

District **Municipality**
Name of Place **Naval Reservations and Ships**
[Proper name and, also, name of class, as city, town, village, barrio, etc]

Enumeration District No. **13**
Enumerated by me on **April 10, 1930** **Susan W. Bradley**, Enumerator

	PLACE OF ABODE			NAME	RELATION	PERSONAL DESCRIPTION				EDUCATION		NATIVITY		OCCUPATION
	Street, avenue, road, etc.	Number of dwelling house is order of visitation	Number of family in order of visitation	of each person whose place of abode on April 1, 1930, was in this family. Enter surname, first, then given name and middle initial. If any. Include every person living on April 1, 1930. Omit children born since April 1, 1930.	Relationship of this Person to the head of the family.	Sex	Color or race	Age at last birthday	Single, married, widowed or divorced	Attended school any time since Sept. 1, 1929	Whether able to read and write.	Place of birth of this person.	Whether able to speak English.	
	1	2	3	4	5	6	7	8	9	10	11	12	13	14
1	[blank]			Kelly, David H		M	W	39	S	N	Y	New York	Y	U.S. Navy
2				Manibusan, Antonio M		M	Cha	25	M	N	Y	Guam	Y	U.S. Navy
3				Rosario, Jose		M	Cha	36	M	N	Y	Guam	Y	U.S. Navy
4				Sanchez, Pablo		M	Cha	40	M	N	Y	Guam	Y	U.S. Navy
5				Siguenza, Jose		M	Cha	29	M	N	Y	Guam	Y	U.S. Navy
6				Wackman, Donald T		M	W	38	M	N	Y	Iowa	Y	U.S. Navy
7	Navy Yard, Piti	26		Aflleje, Juan		M	Cha	25	M	N	Y	Guam	Y	U.S. Navy
8				Aguon, Jesus L		M	Cha	20	S	N	Y	Guam	Y	U.S. Navy
9				Aguon, Jose L		M	Cha	29	M	N	Y	Guam	Y	U.S. Navy
10				Anderson, Juan		M	Cha	38	M	N	Y	Guam	Y	U.S. Navy
11				Arceo, Gregorio C		M	Cha	37	M	N	Y	Guam	Y	U.S. Navy
12				Blaz, Francisco A		M	Cha	31	M	N	Y	Guam	Y	U.S. Navy
13				Borja, Jose M		M	Cha	28	M	N	Y	Guam	Y	U.S. Navy
14				Camacho, Enrique G		M	Cha	29	M	N	Y	Guam	Y	U.S. Navy
15				Camacho, Vincente		M	Cha	31	M	N	Y	Guam	Y	U.S. Navy
16				Carbullido, Juan		M	Cha	33	M	N	Y	Guam	Y	U.S. Navy
17				Castro, Jesus C		M	Cha	33	M	N	Y	Guam	Y	U.S. Navy
18				Chaco, Joaquin R		M	Cha	26	M	N	Y	Guam	Y	U.S. Navy
19				Chaco, Juan R		M	Cha	24	S	N	Y	Guam	Y	U.S. Navy
20				Champaco, Vincente A		M	Cha	29	M	N	Y	Guam	Y	U.S. Navy
21				Concepcion, Antonio		M	Cha	26	M	N	Y	Guam	Y	U.S. Navy
22				Concepcion, Manuel C		M	Cha	25	M	N	Y	Guam	Y	U.S. Navy
23				Cruz, Jose A		M	Cha	20	S	N	Y	Guam	Y	U.S. Navy
24				Cruz, Jose C		M	Cha	34	M	N	Y	Guam	Y	U.S. Navy
25				Cruz, Jose Q		M	Cha	30	M	N	Y	Guam	Y	U.S. Navy

DEPARTMENT OF COMMERCE-BUREAU OF THE CENSUS
WASHINGTON

FIFTEENTH CENSUS OF THE UNITED STATES: 1930-POPULATION

THE ISLAND OF GUAM

Sheet No. 14B

299B

District **Municipality**
Name of Place **Naval Reservations and Ships**
[Proper name and, also, name of class, as city, town, village, barrio, etc]

Enumeration District No. **13**
Enumerated by me on **April 11, 1930** **Susan W. Bradley**, Enumerator

	PLACE OF ABODE			NAME	RELATION	PERSONAL DESCRIPTION				EDUCATION		NATIVITY		OCCUPATION
	Street, avenue, road, etc.	Number of dwelling house is order of visitation	Number of family in order of visitation	of each person whose place of abode on April 1, 1930, was in this family. Enter surname, first, then given name and middle initial. If any. Include every person living on April 1, 1930. Omit children born since April 1, 1930.	Relationship of this Person to the head of the family.	Sex	Color or race	Age at last birthday	Single, married, widowed or divorced	Attended school any time since Sept. 1, 1929	Whether able to read and write.	Place of birth of this person.	Whether able to speak English.	
	1	2	3	4	5	6	7	8	9	10	11	12	13	14
26	Navy Yard, Piti			Cruz, Jesus V		M	Cha	35	M	N	Y	Guam	Y	U.S. Navy
27				Cruz, Pedro S		M	Cha	30	M	N	Y	Guam	Y	U.S. Navy
28				De Leon, Francisco Q		M	Cha	28	M	N	Y	Guam	Y	U.S. Navy
29				Duenas, Pedro S		M	Cha	28	M	N	Y	Guam	Y	U.S. Navy
30				Fejeran, Enrique P		M	Cha	30	M	N	Y	Guam	Y	U.S. Navy
31				Fejeran, Joaquin C		M	Cha	23	M	N	Y	Guam	Y	U.S. Navy
32				Fejeran, Joaquin P		M	Cha	28	M	N	Y	Guam	Y	U.S. Navy
33				Flores, Lorenzo P		M	Cha	28	M	N	Y	Guam	Y	U.S. Navy
34				Gibson, Norman M		M	W	31	M	N	Y	Oregon	Y	U.S. Navy
35				Gomez, Vincente S		M	Cha	29	M	N	Y	Guam	Y	U.S. Navy
36				Herrera, Jesus S		M	Cha	32	M	N	Y	Guam	Y	U.S. Navy
37				Indalecio, Vincete I		M	Cha	31	M	N	Y	Guam	Y	U.S. Navy
38				Lujan, Jose G		M	Cha	28	M	N	Y	Guam	Y	U.S. Navy
39				McLean, James W		M	W	32	M	N	Y	Massachusetts	Y	U.S. Navy
40				Mendiola, Francisco U		M	Cha	30	M	N	Y	Guam	Y	U.S. Navy
41				Mesa, Juan C		M	Cha	31	M	N	Y	Guam	Y	U.S. Navy
42				Nauta, Vincente Q		M	Cha	22	M	N	Y	Guam	Y	U.S. Navy
43				Nededog, Felix P		M	Cha	29	M	N	Y	Guam	Y	U.S. Navy
44				Pangelinan, Felix U		M	Cha	28	M	N	Y	Guam	Y	U.S. Navy
45				Perez, Jose R		M	Cha	28	Wd	N	Y	Guam	Y	U.S. Navy
46				Perez, Juan T		M	Cha	31	M	N	Y	Guam	Y	U.S. Navy
47				Perez, Juan Q		M	Cha	24	M	N	Y	Guam	Y	U.S. Navy
48				Quinata, Antonio A		M	Cha	30	M	N	Y	Guam	Y	U.S. Navy
49				Quitugua, Enrique R		M	Cha	31	M	N	Y	Guam	Y	U.S. Navy
50				Sablan, Antonio C		M	Cha	28	M	N	Y	Guam	Y	U.S. Navy

(CHAMORRO ROOTS GENEALOGY PROJECT™ TRANSCRIPTION)
(BERNARD T. PUNZALAN / HTTP://WWW.CHAMORROROOTS.COM)

DEPARTMENT OF COMMERCE-BUREAU OF THE CENSUS
WASHINGTON

FIFTEENTH CENSUS OF THE UNITED STATES: 1930-POPULATION

THE ISLAND OF GUAM

Sheet No. 15A

District **Municipality**
Name of Place **Naval Reservations and Ships**
[Proper name and, also, name of class, as city, town, village, barrio, etc]

Enumeration District No. **13**
Enumerated by me on **April 11, 1930** **Susan W. Bradley**
Enumerator

	PLACE OF ABODE			NAME	RELATION	PERSONAL DESCRIPTION				EDUCATION		NATIVITY		OCCUPATION
	Street, avenue, road, etc.	Number of dwelling house is order of visitation	Number of family in order of visitation	of each person whose place of abode on April 1, 1930, was in this family. Enter surname, first, then given name and middle initial. If any. Include every person living on April 1, 1930. Omit children born since April 1, 1930.	Relationship of this Person to the head of the family.	Sex	Color or race	Age at last birthday	Single, married, widowed or divorced	Attended school any time since Sept. 1, 1929	Whether able to read and write.	Place of birth of this person.	Whether able to speak English.	
	1	2	3	4	5	6	7	8	9	10	11	12	13	14
1	Navy Yard, Piti			Sablan, Enrique		M	Cha	39	M	N	Y	Guam	Y	U.S. Navy
2				Sablan, Francisco C		M	Cha	33	M	N	Y	Guam	Y	U.S. Navy
3				Sablan, Honorato A		M	Cha	26	M	N	Y	Guam	Y	U.S. Navy
4				Sablan, Jose P		M	Cha	31	M	N	Y	Guam	Y	U.S. Navy
5				San Nicolas, Antonio D		M	Cha	30	M	N	Y	Guam	Y	U.S. Navy
6				San Nicolas, Florencio A		M	Cha	23	S	N	Y	Guam	Y	U.S. Navy
7				San Nicolas, Joaquin P		M	Cha	27	S	N	Y	Guam	Y	U.S. Navy
8				Santos, Jesus B		M	Cha	24	M	N	Y	Guam	Y	U.S. Navy
9				Santos, Joaquin Q		M	Cha	29	M	N	Y	Guam	Y	U.S. Navy
10				Santos, Jose S		M	Cha	30	M	N	Y	Guam	Y	U.S. Navy
11				Santos, Santiago C		M	Cha	27	M	N	Y	Guam	Y	U.S. Navy
12				Santos, Vincente C		M	Cha	24	S	N	Y	Guam	Y	U.S. Navy
13				Siguenza, Jesus S		M	Cha	29	M	N	Y	Guam	Y	U.S. Navy
14				Terlaje, Vincente B		M	Cha	31	M	N	Y	Guam	Y	U.S. Navy
15				Thomas, Hurley A		M	W	34	M	N	Y	Missouri	Y	U.S. Navy
16				Torres, Jose P		M	Cha	30	M	N	Y	Guam	Y	U.S. Navy
17				Unpingco, Jesus A		M	Cha	23	S	N	Y	Guam	Y	U.S. Navy
18				Unpingco, Jose A		M	Cha	28	M	N	Y	Guam	Y	U.S. Navy
19				Untalan, Joaquin G		M	Cha	24	M	N	Y	Guam	Y	U.S. Navy
20				Untalan, Joaquin P		M	Cha	25	S	N	Y	Guam	Y	U.S. Navy
21	Navy [illegible]	27		Achaigua, Felix S		M	Cha	28	M	N	Y	Guam	Y	U.S. Navy
22				Bautista, Leocadio		M	Fil	29	M	N	Y	Philippine Island	Y	U.S. Navy
23				Camacho, Jose S		M	Cha	20	S	N	Y	Guam	Y	U.S. Navy
24				Cepeda, Pedro		M	Cha	40	M	N	Y	Guam	Y	U.S. Navy
25				Cruz, Luis T		M	Cha	19	S	N	Y	Guam	Y	U.S. Navy

DEPARTMENT OF COMMERCE-BUREAU OF THE CENSUS
WASHINGTON

FIFTEENTH CENSUS OF THE UNITED STATES: 1930-POPULATION

THE ISLAND OF GUAM

Sheet No. 15B

300B

District **Municipality**
Name of Place **Naval Reservations and Ships**
[Proper name and, also, name of class, as city, town, village, barrio, etc]

Enumeration District No. 13
Enumerated by me on April 11, 1930 Susan W. Bradley
Enumerator

	PLACE OF ABODE			NAME	RELATION	PERSONAL DESCRIPTION				EDUCATION		NATIVITY		OCCUPATION
	Street, avenue, road, etc.	Number of dwelling house is order of visitation	Number of family in order of visitation	of each person whose place of abode on April 1, 1930, was in this family. Enter surname, first, then given name and middle initial. If any. Include every person living on April 1, 1930. Omit children born since April 1, 1930.	Relationship of this Person to the head of the family.	Sex	Color or race	Age at last birthday	Single, married, widowed or divorced	Attended school any time since Sept. 1, 1929	Whether able to read and write.	Place of birth of this person.	Whether able to speak English.	
	1	2	3	4	5	6	7	8	9	10	11	12	13	14
26	Navy [illegible]			Damian, Candido B		M	Fil	20	S	N	Y	Guam	Y	U.S. Navy
27				Guerrero, Matias D		M	Cha	44	M	N	Y	Guam	Y	U.S. Navy
28				Mesa, Jose M		M	Cha	32	M	N	Y	Guam	Y	U.S. Navy
29				Pangelinan, Tomas M		M	Cha	23	S	N	Y	Guam	Y	U.S. Navy
30				Perez, Jesus M		M	Cha	21	S	N	Y	Guam	Y	U.S. Navy
31				Sablan, Jose M		M	Cha	25	M	N	Y	Guam	Y	U.S. Navy
32				Salas, Jesus Q		M	Cha	20	S	N	Y	Guam	Y	U.S. Navy
33				San Nicolas, Juan A		M	Cha	31	M	N	Y	Guam	Y	U.S. Navy
34				Terbure, Ernest W		M	W	41	M	N	Y	Kansas	Y	U.S. Navy
35				Torres, Jose A		M	Cha	43	M	N	Y	Guam	Y	U.S. Navy
36				Velasco, Sebastian		M	Fil	49	S	N	Y	Guam	Y	U.S. Navy
37	Government House	28		Bradley, William W Jr		M	W	45	M	N	Y	New York	Y	U.S. Navy
38				Bradley, Sue Worthingtno		F	W	43	M	N	Y	Maryland	Y	None
39				Bradley, Sue Worthingtno		F	W	17	S	N	Y	Maryland	Y	None
40				Bradley, Anne W		F	W	14	S	N	Y	California	Y	None
41				Bradley, Josephine W		F	W	8	S	N	Y	[illegible]	Y	None
42	Naval Station Guam	30		Melendez, Franz B		M	W	39	S	N	Y	Indiana	Y	U.S. Navy
43				Dees, Randal E		M	W	36	M	N	Y	Mississippi	Y	U.S. Navy
44				Best, William A		M	W	36	M	N	Y	New York	Y	U.S. Navy
45				Masterton, George W		M	W	35	M	N	Y	Maine	Y	U.S. Navy
46				Carroll, John J		M	W	46	M	N	Y	Pennsylvania	Y	U.S. Navy
47				Brady, Thomas J Jr		M	W	45	M	N	Y	New York	Y	U.S. Navy
48				Martin, Alexander Jr.		M	W	37	M	N	Y	Oregon	Y	U.S. Navy
49				Miller, Thornton C		M	W	34	M	N	Y	Kansas	Y	U.S. Navy
50				Gurnan, Ermette F		M	W	41	M	N	Y	Missouri	Y	U.S. Navy

DEPARTMENT OF COMMERCE-BUREAU OF THE CENSUS
WASHINGTON

FIFTEENTH CENSUS OF THE UNITED STATES: 1930-POPULATION

THE ISLAND OF GUAM

Sheet No. 16A

District **Municipality**
Name of Place **Naval Reservations and Ships**
[Proper name and, also, name of class, as city, town, village, barrio, etc]

Enumeration District No. **13**
Enumerated by me on **April 11, 1930** **Susan W. Bradley**
Enumerator

	PLACE OF ABODE			NAME	RELATION	PERSONAL DESCRIPTION				EDUCATION		NATIVITY		OCCUPATION
	Street, avenue, road, etc.	Number of dwelling house is order of visitation	Number of family in order of visitation	of each person whose place of abode on April 1, 1930, was in this family. Enter surname, first, then given name and middle initial. If any. Include every person living on April 1, 1930. Omit children born since April 1, 1930.	Relationship of this Person to the head of the family.	Sex	Color or race	Age at last birthday	Single, married, widowed or divorced	Attended school any time since Sept. 1, 1929	Whether able to read and write.	Place of birth of this person.	Whether able to speak English.	
	1	2	3	4	5	6	7	8	9	10	11	12	13	14
1	Navy Station			Waidner, Charle M		M	W	30	M	N	Y	Indiana	Y	U.S. Navy
2				McAllister, William R		M	W	34	M	N	Y	Colorado	Y	U.S. Navy
3				Walton, George E		M	W	33	M	N	Y	Indiana	Y	U.S. Navy
4	Commissary Store	31		Dembroker, Michael Z		M	W	49	M	N	Y	Pennsylvania	Y	U.S. Navy
5				Fender, Albert		M	W	43	M	N	Y	Kentucky	Y	U.S. Navy
6				Atoigue, Vincente U		M	Cha	39	M	N	Y	Guam	Y	U.S. Navy
7				Blaz, Jose		M	Cha	32	M	N	Y	Guam	Y	U.S. Navy
8				Burnham, Harry J		M	W	39	M	N	Y	Washington	Y	U.S. Navy
9				Carlide, Charles H		M	W	34	M	N	Y	Maryland	Y	U.S. Navy
10				Crowley, Joseph F		M	W	29	S	N	Y	Maine	Y	U.S. Navy
11				Cruz, Eugene P		M	Cha	30	M	N	Y	Guam	Y	U.S. Navy
12				Duenas, Jesus C		M	Cha	20	M	N	Y	Guam	Y	U.S. Navy
13				Franquez, Pedro T		M	Cha	19	S	N	Y	Guam	Y	U.S. Navy
14				Mendiola, Jose A		M	Cha	22	S	N	Y	Guam	Y	U.S. Navy
15				Palumbo, Carmine		M	W	29	M	N	Y	New York	Y	U.S. Navy
16				Perez, Jesus F		M	Cha	18	S	N	Y	Guam	Y	U.S. Navy
17				Ramos, Juan H		M	Cha	26	M	N	Y	Guam	Y	U.S. Navy
18				Rosario, Vincente		M	Cha	36	M	N	Y	Guam	Y	U.S. Navy
19				Santos, Joaquin Q		M	Cha	25	S	N	Y	Guam	Y	U.S. Navy
20	Radio	32		Sharkey, William P		M	W	21	S	N	Y	Rhode Island	Y	U.S. Navy
21				Duicid, Clarence R		M	W	30	M	N	Y	Illinois	Y	U.S. Navy
22				Schell, Charlie W		M	W	32	M	N	Y	Georgia	Y	U.S. Navy
23				Thomas, William B		M	W	27	S	N	Y	Iowa	Y	U.S. Navy
24				Twentey, Louis C		M	W	21	S	N	Y	Indiana	Y	U.S. Navy
25				Vandeberg, Marten A		M	W	29	S	N	Y	Pennsylvania	Y	U.S. Navy

DEPARTMENT OF COMMERCE-BUREAU OF THE CENSUS
WASHINGTON

FIFTEENTH CENSUS OF THE UNITED STATES: 1930-POPULATION

THE ISLAND OF GUAM

Sheet No. 16B

District **Municipality**
Name of Place **Naval Reservations and Ships**
[Proper name and, also, name of class, as city, town, village, barrio, etc]

Enumeration District No. **13**
Enumerated by me on **April 12, 1930** **Susan W. Bradley**
Enumerator

	PLACE OF ABODE			NAME	RELATION	PERSONAL DESCRIPTION				EDUCATION		NATIVITY		OCCUPATION
	Street, avenue, road, etc.	Number of dwelling house in order of visitation	Number of family in order of visitation	of each person whose place of abode on April 1, 1930, was in this family. Enter surname, first, then given name and middle initial. If any. Include every person living on April 1, 1930. Omit children born since April 1, 1930.	Relationship of this Person to the head of the family.	Sex	Color or race	Age at last birthday	Single, married, widowed or divorced	Attended school any time since Sept. 1, 1929	Whether able to read and write.	Place of birth of this person.	Whether able to speak English.	
	1	2	3	4	5	6	7	8	9	10	11	12	13	14
26	Radio			Ward, John C		M	W	24	S	N	Y	Kentucky	Y	U.S. Navy
27				Wood, Murrel D		M	W	26	M	N	Y	Indiana	Y	U.S. Navy
28				Punzalan, Bernardo		M	Fil	32	M	N	Y	Philippine Islands	Y	U.S. Navy
29				Lang, Harry J		M	W	43	D	N	Y	Iowa	Y	U.S. Navy
30				Aflague, Juan S		M	Cha	29	M	N	Y	Guam	Y	U.S. Navy
31				Barcinas, Ignacio		M	Cha	31	M	N	Y	Guam	Y	U.S. Navy
32				Barton, Lawrence K		M	W	42	S	N	Y	Kansas	Y	U.S. Navy
33				Daniels, Charles E		M	W	26	M	N	Y	Ohio	Y	U.S. Navy
34				Dannson, John S		M	W	22	S	N	Y	Kentucky	Y	U.S. Navy
35				Edwing, Alfred E		M	W	29	S	N	Y	Vermont	Y	U.S. Navy
36				English, Floyd E		M	W	24	S	N	Y	Indiana	Y	U.S. Navy
37				Flores, Joaquin L		M	Fil	31	M	N	Y	Philippine Islands	Y	U.S. Navy
38				French, Vernes H		M	W	30	M	N	Y	Connecticut	Y	U.S. Navy
39				Goodwin, Keith E		M	W	28	M	N	Y	Michigan	Y	U.S. Navy
40				Grandy, Harry R		M	W	21	S	N	Y	South Carolina	Y	U.S. Navy
41				Gunn, Max C		M	W	28	M	N	Y	Indiana	Y	U.S. Navy
42				Kimball, Lloyd B		M	W	31	Wd	N	Y	Massachusetts	Y	U.S. Navy
43				Kuernmich, Robert H		M	W	21	S	N	Y	Indiana	Y	U.S. Navy
44				Larry, Joseph McG		M	W	20	S	N	Y	Missouri	Y	U.S. Navy
45				Lusk, Truett C		M	W	30	M	N	Y	Texas	Y	U.S. Navy
46				Messick, John E		M	W	25	S	N	Y	Delaware	Y	U.S. Navy
47				Miner, Jose A		M	Cha	33	M	N	Y	Guam	Y	U.S. Navy
48				Morris, Robert A		M	W	36	D	N	Y	Pennsylvania	Y	U.S. Navy
49				Nelson, Claude L		M	W	20	S	N	Y	Alabama	Y	U.S. Navy
50				Phillips, Edgar		M	W	30	M	N	Y	California	Y	U.S. Navy

(CHAMORRO ROOTS GENEALOGY PROJECT™ TRANSCRIPTION)
(BERNARD T. PUNZALAN / HTTP://WWW.CHAMORROROOTS.COM)

DEPARTMENT OF COMMERCE-BUREAU OF THE CENSUS
WASHINGTON

FIFTEENTH CENSUS OF THE UNITED STATES: 1930-POPULATION

THE ISLAND OF GUAM

Sheet No. 17A

302

District **Municipality**
Name of Place **Naval Reservations and Ships**
[Proper name and, also, name of class, as city, town, village, barrio, etc]

Enumeration District No. **13**
Enumerated by me on **April 12, 1930** **Susan W. Bradley**
Enumerator

	PLACE OF ABODE			NAME	RELATION	PERSONAL DESCRIPTION				EDUCATION		NATIVITY		OCCUPATION
	Street, avenue, road, etc.	Number of dwelling house is order of visitation	Number of family in order of visitation	of each person whose place of abode on April 1, 1930, was in this family. Enter surname, first, then given name and middle initial. If any. Include every person living on April 1, 1930. Omit children born since April 1, 1930.	Relationship of this Person to the head of the family.	Sex	Color or race	Age at last birthday	Single, married, widowed or divorced	Attended school any time since Sept. 1, 1929	Whether able to read and write.	Place of birth of this person.	Whether able to speak English.	
	1	2	3	4	5	6	7	8	9	10	11	12	13	14
1	Radio			Rusnold, Clarence E		M	W	33	M	N	Y	Missouri	Y	U.S. Navy
2				Rufio, Robert G		M	W	21	S	N	Y	New York	Y	U.S. Navy
3				Robert, Wiley D		M	W	30	S	N	Y	Georgia	Y	U.S. Navy
4	U.S.S. Penguin	33		Adamos, Ireneo		M	Fil	29	M	N	Y	Philippine Islands	Y	U.S. Navy
5				Aflague, Jose		M	Cha	35	M	N	Y	Guam	Y	U.S. Navy
6				Arroyo, Brigidio		M	Fil	29	M	N	Y	Philippine Islands	Y	U.S. Navy
7				Barries, Jose G		M	W	29	S	N	Y	Illinois	Y	U.S. Navy
8				Behind, Gerst		M	W	39	S	N	Y	Pennsylvania	Y	U.S. Navy
9				Blaz, Jose		M	Cha	29	M	N	Y	Guam	Y	U.S. Navy
10				Bukikosa, Sacarias		M	Fil	35	D	N	Y	Philippine Islands	Y	U.S. Navy
11				Presignand, William E		M	W	27	M	N	Y	Germany	Y	U.S. Navy
12				Bushell, Alfred		M	W	24	S	N	Y	New York	Y	U.S. Navy
13				Carbullido, Felix		M	Cha	31	M	N	Y	Guam	Y	U.S. Navy
14				Camacho, Mendiola A		M	Cha	39	M	N	Y	Guam	Y	U.S. Navy
15				Castro, Juan S		M	Cha	36	M	N	Y	Guam	Y	U.S. Navy
16				Chargualaf, Rafael		M	Cha	33	M	N	Y	Guam	Y	U.S. Navy
17				Concepcion, Jose C		M	Cha	31	M	N	Y	Guam	Y	U.S. Navy
18				Concepcion, Juan C		M	Cha	36	M	N	Y	Guam	Y	U.S. Navy
19				Carring, Chelaca M		M	W	28	D	N	Y	Ohio	Y	U.S. Navy
20				DiBaun, William G		M	W	19	S	N	Y	Wyoming	Y	U.S. Navy
21				Devenport, William D		M	W	20	S	N	Y	Kentucky	Y	U.S. Navy
22				Dela Torre, Juan N		M	Cha	26	M	N	Y	Guam	Y	U.S. Navy
23				Fejeran, Justo		M	Cha	45	M	N	Y	Guam	Y	U.S. Navy
24				Fox, Donald A		M	W	31	S	N	Y	South Dakota	Y	U.S. Navy
25				Gusbino, John R		M	W	32	S	N	Y	New York	Y	U.S. Navy

DEPARTMENT OF COMMERCE-BUREAU OF THE CENSUS
WASHINGTON
FIFTEENTH CENSUS OF THE UNITED STATES: 1930-POPULATION

THE ISLAND OF GUAM

Sheet No. 17B

302B

District **Municipality**
Name of Place **Naval Reservations and Ships** [Proper name and, also, name of class, as city, town, village, barrio, etc]

Enumeration District No. 13
Enumerated by me on **April 12, 1930** **Susan W. Bradley** Enumerator

	PLACE OF ABODE			NAME	RELATION	PERSONAL DESCRIPTION				EDUCATION		NATIVITY		OCCUPATION
	Street, avenue, road, etc.	Number of dwelling house is order of visitation	Number of family in order of visitation	of each person whose place of abode on April 1, 1930, was in this family. Enter surname, first, then given name and middle initial. If any. Include every person living on April 1, 1930. Omit children born since April 1, 1930.	Relationship of this Person to the head of the family.	Sex	Color or race	Age at last birthday	Single, married, widowed or divorced	Attended school any time since Sept. 1, 1929	Whether able to read and write.	Place of birth of this person.	Whether able to speak English.	
	1	2	3	4	5	6	7	8	9	10	11	12	13	14
26	U.S.S. Penguin			Duenas, Pedro L		M	Cha	39	M	N	Y	Guam	Y	U.S. Navy
27				Iglesias, Antonio		M	Cha	39	M	N	Y	Guam	Y	U.S. Navy
28				Jarry, Benjamin F		M	W	27	M	N	Y	Guam	Y	U.S. Navy
29				Lyorght, John		M	W	38	S	N	Y	Ireland	Y	U.S. Navy
30				Manglona, Vincente		M	Cha	39	M	N	Y	Guam	Y	U.S. Navy
31				Martin, Gilbert		M	W	31	M	N	Y	Colorado	Y	U.S. Navy
32				Matanane, Jose		M	Cha	39	M	N	Y	Guam	Y	U.S. Navy
33				Macos, Hernogenes		M	Fil	28	M	N	Y	Philippine Islands	Y	U.S. Navy
34				Marford, Jessie K		M	W	30	S	N	Y	North Carolina	Y	U.S. Navy
35				McElligott, Les M		M	W	30	S	N	Y	Kentucky	Y	U.S. Navy
36				Perez, Antonio R		M	Cha	31	M	N	Y	Guam	Y	U.S. Navy
37				Pubet, Wlesey O		M	W	32	M	N	Y	Illinois	Y	U.S. Navy
38				Quitugua, Antonio M		M	Cha	31	M	N	Y	Guam	Y	U.S. Navy
39				Robert, Maurice K		M	W	28	S	N	Y	Massachusetts	Y	U.S. Navy
40				Scheuberg, Fred		M	W	35	M	N	Y	California	Y	U.S. Navy
41				Santos, Blas		M	Cha	38	S	N	Y	Guam	Y	U.S. Navy
42				Salas, Vincente		M	Cha	31	M	N	Y	Guam	Y	U.S. Navy
43				Taitano, Francisco		M	Cha	33	M	N	Y	Guam	Y	U.S. Navy
44	Marine Barracks	34		Archerman, Charles F		M	W	29	S	N	Y	Illinois	Y	U.S. Marine Corps
45				Alexanders, Roy T		M	W	22	S	N	Y	Minnesota	Y	U.S. Marine Corps
46				Ascan, James		M	W	19	S	N	Y	Texas	Y	U.S. Marine Corps
47				Atchinson, Wallace J		M	W	18	S	N	Y	Oregon	Y	U.S. Marine Corps
48				Bebich, Michael S		M	W	39	S	N	Y	Ohio	Y	U.S. Marine Corps
49				Becael, Ralph J		M	W	19	S	N	Y	Minnesota	Y	U.S. Marine Corps
50				Beckers, Ralph F		M	W	25	S	N	Y	Wisconsin	Y	U.S. Marine Corps

DEPARTMENT OF COMMERCE-BUREAU OF THE CENSUS
WASHINGTON

FIFTEENTH CENSUS OF THE UNITED STATES: 1930-POPULATION

THE ISLAND OF GUAM

Sheet No. 18A

District **Municipality**
Name of Place **Naval Reservations and Ships**
[Proper name and, also, name of class, as city, town, village, barrio, etc]

Enumeration District No. **13**
Enumerated by me on **April 12, 1930** **Susan W. Bradley**
Enumerator

	PLACE OF ABODE			NAME	RELATION	PERSONAL DESCRIPTION				EDUCATION		NATIVITY		OCCUPATION
	Street, avenue, road, etc.	Number of dwelling house is order of visitation	Number of family in order of visitation	of each person whose place of abode on April 1, 1930, was in this family. Enter surname, first, then given name and middle initial. If any. Include every person living on April 1, 1930. Omit children born since April 1, 1930.	Relationship of this Person to the head of the family.	Sex	Color or race	Age at last birthday	Single, married, widowed or divorced	Attended school any time since Sept. 1, 1929	Whether able to read and write.	Place of birth of this person.	Whether able to speak English.	
	1	2	3	4	5	6	7	8	9	10	11	12	13	14
1	Marine Barracks			Badey, George F		M	W	19	S	N	Y	Pennsylvania	Y	U.S. Marine Corps
2				Barasley, Talph F		M	W	25	S	N	Y	Kansas	Y	U.S. Marine Corps
3				Barnes, Thomas N		M	W	21	S	N	Y	Kentucky	Y	U.S. Marine Corps
4				Batten, Sam		M	W	19	S	N	Y	South Carolina	Y	U.S. Marine Corps
5				Belosers, Bernard		M	W	22	S	N	Y	Illinois	Y	U.S. Marine Corps
6				Blanten, Gus		M	W	20	S	N	Y	Oklahoma	Y	U.S. Marine Corps
7				Borrow, Curtis W		M	W	19	S	N	Y	West Virginia	Y	U.S. Marine Corps
8				Brandt, Lorenzo I		M	W	29	S	N	Y	California	Y	U.S. Marine Corps
9				Baroski, Wilbert C		M	W	19	S	N	Y	Pennsylvania	Y	U.S. Marine Corps
10				Broski, Elden J		M	W	19	S	N	Y	New Hampshire	Y	U.S. Marine Corps
11				Bryan, Harry C		M	W	31	S	N	Y	New York	Y	U.S. Marine Corps
12				Calens, William P		M	W	21	S	N	Y	Pennsylvania	Y	U.S. Marine Corps
13				Carroll, William H		M	W	32	S	N	Y	Mississippi	Y	U.S. Marine Corps
14				Chiyska, Gordon S		M	W	29	S	N	Y	Michigan	Y	U.S. Marine Corps
15				Clark, Francis S		M	W	33	S	N	Y	Iowa	Y	U.S. Marine Corps
16				Cooper, Raymond M		M	W	28	S	N	Y	Missouri	Y	U.S. Marine Corps
17				Cross, Koltis C		M	W	18	S	N	Y	Georgia	Y	U.S. Marine Corps
18				Daneson, Kerafas G		M	W	25	S	N	Y	Texas	Y	U.S. Marine Corps
19				Dexter, Arthur E		M	W	20	S	N	Y	Colorado	Y	U.S. Marine Corps
20				Dillard, Charlie G		M	W	21	S	N	Y	Tennesee	Y	U.S. Marine Corps
21				Darrio, George W		M	W	24	S	N	Y	Indiana	Y	U.S. Marine Corps
22				Dougherty, Gerald J		M	W	20	S	N	Y	Pennsylvania	Y	U.S. Marine Corps
23				Dudley, Reese R		M	W	20	S	N	Y	Virginia	Y	U.S. Marine Corps
24				Erickson, Albert		M	W	40	S	N	Y	Minnesota	Y	U.S. Marine Corps
25				Easton, Charlie H		M	W	41	M	N	Y	Kentucky	Y	U.S. Marine Corps

DEPARTMENT OF COMMERCE-BUREAU OF THE CENSUS
WASHINGTON

FIFTEENTH CENSUS OF THE UNITED STATES: 1930-POPULATION

THE ISLAND OF GUAM

Sheet No. 18B

303B

District **Municipality**
Name of Place **Naval Reservations and Ships**
[Proper name and, also, name of class, as city, town, village, barrio, etc]

Enumeration District No. **13**
Enumerated by me on **April 14, 1930** **Susan W. Bradley**, Enumerator

	PLACE OF ABODE: Street, avenue, road, etc.	Number of dwelling house in order of visitation	Number of family in order of visitation	NAME of each person whose place of abode on April 1, 1930, was in this family. Enter surname, first, then given name and middle initial. If any. Include every person living on April 1, 1930. Omit children born since April 1, 1930.	RELATION Relationship of this Person to the head of the family.	PERSONAL DESCRIPTION: Sex	Color or race	Age at last birthday	Single, married, widowed or divorced	EDUCATION: Attended school any time since Sept. 1, 1929	Whether able to read and write.	NATIVITY Place of birth of this person.	Whether able to speak English.	OCCUPATION
	1	2	3	4	5	6	7	8	9	10	11	12	13	14
26	Marine Barracks			Farley, William T		M	W	29	S	N	Y	California	Y	U.S. Marine Corps
27				Feelings, Antonio G		M	W	23	S	N	Y	New York	Y	U.S. Marine Corps
28				Finkler, Frank S		M	W	18	S	N	Y	Illinois	Y	U.S. Marine Corps
29				Finian, Albert W		M	W	31	S	N	Y	Massachusetts	Y	U.S. Marine Corps
30				Fotheringham, Douglas E		M	W	19	S	N	Y	Utah	Y	U.S. Marine Corps
31				Gauidierg, Dan W		M	W	18	S	N	Y	Georgia	Y	U.S. Marine Corps
32				Gormich, Paul F		M	W	27	S	N	Y	Pennsylvania	Y	U.S. Marine Corps
33				Gracies, Wilbur B		M	W	26	S	N	Y	Massachusetts	Y	U.S. Marine Corps
34				Ganna, Herman		M	W	25	S	N	Y	South Carolina	Y	U.S. Marine Corps
35				Haskins, William R		M	W	25	S	N	Y	Kansas	Y	U.S. Marine Corps
36				Herideig, Wilbur E		M	W	18	S	N	Y	South Carolina	Y	U.S. Marine Corps
37				Herwerdo, Ellis W		M	W	22	S	N	Y	Nebraska	Y	U.S. Marine Corps
38				Herman, Albert		M	W	21	S	N	Y	New York	Y	U.S. Marine Corps
39				Jarvis, Thomas A		M	W	22	S	N	Y	North Carolina	Y	U.S. Marine Corps
40				Kellison, Edward		M	W	49	M	N	Y	West Virginia	Y	U.S. Marine Corps
41				Kennedy, Earnest E		M	W	38	S	N	Y	Texas	Y	U.S. Marine Corps
42				Keepfer, Lawrence H		M	W	25	S	N	Y	Illinois	Y	U.S. Marine Corps
43				Lanais, George J		M	W	29	S	N	Y	Massachusetts	Y	U.S. Marine Corps
44				Lans, Walter R		M	W	19	S	N	Y	Texas	Y	U.S. Marine Corps
45				Letechiers, Herbert G		M	W	20	S	N	Y	Oregon	Y	U.S. Marine Corps
46				Lurney, Merle F		M	W	28	S	N	Y	California	Y	U.S. Marine Corps
47				McBurnie, Herbert C		M	W	30	S	N	Y	Maine	Y	U.S. Marine Corps
48				McDonald, Elmer E		M	W	19	S	N	Y	Washington	Y	U.S. Marine Corps
49				Mihen, John Jr		M	W	22	S	N	Y	Ohio	Y	U.S. Marine Corps
50				Mosick, Joseph W		M	W	29	S	N	Y	New York	Y	U.S. Marine Corps

DEPARTMENT OF COMMERCE-BUREAU OF THE CENSUS
WASHINGTON

FIFTEENTH CENSUS OF THE UNITED STATES: 1930-POPULATION

THE ISLAND OF GUAM

Sheet No. 19A

District **Municipality**
Name of Place **Naval Reservations and Ships**
[Proper name and, also, name of class, as city, town, village, barrio, etc]

Enumeration District No. **13**
Enumerated by me on **April 14, 1930** **Susan W. Bradley**
Enumerator

	PLACE OF ABODE			NAME	RELATION	PERSONAL DESCRIPTION				EDUCATION		NATIVITY		OCCUPATION
	Street, avenue, road, etc.	Number of dwelling house is order of visitation	Number of family in order of visitation	of each person whose place of abode on April 1, 1930, was in this family. Enter surname, first, then given name and middle initial. If any. Include every person living on April 1, 1930. Omit children born since April 1, 1930.	Relationship of this Person to the head of the family.	Sex	Color or race	Age at last birthday	Single, married, widowed or divorced	Attended school any time since Sept. 1, 1929	Whether able to read and write.	Place of birth of this person.	Whether able to speak English.	
	1	2	3	4	5	6	7	8	9	10	11	12	13	14
1	Marine Barracks			Mowers, Gordon E		M	W	21	S	N	Y	Wisconsin	Y	U.S. Marine Corps
2				Nelson, Maxwell		M	W	25	S	N	Y	Ohio	Y	U.S. Marine Corps
3				Nixon, Ivery		M	W	27	S	N	Y	Georgia	Y	U.S. Marine Corps
4				Oakes, George E		M	W	27	S	N	Y	Montana	Y	U.S. Marine Corps
5				O'Brien, Otto T		M	W	24	S	N	Y	Nebraska	Y	U.S. Marine Corps
6				Ogoen, Quentin M		M	W	20	S	N	Y	Connecticut	Y	U.S. Marine Corps
7				Oleson, John W		M	W	21	S	N	Y	Iowa	Y	U.S. Marine Corps
8				Ortan, Frank F		M	W	30	S	N	Y	New York	Y	U.S. Marine Corps
9				Ovlasa, John J		M	W	39	S	N	Y	Illinois	Y	U.S. Marine Corps
10				Peacock, John F		M	W	19	S	N	Y	Montana	Y	U.S. Marine Corps
11				Qualls, Charles E		M	W	20	S	N	Y	California	Y	U.S. Marine Corps
12				Rollins, James Q		M	W	24	S	N	Y	Texas	Y	U.S. Marine Corps
13				Scasoldeo, Adolp R		M	W	27	S	N	Y	Nebraska	Y	U.S. Marine Corps
14				Scolar, Earl F		M	W	19	S	N	Y	Nebraska	Y	U.S. Marine Corps
15				Scott, Claude H		M	W	29	M	N	Y	Ohio	Y	U.S. Marine Corps
16				Shefveland, Carle Q		M	W	24	S	N	Y	Minnesota	Y	U.S. Marine Corps
17				Snider, Henry J		M	W	20	S	N	Y	Wisconsin	Y	U.S. Marine Corps
18				Sorravos, Harland W		M	W	20	S	N	Y	Texas	Y	U.S. Marine Corps
19				Stone, Ewell B		M	W	33	S	N	Y	Texas	Y	U.S. Marine Corps
20				Straight, Jack H		M	W	18	S	N	Y	Oklahoma	Y	U.S. Marine Corps
21				Sutton, John A		M	W	18	S	N	Y	Louisiana	Y	U.S. Marine Corps
22				Sweeney, Paul		M	W	21	S	N	Y	Tennesee	Y	U.S. Marine Corps
23				Talbott, Ralph		M	W	17	S	N	Y	Maryland	Y	U.S. Marine Corps
24				Teagne, Ralph		M	W	26	S	N	Y	North Carolina	Y	U.S. Marine Corps
25				Thompson, George B		M	W	23	S	N	Y	New York	Y	U.S. Marine Corps

(CHAMORRO ROOTS GENEALOGY PROJECT™ TRANSCRIPTION)
(BERNARD T. PUNZALAN / HTTP://WWW.CHAMORROROOTS.COM)

DEPARTMENT OF COMMERCE-BUREAU OF THE CENSUS
WASHINGTON

FIFTEENTH CENSUS OF THE UNITED STATES: 1930-POPULATION

THE ISLAND OF GUAM

Sheet No. 19B

304B

District **Municipality**
Name of Place **Naval Reservations and Ships**
[Proper name and, also, name of class, as city, town, village, barrio, etc]

Enumeration District No. 13
Enumerated by me on **April 14, 1930** **Susan W. Bradley**, Enumerator

	PLACE OF ABODE			NAME	RELATION	PERSONAL DESCRIPTION				EDUCATION		NATIVITY		OCCUPATION
	Street, avenue, road, etc.	Number of dwelling house is order of visitation	Number of family in order of visitation	of each person whose place of abode on April 1, 1930, was in this family. Enter surname, first, then given name and middle initial. If any. Include every person living on April 1, 1930. Omit children born since April 1, 1930.	Relationship of this Person to the head of the family.	Sex	Color or race	Age at last birthday	Single, married, widowed or divorced	Attended school any time since Sept. 1, 1929	Whether able to read and write.	Place of birth of this person.	Whether able to speak English.	
	1	2	3	4	5	6	7	8	9	10	11	12	13	14
26	Marine Barracks			Tickle, Patrick H		M	W	20	S	N	Y	Virginia	Y	U.S. Marine Corps
27				Totten, Charles R		M	W	32	S	N	Y	Ohio	Y	U.S. Marine Corps
28				Tremclay, Albert J		M	W	19	S	N	Y	Massachusetts	Y	U.S. Marine Corps
29				Van Oleck, Florin G		M	W	20	S	N	Y	Kansas	Y	U.S. Marine Corps
30				Ward, Edward M		M	W	22	S	N	Y	Illinois	Y	U.S. Marine Corps
31				Warhol, Alexander		M	W	28	S	N	Y	Minnesota	Y	U.S. Marine Corps
32				Watson, Clarence O		M	W	19	S	N	Y	New York	Y	U.S. Marine Corps
33				Williams, Ralph H		M	W	19	S	N	Y	Missouri	Y	U.S. Marine Corps
34				Wright, Clayton W		M	W	19	S	N	Y	Michigan	Y	U.S. Marine Corps
35				Luedess, Fred		M	W	48	M	N	Y	Australia	Y	U.S. Marine Corps
36				Speese, George N		M	W	45	M	N	Y	Pennsylvania	Y	U.S. Marine Corps
37				Burnbee, Alvin R		M	W	44	M	N	Y	New York	Y	U.S. Marine Corps
38				McCullough, Thomas L		M	W	41	M	N	Y	Nebraska	Y	U.S. Marine Corps
39				Wood, Samuel H		M	W	41	D	N	Y	California	Y	U.S. Marine Corps
40				Blanks, Hugh A		M	W	33	M	N	Y	Virginia	Y	U.S. Marine Corps
41				Burtrow, Joseph H		M	W	33	S	N	Y	Pennsylvania	Y	U.S. Marine Corps
42				Lauren, Jack A		M	W	28	S	N	Y	Washington	Y	U.S. Marine Corps
43				Smith, Gary B		M	W	44	S	N	Y	California	Y	U.S. Marine Corps
44				Sullivan, Frank J		M	W	36	S	N	Y	Mississippi	Y	U.S. Marine Corps
45				Turner, John C		M	W	39	M	N	Y	Mississippi	Y	U.S. Marine Corps
46				Williams, David I		M	W	36	S	N	Y	Pennsylvania	Y	U.S. Marine Corps
47				Wilson, James C		M	W	31	M	N	Y	Virginia	Y	U.S. Marine Corps
48				Woolsey, Kenneth A		M	W	24	S	N	Y	California	Y	U.S. Marine Corps
49				Allison, Frederick		M	W	30	S	N	Y	Montana	Y	U.S. Marine Corps
50				Bealer, Ernest		M	W	29	S	N	Y	Wisconsin	Y	U.S. Marine Corps

(CHAMORRO ROOTS GENEALOGY PROJECT™ TRANSCRIPTION)
(BERNARD T. PUNZALAN / HTTP://WWW.CHAMORROROOTS.COM)

DEPARTMENT OF COMMERCE-BUREAU OF THE CENSUS
WASHINGTON

FIFTEENTH CENSUS OF THE UNITED STATES: 1930-POPULATION

THE ISLAND OF GUAM

Sheet No. 20A

305

District **Municipality**
Name of Place **Naval Reservations and Ships**
[Proper name and, also, name of class, as city, town, village, barrio, etc]

Enumeration District No. **13**
Enumerated by me on **April 15, 1930** **Susan W. Bradley**
Enumerator

	PLACE OF ABODE			NAME	RELATION	PERSONAL DESCRIPTION				EDUCATION		NATIVITY		OCCUPATION
	Street, avenue, road, etc.	Number of dwelling house is order of visitation	Number of family in order of visitation	of each person whose place of abode on April 1, 1930, was in this family. Enter surname, first, then given name and middle initial. If any. Include every person living on April 1, 1930. Omit children born since April 1, 1930.	Relationship of this Person to the head of the family.	Sex	Color or race	Age at last birthday	Single, married, widowed or divorced	Attended school any time since Sept. 1, 1929	Whether able to read and write.	Place of birth of this person.	Whether able to speak English.	
	1	2	3	4	5	6	7	8	9	10	11	12	13	14
1	Marine Barracks			Caruso, Mario		M	W	29	S	N	Y	Massachusetts	Y	U.S. Marine Corps
2				Collier, Zadek		M	W	39	S	N	Y	Guatemala	Y	U.S. Marine Corps
3				Cooper, Charles P		M	W	34	S	N	Y	Mississippi	Y	U.S. Marine Corps
4				Egsnest, John J Jr		M	W	29	S	N	Y	Colorado	Y	U.S. Marine Corps
5				Goff, Alfard B		M	W	28	S	N	Y	Oklahoma	Y	U.S. Marine Corps
6				Jeffer, Larrus		M	W	25	S	N	Y	North Carolina	Y	U.S. Marine Corps
7				Peterson, William C		M	W	38	Wd	N	Y	Pennsylvania	Y	U.S. Marine Corps
8				Bera, Martin W		M	W	25	S	N	Y	New Hampshire	Y	U.S. Marine Corps
9				Bishop, Dewey C		M	W	29	S	N	Y	Alabama	Y	U.S. Marine Corps
10				Brown, Raymond L		M	W	22	S	N	Y	Washington	Y	U.S. Marine Corps
11				Davidson, Arthur J		M	W	22	S	N	Y	Washington	Y	U.S. Marine Corps
12				Evelhoch, Calvin A		M	W	27	S	N	Y	Pennsylvania	Y	U.S. Marine Corps
13				Faith, Dale		M	W	24	D	N	Y	Colorado	Y	U.S. Marine Corps
14				Foster, Frank R		M	W	23	S	N	Y	Nebraska	Y	U.S. Marine Corps
15				Keith, Arley L		M	W	28	S	N	Y	Texas	Y	U.S. Marine Corps
16				Lea, Luther B		M	W	22	S	N	Y	Washington	Y	U.S. Marine Corps
17				Leach, Orsin C		M	W	23	S	N	Y	Illinois	Y	U.S. Marine Corps
18				Narly, Wayne		M	W	24	S	N	Y	Michigan	Y	U.S. Marine Corps
19				Pearson, James C W		M	W	29	S	N	Y	North Dakota	Y	U.S. Marine Corps
20				Perrett, Glenn J		M	W	24	S	N	Y	Michigan	Y	U.S. Marine Corps
21				Powell, Meriem C Jr		M	W	24	S	N	Y	Kansas	Y	U.S. Marine Corps
22				Ratcliff, Arson B		M	W	27	S	N	Y	Kentucky	Y	U.S. Marine Corps
23				Richardson, W R		M	W	29	S	N	Y	Texas	Y	U.S. Marine Corps
24				Retas, Wayne E		M	W	29	S	N	Y	Iowa	Y	U.S. Marine Corps
25				Russell, Carl W		M	W	29	S	N	Y	Iowa	Y	U.S. Marine Corps

(CHAMORRO ROOTS GENEALOGY PROJECT™ TRANSCRIPTION)
(BERNARD T. PUNZALAN / HTTP://WWW.CHAMORROROOTS.COM)

DEPARTMENT OF COMMERCE-BUREAU OF THE CENSUS
WASHINGTON

FIFTEENTH CENSUS OF THE UNITED STATES: 1930-POPULATION

THE ISLAND OF GUAM

Sheet No. 20B

305B

District **Municipality**
Name of Place **Naval Reservations and Ships**
[Proper name and, also, name of class, as city, town, village, barrio, etc]

Enumeration District No. **13**
Enumerated by me on **April 15, 1930** **Susan W. Bradley**
Enumerator

	PLACE OF ABODE			NAME	RELATION	PERSONAL DESCRIPTION				EDUCATION		NATIVITY		OCCUPATION
	Street, avenue, road, etc.	Number of dwelling house is order of visitation	Number of family in order of visitation	of each person whose place of abode on April 1, 1930, was in this family. Enter surname, first, then given name and middle initial. If any. Include every person living on April 1, 1930. Omit children born since April 1, 1930.	Relationship of this Person to the head of the family.	Sex	Color or race	Age at last birthday	Single, married, widowed or divorced	Attended school any time since Sept. 1, 1929	Whether able to read and write.	Place of birth of this person.	Whether able to speak English.	
	1	2	3	4	5	6	7	8	9	10	11	12	13	14
26	Marine Barracks			Russell, Harry M		M	W	22	S	N	Y	Colorado	Y	U.S. Marine Corps
27				Sayre, Francis M		M	W	23	S	N	Y	New Jersey	Y	U.S. Marine Corps
28				Smith, James A		M	W	29	S	N	Y	Texas	Y	U.S. Marine Corps
29				Sprague, Adelbert T		M	W	24	S	N	Y	Kansas	Y	U.S. Marine Corps
30				Stoughton, Charles E		M	W	30	D	N	Y	Pennsylvania	Y	U.S. Marine Corps
31				Thetford, William D		M	W	21	S	N	Y	California	Y	U.S. Marine Corps
32				Walker, Charles W		M	W	24	S	N	Y	Texas	Y	U.S. Marine Corps
33				Williamson, Wesley E		M	W	24	S	N	Y	Missouri	Y	U.S. Marine Corps
34				Barney, Charlie N		M	W	19	S	N	Y	Oregon	Y	U.S. Marine Corps
35				Dickson, Joseph W		M	W	23	S	N	Y	Colorado	Y	U.S. Marine Corps
36				Dodson, James P		M	W	28	S	N	Y	Texas	Y	U.S. Marine Corps
37				Glascott, Rubert		M	W	20	S	N	Y	Illinois	Y	U.S. Marine Corps
38				Nicheo, Mack		M	W	25	S	N	Y	West Virginia	Y	U.S. Marine Corps
39				Parker, Herbert N		M	W	24	S	N	Y	Georgia	Y	U.S. Marine Corps
40				Russell, Cyril R		M	W	22	S	N	Y	Texas	Y	U.S. Marine Corps
41				Wallace, Guy A		M	W	21	S	N	Y	Indiana	Y	U.S. Marine Corps
42				Jackson, Steven M		M	W	20	S	N	Y	Indiana	Y	U.S. Marine Corps
43				Berrings, Yancey A		M	W	22	S	N	Y	Texas	Y	U.S. Marine Corps
44				Borosee, William A		M	W	22	S	N	Y	Pennsylvania	Y	U.S. Marine Corps
45				Bordor, Henry F		M	W	24	S	N	Y	Minnesota	Y	U.S. Marine Corps
46				Casaott, Elvis C		M	W	23	S	N	Y	Colorado	Y	U.S. Marine Corps
47				Chaves, Edward G		M	W	22	S	N	Y	Texas	Y	U.S. Marine Corps
48				Coppersmith, Ora D		M	W	23	S	N	Y	Kansas	Y	U.S. Marine Corps
49				Dahl, Raymond M		M	W	20	S	N	Y	South Dakota	Y	U.S. Marine Corps
50				Fricke, Oliver E		M	W	24	S	N	Y	Indiana	Y	U.S. Marine Corps

(CHAMORRO ROOTS GENEALOGY PROJECT™ TRANSCRIPTION)
(BERNARD T. PUNZALAN / HTTP://WWW.CHAMORROROOTS.COM)

DEPARTMENT OF COMMERCE-BUREAU OF THE CENSUS
WASHINGTON

FIFTEENTH CENSUS OF THE UNITED STATES: 1930-POPULATION

THE ISLAND OF GUAM

Sheet No. 21A

306

District **Municipality**

Name of Place **Naval Reservations and Ships**

[Proper name and, also, name of class, as city, town, village, barrio, etc]

Enumeration District No. **13**

Enumerated by me on **April 15, 1930** **Susan W. Bradley**, Enumerator

	PLACE OF ABODE			NAME	RELATION	PERSONAL DESCRIPTION				EDUCATION		NATIVITY		OCCUPATION
	Street, avenue, road, etc.	Number of dwelling house is order of visitation	Number of family in order of visitation	of each person whose place of abode on April 1, 1930, was in this family. Enter surname, first, then given name and middle initial. If any. Include every person living on April 1, 1930. Omit children born since April 1, 1930.	Relationship of this Person to the head of the family.	Sex	Color or race	Age at last birthday	Single, married, widowed or divorced	Attended school any time since Sept. 1, 1929	Whether able to read and write.	Place of birth of this person.	Whether able to speak English.	
	1	2	3	4	5	6	7	8	9	10	11	12	13	14
1	Marine Barracks			Grover, Archie W		M	W	20	S	N	Y	Kansas	Y	U.S. Marine Corps
2				Gullo, Albert		M	W	25	S	N	Y	Pennsylvania	Y	U.S. Marine Corps
3				Hanna, Roert N		M	W	21	S	N	Y	Missouri	Y	U.S. Marine Corps
4				Hardesty, Charles L		M	W	25	S	N	Y	Ohio	Y	U.S. Marine Corps
5				Hart, Thomas M		M	W	32	S	N	Y	Wisconsin	Y	U.S. Marine Corps
6				Howell, Galen B		M	W	25	S	N	Y	Illinois	Y	U.S. Marine Corps
7				Hoff, Clarence C		M	W	23	S	N	Y	Nebraska	Y	U.S. Marine Corps
8				Johnston, James E		M	W	24	S	N	Y	Arizona	Y	U.S. Marine Corps
9				Julian, Delmar		M	W	23	S	N	Y	California	Y	U.S. Marine Corps
10				Klopz, Harvey F		M	W	25	S	N	Y	Iowa	Y	U.S. Marine Corps
11				Ledwick, Thomas F		M	W	22	S	N	Y	Iowa	Y	U.S. Marine Corps
12				Mable, Sidney C		M	W	22	S	N	Y	Georgia	Y	U.S. Marine Corps
13				Manse, Pack M		M	W	20	S	N	Y	Iowa	Y	U.S. Marine Corps
14				Matheson, Douglas G		M	W	25	S	N	Y	Washington	Y	U.S. Marine Corps
15				Nunn, Clarence		M	W	30	S	N	Y	Oregon	Y	U.S. Marine Corps
16				Osborne, Burton F		M	W	22	S	N	Y	Florida	Y	U.S. Marine Corps
17				Parish, Paul I		M	W	23	S	N	Y	Wisconsin	Y	U.S. Marine Corps
18				Ramstetin, Julian A		M	W	21	S	N	Y	Pennsylvania	Y	U.S. Marine Corps
19				Rosemeice, Vernon W		M	W	24	S	N	Y	Minnesota	Y	U.S. Marine Corps
20				Ripple, Louis McC		M	W	22	S	N	Y	California	Y	U.S. Marine Corps
21				Rosao, Charles		M	W	22	S	N	Y	Colorado	Y	U.S. Marine Corps
22				Schaisun, Emil C		M	W	23	S	N	Y	California	Y	U.S. Marine Corps
23				Tuck, Byron H		M	W	20	S	N	Y	Missouri	Y	U.S. Marine Corps
24				Woodcock, Ronald O		M	W	22	S	N	Y	Missouri	Y	U.S. Marine Corps
25				Quinata, Felisa S		F	Cha	28	S	N	Y	Guam	Y	U.S. Navy

DEPARTMENT OF COMMERCE-BUREAU OF THE CENSUS
WASHINGTON

FIFTEENTH CENSUS OF THE UNITED STATES: 1930-POPULATION

THE ISLAND OF GUAM

Sheet No. 21B

306B

District **Municipality**
Name of Place **Naval Reservations and Ships**
[Proper name and, also, name of class, as city, town, village, barrio, etc]

Enumeration District No. **13**
Enumerated by me on **April 15, 1930** **Susan W. Bradley**
Enumerator

	PLACE OF ABODE			NAME	RELATION	PERSONAL DESCRIPTION				EDUCATION		NATIVITY		OCCUPATION
	Street, avenue, road, etc.	Number of dwelling house is order of visitation	Number of family in order of visitation	of each person whose place of abode on April 1, 1930, was in this family. Enter surname, first, then given name and middle initial. If any. Include every person living on April 1, 1930. Omit children born since April 1, 1930.	Relationship of this Person to the head of the family.	Sex	Color or race	Age at last birthday	Single, married, widowed or divorced	Attended school any time since Sept. 1, 1929	Whether able to read and write.	Place of birth of this person.	Whether able to speak English.	
	1	2	3	4	5	6	7	8	9	10	11	12	13	14
26	U.S. Naval Hospital			San Nicolas, Maria S		F	Cha	23	S	N	Y	Guam	Y	U.S. Navy
27				Aflague, Concepcion S		F	Cha	24	S	N	Y	Guam	Y	U.S. Navy
28				Cruz, Ana Q		F	Cha	27	S	N	Y	Guam	Y	U.S. Navy
29				Mendiola, Ana Q		F	Cha	29	S	N	Y	Guam	Y	U.S. Navy
30				Quinataotao, Virginia N		F	Cha	20	S	N	Y	Guam	Y	U.S. Navy
31				De Leon, Dolores P		F	Cha	28	S	N	Y	Guam	Y	U.S. Navy
32				Terlaje, Consuelo F		F	Cha	29	S	N	Y	Guam	Y	U.S. Navy
33				Gogue, Rita A		F	Cha	26	S	N	Y	Guam	Y	U.S. Navy
34				Lujan, Engracia G		F	Cha	28	S	N	Y	Guam	Y	U.S. Navy
35				Sigenza, Joaquina		F	Cha	20	S	N	Y	Guam	Y	U.S. Navy
36				Castro, Teresa C		F	Cha	23	S	N	Y	Guam	Y	U.S. Navy
37				Rios, Ana L		F	Cha	28	S	N	Y	Guam	Y	U.S. Navy
38				Hong Yee, Concepcion C		F	Cha	24	M	N	Y	Guam	Y	U.S. Navy
39				Mesa, Delores C		F	Cha	24	S	N	Y	Guam	Y	U.S. Navy
40				Taitano, Rosa G		F	Cha	23	S	N	Y	Guam	Y	U.S. Navy
41				Guzman, Amanda P		F	Cha	23	S	N	Y	Guam	Y	U.S. Navy
42				Castro, Ana M		F	Cha	20	S	N	Y	Guam	Y	U.S. Navy
43				Camacho, Delores A		F	Cha	24	S	N	Y	Guam	Y	U.S. Navy
44				Mendiola, Margarita M		F	Cha	23	S	N	Y	Guam	Y	U.S. Navy
45				Siguenza, Ana T		F	Cha	23	S	N	Y	Guam	Y	U.S. Navy
46				Tolentino, Maria L		F	Fil	22	S	N	Y	Guam	Y	U.S. Navy
47	[Illegible]		35	Davis, Lincoln R	Head	M	W	36	M	N	Y	Georgia	Y	U.S. Marine Corps
48				Davis, Oswen	Wife	F	W	29	M	N	Y	Pennsylvania	Y	None
49			36	Jorgensen, Beatrice	Head	F	W	31	M	N	Y	Illinois	Y	None
50				Jorgensen, Helen	Daughter	F	W	7	S	N	Y	California	Y	None

DEPARTMENT OF COMMERCE-BUREAU OF THE CENSUS
WASHINGTON

FIFTEENTH CENSUS OF THE UNITED STATES: 1930-POPULATION

THE ISLAND OF GUAM

Sheet No. 22A

307

District **Municipality**

Name of Place **Naval Reservations and Ships**

[Proper name and, also, name of class, as city, town, village, barrio, etc]

Enumeration District No. **13**

Enumerated by me on **April 15, 1930** **Susan W. Bradley**, Enumerator

	PLACE OF ABODE			NAME	RELATION	PERSONAL DESCRIPTION				EDUCATION		NATIVITY		OCCUPATION
	Street, avenue, road, etc.	Number of dwelling house is order of visitation	Number of family in order of visitation	of each person whose place of abode on April 1, 1930, was in this family. Enter surname, first, then given name and middle initial. If any. Include every person living on April 1, 1930. Omit children born since April 1, 1930.	Relationship of this Person to the head of the family.	Sex	Color or race	Age at last birthday	Single, married, widowed or divorced	Attended school any time since Sept. 1, 1929	Whether able to read and write.	Place of birth of this person.	Whether able to speak English.	
	1	2	3	4	5	6	7	8	9	10	11	12	13	14
1	[Illegible]			Jorgensen, Dorothy	Daughter	F	W	6	S	N		Haiti		None
2				Jorgensen, Joan	Daughter	F	W	4.2	S	N		Haiti		None
3				Jorgensen, Joyce	Daughter	F	W	.2	S	N		Guam		None
4				[Lines 4 through 25 were intentionally left blank by the enumerator.]										
5				[Sheet 22B/307B was intentionally left blank by the enumerator.]										
6														
7														
8														
9														
10														
11														
12														
13			-											
14														
15														
16														
17														
18														
19														
20														
21														
22														
23														
24														
25														

DEPARTMENT OF COMMERCE-BUREAU OF THE CENSUS
WASHINGTON

FIFTEENTH CENSUS OF THE UNITED STATES: 1930-POPULATION

THE ISLAND OF GUAM

Sheet No. 23A

308

District **Municipality**
Name of Place **Naval Reservations and Ships**
[Proper name and, also, name of class, as city, town, village, barrio, etc]

Enumeration District No. **13**
Enumerated by me on **June 25, 1930** **Susan W. Bradley**
Enumerator

	PLACE OF ABODE			NAME	RELATION	PERSONAL DESCRIPTION				EDUCATION		NATIVITY		OCCUPATION
	Street, avenue, road, etc.	Number of dwelling house is order of visitation	Number of family in order of visitation	of each person whose place of abode on April 1, 1930, was in this family. Enter surname, first, then given name and middle initial. If any. Include every person living on April 1, 1930. Omit children born since April 1, 1930.	Relationship of this Person to the head of the family.	Sex	Color or race	Age at last birthday	Single, married, widowed or divorced	Attended school any time since Sept. 1, 1929	Whether able to read and write.	Place of birth of this person.	Whether able to speak English.	
	1	2	3	4	5	6	7	8	9	10	11	12	13	14
1	U.S. Naval Station	37		Bryce, Bascorn D		M	W	20	S	N	Y	Texas	Y	U.S. Navy
2				Casablanca, Robert		M	PR	27	S	N	Y	Porto Rico	Y	U.S. Navy
3				Covington, Edward J		M	W	19	S	N	Y	Indiana	Y	U.S. Navy
4				Cusseh, James I		M	W	29	S	N	Y	New York	Y	U.S. Navy
5				Fradenburg, Lester W		M	W	24	M	N	Y	Washington	Y	U.S. Navy
6				Hall, Claude W		M	W	19	S	N	Y	Kansas	Y	U.S. Navy
7				Horton, Merton T		M	W	19	S	N	Y	Pennsylvania	Y	U.S. Navy
8				Hutchins, Harnes Q		M	W	20	S	N	Y	Texas	Y	U.S. Navy
9				Larson, Robert T		M	W	22	S	N	Y	Minnesota	Y	U.S. Navy
10				Mix, Carl		M	W	21	S	N	Y	South Dakota	Y	U.S. Navy
11				Newby, Homer C		M	W	26	S	N	Y	Kansas	Y	U.S. Navy
12				Phillips, Earl		M	W	19	S	N	Y	Oklahoma	Y	U.S. Navy
13				White, William T		M	W	20	S	N	Y	New York	Y	U.S. Navy
14				Alton, J A		M	W	19	S	N	Y	Louisiana	Y	U.S. Navy
15				Morgan, T G		M	W	26	S	N	Y	New York	Y	U.S. Navy
16				Reames, Wm. L		M	W	29	M	N	Y	Missouri	Y	U.S. Navy
17				Scurry, Valto		M	W	21	S	N	Y	South Carolina	Y	U.S. Navy
18				Shipley, R V		M	W	19	S	N	Y	California	Y	U.S. Navy
19				Cloughly, Sterling T		M	W	32	M	N	Y	California	Y	U.S. Navy
20				Shoeman, Kenneth M		M	W	25	S	N	Y	Iowa	Y	U.S. Navy
21				Kunkel, Edward T		M	W	31	M	N	Y	Indiana	Y	U.S. Navy
22				Dinsmoore, Alfred		M	W	38	M	N	Y	New Jersey	Y	U.S. Navy
23				Goodman, Niel C		M	W	37	M	N	Y	Arkansas	Y	U.S. Marine Corps
24				Cooper, Milton H		M	W	21	S	N	Y	Ohio	Y	U.S. Navy
25				Davison, George		M	W	27	S	N	Y	Michigan	Y	U.S. Navy

DEPARTMENT OF COMMERCE-BUREAU OF THE CENSUS
WASHINGTON

FIFTEENTH CENSUS OF THE UNITED STATES: 1930-POPULATION

THE ISLAND OF GUAM

Sheet No. 23B

308B

District **Municipality**

Name of Place **Naval Reservations and Ships**
[Proper name and, also, name of class, as city, town, village, barrio, etc]

Enumeration District No. **13**

Enumerated by me on **June 25, 1930** **Susan W. Bradley** Enumerator

	PLACE OF ABODE			NAME	RELATION	PERSONAL DESCRIPTION				EDUCATION		NATIVITY		OCCUPATION
	Street, avenue, road, etc.	Number of dwelling house is order of visitation	Number of family in order of visitation	of each person whose place of abode on April 1, 1930, was in this family. Enter surname, first, then given name and middle initial. If any. Include every person living on April 1, 1930. Omit children born since April 1, 1930.	Relationship of this Person to the head of the family.	Sex	Color or race	Age at last birthday	Single, married, widowed or divorced	Attended school any time since Sept. 1, 1929	Whether able to read and write.	Place of birth of this person.	Whether able to speak English.	
	1	2	3	4	5	6	7	8	9	10	11	12	13	14
26	U.S. Naval Station			Penrose, Joseph R		M	W	23	S	N	Y	Iowa	Y	U.S. Marine Corps
27				Silverthorn, Mervin H		M	W	33	M	N	Y	Minnesota	Y	U.S. Officer
28				Silverthorn, Marie A		F	W	35	M	N	Y	Minnesota	Y	None
29				Silverthorn, Mervin H Jr		M	W	9	M	N	Y	California	Y	None
30				Silverthorn, Russell L		M	W	7	S	N	Y	Virginia	Y	None
31				Silverthorn, Robert S		M	W	6.2	S	N	Y	Virginia	Y	None
32				Bennington, James W		M	W	39	M	N	Y	Oklahoma	Y	U.S. Marine Corps
33				Bryant, Welles Y		M	W	30	S	N	Y	Kansas	Y	U.S. Marine Corps
34				Chisinski, Alex		M	W	22	S	N	Y	Wisconsin	Y	U.S. Marine Corps
35				Elliott, Nathaniel L		M	W	34	S	N	Y	Nebraska	Y	U.S. Marine Corps
36				Johnson, Hans		M	W	23	S	N	Y	Finland	Y	U.S. Marine Corps
37				Robert, Charley		M	W	24	S	N	Y	Washington	Y	U.S. Marine Corps
38				Sawyer, Paul F		M	W	19	S	N	Y	Washington	Y	U.S. Marine Corps
39				Taylor, Robert L		M	W	18	S	N	Y	Oklahoma	Y	U.S. Marine Corps
40				Wells, Otto B		M	W	39	S	N	Y	Oklahoma	Y	U.S. Marine Corps
41				Shepherd, James E		M	W	33	S	N	Y	Indiana	Y	U.S. Marine Corps
42				Smith, William C		M	W	19	S	N	Y	Missouri	Y	U.S. Marine Corps
43				Burke, Ralph A		M	W	19	S	N	Y	Oregon	Y	U.S. Marine Corps
44				Coryell, Fred		M	W	39	S	N	Y	Montana	Y	U.S. Marine Corps
45				McKinney, Alfie E Jr		M	W	18	S	N	Y	Montana	Y	U.S. Marine Corps
46				Vugent, David G Jr		M	W	38	S	N	Y	Washington	Y	U.S. Marine Corps
47				Bush, William A		M	W	18	S	N	Y	Kansas	Y	U.S. Marine Corps
48				Avilla, Arthur		M	W	19	S	N	Y	California	Y	U.S. Marine Corps
49				Awls, Harold P		M	W	23	S	N	Y	Minnesota	Y	U.S. Marine Corps
50				Bird, Franklin A Jr		M	W	22	S	N	Y	Missouri	Y	U.S. Marine Corps

(CHAMORRO ROOTS GENEALOGY PROJECT™ TRANSCRIPTION)
(BERNARD T. PUNZALAN / HTTP://WWW.CHAMORROROOTS.COM)

DEPARTMENT OF COMMERCE-BUREAU OF THE CENSUS
WASHINGTON

FIFTEENTH CENSUS OF THE UNITED STATES: 1930-POPULATION

THE ISLAND OF GUAM

Sheet No. 24A

309

District **Municipality**

Name of Place **Naval Reservations and Ships**
[Proper name and, also, name of class, as city, town, village, barrio, etc]

Enumeration District No. **13**

Enumerated by me on **June 25, 1930** **Susan W. Bradley**
Enumerator

	PLACE OF ABODE			NAME	RELATION	PERSONAL DESCRIPTION				EDUCATION		NATIVITY		OCCUPATION
	Street, avenue, road, etc.	Number of dwelling house is order of visitation	Number of family in order of visitation	of each person whose place of abode on April 1, 1930, was in this family. Enter surname, first, then given name and middle initial. If any. Include every person living on April 1, 1930. Omit children born since April 1, 1930.	Relationship of this Person to the head of the family.	Sex	Color or race	Age at last birthday	Single, married, widowed or divorced	Attended school any time since Sept. 1, 1929	Whether able to read and write.	Place of birth of this person.	Whether able to speak English.	
	1	2	3	4	5	6	7	8	9	10	11	12	13	14
1	U.S. Naval Station			Bair, Ernest O		M	W	19	S	N	Y	California	Y	U.S. Marine Corps
2				Curtis, John E		M	W	24	S	N	Y	Iowa	Y	U.S. Marine Corps
3				Easley, William P		M	W	20	S	N	Y	Arkansas	Y	U.S. Marine Corps
4				Farmer, Claude K		M	W	28	S	N	Y	Mississippi	Y	U.S. Marine Corps
5				Franklin, Harold H		M	W	21	S	N	Y	Missouri	Y	U.S. Marine Corps
6				Herdener, Leonard L		M	W	20	S	N	Y	Oregon	Y	U.S. Marine Corps
7				Melingan, Harold H		M	W	21	S	N	Y	Texas	Y	U.S. Marine Corps
8				Pickens, Harry A		M	W	21	S	N	Y	Oklahoma	Y	U.S. Marine Corps
9				Rediens, John A		M	W	21	S	N	Y	Pennsylvania	Y	U.S. Marine Corps
10				Roughton, Clifford		M	W	19	S	N	Y	Missouri	Y	U.S. Marine Corps
11				Simpson, Kenneth		M	W	20	S	N	Y	Nebraska	Y	U.S. Marine Corps
12				William, Kenneth C		M	W	21	S	N	Y	Minnesota	Y	U.S. Marine Corps
13				Darling, Harold N		M	W	35	M	N	Y	Michigan	Y	U.S. Navy
14				Cady, Willam H		M	W	44	M	N	Y	Connecticut	Y	U.S. Navy
15				Wigle, David W		M	W	30	M	N	Y	Oregon	Y	U.S. Navy
16				Mikelson, Paul B		M	W	29	M	N	Y	Alabama	Y	U.S. Navy
17				Freeman, Kenneth M		M	W	25	S	N	Y	Iowa	Y	U.S. Navy
18														
19														
20														
21														
22														
23														
24														
25														

www.ingramcontent.com/pod-product-compliance
Lightning Source LLC
Chambersburg PA
CBHW052128020426
42334CB00023B/2637

* 9 7 8 0 9 8 5 1 2 5 7 1 4 *